# Lab Safety

| Safety symbol | What it means | What to do in the event of an accident |
|---|---|---|
| Eye protection | Wear safety goggles anytime there is the slightest chance that your eyes could be harmed. | If anything gets into your eyes, notify your teacher immediately and flush your eyes with running water for 15 minutes. |
| Clothing protection | Wear your apron whenever you are working with chemicals or whenever you are instructed to do so. | If you spill a corrosive chemical onto your clothing, rinse it off immediately by using a faucet or the safety shower and remove the affected clothing while calling to your teacher. |
| Hand safety | Wear appropriate protective gloves when working with an open flame, chemicals, or plants. Your teacher will provide the type of gloves necessary for a given activity. Wash your hands with soap and hot water at the end of every lab. | If any chemical gets on your hands, rinse it off immediately with water for at least 5 minutes while calling to your teacher. Report any burn of the hands to your teacher no matter how minor it seems. |
| Safety with Gases | Do not inhale any gas or vapor unless directed to do so by your teacher. Handle materials that emit vapors or gases in a well-ventilated area. | Notify your teacher immediately if you have inhaled a gas or vapor, or if your eyes, nose, or throat become irritated. |
| Hygienic Care | Keep you hands away from your face, hair, and mouth while you are working on any activity. Wash your hands thoroughly before you leave the lab or when you finish any activity. Remove contaminated clothing immediately. | Notify your teacher immediately if you spill corrosive substances on your skin or clothing no matter how minor it seems. Use the safety shower or faucet to rinse. Remove affected clothing while you are under the shower and call to your teacher. |
| Sharp/pointed object safety | Use knives and other sharp objects with extreme care. Place objects on a suitable work surface for cutting. | Notify your teacher immediately in the event of a cut or puncture no matter how minor it seems. |
| Animal care and safety | Handle animals only as your teacher directs. Treat animals carefully and respectfully. Wash your hands thoroughly after handling any animal. | Notify your teacher immediately if you injure yourself or any live specimen no matter how minor the injury seems. |
| Glassware Safety | Inspect glassware before use; do not use chipped or cracked glassware. | Notify your teacher immediately if a piece of glassware or a light bulb breaks. |
| Electrical safety | Do not place electrical cords where they could trip someone or cause equipment to fall. Do not use equipment with damaged cords. Do not use electrical equipment near water or when your clothing or hands are wet. Make sure that electrical equipment is in the "off" position before plugging it in. Turn off and unplug electrical equipment when you have finished using it. | Notify your teacher immediately if you notice any abnormal or potentially dangerous equipment. In the event of an electric shock, notify your teacher no matter how minor it seems. |
| Chemical safety | Wear safety goggles, an apron, and gloves whenever working with chemicals. | If a chemical spills onto your skin, rinse it off immediately by using the faucet or safety shower for at least 5 minutes while calling to your teacher. |
| Proper waste disposal | Dispose of contaminated materials in special containers only as directed by your teacher. Dispose of sharp objects in the appropriate sharps container as directed by your teacher. Clean and sanitize all work surfaces and personal protective equipment after each lab period. | Notify your teacher immediately if a piece of glassware or a light bulb breaks. Dispose of broken glass in the appropriate container as directed by your teacher. Notify your teacher immediately if you spill a chemical or culture of microorganisms. Follow your teacher's instructions for clean up. |
| Heating safety | Wear safety goggles when using a heating device or flame. Wear heat-resistant gloves when instructed to do so. When heating materials in a test tube, angle the test tube away from yourself and others. | Notify your teacher immediately in the event of a burn or fire no matter how minor it seems. |
| Plant safety | Do not eat any part of a plant or plant seed. When in nature, do not pick any wild plants unless your teacher instructs you to do so. Wash your hands thoroughly after handling any part of a plant. | Notify your teacher immediately if any potentially dangerous plant material comes into contact with your skin or if any plant matter is inhaled or ingested no matter how minor the event seems. |

# Commonly Used Word Parts

| Word Parts | | |
|---|---|---|
| **Word part** | **Definition** | **Example** |
| *amphi-* | both | amphibian: a type of vertebrate that lives both on land and in water |
| *ante-* | before | anterior: front of an organism |
| *anti-* | against | antibiotic: substance, such as penicillin, capable of killing bacteria |
| *arche-* | ancient | Archaeopteryx: an ancient, fossilized bird |
| *arthro-* | joint | arthritis: a painful disease affecting the joints |
| *bio-* | life | biology: the study of life |
| *chloro-* | green | chlorophyll: green pigment in plants; needed for photosynthesis |
| *chondro-* | cartilage | Chondrichthyes: fish whose skeletons are made of cartilage |
| *cyte-* | cell | cytology: the study of cells |
| *derm-* | skin | dermatology: the study of the skin |
| *ecto-* | outer, outside | ectoderm: the outer tissue layer in many organisms |
| *endo-* | inner, inside | endoderm: the inner tissue layer in many organisms |
| *gastro-* | stomach | gastritis: inflammation of the stomach or stomach lining |
| *gen-* | produce | generate: to make, produce, or bring into being |
| *hemi-* | half | hemisphere: half of a sphere |
| *hetero-* | different | heterogeneous: made of unrelated or various parts |
| *homeo-* | the same | homeostasis: maintaining steady internal conditions |
| *hydro-* | water | hydroponics: growing plants in water instead of soil |
| *hyper-* | above, over | hypertension: blood pressure that is higher than normal |
| *hypo-* | below, under | hypothermic: body temperature that is below normal |
| *inter-* | between, among | interpersonal: relationships between or among people |
| *intra-* | within | intracellular: inside a cell |
| *-logy* | study of | biology: the study of life |
| *macro-* | large | macromolecule: large molecule, such as DNA or a protein |
| *mega-* | large | megaspore: a large spore produced by some ferns and flowering pants |
| *meta-* | change | metamorphosis: change in form |
| *micro-* | small | microscope: a tool for looking at very small objects |
| *morph-* | form | morphology: the study of the form of an organism |
| *neo-* | new | neonatal: newborn |
| *para-* | near, on | parasite: organism that lives on and feeds on another organism |
| *peri-* | around | pericardium: the membrane around the heart |
| *photo-* | light | phototropism: bending of plants toward light |
| *-phyte-* | plant | epiphyte: plant that lives on another plant, as in the branches of trees |
| *poly-* | many | polypeptide: many amino acids joined together to make a protein |
| *pre-* | before | prediction: a forecast of events before they take place |
| *semi-* | partially | semitransparent: allowing some, but not all, light to pass through |
| *sub-* | under | submarine: a boat that travels underwater |
| *syn-* | with | synapse: a place where two or more nerves come together |
| *trans-* | across | transcontinental: going across a continent |

# HOLT NEW YORK BIOLOGY

# THE Living Environment

DeSalle • Heithaus

**HOLT, RINEHART AND WINSTON**
A Harcourt Education Company
Orlando • Austin • New York • San Diego • London

Printed in the United States of America

ISBN-13: 978-0-03-093459-9
ISBN-10: 0-03-093459-1

8 9 10 11 12 0868 14 13 12 11 10 4500255518

# Authors

## Robert DeSalle, Ph.D.

is a curator in the Division of Invertebrate Zoology at the American Museum of Natural History in New York City. He is an adjunct professor at Columbia University and City University of New York, and is a Distinguished Research Professor at New York University. His current research focuses on molecular evolution in various organisms, including pathogenic bacteria and insects. He coauthored *Welcome to the Genome: A User's Guide to the Genetic Past, Present, and Future* (Wiley) and *The Science of Jurassic Park and the Lost World* (HarperCollins), and he edited *Epidemic! The World of Infectious Diseases* (W. W. Norton), which are all aimed at nontechnical readers.

## Michael R. Heithaus, Ph.D.

is an assistant professor of biological sciences at Florida International University and a former host of National Geographic's *Crittercam* television program. He currently works with the National Geographic Channel to develop programming and educational materials and to give talks to students. His current research centers on predator-prey interactions among marine vertebrates. Mike's research in animal behavior has taken him all over the world to deploy Crittercam on a host of marine and terrestrial animal species, including dolphins, sharks, seals, sea turtles, whales, lions, hyenas, and, most recently, penguins.

# Contributing Authors

**Linda K. Gaul, Ph.D.**
is an epidemiologist at the Texas Department of State Health Services. She conducts surveillance and epidemiological investigations related to infectious diseases. She has taught both biology and epidemiology at the college level.

**Shubha Govind, Ph.D.**
is a professor of biology at City College, New York. Her current research focuses on the function of proteins as cellular signaling molecules in the immune response and in animal development.

**Ann Lumsden, Ph.D.**
is a professor of biological science at Florida State University, where she is the coordinator of biology classes for nonmajors. She is a former president of the National Association of Biology Teachers.

**Ellen Mandel**
is the assistant principal and supervisor for Science at a New York City public high school. She is also a New York Biology Mentor, and an active science administrator in many state organizations.

**Alan Seidman**
is a teacher of biology, chemistry, and current topics in science at Margaretville Central School in Margaretville, New York. He is also a Fellow of the Science Teachers Association of New York State.

**Erika Zavaleta, Ph.D.**
is an assistant professor in the environmental-studies department of the University of California, Santa Cruz. Her current research centers on how changes in levels of biodiversity affect society.

# BIOLOGY CAREER

## Ecologist

**Erika Zavaleta**

UNIT 2

Erika Zavaleta is an assistant professor in the Environmental Studies department of the University of California, Santa Cruz. Her current research focuses on changes in levels of biodiversity in biological communities and ecosystems that result from environmental challenges and changes.

A high school science teacher, Dr. Roberts, inspired Zavaleta to become a scientist. Roberts used scientific nonfiction and an inquiry-based approach to inspire her students. Zavaleta still loves to read and engage scientific problems with a creative and open mind.

Zavaleta considers her greatest accomplishment in science to be bridging scientific disciplines to explore changes from many angles. These changes include climate change, the invasive species, the ecological and socioeconomic implications of losing biodiversity, and woodland restoration.

Apart from science, Zavaleta enjoys traveling, reading, and outdoor activities such as surfing, bodyboarding, bicycling, hiking, and backpacking.

Hamster and grasshopper predator-prey relationship

# Chapter 4 Ecosystems

## Preview



## Why It Matters

An ecosystem is a community of organisms that interact with one another and their physical environment. Humans are part of ecosystems and are dependent on healthy ecosystems. However, humans can disrupt ecosystems, and the disruption may harm the organisms of the ecosystems and humans themselves.

***The Living Environment***

**Standard 4** Students will understand and apply scientific concepts, principles, and theories pertaining to the physical setting and living environment and recognize the historical development of ideas in science.

**Key Idea 1** Living things are both similar to and different from each other and from nonliving things. ***Major Understandings*** **- 1.1a, 1.1b, 1.1e**

**Key Idea 5** Organisms maintain a dynamic equilibrium that sustains life. ***Major Understandings*** **- 5.1a**

**Key Idea 6** Plants and animals depend on each other and their physical environment. ***Major Understandings*** **- 6.1a, 6.1b, 6.1c, 6.1e, 6.3b, 6.3c**

**Key Idea 7** Human decisions and activities have had a profound impact on the physical and living environment. ***Major Understandings*** **- 7.1b**

**Organisms in ecosystems interact with each other. This small fish has an unusual predator—a spider. This fishing spider from French Guiana waits at the surface of the water for its prey.**

Some species of fishing spiders can walk on the water's surface, aided by fine hairs on the legs which trap air and act as buoys.

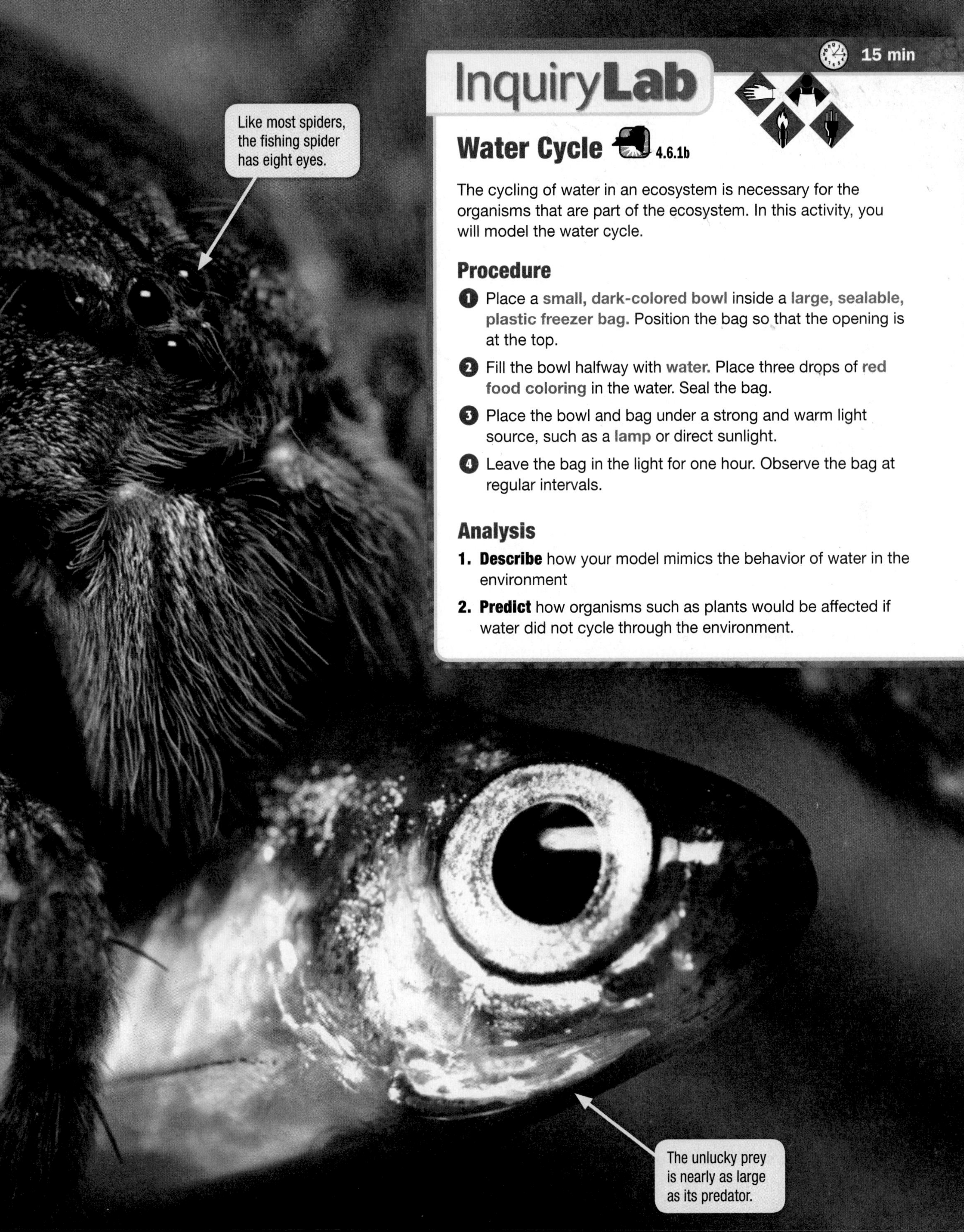

Like most spiders, the fishing spider has eight eyes.
The unlucky prey is nearly as large as its predator.

15 min

# InquiryLab

## Water Cycle 4.6.1b

The cycling of water in an ecosystem is necessary for the organisms that are part of the ecosystem. In this activity, you will model the water cycle.

### Procedure

1. Place a **small, dark-colored bowl** inside a **large, sealable, plastic freezer bag.** Position the bag so that the opening is at the top.
2. Fill the bowl halfway with **water.** Place three drops of **red food coloring** in the water. Seal the bag.
3. Place the bowl and bag under a strong and warm light source, such as a **lamp** or direct sunlight.
4. Leave the bag in the light for one hour. Observe the bag at regular intervals.

### Analysis

1. **Describe** how your model mimics the behavior of water in the environment
2. **Predict** how organisms such as plants would be affected if water did not cycle through the environment.

These reading tools can help you learn the material in this chapter. For more information on how to use these and other tools, see **Appendix: Reading and Study Skills.**

## Using Words

**Word Families** Word families include words that can be combined to create a meaning that differs from the meaning of each word in the combination. The names of natural cycles of Earth are formed from word families that you will find in this chapter.

**Your Turn** Use the information in the table to answer the following questions.

1. What do you think happens in the carbon, water, and phosphorus cycles?
2. How do the three cycles differ?

**Word Parts**

| Word part | Type | Meaning |
|---|---|---|
| *carbon* | noun | an element common to all living things |
| *water* | noun | a liquid necessary for life |
| *phosphorus* | noun | a chemically reactive, nonmetallic element |
| *cycle* | noun | a circular process |

## Using Language

**Word Problems** Read word problems several times before trying to solve them. After you understand what the problems are asking, write down all of the relevant information on a piece of paper. Then, use the mathematical processes that apply to the situation.

**Your Turn** Solve the following word problem about energy.

1. When a snake a eats a mouse, only about 10% of the energy stored in the mouse's body is stored in the snake. If the body of a mouse contains 2000 kcal of energy, how much energy is stored in the snake?

## Using FoldNotes

**Layered Book** A layered book is a useful tool for taking notes as you read a chapter. The four flaps of the layered book can summarize information into four categories. Write details of each category on the appropriate flap to create a summary of the chapter.

**Your Turn** Create a layered book FoldNote.

1. Lay one sheet of paper on top of another sheet. Slide the top sheet up so that 2 cm of the bottom sheet is showing.
2. Holding the two sheets together, fold down the top of the two sheets so that you see four 2 cm tabs along the bottom.
3. Using a stapler, staple the top of the FoldNote.
4. On each tab, write the category of the information that will appear on that layer.

Section 1

# What Is an Ecosystem?

| Key Ideas | Key Terms | Why It Matters |
|---|---|---|
| ❯ What are the parts of an ecosystem?<br>❯ How does an ecosystem respond to change?<br>❯ What two key factors of climate determine a biome?<br>❯ What are the three major groups of terrestrial biomes?<br>❯ What are the four kinds of aquatic ecosystems? | community<br>ecosystem<br>habitat<br>biodiversity<br>succession<br>climate<br>biome | Ecosystems are important units of the natural world. Humans are part of ecosystems and depend on ecosystems for food and many products. Without healthy ecosystems, humans would be in trouble! |

When you walk through a forest, you see many different organisms. There are trees, birds, ants, mushrooms, and much more. You may not see many of these organisms interact. But all organisms, including humans, that live together are interdependent.

## Ecosystems

A species never lives alone. A group of various species that live in the same place and interact with one another is called a **community.** The group, along with the living and nonliving environment, make up an **ecosystem.** ❯ **An ecosystem includes a community of organisms and their physical environment.**

**Community of Organisms** A community of organisms is a web of relationships. One relationship is that of a predator eating its prey. For example, some fish eat spiders, as **Figure 1** shows. Some species help each other. For example, some bacteria fix nitrogen into a form that plants can use to grow. Relationships between organisms are examples of biotic factors that affect an ecosystem. *Biotic* describes living factors in an ecosystem. Biotic factors also include once-living things, such as dead organisms and the waste of organisms.

***The Living Environment***
**Standard 4**
**1.1b** An ecosystem is shaped by the nonliving environment as well as its interacting species. The world contains a wide diversity of physical conditions, which creates a variety of environments.
**1.1e** Ecosystems, like many other complex systems, tend to show cyclic changes around a state of approximate equilibrium.
**6.1e** In any particular environment, the growth and survival of organisms depend on the physical conditions including light intensity, temperature range, mineral availability, soil/rock type, and relative acidity (pH).
**6.3b** Through ecological succession, all ecosystems progress through a sequence of changes during which one ecological community modifies the environment, making it more suitable for another community. These long-term gradual changes result in the community reaching a point of stability that can last for hundreds or thousands of years.
**6.3c** A stable ecosystem can be altered, either rapidly or slowly, through the activities of organisms (including humans), or through climatic changes or natural disasters. The altered ecosystem can usually recover through gradual changes back to a point of longterm stability.

**community** a group of various species that live in the same habitat and interact with each other

**ecosystem** a community of organisms and their abiotic environment

**Figure 1** In this relationship, the fish is the predator, and the spider is the prey. ❯ **Give another example of a relationship between two species in a community.**

Hands-On

30 min

## Biodiversity Evaluation 4.1.1b, 4.6.1.d

By making simple observations, you can draw some conclusions about biodiversity in an ecosystem.

### Procedure

**CAUTION: Follow your teacher's instructions about sun protection handling organisms.** Prepare a list of biotic and abiotic factors to observe around your home or in a nearby park, and record your observations.

### Analysis

1. **Identify** the habitat and community that you observed.
2. **Calculate** the number of different species as a percentage of the total number of organisms that you saw.
3. **Rank** the importance of biotic factors within the ecosystem that you observed.
4. **Infer** what the relationships are between biotic factors and abiotic factors in the observed ecosystem.

**habitat** a place where an organism usually lives

**biodiversity** the variety of organisms in a given area, the genetic variation within a population, the variety of species in a community, or the variety of communities in an ecosystem

**succession** the replacement of one type of community by another at a single location over a period of time

**Physical Factors** The physical or nonliving factors of an environment are called *abiotic factors*. Examples of abiotic factors are oxygen, water, rocks, sand, sunlight, temperature, and climate. These physical factors shape organisms. For example, plants and animals in deserts are small because deserts do not have enough water to support large organisms. Water supply also affects the number of individuals and variety of species that an ecosystem can support. A crop of corn will have a higher yield in a wetter habitat than in a drier habitat. A **habitat** is the place where an organism lives.

**Biodiversity** Suppose you counted the various species in a pine forest. Then, you counted the number of species in a tropical rain forest. Do you think the number of species in each ecosystem would be the same? No, a tropical rain forest has many more species than a pine forest does. The variety of organisms in a given area is called **biodiversity.**

Physical factors can have a big influence on biodiversity. In places that have very high or very low temperatures, biodiversity is often lower. Limited water and food also cause lower biodiversity. The biodiversity of habitats and ecosystems varies greatly. The vast expanse of the open ocean has very low biodiversity. In contrast, rain forests and coral reefs have very high biodiversity. When ecosystems have high biodiversity, they are often more able to resist damage. Damage to ecosystems can be caused by severe weather events or human activities. Systems with low biodiversity can be severely damaged easily. When biodiversity decreases in any ecosystem, that ecosystem is not as healthy as it could be.

› **Reading Check** *List three examples of physical parts of an ecosystem. (See the Appendix for answers to Reading Checks.)*

## Succession

When we observe an ecosystem, it may look like an unchanging feature of the landscape. However, all ecosystems change. As an ecosystem changes, the kinds of species that the ecosystem supports change. The replacement of one community by another at a single place over a period of time is called **succession.**

**Change in an Ecosystem** When a volcano forms a new island or a fire burns the vegetation of an area, new opportunities are made for organisms. The first organisms to appear in a newly made habitat are called *pioneer species*. Pioneer species are often small, fast-growing plants that reproduce quickly. They change the habitat in such a way that other species can live in the ecosystem. For example, pioneer species such as lichens and mosses will break down volcanic rock on a new island to help form soil. Other species can then grow on the soil. For example, after lichens and mosses have formed soil, grasses and weeds may then cover a volcanic island. Even later, shrubs and trees often outcompete and replace the grass. Then, the grassland turns into a forest. **Figure 2** shows an example of succession in response to the receding of a glacier.

**Equilibrium** If a major disruption strikes a community, many of the organisms may be wiped out. But the ecosystem reacts to the change. ❯ **An ecosystem responds to change in such a way that the ecosystem is restored to equilibrium.** When a tree falls down in a rain forest, for example, the newly vacant patch proceeds through succession until the patch returns to its original state. Sometimes, the ecosystem will find an equilibrium in which different species dominate after a change. In the grasslands of Africa, for example, weather conditions can lead to succession. When there is a lot of rain in the grasslands, one species of grass dominates the savanna. But when conditions are drier, a drought-resistant species of grass will dominate.

❯ **Reading Check** ***Why are pioneer species helpful to other species?***

**Figure 2** At Glacier Bay in Alaska, a receding glacier makes succession possible.

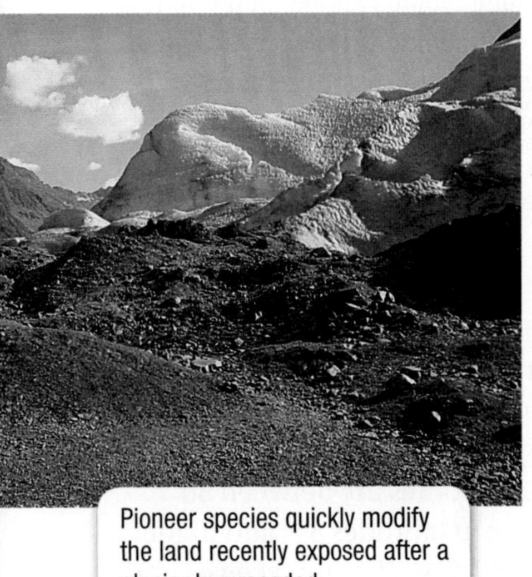

Pioneer species quickly modify the land recently exposed after a glacier has receded.

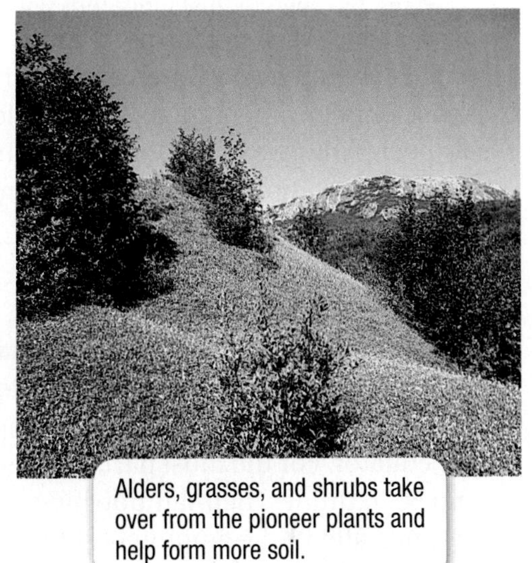

Alders, grasses, and shrubs take over from the pioneer plants and help form more soil.

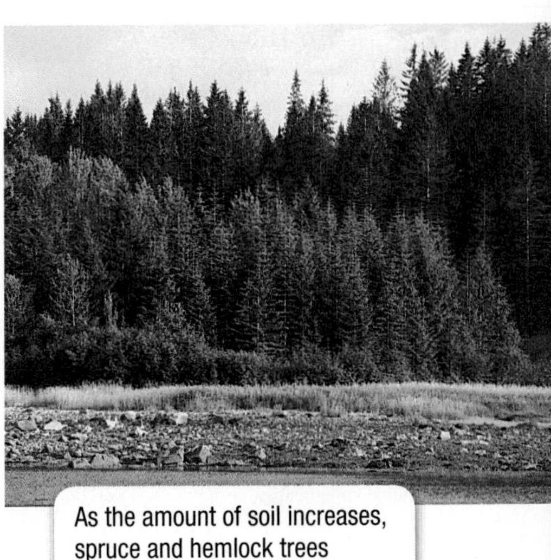

As the amount of soil increases, spruce and hemlock trees become plentiful.

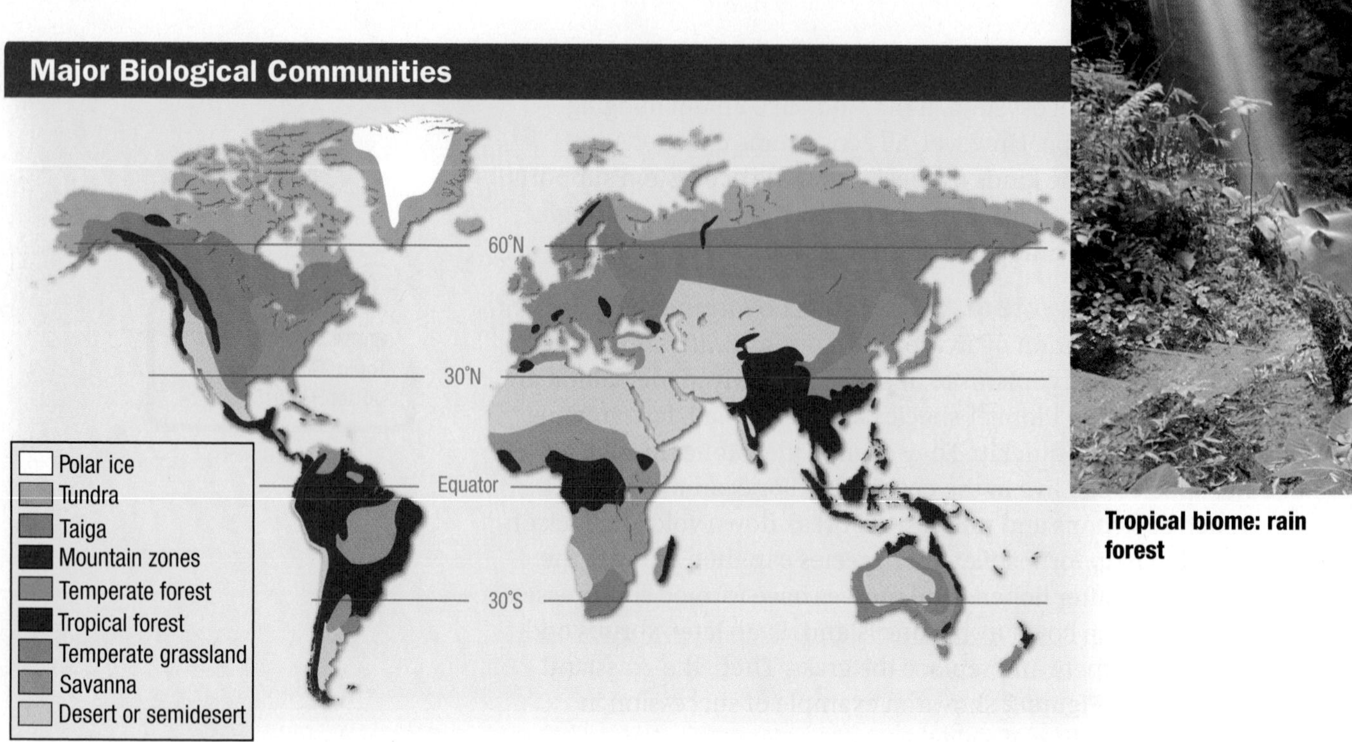


**Figure 3** Biomes cover most of Earth's land surface. Because mountainous areas do not belong to any one biome, they are given their own designation. Polar ice covers Greenland and Antarctica, which is not shown in the map. **❯ Identify the biome that you live in.**

## Major Biological Communities

If you drive across the United States, you notice a change in the kinds of plants and animals. The kinds of species that live in a particular place are determined partly by climate. **Climate** is the average weather conditions in an area over a long period of time. At places near the North Pole, you may see polar bears. Polar bears have thick, white fur and insulating fat that keep them warm on the frozen tundra. The same adaptations that help polar bears in the tundra would hurt polar bears in a tropical forest. Polar bears must live in a biome to which they are adapted. A **biome** is a large region characterized by a specific kind of climate and certain kinds of plant and animal communities.

**❯ Two key factors of climate that determine biomes are temperature and precipitation.** Most organisms are adapted to live within a particular range of temperatures and cannot survive at temperatures too far above or below that range. Precipitation also determines the kinds of species that are found in a biome. In biomes where precipitation is low, for example, the vegetation is made up mostly of plants that need little water, such as cactuses.

**Academic Vocabulary**

**range** a scale or series between limits

**climate** the average weather conditions in an area over a long period of time

**biome** a large region characterized by a specific type of climate and certain types of plant and animal communities

## Terrestrial Biomes

There are many different biomes on land. **❯ Earth's major terrestrial biomes can be grouped by latitude into tropical, temperate, and high-latitude biomes.** As **Figure 3** shows, tropical biomes are generally near the equator. For the most part, temperate biomes are between 30° and 60° latitude. High-latitude biomes are at latitudes 60° and higher. Latitude affects the amount of solar energy that a biome receives and thus affects a biome's temperature range.

Temperate biome: temperate grasslands

Polar biome: taiga

**Tropical Biomes** Because they are located at low latitudes near the equator, all tropical biomes are warm. However, each tropical biome receives a different amount of rain. *Tropical rain forests* receive large amounts of rain and are warm all year. They have the greatest biodiversity of any land biome. At least half of Earth's species of land organisms live in tropical rain forests. *Savannas* are tropical grasslands. They get less rain than tropical rain forests do. Savannas also have long dry seasons and shorter wet seasons. The most well-known savannas are in eastern Africa, where zebras, giraffes, lions, and elephants roam the grasslands. *Tropical deserts* get very little rain. Because the deserts have less water, they have fewer plants and animals than other biomes do.

**Temperate Biomes** Biomes at mid-latitudes have a wide range of temperatures throughout the year. *Temperate grasslands* have moderate precipitation and cooler temperatures than savannas do. Temperate grasslands are often highly productive when used for agriculture. Herds of grazing animals, like bison, used to live on the temperate grasslands of North America. *Temperate forests* grow in mild climates that receive plenty of rain. Trees of the temperate deciduous forests shed their leaves in the fall because of the cold winters. Trees of temperate evergreen forests do not lose their leaves or needles during the winter. Temperate forests are home to deer, bears, beavers, and raccoons. Like tropical deserts, *temperate deserts* receive little precipitation. However, unlike tropical deserts, temperate deserts have a wide temperature range throughout the year.

**High-Latitude Biomes** Biomes at high latitudes have cold temperatures. Coniferous forests in cold, wet climates are called *taiga*. Winters are long and cold. Most of the precipitation falls in the summer. Moose, wolves, and bears live in the taiga. The *tundra* gets very little rain, so plants are short. Much of the water in the soil is not available because the water is frozen for most of the year. Foxes, lemmings, owls, and caribous live in the tundra.

› **Reading Check** ***In what latitudes are savannas found?***

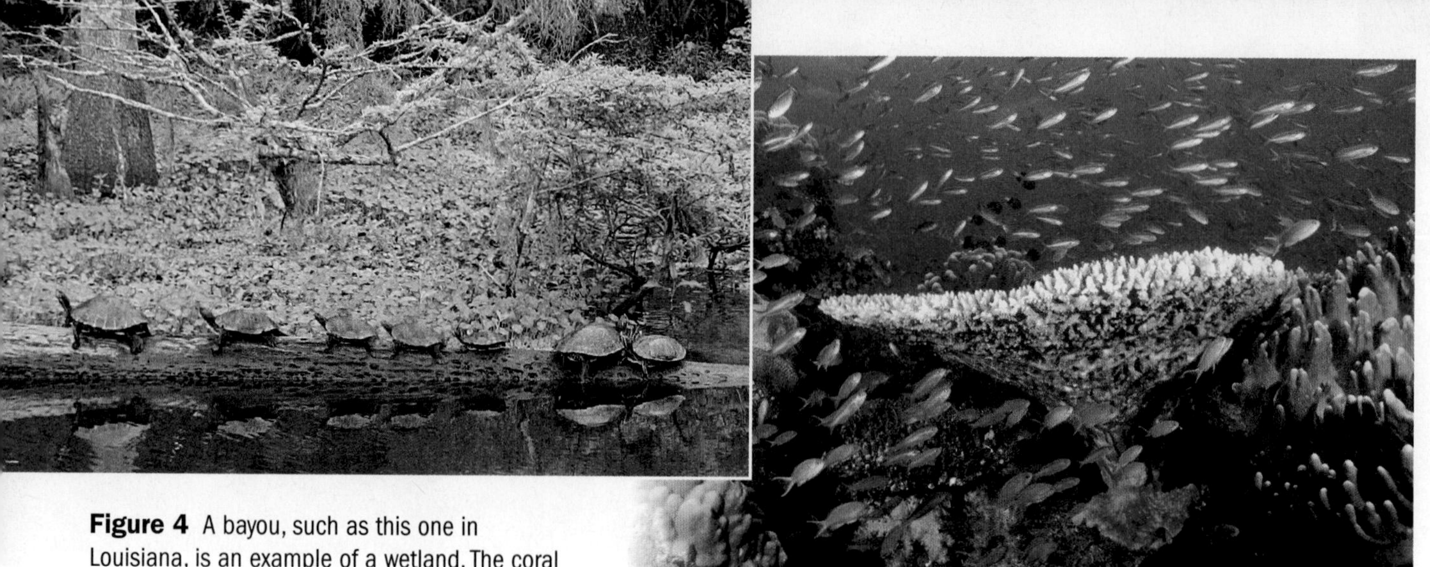

**Figure 4** A bayou, such as this one in Louisiana, is an example of a wetland. The coral reef is an example of a marine ecosystem.

## Aquatic Ecosystems

The diverse regions in the world's bodies of water are not usually called *biomes*. They are often called *aquatic ecosystems*. **Aquatic ecosystems are organized into freshwater ecosystems, wetlands, estuaries, and marine ecosystems.**

*Freshwater ecosystems* are located in bodies of fresh water, such as lakes, ponds, and rivers. These ecosystems have a variety of plants, fish, arthropods, mollusks, and other invertebrates.

*Wetlands* provide a link between the land and fully aquatic habitats. Water-loving plants dominate wetlands. This ecosystem supports many species of birds, fishes, and plants, as shown in **Figure 4.** Wetlands are important because they moderate flooding and clean the water that flows through them.

An *estuary* is an area where fresh water from a river mixes with salt water from an ocean. Estuaries are productive ecosystems because they constantly receive fresh nutrients from the river and the ocean.

*Marine ecosystems* are found in the salty waters of the oceans. Kelp forests, seagrass communities, and coral reefs are found near land. The open ocean, far from land, has plankton and large predators, such as dolphins, whales, and sharks.

**Reading Check** ***Which aquatic ecosystems have salt water?***

**READING TOOLBOX**

**Word Families** Use a dictionary to find the meanings of the words *aquatic* and *ecosystem*. Then, use the definitions to write your own definition of *aquatic ecosystem*.

SCILINKS.
**www.scilinks.org**
Topic: Estuaries
Code: HX80536

## Section 1 Review

### KEY IDEAS

1. **Describe** the difference between an ecosystem and a community.
2. **Explain** how an ecosystem responds to change.
3. **Identify** the three major groups of terrestrial biomes.
4. **Describe** the four types of aquatic ecosystems.
5. **Identify** two factors of climate that determine a biome.

### CRITICAL THINKING

6. **Relating Concepts** If two areas on separate continents have similar climates, do they have similar communities? Explain your answer.

### WRITING FOR SCIENCE

7. **Essay** Identify a biome in which the plants are short and require little water and the animals are small. Then, write a one page description of this biome.

Why It Matters

# Maintained by Fire

REAL WORLD

When a fire sweeps through a forest, the fire destroys just about everything in its path. But did you know that fire can actually be a good thing for certain communities? In fact, fire is important for preserving many plant communities and the animals that depend on them.

## Fire Lovers

Some plants benefit from fire. Fireweed, a plant with purple flowers as shown in this burned forest in Alaska, is one such plant. Fireweed gets its name because it quickly colonizes burned land without competition from other species. Other species of plants need fire in order to reproduce! The jack pine is one such species. The jack pine can release seeds only after it is exposed to the intense heat of a fire.

**Ecosystem on Fire**
Firefighters often light fires on purpose. This firefighter in South Dakota is setting a controlled fire because burned vegetation helps bring nutrients to the soil.

**Research** Find out more about controlled fires. Why must controlled fires be set in some ecosystems? What are the advantages and disadvantages of controlled fires?

Section 2

# Energy Flow in Ecosystems

| Key Ideas | Key Terms | Why It Matters |
|---|---|---|
| ❯ How does energy flow through an ecosystem?<br>❯ What happens to energy as it is transferred between trophic levels in a community? | producer<br>consumer<br>decomposer<br>trophic level<br>energy pyramid | The way in which energy flows through an ecosystem is critical to the ecosystem's productivity and ability to support its species. By understanding this flow of energy, we can learn how to develop food more efficiently. |

***The Living Environment***
**Standard 4**

**1.1a** Populations can be categorized by the function they serve. Food webs identify the relationships among producers, consumers, and decomposers carrying out either autotropic or heterotropic nutrition.

**5.1.a** The energy for life comes primarily from the Sun. Photosynthesis provides a vital connection between the Sun and the energy needs of living systems.

**6.1a** Energy flows through ecosystems in one direction, typically from the Sun, through photosynthetic organisms including green plants and algae, to herbivores to carnivores and decomposers.

**6.1b** Carbon dioxide and water molecules used in photosynthesis to form energy-rich organic compounds are returned to the environment when the energy in these compounds is eventually released by cells. Continual input of energy from sunlight keeps the process going. This concept may be illustrated with an energy pyramid.

**6.1c** At each link in a food web, some energy is stored in newly made structures but much is dissipated into the environment as heat.

SCiLINKS.
**www.scilinks.org**
Topic: Food Webs
Code: HX80600

Everything that organisms do requires energy. Running, breathing, and even sleeping require energy. Every species must somehow get food for energy. A zebra grazes on savanna grass. A lion chases down the zebra and eats it. The lion eventually dies and is eaten by scavengers. The rest of the carcass is decomposed by bacteria and other microbes. At each step in this process, energy flows through the ecosystem.

## Trophic Levels

An organism eating another organism is the most obvious interaction in a community. This interaction transfers energy through an ecosystem. The way in which energy flows through an ecosystem determines how many species and individuals live in the ecosystem.

The primary source of energy for an ecosystem is the sun. Photosynthetic organisms, such as plants and algae, change light energy from the sun into energy that they can use to grow. These photosynthetic organisms are **producers,** the basic food source for an ecosystem. **Consumers** are organisms that eat other organisms instead of producing their own food. **Decomposers,** such as bacteria and fungi, are organisms that break down the remains of animals. **❯ In an ecosystem, energy flows from the sun to producers to consumers to decomposers.** Each step in the transfer of energy through an ecosystem is called a **trophic level. Figure 5** shows the trophic levels through which energy passes to a blue jay.

**❯ Reading Check** ***Where do consumers get their energy?***

**Figure 5** Each step in the transfer of energy through an ecosystem is called a *trophic level.*

The sun is the primary energy source.

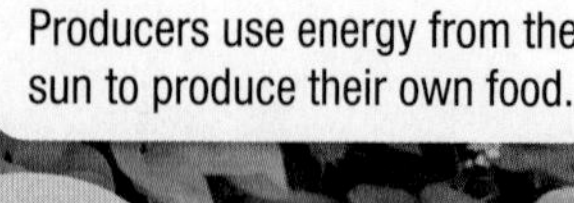

Producers use energy from the sun to produce their own food.

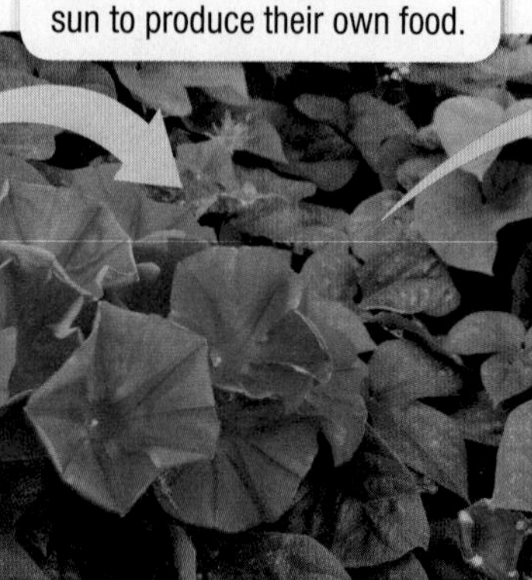

Some consumers eat producers to get energy.

Some consumers eat other consumers.

**Food Chains** In ecosystems, energy flows from one trophic level to the next, forming a *food chain.* The first trophic level of ecosystems is made up of producers. Plants, algae, and some bacteria use the energy in sunlight to build energy-rich carbohydrates. The second trophic level of a food chain is made up of *herbivores,* which eat producers. Cows are an example of an herbivore. The third trophic level includes animals that eat herbivores. Any animal that eats another animal is a *carnivore.* Some carnivores are on the third trophic level because they eat herbivores. For example, small birds eat caterpillars, which feed on plant leaves. Other carnivores are on the fourth trophic level or an even higher trophic level because they eat other carnivores. For example, hawks eat small birds. *Omnivores,* such as bears, are animals that are both herbivores and carnivores.

**Food Web** In most ecosystems, energy does not follow a simple food chain. Energy flow is much more complicated. Ecosystems almost always have many more species than a single food chain has. In addition, most organisms eat more than one kind of food. For example, hawks eat fish, small birds, and rabbits. Rabbits are food not only for hawks but also for wolves, mountain lions, and many other carnivores. This complicated, interconnected group of food chains, such as the group in **Figure 6,** is called a *food web.*

**producer** a photosynthetic or chemosynthetic autotroph that serves as the basic food source in an ecosystem

**consumer** an organism that eats other organisms or organic matter instead of producing its own nutrients or obtaining nutrients from inorganic sources

**decomposer** an organism that feeds by breaking down organic matter from dead organisms

**trophic level** one of the steps in a food chain or food pyramid

**Figure 6** A food web shows a more complete picture of the feeding relationships in an ecosystem. The arrows show the direction in which energy travels. **❯ In the diagram, identify the animals that receive energy from the rabbit.**

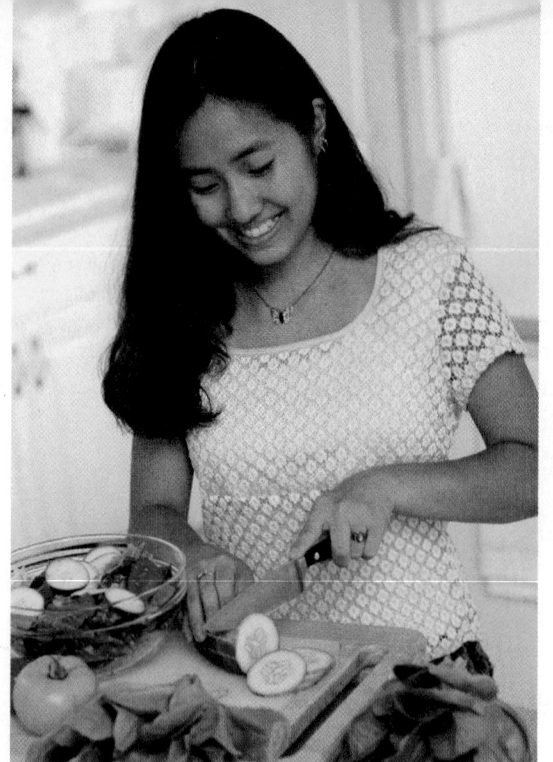

Figure 7 This girl is eating producers, which form the base of an energy pyramid.

## Loss of Energy

When a zebra eats 20 lb of grass, the zebra does not gain 20 lb. A lot of the energy that was stored in the grass is lost. Where did the energy go? **Energy is stored at each link in a food web. But some energy that is used dissipates as heat into the environment and is not recycled.**

**The Ten Percent Rule** When a zebra eats grass, some of the energy in the grass is stored in the zebra. The energy may be stored as fat or as tissue. However, most of the energy does not stay in the zebra. As the zebra uses energy from the grass to run and grow, the energy is changed into heat energy. Then, the heat energy is dispersed into the environment. Thus, the zebra does not keep 90% of the energy that it gets from the grass. Only about 10% of the energy in the grass becomes part of the zebra's body. This amount of stored energy is all that is available to organisms at the next trophic level that consume the zebra. For example, a 100 kg lion needs 1,000 kg of zebras. And combined, the zebras need 10,000 kg of plants!

By understanding energy flow between trophic levels, we can learn how to feed more people. If people eat big fish that are in the third trophic level, it takes 1,000 kg of producers to build 1 kg of human. If people eat cows that are in the second trophic level, 100 kg of producers are needed for 1 kg of human. If people, such as the girl in **Figure 7,** eat producers—such as vegetables, fruits, and grains—only 10 kg of producers are needed to produce 1 kg of human.

**Reading Check** ***When energy is transferred from one trophic level to another, where does 90% of the energy go?***

## Math Skills Energy Pyramid

This energy pyramid shows the trophic levels in a marine ecosystem. You can use the pyramid to help you understand how energy is transferred from one trophic level to another.

The base of a pyramid is the producer, which contains the most energy. Phytoplankton is the base of this pyramid. As energy is transferred from one trophic level to the next trophic level, 90% of the energy is lost. Only 10% of the energy is available to the next trophic level.

If the phytoplankton level has 10,000 units of energy, the amount of energy stored in the copepod level can be calculated as follows:

*10,000 units of energy × 10% = 1,000 units of energy*

The amount of energy stored in the herring level can be calculated as follows:

*1,000 units of energy × 10% = 100 units of energy*

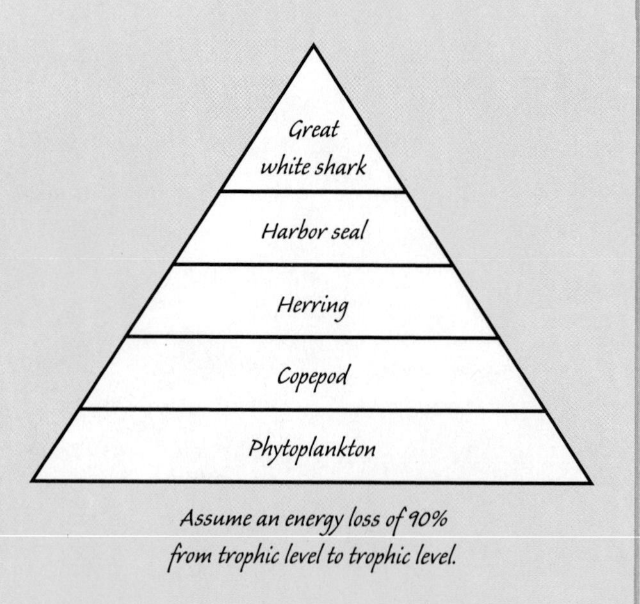

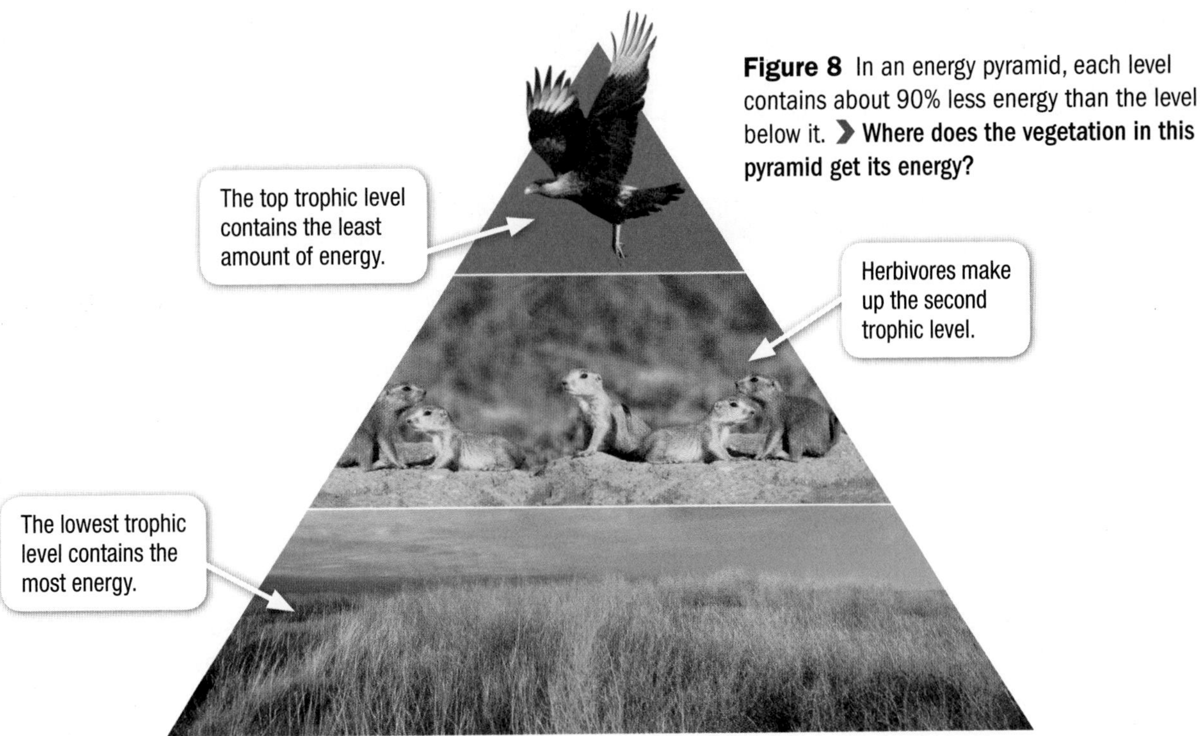
The top trophic level contains the least amount of energy.
Herbivores make up the second trophic level.
The lowest trophic level contains the most energy.

**Figure 8** In an energy pyramid, each level contains about 90% less energy than the level below it. **Where does the vegetation in this pyramid get its energy?**

**Energy Pyramid** A triangular diagram that shows an ecosystem's loss of energy, which results as energy passes through the ecosystem's food chain, is called an **energy pyramid.** An energy pyramid is shown in **Figure 8.** Each layer in the energy pyramid represents one trophic level. Producers form the pyramid's base, which is the lowest trophic level. The lowest level has the most energy in the pyramid. Herbivores have less energy and make up the second level. Carnivores that feed on herbivores make up the higher level. The energy stored by the organisms at each trophic level is about one-tenth the energy stored by the organisms in the level below. So, the diagram takes the shape of a pyramid.

Big predators, such as lions, are rare compared to herbivores. Big predators are rare because a lot more energy is required to support a single predator than a single herbivore. Many ecosystems do not have enough energy to support a large population of predators.

**energy pyramid** a triangular diagram that shows an ecosystem's loss of energy, which results as energy passes through the ecosystem's food chain

READING TOOLBOX

**Word Problem** If the prairie dog level in a food pyramid contains 35,000 units of energy, how much of that energy can be stored in the eagle level of the food pyramid?

## Section 2 Review

### KEY IDEAS

1. **Describe** how energy flows in an ecosystem.
2. **Explain** why only 10% of energy is transferred from one trophic level to the next.
3. **Describe** the difference between a herbivore, a carnivore, and an omnivore.

### CRITICAL THINKING

4. **Justifying Conclusions** What limits the length of food chains in an ecosystem?
5. **Evaluating an Argument** Explain why scientists believe that most animals would become extinct if all plants died.
6. **Analyzing Data** Which trophic level contains more energy: a trophic level of herbivores or a trophic level of carnivores? Why?

### USING SCIENCE GRAPHICS

7. **Creating Diagrams** Draw a diagram of a food web that has four trophic levels and at least one species that is an omnivore. Be sure to label producers, consumers, omnivores, and top predators. Label each trophic level.

Section

# 3 Cycling of Matter

| Key Ideas | Key Terms | Why It Matters |
|---|---|---|
| › What is the water cycle?<br>› Why are plants and animals important for carbon and oxygen in an ecosystem?<br>› Why must nitrogen cycle through an ecosystem?<br>› Why must phosphorus cycle through an ecosystem? | carbon cycle<br>respiration<br>nitrogen cycle<br>phosphorus cycle | Water, carbon, phosphorus, and nitrogen are critical resources for organisms, including humans. Natural cycles of these resources are important to ecosystems, but humans can disrupt these cycles. |

***The Living Environment***
**Standard 4**

**6.1b** The atoms and molecules on the Earth cycle among the living and nonliving components of the biosphere. For example, carbon dioxide and water molecules used in photosynthesis to form energy-rich organic compounds are returned to the environment when the energy in these compounds is eventually released by cells. Continual input of energy from sunlight keeps the process going. This concept may be illustrated with an energy pyramid.

**6.1c** The chemical elements, such as carbon, hydrogen, nitrogen, and oxygen, that make up the molecules of living things pass through food webs and are combined and recombined in different ways. At each link in a food web, some energy is stored in newly made structures but much is dissipated into the environment as heat.

**7.1b** Natural ecosystems provide an array of basic processes that affect humans. Those processes include but are not limited to: maintenance of the quality of the atmosphere, generation of soils, control of the water cycle, removal of wastes, energy flow, and recycling of nutrients. Humans are changing many of these basic processes and the changes may be detrimental.

Water, carbon, oxygen, nitrogen, and phosphorus are five of the most important substances for life. An ecosystem must be able to cycle these kinds of matter in order to support life.

## Water Cycle

Life could not exist without the *water cycle.* › **The water cycle continuously moves water between the atmosphere, the land, and the oceans.** As **Figure 9** shows, water vapor *condenses* and falls to Earth's surface as *precipitation*. Some of this water *percolates* into the soil and becomes groundwater. Other water runs across the surface of Earth into rivers, lakes, and oceans. Then, the water is heated by the sun and reenters the atmosphere by *evaporation*. Water also evaporates from trees and plants in a process called *transpiration*.

go.hrw.com
interact online
Keyword: HX8ECOF9

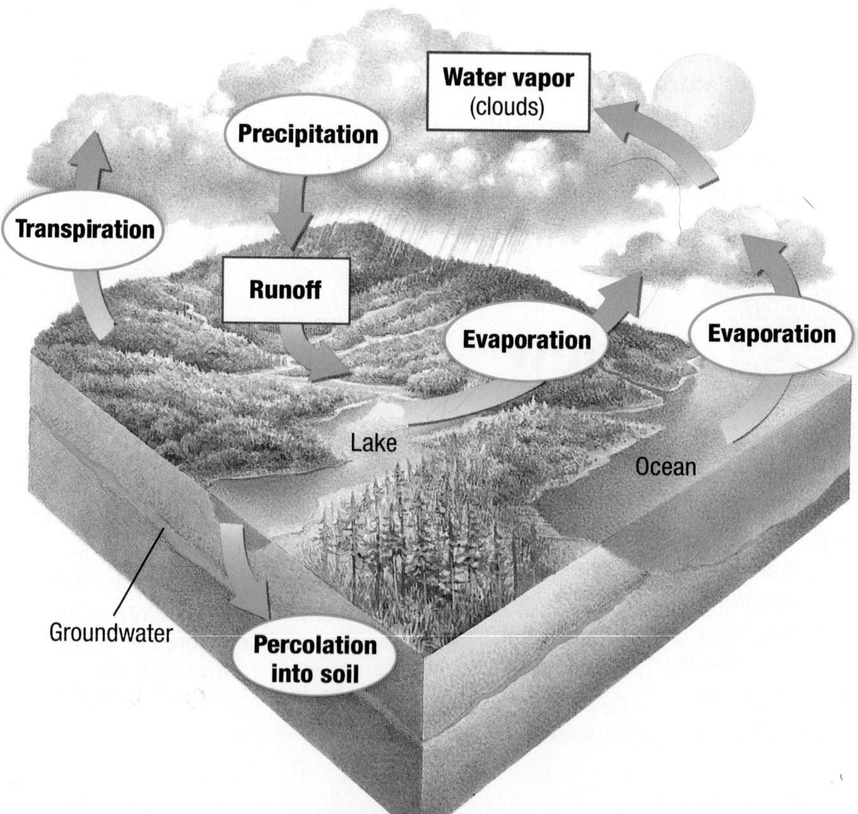


**Figure 9** Water cycles through ecosystems by the processes of transpiration, evaporation, condensation, precipitation and percolation.

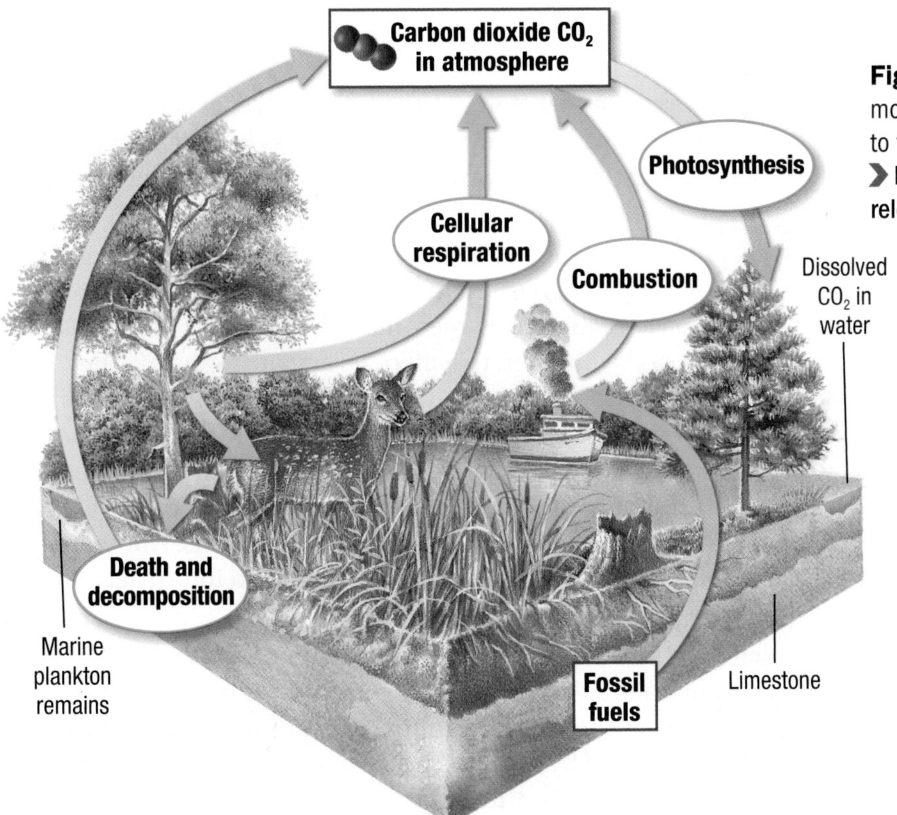


**Figure 10** In the carbon cycle, carbon moves from organisms to the atmosphere, to the soil, and to other living things. **› How is the carbon in fossil fuels released into the atmosphere?**

SCILINKS. www.scilinks.org Topic: Carbon Cycle Code: HX80216

## Carbon and Oxygen Cycles

Carbon and oxygen are critical for life on Earth, and their cycles are tied closely together. The **carbon cycle** is the continuous movement of carbon from the nonliving environment into living things and back. The carbon cycle is shown in **Figure 10.**

**› Animals, plants, and other photosynthesizing organisms play an important role in cycling carbon and oxygen through an ecosystem.** Plants use the carbon dioxide, $CO_2$, in air to build organic molecules during the process of photosynthesis. During photosynthesis, oxygen is released into the surroundings. Many organisms, such as animals, use this oxygen to help break down organic molecules, which releases energy and $CO_2$. Then, plants can use the $CO_2$ in photosynthesis. The process of exchanging oxygen and $CO_2$ between organisms and their surroundings is called **respiration.**

Carbon is also released into the atmosphere in the process of combustion. *Combustion* is the burning of a substance. All living things are made of carbon. When living things or once-living things are burned, they release carbon into the atmosphere. For example, the burning of trees releases carbon into the atmosphere as $CO_2$. Fossil fuels are formed from the remains of dead plants and animals. Thus, the burning of fossil fuels releases $CO_2$ into the atmosphere. Humans burn fossil fuels to generate electricity and to power vehicles. Examples of fossil fuels that humans burn are oil and coal.

**› Reading Check** ***How does respiration play a role in cycling carbon and oxygen through an ecosystem?***

**carbon cycle** the movement of carbon from the nonliving environment into living things and back

**respiration** the exchange of oxygen and carbon dioxide between living cells and their environment

**Word Families** Explain how the carbon cycle and the oxygen cycle are similar. Explain how they are different.

**nitrogen cycle** the cycling of nitrogen between organisms, soil, water, and the atmosphere

**phosphorus cycle** the cyclic movement of phosphorus in different chemical forms from the environment to organisms and then back to the environment

## Nitrogen Cycle

All organisms, including you, need nitrogen. **❯ Nitrogen must be cycled through an ecosystem so that the nitrogen is available for organisms to make proteins.** The **nitrogen cycle** is the process in which nitrogen circulates among the air, soil, water, and organisms in an ecosystem. The nitrogen cycle is shown in **Figure 11.**

The atmosphere is about 78% nitrogen gas, $N_2$. But most organisms cannot use nitrogen gas. It must be changed into a different form. A few bacteria have enzymes that can break down $N_2$. These bacteria supply the nitrogen that all other organisms need. The bacteria split $N_2$ and then bind nitrogen atoms to hydrogen to form ammonia, $NH_3$. The process of combining nitrogen with hydrogen to form ammonia is called *nitrogen fixation.* Nitrogen may be fixed by lightning. But more nitrogen is fixed by bacteria. Nitrogen-fixing bacteria live in the soil and on the roots of some plants. Nitrogen is also fixed when humans burn fuels in vehicles and industrial plants.

Plants get nitrogen by assimilation. *Assimilation* is the process in which plants absorb nitrogen. When an animal eats a plant, nitrogen compounds become part of the animal's body. During *ammonification,* nitrogen from animal waste or decaying bodies is returned to the soil by bacteria. Ammonia is then converted to nitrite and then nitrate by the process of *nitrification.* Finally, in *denitrification,* nitrate is changed to nitrogen gas, $N_2$, which returns to the atmosphere.

**ACADEMIC VOCABULARY**

**convert** to change from one form to another

**❯ Reading Check** ***Explain the role of bacteria in the nitrogen cycle.***

**Figure 11** Bacteria carry out many of the important steps in the nitrogen cycle, including the conversion of atmospheric nitrogen into a usable form, such as ammonia.

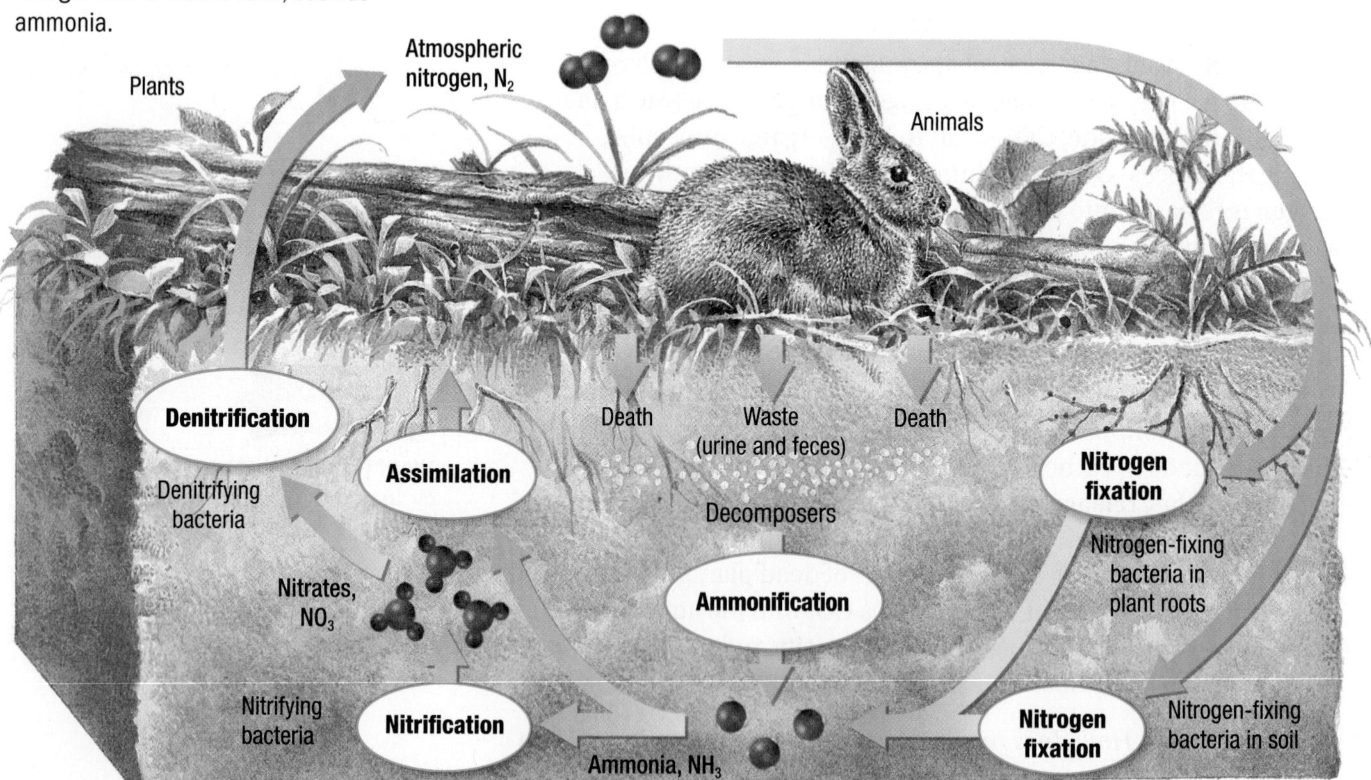

Hands-On

# QuickLab

## The Carbon Cycle 4.6.1.c

You are part of the carbon cycle. Every time that you exhale, you release $CO_2$ into the atmosphere. But the $CO_2$ does not stay as $CO_2$ for very long.

### Procedure

1. Pour **100 mL of water** into a **250 mL beaker.** Add **several drops of bromthymol blue** to the water. Add enough drops to make the solution dark blue.
2. **CAUTION: Be sure not to inhale or ingest the solution.** Exhale through a **straw** into the solution until the $CO_2$ in your breath turns the solution yellow.
3. Pour the yellow solution into a **large test tube** that contains a **sprig of Elodea.**
4. Use a **stopper** to seal the test tube. Then, place the test tube in a sunny location.
5. Observe the solution in the test tube after 15 min.

### Analysis

1. CRITICAL THINKING **Inferring Conclusions** What do you think happened to the carbon dioxide that you exhaled into the solution?
2. CRITICAL THINKING **Analyzing Methods** How do plants, such as the *Elodea,* affect the carbon cycle?

## Phosphorus Cycle

**Phosphorus is an important part of ATP and DNA and must be cycled in order for an ecosystem to support life.** The **phosphorus cycle** is the movement of phosphorus in different chemical forms from the surroundings to organisms and then back to the surroundings. Phosphorus is often found in soil and rock as calcium phosphate, which dissolves in water to form phosphate. The roots of plants absorb phosphate. Humans and animals that eat the plants reuse the organic phosphorus. When the humans and animals die, phosphorus is returned to the soil.

**Reading Check** *How is phosphorus passed from soil to plants?*

## Section 3 Review

### KEY IDEAS

1. **Explain** how carbon and oxygen are cycled through an ecosystem.
2. **Describe** why nitrogen must cycle through an ecosystem.
3. **Explain** why it is important that phosphorus be cycled through an ecosystem.
4. **Summarize** the steps of the water cycle.

### CRITICAL THINKING

5. **Making Connections** Explain why the oxygen and carbon cycles are tied so closely together.
6. **Predicting Outcomes** Describe what would happen if matter could not cycle through ecosystems.
7. **Analyzing Processes** Defend the argument that nutrients can cycle but energy cannot.

### METHODS OF SCIENCE

8. **Designing an Experiment** Design an experiment in which you would determine whether nitrogen-fixing bacteria really help plants grow faster.

Inquiry

# Chapter 4 Lab

1.2.4, 1.3.1a, 4.6.1.e

### Objectives

- Construct an ecosystem model.
- Observe interactions of organisms in an ecosystem model.
- Compare an ecosystem model with a natural ecosystem.

### Materials

- goggles, gloves, and lab apron
- coarse sand or pea gravel
- terrarium or glass jar, large, with a lid
- soil
- grass seeds, a pinch of
- clover seeds, a pinch of
- water, 150 mL
- rolled oats
- mealworms (beetle larvae)
- mung bean seeds
- earthworms
- isopods (pill bugs)
- crickets

### Safety

## Ecosystem Change

Organisms in an ecosystem interact with one another and with their environment. Feeding is one interaction that occurs among the organisms in an ecosystem. A food web describes the feeding relationships among the organisms in an ecosystem. In this lab, you will use a terrarium or a jar to model a closed ecosystem. A *closed ecosystem* is a system that allows energy to enter but that is closed to the transfer of matter.

### Preparation

1. SCIENTIFIC METHODS **State the Problem** How might the different organisms interact in an ecosystem model?
2. SCIENTIFIC METHODS **Form a Hypothesis** Form a testable hypothesis about how the number of individuals of each species in an ecosystem model will change over time.

### Procedure

**Build an Ecosystem in a Jar**

1. **CAUTION: Glassware is fragile. Notify your teacher promptly of any broken glass or cuts. Do not clean up broken glass or spills that contain broken glass unless your teacher tells you to do so.** Place 5 cm of sand or pea gravel in the bottom of a large, clean, glass jar that has a lid. Cover the gravel with 5 cm of soil.
2. Sprinkle the seeds of two or three kinds of small plants, such as grasses and clovers, onto the surface of the soil. Add about 150 mL of water. Put the lid on the jar loosely, and place the jar in indirect sunlight. Let the jar remain undisturbed for one week.
3. **CAUTION: Handle animals carefully.** Do not allow animals to escape from containers. After one week, place a handful of rolled oats into the jar. Place the mealworms in the oats. Then, place the other animals into the jar, and replace the lid. Place the lid on the jar loosely so that air can enter the jar.

### Design an Experiment

4. Work with the members of your lab group to design an experiment that will test the hypothesis that you recorded previously. Design your experiment to use the ecosystem model that you built.
5. Write a procedure for your experiment. Make a list of all of the safety precautions that you will take. Have your teacher approve your procedure and safety precautions before you begin the experiment.
6. Set up your group's experiment. Conduct your experiment for at least 14 days.

### Cleanup and Disposal

7. Dispose of solutions, broken glass, and other materials in the designated waste containers. Do not put lab materials in the trash unless your teacher tells you to do so.
8. Clean up your lab materials according to your teacher's instructions. Wash your hands before you leave the lab.

## Analyze and Conclude

1. **Summarizing Results** Make graphs showing how the number of individuals of each species in your ecosystem changed over time. Be sure to count both plants and animals. Plot time on the *x*-axis and the number of organisms on the *y*-axis.
2. SCIENTIFIC METHODS **Analyzing Data** Compare your results with your hypothesis. Explain any differences.
3. **Inferring Conclusions** Construct a food web for the ecosystem that you observed.
4. SCIENTIFIC METHODS **Recognizing Relationships** Does your ecosystem model resemble a natural ecosystem? Explain your answer.
5. **Analyzing Methods** How can you build an ecosystem model that better represents a natural ecosystem?
6. **Critiquing Models** Was your ecosystem model truly a closed ecosystem? List your model's strengths and weaknesses as a closed ecosystem.
7. **Analyzing Data** List the biotic and abiotic factors in your ecosystem model.

## Extensions

8. **Further Inquiry** Write a new question to explore with another investigation using an ecosystem model.
9. **Making Comparisons** Use the library or Internet to learn about Biosphere 2. What problems did the Biosphere 2 crew encounter during the 1991–1993 project?

# Chapter 4 Summary

| Key Ideas | Key Terms |
|---|---|

## 1 What Is an Ecosystem?

- An ecosystem is a community of organisms and their abiotic environment.
- An ecosystem responds to change in such a way that the ecosystem is restored to equilibrium.
- Two key factors of climate that determine biomes are temperature and precipitation.
- Earth's major terrestrial biomes can be grouped by latitude into tropical, temperate biomes, and high-latitude.
- Aquatic ecosystems are organized into freshwater ecosystems, wetlands, estuaries, and marine ecosystems.

**Key Terms:** **community** (79), **ecosystem** (79), **habitat** (80), **biodiversity** (80), **succession** (81), **climate** (82), **biome** (82)

## 2 Energy Flow in Ecosystems

- In an ecosystem, energy flows from the sun to producers to consumers to decomposers.
- Energy is stored at each link in a food web, but some energy that is used dissipates as heat into the environment and is not recycled.

**Key Terms:** **producer** (86), **consumer** (86), **decomposer** (86), **trophic level** (86), **energy pyramid** (89)

## 3 Cycling of Matter

- The water cycle is the continuous movement of water between the atmosphere, the land, and the oceans.
- Animals, plants, and other photosynthesizing organisms play an important role in cycling carbon and oxygen through an ecosystem.
- Nitrogen must be cycled through an ecosystem so that the nitrogen is available for organisms to make proteins.
- Like water, carbon, oxygen, and nitrogen, phosphorus must be cycled in order for an ecosystem to support life.

**Key Terms:** **carbon cycle** (91), **respiration** (91), **nitrogen cycle** (92), **phosphorus cycle** (93)

The Living Environment

# Regents Exam Practice

**PART A: Answer all questions in this part.**

*Directions:* For each statement or question, write on your separate answer sheet the number of the word or expression that best completes the statement or answers the question.

**1** Many years ago, a volcanic eruption killed many plants and animals on an island. Today the island looks much as it did before the eruption. Which statement is the best possible explanation for this?

(1) Altered ecosystems regain stability through the evolution of new plant species.
(2) Destroyed environments can recover as a result of the process of ecological succession.
(3) Geographic barriers prevent the migration of animals to island habitats.
(4) Destroyed ecosystems always return to their original state.

**2** A fire burns an oak forest down to bare ground. Over the next 150 years, if the climate remains constant, this area will most likely

(1) remain bare ground
(2) return to an oak forest
(3) become a rain forest
(4) become a wetland

**3** What impact do the amounts of available energy, water, and oxygen have on an ecosystem?

(1) They act as limiting factors.
(2) They are used as nutrients.
(3) They recycle the residue of dead organisms.
(4) They control environmental temperature.

**4** As succession proceeds from a shrub community to a forest community, the shrub community modifies its environment, eventually making it

(1) more favorable for itself and less favorable for the forest community
(2) more favorable for itself and more favorable for the forest community
(3) less favorable for itself and more favorable for the forest community
(4) less favorable for itself and less favorable for the forest community

**5** Nutritional relationships between organisms are shown in the diagram below.

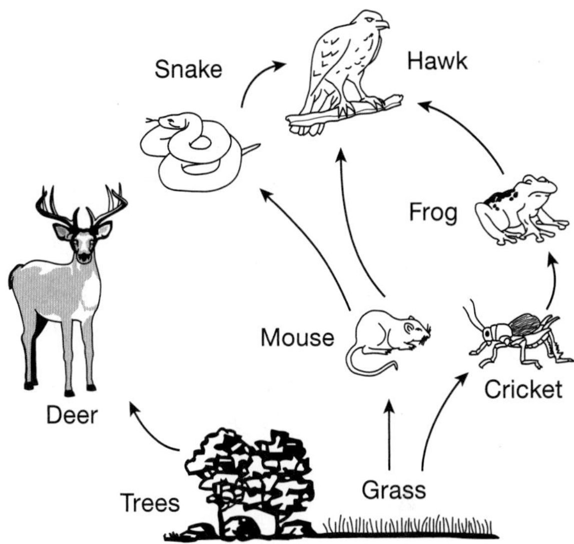


The mouse population would most likely decrease if there were

(1) an increase in the frog and tree populations
(2) a decrease in the snake and hawk populations
(3) an increase in the number of decomposers in the area
(4) a decrease in the amount of available sunlight

**6** In the diagram below, what does X most likely represent?

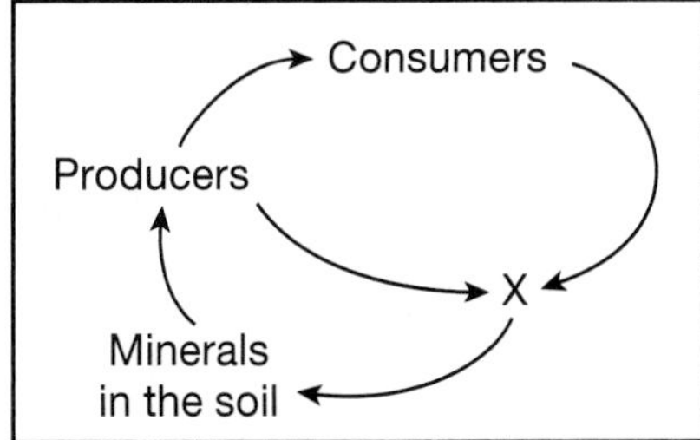


(1) autotrophs
(2) herbivores
(3) decomposers
(4) carnivores

**7** Which diagram best illustrates the relationship between humans (H) and ecosystems (E)?

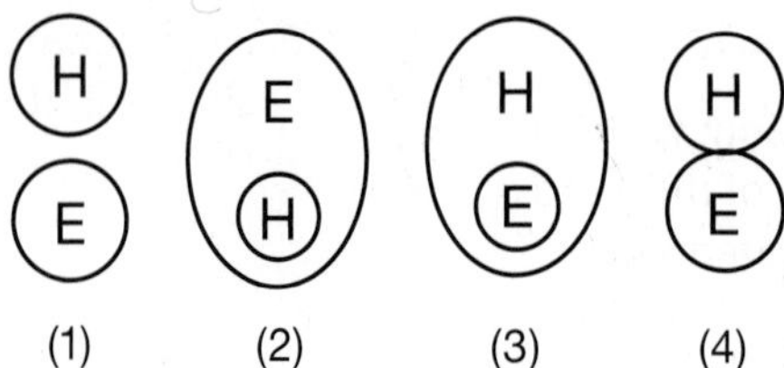


**PART B**

**Base your answers to questions 8 through 10 on the passage below which describes an ecosystem in New York State and on your knowledge of biology.**

The Pine Bush ecosystem near Albany, New York, is one of the last known habitats of the nearly extinct Karner Blue butterfly. The butterfly's larvae feed on the wild green plant, lupine. The larvae are in turn consumed by predatory wasps. The four groups below represent other organisms living in this ecosystem.

| Group A | Group B | Group C | Group D |
|---|---|---|---|
| algae<br>mosses<br>ferns<br>pine trees<br>oak trees | rabbits<br>tent caterpillars<br>moths | hawks<br>moles<br>hognosed snakes<br>toads | soil bacteria<br>molds<br>mushrooms |

**8** Which group contains decomposers?

(1) A  (3) C
(2) B  (4) D

**9** Which food chain best represents information in the passage?

(1) lupine → Karner Blue larvae → wasps
(2) wasps → Karner Blue larvae → lupine
(3) Karner Blue larvae → lupine → wasps
(4) lupine → wasps → Karner Blue larvae

**10** The Karner Blue larvae belong in which group?

(1) A  (3) C
(2) B  (4) D

**11** What would most likely happen if most of the bacteria and fungi were removed from an ecosystem?

(1) Nutrients resulting from decomposition would be reduced.
(2) Energy provided for autotrophic nutrition would be reduced.
(3) The rate of mutations in plants would increase.
(4) Soil fertility would increase.

**12** Which level of the energy pyramid below would contain the plant species of a salt marsh?

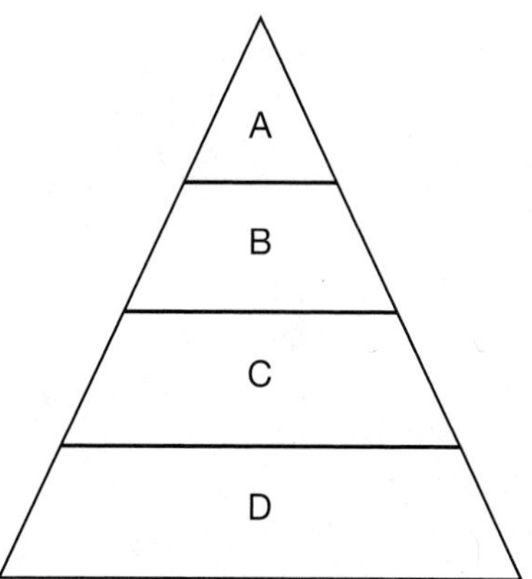


(1) A
(2) B
(3) C
(4) D

**13** The graph below shows the effect of moisture on the number of trees per acre of five three species. Which observation best represents information shown in the graph?

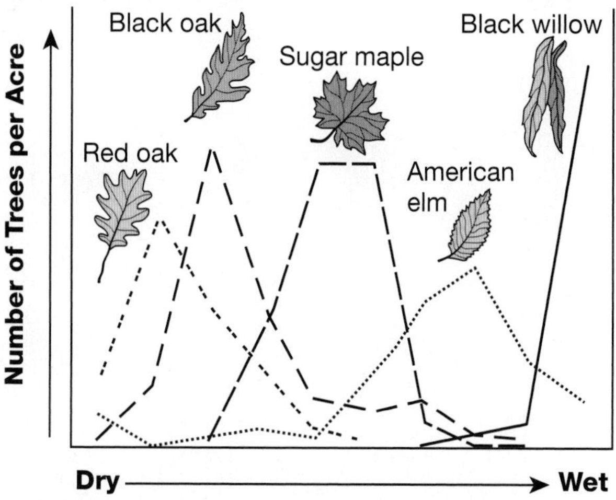


(1) All five species grow in the same habitat.
(2) The American elm grows in the widest range of moisture conditions.
(3) Red oaks can grow in wetter conditions than black willows.
(4) Sugar maples can grow anywhere black oaks can grow.

# Chapter 5 Populations and Communities

## Preview



## Why It Matters

How many species are in an area, how their populations grow, and how they interact with other species, including humans, are major factors that shape ecosystems and the environment's resources.

This crab and iguana have a relationship in which both benefit. The crab eats the iguana's dead skin. The iguana gets the irritating, dead, flaky skin removed, and the crab gets a meal.

The sally lightfoot crab is a scavenger and will feed on just about anything, including dead skin.


***The Living Environment***

**Standard 4** Students will understand and apply scientific concepts, principles, and theories pertaining to the physical setting and living environment and recognize the historical development of ideas in science.

**Key Idea 1** Living things are both similar to and different from each other and from nonliving things. **Major Understandings** - ***1.1c, 1.1d, 1.1f***

**Key Idea 6** Plants and animals depend on each other and their physical environment. ***Major Understandings*** **– 6.1d, 6.1e, 6.1f, 6.1g, 6.2a, 6.3a**

30 min

# Inquiry**Lab**

## Population Size  4.6.1f

In this activity, you will model the change in size of a population.

### Procedure

1. Using **110 g of dry beans,** count out five beans to represent the starting population of a species.
2. Assume that each year, 20% of the beans have two offspring. Also, assume that 20% of the beans die each year.
3. Calculate the number of beans to add or subtract for 1 year.
4. Add to or remove beans from your population as appropriate. Record the new population size.
5. Continue modeling your population changes over the course of 10 years. Record the population size for each year.

### Analysis

1. **Calculate** the final population size after 10 years.
2. **Graph** your data. Describe the changes in your population.

The marine iguana and the sally lightfoot crab live on the Galápagos Islands in the Pacific Ocean.

The marine iguana is the only true saltwater lizard. It is an excellent swimmer and feeds on marine algae.

These reading tools can help you learn the material in this chapter. For more information on how to use these and other tools, see **Appendix: Reading and Study Skills.**

## Using Words

**Word Origins** Many common English words derive from Greek or Latin words. Learning the meanings of some Greek or Latin words can help you understand the meaning of many modern English words.

**Your Turn** Answer the following questions.

1. Why might an organism's role be called its *niche?*
2. Why might a tick on a dog be considered a parasite?

**Word Origins**

| Word | Origin | Meaning |
|---|---|---|
| *niche-* | Latin (*nidus*) | nest |
| *para-* | Greek | beside |
| *-site* | Greek | food |

## Using Language

**Predictions** Some predictions are conditional: Something might happen, but only if something else happens first. For example, if the temperature drops below freezing, snow might fall. The prediction is that snow might fall tonight. But snow might fall under one condition. First, the temperature has to drop below freezing.

**Your Turn** In the following sentences, identify the condition and the prediction.

1. After the deer population reaches 600 individuals on the island, the deer will eat most of the vegetation, and the number of deer will decrease.
2. If the otters are removed from the ecosystem, the sea urchins will eat all of the kelp.

## Using Graphic Organizers

**Venn Diagram** A Venn diagram is a useful tool for comparing two or three topics in science. A Venn diagram shows which characteristics are shared by the topics and which characteristics are unique to each topic.

**Your Turn** Create a Venn diagram that compares the characteristics of communities, ecosystems, and populations.

1. Draw a diagram like the one shown here. Draw one circle for each topic. Make sure that each circle partially overlaps the other circles.
2. In each circle, write a topic that you want to compare with the topics in the other circles.
3. In the areas of the diagram where circles overlap, write the characteristics that the topics in the overlapping circles share.
4. In the areas of the diagram where circles do not overlap, write the characteristics that are unique to the topic of the particular circle.

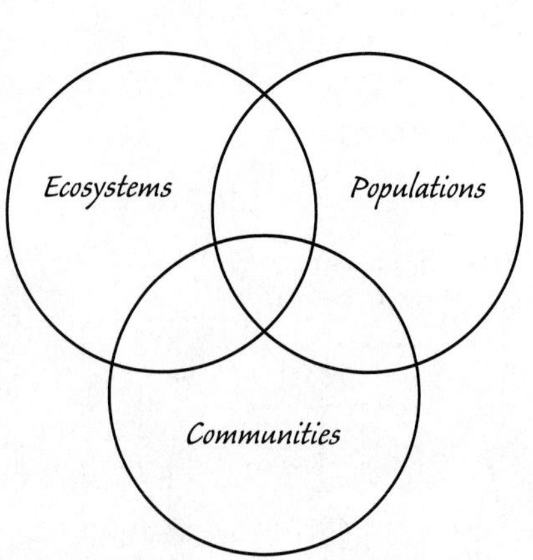

Section

# 1 Populations

| Key Ideas | Key Terms | Why It Matters |
|---|---|---|
| ❯ Why is it important to study populations?<br>❯ What is the difference between exponential growth and logistic growth?<br>❯ What factors affect population size?<br>❯ How have science and technology affected human population growth? | population<br>carrying capacity | Understanding how populations grow and shrink is critical to managing agricultural pests and diseases and also for knowing how to protect ecosystems. |

In the 1850s, about two dozen rabbits from Europe were introduced into Australia. The rabbits had plenty of vegetation to eat, no competition, and no predators. Their numbers increased rapidly. By the 1950s, there were 600 million rabbits! The rabbits ate so much vegetation that the numbers of native plants and animals declined and crops were damaged.

***The Living Environment***

**Standard 4**

**1.1c** In all environments, organisms compete for vital resources. The linked and changing interactions of populations and the environment compose the total ecosystem.

**1.1d** The interdependence of organisms in an established ecosystem often results in approximate stability over hundreds and thousands of years. For example, as one population increases, it is held in check by one or more environmental factors or another species.

**6.1d** The number of organisms any habitat can support (carrying capacity) is limited by the available energy, water, oxygen, and minerals, and by the ability of ecosystems to recycle the residue of dead organisms through the activities of bacteria and fungi.

**6.1e** In any particular environment, the growth and survival of organisms depend on the physical conditions including light intensity, temperature range, mineral availability, soil/rock type, and relative acidity (pH).

**6.1f** Living organisms have the capacity to produce populations of unlimited size, but environments and resources are finite. This has profound effects on the interactions among organisms.

## What Is a Population?

As Australia learned, understanding populations is important for protecting ecosystems. A **population** is made up of a group of organisms of the same species that live together in one place at one time and interbreed. **Figure 1** shows members of a zebra population. As new zebras are born, the population size increases. As other zebras fall prey to predators, the population decreases. Hundreds of miles away, there may be another zebra population that lives together and interbreeds.

**population** a group of organisms of the same species that live in a specific geographical area and interbreed

Populations can be small or large. Some populations stay at nearly the same number for years at a time. Some populations die out from lack of resources. Other populations grow rapidly, such as the rabbit population in Australia. The rapid growth of the rabbit population caused problems with Australia's ecosystems, other species, and farmland. ❯ **Understanding population growth is important because populations of different species interact and affect one another, including human populations.**

❯ **Reading Check** ***What distinguishes one zebra population from another zebra population? (See Appendix for answers to Reading Checks.)***

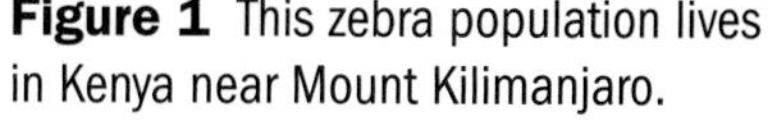

**Figure 1** This zebra population lives in Kenya near Mount Kilimanjaro.

## Exponential Growth

**Figure 2** Exponential growth is characterized by a J-shaped curve. Rabbits and bacteria are two examples of populations that can grow exponentially.

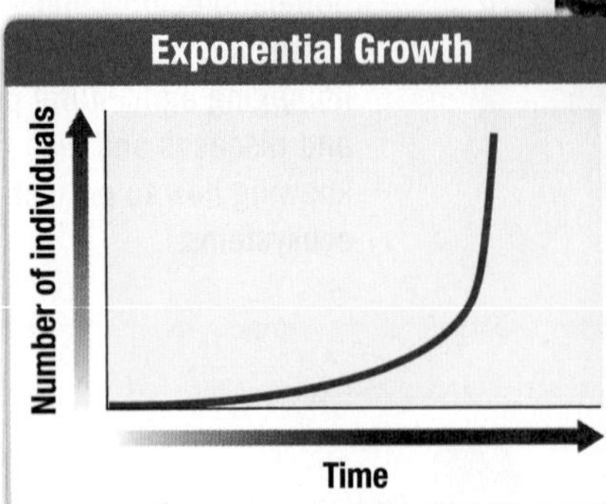


**carrying capacity** the largest population that an environment can support at any given time

www.scilinks.org
Topic: Population Growth Factors
Code: HX81187

## Population Growth

One of the most basic questions ecologists ask is "How do populations grow and shrink?" To help answer this question, biologists make population models. A population model attempts to show key growth characteristics of a real population.

Whether a population grows or shrinks depends on births, deaths, immigration, and emigration. *Immigration* is the movement of individuals into a population. *Emigration* is the movement of individuals out of a population. So, a simple population model describes the rate of population growth as the difference between birthrate, death rate, immigration, and emigration. Plotting population changes against time on a graph creates a model in the form of a curve. Two major models of population growth are *exponential growth* and *logistic growth.*

**Exponential Growth** One important part of a population model is the growth rate. When more individuals are born than die, a population grows. In exponential growth, there are always more births than deaths. As time goes by, more and more individuals enter the population. › ***Exponential growth*** **occurs when numbers increase by a certain factor in each successive time period.** This type of increase causes the J-shaped curve of exponential growth seen in **Figure 2.**

In exponential growth, population size grows slowly when it is small. But as the population gets larger, growth speeds up. Bacteria are an example of a population that can grow exponentially. Populations of bacteria grow very fast. A single bacterial cell that divides every 30 minutes will have produced more than 1 million bacteria in 10 hours. Some populations, such as the rabbits shown in **Figure 2,** may grow exponentially for a while. If they continued to grow exponentially forever, the world would fill up with rabbits!

› **Reading Check** ***What are the characteristics of a population that grows exponentially?***

Data

# QuickLab

4.6.1f

30 min

## Population Growth

You can learn a lot about a population by plotting its changes on a graph. In this activity, you will plot the growth of a deer population.

### Procedure

1. On a graph, plot the data from the table.
2. Title the graph. Then, label the *x*-axis and the *y*-axis.

### Analysis

1. **Identify** the dependent and independent variables.
2. **Describe** the growth curve. Does the population increase logistically or exponentially?
3. **Identify** the point at which the population is growing fastest.
4. CRITICAL THINKING **Analyzing Results** Are you able to determine the carrying capacity from this graph? If so, label it on the graph. What is its value?

| Year | Number of individuals |
|---|---|
| 1930 | 30 |
| 1935 | 50 |
| 1940 | 98 |
| 1945 | 175 |
| 1950 | 250 |
| 1955 | 273 |
| 1960 | 201 |
| 1965 | 159 |
| 1970 | 185 |
| 1975 | 205 |
| 1980 | 194 |
| 1985 | 203 |

**Logistic Growth** Populations do not grow unchecked forever. Factors such as availability of food, predators, and disease limit the growth of a population. Eventually, population growth slows and may stabilize.

An ecosystem can support only so many organisms. The largest population that an environment can support at any given time is called the **carrying capacity.** *Density-dependent factors* are variables affected by the number of organisms present in a given area. An example of a density-dependent factor is the availability of nesting sites. As the number of adult birds increases, there are no longer enough nesting sites for the entire population. So, many birds will not have young, and growth of the population is limited. *Density-independent factors* are variables that affect a population regardless of the population density. Examples of density-independent factors are weather, floods, and fires.

The logistic model takes into account the declining resources available to populations. ➤ ***Logistic growth* is population growth that starts with a minimum number of individuals and reaches a maximum depending on the carrying capacity of the habitat.** When a population is small, the growth rate is fast because there are plenty of resources. As the population approaches the carrying capacity, resources become scarce. Competition for food, shelter, and mates increases between individuals of a population. As a result, the rate of growth slows. The population eventually stops growing when the death rate equals the birthrate. On a graph, logistic growth is characterized by an S-shaped curve, as **Figure 3** shows. Most organisms, such as the macaws shown in **Figure 3,** show a logistic growth pattern.

**Figure 3** Logistic growth is characterized by an S-shaped curve.

## Factors That Affect Population Size

Most populations increase or decrease. Some change with the seasons. Others have good years and bad years. Many factors cause populations to grow and shrink. ❯ **Water, food, predators, and human activity are a few of many factors that affect the size of a population.**

**ACADEMIC VOCABULARY**

**affect** to act upon

**Abiotic Factors** Nonliving factors that affect population size are called *abiotic factors.* Weather and climate are the most important abiotic factors. For example, the population size of the penguins shown in **Figure 4** is affected by the climate of Antarctica. Unusually low temperatures can reduce the number of young penguins that survive. The amount of water available can also influence populations. Kangaroo populations in Australia grew when farmers gave water to their livestock that was also available for kangaroos to drink.

**Word Origins** Write down the definitions of the words *biotic* and *abiotic*. Then, write down what you think that *bio-* means. Use a dictionary to check your answer.

**Biotic Factors** A factor that is related to the activities of living things is called a *biotic factor.* Food, such as grass or other animals, is a biotic factor. When there is plenty of food, populations tend to grow. When food is scarce, populations decline. Predators are another kind of biotic factor. When populations of Canadian lynx grow, they eat a lot of snowshoe hares. The population of hares is then reduced. Diseases and parasites, when they infect many individuals, can also cause populations to decline. Biotic factors are often density dependent because they can have a stronger influence when crowding exists. As the density of a population increases, the effects of starvation, predators, and disease often also increase.

Humans affect populations of many species. Most of the time, humans cause populations to drop by disrupting habitats, introducing diseases, or introducing nonnative species. But some organisms do better around humans. Elk thrive near some Canadian towns because wolves will not come close to humans.

❯ **Reading Check** ***Describe the difference between biotic and abiotic factors.***

**Figure 4** Climate is an abiotic factor that affects the population size of these emperor penguins in Antarctica. ❯ **Name another abiotic factor that may affect the population size of these penguins.**

## Human Population

Today, the world population is more than 6 billion people and is increasing. **› Better sanitation and hygiene, disease control, and agricultural technology are a few ways that science and technology have decreased the death rate of the human population.** As more humans live on the planet, more resources will be needed to support them. As demand for resources increases, more pressure will be put on Earth's ecosystems.

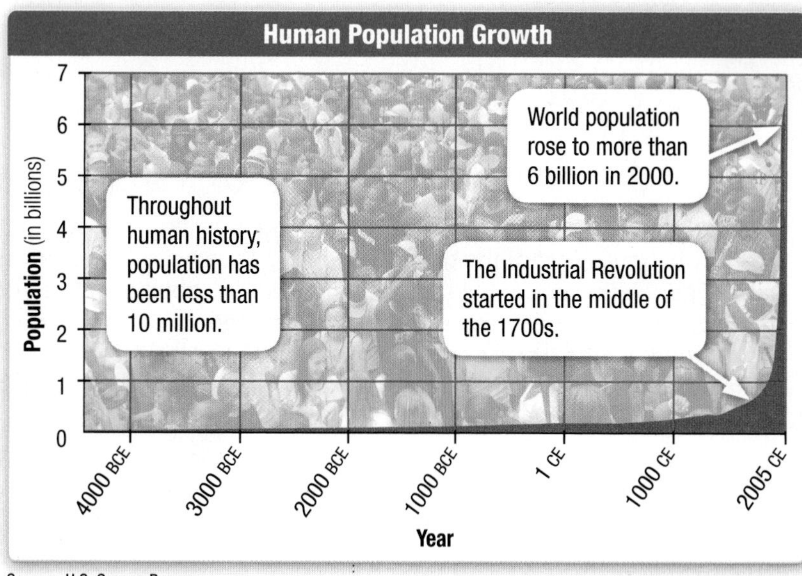


Source: U.S. Census Bureau.

**Figure 5** During the last 200 years, the human population has grown exponentially.

**Historic Growth** For most of human history, there have been fewer than 10 million people. Once agriculture was developed, the population began to grow, but relatively slowly. Two thousand years ago, there were only 10 million people. Around the time of the Industrial Revolution, the human population started to accelerate rapidly. **Figure 5** shows the human population accelerating exponentially starting in the late 1700s. Now, there are more than 6 billion people, and some scientists think that the population will grow to 9 billion in 50 years. How many people Earth can support depends in part on science and technology.

**Science and Technology** Science and technology are major reasons why the human population is growing so rapidly. Advances in agricultural technology have allowed efficient production of crops and other foods. More food supports more people. As a result, the human population has begun to grow faster. Medical advances have also allowed the human population to increase. Vaccines have lowered the death rate. More children are surviving to adulthood. Other medical advances have allowed adults to live longer lives.

**› Reaching Check** ***How have advances in technology allowed the human population to grow faster?***

### Section 1 Review

**› KEY IDEAS**

1. **Explain** the importance of studying populations.
2. **Compare** exponential growth with logistic growth.
3. **Identify** an abiotic factor that affects populations.
4. **Explain** how science and technology have affected human population growth.

**CRITICAL THINKING**

5. **Relating Concepts** A small species of mouse lives in a desert in Arizona. What factors do you think influence the size of this mouse population?
6. **Predicting Outcomes** Identify a biotic factor that could affect the size of the human population. Predict the effect of this biotic factor.

**USING SCIENCE GRAPHICS**

7. **Making Graphs** Draw a graph with a growth curve for a population that starts at 10 individuals and experiences exponential growth. Draw a second graph with a growth curve for a population that starts with 10 individuals and undergoes logistic growth. The second graph should have a carrying capacity of 100 individuals.

Why It Matters

# Growth in Asia

The world population is more than 6 billion and growing by about 9,000 people per hour. Most of the growth is coming from Asia. Because Asia's current population is already so large, one child per couple in Asia adds more to the world population than two children per couple in other areas of the world. As the world population continues to grow, pressure will increase on availability of food, energy, livable space, and landfill space.

REAL WORLD

## A Recycling Society

As landfills quickly approach full capacity, the Japanese government has become a world leader in waste-recycling measures. Japan recycles refrigerators, washing machines, televisions, and even air conditioners. By 2015, Japan plans to recycle 95% of discarded cars. In the United States, 60% to 70% of waste is sent to landfills. In Japan, only 16% of waste is sent to landfills!

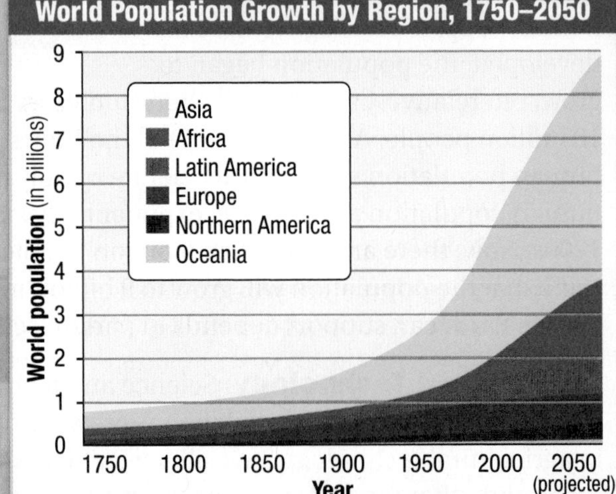

Source: National Geographic

**Old to New** These workers in Tokyo, Japan, are dismantling computers and sorting the parts for recycling.

**Crowed City** With 6,380 people per square kilometer, Hong Kong, China, shown here, is one of the most densely populated regions of the world.

**Research** Identify four strategies used by various countries to slow the rate of population growth.

Section

# 2 Interactions in Communities

| Key Ideas | Key Terms | Why It Matters |
|---|---|---|
| ➤ How do predator-prey interactions influence both predators and prey?<br>➤ What are two other types of interaction in a community? | predation<br>coevolution<br>parasitism<br>symbiosis<br>mutualism<br>commensalism | Interactions between organisms are the basis of communities and are shaped by evolution. |

Interactions in communities can take many forms. Predators and prey are locked in a struggle for survival. Organisms with the same needs compete for food. Parasites and hosts try to get ahead of one another. Some organisms even depend on one another for survival.

## Predator-Prey Interactions

One of the most common interactions in communities is that between predators and their prey. **Predation** is the act of one organism killing another for food. As **Figure 6** shows, predators try to get a meal, and prey do their best not to become one! We often think of predators as big animals, such as lions chasing zebras or sharks eating fish. Predators come in all sizes. Even microscopic organisms can be predators. In fact, most animals are both predators and prey. Only a few species, such as killer whales, are not hunted by any other animals.

Many interactions between species are the result of a long evolutionary history. Evolutionary changes in one species can result in changes in another species. **➤ Species that involve predator-prey or parasite-host relationships often develop adaptations in response to one another.** For example, predators evolve to be more cunning to catch their prey. In response, prey evolve to be faster runners to escape more easily. Back-and-forth evolutionary adjustment between two species that interact is called **coevolution.**

***The Living Environment***
**Standard 4**
**6.1g** Relationships between organisms may be negative, neutral, or positive. Some organisms may interact with one another in several ways. They may be in a producer/consumer, predator/prey, or parasite/host relationship; or one organism may cause disease in, scavenge, or decompose another.
**6.2a** As a result of evolutionary processes, there is a diversity of organisms and roles in ecosystems. This diversity of species increases the chance that at least some will survive in the face of large environmental changes. Biodiversity increases the stability of the ecosystem.

**predation** an interaction between two organisms in which one organism, the predator, kills and feeds on the other organism, the prey

**coevolution** the evolution of two or more species that is due to mutual influence

**Figure 6** This lion is hoping to have the zebra for lunch.

Data

# QuickLab

15 min

## The Effects of Herbivores on a Plant Species 4.6.1g

### Background

Some plant species, such as *Gilia,* respond to grazing by growing new stems. Consider the three images of *Gilia* to the right. Then, answer the statements below.

### Analysis

1. **Identify** the plant that is likely to produce more seeds.
2. **Explain** how grazing affects this plant species.
3. **Evaluate** the significance to its environment of the plant's regrowth pattern.
4. **Hypothesize** how this plant species might be affected if individual plants did not produce new stems in response to grazing.

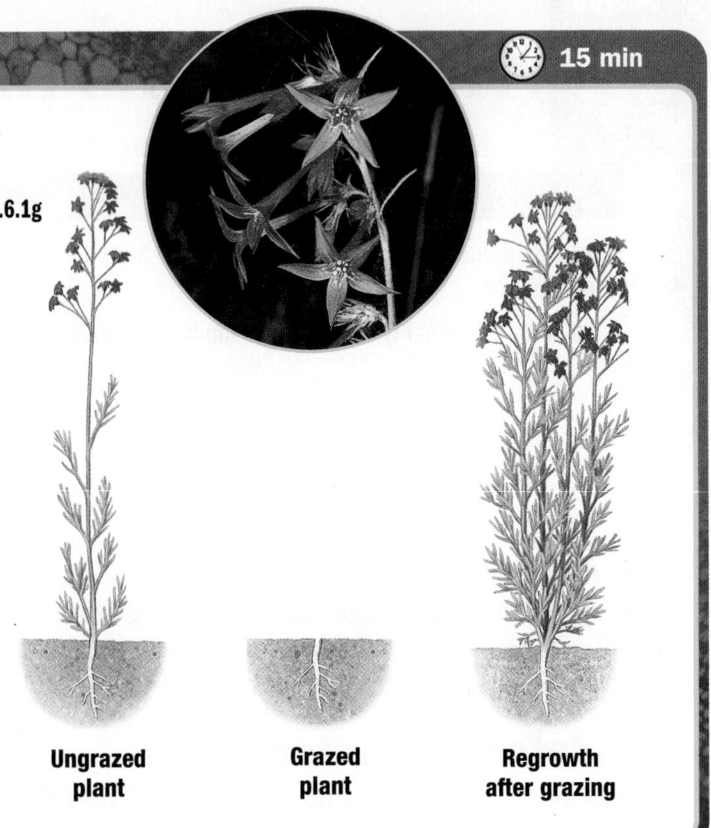

**Venn Diagram** Make a Venn diagram to help you compare the similarities and differences between predators, parasites, and herbivores.

**Parasitism** In **parasitism,** one organism feeds on another organism called a *host.* The host is almost always larger than the parasite and is usually harmed but not killed. Parasites often live on or in their host. Therefore, the parasite depends on its host not only for food but for a place to live as well. For example, tapeworms live in the digestive system of their hosts. Fleas that live on the skin of their host are another example.

Hosts try to keep parasites from infecting them. Hosts can defend themselves with their immune systems or behaviors such as scratching. In response, parasites may evolve ways to overcome the host's defenses.

**parasitism** a relationship between two species in which one species, the parasite, benefits from the other species, the host, which is harmed

**symbiosis** (SIM bie OH sis) a relationship in which two different organisms live in close association with each other

**mutualism** a relationship between two species in which both species benefit

**commensalism** a relationship between two organisms in which one organism benefits and the other is unaffected

**Herbivory** Herbivores are animals that eat plants. Unlike predators, herbivores do not often kill the plants. But plants do try to defend themselves. Some plants have thorns or spines that cause pain for herbivores that try to eat them. Other plants have chemical compounds inside them that taste bad. Some chemical compounds can make an herbivore sick or kill the herbivore.

Some herbivores have evolved ways to overcome plant defenses. For example, monarch butterfly caterpillars feed on milkweed, which is a plant that is toxic to many herbivores. Not only can the caterpillars survive eating the toxic milkweed but the plant toxins then make the monarch butterfly inedible to bird predators.

› **Reading Check** ***Identify one way in which herbivores and plants coevolve.***

Cleaner fish eat
parasites from
the eel's mouth.
Orchids receive
more sunlight when
attached to trees.

**Figure 7** This yellow-edged moray eel is getting its mouth cleaned by a humpback cleaner shrimp. Orchids avoid the dark forest floor by attaching themselves to the trunks of trees. **❯ Name another symbiotic relationship.**

## Other Interactions

Not all interactions between organisms result in a winner and a loser. **Symbiosis** is a relationship in which two species live in close association with each other. In some forms of symbiosis, a species may benefit from the relationship. **❯ Mutualism and commensalism are two kinds of symbiotic relationships in which at least one species benefits.**

**Mutualism** A relationship between two species in which both species benefit is called **mutualism.** Some shrimp and fishes on coral reefs clean the bodies of large fish and turtles. The cleaners even venture into the mouths of big predators that could easily swallow them, as **Figure 7** shows. Why don't the cleaners become an easy meal? The reason is that the big fish is having parasites removed by the cleaner. Because the cleaner gets a meal, both species win.

**Commensalism** In **commensalism,** two species have a relationship in which one species benefits and the other is neither harmed nor helped. **Figure 7** shows an example of commensalism between orchids and trees. In thick, tropical forests, little sunlight reaches the forest floor. Orchids need sunlight to survive. To reach the sunlight, orchids get a boost from the forest trees. Orchids will attach themselves and grow on the trunks of the trees. In this way, the orchids move up off the dark forest floor and closer to the sunny canopy.

SciLinks.
www.scilinks.org
Topic: Symbiosis
Code: HX81486

**❯ Reading Check** *Compare mutualism and commensalism.*

## Section 2 Review

### ❯ KEY IDEAS

1. **Explain** how predator-prey interactions influence both predators and prey.
2. **Define** symbiosis.
3. **Describe** two types of relationships in a community.

### CRITICAL THINKING

4. **Analyzing Results** The cookie-cutter shark feeds by taking a bite of flesh out of whales and large fish. The shark does not kill the larger fish it feeds on. Is the shark a predator or a parasite? Why?
5. **Relating Concepts** In commensalism, would both species coevolve?

### WRITING FOR SCIENCE

6. **Essay** In a report, explain what might happen to an ecosystem if one species in a mutualistic relationship disappeared. What would happen if a new predator were introduced to prey with which it has not coevolved?

Section 3

# Shaping Communities

| Key Ideas | Key Terms | Why It Matters |
|---|---|---|
| ❯ How does a species' niche affect other organisms?<br>❯ How does competition for resources affect species in a community?<br>❯ What factors influence the resiliency of an ecosystem? | niche<br>fundamental niche<br>realized niche<br>competitive exclusion<br>keystone species | The interactions among organisms in communities shape the ecosystem and the organisms that live there. |

***The Living Environment***
**Standard 4**

**1.1c** In all environments, organisms compete for vital resources. The linked and changing interactions of populations and the environment compose the total ecosystem.

**1.1d** The interdependence of organisms in an established ecosystem often results in approximate stability over hundreds and thousands of years. For example, as one population increases, it is held in check by one or more environmental factors or another species.

**1.1f** Every population is linked, directly or indirectly, with many others in an ecosystem. Disruptions in the numbers and types of species and environmental changes can upset ecosystem stability.

**6.2a** As a result of evolutionary processes, there is a diversity of organisms and roles in ecosystems. This diversity of species increases the chance that at least some will survive in the face of large environmental changes. Biodiversity increases the stability of the ecosystem.

**6.3a** The interrelationships and interdependencies of organisms affect the development of stable ecosystems.

No organism can live everywhere. Each organism has its own set of conditions where it can live and where it does best. Some plants, such as cactuses, can survive in deserts, but other plants need a lot of water. The desert plants cannot live in areas that have a lot of water because other plants outcompete them.

## Carving a Niche

Think of your favorite plant or animal. How does it use the physical environment? How does it interact with other species? The unique position occupied by a species, both in terms of its physical use of its habitat and its function in an ecological community, is called a **niche.** A niche is not the same as a habitat. A *habitat* is the place where an organism lives. ❯ **A niche includes the role that the organism plays in the community. This role affects the other organisms in the community.** For example, the beaver shown in **Figure 8** cuts down trees with its sharp teeth. The beaver then uses the trees to make dams that divert, or redirect, water flow in rivers and streams. These actions directly affect the trees by killing the trees. These actions also affect organisms that depend on the trees for shelter or food. However, some plants would benefit: fewer trees would allow the plants access to more sunlight. Diverting water flow in a stream could be beneficial to some forms of aquatic life. For others, a dam in a stream could prevent them from traveling upstream to mating grounds. The beaver's role affects many other organisms. If you took the beaver out of this ecosystem, the community would be very different.

❯ **Reading Check** ***How is a niche different from a habitat?***

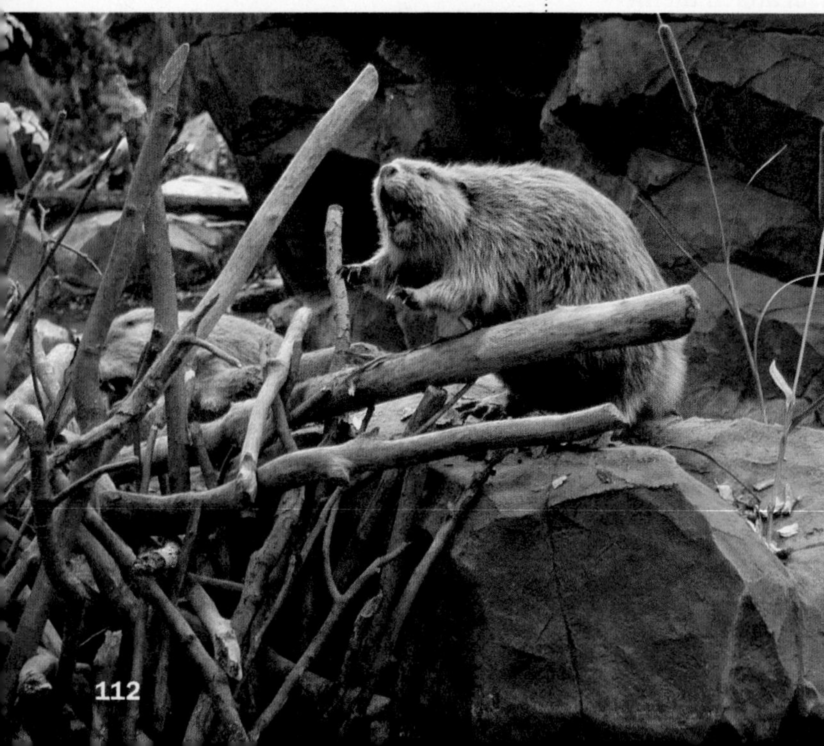

**Figure 8** Beavers build dams from trees and tree branches that they cut with their sharp, powerful teeth. ❯ **How might these dams affect other organisms in the community?**

Data

# QuickLab

4.1.1c, 4.6.3b

15 min

## Changes in a Realized Niche

This graph shows the location where species A feeds and the size of its preferred prey. The darkest shade in the center of the graph indicates the prey size and feeding location most frequently selected by species A.

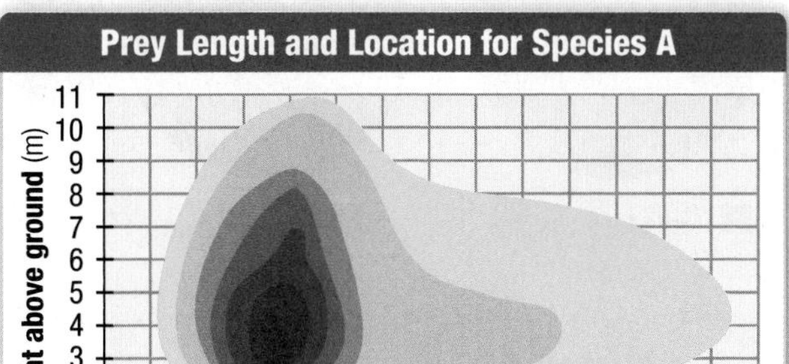


### Analysis

1. **State** the range of lengths of prey on which species A prefers to feed.
2. **Identify** the maximum height above ground at which species A feeds.
3. **Describe** what the palest shade at the edge of the contour lines represents.
4. CRITICAL THINKING **Predicting Outcomes** Species B is introduced into species A's ecosystem. Species B has the same feeding preferences but hunts at a different time of day. How might this affect species A?
5. CRITICAL THINKING **Interpreting Graphics** Species C is now introduced into species A's feeding range. Species C feeds at the same time of day as species A but prefers prey that are between 10 and 13 mm long. How might this change affect species A?

## Competing for Resources

The entire range of conditions where an organism or species could survive is called its **fundamental niche.** Many species share parts of their fundamental niche with other species. Sometimes, species compete for limited resources. Because of this competition, a species almost never inhabits its entire fundamental niche. **› Competition for resources between species shapes a species' fundamental niche.** The actual niche that a species occupies in a community is called its **realized niche.**

Sometimes, competition results in fights between rivals. Hyenas and lions will even steal food from one another. The stealing of food is called *kleptoparasitism.* Many competitive interactions do not involve direct contests. But when one individual takes a resource, the resource is no longer available for another individual. Many plants compete fiercely for access to light. Some do so by growing quickly to get above other plants. Other plants can tolerate periods of shade and grow slowly. As the slow-growing plants become larger, they eventually shade out other plants.

Competition has several possible outcomes. Sometimes, one species wins, and the other loses. The loser is eliminated from the habitat. Other times, competitors can survive together in the same habitat. They are able to survive together because they divide the resources.

**› Reading Check** ***Why do organisms rarely occupy their entire fundamental niche?***

**niche** the unique position occupied by a species, both in terms of its physical use of its habitat and its function within an ecological community

**fundamental niche** the largest ecological niche where an organism or species can live without competition

**realized niche** the range of resources that a species uses, the conditions that the species can tolerate, and the functional roles that the species plays as a result of competition in the species' fundamental niche

**Figure 9** Each of these five warbler species feeds on insects in a different portion of the same tree, as indicated by the five colors shown in the figure.

**Competitive Exclusion** No two species that are too similar can coexist. Why? If species are too similar in their needs, one will be slightly better at getting the resources on which they both depend. The more successful species will dominate the resources. The less successful species will either die off or have to move to another ecosystem. Eventually, the better competitor will be the only one left. One species eliminating another through competition is called **competitive exclusion.**

**competitive exclusion** the exclusion of one species by another due to competition

**keystone species** a species that is critical to the functioning of the ecosystem in which it lives because it affects the survival and abundance of many other species in its community

Competitive exclusion is seen in many places. When there are no predators around, mussels take over all of the space on rocks in the surf zone. The mussels eliminate barnacles from the surf-zone rocks that are part of the mussels' fundamental niche. Introduced species can also competitively exclude native species. When introduced species multiply quickly, they can use up all of the available resources. When resources are used up, other species that depend on the resources may become extinct.

**Dividing Resources** Sometimes, competitors eat the same kinds of food and are found in the same places. How do these species live together? Some competitors divide resources by feeding in slightly different ways or slightly different places. The five warblers shown in **Figure 9** are all potential competitors. All five species feed on insects in the same spruce trees at the same time. But they divide the habitat so that they do not compete. Each species feeds in a different part of the tree. Every one of the warbler species would feed everywhere in the tree if it had the tree to itself. Therefore, all the warbler species have the same fundamental niche. But when they are all present in the tree, they each have a smaller realized niche.

**Academic Vocabulary**

**potential** possible

> **Reading Check** ***How might two different species divide resources?***

## Ecosystem Resiliency

Ecosystems can be destroyed or damaged by severe weather, humans, or introduced species. Some factors can help keep an ecosystem stable. **› Interactions between organisms and the number of species in an ecosystem add to the resiliency of an ecosystem.**

**Figure 10** Sea otters off the coast of California are a threatened species. The decrease in their population has affected the stability of the ecosystem. **› Why is the sea otter considered a keystone species?**

**Predation and Competition** Predation can reduce the effects of competition among species. Many aquatic species compete for space in the intertidal zone along the Pacific coast. Mussels are fierce competitors that can take over that space. All other species are excluded. However, sea stars eat mussels. When sea stars eat the mussels, a variety of species can live in the intertidal zone.

Predators can influence more than their prey. Sea otters, as shown in **Figure 10,** eat sea urchins. Sea urchins eat kelp. When sea otters are present, lush kelp forests grow along the west coast of North America. These kelp forests provide habitat for many fishes and aquatic animals. When sea otters disappeared because of overhunting, the sea urchins ate all of the kelp. All of the species that depended on the kelp also disappeared. Sea otters are an example of a keystone species. A **keystone species** is a species that is critical to an ecosystem because the species affects the survival and number of many other species in its community.

**Biodiversity and Resiliency** One community has 50 species. Another community has 100 species. If a severe drought affected both communities equally, the community with 100 species would be more likely to recover quickly. The reason is that higher biodiversity often helps make an ecosystem more resilient. Predation helps increase biodiversity. The sea stars prevented the mussels from excluding other species. In response, the inter tidal zone had a higher biodiversity.

**› Reading Check** ***List two factors that contribute to the resiliency of an ecosystem.***

**Predictions** Using the term *keystone species,* write a sentence with a prediction based on a condition.

### Section 3 Review

**› KEY IDEAS**

1. **Explain** why an organism's role is important for a community.
2. **Describe** one example of how competition for resources affects species in a community.
3. **Explain** how predation can help make an ecosystem resilient.
4. **Compare** niche and habitat.

**CRITICAL THINKING**

5. **Inferring Conclusions** Two predators feed on small antelope. One predator weighs 100 kg, and the other weighs 35 kg. Explain what might happen if the two predators share the same area.
6. **Evaluating Results** Wolves are reintroduced into a park. As a result, the vegetation changes. Explain how the changes to the vegetation happened.

**ALTERNATIVE ASSESSMENT**

7. **Essay** Search the Internet to find out about the niche of wolves in their community. Determine if they are a keystone species. Then, write a one-page essay describing their role in their ecosystem.

Skills Practice

# Chapter 5 Lab

## Objectives

- Observe the growth and decline of a population of yeast cells.
- Determine the carrying capacity of a yeast culture.

## Materials

- lab apron, safety goggles, and gloves
- yeast cell culture
- test tube (2)
- pipets, 1 mL (2)
- methylene blue solution, 1%
- microscope slide, ruled
- coverslip
- microscope, compound

## Safety

# Yeast Population Growth

You have learned that a population will keep growing until limiting factors slow or stop this growth. In this lab, you will observe the changes in a population of yeast cells. The cells will grow in a container and have limited food over several days.

## Procedure

### Collecting Data

1. **CAUTION: Do not touch or taste any chemicals. Know the location of the emergency shower and eyewash station and how to use them. Methylene blue will stain your skin and clothing.** Transfer 1 mL of yeast culture to a test tube. Add two drops of methylene blue to the test tube. The methylene blue will remain blue in dead cells but will turn colorless in living cells.
2. Make a wet mount by placing 0.1 mL, or about one drop, of the yeast culture and methylene blue mixture on a ruled microscope slide. Cover the slide with a coverslip.
3. Observe the wet mount under low power of a compound microscope. Notice the squares on the slide. Then, switch to high power. (Note: Adjust the light so that you can clearly see both stained and unstained cells.) Move the slide so that the top left-hand corner of one square is in the center of your field of view. This area will be area 1, as shown in the diagram.

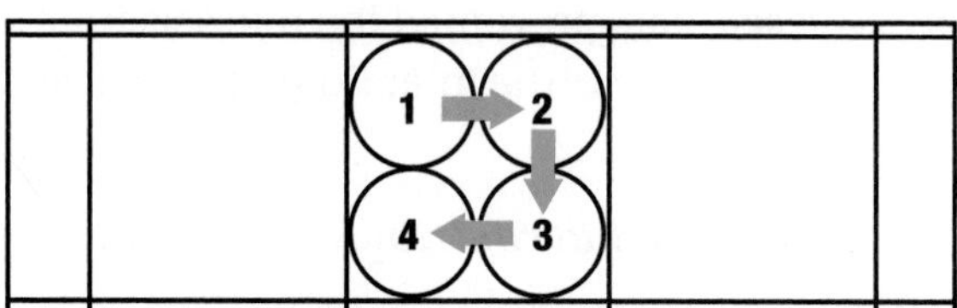


4. Make two data tables like the one shown. One table will contain your observations of living cells. The other table will contain your observations of dead cells.

Number of cells

| Time (h) | 1 | 2 | 3 | 4 | 5 | 6 | Average |
|---|---|---|---|---|---|---|---|
| 0 | | | | | | | |
| 24 | | | | | | | |
| 48 | | | | | | | |
| 72 | | | | | | | |
| 96 | | | | | | | |

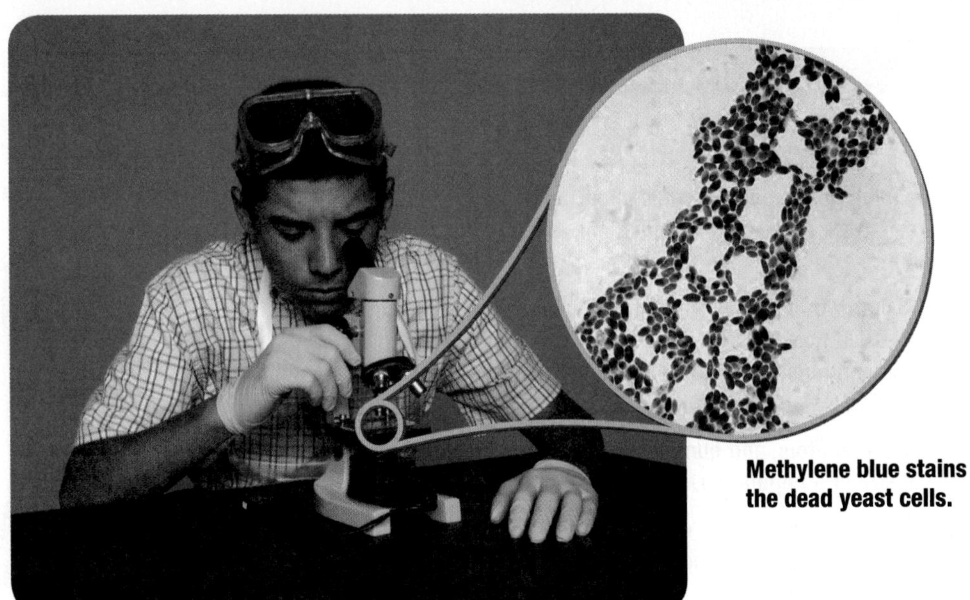

Methylene blue stains the dead yeast cells.

5 Count the live (unstained) cells and the dead (stained) cells in the four corners of a square by using the pattern shown in the diagram in step 3. Record the number of live cells and dead cells that you counted in the entire square.

6 Repeat step 5 until you have counted all six squares on the slide.

7 Clean up your lab materials according to your teacher's instructions. Wash your hands before leaving the lab.

### Compiling Data

8 Refer to your first data table. Find the total number of live cells in the six squares. Divide this total by 6 to find the average number of live cells per square. Record this number in your data table. Repeat this procedure for the dead cells.

9 Repeat steps 1 through 5 each day for four more days.

SCILINKS.
www.scilinks.org
Topic: Characteristics of Populations
Code: HX80260

## Analyze and Conclude

1. **Evaluating Methods** Explain why several areas were counted and averaged each day.
2. **Analyzing Data** Graph the changes in the numbers of live yeast cells and dead yeast cells over time. Plot the number of cells in 1 mL of yeast culture on the *y*-axis and the time (in hours) on the *x*-axis.
3. **Evaluating Results** Describe the general population changes that you observed in the yeast cultures over time.
4. SCIENTIFIC METHODS **Inferring Conclusions** Did the yeast population appear to reach a certain carrying capacity? What limiting factors probably caused the yeast population to decline?

## Extensions

5. **Designing an Investigation** Write a question about population growth that could be explored in another investigation. Design an investigation that could help answer that question.

# Chapter 5 Summary

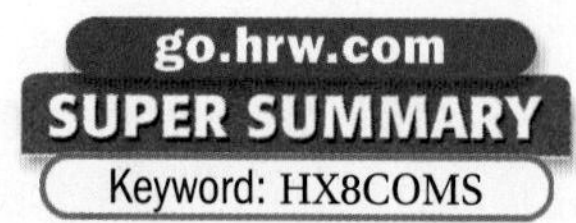


| Key Ideas | Key Terms |
|---|---|

## 1 Populations

- Understanding population growth is important because populations of different species interact and affect one another, including human populations.
- Exponential growth occurs when numbers increase by a certain factor in each successive time period. Logistic growth is population growth that starts with a minimum number of individuals and reaches a maximum depending on the carrying capacity of the habitat.
- Water, food, predators, and human activity are a few of many factors that affect the size of a population.
- Better sanitation and hygiene, disease control, and agricultural technology are a few ways that science and technology have decreased the death rate of the human population.

**Key Terms**

**population** (103)
**carrying capacity** (105)

## 2 Interactions in Communities

- Species that involve predator-prey or parasite-host relationships often develop adaptations in response to one another.
- Mutualism and commensalism are two types of symbiotic relationships in which one or both of the species benefit.

**Key Terms**

**predation** (109)
**coevolution** (109)
**parasitism** (110)
**symbiosis** (111)
**mutualism** (111)
**commensalism** (111)

## 3 Shaping Communities

- A niche includes the role that the organism plays in the community. This role affects the other organisms in the community.
- Competition for resources between species shapes a species' fundamental niche.
- Interactions between organisms and the number of species in an ecosystem add to the stability of an ecosystem.

**Key Terms**

**niche** (112)
**fundamental niche** (113)
**realized niche** (113)
**competitive exclusion** (114)
**keystone species** (115)

The Living Environment

# Regents Exam Practice

**PART A: Answer all questions in this part.**

*Directions:* For each statement or question, write on your separate answer sheet the number of the word or expression that best completes the statement or answers the question.

**1** When habitats are destroyed, there are usually fewer niches for animals and plants. This action would most likely not lead to a change in the amount of

(1) biodiversity
(2) competition
(3) interaction between species
(4) solar radiation reaching the area

**2** The growth of a population is shown in the graph below. Which letter indicates the carrying capacity of the environment for this population?

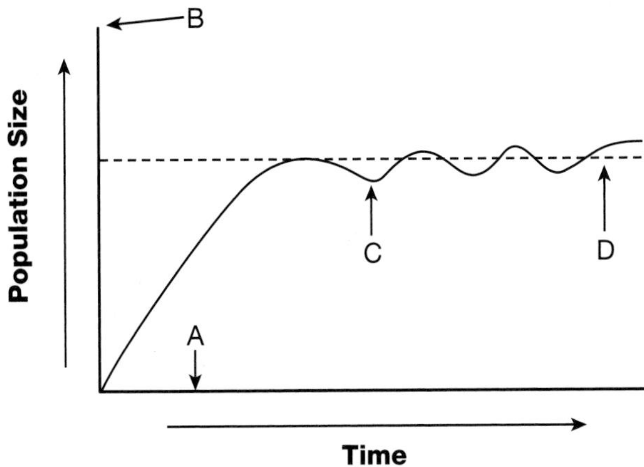


(1) A
(2) B
(3) C
(4) D

**3** The removal of nearly all the predators from an ecosystem would most likely result in

(1) an increase in the number of carnivore species
(2) a decrease in new predators migrating into the ecosystem
(3) a decrease in the size of decomposers
(4) an increase in the number of herbivores

**4** Ten breeding pairs of rabbits are introduced onto an island with no natural predators and a good supply of water and food. What will most likely happen to the rabbit population?

(1) It will remain relatively constant due to equal birth and death rates.
(2) It will die out due to an increase in the mutation rate.
(3) It will increase until it exceeds carrying capacity.
(4) It will decrease and then increase indefinitely.

**5** The graph below shows how the human population has grown over the last several thousand years. Which statement is a valid inference that can be made if the human population continues to grow at a rate similar to the rate shown between 1000 A.D. and 2000 A.D.?

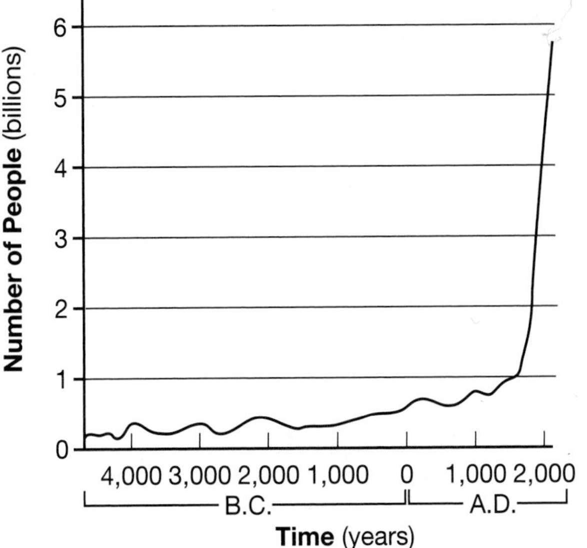


(1) Future ecosystems will be stressed and many animal habitats may be destroyed.
(2) Global warming will decrease as a result of a lower demand for fossil fuels.
(3) One hundred years after all resources are used up, the human population will level off.
(4) All environmental problems can be solved without a reduction in the growth rate of the human population.

**6** Which graph illustrates changes that indicate a state of dynamic equilibrium in a mosquito population?

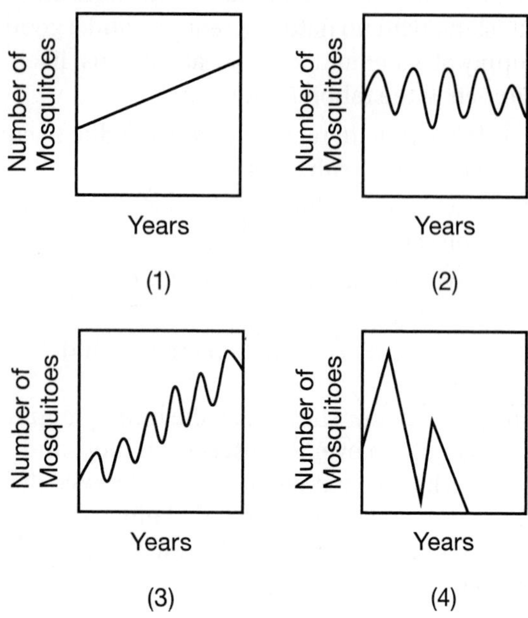


**7** Which statement best describes the fruit fly population in the part of the curve labeled X in the graph shown below?

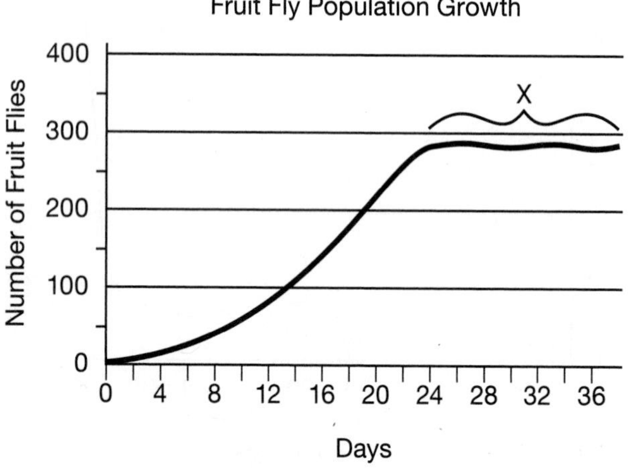


(1) The fruit fly population has reached the number of organisms the habitat can support.
(2) The fruit fly population can no longer mate and produce fertile offspring.
(3) The fruit fly population has an average life span of 36 days.
(4) The fruit fly population is no longer able to adapt to the changing environmental conditions.

**8** The ecological niches of three bird species are shown in the diagram below. What is the advantage of each bird species having a different niche?

Cape May warblers feed in the upper area of the tree.
Bay-breasted warblers feed in the middle of the tree.
Yellow-rumped warblers feed in the lower part of the tree.

(1) As the birds feed higher in the tree, available energy increases.
(2) More abiotic resources are available for each bird.
(3) Predators are less likely to feed on birds in a variety of locations.
(4) There is less competition for food.

**9** Two closely related species of birds live in the same tree. Species A feeds on ants and termites, while species B feeds on caterpillars. The two species coexist successfully because

(1) each occupies a different niche
(2) they interbreed
(3) they use different methods of reproduction
(4) birds compete for food

## PART B

**Base your answers to questions 10 and 11 on the information and graph below and on your knowledge of biology.**

A population of paramecia (single-celled aquatic organisms) was grown in a 200-mL beaker of water containing some smaller single-celled organisms. Population growth of the organisms for 28 hours is shown in the graph below.

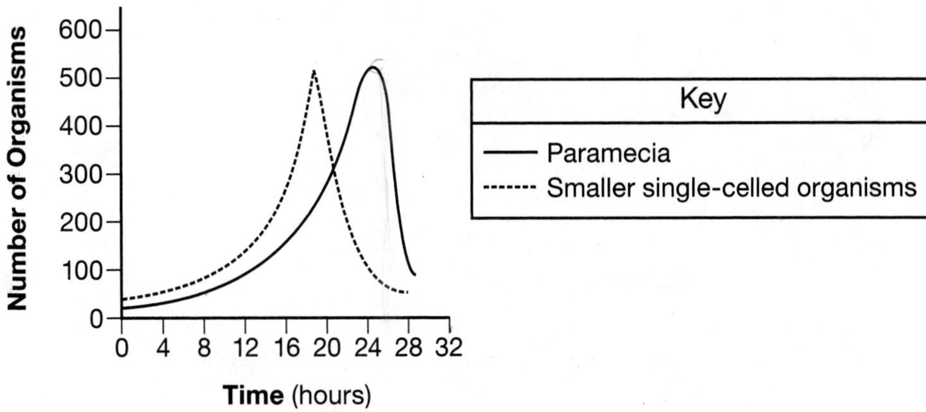


**10** Which factor most likely accounts for the change in the paramecium population from 8 to 20 hours?

(1) an increase in the nitrogen content of water
(2) an increase in wastes produced
(3) an increase in available food
(4) an increase in water pH

**11** One likely explanation for the change in the paramecium population from 26 hours to 28 hours is that the

(1) carrying capacity of the beaker was exceeded
(2) rate of reproduction increased
(3) time allowed for growth was not sufficient
(4) oxygen level was too high

## PART C

**Base your answers to question 12 on the information below and on your knowledge of biology.**

A student uses a covered aquarium to study the interactions of biotic and abiotic factors in an ecosystem. The aquarium contains sand, various water plants, algae, small fish, snails, and decomposers. The water contains dissolved oxygen and carbon dioxide, as well as tiny amounts of minerals and salts.

**12** Explain how oxygen is cycled between organisms in this ecosystem.

# Chapter 6 The Environment

The Neversink Pit in Alabama has recently been bought by local cavers who plan to preserve its ecosystem.

Neversink is an open air pit that is 162 ft deep.

A rare species of fern lives in the Neversink Pit.

## Preview

**1 An Interconnected Planet**
- Humans and the Environment
- Resources
- The Environment and Health

**2 Environmental Issues**
- Air Pollution
- Global Warming
- Water Pollution
- Soil Damage
- Ecosystem Disruption

**3 Environmental Solutions**
- Conservation and Restoration
- Reducing Resource Use
- Technology
- Environmental Awareness
- Planning for the Future

## Why It Matters

The environment provides the basic support system for all life on Earth, including humans. By taking care of the environment, we take care of ourselves and all other life on Earth.

***The Living Environment***

**Standard 4** Students will understand and apply scientific concepts, principles, and theories pertaining to the physical setting and living environment and recognize the historical development of ideas in science.

**Key Idea 6** Plants and animals depend on each other and their physical environment. ***Major Understandings*** **- 6.2b**

**Key Idea 7** Human decisions and activities have had a profound impact on the physical and living environment. ***Major Understandings*** **- 7.1a, 7.1b, 7.1c, 7.2a, 7.2b. 7.2c, 7.3a, 7.3b**

A person who explores caves is a spelunker.

15 min

# InquiryLab

## The Greenhouse Effect

Gases in the atmosphere trap heat and keep Earth warm. In this activity, you will model this process called the *greenhouse effect.*

### Procedure

1. **CAUTION: Handle the glass thermometer and jar with care.** Insert a thermometer through a hole in the lid of a quart jar. Tape the thermometer in place.
2. Place the jar about 30 cm from a heat source, such as a sunlit window.
3. Record the temperature inside and outside the jar every 30 s for 5 min.
4. Remove the jar from the heat source. Record the temperature inside and outside the jar every 30 s for another 5 min.

### Analysis

1. **Compare** the change in temperature inside the jar with the change in temperature outside the jar.
2. **Identify** the part of your model that represents the gases in the atmosphere.
3. **Explain** a possible reason why global temperatures on Earth have increased. Include what you learned from your model of the greenhouse effect.

These reading tools can help you learn the material in this chapter. For more information on how to use these and other tools, see **Appendix: Reading and Study Skills.**

## Using Words

**Word Parts** You can tell a lot about a word by taking it apart and examining its prefix, root, and suffix.

**Your Turn** Use the information in the table to define the following words.

1. biodiversity
2. deforestation

**Word Parts**

| Word Part | Type | Meaning |
|---|---|---|
| *bio-* | prefix | life |
| versi | root | various |
| *de-* | prefix | remove |
| *-ation* | suffix | a state of being |

## Using Language

**Hypothesis or Theory?** To scientists, a theory is a well-supported scientific explanation that makes useful predictions. The main difference between a theory and a hypothesis is that a hypothesis has not been tested, and a theory has been tested repeatedly and seems to correctly explain all the available data.

**Your Turn** Use information from the chapter to answer the following questions.

1. Is the greenhouse effect a hypothesis or theory? Explain.
2. Write your own hypothesis that explains the increase in global temperatures.

## Using Graphic Organizers

**Venn Diagrams** A Venn diagram is a useful tool for comparing two or three topics in science. A Venn diagram shows which characteristics the topics share and which characteristics are unique to each topic.

**Your Turn** Create a Venn diagram that describes the characteristics of renewable and nonrenewable resources.

1. Draw a diagram like the one shown here. Draw one circle for each topic. Make sure that each circle partially overlaps the other circles.
2. In each circle, write a topic that you want to compare with the topics in the other circles.
3. In the areas of the diagram where circles overlap, write the characteristics that the topics in the overlapping circles share.
4. In the areas of the diagram where circles do not overlap, write the characteristics that are unique to the topic of the particular circle.

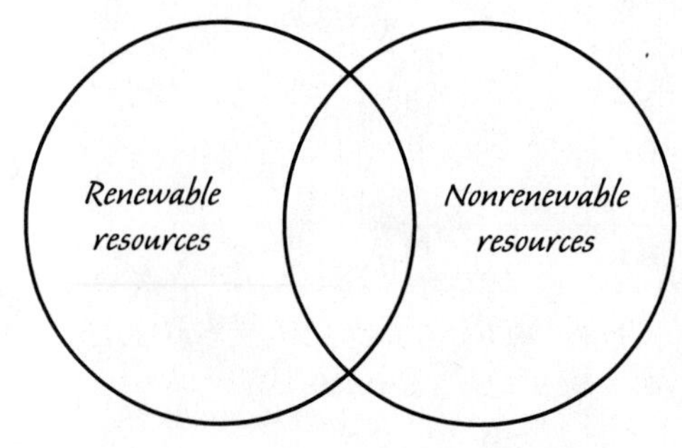

Section 1

# An Interconnected Planet

| Key Ideas | Key Terms | Why It Matters |
|---|---|---|
| ➤ How are humans and the environment connected?<br>➤ What is the difference between renewable resources and nonrenewable resources?<br>➤ How can the state of the environment affect a person's health and quality of life? | fossil fuel | The environment provides the resources that we need to live. When the environment is damaged, our resources are damaged. |

We depend on the environment for food, water, air, shelter, fuel, and many other resources. However, human actions can affect the quality and availability of these important resources. The study of the impact of humans on the environment is called *environmental science.*

***The Living Environment***
**Standard 4**
**7.1a** The Earth has finite resources; increasing human consumption of resources places stress on the natural processes that renew some resources and deplete those resources that cannot be renewed.
**7.1b** Natural ecosystems provide an array of basic processes that affect humans. Those processes include but are not limited to: maintenance of the quality of the atmosphere, generation of soils, control of the water cycle, removal of wastes, energy flow, and recycling of nutrients. Humans are changing many of these basic processes and the changes may be detrimental.
**7.1c** Human beings are part of the Earth's ecosystems. Human activities can, deliberately or inadvertently, alter the equilibrium in ecosystems. Humans modify ecosystems as a result of population growth, consumption, and technology.
**7.2a** Human activities that degrade ecosystems result in a loss of diversity of the living and nonliving environment.
**7.2b** When humans alter ecosystems either by adding or removing specific organisms, serious consequences may result.

## Humans and the Environment

10,000 years ago, there were only about 5 million people on Earth. The development of dependable food supplies, sanitation, and medical care have allowed the population to grow to more than 6 billion. The population will likely exceed 10 billion before it stabilizes. All 10 billion of these people will need a place to live. Humans now live in almost every kind of ecosystem on Earth. **Figure 1** shows one type of ecosystem in which humans live. As human population increases, the impact of humans on the environment increases. ➤ **Humans are a part of the environment and can affect the resilience of the environment.** The more that the human population grows, the more resources from the environment we will need to survive. Today's humans consume more resources than their ancestors did. The environment does not have an infinite amount of resources with which to meet humans' demand.

Earth is an interconnected planet: we depend on the environment, and the environment is affected by our actions. Learning about this connectedness helps us care for the environment and helps ensure that the environment will continue to support us and other species on Earth.

➤ **Reading check** ***How is Earth an interconnected planet? (See the Appendix for answers to Reading Checks.)***

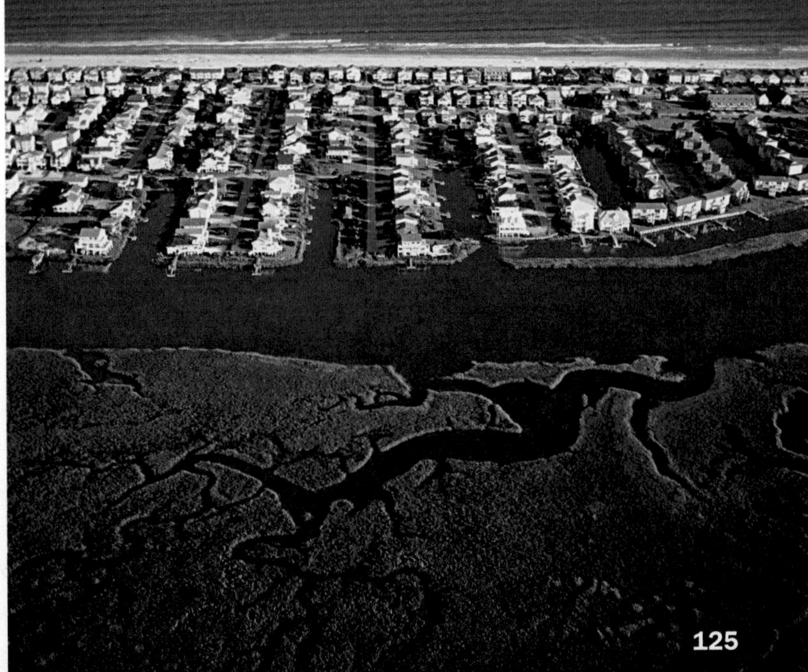

**Figure 1** This housing development lies in the marshlands along Myrtle Beach, South Carolina. ➤ **Can you describe another ecosystem that humans live in?**

## Resources

What would your day be like if you didn't have water to drink or electricity to provide lighting and heat? Water and fuel that generates electricity are two of Earth's many resources. Earth's resources are described as renewable or nonrenewable, as shown in **Figure 2.**

**ACADEMIC VOCABULARY**

**resource** anything that can be used to take care of a need

**Renewable Resources** Fresh water, solar energy, and fish are examples of renewable resources. ❯ ***Renewable resources* are natural resources that can be replaced at the same rate at which they are consumed.** A renewable resource's supply is either so large or so constantly renewed that it will never be used up. However, a resource can be renewable but still be used up if it is used faster than it can be renewed. For example, trees are renewable. But, some forests are being cut down faster than new forests can grow to replace them.

SCILINKS.
www.scilinks.org
Topic: Renewable and nonrenewable resources
Code: HX81290

**Nonrenewable Resources** Many resources that we depend on, such as minerals, coal and oil, are nonrenewable resources. ❯ ***Nonrenewable resources* are resources that form at a rate that is much slower than the rate at which they are consumed.** Most of our energy today comes from fossil fuels. **Fossil fuels** are nonrenewable energy resources that formed from the remains of organisms that lived long ago. Examples of fossil fuels are coal, oil, and natural gas. Coal, oil, and natural gas are nonrenewable resources because it takes millions of years for them to form. They form from the remains of organisms that were buried by sediment millions of years ago. As sediment accumulated over the remains, heat and pressure increased. Over time, the heat and pressure caused chemical changes that changed the remains into oil and natural gas. We use fossil fuels at a rate that is faster than the rate at which they form. So, when these resources are gone, millions of years will pass before more have formed.

**fossil fuel** a nonrenewable energy resource formed from the remains of organisms that lived long ago; examples include oil, coal, and natural gas

❯ **Reading check** ***Explain why natural gas is a nonrenewable resource.***

**Figure 2** Windmills produce renewable wind energy, while the oil rig extracts a nonrenewable energy resource. ❯ **Can you think of another example for each renewable and nonrenewable resource?**

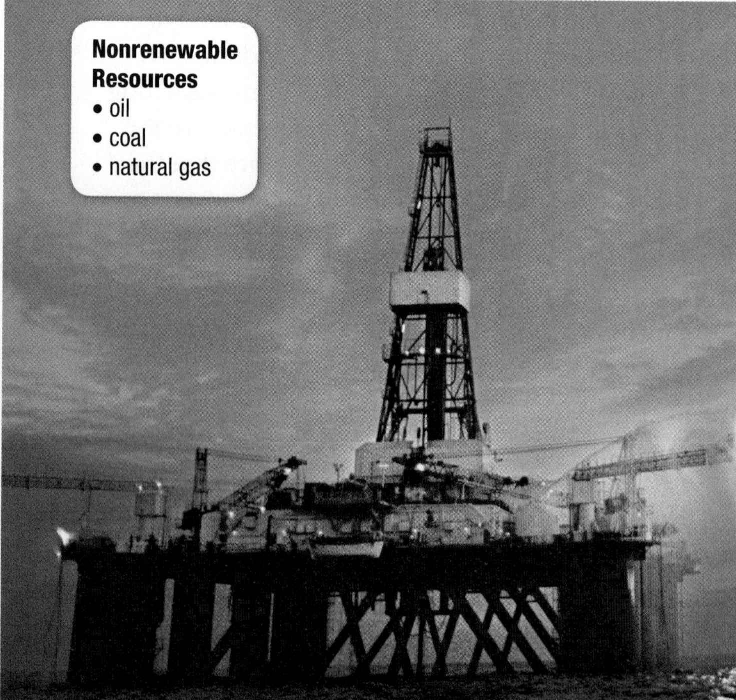

Hands-On

# QuickLab

15 min

## Contaminated Water 4.7.1c, 4.7.1b

In this activity, you will learn how contaminated water can spread an infectious disease.

### Procedure

1. **CAUTION: Do not taste or touch the fluids used in this lab.** Obtain one test tube of fluid from your teacher. Some test tubes contain pure water. One test tube contains water that has been "contaminated".
2. Pour half your fluid into the test tube of a classmate. Your classmate will then pour an equal amount back into your test tube. Exchange water with three classmates in this way.
3. Your teacher will now put a small amount of a test chemical into your test tube. If your water turns cloudy, you have been "contaminated."

### Analysis

1. CRITICAL THINKING **Analyzing Conclusions** Who had the test tube that started the "infection?"
2. **Identify** a disease that could be spread in water.

## The Environment and Health

Our health and quality of life are affected by the state of the environment. **Pollution and habitat destruction destroy the resources we need to live, such as the air we breathe, the water we drink, and the food we eat.** Air pollution can cause headaches, sore throats, nausea, and upper respiratory infections. Air pollution has also been connected to lung cancer and heart disease. Some chemical pollutants in drinking water can lead to birth defects and cancer. Many infectious diseases, such as cholera, are spread by water polluted by sewage. Habitat destruction can also affect our safety. The root networks of trees help hold soil in place. Cutting down trees increases the number of landslides and floods, which can cause deaths and injuries.

READING TOOLBOX

**Word Parts** Look up the suffix *-tion* in the dictionary. Also, look up the words *pollute* and *destroy* in a dictionary. Then, write your own definition for *pollution* and *destruction.*

## Section 1 Review

### KEY IDEAS

1. **Explain** how human population affects the environment.
2. **Describe** the difference between renewable resources and nonrenewable resources.
3. **State** a nonrenewable resource that you used today.
4. **State** three ways that environmental problems may affect human health.

### CRITICAL THINKING

5. **Inferring relationships** Events such as floods and landslides are commonly called *natural disasters.* Explain how both natural events and human actions might have contributed to a natural disaster that you have learned about.
6. **Analyzing data** Consider a 1,000-year-old forest and a 30-year-old tree farm. How do differences between these resources affect how renewable the resources are?

### WRITING FOR SCIENCE

7. **Evaluating viewpoints** A classmate argues that pollution is a necessary evil to produce food, jobs, and a high standard of living. Write a one-page paper describing your opinion of your classmates argument. Support your opinion with facts.

Section

# 2 Environmental Issues

| Key Ideas | Key Terms | Why It Matters |
|---|---|---|
| ➤ What are the effects of air pollution?<br>➤ How might burning fossil fuels lead to climate change?<br>➤ What are some sources of water pollution?<br>➤ Why is soil erosion a problem?<br>➤ How does ecosystem disruption affect humans? | acid rain<br>global warming<br>greenhouse effect<br>erosion<br>deforestation<br>biodiversity<br>extinction | In the course of meeting their basic needs, humans can unintentionally damage the global environment. |

***The Living Environment***
**Standard 4**

**6.2b** Biodiversity also ensures the availability of a rich variety of genetic material that may lead to future agricultural or medical discoveries with significant value to humankind. As diversity is lost, potential sources of these materials may be lost with it.

**7.1c** Human destruction of habitats through direct harvesting, pollution, atmospheric changes, and other factors is threatening current global stability, and if not addressed, ecosystems may be irreversibly affected.

**7.2a** Human activities that degrade ecosystems result in a loss of diversity of the living and nonliving environment. For example, the influence of humans on other organisms occurs through land use and pollution. Land use decreases the space and resources available to other species, and pollution changes the chemical composition of air, soil, and water.

**7.2b** When humans alter ecosystems either by adding or removing specific organisms, serious consequences may result. For example, planting large expanses of one crop reduces the biodiversity of the area.

**7.2c** Industrialization brings an increased demand for and use of energy and other resources including fossil and nuclear fuels. This usage can have positive and negative effects on humans and ecosystems.

Human activities can affect every ecosystem on Earth. Understanding these effects and the problems that they can cause is the first step to successfully solving them.

## Air Pollution

Have you ever breathed air that smelled bad or made your lungs burn? The bikers in **Figure 3** have. Natural processes, such as volcanic activity, can affect air quality. However, most air pollution is caused by human activities. Industries, power plants, and vehicles must burn fossil fuels for energy. The burning of fossil fuels releases the pollutants carbon dioxide ($CO_2$), sulfur dioxide ($SO_2$), and nitrogen oxides ($NO_2$ and $NO_3$) into the air. **➤ Air pollution causes respiratory problems for people, results in acid rain, damages the ozone layer, and may affect global temperature.**

**Acid rain** is precipitation that has an unusually high concentration of sulfuric or nitric acids, which is caused by pollution. Acid rain damages forests and lakes. The ozone layer protects life on Earth from the sun's damaging ultraviolet (UV) rays. The ozone layer has been damaged by *chlorofluorocarbons (CFCs)*. CFCs are human-made chemicals that are used as coolants in refrigerators and air conditioners and as propellants in spray cans. Global temperature may be affected by air pollutants. **Global warming** is the gradual increase in the average global temperature.

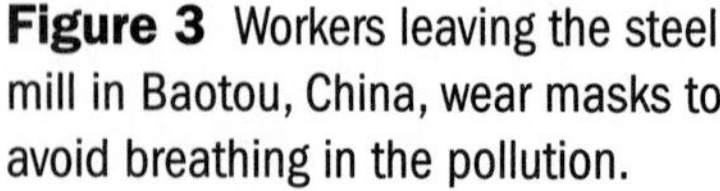

**Figure 3** Workers leaving the steel mill in Baotou, China, wear masks to avoid breathing in the pollution.

1 Solar radiation passes through the atmosphere and warms Earth's surface.
2 Some heat radiates away from Earth into the atmosphere. Some heat escapes into space.
3 Greenhouse gases also absorb some of the sun's energy and radiate it back toward Earth's surface.


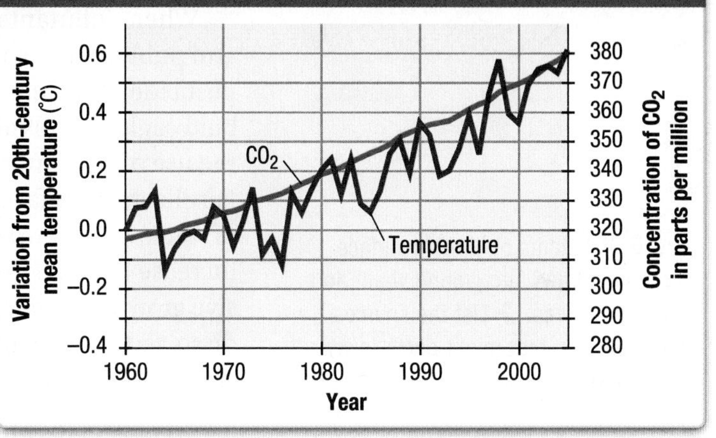


Source: Scripps Institute of Oceanography and National Oceanic & Atmospheric Administration.

## Global Warming

What does it feel like to climb into a car on a hot, sunny day? The inside of the car is hot because the sun's energy passes through the glass windows. The inside of the car absorbs the solar energy and changes it to heat energy. The heat energy cannot easily pass back through the glass windows. Therefore, the heat is trapped and makes the inside of the car hot. The atmosphere traps heat and warms the Earth in a similar way. The **greenhouse effect** is the warming of the surface and lower atmosphere of Earth that happens when greenhouse gases in the air absorb and reradiate heat. Examples of greenhouse gases are $CO_2$ and water vapor. **Figure 4** shows how this process works.

**Figure 4** The greenhouse effect is a natural process that keeps Earth warm.
**› How does the increase in $CO_2$ relate to global warming?**

The greenhouse effect is necessary to keep Earth's temperatures stable. However, Earth's global temperatures have been rising steadily for many decades. Most scientists think that this increase in temperatures is caused by an increase in $CO_2$. **› Burning fossil fuels increases the amount of $CO_2$ in the atmosphere. Increases in atmospheric $CO_2$ may be responsible for an increase in global temperatures.**

**Effects of Global Warming** A continued increase in global temperatures has the potential to cause a number of serious environmental problems. For example, ice sheets over Antarctica and Greenland have already started to melt. If these ice sheets continue to melt, they could raise sea levels around the world. Coastal ecosystems would be destroyed. People who live along a coast could lose their homes. Global weather patterns would also be affected. For example, warmer oceans make hurricanes and typhoons more intense and could make such storms more common. Droughts could become more frequent, causing damage to crops. The equilibrium in ecosystems could be altered. Migration patterns of some birds have already changed.

**› Reading check** *How might the burning of fossil fuels affect climate?*

**acid rain** precipitation that has a pH below normal and has an unusually high concentration of sulfuric or nitric acids, often as a result of chemical pollution of the air from sources such as automobile exhausts and the burning of fossil fuels

**global warming** a gradual increase in the average global temperature

**greenhouse effect** the warming of the surface and lower atmosphere of Earth that occurs when carbon dioxide, water vapor and other gases in the air absorb and reradiate infrared radiation

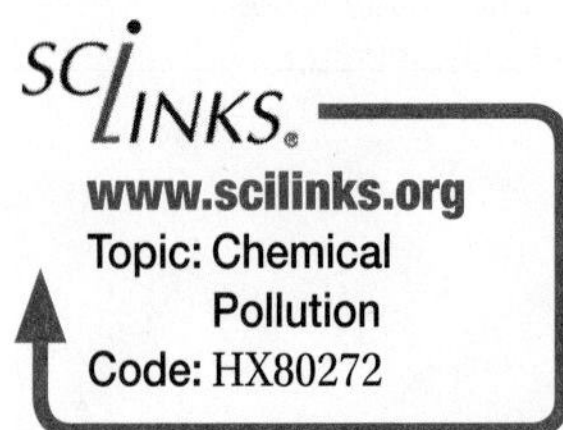

## Water Pollution

Every person needs 20–70 L (5–18 gal) of clean water each day to meet his or her drinking, washing, and sanitation needs. Unfortunately, many sources of water are polluted. **Figure 5** shows major sources of water pollution. **› Water pollution can come from fertilizers and pesticides used in agriculture, livestock farms, industrial waste, oil runoff from roads, septic tanks, and unlined landfills.** Pollution enters groundwater when polluted surface water percolates down through the soil. Oil on roads can be washed into the ground by rain. Pesticides, fertilizers, and livestock waste seep into the ground in a similar way. Landfills and leaking underground septic tanks are also major sources of groundwater pollution.

When pollutants run off land and into rivers, both aquatic habitats and public water sources may be contaminated. For example, the pesticide, DDT, harmed many species, such as the bald eagle. The bald eagle was in danger of becoming extinct until the U.S. restricted the use of DDT in 1972. Pollution can also affect ecosystems. Fertilizers from farms, lawns, and golf courses can run off into a body of water, which increases the amount of nutrients in the water. An increase in some nutrients in a body of water can lead to an excessive growth of algae called a "bloom." Algal blooms can deplete the dissolved oxygen in a body of water. Fish and other organisms then suffocate in the oxygen-depleted water.

**› Reading check** ***List three sources of water pollution.***

SCILINKS.
www.scilinks.org
Topic: Chemical Pollution
Code: HX80272

**Figure 5** Pollutants on Earth's surface run off the land and into ground water and other water systems. **› List the sources of water pollution that might occur in your neighborhood.**

go.hrw.com
interact online
Keyword: HX8ENVF5

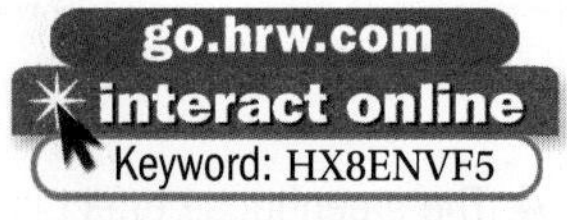

Industrial waste
Wastewater plant
Urban pollutants
Pesticides
Runoff
City of
Hazardous waste injection well
Lawn fertilizer
Private well
Road salt
Landfill
Petroleum storage tank
Septic system
Municipal well
Percolation
Water table
Aquifer

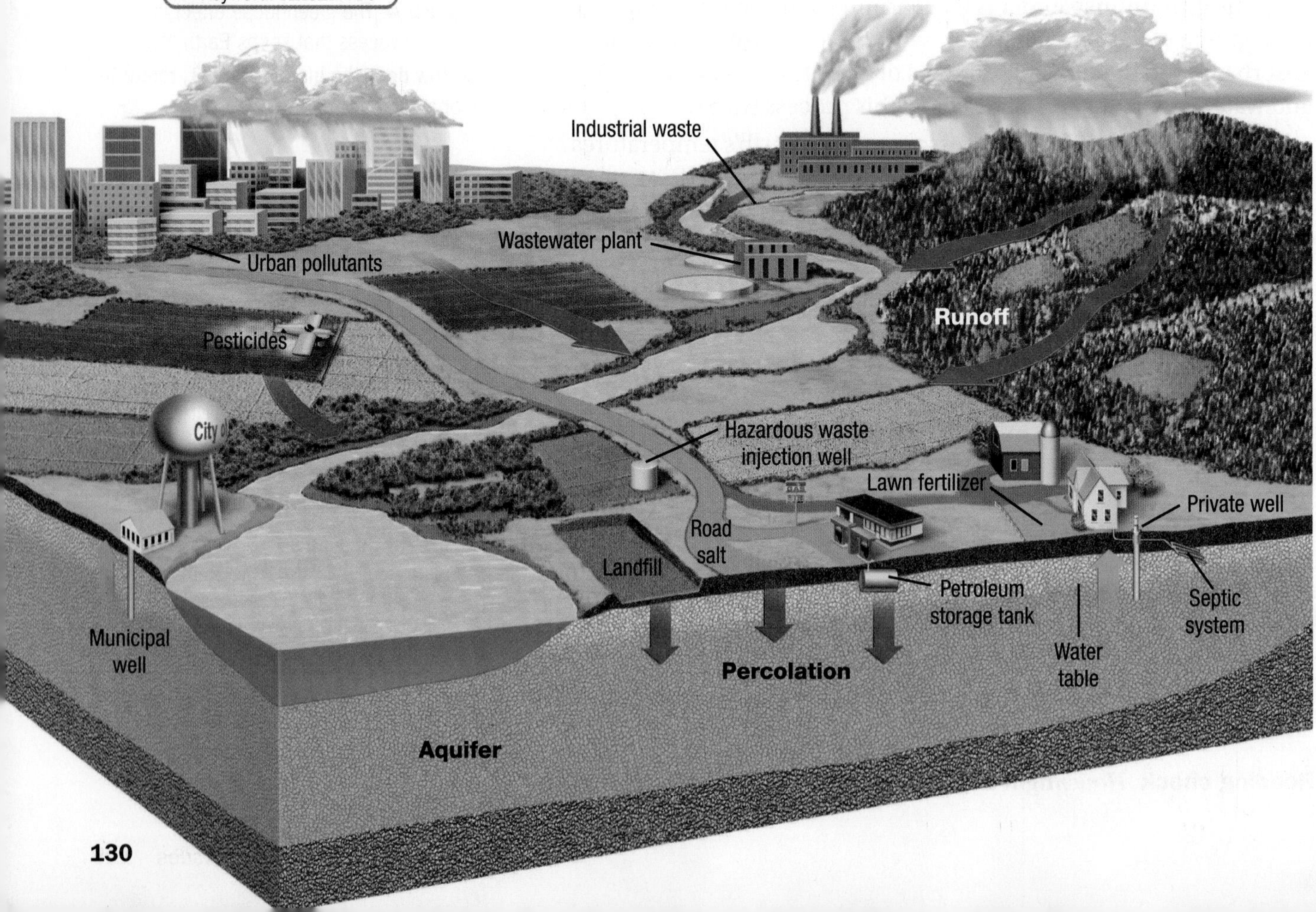

Hands-On

# QuickLab

## Soil Erosion  4.7.1b, 4.7.2a

In this lab you will investigate factors that affect erosion.

### Procedure

1. Fill **three trays:** one with **sod,** one with **topsoil,** and one with a type of **mulch.**
2. Place each tray at an angle on a "hill" of stacked **textbooks.** Place the same type of **large bowl** at the bottom of each tray to catch the runoff.
3. Pour **2 L of water** slowly and evenly on each tray to simulate heavy rainfall.
4. Use a **scale** to weigh the runoff of soil and water that collected in each bowl.

### Analysis

1. **Determine** which tray had the most soil erosion and water runoff. Which tray had the least? Why?
2. CRITICAL THINKING **Inferring Conclusions** What does this lab demonstrate about soil erosion?

## Soil Damage

Fertile soil allows agriculture to supply the world with food. The United States is one of the most productive farming countries, largely because of its fertile soils. Fertile soil forms from rock that is broken down by weathering. Nutrients that make soil fertile come from the weathered rock as well as from bacteria, fungi and the remains of plants and animals. The processes that form just a few centimeters of fertile soil can take thousands of years. Without fertile soil, we cannot grow crops to feed ourselves or the livestock we depend on.

**Soil Erosion** The greatest threat to soil is soil erosion. **Erosion** is a process in which the materials of Earth's surface are worn away and transported from one place to another by wind, gravity, or water. **❯ Soil erosion destroys fertile soil that we need in order to produce food.** Roots from plants and trees help hold soil together and protect it from erosion. When vegetation is removed, soil is left vulnerable to erosion. Many farming methods can lead to soil erosion. Plowing loosens the topsoil and removes plants that hold the soil in place. The topsoil can then be washed away by wind or rain.

**Soil Conservation** Sustainable agricultural practices can help conserve fertile soil. For example, *terracing* changes a steep field into a series of flat steps that stop gravity from eroding the soil. Planting a *cover crop,* such as soybeans, restores nutrients to the soil. *Crop rotation,* or planting a different crop every year, slows down the depletion of nutrients in the soil. In *contour plowing,* rows are plowed in curves along hills instead of in straight lines. The rows then act as a series of dams, which prevent water from eroding the soil.

**❯ Reading check** *How does erosion damage soil?*

**erosion** a process in which the materials of Earth's surface are loosened, dissolved, or worn away and transported from one place to another by a natural agent, such as wind, water, ice, or gravity

**Hypothesis or Theory?** A lake in your state has had hundreds of dead fish wash up on shore. Write your own hypothesis that might explain why so many fish in the lake died.

## Ecosystem Disruption

We share Earth with about 5 million to 15 million species. We depend on many of these species for fulfillment of our basic needs. We get food, clothing, medicines, and building material from many plants and animals. Yet as the human population has grown and affected every ecosystem, this wondrous diversity of life has suffered. **❯ Ecosystem disruptions can result in loss of biodiversity, food supplies, potential cures for diseases, and the balance of ecosystems that supports all life on Earth.** We cannot avoid disrupting ecosystems as we try to meet the needs of a growing human population. But we can learn about how our actions affect the environment so that we can create ways to conserve it.

**Habitat Destruction** Over the last 50 years, about half of the world's tropical rain forests have been cut down or burned. The forests have been cleared for timber, pastureland, or farmland, as shown in **Figure 6.** This process of clearing forests is called **deforestation.** Many more thousands of square miles of forest will be destroyed this year. Some of the people who cut down the trees are poor farmers trying to make a living. The problem with deforestation is that as the rain forests and other habitats disappear, so do their inhabitants. In today's world, habitat destruction and damage cause more extinction and loss of biodiversity than any other human activities do.

**deforestation** the process of clearing forests

**biodiversity** the variety of organisms in a given area, the genetic variation within a population, the variety of species in a community, or the variety of communities in an ecosystem

**extinction** the death of every member of a species

**Loss of Biodiversity** Ecosystem disruption decreases the number of Earth's species. Biodiversity affects the stability of ecosystems and the sustainability of populations. **Biodiversity** is the variety of organisms in a given area. Every species plays an important role in the cycling of energy and nutrients in an ecosystem. Each species either depends on or is dependent on by at least one other species. When a species disappears, a strand in a food web disappears. If a keystone species disappears, other species may also disappear. The species that disappears may be one that humans depend on.

**ACADEMIC VOCABULARY**

**sustain** to maintain or keep in existence

There are many ways in which humans benefit from a variety of life forms on Earth. Humans have used a variety of organisms on Earth for food, clothing, shelter, and medicine. At least one-fourth of the medicines prescribed in the world are derived from plants. Fewer species of plants could mean fewer remedies for illnesses.

**Figure 6** This forest in Brazil was slashed and burned to provide land for cattle and crops. **❯ How does deforestation decrease biodiversity?**

**Figure 7** The zebra mussel (left) is an invasive species that has disrupted the ecosystems of the Great Lakes region. The red panda (right) is an endangered species because its habitat, located in China and Myanmar, is being disrupted. **› Name another example of an invasive species. Name three other endangered species.**

**Invasive Species** Humans have disrupted ecosystems by intentionally and unintentionally introducing nonnative species. One example of an invasive species is the zebra mussel, shown in **Figure 7.** In the 1980s, the zebra mussel was unintentionally introduced to the Great Lakes by ships traveling from the Black and Caspian Seas. The zebra mussel disrupted the Great Lakes ecosystem, causing some species to struggle while others flourished. Zebra mussels have also had a negative impact on humans. Zebra mussels clog the pipes of water treatment facilities which costs the public millions of dollars a year.

**Extinction** Many species are on the edge of extinction. **Extinction** is the death of every member of a species. One species that is at risk of extinction is the red panda. A red panda is shown in **Figure 7.** When a species becomes extinct, we lose forever the knowledge and benefits that we might have gained from the species. For example, two anticancer drugs have been developed from the rosy periwinkle, a flower in Madagascar that is threatened by deforestation. If this flower becomes extinct, a possible source of new drugs is gone.

**› Reading Check** ***How has the introduction of the zebra mussel into the Great Lakes affected humans?***

## Section 2 Review

### › KEY IDEAS

1. **Identify** the affects of air pollution.
2. **Explain** how the burning of fossil fuels, such as oil, might lead to climate change.
3. **Identify** five sources of water pollution.
4. **Explain** why soil erosion is a problem.
5. **List** four ways ecosystem disruption affects humans.

### CRITICAL THINKING

6. **Evaluating Viewpoints** A classmate asserts that extinction is not a problem because everything goes extinct eventually. Explain how extinction can be both a natural process and a current problem for society.

### USING SCIENCE GRAPHICS

7. **Predicting Patterns** Using the chart, "$CO_2$ and Global Temperature Trends, 1960–2005," predict temperature and $CO_2$ levels for the year 2020. Describe how the temperature you predict would affect humans.

Section 3

# Environmental Solutions

| Key Ideas | Key Terms | Why It Matters |
|---|---|---|
| ❯ How do conservation and restoration solve environmental issues?<br>❯ What are three ways that people can reduce the use of environmental resources?<br>❯ How can research and technology affect the environment?<br>❯ How do education and advocacy play a part in preserving the environment?<br>❯ Why is it important for societies to consider environmental impact when planning for the future? | recycling<br>ecotourism | Everyone can play an important role in sustaining a healthy environment for all of us. |

***The Living Environment***
**Standard 4**

**7.3a** Societies must decide on proposals which involve the introduction of new technologies. Individuals need to make decisions which will assess risks, costs, benefits, and trade-offs.

**7.3b** The decisions of one generation both provide and limit the range of possibilities open to the next generation.

Protecting the environment is critical to human well-being. With new technologies and the effort of individuals and governments, many environmental problems can be solved.

## Conservation and Restoration

Two major techniques for dealing with environmental problems are conservation and restoration. ❯ ***Conservation*** **involves protecting existing natural habitats.** ***Restoration*** **involves cleaning up and restoring damaged habitats.** The best way to deal with environmental problems is to prevent them from happening. Conserving habitats prevents environmental issues that arise from ecosystem disruption. For example, parks and reserves protect a large area in which many species live.

Restoration reverses damage to ecosystems. Boston Harbor, shown in **Figure 8,** is one restoration success story. Since the colonial period, the city dumped sewage directly into the harbor. The buildup of waste caused outbreaks of disease. Beaches were closed. Most of the marine life disappeared and as a result, the shellfish industry shut down. To solve the problem, the city built a sewage-treatment complex. Since then, the harbor waters have cleared up. Plants and fish have returned, and beaches have been reopened.

❯ **Reading check** ***What is the difference between restoration and conservation?***

**Figure 8** Once considered one of the most polluted harbors in the world, Boston Harbor has been cleaned up as part of a restoration project. ❯ **Name a restoration project or natural preserve in your state.**

Hands-On

# QuickLab

30 min

## Recycled Paper 4.7.3a

In this activity, you will learn how to recycle paper.

### Procedure

1. Tear two sheets of used paper into small pieces.
2. Put the pieces in a blender with 1 L of water. Cover and blend until the mixture is soupy.
3. Fill a square pan with 2–3 cm of water. Place a wire screen in the pan.
4. Pour 250 mL of the paper mixture onto the screen and spread the mixture evenly.
5. Lift the screen and paper mixture out of the water.
6. Place the screen inside a section of newspaper. Close the newspaper and turn it over so that the screen is on top of the mixture.
7. Cover the newspaper with a flat board and press on the board to squeeze out the water.
8. Open the newspaper and let your paper dry overnight.

### Analysis

1. **Evaluate** whether the paper you made is as strong as the paper that it was made from.
2. CRITICAL THINKING **Analyzing Methods** How might you improve your technique to produce stronger paper?

## Reduce Resource Use

The impact of humanity on the environment depends on how many resources we use. We can decrease our impact by using fewer resources. **We can reduce our use of resources, such as water and fossil fuels for energy. We can reuse goods rather than disposing of them. Furthermore, we can recycle waste to help protect the environment.**

**Reduce** One of the best ways that you can help solve environmental problems is by reducing the amount of energy that you use and the amount of waste that you produce. You can use ceramic plates instead of a disposable paper plate. Low-flow toilets and shower heads can decrease the amount of water used.

**Reuse** The reuse of goods saves both money and resources. Many things are thrown away and wasted though they are still useful. Plastic bags and utensils can be used several times, rather than only once before disposal.

**Recycle** The process of reusing things instead of taking more resources from the environment is called **recycling.** Recycling existing products generally costs less than making new ones from raw materials does. For example, recycling aluminum uses about 95 percent less energy than mining and processing the aluminum from Earth does. Recycling also prevents pollution. For example, recycling motor oil keeps toxic substances out of landfills.

**Reading Check** *What are three ways that you can reduce your use of resources?*

ACADEMIC VOCABULARY

**impact** the effect of one thing on another

**recycling** the process of recovering valuable or useful materials from waste or scrap

## Technology

Advances in technology have lead to the production of cars and the development of industry. Both of these processes have contributed to the problem of pollution. But, technology brings not only problems but also environmental solutions. **› Research and technology can help protect our environment by providing cleaner energy sources, better ways to deal with waste, and improved methods for cleaning up pollution.**

SCILINKS.
www.scilinks.org
Topic: Environment
Code: HX80524

Solar panels, shown in **Figure 9,** hybrid cars, and scrubbers are examples of advances in technology. Hybrid cars use a combination of electricity and gasoline as their source of energy. Hybrid cars designed to be fuel-efficient, burn less gasoline and release less pollution into the atmosphere than the average car. Scrubbers are devices that reduce harmful sulfur emissions from industrial smoke-stacks. Scrubbers have decreased emissions of sulfur dioxide, carbon monoxide, and soot by more than 30%!

**Researching Solutions** Researchers must determine the cause of an environmental problem before they can provide a solution to it. Researching such problems requires the use of scientific methods. Scientists make observations and collect data. After analyzing the data, a scientist may propose a solution to the environmental problem that was studied. Proposals should take into account the costs, risks, and benefits of implementing the solution. Mario Molina is a scientist who researched the effects of CFCs on the ozone layer of the atmosphere. He determined that CFCs damage the ozone layer, which protects us from the sun's harmful ultra-violet radiation. His research convinced the nations of the world to limit the use of CFCs.

Research by students can also help solve environmental problems. **Figure 9** shows students trying to find out why the dwarf wedge mussel is disappearing from rivers.

**› Reading Check** ***How can fuel-efficient hybrid cars help solve environmental problems?***

**Figure 9** Students at Keene High School in New Hampshire do field research on dwarf wedge mussels (left). Solar panels in California generate energy without producing pollution (right).

**Figure 10** From a skybridge, ecotourists learn about the unique ecosystems at Monteverde Biological Cloud Forest Preserve in Costa Rica, without disturbing wildlife.

## Environmental Awareness

Addressing environmental issues requires cooperation among conservation groups, individuals, and governments. Education and advocacy help more individuals take an active role in this process. **❯ Education makes people more aware of environmental issues. Education also shows people how they can help address such issues. Expressing support, or *advocating*, for efforts to protect the environment can help get more people involved in these efforts.**

**Advocacy** Many environmental problems have been solved because of the efforts of those who advocate for a solution. Conservation groups make efforts to educate people, protect land, and influence laws through advocacy. Some organizations work on an international level. Others work on local environmental problems. Some groups help farmers, ranchers, and other landowners ensure the long-term conservation of their land.

Individuals and the media also play an important role in raising awareness of environmental issues. With her 1962 book *Silent Spring,* biologist Rachel Carson made millions of people aware of the dangers of pesticides. Her efforts contributed to the restriction on the use of the dangerous pesticide DDT.

**Venn Diagram** Make a Venn diagram to help you compare the similarities and differences between advocacy and education relating to environmental science.

**Education** Educating the public about the environment helps gain public support for solving environmental issues. Environmental education can enrich people's experience of their world and empower them to care for it. Ecotourism is one way to educate the public about the environment. **Ecotourism** is a form of tourism that supports conservation of the environment. **Figure 10** shows ecotourists in Costa Rica. Ecotourists may learn about the particular environmental problems of an area. Often, an ecotourist is given an opportunity to help solve environmental problems as part of his or her tour.

**ecotourism** a form of tourism that supports the conservation and sustainable development of ecologically unique areas

**❯ Reading check** ***How can advocacy and education help solve environmental problems?***

**Figure 11** The Fresh Kills landfill (left) occupies 2,200 acres on Staten Island. To the right is the plan for the Fresh Kills of tomorrow. **› In what ways does your community plan to conserve or restore the environment?**

## Planning for the Future

What will our planet look like in 50 years? Will it still supply the basic needs and quality of life that we enjoy today, or will we lack the resources we need? **› Careful planning for the future can help us avoid damaging the environment and can help us solve the environmental issues that we face.** If we want a safe, healthy, bright future, we need to actively aim for it. **Figure 11** shows how Staten Island is planning for the future by turning a landfill into a park.

Society can plan by noting the effects of certain activities, such as development and resource use. For example, if a builder wants to develop an area that is near an aquifer's recharge zone, the local government may evaluate the effects of development on the aquifer. After analyzing risks, costs, and benefits to the community, the government may choose to enforce limitations on the development. When governments plan for the future, they can protect resources for the community for years to come.

**› Reading check** ***Why do we need to evaluate effects of development before following through with the development?***

SCILINKS.
www.scilinks.org
Topic: Solving Environmental Problems
Code: HX81424

## Section 3 Review

### › KEY IDEAS

1. **Explain** how conservation might help an endangered species.
2. **Describe** three ways you can reduce the use of environmental resources.
3. **Describe** how research and technology affect the environment.
4. **Explain** how education on the resources that we use can help preserve the environment.
5. **Describe** how planning can prevent damage to the environment.

### CRITICAL THINKING

6. **Analyzing Methods** To join a global agreement to fight climate change, the United States must reduce $CO_2$ levels by 10%. What would be the positive and negative effects on society of such a reduction in $CO_2$?

### METHODS OF SCIENCE

7. **Predicting Outcomes** A land manager proposes planting shrubs to help restore land damaged by erosion. Describe a study or experiment that you could carry out to evaluate whether this proposal will work.

Why It Matters

WEIRD SCIENCE

# Cars of the Future

For many Americans, a car is a necessity. People rely on cars to get to work, to school, and to run errands. However, most cars are the main contributor of pollutants, such as $CO_2$, in the atmosphere. To help reduce the amount of pollutants released into the atmosphere, scientists have been developing cars that use nonpolluting forms of energy.

## Different Forms of Energy

Scientists have developed many cars of the future that are more fuel efficient than other cars of today or that use nonpolluting forms of energy. The hybrid, a type of car that is becoming popular in the United States, uses electricity as well as gasoline. Some cars of the future run on only solar power! Solar-car races, as shown in the image above right, inspire advancements in car technology through friendly competitions. The FIA Alternative Energies Cup in Japan has solar cars compete in an eight-hour endurance race. Scientists have also developed cars that can run on ethanol and hydrogen. Some day, you may be riding in one of these cars.

**Research** Many technical universities have teams that compete in solar car races. Conduct Internet research and investigate some of the more successful teams. Create a Web site or poster supporting one of the teams you learn about.

**Obvio!—Gas or Ethanol** This fuel-efficient Brazilian minicar can run on either gas or ethanol. Ethanol produces less pollution than gas and is renewable. Ethanol is formed from biomass, such as corn or potatoes.

**Toyota Fine-N Fuel Cell Hybrid (FCHV)** The FCHV doesn't burn fossil fuels. It gets its energy from a fuel cell that produces chemical energy by combining oxygen and hydrogen. The best thing about the fuel cell is that it doesn't produce any pollution. The only byproduct of the fuel cell is water!

Inquiry

# Chapter 6 Lab

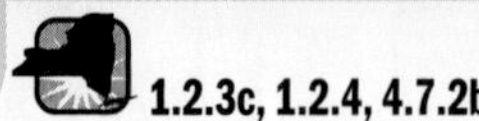


## Objectives

- Simulate an environmental condition in the laboratory.
- Measure the difference between treated and untreated seedlings.
- Analzye the effects of acidic conditions on plants.

## Materials

- seeds (50)
- beaker (250 mL)
- mold inhibitor (20 mL)
- water, distilled
- paper towels
- solutions of various pH
- pencil, wax (or marker)
- bags, plastic, resealable
- metric ruler
- graph paper

## Safety

*Effects of Acid Rain*

| Solution | Date | Observations |
|---|---|---|
| | | |
| | | |
| | | |

# Effects of Acid Rain on Seeds

Living things, such as salamander embryos, can be damaged by acid rain at certain times during their lives. In this lab, you will design an experiment to investigate the effects of acidic solutions on seeds. To do this, you will germinate seeds under various experimental conditions that you determine.

## Preparation

1. SCIENTIFIC METHODS **State the Problem** How does acid rain affect plants?
2. SCIENTIFIC METHODS **Form a Hypothesis** Form a testable hypothesis that explains how a germinating plant might be affected by acid rain. Record your hypothesis.

## Procedure

### Design an Experiment

1. Design an experiment that tests your hypothesis and that uses the materials listed for this lab. Predict what will happen during your experiment if your hypothesis is supported.
2. Write a procedure for your experiment. Identify the variables that you will control, the experimental variables, and the responding variables. Construct any tables that you will need to record your data. Make a list of all of the safety precautions that you will take. Have your teacher approve your procedure before you begin.

### Conduct Your Experiment

3. Put on safety goggles, gloves, and a lab apron.
4. **CAUTION: The mold inhibitor contains household bleach, which is a toxic chemical and a base.** Place your seeds in a 250 mL beaker, and slowly add enough mold inhibitor to cover the seeds. Soak the seeds for 10 minutes, and then pour the mold inhibitor into the proper waste container. Gently rinse the seeds with distilled water, and place them on clean paper towels.
5. **CAUTION: Solutions that have a pH below 7.0 are acids.** Carry out your experiment for 7–10 days. Make observations every 1–2 days, and note any changes. Record your observations each day in a data table, similar to the one shown.
6. Clean up your lab materials according to your teacher's instructions. Wash your hands before leaving the lab.

## Analyze and Conclude

1. **Summarizing Results** Describe any changes in the look of your seeds during the experiment. Discuss seed type, average seed size, number of germinated seeds, and changes in seedling length.
2. **Analyzing Results** Were there any differences between the solutions? Explain.
3. **Analyzing Methods** What was the control group in your experiment?
4. **Analyzing Data** Make graphs of your group's data. Plot seedling growth (in millimeters) on the *y*-axis. Plot number of days on the *x*-axis.
5. SCIENTIFIC METHODS **Interpreting Data** How do acidic conditions appear to affect seeds?
6. **Predicting Outcomes** How might acid rain affect the plants in an ecosystem?
7. SCIENTIFIC METHODS **Critiquing Procedures** How could your experiment be improved?
8. SCIENTIFIC METHODS **Formulating Scientific Questions** Write a new question about the effect of acid rain that could be explored with another investigation.

## Extensions

9. **Inferring Relationships** Research to identify the parts of the United States that are most affected by acid rain. Explain why acid rain affects these areas more than it affects other areas.
10. **Analyzing Methods** Describe how factories have changed to reduce the amount of acid rain.

# Chapter 6 Summary

| Key Ideas | Key Terms |
|---|---|

## 1 An Interconnected Planet

- Humans are a part of the environment and can affect the resilience of the environment.
- Renewable resources are natural resources that can be replaced at the same rate at which they are consumed.
- Nonrenewable resources are resources that form at a rate that is much slower than the rate at which they are consumed.
- Pollution and habitat destruction destroy the resources we need to live, such as the air we breathe, the water we drink, and the food we eat.

**Key Terms:** **fossil fuel** (126)

## 2 Environmental Issues

- Air pollution causes respiratory problems for people, results in acid rain, damages the ozone layer, and affects global temperature.
- Burning fossil fuels increases the amount of $CO_2$ in the atmosphere. Increases in atmospheric $CO_2$ may be responsible for an increase in global temperatures.
- Water pollution can come from fertilizers and pesticides used in agriculture and from livestock farms, industrial waste, oil runoff from roads, septic tanks, and unlined landfills.
- Soil erosion destroys fertile soil that we need in order to produce food.
- Ecosystem disruptions can result in loss of biodiversity, food supplies, potential cures for diseases, and the balance of ecosystems that supports all life on Earth.

**Key Terms:**
**acid rain** (128)
**global warming** (128)
**greenhouse effect** (129)
**erosion** (131)
**deforestation** (132)
**biodiversity** (132)
**extinction** (133)

## 3 Environmental Solutions

- Conservation involves protecting existing natural habitats. Restoration involves cleaning up and restoring damaged habitats.
- We can reduce our use of natural resources, such as water and fossil fuels for energy. We can reuse goods rather than disposing of them. Furthermore, we can recycle waste to help protect the environment.
- Research and technology can help protect our environment by providing cleaner energy sources, better ways to deal with waste, and improved methods for cleaning up pollution.
- Education makes people more aware of environmental issues and of ways that they can help. Expressing support, or *advocating,* for efforts to protect the environment can help get more people involved.
- Careful planning for the future can help us avoid damaging the environment and solve environmental issues that we currently face.

**Key Terms:**
**recycling** (135)
**ecotourism** (137)

The Living Environment

# Regents Exam Practice

**PART A: Answer all questions in this part.**

*Directions:* For each statement or question, write on your separate answer sheet the number of the word or expression that best completes the statement or answers the question.

**1** Which human activity would have the most positive effect on the environment of an area?

(1) using fire to eliminate most plants in the area
(2) clearing the area to eliminate weed species
(3) protecting native flowers and grasses in the area
(4) introducing a foreign plant species to the area

**2** A forest is cut down and is replaced by a cornfield. A negative consequence of this practice is

(1) an increase in the carbon dioxide released into the atmosphere
(2) an increase in the size of predators
(3) a decrease in biodiversity
(4) a decrease in the amount of soil that is washed away during rainstorms

**3** A change in the acidity of mountain lakes would most likely be a result of

(1) ecological succession of the area at the top of the mountain
(2) the introduction of new species into the lakes
(3) air pollution from smoke stacks miles away
(4) planting grasses and shrubs around the lakes

**4** Continued depletion of the ozone layer will most likely result in

(1) an increase in skin cancer among humans
(2) a decrease in atmospheric pollutants
(3) an increase in marine ecosystem stability
(4) a decrease in climatic changes

**5** Which human activity would have the least negative impact on the quality of the environment?

(1) adding animal wastes to rivers
(2) cutting down tropical rain forests for plywood
(3) using species-specific sex attractants to trap and kill insect pests
(4) releasing chemicals into the groundwater

**6** Which long-term change could directly cause the other three?

(1) pollution of air and water
(2) increasing human population
(3) scarcity of suitable animal habitats
(4) depletion of resources

**7** Water from nearby rivers or lakes is usually used to cool down the reactors in nuclear power plants. The release of this heated water back into the river or lake would most likely result in

(1) an increase in the sewage content in the water
(2) a change in the biodiversity in the water
(3) a change in the number of mutations in plants growing near the water
(4) a decrease in the amount of sunlight necessary for photosynthesis in the water

**8** Some organizations are buying up sections of forest land. Once purchased, these sections of forest will never be cut down. The main reason for protecting these sections of forest is to

(1) cause the extinction of undesirable animal species.
(2) prevent these trees from reproducing too fast.
(3) maintain the diversity of the living environment.
(4) provide more land for agricultural purposes.

**9** The rapid destruction of tropical rain forests may be harmful because

(1) removing trees will prevent scientists from studying ecological succession.
(2) genetic material that may be useful for future medical discoveries will be lost.
(3) energy cycling in the environment will stop.
(4) the removal of trees will limit the construction of factories that will pollute the environment.

**10** Which of the following is a result of ecosystem disruption?

(1) acid rain
(2) global warming
(3) greenhouse effect
(4) loss of biodiversity

## PART B

**11** Bacteria that are removed from the human intestine are genetically engineered to feed on organic pollutants in the environment and convert them into harmless inorganic compounds. Which row in the table below best represents the most likely negative and positive effects of this technology on the ecosystem?

| Row | Negative Effect | Positive Effect |
|---|---|---|
| (1) | Inorganic compounds interfere with cycles in the environment. | Human bacteria are added to the environment. |
| (2) | Engineered bacteria may out-compete native bacteria. | The organic pollutants are removed. |
| (3) | Only some of the pollutants are removed. | Bacteria will make more organic pollutants. |
| (4) | The bacteria will cause diseases in humans. | The inorganic compounds are buried in the soil. |

(1) 1
(2) 2
(3) 3
(4) 4

## PART C

**12** Mosquitoes are eaten by many birds and bats. In the New York City area, mosquitoes have been found to transmit West Nile Virus to some people who have been bitten by a mosquito carrying this virus. As a result, New York City health officials have sprayed pesticides into the air in order to kill as many mosquitoes as possible.

Discuss the use of pesticides to control the mosquito population. In your answer be sure to:

- state *one* advantage of killing all of the mosquitoes
- state *one* disadvantage of killing all of the mosquitoes
- state *one* danger to humans of spraying pesticides in the air

**13** Deforestation is viewed as a problem in the world today. Describe a cause and an effect of deforestation and a way to lessen this effect. In your answer, be sure to:

- state *one* reason deforestation is occurring
- state *one* environmental problem that results from widespread deforestation
- state *one* way to lessen the effects of deforestation, other than planting trees

**14** Currently, Americans rely heavily on the burning of fossil fuels as sources of energy. As a result of increased demand for energy sources, there is a continuing effort to find alternatives to burning fossil fuels. Discuss fossil fuels and alternative energy sources. In your answer be sure to:

- state one disadvantage of burning fossil fuels for energy
- identify one energy source that is an alternative to using fossil fuels
- state one advantage of using this alternative energy source
- state one disadvantage of using this alternative energy source

**15** For over 100 years scientists have monitored the carbon dioxide concentrations in the atmosphere in relation to changes in the atmospheric temperature. The graphs below show the data collected for these two factors.

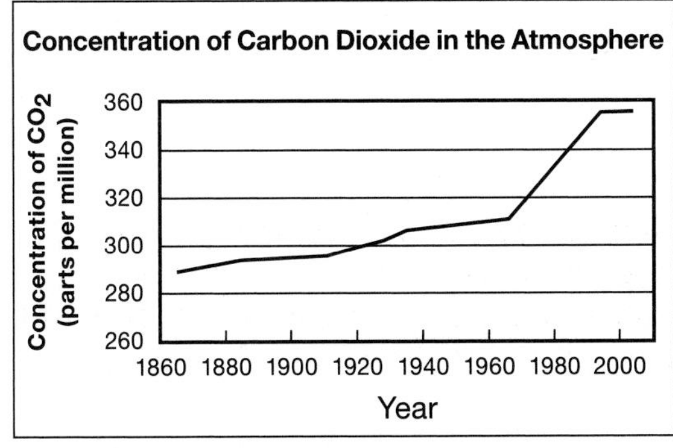


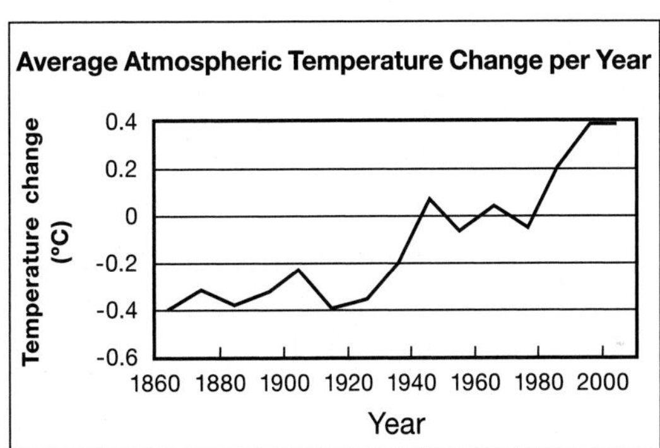


On a separate piece of paper, discuss the overall relationship between carbon dioxide concentration and changes in atmospheric temperature and the effect of these factors on ecosystems. Your answer must include:

- a statement identifying the overall relationship between the concentration of carbon dioxide and changes in atmospheric temperature
- one way in which humans have contributed to the increase in atmospheric carbon dioxide
- one specific negative effect the continued rise in temperature would be likely to have on an ecosystem
- one example of how humans are trying to reduce the problem of global warming

# UNIT 3 Cells

***The Living Environment***

**Standard 4** Students will understand and apply scientific concepts, principles, and theories pertaining to the physical setting and living environment and recognize the historical development of ideas in science.

**Key Idea 1** Living things are both similar to and different from each other and from nonliving things.

**Key Idea 2** Organisms inherit genetic information in a variety of ways that result in continuity of structure and function between parents and offspring.

**Key Idea 3** Individual organisms and species change over time.

**Key Idea 5** Organisms maintain a dynamic equilibrium that sustains life.

**Key Idea 6** Plants and animals depend on each other and their physical environment.

Sex chromosomes of a human male: Y (left) and X (right)

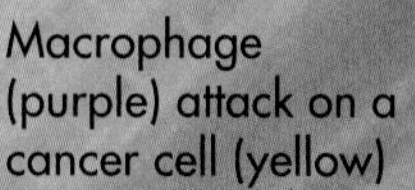

Macrophage (purple) attack on a cancer cell (yellow)

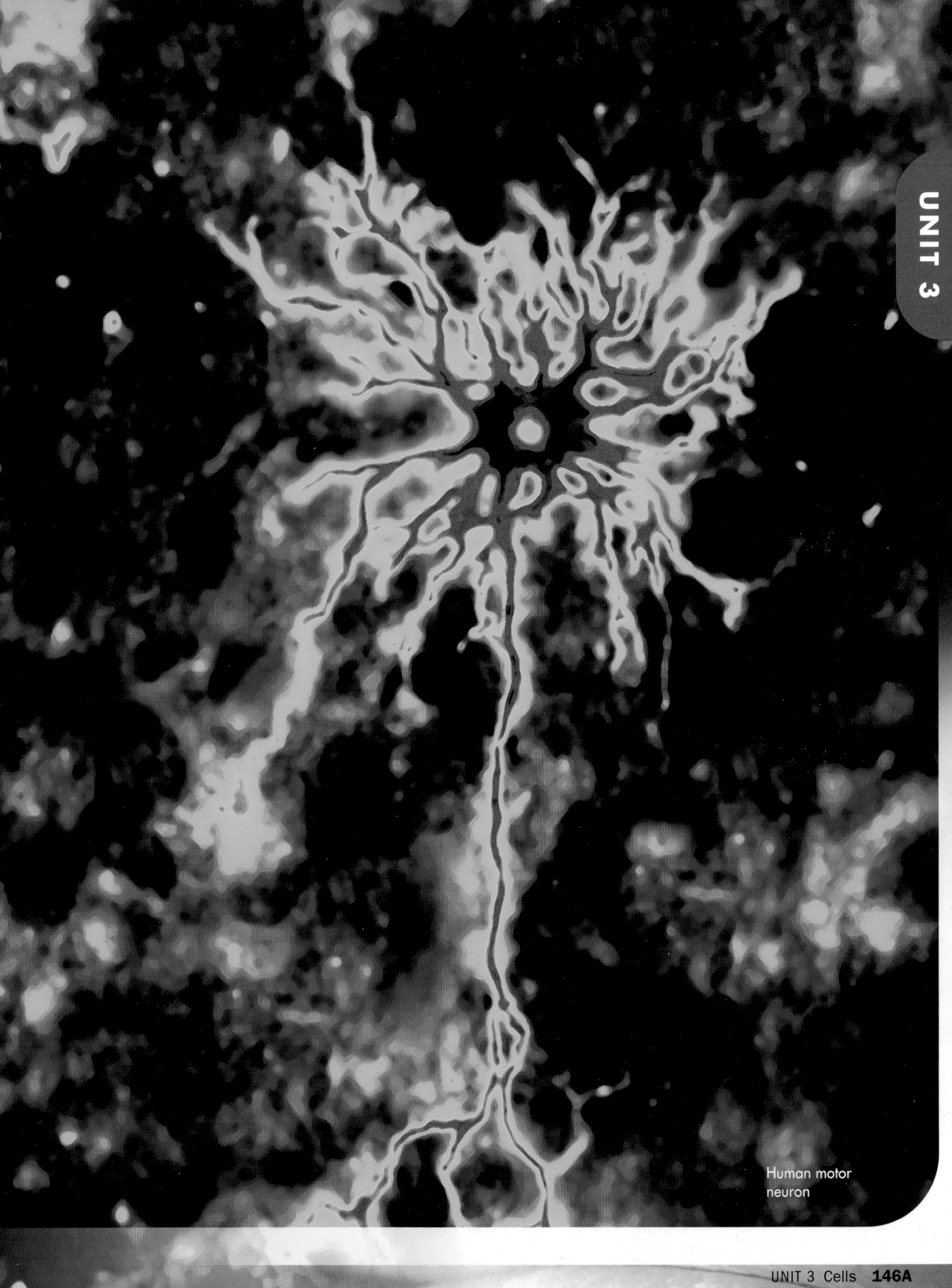

Human motor neuron

# DISCOVERIES IN SCIENCE

# Cell Biology

## 1665

Robert Hooke builds a microscope to look at tiny objects. He discovers cells after observing a thin piece of cork under a microscope. He also finds cells in plants and fungi.

Hooke's microscope

## 1772

British clergyman and chemist, Joseph Priestly, presents his paper, *On Different Kinds of Air,* in which he describes his discovery of oxygen and other previously-unknown gases found in air. He also demonstrates that oxygen is produced by plants.

## 1839

Theodor Schwann shows that all animal tissue is made of cells. With plant biologist, Matthias Schleiden, Schwann identifies cell components, such as membranes and a nucleus common, to many eukaryotic cells.

## 1855

Rudolf Virchow publishes a theory stating that all cells come from another cells. He explains, "Where a cell exists, there must have been a preexisting cell."

Animal cells

## 1945

Keith R. Porter, Albert Claude, and Ernest F. Fullam publish the first electromicrograph of a cell. Small organelles, such as the endoplasmic reticulum and the Golgi apparatus, are visible for the first time.

## LATE 1950s

Canadian scientists Ernest McCulloch and James Till begin research on stem cells in rodents. Bone marrow stem cells can produce several types of blood cells.

Bone marrow stem cell

## 1971

Lynn Margulis proposes the endosymbiotic theory of the origins of cell organelles. This theory states that chloroplasts and mitochondria in eukaryotes evolved from prokaryotes.

Lynn Margulis

## 2004

Richard Axel, and Linda Buck earn the Noble Prize in Medicine or Physiology for their discovery of how olfactory cells detect odors and how the brain processes information to provide a sense of smell.

Microtubules (green) and chromosomes (blue) in a dividing cell

# BIOLOGY CAREER



## Cell Biologist

**Shubha Govind**

Shubha Govind is a professor of biology at City College, City University of New York. Govind considers her most important scientific contribution to be developing a model system for using genetic tools to study the molecular basis of host-parasite interaction in fruit flies. She is studying how blood cells of fruit flies are formed and how they guard against infections when flies are attacked by parasites. She is also studying how parasites have evolved to overcome the immune reactions of the fly.

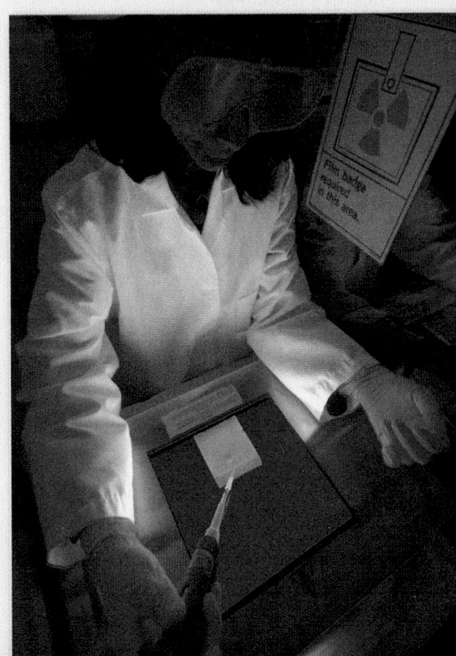

Govind grew up in India, and her family traveled a lot. As she traveled, she was impressed with the diversity of flora and fauna in different parts of the country. By the time she reached middle school, she knew that she wanted to be a biologist.

Apart from science, Govind enjoys reading, listening to music and spending time with family and friends.

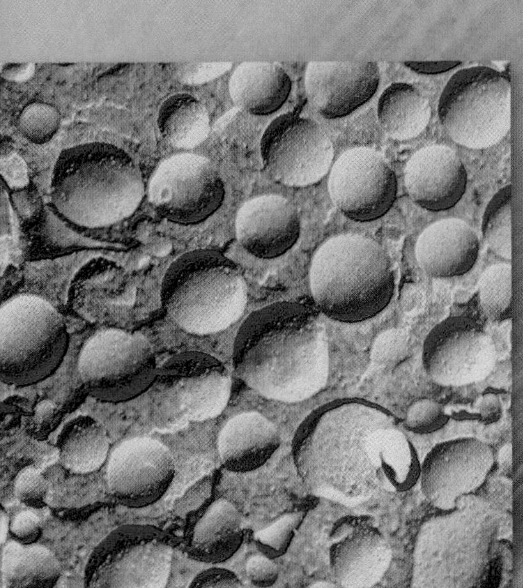

Freeze fracture of cell

# Chapter 7 Cell Structure

## Preview



## Why It Matters

All living things are made of cells. Scientists study how cells work to understand life.

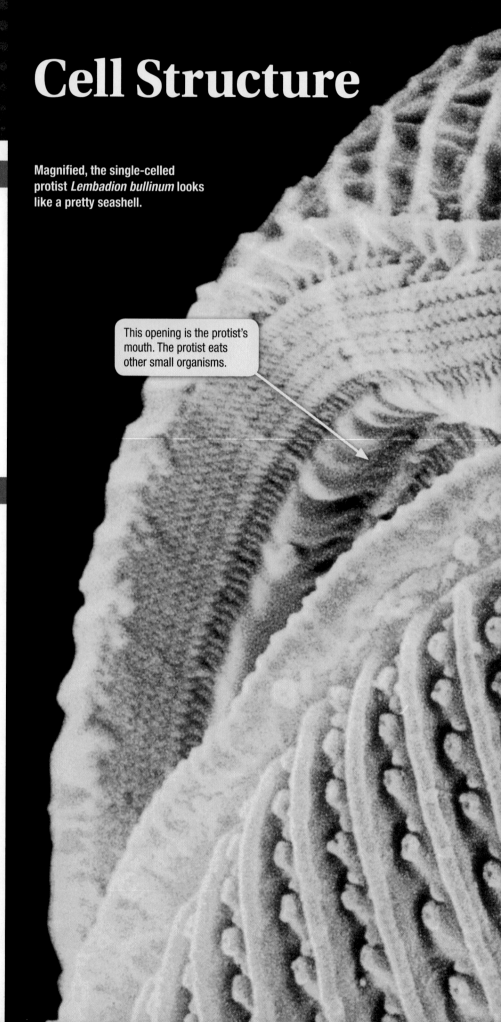

Magnified, the single-celled protist *Lembadion bullinum* looks like a pretty seashell.

This opening is the protist's mouth. The protist eats other small organisms.

***The Living Environment***

**Standard 4** Students will understand and apply scientific concepts, principles, and theories pertaining to the physical setting and living environment and recognize the historical development of ideas in science.

**Key Idea 1** Living things are both similar to and different from each other and from nonliving things. ***Major Understandings* - 1.2a, 1.2e, 1.2f, 1.2g, 1.2i**

**Key Idea 2** Organisms inherit genetic information in a variety of ways that result in continuity of structure and function between parents and offspring. ***Major Understandings* - 2.1f, 2.1k**

**Key Idea 3** Individual organisms and species change over time. ***Major Understandings* - 3.1j**

**Key Idea 5** Organisms maintain a dynamic equilibrium that sustains life. ***Major Understandings* - 5.1b, 5.1d, 5.3a**

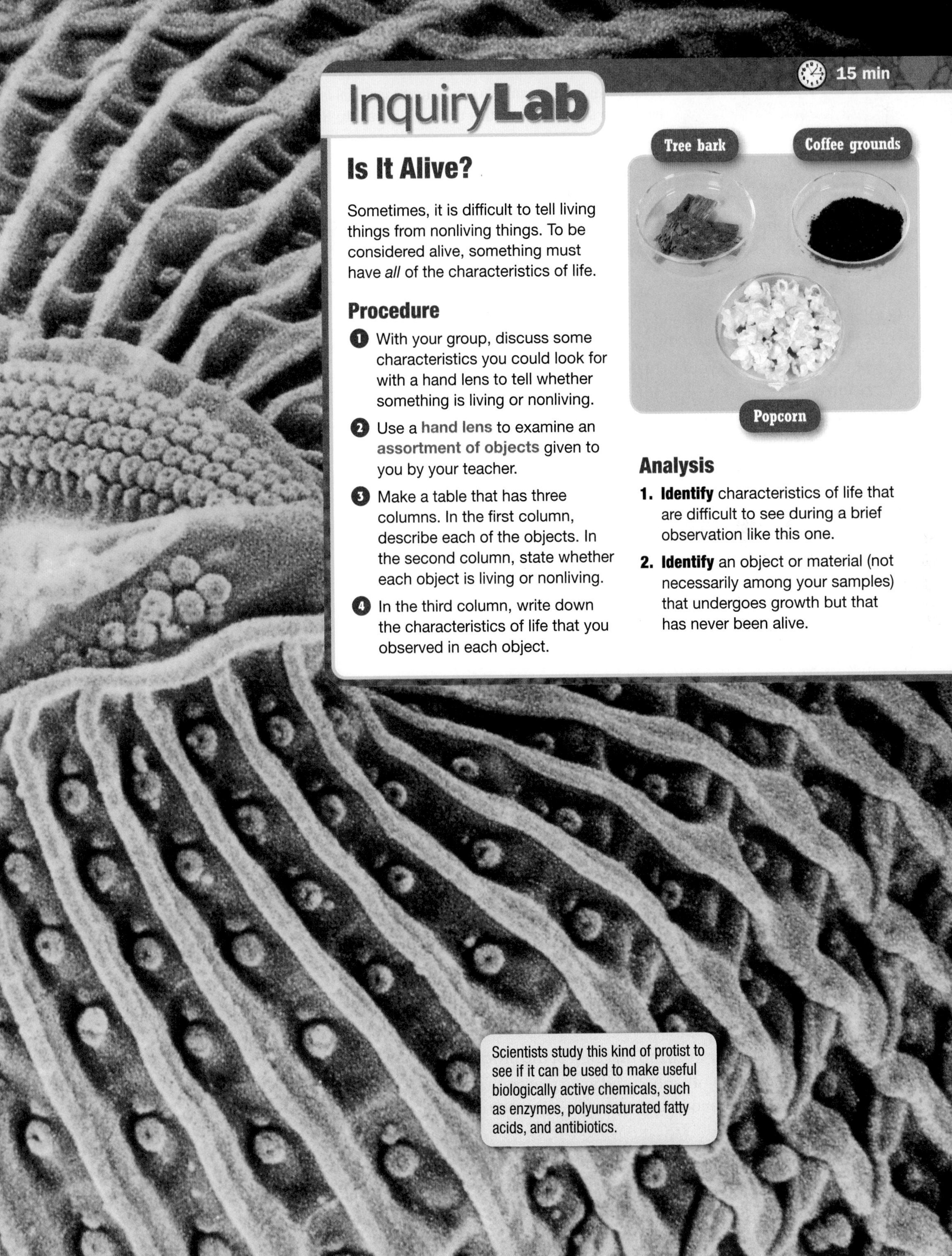


# Inquiry**Lab**

## Is It Alive?

Sometimes, it is difficult to tell living things from nonliving things. To be considered alive, something must have *all* of the characteristics of life.

### Procedure

1. With your group, discuss some characteristics you could look for with a hand lens to tell whether something is living or nonliving.
2. Use a **hand lens** to examine an **assortment of objects** given to you by your teacher.
3. Make a table that has three columns. In the first column, describe each of the objects. In the second column, state whether each object is living or nonliving.
4. In the third column, write down the characteristics of life that you observed in each object.

### Analysis

1. **Identify** characteristics of life that are difficult to see during a brief observation like this one.
2. **Identify** an object or material (not necessarily among your samples) that undergoes growth but that has never been alive.

Scientists study this kind of protist to see if it can be used to make useful biologically active chemicals, such as enzymes, polyunsaturated fatty acids, and antibiotics.

These reading tools can help you learn the material in this chapter. For more information on how to use these and other tools, see **Appendix: Reading and Study Skills.**

## Using Words

**Word Parts** Knowing the meanings of word parts can help you figure out the meanings of words that you do not know.

**Your Turn** Use the information in the table to answer the questions that follow.

1. Use the table to write your own definition for *organize.*
2. What do you think an organelle does in a cell?

**Word Parts**

| Word part | Type | Meaning |
|---|---|---|
| *organ* | root | a group of parts that work together |
| *-ize* | suffix | to make or become |
| *-elle* | suffix | small part |

## Using Language

**Similes** Similes help relate new ideas to ideas that you already know. Often, similes use the terms *like* or *as.* For example, if you were describing a motorcycle to someone who had never seen one, you might say that it is like a bicycle that has a motor.

**Your Turn** Use information in the chapter to answer the questions that follow.

1. Find a simile to describe a cytoskeleton.
2. Write a simile to describe the function of a mitochondrion.

## Using Science Graphics

**Process Chart** Science is full of processes. A process chart shows the steps that a process takes to get from one point to another point. This tool can help you visualize a process and remember the steps.

**Your Turn** Make a process chart to help you remember the steps of protein packaging.

1. Draw a box. In the box, write the first step of the process.
2. Under the box, draw another box and an arrow connecting the two boxes. In the second box, write the next step of the process.
3. Keep adding boxes and arrows until each step of the process has been included.

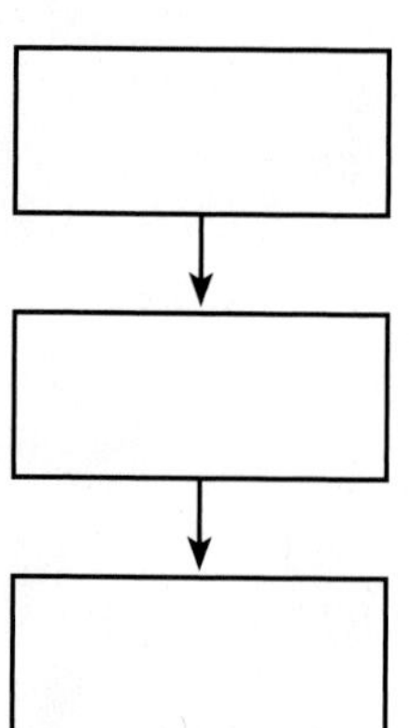

Section 1

# Introduction to Cells

| Key Ideas | Key Terms | | Why It Matters |
|---|---|---|---|
| ❯ How were cells discovered?<br>❯ What defines cell shape and size?<br>❯ What enables eukaryotes to perform more specialized functions than prokaryotes do? | cell membrane<br>cytoplasm<br>ribosome | prokaryote<br>eukaryote<br>nucleus<br>organelle | Cells are the basic unit of life. By studying cells, biologists can better understand life's processes. |

All life-forms on our planet are made up of cells. The bacteria that live in our gut and the cells that make up our body are built from the same chemical machinery. This machinery allows living things to obtain and use energy, to respond to their environment, and to reproduce. In all organisms, cells have the same basic structure.

***The Living Environment***
**Standard 4**

**1.2f** Cells have particular structures that perform specific jobs. These structures perform the actual work of the cell. Just as systems are coordinated and work together, cell parts must also be coordinated and work together.

**1.2g** Each cell is covered by a membrane that performs a number of important functions for the cell. These include: separation from its outside environment, controlling which molecules enter and leave the cell, and recognition of chemical signals. The processes of diffusion and active transport are important in the movement of materials in and out of cells.

**1.2i** Inside the cell a variety of specialized structures, formed from many different molecules, carry out the transport of materials (cytoplasm), extraction of energy from nutrients (mitochondria), protein building (ribosomes), waste disposal (cell membrane), storage (vacuole), and information storage (nucleus).

**2.1f** In all organisms, the coded instructions for specifying the characteristics of the organism are carried in DNA, a large molecule formed from subunits arranged in a sequence with bases of four kinds (represented by A, G, C, and T).

**3.1j** Billions of years ago, life on Earth is thought by many scientists to have begun as simple, single-celled organisms. About a billion years ago, increasingly complex multicellular organisms began to evolve.

## The Discovery of Cells

How do living things differ from nonliving things? The discovery of cells was an important step toward answering this question. Most cells are too small to see with the naked eye. As **Figure 1** shows, microscopes have become an important tool for studying biology. **❯ Microscope observations of organisms led to the discovery of the basic characteristics common to all living things.**

In 1665, Robert Hooke, an English scientist, used a crude microscope to look at a thin slice of cork. His microscope could magnify objects to only 30 times their normal size. Hooke saw many "little boxes" in the cork. They reminded him of the small rooms in which monks lived, so he called them *cells*. Hooke later discovered cells in the stems and roots of plants. Ten years later, Anton van Leeuwenhoek, a Dutch scientist, used a more powerful microscope that could magnify objects 300-fold. He discovered many living creatures in pond water. He named them *animalcules,* or "tiny animals." Today, we know that they were not animals. They were single-celled organisms.

**❯ Reading Check** ***How powerful was Hooke's microscope? (See the Appendix for answers to Reading Checks.)***

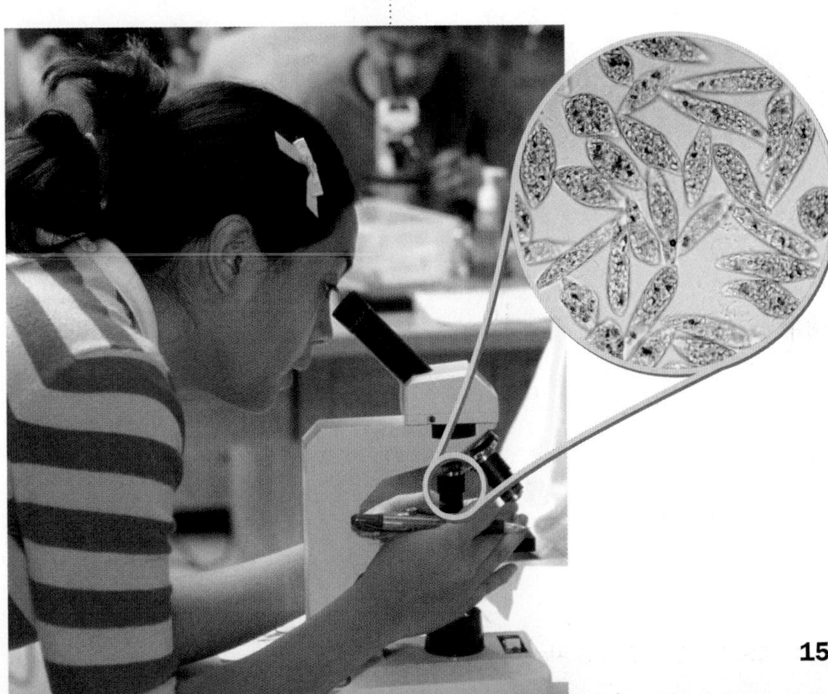

**Figure 1** A student looks through a light microscope. Euglena (inset) are single-celled organisms that are commonly found in pond water.

**Cell Theory** It took more than 150 years for scientists to fully appreciate the discoveries of Hooke and Leeuwenhoek. By the 1830s, microscopes were powerful enough to resolve structures only 1 μm apart. In 1838, Matthias Schleiden, a German botanist, concluded that cells make up every part of a plant. A year later, Theodor Schwann, a German zoologist, discovered that animals are also made up of cells. In 1858, Rudolph Virchow, a German physician, proposed that cells come only from the division of existing cells. The observations of Schleiden, Schwann, and Virchow form the *cell theory:*

- All living things are made up of one or more cells.
- Cells are the basic units of structure and function in organisms.
- All cells arise from existing cells.

The cell theory has withstood the rigorous examination of cells by scientists equipped with today's high-powered microscopes. As new tools and techniques are invented, scientists will learn more about the characteristics of cells.

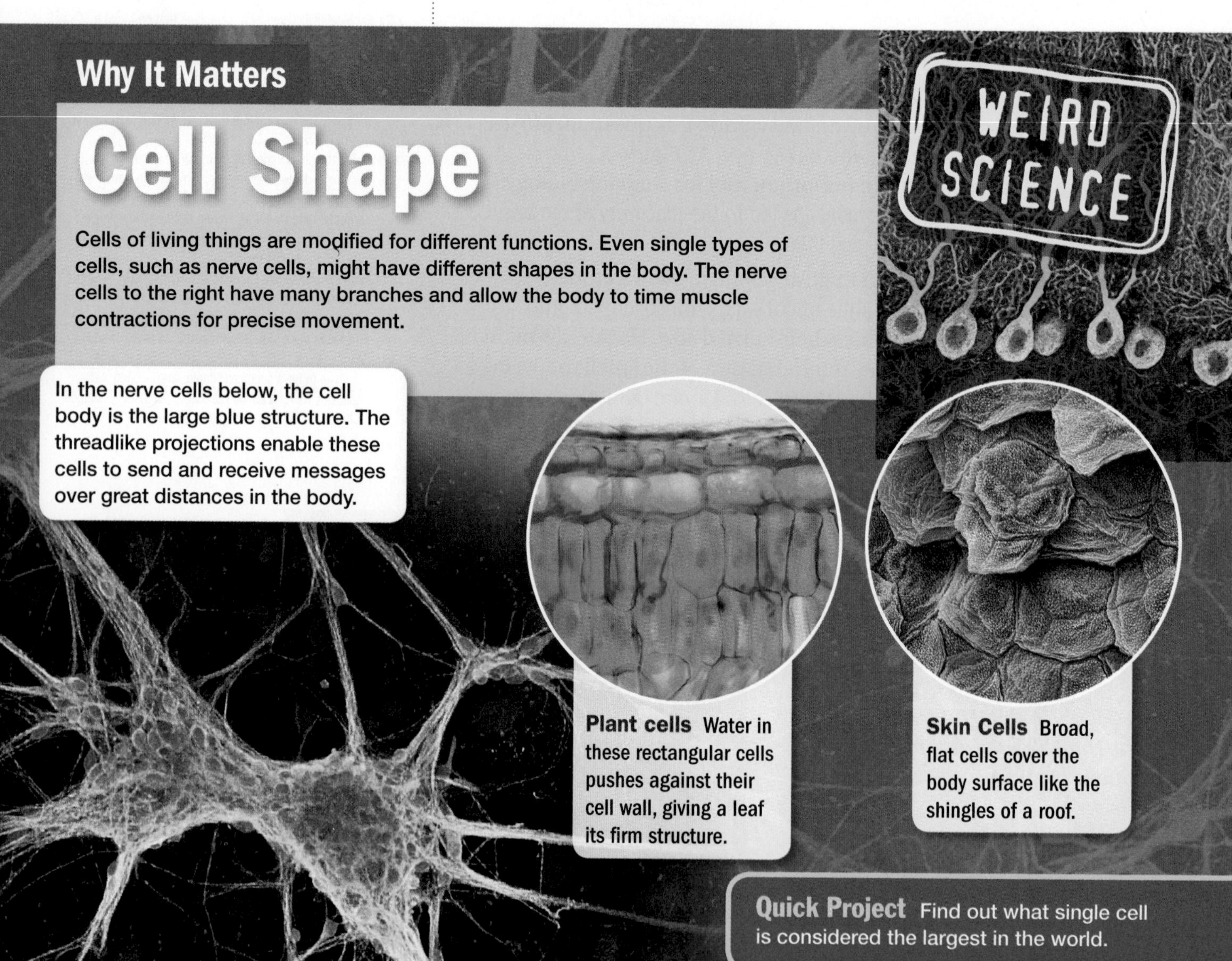


Cells of living things are modified for different functions. Even single types of cells, such as nerve cells, might have different shapes in the body. The nerve cells to the right have many branches and allow the body to time muscle contractions for precise movement.

In the nerve cells below, the cell body is the large blue structure. The threadlike projections enable these cells to send and receive messages over great distances in the body.

**Plant cells** Water in these rectangular cells pushes against their cell wall, giving a leaf its firm structure.

**Skin Cells** Broad, flat cells cover the body surface like the shingles of a roof.

**Quick Project** Find out what single cell is considered the largest in the world.

## Math Skills Ratio of Surface Area and Volume

A ratio compares two numbers by dividing one number by the other number. A ratio can be expressed in three ways:

$x$ to $y$ $\frac{x}{y}$ $x:y$

You can improve your understanding of a cell's surface area–to-volume ratio by practicing with cubes of various sizes. What is the surface area–to-volume ratio of a cube that has a side length ($l$) of 4 mm?

**1** Find the surface area of the cube. A cube has six square faces. The surface area of one face is $l \times l$, or $l^2$.

- *total surface area of cube* = $6 \times l^2$
- *total surface area of cube* = $6 \times (4 \text{ mm})^2 = 96 \text{ mm}^2$

**2** Find the volume of the cube.

- *volume of cube* = $l^3$
- *volume of cube* = $(4 \text{ mm})^3 = 64 \text{ mm}^3$

**Surface Area and Volume**

| Side length | Surface area | Volume | Surface area–to-volume |
|---|---|---|---|
| 1 mm | 6 $mm^2$ | 1 $mm^3$ | 6:1 |
| 2 mm | 24 $mm^2$ | 8 $mm^3$ | 3:1 |
| 4 mm | 96 $mm^2$ | 64 $mm^3$ | 3:2 |

**3** Divide the total surface area by volume:

- *surface area–to-volume ratio* = $\frac{\textit{total surface area}}{\textit{volume}}$

Reduce both numbers by their greatest common factor:

- *surface area–to-volume ratio* = $\frac{(96 \div 32)}{(64 \div 32)} = \frac{3}{2}$

## Looking at Cells

Cells vary greatly in size and in shape. **› A cell's shape reflects the cell's function.** Cells may be branched, flat, round, or rectangular. Some cells have irregular shapes, while other cells constantly change shapes. These differences enable different cells to perform highly specific functions in the body. There are at least 200 types of cells. The human body is made up of about 100 trillion cells, most of which range from 5 to 20 µm in diameter. Why are cells so small?

**Cell Size** All substances that enter or leave a cell must pass through the surface of the cell. As a cell gets larger, it takes up more nutrients and releases more wastes. These substances must move farther to reach their destination in a larger cell. **› Cell size is limited by a cell's surface area–to-volume ratio.**

Scientists can estimate a cell's ability to exchange materials by calculating the cell's surface area–to-volume ratio. Cells with greater surface area–to-volume ratios can exchange substances more efficiently. When cells that are the same shape as one another are compared, the smaller cells have greater surface area–to-volume ratios than larger cells do.

**Cell Shape** Larger cells often have shapes that increase the surface area available for exchange. A cell may grow large in one or two dimensions but remain small in others. For example, some skin cells are broad and flat. Some nerve cells are highly extended and can be more than 10,000 times as long as they are thick. In both of these types of cells, the surface area–to-volume ratio is larger than it would be if the cells were spheres.

**› Reading Check** *How does a cell's size affect the cell's function?*

**Academic Vocabulary**

**dimension** a measurement in a particular direction

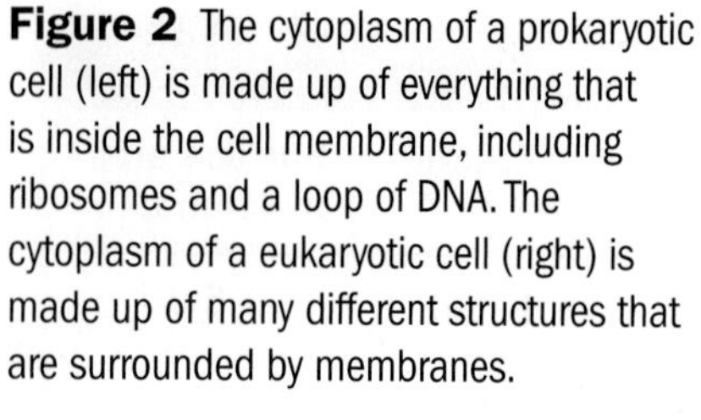

**Figure 2** The cytoplasm of a prokaryotic cell (left) is made up of everything that is inside the cell membrane, including ribosomes and a loop of DNA. The cytoplasm of a eukaryotic cell (right) is made up of many different structures that are surrounded by membranes.

**Features of Prokaryotic and Eukaryotic Cells**

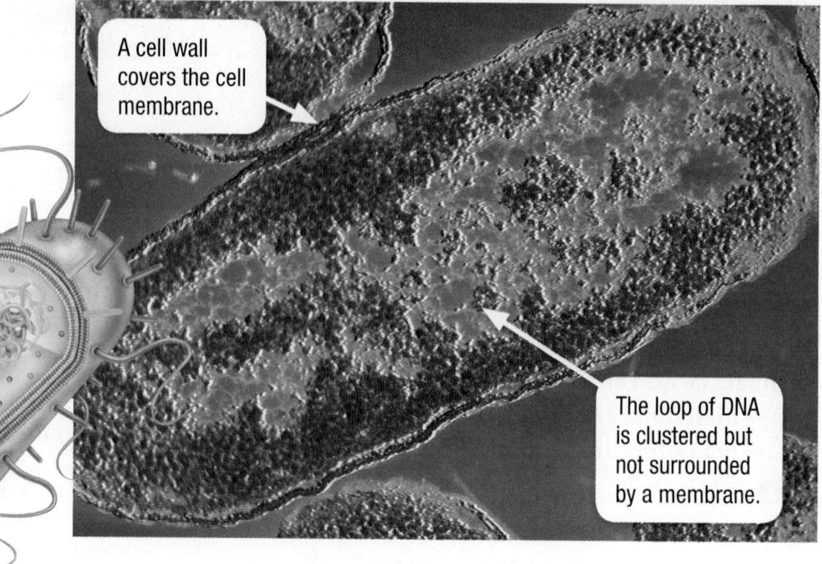
A cell wall covers the cell membrane.
The loop of DNA is clustered but not surrounded by a membrane.
Bacterium (Prokaryotic cell)

SCILINKS.

www.scilinks.org
Topic: Cell Features
Code: HX80238

## Cell Features

All cells—from bacteria to those in a berry, bug, or bunny—share common structural features. All cells have a cell membrane, cytoplasm, ribosomes, and DNA. The **cell membrane** is the cell's outer boundary. It acts as a barrier between the outside environment and the inside of the cell. The *cytosol,* the fluid inside the cell, is full of dissolved particles. The **cytoplasm** includes this fluid and almost all of the structures that are suspended in the fluid. Many ribosomes are found in the cytoplasm. A **ribosome** is a cellular structure on which proteins are made. All cells also have DNA, the genetic material. DNA provides instructions for making proteins, regulates cellular activities, and enables cells to reproduce.

**Features of Prokaryotic Cells** The bacterium shown in **Figure 2** is an example of a **prokaryote,** an organism that is a single prokaryotic cell. A prokaryotic cell is quite simple in its organization. The genetic material is a single loop of DNA, which looks like a tangled string and usually lies near the center of the cell. Ribosomes and enzymes share the cytoplasm with the DNA.

Prokaryotic cells have a cell wall that surrounds the cell membrane and that provides structure and support. Some prokaryotic cell walls are surrounded by a *capsule,* a structure that enables prokaryotes to cling to surfaces, including teeth, skin, and food.

Scientists think that the first prokaryotes may have lived 3.5 billion years ago or more. For millions of years, prokaryotes were the only organisms on Earth. They were very simple and small (1 to 2 μm in diameter). Like their ancestors, modern prokaryotes are also very small (1 to 15 μm), and they live in a wide range of habitats. Prokaryotes make up a very large and diverse group of cells.

› **Reading Check** ***What is a ribosome?***

**cell membrane** a phospholipid layer that covers a cell's surface and acts as a barrier between the inside of a cell and the cell's environment

**cytoplasm** (SIET oh PLAZ uhm) the region of the cell within the membrane

**ribosome** (RIE buh SOHM) a cell organelle where protein synthesis occurs

**prokaryote** a single-celled organism that does not have a nucleus or membrane-bound organelles

**eukaryote** an organism made up of cells that have a nucleus and membrane-bound organelles

**nucleus** in a eukaryotic cell, a membrane-bound organelle that contains the cell's DNA

**organelle** one of the small bodies that are found in the cytoplasm of a cell and that are specialized to perform a specific function

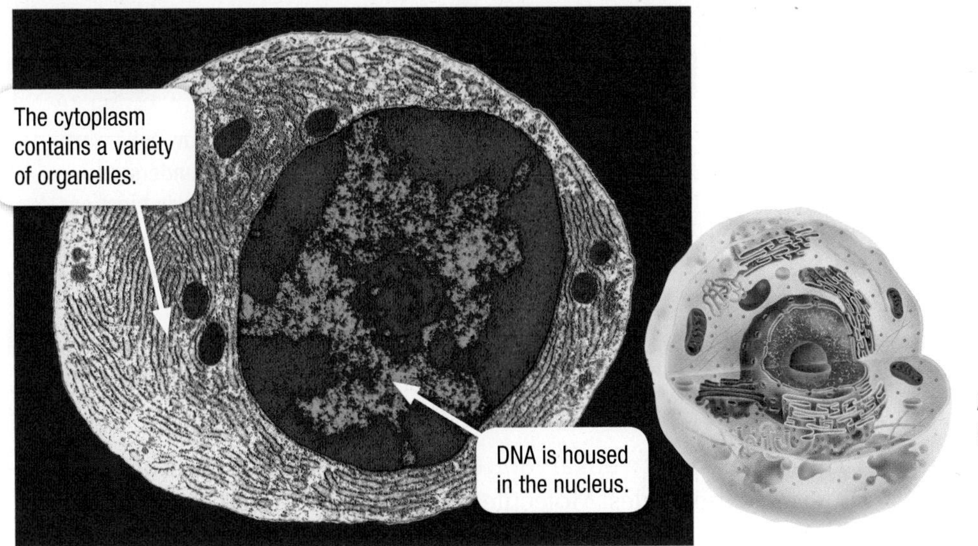
The cytoplasm contains a variety of organelles.
DNA is housed in the nucleus.
Animal cell
(Eukaryotic cell)

**Features of Eukaryotic Cells** A **eukaryote** is an organism that is made up of one or more eukaryotic cells. Some eukaryotes live as single cells. Others are multicellular organisms. In fact, all multicellular organisms are made up of eukaryotic cells. **Because of their complex organization, eukaryotic cells can carry out more specialized functions than prokaryotic cells can.**

Primitive eukaryotic cells first appeared about 1.5 billion years ago. As shown in the animal cell in **Figure 2,** a eukaryotic cell contains compartments that are separated by membranes. The cell's DNA is housed in an internal compartment called the **nucleus.**

In addition to having a membrane, cytoplasm, ribosomes, and a nucleus, all eukaryotic cells have membrane-bound organelles. An **organelle** is a structure that carries out specific activities inside the cell. The animal cell in **Figure 2** shows many of the organelles found in eukaryotic cells. Each organelle performs distinct functions. Many organelles are surrounded by a membrane. Some of the membranes are connected by channels that help move substances within the cell.

READING TOOLBOX

**Word Parts** The root *kary* means "kernel," which describes the nucleus. *Eu-* means "true," so a eukaryotic cell has a true nucleus. If *pro-* means "before," what does prokaryotic mean?

## Section 1 Review

### KEY IDEAS

1. **List** the three parts of the cell theory.
2. **Describe** the importance of a cell's surface area–to-volume ratio.
3. **Compare** the structure of a eukaryotic cell with that of a prokaryotic cell.

### CRITICAL THINKING

4. **Explaining Relationships** The development of the cell theory is directly related to advances in microscope technology. Why are these two developments related?
5. **Making Comparisons** How do the membrane-bound organelles of a eukaryotic cell act in a manner similar to the organs in a multicellular organism?

### METHODS OF SCIENCE

6. **Extraterrestrial Cells** You are a scientist with NASA. Some samples of extraterrestrial material containing living things have arrived on your spaceship. Your first job is to determine if the samples contain prokaryotic or eukaryotic cells. How will you proceed?

Section 2

# Inside the Eukaryotic Cell

| Key Ideas | Key Terms | Why It Matters |
|---|---|---|
| ❯ What does the cytoskeleton do?<br>❯ How does DNA direct activity in the cytoplasm?<br>❯ What organelles participate in protein production?<br>❯ What is the role of vesicles in cells?<br>❯ How do cells get energy? | vesicle<br>endoplasmic reticulum<br>Golgi apparatus<br>vacuole<br>chloroplast<br>mitochondrion | Knowing how cells work helps you understand how your body functions and what goes wrong when you get sick. |

***The Living Environment***
**Standard 4**

**1.2f** Cells have particular structures that perform specific jobs. These structures perform the actual work of the cell. Just as systems are coordinated and work together, cell parts must also be coordinated and work together.

**1.2i** Inside the cell a variety of specialized structures, formed from many different molecules, carry out the transport of materials (cytoplasm), extraction of energy from nutrients (mitochondria), protein building (ribosomes), waste disposal (cell membrane), storage (vacuole), and information storage (nucleus).

**5.1b** Plant cells and some one-celled organisms contain chloroplasts, the site of photosynthesis.

**5.1d** In all organisms, the energy stored in organic molecules may be released during cellular respiration. This energy is temporarily stored in ATP molecules. In many organisms, the process of cellular respiration is concluded in mitochondria, in which ATP is produced more efficiently, oxygen is used, and carbon dioxide and water are released as wastes.

**5.3a** Dynamic equilibrium results from detection of and response to stimuli. Organisms detect and respond to change in a variety of ways both at the cellular level and at the organismal level.

The cytoplasm of a eukaryotic cell is packed with all sorts of structures and molecules. Molecules can be concentrated in certain parts of the cell because of the membranes that divide the cytoplasm into compartments. This organization enables each organelle to perform highly sophisticated and specialized functions.

## The Framework of the Cell

The *cytoskeleton* is a web of protein fibers, shown in **Figure 3,** found in eukaryotic cells. The cytoskeleton supports the cell in much the same way that bones support your body. **❯ The cytoskeleton helps the cell move, keep its shape, and organize its parts.** There are three kinds of cytoskeleton fibers.

*Microfilaments* are long, thin fibers that are made of the protein actin. Some are attached to the cell membrane. They contract to pull the membrane in some places and expand to push it out in others. *Microtubules* are thick, hollow fibers that are made of the protein tubulin. Information molecules move through these tubes to various parts of the cell. *Intermediate fibers* are moderately thick and mainly anchor organelles and enzymes to certain parts of the cell.

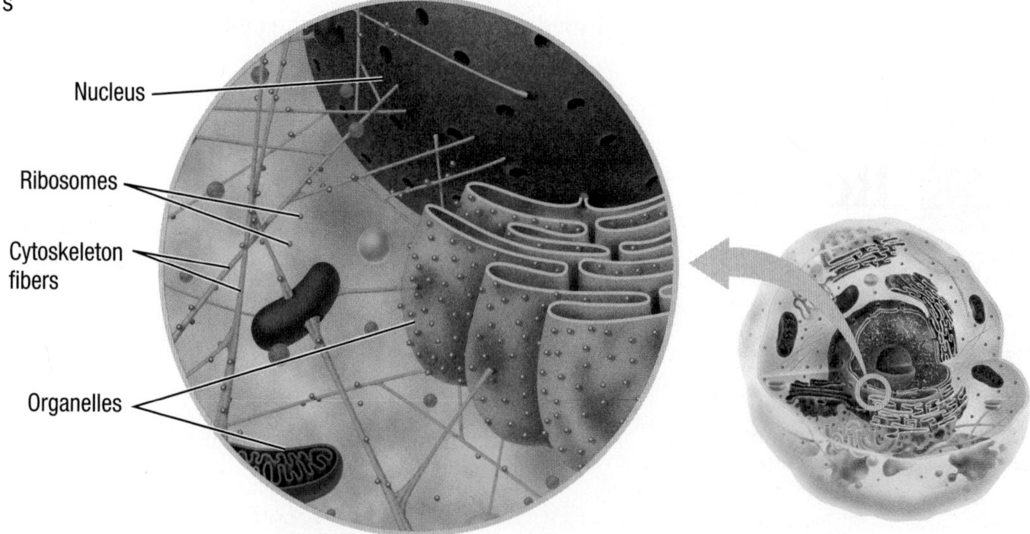


**Figure 3** The cytoskeleton's network of protein fibers anchors cell organelles and other components of the cytoplasm. **❯ What are the three types of cytoskeleton fibers?**

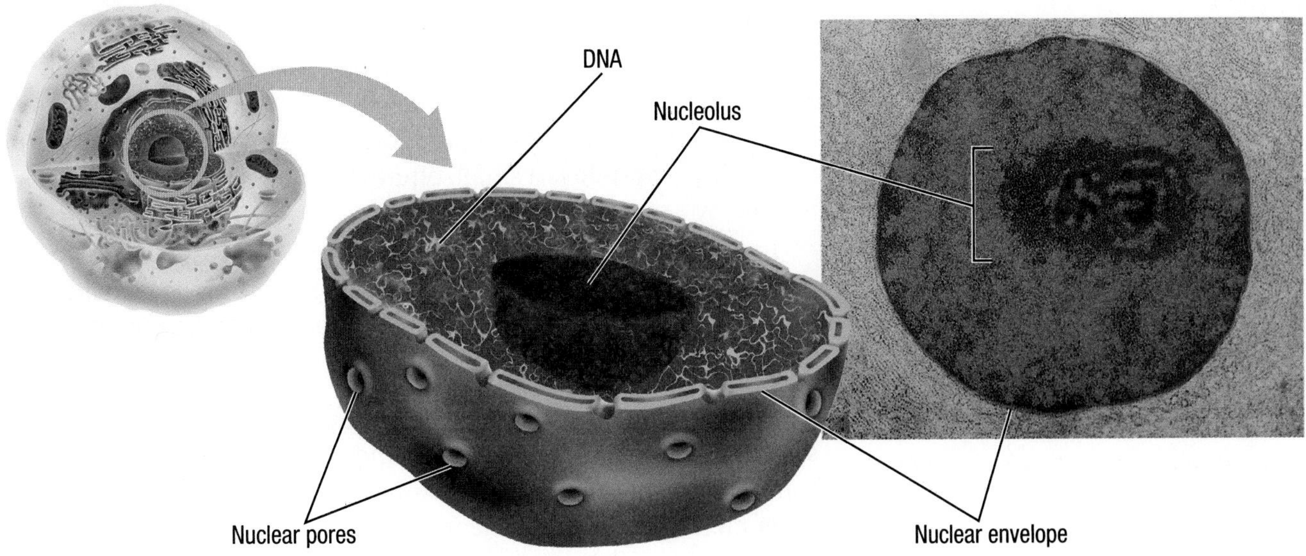


**Figure 4** The nucleus stores the cell's DNA. The nuclear envelope is a double membrane that surrounds the nucleus of a cell. Ribosomes are made in the nucleolus. ❯ **How do molecules move from the nucleus to the cytoplasm?**

## Directing Cellular Activity

Almost all cellular activity depends on the proteins that the cell makes. The instructions for making proteins are stored in the DNA. In a eukaryotic cell, the DNA is packed into the nucleus. This location separates the DNA from the activity in the cytoplasm and helps protect the information from getting lost or destroyed. ❯ **DNA instructions are copied as RNA messages, which leave the nucleus. In the cytoplasm, ribosomes use the RNA messages to assemble proteins.**

**ACADEMIC VOCABULARY**

**assemble** to fit together parts or pieces; to build

**Nucleus** As **Figure 4** shows, the nucleus is surrounded by a double membrane called the *nuclear envelope*. The nuclear envelope has many nuclear pores. Nuclear pores are small channels that allow certain molecules to move into and out of the nucleus. Even though the inside of the nucleus appears to be quite jumbled, the DNA is very organized. Within the nucleus is a prominent structure called the *nucleolus*. The nucleolus is the region where ribosome parts are made. These "preassembled" parts of ribosomes pass through the nuclear pores into the cytoplasm. Outside the nucleus, the parts are assembled to form a complete ribosome.

**Ribosomes** Each ribosome is made of RNA and many proteins. Some ribosomes in a eukaryotic cell are suspended in the cytosol, as they are in prokaryotic cells. These "free" ribosomes make proteins that remain inside the cell, such as proteins that build new organelles or enzymes to speed chemical reactions. Other ribosomes are attached to the membrane of another organelle. These "bound" ribosomes make proteins that are exported from the cell. Some of these proteins are important in cell communication. Bound ribosomes also make proteins that must be kept separate from the rest of the cytoplasm. Ribosomes can switch between being bound or free depending on the kind of protein that the cell needs to make.

❯ **Reading Check** ***What kind of protein do "free" ribosomes make?***

**vesicle** a small cavity or sac that contains materials in a eukaryotic cell

**endoplasmic reticulum** (EN doh PLAZ mik ri TIK yuh luhm) a system of membranes that is found in a cell's cytoplasm and that assists in the production, processing, and transport of proteins and in the production of lipids

**Golgi apparatus** (GOHL jee) a cell organelle that helps make and package materials to be transported out of the cell

**Process Chart** Make a process chart that shows how the cell digests food particles.

## Protein Processing

The proteins produced by cells have many uses. The proteins that are sent outside the cell must be kept separate from the rest of the cytoplasm. To achieve this separation, the cell packages the proteins in vesicles. A **vesicle** is a small, often spherical-shaped sac that is formed by a membrane.

In a eukaryotic cell, two structures are mainly responsible for modifying, packaging, and transporting proteins for use outside the cell. **The endoplasmic reticulum and the Golgi apparatus are organelles that prepare proteins for extracellular export.**

**Endoplasmic Reticulum** The **endoplasmic reticulum** (ER) is a system of internal membranes that moves proteins and other substances through the cell. The membrane of the ER is connected to the outer membrane of the nuclear envelope.

**Rough ER** Ribosomes are attached to some parts of the surface of the ER. This *rough ER* has a bumpy appearance when viewed with an electron microscope, as shown in **Figure 5.** ❶ As proteins are made, they cross the ER membrane, entering the ER. Then, the ER membrane pinches off to form a vesicle around the proteins.

**Smooth ER** The rest of the ER, called *smooth ER,* has no attached ribosomes. Thus it appears smooth when viewed with an electron microscope. Enzymes of the smooth ER performs various functions, such as making lipids and breaking down toxic substances.

**Golgi Apparatus** The **Golgi apparatus** is a set of flattened, membrane-bound sacs. Cell products enter one side of the Golgi apparatus, which modifies, sorts, and packages them for distribution.

**Repackaging** Vesicles that contain newly made proteins move through the cytoplasm from the ER to the Golgi apparatus. ❷ The vesicle membrane fuses with the Golgi membrane. Inside the Golgi apparatus, enzymes modify the proteins as they move through the organelle. On the other side, the finished proteins are enclosed in new vesicles that bud from the surface of the Golgi apparatus.

**Exporting** Many of these vesicles then migrate to the cell membrane. ❸ As the vesicle membrane fuses with the cell membrane, the completed proteins are released to the outside the cell.

## Storage and Maintenance

Vesicles have many functions in the cell. Some transport materials within the cell. Others have important storage roles. **Vesicles help maintain homeostasis by storing and releasing various substances as the cell needs them.**

**Lysosome** A lysosome is a vesicle that contains specific enzymes that break down large molecules. These enzymes can digest food particles to provide nutrients for the cell. They also help recycle materials in the cell by digesting old, damaged, or unused organelles. Lysosomes work by fusing with other vesicles. Lysosomes, made by the Golgi apparatus, prevent the enzymes from destroying the cell.

go.hrw.com
interact online
Keyword: HX8CSFF5

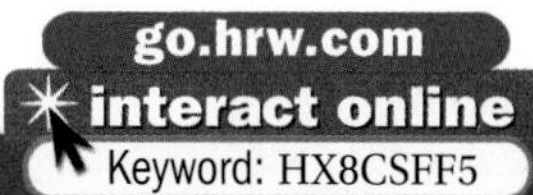

## Making and Exporting Proteins

**Figure 5** The cell manufactures many proteins. Some proteins are used outside the cell that makes them. Many organelles play a role in producing, processing, and packaging these proteins.

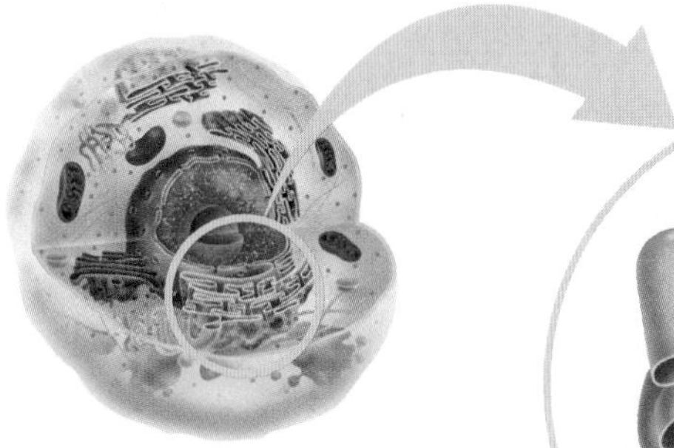

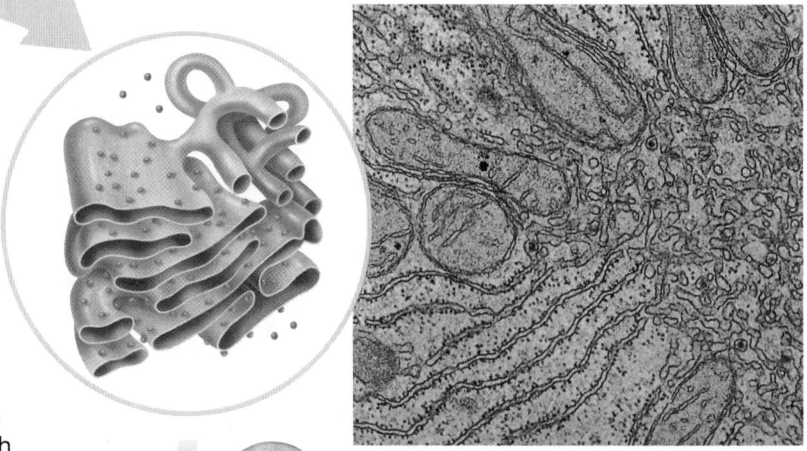

**1 Endoplasmic Reticulum** Proteins are made by ribosomes on the rough ER, which packages the proteins into vesicles. The vesicles transport the newly made proteins from the rough ER to the Golgi apparatus.

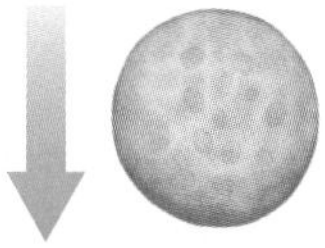

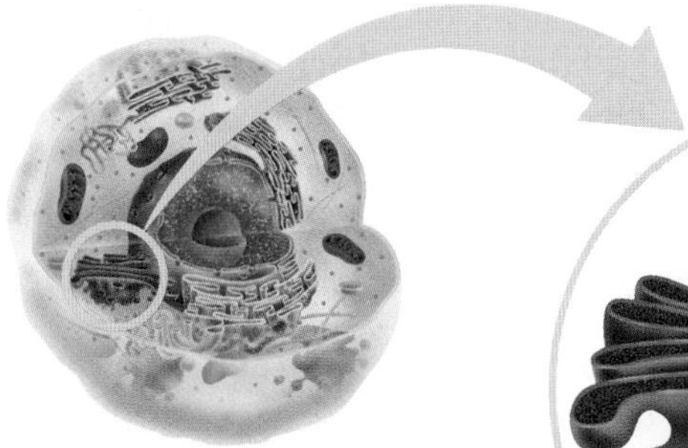

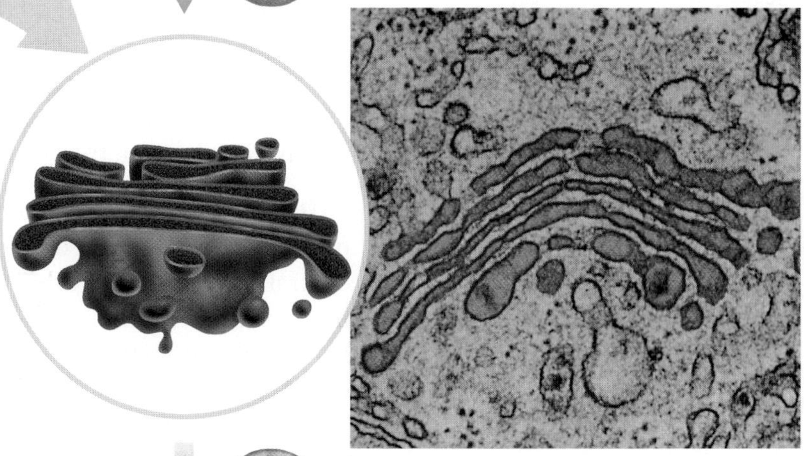

**2 Golgi Apparatus** The vesicle enters one side of the Golgi apparatus. As the proteins move through the folds, they are changed and repackaged into new vesicles. These new vesicles then move to the cell membrane.

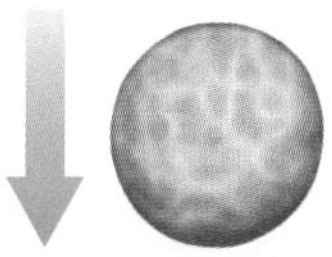

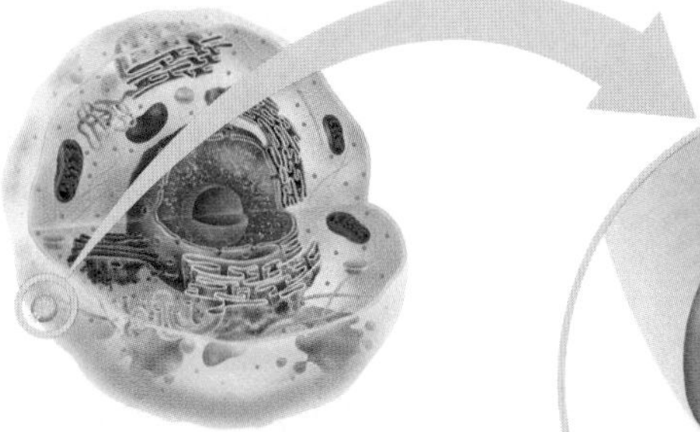

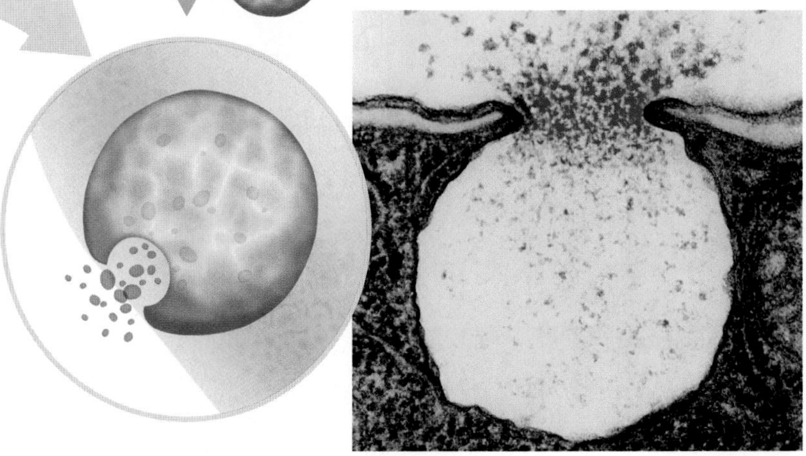

**3 Cell Membrane** The vesicles move to the cell membrane and release their contents (modified proteins) outside the cell. The vesicle membrane becomes part of the cell membrane.

Hands-On

# QuickLab

10 min

## Cell Parts Model 4.1.2f, 4.1.2i

No space is wasted inside a cell. Packed into the cell are all parts essential to its survival.

### Procedure

1. Fill a **sealable plastic sandwich bag** halfway with **tap water.** Add several drops of **blue food dye.** Before you seal the bag, push out any remaining air.
2. Roll this water-filled bag into a cylindrical shape. Use two long strips of **tape** to secure this shape.
3. Fill **two small plastic jewelry bags** with water. Before sealing the bags, add several drops of **green food coloring** to each bag.
4. Place the water-filled sandwich bag and the two small jewelry bags into a **gallon-size plastic bag.**
5. Fill this outer bag two-thirds full with water. Push out any remaining air, and seal the bag.

### Analysis

1. **State** what each plastic bag in this model represented.
2. **Describe** how the "central vacuole" affects the contents of your cell model.
3. CRITICAL THINKING **Predicting Outcomes** Explain how removing water from the model's central bag might affect the tension and shape of the outer plastic bag.

**Central Vacuole** Many plant cells contain a large, membrane-bound compartment called the central **vacuole.** This large vacuole stores water, ions, nutrients, and wastes. It can also store toxins or pigments. When water fills the central vacuole, as shown in **Figure 6,** it makes the cell rigid, allowing the plant to stand upright. When the vacuole loses water, the cell shrinks, and the plant wilts.

**Other Vacuoles** Some protists have contractile vacuoles, which pump excess water out of the cell. This process controls the concentration of salts and other molecules and helps the cell maintain homeostasis. Another type of vacuole forms when the cell membrane surrounds food particles outside the cell and pinches off to form a vesicle inside the cell. When the food vacuole later fuses with a lysosome, the enzymes that digest the stored food are released.

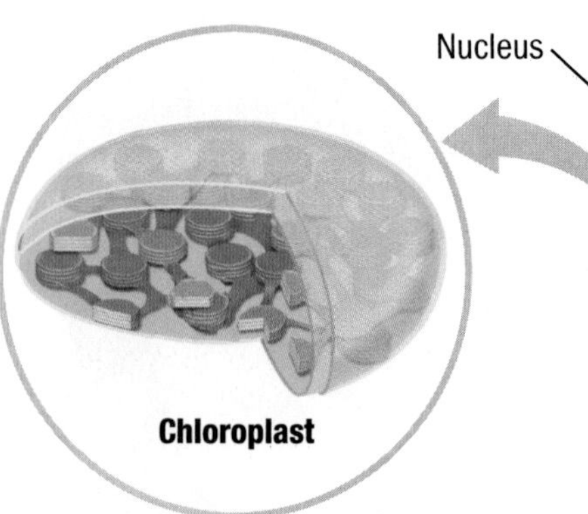


**Figure 6** A plant cell may have a large central vacuole and several chloroplasts. When filled, the central vacuole pushes the other organelles against the membrane. **› In which organelle does photosynthesis occur?**

## Energy Production

Cells need a constant source of energy. **› The energy for cellular functions is produced by chemical reactions that occur in the mitochondria and chloroplasts.** Nearly all eukaryotic cells contain mitochondria. Chloroplasts are found in plants and some plant-like protists, such as seaweed, but not in animal cells. In both organelles, chemical reactions produce adenosine triphosphate (ATP), the form of energy that fuels almost all cell processes.

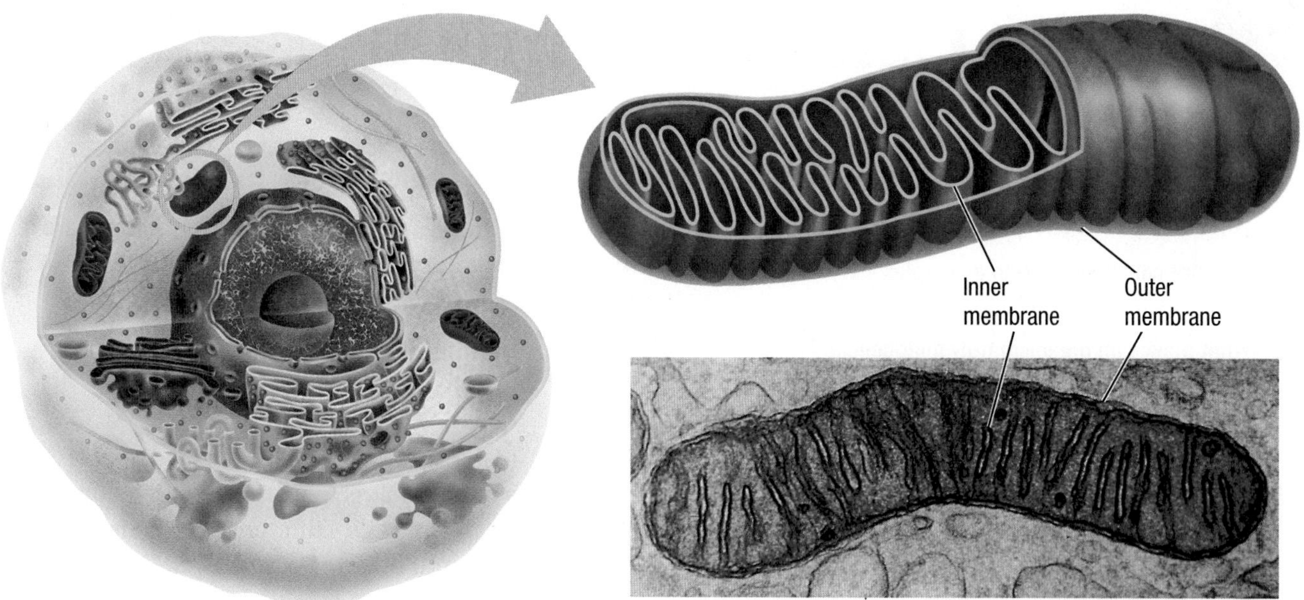


**Figure 7** A mitochondrion uses the energy in organic molecules to make ATP for the cell. The mitochondrion has two membranes. **› Where in the mitochondrion is ATP produced?**

**Chloroplasts** A **chloroplast** is an organelle that uses light energy to make sugar from carbon dioxide and water. As **Figure 6** shows, plant cells may have several chloroplasts. Each chloroplast is surrounded by a pair of membranes. Inside the inner membrane are many stacks of flattened sacs. The ATP-producing chemical reactions take place on the membranes of these sacs.

**Mitochondria** A **mitochondrion** is an organelle that uses energy from organic compounds to make ATP. Although some ATP is made in the cytosol, most of a cell's ATP is made inside mitochondria. Cells that have a high energy requirement, such as muscle cells, may contain hundreds or thousands of mitochondria. As **Figure 7** shows, a mitochondrion has a smooth outer membrane. It also has a greatly folded inner membrane, which divides the organelle into two compartments. Many ATP-producing enzymes are located on the inner membrane.

**› Reading Check** ***In what kinds of cells are mitochondria found?***

**vacuole** (VAK yoo OHL) a fluid-filled vesicle found in the cytoplasm of plant cells or protists

**chloroplast** an organelle found in plant and algae cells where photosynthesis occurs

**mitochondrion** (MIET oh KAHN dree uhn) in eukaryotic cells, the cell organelle that is surrounded by two membranes and that is the site of cellular respiration

## Section 2 Review

### › KEY IDEAS

1. **Compare** the functions of the three types of cytoskeletal fibers.
2. **Describe** the nucleus.
3. **Trace** a protein's path through the cell, from assembly to export.
4. **Contrast** vesicles and vacuoles.
5. **Compare** the role of mitochondria and chloroplasts.

### CRITICAL THINKING

6. **Constructing Explanations** Is it accurate to say that organelles are floating freely in the cytosol? Why or why not?
7. **Real World** Research Tay-Sachs disease, and explain what goes wrong in diseased cells.

### ALTERNATIVE ASSESSMENT

8. **Analogy** Compare the organelles of a eukaryotic cell to the parts of a city. For example, the lysosome could be a recycling center.

Section

# 3 From Cell to Organism

| Key Ideas | Key Terms | Why It Matters |
|---|---|---|
| ❯ What makes cells and organisms different?<br>❯ How are cells organized in a complex multicellular organism?<br>❯ What makes an organism truly multicellular? | flagellum<br>tissue<br>organ<br>organ system<br>colonial organism | Diverse organisms have unique cells and cellular organization. |

***The Living Environment***
**Standard 4**

**1.2a** Important levels of organization for structure and function include organelles, cells, tissues, organs, organ systems, and whole organisms.

**1.2e** The organs and systems of the body help to provide all the cells with their basic needs. The cells of the body are of different kinds and are grouped in ways that enhance how they function together.

**2.1k** The many body cells in an individual can be very different from one another, even though they are all descended from a single cell and thus have essentially identical genetic instructions. This is because different parts of these instructions are used in different types of cells, and are influenced by the cells' environment and past history.

More than 50 million types of organisms live on Earth. Each organism is made up of different types of cells. Differences in cells enable organisms to adapt to their natural environments.

## Diversity in Cells

Prokaryotes are always unicellular and limited in size. Eukaryotes are often larger and can be either unicellular or multicellular. Prokaryotic cells lack a nucleus and membrane-bound organelles, which are found in eukaryotic cells. Within both types, cells can have a variety of shapes and structures. Recall that a cell's shape reflects its function. ❯ **The different organelles and features of cells enable organisms to function in unique ways in different environments.**

**Diversity in Prokaryotes** Prokaryotes can vary in shape, the way that they obtain and use energy, the makeup of their cell walls, and their ability to move. Many prokaryotes have **flagella**—long, threadlike structures that rotate to quickly move an organism through its environment. Many prokaryotes have pili. Pili are short, thick outgrowths that allow prokaryotes to attach to surfaces or to other cells. These features are shown in **Figure 8.**

**flagellum** a long, hairlike structure that grows out of a cell and enables the cell to move

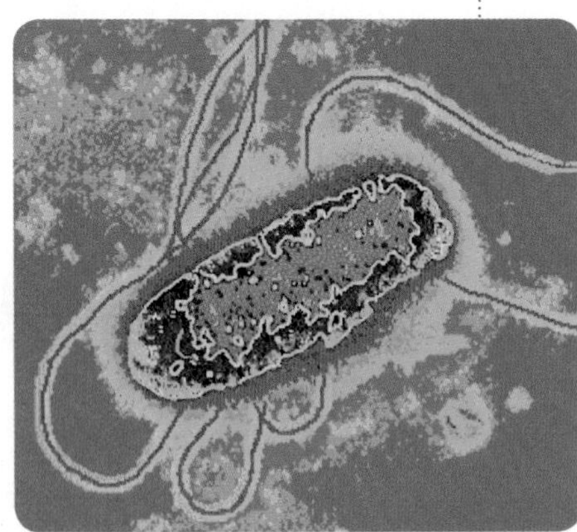

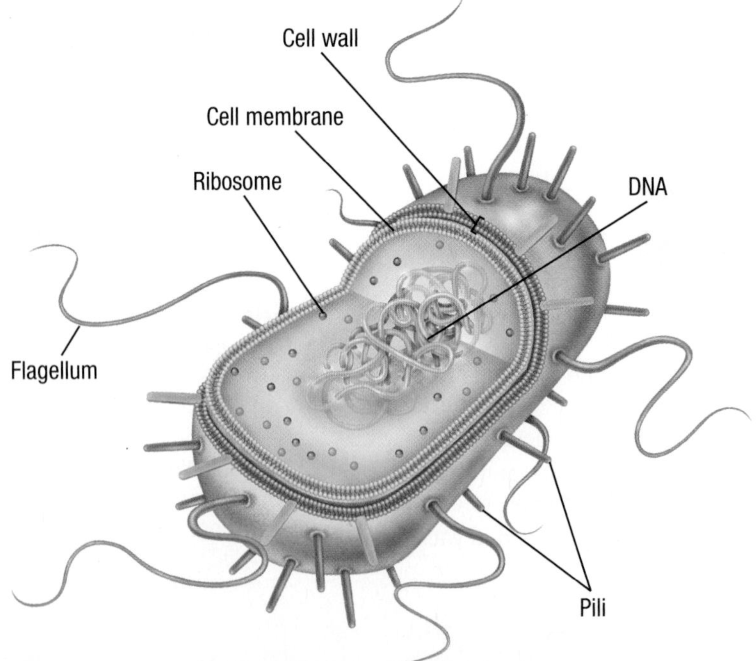


**Figure 8** The bacterium *Escherichia coli* is a rod-shaped prokaryote that has both pili and flagella. ❯ **What do flagella enable prokaryotic cells to do?**

**Diversity in Eukaryotic Cells** Animal and plant cells are two types of eukaryotic cells, as **Figure 9** shows. Both have many of the same organelles, but plant cells also have chloroplasts, a large central vacuole, and a cell wall that surrounds the cell membrane.

Like prokaryotic cells, eukaryotic cells vary in structure according to their function. Also, some organelles are more prominent in some cell types. By varying in their internal makeup, cells can become specialized for certain functions. For example, muscle cells, which use large amounts of energy, have many mitochondria.

› **Reading Check** ***What are flagella?***

## Eukaryotic Cells

**Figure 9** Most eukaryotic cells contain all of the organelles shown here. Depending on their function, cells may have different shapes and different amounts of certain organelles. › **What are three features that plant cells have, but animal cells lack?**

**Animal cell**

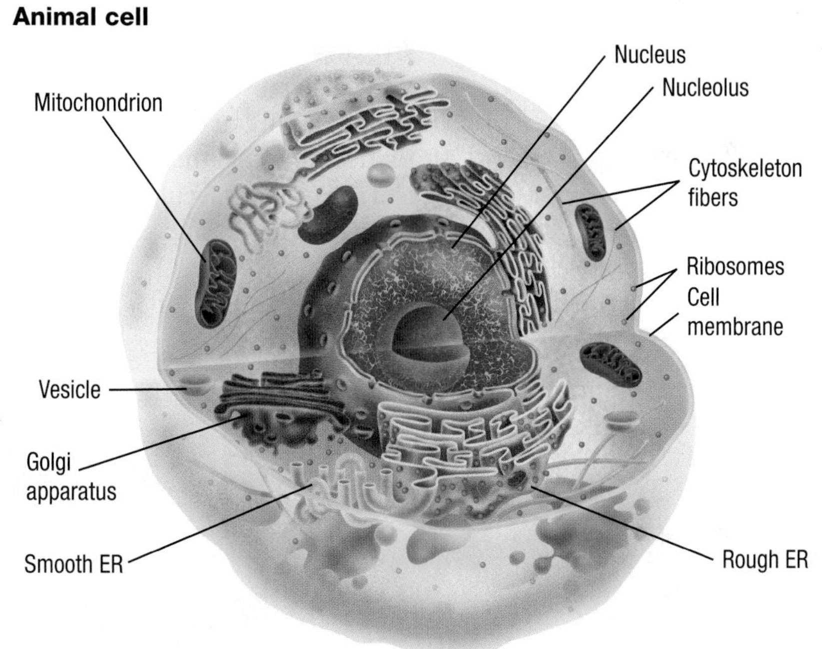


**Plant cell**

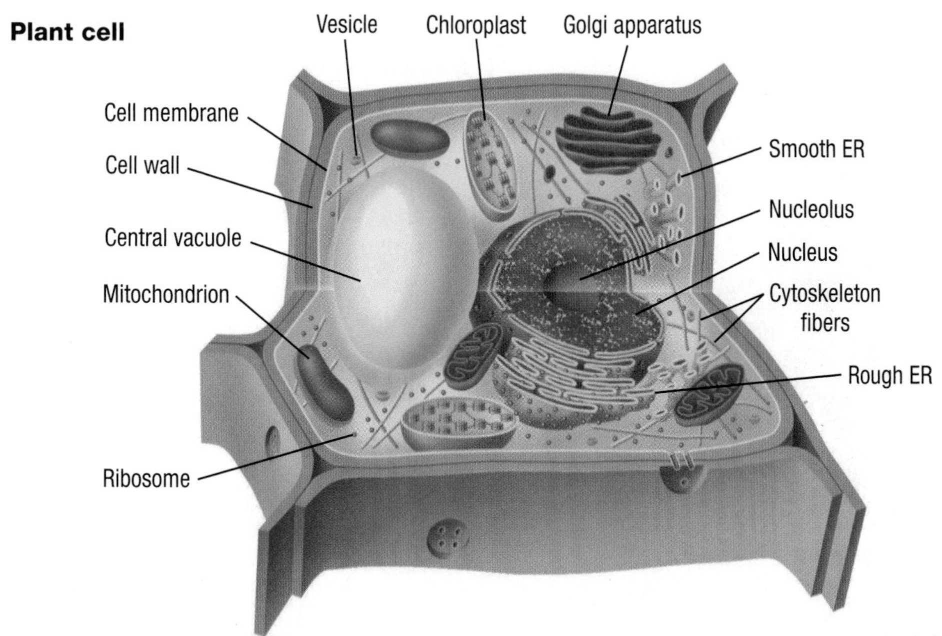

**Similes** Write a simile comparing each level of organization to a part of your textbook. (Hint: Cells are like letters.)

## Levels of Organization

Multicellular organisms, such as plants and animals, are made up of thousands, millions, or even trillions of highly specialized cells. These cells cooperate to perform a specific task. They assemble together to form structures called tissues and organs. ❯ **Plants and animals have many highly specialized cells that are arranged into tissues, organs, and organ systems.** The relationships between tissues, organs, and organ systems are shown in **Figure 10.**

**Tissues** A **tissue** is a distinct group of cells that have similar structures and functions. For example, muscle tissue is a group of many cells that have bundles of cytoskeletal structures. When the bundles contract at the same time, they help animals move. In plants, vascular tissue is made of hollowed cells that are stacked up to make tiny straws. These structures help carry fluids and nutrients to various parts of the plant.

**Organs** Different tissues may be arranged into an **organ,** which is a specialized structure that has a specific function. In animals, the heart is an organ made of muscle, nerve, and other tissues. These tissues work together to pump blood. In plants, a leaf is an organ. A leaf is made of vascular tissue and other types of plant tissues that work together to trap sunlight and produce sugar.

**Figure 10** Cells group together to make tissues, which assemble into organs. A leaf is an example of an organ in plants. A lung is an example of an organ in animals. ❯ **What level of organization is the respiratory system?**

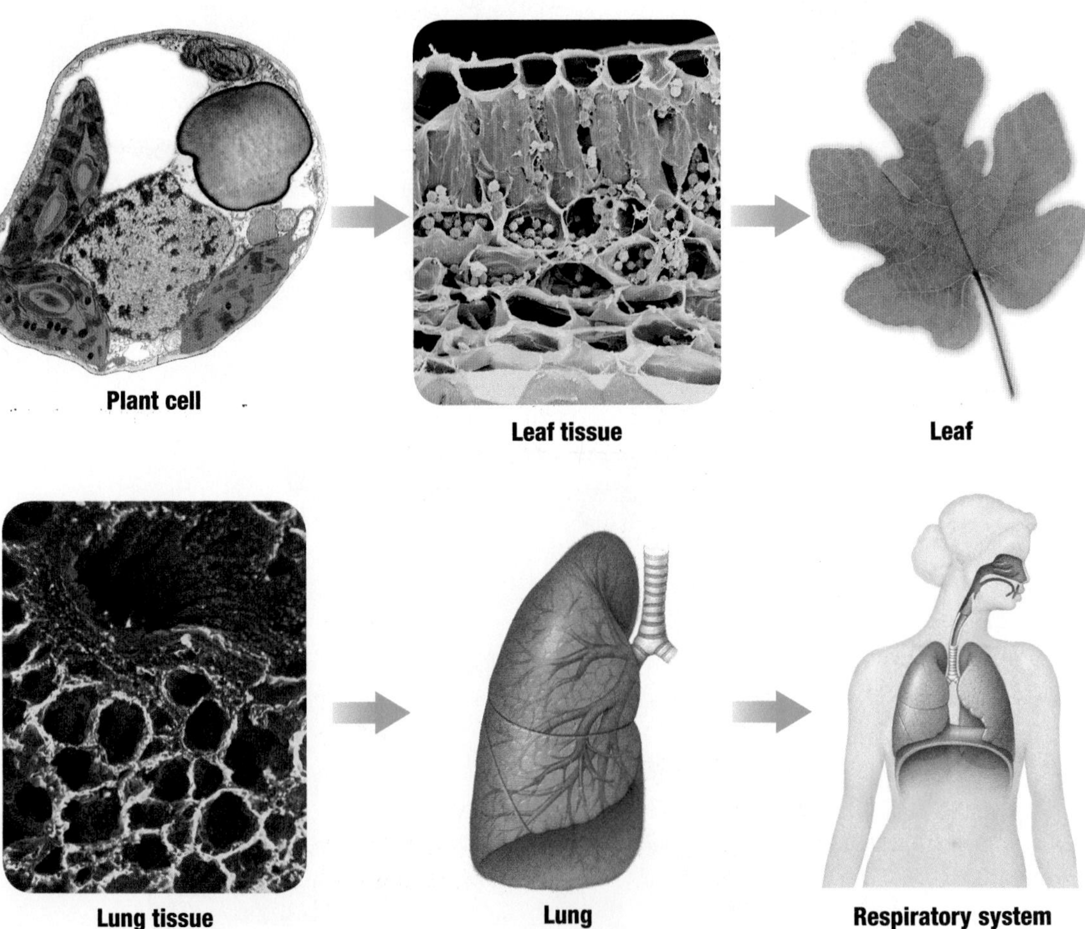

Hands-On

## QuickLab

### Colonies on the Move 1.1.2a, 4.1.2f

10 min

Volvox is a green colonial alga. A single colony may contain over 500 cells and is visible to the unaided eye.

#### Procedure

1. With the unaided eye, examine a **container of Volvox colonies.** What do you see?
2. Use a **dropper** to transfer some of the colonies to a **well slide.**
3. Examine the colonies using a **light microscope.**

#### Analysis

1. **Draw** the shape and structure of Volvox.
2. **Describe** the motion of a Volvox colony.
3. CRITICAL THINKING **Inferring Relationships** From your observations, do you think that the movements of the colony members are coordinated? Explain.

**Organ System** Various organs that carry out a major body function make up an **organ system.** One example of an organ system is the circulatory system, which is made up of the heart, the blood vessels, and blood. In plants, the shoot system consists of stems, leaves, and the vascular tissue that connects them.

## Body Types

Sometimes, the entire body of an organism is made up of a single cell. This cell must carry out all of the organism's activities, including growing, using energy, responding to the environment, and reproducing. More than half of the biomass on Earth is composed of unicellular organisms.

While single cells cannot grow larger than a certain size, multicellular organisms can be large. ➤ **A multicellular organism is composed of many individual, permanently associated cells that coordinate their activities.** Distinct types of cells have specialized functions that help the organism survive. Individual cells cannot survive alone and are dependent on the other cells of the organism.

**Cell Groups** Some unicellular organisms can thrive independently, but others live in groups. Cells that live as a connected group but do not depend on each other for survival are considered **colonial organisms.** For example, the cell walls of some bacteria adhere to one another after dividing. These formations are not considered multicellular, because the cells can survive when separated.

Another type of cell grouping occurs in certain types of slime molds. These organisms spend most of their lives as single-celled amoebas. When starved, the individual cells form a large mass, which produces spores.

**tissue** a group of similar cells that perform a common function

**organ** a collection of tissues that carry out a specialized function of the body

**organ system** a group of organs that work together to perform body functions

**colonial organism** a collection of genetically identical cells that are permanently associated but in which little or no integration of cell activities occurs

**Figure 11** The giant kelp is a multicellular protist. Mushrooms are multicellular fungi. All plants and animals are multicellular organisms. **❯ Can prokaryotes be multicellular?**

**Multicellularity** True multicellularity occurs only in eukaryotes, such as the organisms shown in **Figure 11.** Some protists, most fungi, and all plants and animals have a multicellular body. The cells of a multicellular body perform highly specific functions. Some cells protect the organism from predators or disease. Others may help with movement, reproduction, or feeding.

Most multicellular organisms begin as a single cell. For example, as a chicken develops from an egg, new cells form by cell division. These cells then grow and undergo differentiation, the process by which cells develop specialized forms and functions. The specialized cells are arranged into tissues, organs, and organ systems, making up the entire organism.

**❯ Reading Check** *What is differentiation?*

## Section 3 Review

### ❯ KEY IDEAS

1. **Relate** the structure of a cell to the cell's function.
2. **Describe** the four levels of organization that make up an organism.
3. **Explain** what makes a group of cells a truly multicellular organism.

### CRITICAL THINKING

4. **Comparing** Describe how the circulatory system in animals is similar to the vascular system in plants.
5. **Making Inferences** How would the formation of bacterial colonies be affected if bacterial cells did not contain pili?

### WRITING FOR SCIENCE

6. **Cell Group Therapy** Write a short play set in a therapy group that contains cells belonging to a unicellular colony and cells belonging to a multicellular organism. Have the cells discuss issues such as communication and individuality.

Inquiry

# Chapter 7 Lab

45 min

4.1.2f, 4.1.2i

## Objectives

- Identify the structures that you can see in plant cells.
- Investigate factors that influence the movement of cell contents.

## Materials

- compound light microscope
- elodea sprig
- forceps
- microscope slides and coverslips
- lamp, incandescent
- dropper bottle of Lugol's iodine solution

## Safety

# Plant Cell Observation

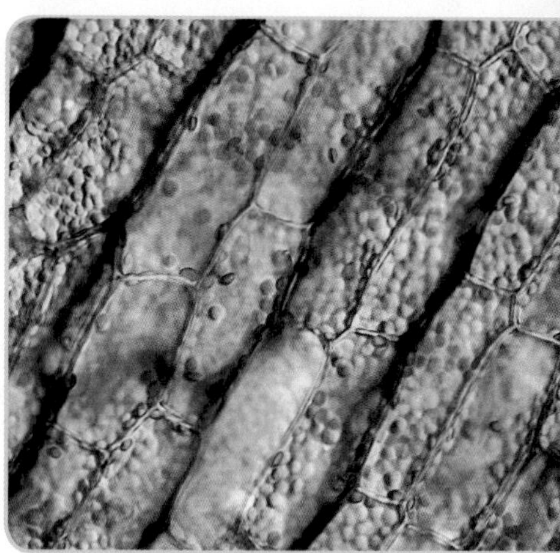

When you look at cells under a microscope, you often can observe cytoplasmic streaming, or movement of cell contents. This effect occurs only in living cells. In this lab, you will investigate factors that influence cytoplasmic streaming.

## Preparation

1. SCIENTIFIC METHODS **State the Problem** How do heat and an iodine solution influence cytoplasmic streaming?
2. SCIENTIFIC METHODS **Form a Hypothesis** Form testable hypotheses that explain how heat and iodine influence cytoplasmic streaming.

## Procedure

1. Put on safety goggles, gloves, and a lab apron.
2. **CAUTION: Handle glass slides and coverslips with care.** Using forceps, remove a small leaf near the top of an elodea sprig. Place the whole leaf in a drop of water on a slide, and add a coverslip.
3. Observe the leaf under low power. Switch to high power.
4. Focus on a cell in which you can see the chloroplasts clearly. Draw this cell. Label the cell parts that you can see.
5. If chloroplasts are not moving in any of the cells, briefly warm the slide under a lamp. Look for movement again under high power.
6. **CAUTION: Lugol's solution is toxic and stains skin and clothing. Promptly wash off spills.** Make a wet mount of another leaf with Lugol's iodine solution. Observe the cells under low and high power.
7. Draw a stained elodea cell and label all visible parts.
8. Clean up your lab materials according to your teacher's instructions. Wash your hands before leaving the lab.

## Analyze and Conclude

1. **Inferring Relationships** What effect did warming the slide have on the movement of cell contents? Why do you think this is so?
2. SCIENTIFIC METHODS **Inferring Conclusions** What can you conclude about the effect of Lugol's iodine solution on plant cells?

# Chapter 7 Summary

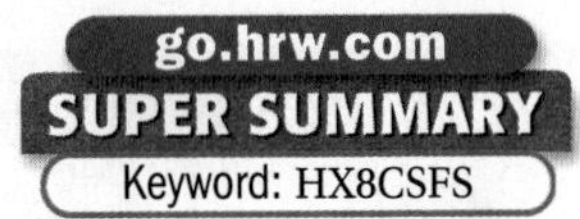


| Key Ideas | Key Terms |
|---|---|

## 1 Introduction to Cells

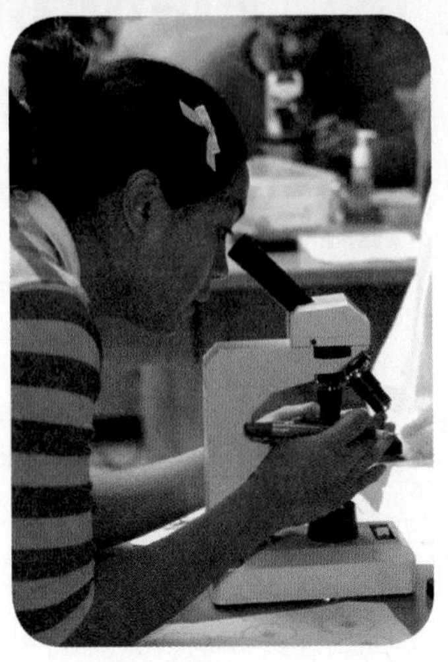

- Microscope observations of organisms led to the discovery of the basic characteristics common to all living things.
- A cell's shape reflects the cell's function. Cell size is limited by a cell's surface area-to-volume ratio.
- Because of their complex organization, eukaryotic cells can carry out more specialized functions than prokaryotic cells can.

**Key Terms:** **cell membrane** (154), **cytoplasm** (154), **ribosome** (154), **prokaryote** (154), **eukaryote** (155), **nucleus** (155), **organelle** (155)

## 2 Inside the Eukaryotic Cell

- The cytoskeleton helps the cell move, keep its shape, and organize its parts.
- DNA instructions are copied as RNA messages, which leave the nucleus. In the cytoplasm, ribosomes use the RNA messages to assemble proteins.
- The endoplasmic reticulum and the Golgi apparatus are organelles that prepare proteins for extracellular export.
- Vesicles help maintain homeostasis by storing and releasing various substances as the cell needs them.
- The energy for cellular functions is produced by chemical reactions that occur in the mitochondria and chloroplasts.

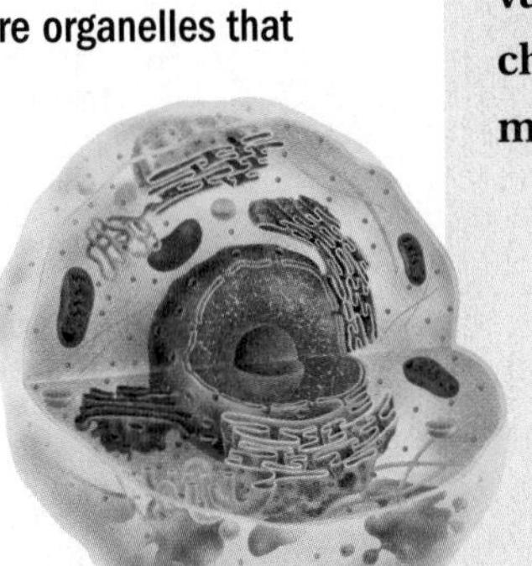

**Key Terms:** **vesicle** (158), **endoplasmic reticulum** (158), **Golgi apparatus** (158), **vacuole** (160), **chloroplast** (161), **mitochondrion** (161)

## 3 From Cell to Organism

- The different organelles and features of cells enable organisms to function in unique ways in different environments.
- Plants and animals have many highly specialized cells that are arranged into tissues, organs, and organ systems.
- A multicellular organism is composed of many individual, permanently associated cells that coordinate their activities.

**Key Terms:** **flagellum** (162), **tissue** (164), **organ** (164), **organ system** (165), **colonial organism** (165)

## The Living Environment

# Regents Exam Practice

**PART A: Answer all questions in this part.**

*Directions:* For each statement or question, write on your separate answer sheet the number of the word or expression that best completes the statement or answers the question.

**1** The diagram below represents levels of organization in living things. Which term would best represent X?

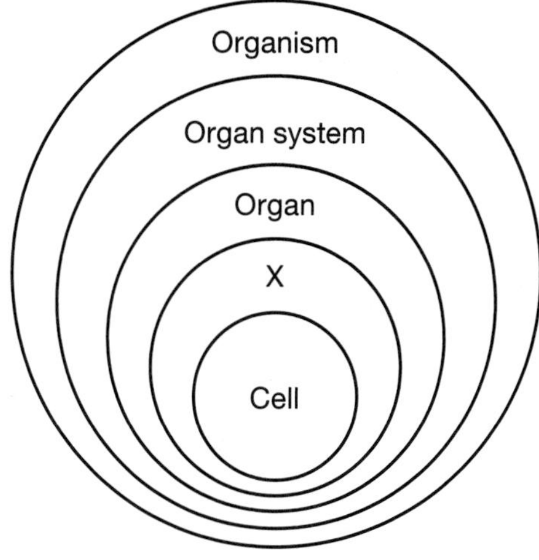


(1) human
(2) tissue
(3) stomach
(4) organelle

**2** Which statement best compares a multicellular organism to a single-celled organism?

(1) A multicellular organism has organ systems that interact to carry out life functions, while a single-celled organism carries out life functions without using organ systems.
(2) A single-celled organism carries out fewer life functions than each cell of a multicellular organism.
(3) A multicellular organism always obtains energy through a process that is different from that used by a single-celled organism.
(4) The cell of a single-celled organism is always much larger than an individual cell of a multicellular organism.

**3** The levels of organization for structure and function in the human body from least complex to most complex are

(1) systems → organs → tissues → cells
(2) cells → organs → tissues → systems
(3) tissues → systems → cells → organs
(4) cells → tissues → organs → systems

**4** The largest amount of DNA in a plant cell is contained in

(1) a nucleus
(2) a chromosome
(3) a protein molecule
(4) an enzyme molecule

**5** The diagram below illustrates the movement of materials involved in a process that is vital for the energy needs of organisms. The process illustrated occurs within

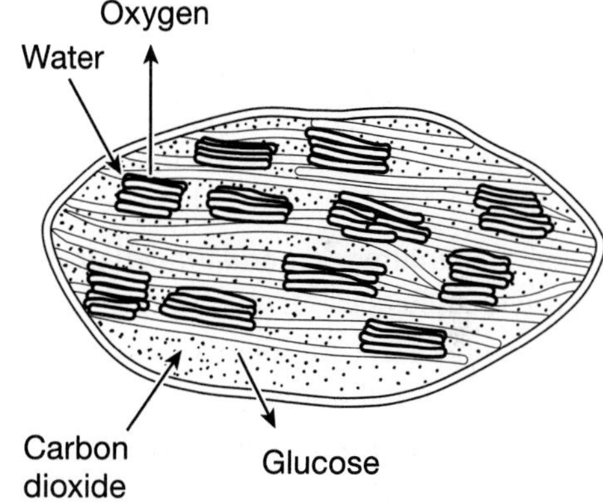


(1) chloroplasts
(2) mitochondria
(3) ribosomes
(4) vacuoles

**6** In a cell, information that controls the production of proteins must pass from the nucleus to the

(1) cell membrane.
(2) chloroplasts.
(3) mitochondria.
(4) ribosomes.

**7** The diagram below represents a portion of an organic molecule. This molecule controls cellular activity by directing the synthesis of

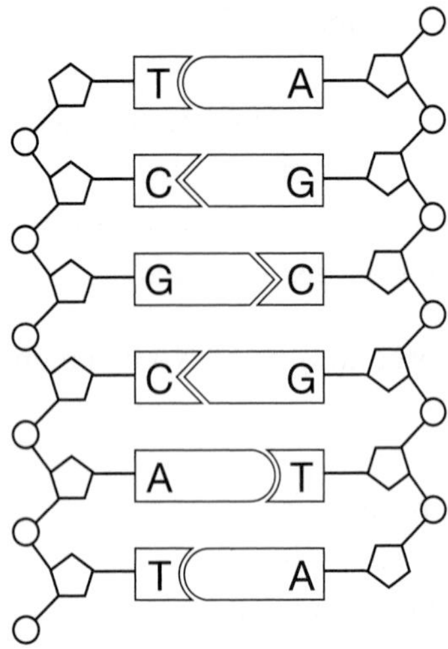


(1) carbohydrates
(2) minerals
(3) fats
(4) proteins

**8** Muscle cells in athletes often have more mitochondria than muscle cells in nonathletes. Based on this observation, it can be inferred that the muscle cells in athletes

(1) have a smaller demand for cell proteins than the muscle cells of nonathletes
(2) reproduce less frequently than the muscle cells of nonathletes
(3) have nuclei containing more DNA than nuclei in the muscle cells of nonathletes
(4) have a greater demand for energy than the muscle cells of nonathletes

**9** Eukaryotic cells differ from prokaryotic cells in that eukaryotic cells

(1) have a nucleus
(2) lack organelles
(3) lack ribosomes
(4) have a cell wall

**10** Two types of human cells are shown in the diagram below. Cell A causes the cells at B to contract. This activity would be most useful for

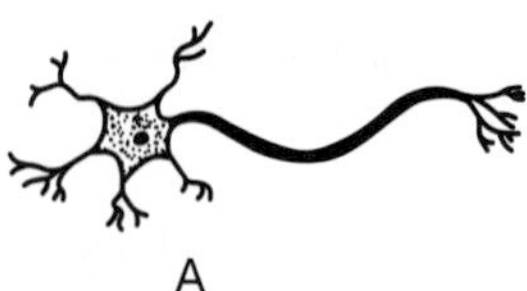


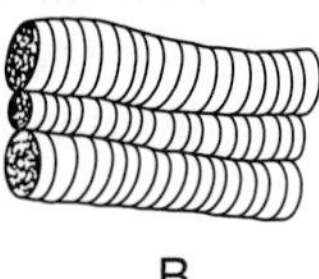


(1) lifting a book from a bookshelf
(2) coordinating the functions of organelles
(3) digesting food in the small intestine
(4) carrying out the process of protein synthesis

**PART B**

**11** Studies of fat cells and thyroid cells show that fat cells have fewer mitochondria than thyroid cells. A biologist would most likely infer that fat tissue

(1) does not require energy
(2) has energy requirements equal to those of thyroid tissue
(3) requires less energy than thyroid tissue
(4) requires more energy than thyroid tissue

**Base your answer to question 12 on the diagram below of a cell associated with coordination and on your knowledge of biology.**

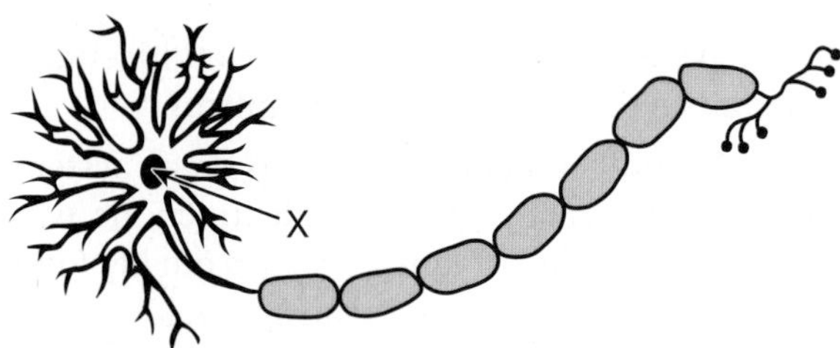


**12** Structure X would be involved in the

(1) storage of digestive enzymes
(2) absorption of energy from the Sun
(3) development of pathogens
(4) synthesis of proteins

**13** Describe how *two* of the cell structures listed below interact to help maintain a balanced internal environment in a cell:

mitochondrion
ribosome
cell membrane
nucleus
vacuole

In your answer be sure to:

- select *two* of these structures, write their names, and state one function of each
- describe how each structure you selected contributes to the functioning of the other

**Base your answer to question 14 on the passage below and on your knowledge of biology.**

. . . Some of the most common and deadly bacteria do their mischief by forming a sticky scum called biofilm. Individually, the microbes are easy to control, but when they organize themselves into biofilms they can become deadly, said Dr. Barbara Iglewski of the University of Rochester. . . .

Biofilms are actually intricately organized colonies of billions of microbes, all working in a coordinated way to defend against attack and to pump out a toxin that can be deadly.

Once they are organized, the bacteria are highly resistant to antibiotics and even strong detergents often cannot wash them away or kill them.

Iglewski and colleagues from Montana State University and the University of Iowa report in *Science* that they discovered how the microbes in the colonies communicate and found that once this conversation is interrupted, the deadly bugs can be easily washed away.

Using *Pseudomonas aeruginosa,* a common bacteria that is a major infection hazard in hospitals and among cystic fibrosis patients, the researchers isolated a gene that the bacteria uses to make a communications molecule. The molecule helps the microbes organize themselves into a biofilm — a complex structure that includes tubes to carry in nutrients and carry out wastes, including deadly toxins.

In their study, the researchers showed that if the gene that makes the communications molecule was blocked, the *Pseudomonas aeruginosa* could form only wimpy [weak], unorganized colonies that could be washed away with just a soap that has no effect on a healthy colony. . . .

Adapted from: Paul Recer, "Researchers find new means to disrupt attack by microbes," *The Daily Gazette,* April 26, 1998.

**14** What is one characteristic of a biofilm?

(1) presence of tubes to transport materials into annd out of the colony
(2) presence of a nervous system for communication within the colony
(3) ease with which colonies can be broken down by detergents
(4) lack of resistance of the bacterial colony to antibiotics

# Chapter 8 Cells and Their Environment

## Preview

**1 Cell Membrane**
- Homeostasis
- Lipid Bilayer
- Membrane Proteins

**2 Cell Transport**
- Passive Transport
- Osmosis
- Active Transport

**3 Cell Communication**
- Sending Signals
- Receiving Signals
- Responding to Signals

## Why It Matters

Cells interact with their environment to exchange nutrients and wastes and to coordinate activities over long distances.

**Did you know that cells drink? This blood capillary cell wraps its cell membrane around the surrounding fluid and takes in a big gulp.**

The lumen (blue) is the hollow part of a capillary.

A row of vesicles forms in the upper cell membrane (purple) and moves toward the bottom of the capillary. These vesicles help transport serum.

***The Living Environment***

**Standard 4** Students will understand and apply scientific concepts, principles, and theories pertaining to the physical setting and living environment and recognize the historical development of ideas in science.

**Key Idea 1** Living things are both similar to and different from each other and from nonliving things. ***Major Understandings* - 1.2c, 1.2g, 1.2i, 1.2j**

**Key Idea 5** Organisms maintain a dynamic equilibrium that sustains life ***Major Understandings* - 5.1e, 5.1g, 5.3a**

10 min

## Salty Cells

4.1.2g

The movement of substances in a living cell can produce observable changes in the cell's appearance.

### Procedure

1. Make **two wet mounts** of the **epidermis of a red onion.** Use **distilled water** for one and **saline solution** for the other.
2. Examine both slides under low power. Carefully switch to high power.
3. Make drawings of representative cells from each slide.

### Analysis

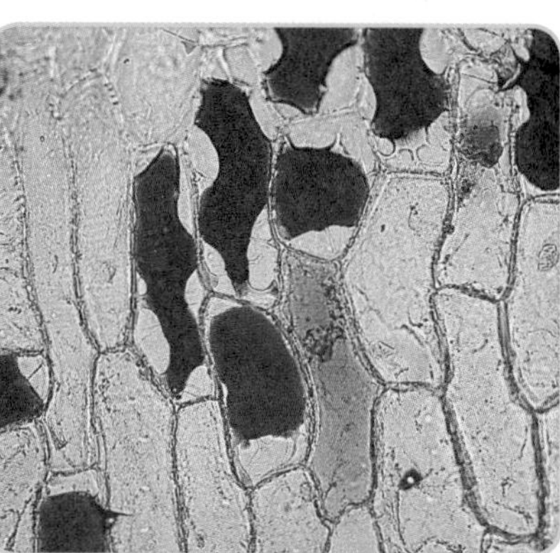

1. **Compare** the appearance of the cells in the two wet mounts.
2. **Predict** what might cause the observed difference in cell appearance.
3. **Infer** whether the onion's cell wall is permeable to water.

This is the nucleus of the cell that lines the inside of a capillary.

These reading tools can help you learn the material in this chapter. For more information on how to use these and other tools, see **Appendix: Reading and Study Skills.**

## Using Words

**Word Parts** You can tell a lot about a word by taking it apart and examining its prefix and root.

**Your Turn** Use the information in the table to predict the meaning of the following words:

1. *phospholipid*
2. *exocytosis*

**Word Parts**

| Word part | Type | Meaning |
|---|---|---|
| *phospho-* | prefix | containing phosphorus |
| *lipid* | root | a fat |
| *exo-* | prefix | outside |
| *cyto* | root | cell |

## Using Language

**Finding Examples** Concrete examples often help clarify new information. Certain words and phrases can help you recognize examples. These words include *for example, such as, like,* and *including.*

**Your Turn** Use what you have learned about examples to answer the following questions.

1. Find the examples in the following sentence: Some cells also use exocytosis to remove infecting microbes, such as bacteria or fungal spores.
2. Find the examples in the introductory paragraph above.

## Using FoldNotes

**Four-Corner Fold** A four-corner fold is useful when you want to compare the characteristics of four topics. The four-corner fold can organize the characteristics of the four topics side by side under the flaps. Similarities and differences between the four topics can then be easily identified.

**Your Turn** Make a four-corner fold to help you learn about four topics in this chapter.

1. Fold a sheet of paper in half from top to bottom. Then, unfold the paper.
2. Fold the top and bottom of the paper to the crease in the center.
3. Fold the paper in half from side to side. Then, unfold the paper.
4. Using scissors, cut the top flap creases made in step 3 to form four flaps.

Section 1

# Cell Membrane

| Key Ideas | Key Terms | Why It Matters |
| --- | --- | --- |
| ❯ How does the cell membrane help a cell maintain homeostasis?<br>❯ How does the cell membrane restrict the exchange of substances?<br>❯ What are some functions of membrane proteins? | phospholipid<br>lipid bilayer | A simple defect in a cell membrane protein can make a life-or-death difference. In people who have cystic fibrosis, the cell membrane is does not work properly. |

Every cell is surrounded by a cell membrane. The cell membrane protects the cell and helps move substances and messages in and out of the cell. By regulating transport, the membrane helps the cell maintain constancy and order.

## Homeostasis

All living things respond to their environments. For example, we sweat when we are hot and shiver when we are cold. These reactions help our bodies maintain homeostasis. Recall that homeostasis is the maintenance of stable internal conditions in a changing environment. Individual cells, as well as organisms, must maintain homeostasis in order to live. ❯ **One way that a cell maintains homeostasis is by controlling the movement of substances across the cell membrane.**

Like the swimmer and the jellyfish in **Figure 1,** cells are suspended in a fluid environment. Even the cell membrane is fluid. It is made up of a "sea" of lipids in which proteins float. By allowing some materials but not others to enter the cell, the cell membrane acts as a gatekeeper. In addition, it provides structural support to the cytoplasm, recognizes foreign material, and communicates with other cells. These functions also contribute to maintaining homeostasis.

❯ **Reading Check** *What are some roles of the cell membrane? (See the Appendix for answers to Reading Checks.)*

***The Living Environment***

**Standard 4**

**1.2c** The components of the human body, from organ systems to cell organelles, interact to maintain a balanced internal environment. To successfully accomplish this, organisms possess a diversity of control mechanisms that detect deviations and make corrective actions.

**1.2g** Each cell is covered by a membrane that performs a number of important functions for the cell. These include: separation from its outside environment, controlling which molecules enter and leave the cell, and recognition of chemical signals. The processes of diffusion and active transport are important in the movement of materials in and out of cells.

**5.3a** Dynamic equilibrium results from detection of and response to stimuli. Organisms detect and respond to change in a variety of ways both at the cellular level and at the organismal level.

SCILINKS.
www.scilinks.org
Topic: Homeostasis
Code: HX80753

Cells in this jellyfish exchange substances with the water.
The skin of the swimmer forms a watertight seal.

**Figure 1** The cells of the jellyfish exchange materials more freely with the sea water than do the cells of the swimmer.

**phospholipid** (FAHS foh LIP id) a lipid that contains phosphorus and that is a structural component in cell membranes

**lipid bilayer** (LIP id BIE LAY uhr) the basic structure of a biological membrane, composed of two layers of phospholipids

## Lipid Bilayer

The cell membrane is made of a "sea" of phospholipids. As **Figure 2** shows, a **phospholipid** is a specialized lipid made of a phosphate "head" and two fatty acid "tails." The phosphate head is polar and is attracted to water. In contrast, the fatty acid tails are nonpolar and are repelled by water.

**Structure** Because there is water inside and outside the cell, the phospholipids form a double layer called the **lipid bilayer.** The non-polar tails, repelled by water, make up the interior of the lipid bilayer. The polar heads are attracted to the water, so they point toward the surfaces of the lipid bilayer. One layer of polar heads faces the cytoplasm, while the other layer is in contact with the cell's immediate surroundings.

**Barrier** Only certain substances can pass through the lipid bilayer. **› The phospholipids form a barrier through which only small, nonpolar substances can pass.** Ions and most polar molecules are repelled by the nonpolar interior of the lipid bilayer.

## Membrane Proteins

Various proteins can be found in the cell membrane. Some proteins face inside the cell, and some face outside. Other proteins may stretch across the lipid bilayer and face both inside and outside.

**Proteins in Lipids** What holds these proteins in the membrane? Recall that proteins are made of amino acids. Some amino acids are polar, and others are nonpolar. Nonpolar portions of a protein are attracted to the interior of the lipid bilayer but are repelled by water on either side of the membrane. In contrast, polar parts of the protein are attracted to the water on both sides of the lipid bilayer. These opposing attractions help hold the protein in the membrane.

**› Reading Check** ***Why can't ions pass through the lipid bilayer?***

**Figure 2** The membrane that surrounds the cell is made of a lipid bilayer, a double layer of phospholipids.

The lipid bilayer is the foundation of the cell membrane.

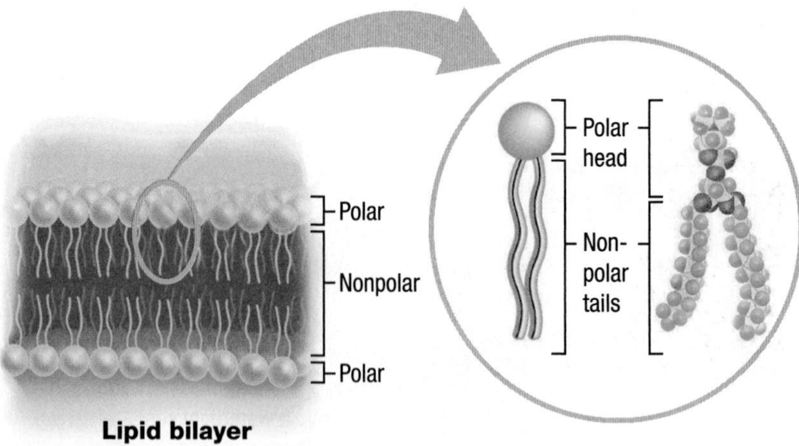


The arrangement of phospholipids in the lipid bilayer makes the cell membrane selectively permeable.

A phospholipid's "head" is polar, and its two fatty acid "tails" are nonpolar.

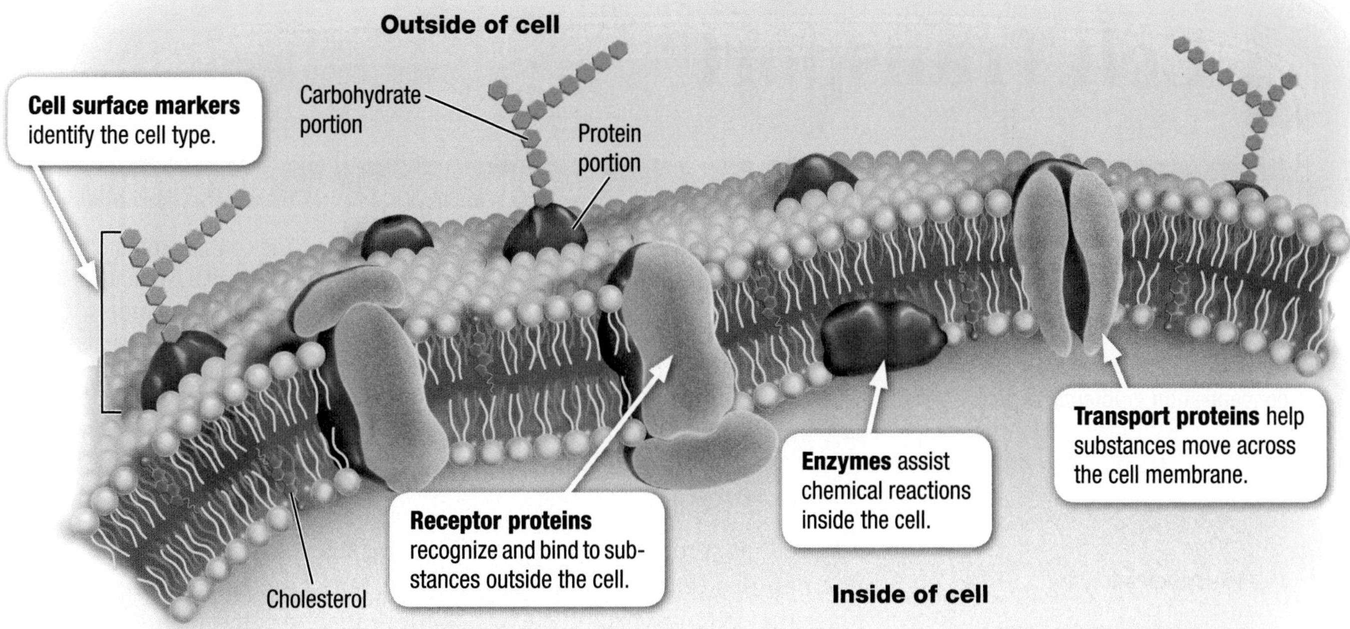
Outside of cell
Cell surface markers identify the cell type.
Carbohydrate portion
Protein portion
Transport proteins help substances move across the cell membrane.
Enzymes assist chemical reactions inside the cell.
Receptor proteins recognize and bind to substances outside the cell.
Cholesterol
Inside of cell

**Figure 3** The cell membrane contains various proteins that have specialized functions.

**Types of Proteins** As **Figure 3** shows, membranes contain different types of proteins. **› Proteins in the cell membrane include cell-surface markers, receptor proteins, enzymes, and transport proteins.**

- **Cell-Surface Markers** Like a name tag, a chain of sugars acts as a marker to identify each type of cell. Liver cells have a different chain of sugars from heart cells. These sugars (carbohydrates) are attached to the cell surface by proteins called *glycoproteins*. Glycoproteins help cells work together.
- **Receptor Proteins** Receptor proteins enable a cell to sense its surroundings by binding to certain substances outside the cell. When this happens, it causes changes inside the cell.
- **Enzymes** Many proteins in the cell membrane help with important biochemical reactions inside the cell.
- **Transport Proteins** Many substances that the cell needs cannot pass through the lipid bilayer. Transport proteins aid the movement of these substances into and out of the cell.

READING TOOLBOX

**Four-Corner Fold** Make a four-corner fold to compare four types of proteins found in the cell membrane.

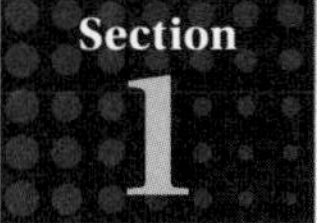
Section 1

## Review

### › KEY IDEAS

1. **Relate** the functions of the cell membrane to homeostasis.
2. **Describe** the types of substances that can pass through the lipid bilayer of the cell membrane.
3. **Outline** four functions of proteins within the cell membrane.

### CRITICAL THINKING

4. **Applying Logic** What would happen if the cell membrane were fully permeable to all substances in the cell's environment?
5. **Predicting Outcomes** What would happen if the cell were exposed to a drug that disabled the transport proteins in the cell membrane?

### ALTERNATIVE ASSESSMENT

6. **Making Models** Create a model of the lipid bilayer, including its associated proteins. Your model may be made of clay or household items. Present your model to the class. Indicate the role of each type of protein in maintaining homeostasis.

Section

# 2 Cell Transport

| Key Ideas | Key Terms | Why It Matters |
|---|---|---|
| ❯ What determines the direction in which passive transport occurs?<br>❯ Why is osmosis important?<br>❯ How do substances move against their concentration gradients? | equilibrium<br>concentration gradient<br>diffusion<br>carrier protein<br>osmosis<br>sodium-potassium pump | The cell's membrane is a little like a country's border. Both barriers regulate who or what enters and who or what leaves. |

*The Living Environment*
**Standard 4**

**1.2g** Each cell is covered by a membrane that performs a number of important functions for the cell. These include: separation from its outside environment, controlling which molecules enter and leave the cell, and recognition of chemical signals. The processes of diffusion and active transport are important in the movement of materials in and out of cells.

**1.2i** Inside the cell a variety of specialized structures, formed from many different molecules, carry out the transport of materials (cytoplasm), extraction of energy from nutrients (mitochondria), protein building (ribosomes), waste disposal (cell membrane), storage (vacuole), and information storage (nucleus).

**5.1e** The energy from ATP is used by the organism to obtain, transform, and transport materials, and to eliminate wastes.

The cell must move substances of varying size, electrical charge, and composition into and out of the cell. Substances may enter and leave the cell in a variety of ways. Sometimes the cell must use energy to move a substance across the cell membrane. In *active transport,* the cell is required to use energy to move a substance. In *passive transport,* the cell does not use energy.

## Passive Transport

In a solution, randomly moving molecules tend to fill up a space. When the space is filled evenly, a state called **equilibrium** is reached. The amount of a particular substance in a given volume is called the *concentration* of the substance. When one area has a higher concentration than another area does, as **Figure 4** shows, a **concentration gradient** exists. Substances move from an area of higher concentration to an area of lower concentration. This movement down the concentration gradient is called **diffusion.**

The cell membrane separates the cytoplasm from the fluid outside the cell. Some substances enter and leave the cell by diffusing across the cell membrane. The direction of movement depends on the concentration gradient and does not require energy. ❯ **In passive transport, substances cross the cell membrane down their concentration gradient.** Some substances diffuse through the lipid bilayer. Others diffuse through transport proteins.

**Figure 4** If people acted like molecules, they would fill up the space in this room evenly over time. ❯ **What area of this room has a high concentration of people?**

**Simple Diffusion** Small, nonpolar molecules can pass directly through the lipid bilayer. This type of movement is called *simple diffusion.* As **Figure 5** shows, oxygen diffuses into the cell through the lipid bilayer. The concentration of oxygen is higher outside the cell than it is inside. Thus, oxygen moves down its concentration gradient into the cell. In contrast, the concentration of carbon dioxide is often higher inside the cell than it is outside. So, carbon dioxide diffuses out of the cell. Natural steroid hormones, which are nonpolar and fat soluble, can also diffuse across the lipid bilayer.

**Facilitated Diffusion** Many ions and polar molecules that are important for cell function do not diffuse easily through the nonpolar lipid bilayer. During *facilitated diffusion,* transport proteins help these substances diffuse through the cell membrane. Two types of transport proteins are channel proteins and carrier proteins.

**Channel Proteins** Ions, sugars, and amino acids can diffuse through the cell membrane through channel proteins. These proteins, sometimes called *pores,* serve as tunnels through the lipid bilayer. Each channel allows the diffusion of specific substances that have the right size and charge. For example, only sodium ions can pass through the sodium ion channel shown in **Figure 5.**

**Carrier Proteins** Carrier proteins transport substances that fit within their binding site, as **Figure 6** shows. A carrier protein binds to a specific substance on one side of the cell membrane. This binding causes the protein to change shape. As the protein's shape changes, the substance is moved across the membrane and is released on the other side.

**› Reading Check** *Why does oxygen diffuse into the cell?*

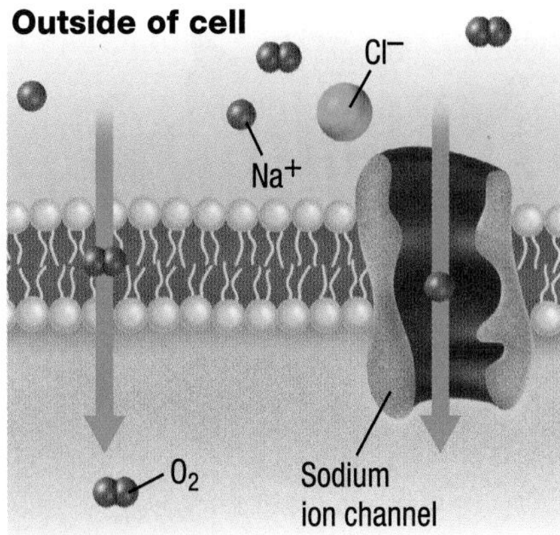


**Figure 5** Nonpolar molecules, such as $O_2$, diffuse through the lipid bilayer. Channel proteins allow certain ions, such as $Na^+$, to diffuse through the cell membrane. $Cl^-$ ions cannot pass through the sodium ion channel.

**equilibrium** a state that exists when the concentration of a substance is the same throughout a space

**concentration gradient** a difference in the concentration of a substance across a distance

**diffusion** the movement of particles from regions of higher density to regions of lower density

**carrier protein** a protein that transports substances across a cell membrane

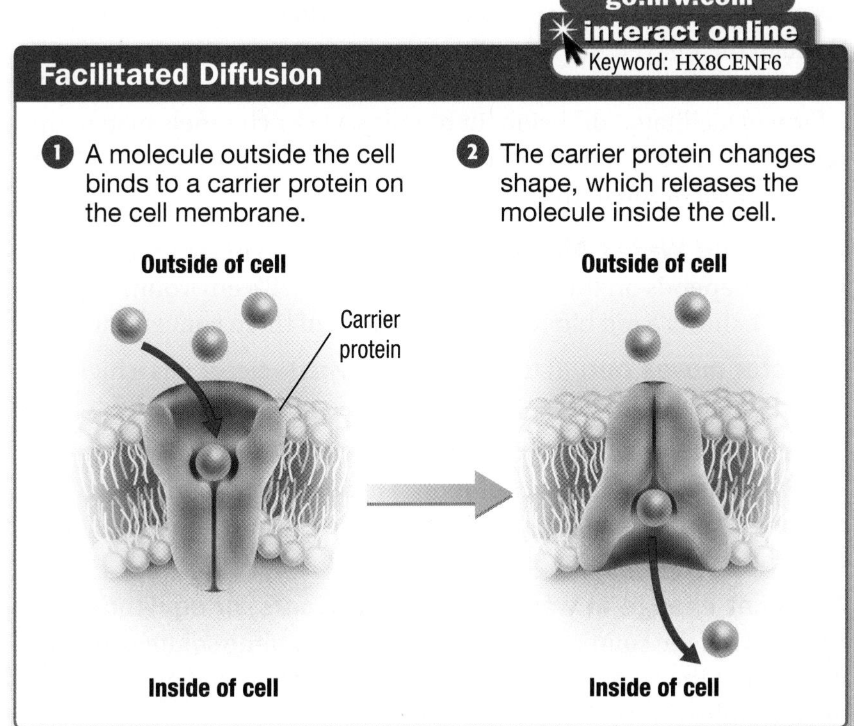


**Figure 6** Carrier proteins allow the diffusion of specific molecules by binding the molecules on one side of the cell membrane and releasing them on the other side.
**›** **Which side of this membrane has a higher concentration of molecules?**

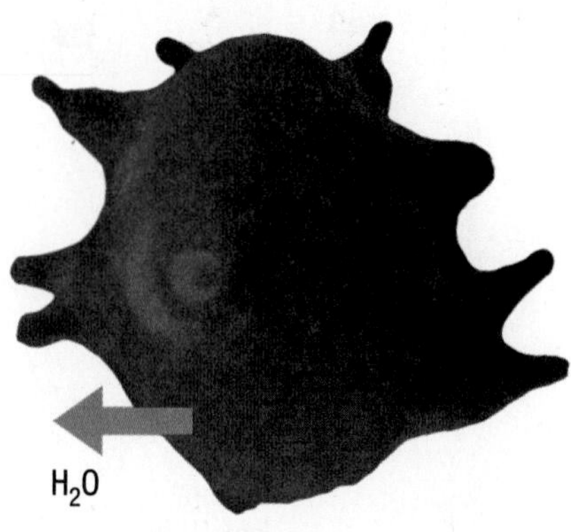


**Hypertonic Solution** The fluid outside is more concentrated. As water moves out of the cell, the cell shrinks.

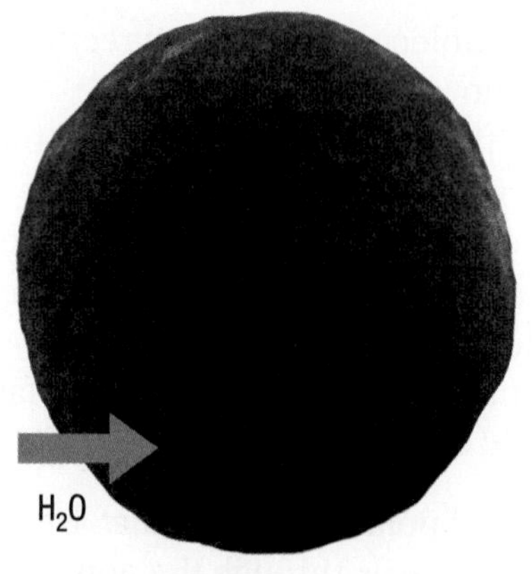


**Hypotonic Solution** The fluid outside is less concentrated. As water moves into the cell, the cell swells.

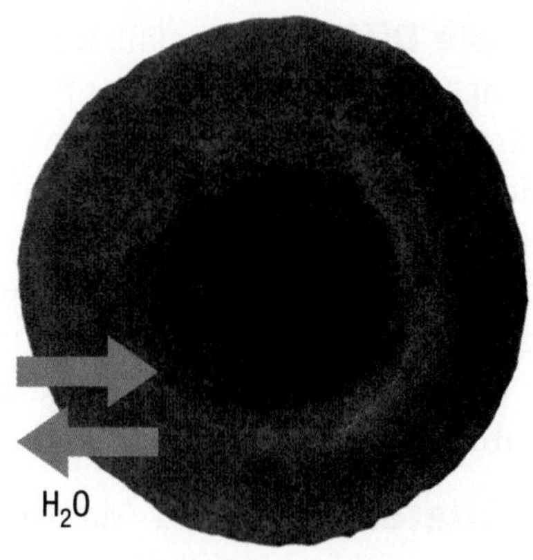


**Isotonic Solution** Water moves into and out of the cell at the same rate. The cell stays the same size.

**Figure 7** Red blood cells change shape due to the movement of water. The direction of water movement depends on the difference between the concentration of the solution outside the cell and the concentration of the cytosol.

## Osmosis

Water can diffuse across a selectively permeable membrane in a process called **osmosis.** Osmosis is a type of passive transport that is very important to keeping cells functional. **> Osmosis allows cells to maintain water balance as their environment changes.**

When ions and polar substances dissolve in water, they attract and bind some water molecules. The remaining water molecules are free to move around. If a concentration gradient exists across a membrane for solutes, a concentration gradient also exists across the membrane for free water molecules. Osmosis occurs as free water molecules move down their concentration gradient into the solution that has the lower concentration of free water molecules.

**Word Parts** The prefix *hyper-* means "higher than," and *hypertonic* means "higher concentration." If *hypo-* means "lower than," what does *hypotonic* mean?

**Water Channels** Polar water molecules do not diffuse directly through the bilayer. But the cell membrane contains channel proteins that only water molecules can pass through. Thus, osmosis in cells is a form of facilitated diffusion. In humans, water channels help in the regulation of body temperature, in digestion, in reproduction, and in water conservation in the kidneys.

**Predicting Water Movement** The direction of water movement in a cell depends on the concentration of the cell's environment. **Figure 7** shows a red blood cell in solutions of three concentrations.

**1. Water moves out.** If the solution is *hypertonic,* or has a higher solute concentration than the cytoplasm does, water moves out of the cell. The cell loses water and shrinks.

**2. Water moves in.** If the solution is *hypotonic,* or has a lower solute concentration than the cytoplasm does, water moves into the cell. The cell gains water and expands in size.

**3. No net change in water movement occurs, or equilibrium is reached.** If the solution is *isotonic,* or has the same solute concentration that the cytoplasm does, water diffuses into and out of the cell at equal rates. The cell stays the same size.

**osmosis** the diffusion of water or another solvent from a more dilute solution (of a solute) to a more concentrated solution (of the solute) through a membrane that is permeable to the solvent

Hands-On

# QuickLab

MULTI-DAY 15 min

## Osmosis 4.1.2g

You will observe the movement of water into or out of a grape under various conditions.

### Procedure

1. Make a data table with four columns and three rows.
2. Fill **one jar** with a **sugar solution.** Fill a **second jar** with **grape juice.** Fill a **third jar** with **tap water.** Label each jar with the name of the solution that it contains.
3. Use a **balance** to find the mass of each of **three grapes.** Place one grape in each jar, and put the lids on the jars.
4. Predict whether the mass of each grape will increase or decrease over time. Explain your predictions.
5. After 24 h, remove each grape from its jar, and dry the grape gently with a **paper towel.** Using the balance, find each grape's mass again. Record your results.

### Analysis

1. **Identify** the solutions in which osmosis occurred.
2. CRITICAL THINKING **Evaluating Conclusions** How did you determine whether osmosis occurred in each of the three solutions?
3. CRITICAL THINKING **Evaluating Hypotheses** Did the mass of each grape change as you had predicted? Why or why not?

**Effects of Osmosis** If left unchecked, the swelling caused by a hypotonic solution could cause a cell to burst. The rigid cell walls of plants and fungi prevent the cells of these organisms from expanding too much. In fact, many plants are healthiest in a hypotonic environment, as **Figure 8** shows. Some unicellular eukaryotes have *contractile vacuoles,* which collect excess water inside the cell and force the water out of the cell. Animal cells have neither cell walls nor contractile vacuoles. However, many animal cells can avoid swelling caused by osmosis by actively removing solutes from the cytoplasm. The removal of dissolved solutes from a cell increases the concentration of free water molecules inside the cell.

**Figure 8** Plant cells are healthiest in a hypotonic environment. When its cells swell, the plant stands rigid. In an isotonic environment, a plant wilts. **› What would happen if you added water to the plant on the right?**

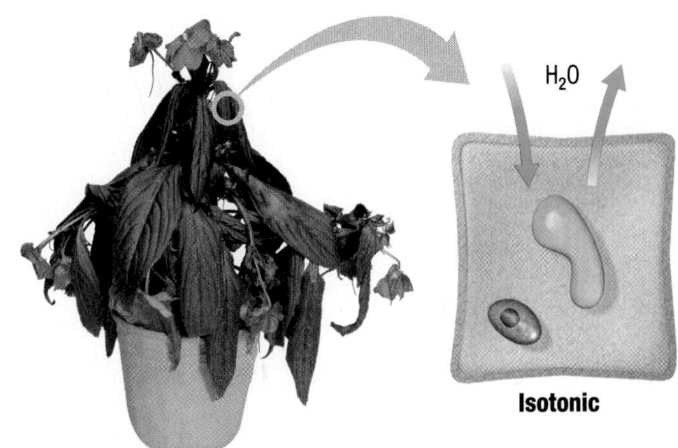

## Active Transport

Sometimes, cells must transport substances against their concentration gradients. This movement is called *active transport* because the cell must use energy to move these substances. **Active transport requires energy to move substances against their concentration gradients.** Most often, the energy needed for active transport is supplied directly or indirectly by ATP.

**Pumps** Many active transport processes use carrier proteins to move substances. In facilitated diffusion, the carrier proteins do not require energy. In active transport, the carrier proteins do require energy to "pump" substances against their concentration gradient.

One of the most important carrier proteins in animal cells is the **sodium-potassium pump,** shown in **Figure 9.** Sodium ions inside the cell bind to the carrier protein. A phosphate group from ATP transfers energy to the protein. The protein changes shape and releases the sodium ions outside the cell membrane. Outside the cell, potassium ions bind to the pump. As a result, the phosphate group is released from the pump. The pump returns to its original shape and releases the potassium ions inside the cell membrane. For every three sodium ions taken out, two potassium ions are brought inside.

**sodium-potassium pump** a carrier protein that uses ATP to actively transport sodium ions out of a cell and potassium ions into the cell

This pump prevents sodium ions from building up in the cell. Osmosis results when sodium ion levels are high. The cell could swell or even burst if too much water enters. The concentration gradients of sodium ions and potassium ions also help transport other substances, such as glucose, across the cell membrane.

**Figure 9** The sodium-potassium pump actively transports both $Na^+$ and $K^+$ ions across the cell membrane. **In this figure, is the concentration of sodium ions higher inside the cell or outside the cell?**

go.hrw.com
interact online
Keyword: HX8CENF9

### Sodium-Potassium Pump

1. Three sodium ions bind to the pump. A phosphate from ATP also binds, which transfers energy.
2. The pump changes shape, releasing the three sodium ions on the other side of the membrane.
3. Two potassium ions bind to the pump and are tranported across the cell membrane.
4. The phosphate group is released. The pump returns to its original shape, releasing the two potassium ions.

Outside of cell

Sodium ion, Na+

Potassium ion, K+

ATP

P + ADP

Phosphate group

P

P

Inside of cell

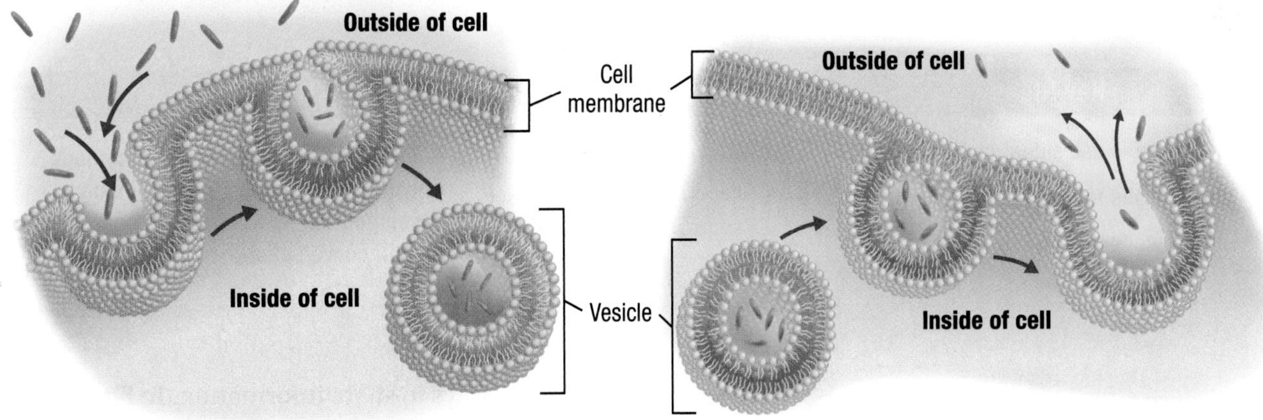


**Figure 10** A cell moves large substances or large amounts of materials in vesicles. Vesicles can fuse with the cell membrane to take in and release substances.

**Vesicles** Many substances, such as proteins and polysaccharides, are too large to be transported by carrier proteins. Instead, they cross the cell membrane in vesicles. Recall that vesicles are membrane-bound sacs. The vesicle membrane is a lipid bilayer, like the cell membrane. Therefore, vesicles can bud off from the membrane, fuse with it, or fuse with other vesicles.

The movement of a large substance into a cell by means of a vesicle is called *endocytosis.* During endocytosis, shown in **Figure 10,** the cell membrane forms a pouch around the substance. The pouch then closes up and pinches off from the membrane to form a vesicle inside the cell. Vesicles that form by endocytosis may fuse with lysosomes or other organelles.

The movement of material out of a cell by means of a vesicle is called *exocytosis.* During exocytosis, shown in **Figure 10,** vesicles inside the cell fuse with the cell membrane. From the cell membrane, the contents of the vesicle are released to the outside of the cell. Cells use exocytosis to export proteins modified by the Golgi apparatus. Some protists release their waste products through this process. Some cells also use exocytosis to remove bacteria or other microbes.

**ACADEMIC VOCABULARY**

**release** to set free

**› Reading Check** ***What is the structure of the vesicle membrane?***

## Section 2 Review

### › KEY IDEAS

1. **Compare** the functions of channel proteins and carrier proteins in facilitated diffusion.
2. **Explain** why the presence of dissolved particles on one side of a membrane results in diffusion of water across the membrane.
3. **List** two ways that a cell can move a substance against its concentration gradient.

### CRITICAL THINKING

4. **Applying Logic** Based on have learned about homeostasis and osmosis, why should humans avoid drinking sea water?
5. **Predicting Outcomes** If a cell were unable to make ATP, how would the cell membrane's transport processes be affected?

### METHODS OF SCIENCE

6. **Designing an Experiment** What data would a biologist need to collect to determine whether a specific molecule is transported into cells by diffusion, by facilitated diffusion, or by active transport?

Section

# 3 Cell Communication

| Key Ideas | Key Terms | Why It Matters |
|---|---|---|
| ❯ How do cells use signal molecules?<br>❯ How do cells receive signals?<br>❯ How do cells respond to signaling? | signal<br>receptor protein<br>second messenger | Cells developed sophisticated methods of communication long before humans developed the Internet, cell phones, or even regular conversation. |

***The Living Environment***
**Standard 4**

**1.2g** Each cell is covered by a membrane that performs a number of important functions for the cell. These include: separation from its outside environment, controlling which molecules enter and leave the cell, and recognition of chemical signals. The processes of diffusion and active transport are important in the movement of materials in and out of cells.

**1.2j** Receptor molecules play an important role in the interactions between cells. Two primary agents of cellular communication are hormones and chemicals produced by nerve cells. If nerve or hormone signals are blocked, cellular communication is disrupted and the organism's stability is affected.

**5.1g** Enzymes and other molecules, such as hormones, receptor molecules, and antibodies, have specific shapes that influence both how they function and how they interact with other molecules.

We communicate in many ways to share information. In **Figure 11,** one person is surfing the Internet, another is talking on her cell phone, and two are having a face-to-face conversation. All of these are forms of communication. To coordinate activities, information must be shared. Cells in multicellular organisms depend on the activities of other cells to survive. Even unicellular organisms need to communicate—for example, to find a mate.

## Sending Signals

You use different methods to communicate in different ways. You may whisper a secret to a trusted friend, or you may shout a warning to several people nearby. You may phone a friend who is far away, or you may put an ad in the newspaper for everyone to see.

Cells also use various methods of communication. These methods vary depending on whether the target is specific or general. They also depend on whether the target is nearby or far away. ❯ **Cells communicate and coordinate activity by sending chemical signals that carry information to other cells.** A *signaling cell* produces a **signal,** often a molecule, that is detected by the *target cell.* Typically, target cells have specific proteins that recognize and respond to the signal.

**Targets** Neighboring cells can communicate through direct contact between their membranes. Short-distance signals may act locally, a few cells away from the originating cell. Long-distance signals are carried by hormones and nerve cells. Hormones are signal molecules that are made in one part of the body. Hormones are distributed widely in the bloodstream throughout the body, but they affect only specific cells. Nerve cells also signal information to distant locations in the body, but their signals are not widely distributed.

**Environmental Signals** While most signal molecules originate within the body, some signals come from outside. For example, light has a great effect on the action of hormones in plants. The length of the day determines when some plants flower.

❯ **Reading Check** ***Compare the targets of signaling hormones and nerve cells.***

**Figure 11** This young man dials a phone number, which sends a signal to a target. ❯ **Is this target general or specific?**

Hands-On

# QuickLab

## Sensitive Plants 4.1.2j

10 min

The sensitive plant *(Mimosa pudica)* reacts to touch. This reaction results from rapid cell-to-cell communication.

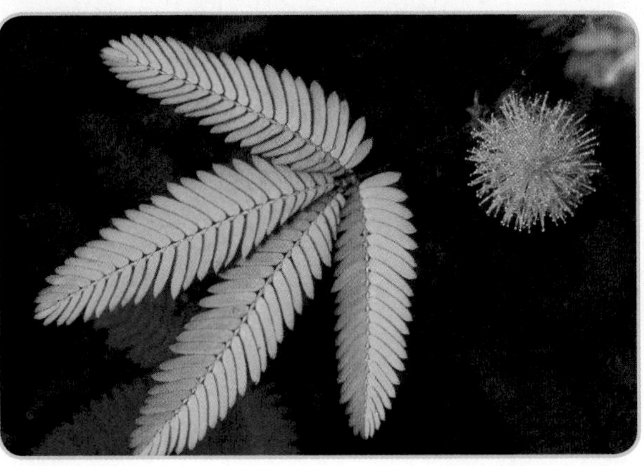

### Procedure

1. Observe and sketch the extended leaves on the *Mimosa* plant branch.
2. Touch the tip of the end leaf on this branch. Observe the plant's reaction.
3. Make a sketch showing the branch's new appearance.

### Analysis

1. **Identify** what stimulus produced the plant's response.
2. **Describe** the plant's response.
3. **Explain** whether the reaction behavior was communicated beyond the leaf that was touched.
4. **CRITICAL THINKING** **Making Inferences** Plants can respond to touch, although they lack a nervous system. Propose a mechanism for the response you observed.

## Receiving Signals

A target cell is bombarded by hundreds of signals. But it recognizes and responds only to the few signals that are important for its function. This response to some signals, but not to others, is made possible by **receptor proteins,** such as the ones in the cell's membrane.

**signal** anything that serves to direct, guide, or warn

**receptor protein** a protein that binds specific signal molecules, which causes the cell to respond

**Binding Specificity** A receptor protein binds specific substances, such as signal molecules. The outer part of the protein is folded into a unique shape, called the *binding site.* **A receptor protein binds only to signals that match the specific shape of its binding site.** As **Figure 12** shows, only signal molecules that have the "right" shape can fit into the receptor protein. Signal molecules that have the "wrong" shape have no effect on that particular receptor protein. A cell may also have receptor proteins that bind to molecules in its environment. Some cells may have receptor proteins that can detect and respond to light. Receptor proteins enable a cell to detect its environment.

SCILINKS.
www.scilinks.org
Topic: Receptor Proteins
Code: HX81274

**Effect** Once it binds the signal molecule, the receptor protein changes its shape in the membrane. This change in shape relays information into the cytoplasm of the target cell.

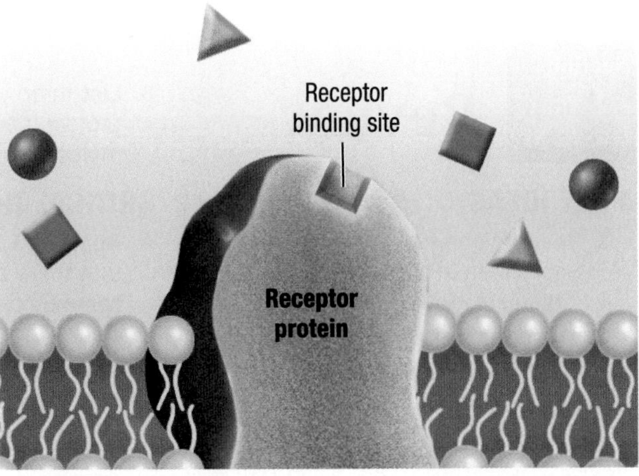


**Figure 12** The binding site of this receptor protein has a specific shape to which only one type of signal molecule can bind. **Which of these molecules would bind with the receptor?**

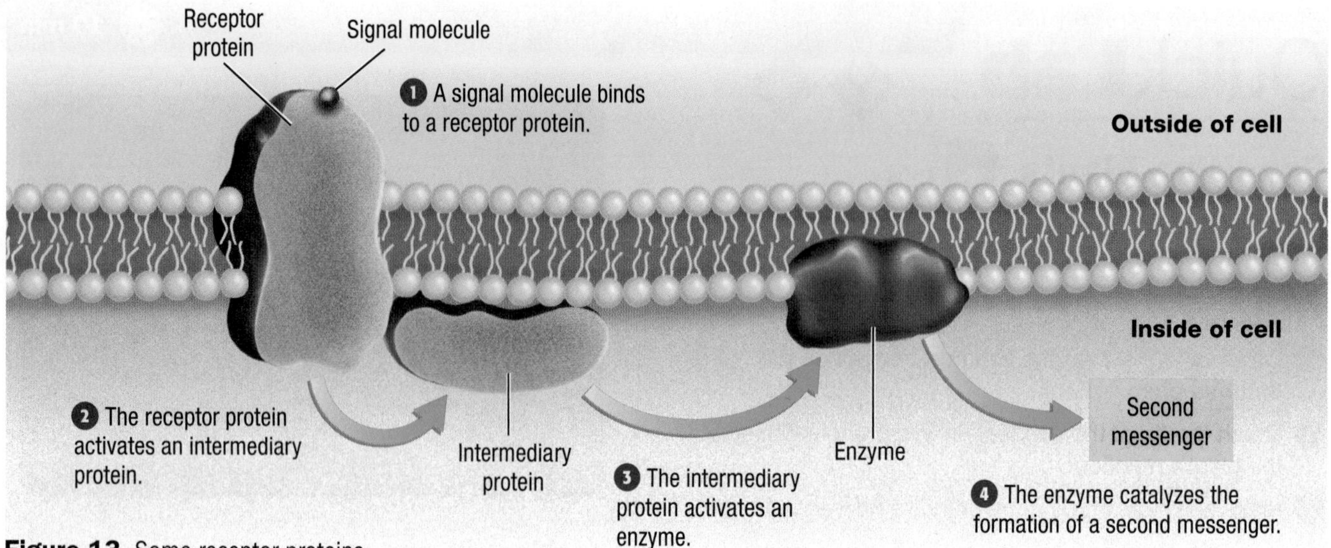
Receptor protein
Signal molecule
1 A signal molecule binds to a receptor protein.
Outside of cell
Inside of cell
2 The receptor protein activates an intermediary protein.
Intermediary protein
3 The intermediary protein activates an enzyme.
Enzyme
Second messenger
4 The enzyme catalyzes the formation of a second messenger.

**Figure 13** Some receptor proteins trigger the production of second messengers.

## Responding to Signals

When a signal molecule binds to a receptor protein, the protein changes shape, which triggers changes in the cell membrane. **› The cell may respond to a signal by changing its membrane permeability, by activating enzymes, or by forming a second messenger.**

- **Permeability Change** Transport proteins may open or close in response to a signal. For example, a nerve impulse may result when ion channels in nerve cells open after receiving a signal.
- **Enzyme Activation** Some receptor proteins activate enzymes in the cell membrane. Some receptors are enzymes themselves and are activated by the binding of a signal molecule. Enzymes trigger chemical reactions in the cell.
- **Second Messenger** Binding of a signal molecule outside the cell may cause a second messenger to form, as **Figure 13** shows. The **second messenger** acts as a signal molecule within the cell and causes changes in the cytoplasm and nucleus.

**› Reading Check** ***How does membrane permeability change?***

READING TOOLBOX

**Finding Examples** Search the text on this page to find an example of the function of a transport protein.

**second messenger** a molecule that is generated when a specific substance attaches to a receptor on the outside of a cell membrane, which produces a change in cellular function

## Section 3 Review

**› KEY IDEAS**

1. **Identify** one function of signal molecules in a multicellular organism.
2. **Describe** the relationship between receptor proteins and signal molecules.
3. **List** three ways that a receptor protein may respond when a signal molecule binds to it.

**CRITICAL THINKING**

4. **Applying Logic** Why do you think that there are many forms of communication between body cells?
5. **Applying Logic** Why is specificity between a receptor protein and a signal molecule important?

**WRITING FOR SCIENCE**

6. **Finding Information** Use library or Internet resources to research a human disease that results from problems in the transport of molecules across the cell membrane. Describe the disease's symptoms and treatments. Summarize your findings in a written report.

# Heady Effects



Many people start their day with a hot cup of coffee. Coffee contains a chemical stimulant, caffeine, that produces a feeling of heightened alertness.

## Caffeine

The shape of the caffeine molecule is similar to the shape of a signal molecule that your body produces naturally. Receptor proteins respond to this signal in a chain of events that increases heart rate, blood flow, and the amount of sugar in the bloodstream.

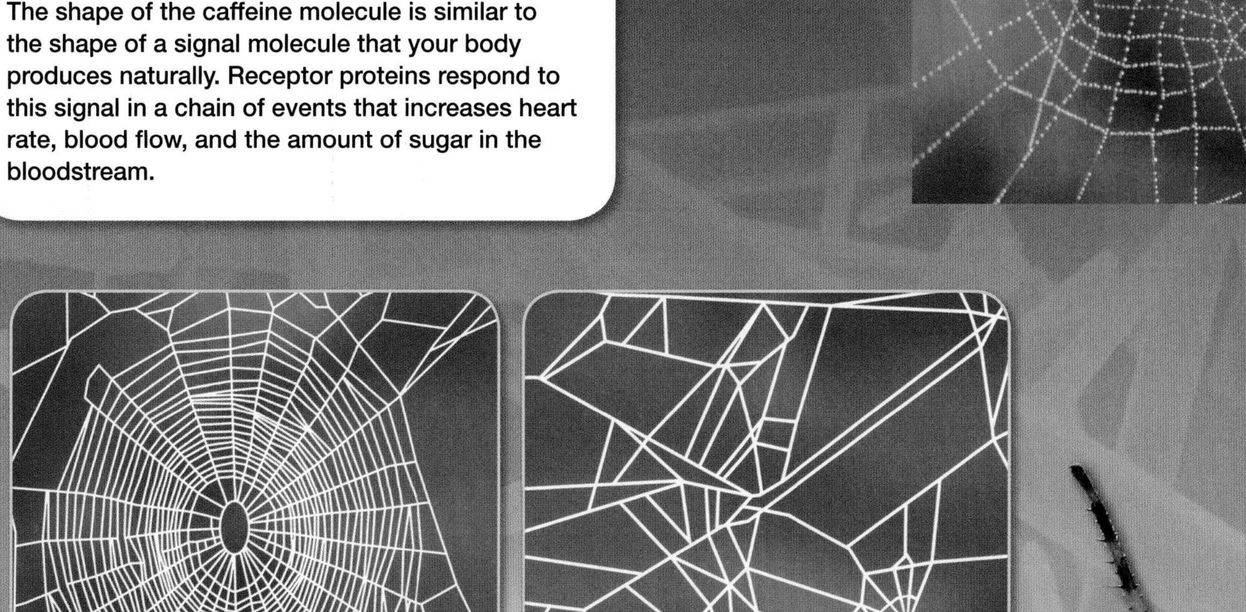

**Wacky Webs** Most spider webs look like the one on the left. This web was created by a common garden spider, *Araneus diadematus*. The web on the right was created by the same spider after it was fed caffeine-dosed flies.

**Quick Project** Find out the average caffeine content in milligrams (mg) of coffee, tea, cola drinks, energy drinks, chocolate milk, dark chocolate, and milk chocolate.

Inquiry

# Chapter 8 Lab

## Cell Size and Diffusion

### Objectives

- Relate a cell's size to its surface area-to-volume ratio.
- Predict how the surface area-to-volume ratio of a cell will affect the diffusion of substances into the cell.

### Materials

- safety goggles
- lab apron
- disposable gloves
- block of phenolphthalein agar (3 cm × 3 cm × 6 cm)
- knife, plastic
- ruler, metric
- beaker, 250 mL
- vinegar, 150 mL
- spoon, plastic
- paper towel

### Safety

Substances enter and leave a cell in several ways, including by diffusion. Substances that a cell needs must come from outside the cell to the cell's center. How easily a cell can exchange substances depends on the ratio of its surface area to its volume (surface area ÷ volume). Surface area is a measure of the exposed outer surface of an object. Volume is the amount of space that an object takes up.

In this lab, you will design an experiment to investigate how a cell's size affects the diffusion of substances into the cell. To do so, you will make cell models using agar that contains phenolphthalein. Phenolphthalein is an indicator that changes color in the presence of an acidic solution.

### Preparation

1. SCIENTIFIC METHODS **State the Problem** How does a cell's size affect the delivery of substances via diffusion to the center of the cell?
2. SCIENTIFIC METHODS **Form a Hypothesis** Form a testable hypothesis that explains how a cell's size affects the rate of diffusion of substances from outside the cell.

### Procedure

#### Design an Experiment

1. Design an experiment that tests your hypothesis and that uses the materials listed for this lab. Predict what will happen during your experiment if your hypothesis is correct.

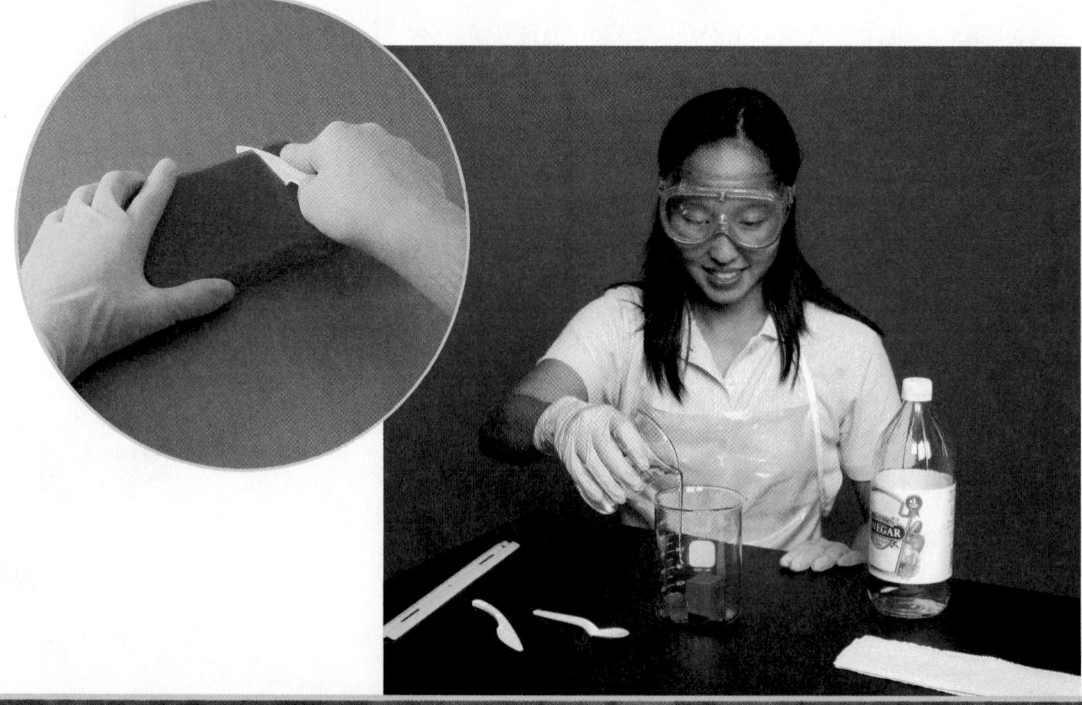

2. Write a procedure for your experiment. Identify the variables that you will control, the experimental variables, and the responding variables. Construct any tables that you will need to record your data. Make a list of all safety precautions that you will take. Have your teacher approve your procedure before you begin.

*Diffusion in Cubes*

| Size (cm) | Ratio | Distance (mm) |
|---|---|---|
| | | |
| | | |
| | | |

### Conduct Your Experiment

3. Put on safety goggles, gloves, and a lab apron.
4. Carry out your experiment. Record your observations in your data table.
5. Follow your teacher's instructions for cleaning up your lab materials. Wash your hands before leaving the lab.

## Analyze and Conclude

1. **Interpreting Observations** Describe any changes in the appearance of the agar cubes. Explain why these changes occurred.
2. **Summarizing Results** Make a graph labeled "Diffusion distance (mm)" on the vertical axis and "Surface area–to-volume ratio" on the horizontal axis. Plot your group's data on the graph.
3. SCIENTIFIC METHODS **Analyzing Results** Using the graph you made in item 2, make a statement relating the surface area–to-volume ratio and the distance that the substance diffuses.
4. **Summarizing Results** Make a second graph using your group's data. Label the vertical axis "Rate of diffusion (mm/min)" (distance that vinegar moved ÷ time). Label the horizontal axis "Surface area–to-volume ratio." Plot your group's data on the graph.
5. **Analyzing Results** Referring to the graph that you made in item 4, write a statement that relates the surface area–to-volume ratio and the rate at which the substance diffuses.
6. SCIENTIFIC METHODS **Evaluating Methods** In what ways do your agar models simplify or fail to simulate the features of cells?
7. **Calculating** Calculate the surface area and the volume of a cube that has a side length of 5 cm. Calculate the surface area and volume of a cube that has a side length of 10 cm. Determine the surface area–to-volume ratio of each cube. Which cube has the greater surface area–to-volume ratio?
8. SCIENTIFIC METHODS **Evaluating Conclusions** How does the size of a cell affect the rate at which substances diffuse into the cell?
9. **Further Inquiry** Write a new question about cell size and diffusion that could be explored in another investigation.

SCILINKS.
www.scilinks.org
Topic: Diffusion
Code: HX80406

## Extensions

10. How does cell transport in prokaryotic cells differ from cell transport in eukaryotic cells?
11. Which of the following can diffuse across the cell membrane without the help of a transport protein: water, carbohydrates, lipids, or proteins?

# Chapter 8 Summary

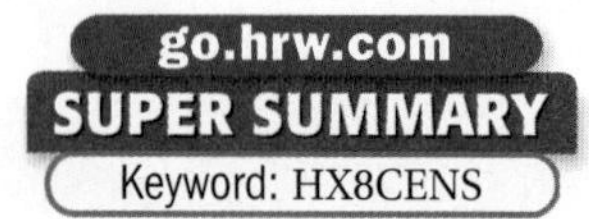


| Key Ideas | Key Terms |
|---|---|

## 1 Cell Membrane

- One way that a cell maintains homeostasis is by controlling the movement of substances across the cell membrane.
- The lipid bilayer is selectively permeable to small, nonpolar substances.
- Proteins in the cell membrane include cell-surface markers, receptor proteins, enzymes, and transport proteins.

**Key Terms:** **phospholipid** (176), **lipid bilayer** (176)

## 2 Cell Transport

- In passive transport, substances cross the cell membrane down their concentration gradient.
- Osmosis allows cells to maintain water balance as their environment changes.
- Active transport requires energy to move substances against their concentration gradients.

**Key Terms:** **equilibrium** (178), **concentration gradient** (178), **diffusion** (178), **carrier protein** (178), **osmosis** (180), **sodium-potassium pump** (182)

## 3 Cell Communication

- Cells communicate and coordinate activity by sending chemical signals that carry information to other cells.
- A receptor protein binds only to the signals that match the specific shape of its binding site.
- The cell may respond to a signal by changing its membrane permeability, by activating enzymes, or by forming a second messenger.

**Key Terms:** **signal** (184), **receptor protein** (185), **second messenger** (186)

Chapter 8

The Living Environment

# Regents Exam Practice

**PART A: Answer all questions in this part.**

*Directions:* For each statement or question, write on your separate answer sheet the number of the word or expression that best completes the statement or answers the question.

**1** Which row in the chart below best describes the active transport of molecule X through a cell membrane?

| Row | Movement of Molecule X | ATP |
|---|---|---|
| (1) | high concentration → low concentration | used |
| (2) | high concentration → low concentration | not used |
| (3) | low concentration → high concentration | used |
| (4) | low concentration → high concentration | not used |

(1) 1 (3) 3
(2) 2 (4) 4

**2** Molecule X moves across a cell membrane by diffusion. Which row in the chart above best indicates the relationship between the relative concentrations of molecule X and the use of ATP for diffusion?

(1) 1 (3) 3
(2) 2 (4) 4

**3** Which letter indicates a cell structure that directly controls the movement of molecules into and out of the cell?

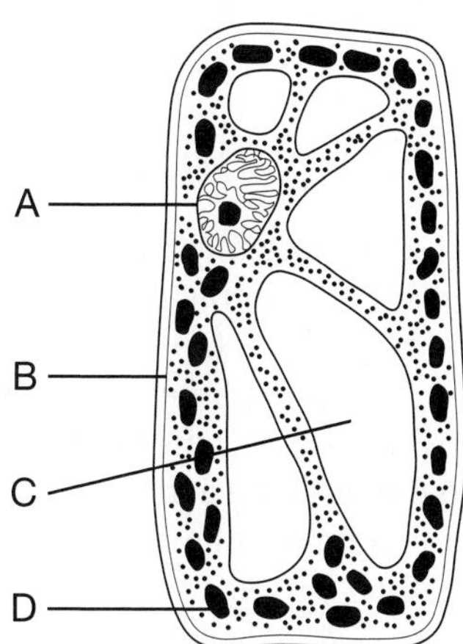


(1) A (3) C
(2) B (4) D

**4** Cellular communication is illustrated in the diagram below.

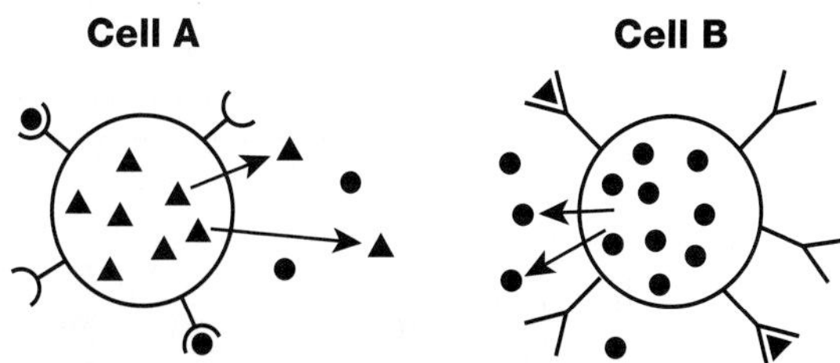


| Key |
|---|
| ● Signal 1 |
| ▲ Signal 2 |

Information can be sent from

(1) cell A to cell B because cell B is able to recognize signal 1
(2) cell A to cell B because cell A is able to recognize signal 2
(3) cell B to cell A because cell A is able to recognize signal 1
(4) cell B to cell A because cell B is able to recognize signal 2

**5** Which substances are found on cell surfaces and respond to nerve and hormone signals?

(1) starches and simple sugars
(2) subunits of DNA
(3) vitamins and minerals
(4) receptor molecules

**6** After a hormone enters the bloodstream, it is transported throughout the body, but the hormone affects only certain cells. The reason only certain cells are affected is that the membranes of these cells have specific

(1) receptors (3) antibodies
(2) tissues (4) carbohydrates

**7** The graph below shows the relative concentrations of different ions inside and outside of an animal cell.

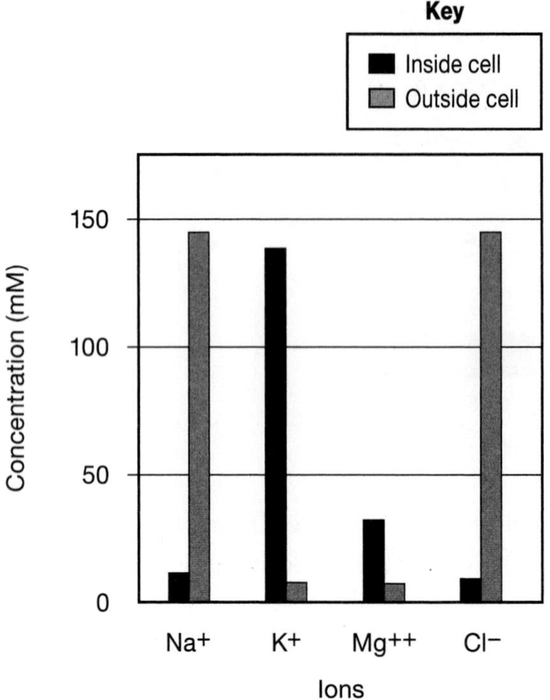


Which process is directly responsible for the net movement of K+ and Mg++ into the animal cell?

(1) electrophoresis
(2) diffusion
(3) active transport
(4) circulation

**8** In the diagram below, the dark dots indicate small molecules. These molecules are moving out of the cells, as indicated by the arrows. The number of dots inside and outside of the two cells represents the relative concentrations of the molecules inside and outside of the cells.

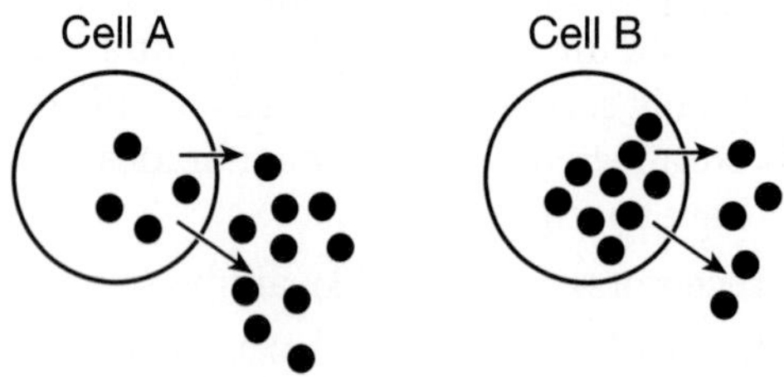


ATP is being used to move the molecules out of the cell by

(1) cell A, only
(2) cell B, only
(3) both cell A and cell B
(4) neither cell A nor cell B

**PART B**

**Base your answers to questions 9 through 11 on the diagram below and on your knowledge of biology.**

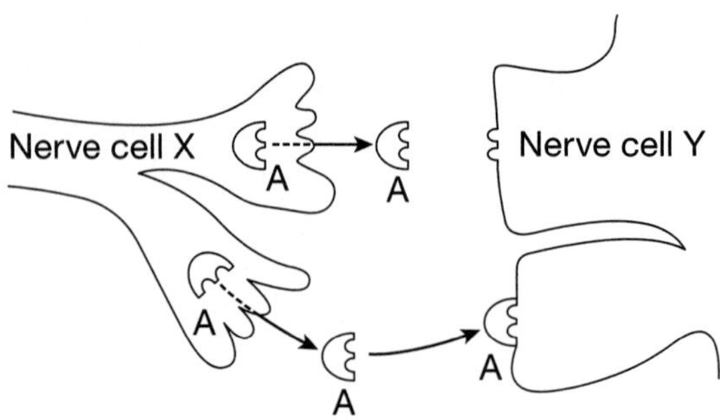


**9** The process represented in the diagram best illustrates

(1) cellular communication
(2) muscle contraction
(3) extraction of energy from nutrients
(4) waste disposal

**10** Which statement best describes the diagram?

(1) Nerve cell X is releasing receptor molecules.
(2) Nerve cell Y is signaling nerve cell X.
(3) Nerve cell X is attaching to nerve cell Y.
(4) Nerve cell Y contains receptor molecules for substance A.

**11** A drug is developed that, due to its molecular shape, blocks the action of substance A. Which shape would the drug molecule most likely resemble?

(1) (2) (3) (4)

**12** Acetylcholine is a chemical secreted at the ends of nerve cells. This chemical helps to send nerve signals across synapses (spaces between nerve cells). After the signal passes across a synapse, an enzyme breaks down the acetylcholine. LSD is a drug that blocks the action of this enzyme. Describe one possible effect of LSD on the action of acetylcholine.

## PART D

**13** The diagram below represents a container of water and two different kinds of molecules, A and B, separated into two chambers by a membrane through which only water and molecule A can pass.

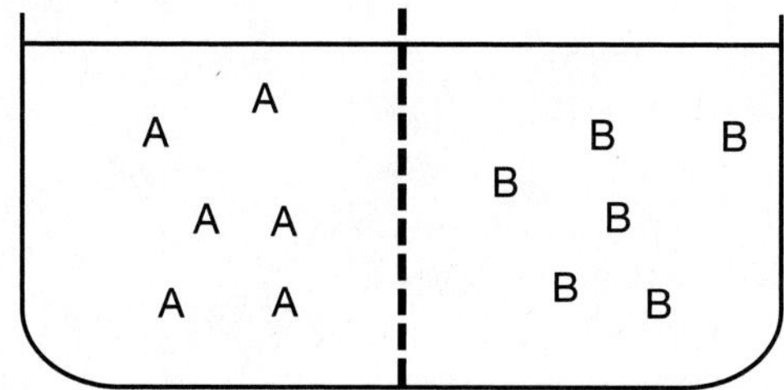


On a seperate piece of paper, copy the diagram of the container below. On your diagram, indicate the distribution of molecules A and B after the net movement of these molecules stops.

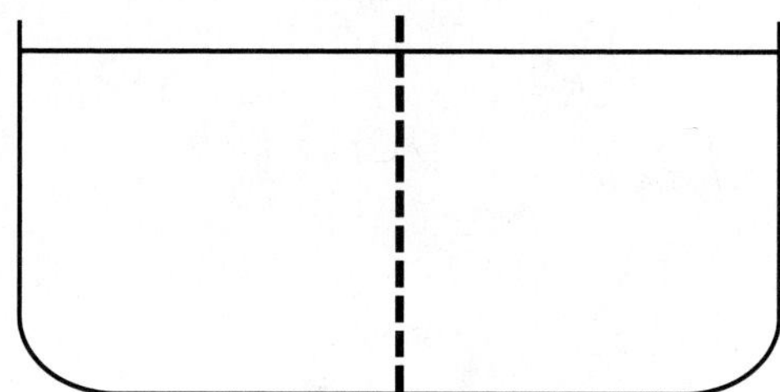

**Base your answers to questions 14 and 15 on the information below and on your knowledge of biology.**

Students prepared four models of cells by using dialysis tubing containing the same blue solution. Each of the model cells originally weighed 10 grams. They then placed each model cell in a beaker containing a different concentration of water. After 24 hours, they recorded the mass of the model cells as shown in the data table below.

| Concentration of Water Surrounding the Model Cell | Mass of Model Cell |
|---|---|
| 100% | 12 grams |
| 90% | 11 grams |
| 80% | 10 grams |
| 70% | 9 grams |

**14** Why did the model cell that was placed in 100% water increase in mass?

**15** What was the concentration of water in the original blue solution? State evidence in support of your answer.

Chapter 9

# Photosynthesis and Cellular Respiration

## Preview

1 **Energy in Living Systems**
- Chemical Energy
- Metabolism and the Carbon Cycle
- Transferring Energy

2 **Photosynthesis**
- Harvesting Light Energy
- Two Electron Transport Chains
- Producing Sugar
- Factors that Affect Photosynthesis

3 **Cellular Respiration**
- Glycolysis
- Aerobic Respiration
- Fermentation

## Why It Matters

Everything you do—from moving, to breathing, to thinking—requires energy. The energy your body uses is mostly derived from the processes of photosynthesis and cellular respiration.

***The Living Environment***

**Standard 4** Students will understand and apply scientific concepts, principles, and theories pertaining to the physical setting and living environment and recognize the historical development of ideas in science.

**Key Idea 1** Living things are both similar to and different from each other and from nonliving things. ***Major Understandings* - 1.2f, 1.2h, 1.2i**

**Key Idea 5** Organisms maintain a dynamic equilibrium that sustains life. ***Major Understandings* - 5.1a, 5.1b, 5.1c, 5.1d, 5.1e, 5.1f**

**Key Idea 6** Plants and animals depend on each other and their physical environment ***Major Understandings* - 6.1c**

**A saturniid caterpillar feeds on a leaf. The leaf provides the energy the caterpillar needs to grow and undergo metamorphosis.**

The caterpillar gets the organic compounds it needs for cellular respiration from the leaf. Caterpillars, like other animals, are *heterotrophs.*

Carbohydrates and oxygen are produced in leaves by photosynthesis. A green pigment called *chlorophyll* gives plants their characteristic green color.

# Inquiry Lab

15 min

## Stored Energy

Have you ever used a hot pack? The way the hot pack works has to do with energy storage and the release of stored heat energy during a chemical reaction.

### Procedure

1. Fill a **plastic foam cup** halfway with **tap water.**
2. Measure and record the water's temperature.
3. Examine the **reusable hot pack.** Then, activate it according to your instructor's directions. Quickly place the pack into the water-filled cup.
4. Measure and record the water's temperature at intervals of 30 s.

### Analysis

1. **Describe** what happened when the hot pack was activated.
2. **Explain** how the activated hot pack affected the temperature of the water.
3. **Explain** where the observed heat energy came from.
4. **Speculate** whether the hot pack can be restored to its activated state by placing the hot pack in direct sunlight.

The veins in leaves are part of a vascular system. Sugars produced by photosynthesis are transported through the veins in leaves to the stems and roots by special tissues called *vascular tissues.*

These reading tools can help you learn the material in this chapter. For more information on how to use these and other tools, see **Appendix: Reading and Study Skills.**

## Using Words

**Key-Term Fold** A key-term fold is useful for studying definitions of key terms in a chapter. Each tab can contain a key term on one side and its definition on the other side.

**Your Turn** Make a key-term fold for the terms in this chapter.

1. Fold a sheet of lined notebook paper in half from left to right.
2. Using scissors, cut along every third line from the right edge of the paper to the center fold to make tabs.

## Using Language

**Describing Space** As you read the chapter, look for language clues that answer the question, "Where does this process take place?" Words such as *inside, outside,* and *between* can help you learn where these processes happen. Knowing where these processes take place can help you better understand them.

**Your Turn** Describe as precisely as you can where the following processes happen.

1. photosynthesis
2. cellular respiration

## Using Graphic Organizers

**Pattern Puzzles** You can use pattern puzzles to help you remember information. Exchanging puzzles with a classmate can help you study.

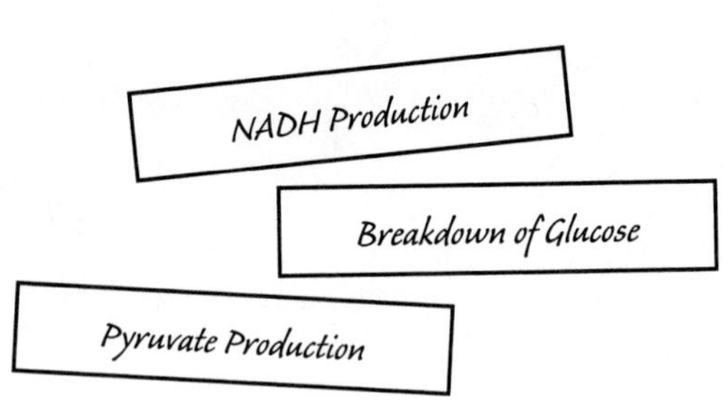


**Your Turn** Make pattern puzzles for the steps of glycolysis.

1. Write down the steps of the process. On a sheet of notebook paper, write down one step per line. Do not number the steps.
2. Cut the sheet of paper into strips with only one step per strip of paper. Shuffle the paper strips so that they are out of sequence.
3. Place the strips in the correct sequence. Confirm the order of the steps of the process by checking your text or class notes.

Section 1

# Energy in Living Systems

| Key Ideas | Key Terms | Why It Matters |
|---|---|---|
| › What type of energy is used in cells, and what is the ultimate source of this energy?<br>› How is an organism's metabolism related to the carbon cycle?<br>› How is energy released in a cell? | photosynthesis<br>cellular respiration<br>ATP<br>ATP synthase<br>electron transport chain | Plants convert sunlight into chemical energy. This chemical energy can be used for biological processes in nearly all living things. |

Imagine an abandoned house that is falling apart. The house, like almost everything else in the universe, breaks down over time. Restoring order to the house would require an input of energy, such as the energy needed to apply a fresh coat of paint. Living things also need energy in order to stay in good repair, or maintain their *homeostasis.* Remember that homeostasis is the process of maintaining internal order and balance even when the environment changes. Every organism must maintain homeostasis as long as it lives. Therefore, organisms require a constant source of energy.

***The Living Environment***
**Standard 4**
**1.2h** Many organic and inorganic substances dissolved in cells allow necessary chemical reactions to take place in order to maintain life.
**5.1a** The energy for life comes primarily from the Sun. Photosynthesis provides a vital connection between the Sun and the energy needs of living systems.
**5.1c** In all organisms, organic compounds can be used to assemble other molecules such as proteins, DNA, starch, and fats. The chemical energy stored in bonds can be used as a source of energy for life processes.
**5.1e** The energy from ATP is used by the organism to obtain, transform, and transport materials, and to eliminate wastes.
**6.1c** The chemical elements, such as carbon, hydrogen, nitrogen, and oxygen, that make up the molecules of living things pass through food webs and are combined and recombined in different ways. At each link in a food web, some energy is stored in newly made structures but much is dissipated into the environment as heat.

## Chemical Energy

**› Organisms use and store energy in the chemical bonds of organic compounds. Almost all of the energy in organic compounds comes from the sun.** Solar energy enters living systems when plants, algae, and certain prokaryotes use sunlight to make organic compounds from carbon dioxide and water through the process of **photosynthesis.** Organisms that are able to perform photosynthesis, such as the wheat plants shown in **Figure 1,** are *autotrophs.* Autotrophs make organic compounds that serve as food for them and for almost all of the other organisms on Earth.

**photosynthesis** the process by which plants, algae, and some bacteria use sunlight, carbon dioxide, and water to produce carbohydrates and oxygen

Most autotrophs have a supply of food as long as sunlight is available. But how do other organisms get food molecules? To survive, organisms that cannot make their own food must absorb food molecules made by autotrophs, eat autotrophs, or eat organisms that consume autotrophs. Food molecules that are made or consumed by an organism are the fuel for its cells. Cells use these molecules to release the energy stored in the molecules' bonds. The energy is used to carry out life processes.

**› Reading Check** ***Why do organisms need a constant supply of energy? (See the Appendix for answers to Reading Checks.)***

**Figure 1** Food crops such as wheat supply humans and other animals with the chemical energy needed to carry out life processes.

Hands-On

# QuickLab

MULTI-DAY 15 min

## Product of Photosynthesis

4.5.1d

Plants use photosynthesis to produce food. One product of photosynthesis is oxygen. In this activity, you will observe the process of photosynthesis in elodea.

### Procedure

1. Add 450 mL of baking-soda-and-water solution to a beaker.
2. Put two or three sprigs of elodea into the beaker. The baking soda will provide the elodea with the carbon dioxide it needs for photosynthesis.
3. Place the wide end of a glass funnel over the elodea. The elodea and the funnel should be completely submerged in the solution.
4. Fill a test tube with the remaining solution. Place your thumb over the end of the test tube. Turn the test tube upside down, taking care that no air enters. Hold the opening of the test tube under the solution, and place the test tube over the small end of the funnel.
5. Place the beaker setup in a well-lit area near a lamp or in direct sunlight, and leave it overnight.

### Analysis

1. **Describe** what happened to the solution in the test tube.
2. CRITICAL THINKING **Predicting Patterns** Explain what may happen if an animal, such as a snail, were put into the beaker with the elodea sprig.

**cellular respiration** the process by which cells produce energy from carbohydrates

**ATP** adenosine triphosphate, an organic molecule that acts as the main energy source for cell processes; composed of a nitrogenous base, a sugar, and three phosphate groups

## Metabolism and the Carbon Cycle

**› Metabolism involves either using energy to build organic molecules or breaking down organic molecules in which energy is stored. Organic molecules contain carbon. Therefore, an organism's metabolism is part of Earth's carbon cycle.** The carbon cycle not only makes carbon compounds continuously available in an ecosystem but also delivers chemical energy to organisms living within that ecosystem.

**Photosynthesis** Energy enters an ecosystem when organisms use sunlight during photosynthesis to convert stable carbon dioxide molecules into glucose, a less stable carbon compound. In plant cells and algae, photosynthesis takes place in chloroplasts. **Figure 2** summarizes the process by which energy from the sun is converted to chemical energy in chloroplasts.

**Cellular Respiration** Organisms extract energy stored in glucose molecules. Through the process of **cellular respiration,** cells make the carbon in glucose into stable carbon dioxide molecules and produce energy. Thus, stable and less stable compounds alternate during the carbon cycle and provide a continuous supply of energy for life processes in an ecosystem.

The breakdown of glucose during cellular respiration is summarized in **Figure 2.** The inputs are a glucose molecule and six oxygen molecules. The final products are six carbon dioxide molecules and six water molecules. Energy is also released and used to make **ATP** (adenosine triphosphate), an organic molecule that is the main energy source for cell processes.

**› Reading Check** ***How is solar energy related to the carbon cycle?***

go.hrw.com
interact online
Keyword: HX8PHRF2

## Photosynthesis and Cellular Respiration

**Figure 2** Photosynthesis and cellular respiration are major steps in the carbon cycle. **› Compare the end results of photosynthesis and cellular respiration.**

ATP produced in cellular respiration provides energy for life processes.

Light energy

Solar energy is converted to chemical energy during photosynthesis.

ATP

$CO_2 + H_2O$

Chloroplast

$C_6H_{12}O_6 + O_2$

Mitochondrion

Chloroplasts contain pigments that absorb light to provide energy for photosynthesis.

Cellular respiration takes place in mitochondria.

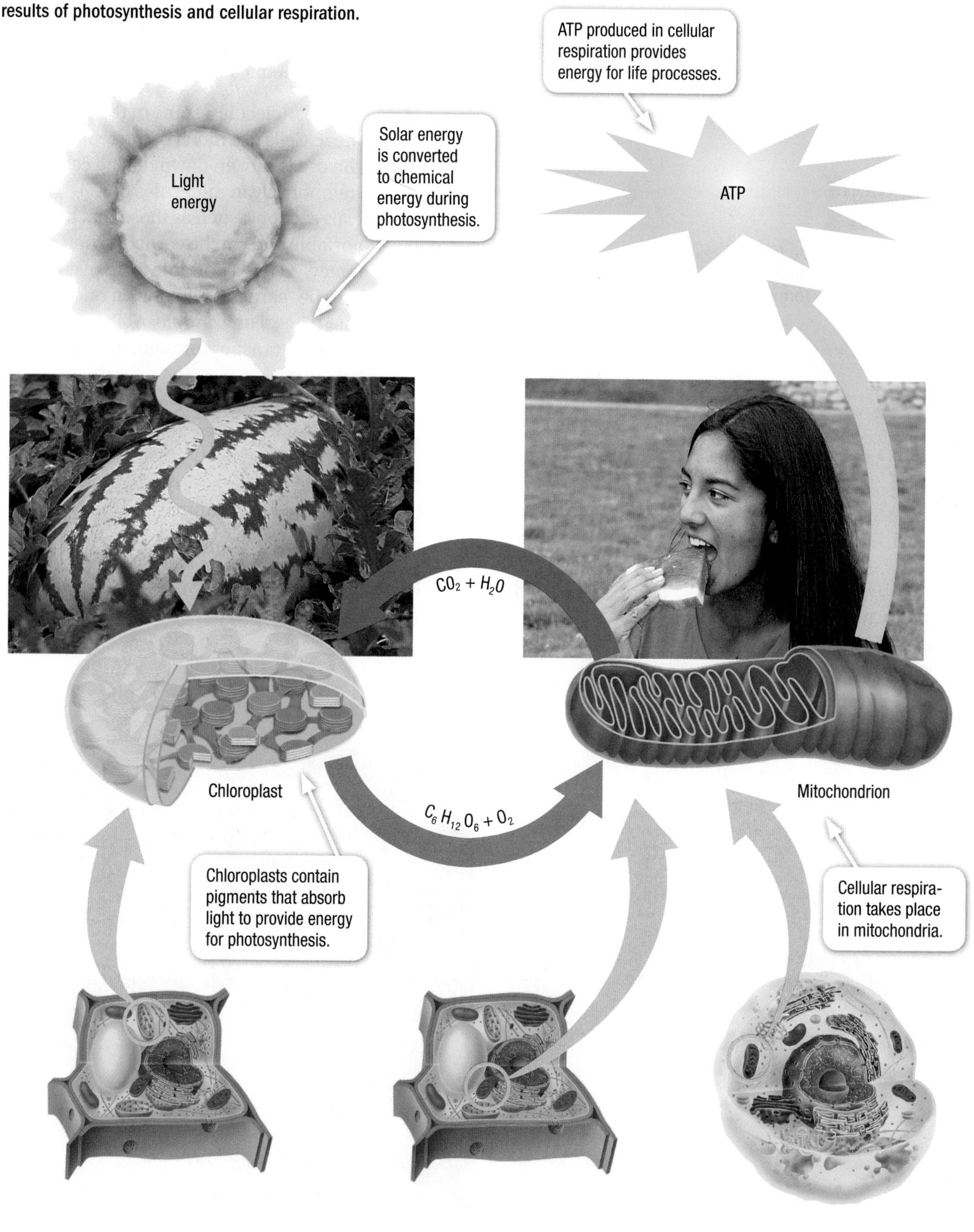

## Transferring Energy

In chemical reactions, energy can be absorbed and released during the breaking and forming of bonds. For example, when a log burns, the energy stored in wood molecules is released in a burst of heat and light. **› In cells, chemical energy is gradually released in a series of chemical reactions that are assisted by enzymes.** Recall that enzymes are proteins that act as catalysts in biochemical reactions.

**READING TOOLBOX**

**Key-Term Fold** On the back of your key-term fold, write a definition in your own words for each key term in this section.

**ATP** When cells break down food molecules, some of the energy in the molecules is released as heat. Cells use much of the remaining energy to make ATP. When glucose is broken down during cellular respiration, energy is stored temporarily in molecules of ATP. ATP can be used to power chemical reactions, such as those that build molecules. Paper money is portable and can be earned in one place and spent in another. Like money, ATP is a portable form of energy "currency" inside cells. ATP can be "earned," or made, in one place and "spent," or used, in another place. For example, ATP can be used to contract a muscle cell, to actively transport protein, or to help make more ATP.

ATP is a nucleotide made up of a chain of three phosphate groups. This chain is unstable because the phosphate groups are negatively charged and thus repel each other. When the bond of the third phosphate group is broken, energy is released. This produces adenosine diphosphate, or ADP. The equation below summarizes the process.

**ACADEMIC VOCABULARY**

**process** a set of steps, events, or changes

$$\text{ATP} \longrightarrow \text{ADP} + \text{P} + \text{energy}$$

The reaction in which ATP is converted to ADP requires a small input of energy. But much more energy is released than is used during the reaction.

**› Reading Check** ***How is ATP used inside a cell?***

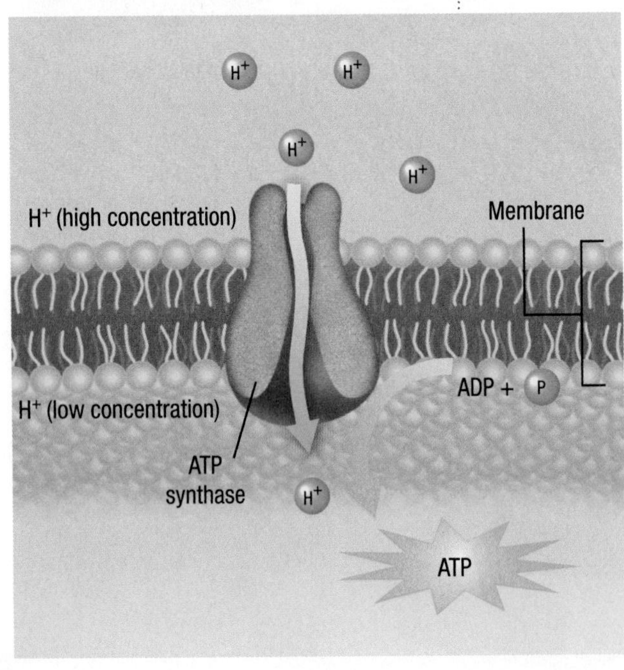

**Figure 3** The energy of falling water can turn a water wheel, which provides energy to do work. In ATP synthase, the movement of hydrogen ions provides energy to convert ADP to ATP.

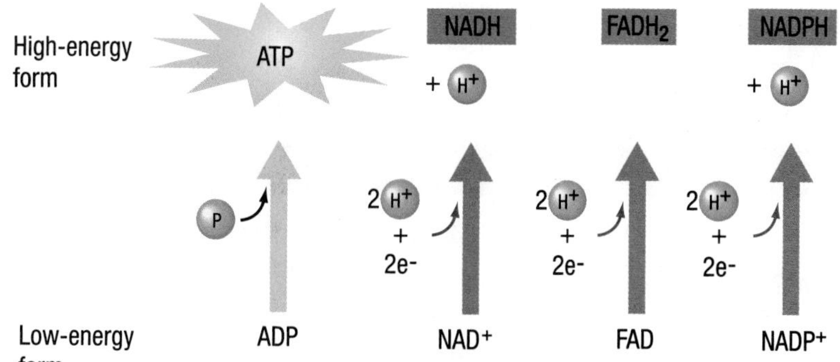


**Figure 4** Electron carriers store energy by bonding with hydrogen, just as ATP stores energy by bonding a third phosphate group. ❯ **Where is the electron transport chain found in animal cells?**

**ATP Synthase** In many cells, **ATP synthase,** an enzyme that catalyzes the synthesis of ATP, recycles ADP by bonding a third phosphate group to the molecule. As **Figure 3** shows, ATP synthase acts as both an enzyme and a carrier protein for hydrogen ($H^+$) ions. The flow of $H^+$ ions through ATP synthase powers the production of ATP. You can think of the $H^+$ ions moving through ATP synthase to produce ATP as falling water turning a water wheel to produce power. As $H^+$ ions flow, ATP synthase catalyzes a reaction in which a phosphate group is added to a molecule of ADP to make ATP.

**ATP synthase** an enzyme that catalyzes the synthesis of ATP

**electron transport chain** a series of molecules, found in the inner membranes of mitochondria and chloroplasts, through which electrons pass in a process that causes protons to build up on one side of the membrane

**Hydrogen Ion Pumps** Recall how diffusion across cell membranes works. Particles of a substance diffuse through a membrane from a region of higher concentration to a region of lower concentration. The inner mitochondrial membrane allows $H^+$ ions to diffuse through only ATP synthase. When glucose is broken down during cellular respiration, $NAD^+$ (nicotinamide adenine dinucleotide) accepts electrons and hydrogen ions, which changes $NAD^+$ to NADH. As **Figure 4** shows, NADH enters an **electron transport chain,** a series of molecules in the inner membrane of a mitochondrion. The electron transport chain allows electrons to drop in energy as they are passed along and uses the energy released to pump $H^+$ ions out of a mitochondrion's inner compartment. This action increases the concentration of $H^+$ ions in the outer compartment. The ions then diffuse back into the inner compartment through ATP synthase.

www.scilinks.org
Topic: ATP
Code: HX80123

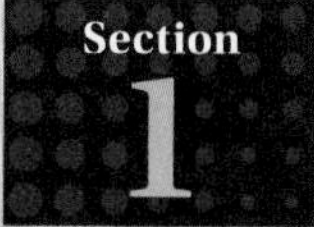


## Review

### ❯ KEY IDEAS

1. **Identify** the primary source of energy that flows through most living systems.
2. **Explain** how an organism's metabolism is related to Earth's carbon cycle.
3. **Describe** how energy is released from ATP.

### CRITICAL THINKING

4. **Analyzing Patterns** Explain how life involves a continuous flow of energy.
5. **Inferring Relationships** How can the energy in the food that a fox eats be traced back to the sun?
6. **Summarizing Information** What is the difference between cellular respiration and the process by which energy is released from a burning log?

### WRITING FOR SCIENCE

7. **Career Connection** Research the educational background that a person needs to become an enzymologist. List the courses required, and describe additional degrees or training that are recommended for this career. Write a report on your findings.

Section

# 2 Photosynthesis

| Key Ideas | Key Terms | Why It Matters |
|---|---|---|
| ❯ What is the role of pigments in photosynthesis?<br>❯ What are the roles of the electron transport chains?<br>❯ How do plants make sugars and store extra unused energy?<br>❯ What are three environmental factors that affect photosynthesis? | thylakoid<br>pigment<br>chlorophyll<br>Calvin cycle | Nearly all of the energy for life processes comes from the sun and is stored in organic molecules during the process of photosynthesis. |

***The Living Environment***
**Standard 4**

**1.2f** Cells have particular structures that perform specific jobs. These structures perform the actual work of the cell. Just as systems are coordinated and work together, cell parts must also be coordinated and work together.

**1.2i** Inside the cell a variety of specialized structures, formed from many different molecules, carry out the transport of materials (cytoplasm), extraction of energy from nutrients (mitochondria), protein building (ribosomes), waste disposal (cell membrane), storage (vacuole), and information storage (nucleus).

**5.1b** Plant cells and some one-celled organisms contain chloroplasts, the site of photosynthesis. The process of photosynthesis uses solar energy to combine the inorganic molecules carbon dioxide and water into energy rich organic compounds (e.g., glucose) and release oxygen to the environment.

**5.1f** Biochemical processes, both breakdown and synthesis, are made possible by a large set of biological catalysts called enzymes. Enzymes can affect the rates of chemical change. The rate at which enzymes work can be influenced by internal environmental factors such as pH and temperature.

Plants, algae, and certain prokaryotes capture about 1% of the energy in the sunlight that reaches Earth and convert it to chemical energy through photosynthesis. Photosynthesis is the process that provides energy for almost all life.

## Harvesting Light Energy

The cells of many photosynthetic organisms have chloroplasts, organelles that convert light energy into chemical energy. Study the diagram of a chloroplast in **Figure 5.**

A chloroplast has an outer membrane and an inner membrane. Molecules diffuse easily through the outer membrane. The inner membrane is much more selective about what substances enter and leave. Both membranes allow light to pass through.

The space inside the inner membrane is the stroma. Within the stroma is a membrane called the *thylakoid membrane.* This membrane is folded in a way that produces flat, disc-like sacs called **thylakoids.** These sacs, which contain molecules that absorb light energy for photosynthesis, are arranged in stacks. The first stage of photosynthesis begins when light waves hit these stacks.

❯ **Reading Check** ***Describe the structure of a chloroplast.***

**Figure 5** Pigments, as well as other molecules that participate in photosynthesis, are embedded in thylakoids. ❯ **Where are thylakoids located?**

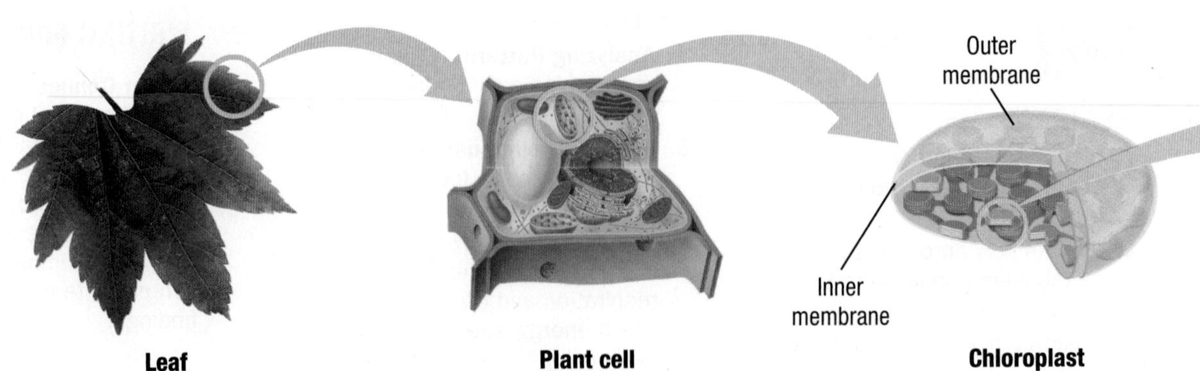

**Electromagnetic Radiation** Light is a form of electromagnetic radiation, energy that can travel through empty space in the form of waves. Radio waves, X-rays, and microwaves are also forms of electromagnetic radiation. The difference between these forms of radiation is that they have different wavelengths. Each wavelength corresponds to a certain amount of energy. The wavelength is the distance between consecutive wave peaks. Sunlight contains all of the wavelengths of visible light. You see these wavelengths as different colors.

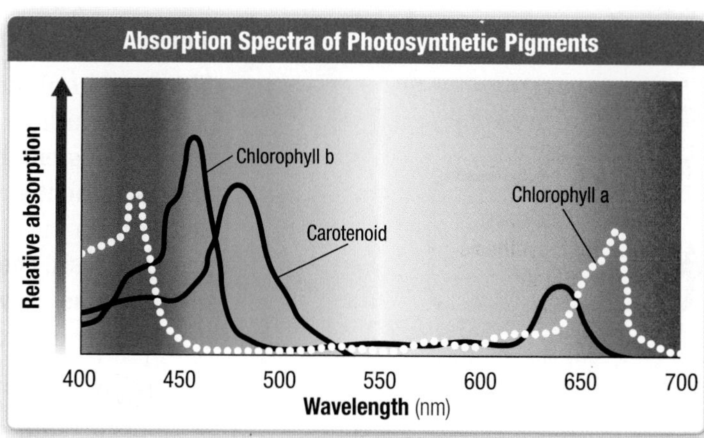


**Figure 6** This graph shows the colors of light that three different pigments absorb. Where a curve peaks, much of the light at that wavelength is absorbed. Where a curve dips, much of the light at that wavelength is reflected or transmitted.

**Pigments** What makes the human eye sensitive to light? Cells in the back of the eye contain pigments. A **pigment** is a substance that absorbs certain wavelengths (colors) of light and commonly reflects all of the others. **› In plants, light energy is harvested by pigments that are located in the thylakoid membrane of chloroplasts.** **Chlorophyll** is a green pigment in chloroplasts that absorbs light energy to start photosynthesis. It absorbs mostly blue and red light and reflects green and yellow light, which makes plants appear green. Plants have two types of chlorophyll: chlorophyll *a* and chlorophyll *b.* Plants also have pigments called *carotenoids.* Carotenoids absorb blue and green light, and they reflect yellow, orange, and red light. When chlorophyll fades away in the fall, the colors of carotenoids are exposed. Carotenoids aid photosynthesis by allowing plants to absorb additional light energy. **Figure 6** shows the wavelengths of light that are absorbed by chlorophyll *a,* chlorophyll *b,* and carotenoids—the pigments found in thylakoid membranes.

**Electron Carriers** When light hits a thylakoid, energy is absorbed by many pigment molecules. They all funnel the energy to a special chlorophyll molecule in a region called the *reaction center,* where the energy causes the electrons to become "excited" and to move to a higher energy level. These electrons are transferred quickly to other nearby molecules and then to an electron carrier.

**thylakoid** (THIE luh KOYD) a membrane system found within chloroplasts that contains the components for photosynthesis

**pigment** a substance that gives another substance or a mixture its color

**chlorophyll** (KLAWR uh FIL) a green pigment that is present in most plant and algae cells and some bacteria, that gives plants their characteristic green color, and that absorbs light to provide energy for photosynthesis

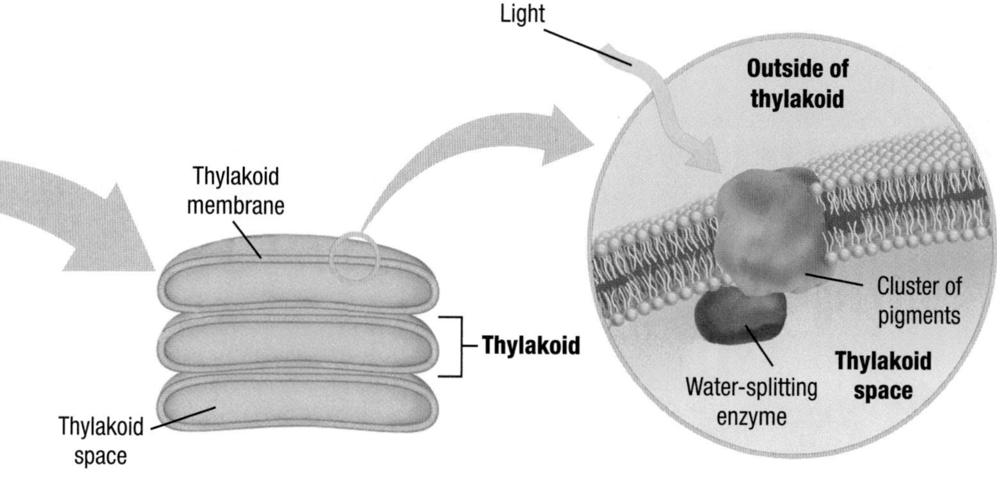

SCILINKS.
www.scilinks.org
Topic: Photosynthesis
Code: HX81140

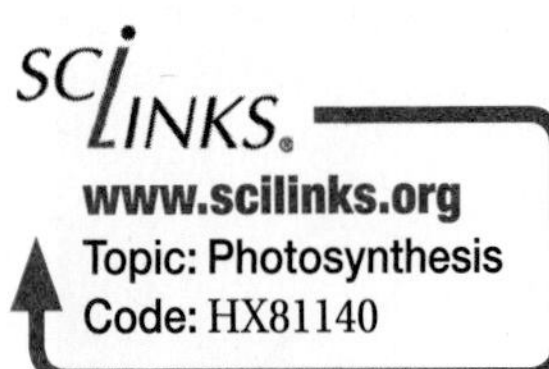

## Two Electron Transport Chains

Electrons from the electron carrier are used to produce new molecules, including ATP, that temporarily store chemical energy. The carrier transfers the electrons to the first of two electron transport chains in the thylakoid membrane. Trace the path taken by the electrons in the electron transport chains shown in **Figure 7.** **During photosynthesis, one electron transport chain provides energy to make ATP, while the other provides energy to make NADPH.** Both chains use energy from electrons excited by light.

**Producing ATP** In mitochondria, electron transport chains pump $H^+$ ions through a membrane, which produces a concentration gradient. This process also happens in chloroplasts.

**Step 1 Water Splitting** The excited electrons that leave chlorophyll molecules must be replaced by other electrons. Plants get these replacement electrons from water molecules, $H_2O$. During photosynthesis, an enzyme splits water molecules inside the thylakoid. When water molecules are split, chlorophyll molecules take the electrons from the hydrogen atoms, H, which leaves $H^+$ ions. The remaining oxygen atoms, O, from the split water molecules combine to form oxygen gas, $O_2$. This oxygen gas is not used for any later steps of photosynthesis, so it is released into the atmosphere.

**Figure 7** Photosynthesis converts light energy to chemical energy. This figure shows key molecules involved in the capture of light, electron transport, and synthesis of ATP and NADPH. **What causes $H^+$ ions to move through the carrier protein that produces ATP?**

go.hrw.com
interact online
Keyword: HX8PHRF7

**Electron Transport Chains of Photosynthesis**

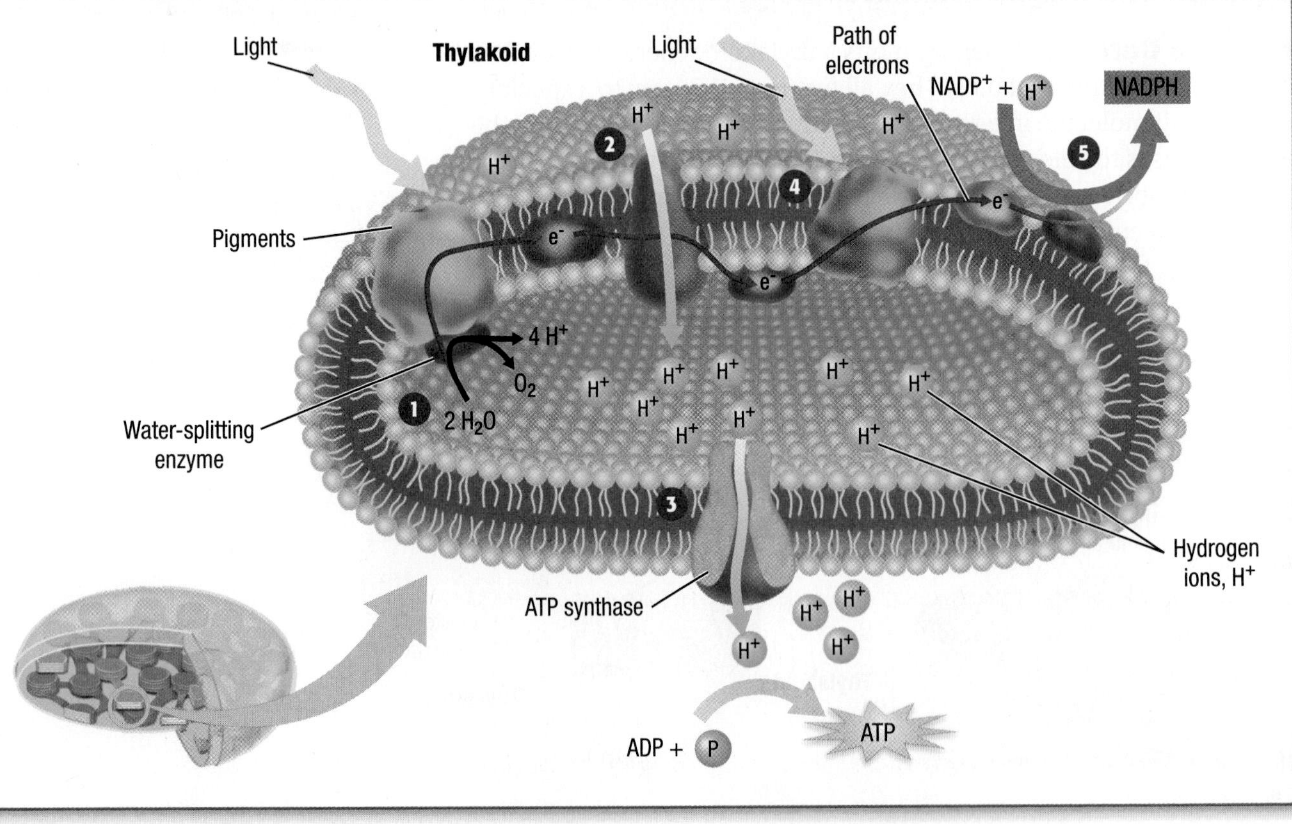

Data

# QuickLab

15 min

## Photosynthetic Rate  4.5.1a

Changes in a plant's surroundings influence photosynthetic rate. The two graphs illustrate how photosynthetic rate responds to changes in light intensity and temperature. Use the graphs to answer the following questions.

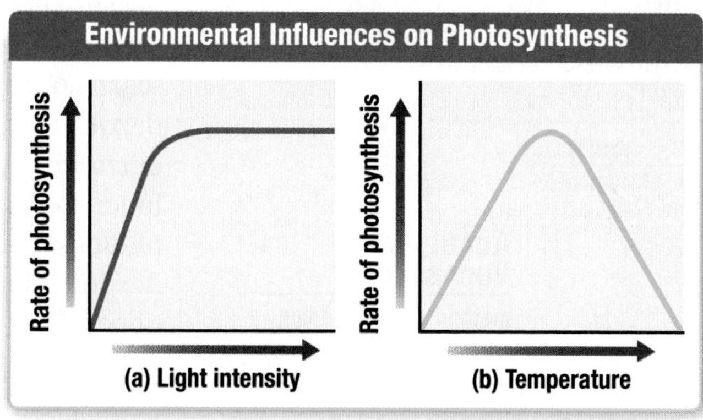


### Analysis

1. **Describe** how increasing light intensity affects the rate of photosynthesis.
2. **Explain** whether continuing to increase light intensity will increase the rate of photosynthesis.
3. **Describe** how increasing temperature affects the rate of photosynthesis.
4. CRITICAL THINKING **Inferring Relationships** Explain how a global temperature increase could affect plants.

**Step 2 Hydrogen Ion Pump** A protein acts as a membrane pump. Excited electrons transfer some of their energy to pump $H^+$ ions into the thylakoid. This process creates a concentration gradient across the thylakoid membrane.

**Step 3 ATP Synthase** The energy from the diffusion of $H^+$ ions through the carrier protein is used to make ATP. These carrier proteins are unusual because they function both as an ion channel and as the enzyme ATP synthase. As hydrogen ions pass through the channel portion of the protein, ATP synthase catalyzes a reaction in which a phosphate group is added to a molecule of ADP. The result of the reaction is ATP, which is used to power the final stage of photosynthesis.

**Producing NADPH** While one electron transport chain provides energy used to make ATP, a second electron transport chain receives excited electrons from a chlorophyll molecule and uses them to make NADPH. The second electron transport chain is to the right of the second cluster of pigment molecules in **Figure 7.**

**Step 4 Reenergizing** In this second chain, light excites electrons in the chlorophyll molecule. The excited electrons are passed on to the second chain. They are replaced by the de-energized electrons from the first transport chain.

**Step 5 Making NADPH** Excited electrons combine with $H^+$ ions and an electron acceptor called $NADP^+$ to form NADPH. NADPH is an electron carrier that provides the high-energy electrons needed to store energy in organic molecules. Both NADPH and the ATP made during the first stage of photosynthesis will be used to provide the energy to carry out the final stage of photosynthesis.

› **Reading Check** ***Summarize how ATP and NADPH are formed during photosynthesis.***

**Describing Space** Use spatial language to describe production of ATP and NADPH during photosynthesis.

## Producing Sugar

The first two stages of photosynthesis depend directly on light because light energy is used to make ATP and NADPH. **In the final stage of photosynthesis, ATP and NADPH are used to produce energy-storing sugar molecules from the carbon in carbon dioxide.** The use of carbon dioxide to make organic compounds is called *carbon dioxide fixation,* or *carbon fixation.* The reactions that fix carbon dioxide are light-independent reactions, sometimes called *dark reactions.* Among photosynthetic organisms, there are several ways in which carbon dioxide is fixed. The most common method of carbon dioxide fixation is the **Calvin cycle,** which is described in the following steps:

**Calvin cycle** a biochemical pathway of photosynthesis in which carbon dioxide is converted into glucose using ATP and NADPH

**ACADEMIC VOCABULARY**

**method** a way of doing something

**Step 1 Carbon Fixation** In carbon dioxide fixation, an enzyme adds a molecule of carbon dioxide, $CO_2$, to a five-carbon compound. This process occurs three times to yield three six-carbon molecules.

**Step 2 Transferring Energy** Each six-carbon compound splits into two three-carbon compounds. Phosphate groups from ATP and electrons from NADPH are added to the three-carbon compounds to form higher energy three-carbon sugars.

**Step 3 Making Sugar** One of the resulting three-carbon sugars leaves the cycle and is used to make organic compounds—including glucose, sucrose, and starch—in which energy is stored for later use by the organism.

**Figure 8** The Calvin cycle is the most common method of carbon dioxide fixation. **What is formed when the three six-carbon molecules split during step 2 of the Calvin cycle?**

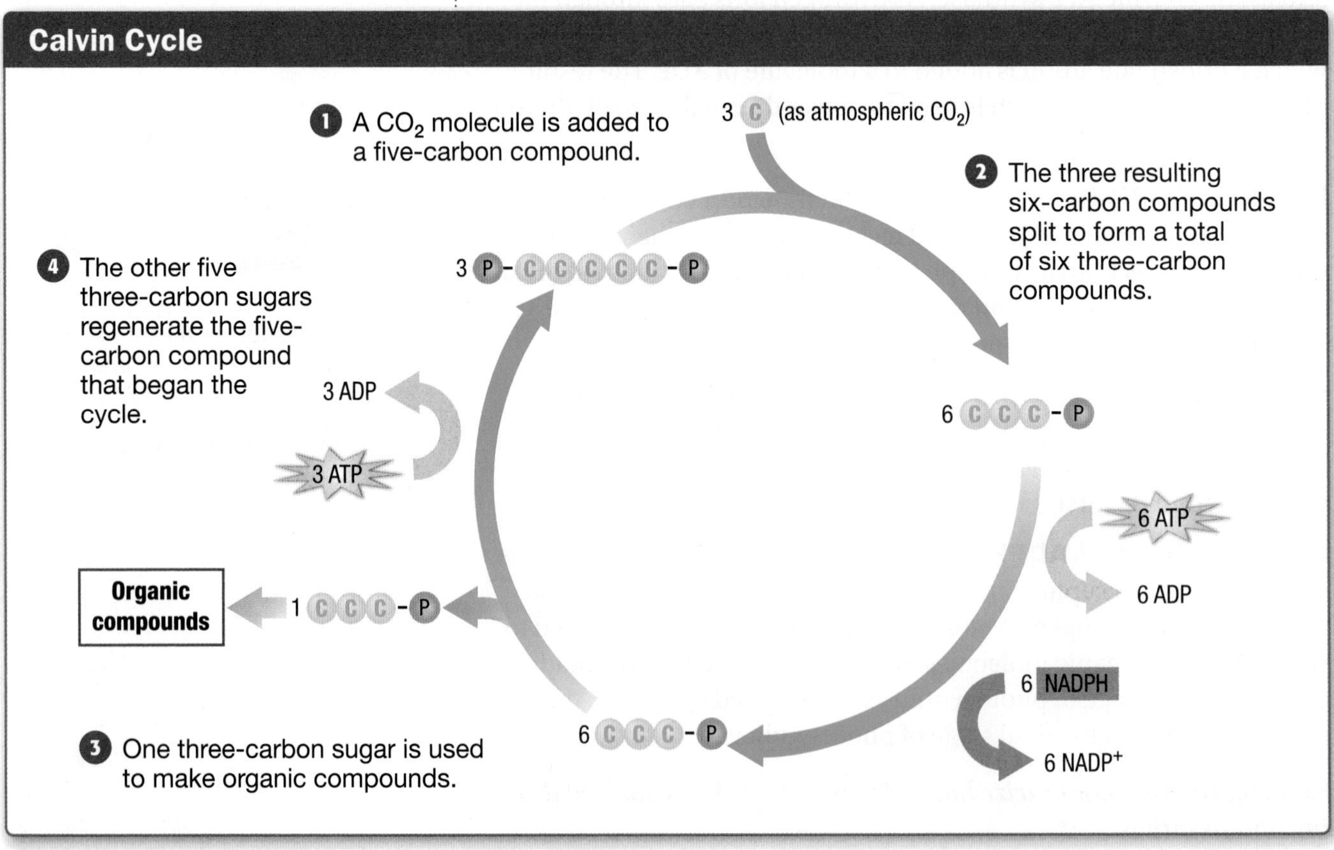

Calvin Cycle
1 A $CO_2$ molecule is added to a five-carbon compound.
3 C (as atmospheric $CO_2$)
2 The three resulting six-carbon compounds split to form a total of six three-carbon compounds.
3 P-CCCCCC-P
6 CCC-P
6 ATP
6 ADP
6 NADPH
6 NADP+
6 CCC-P
3 One three-carbon sugar is used to make organic compounds.
Organic compounds
1 CCC-P
4 The other five three-carbon sugars regenerate the five-carbon compound that began the cycle.
3 ADP
3 ATP

**Figure 9** Some plants, such as a cactus (left), grow in extremely sunny, dry environments. Others, such as the bromeliad (right), are able to grow in shady areas.

**Step 4 Recycling** The remaining five three-carbon sugars are rearranged. Using energy from ATP, enzymes reform three molecules of the initial five-carbon compound. This process completes the cycle. The reformed compounds are used to begin the cycle again.

## Factors that Affect Photosynthesis

**› Light intensity, carbon dioxide concentration, and temperature are three environmental factors that affect photosynthesis.** The most obvious of these factors is light. **Figure 9** shows plants that are adapted to different levels of light. In general, the rate of photosynthesis increases as light intensity increases until all of the pigments in a chloroplast are being used. At this saturation point, the rate of photosynthesis levels off because the pigments cannot absorb more light.

The concentration of carbon dioxide affects the rate of photosynthesis in a way similar to light. Once a certain concentration of carbon dioxide is present, photosynthesis cannot proceed any faster.

Photosynthesis is most efficient in a certain range of temperatures. Like all metabolic processes, photosynthesis involves many enzyme-assisted chemical reactions. Unfavorable temperatures may inactivate certain enzymes so that reactions cannot take place.

**› Reading Check** ***How does temperature affect photosynthesis?***

## Section 2 Review

### › KEY IDEAS

1. **Summarize** how autotrophs capture the energy in sunlight.
2. **Compare** the roles of water molecules and $H^+$ ions in electron transport chains.
3. **Describe** the role of the Calvin cycle in photosynthesis.
4. **Name** the three main environmental factors that affect the rate of photosynthesis in plants.

### CRITICAL THINKING

5. **Organizing Information** Make a table in which you identify the role of each of the following in photosynthesis: light, water, pigments, ATP, NADPH, and carbon dioxide.

### METHODS OF SCIENCE

6. **Inferring Relationships** How do you think photosynthesis will be affected if the sun's rays are blocked by clouds or by smoke from a large fire? How might the levels of atmospheric carbon dioxide and oxygen be affected? What experiments could scientists conduct in the laboratory to test your predictions?

Section

# 3 Cellular Respiration

| Key Ideas | Key Terms | Why It Matters |
|---|---|---|
| ❯ How does glycolysis produce ATP?<br>❯ How is ATP produced in aerobic respiration?<br>❯ Why is fermentation important? | glycolysis<br>anaerobic<br>aerobic<br>Krebs cycle<br>fermentation | Cellular respiration is the process used by humans and most other organisms to release the energy stored in the food they consume. |

***The Living Environment***
**Standard 4**

**1.2i** Inside the cell a variety of specialized structures, formed from many different molecules, carry out the transport of materials (cytoplasm), extraction of energy from nutrients (mitochondria), protein building (ribosomes), waste disposal (cell membrane), storage (vacuole), and information storage (nucleus).

**5.1d** In all organisms, the energy stored in organic molecules may be released during cellular respiration. This energy is temporarily stored in ATP molecules. In many organisms, the process of cellular respiration is concluded in mitochondria, in which ATP is produced more efficiently, oxygen is used, and carbon dioxide and water are released as wastes.

Where do the students shown in **Figure 10** get energy? Most of the foods we eat contain energy. Much of the energy in a hamburger, for example, is stored in proteins, carbohydrates, and fats. But before you can use that energy, it must be released and transferred to ATP. Like cells of most organisms, your cells transfer the energy in organic compounds, especially the glucose made during photosynthesis, to ATP through cellular respiration, which begins with glycolysis.

## Glycolysis

The primary fuel for cellular respiration is glucose, which is formed when carbohydrates, such as starch and sucrose, are broken down. If too few carbohydrates are available to meet an organism's energy needs, other molecules, such as fats, can be broken down to make ATP. In fact, one gram of fat releases more energy than two grams of carbohydrates do. Proteins and nucleic acids can also be used to make ATP, but they are usually used for building important cell parts.

**Figure 10** These students get their energy by eating carbohydrates, fats, proteins, and other organic molecules. **❯ What is the origin of the energy-containing organic molecules in these students' food?**

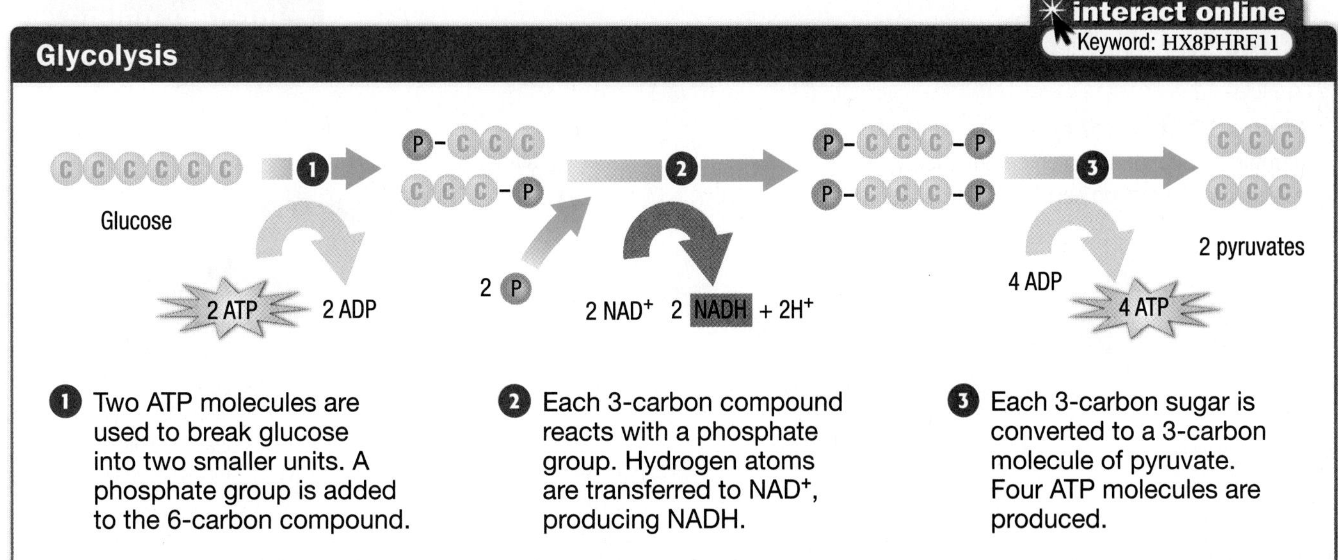
go.hrw.com
interact online
Keyword: HX8PHRF11
Glycolysis
Glucose
2 ATP
2 ADP
2 P
2 NAD+ 2 NADH + 2H+
4 ADP
4 ATP
2 pyruvates
1 Two ATP molecules are used to break glucose into two smaller units. A phosphate group is added to the 6-carbon compound.
2 Each 3-carbon compound reacts with a phosphate group. Hydrogen atoms are transferred to NAD+, producing NADH.
3 Each 3-carbon sugar is converted to a 3-carbon molecule of pyruvate. Four ATP molecules are produced.

**Figure 11** Glycolysis uses two ATP molecules but produces four ATP molecules. The process results in a net gain of ATP. ❯ **What is the starting material in glycolysis?**

**Steps of Glycolysis** In the first stage of cellular respiration, glucose is broken down in the cytoplasm by glycolysis. In **glycolysis,** enzymes break down one six-carbon molecule of glucose into two three-carbon pyruvate molecules, as **Figure 11** shows. Most of the energy that was stored in the glucose molecule is stored in the pyruvate.

**Step 1 Breaking Down Glucose** In the first stage of glycolysis, two ATP molecules are used to break glucose into two smaller units. This stage has four steps with four different enzymes. A phosphate group from ATP is added to the six-carbon compound. This makes the molecule reactive so that an enzyme can break it into two three-carbon sugars, each with a phosphate group. ATP is produced in the next two stages.

**Step 2 NADH Production** In the second stage, each three-carbon compound reacts with another phosphate group (not from ATP). As the two three-carbon sugars react further, hydrogen atoms, including their electrons, are transferred to two molecules of $NAD^+$, which produces two molecules of the electron carrier NADH. NADH is used later in other cell processes, where it is recycled to $NAD^+$.

**Step 3 Pyruvate Production** In a series of four reactions, each three-carbon sugar is converted into a three-carbon molecule of pyruvate. This process produces four ATP molecules. ❯ **Thus, the breaking of a sugar molecule by glycolysis results in a net gain of two ATP molecules.**

Glycolysis is the only source of energy for some prokaryotes. This process is **anaerobic,** so it takes place without oxygen. Other organisms use oxygen to release even more energy from a glucose molecule. Metabolic processes that require oxygen are **aerobic.** In aerobic respiration, the pyruvate product of glycolysis undergoes another series of reactions to produce more ATP molecules.

❯ **Reading Check** *What are the three products of glycolysis?*

**glycolysis** (glie KAHL i sis) the anaerobic breakdown of glucose to pyruvate, which makes a small amount of energy available to cells in the form of ATP

**anaerobic** (AN uhr OH bik) describes a process that does not require oxygen

**aerobic** (er OH bik) describes a process that requires oxygen

SCILINKS.
www.scilinks.org
Topic: Cellular Respiration
Code: HX80244

go.hrw.com
interact online
Keyword: HX8PHRF12

## Krebs Cycle

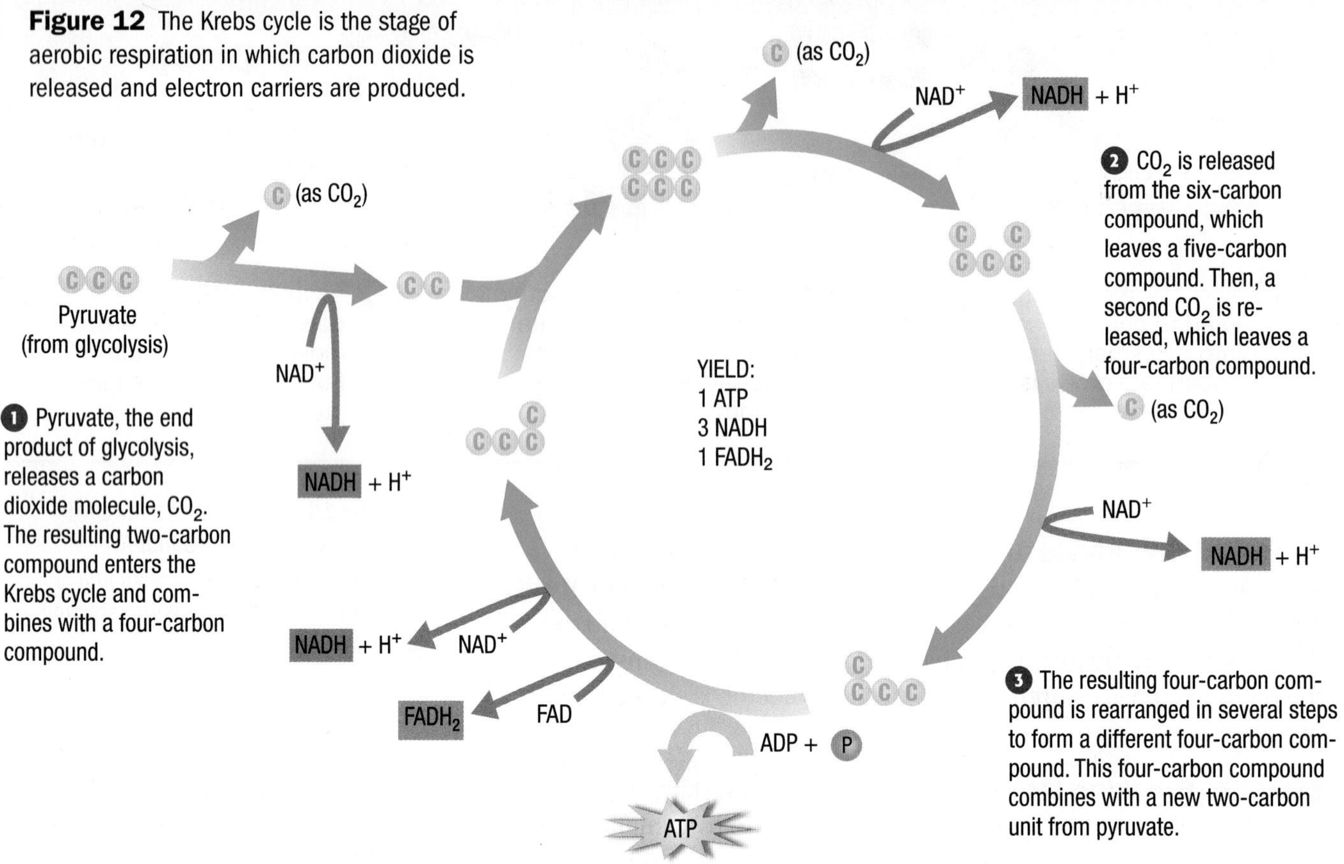
C (as $CO_2$)
C C C
Pyruvate
(from glycolysis)
NAD$^+$
NADH + H$^+$
C C
C C C
C C C
C (as $CO_2$)
NAD$^+$
NADH + H$^+$
C C
C C C
YIELD:
1 ATP
3 NADH
1 $FADH_2$
C (as $CO_2$)
NAD$^+$
NADH + H$^+$
C
C C C
C
C C C
NADH + H$^+$
NAD$^+$
$FADH_2$
FAD
ADP + P
ATP
❶ Pyruvate, the end product of glycolysis, releases a carbon dioxide molecule, $CO_2$. The resulting two-carbon compound enters the Krebs cycle and combines with a four-carbon compound.
❷ $CO_2$ is released from the six-carbon compound, which leaves a five-carbon compound. Then, a second $CO_2$ is released, which leaves a four-carbon compound.
❸ The resulting four-carbon compound is rearranged in several steps to form a different four-carbon compound. This four-carbon compound combines with a new two-carbon unit from pyruvate.

**Figure 12** The Krebs cycle is the stage of aerobic respiration in which carbon dioxide is released and electron carriers are produced.

## Aerobic Respiration

Organisms such as humans can use oxygen to produce ATP efficiently through aerobic respiration. Pyruvate is broken down in the **Krebs cycle,** a series of reactions that produce electron carriers. The electron carriers enter an electron transport chain, which powers ATP synthase. Up to 34 ATP molecules can be produced from one glucose molecule in aerobic respiration.

**Krebs cycle** a series of biochemical reactions that convert pyruvate into carbon dioxide and water

**Krebs Cycle** The first stage of aerobic respiration, the Krebs cycle, is named for Hans Krebs, a German biochemist. He was awarded the Nobel Prize in 1953 for discovering it. As **Figure 12** shows, the Krebs cycle begins with pyruvate, which is produced during glycolysis. Pyruvate releases a carbon dioxide molecule to form a two-carbon compound. An enzyme attaches this two-carbon compound to a four-carbon compound and forms a six-carbon compound.

The six-carbon compound releases one carbon dioxide molecule and then another. Energy is released each time, which forms an electron carrier, NADH. The remaining four-carbon compound is converted to the four-carbon compound that began the cycle. This conversion takes place in a series of steps that produce ATP, then $FADH_2$, and another NADH. The four-carbon compound combines with a new two-carbon unit from pyruvate to continue the cycle.

**Products of the Krebs Cycle** Each time the carbon-carbon bonds are rearranged or broken, energy is released. **› The total yield of energy-storing products from one time through the Krebs cycle is one ATP, three NADH, and one $FADH_2$. Electron carriers transfer energy through the electron transport chain, which ultimately powers ATP synthase.**

**Electron Transport Chain** The second stage of aerobic respiration takes place in the inner membranes of mitochondria. Recall that electrons pass through a series of molecules called an *electron transport chain,* as **Figure 13** shows. ❶ The electrons that are carried by NADH and $FADH_2$ pass through this chain. Energy is transferred into each molecule through which the electrons pass. Some of the molecules are hydrogen ion pumps. ❷ Energy from the electrons is used to actively transport hydrogen ions, $H^+$, out of the inner mitochondrial compartment. As $H^+$ ions accumulate in the outer compartment, a concentration gradient across the inner membrane is created.

**ATP Production** The enzyme ATP synthase is also present on the inner membranes of mitochondria. ❸ Hydrogen ions diffuse through a channel in this enzyme. This movement provides energy, which is used to produce several ATP molecules from ADP.

**The Role of Oxygen** At the end of the electron transport chain, the electrons have given up most of their energy. ❹ An oxygen atom combines with these electrons and two $H^+$ ions to form two water molecules, $H_2O$. If oxygen is not present, the electron transport chain stops. The electron carriers cannot be recycled, so the Krebs cycle also stops. Without oxygen, a cell can produce ATP only by glycolysis.

**› Reading Check** ***Why is glycolysis important to the Krebs cycle?***

**Pattern Puzzles** Make a pattern puzzle to help you remember the steps in aerobic respiration.

**Figure 13** Along the inner mitochondrial membrane, an electron transport chain produces a hydrogen ion gradient. The diffusion of hydrogen ions provides energy for the production of ATP by ATP synthase.

go.hrw.com
interact online
Keyword: HX8PHRF13

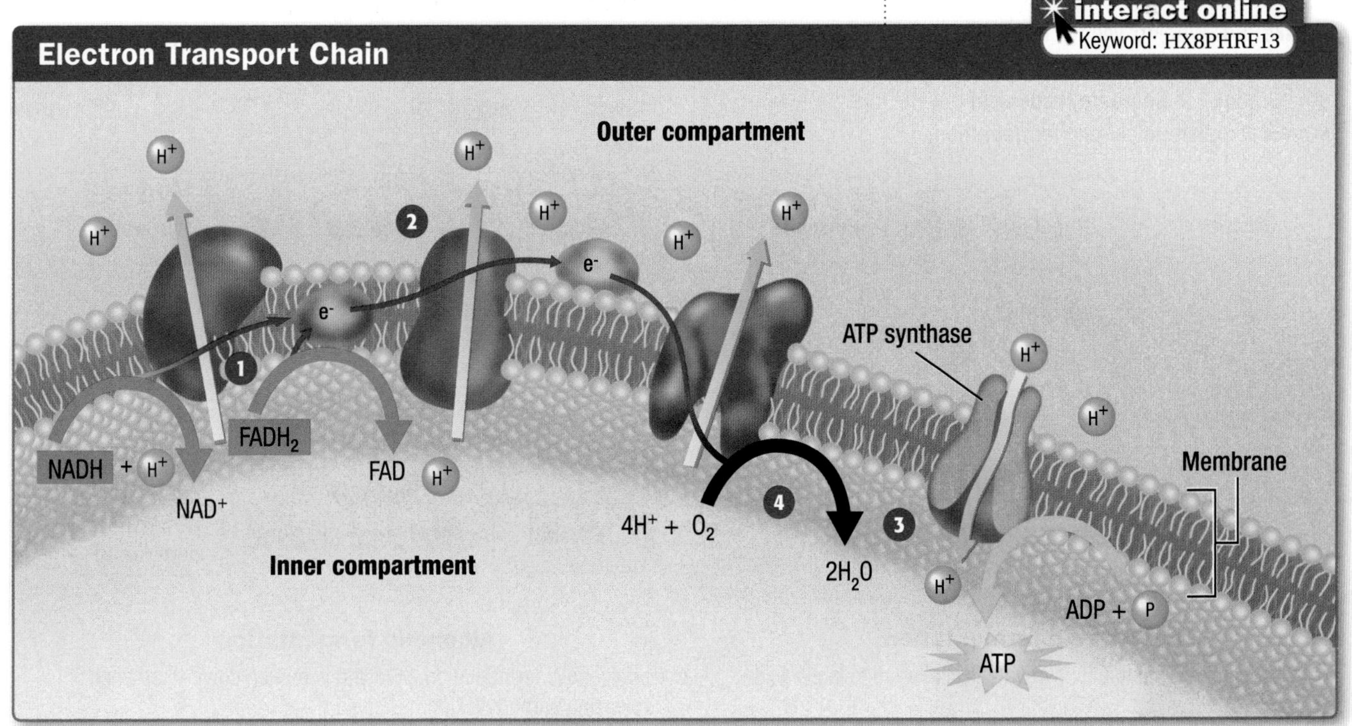

## Fermentation

**ACADEMIC VOCABULARY**

**transfer** to carry or remove something from one thing to another

**fermentation** the breakdown of carbohydrates by enzymes, bacteria, yeasts, or mold in the absence of oxygen

Many prokaryotes live entirely on the energy released in glycolysis. Recall that glycolysis produces two ATP molecules and one molecule of the electron carrier NADH. The NADH must be able to transfer its electrons to an acceptor so that $NAD^+$ is continuously available. Under anaerobic conditions, the electron transport chain, if present, does not work. Organisms must have another way to recycle $NAD^+$. So, electrons carried by NADH are transferred to pyruvate, which is produced during glycolysis. This process in which carbohydrates are broken down in the absence of oxygen, called **fermentation,** recycles the $NAD^+$ that is needed to continue making ATP through glycolysis. **❯ Fermentation enables glycolysis to continue supplying a cell with ATP in anaerobic conditions.** Two types of fermentation are lactic acid fermentation and alcoholic fermentation.

**Lactic Acid Fermentation** Recall that the end products of glycolysis are three-carbon pyruvate molecules. In some organisms, pyruvate accepts electrons and hydrogen from NADH. Pyruvate is converted to lactic acid in a process called *lactic acid fermentation,* as **Figure 14** shows. Lactic acid fermentation also occurs in the muscles of animals, including humans. During vigorous exercise, muscle cells must operate without enough oxygen. So, glycolysis becomes the only source of ATP as long as the glucose supply lasts. For glycolysis to continue, $NAD^+$ is recycled by lactic acid fermentation.

**Alcoholic Fermentation** In other organisms, an enzyme removes carbon dioxide from the three-carbon pyruvate to form a two-carbon molecule. Then, a second enzyme adds electrons and hydrogen from NADH to the molecule to form ethanol (ethyl alcohol) in a process called *alcoholic fermentation.* In this process, $NAD^+$ is recycled and glycolysis can continue to produce ATP.

**❯ Reading Check** ***Explain how fermentation recycles $NAD^+$.***

**Figure 14** When oxygen is not present, cells recycle $NAD^+$ through fermentation. **❯ Compare lactic acid fermentation with alcoholic fermentation.**

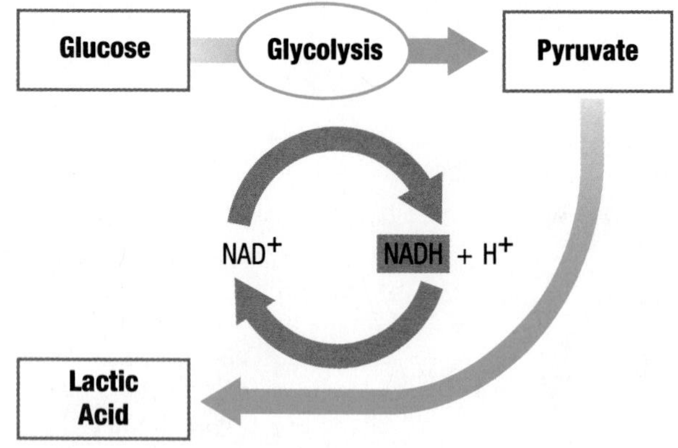


**Lactic acid fermentation**

In lactic acid fermentation, pyruvate is converted to lactic acid.

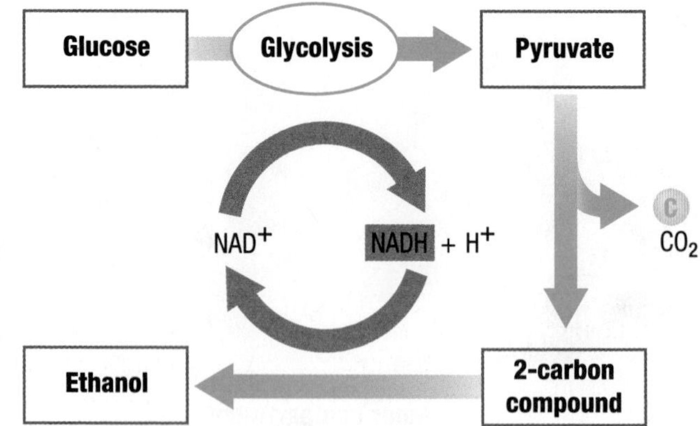


**Alcoholic fermentation**

In alcoholic fermentation, pyruvate is broken down to ethanol, releasing carbon dioxide.

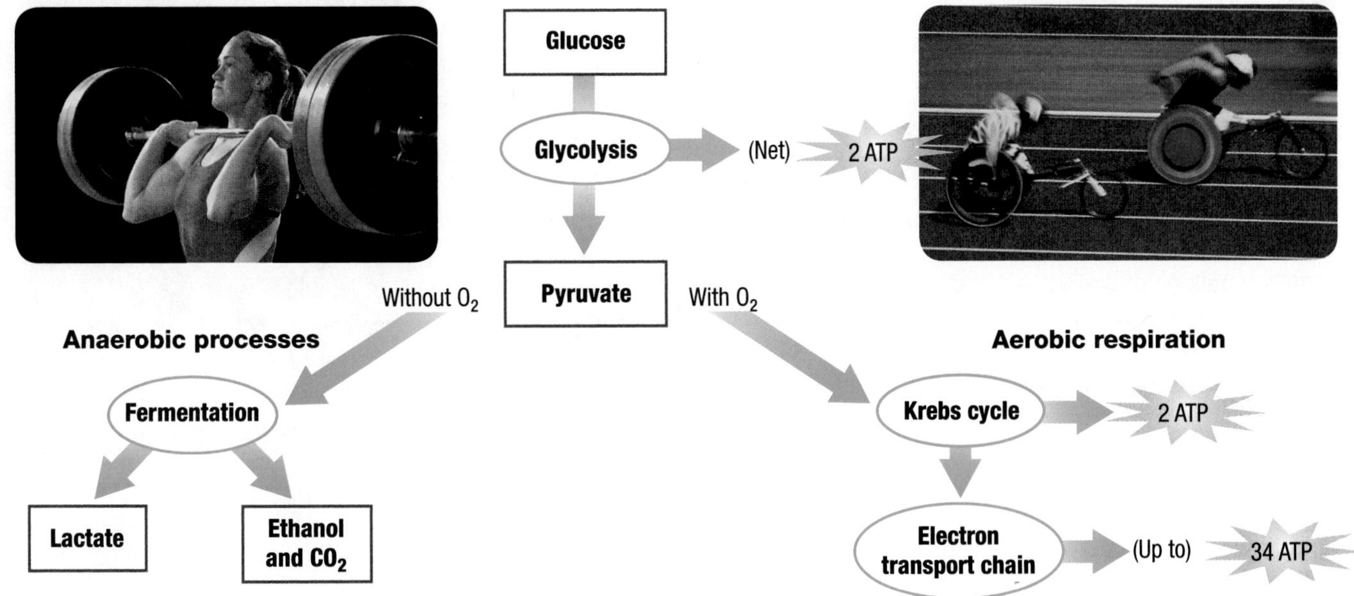


**Figure 15** Most ATP is produced during aerobic respiration. **❯ Which cellular respiration process produces ATP molecules most efficiently?**

**Efficiency of Cellular Respiration** The total amount of ATP that a cell harvests from each glucose molecule depends on the presence or absence of oxygen. **Figure 15** compares the amount of ATP produced in both cases.

In the first stage of cellular respiration, glucose is broken down to pyruvate during glycolysis. Glycolysis is an anaerobic process, and it results in a net gain of two ATP molecules.

In the second stage of cellular respiration, pyruvate either passes through the Krebs cycle or undergoes fermentation. When oxygen is not present, fermentation occurs. The $NAD^+$ that is recycled during fermentation allows glycolysis to continue producing ATP.

Cells release energy most efficiently when oxygen is present because they make most of their ATP during aerobic respiration. For each molecule of glucose that is broken down, as many as two ATP molecules are made during the Krebs cycle. The Krebs cycle feeds NADH and $FADH_2$ to the electron transport chain. The electron transport chain can produce up to 34 ATP molecules.

## Section 3 Review

### ❯ KEY IDEAS

1. **List** the products of glycolysis, and explain the role of each of these products in both aerobic respiration and anaerobic respiration.
2. **Summarize** the roles of the Krebs cycle and the electron transport chain during aerobic respiration.
3. **Describe** the role of fermentation in the second stage of cellular respiration.

### CRITICAL THINKING

4. **Inferring Conclusions** Excess glucose in your blood is stored in your liver as glycogen. How might your body sense when to convert glucose to glycogen and glycogen back to glucose again?

### ALTERNATIVE ASSESSMENT

5. **Analyzing Methods** Research ways that fermentation is used in food preparation. Find out what kinds of microorganisms are used in cultured dairy products, such as yogurt, sour cream, and some cheeses. Research the role of alcoholic fermentation by yeast in bread making. Prepare an oral report to summarize your findings.

Why It Matters

# Life in a Biosphere

The Biosphere 2 research facility has seven ecosystems that mirror those on Earth, including a desert, a savannah, a saltwater ocean that contains a million gallons of water, an Amazonian rain forest, a mangrove marsh, an area of intensive agriculture, and a habitat for humans. The giant, self-contained system of Biosphere 2 is a miniature version of the flows and balances that occur on Earth. But in Biosphere 2, they are occurring at a much faster pace.

## A World Under Glass

Located on 3.15 acres in southern Arizona, this miniature, airtight world is sealed on the bottom by a stainless steel liner and on the top by a steel and glass structure. The seven ecosystems were built from scratch with soils, water, and plant and animal life from around the world. Biosphere 2 has more than 1,000 sensors that monitor the vital statistics of this living laboratory by measuring temperature, humidity, oxygen, carbon dioxide, and other qualities of the air and soil.

**Biospherians** Eight researchers, known as *biospherians,* lived entirely within the facility. They controlled the technical systems and gathered results for more than 60 research projects, including studies of carbon dioxide and oxygen cycles, soil composition, coral reef health, agricultural pest management, and waste and water recycling.

**Quick Project** Biosphere 2 research is being used to help develop environmental technologies for use in space. Find out details about the Mars on Earth Project and its connection to Biosphere 2.

**Biosphere 2** The research facility opened in 1991 as an ecological experiment designed for research, education, and the development of environmental technologies.

# Chapter 9 Lab

45 min

4.5.1d

## Objectives

- Demonstrate how carbon dioxide affects bromothymol blue when added to the indicator solution.
- Describe the effect of temperature on carbon dioxide production by yeast.

## Materials

- safety goggles
- disposable gloves
- lab apron
- plastic cups, clear (4)
- room temperature water
- bromothymol blue
- drinking straw, plastic
- warm water
- ice water
- baker's yeast
- ¼ teaspoon
- hand lens
- sugar

## Safety

# Cellular Respiration

In cellular respiration, sugar is broken down and energy is released. This energy is harnessed and used to produce ATP. In addition to releasing energy, respiration generates reaction byproducts such as carbon dioxide gas. Carbon dioxide readily dissolves in water to produce a mild acid. This change to an acid can be confirmed through the use of an acid-base indicator, such as bromothymol blue. In this activity, you will use bromothymol blue to confirm respiration, and you will explore how temperature may affect this metabolic process.

## Procedure

1. Put on safety goggles, gloves, and a lab apron. Fill a clean plastic cup halfway with room temperature water. Add several drops of bromothymol blue to the water. Swirl to mix the solution. **CAUTION: Bromothymol blue is a skin and eye irritant.**
2. Insert a clean straw into the solution. Gently blow a steady stream of air through the straw. Note any changes in the solution's appearance. **CAUTION: Be careful not to accidentally drink the solution while blowing into the straw.**
3. Label three plastic cups, "A," "B" and "C."
4. Fill cup A with ice water, fill cup B with room temperature water, and fill cup C with warm water. Add several drops of bromothymol blue solution to each cup to ensure a uniform appearance.
5. Add ¼ teaspoon of baker's yeast to each cup. Swirl the cups, and observe the appearance of the solutions every 30 s. After 5 min, examine the surface of each solution with a hand lens.
6. Clean up your lab materials according to your teacher's instructions. Wash your hands before leaving the lab.

## Analyze and Conclude

1. **Drawing Conclusions** What happened to the indicator as exhaled air bubbled through the solution? What caused this change?
2. SCIENTIFIC METHODS **Evaluating Results** Did the yeast produce a similar color change? Explain your answer.
3. SCIENTIFIC METHODS **Evaluating Results** Did temperature affect the yeast's production of carbon dioxide? Explain your answer.
4. SCIENTIFIC METHODS **Summarizing Results** What did you observe on the surface of the solutions?
5. **Predicting Outcomes** Will adding sugar to the yeast solution affect the respiration rate? Make a guess. Then, design a method for inquiry that would test the effects of various sugar concentrations on yeast metabolism.

# Chapter 9 Summary

| Key Ideas | Key Terms |
|---|---|

## 1 Energy in Living Systems

- Organisms use and store energy in the chemical bonds of organic compounds.
- Metabolism involves either using energy to build organic molecules or breaking down organic molecules in which energy is stored. Organic molecules contain carbon. Therefore, an organism's metabolism is part of Earth's carbon cycle.
- In cells, chemical energy is gradually released in a series of chemical reactions that are assisted by enzymes.

**Key Terms:** **photosynthesis** (197), **cellular respiration** (198), **ATP** (198), **ATP synthase** (201), **electron transport chain** (201)

## 2 Photosynthesis

- In plants, light energy is harvested by pigments located in the thylakoid membrane of chloroplasts.
- During photosynthesis, one electron transport chain provides energy used to make ATP, while the other provides energy to make NADPH.
- In the final stage of photosynthesis, chemical energy is stored by being used to produce sugar molecules from the carbon in the gas carbon dioxide.
- Light intensity, carbon dioxide concentration, and temperature are three environmental factors that affect photosynthesis.

**Key Terms:** **thylakoid** (202), **pigment** (203), **chlorophyll** (203), **Calvin cycle** (206)

## 3 Cellular Respiration

- The breaking of a sugar molecule by glycolysis results in a net gain of two ATP molecules.
- The total yield of energy-storing products from one time through the Krebs cycle is one ATP, three NADH, and one $FADH_2$. Electron carriers transfer energy through the electron transport chain, which ultimately powers ATP synthase.
- Fermentation enables glycolysis to continue supplying a cell with ATP in anaerobic conditions.

**Key Terms:** **glycolysis** (209), **anaerobic** (209), **aerobic** (209), **Krebs cycle** (210), **fermentation** (212)

The Living Environment

# Regents Exam Practice

**PART A: Answer all questions in this part.**

*Directions:* For each statement or question, write on your separate answer sheet the number of the word or expression that best completes the statement or answers the question.

**1** Plants in areas with short growing seasons have more chloroplasts in their cells than plants in areas with longer growing seasons. Compared to plants in areas with longer growing seasons, plants in areas with shorter growing seasons most likely

(1) make and store food more quickly.
(2) have a higher rate of protein metabolism.
(3) grow taller.
(4) have a different method of respiration.

**2** Most of the starch stored in the cells of a potato is composed of molecules that originally entered these cells as

(1) enzymes
(2) simple sugars
(3) amino acids
(4) minerals

**3** The dissolved carbon dioxide in a lake is used directly by

(1) autotrophs
(2) parasites
(3) fungi
(4) decomposers

**4** When organisms break the bonds of organic compounds, the organisms can

(1) use the smaller molecules to plug the gaps in the cell membrane to slow diffusion.
(2) use the energy obtained to digest molecules produced by respiration that uses oxygen.
(3) obtain energy or reassemble the resulting materials to form different compounds.
(4) excrete smaller amounts of solid waste materials during vigorous exercise.

**5** Which statement best describes cellular respiration?

(1) It occurs in animal cells but not in plant cells.
(2) It converts energy in food into a more usable form.
(3) It uses carbon dioxide and produces oxygen.
(4) It stores energy in food molecules.

**6** The production of energy-rich ATP molecules is the direct result of

(1) recycling light energy to be used in the process of photosynthesis
(2) releasing the stored energy of organic compounds by the process of respiration
(3) breaking down starch by the process of digestion
(4) copying coded information during the process of protein synthesis

**7** The green aquatic plant represented in the diagram below was exposed to light for several hours. Which gas would most likely be found in the greatest amount in the bubbles?

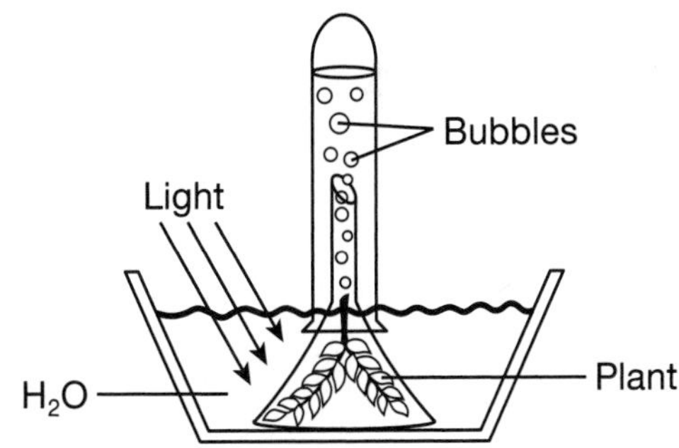


(1) oxygen
(2) nitrogen
(3) ozone
(4) carbon dioxide

**8** Which process is directly used by autotrophs to store energy in glucose?

(1) diffusion
(2) photosynthesis
(3) respiration
(4) active transport

**9** In heterotrophs, energy for the life processes comes from the chemical energy stored in the bonds of

(1) water molecules
(2) oxygen molecules
(3) organic compounds
(4) inorganic compounds

**10** Which set of terms best identifies the letters in the diagram below?

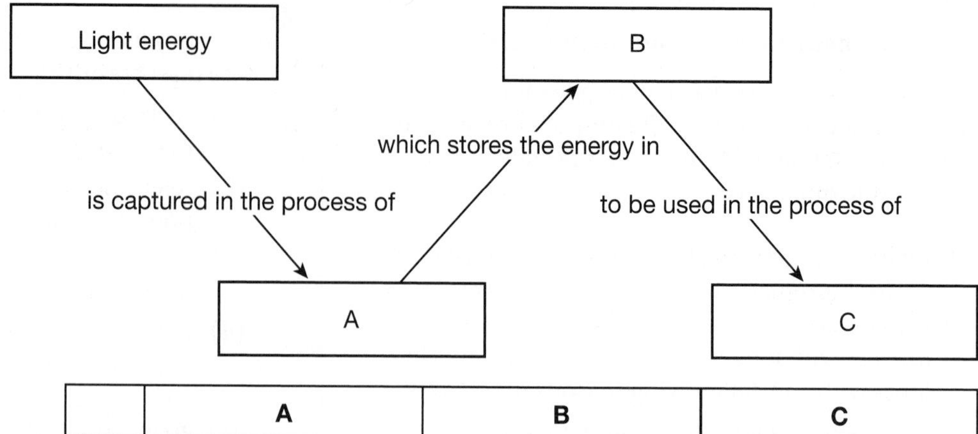


| | A | B | C |
|---|---|---|---|
| (1) | photosynthesis | inorganic molecules | decomposition |
| (2) | respiration | organic molecules | digestion |
| (3) | photosynthesis | organic molecules | respiration |
| (4) | respiration | inorganic molecules | photosynthesis |

**PART B**

**11** An experimental setup is shown in the diagram below. Which hypothesis would most likely be tested using this setup?

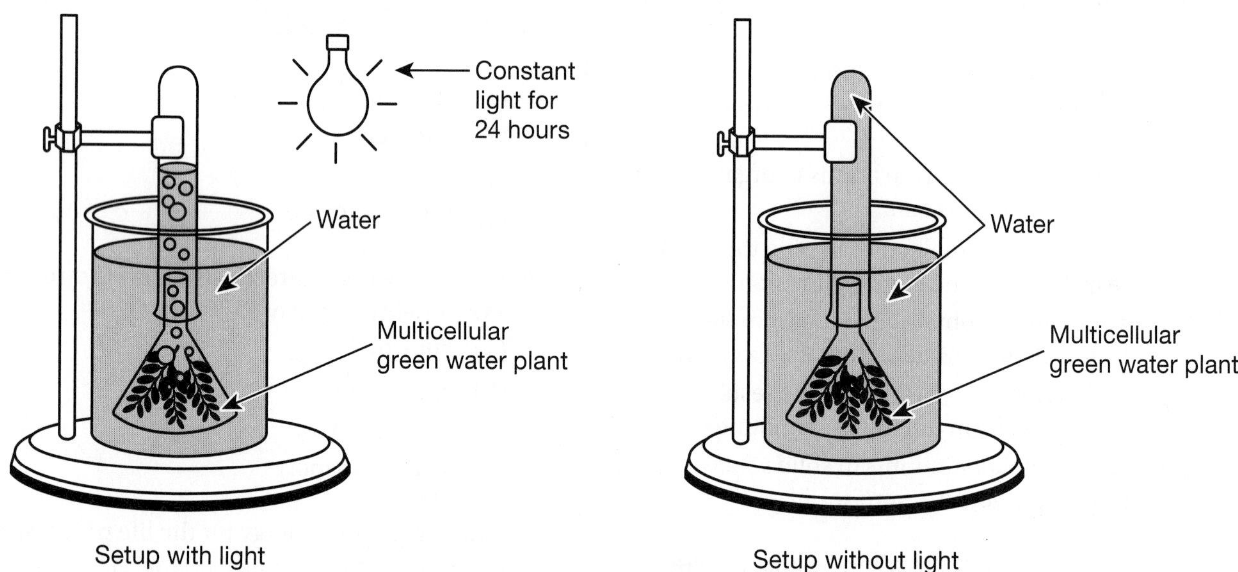


(1) Green water plants release a gas in the presence of light.
(2) Roots of water plants absorb minerals in the absence of light.
(3) Green plants need light for cell division.
(4) Plants grow best in the absence of light.

**Base your answers to questions 12 through 14 on the diagram below and on your knowledge of biology. The arrows in the diagram represent biological processes.**

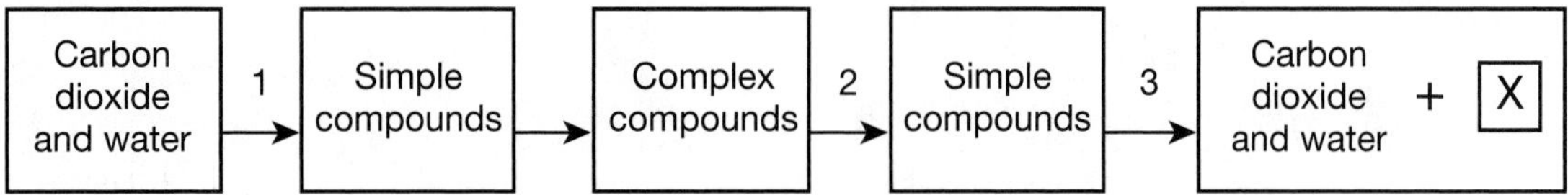


**12** Identify *one* type of organism that carries out process 1.

**13** Identify process 3.

**14** Identify what letter *X* represents.

**PART C**

**15** Photosynthesis and respiration are two important processes. Discuss one of these processes and explain its importance to an organism. In your answer, be sure to:

- identify the process being discussed
- identify the organelle where this process occurs
- identify two raw materials necessary for this process
- identify one energy-rich molecule that is produced by this process
- state how organisms use the energy-rich molecule that is produced
- state how a gas produced by this process is recycled in nature

**Base your answers to question 16 on the statement below and on your knowledge of biology.**

Some internal environmental factors may interfere with the ability of an enzyme to function efficiently.

**16** Identify *two* internal environmental factors that directly influence the rate of enzyme action.

**PART D**

**17** State whether you think the following viewpoint can be supported, and justify your answer. "If Earth's early atmosphere had been rich in oxygen, photosynthetic organisms would not have been able to evolve."

# Chapter 10 Cell Growth and Division

## Preview



## Why It Matters

The cell is the basic unit of life—common to all living things. The growth and division of cells is essential to the continuity of life.

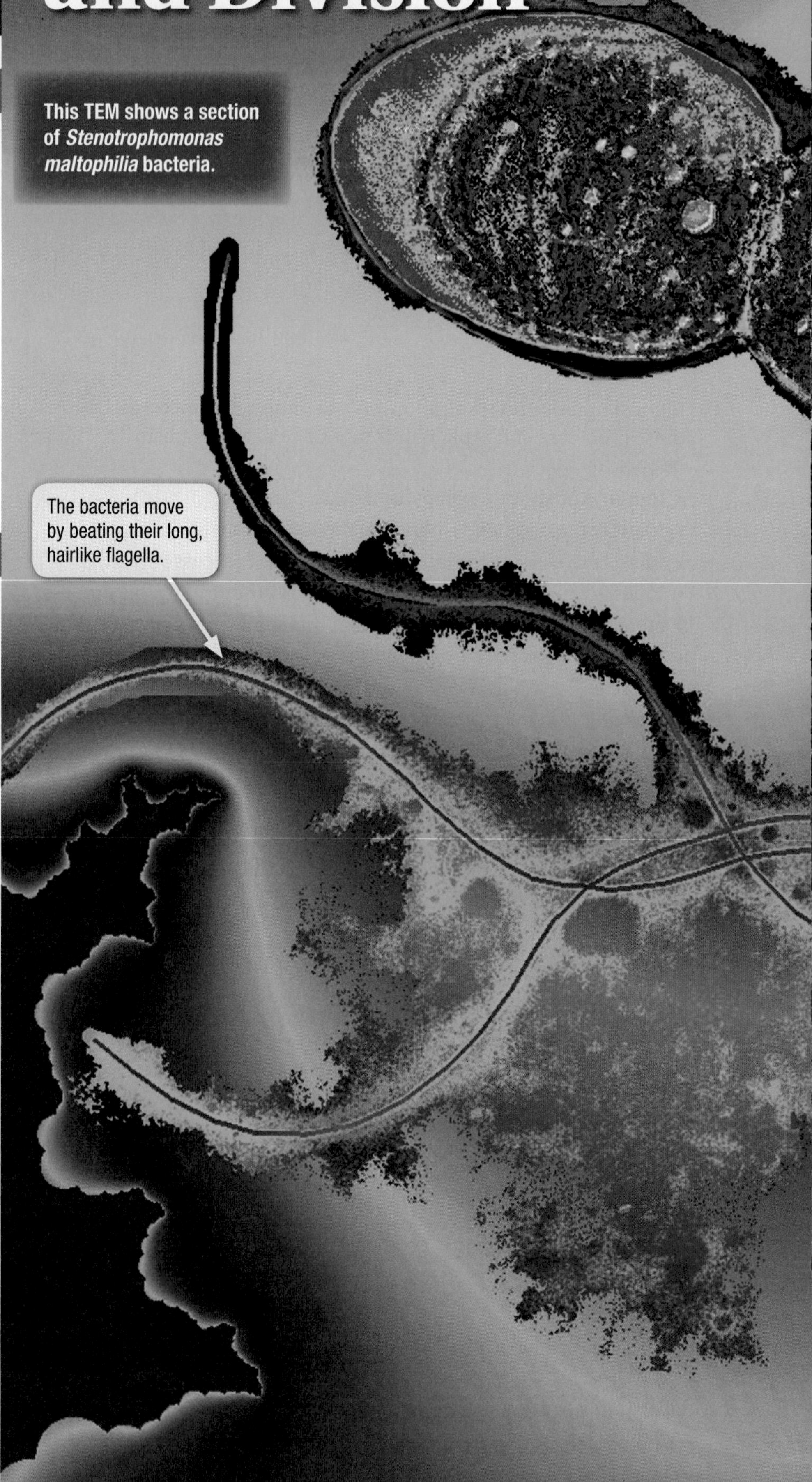

This TEM shows a section of *Stenotrophomonas maltophilia* bacteria.

The bacteria move by beating their long, hairlike flagella.

***The Living Environment***

**Standard 4** Students will understand and apply scientific concepts, principles, and theories pertaining to the physical setting and living environment and recognize the historical development of ideas in science.

**Key Idea 1** Living things are both similar to and different from each other and from nonliving things. ***Major Understandings* - 1.2c**

**Key Idea 5** Organisms maintain a dynamic equilibrium that sustains life. ***Major Understandings* - 5.2i**

# InquiryLab

15 min

## Whitefish Cells

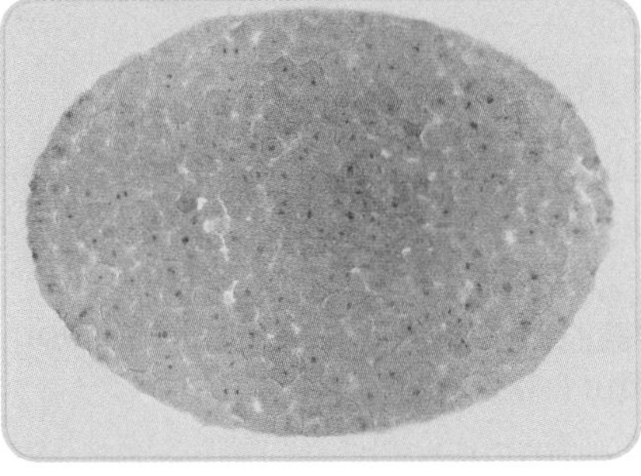

As an embryo develops, its cells divide rapidly. Few of these cells remain in a resting state, so when observing them, you will see groups of these cells in various stages of division.

### Procedure

1. Place a **slide of whitefish cells** on the stage of a **microscope.** Examine the cells under low power. Do all of the cells look alike? If not, how do they differ? Draw several representative cells.
2. Carefully switch to high power. Slowly scan the slide, and look for obvious differences between cells. Pay particular attention to the appearance of the nuclei.
3. Make a sketch of each distinct pattern of cells that you see.

### Analysis

1. **Describe** any differences you observed in the nuclei of these cells.
2. **Determine** whether all the cells you observed had a distinct nucleus. Explain.

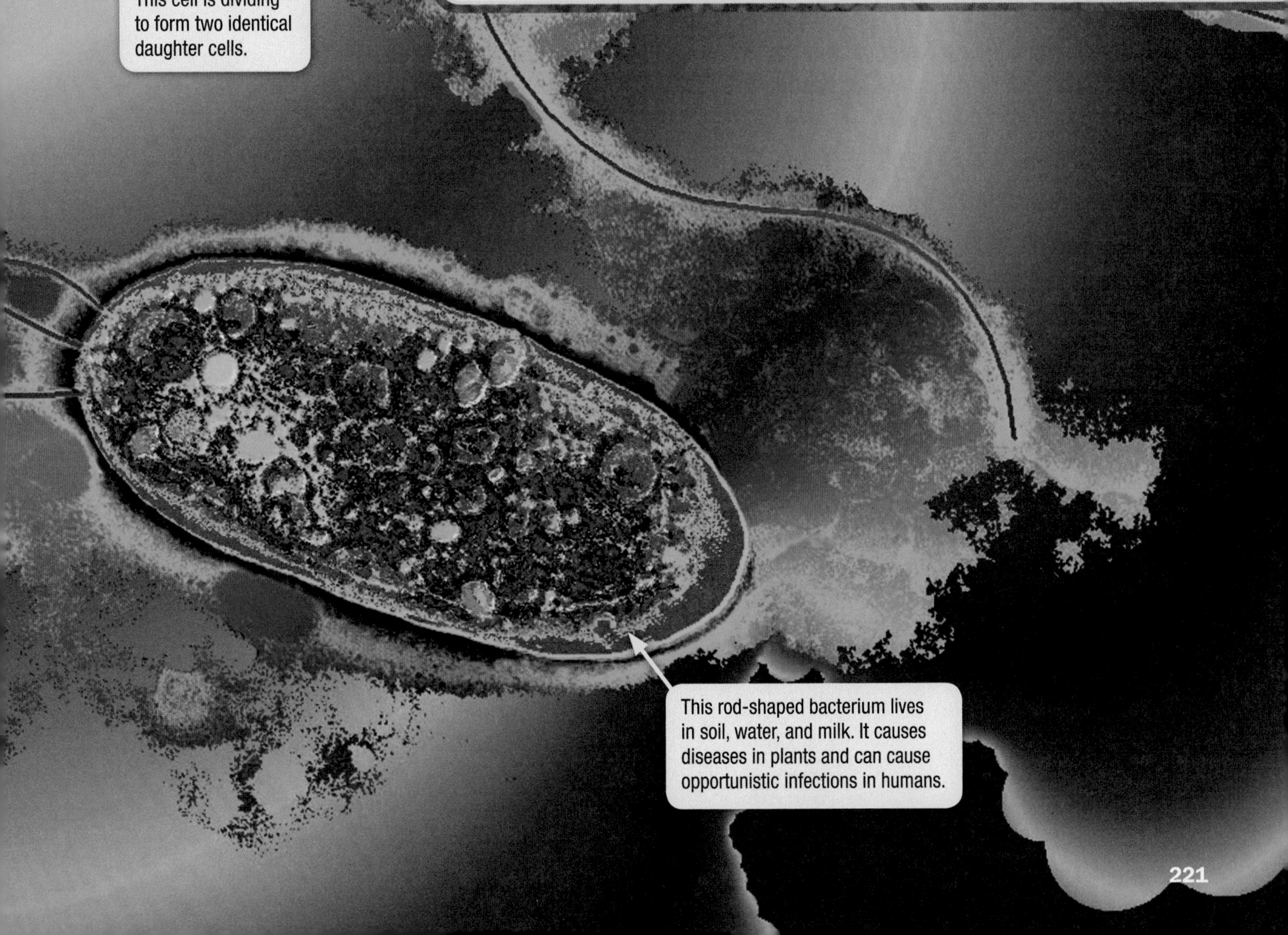

This cell is dividing to form two identical daughter cells.

This rod-shaped bacterium lives in soil, water, and milk. It causes diseases in plants and can cause opportunistic infections in humans.

These reading tools can help you learn the material in this chapter. For more information on how to use these and other tools, see **Appendix: Reading and Study Skills.**

## Using Words

**Word Parts** You can tell a lot about a word by taking it apart and examining its prefix and root.

**Your Turn** Use the information in the table to define the following terms.

1. *chromosome*
2. *mitosis*

**Word Parts**

| Word part | Type | Meaning |
|---|---|---|
| *mito-* | prefix | thread |
| *chromo-* | prefix | color |
| *-osis* | suffix | condition or process |
| *-some* | root | body |

## Using Language

**Cause and Effect** In biological processes, one step leads to another step. When reading, you can often recognize these cause-and-effect relationships by words that indicate a result, such as *so, consequently, if-then,* and *as a result.*

**Your Turn** Identify the cause and effect in the following sentences.

1. People often shiver as a result of being cold.
2. The light got brighter, so the pupil of the eye got smaller.
3. If the cell passes the $G_2$ checkpoint, then the cell may begin to divide.

## Using Graphic Organizers

**Pattern Puzzles** You can use pattern puzzles to help you remember sequential information. Exchanging puzzles with a classmate can help you study.

**Your Turn** Make a pattern puzzle for the stages of mitosis.

1. Write down the steps of the process. On a sheet of notebook paper, write down one step per line. Do not number the steps.
2. Cut the sheet of paper into strips so that each strip of paper has only one step. Shuffle the paper strips so that they are out of sequence.
3. Place the strips in their proper sequence. Confirm the order of the process by checking your text or class notes.

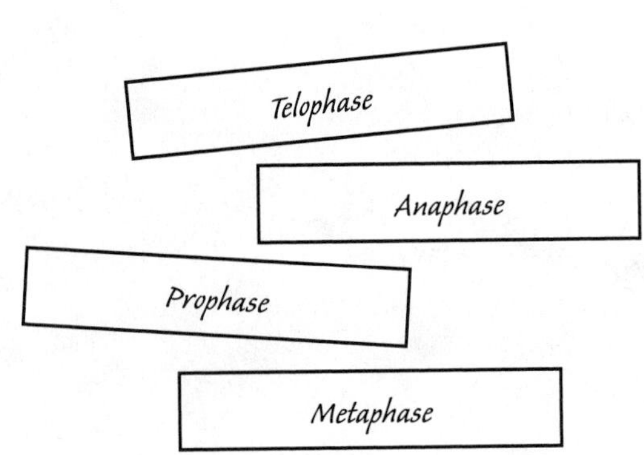

Section 1

# Cell Reproduction

| Key Ideas | Key Terms | Why It Matters |
|---|---|---|
| ❯ Why do cells divide?<br>❯ How is DNA packaged into the nucleus?<br>❯ How do cells prepare for division? | gene, chromosome, chromatin, histone, nucleosome, chromatid, centromere | Cells are busy making more cells. The reproduction of cells allows you to grow and heal. |

The adult human body produces roughly 2 trillion cells per day. The new cells are exact copies of the cells they replace. This process is called *cell reproduction*. Some cells, such as hair and skin cells, are replaced frequently throughout your life. Other cells, such as brain and nerve cells, are rarely produced after infancy.

***The Living Environment***
**Standard 4**
**1.2c** The components of the human body, from organ systems to cell organelles, interact to maintain a balanced internal environment. To successfully accomplish this, organisms possess a diversity of control mechanisms that detect deviations and make corrective actions.

## Why Cells Reproduce

As the body of a multicellular organism grows larger, its cells do not also grow large. Instead, the body grows by producing more cells. New cells are needed to help tissues and organs grow. Even after organisms reach adulthood, old cells die and new cells take their place. This replacement and renewal is important for keeping the body healthy. New cells also replace damaged cells. As **Figure 1** shows, the body repairs a wound by making more cells.

**Cell Size** A cell grows larger by building more cell products. To do this, the cell must take in more nutrients, process them, and get rid of wastes. Recall that a cell's ability to exchange substances is limited by its surface area-to-volume ratio. As a cell gets larger, substances must travel farther to reach where they are needed.

**Cell Maintenance** The work of cells is done by proteins. As a cell gets larger, more proteins are required to maintain its function. Recall that the instructions for making these proteins are copied from the cell's DNA. If the cell gets too large, DNA instructions cannot be copied quickly enough to make the proteins that the cell needs to support itself. Thus, cell size is also limited by the cell's DNA.

**Making New Cells** Cell division can solve the problems of cell size. Each "daughter" cell has a higher surface area-to-volume ratio than its parent does. Each new cell also gets an entire copy of the cell's DNA. ❯ **Because larger cells are more difficult to maintain, cells divide when they grow to a certain size.**

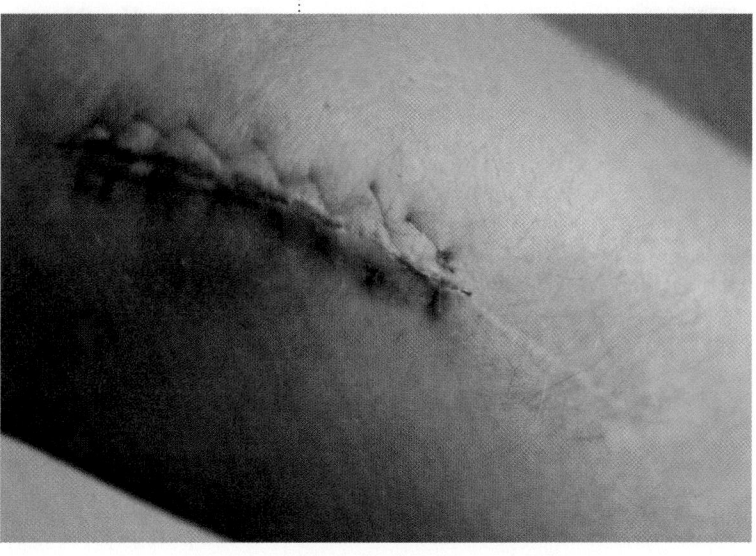

**Figure 1** When these stitches are removed, this cut will be healed. Cell division enables the body to repair a wound.

Hands-On

# QuickLab

15 min

## Chromosome Package

DNA is condensed to reduce the space that it occupies in the cell. In eukaryotic cells, the linear DNA molecule is condensed by being wrapped around a core of proteins.

### Procedure

1. Scrunch a **1 m length of kite string** into a wad. Cover this wad with a piece of **plastic wrap.**
2. Wind another **1 m length of string** tightly and uniformly around a **paper clip.** Cover this shape with another piece of plastic wrap.

### Analysis

1. **Identify** what the string, the plastic wrap, and the paper clip represent in each model.
2. **Compare** the volumes of space that the two models occupy.
3. CRITICAL THINKING **Evaluating Models** Describe an object that would be more effective than a paper clip as a core to wrap the string around. Explain your answer.

**gene** a unit of heredity that consists of a segment of nucleic acid that codes for a functional unit of RNA or protein

**chromosome** in a eukaryotic cell, one of the structures in the nucleus that are made up of DNA and protein; in a prokaryotic cell, the main ring of DNA

**chromatin** the substance of which eukaryotic chromosomes are composed

**histone** a type of protein molecule found in the chromosomes of eukaryotic cells but not prokaryotic cells

**nucleosome** (NOO klee uh SOHM) a eukaryotic structural unit of chromatin that consists of DNA wound around a core of histone proteins

**chromatid** one of the two strands of a chromosome that become visible during meiosis or mitosis

**centromere** the region of the chromosome that holds the two sister chromatids together during mitosis

## Chromosomes

Recall that a cell's activity is directed by its DNA. The large molecule of DNA is organized into hereditary units called **genes.** A gene is a segment of DNA that codes for RNA and protein. The simplest organisms have thousands of genes. Each cell has a large amount of DNA that must be condensed into a very small volume. DNA is organized and packaged into structures called **chromosomes.**

**Prokaryotic Chromosome** A prokaryotic cell has a single circular molecule of DNA. This loop of DNA contains thousands of genes. A prokaryotic chromosome is condensed through repeated twisting or winding, like a rubber band twisted upon itself many times.

**Eukaryotic Chromosome** The challenge of packaging DNA into the eukaryotic nucleus is much greater. Eukaryotic cells contain many more genes arranged on several linear DNA molecules. A human cell contains 46 separate, linear DNA molecules that are packaged into 46 chromosomes. **Eukaryotic DNA is packaged into highly condensed chromosome structures with the help of many proteins.** The DNA and proteins make up a substance called **chromatin.**

**Forms of Chromatin** The first level of packaging is done by a class of proteins called **histones.** A group of eight histones come together to form a disc-shaped histone core. As **Figure 2** shows, the long DNA molecule is wound around a series of histone cores in a regular manner. The structure made up of a histone core and the DNA around it is called a **nucleosome.** Under an electron microscope, this level of packaging resembles beads on a string. The string of nucleosomes line up in a spiral to form a cord that is 30 nm in diameter.

**Packaging During Cell Division** During most of a cell's life, its chromosomes exist as coiled or uncoiled nucleosomes. As the cell prepares to divide, the chromosomes condense even further. This ensures that the extremely long DNA molecules do not get tangled up during cell division. The 30-nm fiber (the nucleosome cord) forms loops that are attached to a protein scaffold. These looped domains then coil into the final, most highly condensed form of the chromosome. Many dense loops of chromatin form the rod-shaped structures that can be seen in regular light microscopes.

**Chromosome Structure** A fully condensed, duplicated chromosome is shown in **Figure 2.** Each of the two thick strands, called a **chromatid,** is made of a single, long molecule of DNA. Identical pairs, called *sister chromatids,* are held together at a region called the **centromere.** During cell division, the sister chromatids are separated at the centromere, and one ends up in each daughter cell. This ensures that each new cell has the same genetic information as the parent cell.

› **Reading Check** *What is a chromatid? (See the Appendix for answers to Reading Checks.)*

**Word Parts** The prefix *tel-* means "end." If *centromere* means a "central part," what do you think *telomere* means?

**Figure 2** A eukaryotic chromosome consists of DNA tightly coiled around proteins. As a cell prepares to divide, the duplicated chromosomes are condensed. › **Why do chromosomes condense during cell division?**

**Eukaryotic Chromosome Structure**

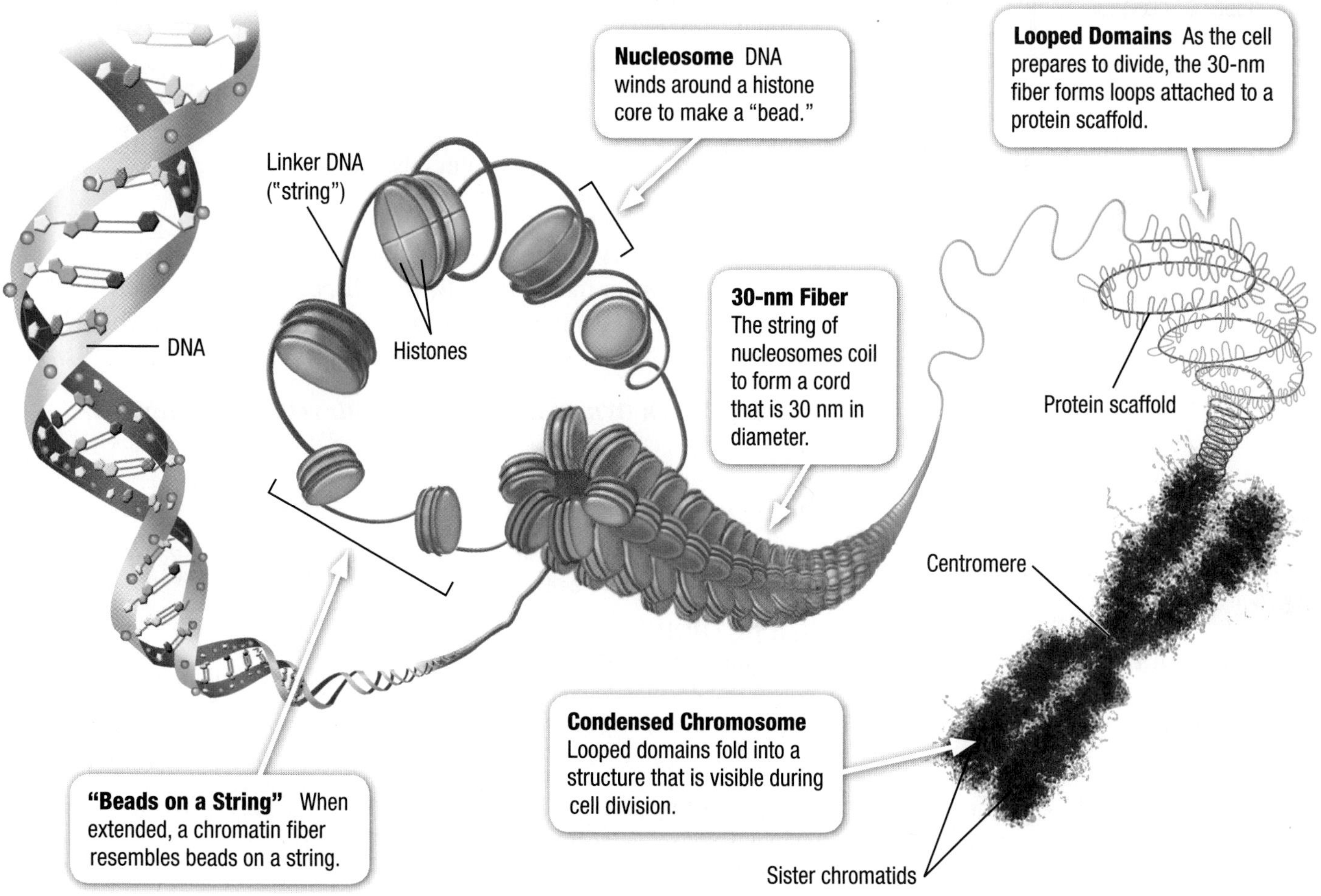

DNA

Linker DNA ("string")

Histones

**Nucleosome** DNA winds around a histone core to make a "bead."

**Looped Domains** As the cell prepares to divide, the 30-nm fiber forms loops attached to a protein scaffold.

**30-nm Fiber** The string of nucleosomes coil to form a cord that is 30 nm in diameter.

Protein scaffold

Centromere

**Condensed Chromosome** Looped domains fold into a structure that is visible during cell division.

**"Beads on a String"** When extended, a chromatin fiber resembles beads on a string.

Sister chromatids

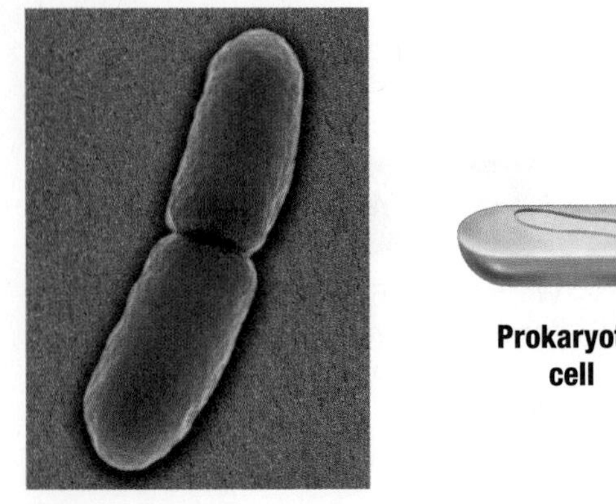
Cell dividing

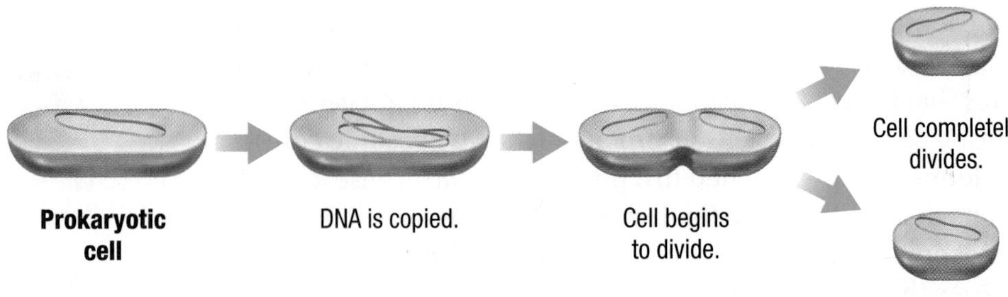
Prokaryotic cell
DNA is copied.
Cell begins to divide.
Cell completely divides.
Two genetically identical cells

**Figure 3** A prokaryotic cell divides by copying its single, circular chromosome and building a cell membrane between the two copies. A new cell wall forms around the membrane, squeezing the cell. Eventually it pinches off into two independent daughter cells.

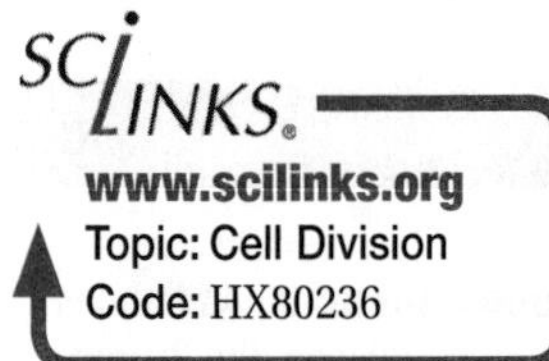
www.scilinks.org
Topic: Cell Division
Code: HX80236

## Preparing for Cell Division

All new cells are produced by the division of preexisting cells. The process of cell division involves more than cutting a cell into two pieces. Each new cell must have all of the equipment needed to stay alive. **› All newly-formed cells require DNA, so before a cell divides, a copy of DNA is made for each daughter cell.** This way, the new cells will function in the same way as the cells that they replace.

**Prokaryotes** In prokaryotic cells, the circular DNA molecule is attached to the inner cell membrane. As **Figure 3** shows, the cytoplasm is divided when a new cell membrane forms between the two DNA copies. Meanwhile the cell continues to grow until it nearly doubles in size. The cell wall also continues to form around the new cell membrane, pushing inward. The cell is constricted in the middle, like a long balloon being squeezed near the center. Eventually the dividing prokaryote is pinched into two independent daughter cells, each of which has its own circular DNA molecule.

**ACADEMIC VOCABULARY**

**complex** having many parts or functions

**Eukaryotes** The reproduction eukaryotic cells is more complex than that of prokaryotic cells. Recall that eukaryotic cells have many organelles. In order to form two living cells, each daughter cell must contain enough of each organelle to carry out its functions. The DNA within the nucleus must also be copied, sorted, and separated.

**› Reading Check** ***Where does a prokaryotic cell begin to divide?***

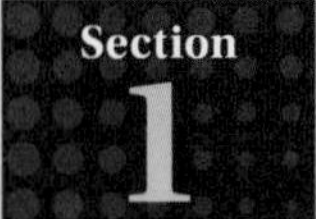

## Section 1 Review

### › KEY IDEAS

1. **List** two reasons for cell reproduction in multicellular organisms.
2. **Describe** three levels of structure in the DNA packaging system found within a eukaryotic nucleus.
3. **Explain** why daughter cells are identical to the parent cell.

### CRITICAL THINKING

4. **Evaluating Conclusions** If cells constantly double in number each time they divide, why doesn't a multicellular organism continue to grow in size?
5. **Inferring Relationships** Why do chromosomes condense before they divide?

### MATH SKILLS

6. **Exponents** Imagine you are observing a cell that divides once every hour for 12 h. Assume that none of the cells die during this period. How many cells would exist after each hour? How many cells would exist after 12 h?

Why It Matters

# Replacement Parts

If you look closely at the camouflaged green anole lizard at right, you will see that it appears to be growing a new tail. The process by which an organism replaces or restores a lost or amputated body part is called *regeneration.* A series of rapid cell divisions allows certain organisms to regenerate certain lost parts.

## Sea Star Comets

To keep sea stars from destroying oyster beds, oyster fishermen used to chop up sea stars and throw the pieces back into the sea. Unfortunately, this practice increased the number of sea stars! Some sea stars can regenerate their entire bodies from just a small piece of arm. Specimens such as the one shown below are sometimes called "comets." The regeneration of these sea stars is possible because they keep their vital organs in their arms.

**Tail Regeneration** Lizards, such as the gecko at left, are well known for their ability to "release" their tails. Lizards use this ability as a defense mechanism to escape predators. The broken piece of tail twists and wiggles, which diverts the attention of the predator while the lizard escapes. When the tail regenerates, it is made up of cartilage, rather than bone.

**Research** Investigate and explain compensatory hypertrophy, a process in mammals that is similar to the regeneration of body parts. Identify an organ in humans that is capable of compensatory hypertrophy.

Sea star "comet"

Section 2

# Mitosis

| Key Ideas | Key Terms | Why It Matters |
|---|---|---|
| ❯ What are the phases of the eukaryotic cell cycle?<br>❯ What are the four stages of mitosis?<br>❯ How does cytokinesis occur? | cell cycle, interphase, mitosis, cytokinesis, spindle, centrosome | The events of the cell cycle ensure that new cells will be just like the old cell. |

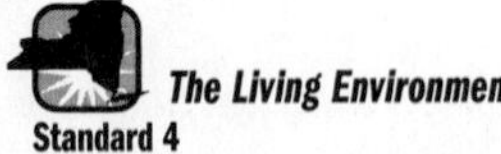
The Living Environment

Standard 4

**5.2i** Gene mutations in a cell can result in uncontrolled cell division, called cancer. Exposure of cells to certain chemicals and radiation increases mutations and thus increases the chance of cancer.

Unlike prokaryotic cells, eukaryotic cells cannot simply be pinched into two new cells. The physical division of one cell into two cells requires many preparations.

## Eukaryotic Cell Cycle

The **cell cycle** is a repeating sequence of cellular growth and division during the life of a cell. ❯ **The life of a eukaryotic cell cycles through phases of growth, DNA replication, preparation for cell division, and division of the nucleus and cytoplasm.** The cell cycle is made up of five phases, shown in **Figure 4.** The first three phases together are known as **interphase.** The remaining two phases make up cell division.

**Interphase** During interphase, the cell is not dividing. It is growing and preparing to divide. Different types of cells spend different amounts of time in interphase. Cells that divide often, such as skin cells, spend less time in interphase. Cells that divide seldom, such as nerve cells, spend most of their time in interphase.

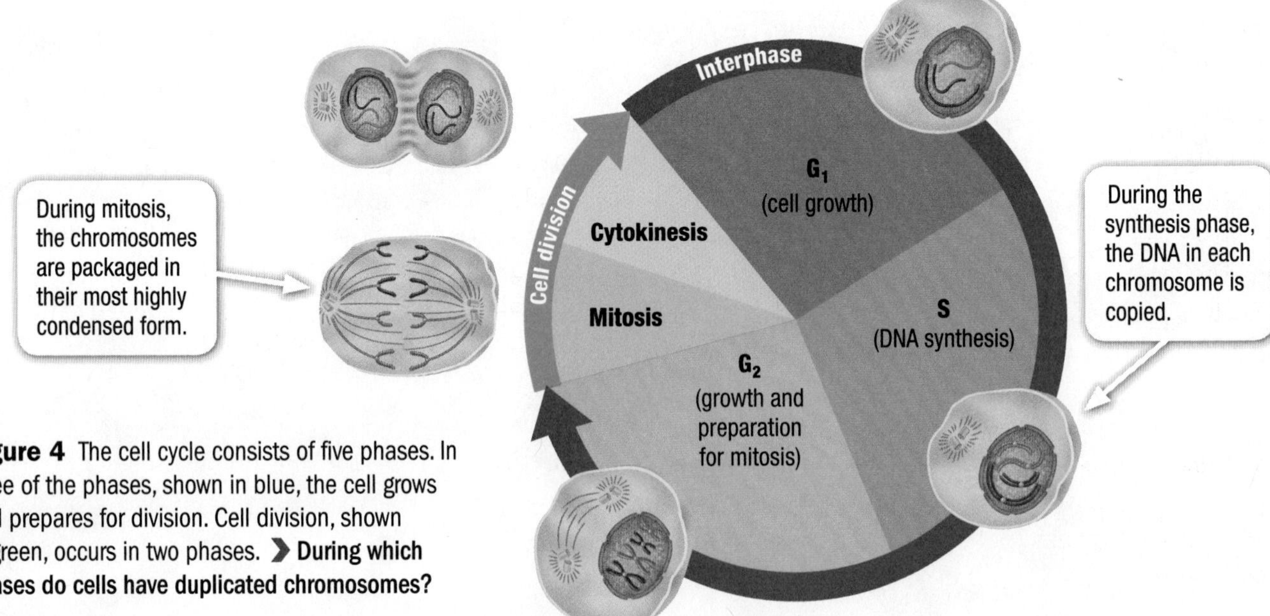
Interphase
Cell division
$G_1$
(cell growth)
Cytokinesis
Mitosis
S
(DNA synthesis)
$G_2$
(growth and preparation for mitosis)
During mitosis, the chromosomes are packaged in their most highly condensed form.
During the synthesis phase, the DNA in each chromosome is copied.

**Figure 4** The cell cycle consists of five phases. In three of the phases, shown in blue, the cell grows and prepares for division. Cell division, shown in green, occurs in two phases. ❯ **During which phases do cells have duplicated chromosomes?**

Data

# QuickLab

5 min

## Number of Cells Resulting from Mitosis

In the human body, the rate of mitosis is about 25 million ($2.5 \times 10^7$) cells produced per second. By using this rate, you can calculate the number of cells produced by mitosis in a given amount of time.

### Procedure

1. Calculate the number of cells produced by mitosis in the time given. For example, to find the number of cells produced in 3 min, determine how many seconds are in 3 min (because the rate is given in seconds).

$$\frac{60 \text{ seconds}}{1 \text{ minute}} \times 3 \text{ minutes} = 180 \text{ seconds}$$

2. Multiply the rate of mitosis by the time (in seconds) given in the problem (180 s).

$$\frac{2.5 \times 10^7 \text{ cells}}{\text{second}} \times 180 \text{ seconds} = 4.5 \times 10^9 \text{ cells}$$

$$4.5 \times 10^9 \text{ cells} = 4{,}500{,}000{,}000 \text{ cells} = 4.5 \text{ billion cells}$$

### Analysis

1. **Calculate** the number of cells that would be produced in 1 h.
2. **Calculate** the number of cells that would be produced in 1 day.
3. CRITICAL THINKING **Predicting Patterns** Identify factors that might increase or decrease the rate of mitosis.

- **$G_1$** During the *first gap phase* ($G_1$), a cell grows rapidly as the cell builds more organelles. For most organisms, this phase occupies the major portion of the cell's life. Cells that are not dividing remain in the $G_1$ phase.
- **S** During the *synthesis phase* (S), a cell's DNA is copied. At the end of the S phase, the cell's nucleus has twice as much DNA as it did in the $G_1$ phase. Each chromosome now consists of two identical chromatids that are attached at the centromere.
- **$G_2$** During the *second gap phase* ($G_2$), the cell continues to grow and prepares to divide. The cell forms some special structures that help the cell divide. Hollow protein fibers called *microtubules* are organized in the cytoplasm during $G_2$ in preparation for division.

**Cell Division** Each new cell requires a complete set of organelles, including a nucleus. The process of dividing the nucleus into two daughter nuclei is called **mitosis.** The process of separating the organelles and the cytoplasm is called **cytokinesis.**

- **Mitosis** During mitosis, the nucleus divides to form two nuclei. Each nucleus contains a complete set of the cell's chromosomes. The nuclear membrane breaks down briefly. The two sister chromatids of each chromosome are pulled to the opposite sides of the dividing cell.
- **Cytokinesis** As the nucleus divides, the cytoplasm also begins to divide. Each daughter cell receives about half of the original cell's organelles. During cytokinesis, the two daughter cells are physically separated.

**❯ Reading Check** ***What phases are included in interphase?***

**cell cycle** the life cycle of a cell

**interphase** the period of the cell cycle during which activities such as cell growth and protein synthesis occur without visible signs of cell division

**mitosis** in eukaryotic cells, a process of cell division that forms two new nuclei, each of which has the same number of chromosomes

**cytokinesis** the division of the cytoplasm of a cell

spindle a network of microtubules that forms during mitosis and moves chromatids to the poles

centrosome an organelle that contains the centrioles and is the center of dynamic activity in mitosis

## Stages of Mitosis

Although mitosis is a continuous process, biologists traditionally divide it into four stages, as shown in **Figure 5.** **❯ Mitosis is a continuous process that can be observed in four stages: prophase, metaphase, anaphase, and telophase.**

**Stage 1 Prophase** Within the nucleus, chromosomes begin to condense and become visible under a light microscope. The nuclear membrane breaks down. Outside the nucleus, a special structure called the **spindle** forms. The spindle is made up of several spindle fibers. Each spindle fiber in turn is made up of an individual microtubule—a hollow tube of protein. Microtubules organize into a spindle that runs at a right angle to the cell's equator.

Cells have an organelle called the **centrosome,** which helps assemble the spindle. In animal cells, the centrosome includes a pair of centrioles, shown in **Figure 5.** Each centriole is made up of nine triplets of microtubules arranged as a short, hollow tube. Before mitosis, the cell's centrosome is duplicated. During prophase, the centrosomes move to opposite poles of the cell.

**Figure 5** During mitosis, the copies (sister chromatids) of each chromosome are separated into two nuclei. **❯ What is the role of the spindle fibers?**

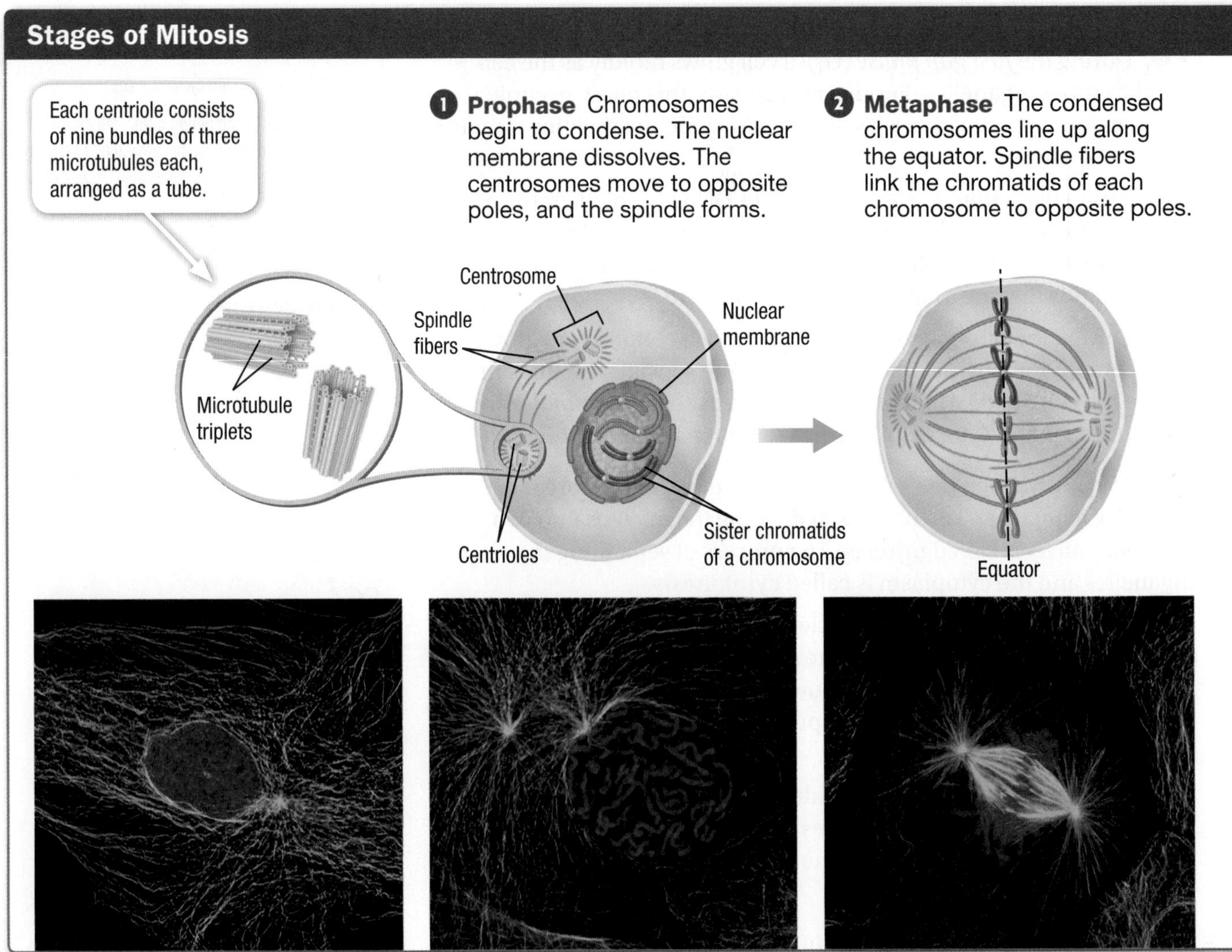

Stages of Mitosis
Each centriole consists of nine bundles of three microtubules each, arranged as a tube.
1 Prophase Chromosomes begin to condense. The nuclear membrane dissolves. The centrosomes move to opposite poles, and the spindle forms.
2 Metaphase The condensed chromosomes line up along the equator. Spindle fibers link the chromatids of each chromosome to opposite poles.
Centrosome
Spindle fibers
Nuclear membrane
Microtubule triplets
Centrioles
Sister chromatids of a chromosome
Equator

**Stage ② Metaphase** During metaphase, the chromosomes are packaged into their most condensed form. The nuclear membrane is fully dissolved, and the condensed chromosomes move to the center of the cell and line up along the cell's equator. Spindle fibers form a link between the poles and the centromere of each chromosome.

**Stage ③ Anaphase** Once all of the chromosomes are lined up, the spindle fibers shorten. The spindle fibers shorten by breaking down the microtubules bit by bit. Sister chromatids move toward opposite poles as the spindle fibers that are attached continue to shorten. Each pole now has a full set of chromosomes.

**Stage ④ Telophase** A nuclear envelope forms around the chromosomes at each pole of the cell. Chromosomes, now at opposite poles, uncoil and change back to their original chromatin form. The spindle dissolves. The spindle fibers break down and disappear. Mitosis is complete.

› **Reading Check** *What is the spindle composed of?*

**READING TOOLBOX**

**Pattern Puzzles** Cut each piece of the pattern puzzle that you made for the stages of mitosis so that each strip describes one of the events that occurs. Shuffle the strips and match the events with the correct stage.

go.hrw.com
interact online
Keyword: HX8CRPF5

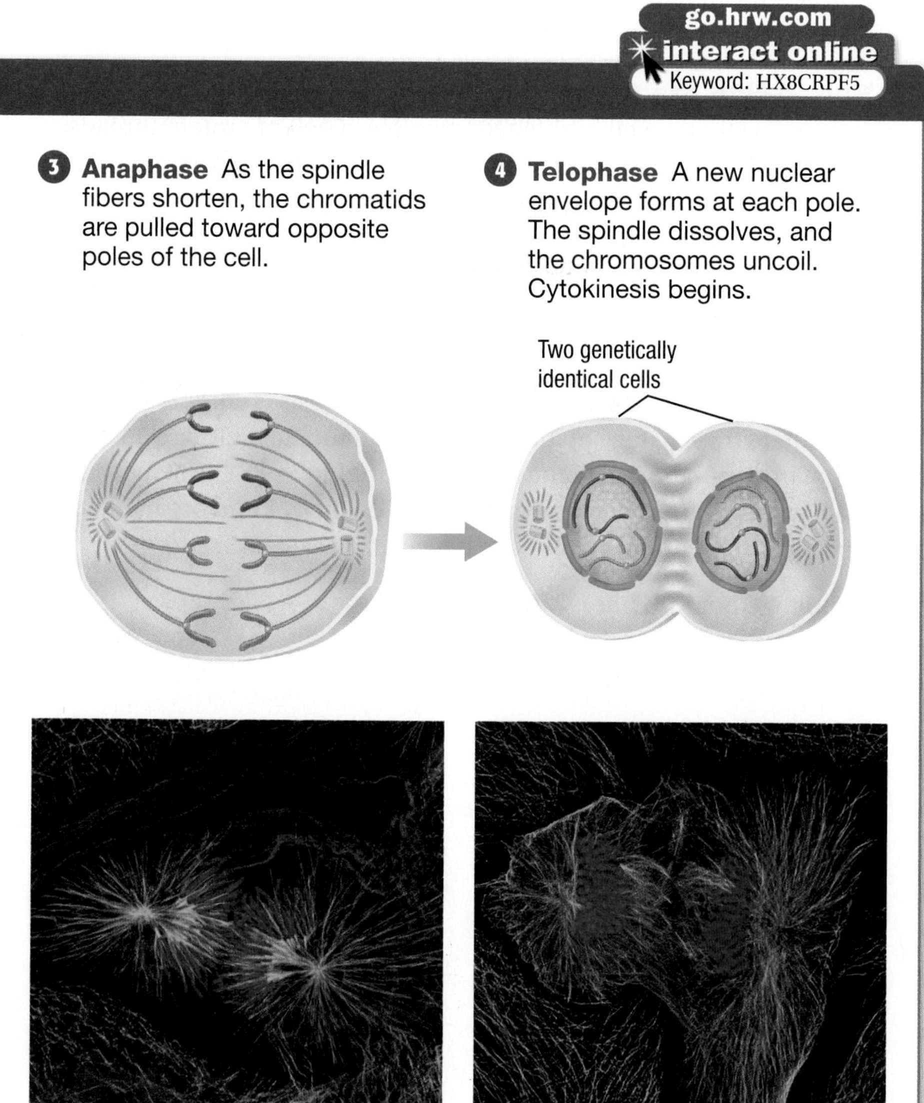


③ **Anaphase** As the spindle fibers shorten, the chromatids are pulled toward opposite poles of the cell.

④ **Telophase** A new nuclear envelope forms at each pole. The spindle dissolves, and the chromosomes uncoil. Cytokinesis begins.

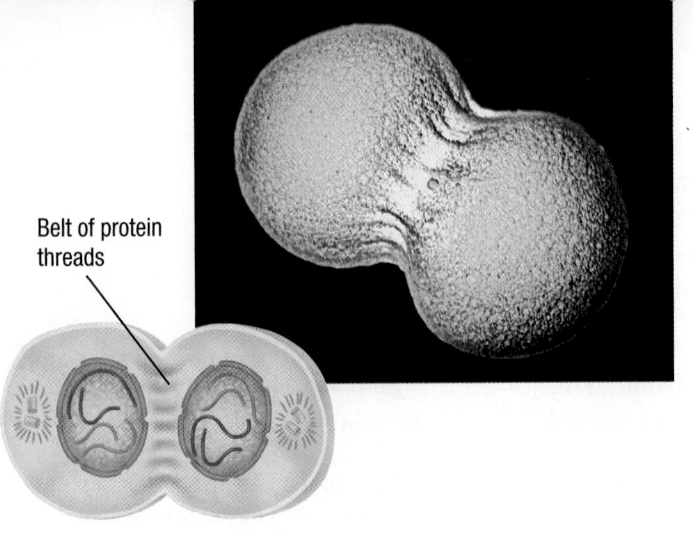


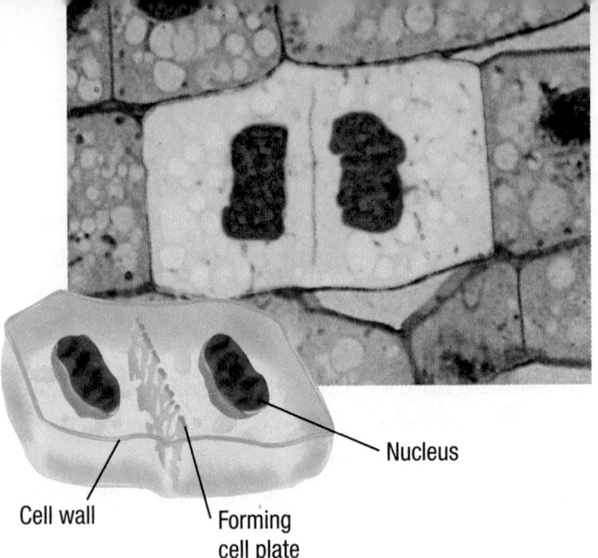


**Figure 6** During cytokinesis in an animal cell (left), the cell membrane is pinched in half by a belt of protein threads. During cytokinesis in plant cells (right), a cell plate forms down the middle of the dividing cell.

## Cytokinesis

As mitosis ends, cytokinesis begins. The cytoplasm is separated, and two cells are formed. **› During cytokinesis, the cell membrane grows into the center of the cell and divides it into two daughter cells of equal size. Each daughter cell has about half of the parent's cytoplasm and organelles.** The end result of mitosis and cytokinesis is two genetically identical cells in place of the original cell.

**Separating the Cytoplasm** In animal cells and other cells that lack cell walls, the cell is pinched in half by a belt of protein threads, as **Figure 6** shows. In plant cells and other cells that have rigid cell walls, the cytoplasm is divided in a different way. Vesicles holding cell wall material line up across the middle of the cell. These vesicles fuse to form a large, membrane-bound cell wall called the *cell plate,* shown in **Figure 6.** When it is completely formed, the cell plate separates the plant cell into two new plant cells.

**ACADEMIC VOCABULARY**

**rigid** stiff, firm, inflexible

**Continuing the Cell Cycle** After cytokinesis is complete, each cell enters the $G_1$ stage of interphase. The daughter cells are about equal in size—about half the size of the original cell. The activity of each cell continues because each has its own DNA and organelles. The cell cycle continues for each new cell.

**› Reading Check** *What is a cell plate?*

## Section 2 Review

**› KEY IDEAS**

1. **Describe** the five phases of the cell cycle.
2. **List** in order the four stages of mitosis and the changes that occur during each stage.
3. **Compare** the products of cytokinesis.

**CRITICAL THINKING**

4. **Evaluating Information** Why are individual chromosomes more difficult to see during interphase than they are during mitosis?
5. **Predicting Results** What would happen if the cell did not have spindle fibers?
6. **Making Connections** Compare cell division in prokaryotic cells with cell division in eukaryotic cells.

**ALTERNATIVE ASSESSMENT**

7. **Animated Flipbook** Make a series of drawings that show the cell cycle of a plant cell. Be sure to include the five phases of the cell cycle and the four stages of mitosis.

Section

# 3 Regulation

| Key Ideas | Key Terms | Why It Matters |
| --- | --- | --- |
| ❯ What are some factors that control cell growth and division?<br>❯ How do feedback signals affect the cell cycle?<br>❯ How does cancer relate to the cell cycle? | cancer<br>tumor | Understanding how to control cell growth could be the key to curing cancer! |

Your body grows when more cells are added to the tissues and organs that make up the body. To stay healthy, cells continue to divide as needed to replace or renew tissues. How is the cell cycle regulated?

***The Living Environment***

**5.2i** Gene mutations in a cell can result in uncontrolled cell division, called cancer. Exposure of cells to certain chemicals and radiation increases mutations and thus increases the chance of cancer.

## Controls

Scientists study the cell cycle by observing cells in a culture medium. When a few healthy cells are placed in a dish with plenty of nutrients, they divide rapidly. But when they come in contact with one another or with the edge of the dish, the cells stop dividing.

These observations apply to real life. For example, when you cut your skin or break a bone, your cells start growing and dividing more rapidly to repair the wounds. The cells shown in **Figure 7** will begin dividing to replace the cells cut by the scalpel. As more cells form, the new cells come into contact with each other and close the wound. When the wound is healed, the cells slow down or stop dividing.

Cell division is highly controlled. ❯ **Cell growth and division depend on protein signals and other environmental signals.** Many proteins within the cell control the phases of the cell cycle. Signals from surrounding cells or even from other organs can also regulate cell growth and division. Environmental conditions, including the availability of nutrients, also affect the cell cycle.

❯ **Reading Check** ***What are two factors that affect the cell cycle?***

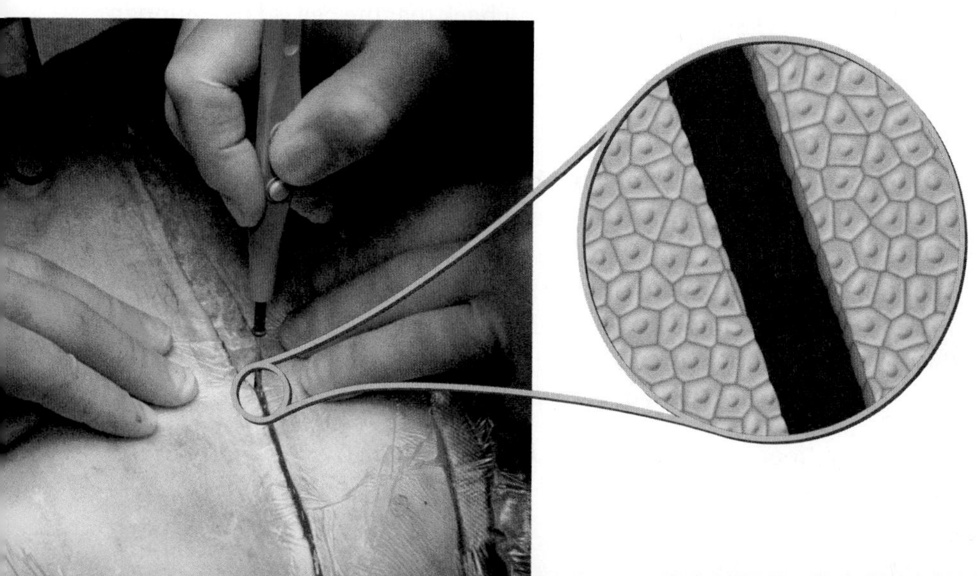

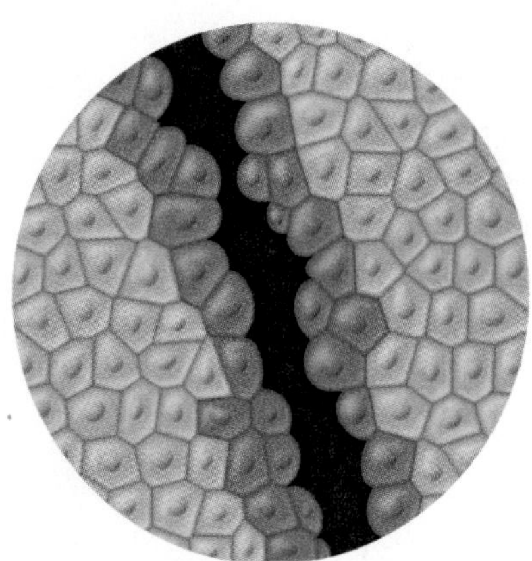

**Figure 7** The cells surrounding this surgical incision will begin dividing more often to fill in the gap. ❯ **What signals the cells to stop dividing when the wound is healed?**

Hands-On

# QuickLab

30 min

## UV and Sunblock

Prolonged exposure to the sun's UV radiation can damage DNA, disrupting the cell cycle and causing skin cancer.

### Procedure

1. In a dimly lit room, expose **UV-sensitive beads** to a bright, incandescent light source. Record any changes that you observe.
2. Thoroughly coat five beads in a thick covering of **sunblock.** Place these beads on one side of a **paper plate.** Place five uncoated beads on the other side.
3. Expose the plate to direct sunlight for a moment. Examine the beads in dim surroundings. Record any changes that you observe.

### Analysis

1. **Describe** the appearance of the beads before they were exposed to bright light sources.
2. **Determine** whether exposure to the artificial light source affected their appearance.
3. **Describe** how direct sunlight affected the beads.
4. CRITICAL THINKING **Making Inferences** How can using sunblock protect you from getting cancer?

READING TOOLBOX

**Cause and Effect** At each checkpoint, identify a cause that would result in a delay of the next phase of the cell cycle.

## Checkpoints

During the cell cycle, a cell undergoes an inspection process to ensure that the cell is ready for the next phase in the cell cycle. **› Feedback signals at key checkpoints in the cell cycle can delay or trigger the next phase of the cell cycle.** There are three main checkpoints in the cell cycle, as **Figure 8** shows.

**$G_1$ Checkpoint** Before the cell copies its DNA, the cell checks its surroundings. If conditions are favorable and the cell is healthy and large enough, the cell enters the synthesis phase. If conditions are not favorable, the cell goes into a resting period. Certain cells, such as some nerve and muscle cells, remain in this resting period for a long time. They do not divide very often.

**Figure 8** The eukaryotic cell cycle has three checkpoints. Many proteins play a role in controlling the cell cycle.

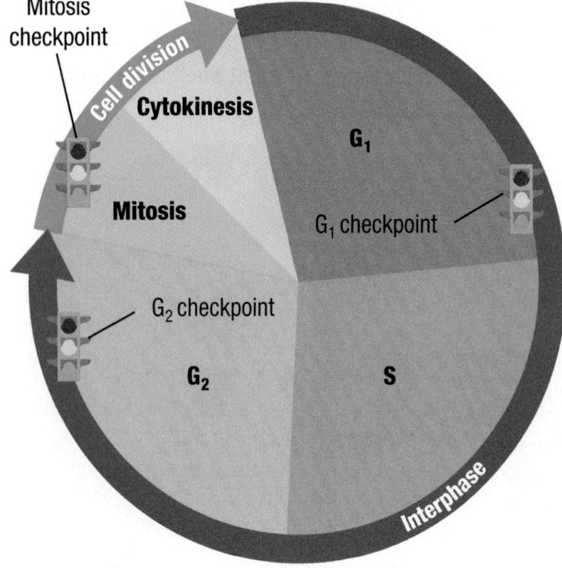


**$G_2$ Checkpoint** Before mitosis begins, the cell checks for any mistakes in the copied DNA. Enzymes correct mistakes that are found. This checkpoint ensures that the DNA of the daughter cells will be identical to the DNA of the original cell. Proteins also double-check that the cell is large enough to divide. If the cell passes the $G_2$ checkpoint, then the cell may begin to divide. Once past this checkpoint, proteins help to trigger mitosis.

**Mitosis Checkpoint** During the metaphase stage of mitosis, chromosomes line up at the equator. At this point, the cell checks that the chromosomes are properly attached to the spindle fibers. Without this point, the sister chromatids of one or more chromosomes may not separate properly. This checkpoint ensures that the genetic material is distributed equally between the daughter cells.

**› Reading Check** ***What happens at the $G_2$ checkpoint?***

## Cancer

Each year, more than 1 million Americans are diagnosed with cancer. **Cancer** is a group of severe and sometimes fatal diseases that are caused by uncontrolled cell growth. **> Uncontrolled cell growth and division can result in masses of cells that invade and destroy healthy tissues.** Preventing or curing cancer requires an understanding of how a healthy person's cells can become cancerous.

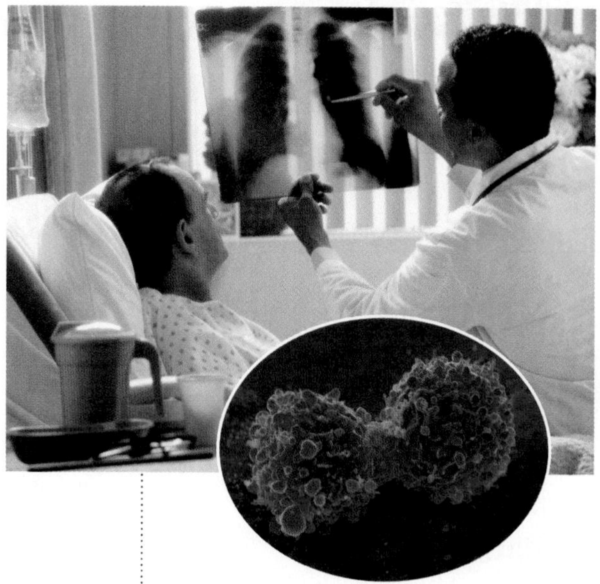

**Figure 9** A doctor often can see a lung tumor on an X ray. Tumors are masses of cells (inset) that divide out of control.

**Loss of Control** Normally, a cell responds properly to signals and controls. However, damage to a cell's DNA can cause the cell to respond improperly or to stop responding. The cell cycle can no longer be controlled. The defective cell divides and produces more defective cells, such as the cells in **Figure 9.** Eventually, these cells can form a mass called a **tumor.**

**Development** A *benign tumor* does not spread to other parts of the body and can often be removed by surgery. A *malignant tumor* invades and destroys nearby healthy tissues and organs. Malignant tumors, or cancers, can break loose from their tissue of origin and grow throughout the body. This process is called *metastasis.* Once a cancer has metastasized, it becomes more difficult to treat.

**cancer** a group of diseases characterized by uncontrolled growth and spread of abnormal cells

**tumor** a growth that arises from normal tissue but that grows abnormally in rate and structure and lacks a function

**Treatment** Some cancers can be treated by using drugs that kill the fast-growing cancer cells. Because drugs are chemicals, this method of treatment is called *chemotherapy,* or "chemo" for short. Some cancers can be treated by surgery to remove the affected organ. In radiation therapy, high-energy rays are focused on an area in order to destroy cancerous cells. Doctors choose the most effective treatment for a particular kind of cancer.

**Prevention** The best way to prevent cancer is to avoid things that can cause cancer. Ultraviolet radiation in sunlight can damage genes that control the cell cycle. Chemicals in cigarette smoke also affect how cell growth and division is regulated.

**> Reading Check** ***What causes cells to lose control of the cell cycle?***

## Section 3 Review

### > KEY IDEAS

1. **Describe** the effect of environmental conditions on the cell cycle.
2. **Summarize** the events of each of the three checkpoints of the cell cycle.
3. **Distinguish** between a benign tumor and a malignant tumor.

### CRITICAL THINKING

4. **Applying Concepts** Propose an example of a situation in which an environmental condition might signal cell division in an organism.
5. **Logical Reasoning** The three checkpoint steps that a cell goes through allow the cell cycle to proceed correctly. What would happen if these steps did not function properly?

### WRITING FOR SCIENCE

6. **Research** Use library resources or the Internet to research factors that increase the risk of cancer and the types of cancer that they could lead to. Why are factors in lifestyle or the environment difficult to identify? How can people protect themselves from exposure to known risk factors?

Skills Practice

# Chapter 10 Lab

## Objectives

- Examine the dividing root-tip cells of an onion.
- Identify the phase of mitosis that each cell in an onion root tip is undergoing.
- Determine the relative length of time each phase of mitosis takes in onion root-tip cells.

## Materials

- compound light microscope
- prepared microscope slide of a longitudinal section of *Allium* (onion) root tip

## Safety

# Mitosis in Plant Cells

Look at the photograph of a longitudinal section of an onion root tip. In the tips of plant roots and shoots, mitosis is ongoing in growth regions called *meristems.* Mitosis occurs in four phases: prophase, metaphase, anaphase, and telophase. In this lab, you will determine the relative length of time each phase of mitosis takes in onion root-tip cells. To do this, you will count the number of cells undergoing each phase of mitosis in the meristem of an onion root section.

## Procedure

### Identify the Phases of Mitosis

1. **CAUTION: Put on safety goggles, gloves, and a lab apron.**
2. **CAUTION: Handle glass slides and cover slips with care.** Using low power on your microscope, bring the meristem region on your slide into focus.
3. Examine the meristem carefully. Choose a sample of about 50 cells. Look for a group of cells that appear to have been actively dividing at the time that the slide was made. The cells will appear to be in rows, so it should be easy to keep track of them. The dark-staining bodies are the chromosomes.
4. For each of the cells in your sample, identify the stage of mitosis. Make a data table of the relative duration of each phase of mitosis. Record your observations in the data table.

*Relative Duration of Each Phase of Mitosis*

| *Phase of mitosis* | *Tally marks* | *Count* | *Percentage of all cells* | *Time (min)* |
|---|---|---|---|---|
| *Prophase* | | | | |
| *Metaphase* | | | | |
| *Anaphase* | | | | |
| *Telophase* | | | | |

### Calculate the Relative Length of Each Phase

5. When you have classified each cell in your sample, count the tally marks for each phase and fill in the "Count" column. In which phase of mitosis was the number of cells the greatest? In which phase of mitosis was the number of cells the fewest?

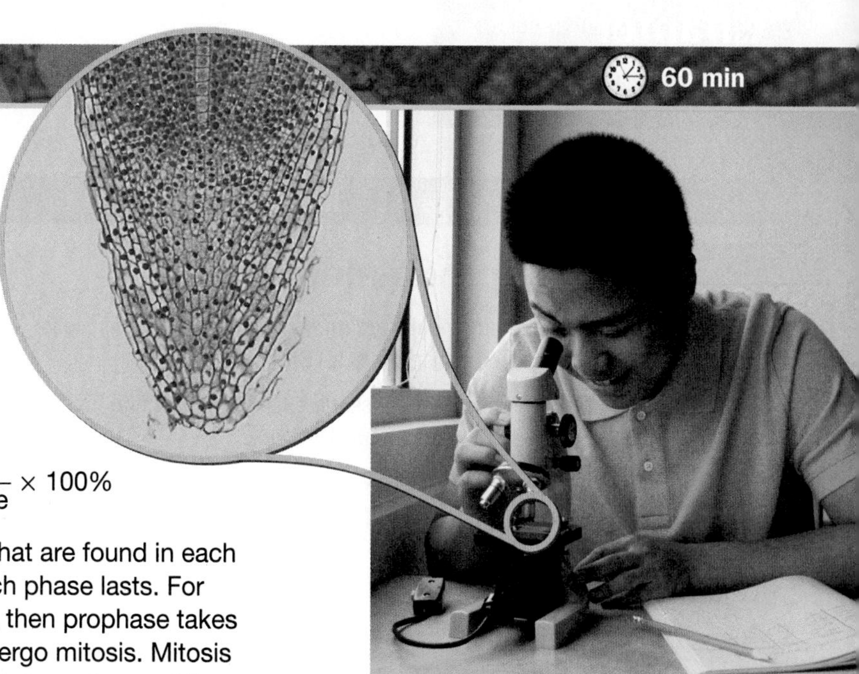

6 Calculate what percentage of all cells were found in each phase. Divide the number of cells in a phase by the total number of cells in your sample, and multiply by 100%. Enter these figures under the "Percentage" column.

$$\text{Percentage} = \frac{\text{number of cells in phase}}{\text{total number of cells in sample}} \times 100\%$$

7 The percentage of the total number of cells that are found in each phase can be used to estimate how long each phase lasts. For example, if 25% of the cells are in prophase, then prophase takes 25% of the total time that a cell takes to undergo mitosis. Mitosis in onion cells takes about 80 min. Using this information and the percentages you have just determined, calculate the time for each phase and record it in your data table.

$$\text{Duration of phase (in minutes)} = \frac{\text{percentage}}{100} \times 80 \text{ min}$$

8 Make another table to record the data for the entire class. Collect and add the counts for each phase of mitosis for the entire class. Fill in the percentage and time information by using these data.

*Class Data*

| *Phase of mitosis* | *Count* | *Percentage of all cells* | *Duration (min)* |
|---|---|---|---|
| *Prophase* | | | |
| *Metaphase* | | | |
| *Anaphase* | | | |
| *Telophase* | | | |

9 Clean up your lab materials according to your teacher's instructions. Wash your hands before leaving the lab.

## Analyze and Conclude

1. **Identifying Structures** What color are the chromosomes stained?
2. **Recognizing Relationships** How can you distinguish between early and late anaphase?
3. SCIENTIFIC METHODS **Making Systematic Observations** According to your data table, which phase takes the least amount of time? Which phase of mitosis lasts the longest? Why might this phase require more time than other phases of mitosis do?
4. SCIENTIFIC METHODS **Summarizing Data** How do your data compare with the data of the entire class?
5. SCIENTIFIC METHODS **Critiquing Procedures** In this investigation, you assumed that the percentage of the total time that any given phase takes is equal to the percentage of the total number of cells in that phase at any moment. Why might this not be true for very small samples of cells?

## Extensions

6. **Applying Methods** Cancerous tissue is composed of cells undergoing uncontrolled, rapid cell division. How could you develop a procedure to identify cancerous tissue by counting the number of cells undergoing mitosis?

# Chapter 10 Summary

| Key Ideas | Key Terms |
|---|---|
| **1 Cell Reproduction**<br>› Because larger cells are more difficult to maintain, cells divide when they grow to a certain size.<br>› Many proteins help package eukaryotic DNA into highly condensed chromosome structures.<br>› All newly-formed cells require DNA, so before a cell divides, a copy of its DNA is made for each daughter cell.<br>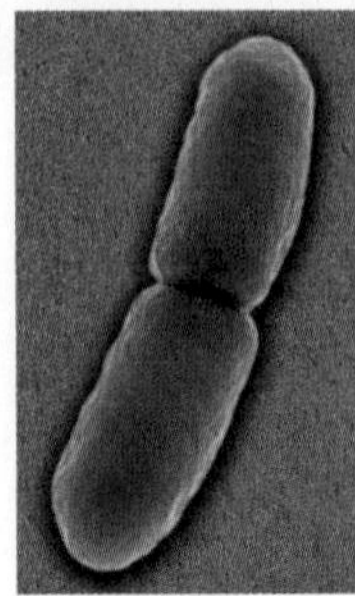 | **gene** (224)<br>**chromosome** (224)<br>**chromatin** (224)<br>**histone** (224)<br>**nucleosome** (224)<br>**chromatid** (225)<br>**centromere** (225) |
| **2 Mitosis**<br>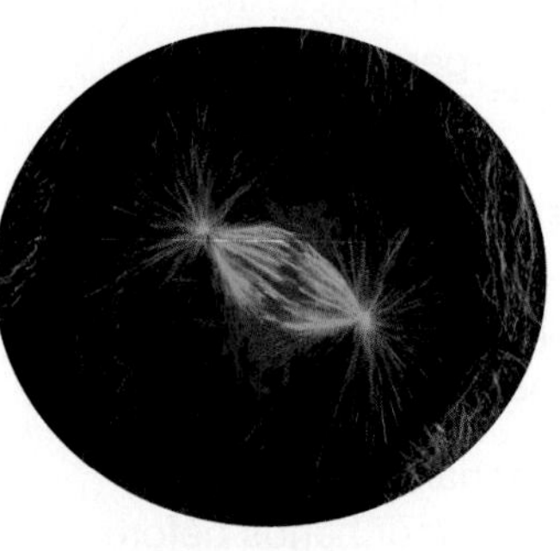<br>› The life of a eukaryotic cell cycles through phases of growth, DNA replication, preparation for cell division, and division of the nucleus and cytoplasm.<br>› Mitosis is a continuous process that can be observed in four stages: prophase, metaphase, anaphase, and telophase.<br>› During cytokinesis, the cell membrane grows into the center of the cell and divides it into two daughter cells of equal size. Each daughter cell has about half of the parent's cytoplasm and organelles. | **cell cycle** (228)<br>**interphase** (228)<br>**mitosis** (229)<br>**cytokinesis** (229)<br>**spindle** (230)<br>**centrosome** (230) |
| **3 Regulation**<br>› Cell growth and division depend on protein signals and other environmental signals.<br>› Feedback signals at key checkpoints in the cell cycle can delay or trigger the next phase of the cell cycle.<br>› Uncontrolled cell growth and division results in tumors, which can invade surrounding tissues and cause cancer.<br>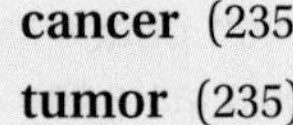<br> | **cancer** (235)<br>**tumor** (235) |

Chapter 10

The Living Environment

# Regents Exam Practice

**PART A: Answer all questions in this part.**

*Directions:* For each statement or question, write on your separate answer sheet the number of the word or expression that best completes the statement or answers the question.

**1** Hereditary information is stored inside the

(1) ribosomes, which have chromosomes that contain many genes
(2) ribosomes, which have genes that contain many chromosomes
(3) nucleus, which has chromosomes that contain many genes
(4) nucleus, which has genes that contain many chromosomes

**2** Which sequence of terms represents a decrease from the greatest number of structures to the least number of structures present in a cell?

(1) nucleus → gene → chromosome
(2) gene → nucleus → chromosome
(3) gene → chromosome → nucleus
(4) chromosome → gene → nucleus

**3** Which statements best describe the relationship between the terms chromosomes, genes, and nuclei?

(1) Chromosomes are found on genes. Genes are found in nuclei.
(2) Chromosomes are found in nuclei. Nuclei are found in genes.
(3) Genes are found on chromosomes. Chromosomes are found in nuclei.
(4) Genes are found in nuclei. Nuclei are found in chromosomes.

**4** Which of the following is a reason that the size of a cell is limited?

(1) Larger cells are easier for an organism to produce than smaller cells.
(2) The cell's ability to exchange substances is limited by its surface area–to-volume ratio.
(3) The larger the cell becomes, the easier it is for substances to reach where they are needed.
(4) The size of a cell has no relationship to the cell's function in a multicellular organism.

**5** What factors can cause cells to divide in a culture medium?

(1) protein signals
(2) lack of nutrients
(3) contact with other cells
(4) contact with the edge of the dish

**6** What is the importance of feedback signals at key checkpoints within the cell cycle?

(1) to indicate the end of the cycle
(2) to indicate the presence of proteins
(3) to identify the meiosis and mitosis indicators
(4) to delay or trigger the next phase of the cycle

**7** What is a gene?

(1) a large molecule of chromosomes
(2) a protein that directs the activity of a cell
(3) a segment of DNA that codes for RNA and protein
(4) a segment of RNA that moves from the nucleus to the cytoplasm

**8** What might happen if cytokinesis were omitted from the cell cycle?

(1) The daughter cells would die.
(2) The cell would lose its mitochondria.
(3) The daughter cells would not have nuclei.
(4) The cell would not divide into two daughter cells.

**9** Mitosis could not proceed if a mutation interrupted the assembly of the

(1) cell wall.
(2) spindle fibers.
(3) cell membrane.
(4) nuclear envelope.

**10** The diagram below illustrates the process of cell division. What is the significance of anaphase in this process?

4 chromosomes

Interphase (parent cell) → Prophase → Metaphase → Anaphase → Telophase → Interphase (daughter cells)

(1) Anaphase usually ensures that each daughter cell has the same number of chromosomes as the parent cell.
(2) Anaphase usually ensures that each daughter cell has twice as many chromosomes as the parent cell.
(3) In anaphase, the cell splits in half.
(4) In anaphase, the DNA is being replicated.

**The chromosome content of a skin cell that is about to form two new skin cells is represented in the diagram below.**

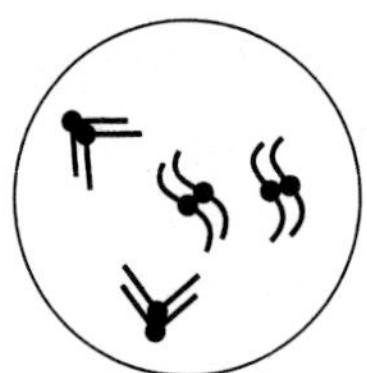

**11** Which diagram best represents the chromosomes that would be found in the two new skin cells produced as a result of this process?

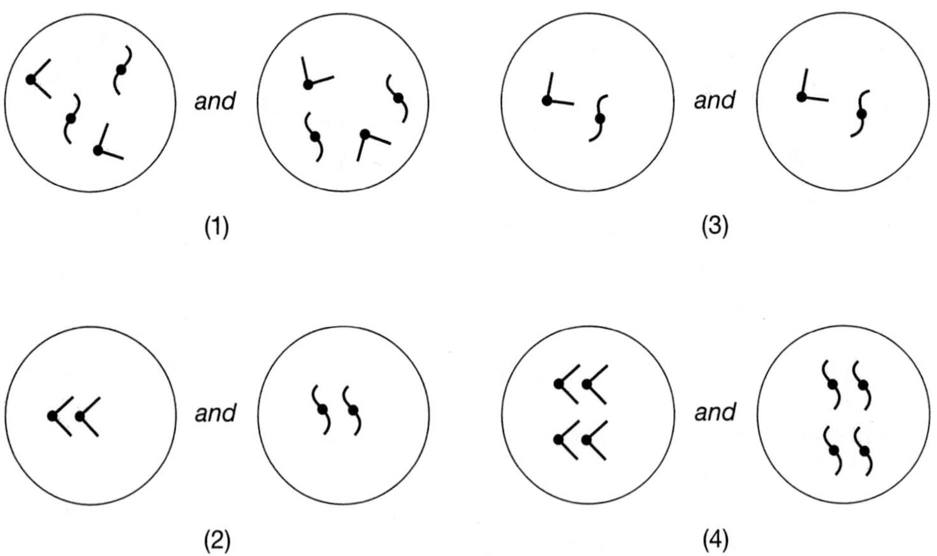

## PART B

**12** Which activity most directly involves the process represented in the diagram below?

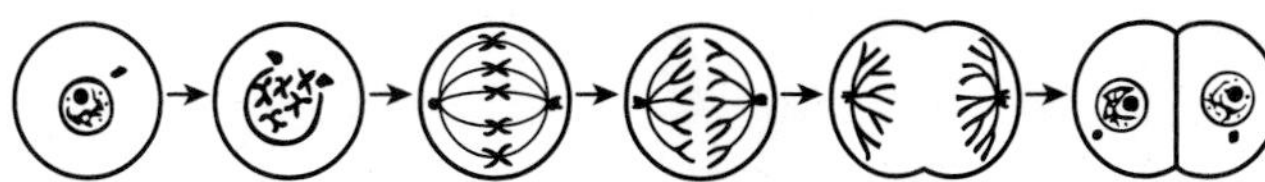

(1) a gamete reproducing sexually
(2) a white blood cell engulfing bacteria
(3) a zygote being produced in an ovary
(4) an animal repairing damaged tissue

**13** The diagram below represents single-celled organism A dividing by mitosis to form cells B and C. Cells A, B, and C all produced protein X. What can best be inferred from this observation?

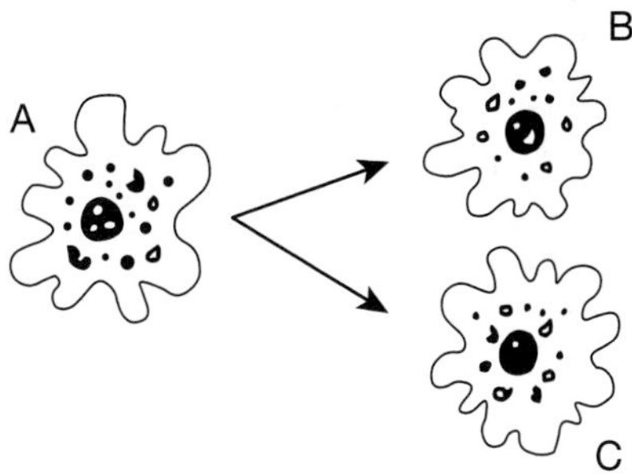


(1) Protein X is found in all organisms.
(2) The gene for protein X is found in single celled organisms, only.
(3) Cells A, B, and C ingested food containing the gene to produce protein X.
(4) The gene to produce protein X was passed from cell A to cells B and C.

**14** Arrange the following structures from largest to smallest.

a chromosome

a nucleus

a gene

Largest

↓

Smallest

UNIT 4

# Heredity

### The Living Environment

**Standard 1** Students will use mathematical analysis, scientific inquiry, and engineering design, as appropriate, to pose questions, seek answers, and develop solutions.

**Key Idea 3** The observations made while testing proposed explanations, when analyzed using conventional and invented methods, provide new insights into natural phenomena.

**Standard 4** Students will understand and apply scientific concepts, principles, and theories pertaining to the physical setting and living environment and recognize the historical development of ideas in science.

**Key Idea 1** Living things are both similar to and different from each other and from nonliving things.

**Key Idea 2** Organisms inherit genetic information in a variety of ways that result in continuity of structure and function between parents and offspring.

**Key Idea 3** Individual organisms and species change over time

**Key Idea 4** The continuity of life is sustained through reproduction and development.

**Key Idea 5** Organisms maintain a dynamic equilibrium that sustains life.

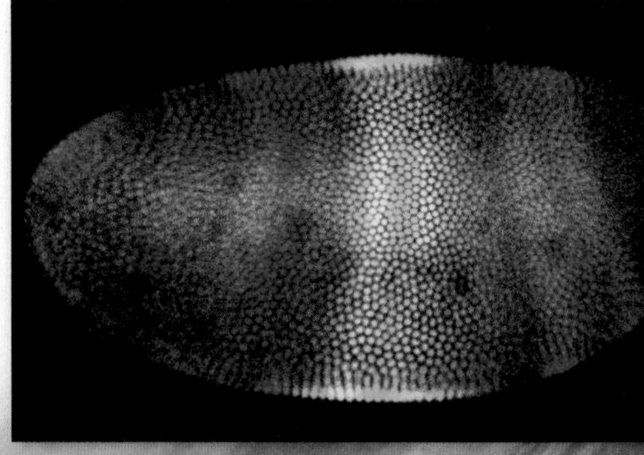

Fruit fly embryo, marked to show pattern of genes being expressed

Eggs of the red-eyed tree frog stuck to the underside of a leaf

Emperor penguin parents with chick

# DISCOVERIES IN SCIENCE

# Heredity and Genetics

## 1865

Gregor Mendel publishes the results of his studies of genetic inheritance in pea plants. Although his work is not widely known until much later, Mendel is remembered as the founder of the science of genetics.

Gregor Mendel

## 1879

After staining cells with Perkins dye and viewing them under a microscope, Walter Fleming identifies chromatin in cells. Soon after, he observes and describes all stages of mitosis, using terms such as *metaphase, anaphase and telophase.*

## 1905

Nettie Maria Stephens describes how human gender is determined by the X and Y chromosomes.

Nettie Stevens

## 1909

*The Elements of Heredity,* by Wilhelm Johannsen, a Danish biologist, is revised and translated into German. In the book, Johannsen develops many of the concepts of modern genetics, particularly phenotype and genotype. This book becomes a founding text of genetics.

## 1913

Alfred Henry Sturtevant, an undergraduate student at Columbia University, determines the relative location of genes on a fruit fly chromosome. He publishes a genetic map showing the order of genes and their relative distance from each other.

## 1915

Thomas Hunt publishes the book *Mechanism of Mendelian Heredity,* which explains the phenomenon of sex-linked traits observed in fruit flies.

***Drosophila melanogaster*** **(fruit fly)**

## 1989

Francis Collins and Lap-Chee Tsui identify a mutant version of a gene on chromosome 7 that causes cystic fibrosis. Discovery of the gene leads to the development of tests that can determine whether potential parents are carriers of the gene.

## 2003

The Human Genome Project is completed. Research teams around the world collaborated to identify all genes and decode the sequence of all DNA in human cells.

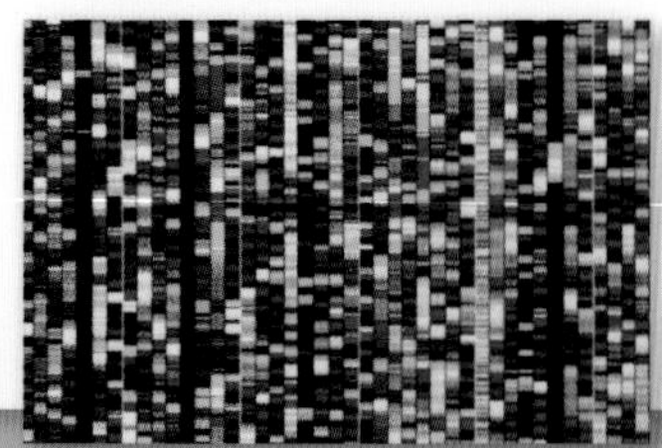

**Genetic sequences on a computer screen**

Albino peacock

# BIOLOGY CAREER



## Genetics Researcher

**Rob Desalle**

Rob DeSalle is a curator in the Division of Invertebrate Zoology at the American Museum of Natural History in New York City. His current research focuses on molecular evolution in a variety of organisms, including pathogenic bacteria and insects.

DeSalle studies molecular evolution through comparative genomics, which is the study of similarities and differences between the genomes of various species or strains within species. Comparing the genomes of species can help determine how the species are related.

DeSalle also helped found the Conservation Genetics Program at the American Museum of Natural History. This program uses the tools of molecular genetics to help protect wildlife around the world. For example, DeSalle helped develop a genetic test to determine if caviar sold in the United States was illegally harvested from endangered species of sturgeon in the Caspian Sea.

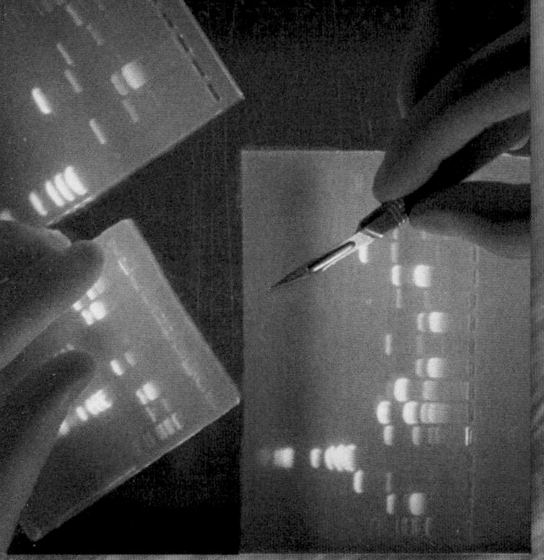

Genetic analysis by gel electrophoresis

Chapter 11

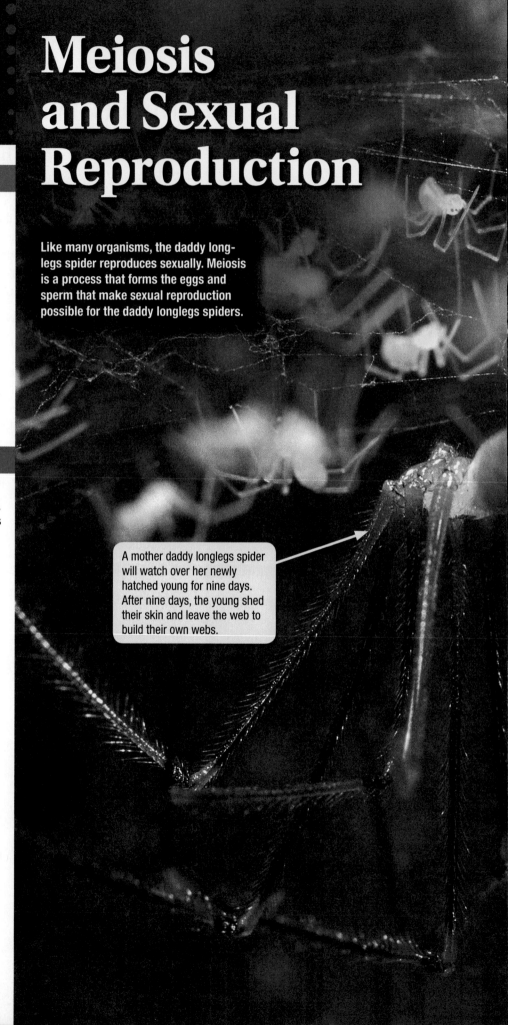

# Meiosis and Sexual Reproduction

## Preview

**1 Reproduction**
- Asexual Reproduction
- Sexual Reproduction
- Chromosome Number

**2 Meiosis**
- Stages of Meiosis
- Comparing Mitosis and Meiosis
- Genetic Variation

**3 Multicellular Life Cycles**
- Diploid Life Cycle
- Haploid Life Cycle
- Alternation of Generations

## Why It Matters

You know that in sexual reproduction, an egg and a sperm combine to form a new organism. But how are eggs and sperm produced? In this chapter, you will learn about a special type of cell division called *meiosis.*

Like many organisms, the daddy long-legs spider reproduces sexually. Meiosis is a process that forms the eggs and sperm that make sexual reproduction possible for the daddy longlegs spiders.

A mother daddy longlegs spider will watch over her newly hatched young for nine days. After nine days, the young shed their skin and leave the web to build their own webs.

***The Living Environment***

**Standard 4** Students will understand and apply scientific concepts, principles, and theories pertaining to the physical setting and living environment and recognize the historical development of ideas in science.

**Key Idea 2** Organisms inherit genetic information in a variety of ways that result in continuity of structure and function between parents and offspring. ***Major Understandings* - 2.1c, 2.1d, 2.1e**

**Key Idea 3** Individual organisms and species change over time. ***Major Understandings* - 3.1c**

**Key Idea 4** The continuity of life is sustained through reproduction and development. ***Major Understandings* - 4.1b, 4.1c**

The newly hatched spiders, or *prenymphs,* may all look alike. However, because they formed from sexual reproduction, they are all genetically different.

# InquiryLab

## Pollen Up Close

Pollen is produced in the male reproductive part of a flower called the *anther*. Pollen develops from cells called *microspores*. The mature pollen grain encloses two nuclei. Each nucleus contains half of the number of chromosomes found in most cells of the mature, flower-producing plant.

### Procedure

1. **CAUTION: Handle glass slides with care.** Place a **prepared slide of a lily anther** on the **microscope** stage. Examine the slide under low power.
2. Identify the large chambers called *pollen sacs*. How many can you find in your cross-sectional view? Are they whole or broken? Make a sketch of what you see.
3. Depending upon the stage of development, the pollen sacs will contain either clustered cells in various stages of division or mature grains of pollen. You can identify a pollen grain by its two stained nuclei and textured coat. Select several representative cells within the pollen sac. Make a sketch of each cell.

### Analysis

1. **Describe** the structure of the lily anther.
2. **Determine** whether the observed pollen sacs contain dividing cells, pollen grains, or both.
3. **Describe** the appearance of the nuclei in either the dividing cells or the pollen grains.
4. **Explain** what advantage is achieved by halving the chromosome number in pollen nuclei.

**These reading tools can help you learn the material in this chapter. For more information on how to use these and other tools, see Appendix: Reading and Study Skills.**

## Using Words

**Key-Term Fold** A key-term fold is a useful tool for studying definitions of key terms in a chapter. Each tab can contain a key term on one side and its definition on the other.

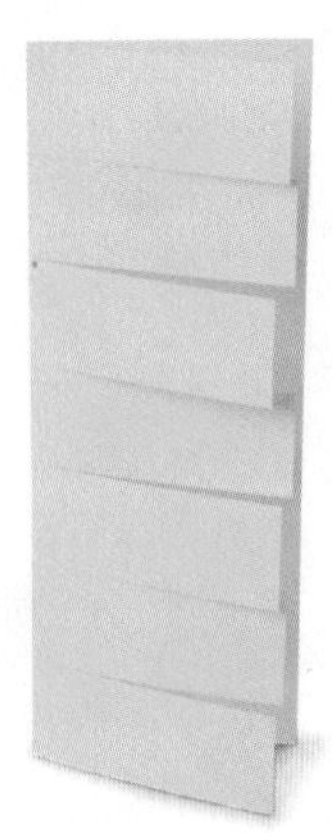

**Your Turn** Make a key-term fold for the terms of this chapter.

1. Fold a sheet of lined notebook paper in half from left to right.
2. Using scissors, cut along every third line from the right edge of the paper to the center fold to make tabs.

## Using Language

**Comparisons** Comparing is a way of looking for the similarities between different things. Contrasting is a way of looking for the differences. Certain words and phrases can help you determine if things are being compared or contrasted. Comparison words include *and, like, just as,* and *in the same way.* Contrast words include *however, unlike, in contrast,* and *on the other hand.*

**Your Turn** In the following sentences, find the things that are being compared or contrasted.

1. Like mitosis, meiosis is a process that reproduces new cells.
2. In contrast to many other reptiles, the Burmese python does not reproduce sexually.

## Taking Notes

**Two-Column Notes** Two-column notes can help you summarize the key ideas of a topic, chapter, or process. The left column of the table contains key ideas. The right column contains details and examples of each main idea.

**Your Turn** As you read the chapter, create two-column notes that summarize the key ideas of this chapter.

1. Write the key ideas in the left-hand column. The key ideas are listed in the section openers. Include one key idea in each row.
2. As you read the section, add detailed notes and examples in the right-hand column. Be sure to put these details and examples in your own words.

*Meiosis and Sexual Reproduction*

| *Key Ideas* | *Details and Examples* |
|---|---|
| | |
| | |
| | |

Section

# 1 Reproduction

| Key Ideas | Key Terms | Why It Matters |
|---|---|---|
| ➤ In asexual reproduction, how does the offspring compare to the parent?<br>➤ In sexual reproduction, how does the offspring compare to the parent?<br>➤ Why are chromosomes important to an organism? | gamete<br>zygote<br>diploid<br>haploid<br>homologous chromosomes | Living organisms produce offspring. How closely the offspring resemble their parents depends on how the organism reproduces. |

*Reproduction* is the process of producing offspring. Some offspring are produced by two parents, and others are produced by just one parent. Some organisms look exactly like their parents, and others look very similar. Whether an organism is identical or similar to its parent is determined by the way that the organism reproduces.

## Asexual Reproduction

In *asexual reproduction,* a single parent passes a complete copy of its genetic information to each of its offspring. ➤ **An individual formed by asexual reproduction is genetically identical to its parent.**

Prokaryotes reproduce asexually by a kind of cell division called *binary fission.* Many unicellular eukaryotes also reproduce asexually. Amoebas reproduce by splitting into two or more individuals of about equal size. Some multicellular eukaryotes, such as starfish, go through fragmentation. *Fragmentation* is a kind of reproduction in which the body breaks into several pieces. Some or all of these fragments regrow missing parts and develop into complete adults.

Other animals, such as the hydra shown in **Figure 1,** go through *budding.* In budding, new individuals split off from existing ones. Some plants, such as potatoes, can form whole new plants from parts of stems. Other plants can reproduce from roots or leaves. Some crustaceans, such as water fleas, reproduce by parthenogenesis. *Parthenogenesis* is a process in which a female makes a viable egg that grows into an adult without being fertilized by a male.

➤ **Reading Check** *What is fragmentation? (See the Appendix for answers to Reading Checks.)*

***The Living Environment***
**Standard 4**

**2.1c** Hereditary information is contained in genes, located in the chromosomes of each cell. An inherited trait of an individual can be determined by one or by many genes, and a single gene can influence more than one trait. A human cell contains many thousands of different genes in its nucleus.

**2.1d** In asexually reproducing organisms, all the genes come from a single parent. Asexually produced offspring are normally genetically identical to the parent.

**2.1e** In sexually reproducing organisms, the new individual receives half of the genetic information from its mother (via the egg) and half from its father (via the sperm). Sexually produced offspring often resemble, but are not identical to, either of their parents.

**4.1b** Some organisms reproduce asexually with all the genetic information coming from one parent. Other organisms reproduce sexually with half the genetic information typically contributed by each parent. Cloning is the production of identical genetic copies.

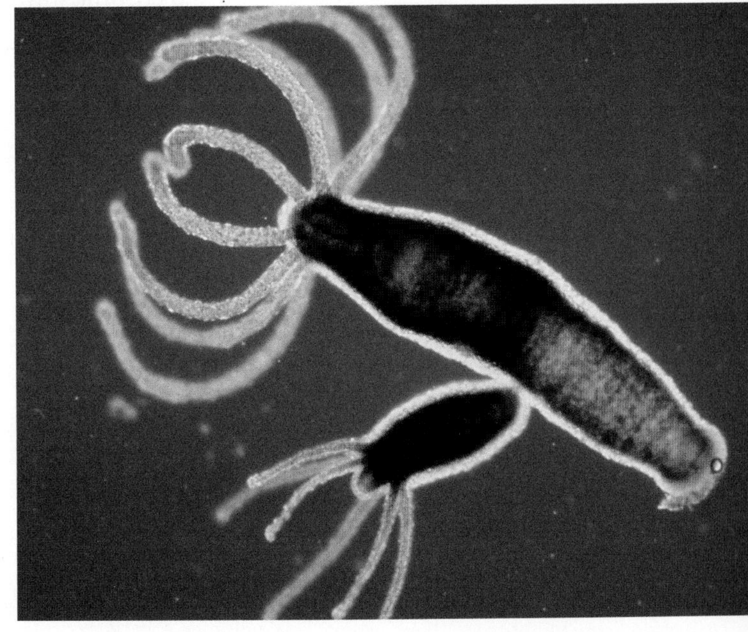

**Figure 1** This hydra is in the process of reproducing asexually. The smaller hydra budding from the parent is genetically identical to the parent.

## Sexual Reproduction

Most eukaryotic organisms reproduce sexually. ➤ **In *sexual reproduction*, two parents give genetic material to produce offspring that are genetically different from their parents.** Each parent produces a reproductive cell, called a **gamete.** A gamete from one parent fuses with a gamete from the other parent, as **Figure 2** shows. The resulting cell, called a **zygote,** has a combination of genetic material from both parents. This process is called *fertilization.* Because both parents give genetic material, the offspring has traits of both parents but is not exactly like either parent.

**gamete** (GAM eet) a haploid reproductive cell that unites with another haploid reproductive cell to form a zygote

**zygote** (ZIE GOHT) the cell that results from the fusion of gametes

**diploid** a cell that contains two haploid sets of chromosomes

**haploid** describes a cell, nucleus, or organism that has only one set of unpaired chromosomes

**homologous chromosomes** (hoh MAHL uh guhs) chromosomes that have the same sequence of genes, that have the same structure, and that pair during meiosis

**Germ Cells and Somatic Cells** Recall that the cells of a multicellular organism are often specialized for certain functions. Muscle cells, for example, contract and move your body. Cells that are specialized for sexual reproduction are called *germ cells.* Only germ cells can produce gametes. Other body cells are called *somatic cells.* Somatic cells do not participate in sexual reproduction.

**Advantages of Sexual Reproduction** Asexual reproduction is the simplest, most efficient method of reproduction. Asexual reproduction allows organisms to produce many offspring in a short period of time without using energy to make gametes or to find a mate. But the genetic material of these organisms varies little between individuals, so they may be at a disadvantage in a changing environment. Sexual reproduction, in contrast, produces genetically diverse individuals. A population of diverse organisms is more likely to have some individuals that survive a major environmental change.

SCI LINKS.
**www.scilinks.org**
Topic: Sexual and Asexual Reproduction
Code: HX81386

## Chromosome Number

Genes are located on chromosomes. ➤ **Each chromosome has thousands of genes that play an important role in determining how an organism develops and functions.** Each species has a characteristic number of chromosomes. As shown in **Figure 3,** mosquitoes have only 6 chromosomes in each cell. Chimpanzees have 48 chromosomes in each cell. Some ferns have more than 500! An organism must have exactly the right number of chromosomes. If an organism has too many or too few chromosomes, the organism may not develop and function properly.

In humans, each cell has two copies of 23 chromosomes for a total of 46. When fertilization happens, two cells combine to form a zygote, which still has only 46 chromosomes. Why is the number the same? The gametes that form a zygote have only *one* copy of each chromosome, or one set of 23 chromosomes. This reduction of chromosomes in gametes keeps the chromosome number of human somatic cells at a constant 46.

➤ **Reading Check** ***What kind of cells do germ cells produce?***

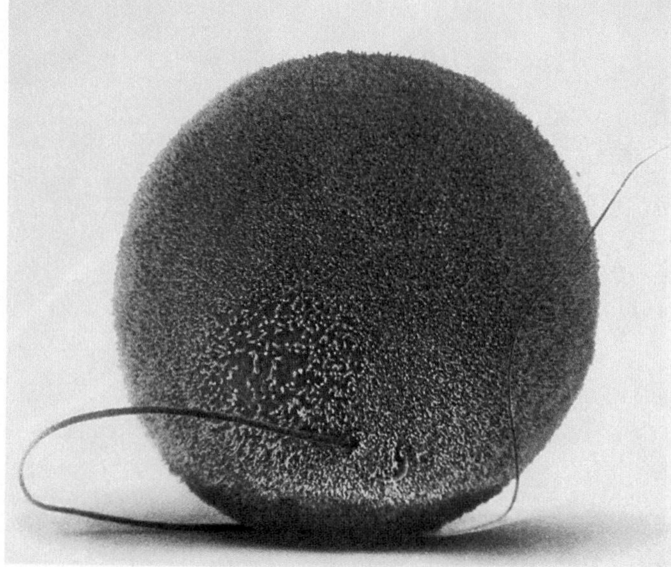

**Figure 2** Two gametes, an egg and a sperm, combine during fertilization to form a zygote. ➤ **What types of cells produce gametes?**

**Haploid and Diploid Cells** A cell, such as a somatic cell, that has two sets of chromosomes is **diploid.** A cell is **haploid** if it has one set of chromosomes. Gametes are haploid cells. The symbol $n$ is used to represent the number of chromosomes in one set. Human gametes have 23 chromosomes, so $n = 23$. The diploid number in somatic cells is written as $2n$. Human somatic cells have 46 chromosomes ($2n = 46$).

**Homologous Chromosomes** Each diploid cell has pairs of chromosomes made up of two homologous chromosomes. **Homologous chromosomes** are chromosomes that are similar in size, in shape, and in kinds of genes that they contain. Each chromosome in a homologous pair comes from one of the two parents. In humans, one set of 23 chromosomes comes from the mother, and one set comes from the father. Homologous chromosomes can carry different forms of genes. For example, flower color in peas is determined by a gene on one of its chromosomes. The form of this gene can be white or purple. The cells of each pea plant will have two flower-color genes, one on each of the chromosomes that carry the flower-color gene. Both could be genes for white flower color, or both could be genes for purple flower color. Or one gene could be for white color, and the other could be for purple color.

**Autosomes and Sex Chromosomes** *Autosomes* are chromosomes with genes that do not determine the sex of an individual. *Sex chromosomes* have genes that determine the sex of an individual. In humans and many other organisms, the two sex chromosomes are referred to as the *X* and *Y chromosomes.* The genes that cause a zygote to develop into a male are located on the Y chromosome. Human males have one X chromosome and one Y chromosome (XY), and human females have two X chromosomes (XX).

**Chromosome Number of Various Organisms**

| Organism | Number (2*n*) of chromosomes |
|---|---|
| *Penicillium* | 1–4 |
| *Saccharomyces* (yeast) | 16 |
| Mosquito | 6 |
| Housefly | 12 |
| Garden pea | 14 |
| Corn | 20 |
| Fern | 480–1,020 |
| Frog | 26 |
| Human | 46 |
| Orangutan | 48 |
| Dog | 78 |

**Figure 3**
Different species have different numbers of chromosomes.

**READING TOOLBOX**

**Key-Term Fold** On the back of your key-term fold, write a definition in your own words for the key terms in this section.

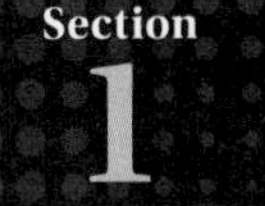

Section 1 Review

**KEY IDEAS**

1. **Compare** the offspring in asexual reproduction with the parent.
2. **Describe** how the offspring in sexual reproduction compares genetically with its parent.
3. **Compare** the number of sets of chromosomes between a haploid cell and a diploid cell.
4. **Explain** why chromosomes are important for organisms.

**CRITICAL THINKING**

5. **Inferring Relationships** Why are haploid cells important in sexual reproduction?
6. **Forming Reasoned Opinions** Do you agree or disagree that homologous chromosomes occur in gametes? Explain.

**METHODS OF SIENCE**

7. **Evaluating Hypotheses** A student states that organisms that reproduce asexually are at a disadvantage in a stable environment. If you agree with this hypothesis, name one or more of its strengths. If you disagree, name one or more of its weaknesses.

Section 2

# Meiosis

| Key Ideas | Key Terms | Why It Matters |
|---|---|---|
| ❯ What occurs during the stages of meiosis?<br>❯ How does the function of mitosis differ from the function of meiosis?<br>❯ What are three mechanisms of genetic variation? | meiosis<br>crossing-over<br>independent assortment | Meiosis allows genetic information from two parents to combine to form offspring that are different from both parents. |

***The Living Environment***
**Standard 4**

**2.1e** In sexually reproducing organisms, the new individual receives half of the genetic information from its mother (via the egg) and half from its father (via the sperm). Sexually produced offspring often resemble, but are not identical to, either of their parents.

**3.1c** Mutation and the sorting and recombining of genes during meiosis and fertilization result in a great variety of possible gene combinations.

**4.1c** The processes of meiosis and fertilization are key to sexual reproduction in a wide variety of organisms. The process of meiosis results in the production of eggs and sperm which each contain half of the genetic information. During fertilization, gametes unite to form a zygote, which contains the complete genetic information for the offspring.

Most cells that divide and produce new cells form two offspring cells that have the same number of chromosomes as the parent cell. How do haploid gametes form from a diploid germ cell? **Meiosis** is a form of cell division that produces daughter cells with half the number of chromosomes that are in the parent cell.

## Stages of Meiosis

Before meiosis begins, the chromosomes in the original cell are copied. Meiosis involves two divisions of the nucleus—meiosis I and meiosis II. ❯ **During meiosis, a diploid cell goes through two divisions to form four haploid cells.** In meiosis I, homologous chromosomes are separated. In meiosis II, the sister chromatids of each homologue are separated. As a result, four haploid cells are formed from the original diploid cell. **Figure 4** illustrates the steps of meiosis.

### Stages of Meiosis I

**1 Prophase I** Chromosomes condense. The nuclear envelope breaks down.

**2 Metaphase I** Pairs of homologous chromosomes move to the cell's equator.

**3 Anaphase I** Homologous chromosomes move to the cell's opposite poles.

**4 Telophase I** Chromosomes gather at the poles. The cytoplasm divides.

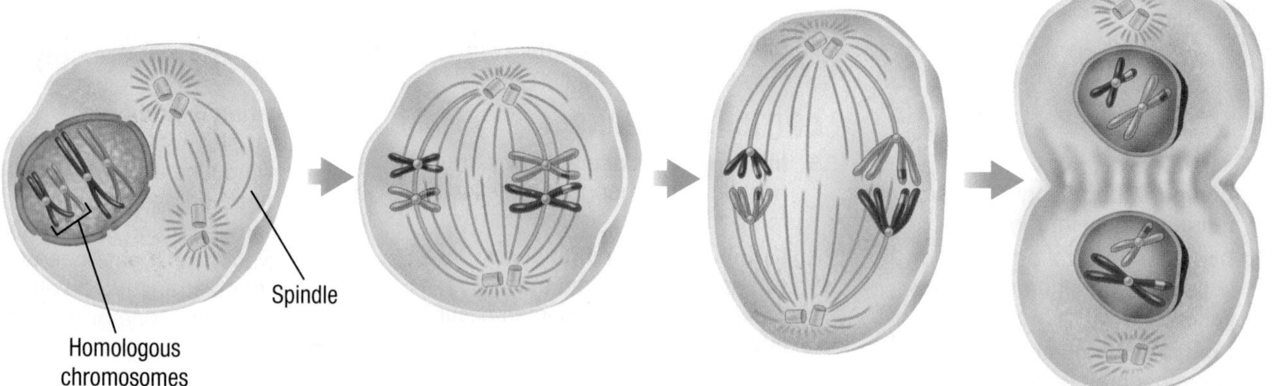

**Meiosis I** Meiosis begins with a diploid cell that has copied its chromosomes. The first phase is prophase I. ❶ During prophase I, the chromosomes condense, and the nuclear envelope breaks down. Homologous chromosomes pair. Chromatids exchange genetic material in a process called **crossing-over.** ❷ In metaphase I, the spindle moves the pairs of homologous chromosomes to the equator of the cell. The homologous chromosomes remain together. ❸ In anaphase I, the homologous chromosomes separate. The spindle fibers pull the chromosomes of each pair to opposite poles of the cell. But the chromatids do not separate at their centromeres. Each chromosome is still made of two chromatids. The genetic material, however, has recombined. ❹ During telophase I, the cytoplasm divides (cytokinesis), and two new cells are formed. Both cells have one chromosome from each pair of homologous chromosomes.

**Meiosis II** Meiosis II begins with the two cells formed at the end of telophase I of meiosis I. The chromosomes are not copied between meiosis I and meiosis II. ❺ In prophase II, new spindles form. ❻ During metaphase II, the chromosomes line up along the equators and are attached at their centromeres to spindle fibers. ❼ In anaphase II, the centromeres divide. The chromatids, which are now called *chromosomes,* move to opposite poles of the cell. ❽ During telophase II, a nuclear envelope forms around each set of chromosomes. The spindle breaks down, and the cell goes through cytokinesis. The result of meiosis is four haploid cells.

**› Reading Check** ***In what phase of meiosis is genetic material exchanged?***

**meiosis** a process in cell division during which the number of chromosomes decreases to half the original number by two divisions of the nucleus, which results in the production of sex cells (gametes or spores)

**crossing-over** the exchange of genetic material between homologous chromosomes during meiosis

**Figure 4** During meiosis, four haploid cells are produced from a diploid cell. ***› What is the difference between anaphase I and anaphase II?***

go.hrw.com
interact online
Keyword: HX8MEIF4

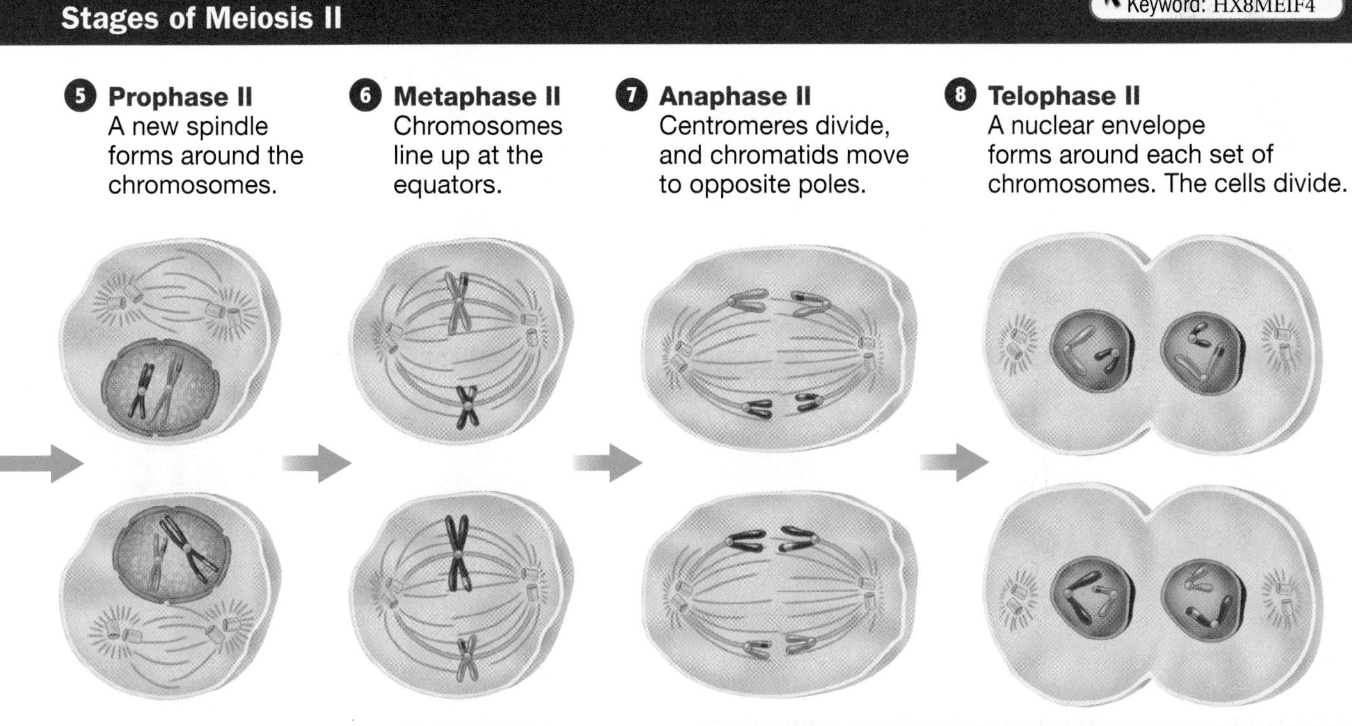

Stages of Meiosis II
❺ Prophase II
A new spindle forms around the chromosomes.
❻ Metaphase II
Chromosomes line up at the equators.
❼ Anaphase II
Centromeres divide, and chromatids move to opposite poles.
❽ Telophase II
A nuclear envelope forms around each set of chromosomes. The cells divide.

## Comparing Mitosis and Meiosis

The processes of mitosis and meiosis are similar but meet different needs and have different results. **› Mitosis makes new cells that are used during growth, development, repair, and asexual reproduction. Meiosis makes cells that enable an organism to reproduce sexually and happens only in reproductive structures.** Mitosis produces two genetically identical diploid cells. In contrast, meiosis produces four genetically different haploid cells. The haploid cells produced by meiosis contain half the genetic information of the parent cell. When two such cells, often an egg cell and a sperm cell, combine, the resulting zygote has the same number of chromosomes as each of the parents' cells.

**Comparisons** Write two sentences that compare and two sentences that contrast meiosis and mitosis.

If you compare meiosis and mitosis, as shown in **Figure 5,** you may think that they are alike. For example, in metaphase of mitosis and metaphase I of meiosis, the chromosomes move to the equator. However, there is a major difference that happens in an earlier stage.

In prophase I of meiosis, every chromosome pairs with its homologue. A pair of homologous chromosomes is called a *tetrad.* As the tetrads form, different homologues exchange parts of their chromatids in the process of crossing-over. The pairing of homologous chromosomes and the crossing-over do not happen in mitosis. Therefore, a main difference between meiosis and mitosis is that in meiosis, genetic information is rearranged. The rearranging of genetic information leads to genetic variation in offspring. Crossing-over is one of several processes that lead to genetic variation.

**› Reading Check** ***How are cells formed by mitosis different from cells formed by meiosis in relation to number of chromosomes?***

**Figure 5** Mitosis produces two diploid daughter cells that are identical to the parent cell. Meiosis produces four haploid cells from a diploid cell. **›** ***What is the difference between anaphase in mitosis and anaphase I in meiosis I?***

**Comparing Mitosis and Meiosis**

Mitosis

Prophase | Metaphase | Anaphase | Telophase

2 identical diploid cells

Meiosis

Prophase I | Metaphase I | Anaphase I | Telophase I

Meiosis II

4 nonidentical haploid cells

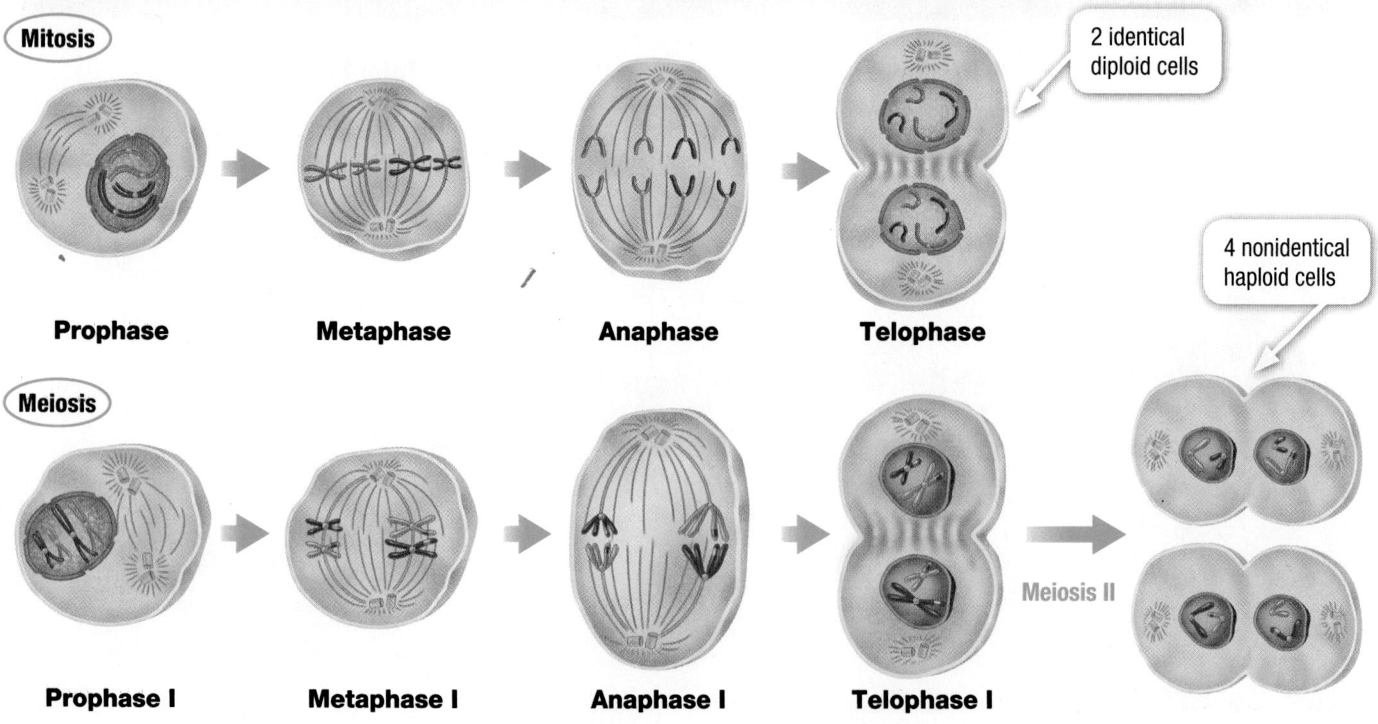

Hands On

# QuickLab

30 min

## Crossing-Over Model

You can use paper strips and pencils to model the process of crossing-over.

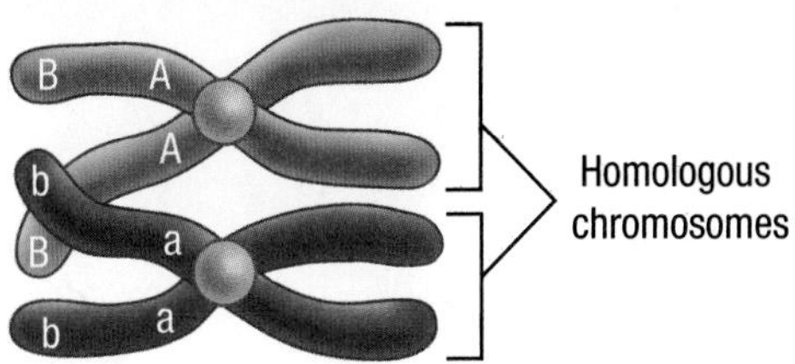


### Procedure

1. Use a colored pencil to write "A" and "B" on two paper strips. These two strips will represent one of the two homologous chromosomes shown.
2. Use a second colored pencil to write "a" and "b" on two paper strips. These two strips will represent the second homologous chromosome shown.
3. **CAUTION: Handle scissors with care.** Use your chromosome models, scissors, and tape to demonstrate crossing-over between two chromatids.

### Analysis

1. **Determine** what the letters *A, B, a,* and *b* represent.
2. **Explain** why the chromosomes that you made are homologous.
3. **Compare** the number of different types of chromatids (combinations of *A, B, a,* and *b*) before crossing-over with the number after crossing-over.
4. CRITICAL THINKING **Analyzing Information** How does crossing-over relate to genetic recombination?

## Genetic Variation

Genetic variation is advantageous for a population. Genetic variation can help a population survive a major environmental change. For example, in the Arctic, if temperatures drop below average, those polar bears with genes that make thicker fur will survive. Polar bears without the genes for thicker fur may die out. The polar bears with the genes for thicker fur reproduce, and the population grows. Now, suppose that all of the individuals in the population have the same genes, but none of the genes are for thicker fur. What do you think will happen if the temperature drops below average? The entire population of polar bears may die out.

Genetic variation is made possible by sexual reproduction. In sexual reproduction, existing genes are rearranged. Meiosis is the process that makes the rearranging of genes possible. Fusion of haploid cells from two different individuals adds further variation. **› Three key contributions to genetic variation are crossing-over, independent assortment, and random fertilization.**

**Crossing-Over** During prophase I, homologous chromosomes line up next to each other. Each homologous chromosome is made of two sister chromatids attached at the centromere. Crossing-over happens when one arm of a chromatid crosses over the arm of the other chromatid, as illustrated in the QuickLab. The chromosomes break at the point of the crossover, and each chromatid re-forms its full length with the piece from the other chromosome. Thus, the sister chromatids of a homologous chromosome no longer have identical genetic information.

**› Reading Check** *How can crossing-over increase genetic variation?*

SCILINKS.
www.scilinks.org
Topic: Genetic Variation
Code: HX80658

**ACADEMIC VOCABULARY**

**exist** to occur or be present

Figure 6 The same cell is shown twice. Because each pair of homologous chromosomes separates independently, four different gametes can result in each case.

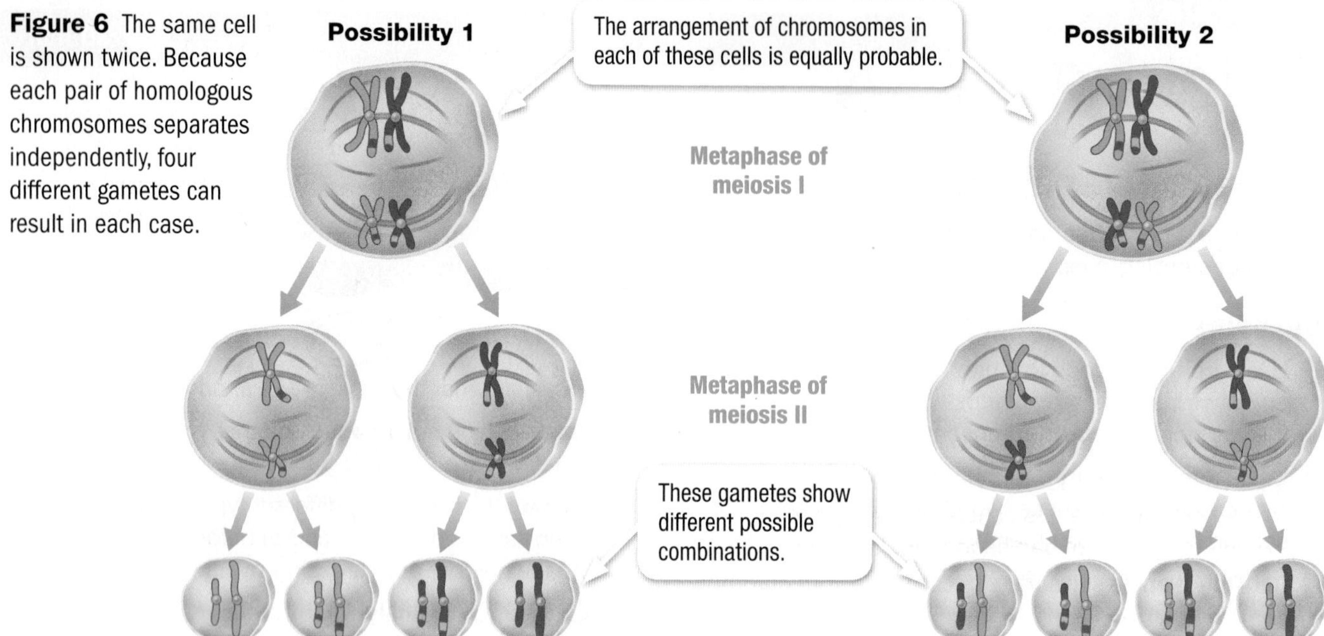
Possibility 1
The arrangement of chromosomes in each of these cells is equally probable.
Possibility 2
Metaphase of meiosis I
Metaphase of meiosis II
These gametes show different possible combinations.

**Independent Assortment** During metaphase I, homologous pairs of chromosomes line up at the equator of the cell. The two pairs of chromosomes can line up in either of two equally probable ways. This random distribution of homologous chromosomes during meiosis is called **independent assortment.** The four haploid cells formed in possibility 1 in **Figure 6** have entirely different combinations of chromosomes than do the four cells made in possibility 2.

**independent assortment** the random distribution of the pairs of genes on different chromosomes to the gametes

In humans, each gamete receives one chromosome from each of 23 pairs of homologous chromosomes. Each of the 23 pairs of chromosomes separates independently. Thus, there are $2^{23}$ (more than 8 million) different possibilities for the gene combinations in gametes that form from a single original cell.

**Random Fertilization** Fertilization is a random process that adds genetic variation. The zygote that forms is made by the random joining of two gametes. Because fertilization of an egg by a sperm is random, the number of possible outcomes is *squared.* In humans, the possibility is $2^{23} \times 2^{23}$, or about 70 trillion, different combinations!

## Section 2 Review

### KEY IDEAS

1. **Summarize** the different phases of meiosis.
2. **Explain** how the function of meiosis differs from the function of mitosis.
3. **Describe** three mechanisms of genetic variation.

### CRITICAL THINKING

4. **Comparing Functions** Compare the processes of crossing-over and independent assortment. How does each contribute to genetic variation?
5. **Inferring Conclusions** Why might sexual reproducers better adapt to a changing environment than asexual reproducers?

### ALTERNATIVE ASSESSMENT

6. **Word Problem** If one cell in a dog ($2n = 78$) undergoes meiosis and another cell undergoes mitosis, how many chromosomes will each resulting cell contain?

Why It Matters

# Girls, Girls, Girls

WEIRD SCIENCE

Did you know that some species, such as the predatory brush cricket to the right, and the lupin aphid below, have only females? These species, with only females, reproduce asexually.

## Parthenogenesis

In animals, the process of a female producing an egg that can grow into a new individual without being fertilized by a male is called *parthenogenesis*. The major advantage of parthenogenesis is that every individual can reproduce and the population can grow quickly. The disadvantage is that every individual has the same genes. The animals may not have the genes that produce the traits that are necessary for adaptation. If a species cannot adapt, it could become extinct.

**Apomixis** Asexual reproduction in plants in which embryos develop in the absence of fertilization by pollen is called *apomixis*. There are more than 300 apomictic plant species, such as dandelions. Apomictic plants still produce seeds, and the offspring are genetically identical to the mother plant.

**New Discovery** Until recently, scientists believed that all snakes reproduced sexually. However, this Burmese python is parthenogenetic. Scientists discovered that the Burmese python was parthenogenetic only after an isolated female in a zoo had offspring.

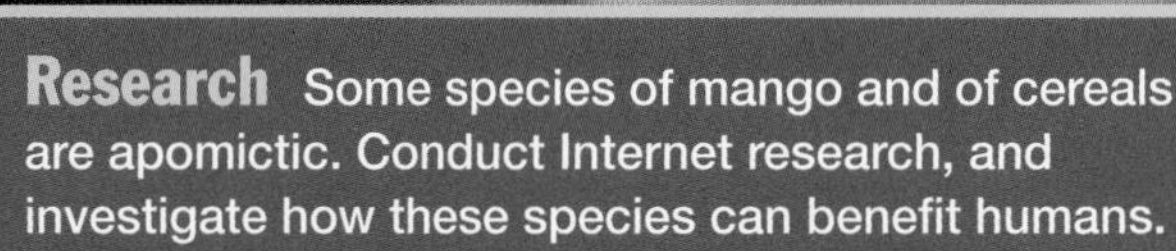

**Research** Some species of mango and of cereals are apomictic. Conduct Internet research, and investigate how these species can benefit humans.

Section 3

# Multicellular Life Cycles

| Key Ideas | Key Terms | Why It Matters |
|---|---|---|
| ❯ What is a diploid life cycle?<br>❯ What is a haploid life cycle?<br>❯ What is alternation of generations? | life cycle<br>sperm<br>ovum | Some life cycles are mainly diploid, others are mainly haploid, and still others alternate between haploid and diploid phases. |

Standard 4

**2.1e** In sexually reproducing organisms, the new individual receives half of the genetic information from its mother (via the egg) and half from its father (via the sperm). Sexually produced offspring often resemble, but are not identical to, either of their parents.

**4.1b** Some organisms reproduce asexually with all the genetic information coming from one parent. Other organisms reproduce sexually with half the genetic information typically contributed by each parent. Cloning is the production of identical genetic copies.

**4.1c** The processes of meiosis and fertilization are key to sexual reproduction in a wide variety of organisms. The process of meiosis results in the production of eggs and sperm which each contain half of the genetic information. During fertilization, gametes unite to form a zygote, which contains the complete genetic information for the offspring.

All of the events in the growth and development of an organism until the organism reaches sexual maturity are called a **life cycle.** All organisms that reproduce sexually have both diploid stages and haploid stages.

## Diploid Life Cycle

Most animals have a diploid life cycle. **Figure 7** illustrates this type of life cycle. Most of the life cycle is spent in the diploid state. All of the cells except the gametes are diploid.

A diploid germ cell in a reproductive organ goes through meiosis and forms gametes. The gametes, the sperm and the egg, join during fertilization. The result is a diploid zygote. This single diploid cell goes through mitosis and eventually gives rise to all of the cells of the adult, which are also diploid. **❯ In diploid life cycles, meiosis in germ cells of a multicellular diploid organism results in the formation of haploid gametes.**

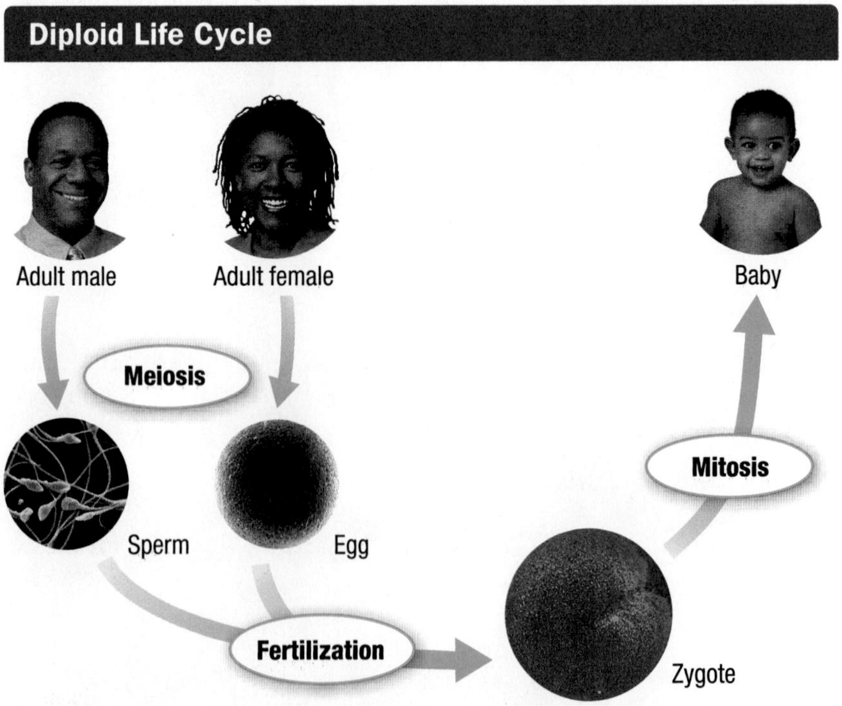

**Figure 7** Humans and most other animals have a life cycle dominated by a diploid individual. **❯ *What are the only haploid cells in a diploid life cycle?***

**Diploid Life Cycle**

Adult male

Adult female

Baby

Meiosis

Mitosis

Sperm

Egg

Fertilization

Zygote

**life cycle** all of the events in the growth and development of an organism until the organism reaches sexual maturity

**sperm** the male gamete (sex cell)

**ovum** a mature egg cell

### Meiosis and Gamete Formation

Male animals produce gametes called **sperm.** As **Figure 8** illustrates, a diploid germ cell goes through meiosis I. Two cells are formed, each of which goes through meiosis II. The result is four haploid cells. The four cells change in form and develop a tail to form four sperm.

Female animals produce gametes called eggs, or ova (singular, **ovum**). A diploid germ cell begins to divide by meiosis. Meiosis I results in the formation of two haploid cells that have unequal amounts of cytoplasm. One of the cells has nearly all of the cytoplasm. The other cell, called a *polar body,* is very small and has a small amount of cytoplasm. The polar body may divide again, but its offspring cells will not survive. The larger cell goes through meiosis II, and the division of the cell's cytoplasm is again unequal. The larger cell develops into an ovum. The smaller cell, the second polar body, dies. Because of its larger share of cytoplasm, the mature ovum has a rich storehouse of nutrients. These nutrients nourish the young organism that develops if the ovum is fertilized.

**Reading Check** *How many gametes are formed from one female germ cell?*

Data

## Chromosome Combinations 4.4.1a

When a sperm and egg fuse, two sets of chromosomes are combined. In this lab, you will model this cross between two sets of chromosomes.

### Procedure

1. **Write** "F1F2 X M1M2" on a sheet of paper. F1 and F2 represent the father's chromosomes. M1 and M2 represent the mother's chromosomes.
2. **Determine** all of the possible chromosome combinations in the zygote that forms from the fusion of the gametes with the chromosomes that you wrote in step 1.

### Analysis

1. **Calculate** the number of chromosome combinations that are possible in the zygote.
2. CRITICAL THINKING **Analyzing Data** List all of the possible chromosome combinations.

**Figure 8** Meiosis of diploid germ cells results in haploid gametes.

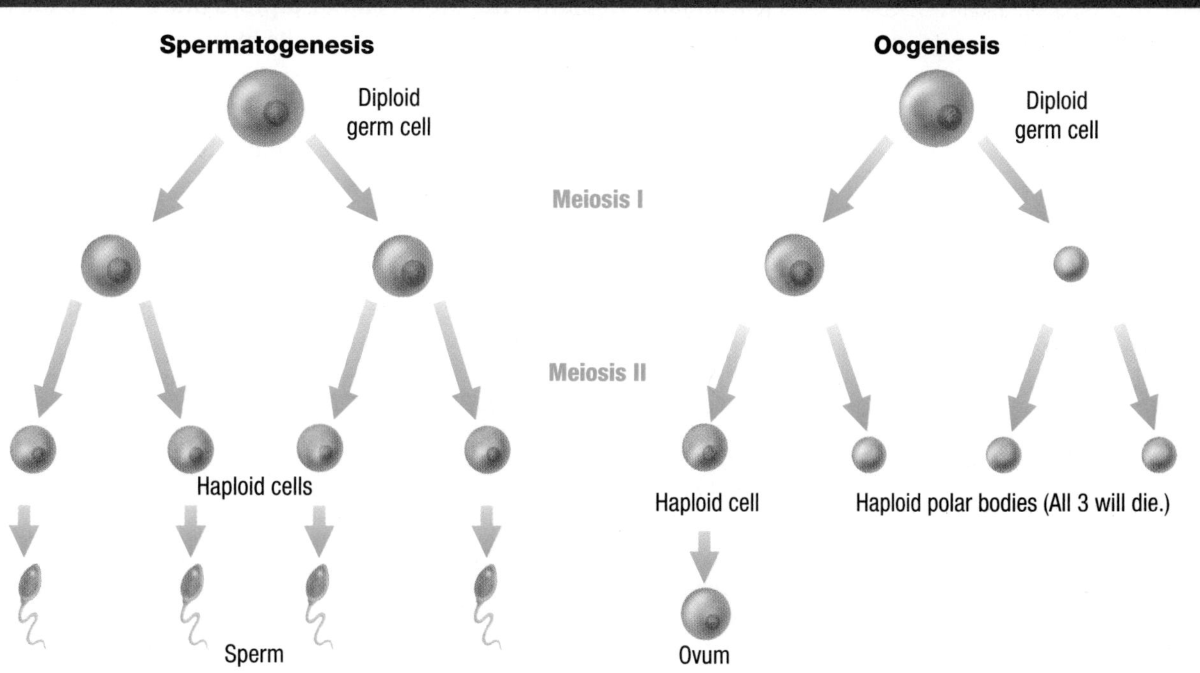

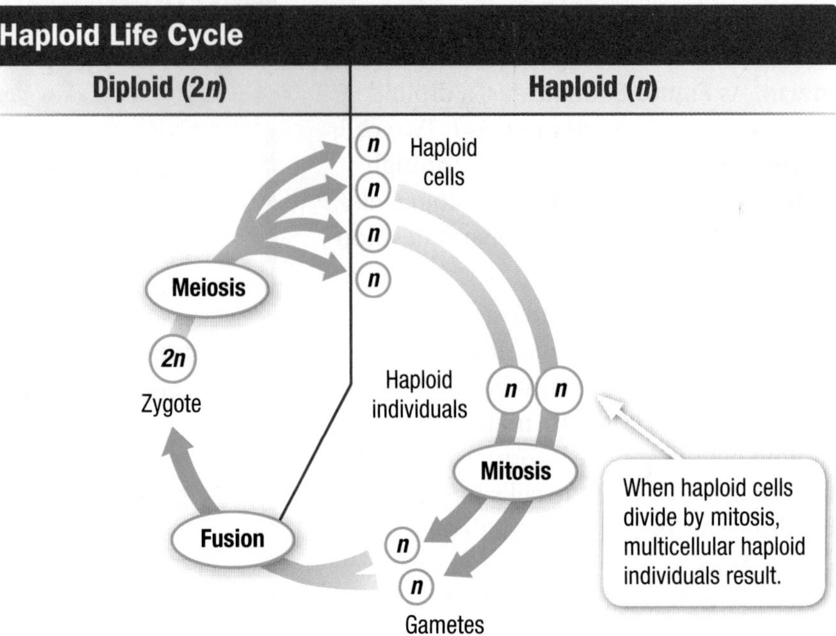


**Figure 9** Some organisms, such as fungi, have haploid cells as a major portion of their life cycles.

## Haploid Life Cycle

The haploid life cycle, shown in **Figure 9,** happens in most fungi and some protists. Haploid stages make up the major part of this life cycle. The zygote, the only diploid structure, goes through meiosis immediately after it is formed and makes new haploid cells. The haploid cells divide by mitosis and give rise to multicellular haploid individuals. **› In haploid life cycles, meiosis in a diploid zygote results in the formation of the first cell of a multicellular haploid individual.**

**Two-column notes** Use two-column notes to summarize the stages and details of the haploid life cycle.

## Alternation of Generations

**› Plants and most multicellular protists have a life cycle that alternates between a haploid phase and a diploid phase called *alternation of generations.*** In plants, the multicellular diploid phase in the life cycle is called a *sporophyte.* Spore-forming cells in the sporophyte undergo meiosis and produce spores. A spore forms a multicellular gametophyte. The *gametophyte* is the haploid phase that produces gametes by mitosis. The gametes fuse and give rise to the diploid phase.

## Section 3 Review

### › KEY IDEAS

1. **Summarize** the process in a diploid life cycle.
2. **Describe** what happens in a haploid life cycle.
3. **Describe** what happens to the polar bodies formed during meiosis of a female diploid cell in animal.
4. **Explain** the alternation of generations life cycle.

### CRITICAL THINKING

5. **Evaluating Processes** How does the formation of sperm through meiosis of a diploid germ cell differ from the formation of an ovum from a diploid germ cell?
6. **Analyzing Information** What type of cell or structure is the first stage of every sexual life cycle?

### WRITING IN SCIENCE

7. **Lesson Plan** Write a lesson plan that you can use to teach a classmate the difference between a haploid and a diploid life cycle. In your own words, write a summary of each. Include diagrams with your explanation.

Skills Practice

# Chapter 11 Lab

4.4.1c

45 min

## Objectives

- Model the stages of meiosis.
- Describe the events that occur in each stage of the process of meiosis.
- Compare your meiosis model to meiosis stages in a set of prepared slides of lily anther microsporocytes.

## Materials

- beads, wooden (40)
- index cards (8)
- marker
- microscope
- microscope slides of lilium anther, 1st and 2nd meiotic division
- scissors
- tape, masking
- yarn

## Safety

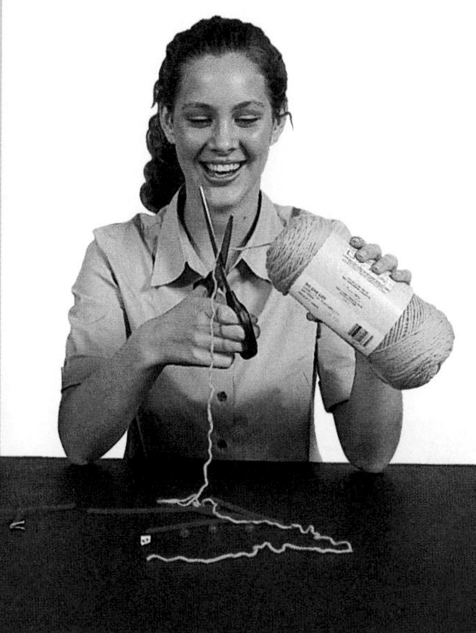

# Meiosis Model

In this laboratory, you will work with a partner to develop a meiosis model. You will also have the opportunity to compare your model to the stages of meiosis found in the sacs of a lily anther.

## Procedure

### Build a Model

1. Work in a team of two. Review the stages of meiosis I and meiosis II. Note the structures and organization that are characteristic of each stage. Pay particular attention to the appearance and behavior of the chromosomes.
2. Work with your partner to design a model of a cell by using the materials listed for this lab. Select and assign a different material to represent each cell structure and keep this consistent in all models. Have your teacher approve the plan.
3. Label each of eight index cards with a specific stage of meiosis, such as "Prophase II."
4. Using your model plan that you designed in step 2, you or your partner will construct a set of models representing the four stages of meiosis I. The other team member will construct another set of models representing the four stages of meiosis II.
5. Once you have completed your set of models, position the cards in two horizontal rows. The top row illustrates the stages of meiosis I. The bottom row illustrates the stages of meiosis II. Compare and contrast the corresponding stages.

### Observe Meiosis

6. **CAUTION: Handle glass slides with care.** Obtain a set of prepared slides of lily anther microsporocytes that include a variety of meiotic stages.
7. Use your microscope to view each slide. Locate the various stages of meiosis within the anther sacs.
8. Compare what you observe in the prepared slides to the models that you have constructed.

## Analyze and Conclude

1. **Analyzing Processes** Identify and label each stage of meiosis as a haploid stage or a diploid stage.
2. **Comparing Functions** How does anaphase I differ from anaphase II?
3. SCIENTIFIC METHODS **Critiquing Models** Based upon the observations of real cells, evaluate your model. How would you improve your model?

# Chapter 11 Summary

| Key Ideas | Key Terms |
|---|---|
| **1 Reproduction**<br>› An individual formed by asexual reproduction is genetically identical to its parent.<br>› In sexual reproduction, two parents give genetic material to produce offspring that are genetically different from their parents.<br>› Each chromosome has thousands of genes that play an important role in determining how an organism develops and functions. | **gamete** (248)<br>**zygote** (248)<br>**diploid** (249)<br>**haploid** (249)<br>**homologous chromosomes** (249) |
| **2 Meiosis**<br>› During meiosis, a diploid cell goes through two divisions to form four haploid cells.<br>› Mitosis produces cells that are used during growth, development, repair, and asexual reproduction. Meiosis makes cells that enable an organism to reproduce sexually and it only happens in reproductive structures.<br>› Three key contributions to genetic variation are crossing-over, independent assortment, and random fertilization. 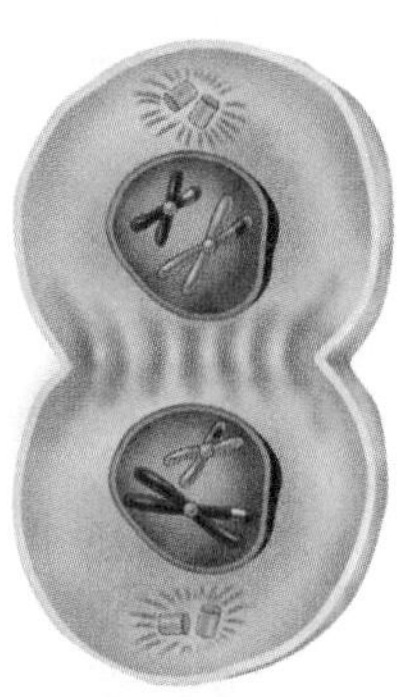 | **meiosis** (250)<br>**crossing-over** (251)<br>**independent assortment** (254) |
| **3 Multicellular Life Cycles**<br>› In diploid life cycles, meiosis in germ cells of a multicellular diploid organism results in the formation of haploid gametes.<br>› In haploid life cycles, meiosis in a diploid zygote results in the formation of the first cell of a multicellular haploid individual.<br>› Plants and most multicellular protists have a life cycle that alternates between a haploid phase and a diploid phase called *alternation of generations*. 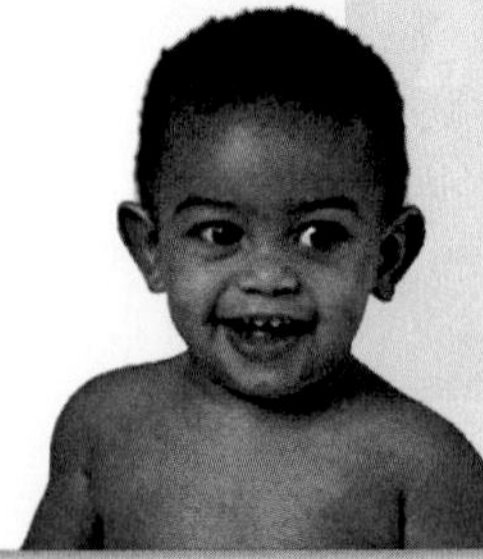 | **life cycle** (256)<br>**sperm** (257)<br>**ovum** (257) |

# Chapter 11 The Living Environment Regents Exam Practice

**PART A: Answer all questions in this part.**

*Directions:* For each statement or question, write on your separate answer sheet the number of the word or expression that best completes the statement or answers the question.

**1** Offspring that result from meiosis and fertilization each have

(1) twice as many chromosomes as their parents
(2) one-half as many chromosomes as their parents
(3) gene combinations different from those of either parent
(4) gene combinations identical to those of each parent

**2** Which diagram best illustrates an event in sexual reproduction that would most directly lead to the formation of a human embryo?

(1) 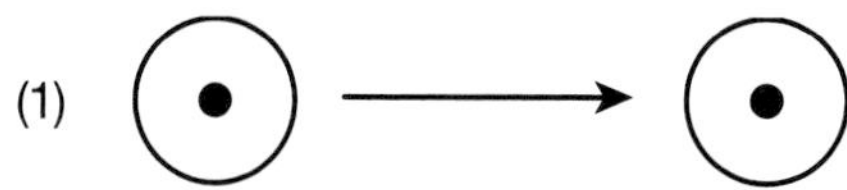

(2) 

(3) 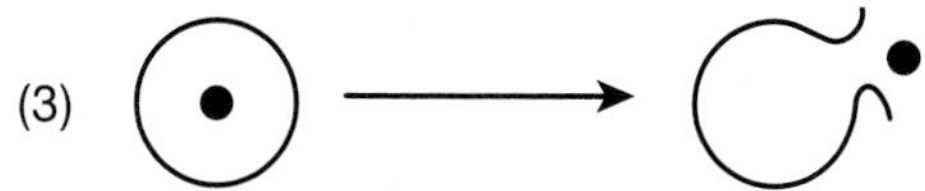

(4) 

**3** Certain bacteria produce a chemical that makes them resistant to penicillin. Since these bacteria reproduce asexually, they usually produce offspring that

(1) can be destroyed by penicillin
(2) mutate into another species
(3) are genetically different from their parents
(4) survive exposure to penicillin

**4** Which statement about the gametes represented in the diagram below is correct?

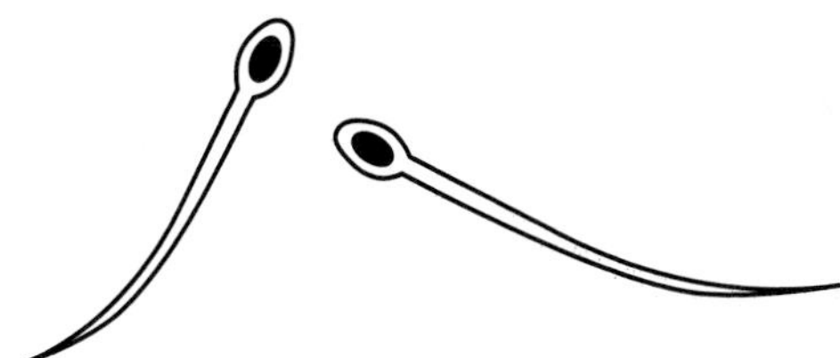

(1) They are produced by females.
(2) They are fertilized in an ovary.
(3) They transport genetic material.
(4) They are produced by mitosis.

**5** Which of the following is a difference between a sporophyte and a gametophyte?

(1) A sporophyte is diploid, and a gametophyte is haploid.
(2) A sporophyte is a plant, and a gametophyte is an animal.
(3) A sporophyte is multicellular, and a gametophyte is unicellular.
(4) A sporophyte undergoes only mitosis, and a gametophyte undergoes both mitosis and meiosis.

**6** Compared to human cells resulting from mitotic cell division, human cells resulting from meiotic cell division would have

(1) twice as many chromosomes
(2) the same number of chromosomes
(3) one-half the number of chromosomes
(4) one-quarter as many chromosomes

**7** In an environment that undergoes frequent change, species that reproduce sexually may have an advantage over species that reproduce asexually because the sexually reproducing species produce

(1) more offspring in each generation
(2) identical offspring
(3) offspring with more variety
(4) new species of offspring in each generation

**8** Which statement correctly describes the genetic makeup of the sperm cells produced by a human male?

(1) Each cell has pairs of chromosomes and the cells are usually genetically identical.
(2) Each cell has pairs of chromosomes and the cells are usually genetically different.
(3) Each cell has half the normal number of chromosomes and the cells are usually genetically identical.
(4) Each cell has half the normal number of chromosomes and the cells are usually genetically different.

**9** Which statement describes asexual reproduction?

(1) Adaptive traits are usually passed from parent to offspring without genetic modification.
(2) Mutations are not passed from generation to generation.
(3) It always enables organisms to survive in changing environmental conditions.
(4) It is responsible for many new variations in offspring.

**10** Reproduction in humans usually requires

(1) the process of cloning
(2) mitotic cell division of gametes
(3) gametes with chromosomes that are not paired
(4) the external fertilization of sex cells

**11** Meiosis and fertilization are important for the survival of many species because these two processes result in

(1) large numbers of gametes
(2) increasingly complex multicellular organisms
(3) cloning of superior offspring
(4) genetic variability of offspring

**12** Strawberries can reproduce by means of runners, which are stems that grow horizontally along the ground. At the region of the runner that touches the ground, a new plant develops. The new plant is genetically identical to the parent because

(1) it was produced sexually.
(2) nuclei traveled to the new plant through the runner to fertilize it.
(3) it was produced asexually.
(4) there were no other strawberry plants in the area to provide fertilization.

**13** During meiosis, crossing-over (gene exchange between chromosomes) may occur. Crossing-over usually results in

(1) overproduction of gametes
(2) fertilization and development
(3) the formation of identical offspring
(4) variation within the species

**14** Which statement is true of both mitosis and meiosis?

(1) Both are involved in asexual reproduction.
(2) Both occur only in reproductive cells.
(3) The number of chromosomes is reduced by half.
(4) DNA replication occurs before the division of the nucleus.

**15** Human egg cells are most similar to human sperm cells in their

(1) degree of motility.
(2) amount of stored food.
(3) chromosome number.
(4) shape and size.

**16** The arrows in the diagram below illustrate processes in the life of a species that reproduces sexually. Which processes result directly in the formation of cells with half the amount of genetic material that is characteristic of the species?

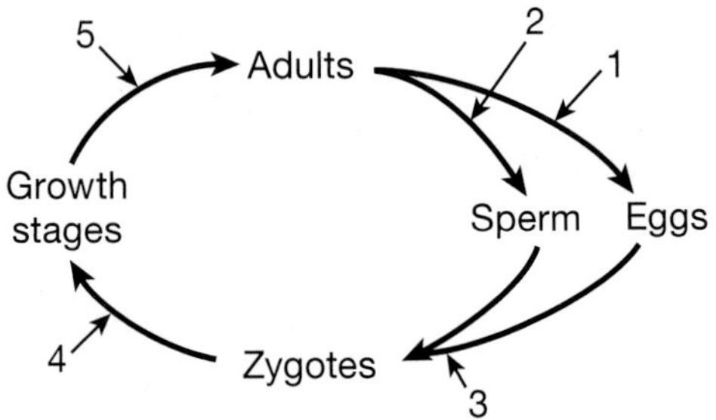


(1) 1 and 2
(2) 2 and 3
(3) 3 and 4
(4) 4 and 5

**17** The diagram below shows a process that can occur during meiosis. The most likely result of this process is

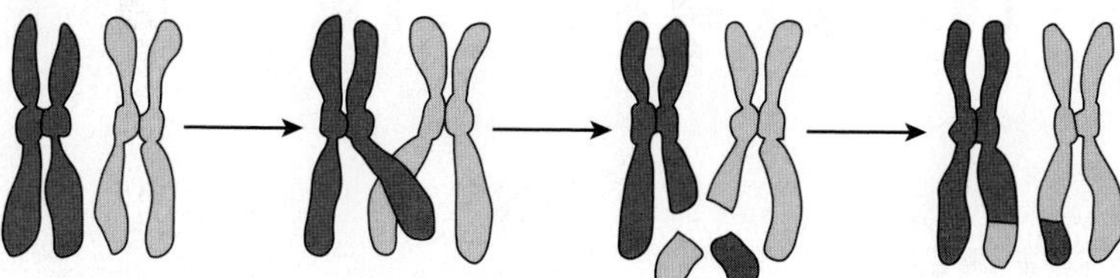

(1) a new combination of inheritable traits that can appear in the offspring
(2) an inability to pass either of these chromosomes on to offspring
(3) a loss of genetic information that will produce a genetic disorder in the offspring
(4) an increase in the chromosome number of the organism in which this process occurs

**PART B**

**18** A sperm cell from an organism is represented in the diagram below. Which statement regarding this sperm cell is not correct?

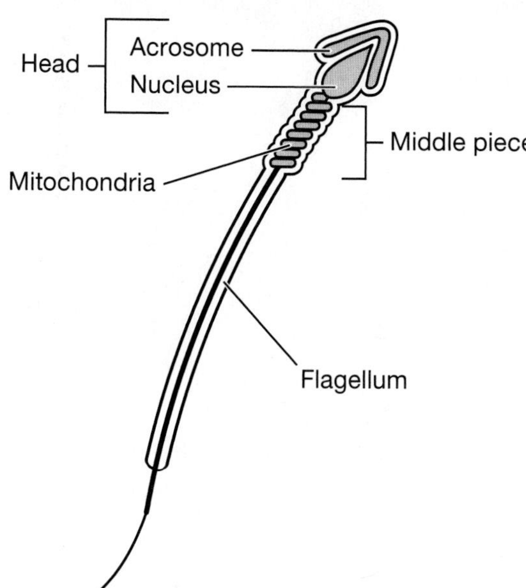


(1) The acrosome contains half the normal number of chromosomes.
(2) Energy to move the flagellum originates in the middle piece.
(3) The head may contain a mutation.
(4) This cell can unite with another cell resulting in the production of a new organism.

**19** Sexually produced offspring often resemble, but are not identical to, either of their parents. Explain why they resemble their parents but are not identical to either parent.

# Chapter 12 Mendel and Heredity

## Preview



## Why It Matters

Your genetic makeup influences your appearance, your personality, your abilities, and your health. We now know that many human traits, such as talents and diseases, have their origins in genes. As we come to understand how traits are inherited, we can use this information to better our lives.

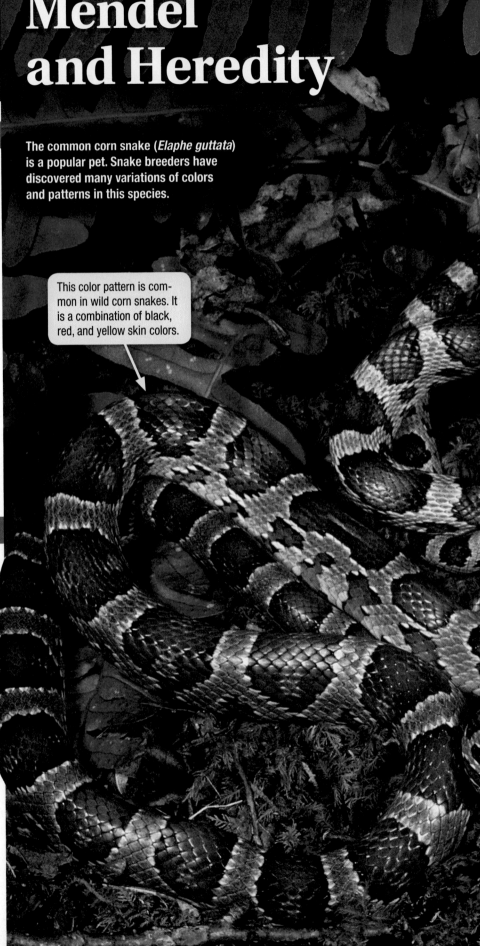

The common corn snake (*Elaphe guttata*) is a popular pet. Snake breeders have discovered many variations of colors and patterns in this species.

This color pattern is common in wild corn snakes. It is a combination of black, red, and yellow skin colors.

***The Living Environment***

**Standard 1** Students will use mathematical analysis, scientific inquiry, and engineering design, as appropriate, to pose questions, seek answers, and develop solutions.

**Key Idea 3** The observations made while testing proposed explanations, when analyzed using conventional and invented methods, provide new insights into natural phenomena.

**Standard 4** Students will understand and apply scientific concepts, principles, and theories pertaining to the physical setting and living environment and recognize the historical development of ideas in science.

**Key Idea 2** Organisms inherit genetic information in a variety of ways that result in continuity of structure and function between parents and offspring. ***Major Understandings* - 2.1a, 2.1b, 2.1c, 2.1j, 2.2a**

15 min

# InquiryLab

## What Are the Chances? 1.3.2

Do you think you can predict the result of a coin toss? What if you flip the coin many times? In this activity, you will test your predictions.

### Procedure

1. Read steps 2 and 3. Predict the results, and write down your prediction.
2. Flip a **coin**, and let it land. Record which side is up (heads or tails). Repeat this step 10 times.
3. Calculate what fraction of the total number of flips resulted in heads. Calculate what fraction of flips resulted in tails.
4. Read steps 5 and 6. Predict the results, and write down your prediction.
5. Tally the flip results of the entire class.
6. Calculate the fraction of heads and the fraction of tails in step 5.

### Analysis

1. **Compare** your predictions from steps 1 and 4 with the results in steps 3 and 6.
2. **Compare** your own results in step 3 to those of other individuals in your class. Identify how closely each individual result matches the total class results.

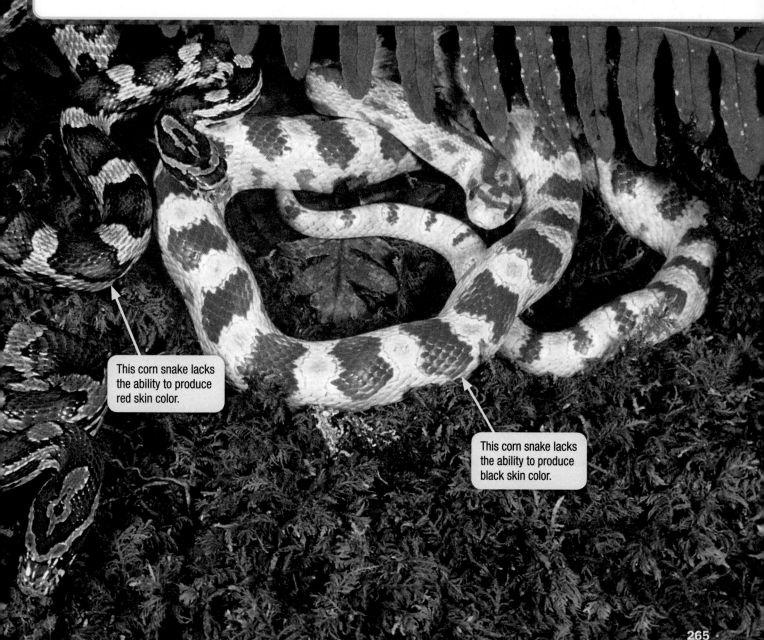

This corn snake lacks the ability to produce red skin color.

This corn snake lacks the ability to produce black skin color.

These reading tools can help you learn the material in this chapter. For more information on how to use these and other tools, see **Appendix: Reading and Study Skills.**

## Using Words

**Word Parts** Knowing the meanings of word parts can help you figure out the meaning of words that you do not know.

**Your Turn** Use the table to answer the following.

1. Heritage is something handed down from one's ancestors. What do you think *heredity* is?
2. Use the meaning of the prefix *phen-* and the suffix *-type* to figure out what *phenotype* means.

**Word Parts**

| Word part | Type | Meaning |
|---|---|---|
| *gen-* | prefix | born; to become; to produce |
| *her-* | prefix | heir; remains; to be left behind |
| *phen-* | prefix | to show |
| *-type* | suffix | form; mark; kind |

## Using Language

**Analogies** An analogy question asks you to analyze the relationship between two words in one pair and to identify a second pair of words that have the same relationship. Colons are used to express the analogy for this type of question. For example, the analogy "up is to down as top is to bottom" is written "up : down :: top : bottom. In this example, the relationship between the words in each pair is the same.

**Your Turn** Use information in the chapter to complete this analogy.

allele : gene :: trait : __________

(*Hint:* Finding out how alleles and genes are related will help you figure out which word to use to fill in the blank.)

## Using Science Graphics

**Punnett Squares** A Punnett square is a tool that is used to figure out possible combinations when combining items from a group. For example, if you have a red shirt, a green shirt, and a yellow shirt that you could wear with either blue jeans or shorts, how many combinations could you make?

**Your Turn** Finish filling in the Punnett square shown here to answer the following questions.

1. How many combinations include a red shirt?
2. What combination of shirt and pants do you find in the bottom right corner of this Punnett square?
3. How many combinations would you have if you added a pair of brown pants to the group?

| | Red shirt | Green shirt | Yellow shirt |
|---|---|---|---|
| Blue jeans | Red shirt with blue jeans | | |
| Shorts | | Green shirt with shorts | |

Section 1

# Origins of Hereditary Science

| Key Ideas | Key Terms | Why It Matters |
|---|---|---|
| ❯ Why was Gregor Mendel important for modern genetics?<br>❯ Why did Mendel conduct experiments with garden peas?<br>❯ What were the important steps in Mendel's first experiments?<br>❯ What were the important results of Mendel's first experiments? | character<br>trait<br>hybrid<br>generation | Our understanding of genetics, including what makes us unique, can be traced back to Mendel's discoveries. |

Since they first learned how to breed plants and animals, people have been interested in heredity. In the 1800s, one person figured out some of the first key ideas of genetics. Recall that *genetics* is the science of heredity and the mechanism by which traits are passed from parents to offspring.

***The Living Environment***
**Standard 4**
**2.2a** For thousands of years new varieties of cultivated plants and domestic animals have resulted from selective breeding for particular traits.

## Mendel's Breeding Experiments

A monk named Gregor Johann Mendel lived in the 1800s in Austria. Mendel did breeding experiments with the garden pea plant, *Pisum sativum,* shown in **Figure 1.** Farmers had done similar experiments before, but Mendel was the first person to develop rules that accurately predict the patterns of heredity in pea plants. ❯ **Modern genetics is based on Mendel's explanations for the patterns of heredity in garden pea plants.**

As a young man, Mendel studied to be a priest. Later, he went to the University of Vienna. There, he learned how to study science through experimentation and how to use mathematics to explain natural events. Mendel lived the rest of his life in a monastery, where he taught high school and cared for a garden. It was in this garden that he completed his important experiments.

Most of Mendel's experiments involved crossing different types of pea plants. In this case, the word *cross* means "to mate or breed two individuals." Mendel crossed a type of garden pea plant that had purple flowers with a type that had white flowers. All of the offspring from that cross had purple flowers. However, when two of these purple-flowered offspring were crossed, some offspring had white flowers and some had purple flowers.

The white color had reappeared in the second group of offspring! Mendel decided to investigate this strange occurrence. So, he carefully crossed different types of pea plants and recorded the numbers of each type of offspring. He did this experiment many times.

❯ **Reading Check** ***How did Mendel experiment with pea plants? (See the Appendix for answers to Reading Checks.)***

**Figure 1** To cross plants that each had flowers of a different color, Mendel controlled the pollen that fertilized each flower.

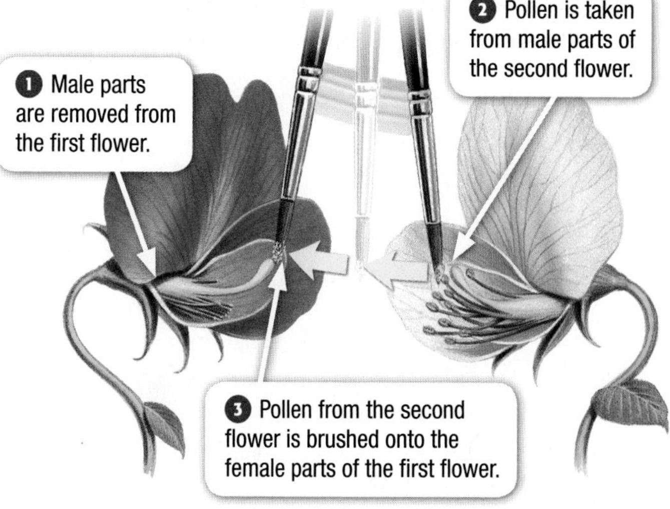

1 Male parts are removed from the first flower.
2 Pollen is taken from male parts of the second flower.
3 Pollen from the second flower is brushed onto the female parts of the first flower.

## Features of Pea Plants

Mendel studied seven features in his pea plants, as **Figure 2** shows. **❯The garden pea plant is a good subject for studying heredity because the plant has contrasting traits, usually self-pollinates, and grows easily.**

**Contrasting Traits** In the study of heredity, physical features that are inherited are called **characters.** Several characters of the garden pea plant exist in two clearly different forms. The plant's flower color is either purple or white—there are no intermediate forms. A **trait** is one of several possible forms of a character. Purple is one of two possible traits for the flower-color character in pea plants. Other contrasting traits of pea plants are shown in **Figure 2.** (For some characters, more than two traits may be possible). Mendel wanted to see what would happen when he crossed individuals that have different traits. In such a cross, the offspring that result are called **hybrids.**

**Academic Vocabulary**

**contrast** to show differences when compared.

**character** a recognizable inherited feature or characteristic of an organism

**trait** one of two or more possible forms of a character; a recognizable feature or characteristic of an organism

**hybrid** the offspring of a cross between parents that have contrasting traits

**generation** the entire group of offspring produced by a given group of parents

**Self-Pollination** In garden pea plants, each flower contains both male and female reproductive parts. This arrangement allows the plant to *self-pollinate,* or fertilize itself. Pea plants can also reproduce through *cross-pollination.* This process occurs when pollen from the flower of one plant is carried by insects or by other means to the flower of another plant. To cross-pollinate two pea plants, Mendel had to make sure that the plants could not self-pollinate. So, he removed the male parts (which produce pollen) from some of the flowers. But he did not remove the female parts (which produce eggs, fruit, and seeds). Then, he dusted the female parts of one plant with pollen from another plant.

**Easy to Grow** The garden pea is a small plant that needs little care and matures quickly. Also, each plant produces many offspring. Thus, many results can be compared for each type of cross. Recall that collecting repeated data is an important scientific method.

**❯ Reading Check** ***What is the difference between a trait and a character?***

**Figure 2** In the experiments in his garden, Mendel grew and studied many kinds of pea plants. **❯ Why did Mendel study pea plants?**

**Seven Characters with Contrasting Traits Studied by Mendel**

| Flower color | Seed color | Seed shape | Pod color | Pod Shape | Flower position | Plant height |
|---|---|---|---|---|---|---|
| purple | yellow | round | green | smooth | mid-stem | tall |
| white | green | wrinkled | yellow | bumpy | end of stem | short |

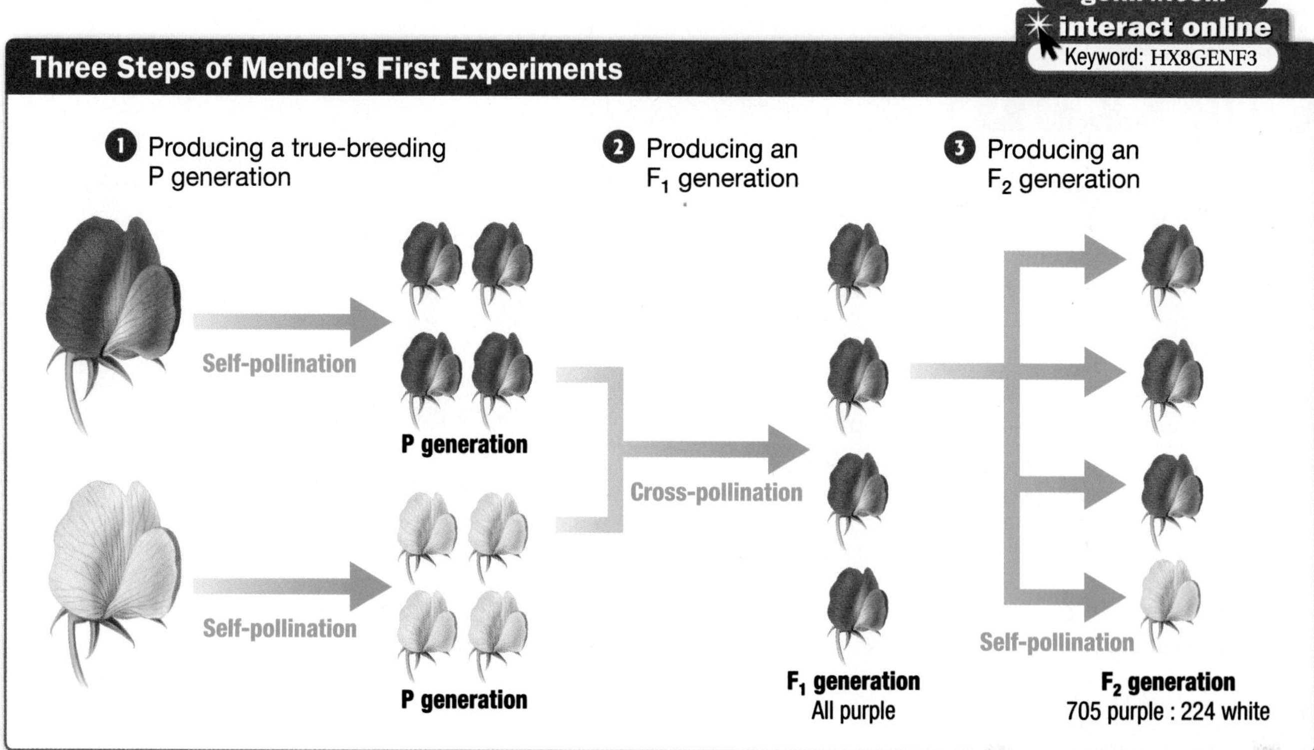


**Figure 3** In his garden experiments, Mendel carefully selected and grew specific kinds of pea plants. **› What is the relationship between each generation in these experiments?**

## Mendel's First Experiments

A *monohybrid cross* is a cross that is done to study one pair of contrasting traits. For example, crossing a plant that has purple flowers with a plant that has white flowers is a monohybrid cross. **› Mendel's first experiments used monohybrid crosses and were carried out in three steps.** The three steps are shown in **Figure 3.** Each step involved a new generation of plants. A **generation** is a group of offspring from a given group of parents.

**Step 1** Mendel allowed plants that had each type of trait to self-pollinate for several generations. This process ensured that each plant always produced offspring of the same type. Such a plant is said to be *true-breeding* for a given trait. For example, every time a true-breeding plant that has purple flowers self-pollinates, its offspring will have purple flowers. Mendel used true-breeding plants as the first generation in his experiments. The first group of parents that are crossed in a breeding experiment are called the *parental generation,* or *P generation.*

**Step 2** Mendel crossed two P generation plants that had contrasting traits, such as purple flowers and white flowers. He called the offspring of the P generation the *first filial generation,* or *$F_1$ generation.* He recorded the number of $F_1$ plants that had each trait.

**Step 3** Mendel allowed the $F_1$ generation to self-pollinate and produce new plants. He called this new generation of offspring the *second filial generation,* or *$F_2$ generation.* He recorded the number of $F_2$ plants that had each trait.

**› Reading Check** ***What is a monohybrid cross?***

**Word Parts** The word *filial* is from the Latin *filialis,* which means "of a son or daughter." Thus, F (filial) generations are all of the generations that follow a P (parental) generation. What do you think *filiation* means?

Data

# QuickLab

10 min

## Mendel's Ratios

You can calculate and compare the $F_2$ generation ratios that Mendel obtained from his first experiments.

### Procedure

1. Copy this partially complete table onto a separate sheet of paper. Then, fill in the ratios of $F_2$ traits.
2. Simplify the ratios, and round the terms in each ratio to the nearest hundredth digit.

| Character | Traits in $F_2$ generation | | Ratio |
|---|---|---|---|
| Flower color | 705 purple | 224 white | 705:224 or 3.15:1.00 |
| Seed color | 6,022 yellow | 2,001 green | |
| Seed shape | 5,474 round | 1,850 wrinkled | |
| Pod color | 428 green | 152 yellow | |
| Pod shape | 882 smooth | 299 bumpy | |
| Flower position | 651 mid-stem | 207 end of stem | |
| Plant height | 787 tall | 277 short | |

### Analysis

1. **Identify** the similarities between the ratios by rounding each term to the nearest whole number.
2. CRITICAL THINKING **Analyzing Data** Why weren't all of the ratios exactly the same?

## Ratios in Mendel's Results

All of Mendel's $F_1$ plants expressed the same trait for a given character. The contrasting trait had disappeared! But when the $F_1$ plants were allowed to self-pollinate, the missing trait reappeared in some of the $F_2$ plants. Noticing this pattern, Mendel compared the ratio of traits that resulted from each cross.

When $F_1$ plants that had purple flowers were crossed with one another, 705 of the $F_2$ offspring had purple flowers and 224 had white flowers. So, the $F_2$ ratio of purple-flowered plants to white-flowered plants was 705:224, or about 3:1. Mendel's studies of the other characters gave a similar pattern. **For each of the seven characters that Mendel studied, he found a similar 3-to-1 ratio of contrasting traits in the $F_2$ generation.** As you will learn, Mendel tried to explain this pattern.

**Reading Check** ***What was the important difference between Mendel's $F_1$ and $F_2$ generations?***

## Section 1 Review

### KEY IDEAS

1. **Identify** Gregor Mendel's contribution to modern genetics.
2. **Describe** why garden pea plants are good subjects for genetic experiments.
3. **Summarize** the three major steps of Mendel's first experiments.
4. **State** the typical ratio of traits in Mendel's first experiments.

### CRITICAL THINKING

5. **Using Scientific Methods** Why did Mendel record the results of so many plant crosses?
6. **Predicting Outcomes** Squash plants do not usually self-pollinate. If Mendel had used squash plants, how might his experiments have differed?

### WRITING FOR SCIENCE

7. **Technical Writing** Imagine that you are Gregor Mendel and you need to document your first experiments for a science magazine. Write out your procedure for breeding pea plants. Be sure to explain how you controlled variables and assured that data was reliable.

Why It Matters

WEIRD SCIENCE

# Amazing Mutants

Fruit flies are widely used in genetic research because "mutant" forms provide clues about how genes work. One fly species, *Drosophila melanogaster,* has been studied so much that scientists understand its genes better than those of most other organisms. Still, there are many bizarre mutations yet to be understood.

## Popular in the Lab

Fruit flies are popular with scientists because the flies are easy to breed and raise in a laboratory. The flies grow and reproduce quickly and reproduce in large numbers. Also, the flies have been used in important genetic experiments since 1910.

## Many Mutations

Most scientists who study fruit flies are interested in genetic variation and mutations. Thousands of "mutant" forms that have unique *alleles* (versions of a gene) have been observed in species of the genus *Drosophila*. Databases on the Internet are used to share information on over 14,000 fruit fly genes. Just a few of the many kinds of fruit fly "mutants" are described here.

Normal "wild" fruit fly

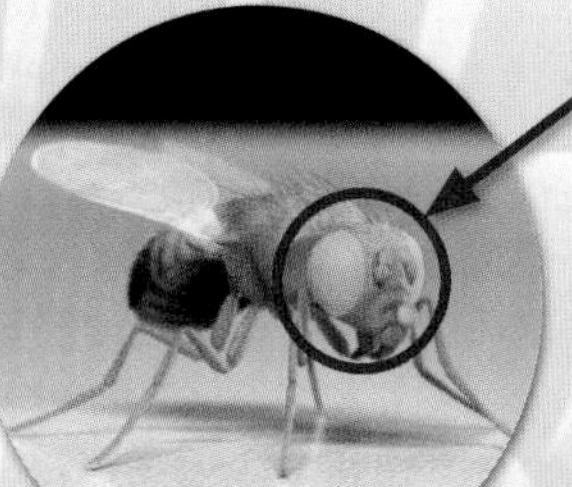

Fly lacking eye color

**Different Colors** Differences in color are easy to recognize in a lab. Some fruit fly mutations affect eye color and body patterns. Some of the genes for coloration in flies show simple inheritance patterns, like the patterns that Mendel observed in garden pea plants.

**Research** Find out more about *Drosophila,* such as its life cycle, size, and use in research.

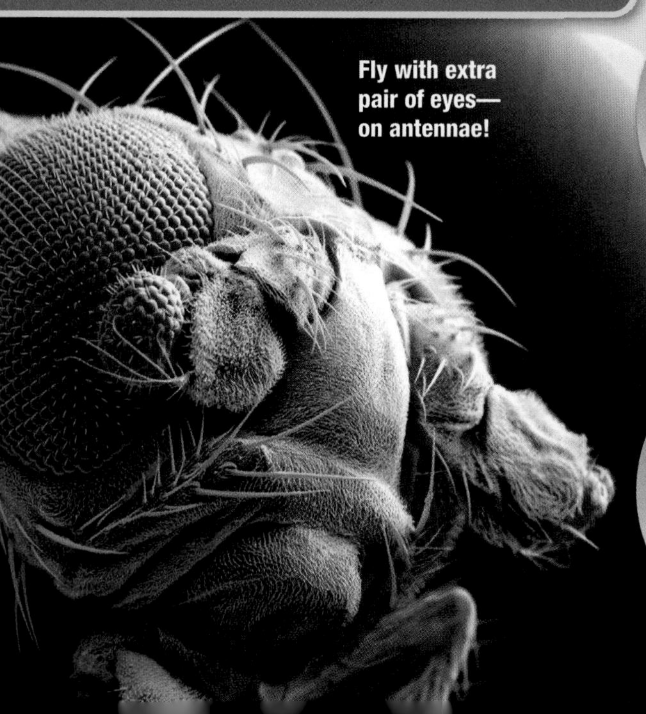

**Fly with extra pair of eyes—on antennae!**

Fly with malformed wings

**Malformed Body Parts** Some genes control the development of body parts. Mutations in such genes often cause body parts to develop improperly, as did the malformed wings shown here. This particular trait is seen only when a fly has a normal allele paired with the malformed-wing allele. A fly that has two such alleles will not survive.

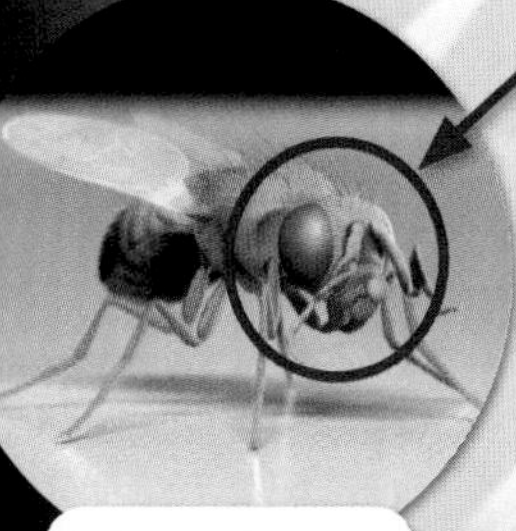

Fly with legs in place of antennae

**Misplaced Body Parts** Imagine growing legs from your head! Some mutations cause legs, antennae, mouthparts, and wings to grow in various places on a fly's body. By studying these oddities, scientists have begun to understand the genes that control the arrangement of body parts in insects and other animals.

Section 2

# Mendel's Theory

| Key Ideas | Key Terms | Why It Matters |
|---|---|---|
| ❯ What patterns of heredity were explained by Mendel's hypotheses?<br>❯ What is the law of segregation?<br>❯ How does genotype relate to phenotype?<br>❯ What is the law of independent assortment? | allele<br>dominant<br>recessive<br>genotype<br>phenotype<br>homozygous<br>heterozygous | Mendel's theory explains why you have some, but not all, of the traits of your parents. |

***The Living Environment***
**Standard 4**

**2.1b** Every organism requires a set of coded instructions for specifying its traits. For offspring to resemble their parents, there must be a reliable way to transfer information from one generation to the next. Heredity is the passage of these instructions from one generation to another.

**2.1c** Hereditary information is contained in genes, located in the chromosomes of each cell. An inherited trait of an individual can be determined by one or by many genes, and a single gene can influence more than one trait. A human cell contains many thousands of different genes in its nucleus.

**2.1j** Offspring resemble their parents because they inherit similar genes that code for the production of proteins that form similar structures and perform similar functions.

## Explaining Mendel's Results

Mendel developed several hypotheses to explain the results of his experiments. His hypotheses were basically correct but have been updated with newer terms and more-complete knowledge. Mendel's hypotheses, collectively called the *Mendelian theory of heredity,* form the foundation of modern genetics. ❯ **Mendelian theory explains simple patterns of inheritance. In these patterns, two of several versions of a gene combine and result in one of several possible traits.**

**Alternate Versions of Genes** Before Mendel's experiments, many people thought that the traits of offspring were always a blend of the traits from parents. If this notion were true, a tall plant crossed with a short plant would result in offspring of medium height. But Mendel's results did not support the blending hypothesis. Mendel noticed that his pea plants would express only one of two traits for each character, such as purple or white flower color. Today, scientists know that different traits result from different versions of genes. Each version of a gene is called an **allele.**

❯ **Reading Check** *What is the "blending" hypothesis?*

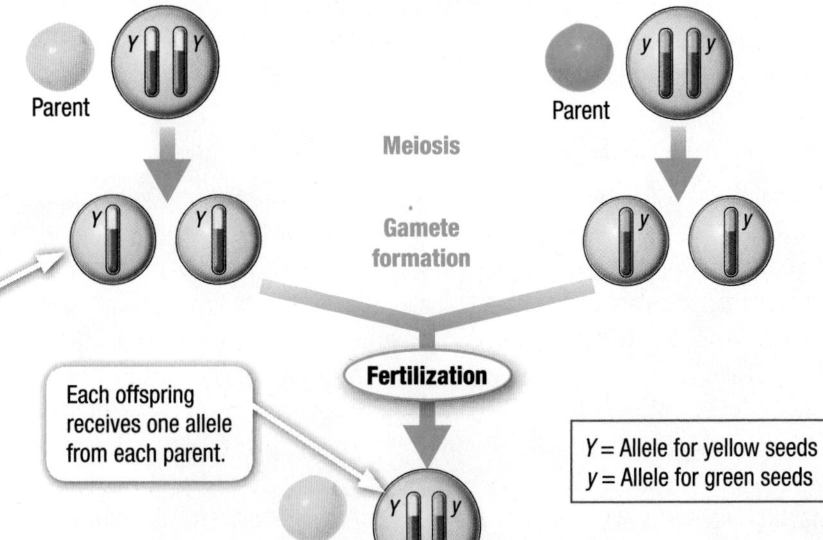


**Figure 4** Each individual has two alleles for a given character. A single gamete carries only one of the two alleles. ❯ **In pea plants, how many alleles for seed color does each parent pass on to each offspring?**

Data

# QuickLab

15 min

## Dominant and Recessive Traits 4.2.1j

Can you find Mendelian patterns in humans? Look for ratios between these contrasting traits.

### Procedure

1. On a separate sheet of paper, draw a table like the one shown here. For each character, circle the trait that best matches your own trait.
2. Tally the class results to determine how many students in your class share each trait.

| Dominant trait | Recessive trait |
|---|---|
| freckles | no freckles |
| no cleft | cleft chin |
| dimples | no dimples |

### Analysis

1. **Summarize** the class results for each character.
2. **Calculate** the ratio of dominant traits to recessive traits for each character.
3. CRITICAL THINKING **Mathematical Reasoning** Are each of the ratios the same? Why is this unlikely to happen?
4. CRITICAL THINKING **Analyzing Results** For which traits must a person who has the given trait receive the same allele from both parents? Explain your answer.

**One Allele from Each Parent** Mendel also noticed that traits can come from either parent. The reason is related to meiosis, as **Figure 4** shows. When gametes form, each pair of alleles is separated. Only one of the pair is passed on to offspring.

**Dominant and Recessive Alleles** For every pair of traits that Mendel studied, one trait always seemed to "win" over the other. That is, whenever both alleles were present, only one was fully expressed as a trait. The other allele had no effect on the organism's physical form. In this case, the expressed allele is called **dominant.** The allele that is not expressed when the dominant allele is present is called **recessive.** Traits may also be called *dominant* or *recessive.* For example, in pea plants, the yellow-seed trait is dominant, and the green-seed trait is recessive.

**allele** (uh LEEL) one of two or more alternative forms of a gene, each leading to a unique trait

**dominant** (DAHM uh nuhnt) describes an allele that is fully expressed whenever the allele is present in an individual

**recessive** (ri SES iv) describes an allele that is expressed only when there is no dominant allele present in an individual

## Random Segregation of Alleles

Mendel did not understand how chromosomes separate during meiosis, but he learned something important about this process. Because chromosome pairs split up randomly, either one of a pair of homologous chromosomes might end up in any one gamete. As **Figure 4** shows, offspring receive one allele from each parent. But only chance decides which alleles will be passed on through gametes. Mendel showed that segregation is random, and he stated his hypothesis as a law. **In modern terms, the *law of segregation* holds that when an organism produces gametes, each pair of alleles is separated and each gamete has an equal chance of receiving either one of the alleles.**

**ACADEMIC VOCABULARY**

**random** without aim

**Word Parts** Look up the word *phenomenon* in a dictionary. What is the meaning of the Greek root of this word? How does this meaning apply to the word *phenotype* as used in biology?

**genotype** (JEE nuh TIEP) a specific combination of alleles in an individual

**phenotype** (FEE noh TIEP) the detectable trait or traits that result from the genotype of an individual

**homozygous** (HOH moh ZIE guhs) describes an individual that carries two identical alleles of a gene

**heterozygous** (HET uhr OH ZIE guhs) describes an individual that carries two different alleles of a gene

## Mendel's Findings in Modern Terms

Although Mendel did not use the term allele, he used a code of letters to represent the function of alleles. Today, scientists use such a code along with modern terms, as shown in **Figure 5.** A dominant allele is shown as a capital letter. This letter is usually the first letter of the word for the trait. For example, purple flower color is a dominant trait in pea plants, so the allele is written as *P*. A recessive allele is shown as a lowercase letter. The letter is usually the same as the one used for the dominant allele. So, white flower color is written as *p*.

**Genotype and Phenotype** Mendel's experiments showed that an offspring's traits do not match one-to-one with the parents' traits. In other words, offspring do not show a trait for every allele that they receive. Instead, combinations of alleles determine traits. The set of alleles that an individual has for a character is called the **genotype.** The trait that results from a set of alleles is the **phenotype.** In other words, **genotype determines phenotype.** For example, if the genotype of a pea plant is *pp*, the phenotype is white flowers. If the genotype is *Pp* or *PP*, the phenotype is purple flowers, as shown in **Figure 5.**

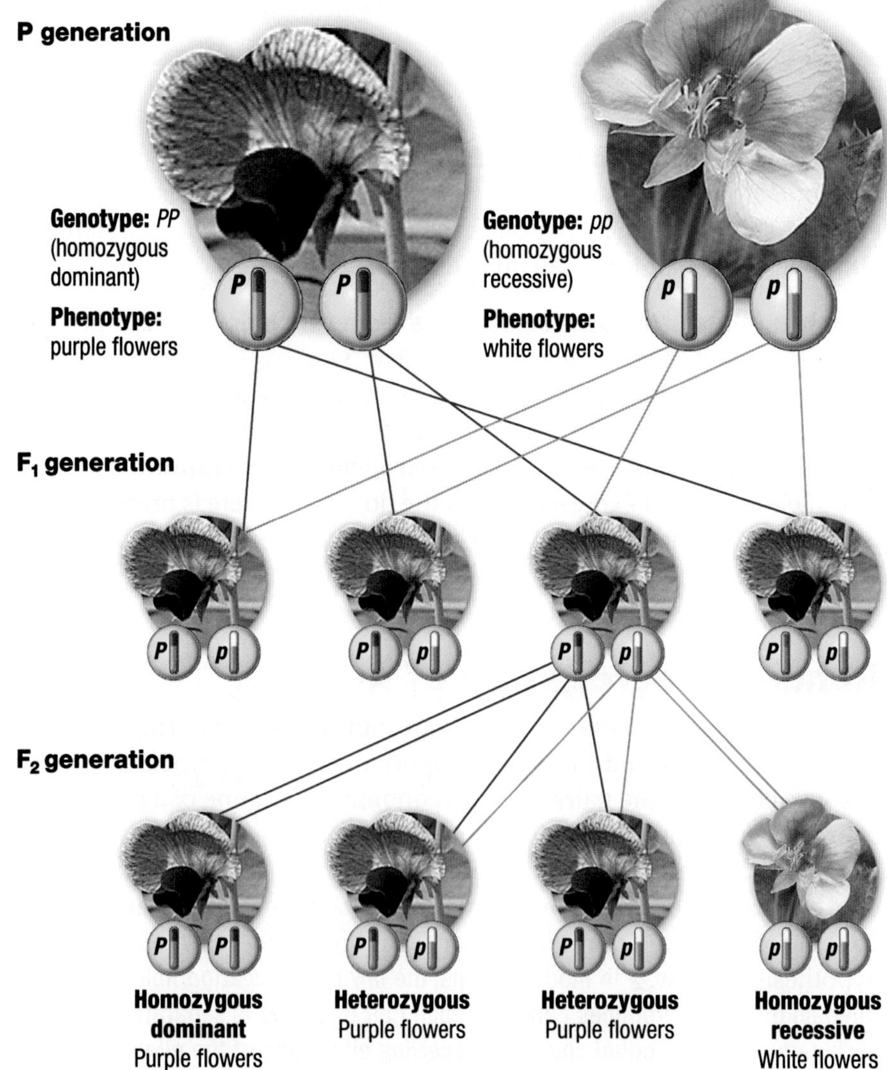


**Figure 5** Mendel's first experiments demonstrated dominance, segregation, genotype, and phenotype. **What is the relationship between the genotypes and phenotypes in each generation shown here?**

**Homozygous and Heterozygous** If an individual has two of the same alleles of a certain gene, the individual is **homozygous** for the related character. For example, a plant that has two white-flower alleles (*pp*) is homozygous for flower color. On the other hand, if an individual has two different alleles of a certain gene, the individual is **heterozygous** for the related character. For example, a plant that has one purple-flower allele and one white-flower allele (*Pp*) is heterozygous for flower color. In the heterozygous case, the dominant allele is expressed. This condition explains Mendel's curious results, as **Figure 5** shows.

## Mendel's Second Experiments

Mendel not only looked for patterns, he also looked for a lack of patterns. For example, the round-seed trait did not always show up in garden pea plants that had the yellow-seed trait. Mendel made dihybrid crosses to study these results. A *dihybrid cross*, shown in **Figure 6,** involves two characters, such as seed color and seed shape.

Parents
Yellow and round seeds — *YyRr*
Green and wrinkled seeds — *yyrr*

*YyRr* — Yellow and round
*Yyrr* — Yellow and wrinkled
*yyRr* — Green and round
*yyrr* — Green and wrinkled
Offspring

**Figure 6** Mendel used dihybrid crosses in his second experiments. He found that the inheritance of one character, such as seed color, did not affect the inheritance of another character, such as seed shape. **› What law did Mendel propose to explain these findings?**

**Independent Assortment** In these crosses, Mendel found that the inheritance of one character did not affect the inheritance of any other. He proposed another law. **› In modern terms, the *law of independent assortment* holds that during gamete formation, the alleles of each gene segregate independently.** For example, in **Figure 6,** the alleles for seed color (*Y* and *y*) can "mix and match" with the alleles for seed shape (*R* and *r*). So, round seeds may or may not be yellow.

**Genes Linked on Chromosomes** Mendel's second law seems to say that each gene has nothing to do with other genes. But we now know that many genes are linked to each other as parts of chromosomes. So, genes that are located close together on the same chromosome will rarely separate independently. Thus, genes are said to be *linked* when they are close together on chromosomes. The only genes that follow Mendel's law are those that are far apart.

**› Reading Check** ***What is a dihybrid cross?***

SciLINKS.
www.scilinks.org
Topic: Mendel's Laws
Code: HX80938


## Section 2 Review

### › KEY IDEAS

1. **Describe** the patterns that Mendelian theory explains.
2. **Summarize** the law of segregation.
3. **Relate** genotype to phenotype, using examples from Mendel's experiments with pea plants.
4. **Summarize** the law of independent assortment.

### CRITICAL THINKING

5. **Analyzing Data** The term *gene* did not exist when Mendel formed his hypotheses. What other genetic terms are used today that Mendel did not likely use?
6. **Arguing Logically** Would it be correct to say that a genotype is heterozygous recessive? Explain.
7. **Critiquing Explanations** Identify the strengths and weaknesses of Mendel's law of independent assortment.

### METHODS OF SCIENCE

8. **Testing an Hypothesis** How did Mendel test his hypothesis that the inheritance of one character does not affect the inheritance of another character?

Section 3

# Modeling Mendel's Laws

| Key Ideas | Key Terms | Why It Matters |
|---|---|---|
| ❯ How can a Punnett square be used in genetics?<br>❯ How can mathematical probability be used in genetics?<br>❯ What information does a pedigree show? | Punnett square<br>probability<br>pedigree<br>genetic disorder | Mendel's laws can be used to help breed exotic pets, thoroughbred livestock, and productive crops. |

*The Living Environment*

**Standard 1**

**3.2** Apply statistical analysis techniques when appropriate to test if chance alone explains the results.

**Standard 4**

**2.1c** Hereditary information is contained in genes, located in the chromosomes of each cell. An inherited trait of an individual can be determined by one or by many genes, and a single gene can influence more than one trait. A human cell contains many thousands of different genes in its nucleus.

Why are Mendel's laws so important? Mendel's laws can be used to predict and understand the results of certain kinds of crosses. Farmers, gardeners, animal keepers, and biologists need to make predictions when they try to breed organisms that have desired characteristics. Medical professionals need to know about the inheritance of traits in their patients. Graphical models that can help with these tasks include Punnett squares and pedigrees.

## Using Punnett Squares

A **Punnett square** is a model that predicts the likely outcomes of a genetic cross. The model is named for its inventor, Reginald Punnett. **❯ A Punnett square shows all of the genotypes that could result from a given cross.**

The simplest Punnett square consists of a square divided into four boxes. As **Figure 7** shows, the possible alleles from one parent are written along the top of the square. The possible alleles from the other parent are written along the left side. Each box inside the square holds two letters. The combination of letters in each box represents one possible genotype in the offspring. The letters in each box are a combination of two alleles—one from each parent.

**Punnett square** (PUHN uht SKWER) a graphic used to predict the results of a genetic cross

**Figure 7** Each of these Punnett squares shows a monohybrid cross involving seed color in peas. **❯ How does a Punnett square predict the outcome of a cross?**

YY = homozygous dominant

Yy = heterozygous

yy = homozygous recessive

**Homozygous Cross** In a cross of homozygous parents that have contrasting traits, 100% of the offspring will be heterozygous and will show the dominant trait.

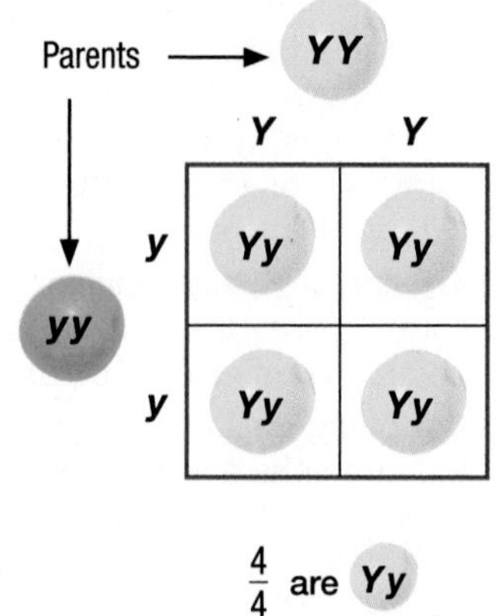


**Heterozygous Cross** In a cross of heterozygous parents that have the same traits, the ratio of genotypes will be 1:2:1. The ratio of phenotypes will be 3:1.

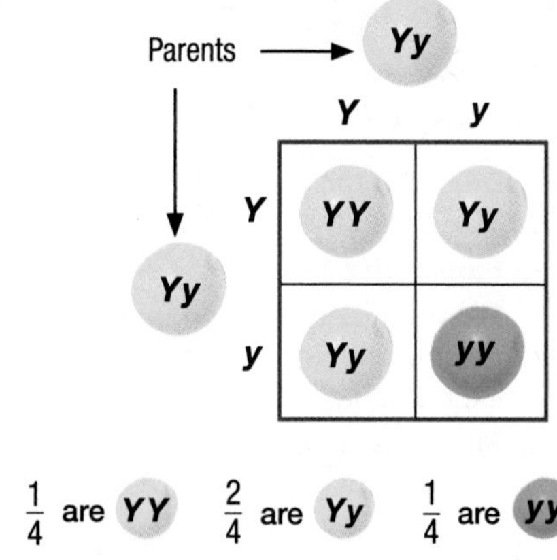

Data

# QuickLab

10 min

## Testcross

When genotypes are known, Punnett squares can be used to predict phenotypes. But can genotypes be determined if only phenotypes are known?

Suppose a breeder has a rabbit that has a dominant phenotype, such as black fur (as opposed to recessive brown fur). How could the breeder know whether the rabbit is homozygous (*BB*) or heterozygous (*Bb*) for fur color? The breeder could perform a testcross.

A *testcross* is used to test an individual whose phenotype for a characteristic is dominant but whose genotype is not known. This individual is crossed with an individual whose genotype is known to be homozygous recessive. In our example, the breeder would cross the black rabbit (*BB* or *Bb*) with a brown rabbit (*bb*).

### Procedure

On a separate sheet of paper, copy the two Punnett squares shown here. Write the appropriate letters in the boxes of each square.

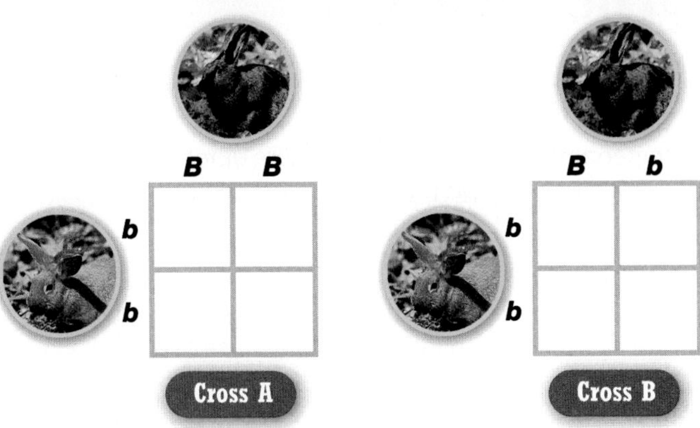


### Analysis

1. **Label** what each pair of letters represents in each of the Punnett squares.
2. **Identify** which figure represents a testcross involving a heterozygous parent.
3. **Identify** which figure shows a cross in which all offspring will have black fur.
4. CRITICAL THINKING **Applying Models** If half of the offspring in a testcross have brown fur, what is the genotype of the parent that has black fur?

**Analyzing Monohybrid Crosses** Two kinds of monohybrid crosses are shown in **Figure 7.** A simple Punnett square can be used to analyze a monohybrid cross. Recall that this cross involves parents who each have a trait that contrasts with the trait of the other parent. The parents may be homozygous or heterozygous.

**Monohybrid Homozygous Crosses** Consider a cross between a pea plant that is homozygous for yellow seed color (*YY*) and a pea plant that is homozygous for green seed color (*yy*). The first Punnett square in **Figure 7** shows that all of the offspring in this type of cross will be heterozygous (*Yy*) and will express the dominant trait of yellow seed color. Other results are not possible in this case.

**Monohybrid Heterozygous Crosses** The second Punnett square in **Figure 7** predicts the results of a monohybrid cross between two pea plants that are heterozygous (*Yy*) for seed color. This cross is more complex than a homozygous cross. About one-fourth of the offspring will be *YY*. About two-fourths (or one-half) will be *Yy*. And about one-fourth will be *yy*. Another way to express this prediction is to say that the genotypic ratio will be 1 *YY* : 2 *Yy* : 1 *yy*. Because the *Y* allele is dominant, three-fourths of the offspring will be yellow (*YY* or *Yy*) and one-fourth will be green (*yy*). Thus, the phenotypic ratio will be 3 yellow : 1 green.

**› Reading Check** ***Explain the boxes inside a Punnett square?***

**ACADEMIC VOCABULARY**

**contrast** different when compared

**Analogies** Use the information on this page to solve the following analogy.

yy : Yy :: Homozygous : _______

Data

# QuickLab

15 min

## Probabilities

Some people are born with extra fingers or toes. This condition, known as *polydactyly,* is rare. However, it is usually the result of a dominant allele.

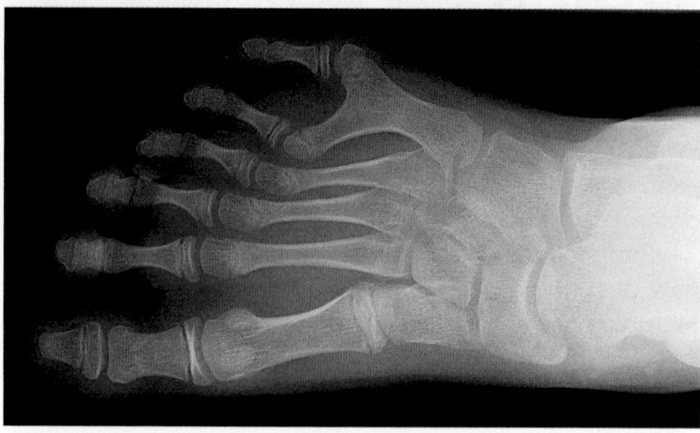

▲ Polydactyly (extra fingers or toes) is usually a dominant trait.

### Procedure

Draw Punnett squares to represent all possible combinations of alleles for each the crosses discussed below. Use *Z* to represent a dominant allele and *z* to represent a recessive allele.

### Analysis

1. **Calculate** the probability that a cross of two heterozygous (*Zz*) parents will produce homozygous dominant (*ZZ*) offspring.
2. **Determine** the probability that a cross of a heterozygous parent (Zz) and a homozygous recessive *(zz)* parent will produce heterozygous offspring.
3. **Calculate** the probability that a cross of a homozygous dominant parent and a homozygous recessive parent will produce heterozygous offspring.
4. **Determine** the probability that a cross between a heterozygous parent and a homozygous recessive parent will produce homozygous dominant offspring.

## Using Probability

Punnett squares allow direct and simple predictions to be made about the outcomes of genetic crosses, but those predictions are not certain. A Punnett square shows the possible outcomes of a cross, but it can also be used to calculate the probability of each outcome. **Probability** is the likelihood that a specific event will occur.

**ACADEMIC VOCABULARY**

**occur** to take place

**Calculating Probability** Punnett squares are one simple way to demonstrate probability. Probability can be calculated and expressed in many ways. Probability can be expressed in words, as a decimal, as a percentage, or as a fraction. For example, if an event will definitely occur, its probability can be expressed as either 1 out of 1 (in words), 100 % (as a percentage), 1.0 (as a decimal), or $\frac{1}{1}$ (as a fraction). If an event is just as likely to occur as to not occur, its probability can be expressed as either 1 out of 2, 50 %, 0.5, or $\frac{1}{2}$. Probability can be determined by the following formula:

**probability** (PRAHB uh BIL uh tee) the likelihood that a specific event will occur; expressed in mathematical terms

$$\textit{probability} = \frac{\textit{number of one kind of possible outcome}}{\textit{total number of all possible outcomes}}$$

Consider the example of a coin tossed into the air. The total number of possible outcomes is two—heads or tails. Landing on heads is one possible outcome. Thus, the probability that the coin will land on heads is $\frac{1}{2}$. Likewise, the probability that it will land on tails is $\frac{1}{2}$. Of course, the coin will not land on tails exactly half of the time, but it will tend to do so. The average number of total flips that result in tails will tend to be $\frac{1}{2}$.

**Probability of a Specific Allele in a Gamete** Recall the law of segregation, which states that each gamete has an equal chance of receiving either one of a pair of alleles. If a pea plant has two alleles for seed color, only one of the two alleles (yellow or green) can end up in a gamete. **Probability formulas can be used to predict the probabilities that specific alleles will be passed on to offspring.** For a plant that has two alleles for seed color, the total number of possible outcomes is two—green or yellow. The probability that a gamete from this plant will carry the allele for green seed color is $\frac{1}{2}$. The probability that a gamete will carry the allele for yellow seed color is also $\frac{1}{2}$.

**Probability in a Heterozygous Cross** The possible results of a heterozygous cross are similar to those of flipping two coins at once. Consider the possible results of a cross of two pea plants that are heterozygous for seed shape (*Rr*). Either parent is equally likely to pass on a gamete that has either an *R* allele or an *r* allele. So, the chance of inheriting either allele is $\frac{1}{2}$. Multiplying the probabilities for each gamete shows that the probability that the offspring will have *RR* alleles is $\frac{1}{4}$. The probability that the offspring will have *rr* alleles is also $\frac{1}{4}$. The combination *Rr* has two possible outcomes, so the probability that the offspring will have *Rr* alleles is $\frac{2}{4}$, or $\frac{1}{2}$.

**Reading Check** ***What is the probability that a heterozygous cross will produce homozygous recessive offspring?***

SCILINKS®
**www.scilinks.org**
Topic: Probability
Code: HX81217

## Math Skills Probability of Two Independent Events

Because two parents are involved in a genetic cross, both parents must be considered when predicting the probable outcomes. Consider the example of tossing two coins at the same time. The probability that a penny will land on heads is $\frac{1}{2}$, and the probability that a nickel will land on heads is $\frac{1}{2}$. How one coin falls does not affect how the other coin falls.

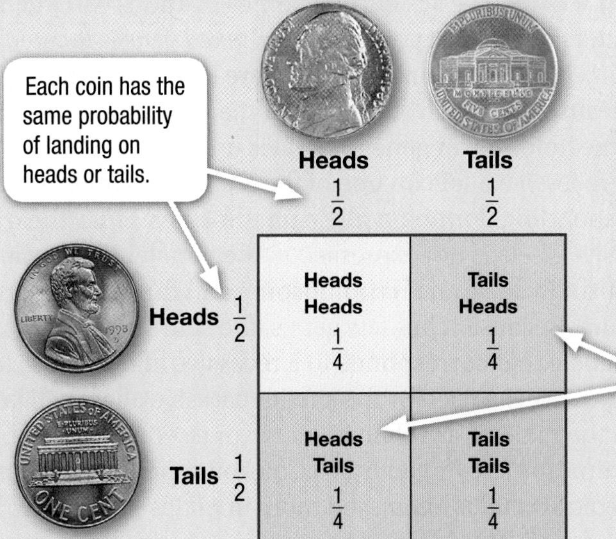
Each coin has the same probability of landing on heads or tails.
Heads 1/2
Tails 1/2
Heads 1/2
Tails 1/2
Heads Heads 1/4
Tails Heads 1/4
Heads Tails 1/4
Tails Tails 1/4
The green boxes have the same combination (heads and tails), so these two probabilities can be added together.

What is the probability that the nickel and the penny will both land on heads at the same time? To find the probability that a specific combination of two independent events will occur, multiply the probabilities of each event. Thus, the probability that both coins will land on heads is

$$\frac{1}{2} \times \frac{1}{2} = \frac{1}{4}$$

What about the probability that one coin will land on heads while the other coin lands on tails? Because the combination of heads and tails has two possible outcomes, the probabilities of each possible combination are added together:

$$\frac{1}{4} + \frac{1}{4} = \frac{2}{4} = \frac{1}{2}$$

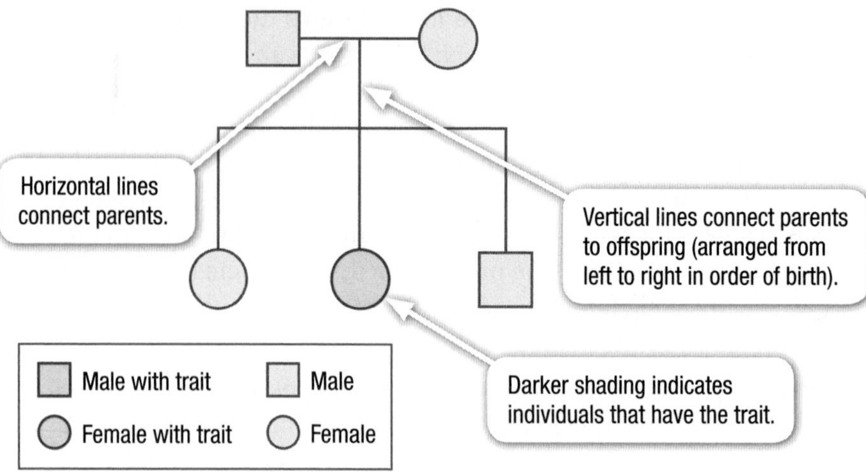
Horizontal lines connect parents.
Vertical lines connect parents to offspring (arranged from left to right in order of birth).
Darker shading indicates individuals that have the trait.
Male with trait
Male
Female with trait
Female

**Figure 8** Albinism is a genetic disorder carried by a recessive allele. Because of this disorder, this baby koala's skin and hair cells do not produce pigments, so the baby is mostly white. The pedigree (top right) shows the presence of the albinism trait in a family.

## Using a Pedigree

Mendel observed several generations of pea plants to see patterns in the inheritance of traits. A simple way to model inheritance is to use a pedigree. A **pedigree** is a family history that shows how a trait is inherited over several generations. A healthcare worker may use a pedigree to help a family understand a genetic disorder. A **genetic disorder** is a disease or disorder that can be inherited. If a family has a history of a genetic disorder, the parents may want to know if their children could inherit the disorder. Some parents are carriers. Carriers have alleles for a disorder but do not show symptoms. Carriers can pass the allele for the disorder to their offspring.

**Figure 8** shows a pedigree for a family in which albinism is present. A body affected by the genetic disorder albinism is unable to produce the pigment that gives dark color to skin, eyes, and hair. Without this pigment, the body may appear white or pink. A recessive allele causes albinism. The pedigree helps show how this trait is inherited. ❯ **A pedigree can help answer questions about three aspects of inheritance: sex linkage, dominance, and heterozygosity.**

**Sex-Linked Gene** The sex chromosomes, X and Y, carry genes for many characters other than gender. A *sex-linked gene* is located on either an X or a Y chromosome, but most are located on the X chromosome. Because it is much shorter than the X chromosome, the Y chromosome holds fewer genes. Females usually have two X chromosomes. A recessive allele on one of the X chromosomes will often have a corresponding dominant allele on the other. Thus, the trait for the recessive allele is not expressed in the female. Males, on the other hand, usually have an X chromosome and the much shorter Y chromosome. Because it has few genes, the shorter Y chromosome may lack an allele that corresponds to a recessive allele on the longer X chromosome. So, the trait for the single recessive allele will be expressed in the male. Traits that are not expressed equally in both sexes are commonly sex-linked traits. Colorblindness is an example of a sex-linked trait that is expressed more in males than in females.

❯ **Reading Check** ***How can one identify a sex-linked trait?***

**pedigree** (PED i GREE) a diagram that shows the occurrence of a genetic trait in several generations of a family

**genetic disorder** an inherited disease or disorder that is caused by a mutation in a gene or by a chromosomal defect

Data

# QuickLab

15 min

## Pedigree Analysis  4.2.1j

You will practice interpreting a pedigree. The pedigree to the right shows the presence or absence of a specific trait in several generations of a family.

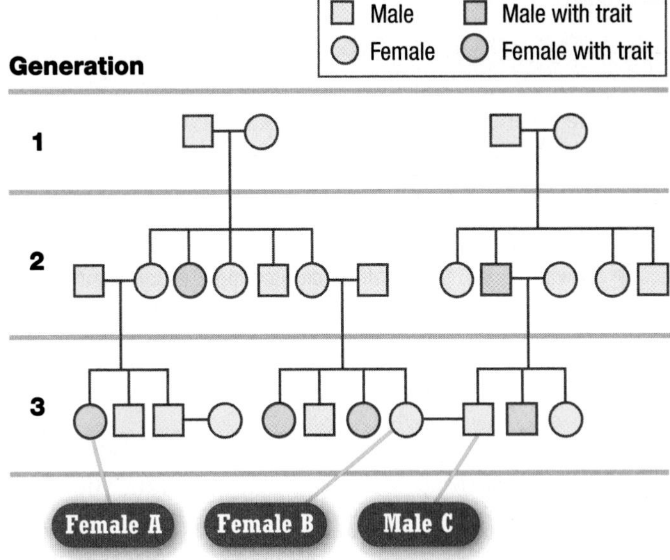


### Analysis

1. **Determine** whether the trait is dominant or recessive. Explain your reasoning.
2. **Determine** if Female A could be heterozygous for the trait. Do the same for Female B.
3. CRITICAL THINKING **Applying Information** Suppose that Female B is homozygous and produces children with Male C. If Male C is heterozygous, what is the probability that the children will have the trait?

**Dominant or Recessive?** If a person has a trait that is autosomal and dominant and has even one dominant allele, he or she will show the trait. A dominant allele is needed to pass on the trait. If a person has a recessive trait and only one recessive allele, he or she will not show the trait but may pass it on. So, if a trait appears in a child whose parents lack the trait, it is most likely recessive.

**Heterozygous or Homozygous?** If a person is either heterozygous or homozygous dominant for an autosomal gene, his or her phenotype will show the dominant trait. If a person is homozygous recessive, his or her phenotype will show the recessive trait. Heterozygous parents can produce a child who is homozygous recessive. Thus, a recessive trait in the child shows that both parents were heterozygous carriers of the recessive allele.

## Section 3 Review

### KEY IDEAS

1. **Describe** how a Punnett square is used in genetics.
2. **List** ways to express mathematical probability in genetics.
3. **Sketch** a pedigree for an imaginary family of three generations and describe what the pedigree shows.

### CRITICAL THINKING

4. **Scientific Methods** How can you determine the genotype of a pea plant that has purple flowers?
5. **Mathematical Reasoning** If you flip two coins at once, will at least one coin land on heads? Explain.
6. **Analyzing Graphics** When analyzing a pedigree, how can you determine if an individual is a carrier (heterozygous) for the trait being studied?

### USING SCIENCE GRAPHICS

7. **Pedigree** Some kinds of colorblindness are sex-linked traits carried on the X chromosome. So, males can inherit the trait from mothers that are not colorblind. Draw a pedigree that demonstrates this pattern of inheritance.

Section

# 4 Beyond Mendelian Heredity

| Key Ideas | Key Terms | Why It Matters |
|---|---|---|
| ➤ Are there exceptions to the simple Mendelian pattern of inheritance?<br>➤ How do heredity and the environment interact to influence phenotype?<br>➤ How do linked genes affect chromosome assortment and crossover during meiosis? | polygenic character<br>codominance<br>linked | Some inheritance is more complex than Mendel showed. This complexity helps explain the large variety of human traits. |

*The Living Environment*
**Standard 4**

**2.1a** Genes are inherited, but their expression can be modified by interactions with the environment.

**2.1c** Hereditary information is contained in genes, located in the chromosomes of each cell. An inherited trait of an individual can be determined by one or by many genes, and a single gene can influence more than one trait. A human cell contains many thousands of different genes in its nucleus.

Suppose a horse that has red hair mates with a horse that has white hair. The offspring of the horses has both red and white hair on its body. How can this be? Shouldn't the colt's hair be one color or the other? Not always! In fact, most characters are not inherited in the simple patterns identified by Mendel. Although Mendel was correct about the inheritance of the traits that he studied, most patterns of inheritance are more complex than those that Mendel identified.

## Many Genes, Many Alleles

If you look at people and animals around you, you will notice a variety of physical features, as **Figure 9** shows. Why do so few of these features have only two types? First, not all genes have only two alleles. Second, not all characters are controlled by one gene. ➤ **The Mendelian inheritance pattern is rare in nature; other patterns include polygenic inheritance, incomplete dominance, multiple alleles, and codominance.**

**Polygenic Inheritance** When several genes affect a character, it is called a **polygenic character.** For example, eye color is affected by several genes. One gene controls the relative amount of greenness of the eye, and another gene controls brownness. (The recessive condition in both cases is blue eyes.) Other genes also affect eye color. Sorting out the effects of each gene is difficult. The genes may be on the same or different chromosomes. Other examples of polygenic characters in humans are height and skin color. In fact, most characters are polygenic.

**Figure 9** A physical feature—such as height, weight, hair color, and eye color—is often influenced by more than one gene.

**Incomplete Dominance** Recall that in Mendel's pea-plant crosses, one allele was completely dominant over the other. In some cases, however, an offspring has a phenotype that is intermediate between the traits of its two parents. This pattern is called *incomplete dominance.*

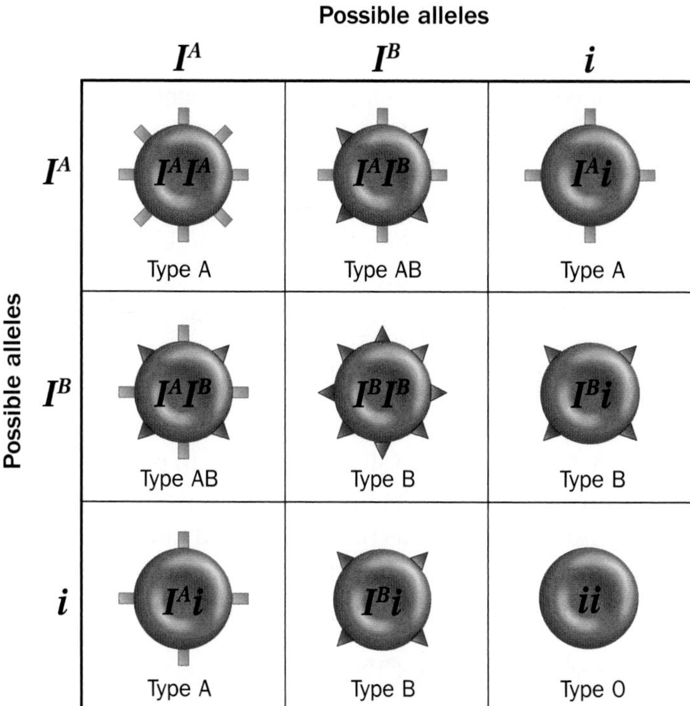


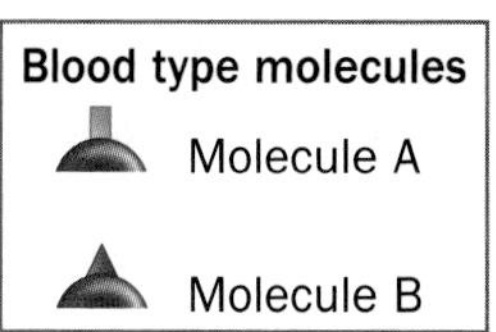


**Figure 10** Multiple alleles control the ABO blood groups. Different combinations of three alleles ($I^A$, $I^B$, and $i$) result in four blood phenotypes (A, AB, B, and O). For example, a person who has the alleles $I^A$ and $i$ has type A blood. **› What is another kind of inheritance pattern demonstrated by the ABO blood groups?**

When a snapdragon that has red flowers is crossed with a snapdragon that has white flowers, the offspring have pink flowers. Neither the red allele nor the white allele is completely dominant over the other. The pink flowers simply have less red pigment than the red flowers do.

**Multiple Alleles** Genes that have three or more possible alleles are said to have *multiple alleles*. For example, multiple alleles exist for hair color in cats. Still, only two alleles for a gene can be present in one individual. The determination of dominance may be complex.

In humans, the ABO blood groups (blood types) are determined by three alleles: $I^A$, $I^B$, and $i$. **Figure 10** shows how various combinations of the three alleles can produce four blood types: A, B, AB, and O. The $I^A$ and $I^B$ alleles cause red blood cells to make certain molecules. The letters *A* and *B* refer to the two kinds of molecules. The $i$ allele does not cause either molecule to be made. So, both the $I^A$ and $I^B$ alleles are dominant over $i$. But $I^A$ and $I^B$ are not dominant over each other. So, a person who has both $I^A$ and $I^B$ alleles has type AB blood. A person who has two $i$ alleles has type O blood.

**Codominance** For some characters, two traits can appear at the same time. **Codominance** is a condition in which both alleles for the same gene are fully expressed.

The genetics of human blood groups, which was discussed above, is also an example of codominance. A person who has $I^A I^B$ alleles will have type AB blood because neither allele is dominant over the other. Type AB blood cells make both A-type and B-type molecules.

**› Reading Check** ***How does codominance differ from incomplete dominance?***

**polygenic** (PAHL uh JEN ik ) **character**
a character that is influenced by more than one gene

**codominance** (KOH DAHM uh nuhns)
a condition in which both alleles for a gene are fully expressed

**ACADEMIC VOCABULARY**

**various** many kinds of

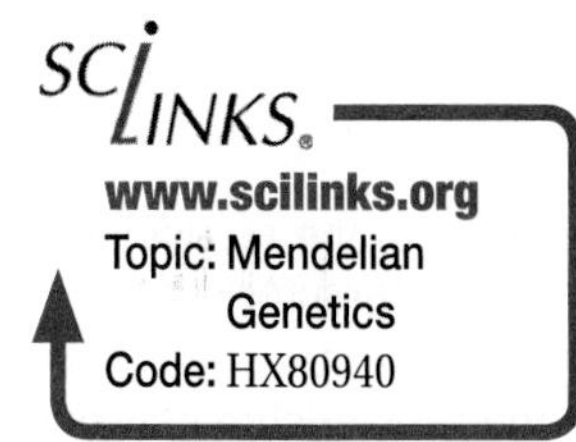

**Figure 11** Many Arctic mammals, such as the Arctic fox, develop white fur during the winter and dark fur during the summer. **❯ What does this change indicate about the character for fur color in these animals?**

## Genes Affected by the Environment

Genes are the key to life, but there is more to life than genes. **❯ Phenotype can be affected by conditions in the environment, such as nutrients and temperature.** For example, temperature affects the fur color of the Arctic fox, shown in **Figure 11.** During summer, genes in the fox's skin cells cause pigments to be made. These pigments make the fox's coat darker. Dark fur color helps the fox blend in with grass or woods. But during cold weather, the genes stop causing pigment to be made. Then, the fox's fur grows white, and the fox can blend in with the winter snow.

In humans, many of the characters that are partly determined by heredity are also affected by the environment. For example, a person's height is partly hereditary. Tall parents tend to produce tall children. But nutrition also affects height. A person who has an unhealthy diet may not grow as tall as he or she could have. Many aspects of human personality and behavior are strongly affected by the environment, but genes also seem to play an important role.

## Genes Linked Within Chromosomes

Many traits do not follow Mendel's laws, but Mendel's pea traits did. Why? One reason is that Mendel studied the simplest kinds of heredity: characters determined by one gene that has two alleles. Also, he studied characters that are determined by independent genes.

Recall how meiosis relates to the *law of independent assortment.* If genes are on different chromosomes, the alleles for each gene can be sorted independently. Then, each set of alleles can be recombined in any way. For example, in the pea plants, the two alleles for seed color could be combined in any way with the two alleles for seed shape.

Some genes are close together on the same chromosome. **❯ During meiosis, genes that are close together on the same chromosome are less likely to be separated than genes that are far apart.** Genes that are close together, as well as the traits that they determine, are said to be **linked.**

**linked** in genetics, describes two or more genes that tend to be inherited together

**❯ Reading Check** ***What term describes genes that are close together on the same chromosome and that are unlikely to be separated?***

## Section 4 Review

**❯ KEY IDEAS**

1. **List** exceptions to the Mendelian pattern of one character controlled by two alleles.
2. **Describe** the relationship between heredity and the environment.
3. **Relate** gene linkage to chromosome assortment and crossover during meiosis.

**CRITICAL THINKING**

4. **Evaluating an Argument** A classmate states that Mendel's hypotheses are incorrect because they do not consider intermediate forms of a character. Evaluate this argument.
5. **Applying Concepts** Propose another example of a character in humans that seems to be partly affected by heredity and partly affected by environment. Explain your reasoning.

**USING SCIENCE GRAPHICS**

6. **Punnett Square** Predict the ratios of each of the ABO blood groups in an average population. Use a Punnett square like the one shown in Figure 10 and explain your results. Assume that the population has equal numbers of $I^A$, $I^B$, and $i$ alleles.

# Chapter 12 Lab

MULTI-DAY 45 min

1.2.4

## Plant Genetics

In plants, albinism is characterized by the failure to produce chlorophyll, a plant pigment necessary for photosynthesis. Because the trait is recessive, parent plants with the normal phenotype may produce offspring (seeds) that carry the alleles for albinism. In this lab, you will investigate a question about albinism alleles in plants.

### Objectives

- Develop a hypothesis to predict the yield of a corn crop.
- Design and conduct an experiment to test your hypothesis.
- Compare germination and survival rates of three lots of corn seeds.

### Materials

- lab apron, disposable gloves
- corn seeds, normal (10 from lot A and 10 from lot B)
- corn seeds, 3:1 mix of normal and albino (10 from lot C)
- plant tray or pots
- soil, potting (3 kg)
- water

### Safety

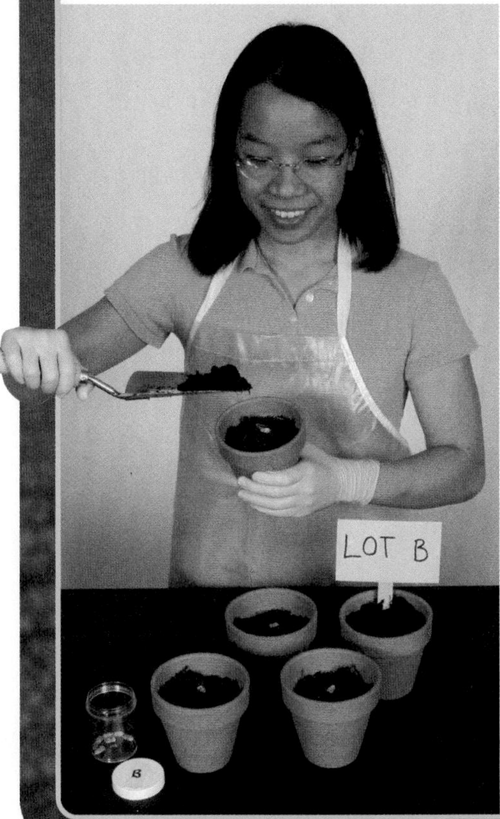


### Preparation

1. SCIENTIFIC METHODS **State the Problem** What might happen to a seed that has one or more albinism alleles?
2. SCIENTIFIC METHODS **Form a Hypothesis** Form a hypothesis about how albinism affects the success of plants grown from seed.

### Procedure

#### Design an Experiment

1. Design an experiment that will determine the germination and survival rates of three lots of corn seeds. Write out a procedure for your experiment on a separate sheet of paper. Be sure to include safety procedures, and construct tables to organize your data. Have your teacher approve your plan before you begin.
2. Predict the outcome of your experiment, and record this prediction.

#### Conduct Your Experiment

3. **CAUTION: Wear gloves and a lab apron whenever handling soil, seeds, or plants.**
4. Follow your written procedure. Make note of any changes.
5. Record all data in your tables. Also record any other observations.
6. At the end of the experiment, present your results to the class. Devise a way to collect the class data in a common format.
7. Clean up your lab materials according to your teacher's instructions. Wash your hands before leaving the lab.

### Analyze and Conclude

1. SCIENTIFIC METHODS **Evaluating Experimental Design** Did you get clear results? How might you improve your design?
2. SCIENTIFIC METHODS **Analyzing Results** Did your results support your hypothesis? Explain your answer.
3. **Analyzing Data** Use the class data to calculate the average germination rate and survival rate for each lot of corn seeds. Describe any patterns that you notice.

# Chapter 12 Summary

| Key Ideas | Key Terms |
|---|---|
| **1 Origins of Hereditary Science**<br>› Modern genetics is based on Mendel's explanations for the patterns of heredity that he studied in garden pea plants.<br>› The garden pea plant is a good subject for studying heredity because the plant has contrasting traits, usually self-pollinates, and grows easily.<br>› Mendel's first experiments used monohybrid crosses and were carried out in three steps.<br>› For each of the seven characters that Mendel studied, he found a similar 3-to-1 ratio of contrasting traits in the $F_2$ generation. | **character** (268)<br>**trait** (268)<br>**hybrid** (268)<br>**generation** (269) |
| **2 Mendel's Theory**<br>› Mendelian theory explains simple patterns of inheritance in which each possible combination of alleles results in one of several possible traits.<br>› In modern terms, the *law of segregation* holds that when an organism produces gametes, each pair of alleles is separated and each gamete has an equal chance of receiving either one of the alleles.<br>› Genotype determines phenotype.<br>› In modern terms, the *law of independent assortment* holds that during gamete formation, the alleles of each gene segregate independently. | **allele** (272)<br>**dominant** (273)<br>**recessive** (273)<br>**genotype** (274)<br>**phenotype** (274)<br>**homozygous** (275)<br>**heterozygous** (275) |
| **3 Modeling Mendel's Laws**<br>› A Punnett square shows all of the genotypes that could result from a given cross.<br>› Probability formulas can be used to predict the probabilities that specific alleles will be passed on to offspring.<br>› A pedigree can help answer questions about three aspects of inheritance: sex linkage, dominance, and heterozygosity. | **Punnett square** (276)<br>**probability** (278)<br>**pedigree** (280)<br>**genetic disorder** (280) |
| **4 Beyond Mendelian Heredity**<br>› Mendelian inheritance is rare in nature; other patterns include polygenic inheritance, incomplete dominance, multiple alleles, and codominance.<br>› Phenotype can be affected by conditions in the environment, such as nutrients and temperature.<br>› Genes that are close together on the same chromosome are linked. | **polygenic character** (282)<br>**codominance** (283)<br>**linked** (284) |

Chapter 12

The Living Environment

# Regents Exam Practice

**PART A: Answer all questions in this part.**

*Directions:* For each statement or question, write on your separate answer sheet the number of the word or expression that best completes the statement or answers the question.

**1** Which statement provides accurate information about the technique illustrated below?

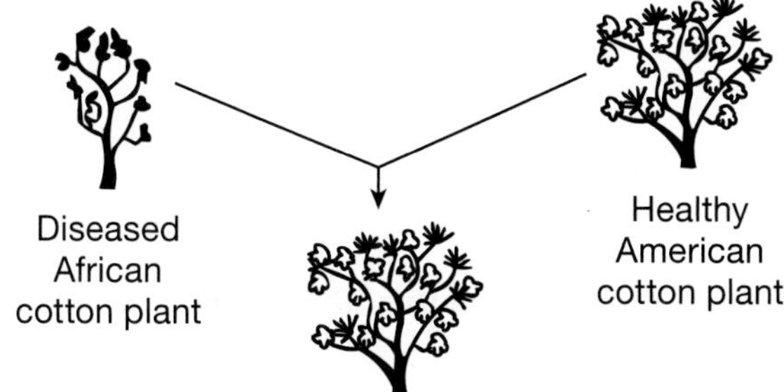


(1) This technique results in offspring that are genetically identical to the parents.
(2) New varieties of organisms can be developed by this technique known as selective breeding.
(3) This technique is used by farmers to eliminate mutations in future members of the species.
(4) Since the development of cloning, this technique is no longer used in agriculture.

**2** Which statement best explains the fact that some identical twins appear different from one another?

(1) Their DNA is essentially the same and the environment plays little or no role in the expression of their genes.
(2) Their DNA is very different and the environment plays a significant role in the expression of their genes.
(3) Their DNA is very different and the environment plays little or no role in the expression of their genes.
(4) Their DNA is essentially the same and the environment plays a significant role in the expression of their genes.

**3** Genes are inherited, but their expressions can be modified by the environment. This statement explains why

(1) some animals have dark fur only when the temperature is within a certain range
(2) offspring produced by means of sexual reproduction look exactly like their parents
(3) identical twins who grow up in different homes have the same characteristics
(4) animals can be cloned, but plants cannot

**4** Scientific studies show that identical twins who were separated at birth and raised in different homes may vary in height, weight, and intelligence. The most probable explanation for these differences is that

(1) original genes of each twin increased in number as they developed
(2) one twin received genes only from the mother while the other twin received genes only from the father
(3) environments in which they were raised were different enough to affect the expression of their genes
(4) environments in which they were raised were different enough to change the genetic makeup of both individuals

**5** In a particular variety of corn, the kernels turn red when exposed to sunlight. In the absence of sunlight, the kernels remain yellow. Based on this information, it can be concluded that the color of these corn kernels is due to

(1) a different type of DNA that is produced when sunlight is present
(2) a different species of corn that is produced in sunlight
(3) the effect of sunlight on the number of chromosomes inherited
(4) the effect of environment on gene expression

6 One variety of strawberry is resistant to a damaging fungus, but produces small fruit. Another strawberry variety produces large fruit, but is not resistant to the same fungus. The two desirable qualities may be combined in a new variety of strawberry plant by

(1) cloning
(2) asexual reproduction
(3) direct harvesting
(4) selective breeding

7 Some people are born with an extra finger or toe. People who have this trait have inherited either one or two of the same allele. So, the trait is

(1) recessive.
(2) dominant.
(3) phenotypic.
(4) independent.

**Base your answers to the following questions on the table below and on your knowledge of biology.**

| Experimental group | Dominant trait | Recessive trait |
| --- | --- | --- |
| Group 1 | 77 | 23 |
| Group 2 | 74 | 26 |
| Group 3 | 75 | 25 |
| Group 4 | 73 | 27 |

8 What is the approximate average ratio of dominant traits to recessive traits?

(1) 1:0
(2) 2:1
(3) 1:2
(4) 3:1

9 What kind of cross would result in these ratios?

(1) two heterozygous parents
(2) two homozygous recessive parents
(3) two homozygous dominant parents
(4) one heterozygous parent and one homozygous recessive parent

## PART B

**Base your answer to question 10 on the passage below and on your knowledge of biology.**

### In Search of a Low-Allergy Peanut

Many people are allergic to substances in the environment. Of the many foods that contain allergens (allergy-inducing substances), peanuts cause some of the most severe reactions. Mildly allergic people may only get hives. Highly allergic people can go into a form of shock. Some people die each year from reactions to peanuts.

A group of scientists is attempting to produce peanuts that lack the allergy-inducing proteins by using traditional selective breeding methods. They are searching for varieties of peanuts that are free of the allergens. By crossing those varieties with popular commercial types, they hope to produce peanuts that will be less likely to cause allergic reactions and still taste good. So far, they have found one variety that has 80 percent less of one of three complex proteins linked to allergic reactions. Removing all three of these allergens may be impossible, but even removing one could help.

Other researchers are attempting to alter the genes that code for the three major allergens in peanuts. All of this research is seen as a possible long-term solution to peanut allergies.

**10** Explain how selective breeding is being used to try to produce commercial peanuts that will not cause allergic reactions in people.

**Base your answer to question 11 on the passage below and on your knowledge of biology.**

### Better Rice

The production of new types of food crops will help raise the quantity of food grown by farmers. Research papers released by the National Academy of Sciences announced the development of two new superior varieties of rice—one produced by selective breeding and the other by biotechnology.

One variety of rice, called Nerica (New Rice for Africa), is already helping farmers in Africa. Nerica combines the hardiness and weed resistance of rare African rice varieties with the productivity and faster maturity of common Asian varieties.

Another variety, called Stress-Tolerant Rice, was produced by inserting a pair of bacterial genes into rice plants for the production of trehalose (a sugar). Trehalose helps plants maintain healthy cell membranes, proteins, and enzymes during environmental stress. The resulting plants survive drought, low temperatures, salty soils, and other stresses better than standard rice varieties.

**11** Nerica was most likely produced by

(1) crossing a variety of African rice with a variety of Asian rice
(2) cloning genes for hardiness and weed resistance from Asian rice
(3) using Asian rice to compete with rare African varieties
(4) inserting genes for productivity and faster maturity into Asian rice

Chapter 13

# DNA, RNA, and Proteins

## Preview



## Why It Matters

Did you know that DNA is found in the cells of all organisms? A unique set of genes makes one organism different from another, but DNA is the universal molecule found in all genes.

The shape of a DNA molecule is called a *double helix,* which looks a bit like a twisted ladder. The rails and the rungs of the ladder are each composed of different parts.

Nucleotide bases pair together to form the rungs of the ladder. Hydrogen bonds hold the bases together.

***The Living Environment***

**Standard 4** Students will understand and apply scientific concepts, principles, and theories pertaining to the physical setting and living environment and recognize the historical development of ideas in science.

**Key Idea 1** Living things are both similar to and different from each other and from nonliving things. ***Major Understandings*** **- 1.2i**

**Key Idea 2** Organisms inherit genetic information in a variety of ways that result in continuity of structure and function between parents and offspring. ***Major Understandings*** **– 2.1a, 2.1b, 2.1c, 2.1f, 2.1g, 2.1h, 2.1i**

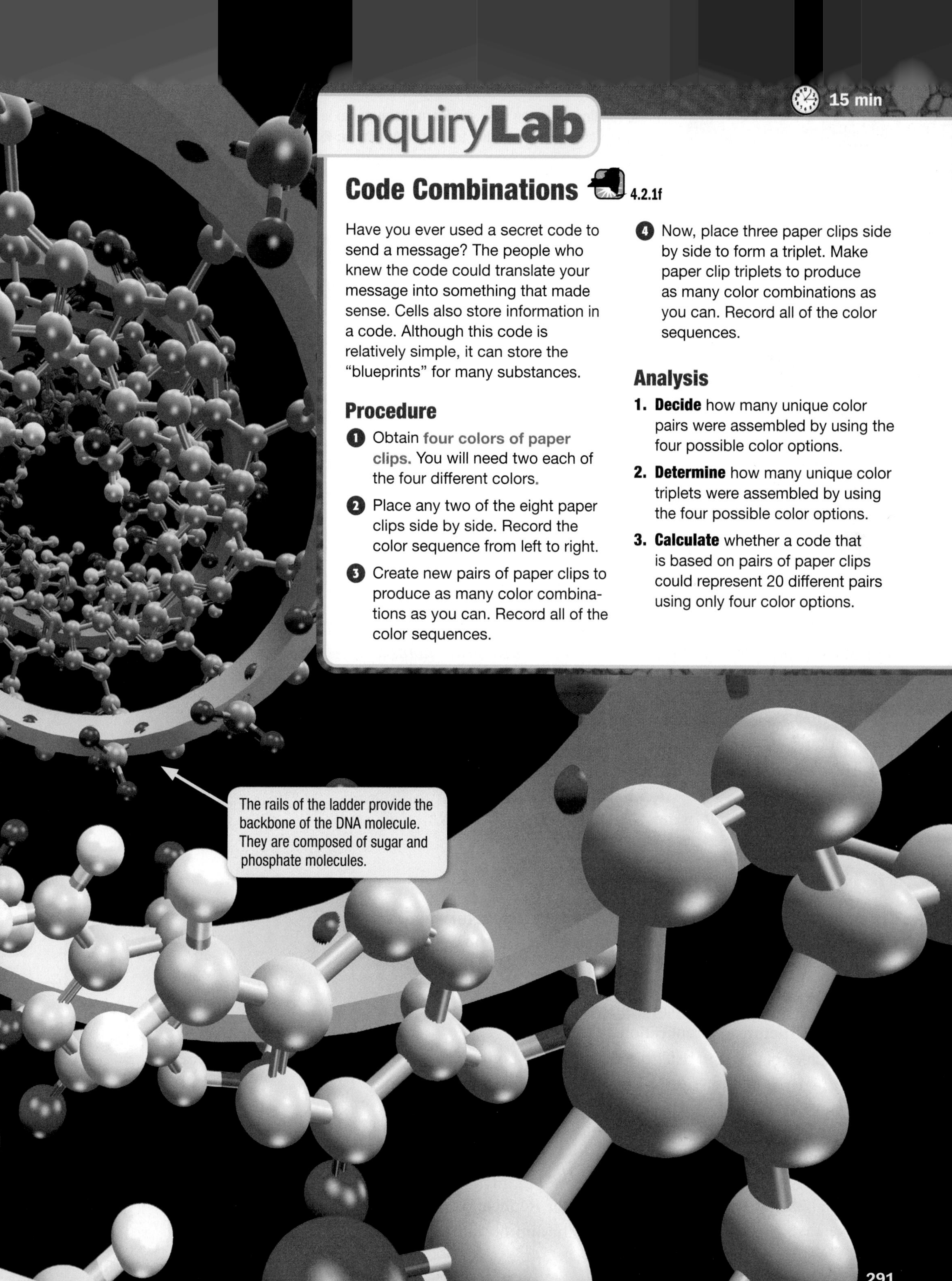

The rails of the ladder provide the backbone of the DNA molecule. They are composed of sugar and phosphate molecules.

15 min

# InquiryLab

## Code Combinations 4.2.1f

Have you ever used a secret code to send a message? The people who knew the code could translate your message into something that made sense. Cells also store information in a code. Although this code is relatively simple, it can store the "blueprints" for many substances.

### Procedure

1. Obtain **four colors of paper clips.** You will need two each of the four different colors.
2. Place any two of the eight paper clips side by side. Record the color sequence from left to right.
3. Create new pairs of paper clips to produce as many color combinations as you can. Record all of the color sequences.
4. Now, place three paper clips side by side to form a triplet. Make paper clip triplets to produce as many color combinations as you can. Record all of the color sequences.

### Analysis

1. **Decide** how many unique color pairs were assembled by using the four possible color options.
2. **Determine** how many unique color triplets were assembled by using the four possible color options.
3. **Calculate** whether a code that is based on pairs of paper clips could represent 20 different pairs using only four color options.

**These reading tools can help you learn the material in this chapter. For more information on how to use these and other tools, see Appendix: Reading and Study Skills.**

## Using Words

**Word Parts** Knowing the meanings of word parts can help you figure out the meanings of unknown words.

**Your Turn** Use the table to answer the following questions.

1. The root *-ptera* means "wing." What familiar machine is named for its spiral wing?
2. *Helicobacter* is a genus of bacteria. What shape is a bacterium of this genus?
3. In your own words, write a definition for *bacteriophage*.

**Word Parts**

| Part | Type | Meaning |
|---|---|---|
| *bacterio* | root | involving bacteria |
| *helic* | root | spiral |
| *-ase* | suffix | enzyme |
| *phage* | root | to eat or destroy |

## Using Language

**Describing Time** Certain words and phrases can help you understand when something happened and how long it took. These words and phrases are called *specific time markers*. Specific time markers include words and phrases such as *first, next, 1 hour, yesterday, the twentieth century,* and *30 years later.*

**Your Turn** Read the sentences below and write down the specific time markers.

1. Early in the morning, before the sun rises, Emilio gets up to take his dogs for a walk.
2. Before a cell can divide, it must first make a copy of its DNA.

## Using FoldNotes

**Three-Panel Flip Chart** A three-panel flip chart is useful when you want to organize notes about three topics. It can help you organize the characteristics of the topics side by side.

**Your Turn** Make a three-panel flip chart to organize your notes about DNA structure and replication.

1. Fold a piece of paper in half from the top to the bottom.
2. Fold the paper in three sections from side to side. Unfold the paper so that you can see the three sections.
3. From the top of the paper, cut along the vertical fold lines to the fold in the middle of the paper. You will now have three flaps.
4. Label the flaps of the three-panel flip chart "Identifying the Genetic Material," "The Structure of DNA," and "The Replication of DNA."
5. Under each flap, write your notes about the appropriate topic.

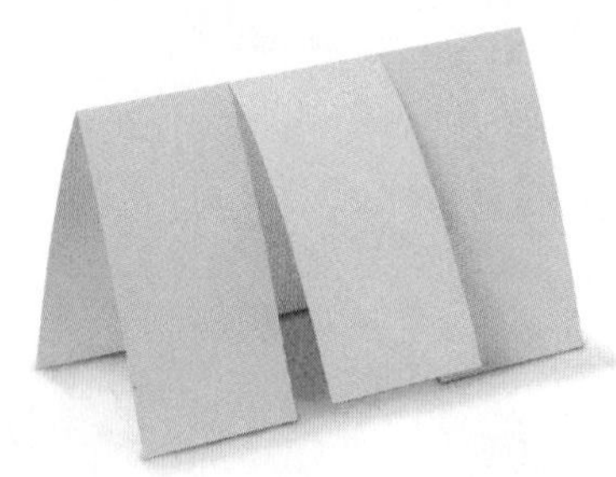

Section 1

# The Structure of DNA

| Key Ideas | Key Terms | Why It Matters |
|---|---|---|
| ❯ What is genetic material composed of?<br>❯ What experiments helped identify the role of DNA?<br>❯ What is the shape of a DNA molecule?<br>❯ How is information organized in a DNA molecule?<br>❯ What scientific investigations led to the discovery of DNA's structure? | gene<br>DNA<br>nucleotide<br>purine<br>pyrimidine | DNA is the "blueprint" from which all living things are made, so understanding DNA is key to understanding life. |

Unless you have an identical twin, you—like the sisters in **Figure 1**—share some, but not all, characteristics with family members.

## DNA: The Genetic Material

In the 1800s, Gregor Mendel showed that traits are passed from parents to offspring. Many years later, scientists have discovered how these traits are passed on. The instructions for inherited traits are called **genes.** Before the 1950s, however, scientists did not know what genes were made of. We now know that genes are made of small segments of deoxyribonucleic acid, or **DNA.** ❯ **DNA is the primary material that causes recognizable, inheritable characteristics in related groups of organisms.**

DNA is a relatively simple molecule, composed of only four different subunits. For this reason, many early scientists did not consider DNA to be complex enough to be genetic material. A few key experiments led to the discovery that DNA is, in fact, genetic material.

❯ **Reading Check** *What are genes composed of? (See Appendix for answers to Reading Checks.)*

***The Living Environment***
**Standard 4**

**2.1c** Hereditary information is contained in genes, located in the chromosomes of each cell. An inherited trait of an individual can be determined by one or by many genes, and a single gene can influence more than one trait. A human cell contains many thousands of different genes in its nucleus.

**2.1f** In all organisms, the coded instructions for specifying the characteristics of the organism are carried in DNA, a large molecule formed from subunits arranged in a sequence with bases of four kinds (represented by A, G, C, and T). The chemical and structural properties of DNA are the basis for how the genetic information that underlies heredity is both encoded in genes (as a string of molecular bases) and replicated by means of a template.

**2.1h** Genes are segments of DNA molecules. Any alteration of the DNA sequence is a mutation. Usually, an altered gene will be passed on to every cell that develops from it.

**gene** a segment of DNA that is located in a chromosome and that codes for a specific hereditary trait

**DNA** deoxyribonucleic acid, the material that contains the information that determines inherited characteristics

**Figure 1** These sisters share many traits but also have differences. ❯ **What role do genes play in passing traits from parents to offspring?**

## Searching for the Genetic Material

Once scientists discovered DNA, they began to search for its location. By the 1900s, scientists had determined that genetic material was located in cells, but they did not know exactly where. **❯ Three major experiments led to the conclusion that DNA is the genetic material in cells. These experiments were performed by Griffith, Avery, Hershey, and Chase.**

**Griffith's Discovery of Transformation** In 1928, Frederick Griffith was working with two related strains of bacteria. The S strain causes pneumonia and is covered by a capsule of polysaccharides. The R strain has no capsule and does not cause pneumonia. Mice that are infected with the S bacteria get sick and die. Griffith injected mice with heat-killed S bacteria. The bacteria were dead, but the capsule was still present. The mice lived. Griffith concluded that the S bacteria cause disease.

However, when harmless, live R bacteria were mixed with the harmless, heat-killed S bacteria and were injected into mice, the mice died. Griffith had discovered *transformation,* which is a change in genotype that is caused when cells take up foreign genetic material. Griffith's experiments, shown in **Figure 2,** led to the conclusion that genetic material could be transferred between cells. But no one knew that this material was DNA.

**Describing Time** Use specific time markers and **Figure 2** to describe Griffith's experiment.

**Avery's Experiments with Nucleic Acids** In the 1940s, Oswald Avery wanted to determine whether the transforming agent in Griffith's experiments was protein, RNA, or DNA. Avery and his colleagues used enzymes to destroy each of these molecules in heat-killed S bacteria. They found that bacteria that were missing protein and RNA were able to transform R cells into S cells. However, bacteria that were missing DNA did not transform R cells. The scientists concluded that DNA is responsible for transformation in bacteria.

In 1952, Alfred Hershey and Martha Chase thought that they could support Avery's conclusions by showing how DNA and proteins cross the cell membrane. Their experiment would determine how DNA affected other cells.

**Figure 2** Griffith discovered that harmless bacteria could cause disease when they were mixed with killed disease-causing bacteria. **❯ What were the variables in Griffith's experiments?**

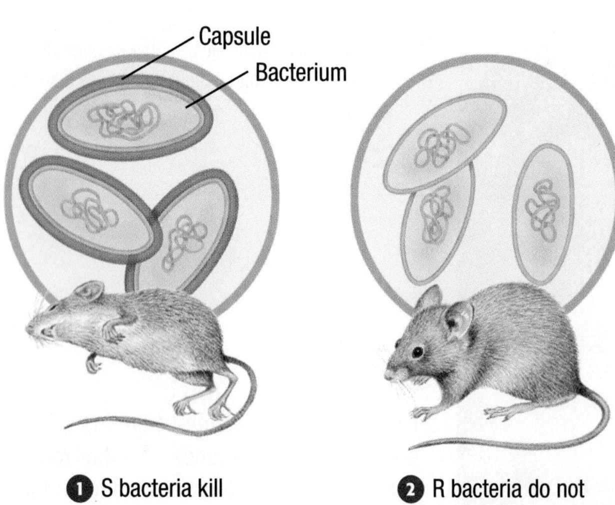


❶ S bacteria kill the mouse.

❷ R bacteria do not kill the mouse.

❸ Heat-killed S bacteria do not kill the mouse.

❹ R bacteria and heat-killed S bacteria kill the mouse.

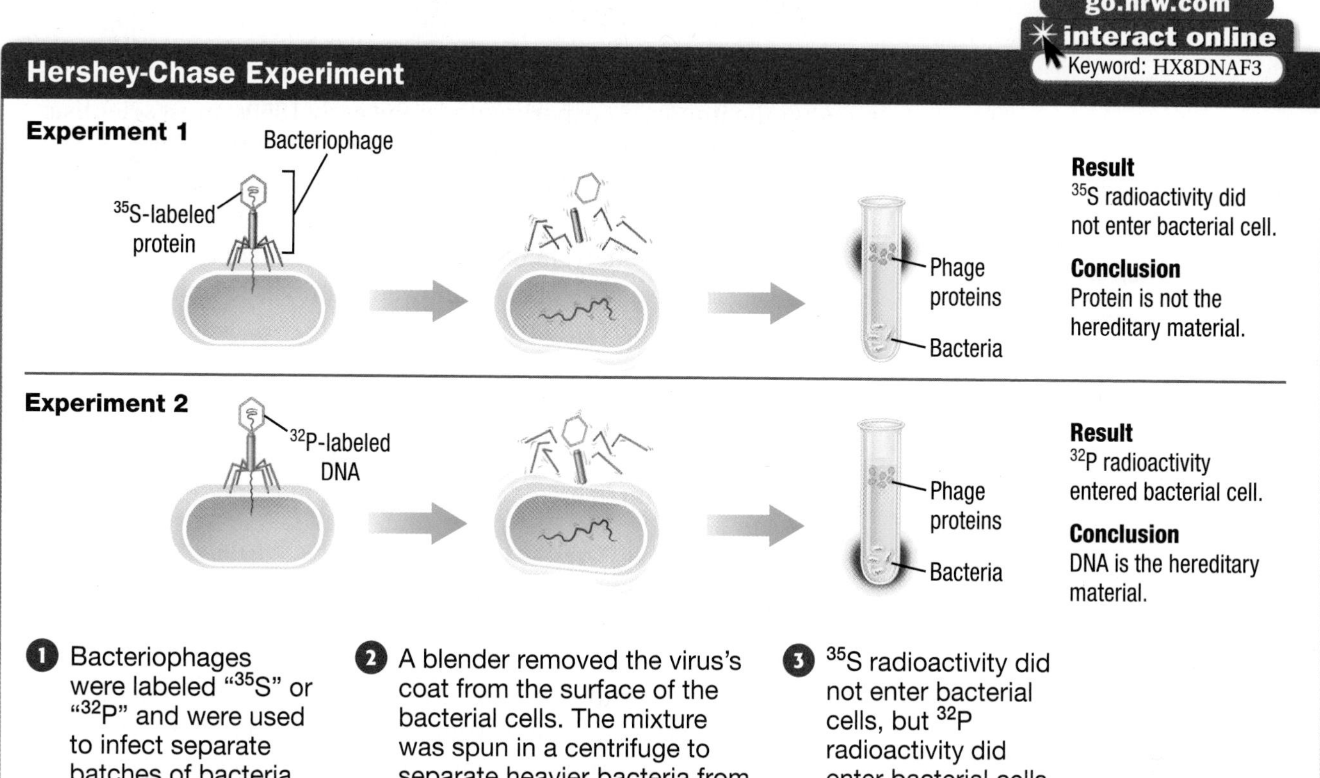
go.hrw.com
interact online
Keyword: HX8DNAF3
Hershey-Chase Experiment
Experiment 1
Bacteriophage
35S-labeled protein
Phage proteins
Bacteria
Result
35S radioactivity did not enter bacterial cell.
Conclusion
Protein is not the hereditary material.
Experiment 2
32P-labeled DNA
Phage proteins
Bacteria
Result
32P radioactivity entered bacterial cell.
Conclusion
DNA is the hereditary material.
1 Bacteriophages were labeled "35S" or "32P" and were used to infect separate batches of bacteria.
2 A blender removed the virus's coat from the surface of the bacterial cells. The mixture was spun in a centrifuge to separate heavier bacteria from the lighter bacteriophages.
3 35S radioactivity did not enter bacterial cells, but 32P radioactivity did enter bacterial cells.

**Figure 3** Bacteriophages were used to show that DNA, not protein, is the genetic material in viruses.

**Hershey-Chase Experiment** Hershey and Chase studied bacteriophages, viruses that infect bacterial cells and cause the cells to produce viruses. Bacteriophages are made up of proteins and DNA, but which of these two molecules is the genetic material in viruses? **Figure 3** illustrates their experiment.

**Step 1** First, Hershey and Chase knew that proteins contain some sulfur but no phosphorus and that DNA contains phosphorus but no sulfur. The scientists grew two sets of viruses in environments that were enriched with different radioactive isotopes. One set of viruses had radioactive sulfur ($^{35}S$) atoms attached to proteins. The other set had radioactive phosphorus ($^{32}P$) atoms attached to DNA.

**Step 2** Second, each set of viruses was allowed to infect separate batches of nonradioactive bacteria. Because radioactive elements release particles that can be detected with machines, they can be tracked in a biological process. Each of the batches was then separated into parts that contained only bacteria or only viruses.

**Step 3** The infected bacteria from the $^{35}S$ batch did not contain radioactive sulfur, so proteins could not have infected the bacteria. However, the infected bacteria from the $^{32}P$ batch did contain radioactive phosphorus. DNA had infected the bacteria.

Hershey and Chase concluded that only the DNA of viruses is injected into bacterial cells. The injected DNA caused the bacteria to produce viral DNA and proteins. This finding indicated that rather than proteins, DNA is the hereditary material, at least in viruses.

## The Shape of DNA

After the important experiments in the early 1950s, most scientists were convinced that genes were made of DNA, but nothing was known about DNA's structure. The research of many scientists led James Watson and Francis Crick, two young researchers at Cambridge University, to piece together a model of DNA's structure. Knowing the structure of DNA allowed scientists to understand how DNA could serve as genetic material.

**A Winding Staircase** ❯ **A DNA molecule is shaped like a spiral staircase and is composed of two parallel strands of linked subunits.** This spiral shape is known as a *double helix,* as **Figure 4** shows. Each strand is made up of linked subunits called nucleotides.

**Parts of the Nucleotide Subunits** Each **nucleotide** is made up of three parts: a phosphate group, a five-carbon sugar molecule, and a nitrogen-containing base. **Figure 4** shows how these three parts are arranged to form a nucleotide. The phosphate groups and the sugar molecules of nucleotides link together to form a "backbone" for a DNA strand. The five-carbon sugar in DNA is called *deoxyribose,* from which DNA gets its full name, *deoxyribonucleic acid.* The bases of nucleotides pair together to connect the two strands.

**Figure 4** Watson and Crick's model of DNA is a double helix that is composed of two nucleotide chains. The chains are twisted around a central axis and are held together by hydrogen bonds.

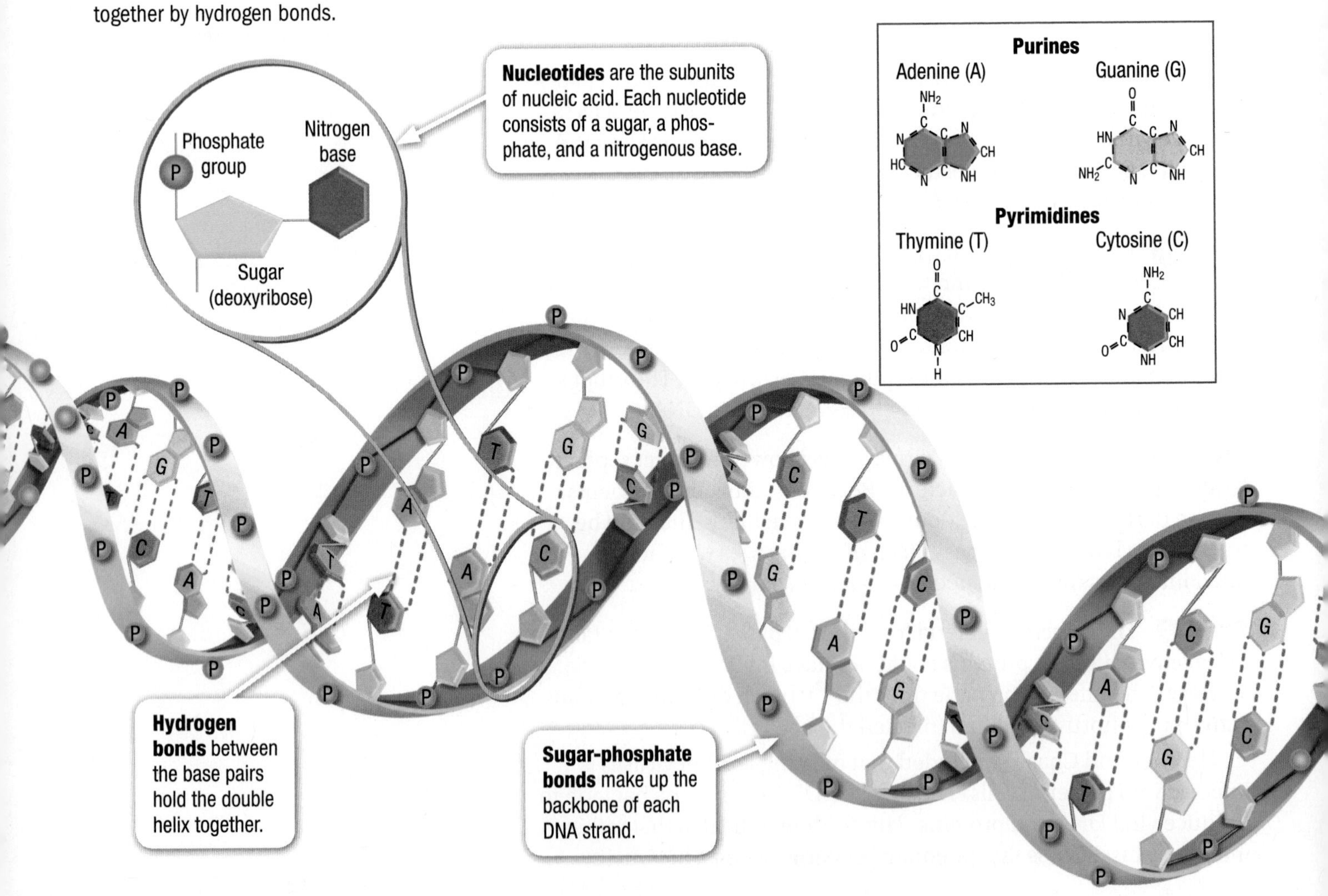

Phosphate group
Nitrogen base
Sugar (deoxyribose)

**Nucleotides** are the subunits of nucleic acid. Each nucleotide consists of a sugar, a phosphate, and a nitrogenous base.

**Purines**
Adenine (A)
Guanine (G)
**Pyrimidines**
Thymine (T)
Cytosine (C)

**Hydrogen bonds** between the base pairs hold the double helix together.

**Sugar-phosphate bonds** make up the backbone of each DNA strand.

Hands-On

# QuickLab

15 min

## DNA's Structure  4.2.1f

Build a model to help you understand the structure of DNA.

### Procedure

1. Use the following materials to build a model of DNA: **plastic straws** cut into 3 cm sections, a **metric ruler, scissors, pushpins (four different colors),** and **paper clips.** Your model should have at least 12 nucleotides on each strand.
2. As you design your model, decide how to use the straws, pushpins, and paper clips to represent the three components of a nucleotide and how to link the nucleotides together.

### Analysis

1. **Describe** your model by using words or drawings. Are the two strands in your model identical? Explain why or why not.
2. **Explain** how you determined which nucleotides were placed on each strand of DNA in your model.
3. CRITICAL THINKING **Inferring Relationships** How might the structure of DNA be beneficial when a cell copies its DNA before cell division?

## The Information in DNA

The structure of DNA is very important in the transfer of genetic information. ❯ **The information in DNA is contained in the order of the bases, while the base-pairing structure allows the information to be copied.**

**Nitrogenous Bases** In DNA, each nucleotide has the same sugar molecule and phosphate group, but the nucleotide can have one of four nitrogenous bases. The four kinds of bases, shown in **Figure 4,** are *adenine* (A), *guanine* (G), *thymine* (T), and *cytosine* (C). Bases A and G are classified as **purines.** Purines have two rings of carbon and nitrogen atoms per base. Bases T and C are **pyrimidines.** Pyrimidines have one ring of carbon and nitrogen atoms per base.

**Base-Pairing Rules** A purine on one strand of a DNA molecule is always paired with a pyrimidine on the other strand. More specifically, adenine always pairs with thymine, and guanine always pairs with cytosine. These *base-pairing rules* are dictated by the chemical structure of the bases. The structure and size of the nitrogenous bases allow for only these two pair combinations. The base pairs are held together by weak hydrogen bonds. Adenine forms two hydrogen bonds with thymine, while cytosine forms three hydrogen bonds with guanine. The hydrogen bonds are represented by dashed lines in **Figure 4.** The hydrogen bonds between bases keep the two strands of DNA together.

❯ **Reading Check** *How are base-pairs held together?*

**nucleotide** (NOO klee oh TIED) in a nucleic acid chain, a subunit that consists of a sugar, a phosphate, and a nitrogenous base

**purine** (PYOOR EEN) a nitrogenous base that has a double-ring structure; adenine or guanine

**pyrimidine** (pi RIM uh DEEN) a nitrogenous base that has a single-ring structure; in DNA, either thymine or cytosine

**Academic Vocabulary**

**complementary** being separate parts that improve or enhance each other

**Complementary Sides** **Figure 5** shows a simpler way to represent base-pairing. Paired bases are said to be complementary because they fit together like puzzle pieces. For example, if the sequence of nitrogen bases on one strand is TATGAGAGT, the sequence of nitrogen bases on the other strand must be ATACTCTCA. The pairing structure ensures that each strand of a DNA molecule contains the same information. However, the information on one strand is in reverse order from that on the other strand.

## Discovering DNA's Structure

How were James Watson and Francis Crick able to determine the double-helical structure of DNA? **Watson and Crick used information from experiments by Chargaff, Wilkins, and Franklin to determine the three-dimensional structure of DNA.**

**Observing Patterns: Chargaff's Observations** In 1949, biochemist Erwin Chargaff made an interesting observation about DNA. His data showed that for each organism that he studied, the amount of adenine always equaled the amount of thymine (A = T). Similarly, the amount of guanine always equaled the amount of cytosine (G = C). **Figure 6** shows some of Chargaff's data. Watson and Crick used this information to determine how nucleotides are paired in DNA.

**Using Technology: Photographs of DNA** The significance of Chargaff's data became clear when scientists began using X rays to study the structures of molecules. In 1952, Rosalind Franklin, shown in **Figure 6,** and Maurice Wilkins developed high-quality X-ray diffraction images of strands of DNA. These photographs suggested that the DNA molecule resembled a tightly coiled helix and was composed of two chains of nucleotides.

**Figure 5** The diagram of DNA below the double helix simplifies the base pairing that occurs between DNA strands.

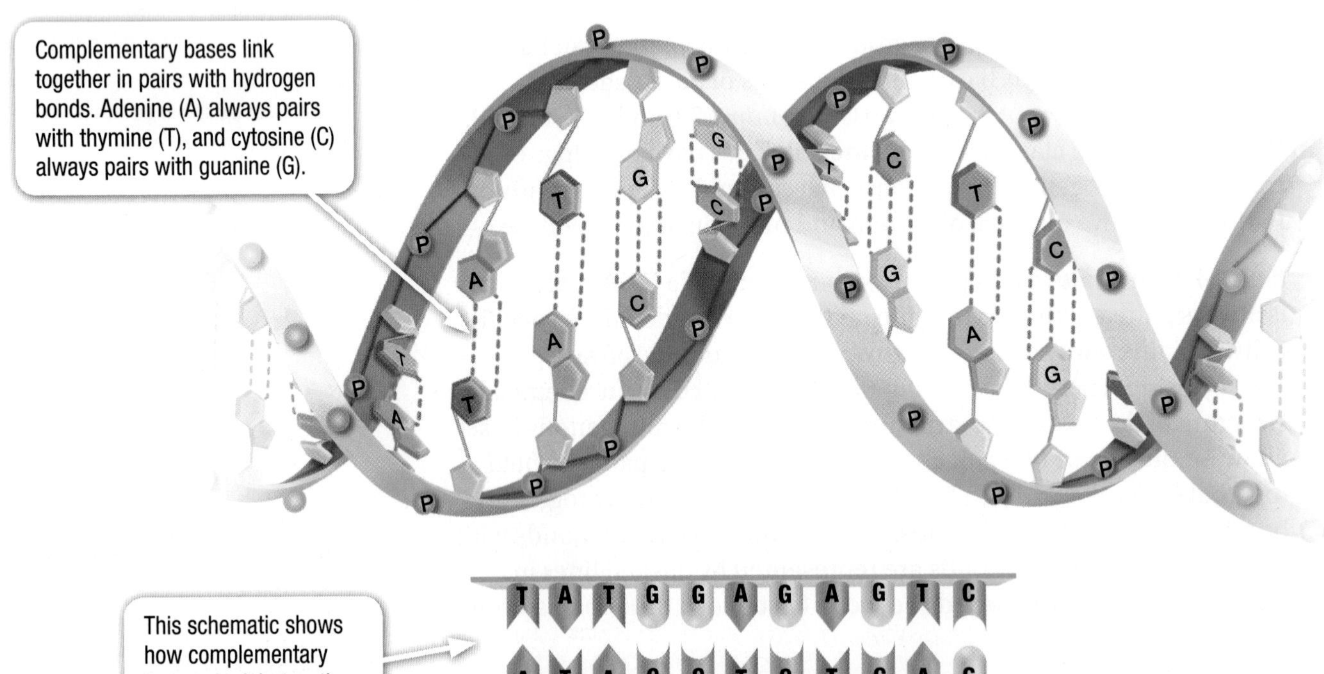

Complementary bases link together in pairs with hydrogen bonds. Adenine (A) always pairs with thymine (T), and cytosine (C) always pairs with guanine (G).
This schematic shows how complementary base pairs join together.
T A T G G A G A G T C
A T A C C T C T C A G

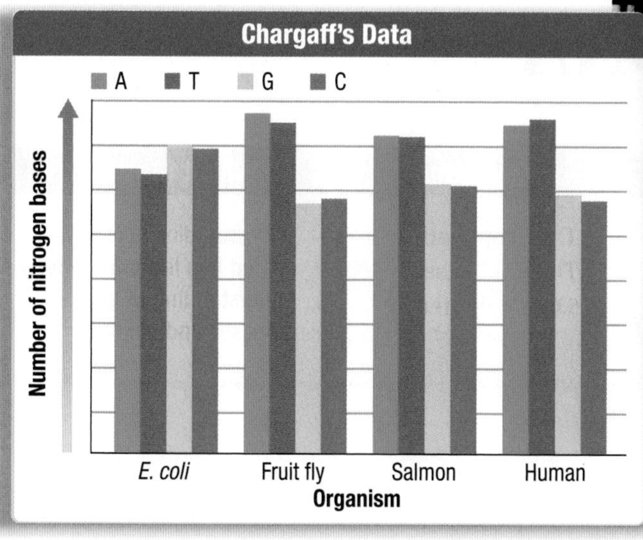


**Watson & Crick**

**Franklin**

**Figure 6** Chargaff's data and Franklin's X-ray diffraction studies were instrumental in the discovery of DNA's structure. Watson and Crick are shown with their tin and wire model of DNA.

**Watson and Crick's Model of DNA** To determine the three-dimensional structure of DNA, Watson and Crick set out to build a model of DNA. They knew that any model would have to take into account both Chargaff's data and the findings from Franklin's X-ray diffraction studies. In 1953, Watson and Crick used these findings, along with knowledge of chemical bonding, to create a complete three-dimensional model of DNA. By using paper models of the bases, Watson and Crick worked out the pairing structure of purines with pyrimidines. Then, they built a large model of a DNA double helix by using tin, wire, and other materials. Their model showed a "spiral staircase" in which two strands of nucleotides twisted around a central axis. **Figure 6** shows Watson and Crick with their model.

Nine years later, in 1962, the Nobel Prize was awarded to Watson, Crick, and Wilkins for their discovery. Rosalind Franklin died in 1958 and was not named in the award.

› **Reading Check** ***How was X-ray diffraction used to model the structure of DNA?***

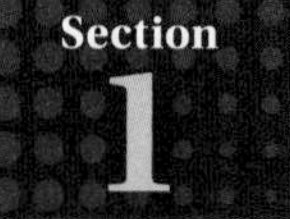


## Review

### › KEY IDEAS

1. **Identify** the substance that makes up genetic material.
2. **Name** the experiments that identified the role of DNA.
3. **Draw** the shape of a DNA molecule.
4. **Relate** the structure of DNA to the function of DNA as a carrier of information.
5. **Name** the studies that led to the discovery of DNA's structure.

### CRITICAL THINKING

6. **Applying Information** If a DNA strand has the nucleotide sequence of CCGAGATTG, what is the nucleotide sequence of the complementary strand?
7. **Applying Information** What might Hershey and Chase have concluded if they had found $^{35}S$ instead of $^{32}P$ in bacterial cells? Explain your answer.

### USING SCIENCE GRAPHICS

8. **Evaluating Graphics** Look at the graph of Chargaff's data in **Figure 6.** How do the amounts of adenine compare with the amounts of thymine across species? How do the amounts of cytosine and guanine compare? How did these data lead to the discovery of the base-pairing rules by Chargaff? How was this discovery used to determine DNA's structure?

Section

# 2 Replication of DNA

| Key Ideas | Key Terms | Why It Matters |
|---|---|---|
| ➤ How does DNA replicate, or make a copy of itself?<br>➤ What are the roles of proteins in DNA replication?<br>➤ How is DNA replication different in prokaryotes and eukaryotes? | DNA replication<br>DNA helicase<br>DNA polymerase | Understanding how DNA is copied has led to a better understanding of genetic diseases and cancer. |

*The Living Environment*
**Standard 4**

**2.1b** Every organism requires a set of coded instructions for specifying its traits. For offspring to resemble their parents, there must be a reliable way to transfer information from one generation to the next. Heredity is the passage of these instructions from one generation to another.

**2.1f** In all organisms, the coded instructions for specifying the characteristics of the organism are carried in DNA, a large molecule formed from subunits arranged in a sequence with bases of four kinds (represented by A, G, C, and T). The chemical and structural properties of DNA are the basis for how the genetic information that underlies heredity is both encoded in genes (as a string of molecular bases) and replicated by means of a template.

When cells divide, each new cell contains an exact copy of the original cell's DNA. How is this possible?

## DNA Replication

Remember that DNA is made of two strands of complementary base pairs. Adenine always pairs with thymine, and guanine always pairs with cytosine. If the strands of DNA are separated, as shown in **Figure 7**, each strand can serve as a pattern to make a new complementary strand. This separation allows two exact copies of DNA to be made from the original DNA molecule. Copying the DNA before cell division allows each new cell to have DNA identical to the original cell's.

The process of making a copy of DNA is called **DNA replication.** ➤ **In DNA replication, the DNA molecule unwinds, and the two sides split. Then, new nucleotides are added to each side until two identical sequences result.** DNA replication occurs before a cell divides so that each cell has a complete copy of DNA. The basic steps of DNA replication are described below and are illustrated in **Figure 8** on the next page.

**Step 1 Unwinding and Separating DNA Strands** Before DNA replication can begin, the double helix unwinds. The two complementary strands of DNA separate from each other and form Y shapes. These Y-shaped areas are called *replication forks.* **Figure 7** shows two replication forks in a molecule of DNA.

**Step 2 Adding Complementary Bases** At the replication fork, new nucleotides are added to each side and new base pairs are formed according to the base-pairing rules. For example, if one of the original strands has thymine, then adenine will be paired with thymine as the new strand forms. Thus, the original two strands serve as a template for two new strands. As more nucleotides are added, two new double helixes begin to form. The process continues until the whole DNA sequence has been copied.

**Step 3 Formation of Two Identical DNA Molecules** This process of DNA replication produces two identical DNA molecules. Each double-stranded DNA helix is made of one new strand of DNA and one original strand of DNA. The nucleotide sequences in both of these DNA molecules are identical to each other and to the original DNA molecule.

**Figure 7** When the two strands of the DNA helix separate, Y-shaped replication forks form.

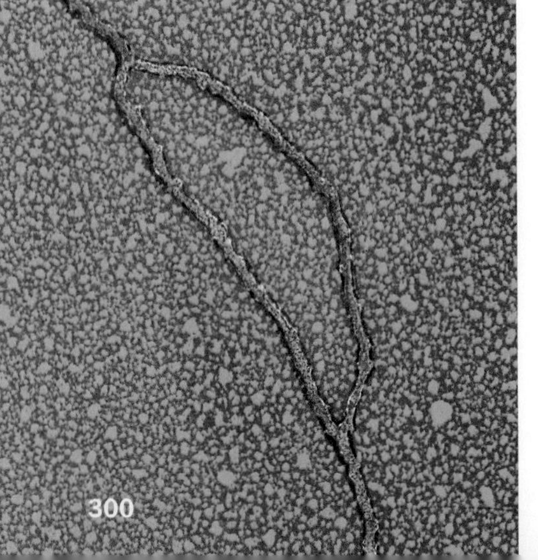

go.hrw.com
interact online
Keyword: HX8DNAF8

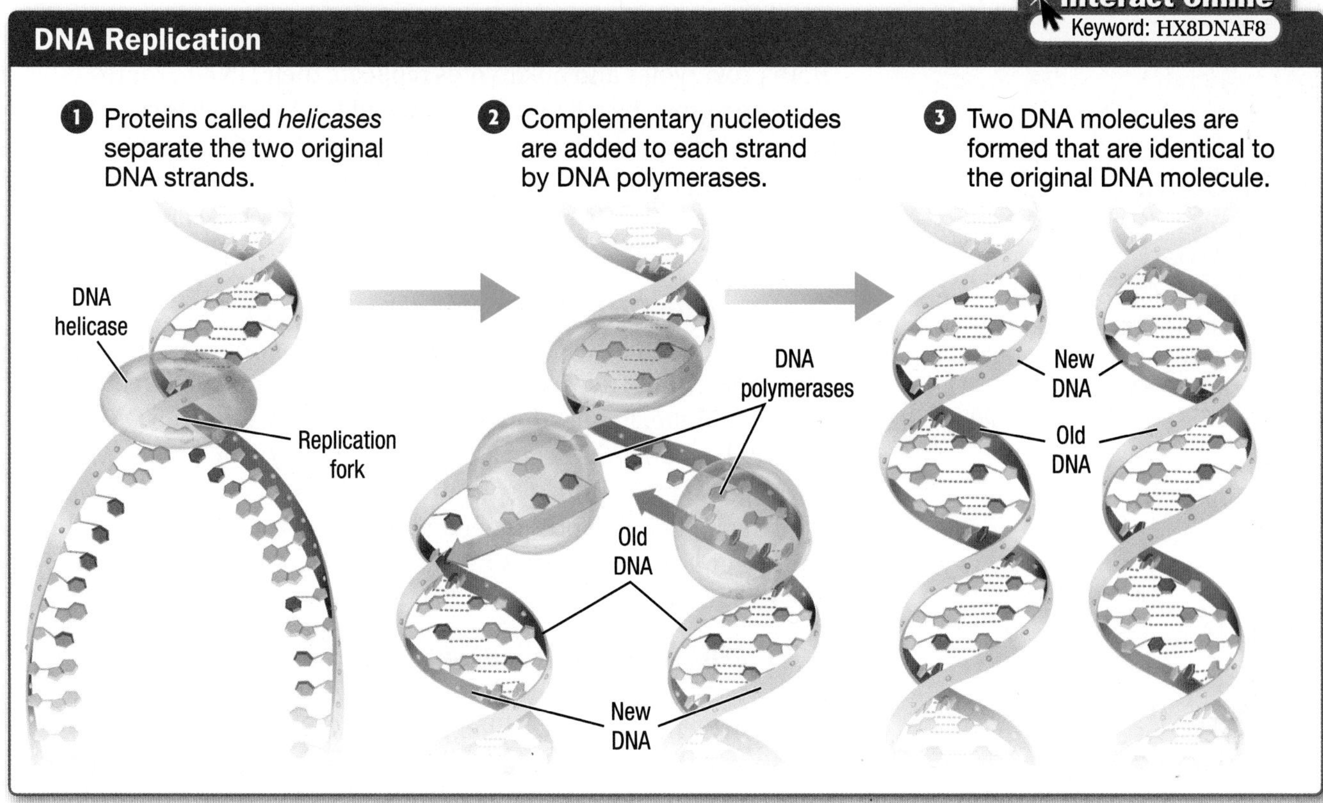
DNA Replication
1 Proteins called helicases separate the two original DNA strands.
2 Complementary nucleotides are added to each strand by DNA polymerases.
3 Two DNA molecules are formed that are identical to the original DNA molecule.
DNA helicase
Replication fork
DNA polymerases
Old DNA
New DNA
New DNA
Old DNA

**Figure 8** DNA replication results in two identical DNA strands.

## Replication Proteins

**› During the replication of DNA, many proteins form a machinelike complex of moving parts.** Each protein has a specific function.

**DNA Helicase** Proteins called **DNA helicases** unwind the DNA double helix during DNA replication. These proteins wedge themselves between the two strands of the double helix and break the hydrogen bonds between the base pairs. This process causes the helix to unwind and forms a replication fork, as **Figures 7** and **8** show. Additional proteins keep the two strands separated so that replication can occur.

**DNA Polymerase** Proteins called **DNA polymerases** catalyze the formation of the DNA molecule. At the replication fork, DNA polymerases move along each strand. The polymerases add nucleotides that pair with each base to form two new double helixes. After all of the DNA has been copied, the polymerases are released.

DNA polymerases also have a "proofreading" function. During DNA replication, errors sometimes occur, and the wrong nucleotide is added to the new strand. DNA polymerases cannot add another nucleotide unless the previous nucleotide is correctly paired with its complementary base. If a mismatch occurs, the DNA polymerase can backtrack, remove the incorrect nucleotide, and replace it with the correct one. Proofreading reduces the replication errors to about one per 1 billion nucleotides.

**› Reading Check** *Why is proofreading critical during replication?*

**DNA replication** the process of making a copy of DNA

**DNA helicase** (HEEL uh KAYS) an enzyme that unwinds the DNA double helix during DNA replication

**DNA polymerase** (puh LIM uhr AYS) an enzyme that catalyzes the formation of the DNA molecule

**Word Parts** In your own words, write a definition of *helicase* and *polymerase,* the names of the enzymes involved in DNA replication, based on the meanings of each term's word parts.

## Prokaryotic and Eukaryotic Replication

Both prokaryotes and eukaryotes replicate their DNA to reproduce and grow. Recall that the packaged DNA in a cell is called a *chromosome.* All cells have chromosomes, but eukaryotes and prokaryotes replicate their chromosomes differently. ❯ **In prokaryotic cells, replication starts at a single site. In eukaryotic cells, replication starts at many sites along the chromosome.**

**Prokaryotic DNA Replication** Prokaryotic cells usually have a single DNA molecule, or chromosome. Prokaryotic chromosomes are a closed loop, may contain protein, and are attached to the inner cell membrane. Replication begins at one place along the DNA loop. Two replication forks begin at that single point, which is known as the origin of replication. Replication occurs in opposite directions until the replication forks meet on the opposite side of the DNA loop and the entire molecule has been copied. **Figure 9** shows prokaryotic DNA replication.

**Eukaryotic DNA Replication** While prokaryotes have a single chromosome, eukaryotic cells often have several chromosomes. Eukaryotic chromosomes differ from the simple, looped chromosomes found in prokaryotic cells. Eukaryotic chromosomes are linear, and they contain both DNA and protein. Recall that the long molecules of DNA are tightly wound around proteins called *histones* and are packaged into thick chromosome fibers.

**ACADEMIC VOCABULARY**

**distinct** separate; not the same

By starting replication at many sites along the chromosome, eukaryotic cells can replicate their DNA faster than prokaryotes can. As in prokaryotic replication, two distinct replication forks form at each start site, and replication occurs in opposite directions. This process forms replication "bubbles" along the DNA molecule. The replication bubbles continue to get larger as more of the DNA is copied. As **Figure 9** shows, they eventually meet to form two identical, linear DNA molecules. Because multiple replication forks are working at the same time, an entire human chromosome can be replicated in about eight hours. Then, the cell will be ready to divide.

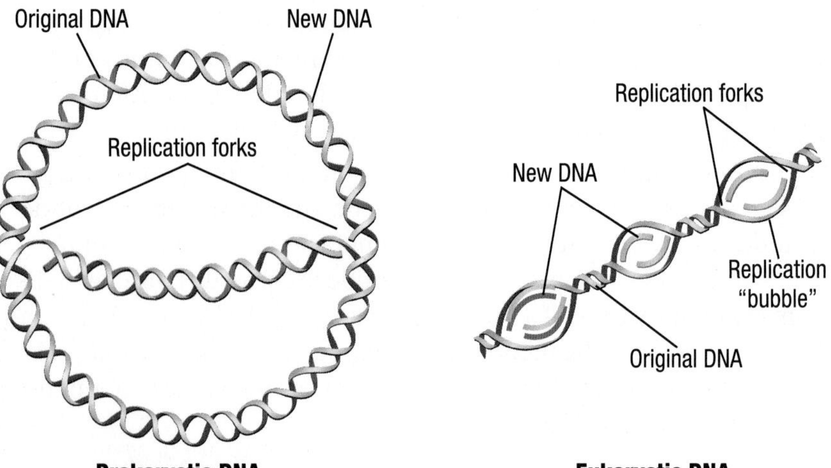


**Figure 9** Prokaryotic and eukaryotic DNA have different numbers of replication forks. ❯ **Why does replication in eukaryotes involve more replication forks?**

Data

# QuickLab

15 min

## DNA Replication Rate

Cancer is a disease caused by cells that divide uncontrollably. Scientists studying drugs that prevent cancer often measure the effectiveness of a drug by its effect on DNA replication. During normal DNA replication, nucleotides are added at a rate of about 50 nucleotides per second in mammals and 500 nucleotides per second in bacteria.

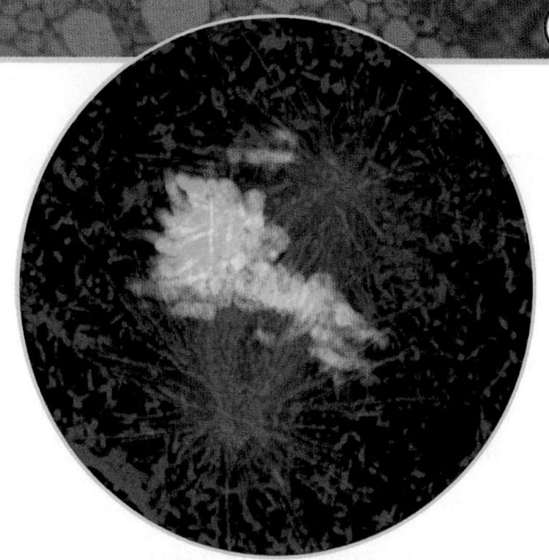

### Analysis

1. **Calculate** the time it would take a bacterium to add 4,000 nucleotides to one DNA strand undergoing replication.
2. **Calculate** the time it would take a mammalian cell to add 4,000 nucleotides to one DNA strand undergoing replication.
3. CRITICAL THINKING **Predicting Outcomes** How would the total time needed to add the 4,000 nucleotides be affected if a drug that inhibits DNA polymerases were present? Explain your answer.

**Size of Eukaryotic DNA** The smallest eukaryotic chromosomes are often 10 times the size of a prokaryotic chromosome. If a scientist took all of the DNA in a single human cell and laid the DNA in one line (that is, laid the DNA from all 46 chromosomes end to end), the line would be 2 m long. In contrast, if the scientist laid out the DNA from one bacterial chromosome, the line would be only about 0.25 cm long. In fact, the length of eukaryotic chromosomes is so long that replication of a typical human chromosome would take 33 days if there were only one origin of replication.

Each human chromosome is replicated in about 100 sections that are 100,000 nucleotides long, each section with its own starting point. With multiple replication forks working in concert, an entire human chromosome can be replicated in about 8 hours.

SCILINKS.
**www.scilinks.org**
Topic: DNA Replication
Code: HX80420

› **Reading Check** *How is a "replication bubble" formed?*

## Section 2 Review

### › KEY IDEAS

1. **Describe** the steps of DNA replication.
2. **Compare** the roles of DNA helicases and DNA polymerases.
3. **Compare** the process of DNA replication in prokaryotes and in eukaryotes.

### CRITICAL THINKING

4. **Inferring Relationships** What is the relationship between DNA polymerases and mutations in DNA?
5. **Relating Concepts** Cancer is a disease caused by cells that divide uncontrollably. Scientists are researching drugs that inhibit DNA polymerase as potential anticancer drugs. Why would these drugs be useful against cancer?

### ALTERNATIVE ASSESSMENT

6. **Replication Model** Conduct research on the shapes of prokaryotic and eukaryotic chromosomes. Draw a model of each type of chromosome. How does the structure of chromosomes in prokaryotic cells and eukaryotic cells affect the DNA replication processes in a cell?

Section 3

# RNA and Gene Expression

| Key Ideas | Key Terms | Why It Matters |
|---|---|---|
| ❯ What is the process of gene expression?<br>❯ What role does RNA play in gene expression?<br>❯ What happens during transcription?<br>❯ How do codons determine the sequence of amino acids that results after translation?<br>❯ What are the major steps of translation?<br>❯ Do traits result from the expression of a single gene? | RNA<br>gene expression<br>transcription<br>translation<br>codon | Traits, such as eye color, are determined by proteins that are built according to instructions coded in DNA. |

***The Living Environment***
**Standard 4**

**1.2i** Inside the cell a variety of specialized structures, formed from many different molecules, carry out the transport of materials (cytoplasm), extraction of energy from nutrients (mitochondria), protein building (ribosomes), waste disposal (cell membrane), storage (vacuole), and information storage (nucleus).

**2.1a** Genes are inherited, but their expression can be modified by interactions with the environment.

**2.1g** Cells store and use coded information. The genetic information stored in DNA is used to direct the synthesis of the thousands of proteins that each cell requires.

**2.1i** The work of the cell is carried out by the many different types of molecules it assembles, mostly proteins. Protein molecules are long, usually folded chains made from 20 different kinds of amino acids in a specific sequence. This sequence influences the shape of the protein. The shape of the protein, in turn, determines its function.

Proteins perform most of the functions of cells. DNA provides the original "recipe," or information, from which proteins are made in the cell. However, DNA does not directly make proteins. A second type of nucleic acid, ribonucleic acid, or **RNA,** is essential in taking the genetic information from DNA and building proteins.

## An Overview of Gene Expression

**Gene expression** is the manifestation of genes into specific traits. **❯ Gene expression produces proteins by transcription and translation. This process takes place in two stages, both of which involve RNA. Figure 10** illustrates the parts of the cell that play a role in gene expression.

**Transcription: DNA to RNA** The first stage of gene expression, which is making RNA from the information in DNA, is called **transcription.** You can think of transcription as copying (transcribing) notes from the board (DNA) to a notebook (RNA).

**RNA** ribonucleic acid, a natural polymer that is present in all living cells and that plays a role in protein synthesis

**gene expression** the manifestation of the genetic material of an organism in the form of specific traits

**transcription** the process of forming a nucleic acid by using another molecule as a template

**translation** the portion of protein synthesis that takes place at ribosomes and that uses the codons in mRNA molecules to specify the sequence of amino acids in polypeptide chains

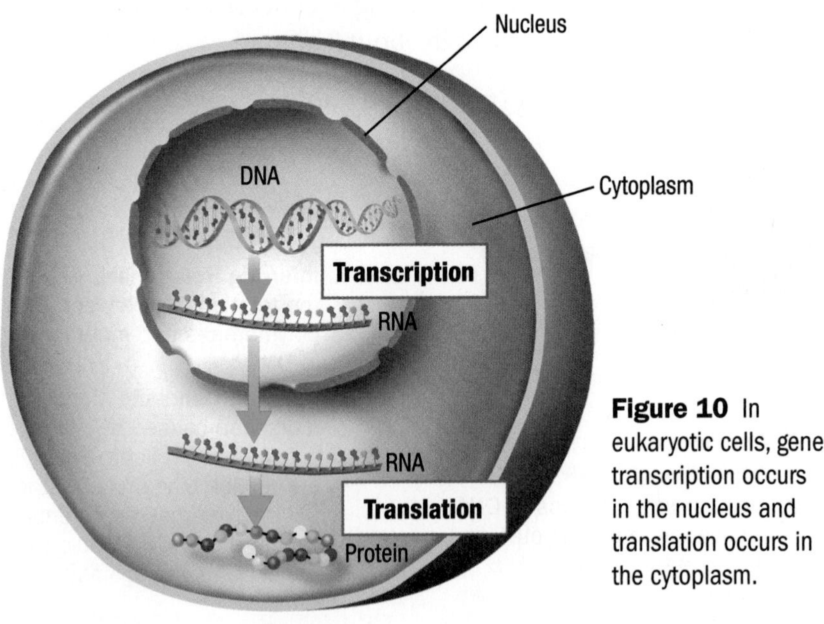


**Figure 10** In eukaryotic cells, gene transcription occurs in the nucleus and translation occurs in the cytoplasm.

**Translation: RNA to Proteins** The second stage of gene expression, called **translation,** uses the information in RNA to make a specific protein. Translation is similar to translating a sentence in one language (RNA, the nucleic acid "language") to another language (protein, the amino acid "language").

## RNA: A Major Player

All of the steps in gene expression involve RNA. Several types of RNA are used in transcription and translation. › **In cells, three types of RNA complement DNA and translate the genetic code into proteins.** But what exactly is RNA, and how does it compare to DNA?

**RNA Versus DNA** Like DNA, RNA is a nucleic acid—a molecule made of nucleotide subunits linked together. Like DNA, RNA has four bases and carries information in the same way that DNA does.

RNA differs from DNA in three ways. First, RNA usually is composed of one strand of nucleotides rather than two strands. The structural difference between the two nucleotides is shown in **Figure 11.** Second, RNA nucleotides contain the five-carbon sugar *ribose* rather than the sugar deoxyribose. Ribose contains one more oxygen atom than deoxyribose does. And third, RNA nucleotides have a nitrogenous base called *uracil* (U) instead of the base thymine (T). Although no thymine (T) bases are found in RNA, the other bases (A, G, and C) are identical to the bases found in DNA. In place of thymine, uracil (U) is complementary to adenine (A) whenever RNA pairs with another nucleic acid.

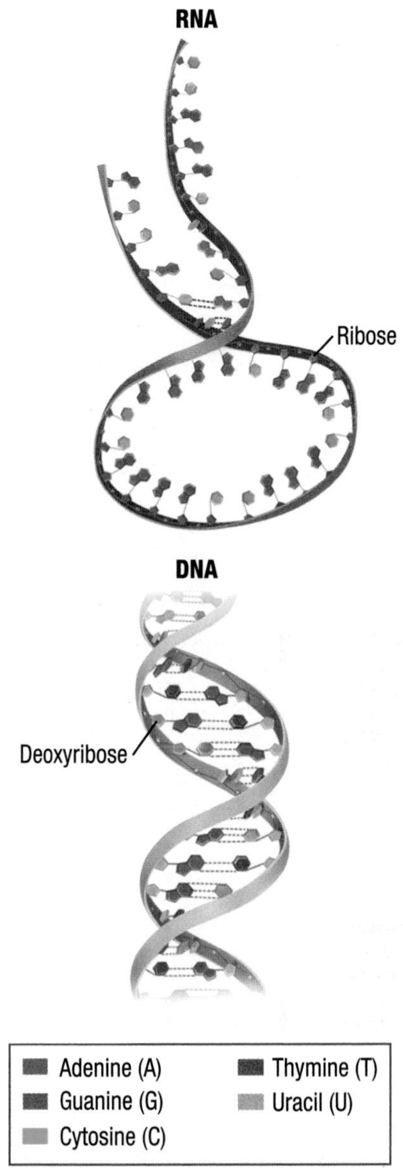


**Figure 11** Both RNA (top) and DNA (bottom) are nucleic acids.

**Types of RNA** There are several types of RNA. Three main types of RNA play a role in gene expression. These types are messenger RNA, transfer RNA, and ribosomal RNA.

**Messenger RNA** When DNA is transcribed into RNA, *messenger RNA* (mRNA) is the type of RNA that is produced. mRNA is complementary to the DNA sequence of a gene. The mRNA carries instructions for making a protein from a gene and delivers them to the site of translation.

**Transfer RNA** During translation, *transfer RNA* (tRNA) "reads" the mRNA sequence. Then, tRNA translates the mRNA sequence into a specific sequence of protein subunits, or amino acids. tRNA molecules have amino acids attached to them, and the tRNA molecules act as decoders by matching the mRNA sequence and placing the amino acids on growing protein chains.

**Ribosomal RNA** Protein production occurs on cellular structures called *ribosomes*. Ribosomes are made up of about 80 protein molecules (ribosomal proteins) and several large RNA molecules. The RNA that is found in ribosomes is called *ribosomal RNA* (rRNA). A cell's cytoplasm contains thousands of ribosomes. In eukaryotic cells, ribosomes are attached to the endoplasmic reticulum (ER), which transports proteins as the proteins are produced.

› **Reading Check** ***What are the structural differences between RNA and DNA?***

go.hrw.com
interact online
Keyword: HX8DNAF12

**Transcription**

1 RNA polymerase binds to the gene's promoter.
2 The two DNA strands unwind and separate.
3 Complementary RNA nucleotides are added.
RNA polymerase
Promoter site on DNA
RNA

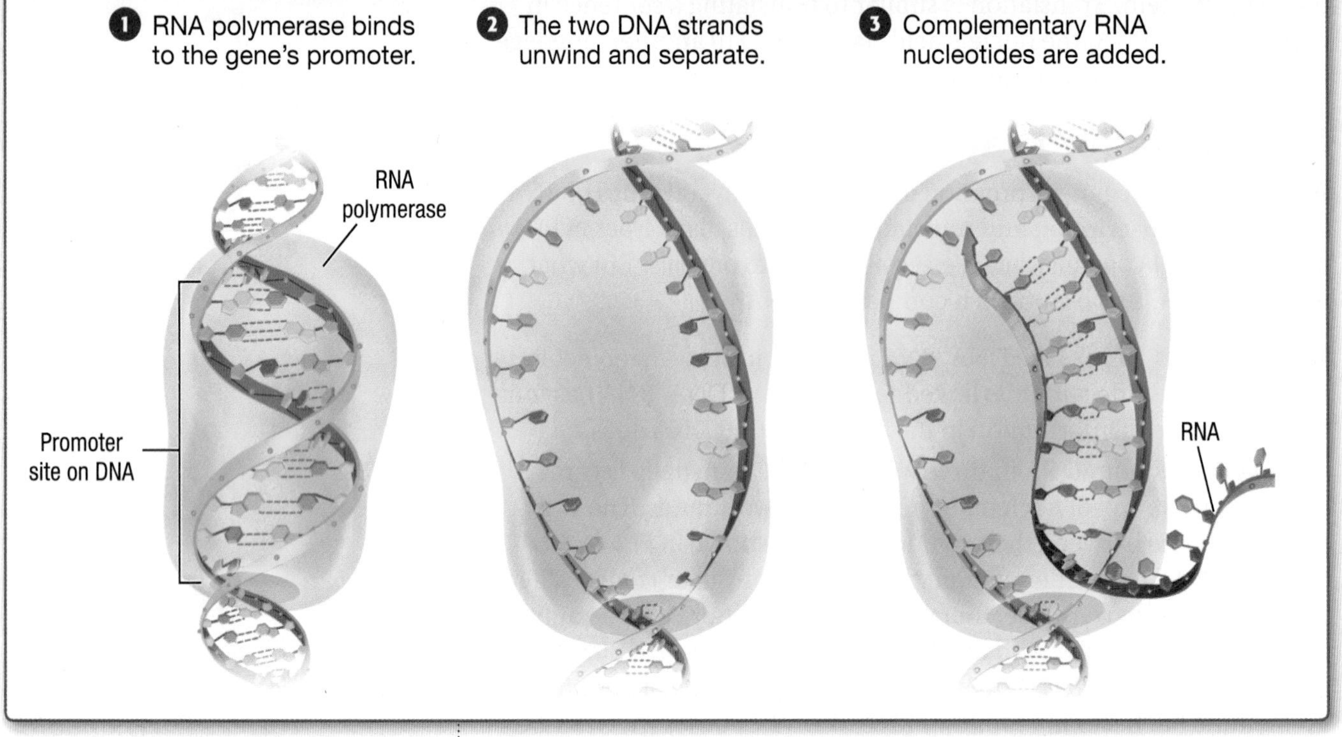

**Figure 12** Transcription is the process in which mRNA is made to complement the DNA of a gene.

## Transcription: Reading the Gene

**❯ During transcription, the information in a specific region of DNA (a gene) is transcribed, or copied, into mRNA.** Transcription is carried out by a protein called *RNA polymerase*. The steps of transcription are described below and are shown in **Figure 12.**

**Step 1** Transcription begins when RNA polymerase binds to the specific DNA sequence in the gene that is called the *promoter*. The promoter site is the "start" location.

**Step 2** RNA polymerase then unwinds and separates the two strands of the double helix to expose the DNA bases on each strand.

**Step 3** RNA polymerase adds and links complementary RNA bases as it "reads" the gene. RNA polymerase moves along the bases on the DNA strand in much the same way that a train moves along a track. Transcription follows the base-pairing rules for DNA replication except that in RNA, uracil—rather than thymine—pairs with adenine. As RNA polymerase moves down the DNA strand, a single strand of mRNA grows. Behind the moving RNA polymerase, the two strands of DNA close up and re-form the double helix.

The RNA polymerase eventually reaches a "stop" location in the DNA. This stop signal is a sequence of bases that marks the end of each gene in eukaryotes or the end of a set of genes in prokaryotes. The result is a single strand of mRNA.

**❯ Reading Check** ***What is the role of a promoter?***

READING TOOLBOX

**Three-Panel Flip Chart** Make a three-panel flip chart to help you compare the roles of the three types of RNA used in gene expression.

**Transcription Versus Replication** Like DNA replication, transcription uses DNA as a template for making a new molecule. In transcription, a new molecule of RNA is made from the DNA. However, in DNA replication, a new molecule of DNA is made from the DNA. Also, in DNA replication, both strands of DNA serve as templates. In contrast, during transcription only part of one of the two strands of DNA (a gene) serves as a template for the new RNA.

SCILINKS.
www.scilinks.org
Topic: Genetic Code
Code: HX80648

## The Genetic Code: Three-Letter "Words"

A gene can be thought of as a "sentence" of "words" that is first transcribed and then translated into a functional protein. Once a section of a gene is transcribed into mRNA, the words can be carried from the nucleus to ribosomes in the cytoplasm. There, the words are translated to make proteins.

**Codons of mRNA** Each of the words in mRNA is made up of three adjacent nucleotide bases. Each three-nucleotide sequence is called a **codon.** Each codon is matched to 1 of 20 amino acids or acts as a start or stop signal for the translation stage. **Figure 13** shows this matching system for each of the possible 64 mRNA codons. For example, the codon GCU specifies the amino acid alanine. Notice that each codon specifies only one amino acid but that several amino acids have more than one codon. This system of matching codons and amino acids is called the *genetic code.* **The genetic code is based on codons that each represent a specific amino acid.**

**codon** in DNA and mRNA, a three-nucleotide sequence that encodes an amino acid or signifies a start signal or a stop signal

**Figure 13** The amino acid coded for by a specific mRNA codon can be determined by following the three steps below. **What amino acid does the codon GAA code for?**

1 Find the first base of the mRNA codon in this column of the table.

2 Follow that row to the column that matches the second base of the codon.

3 Move up or down in that box until you match the third base of the codon with this column of the chart.

**Codons in mRNA**

| First base | Second base: U | Second base: C | Second base: A | Second base: G | Third base |
|---|---|---|---|---|---|
| U | UUU, UUC Phenylalanine; UUA, UUG Leucine | UCU, UCC, UCA, UCG Serine | UAU, UAC Tyrosine; UAA, UAG Stop | UGU, UGC Cysteine; UGA–Stop; UGG–Tryptophan | U C A G |
| C | CUU, CUC, CUA, CUG Leucine | CCU, CCC, CCA, CCG Proline | CAU, CAC Histidine; CAA, CAG Glutamine | CGU, CGC, CGA, CGG Arginine | U C A G |
| A | AUU, AUC, AUA Isoleucine; AUG–Start | ACU, ACC, ACA, ACG Threonine | AAU, AAC Asparagine; AAA, AAG Lysine | AGU, AGC Serine; AGA, AGG Arginine | U C A G |
| G | GUU, GUC, GUA, GUG Valine | GCU, GCC, GCA, GCG Alanine | GAU, GAC Aspartic acid; GAA, GAG Glutamic acid | GGU, GGC, GGA, GGG Glycine | U C A G |

**Translation**

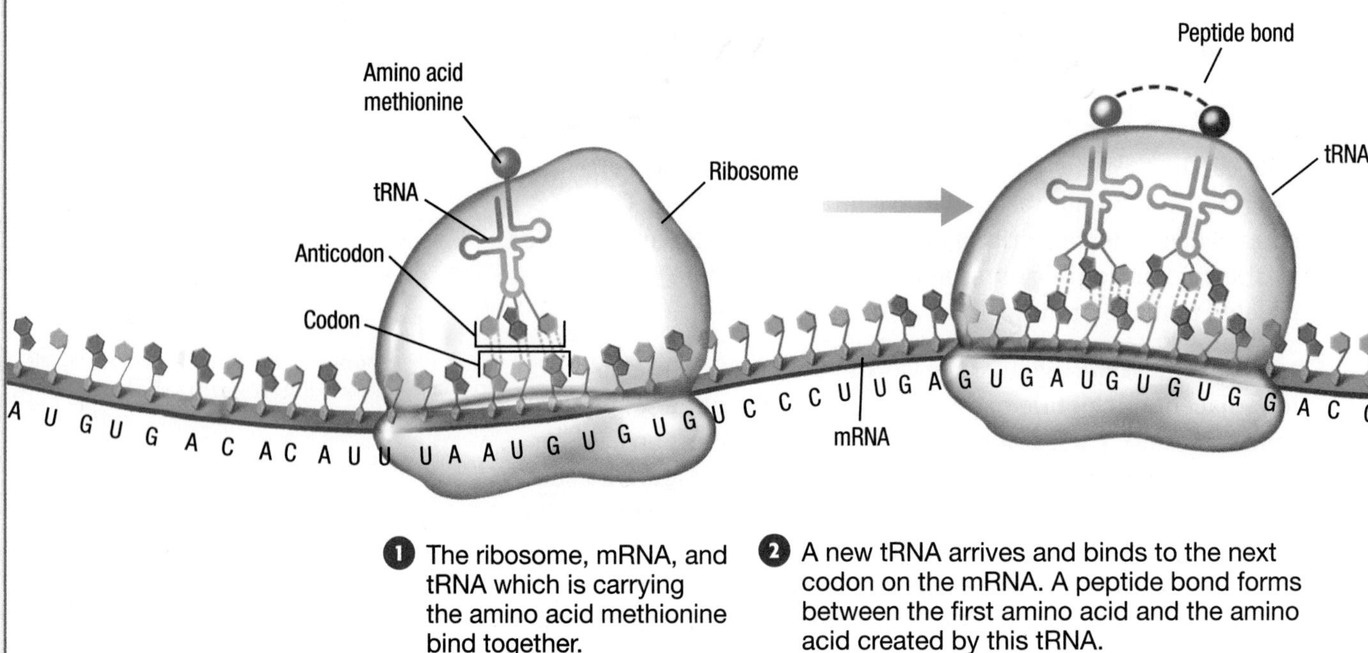


❶ The ribosome, mRNA, and tRNA which is carrying the amino acid methionine bind together.

❷ A new tRNA arrives and binds to the next codon on the mRNA. A peptide bond forms between the first amino acid and the amino acid created by this tRNA.

**Figure 14** During translation, amino acids are assembled from information encoded in mRNA. As the mRNA codons move through the ribosome, tRNAs add specific amino acids to the growing polypeptide chain. This process continues until a stop codon is reached and the newly made protein is released.

## Translation: RNA to Proteins

Translation is the process of converting the "language" of RNA (nucleotide sequences) into the "language" of proteins (amino acid sequences). **› Translation occurs in a sequence of steps, involves three kinds of RNA, and results in a complete *polypeptide.*** In the cytoplasm, ribosomes are formed as tRNA, rRNA, and mRNA interact to assemble amino acid sequences that are based on the genetic code. The process of translation is summarized below and in **Figure 14.**

**Step ❶** Each tRNA is folded into a compact shape, as **Figure 15** shows. An amino acid is added to one end of each tRNA. The other end of the tRNA has an anticodon. An *anticodon* is a three-nucleotide sequence that is complementary to an mRNA codon. Each tRNA molecule carries the amino acid that corresponds with the tRNA's anticodon. After leaving the nucleus, the mRNA joins with a ribosome and tRNA. The mRNA start codon, AUG, signals the beginning of a protein chain. A tRNA molecule carrying methionine at one end and the anticodon, UAC, at the other end binds to the start codon.

**Step ❷** A tRNA molecule that has the correct anticodon and amino acid binds to the second codon on the mRNA. A peptide bond forms between the two amino acids, and the first tRNA is released from the ribosome. The tRNA leaves its amino acid behind.

go.hrw.com
interact online
Keyword: HX8DNAF14

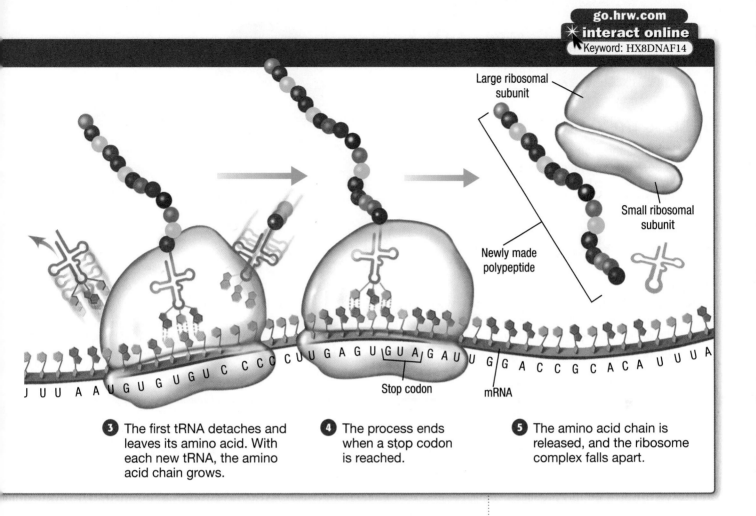

Large ribosomal subunit

Small ribosomal subunit

Newly made polypeptide

Stop codon

mRNA

**3** The first tRNA detaches and leaves its amino acid. With each new tRNA, the amino acid chain grows.

**4** The process ends when a stop codon is reached.

**5** The amino acid chain is released, and the ribosome complex falls apart.

**Step 3** The ribosome moves one codon down the mRNA. Because the anticodon remains attached to the codon, the tRNA molecule and the mRNA molecule move as a unit, which leaves the next mRNA codon open and ready to receive the next tRNA and its amino acid. The amino acid chain continues to grow as each new amino acid binds to the chain and the previous tRNA is released.

**Step 4** This process is repeated until a stop codon is reached. A *stop codon* is one of three codons: UAG, UAA, or UGA. No tRNAs have anticodons for these stop codons, so protein production stops.

**Step 5** The newly made polypeptide falls off the ribosome. The ribosome complex falls apart. The last tRNA leaves the ribosome, and the ribosome moves away from the mRNA. The ribosome is then free to begin translation again on the same mRNA or on another mRNA.

**Repeating Translation** Like replication, translation needs to happen quickly and often. As a segment of mRNA moves through a ribosome, another ribosome can form on the AUG codon on the same mRNA segment and can begin a new translation process. Thus, several ribosomes can translate the same mRNA at the same time, which allows many copies of the same protein to be made rapidly from a single mRNA molecule.

› **Reading Check** ***How do codons and anticodons differ?***

**Figure 15** tRNA folds into this shape such that an anticodon is on one end and a binding site for amino acids is on the other end.

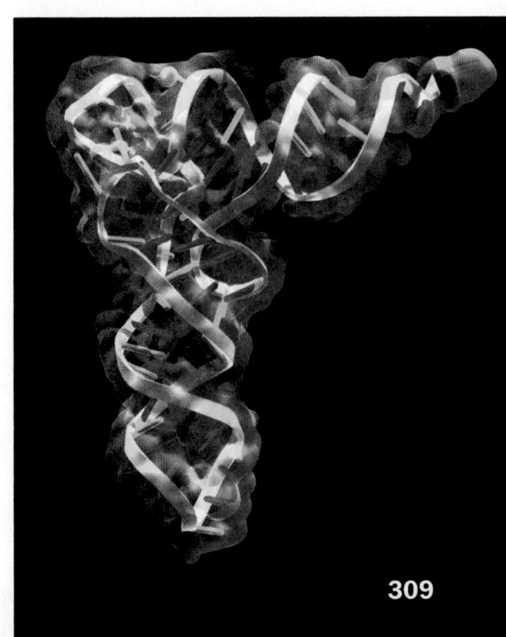

Data

# QuickLab

15 min

## Genetic Code of Keratin  4.2.1g

Keratin is one of the proteins in hair. The gene for keratin is transcribed and translated by certain skin cells. The sequence below is part of the mRNA molecule that is transcribed from the gene for keratin.

U C U C G U G A A U U U U C C

### Analysis

1. **Determine** the sequence of amino acids that will result from the translation of the segment of mRNA above. Use the genetic code in **Figure 13.**
2. **Determine** the anticodon of each tRNA molecule that will bind to this mRNA segment.
3. CRITICAL THINKING **Recognizing Patterns** Determine the sequence of nucleotides in the segment of DNA from which this mRNA strand was transcribed.
4. CRITICAL THINKING **Recognizing Patterns** Determine the sequence of nucleotides in the segment of DNA that is complementary to the DNA segment that is described in item 3.

## Complexities of Gene Expression

**❯ The relationship between genes and their effects is complex. Despite the neatness of the genetic code, every gene cannot be simply linked to a single outcome.** Some genes are expressed only at certain times or under specific conditions. Some traits result from the expression of multiple genes. Variations, mistakes, feedback, and other complex interactions can occur at each of the steps in replication and expression. The final outcome of gene expression is affected by the environment of the cells, the presence of other cells, and the timing of gene expression.

Overall, knowledge of the basic process of gene expression has allowed scientists to better understand the workings of all organisms. The next chapters delve into the exciting results of applying this knowledge.

## Section 3 Review

### ❯ KEY IDEAS

1. **Describe** gene expression.
2. **Explain** the role of RNA in gene expression.
3. **Summarize** transcription.
4. **Explain** how codons determine the amino acid sequence of a protein.
5. **Describe** the steps of translation.
6. **Identify** a complexity of gene expression.

### CRITICAL THINKING

7. **Inferring Relationships** Multiple codons can produce the same amino acid. What is the advantage of this redundancy?
8. **Relating Concepts** What amino acid is coded for by the mRNA codon CCU?

### ALTERNATIVE ASSESSMENT

9. **Gene Poster** Research two methods used to sequence the nucleotides in a gene. Compare the two methods. Give examples of how this technology might be used in a clinical setting. Prepare a poster to summarize the two methods that you researched.

# Chapter 13 Lab

45 min

## Objectives

- Extract DNA from wheat germ.
- Explain the role of detergents, heat, and alcohol in the extraction of DNA.

## Materials

- wheat germ, raw (1 g)
- test tube or beaker (50 mL)
- water, hot tap (55°C, 20 mL)
- salt, table
- soap, liquid dishwashing (1 mL)
- isopropyl alcohol, cold (15 mL)
- glass rod, 8 cm long
- inoculating loop
- glass slide

## Safety

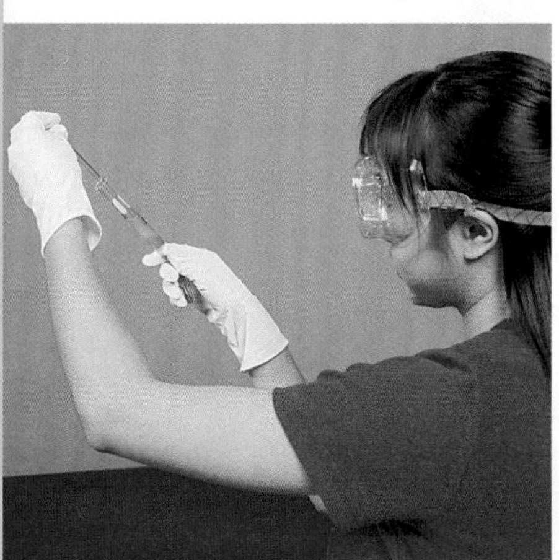

## DNA Extraction from Wheat Germ

The extraction and purification of DNA are the first steps in the analysis and manipulation of DNA. Very pure DNA can be easily extracted from cells in a research laboratory, and somewhat less pure DNA can be extracted with some simple techniques easily performed in a classroom.

The first step in extracting DNA from a cell is to lyse, or break open, the cell. Cell walls, cell membranes, and nuclear membranes are broken down by physical smashing, heating, and the addition of detergents. In water, DNA is soluble. When isopropyl alcohol is added, the DNA uncoils and precipitates, leaving behind many other cell components that are not soluble in isopropyl alcohol. The DNA can be then spooled, or wound onto an inoculating loop, and pulled from the solution. In this lab, you will extract the DNA from wheat germ. Wheat germ is simply the ground-up cells of wheat kernels, or seeds.

### Procedure

1. Put on safety goggles, lab apron, and gloves.
2. **CAUTION: Glassware, such as a test tube, is fragile and can break.** Place 1 g of wheat germ into a clean test tube.
3. Add 20 mL hot (55°C) tap water and stir with glass rod for 2 to 3 min.
4. Next, add a pinch of table salt, and mix well.
5. Add a few drops (1 mL) of liquid dishwashing soap. Stir the mixture with the glass rod for 1 min until it is well mixed.
6. **CAUTION: Isopropyl alcohol is flammable. Bunsen burners and hot plates should be removed from the lab.** Slowly pour 15 mL cold isopropyl alcohol down the side of the tilted tube or beaker. The alcohol should form a top layer over the original solution. Note: Do not pour the alcohol too fast or directly into the wheat germ solution.
7. Tilt the tube upright, and watch the stringy, white material float up into the alcohol layer (this result should occur after 10 to 15 min). This material is the DNA from the wheat germ.
8. Carefully insert the inoculating loop into the white material in the alcohol layer. Gently twist the loop as you wind the DNA around the loop. Remove the loop from the tube, and tap the DNA onto a glass slide.
9. Clean up your lab materials according to your teacher's instructions. Wash your hands before leaving the lab.

### Analyze and Conclude

1. **Describing Events** Describe the appearance of the DNA on the slide.
2. **Interpreting Information** Explain the role of detergent, heat, and isopropyl alcohol in the extraction of DNA.
3. SCIENTIFIC METHODS **Comparing Structures** How do the characteristics of your DNA sample relate to the structure of eukaryotic DNA?
4. SCIENTIFIC METHODS **Designing Experiments** Design a DNA extraction experiment in which you explore the effect of changing the variables.

# Chapter 13 Summary

| Key Ideas | Key Terms |
|---|---|

## 1 The Structure of DNA

- DNA is the primary material that causes recognizable, inheritable characteristics in related groups of organisms.
- Three major experiments led to the conclusion that DNA is the genetic material in cells. These experiments were performed by Griffith, Avery, Hershey, and Chase.
- A DNA molecule is shaped like a spiral staircase and is composed of two parallel strands of linked subunits.
- The information in DNA is contained in the order of the bases, while the base-pairing structure allows the information to be copied.
- Watson and Crick used information from experiments by Chargaff, Wilkins, and Franklin to determine the three-dimensional structure of DNA.

**Key Terms**

**gene** (293)
**DNA** (293)
**nucleotide** (296)
**purine** (297)
**pyrimidine** (297)

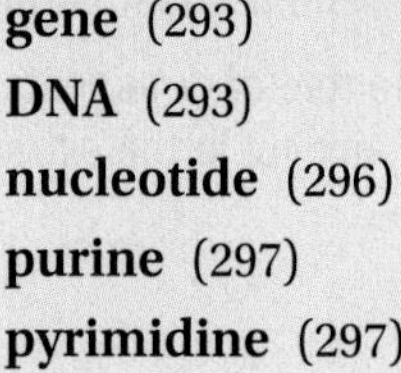

## 2 Replication of DNA

- In DNA replication, the DNA molecule unwinds, and the two sides split. Then, new bases are added to each side until two identical sequences result.
- The replication of DNA involves many proteins that form a machinelike complex of moving parts.
- In prokaryotic cells, replication starts at a single site. In eukaryotic cells, replication starts at many sites along the chromosome.

**Key Terms**

**DNA replication** (300)
**DNA helicase** (301)
**DNA polymerase** (301)

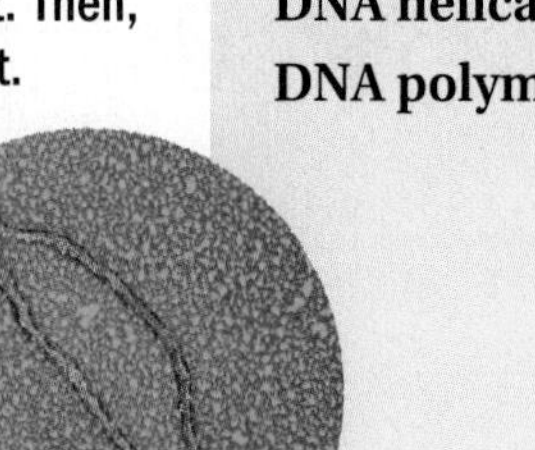

## 3 RNA and Gene Expression

- Gene expression produces proteins by transcription and translation. This process takes place in two stages, both of which involve RNA.
- In cells, three types of RNA complement DNA and translate the genetic code into proteins.
- During transcription, the information in a gene is transcribed, or copied, into mRNA.
- The genetic code is based on codons that each represent a specific amino acid.
- Translation occurs in a sequence of steps, involves three kinds of RNA, and results in a complete polypeptide.
- Despite the neatness of the genetic code, every gene cannot be simply linked to a single outcome.

**Key Terms**

**RNA** (304)
**gene expression** (304)
**transcription** (305)
**translation** (305)
**codon** (307)

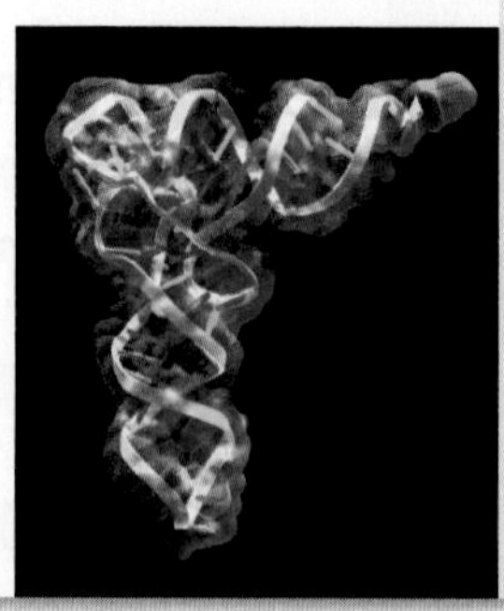

# Chapter 13

The Living Environment

## Regents Exam Practice

**PART A: Answer all questions in this part.**

*Directions:* For each statement or question, write on your separate answer sheet the number of the word or expression that best completes the statement or answers the question.

**1** Hereditary traits are transmitted from generation to generation by means of

(1) specific sequences of bases in DNA in reproductive cells.
(2) proteins in body cells.
(3) carbohydrates in body cells.
(4) specific starches making up DNA in reproductive cells.

**2** Which statement best expresses the relationship between the three structures represented below?

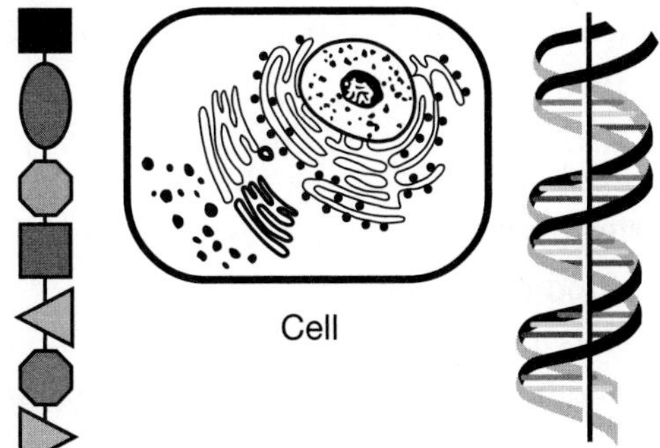


(1) DNA is produced from protein absorbed by the cell.
(2) Protein is composed of DNA that is produced in the cell.
(3) DNA controls the production of protein in the cell.
(4) Cells make DNA by digesting protein.

**3** A characteristic of a DNA molecule that is not characteristic of a protein molecule is that the DNA molecule

(1) can replicate itself.
(2) can be very large.
(3) is found in nuclei.
(4) is composed of subunits.

**4** Synthesis of a defective protein may result from an alteration in

(1) vacuole shape.
(2) the number of mitochondria.
(3) a base sequence code.
(4) cellular fat concentration.

**5** The genetic code of a DNA molecule is determined by a specific sequence of

(1) ATP molecules.
(2) sugar molecules.
(3) chemical bonds.
(4) molecular bases.

**6** The sequence of subunits in a protein is most directly dependent on the

(1) region in the cell where enzymes are produced.
(2) DNA in the chromosomes in a cell.
(3) type of cell in which starch is found.
(4) kinds of materials in the cell membrane.

**7** Most of the hereditary information that determines the traits of an organism is located in

(1) only those cells of an individual produced by meiosis.
(2) the nuclei of body cells of an individual.
(3) certain genes in the vacuoles of body cells.
(4) the numerous ribosomes in certain cells.

**8** The instructions for the traits of an organism are coded in the arrangement of

(1) glucose units in carbohydrate molecules.
(2) bases in DNA in the nucleus.
(3) fat molecules in the cell membrane.
(4) energy-rich bonds in starch molecules.

**9** When DNA separates into two strands, the DNA would most likely be directly involved in

(1) replication.
(2) fertilization.
(3) differentiation.
(4) evolution.

**10** A change in the order of DNA bases that code for a respiratory protein will most likely cause

(1) the production of a starch that has a similar function.

(2) the digestion of the altered gene by enzymes.

(3) a change in the sequence of amino acids determined by the gene.

(4) the release of antibodies by certain cells to correct the error.

**11** A portion of a molecule is shown in the diagram below. Which statement best describes the main function of this type of molecule?

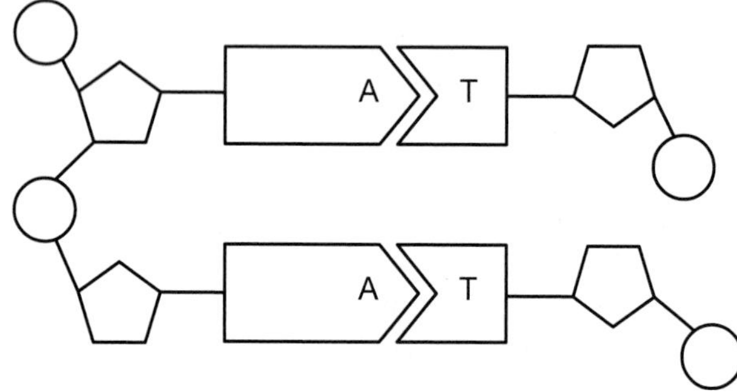


(1) It is a structural part of the cell wall.

(2) It stores energy for metabolic processes.

(3) It determines what traits may be inherited.

(4) It transports materials across the cell membrane.

**12** If a set of instructions that determines all of the characteristics of an organism is compared to a book, and a chromosome is compared to a chapter in the book, then what might be compared to a paragraph in the book?

(1) a starch molecule

(2) an egg

(3) an amino acid

(4) a DNA molecule

**13** Down syndrome is a genetic disorder caused by the presence of an extra chromosome in the body cells of humans. This extra chromosome occurs in a gamete as a result of

(1) an error in the process of cloning.

(2) an error in meiotic cell division.

(3) a gene mutation.

(4) replication of a single chromosome during mitosis.

**14** Some mammals have genes for fur color that produce pigment only when the outside temperature is above a certain level. This pigment production is an example of how the environment of an organism can

(1) destroy certain genes.

(2) cause new mutations to occur.

(3) stop the process of evolution.

(4) influence the expression of certain genes.

**15** What determines the kind of genes an organism possesses?

(1) type of amino acids in the cells of the organism

(2) sequence of the subunits A, T, C, and G in the DNA of the organism

(3) size of simple sugar molecules in the organs of the organism

(4) shape of the protein molecules in the organelles of the organism

**16** What does the process of transcription produce?

(1) tRNA (3) mRNA

(2) RNA (4) DNA

**17** During protein synthesis, transfer RNA (tRNA)

(1) produces a new RNA molecule.

(2) acts as a start signal for protein synthesis.

(3) produces protein subunits by translating the codons on mRNA.

(4) delivers the instructions for protein synthesis to the site of translation.

**18** Erwin Chargaff's data on nitrogeneous bases

(1) suggested that DNA bases are paired.

(2) suggested that DNA is a tightly coiled helix.

(3) suggested that certain bases are found in equal amounts in DNA.

(4) proved that DNA's structure is similar to a twisted ladder.

## PART D

**Base your answers to questions 19 and 20 on the Universal Genetic Code Chart below and on your knowledge of biology. Some DNA, RNA, and amino acid information from four similar sequences of four plant species is shown in the chart below.**

**Universal Genetic Code Chart**
**Messenger RNA Codons and the Amino Acids They Code For**

| FIRST BASE | SECOND BASE: U | SECOND BASE: C | SECOND BASE: A | SECOND BASE: G | THIRD BASE |
|---|---|---|---|---|---|
| **U** | UUU, UUC } **PHE**<br>UUA, UUG } **LEU** | UCU, UCC, UCA, UCG } **SER** | UAU, UAC } **TYR**<br>UAA, UAG } STOP | UGU, UGC } **CYS**<br>UGA } STOP<br>UGG } **TRP** | **U**<br>**C**<br>**A**<br>**G** |
| **C** | CUU, CUC, CUA, CUG } **LEU** | CCU, CCC, CCA, CCG } **PRO** | CAU, CAC } **HIS**<br>CAA, CAG } **GLN** | CGU, CGC, CGA, CGG } **ARG** | **U**<br>**C**<br>**A**<br>**G** |
| **A** | AUU, AUC } **ILE**<br>AUA, AUG } **MET** or START | ACU, ACC, ACA, ACG } **THR** | AAU, AAC } **ASN**<br>AAA, AAG } **LYS** | AGU, AGC } **SER**<br>AGA, AGG } **ARG** | **U**<br>**C**<br>**A**<br>**G** |
| **G** | GUU, GUC, GUA, GUG } **VAL** | GCU, GCC, GCA, GCG } **ALA** | GUA, GAC } **ASP**<br>GAA, GAG } **GLU** | GGU, GGC, GGA, GGG } **GLY** | **U**<br>**C**<br>**A**<br>**G** |

**19** Using the information given, identify the missing mRNA base sequence for species B. Record your answer on a separate sheet of paper in the chart below.

**20** Using the Universal Genetic Code Chart, identify the missing amino acid sequence for species C in the chart below. Record your answer on a separate sheet of paper.

| Species | | | | | | |
|---|---|---|---|---|---|---|
| Species A | DNA base sequence<br>mRNA base sequence<br>Amino acid sequence | CCG<br>GGC<br>**GLY** | TGC<br>ACG<br>**THR** | ATA<br>UAU<br>**TYR** | CAG<br>GUC<br>**VAL** | GTA<br>CAU<br>**HIS** |
| Species B | DNA base sequence<br>mRNA base sequence<br>Amino acid sequence | TGC<br>____<br>**THR** | TGC<br>____<br>**THR** | ATA<br>____<br>**TYR** | CAG<br>____<br>**VAL** | GTA<br>____<br>**HIS** |
| Species C | DNA base sequence<br>mRNA base sequence<br>Amino acid sequence | CCG<br>GGC<br>____ | TGC<br>ACG<br>____ | ATA<br>UAU<br>____ | CAG<br>GUC<br>____ | GTT<br>CAA<br>____ |
| Species D | DNA base sequence<br>mRNA base sequence<br>Amino acid sequence | CCT<br>GGA<br>**GLY** | TGT<br>ACA<br>**THR** | ATG<br>UAC<br>**TYR** | CAC<br>GUG<br>**VAL** | GTC<br>CAG<br>**GLN** |

# Chapter 14 Genes in Action

## Preview



## Why It Matters

Knowing the genetic code is not enough to understand how genes work. To understand our own bodies, we must study thousands of genes, proteins, and other molecules that interact as our bodies grow and develop.

These frogs have extra legs! When many mutated or deformed organisms are found in one area, scientists want to find out why.

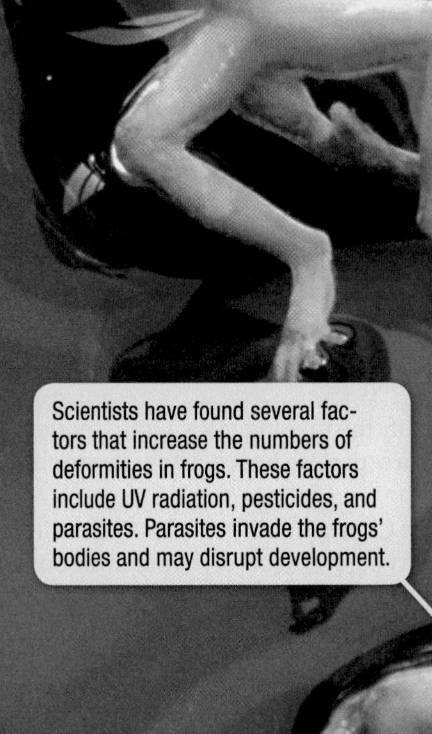

Scientists have found several factors that increase the numbers of deformities in frogs. These factors include UV radiation, pesticides, and parasites. Parasites invade the frogs' bodies and may disrupt development.

***The Living Environment***

**Standard 4** Students will understand and apply scientific concepts, principles, and theories pertaining to the physical setting and living environment and recognize the historical development of ideas in science.

**Key Idea 1** Living things are both similar to and different from each other and from nonliving things. ***Major Understandings*** **- 1.2e**

**Key Idea 2** Organisms inherit genetic information in a variety of ways that result in continuity of structure and function between parents and offspring. ***Major Understandings*** **– 2.1a, 2.1g, 2.1h, 2.1i, 2.1k, 2.2d**

**Key Idea 3** Individual organisms and species change over time. ***Major Understandings*** **– 3.1b, 3.1c, 3.1d**

**Key Idea 5** Organisms maintain a dynamic equilibrium that sustains life. ***Major Understandings*** **– 5.2i**

15 min

# InquiryLab

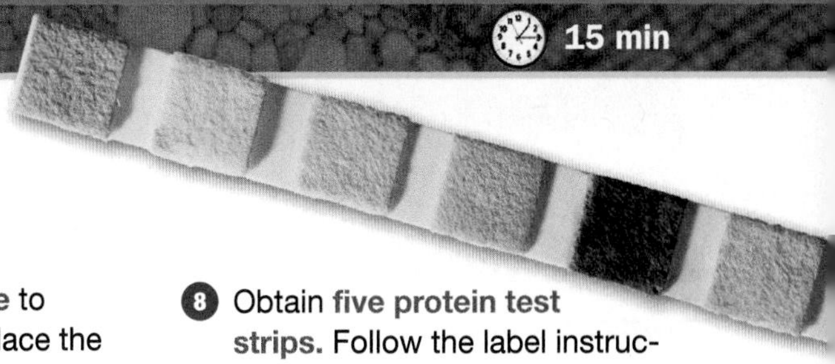

## Where Is the Protein?

Protein test strips are inexpensive and easy-to-use measuring tools. Sold in local pharmacies, these strips are purchased by individuals who must monitor the concentration of protein in their urine. The strips can also be used to confirm the presence of protein in various foods.

### Procedure

1. Work with a partner. Label five small cups "A," "B," "C," "D," and "E."
2. Use a mortar and pestle to crush 20 lentil beans. Place the crushed beans into cup A.
3. Place 1 g of instant oatmeal into cup B.
4. Pour 10 mL of water into cups A and B. Swirl each cup to mix its contents.
5. Pour 10 mL of water into cup C.
6. Pour 10 mL of milk into cup D.
7. Pour 10 mL of fruit juice into cup E.
8. Obtain five protein test strips. Follow the label instructions to detect and measure the presence of protein in each cup.

### Analysis

1. **Identify** the cups in which protein was present.
2. **Identify** the cups that had the most and least amounts of protein.
3. **Identify** the control group in this experiment. Explain its purpose.

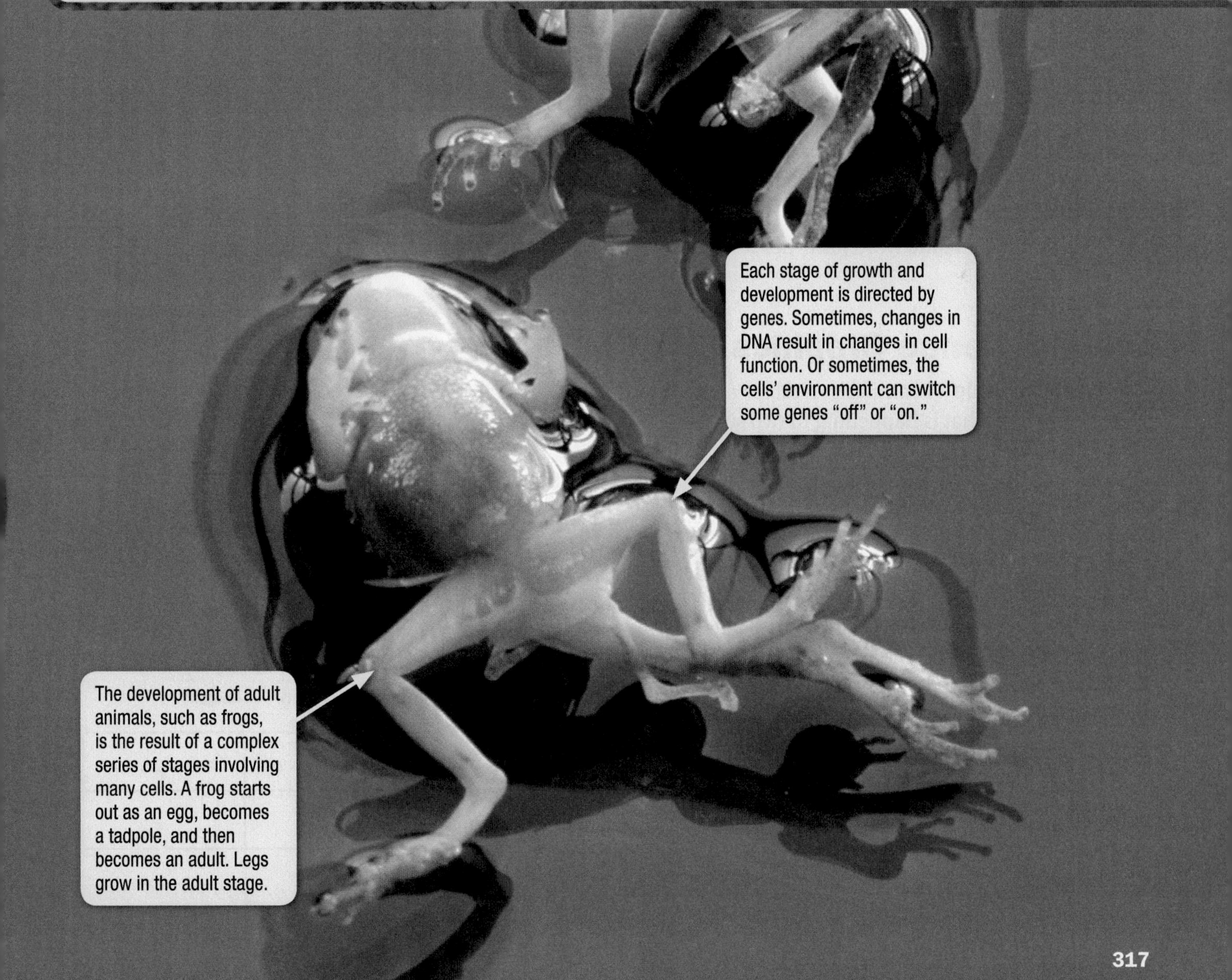

Each stage of growth and development is directed by genes. Sometimes, changes in DNA result in changes in cell function. Or sometimes, the cells' environment can switch some genes "off" or "on."

The development of adult animals, such as frogs, is the result of a complex series of stages involving many cells. A frog starts out as an egg, becomes a tadpole, and then becomes an adult. Legs grow in the adult stage.

These reading tools can help you learn the material in this chapter. For more information on how to use these and other tools, see **Appendix: Reading and Study Skills.**

## Using Words

**Prefixes** A prefix is a word part that is attached to the beginning of a word. Prefixes add to the meaning of words. For example, the prefix *im-* means "not." So, *immovable* means "not able to be moved." This table shows some additional prefixes that you may see in this chapter.

**Your Turn** Use the table to answer the questions that follow.

1. In your own words, define *immutable.*
2. What do you think the word *transmutation* means?

**Prefixes**

| Prefix | Meaning |
|---|---|
| *in-* or *im-* | not |
| *mut-* | change |
| *trans-* | cross |
| *homeo-* | the same |

## Using Language

**Finding Examples** When you are reading scientific explanations, finding examples can help you put a concept into practical terms. Thinking of your own examples will help you remember what you read.

**Your Turn** For each category of items below, brainstorm as many examples as you can think of that could fit into the category.

1. hereditary traits
2. words that include the word part *-her-*.

## Using Science Graphics

**Comparison Table** A comparison table can help you understand what is happening in two similar situations. For example, this graphic shows the effect of lactose on specific genes in some prokaryotic cells. If you compare the two situations shown, you will find similarities and differences.

**Your Turn** Make a comparison table like the one shown here to compare what happens when lactose is present and when lactose is absent.

1. Draw a table with two columns.
2. Label the first column "Lactose absent."
3. Label the second column "Lactose present."
4. Use the graphic as a reference as you list the structures and events that are similar or different.

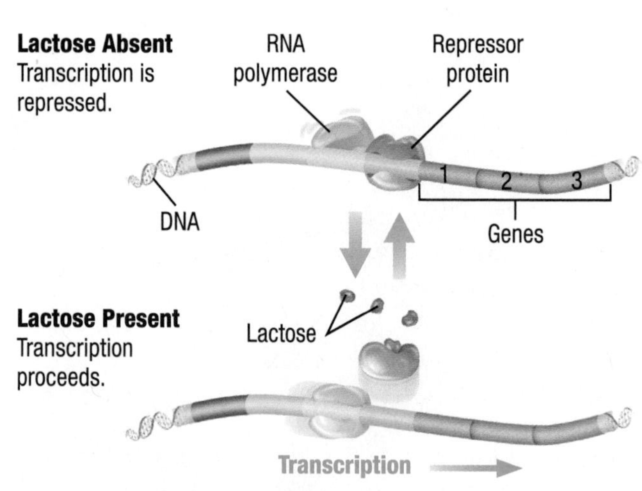


| | *Lactose absent* | *Lactose present* |
|---|---|---|
| *Similarities* | | |
| *Differences* | | |

Section 1

# Mutation and Genetic Change

| Key Ideas | Key Terms | Why It Matters |
|---|---|---|
| ❯ What is the origin of genetic differences among organisms?<br>❯ What kinds of mutations are possible?<br>❯ What are the possible effects of mutations?<br>❯ How can genetic change occur on a larger scale? | mutation<br>nondisjunction<br>polyploidy | Understanding mutation is key to understanding the differences among organisms over time. |

In general, *mutation* simply means "change," and any organism that has changed from some previous or normal state can be called a *mutant*. So, a frog that has extra legs may be called a *mutant,* although the extra legs may or may not have a genetic cause.

## Mutation: The Basis of Genetic Change

In genetics, a **mutation** is a change in the structure or amount of the genetic material of an organism. A genetic *mutant* is an individual whose DNA or chromosomes differ from some previous or normal state. ❯ **For the most part, genetic differences among organisms originate as some kind of genetic mutation.** Every unique allele of every gene began as a mutation of an existing gene.

**Causes of Mutations** Mutations occur naturally as accidental changes to DNA or to chromosomes during the cell cycle. Recall that enzymes repair most DNA that is mismatched during replication, but rarely, some DNA is not repaired. Other kinds of mistakes are possible, as you will learn. Also, the rate of mutation can be increased by some environmental factors. Such factors, called *mutagens,* include many forms of radiation and some kinds of chemicals.

**Effects of Mutations** Because of the way DNA is translated, a mutation can have many possible effects. A small change in DNA may affect just one amino acid in the protein that results from a gene. However, as you will see, other results are possible. A mutation may have no effect, or may harm or help in some way. The effect depends on where and when the mutation occurs. We notice mutations when they cause an unusual trait or disease, such as *sickle cell anemia,* shown in **Figure 1.** However, many mutations may go unnoticed.

❯ **Reading Check** ***Where do new alleles come from? (See the Appendix for answers to Reading Checks.)***

***The Living Environment***
**Standard 4**
**2.1h** Genes are segments of DNA molecules. Any alteration of the DNA sequence is a mutation. Usually, an altered gene will be passed on to every cell that develops from it.
**2.2d** Inserting, deleting, or substituting DNA segments can alter genes. An altered gene may be passed on to every cell that develops from it.
**3.1b** New inheritable characteristics can result from new combinations of existing genes or from mutations of genes in reproductive cells.
**3.1c** Mutation and the sorting and recombining of genes during meiosis and fertilization result in a great variety of possible gene combinations.
**3.1d** Mutations occur as random chance events. Gene mutations can also be caused by such agents as radiation and chemicals. When they occur in sex cells, the mutations can be passed on to offspring; if they occur in other cells, they can be passed on to other body cells only.
**5.2i** Gene mutations in a cell can result in uncontrolled cell division, called cancer. Exposure of cells to certain chemicals and radiation increases mutations and thus increases the chance of cancer.

**mutation** a change in the structure or amount of the genetic material of an organism

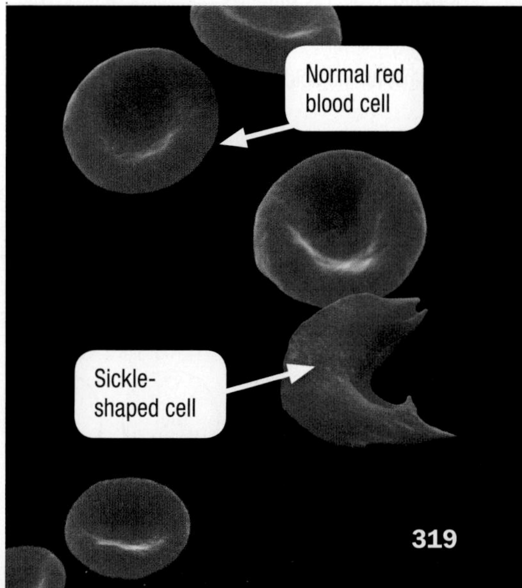


**Figure 1** One out of 500 African Americans has sickle cell anemia, which is caused by a mutation in the gene that produces hemoglobin. Blood cells with the defective hemoglobin tend to bend, rupture, and get stuck.

## Several Kinds of Mutations

DNA and chromosomes are involved in many processes, so there are many kinds of mutations. Most mutations involve a misplacement of a nucleotide in a DNA segment. A mutation may change the results of a gene (when the gene is translated and transcribed), but not all mutations do so. **Different kinds of mutations are recognized as either changes in DNA or changes in the results of genes,** as shown in **Figure 2.**

**READING TOOLBOX**

**Finding Examples** Use the phrase "the cat ate" to create examples of mutations. For example, a point mutation could change the letter *c* to *b* and would result in "the bat ate." The new phrase is also a missense mutation. Use the original phrase to make examples of an insertion, a deletion, and a nonsense mutation.

### Mutations as Changes in DNA

During DNA replication, the wrong nucleotide may be paired or placed in a sequence.

**Point Mutation** A *point* mutation is a change of a single nucleotide in a sequence from one kind of base to another.

**Insertion or Deletion** Rarely, errors in replication can cause the *insertion* or *deletion* of one or more nucleotides in a sequence.

### Mutations as Changes in Results of Genes

Changes in a DNA sequence may affect the results of genes in many ways.

**Silent Mutation** A mutation is *silent* when it has no effect on a gene's function. Point mutations are often silent because the genetic code is redundant (each amino acid has multiple codons).

**Missense Mutation** A *missense* mutation results when a codon is changed such that the new codon codes for a different amino acid. This kind of mutation is also called a *replacement* mutation.

**Frameshift Mutation** Recall that the genetic code is "read" in "words" of three letters each (codons). The *reading frame* of a sequence depends on the starting point for reading. An insertion or deletion can shift the reading frame, or cause a *frameshift*. In this case, the remaining sequence may be "read" as different codons.

go.hrw.com
interact online
Keyword: HX8GNXF2

**Kinds of Mutations**

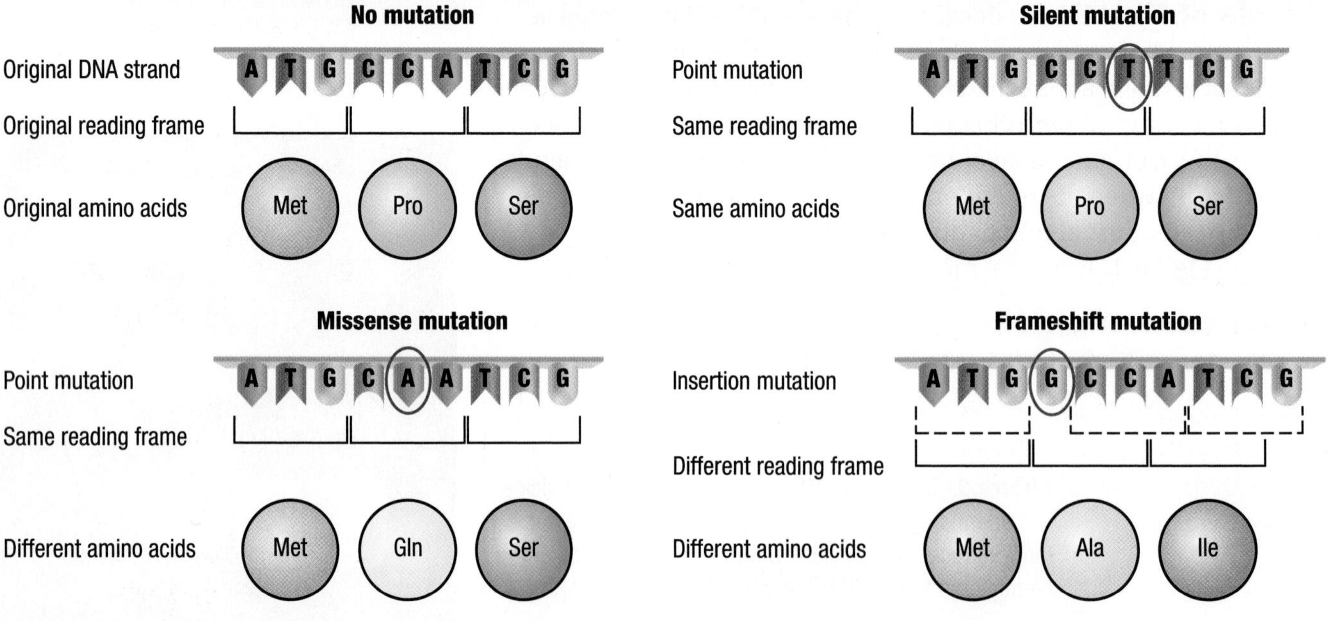

**Figure 2** A mutation is a change, insertion, or deletion of one or more nucleotides in a gene. The change may or may not result in a different amino acid sequence within a protein.

Hands-On

# QuickLab

15 min

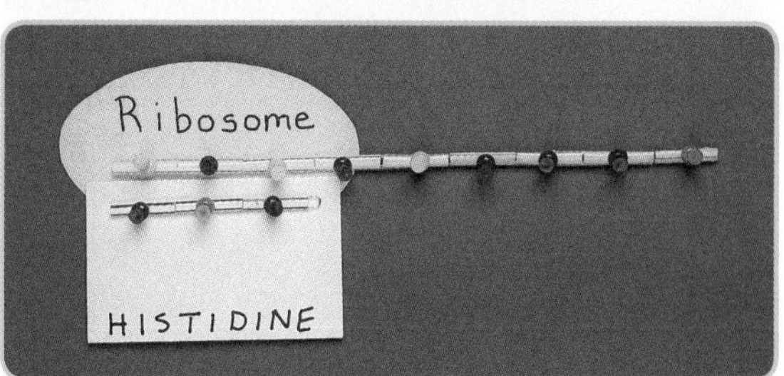


## Make a Model of Mutations  4.2.1h

You have learned about (and may have built models of) DNA replication and gene expression. Now, challenge yourself to build (or add to) a model that demonstrates each type of mutation described in this section.

### Analysis

1. **List** each mutation type on 12 separate sheets of paper. Work with a partner.
2. **Demonstrate** each mutation type by using assorted materials (or models that you have built previously).
3. **Draw** the "before" and "after" state for each mutation.
4. CRITICAL THINKING **Critiquing Models** Trade your drawings with another group. What is accurate and useful about their model? What could be improved? Write down your comments for the other group.

**Nonsense Mutation** A *nonsense* mutation results when a codon is changed to a "stop" signal. In this case, the resulting string of amino acids may be cut short, and the protein may fail to function.

**More or Fewer Amino Acids** If an insertion or deletion is a multiple of 3, the reading frame will be preserved. However, the protein that results may have a few more or less amino acids in it. An insertion or deletion of many codons is likely to disrupt the resulting protein's structure and function.

**Chromosomal Mutations** **› In eukaryotic cells, the process of meiosis creates the chance of mutations at the chromosomal level.** Recall that during this process, chromosomes pair up and may undergo *crossover*. Usually, the result is an equal exchange of alleles between homologous chromosomes. But errors in the exchange can cause *chromosomal mutations*, as shown in **Figure 3.**

**Deletion** A *deletion* occurs when a piece of a chromosome is lost. At the end of meiosis, one of the cells will lack the genes from that missing piece. Such deletions are usually harmful.

**Duplication** A *duplication* occurs when a piece remains attached to its homologous chromosome after meiosis. One chromosome will then carry both alleles for each of the genes in that piece.

**Inversion** An *inversion* occurs when a piece reattaches to its original chromosome, but in a reverse direction.

**Translocation** A *translocation* occurs when a chromosome piece ends up in a completely different, nonhomologous chromosome.

**Gene Rearrangement** A chromosomal mutation can move an entire gene to a new location. Such a change, called a *gene rearrangement,* is likely to disrupt the gene's function in other ways, as you will learn.

**› Reading Check** ***Why are point mutations often silent?***

**Figure 3** Four kinds of chromosomal mutations can result from errors in crossover during meiosis. **› How are the types of chromosomal mutations similar to the types of smaller-scale mutations?**

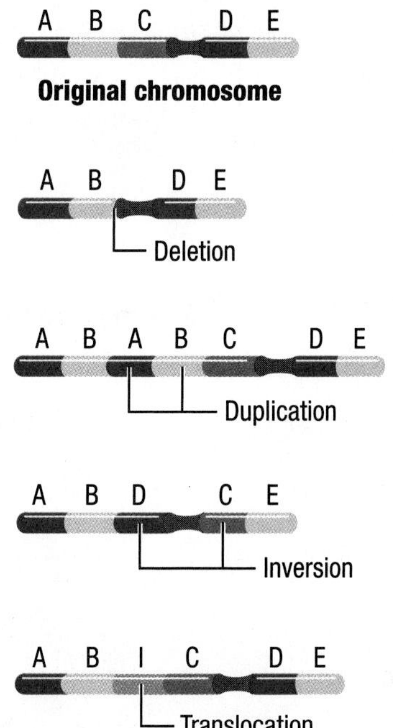

## Effects of Genetic Change

Many genetic changes will cause no change in the appearance or function of organisms. Moreover, many changes in the DNA of cells may not be passed on to other cells by mitosis or meiosis. ❯ **The results of genetic change may be harmful, beneficial, or neutral; most changes are neutral and may not be passed on to offspring.** Mutations that occur in gametes can be passed on to offspring, but mutations in body cells affect only the individual in which they occur.

**Heritable or Not** Multicellular eukaryotes have two primary cell types: germ cells and somatic cells. *Germ cells* make up gametes, and *somatic cells* make up the rest of the body. Mutations can occur in either type of cell. However, if a mutation occurs in a somatic cell, that genetic change will be lost when the owner of the cell dies. For example, a mutation in a person's lung cell could cause the cell to grow into lung cancer. The mutated genes in the cancer cells will not be transferred to the person's children.

**Academic Vocabulary**

**dramatic** vivid or striking

Only a mutation in a germ cell may be passed on to the next generation. However, any such mutation may be silent or have little effect. Only rarely do mutations cause dramatic changes in future generations.

If a mutation occurs in a somatic cell, the change may be silent or it may change the function of the cell. Recall that most tissues are derived from a few parent cells. So, if a mutation occurs in a parent cell, all cells that arise by mitosis from that cell will have copies of the mutation. If the new cells can function at all, each will have the altered structure or function caused by the mutation. If the other parent cells were normal, the resulting tissue may include both normal tissue and mutant tissue.

**Figure 4** Melanoma is a type of skin cancer caused by mutations in melanocytes, the cells that make skin pigment. Melanoma is an example of a somatic cell cancer. ❯ **Can this kind of cancer be passed on to offspring?**

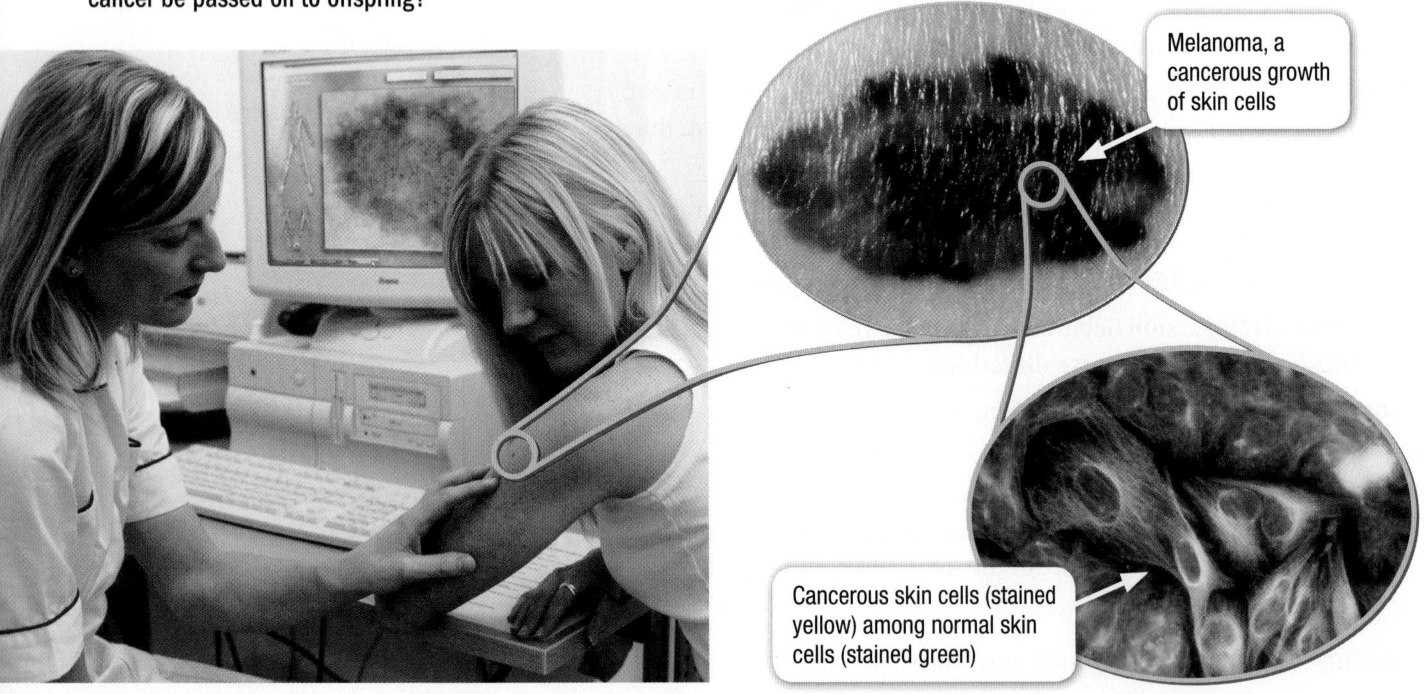

**Some Human Genetic Disorders**

| Disorder | Inheritance pattern | Major physical symptoms | Genetic effect of mutant allele | Number of cases (United States) |
|---|---|---|---|---|
| Sickle cell anemia | recessive | poor blood circulation; pain; damage to organs such as liver, kidney, lungs, and heart | abnormal hemoglobin in red blood cells | 72,000 |
| Tay-Sachs disease | recessive in most cases | deterioration of central nervous system; death in early childhood | defective form of an enzyme in nerve cells | < 100 |
| Cystic fibrosis | recessive | mucus buildup in organs such as lungs, liver, and pancreas; difficulty breathing and digesting; shortened life span | defective form of an enzyme in secretory cells | 30,000 |
| Hemophilia A (classical) | recessive, sex-linked | failure of blood to clot; excessive bleeding and bruising when injured | defective form of a protein for blood clotting | 18,000 |
| Huntington disease | dominant | gradual deterioration of brain tissue in middle age; shortened life expectancy | abnormal protein in brain cells | 30,000 |

**Figure 5** Genetic disorders are caused by inherited mutations that disrupt the normal function of a gene. **› Why are genetic disorders relatively rare?**

**Tumors and Cancers** Certain genes control the normal growth, division, and specialization of cells in bodies. Mutations in these genes can cause a normal somatic cell to "lose control" and begin growing and dividing abnormally. The group of cells that grows will become a *tumor.* If the tumor cells begin to invade other parts of the body, they become a form of *cancer*. An example of a somatic cell tumor is shown in **Figure 4.** Note that although cancers result from somatic cell mutations, not all somatic cell mutations cause cancer.

**New Alleles** You previously learned that for any given gene, many alleles, or variations, may exist. Now, you should see that any new allele must begin as a mutation of an existing allele. Most new alleles are simply the result of silent mutations, so these changes make little difference to the organisms in which they occur. However, sometimes a new allele can cause a change in a gene's function. Depending on the gene, the result may be harmful or beneficial to the organism.

**Genetic Disorders** Harmful effects produced by inherited mutations (defective alleles) are called *genetic disorders*. Several human genetic disorders are summarized in **Figure 5.** Often, such a disorder results because a mutation has altered the normal function of a gene. However, a person may still have one allele of the original, functioning gene. For this reason, many disorders are recessive—that is, the disorder develops only in a person who is homozygous for the mutated allele. So, two heterozygous people may be healthy, yet have children who develop a genetic disorder. A person who is heterozygous for such an allele is said to be a *carrier* of the disorder.

**› Reading Check** *How are mutations related to cancer?*

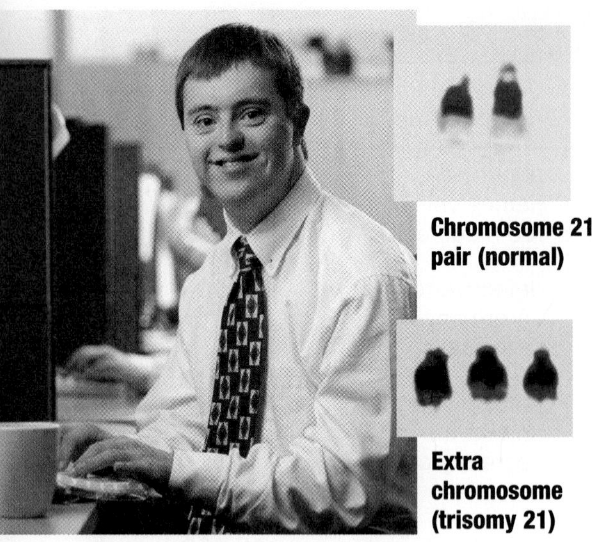


**Figure 6** Most people with Down syndrome have an extra copy of chromosome 21. The extra chromosome can be seen in a karyotype. ❯ **What other conditions can result from accidents in chromosome sorting?**

## Large-Scale Genetic Change

At another scale, accidents can happen to entire sets of chromosomes. ❯ **Very large-scale genetic change can occur by misplacement, recombination, or multiplication of entire chromosomes.**

**Recombination During Crossover** Genetic recombination through sexual reproduction has many important consequences. Recall that during the *crossover* step of meiosis, the alleles from one parent are recombined with the alleles from the other parent. So, meiosis creates new combinations of alleles in offspring. Over time, sexual reproduction and meiotic recombination maintain genetic variety within a population.

**Errors in Sorting Chromosomes** Each of your chromosomes has thousands of genes. Together, these genes control cell structure and function. So, all 46 chromosomes (23 pairs) are needed for your body to develop and function normally. Human embryos with missing chromosomes rarely survive. Humans with an extra chromosome may survive but do not develop normally.

**Nondisjunction** Recall that when gametes form by meiosis, each pair of chromosomes separates in the step called *disjunction.* When the pairs fail to separate properly, the error is called **nondisjunction.** For example, nondisjunction of chromosome 21 can lead to a disabling condition called *Down syndrome,* or *trisomy 21,* as shown in **Figure 6.** In this case, one of the parent's gametes received both copies of chromosome 21 instead of one. When that gamete joined with a normal gamete, the child received three copies instead of two.

**Polyploidy** The largest scale of genetic change can happen if the entire genome is duplicated. Such duplication can occur—rarely—during meiosis, by nondisjunction of *all* chromosomes. The result is a cell with multiple sets of chromosomes, a condition known as **polyploidy.** A polyploid cell has genetic material "to spare." In future offspring, mutations can happen in some genes without losing the functions of the original genes. Thus, polyploidy is another way that organisms can change over time. Polyploidy is common in plants.

**nondisjunction** (NAHN dis JUHNK shuhn) a failure of homologous chromosomes to separate during meiosis I or the failure of sister chromatids to separate during mitosis or meiosis II

**polyploidy** (PAH lee PLOY dee) an abnormal condition of having more than two sets of chromosomes

❯ **Reading Check** ***How can a child be born with extra chromosomes?***

## Section 1 Review

### ❯ KEY IDEAS

1. **Identify** the primary mechanism for genetic change and differences among organisms.
2. **List** the kinds of mutations.
3. **Relate** the possible kinds of mutations to their effects.
4. **Relate** changes in chromosome number to possible results.

### CRITICAL THINKING

5. **Evaluating Significance** Compare DNA mutations with chromosomal mutations in terms of the severity of the results of each.
6. **Justifying Conclusions** You read in a magazine that all mutations are bad. Do you agree? Explain.

### USING SCIENCE GRAPHICS

7. **Visualizing** Look at **Figure 2** in this section. Notice that it shows only a single strand of the original DNA sequence and a final amino acid sequence. Sketch the matching DNA and RNA strands for the steps in between. Review the steps of gene expression if needed.

Section 2

# Regulating Gene Expression

| Key Ideas | Key Terms | Why It Matters |
|---|---|---|
| ❯ Can the process of gene expression be controlled?<br>❯ What is a common form of gene regulation in prokaryotes?<br>❯ How does gene regulation in eukaryotes differ from gene regulation in prokaryotes?<br>❯ Why are proteins so important and versatile? | operon<br>transcription factor<br>intron<br>exon<br>domain | Understanding gene regulation may enable us to treat or prevent diseases that were previously unbeatable. |

How do butterflies develop from caterpillars? We now know that genes determine traits such as patterns on butterfly wings, as shown in **Figure 7.** And we know that every cell in an individual starts with the same genes. So, in a butterfly's lifetime, every trait of every gene is not always "at work."

***The Living Environment***
**Standard 4**

**2.1a** Genes are inherited, but their expression can be modified by interactions with the environment.

**2.1g** Cells store and use coded information. The genetic information stored in DNA is used to direct the synthesis of the thousands of proteins that each cell requires.

**2.1i** The work of the cell is carried out by the many different types of molecules it assembles, mostly proteins. Protein molecules are long, usually folded chains made from 20 different kinds of amino acids in a specific sequence. This sequence influences the shape of the protein. The shape of the protein, in turn, determines its function.

**2.1k** The many body cells in an individual can be very different from one another, even though they are all descended from a single cell and thus have essentially identical genetic instructions. This is because different parts of these instructions are used in different types of cells, and are influenced by the cells' environment and past history.

## Complexities of Gene Expression

Scientists have learned that gene expression (transcription and translation) can be regulated. It is now clear that not all genes are expressed in every cell, nor are many genes expressed all of the time. **❯ Cells have complex systems that regulate whether or not specific genes are expressed. Expression depends on the cell's needs and environment.**

Through *gene regulation,* a given genetic sequence can be expressed in different ways—in different bodies or tissues, under different conditions, or at different times. Thus, gene regulation accounts for changes during development as well as differences among organisms that have similar genes. One benefit of gene regulation is that cells can use energy and materials efficiently.

Recall that many steps take place in the expression of a gene. Also, other molecules play a role in the processes. Because complex interactions happen at each step, there are many opportunities to regulate gene expression. So, nearly every step in the process of gene expression can be regulated or controlled.

A molecular system that controls the expression of a specific gene is called a *genetic switch.* Like a light switch, a genetic switch can be turned "on" or "off." Often, the switch is triggered by factors or conditions outside the cell. Also, the product of one gene may serve to regulate another gene in the same organism.

**❯ Reading Check** ***Are all genes expressed all of the time?***

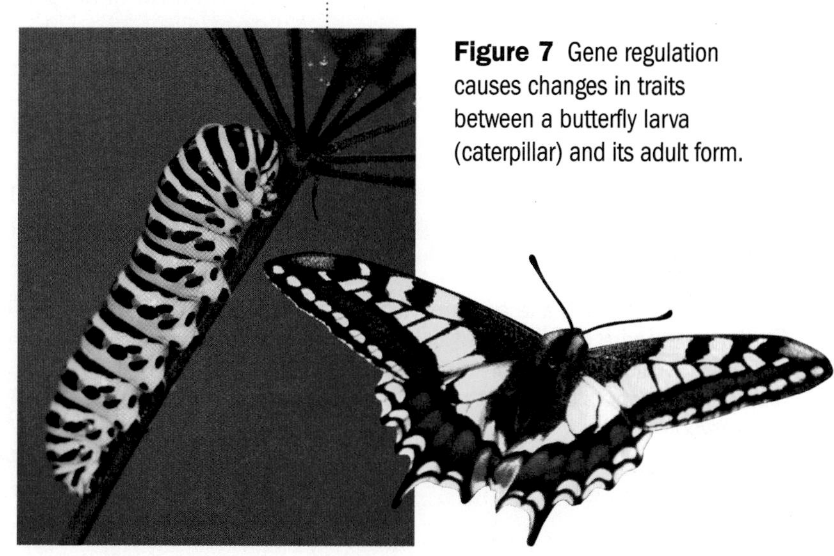

**Figure 7** Gene regulation causes changes in traits between a butterfly larva (caterpillar) and its adult form.

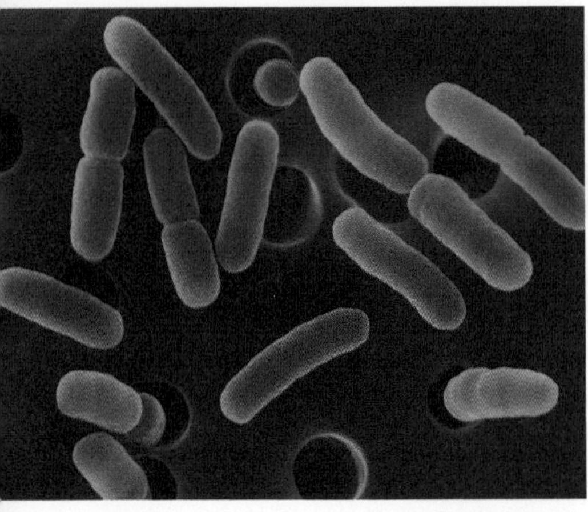

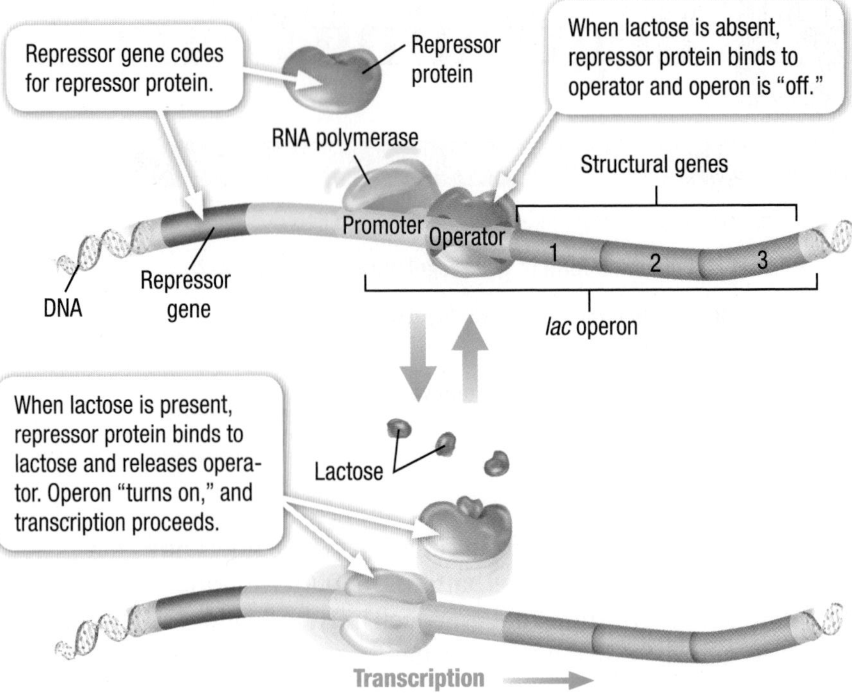
Repressor gene codes for repressor protein.
Repressor protein
When lactose is absent, repressor protein binds to operator and operon is "off."
RNA polymerase
Structural genes
Promoter
Operator
1
2
3
DNA
Repressor gene
lac operon
When lactose is present, repressor protein binds to lactose and releases operator. Operon "turns on," and transcription proceeds.
Lactose
Transcription

**Figure 8** The *lac* operon controls the genes that code for the proteins that help a bacterium use lactose. The operon "turns on" and expresses the genes only in the presence of lactose. **❯ How common are operons?**

## Gene Regulation in Prokaryotes

Scientists have studied and compared gene expression in prokaryotes and eukaryotes. Each has very different ways of regulating how genes are expressed. One reason for the differences can be found in the structure of genes in the two kinds of organisms.

**❯ The major form of gene regulation in prokaryotes depends upon operons that respond to environmental factors.** An **operon** is a gene-regulation system in which adjacent DNA segments control the expression of a group of genes with closely related functions. Operons are common in bacteria but uncommon in eukaryotes.

**Interactions with the Environment** Recall that bacteria are single cells that must get food directly from the environment. Given a stable environment, a bacterium will need a steady supply of proteins and will tend to keep expressing the same genes in the same way. But if the environment changes, a cascade of changes in gene expression may result. In a way, the environment "flips a switch."

**The *lac* Operon Example** An example of gene regulation is found in the bacterium *Escherichia coli*. Usually, when you eat or drink a dairy product, the chemical lactose ("milk sugar") is digested by *E. coli* cells living in your gut. These cells can use the lactose for energy or for other needs. But first, the cells must attach to, absorb, and then break down the lactose. These tasks require three different enzymes, each of which is coded for by a different gene.

The system that involves the *lac* genes is called the *lac operon* and is shown in **Figure 8.** This system includes the three genes plus a *promoter* site and an *operator* site. When lactose is available, the system "turns on" and the three genes are transcribed. When lactose is absent, the system "turns off" and transcription is blocked.

READING TOOLBOX

**Comparison Table** Make a comparison table to compare **Figure 8** and **Figure 9.** Which roles do proteins have in the eukaryotic system but not in the prokaryotic system?

## Gene Regulation in Eukaryotes

Eukaryotic cells, too, must turn genes on and off in response to signals from their environment. However, ❯ **gene regulation in eukaryotes is more complex and variable than gene regulation in prokaryotes.** To begin with, gene expression in eukaryotes involves more steps and interactions than gene expression in prokaryotes.

As you shall see, regulation can occur before transcription, after transcription, or after translation. Furthermore, in eukaryotes, a nuclear membrane separates these processes. So, each process can be regulated separately.

Eukaryotic gene regulation is unique in other ways. Operons are very rare in eukaryotic cells. Also, groups of genes with related functions may be scattered on different chromosomes and controlled by multiple factors. Finally, much of the DNA in eukaryotes may never be transcribed, and even less is ultimately translated into proteins.

**operon** (AHP uhr AHN) a unit of adjacent genes that consists of functionally related structural genes and their associated regulatory genes

**transcription factor** an enzyme that is needed to begin and/or continue genetic transcription

**Controlling Transcription** Like prokaryotic cells, eukaryotic cells have proteins that regulate transcription. But many more proteins are involved, and the interactions are more complex. Most often, the genetic switch involves the first step of transcription, when RNA polymerase binds to the promoter region. The proteins involved in this kind of genetic switch are called **transcription factors.**

**Academic Vocabulary**

**regulate** to control, direct, or govern; to adjust

As shown in **Figure 9,** transcription factors interact with RNA polymerases around promoter regions of DNA. A given gene can be influenced by many transcription factors. Some transcription factors act as *activators,* and some act as *repressors.*

One kind of DNA sequence that can be bound by an activator is called an *enhancer*. Enhancers are often located thousands of bases away from the promoter. A loop in the DNA forms as the factors interact at the promoter site. Each factor may also affect other factors.

❯ **Reading Check** ***Which parts of gene expression can be regulated?***

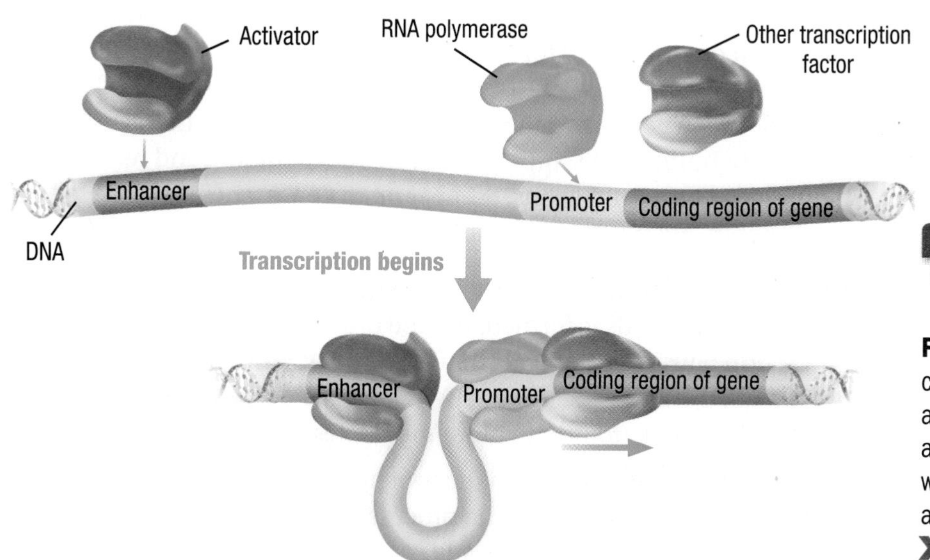


go.hrw.com
interact online
Keyword: HX8GNXF9

**Figure 9** Control of transcription is complex in eukaryotes. For example, an activator may bind to an enhancer site and also to RNA polymerase. This action will activate another transcription factor, and finally transcription will begin.
❯ **Why is gene regulation more complex in eukaryotes than in prokaryotes?**

Hands-On

# QuickLab

## A Model of Introns and Exons

appropriately joined

You can model introns and exons with masking tape.

### Procedure

1. Place a **15 to 20 cm strip of masking tape** on your desk. The tape represents a gene.
2. Use **two colored pens** to write letters on the tape, exactly as shown in the example here. Space the letters to take up the entire length of the tape. The segments in one color represent introns; those in the other color represent exons.
3. Lift the tape. Working from left to right, use **scissors** to cut apart each group of letters of the same color.
4. Stick the pieces of tape to your desk as you cut them. Make two strips of matching colors, and join the pieces in their original order.

### Analysis

1. **Determine** from the resulting two strips which strip represents "introns" and which represents "exons."
2. CRITICAL THINKING **Predicting Results** What might happen to the protein if an intron were not removed?

**Processing RNA After Transcription** It is simplest to think of a gene as a string of nucleotides that code for a protein. However, this simple arrangement is usually found only in prokaryotes. In eukaryotes, many genes contain *noncoding* sequences, or segments of code that will not be translated into amino acids. The noncoding segments are called **introns,** while those portions of the gene that *do* code for amino acids and will be translated are called **exons.**

**RNA Splicing** Exons and introns are handled in a process called *RNA splicing,* as shown in **Figure 10.** After a eukaryotic gene is transcribed, the introns are removed with the help of certain proteins. The exons that remain are *spliced,* or rejoined together, to form a smaller mRNA molecule. Finally, the spliced mRNA leaves the nucleus and is then translated.

**Alternative Splicing** The splicing of eukaryotic genes creates additional opportunities for variation over time. Because each exon encodes a different part of a protein, cells can occasionally shuffle exons between genes and thus make new proteins. The thousands of proteins in human cells appear to result from shuffling and recombining a few thousand exons. Some human genes, such as those for hemoglobin, are made up of multiple copies of similar exons.

**Figure 10** After transcription in eukaryotes, the entire new mRNA segment may not be translated into proteins. Instead, introns are removed, and only exons are translated.

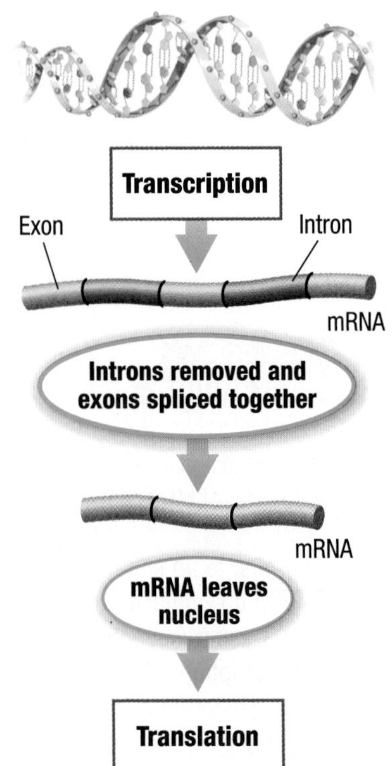


**Processing Proteins After Translation** After translation, a chain of amino acids is formed, but the protein may not go directly into action. Further chemical changes may alter the structure and function of the protein. Such changes may affect the protein's shape, stability, or interactions with other molecules.

**Final Destination** A newly made protein may be needed in a specific location within the cell. The process of getting proteins to their correct destination is called *protein sorting.* Protein sorting occurs in many parts of the cell, such as the Golgi apparatus.

**Sorting Signals** Protein sorting is often directed by *sorting signals,* small parts of a protein that bind to other molecules within the cell. Some signals bind the protein to its final location in the cell. Some signals bind proteins to ribosomes while translation is in progress, and sends them together to the ER for further processing. This variation is another example of the complexity of genes.

## The Many Roles of Proteins

Recall that proteins are complex strings of amino acids that do much of the work in cells. The diversity of protein structures relates to the many functions that proteins serve in cells. These functions range from forming the cell's shape to regulating gene expression. Proteins range in size from about 50 amino acids to more than 25,000 amino acids. The average protein is about 250 amino acids.

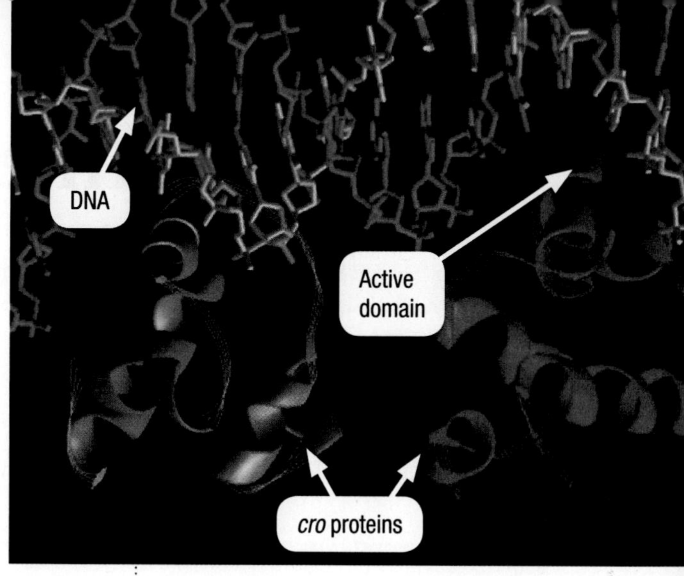


**Figure 11** Many of the proteins involved in gene regulation have a shape that fits closely with DNA or RNA molecules. The example shown here is a model of two molecules of bacterial *cro* protein (orange and red) binding to a molecule of DNA (blue and purple). The parts of the protein molecules that are chemically active are called *active domains.*

**Protein Structure** Because they can form many shapes, proteins can serve many roles. **› The sequence of amino acids in a protein determines its three-dimensional structure and chemical behavior.** In turn, this folding determines the function of the protein, as shown in **Figure 11.** Some parts of a protein that have a specific chemical structure and function are protein **domains.** A protein may have several domains, each with a specific function. In eukaryotes, each domain is usually the result of a specific exon. Finally, large proteins may be made up of several smaller proteins, or *subunits.*

**Proteins in Gene Expression** Proteins serve important roles in gene expression. For example, several forms of RNA polymerase function to make mRNA, tRNA, and rRNA. Other proteins serve as *regulatory proteins* by binding to genetic switches in specific genes.

Because transcription is more complex in eukaryotes than in prokaryotes, more proteins are involved in the process. Likewise, more enzymes and structural proteins are required for translation in eukaryotes. Even after translation, additional steps may be needed to make a protein fully active in its proper place in a cell.

**› Reading Check** ***What determines a protein's shape?***

**intron** a nucleotide sequence that is part of a gene and that is transcribed from DNA into mRNA but not translated into amino acids

**exon** one of several nonadjacent nucleotide sequences that are part of one gene and that are transcribed, joined together, and then translated

**domain** in proteins, a functional unit that a has a distinctive pattern of structural folding

## Section 2 Review

### › KEY IDEAS

1. **Generalize** the ways that gene expression can be regulated.
2. **Describe** an example of gene regulation in prokaryotes.
3. **Identify** how gene regulation in eukaryotes is unique.
4. **Relate** protein structure to function in gene expression and regulation.

### CRITICAL THINKING

5. **Proposing Mechanisms** Propose one other mechanism, not yet mentioned, for gene regulation in either prokaryotes or eukaryotes.
6. **Using Models** Use letters and words to show how a sequence could be spliced in several ways.

### ALTERNATIVE ASSESSMENT

7. **Electronic Research** Use electronic resources to find three-dimensional computer models of proteins. Be sure that the models are based on scientific research. Make a display of several models.

Section

# 3 Genome Interactions

| Key Ideas | Key Terms | Why It Matters |
| --- | --- | --- |
| ❯ What can we learn by comparing genomes?<br>❯ Can genetic material be stored and transferred by mechanisms other than chromosomes?<br>❯ What are the roles of genes in multicellular development? | genome<br>plasmid<br>transposon<br>cell differentiation<br>apoptosis | We can understand how our own bodies work by comparing our genetic systems to those of other organisms. |

**Standard 4**

**1.2e** The organs and systems of the body help to provide all the cells with their basic needs. The cells of the body are of different kinds and are grouped in ways that enhance how they function together.

**2.1k** The many body cells in an individual can be very different from one another, even though they are all descended from a single cell and thus have essentially identical genetic instructions. This is because different parts of these instructions are used in different types of cells, and are influenced by the cells' environment and past history.

**3.1b** New inheritable characteristics can result from new combinations of existing genes or from mutations of genes in reproductive cells.

Do you share genes with bacteria? In a way, you do. About 10% of human genes are nearly identical to bacterial genes. **Figure 12** shows the similarity between human genes and genes of other organisms.

## Genomes and the Diversity of Life

Studying genomes has revolutionized how we look at gene regulation and gene expression. Recall that a **genome** is all of the DNA that an organism or species has within its chromosomes. A genome contains all the genes needed to make more of that organism. Today, the genomes of hundreds of organisms have been extensively studied. **❯ Comparisons among the genetic systems of many organisms reveal basic biological similarities and relationships.**

**Universal Code** With few exceptions, the genetic code is the same in all organisms. For example, the codon GUC codes for the amino acid valine in bacteria, in eagles, in plants, and in your own cells. For this reason, the genetic code is often described as being universal. However, some exceptions exist to the universal aspects of the genetic code. For example, some bacteria use a slightly different set of amino acids in making proteins.

**Figure 12** This graph shows the ratios of human genes that are nearly identical to genes in each of these species. **❯ What can we learn from such comparisons?**

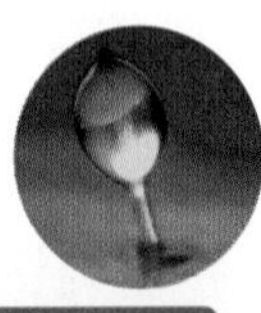

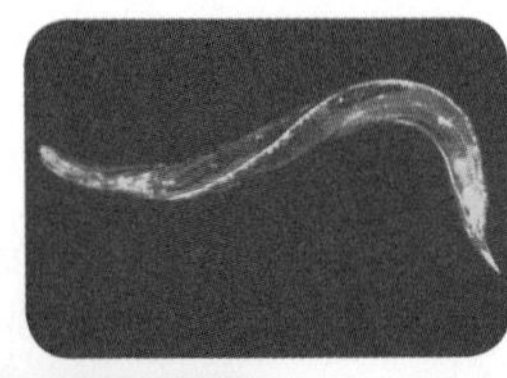

Slime mold 16%
Mouse-ear cress 17%
Nematode 31%
Fruit fly 39%

**Genome Sizes** Genome size can be measured as an amount of DNA or a number of genes. Either way, genome size is only roughly related to complexity. Genomes in microbes range from 400,000 to millions of base pairs and include from 400 to 9,300 genes. Eukaryote genomes range from 100 million to more than 3 billion base pairs with 6,000 to 100,000 genes. The human genome has about 25,000 genes. Some plants have more than 100,000 genes.

**DNA Versus Genes** Not all DNA in a cell is part of a gene or even part of a chromosome. Special kinds of DNA include the following:

- **Plasmids in Prokaryotes** Recall that bacterial DNA is usually stored in one long, circular chromosome. However, most bacteria have extra pieces of DNA called **plasmids.** These small, circular DNA segments are replicated independently and can be transferred between cells. So, plasmids are an important source of genetic variation in bacteria.
- **Noncoding DNA in Eukaryotes** Eukaryotes have a great deal of *noncoding* DNA. For example, introns are transcribed but never translated. Also, long stretches of repeating sequences exist that are never transcribed. The function of most noncoding DNA is unclear.
- **DNA in Cell Organelles** Recall that mitochondria and chloroplasts, shown in **Figure 13,** are organelles that have special roles in eukaryotic cells. Chloroplasts enable plants to harvest energy from sunlight. Mitochondria act as the source of energy for cell function. Each of these organelles has its own small genome that is separate from that in the nucleus. These genomes code for proteins and RNAs (rRNA and tRNA) that assist in the function of each organelle.

**Endosymbiotic Theory** Why do mitochondria and chloroplasts have their own DNA? Scientists suspect that each organelle had its origin in ancient bacterial cells. This idea is known as the *endosymbiotic theory*. For example, chloroplast-like bacteria could have been engulfed, but not killed, by larger cells. Each kind of cell may have benefited from this relationship. Over time, the cells would live together in a close relationship called *symbiosis*.

› **Reading Check** ***What kinds of organisms have large genomes?***

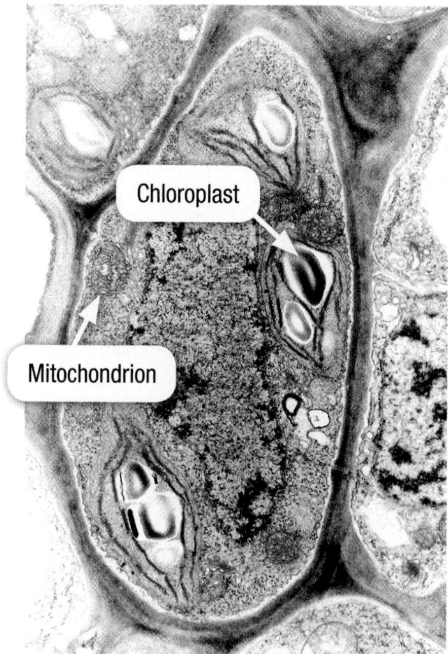


**Figure 13** Chloroplasts and mitochondria have their own DNA. Each organelle's genome is stored and replicated separately from the chromosomes of the cell.

**genome** (JEE NOHM) the complete genetic material contained in an individual or species

**plasmid** (PLAZ mid) a genetic structure that can replicate independently of the main chromosome(s) of a cell

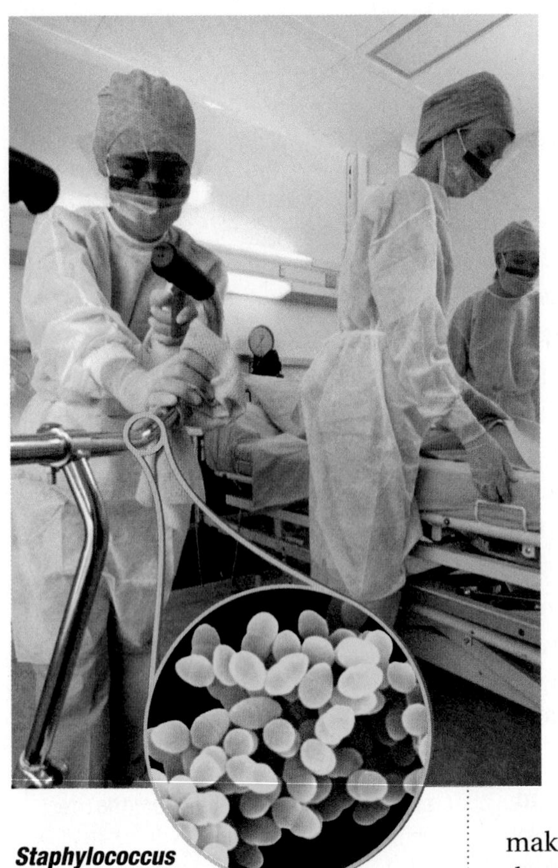

**Staphylococcus bacteria**

**Figure 14** We use antibiotic chemicals in drugs and cleaning products in an attempt to kill bacteria. However, some bacteria have become resistant to most antibiotics. **› What is the role of mobile genetic elements in antibiotic resistance?**

SCILINKS.
**www.scilinks.org**
Topic: Antibiotic Resistance
Code: HX80081

## Moving Beyond Chromosomes

We now know that cells can interact at the genetic level. And we know that genetic material exists outside of chromosomes. The closer we study genetics, the more complexities we find. **› Small bits of genetic material can be stored, moved, and changed by a variety of interactions.**

**Mobile Genetic Elements** Plasmids are just one kind of *mobile genetic element (MGE).* MGEs are units of DNA or RNA that are sometimes *transposed,* or moved as a functional unit, from one place to another in a genome. Other MGEs are transposons and viruses.

**Transposons** Sets of genes that are transposed randomly are *jumping genes,* or **transposons.** When a transposon moves to a new place, it may inactivate a nearby gene, much like an operon does. All organisms seem to have transposons in their genomes. Some bacteria have transposons that jump between plasmids and chromosomes.

**Viruses** In terms of structure and function, transposons are similar to viruses. *Viruses* are very small, nonliving particles that consist of DNA or RNA inside a protein coating. Viruses infect cells by using the cells' own replication processes to make new virus copies. Sometimes, viruses take away copies of the cells' DNA or leave some DNA behind. Thus, viruses can move genetic material between cells. Certain kinds of RNA viruses, called *retroviruses,* produce DNA that becomes part of the host cell's genome.

**Genetic Change** The discovery of MGEs has helped us further understand genetic change. It has also enabled us to manipulate genetic change for our own purposes, as you will learn. MGEs cause genetic change by bringing together new combinations of genes. Furthermore, MGEs can transfer genetic material between individuals and even between species. For example, the genome of *Escherichia coli* (common gut bacteria) is about 15% similar to that of *Salmonella* (food-borne, illness-causing bacteria). Scientists suspect that the similar genetic sequences are the result of MGEs being passed between the species.

**Antibiotic Resistance** Like mutations, transpositions may have helpful or harmful effects. And what helps one organism may harm another. An effect that is helpful to bacteria but harmful to humans is the evolution of antibiotic resistance. Antibiotic chemicals are often used to prevent or combat bacterial infections, as shown in **Figure 14.** But if just one bacterial cell has a gene that makes the cell resist the effect of a particular antibiotic, that cell may survive and reproduce. Furthermore, the gene could be passed to other bacteria as part of an MGE. Scientists fear that this process is indeed happening, because increasing numbers and kinds of bacteria are becoming resistant to each of the antibiotics that have been produced.

**› Reading Check** ***How are transposons and viruses similar?***

## Multicellular Development and Aging

You have learned that external or environmental cues can regulate gene expression in cells. In multicellular eukaryotes, gene regulation can also happen because of internal cues. In particular, the development of an embryo involves complex gene regulation. Many cells will develop from one beginning cell. And different kinds of cells will develop to have different functions in different parts of the body. **❯ Each cell within a developing body will express specific genes. Gene expression depends on the cell's age and location within the body.**

**transposon** (trans POH ZAHN) a genetic sequence that is randomly moved, in a functional unit, to new places in a genome

**cell differentiation** the process by which a cell becomes specialized for a specific structure or function during multicellular development

**Cell Differentiation** In the process of **cell differentiation,** each new cell is modified and specialized as the cells multiply to form a body. Gene regulation plays an important role in this process. *Homeotic* genes are examples of genes that regulate differentiation. Scientists first discovered these genes in fruit flies. Mutations in these genes can cause one body part, such as a leg, to develop in place of another body part, such as an antenna.

As scientists studied many genomes, they found that many kinds of organisms have homeotic genes. And these genes always seem to control similar developmental processes by similar mechanisms. All homeotic genes code for proteins that regulate the expression of other genes. Many homeotic genes contain a similar sequence of 180 bases. This sequence, called a *homeobox,* codes for a DNA-binding domain in the resulting protein.

In general, the genetic regulation of development seems to be similar in all animals. A specific set of homeotic genes, called *hox,* is found in all animals that have a head end and a tail end. Hox genes direct development relative to body position, as shown in **Figure 15.**

**Prefixes** The prefix *homeo-* is used several times on this page. Use the Reading Toolbox page to find the meaning of the prefix *homeo-*. Write a definition for *homeotic* and *homeobox* in your own words.

**❯ Reading Check** *What is a homeobox?*

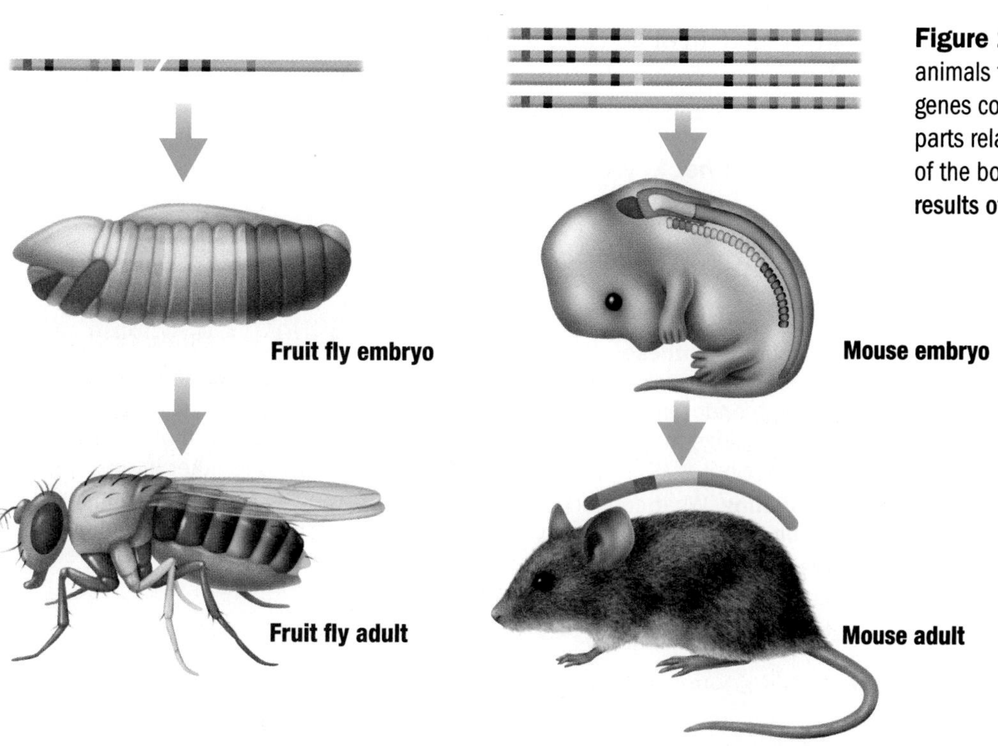


**Figure 15** *Hox* genes are found in animals from insects to mammals. These genes control the development of body parts relative to the head and tail ends of the body. **❯ What are some possible results of mutations in these genes?**

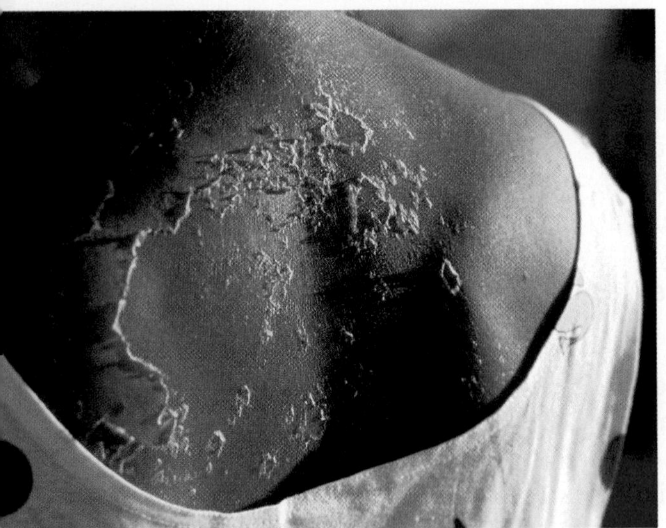

**Figure 16** Sunburn is the result of apoptosis—or cell suicide. When skin cells are heavily damaged by overexposure to the sun, a genetic switch in the cells may signal the cells to stop functioning. **› Why is apoptosis important in multicellular organisms?**

**Cell Growth and Maintenance** Although scientists have long been aware of the *cell cycle*, only recently have they begun to understand how genes regulate the cell cycle and cell growth. In 2001, three scientists received the Nobel Prize for discovering the genetic systems that regulate the cell cycle. The scientists identified two kinds of proteins that regulate the cell cycle: *CDK* and *cyclin*. These proteins are present in all eukaryotes and drive the cell cycle forward. The CDK molecules function like an engine, and the cyclins function like gears. Together, they control the speed of the cell cycle. Cancer results when control of cells has been lost because either the "engine" or the "gears" malfunction.

**Cell Death and Aging** In multicellular organisms, all cells have arisen from the division of other cells. But most of these cells stop dividing once the organism is mature. In fact, almost all body cells are "programmed" to age and die. At some point, the cell will simply shut down all functioning, gradually shrink, and eventually fall apart. This process of cellular "suicide" is known as **apoptosis.** Apoptosis seems to occur in consistent steps, much like other cellular processes, such as mitosis. Scientists are still studying the genetic systems that may control apoptosis.

**apoptosis** (AP uhp TOH sis) in multicellular organisms, a genetically controlled process that leads to the death of a cell; programmed cell death

**Function of Apoptosis** Why do some cells need to die? In some cases, the full development of a body part requires the removal of some cells. For example, apoptosis is responsible for the loss of a tadpole's tail as the tadpole becomes an adult. Likewise, human fingers and toes are formed through the loss of in-between tissue in the embryonic limbs. Also, apoptosis is at work when sunburned skin begins to peel off, as shown in **Figure 16.**

**Telomeres** Aging has many effects on cells. An example is the effect of aging on the ends of chromosomes (called *telomeres*). As cells divide repeatedly, the telomeres lose nucleotides and become shortened. In older cells, this shortening may cause mishandling of the chromosomes during mitosis and thus result in nonfunctioning cells. However, telomere shortening is not the only cause of aging.

**› Reading Check** ***What are the roles of proteins in the cell cycle?***

## Section 3 Review

### › KEY IDEAS

1. **Justify** comparing the genetic systems of various life-forms.
2. **List** mechanisms other than chromosomes by which genetic material may be stored and moved.
3. **Relate** gene expression to multicellular development.

### CRITICAL THINKING

4. **Forming Hypotheses** Could any other cell organelles have arisen through endosymbiosis? If so, what findings may support such a hypothesis?
5. **Predicting** What could be the result of a mutation in a hox gene?
6. **Logical Reasoning** Is apoptosis a useful mechanism for prokaryotes? Explain your answer.

### ALTERNATIVE ASSESSMENT

7. **Gallery of Genetic Curiosities** Create a poster, slide show, or other display that exhibits mutants and other interesting examples of genetic complexity. Be sure to provide a caption and a reference source for each of your images.

Why It Matters

# Forensic Genealogy

BIOTECHNOLOGY

Genealogy (JEE nee AHL uh jee) is the study of family histories. Forensic genealogy can involve finding lost relatives, identifying bodies, or confirming a claim of parenthood.

## Clues in DNA

Because DNA is passed from parents to offspring, scientists can use DNA to find hereditary links between people. Samples of DNA can be analyzed to find similarities and differences. People who are related by birth will share at least some of the DNA of their common ancestors. DNA can be extracted from living cells and from dead cells in hair or bone.

## Mother's or Father's DNA

Every cell in a person's body contains DNA from both parents. However, chromosome recombination makes it hard to tell which DNA came from which parent. But two kinds of DNA are unique. One kind is the DNA in a Y chromosome in males. The Y chromosome always comes from the father.

Mitochondrial DNA is also unique. The DNA in the mitochondria of cells is unrelated to the DNA in the nucleus. In humans, the mitochondria in all cells have been copied from the mother's egg cell. So, your mitochondrial DNA is the same as your mother's.

Analyses of these two kinds of DNA have solved crimes and mysteries. In some cases, people have been able to learn their true family history. In other cases, the identity of a dead body has been confirmed (or not) based on DNA comparisons with living or dead relatives.

**Who is buried here?** This tomb in the Cathedral of Seville, Spain, is supposed to contain the remains of Christopher Columbus. But the history of the remains is disputed, and some people claim that the true remains lie elsewhere. DNA analysis may solve the case.

**Whose coffin is this?** In 2005, Hurricane Katrina caused disastrous flooding in areas along the coast of the Gulf of Mexico. Many coffins floated out of burial sites. To help find the living or dead relatives of unidentified bodies, scientists could compare DNA samples. For example, mitochondrial DNA will be identical among siblings.

**Quick Project** Find out the latest findings from DNA analyses of the supposed remains of Christopher Columbus.

Skills Practice

# Chapter 14 Lab

4.2.1i

## Objectives

- Perform a protein assay to detect the results of gene expression.
- Use gel electrophoresis and staining to detect size differences.
- Infer the presence of similar genes in different species.

## Materials

- lab apron, safety goggles, and disposable gloves
- fish muscle samples (3 to 6 unknowns)
- microtubes, flip-top or screw-top (6 to 12)
- protein buffer solution with dye
- water bath
- precast gel for electrophoresis chamber
- micropipettes or tips, sterile, disposable (3 to 6)
- electrophoresis chamber with power supply and wires
- running buffer solution
- gel staining tray
- protein stain solution
- water, distilled

## Safety

# Protein Detection

Because genes code for proteins, the presence of specific proteins in cells indicates the presence of specific genes. In this lab, you will detect the presence of specific proteins in several species of fishes. You will separate the different proteins by using gel electrophoresis.

*Electrophoresis* relies on a simple fact of biochemistry: opposite charges attract one another, and like charges repel. So, molecules that have a charge can be pulled around by an electric field. To separate molecules by electrophoresis, the molecules can be pulled through a microscopic "obstacle course" that will slow down larger molecules. If the "course" is "run" for a time, the molecules will be sorted by size.

In *gel electrophoresis*, the "obstacle course" is a slab of jellylike material, simply referred to as a *gel*. Several types of gels can be used to separate samples of DNA, RNA, or proteins. The samples can be stained to see where the parts ended up.

## Procedure

### Prepare Protein Samples

1. Put on a lab apron, safety goggles, and gloves. Read all procedures, and prepare to collect your data. For each sample of fish muscle, record the type of fish, and assign it a code letter. Then, mark the letter onto two microtubes.

2. **CAUTION: Never eat or taste food in the lab.** Obtain a small piece of each fish muscle sample. Place each piece in a microtube that has the correct code label.

3. **CAUTION: Never taste chemicals or allow them to contact your skin.** For each sample, add enough protein buffer solution to cover the sample piece. Cap the tube, then gently flick it to mix the contents. The buffer will cause some of the proteins from each fish muscle sample to become suspended in the solution.

4. Let the tubes sit at room temperature for 5 min. Then, pour just the liquid from each into the second tube with the matching label. Keep the samples on ice until used.

5. **CAUTION: Use extreme caution when working with heating devices.** Heat the samples in the water bath at 95 °C for 5 min. The heat will cause the proteins from each fish muscle sample to denature.

### Separate Proteins by Gel Electrophoresis

6. Examine the gel that is precast within its chamber. Note the row of small wells along one edge. These wells are where you will place the samples to be separated. Keep the gel level as you work.

7. Slowly add running buffer solution to the chamber. Add just enough to flood the wells and to cover the gel surface with buffer about 2 mm deep. Be careful not to damage the gel while pouring.

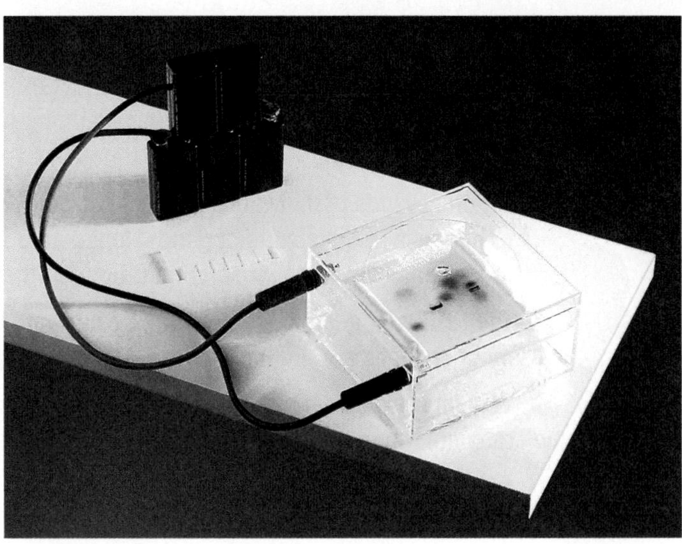

8 Using a clean micropipette, transfer 10 µL of one sample solution into one well. Be careful not to overflow the well or puncture the gel with the pipette tip. Record the sample's "lane" position.

9 Repeat step 8 for each sample. Make sure to use a clean pipette for each transfer.

10 **CAUTION: Use caution when working with electrical equipment.** Assemble the electrophoresis chamber and power source as directed by your teacher. With your teacher's approval, connect the power supply to the chamber electrodes. The negative terminal should be connected to the electrode closest to the wells, and the positive terminal should be connected to the opposite electrode.

11 Leave the chamber running but undisturbed for the amount of time specified by your teacher. During this time, the samples and dye should move toward the positive side of the gel.

### View the Separated Proteins

12 When the moving front of the dye has migrated across the entire gel, disconnect the electrodes from the power source. Gently transfer the gel to the staining tray.

13 **CAUTION: Dispose of materials as directed by your teacher.** Gently pour off the buffer solution into an appropriate container as directed by your teacher.

14 Slowly pour the protein stain solution over the staining tray, and then wait for the amount of time specified by your teacher.

15 Destain the gel by soaking and rinsing it several times in distilled water. Dispose of the rinse water as directed by your teacher. Some of the stain will remain on the proteins in the gel. Draw, photograph, or photocopy the gel for analysis.

16 Clean up and dispose of your lab materials and waste according to your teacher's instructions. Wash your hands before leaving the lab.

SCILINKS.
www.scilinks.org
Topic: Gene Expression
Code: HX80642

## Analyze and Conclude

1. SCIENTIFIC METHODS **Organizing Data** On your picture of the gel, mark the position of each visible band in each lane of the unknown samples.
2. SCIENTIFIC METHODS **Analyzing Data** Compare the numbers and positions of visible bands among all lanes. Identify which bands of the unknown samples appear to match each other. Identify which of the samples share the most similarities.

## Extension

3. **Evolutionary Relationships** Make a table to compare the protein bands from each fish. Use the table to infer which fish are most closely related by heredity and which are least related. Try to draw a "family tree" showing the evolutionary relationships among these fish.

# Chapter 14 Summary

| Key Ideas | Key Terms |
|---|---|

## 1 Mutation and Genetic Change

- For the most part, genetic differences among organisms originate as some kind of mutation.
- Different kinds of mutations are recognized as either changes in DNA or changes in the results of genes. In eukaryotic cells, the process of meiosis creates the chance of mutations at the chromosome level.
- The results of genetic change may be harmful, beneficial, or neutral; most changes are neutral and may not be passed on to offspring.
- Very large-scale genetic change can occur by misplacement, recombination, or multiplication of entire chromosomes.

**Key Terms:** **mutation** (319), **nondisjunction** (324), **polyploidy** (324)

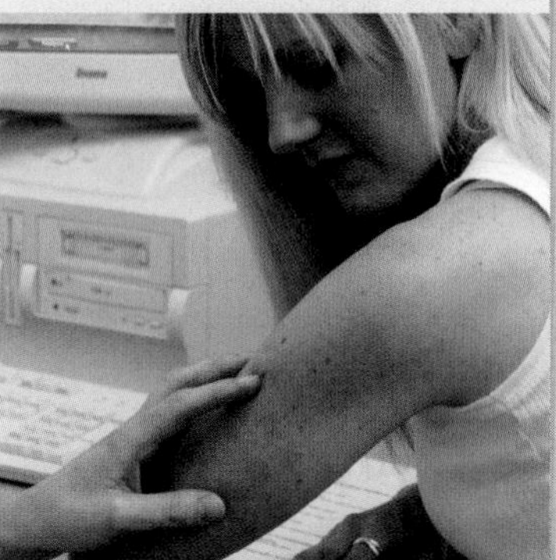

## 2 Regulating Gene Expression

- Cells have complex systems that regulate whether or not specific genes are expressed, depending on the cell's needs and environment.
- The major form of gene regulation in prokaryotes depends upon operons that respond to environmental factors.
- Gene regulation in eukaryotes is more complex and variable than gene regulation in prokaryotes.
- The sequence of amino acids in a protein determines its three-dimensional structure and chemical behavior.

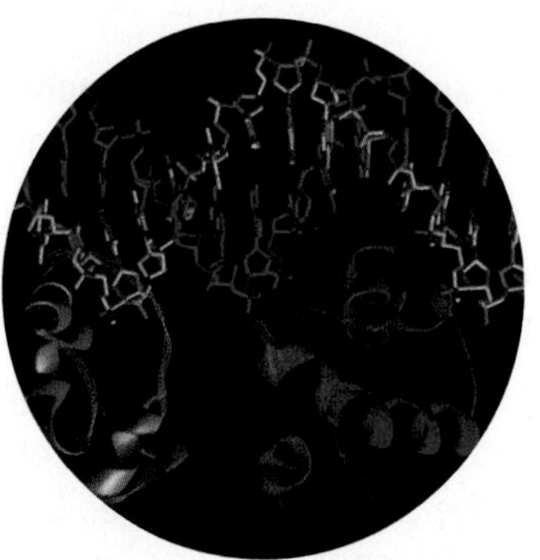

**Key Terms:** **operon** (326), **transcription factor** (327), **intron** (328), **exon** (328), **domain** (329)

## 3 Genome Interactions

- Comparisons among the genetic systems of many organisms reveal basic biological similarities and relationships.
- Small bits of genetic material can be stored, moved, and changed by a variety of interactions.
- Each cell within a developing body will express specific genes, depending on the cell's age and location within the body.

**Key Terms:** **genome** (370), **plasmid** (331), **transposon** (332), **cell differentiation** (333), **apoptosis** (334)

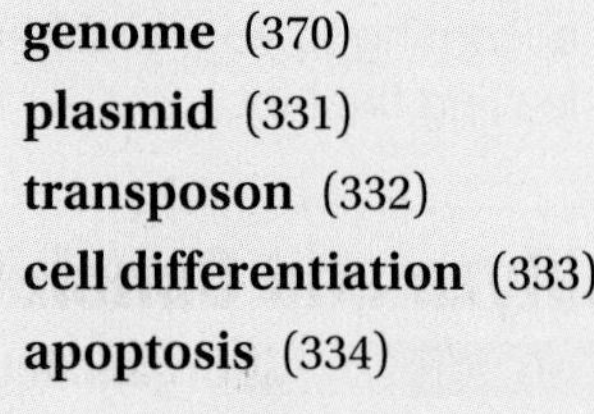

Chapter 14

The Living Environment

# Regents Exam Practice

**PART A: Answer all questions in this part.**

*Directions:* For each statement or question, write on your separate answer sheet the number of the word or expression that best completes the statement or answers the question.

**1** Mutations that occur in skin or lung cells have little effect on the evolution of a species because mutations in these cells

(1) usually lead to the death of the organism.
(2) cannot be passed on to offspring.
(3) are usually beneficial to the organism.
(4) lead to more serious mutations in offspring.

**2** Which statement indicates that different parts of the genetic information are used in different kinds of cells, even in the same organism?

(1) The cells produced by a zygote usually have different genes.
(2) As an embryo develops, various tissues and organs are produced.
(3) Replicated chromosomes separate during gamete formation.
(4) Offspring have a combination of genes from both parents.

**3** Plants inherit genes that enable them to produce chlorophyll, but this pigment is not produced unless the plants are exposed to light. This is an example of how the environment can

(1) cause mutations to occur.
(2) influence the expression of a genetic trait.
(3) result in the appearance of a new species.
(4) affect one plant species, but not another.

**4** Genes involved in the production of abnormal red blood cells have an abnormal sequence of

(1) ATP molecules.
(2) amino acids.
(3) sugars.
(4) bases.

**5** A mutation occurs in the liver cells of a certain field mouse. Which statement concerning the spread of this mutation through the mouse population is correct?

(1) It will spread because it is beneficial.
(2) It will spread because it is a dominant gene.
(3) It will not spread because it is not in a gamete.
(4) It will not spread because it is a recessive gene.

**6** A sudden change in the DNA of a chromosome can usually be passed on to future generations if the change occurs in a

(1) skin cell.
(2) liver cell.
(3) sex cell.
(4) brain cell.

**7** The ozone layer of Earth's atmosphere helps to filter ultraviolet radiation. As the ozone layer is depleted, more ultraviolet radiation reaches Earth's surface. This increase in ultraviolet radiation may be harmful because it can directly cause

(1) photosynthesis to stop in all marine organisms.
(2) abnormal migration patterns in waterfowl.
(3) mutations in the DNA of organisms.
(4) sterility in most species of mammals and birds.

**8** How does the karyotype of a person with Down syndrome differ from a normal karyotype?

(1) It lacks a chromosome.
(2) It has two sex chromosomes.
(3) It has twice the number of chromosomes.
(4) It has an extra copy of a single chromosome.

**9** A human liver cell is very different in structure and function from a nerve cell in the same person. This is best explained by the fact that

(1) different genes function in each type of cell.
(2) liver cells can reproduce while the nerve cells cannot.
(3) liver cells contain fewer chromosomes than nerve cells.
(4) different DNA is present in each type of cell.

10 Which process can produce new inheritable characteristics within a multicellular species?
(1) cloning of the zygote
(2) mitosis in muscle cells
(3) gene alterations in gametes
(4) differentiation in nerve cells

11 Which statement is true regarding an alteration or change in DNA?
(1) It is always known as a mutation.
(2) It is always advantageous to an individual.
(3) It is always passed on to offspring.
(4) It is always detected by the process of chromatography.

12 The development of specialized tissues and organs in a multicellular organism directly results from
(1) cloning
(2) differentiation
(3) meiosis
(4) evolution

**PART B**

13 A mutation occurs in a cell. Which sequence best represents the correct order of the events involved for this mutation to affect the traits expressed by this cell?
(1) a change in the sequence of DNA bases → joining amino acids in sequence →appearance of characteristic
(2) joining amino acids in sequence → a change in the sequence of DNA bases → appearance of characteristic
(3) appearance of characteristic → joining amino acids in sequence → a change in the sequence of DNA bases
(4) a change in the sequence of DNA bases → appearance of characteristic → joining amino acids in sequence

14 The Y-chromosome carries the SRY gene that codes for the production of testosterone in humans. Occasionally a mutation occurs resulting in the SRY gene being lost from the Y-chromosome and added to the X-chromosome, as shown in the diagram below. Based on the diagram, which statement is correct?

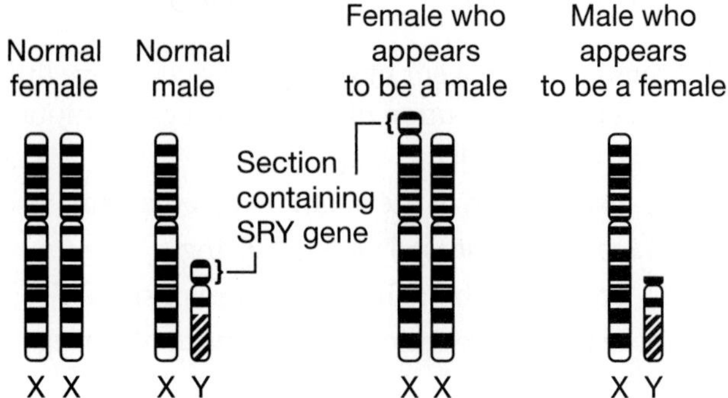


(1) The production of testosterone influences the development of male characteristics.
(2) Reproductive technology has had an important influence on human development.
(3) Normal female characteristics develop from a single X-chromosome.
(4) Male characteristics only develop in the absence of X-chromosomes.

15 Fruit flies with the curly-wing trait will develop straight wings if kept at a temperature of 16°C during development and curly wings if kept at 25°C. The best explanation for this change in the shape of wings is that the
(1) genes for curly wings and genes for straight wings are found on different chromosomes.
(2) type of genes present in the fruit fly is dependent on environmental temperature.
(3) environment affects the expression of the genes for this trait.
(4) higher temperature produces a gene mutation.

16 An example of a mobile genetic element is
(1) a transposon.
(2) a bacterium.
(3) a cancer cell.
(4) a hox gene.

17 Programmed cell death is called
(1) aging.
(2) cyclin.
(3) apoptosis.
(4) transposition.

**18** The types of human cells shown below are different from one another, even though they all originated from the same fertilized egg and contain the same genetic information. Explain why these genetically identical cells can differ in structure and function.

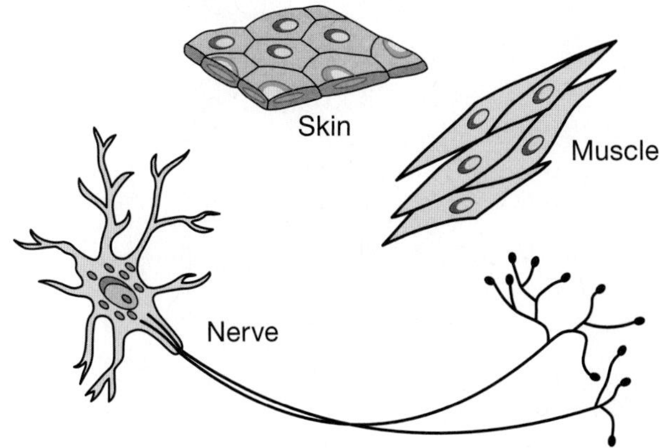


**PART D**

**Base your answer to question 19 on the portion of the mRNA codon chart and information below.**

| | | | |
|---|---|---|---|
| AUU, AUC, AUA } **ILE** (Isoleucine)<br>AUG } **MET** (Methionine) | ACU, ACC, ACA, ACG } **THR** (Threonine) | AAU, AAC } **ASN** (Asparagine)<br>AAA, AAG } **LYS** (Lysine) | AGU, AGC } **SER** (Serine)<br>AGA, AGG } **ARG** (Arginine) |

Series I represents three mRNA codons. Series II includes a mutation of series I.

**19** How would the amino acid sequence produced by the mutant strand (series II) compare to the amino acid sequence produced by series I?

(1) The amino acid sequence would be shorter.

Series I AGAUCGAGU
Series II ACAUCGAGU

(2) One amino acid in the sequence would change.
(3) The amino acid sequence would remain unchanged.
(4) More than one amino acid in the sequence would change.

Chapter 15

# Gene Technologies and Human Applications

## Preview



## Why It Matters

Gene technologies aid the study of basic biology. They have many other applications, such as producing food and treating disease.

Why would scientists make a pig that glows green? So they can study how genes work.

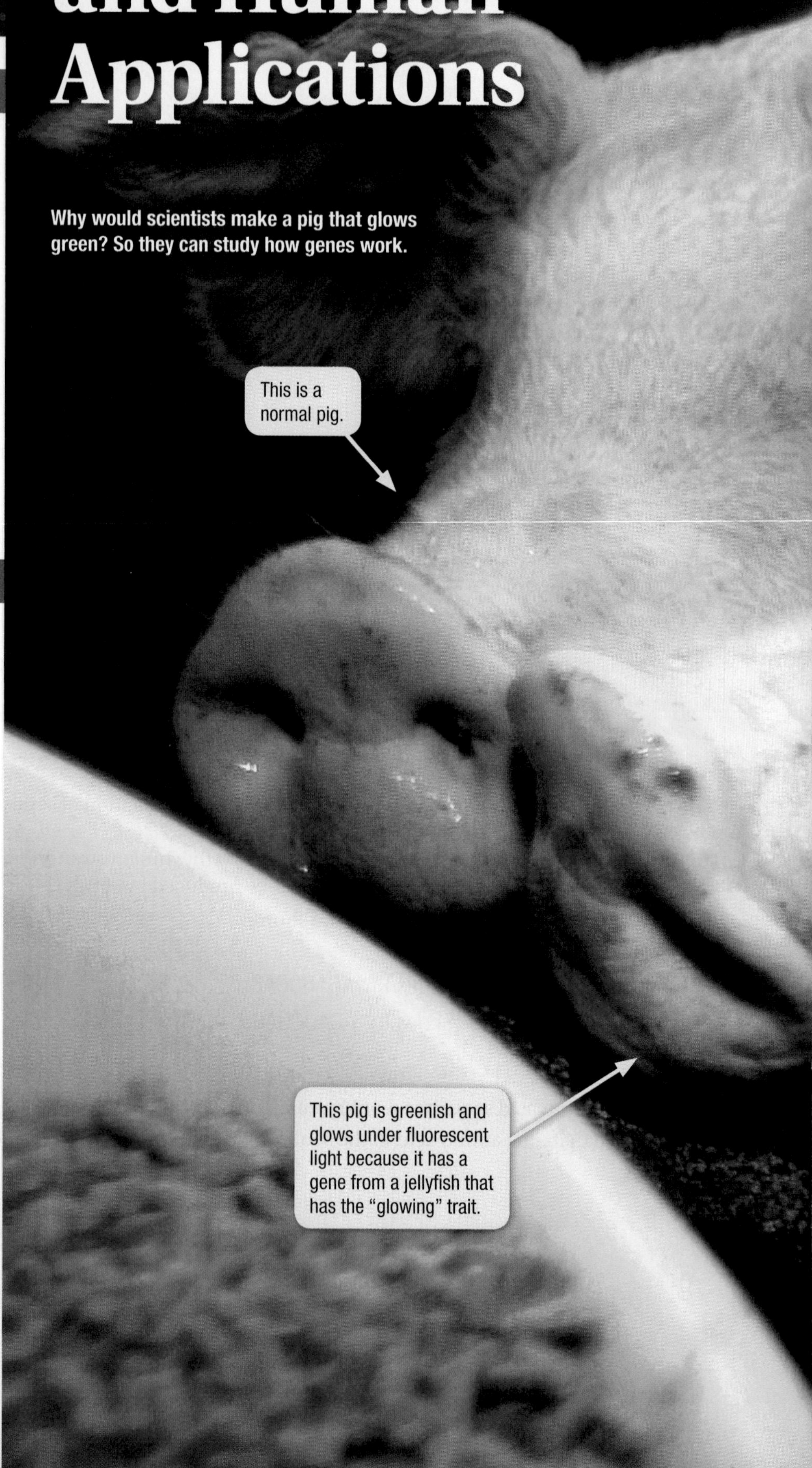

This is a normal pig.

This pig is greenish and glows under fluorescent light because it has a gene from a jellyfish that has the "glowing" trait.

***The Living Environment***

**Standard 1** Students will use mathematical analysis, scientific inquiry, and engineering design, as appropriate, to pose questions, seek answers, and develop solutions.

**Key Idea 1** The central purpose of scientific inquiry is to develop explanations of natural phenomena in a continuing and creative process. ***Major Understandings* - 1.1c**

**Standard 4** Students will understand and apply scientific concepts, principles, and theories pertaining to the physical setting and living environment and recognize the historical development of ideas in science.

**Key Idea 2** Organisms inherit genetic information in a variety of ways that result in continuity of structure and function between parents and offspring. ***Major Understandings* - 2.2b, 2.2c, 2.2d, 2.2e**

**Key Idea 4** The continuity of life is sustained through reproduction and development. ***Major Understandings* - 4.1b**

**Key Idea 5** Organisms maintain a dynamic equilibrium that sustains life. ***Major Understandings* - 5.2e, 5.2j**

# InquiryLab

15 min

## Code Comparison

4.2.1f

All humans have very similar DNA, with slight individual variations. The differences that are easiest to observe are among DNA stretches that have many short, repeating base sequences, as shown below. Different people have different numbers of repeats.

**GATATATAGACTACTACTACTA**

**AGATATAGACTACTACTGACTT**

**GATATAGACTACTACTACTAGC**

### Procedure

1. Copy and then examine the three DNA sequences shown here.
2. Mark the portions of the code that include repeating bases.

### Analysis

1. **Identify** what the four letters in the code sequences represent.
2. **State** how many kinds of repeating sequences you find.
3. **Identify** the basic repeating unit(s) among all segments.
4. **Explain** how each person can have a unique genetic code, even though some people may share an identical pattern of repeating base sequences.

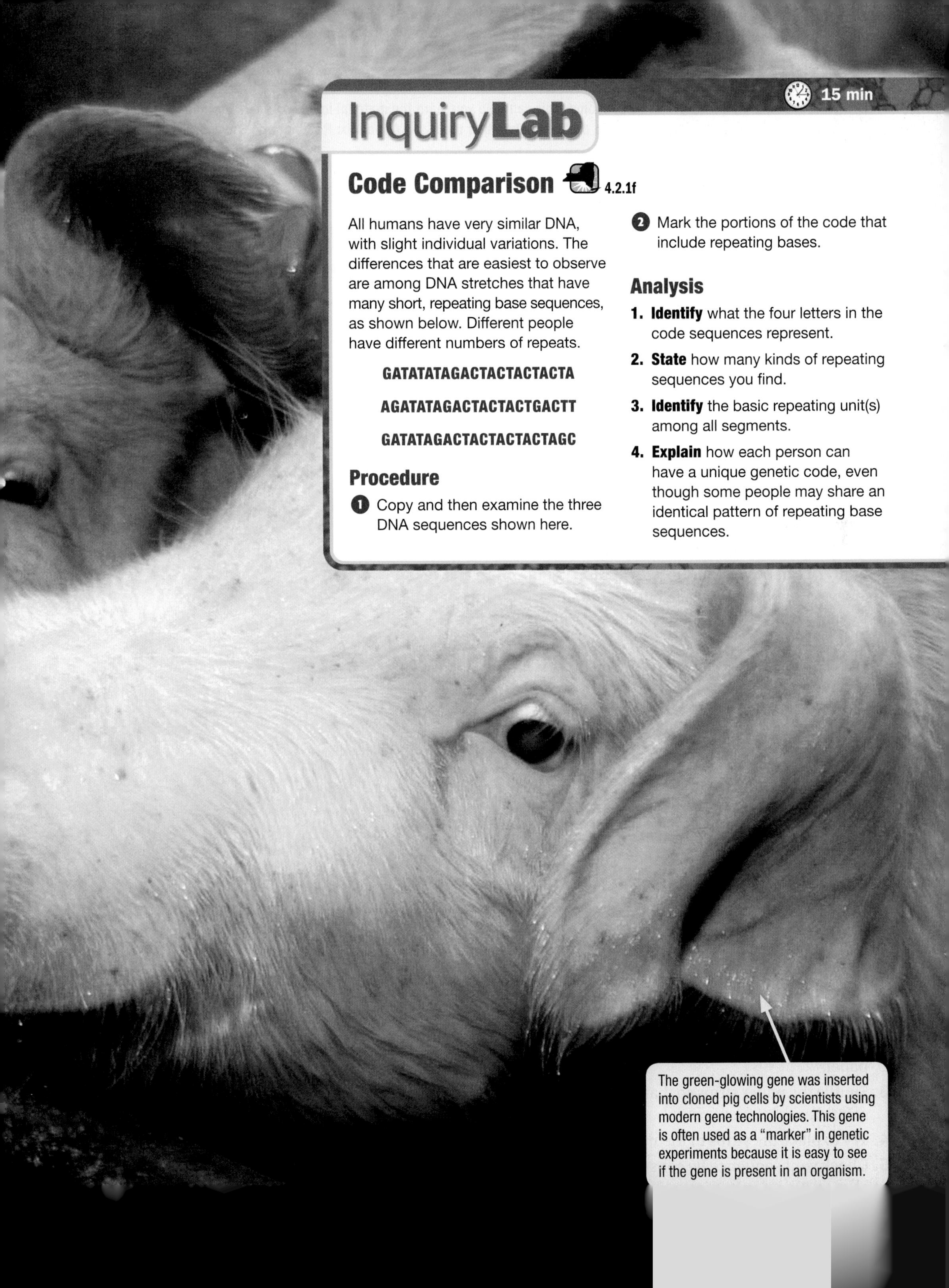

The green-glowing gene was inserted into cloned pig cells by scientists using modern gene technologies. This gene is often used as a "marker" in genetic experiments because it is easy to see if the gene is present in an organism.

These reading tools can help you learn the material in this chapter. For more information on how to use these and other tools, see **Appendix: Reading and Study Skills.**

## Using Words

**Word Parts** You can tell a lot about a word by taking it apart and examining its parts, such as the prefix and root.

**Your Turn** Use the information in the table to define the following terms:

1. *electrophoresis*
2. *microarray*

**Word Parts**

| Word Part | Meaning |
|---|---|
| *electro-* | using electricity |
| *phore* | to carry |
| *micro-* | very small |
| *array* | orderly arrangement |

## Using Language

**Analogies** Analogies compare words with similar relationships. You can write analogies with words or with colons. For example, the analogy "up is related to down in the same way that top is related to bottom" can be written "up : down :: top : bottom." To answer an analogy problem, you must figure out how the words are related. In this example, up is above down, and top is above bottom.

**Your Turn** Use information found in prior chapters to complete the following analogy:

transcription : RNA :: translation : ___.

## Using Graphic Organizers

**Pattern Puzzles** You can use pattern puzzles to help you remember sequential information. Exchanging puzzles with a classmate can help you study.

**Your Turn** Make a pattern puzzle for the steps of a recombinant gene cloning process, as shown in this chapter.

1. Write the steps of the process on a sheet of notebook paper, one step per line. Do not number the steps.
2. Cut the paper so that there is one step per strip of paper.
3. Shuffle the paper strips so that they are out of sequence.
4. Try to place the strips in their proper sequence.
5. Check your sequence by consulting your textbook, class notes, or a classmate.

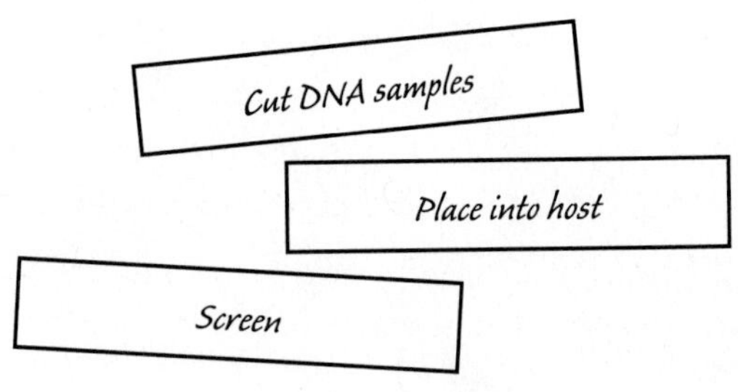

Section 1

# The Human Genome

| Key Ideas | Key Terms | Why It Matters |
|---|---|---|
| ❯ Why is the Human Genome Project so important?<br>❯ How do genomics and gene technologies affect our lives?<br>❯ What questions about the human genome remain to be studied? | genomics<br>microarray<br>DNA fingerprint | Many diseases may someday be cured by genetic technologies. |

In 2000, headlines announced that scientists had deciphered the "book of life" by listing almost the entire sequence of bases in human DNA. This major feat was only the beginning of a new era.

## Secrets of the Human Genome

The term *genome* refers to all of the genetic material in an organism, population, or species. **Genomics** is the study of entire genomes, especially by using technology to compare genes within and between species. A major part of genomics is to *sequence* genomes, or to identify every DNA base pair that makes up each genome. Only recently has it been possible to sequence the human genome.

The *Human Genome Project* (HGP) was an international cooperative effort to sequence the human genome. More than 20 laboratories in six countries worked together to sequence the 2.9 billion DNA base pairs that make up the human genome. ❯ **The sequencing of the human genome has advanced the study of human biology yet created new questions.**

**Surprising Findings** The major draft of the human genome sequence was completed and reported in 2003. Scientists were surprised and excited by findings such as these:

- **Humans have few genes.** Scientists expected to find 120,000 genes but found only about 25,000.
- **Most human DNA is noncoding.** Less than 2% of human DNA seems to code for proteins. The rest is either introns or is not yet fully explained.
- **Many human genes are identical to those of other species.** Much of what we learn about mice and flies can be used to understand ourselves.
- **All humans are genetically close.** If the DNA of any two people is compared, 99.9% is identical.

❯ **Reading Check** ***How big is the human genome? (See the Appendix for answers to Reading Checks.)***

***The Living Environment***

**Standard 1**

**1.1c** Science provides knowledge, but values are also essential to making effective and ethical decisions about the application of scientific knowledge.

**Standard 4**

**2.2e** Knowledge of genetics is making possible new fields of health care; for example, finding genes which may have mutations that can cause disease will aid in the development of preventive measures to fight disease. Substances, such as hormones and enzymes, from genetically engineered organisms may reduce the cost and side effects of replacing missing body chemicals.

**5.2e** Vaccinations use weakened microbes (or parts of them) to stimulate the immune system to react. This reaction prepares the body to fight subsequent invasions by the same microbes.

**5.2j** Biological research generates knowledge used to design ways of diagnosing, preventing, treating, controlling, or curing diseases of plants and animals.

**genomics** (juh NOH miks) the study of entire genomes, especially by using technology to compare genes within and between species

**Figure 1** Despite differences in appearance, the DNA of any two humans is 99.9% similar.

## Applications of Human Genetics

Studying the human genome opens new doors to understanding our bodies. In addition, we have new ways to apply this knowledge. *Gene technologies* allow us to find genes, copy them, turn them on or off, and even move them between organisms. **› Genomics and gene technologies have many applications in human healthcare and society.**

A major part of gene technologies is *genetic engineering,* which usually refers to the transfer of genes from one organism to another. For example, the human gene for insulin has been inserted into bacteria. Insulin is lacking in people with some forms of diabetes. So, the engineered bacteria are used to produce insulin to treat diabetes.

**Diagnosing and Preventing Disease** The first challenge to fighting disease is simply to diagnose, or identify, the problem. Modern gene technologies can help. For example, a **microarray,** shown in **Figure 2,** shows which genes are being actively transcribed in a sample from a cell. Some patterns of gene activity can be recognized as signs of genetic disorders or cancer.

**microarray** (MIE kroh uh RAY) a device that contains a micro-scale, orderly arrangement of biomolecules; used to rapidly test for the presence of a range of similar substances, such as specific DNA sequences

**DNA fingerprint** a pattern of DNA characteristics that is unique, or nearly so, to an individual organism

Although most genetic disorders cannot be cured, they may be avoided in the future. For example, a person with a family history of genetic disorders may wish to undergo genetic counseling before becoming a parent. *Genetic counseling* informs people about the risk of genetic problems that could affect them or their offspring.

Many viral diseases are best prevented by vaccination. However, vaccines can be dangerous because they are made from disease-causing agents. Vaccines made through genetic engineering may limit such dangers by being more carefully designed. Various vaccines are now produced through genetic engineering. Some of these vaccines prevent diseases that were not preventable before.

**› Reading Check** ***When might a person seek genetic counseling?***

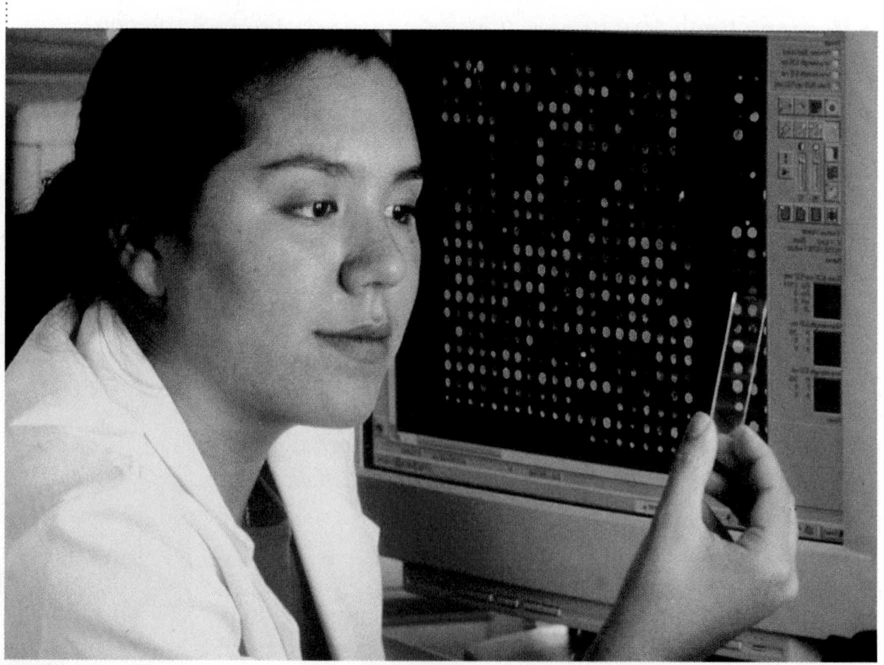

**Figure 2** A microarray contains an assortment of gene sequences, each set in a dot. The colors indicate whether a sample of genetic material has bound to the sequence at that dot. Thus, a pattern of gene expression can be seen. **› What conditions could be detected this way?**

Data

# QuickLab

## Forensic DNA Fingerprints

DNA "fingerprinting" is useful in forensics because it can be performed on a sample of DNA from body tissues such as hair or blood. Samples can be compared to find genetically identical or closely related people. Identical segments of DNA will form identical patterns of bands in the columns of a DNA fingerprint, as shown here.

1 Control
3 Sample from crime scene
4 Victim
6 Standard size marker
8 Suspect A
9 Suspect B
10 Suspect C
12 Suspect D

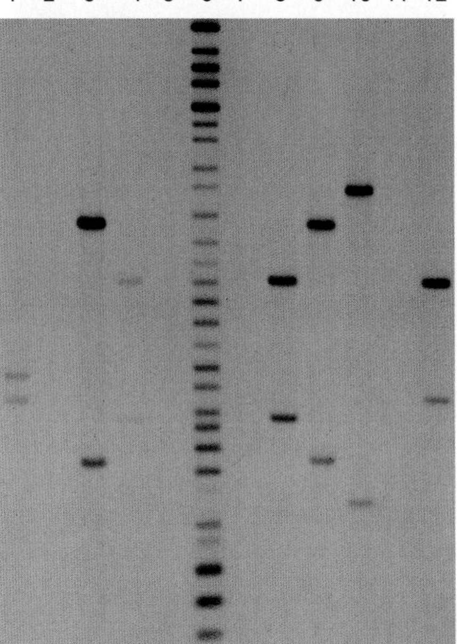


### Analysis

1. **Identify** the number of individuals whose DNA samples are being analyzed in this DNA fingerprint.
2. CRITICAL THINKING **Interpreting Graphics** Identify the suspect sample that matches the sample from the crime scene.
3. CRITICAL THINKING **Analyzing Methods** Column 6 shows an array of DNA segments sorted by increasing length. Propose a purpose for these columns in this method.

**Treating Disease** Many genetic disorders occur when a specific protein, such as insulin, is missing or malformed because a gene has been mutated. So, the disorder can often be treated by supplying the needed protein. Many drug companies are now genetically engineering organisms to produce specific proteins for human use.

Another possible treatment for genetic disorders is to insert a functional "replacement" gene into a person's cells by using a genetically engineered virus. This technique is called *gene therapy.* However, gene therapy has had limited success because the human body has many protections against the invasion and genetic change that viruses cause.

The use of genomics to produce drugs is called *pharmacogenomics.* Currently, most drugs are made to combat diseases in a broad way. The drugs are generally effective for many people but not tailored to individuals. Soon, drugs could be custom-made for individuals based on a personal genetic profile. Such a profile could be produced by technologies that rapidly sequence a person's DNA.

**Identifying Individuals** Each person (other than identical twins) has some parts of the DNA sequence that are unique. So, samples of DNA can be compared to determine if the samples came from the same person or from people related by ancestry. These samples of DNA are cut, sorted, and "tagged" to produce a pattern of banding called a **DNA fingerprint.** DNA fingerprints are now used regularly to confirm the identity of criminals, family members, or dead bodies.

**Reading Check** *Why is insulin used to treat genetic diabetes?*

**Word Parts** The prefix *pharma-* means "medicine" or "drug." Use this information to analyze the meaning of the term *pharmacogenomics*.

**Figure 3** The human genome contains as much information as 180 phone books from different major cities.

SciLinks®
www.scilinks.org
Topic: Human Genome Project
Code: HX80770

## Ongoing Work

Making a list of all of the bases in the human genome was only a first step. Understanding this "book of life" will take much more work. First, a huge amount of information is involved, as **Figure 3** shows. Second, although we know how to read the "letters" of this "book," we do not understand most of its meaning. We have compiled a long list of genes, but we do not know what many of the genes actually do. **› Many important questions about the human genome remain to be investigated or decided.** These questions include the following:

- **How do our genes interact?** To understand how genes interact, scientists are looking closely at the processes of gene expression. For example, they study how the protein that results from one gene may regulate the expression of other genes.
- **How unique are we?** Scientists are increasingly comparing our genome to those of other organisms to find out how small differences in genomes result in different species. Genome projects for many other species have been completed or are under way.
- **Can genetics help us live longer?** Gene technologies and genomics are thus leading to increased knowledge of how we could live longer, healthier lives. We are just beginning to find genetic clues about complex conditions such as asthma, obesity, schizophrenia, cancer, and aging. These conditions are affected by complex interactions between many genes as well as our environment. For many disorders, we are not likely to find a single cause, much less a simple cure.
- **How should we deal with ethical issues?** With so much information about human DNA being recorded, many questions arise that cannot be answered by scientific lab work. For example, Who should get the information? Who owns it? Should it be used to make decisions about individuals? Scientists and governments expect these issues to arise. In the United States, a portion of the federal funds for the HGP are dedicated to a special program of the HGP called *Ethical Legal and Social Implications* (ELSI).

**Academic Vocabulary**

**implication** something involved or resulting from

**› Reading Check** *Why is asthma difficult to cure?*

## Section 1 Review

**› KEY IDEAS**

1. **Describe** the major findings of the Human Genome Project.
2. **Identify** some applications of genomics and genetic engineering that benefit humans.
3. **List** remaining questions about the human genome.

**CRITICAL THINKING**

4. **Proposing Explanations** Propose some possible explanations for the large volume of noncoding DNA in the human genome.
5. **Applying Logic** Scientists say that knowing the sequence of nucleotides in the human genome is only the first step in understanding the genome. What are some possible next steps?

**WRITING FOR SCIENCE**

6. **Genetics on Trial** When were gene technologies first used as evidence in criminal cases? Research the early history of this field, and summarize your findings in a news-style oral report.

Why It Matters

# Cleanup Microbes

Using microbes for environmental cleanup is called *bioremediation*. For example, oil-devouring microbes are used to help clean up oil spills. Increasingly, genetically modified organisms (GMOs) are being engineered for use in bioremediation.

## Oil Spills

Spills of fuel oil can be devastating to environments because the oil is toxic, floats on water, and soaks into soils. Fortunately, scientists have found that some marine bacteria are capable of using oil as food. Some of the first genetically modified (GM) microbes were derived from such bacteria. In fact, the first organism to be patented was an oil-eating, genetically engineered bacterium.

## Radioactive Waste

Nuclear waste is another bioremediation challenge with which GM microbes may help. Water near nuclear waste dumps may become polluted with radioactive substances. Again, bacteria naturally exist that can break down most of these substances, but those bacteria cannot survive high levels of radiation. So, scientists have turned to another kind of bacteria that can withstand 3,000 times the normal radiation levels. They hope to engineer a solution by transferring genes between these species.

**An impossible job?** Cleaning oil and dangerous chemical spills out of sand or soil can be nearly impossible for humans, even with tools. However, this cleanup is simple work for a microbe.

**An Enormous Mess** Oil spills at sea are dangerous to wildlife, dangerous to the people involved in fighting them, and difficult to contain.

**Quick Project** Find out the date that the first patent for a GMO was awarded in the United States. Also find out the name of the scientist to whom it was awarded.

Section 2

# Gene Technologies in Our Lives

| Key Ideas | Key Terms | Why It Matters |
|---|---|---|
| ❯ For what purposes are genes and proteins manipulated?<br>❯ How are cloning and stem cell research related?<br>❯ What ethical issues arise with the uses of gene technologies? | genetic engineering<br>recombinant DNA<br>clone<br>stem cell | Gene technologies have many applications in modern life, but ethical issues exist for each of these applications. |

***The Living Environment***

**Standard 1**

**1.1c** Science provides knowledge, but values are also essential to making effective and ethical decisions about the application of scientific knowledge.

**Standard 4**

**2.2b** In recent years new varieties of farm plants and animals have been engineered by manipulating their genetic instructions to produce new characteristics.

**2.2c** Different enzymes can be used to cut, copy, and move segments of DNA. Characteristics produced by the segments of DNA may be expressed when these segments are inserted into new organisms, such as bacteria.

**2.2d** Inserting, deleting, or substituting DNA segments can alter genes. An altered gene may be passed on to every cell that develops from it.

**2.2e** Knowledge of genetics is making possible new fields of health care; for example, finding genes which may have mutations that can cause disease will aid in the development of preventive measures to fight disease. Substances, such as hormones and enzymes, from genetically engineered organisms may reduce the cost and side effects of replacing missing body chemicals.

**4.1b** Cloning is the production of identical genetic copies.

Recall that a gene has a DNA sequence that is translated into the sequence of amino acids in a protein. In a sense, proteins are the "actors" in biology, and genes are the "directors." To understand how genes work, scientists have studied both the instructions in the genes and the actions of the proteins. Meanwhile, some have tried to modify the instructions to change the actions that result.

## Manipulating Genes

*Gene technologies* include a wide range of procedures that analyze, decode, or manipulate genes from organisms. ❯ **Gene technologies are now widely applied to study organisms in new ways, to alter organisms for human use, and to improve human lives.** Gene technologies have rapidly changed over the past two decades, yet the basic applications are not so new. Human beings have been influencing the lives and genes of organisms for thousands of years. The first farmers and herders did so when they selected plants and animals to breed. But today, we have more specific knowledge, molecular tools, and the ability to move genes between organisms.

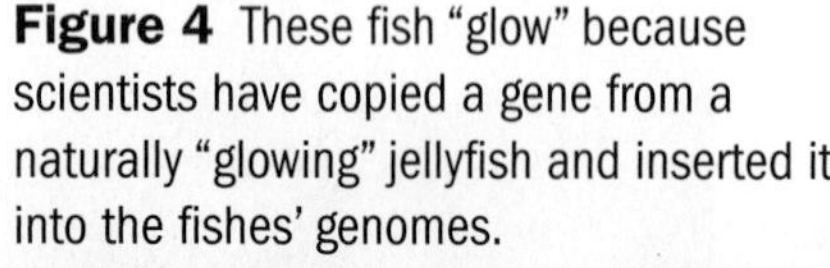

**Figure 4** These fish "glow" because scientists have copied a gene from a naturally "glowing" jellyfish and inserted it into the fishes' genomes.

**Genetic Engineering** The application of science for specific purposes is often referred to as *engineering.* **Genetic engineering** is the deliberate alteration of the genetic material of an organism. The process often involves inserting copies of a gene from one organism into another. DNA that has been recombined by genetic engineering is called **recombinant DNA.** Organisms with recombinant genes may be called *recombinant, transgenic,* or *genetically modified.* In everyday use, they are often referred to as *genetically modified organisms* (GMOs). An example of a GMO is shown in **Figure 4.**

Many applications of gene technologies have become part of our everyday lives, from food to healthcare. In some ways, we are starting to depend on gene technologies, just as we depend on electricity and telephones. As with other technologies, gene technologies raise new social and ethical issues.

❯ **Reading Check** ***What is a GMO?***

**Everyday Applications** Genetic engineering was first applied to bacteria, viruses, and plants and is now applied to many life-forms. Today, GMOs are widely used in agriculture, medicine, industry, and basic research. Following are examples of the many uses of GMOs.

- **Food Crops** Most corn and soybean products sold in grocery stores in the United States are made from GMOs. In many cases, the crops have a gene added from the bacterium *Bacillus thuringiensis* (*Bt*). The gene produces an insecticide and thus benefits the crop grower. Many food crops are engineered to be easier to grow or to be more nutritious.
- **Livestock** New breeds of livestock are being engineered to grow faster or to have more muscle or less fat. Some are made to produce milk with specific proteins. Some GMOs are sold as unusual pets.
- **Medical Treatment** As you have learned, many genetic disorders, such as hemophilia and diabetes, result from a missing or abnormal protein. If the normal human gene for needed protein has been identified, the gene can be spliced into bacterial cells. Then, the recombinant bacteria will rapidly produce the human protein in large quantities. People with hemophilia and diabetes are being treated with proteins produced in this way.
- **Basic Research Tools** A variety of GMOs have been made just for laboratory research. Some plants and animals have been engineered with genes from other organisms that "glow." Often, this engineering is done so that researchers can study another, less obvious gene. In this case, the two foreign genes are spliced into the GMO at the same time. The "glow" gene then serves as a "marker" of the presence of the second gene being studied.

**genetic engineering** a technology in which the genome of a living cell is modified for medical or industrial use

**recombinant DNA** (ree KAHM buh nuhnt) DNA molecules that are artificially created by combining DNA from different sources

**Manipulating Cell Interactions** Gene technologies involve more than just inserting genes. Cells and bodies are affected by when and where each gene is expressed. So, gene technologies are also used to control the expression of genes or to redirect the products.

The study of how proteins interact within cells is called *proteomics* (PROH tee OHM iks). As you have learned, these interactions are very complex. Gene technologies can be used to manipulate the production of specific proteins at specific times and in specific cells, tissues, organs, or individuals. This manipulation can be done for medical treatment or simply for research.

One way to study the actions of genes in cells is to work with living tissues. To do so, scientists can remove living cells from an organism and grow them in a laboratory as tissue culture, as **Figure 5** shows. Then, the cells can be studied closely and experimentally controlled.

› **Reading Check** *What is the* Bt *gene used for?*

**Figure 5** Tissue culture is often used to study living cells. › **What can we learn about genes from tissue culture?**

## Manipulating Bodies and Development

Biologists still have much to learn about the development of multicellular organisms. To do so, they must study cells in the process of multiplying and differentiating into the many types of cells found in a body. **› Cloning and stem cell techniques are used in research on animal development and have potential for treating certain diseases.**

**clone** an organism, cell, or piece of genetic material that is genetically identical to one that was preexisting; to make a genetic duplicate

**stem cell** a cell that can divide repeatedly and can differentiate into specialized cell types

**Cloning** A **clone** is an organism or piece of genetic material that is genetically identical to one that was preexisting. Making a clone in a lab is called *cloning,* but the process does occur in nature. Organisms clone themselves whenever they reproduce asexually. Single-celled organisms clone themselves by simple division. Multicellular organisms may clone themselves by budding off parts, as some plants and fungi do, or by self-fertilization, as many plants and some animals do.

Very few large animals can clone themselves. Also, animals have complex processes of fertilization and embryo development. So, scientists are still experimenting with cloning animals. The first such experiments made clones from eggs or embryos. Then, a clone was made from an adult mammal, as **Figure 6** shows. The clone was made using a process called *somatic-cell nuclear transfer* (SCNT). In this process, the nucleus of an egg cell is replaced with the nucleus of an adult cell. Then, the egg begins to develop into an embryo.

**Problems with Cloning** Although scientists have successfully cloned many kinds of animals, only a few of the cloned offspring have survived for long. In some cases, the fetuses have grown beyond normal size. Many have failed to develop normally with age. Because of such problems and because of ethical issues, efforts to clone humans are illegal in most countries.

**Genomic Imprinting** Some problems with cloning may be related to the ways that eggs and sperm normally develop. Chemicals in the reproductive system turn "on" or "off" certain genes in the developing gametes. These genes later affect development from embryo to adult. Such an effect, called *genomic imprinting,* is altered when animals are cloned in a lab. So, different genes may be activated early on, and the remaining development may be altered.

**Figure 6** Dolly, a cloned sheep, was born in 1997. Dolly was the first successful clone produced from the nucleus of an adult somatic cell.

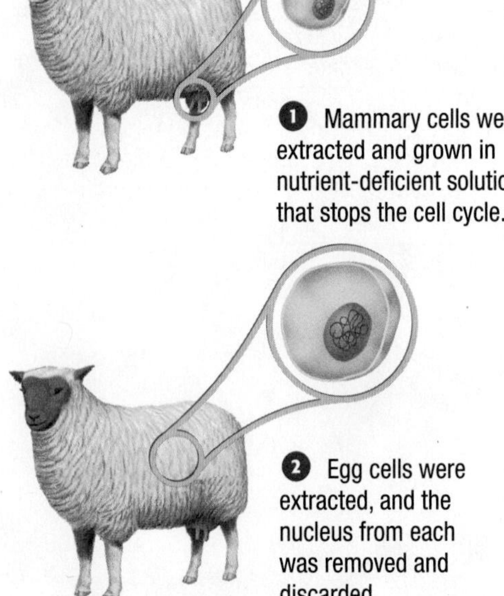

1 Mammary cells were extracted and grown in nutrient-deficient solution that stops the cell cycle.
2 Egg cells were extracted, and the nucleus from each was removed and discarded.

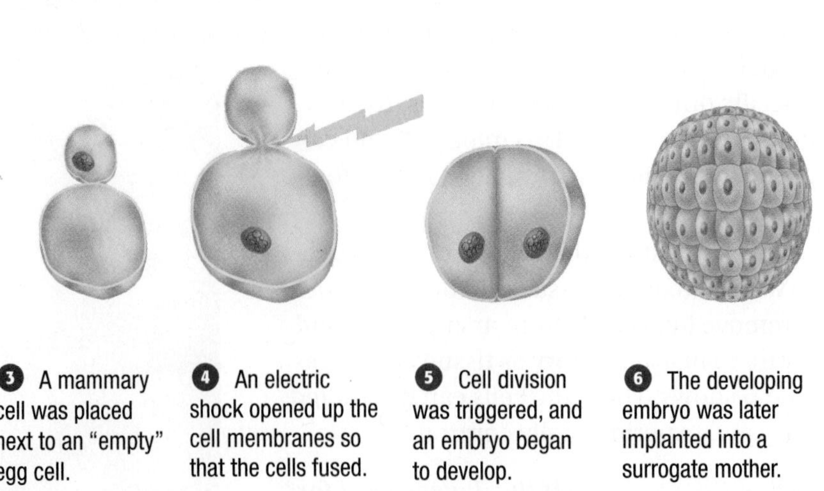

3 A mammary cell was placed next to an "empty" egg cell.
4 An electric shock opened up the cell membranes so that the cells fused.
5 Cell division was triggered, and an embryo began to develop.
6 The developing embryo was later implanted into a surrogate mother.

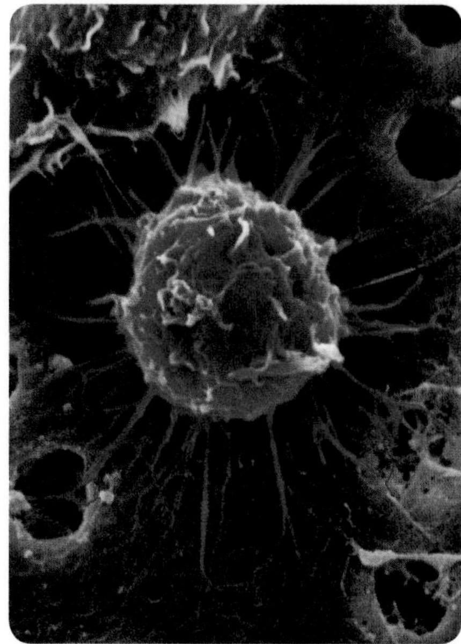

① An adult stem cell can be removed from a specific tissue, such as bone marrow.

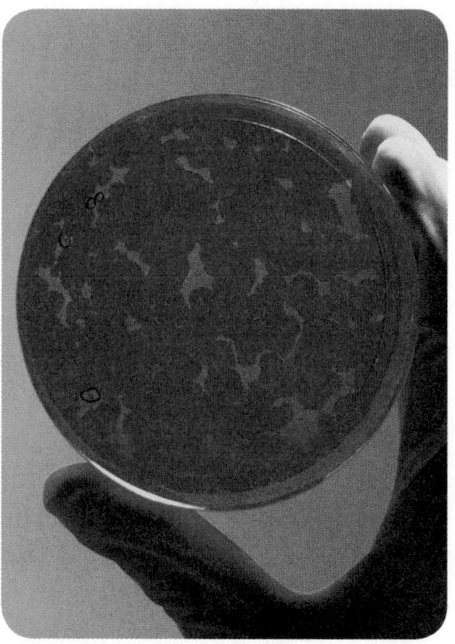

② The cell can be grown in tissue culture to produce more cells of a specific tissue type.

③ The cells can be re-implanted into a patient whose tissues are lacking or damaged.

**Figure 7** Adult stem cells can be removed and used to grow more cells of specific tissue types. This kind of therapy can replace tissue that is damaged or deficient due to disease or other medical treatment. **› How do adult stem cells differ from embryonic stem cells?**

**Using Stem Cells** A **stem cell** is a cell that can continuously divide and differentiate into various tissues. Some stem cells have more potential to differentiate than others. *Totipotent* cells can give rise to any cell or tissue type, *pluripotent* cells can give rise to all types except germ cells, and *multipotent* cells can give rise to just a few other cell types. The state of the cell depends on the stage of development of the body and the tissue of which the cell is part.

Adults' bodies have some multipotent cells, such as bone marrow cells, that give rise to various blood cells. These cells can be removed, frozen or cultured, and used for medical treatments, as **Figure 7** shows. The cells of new embryos have more potential uses. These cells are totipotent at first and pluripotent during development.

**Issues with Stem Cell Research** The first major source of human embryos for stem cell research was fertility clinics. Such clinics help people have children, often by uniting people's gametes and culturing embryos in a lab. Many extra embryos are stored in a frozen state in clinics. In some cases, the parents have given scientists permission to use the embryos for research. But such uses of human embryos pose ethical problems. In the United States, there have been strong debates about the use of federal funds for this kind of research.

**Stem Cells from SCNT** A newer source of embryonic stem cells is through cloning using SCNT. Some people believe that using this kind of stem cell for medical research and treatment should be ethically acceptable. One reason is that an embryo made through SCNT does not have true parents. Another reason is that the cells of the embryo are separated early in its development, so there is no chance of the embryo developing further.

**› Reading Check** ***What are the two main types of stem cells?***

READING TOOLBOX

**Analogies** Use the information in this section to help you write an analogy that relates adult stem cells to embryonic stem cells. Try to use the terms *pluripotent* and *multipotent* in your analogy.

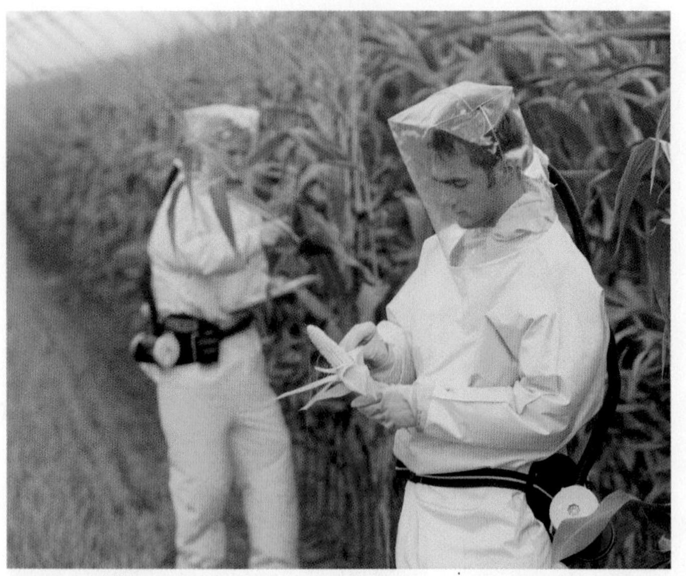

**Figure 8** This corn has been genetically modified to carry the *Bt* gene, which causes the corn plant to produce an insect-killing chemical. As with any use of pesticides, this practice presents risks. An additional danger is that the gene may be transferred to other plants.

## Ethical and Social Issues

Ethical issues involve differing values and perspectives. For example, the use of GMOs is prohibited or tightly controlled by laws in some countries. In others, GMOs are widely used, and GM foods are sold with few restrictions. › **Ethical issues can be raised for every use of gene technologies.**

**Safety** One danger of GMOs is that they can "escape" and have unforeseen effects. For example, the *Bt* toxin gene from GM corn crops, such as those in **Figure 8,** has been transferred to other plants. In addition, the toxic corn pollen seems to be harming populations of the monarch butterfly. Ecologists worry that we do not know enough to safely manipulate genes on a large scale.

**Human Rights** Being able to predict disease before it happens is a major achievement of modern medicine. Today, the DNA of individuals can be tested to find the risk of genetic disorders. But what should we do with this information? Many decisions could be influenced by such genetic information, such as whom to marry or what to eat. Who should have this information? Who should make these decisions? How can future probabilities be weighed against current human needs and rights? There are no easy answers to these ethical questions, but the questions need to be considered carefully.

**Academic Vocabulary**

**ethical** conforming to moral standards

**Property Laws** Gene technologies have also created new issues for old laws, especially those related to intellectual property and patents. Intellectual property (IP) is the ownership of the ideas or plans that a person creates. A patent is a specific set of rights that allows an inventor to control and profit from the uses of his or her idea. In the 1980s, the first patent for a GMO was awarded to a scientist who had engineered an oil-eating bacterium. Before this event, living organisms were considered a part of nature and, as such, were not patentable. Now, specific DNA sequences can be patented.

› **Reading Check** ***What issues does the use of genetic testing raise?***

## Section 2 Review

### › KEY IDEAS

1. **Identify** applications of manipulating genes and proteins.
2. **Relate** stem cell research to the potential use of cloning.
3. **Describe** a specific ethical issue related to a gene technology.

### CRITICAL THINKING

4. **Inferring Relationships** How can manipulating gene expression help advance the study of proteomics?
5. **Evaluating Risks** Given the difficulties that researchers have had with raising cloned animals, do you think it is safe to grow tissues or organs from cloned embryonic stem cells for the purpose of transplanting? Explain.

### ALTERNATIVE ASSESSMENT

6. **Debate** Suppose that genetic analysis could predict a person's ability in sports, math, or music. Should genetic screening be used to determine the course selections and team assignments of every student in school? Prepare and conduct a formal debate on the subject.

Section 3

# Gene Technologies in Detail

| Key Ideas | Key Terms | | Why It Matters |
|---|---|---|---|
| ❯ What are the basic tools of genetic manipulation?<br>❯ How are these tools used in the major processes of modern gene technologies?<br>❯ How do scientists study entire genomes? | restriction enzyme<br>DNA polymorphisms<br>electrophoresis<br>polymerase chain reaction (PCR) | DNA sequencing<br>bioinformatics<br>genome mapping<br>genetic library | Humans now have the ability to identify and manipulate genes in many organisms. |

How do you find a needle in a haystack? This phrase is often used to speak of a nearly impossible task. But if the haystack is a genome and the needle is a gene, the task is now possible!

***The Living Environment***
**Standard 4**
**2.2c** Different enzymes can be used to cut, copy, and move segments of DNA. Characteristics produced by the segments of DNA may be expressed when these segments are inserted into new organisms, such as bacteria.

## Basic Tools for Genetic Manipulation

Molecular biologists spent many years developing tools and methods to manipulate genetic material. The methods continue to be used and adapted for a wide range of applications, but the basic tools are similar. ❯ **The basic tools of DNA manipulation rely on the chemical nature of genetic material and are adapted from natural processes discovered in cells.** These tools include restriction enzymes, polymorphisms, gel electrophoresis, denaturation, and hybridization. For example, the first GMOs were made by using plasmids and enzymes that are naturally present in some bacterial cells.

**Restriction Enzymes** Among the first tools used to manipulate DNA were enzymes that are made by bacteria as a defense. The enzymes serve to slice up any invading DNA sequences or genes from other organisms. These **restriction enzymes** recognize a specific sequence of DNA, called a *restriction site*. The enzymes will cut DNA strands at all such sites, as **Figure 9** shows.

**restriction enzyme** an enzyme that cuts double-stranded DNA into fragments by recognizing specific nucleotide sequences and cutting the DNA at those sequences

These enzymes are useful in two ways. First, different enzymes recognize different sequences, so the enzymes can be used to cut up a DNA sample in specific ways. Second, the cuts of most restriction enzymes create sticky ends. A *sticky end* has a few bases on one strand that are unpaired but complementary to unpaired bases on other sticky ends. So, sticky ends will easily bind to one another.

❯ **Reading Check** ***Which basic genetic tools were used to make the first GMOs?***

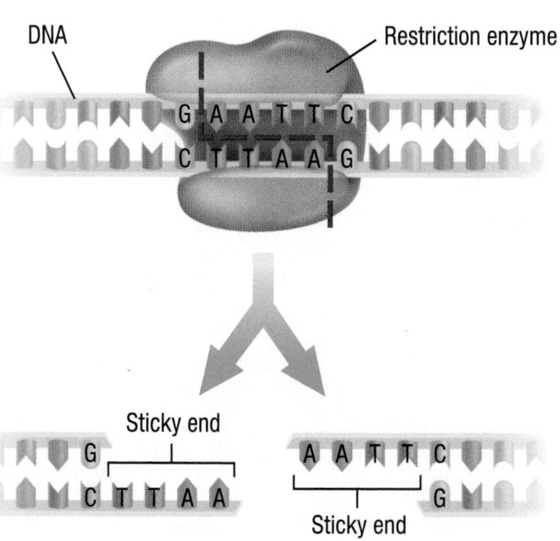


**Figure 9** Restriction enzymes recognize and cut DNA at specific sequences. Usually, complementary ("sticky") ends are created. ❯ **In what ways are restriction enzymes useful?**

Hands-On

QuickLab

15 min

## Gel Electrophoresis Model

You can use beads to model how DNA fragments are separated in a gel during electrophoresis.

### Procedure

1. Fill a **large jar** with the largest of **three sets of beads** (each set should be a different size and different color). The filled jar represents a gel.
2. Mix the smaller sets of beads in a **plastic cup,** and then pour them slowly on top of the "gel." The smaller beads represent DNA fragments.
3. Observe the flow of the beads through the "gel." Lightly agitate the jar if the beads do not flow easily.

### Analysis

1. **Identify** which beads flowed through faster.
2. **Relate** this model to how electrophoresis works.
3. CRITICAL THINKING **Using Models** Why did the beads identified in item 1 pass through the "gel" more quickly?

**Polymorphisms** Differences between the DNA sequences of individuals are called **DNA polymorphisms.** These differences may be slight but can be compared and analyzed for several purposes, as you will learn. Differences of just one nucleotide are called *single nucleotide polymorphisms* (SNPs). SNPs result from point mutations and are usually unique to individuals or populations. At a broader level, each species has a unique pattern of restriction sites. When different DNA samples are cut with the same restriction enzyme, the segments that result will have different lengths. These differences are called *restriction fragment length polymorphisms* (RFLPs).

ACADEMIC VOCABULARY

**slight** very small or barely detectable

**Gel Electrophoresis** DNA carries an electric charge, so an electric current can be used to push or pull DNA fragments. This process is called **electrophoresis.** Often, the DNA fragments are forced though a *gel,* a semisolid that allows molecules to move slowly through it. When a current is applied, shorter fragments will move faster through the gel than longer fragments will. The result is a lane of fragments sorted by size, as shown in **Figure 10.** If the fragments separate clearly, each lane is called a *ladder*. If the fragments have overlapping sizes and do not separate clearly, each lane is called a *smear*.

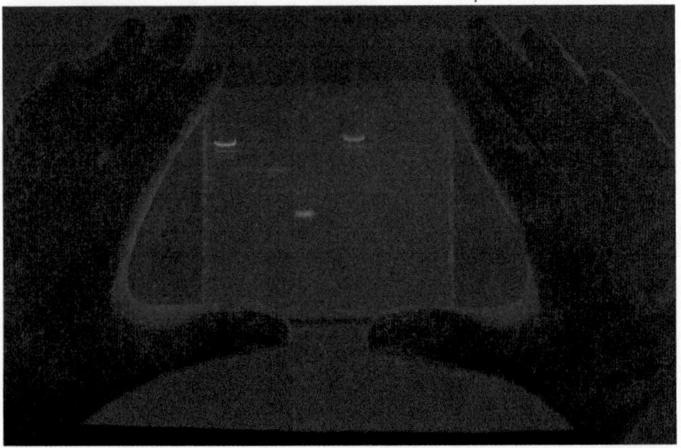

**Figure 10** Gel electrophoresis separates samples of molecules, such as DNA or proteins, into bands that are ordered by size. **› What is the role of the gel?**

There are many types of electrophoresis. Different kinds of gels are used to sort different sizes of DNA fragments, and other methods are used to sort RNA or proteins. Newer methods use tiny tubes of gel to sort tiny samples that can then be "read" by a machine and analyzed by a computer.

**› Reading Check** ***What property of a gel does gel electrophoresis depend upon?***

**Denaturation** Recall that DNA in cells is usually double stranded, twisted, and often associated with proteins. Some conditions, such as heat or strong chemicals, can cause DNA to denature, or untwist and split into single strands. Scientists can easily denature and renature DNA and use the single strands for further manipulations.

**Hybridization** When single-stranded segments of DNA or RNA are mixed together under the right conditions, complementary segments will bind together, or hybridize. Genetic tools that take advantage of this natural process include the following:

- **Primers** *Primers* are short, single strands of DNA that will hybridize with a specific sequence. For this use, the sequence is one that will be recognized by an enzyme, such as DNA polymerase. Thus, primers can be used to initiate replication of single strands of DNA.
- **Probes** When DNA samples are sorted in a gel, probes are used to "tag" and find specific sequences. Probes are much like primers but carry radioactive or fluorescent materials that can be detected.
- **cDNA** Complementary DNA (cDNA) is DNA that has been made to match mRNA from cells. Recall that this mRNA is the result of transcription and has exons removed. So, making cDNA is a shortcut to getting just the expressed DNA of complete genes.

**DNA polymorphisms** (PAHL ee MAWR FIZ uhmz) variations in DNA sequences; used as a basis for comparing genomes

**electrophoresis** (ee LEK troh fuh REE sis) the process by which electrically charged particles suspended in a liquid move through the liquid because of the influence of an electric field

**polymerase chain reaction** (puh LIM uhr ays) a technique that is used to make many copies of selected segments of DNA (abbreviation, PCR)

## Major Gene Technology Processes

**❯ The major methods for working with genes use some combination of the basic tools and mechanisms of cellular machinery.** These methods include PCR, blotting, DNA sequencing, and gene recombination.

**Polymerase Chain Reaction (PCR)** The **polymerase chain reaction (PCR)** process is widely used to clone DNA sequences for further study or manipulation. PCR imitates the normal process of DNA replication in cells. So, using PCR is as simple as combining the right components in a test tube and then controlling the temperature, as **Figure 11** shows. The process is called a *chain reaction* because it is repeated over and over.

**Figure 11** PCR rapidly produces many copies of a DNA sample. The process can make 1 billion copies of a DNA sample within a few hours!

**Polymerase Chain Reaction (PCR)**

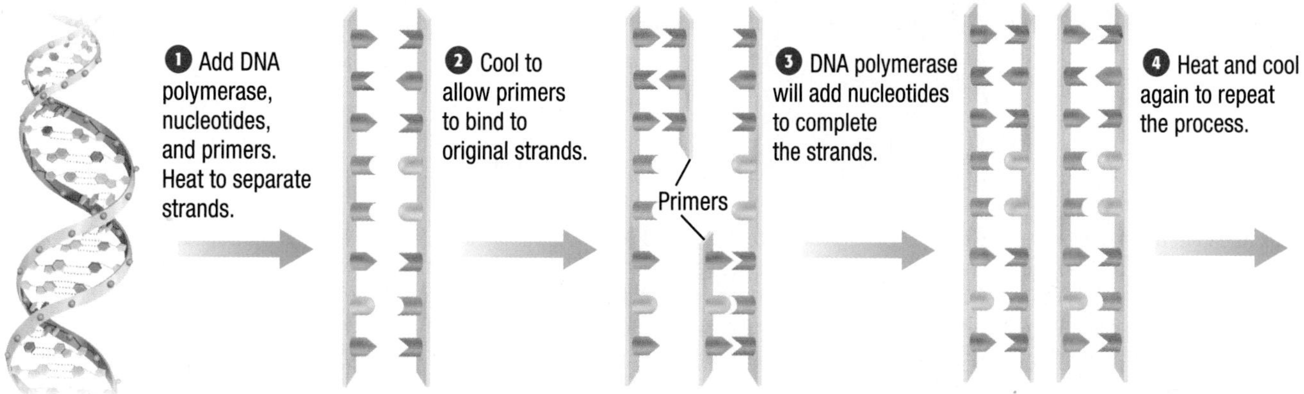

1 Add DNA polymerase, nucleotides, and primers. Heat to separate strands.
2 Cool to allow primers to bind to original strands.
Primers
3 DNA polymerase will add nucleotides to complete the strands.
4 Heat and cool again to repeat the process.

SCILINKS.
www.scilinks.org
Topic: Gene Technologies
Code: HX80539

**Blotting Processes and Applications** Several gene technologies use a combination of restriction enzymes, gel electrophoresis, and hybridization with probes. The goal is to find or compare sequences of DNA or RNA. Many include a blotting step in which sorted segments are preserved by transferring from the gel to another surface or grid (such as a sheet of special paper). Then, probes are used to reveal the location of specific sequences.

**Southern Blot** The Southern blot process, shown in **Figure 12,** is used specifically for DNA, and especially for DNA fingerprints. The process may vary by using either different restriction enzymes on one DNA sample or different DNA samples with the same enzyme.

**Fingerprints and Bar Codes** DNA polymorphisms can be used to identify individuals or species. When restriction fragments are sorted through a Southern blot process, each person's DNA will have a unique pattern of banding called a *DNA fingerprint.* Similarly, a *DNA bar code* can be made to help identify species.

**Northern Blot** The Northern blot process differs from Southern blot in that the sample fragments are mRNA instead of DNA. Recall that mRNA in cells comes from genes being transcribed. So, Northern blot can be used to tell which genes in a cell are "turned on" (being expressed) or to tell the size of the expressed parts of a gene (after exons are removed).

**Microarrays** A *microarray* is a device that enables thousands of tiny Northern blots to be done at once. Microarrays can be used to show patterns of gene expression. For example, a cancer cell will have certain genes turned on or off. The pattern of gene activity seen in a microarray can help identify specific kinds of cancer.

**› Reading Check** ***What does "blotting" refer to?***

**Figure 12** In this example, a DNA sample is analyzed by using the Southern blot process. **› Which basic genetic tools are used as part of this process?**

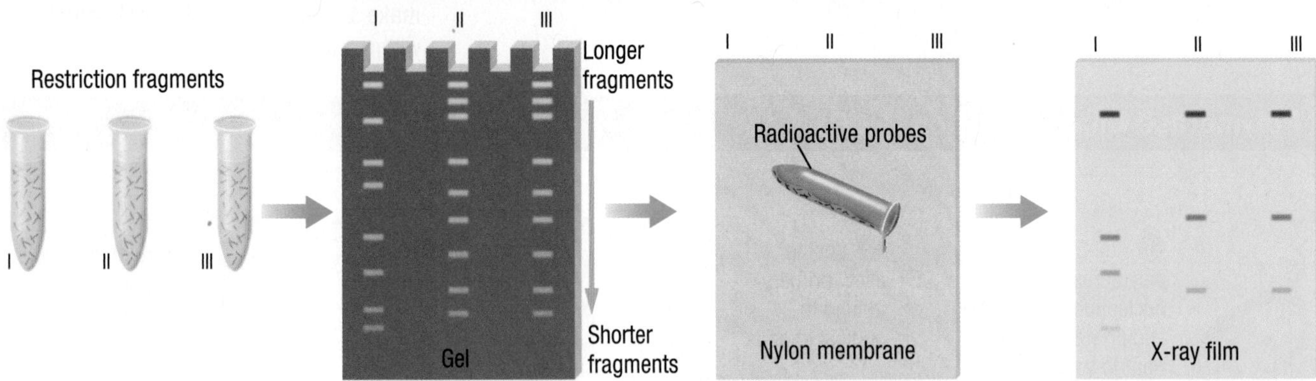
Southern Blot Process
Restriction fragments
I
II
III
Longer fragments
Shorter fragments
Gel
Radioactive probes
Nylon membrane
X-ray film
1 The Southern blot process begins with a sample of DNA. The DNA is cut into fragments using restriction enzymes. A unique enzyme may be used to create several batches of sample DNA.
2 The DNA fragments are sorted by gel electrophoresis. One lane in the gel is used for each batch. Then, a chemical splits all fragments into single-stranded form.
3 The DNA strands are transferred (blotted) onto a piece of nylon paper. A solution containing probes is applied to the nylon paper. The probes bind to specific sites on the single strands.
4 The exposure of photographic or X-ray film to the nylon paper reveals the location of those sample strands that hybridized with the probe. Each person's DNA will make a unique pattern.

go.hrw.com
interact online
Keyword: HX8GTCF13

## Chain Termination Sequencing

**1 Copy** The unknown DNA sequence is copied, denatured, and incubated with specific genetic molecules.

**2 Terminate** New copies of the original sequence begin to form, but some are terminated randomly by tagged nucleotides.

**3 Sort** The resulting strands are denatured and sorted in a gel. The color-coded bands in the gel will match the orginal sequence.

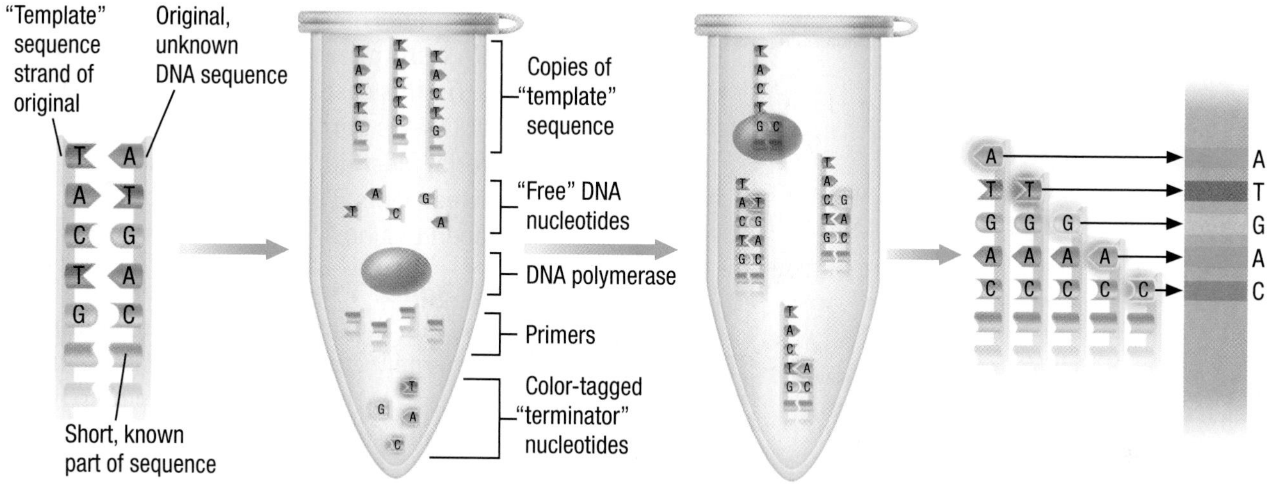

"Template" sequence strand of original
Original, unknown DNA sequence
Short, known part of sequence
Copies of "template" sequence
"Free" DNA nucleotides
DNA polymerase
Primers
Color-tagged "terminator" nucleotides
A
T
G
A
C

**Figure 13** Chain termination sequencing modifies DNA replication processes in order to deduce a DNA sequence. **❯ Why is this method so important?**

**DNA Sequencing** Among the great achievements of modern biology are DNA sequencing methods. **DNA sequencing** is the process of determining the exact order of every nucleotide in a gene. The major modern method is *chain termination sequencing*, as shown in **Figure 13.** This method has been improved over time.

**Step 1 Start Copying a Template** The gene (DNA segment) of interest is copied (using PCR) and split into single strands. The copies are placed in solution with primers, DNA polymerase, and an assortment of bases. The primers will bond to the "template" strand, and then DNA polymerase will begin to add bases to the "copy" strand, as in normal DNA replication.

**Step 2 Randomly Terminate the Copies** Some of the bases act as "terminator" bases. When one of these bases is placed in one of the growing copy strands, copying will stop on that strand. Thus, an assortment of randomly "cut-off" sequence copies is produced.

**Step 3 Sort the Copies by Size** At this point, the sequence of bases can be deduced by sorting the segments by size. When sequencing was first developed, scientists would use four batches of radioactively tagged "terminators" (one for each base type). Then, they would perform electrophoresis in four lanes, side by side, which would reveal the relative order of each end-base. Today, scientists use color-coded fluorescent tags (one color for each base type) and run a single batch through a tiny tube of gel. A machine with a laser can detect the wavelengths of the tags and thus "read" the sequence.

**❯ Reading Check** *When are primers used in DNA sequencing?*

**DNA sequencing** (SEE kwuhns ing) the process of determining the order of every nucleotide in a gene or genetic fragment

**Figure 14** The earliest gene cloning and recombination methods used the steps shown here. The first GMOs were produced in this way.

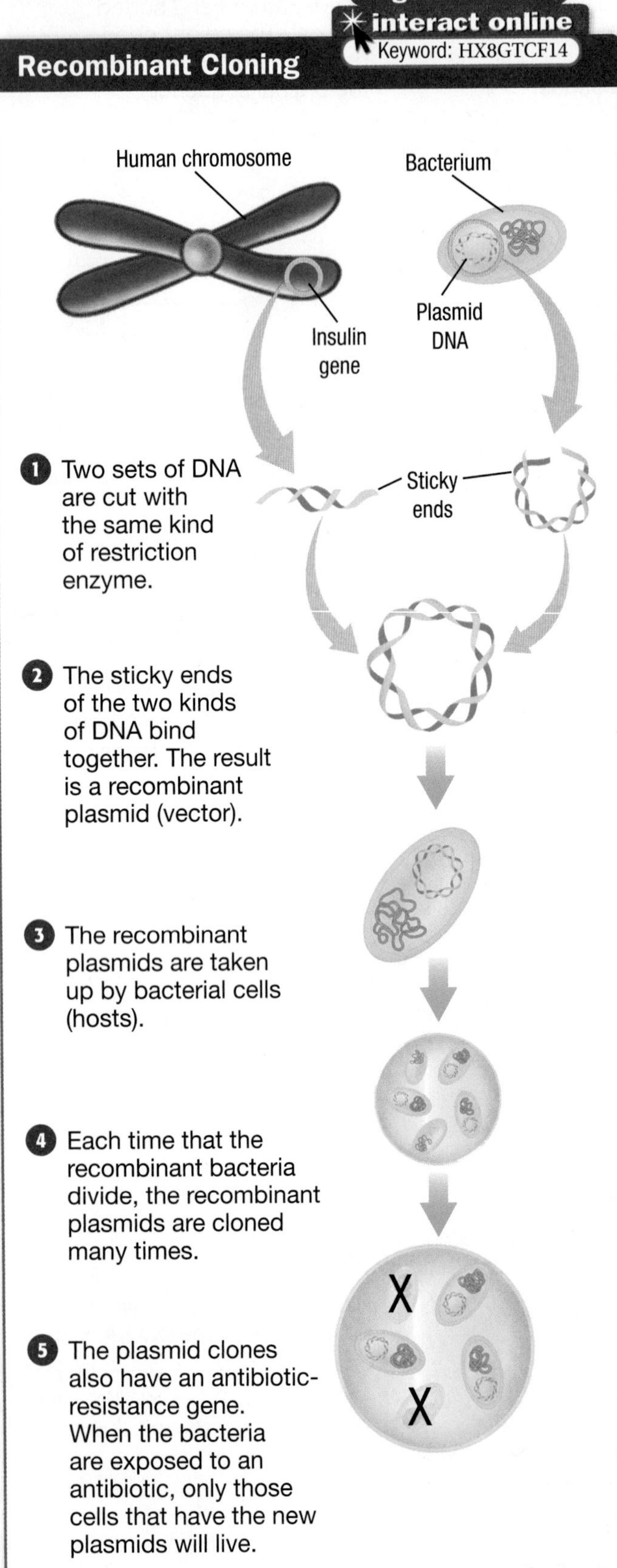

go.hrw.com
interact online
Keyword: HX8GTCF14
Recombinant Cloning
Human chromosome
Bacterium
Insulin gene
Plasmid DNA
Sticky ends
1 Two sets of DNA are cut with the same kind of restriction enzyme.
2 The sticky ends of the two kinds of DNA bind together. The result is a recombinant plasmid (vector).
3 The recombinant plasmids are taken up by bacterial cells (hosts).
4 Each time that the recombinant bacteria divide, the recombinant plasmids are cloned many times.
5 The plasmid clones also have an antibiotic-resistance gene. When the bacteria are exposed to an antibiotic, only those cells that have the new plasmids will live.
X
X


**Gene Recombination and Cloning** The first attempts at gene recombination and cloning were done by inserting a gene into an organism that replicates easily, as shown in **Figure 14.** Other methods may use similar steps.

**Step 1 Cut DNA Samples** Two sets of DNA are cut by the same kind of restriction enzyme so that all fragments have matching sticky ends. One set of DNA is from an organism containing a specific gene (in this case, the human insulin gene). The other DNA is part of a vector, such as a virus or a bacterial plasmid, that can carry or move DNA between cells. The vector will be replicated when placed in a host, such as a bacterial cell.

**Step 2 Splice Pieces Together** The DNA fragments from the first organism are combined with the fragments from the vector. Then, an enzyme called *DNA ligase* is added to help bond the sticky ends of all the fragments together.

**Step 3 Place into Host** At this point, some plasmids are recombinant with human DNA. When the plasmids are placed in a culture of bacteria, some cells take up the plasmids. The cells are allowed to replicate normally.

**Step 4 Replicate Gene** Each time that a bacterial cell divides, its plasmids are copied many times. In a few generations, the cells make millions of clones of the recombinant plasmids.

**Step 5 Screen for Gene** At this point, only some of the bacterial cells contain the recombinant plasmids. These cells must be identified in some way. One clever solution is to use vectors that contain another gene that is easy to detect. In this example, the original plasmids contained a gene that makes bacteria resistant to an antibiotic chemical. When the bacteria from step 4 are exposed to that chemical, only the cells that have taken up the vectors will survive.

These steps are just the beginning of genetic-engineering applications. Before PCR, this process of recombination was the main way to clone genes for further research. Another use is simply to produce a protein, such as insulin, from a cloned gene. As you have learned, recombinant organisms are created for many applications, from agriculture to medicine.

› **Reading Check** *What is a vector?*

## Exploring Genomes

Until recently, the human genome was largely "unexplored." But now, specific genes are being identified and their locations "mapped." These first steps lead to understanding how each gene works. Like geographic maps, maps of genetic data can have different levels of detail or scale. For example, one can view a map of an entire nation or "zoom in" to view a particular state, city, neighborhood, or street. In a similar way, ❯ **one can explore and map a genome at many levels, including species, individual, chromosome, gene, or nucleotide.**

**bioinformatics** the application of information technologies in biology, especially in genetics

**Managing Genomic Data** Your school library has a system for organizing and keeping track of books, as **Figure 15** shows. Similarly, scientists need systems for managing the vast amounts of data in a genome. Today, they use information technologies. The application of information technologies in biology is **bioinformatics.** ❯ **Genomic bioinformatics starts with the mapping and assembly of the many parts of each genome.** The major stages of this work include the following:

- **Mapping and Assembly** Many genes have been "mapped" to reveal their location relative to other genes. In addition, large collections of sequences are being pieced together like a puzzle.
- **Organized Storage** Genomic information is stored in a logical system or database. This way, the information can be sorted and searched, and new information can be added easily.
- **Annotation** Each gene or sequence is named and categorized according to its location, structure, or function in each genome.
- **Analysis** The ultimate goal of genomics is to understand the exact function of each gene or sequence. This analysis includes studying the complex interactions among genes and proteins.

❯ **Reading Check** ***What are the first steps of studying genomes?***

**Learning Steps** If you have not yet completed your pattern puzzle for **Figure 14,** do so now. Then, close your book, scramble the pieces, and see if you can put them in order.

**Figure 15** Like a library full of books, genomic data must be organized in order to be useful. ❯ **What other actions are needed to manage genomic data?**

**genome mapping** the process of determining the relative position of genes in a genome

**genetic library** a collection of genetic sequence clones that represent all of the genes in a given genome

**Mapping Methods** **Genome mapping** is the process of determining the relative position of all of the genes on chromosomes in an organism's genome. To make a city map from scratch, you might start with landmarks that are easy to find and recognize. Similarly, genome mapping methods use *genetic markers,* or traits that can be easily detected, to trace the movement and location of genes. Examples are shown in **Figure 16.** Any detectable physical, behavioral, or chemical trait can be used as a marker. As the next step in making a map, you might try to determine the location of each thing relative to other things. Similarly, genome mapping uses several methods.

**Linkage Mapping** Linkage mapping methods identify the relative order of genes along a chromosome. Recall that the closer together that two genes are, the less frequently they will be separated during chromosome crossover. So, closely linked genes are more often associated, or found together, in the same individual. By comparing how often genes are associated, scientists can deduce their location relative to one another, as **Figure 16** shows.

**Physical Mapping** Physical mapping methods determine the exact number of base pairs between specific genes. These methods manipulate DNA to deduce exactly how close together genes are.

**Human Chromosome Mapping** Early attempts to map human genes used historical family records. By studying the patterns of inheritance of specific traits, scientists could infer which genes tend to be inherited together. This method was especially useful for initial mapping of the X chromosome. Such maps have since been filled in with data from physical mapping, as **Figure 16** shows.

**Figure 16** Each of these maps shows the relative positions of genes on chromosomes. The physical map is more specific than the linkage map. **❯ Why was the X chromosome mapped more easily than other chromosomes?**

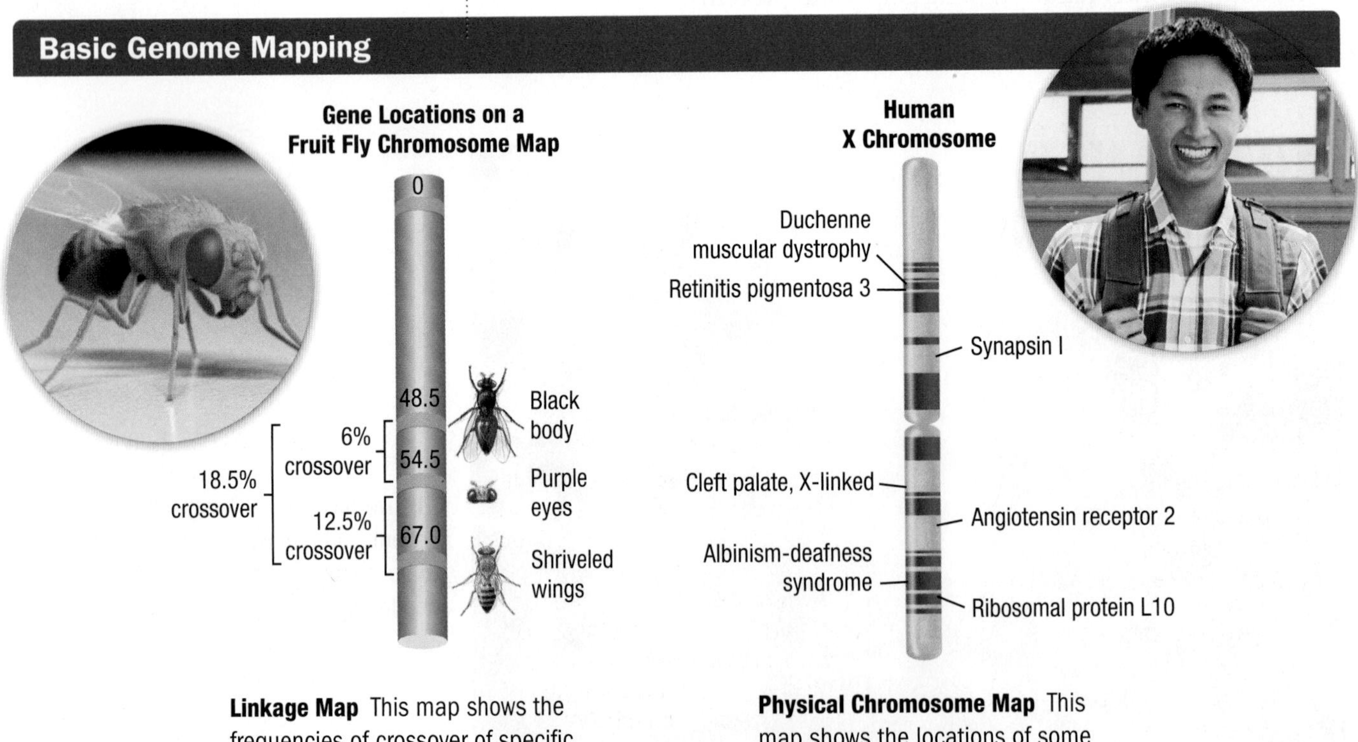


**Linkage Map** This map shows the frequencies of crossover of specific genes in the *Drosophila* genome.

**Physical Chromosome Map** This map shows the locations of some genes on the human X chromosome.

**Genome Sequence Assembly** As they zoom in on the map of genes, scientists want to record all of the nucleotide sequences in a genome. The process of deducing and recording the exact order of every base and gene in a genome is called *sequence assembly.* The process involves collecting, sorting, and comparing large samples of genetic material.

**Genetic Libraries** To study an entire genome, scientists break up the genome into small fragments and clone all of the fragments. A collection of clones that represent all of the genes in a given genome is called a **genetic library.** Two kinds of genetic libraries are made. A *genomic library* is made by cloning all of the DNA in a cell. A genomic library includes all functional genes as well as all noncoding DNA. An *expressed sequence tag* (EST) *library* starts with the mRNA that results from transcription. The mRNA is used to make cDNA segments, which are then cloned to make the library.

**Using the Libraries** Once the clones are assembled, they can be sequenced, sorted, and organized. Early methods involved sorting through libraries one gene at a time by repeated probing and deduction. More recently, a method called *shotgun sequencing* was developed. In this method, an entire genome is cut up randomly into segments of varying size. All resulting segments are cloned and sequenced. Then, by looking for overlapping parts, researchers put together the entire sequence like a puzzle. The resulting genome sequence is stored as data and can be searched for specific genes or sequences of any size.

**Automated Sequencing** Robotic devices are now used to sequence a genome in a fraction of the time that it took to complete such a project only decades ago. Automated sequencing devices can quickly "read" many tiny sequence gels at one time. In such a device, a laser beam scans each gel tube, and detectors identify each of the four kinds of tags. Finally, a computer compiles the data into a string of letters, as **Figure 17** shows.

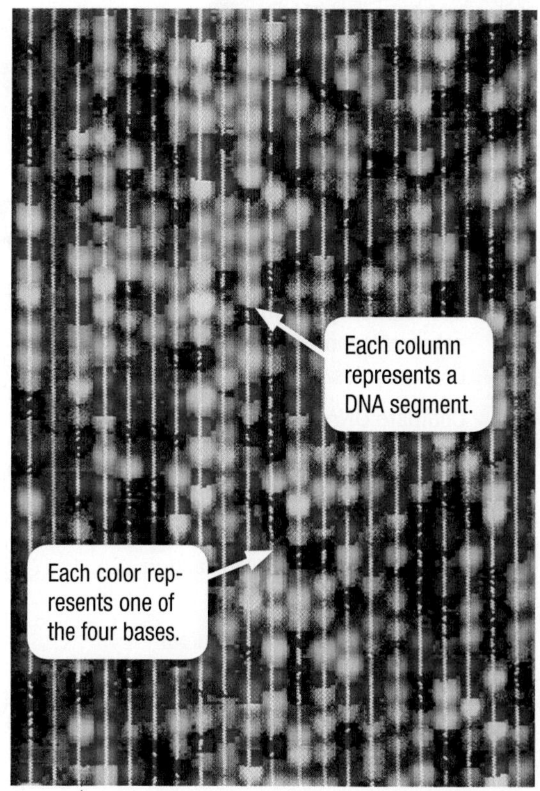

Each column represents a DNA segment.
Each color represents one of the four bases.

**Figure 17** This computer screen shows the output of an automated sequencing device. The device "reads" DNA sequences by detecting color-coded, "tagged" bases in tiny gel-electrophoresis tubes. ❯ **What advantages do computers provide?**

❯ **Reading Check** *What are the two kinds of genetic libraries?*

## Section 3 Review

### ❯ KEY IDEAS

1. **Identify** the basic tools of genetic manipulation.
2. **Outline** any one of the major processes of modern gene technologies.
3. **Identify** the major stages of the work of genomics, in terms of bioinformatics.

### CRITICAL THINKING

4. **Relating Concepts** Differentiate between SNPs and RFLPs.
5. **Predicting Outcomes** If samples of nerve cells and bone cells from the same person were run through the same type of microarray, would the results differ? Explain.
6. **Analyzing Information** Why is *expressed sequence tag library* a fitting name for a collection of clones made from mRNA?

### METHODS OF SCIENCE

7. **Choosing Appropriate Tools** Suppose that you are a genetic scientist who has been asked to help stop the illegal killing of some tropical bird species. These birds are being killed so that their feathers can be sold for fashionable hat decorations. Propose some ways that you could use gene technologies to help protect these birds.

Skills Practice

# Chapter 15 Lab

## Objectives

- Model the forensic analysis of evidence from a crime scene.
- Use restriction enzymes, PCR, and gel electrophoresis to manipulate DNA samples.
- Compare DNA fingerprints to match identical DNA samples.

## Materials

- lab apron, safety goggles, and disposable gloves
- marker, permanent, waterproof
- microcentrifuge tubes (5)
- micropipettes, sterile, disposable (25)
- DNA samples (5)
- restriction enzyme buffer
- restriction enzyme
- incubator or hot water bath
- ice, crushed
- cup, plastic-foam
- gel, agarose, precast for electrophoresis chamber
- electrophoresis chamber with power supply and wires
- running buffer
- loading dye
- bag, plastic, resealable
- DNA staining solution
- tray for staining gel
- water, distilled
- paper, white, or light table

## Safety

# DNA Fingerprint Analysis

Each person's DNA is unique. This fact can be used to match crime suspects to DNA samples taken from crime scenes. *DNA fingerprints* can be made by using restriction enzymes and gel electrophoresis to reveal unique patterns in each individual's DNA.

## Procedure

### Cut DNA with Restriction Enzyme

1. Read all procedures, and prepare to collect your data. Label each microcentrifuge tube with a code for each DNA sample provided. For example, label one tube "C" for "crime scene sample" and the remaining tubes "S1" to "S4," one for each suspect.
2. Wear a lab apron, safety goggles, and gloves during all parts of this lab.
3. **CAUTION: Never taste chemicals or allow them to contact your skin.** Using a clean pipette each time, transfer 10 µL of each DNA sample to the microcentrifuge tube that has the matching label.
4. Using a clean pipette each time, transfer 2 µL of restriction enzyme buffer to each of the tubes.
5. Using a clean pipette each time, transfer 2 µL of restriction enzyme to each of the tubes. Close all of the tubes. Gently flick the bottom of each tube to mix the DNA and reagents.
6. **CAUTION: Use caution when working with heating devices.** Transfer the tubes to the incubator or water bath set at 37 °C. Let the samples incubate for one hour.
7. Stand the tubes in crushed ice in the plastic-foam cup.
8. If you need to pause this lab at this point, store the cup at 4 °C.

### Separate Fragments by Gel Electrophoresis

9. Place the precast gel on the level surface of the electrophoresis chamber. The wells in the gel should be closest to the black, or negative, electrode. Keep the gel level and flat at all times.
10. Fill the chamber with enough buffer to barely cover the gel. Do not pour the buffer directly onto the gel. Sketch a diagram of your gel in your lab notebook, as the sample diagram shows.
11. Using a clean pipette each time, transfer 2 µL of loading dye to each of the tubes. Gently flick the tubes to mix the contents.
12. Using a clean pipette, load the crime scene DNA into the well for Lane 1 of your gel. Be careful not to overflow or puncture the well.
13. Repeat step 12 for the remaining DNA samples and gel lanes. End with the DNA from Suspect 4. Use a clean pipette for each transfer.

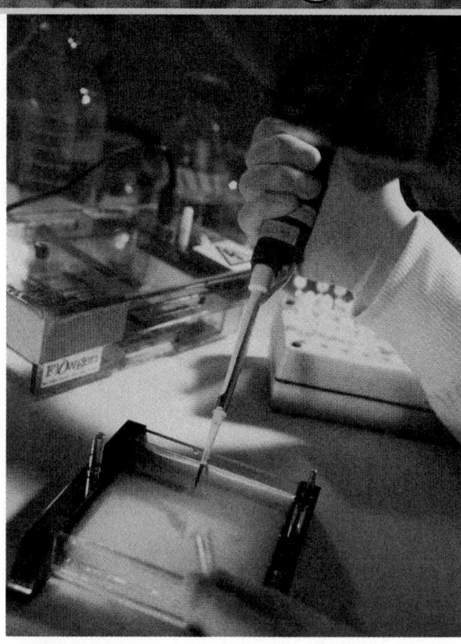
Loading the gel

14 **CAUTION: Use caution when working with electrical equipment; use only as directed by your teacher.** Make sure that everything outside the chamber is dry before proceeding. Attach the power connectors to the chamber and power supply as directed by your teacher. Set the power supply to the voltage determined by your teacher, and turn on the power supply.

15 Allow the gel to run undisturbed for the time directed by your teacher. Observe the gel periodically, and stop the process when the dye front is about 3 cm away from the end of the gel. At that point, turn off the power supply. Then, disconnect the power connectors from the power supply and chamber.

16 **CAUTION: Dispose of all waste materials as directed by your teacher.** Carefully remove the casting tray from the chamber. Pour off the running buffer according to your teacher's instructions.

17 If you need to pause this lab at this point, carefully slide the gel into a resealable bag. Add 2 mL running buffer, seal the bag, and store the bag in a refrigerator. Remember to keep the gel flat.

### View Separated DNA Fragments

18 Gently slide the gel onto the staining tray. Pour enough stain into the tray to barely cover the gel. Do not pour the stain directly onto the gel. Let the gel sit for at least 30 min.

19 Carefully pour off the stain as directed by your teacher.

20 Gently pour distilled water into the tray to cover the gel. Do not pour the water directly onto the gel. After 5 min, carefully pour off the water as directed by your teacher.

21 Repeat step 20 until bands are clearly visible on the gel.

22 Gently transfer the gel to a white sheet of paper or to a light table. Sketch and describe your observations in your lab notebook.

23 Clean up your lab materials according to your teacher's instructions. Wash your hands before leaving the lab.

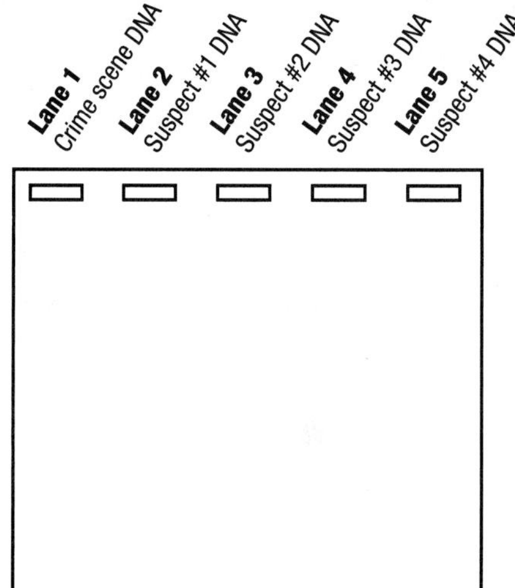

**Sample gel diagram**

## Analyze and Conclude

1. SCIENTIFIC METHODS **Organizing Data** Organize your data into a table. How many different fragment sizes resulted from the treatment of each DNA sample?
2. **Analyzing Data** Identify any bands of fragments that are the same size among any of the samples. Mark these bands on your sketch.
3. **Forming Conclusions** Use this evidence to determine which suspect most likely committed the crime. Explain your answer.
4. SCIENTIFIC METHODS **Evaluating Methods** Do these results provide enough evidence to convict the suspect? Explain your answer.

## Extension

5. **Applying Concepts** Some bands appeared in the same position in several lanes. Propose an explanation for this result.
6. **Predicting Results** How might the results have been affected if a different restriction enzyme had been used? Explain your answer.

# Chapter 15 Summary

| Key Ideas | Key Terms |
|---|---|
| **1 The Human Genome**<br>❯ The sequencing of the human genome has advanced the study of human biology yet created new questions<br>❯ Genomics and gene technologies have many applications in human healthcare and society.<br>❯ Many important questions about the human genome remain to be investigated or decided. | **genomics** (345)<br>**microarray** (346)<br>**DNA fingerprint** (347) |
| **2 Gene Technologies in Our Lives**<br>❯ Today, gene technologies are widely applied to study organisms in new ways, to alter organisms for human use, and to improve human lives.<br>❯ Cloning and stem cell techniques are used in research on animal development and have potential for treating certain diseases.<br>❯ Ethical issues can be raised for every use of gene technologies. | **genetic engineering** (350)<br>**recombinant DNA** (350)<br>**clone** (352)<br>**stem cell** (353) |
| **3 Gene Technologies in Detail**<br>❯ The basic tools of DNA manipulation rely on the chemical nature of genetic material and are adapted from natural processes discovered in cells. These tools include restriction enzymes, polymorphisms, gel electrophoresis, denaturation, and hybridization.<br>❯ The major methods for working with genes use some combination of the basic tools of cellular machinery. These methods include PCR, blotting, DNA sequencing, and gene recombination.<br>❯ One can explore and map a genome at many levels, including species, individual, chromosome, gene, or nucleotide. Genomic bioinformatics starts with the mapping and assembly of the many parts of each genome. | **restriction enzyme** (355)<br>**DNA polymorphisms** (356)<br>**electrophoresis** (356)<br>**polymerase chain reaction (PCR)** (357)<br>**DNA sequencing** (359)<br>**bioinformatics** (361)<br>**genome mapping** (362)<br>**genetic library** (363) |

Chapter 15

The Living Environment

# Regents Exam Practice

**PART A: Answer all questions in this part.**

*Directions:* For each statement or question, write on your separate answer sheet the number of the word or expression that best completes the statement or answers the question.

**1** Steps in a preproductive process used to produce a sheep with certain traits are listed below. Which sheep would be most genetically similar to sheep D?

**Step 1:** The nucleus was removed from an unfertilized egg taken from sheep *A*;

**Step 2:** The nucleus of a body cell taken from sheep *B* was then inserted into this unfertilized egg from sheep *A*;

**Step 3:** The resulting cell was then implanted into the uterus of sheep *C*;

**Step 4:** Sheep *C* gave birth to sheep *D*.

(1) sheep A, only
(2) sheep B, only
(3) both sheep A and B
(4) both sheep A and C

**2** Which transplant method would prevent the rejection of tissue after an organ transplant?

(1) using organs cloned from the cells of the patient
(2) using organs produced by genetic engineering to get rid of all proteins in the donated organs
(3) using organs only from pigs or monkeys
(4) using an organ donated by a close relative because the proteins will always be identical to those of the recipient

**3** People with cystic fibrosis inherit defective genetic information and cannot produce normal CFTR proteins. Scientists have used gene therapy to insert normal DNA segments that code for the missing CFTR protein into the lung cells of people with cystic fibrosis. Which statement does not describe a result of this therapy?

(1) Altered lung cells can produce the normal CFTR protein.
(2) Altered lung cells can divide to produce other lung cells with the normal CFTR gene.
(3) The normal CFTR gene may be expressed in altered lung cells.
(4) Offspring of someone with altered lung cells will inherit the normal CFTR gene.

**4** The diagram below represents a common laboratory technique in molecular genetics. One common use of this technology is the

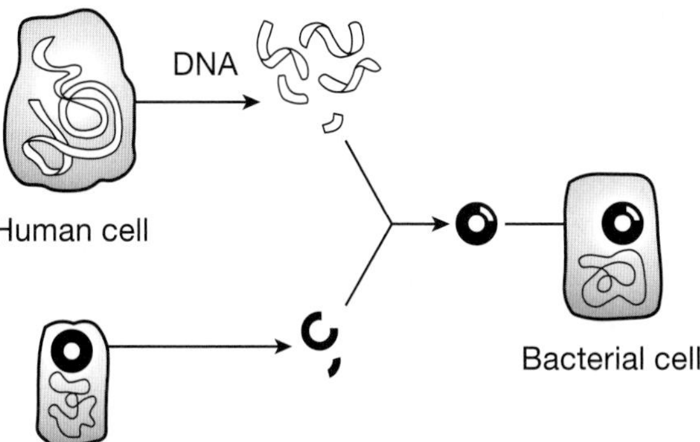


(1) production of a human embryo to aid women who are unable to have children.
(2) change of single-celled organisms to multicellular organisms.
(3) introduction of a toxic substance to kill bacterial cells.
(4) production of hormones or enzymes to replace missing human body chemicals.

**5** A product of genetic engineering technology is represented below. Which substance was needed to join the insulin gene to the bacterial DNA as shown?

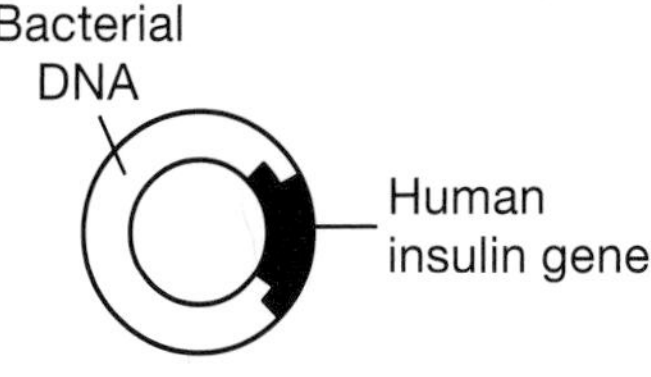


(1) a specific carbohydrate
(2) a specific enzyme
(3) hormones
(4) antibodies

**6** Researchers Cohn and Boyer transferred a gene from an African clawed frog into a bacterium. To accomplish this, these scientists had to use

(1) enzymes to cut out and insert the gene.
(2) hereditary information located in amino acids.
(3) radiation to increase the gene mutation rate of the bacterial cells.
(4) cancer cells to promote rapid cell division.

7 Cloning an individual usually produces organisms that

(1) contain dangerous mutations.
(2) contain identical genes.
(3) are identical in appearance and behavior.
(4) produce enzymes different from the parent.

8 The production of certain human hormones by genetically engineered bacteria results from

(1) inserting a specific group of amino acids into the bacteria.
(2) combining a portion of human DNA with bacterial DNA and inserting this into bacteria.
(3) crossing two different species of bacteria.
(4) deleting a specific amino acid from human DNA and inserting it into bacterial DNA.

9 To produce large tomatoes that are resistant to cracking and splitting, some seed companies use the pollen from one variety of tomato plant to fertilize a different variety of tomato plant. This process is an example of

(1) selective breeding.
(2) DNA sequencing.
(3) direct harvesting.
(4) cloning.

10 A variation causes the production of an improved variety of apple. What is the best method to use to obtain additional apple trees of this variety in the shortest period of time?

(1) selective breeding
(2) natural selection
(3) asexual reproduction
(4) hormone therapy

11 A biotechnology firm has produced tobacco plants that synthesize human antibodies that prevent bacterial diseases. One of the first steps in the production of these plants required

(1) using natural selection to increase the survival of antibody-producing tobacco plants.
(2) inserting human DNA segments into the cells of tobacco plants.
(3) using selective breeding to increase the number of antibody genes in tobacco plants.
(4) growing tobacco plants in soil containing a specific fertilizer.

12 A gene that codes for resistance to glyphosate, a biodegradable weedkiller, has been inserted into certain plants. As a result, these plants will be more likely to

(1) produce chemicals that kill weeds growing near them.
(2) die when exposed to glyphosate.
(3) convert glyphosate into fertilizer.
(4) survive when glyphosate is applied to them.

13 Which statement best describes human insulin that is produced by genetically engineered bacteria?

(1) This insulin will not function normally in humans because it is produced by bacteria.
(2) This insulin is produced as a result of human insulin being inserted into bacteria cells.
(3) This insulin is produced as a result of exposing bacteria cells to radiation, which produces a mutation.
(4) This insulin may have fewer side effects than the insulin previously extracted from the pancreas of other animals.

14 A great deal of information can now be obtained about the future health of people by examining the genetic makeup of their cells. There are concerns that this information could be used to deny an individual health insurance or employment. These concerns best illustrate that

(1) scientific explanations depend upon evidence collected from a single source.
(2) scientific inquiry involves the collection of information from a large number of sources.
(3) acquiring too much knowledge in human genetics will discourage future research in that area.
(4) while science provides knowledge, values are essential to making ethical decisions using this knowledge.

15 What do linkage mapping methods identify?

(1) only genes that are inherited together
(2) the exact nucleotide sequence of a chromosome
(3) the relative position of genes along a chromosome
(4) the exact number of base pairs between specific genes

**16** The diagrams below represent some steps in a procedure used in biotechnology. Letters X and Y represent the

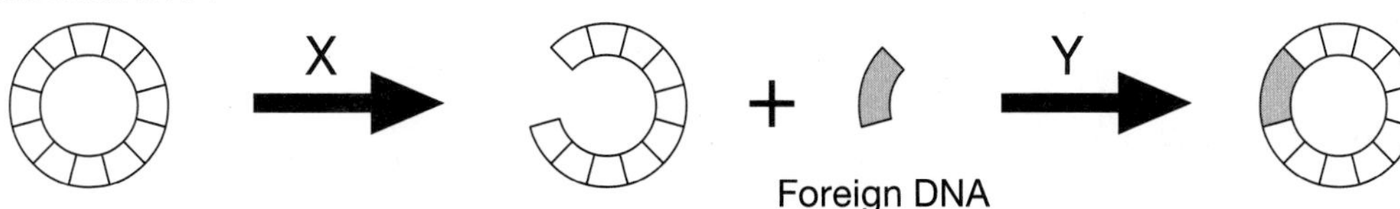


(1) hormones that stimulate the replication of bacterial DNA.
(2) biochemical catalysts involved in the insertion of genes into other organisms.
(3) hormones that trigger rapid mutation of genetic information.
(4) gases needed to produce the energy required for gene manipulation.

**PART D**

**17** Gel electrophoresis is used to separate DNA fragments on the basis of their

(1) size.
(2) color.
(3) functions.
(4) chromosomes.

**Base your answers to question 18 on the information and diagram below and on your knowledge of biology.**

The DNA of three different species of birds was analyzed to help determine if there is an evolutionary relationship between these species. The diagram shows the results of this analysis.

**18** Identify the technique normally used to separate the DNA fragments to produce the patterns shown in the diagram.

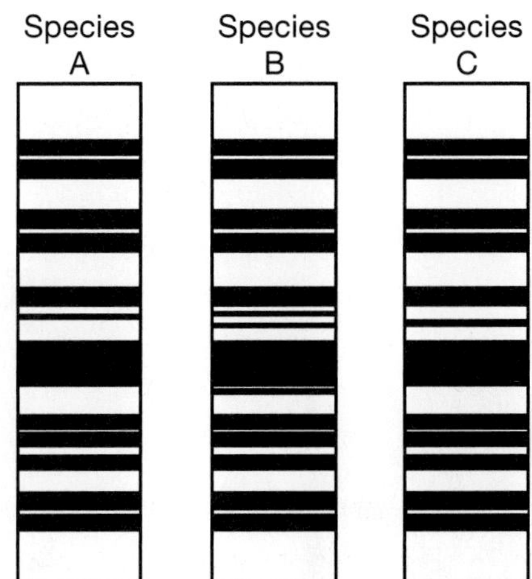

# UNIT 5 Evolution

***The Living Environment***

**Standard 1** Students will use mathematical analysis, scientific inquiry, and engineering design, as appropriate, to pose questions, seek answers, and develop solutions.

**Key Idea 1** The central purpose of scientific inquiry is to develop explanations of natural phenomena in a continuing and creative process.

**Key Idea 2** Beyond the use of reasoning and consensus, scientific inquiry involves the testing of proposed explanations involving the use of conventional techniques and procedures and usually requiring considerable ingenuity.

**Standard 4** Students will understand and apply scientific concepts, principles, and theories pertaining to the physical setting and living environment and recognize the historical development of ideas in science.

**Key Idea 2** Organisms inherit genetic information in a variety of ways that result in continuity of structure and function between parents and offspring.

**Key Idea 3** Individual organisms and species change over time

**Key Idea 4** The continuity of life is sustained through reproduction and development.

**Key Idea 6** Plants and animals depend on each other and their physical environment.

Insect of the newly named order Mantophasmatodea

Kingfisher male with courtship gift

Poison dart frogs

## DISCOVERIES IN SCIENCE

# Evolution and Life on Earth

### 1753

Carolus Linnaeus publishes the first of two volumes containing the classification of all known species. In doing so, Linnaeus establishes a consistent system for naming and classifying species. The system is widely used thereafter.

### 1859

Charles Darwin suggests that natural selection is the mechanism of evolution. Within months, public debates regarding the truth and significance of his theory ensue.

**Galápagos tortoises**

### 1907

In his book, *Plant Breeding,* Hugo de Vries, Dutch botanist, joins Mendel's laws of heredity with the newer theory of mutation. De Vries asserts that inheritable mutations are the mechanism by which species change and new species form.

### 1960

Mary and Jonathan Leakey discover fossil bones of a human ancestor, *Homo habilis,* in Olduvai Gorge, Tanzania.

**Mary Leakey, paleoanthropologist**

### 1974

Donald Johansen discovers a fossilized skeleton of one of the first hominids, *Australopithecus afarensis.* This specimen was nicknamed "Lucy."

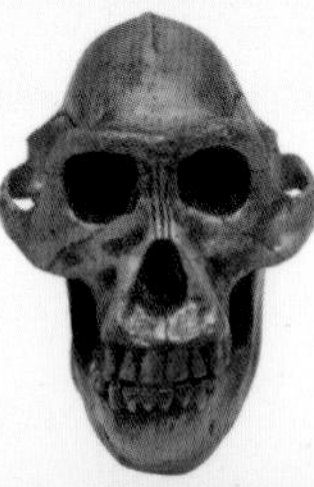

**Skull of *A. afarensis***

### 1980

Walter and Luis Alvarez, Frank Asaro, and Helen Michel publish a paper providing evidence that 65 million years ago, an asteroid collided with Earth and caused severe environmental changes. The changes may have led to the extinction of the majority of species that lived during that time.

### 1994

Reinhardt Kristensen and Peter Funch discover a tiny animal living on the lips of lobsters. They name the new species *Symbion pandora.* This species is so different from other animals that scientists classify it within a new phylum, Cycliophora, within kingdom Animalia.

### 2006

A team of biologists announces a study of Camiguin Island, the smallest island of the Philippines. They find 54 species of birds and 24 of species of mammals.

**As-yet-unnamed parrot species**

Beetles—one of the most diverse groups of animals on Earth

# BIOLOGY CAREER



## Museum Curator

### Rob DeSalle

Rob DeSalle is a curator in the Division of Invertebrate Zoology at the American Museum of Natural History in New York City. He is an adjunct professor at Columbia University and City University of New York and is a Distinguished Research Professor at New York University. His current research focuses on molecular evolution in various organisms, including pathogenic bacteria and insects.

DeSalle enjoys being a scientist because he can investigate the diversity of life every day. He also enjoys the opportunity to serve as a mentor to students. Most of all, he enjoys the thrill of discovering something that no one else on the planet has found.

He considers his most significant accomplishment in science to be his work communicating scientific ideas through his writing and museum exhibitions.

Besides his work, DeSalle loves baseball and is a passionate fan of the Chicago Cubs.

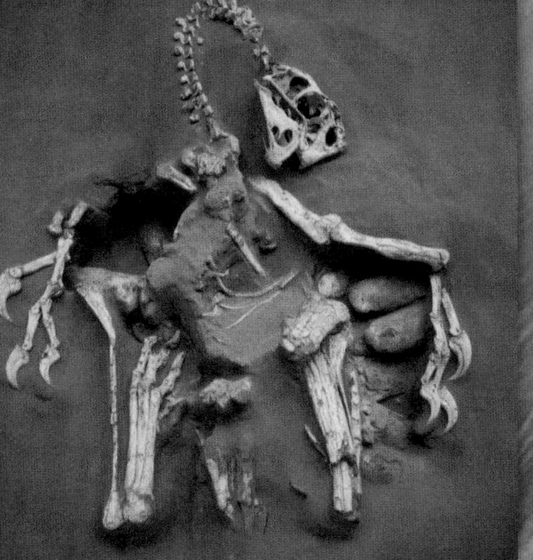

Fossil and eggs of dinosaur called *oviraptor*

# Chapter 16 Evolutionary Theory

## Preview



## Why It Matters

Modern evolutionary theory provides strong and detailed explanations for many aspects of biology, such as anatomy and behavior.

***The Living Environment***

**Standard 1** Students will use mathematical analysis, scientific inquiry, and engineering design, as appropriate, to pose questions, seek answers, and develop solutions.

**Key Idea 1** The central purpose of scientific inquiry is to develop explanations of natural phenomena in a continuing and creative process. ***Major Understandings* - 1.1a, 1.4a**

**Key Idea 2** Beyond the use of reasoning and consensus, scientific inquiry involves the testing of proposed explanations involving the use of conventional techniques and procedures and usually requiring considerable ingenuity. ***Major Understandings* - 2.2a**

**Standard 4** Students will understand and apply scientific concepts, principles, and theories pertaining to the physical setting and living environment and recognize the historical development of ideas in science.

**Key Idea 3** Individual organisms and species change over time. ***Major Understandings* – 3.1a, 3.1b, 3.1e, 3.1f, 3.1g, 3.1h, 3.1k, 3.1l**

**This pygmy sea horse is smaller than your fingernail. It lives exclusively among certain kinds of coral in coral reefs of the western Pacific Ocean.**

The pygmy sea horse looks very similar to the coral among which it lives. This camouflage is an inherited characteristic that may keep other animals from seeing the sea horse.

Several other species of pygmy sea horses live among other kinds of corals. Each species resembles the specific kind of coral among which it lives. Camouflage is a characteristic of many organisms.

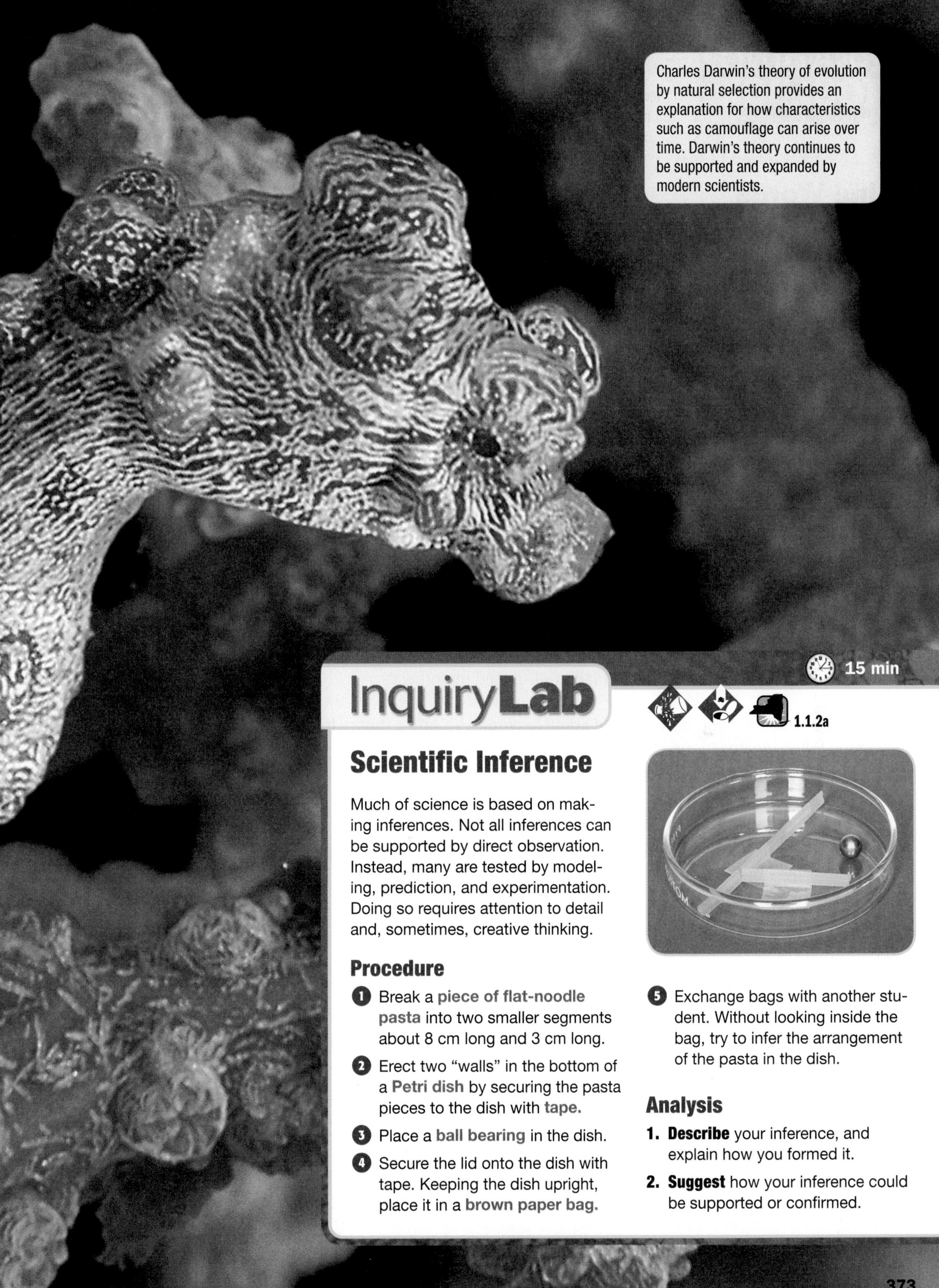

Charles Darwin's theory of evolution by natural selection provides an explanation for how characteristics such as camouflage can arise over time. Darwin's theory continues to be supported and expanded by modern scientists.

# InquiryLab

15 min

1.1.2a

## Scientific Inference

Much of science is based on making inferences. Not all inferences can be supported by direct observation. Instead, many are tested by modeling, prediction, and experimentation. Doing so requires attention to detail and, sometimes, creative thinking.

### Procedure

1. Break a **piece of flat-noodle pasta** into two smaller segments about 8 cm long and 3 cm long.
2. Erect two "walls" in the bottom of a **Petri dish** by securing the pasta pieces to the dish with **tape.**
3. Place a **ball bearing** in the dish.
4. Secure the lid onto the dish with tape. Keeping the dish upright, place it in a **brown paper bag.**
5. Exchange bags with another student. Without looking inside the bag, try to infer the arrangement of the pasta in the dish.

### Analysis

1. **Describe** your inference, and explain how you formed it.
2. **Suggest** how your inference could be supported or confirmed.

These reading tools can help you learn the material in this chapter. For more information on how to use these and other tools, see **Appendix: Reading and Study Skills.**

## Using Words

**Key-Term Fold** A key-term fold is useful for studying definitions of key terms in a chapter. Each tab can contain a key term on one side and the term's definition on the other.

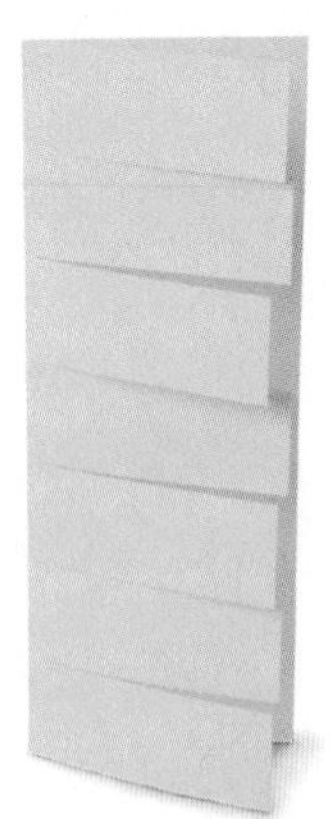

**Your Turn** Prepare a key-term fold for the key terms in this chapter. Fill it in as you read. Use it later to quiz yourself on the definitions.

1. Fold a sheet of lined notebook paper in half from left to right.
2. Using scissors, cut along every third line from the right edge of the paper to the center fold to make tabs.

## Using Language

**Hypothesis or Theory?** In everyday language, there is little difference between a *hypothesis* and a *theory*. But in science, the meanings of these words are more distinct. A *hypothesis* is a specific, testable prediction for a limited set of conditions. A *theory* is a general explanation for a broad range of data. A theory can include hypotheses that have been tested and can also be used to generate new hypotheses. The strongest scientific theories explain the broadest range of data and incorporate many well-tested hypotheses.

**Your Turn** Use what you have learned about a hypothesis and a theory to answer the following questions.

1. List some scientific theories that you have heard of.
2. Make a simple concept map or Venn diagram to show the relationship between hypotheses and theories.
3. The word *theory* may also be used to describe general trends and areas of active investigation in a scientific field. In this context, what does the term *evolutionary theory* mean?

## Taking Notes

**Summarizing Ideas** Summarizing ideas helps you condense important information. When you summarize, use your own words and keep your sentences short. Focus on key ideas.

**Your Turn** Prepare to take notes for this chapter. Use this table as an example. As you read, be sure to summarize the following concepts:

1. natural selection
2. macroevolution
3. microevolution

| Notes about Evolution | | |
|---|---|---|
| *Natural selection* | *Macroevolution* | *Microevolution* |
| | | |

Section 1

# Developing a Theory

| Key Ideas | Key Terms | Why It Matters |
|---|---|---|
| ❯ Why is evolutionary theory associated with Charles Darwin?<br>❯ How was Darwin influenced by his personal experiences?<br>❯ How was Darwin influenced by the ideas of others? | evolution<br>artificial selection | Many aspects of biology are best explained by evolutionary theory. |

Recall that in biology, **evolution** is the process by which species change over time. The idea that life evolves is not new. Yet for centuries, scientists lacked clear evidence that evolution happens. They also lacked a strong theory to explain how evolution happens. In 1859, Charles Darwin pulled together these missing pieces. Darwin, shown in **Figure 1,** was an English naturalist who studied the diversity of life and proposed a broad explanation for it.

***The Living Environment***

**Standard 1**

**1.1a** Scientific explanations are built by combining evidence that can be observed with what people already know about the world.

**1.4a** Well-accepted theories are ones that are supported by different kinds of scientific investigations often involving the contributions of individuals from different disciplines.

**Standard 4**

**2.2a** For thousands of years new varieties of cultivated plants and domestic animals have resulted from selective breeding for particular traits.

**3.1a** The basic theory of biological evolution states that the Earth's present-day species developed from earlier, distinctly different species.

## A Theory to Explain Change over Time

Recall that in science, a *theory* is a broad explanation that has been scientifically tested and supported. ❯ **Modern evolutionary theory began when Darwin presented evidence that evolution happens and offered an explanation of how evolution happens.** Like most scientific theories, evolutionary theory keeps developing and expanding. Many scientists since Darwin have tested and added to his ideas. Most of Darwin's ideas, including his main theory, remain scientifically supported.

**evolution** the process of change by which new species develop from preexisting species over time

❯ **Reading Check** *What does* **evolution** *mean in biology? (See the Appendix for answers to Reading Checks.)*

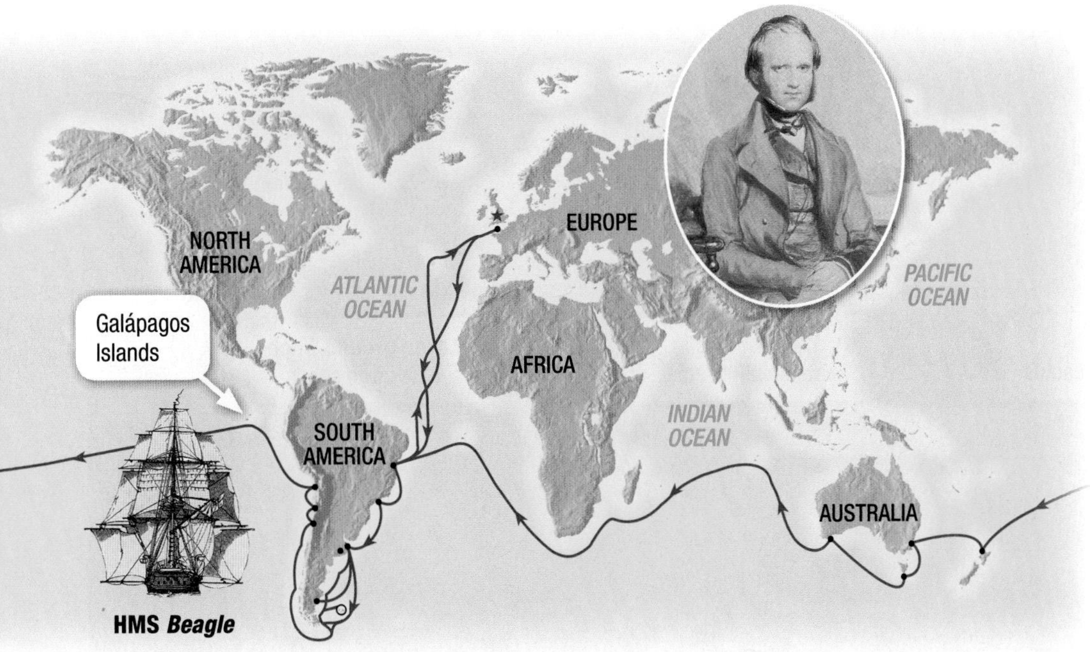


**Figure 1** Charles Darwin took many years to publish his theory of evolution by natural selection. Many of his ideas were first inspired by his 1831 global voyage on a ship called the *Beagle*.

## Darwin's Ideas from Experience

In Darwin's time, most people did not think that living things had changed over time. In fact, many doubted that Earth itself had ever changed. But Darwin saw evidence of gradual change. ❯ **Darwin's experiences provided him with evidence of evolution at work.**

**READING TOOLBOX**

**Key-Term Fold** On the back half of your key-term fold, under each flap, write your own definition for the key terms in this section.

**The Voyage of the *Beagle*** Darwin's first evidence was gathered during a global voyage on a ship called the *Beagle*. As part of his work as a naturalist, Darwin collected natural objects from each place that he visited. For example, in South America, he collected fossils of giant, extinct armadillos. Darwin noticed that these fossils were similar, but not identical, to the living armadillos in the area.

Darwin also visited the Galápagos Islands in the Pacific Ocean. There, he collected several different species of birds called *finches*. Each of the finches are very similar, but differences can be seen in the size and shape of the bill (or beak), such as those shown in **Figure 2.** Each finch has a bill that seems suited to the finch's usual food.

Darwin noticed that many of the islands' plants and animals were similar, but not identical, to the plants and animals he saw in South America. Later, Darwin proposed that the Galápagos species had descended from species that came from South America. For example, he suggested that all of the finch species descended from one ancestral finch species that migrated from South America. Then, the descendant finches were modified over time as different groups survived by eating different types of food. Darwin called such change *descent with modification*. This idea was a key part of his theory.

**artificial selection** the human practice of breeding animals or plants that have certain desired traits

**Years of Reflection** After returning from his voyage at the age of 27, Darwin spent years studying his data. He also continued studying many sciences. As he studied, his confidence grew stronger that evolution must happen. But Darwin did not report his ideas about evolution until much later. Instead, he took time to gather more data and to form a strong explanation for how evolution happens.

**Figure 2** Darwin eventually learned that all Galápagos finch species were similar to each other and to one particular South American finch. ❯ **What explanation did Darwin propose for this similarity?**

**Breeding and Selection** Darwin took interest in the practice of breeding, especially the breeding of exotic pigeons. He bred pigeons himself and studied the work of those who bred other kinds of animals and plants, such as dogs, orchids, and food crops. Eventually, Darwin gained a new insight: breeders take advantage of natural variation in traits within a species. If a trait can be inherited, breeders can produce more individuals that have the trait. Breeders simply select individuals that have desirable traits to be the parents of each new generation. Darwin called this process **artificial selection** because the selection is done by humans and not by natural causes.

**Academic Vocabulary**

**insight** a clear understanding of something

› **Reading Check** *When did Darwin first see evidence of evolution?*

Why It Matters

## Breeding

The power of artificial selection can be seen today in the amazing variety of pets, show animals, and agricultural food crops. For example, more than 400 breeds of dogs exist today, from tiny Chihuahuas to Great Danes. All of these breeds, including wolves, are considered part of the same species (*Canis lupus*) because most can interbreed.

### Dog Diversity

People have lived with dogs—or the wolf ancestors of dogs—throughout history. Over time, people learned to selectively breed dogs by choosing certain individuals to become parents. People have selected dogs that have various kinds of physical and behavioral traits. So today, each breed of dog is known for its appearance as well as its degree of playfulness, friendliness, watchfulness, or cleverness. Some breeds are also known for certain quirks or problems.

**Quick Project** Visit a local pet store, and ask which breeds are most popular or most expensive. Ask why.

Hands-On

# QuickLab

15 min

## Two Kinds of Growth

Can you visualize the difference between linear growth and exponential growth?

### Procedure

1. Place **grains of rice** in the cups of an **egg carton** in the following sequence: Place one grain in the first cup. Place two grains in the second cup. Place three grains in the third cup. In each of the remaining cups, place *one more* grain of rice than in the cup before.
2. Use a line graph to graph the results of step 1.
3. Repeat step 1, but use the following sequence: Place one grain in the first cup, two in the second cup, and four in the third cup. In each remaining cup, place twice as many grains as placed in the cup before.
4. Use a line graph to graph the results of step 3.

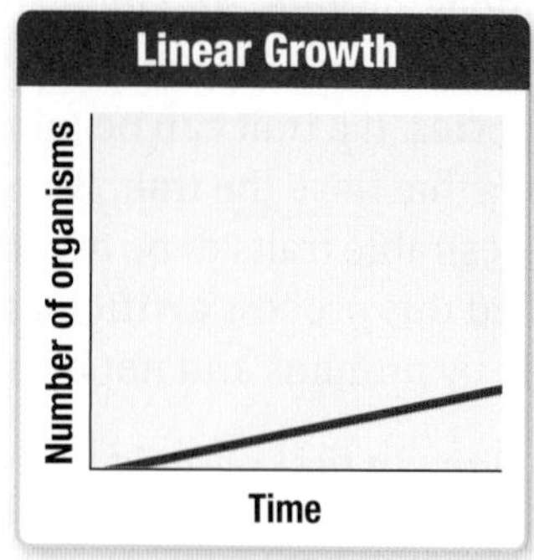


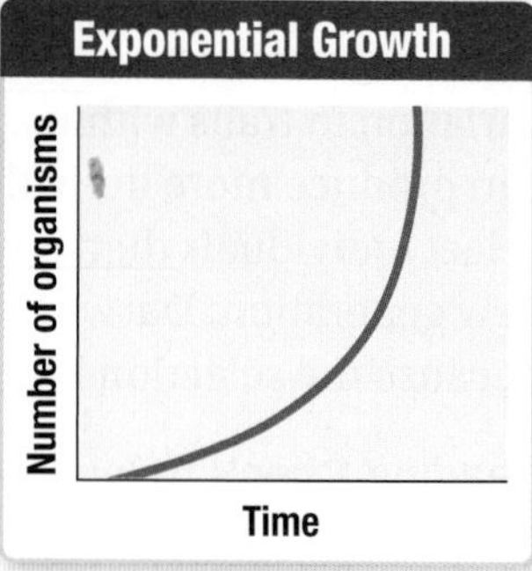


### Analysis

1. **Match** your graphs to the graphs shown.
2. CRITICAL THINKING **Analyzing Terminology** Linear growth is also called *arithmetic growth,* and exponential growth is also called *geometric growth*. Propose an explanation for the use of these terms.

## Darwin's Ideas from Others

In Darwin's time, most people—including scientists—believed that each species was created once and stayed the same forever. But this view could not explain fossils of organisms that no longer exist, such as dinosaurs. Some scientists tried to explain such observations by saying that species could die out but never change. Others, including Darwin's own grandfather, proposed various mechanisms to explain how species may change over time. **Darwin was influenced by ideas from the fields of natural history, economics, and geology.** The ideas of Lamarck, Malthus, Cuvier, and Lyell were especially important.

**Figure 3** According to Lamarck's idea of inheritance, this baseball player's children would inherit strong arm muscles. **Why was this idea important to Darwin?**

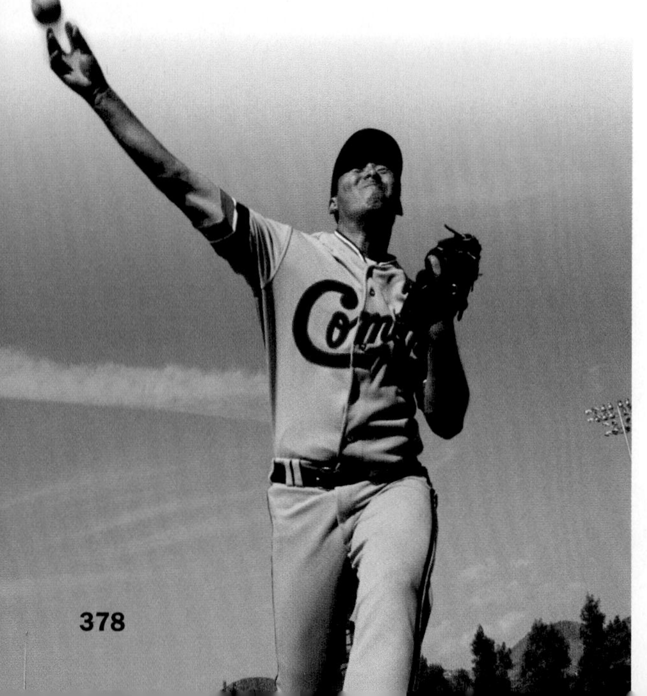

**Lamarckian Inheritance** In 1809, the French scientist Jean Baptiste Lamarck proposed an explanation for how organisms may change over generations. Like Darwin and others, Lamarck noticed that each organism is usually well adapted to its environment. He proposed, as Darwin would later, that organisms change over time as they adapt to changing environments.

However, Lamarck had an incorrect idea about inheritance. He proposed that changes due to use or disuse of a characteristic would be passed on to offspring. For example, he knew that a person's muscles may decrease in size because of disuse or may increase in size because of use, as shown in **Figure 3.** He believed that offspring inherited these kinds of changes. This idea was eventually disproved, but not in Darwin's time. Darwin once accepted this idea because it proposed a role for inheritance in evolution.

**Population Growth** Another key influence on Darwin's thinking about evolution was an essay by Thomas Malthus. In 1798, this English economist observed that human populations were increasing faster than the food supply. Malthus pointed out that food supplies were increasing *linearly*. More food was being produced each year, but the amount by which the food increased was the same each year. In contrast, the number of people was increasing *exponentially*. More people were added each year than were added the year before. Malthus noted that the number of humans could not keep increasing in this way, because many people would probably die from disease, war, or famine.

Darwin simply applied Malthus's idea to all populations. Recall that a *population* is all of the individuals of the same species that live in a specific place. Darwin saw that all kinds of organisms tend to produce more offspring than can survive. So, all populations must be limited by their environments.

**Figure 4** Layers of rock contain evidence of changes occurring over millions of years in organisms and environments on Earth. Darwin realized that such evidence supported his ideas about evolution.

**Geology and an Ancient Earth** In Darwin's time, scientists had become interested in the study of rocks and landforms, and thus began the science of *geology*. In particular, scientists such as Georges Cuvier, James Hutton, and Charles Lyell studied fossils and rock layers, such as those shown in **Figure 4.** Cuvier argued that fossils in rock layers showed differences in species over time and that many species from the past differed from those of the present. But Cuvier did not see species as changing gradually over time. He thought that changes in the past must have occurred suddenly.

Hutton and Lyell, on the other hand, thought that geologic processes—such as those that wear away mountains and form new rocks and fossils—work gradually and constantly. Lyell carefully and thoroughly presented his ideas in a book, which Darwin read. Lyell's ideas fit well with Darwin's observations and showed that Earth's history was long enough for species to have evolved gradually.

SCILINKS.
www.scilinks.org
Topic: Charles Darwin
Code: HX80262

› **Reading Check** ***What idea did Darwin and Lamarck once share?***

## Section 1 Review

### › KEY IDEAS

1. **Describe** Darwin's relationship to modern evolutionary theory.
2. **Identify** personal experiences that contributed to Darwin's thinking about evolution.
3. **Identify** other scientists that influenced Darwin's thinking.

### CRITICAL THINKING

4. **Applying Process Concepts** Darwin observed that artificial selection can produce specific traits. Suppose a farmer has a corn crop in which each ear of corn has some yellow kernels and some white kernels. Describe how the farmer could produce a variety of corn that has all white kernels.

### METHODS OF SCIENCE

5. **Scientific Testing** According to Lamarck's idea of inheritance, an individual that developed an improved trait within its lifetime, especially through repeated use, could pass that trait on to its offspring. Propose a way to test the accuracy of this idea.

Section

# 2 Applying Darwin's Ideas

| Key Ideas | Key Terms | Why It Matters |
|---|---|---|
| ❯ What does Darwin's theory predict?<br>❯ Why are Darwin's ideas now widely accepted?<br>❯ What were the strengths and weaknesses of Darwin's ideas? | natural selection<br>adaptation<br>fossil<br>homologous | The principles of evolution are used daily in medicine, biology, and other areas of modern life to understand, predict, and develop advancements in each area. |

***The Living Environment***

**Standard 4**

**3.1e** Natural selection and its evolutionary consequences provide a scientific explanation for the fossil record of ancient life-forms, as well as for the molecular and structural similarities observed among the diverse species of living organisms.

**3.1f** Species evolve over time. Evolution is the consequence of the interactions of (1) the potential for a species to increase its numbers, (2) the genetic variability of offspring due to mutation and recombination of genes, (3) a finite supply of the resources required for life, and (4) the ensuing selection by the environment of those offspring better able to survive...

**3.1g** Some characteristics give individuals an advantage over others in surviving and reproducing...

**3.1h** The variation of organisms within a species increases the likelihood that at least some members of the species will survive under changed environmental conditions.

**3.1l** Extinction of a species occurs when the environment changes and the adaptive characteristics of a species are insufficient to allow its survival. Fossils indicate that many organisms that lived long ago are extinct. Extinction of species is common; most of the species that have lived on Earth no longer exist.

Darwin applied Malthus's idea to all species. Every living thing has the potential to produce many offspring, but not all of those offspring are likely to survive and reproduce.

## Evolution by Natural Selection

Darwin formed a key idea: Individuals that have traits that better suit their environment are more likely to survive. For example, the insect in **Figure 5** is less likely to be seen (and eaten) than a brightly colored insect is. Furthermore, individuals that have certain traits tend to produce more offspring than others do. These differences are part of **natural selection.** Darwin proposed that natural selection is a cause of evolution. In this context, *evolution* is a change in the inherited characteristics of a population from one generation to the next.

**Steps of Darwin's Theory** Darwin's explanation is often called the *theory of evolution by natural selection.* ❯ **Darwin's theory predicts that over time, the number of individuals that carry advantageous traits will increase in a population.** As shown in **Figure 6,** this theory can be summarized in the following four logical steps:

**Step ❶ Overproduction** Every population is capable of producing more offspring than can possibly survive.

**Step ❷ Variation** Variation exists within every population. Much of this variation is in the form of inherited traits.

**Step ❸ Selection** In a given environment, having a particular trait can make individuals more or less likely to survive and have successful offspring. So, some individuals leave more offspring than others do.

**Step ❹ Adaptation** Over time, those traits that improve survival and reproduction will become more common.

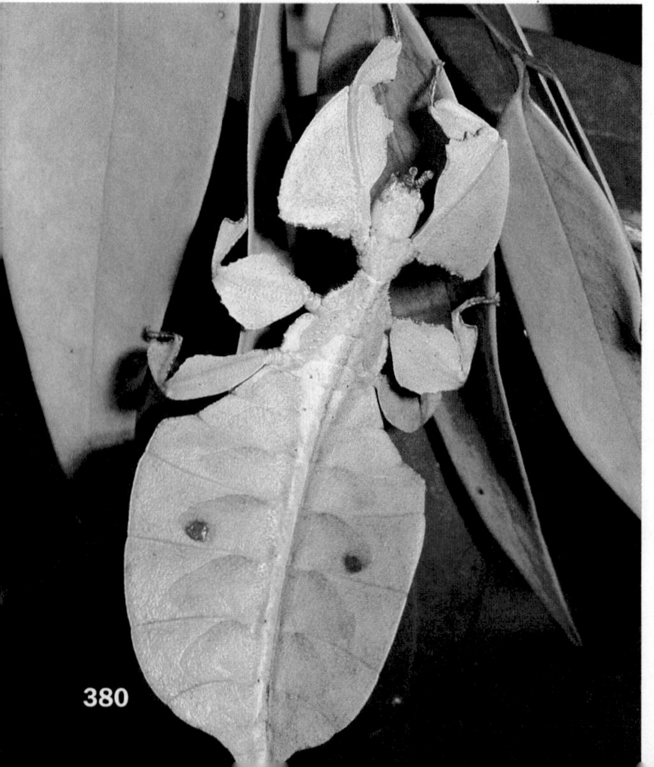

**Figure 5** This insect is well adapted to its environment. ❯ **How does Darwin's theory help explain this observation?**

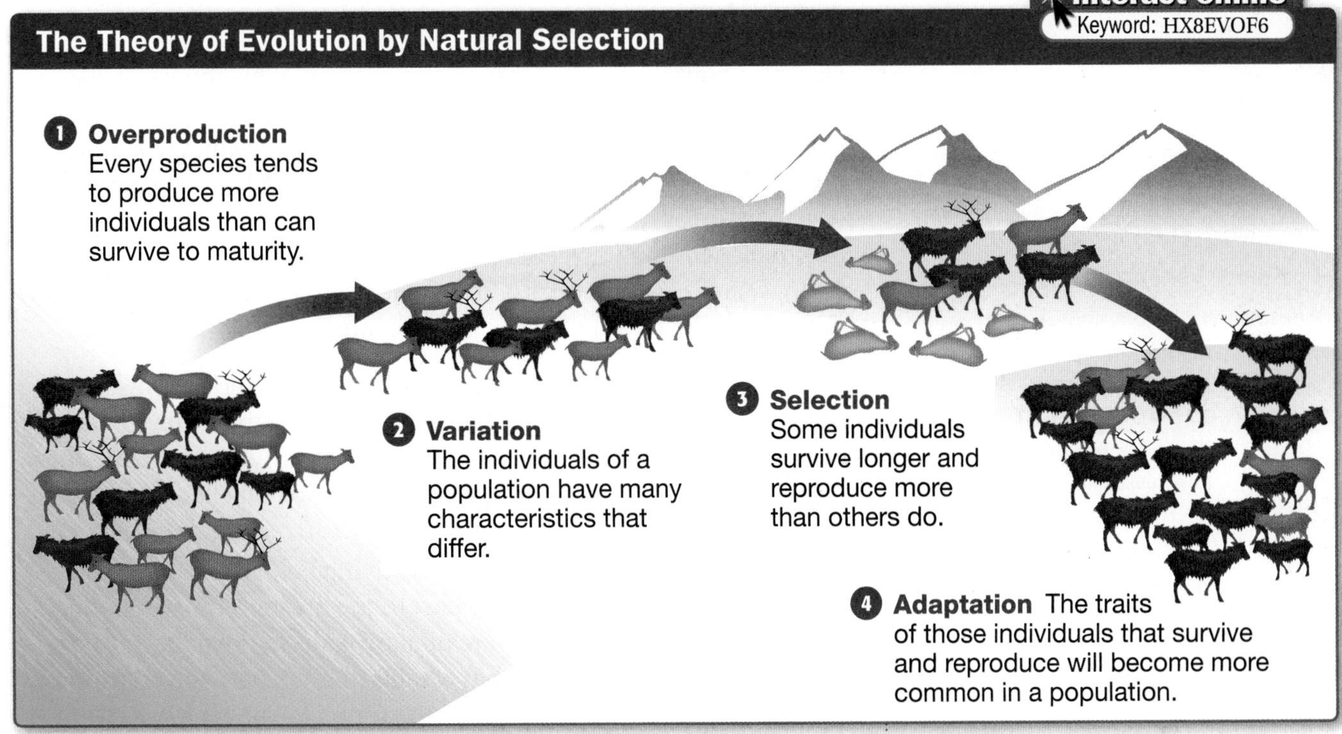

go.hrw.com
interact online
Keyword: HX8EVOF6
The Theory of Evolution by Natural Selection
1 Overproduction Every species tends to produce more individuals than can survive to maturity.
2 Variation The individuals of a population have many characteristics that differ.
3 Selection Some individuals survive longer and reproduce more than others do.
4 Adaptation The traits of those individuals that survive and reproduce will become more common in a population.


**Figure 6** Darwin proposed a logical process by which evolution may occur.
**› Can this process act on individuals?**

**Selection and Adaptation** Darwin's theory explains why living things vary in form yet seem to fit their environment. Each habitat presents unique challenges and opportunities to survive and reproduce. So, each species evolves because of the "selection" of those individuals that survive the challenges or make best use of the opportunities. Put another way, each species becomes *adapted* to its environment as a result of living in it over time. An **adaptation** is an inherited trait that is present in a population because the trait helps individuals survive and reproduce in a given environment.

In sum, Darwin's theory explains evolution as a gradual process of adaptation. Note that Darwin's theory refers to *populations* and *species*—not *individuals*—as the units that evolve. Also, keep in mind that a species is a group of populations that can interbreed.

**Hypothesis or Theory?** Why isn't Darwin's explanation simply called *the theory of evolution*? Why isn't it called a *hypothesis*?

**Publication of the Theory** In 1844, Darwin finally wrote an outline of his ideas about evolution and natural selection. But he showed it only to a few scientists that he knew well. He was afraid that his ideas would be controversial. Then in 1858, he received a letter from another young English naturalist named Alfred Russel Wallace. Wallace asked for Darwin's opinion on a new theory—a theory much like Darwin's! Because of this similarity, Darwin and Wallace jointly presented their ideas to a group of scientists. Darwin was finally motivated to publish a full book of his ideas within the next year.

Darwin's book *On the Origin of Species by Means of Natural Selection* presented evidence that evolution happens and offered a logical explanation of how it happens. Biologists began to accept that evolution occurs and that natural selection helps explain it.

**natural selection** the process by which individuals that are better adapted to their environment survive and reproduce more successfully than less well adapted individuals do

**adaptation** a trait that improves an organism's ability to survive and reproduce; the process of becoming adapted

**› Reading Check** ***Is natural selection the same thing as evolution?***

## What Darwin Explained

Darwin's book was more than an explanation of his theory. It also included a thorough presentation of the evidence that living species evolved from organisms that lived in the past. Darwin had studied much of the data that was available in his time. ❯ **Darwin presented a unifying explanation for data from multiple fields of science.** Today, these sciences include geology, geography, ecology, developmental biology, anatomy, genetics, and biochemistry. Scientists continue to draw upon the power of Darwin's explanations.

**fossil** the trace or remains of an organism that lived long ago, most commonly preserved in sedimentary rock

**The Fossil Record** Have you ever looked at a series of historical maps of a city? You can infer that buildings and streets have been added, changed, or destroyed over time. Similarly, you can infer past events by looking at **fossils,** traces of organisms that lived in the past. All fossils known to science make up the *fossil record.*

**ACADEMIC VOCABULARY**

**infer** to derive by reasoning

Sometimes, comparing fossils and living beings reveals a pattern of gradual change from the past to the present. Darwin noticed these patterns, but he was aware of many gaps in the patterns. For example, Darwin suggested that whales might have evolved from a mammal that lived on land. But at the time, no known fossils were "in between" a land mammal and a whale.

**Figure 7** Darwin once hypothesized that modern whales evolved from ancient, four-legged, land-dwelling, meat-eating mammals. Over the years since, scientists have collected a series of fossil skeletons that support this hypothesis.

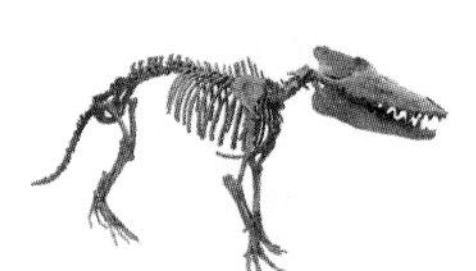

❶ ***Pakicetus* (PAK uh SEE tuhs)** Scientists think that whales evolved from land-dwelling mammals such as those in the genus *Pakicetus.* The fossil skeleton of a pakicetid is shown here. These mammals lived about 50 million years ago, walked or ran on four legs, and ate meat.

❷ ***Ambulocetus* (AM byoo loh SEE tuhs)** Mammals of this genus lived in coastal waters about 49 million years ago. These mammals could swim by kicking their legs and using their tail for balance. They could also use their short legs to waddle on land. They breathed air through their mouth.

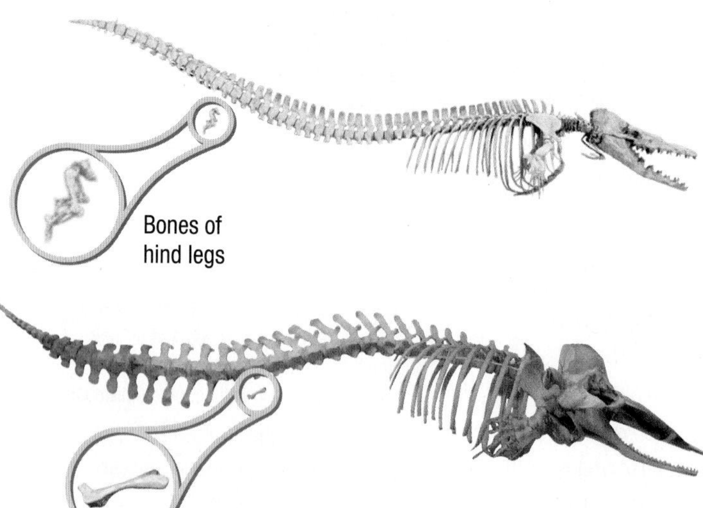


❸ ***Dorudon* (DOHR oo DAHN)** Mammals of this genus lived in the oceans about 40 million years ago. They resembled giant dolphins in the way that they swam and breathed. They had tiny hind limbs that were of no use in swimming.

❹ **Modern Whales** All modern whales have forelimbs that are flippers used for swimming. No whales have hind legs, but some toothed whales have tiny hipbones. All modern whales must come to the surface of the water to breathe through a hole at the top of their head.

Rhea (South America)

Ostrich (Africa)

Emu (Australia)

**Figure 8** Three unique bird species are shown here. Each of these is similar in size, shape, eating habits, and habitat. However, each species lives on a separate continent. › **What does this pattern suggest about evolution?**

Darwin predicted that *intermediate forms* between groups of species might be found. And indeed, many new fossils have been found, such as those shown in **Figure 7.** But the conditions that create fossils are rare, so we will never find fossils of every species that ever lived. The fossil record will grow but will never be complete.

**Biogeography** *Biogeography* is the study of the locations of organisms around the world. When traveling, Darwin and Wallace saw evolution at work when they compared organisms and environments. For example, Darwin saw the similarity of the three species of large birds in **Figure 8.** He found each bird in a similar grassland habitat but on a separate continent. This finding was evidence that similar environments shape the evolution of organisms in similar ways.

Sometimes, geography separates populations. For example, a group of organisms may become separated into two groups living on two different islands. Over time, the two groups may evolve in different patterns. Generally, geologists and biologists have found that the movement of landforms in Earth's past helps to explain patterns in the types and locations of both living and fossil organisms.

**Developmental Biology** The ancestry of organisms is also evident in the ways that multicellular organisms develop from embryos. The study of such development is called *embryology*. This study is interesting because embryos undergo many physical and genetic changes as they develop into mature forms.

Scientists may compare the embryonic development of species to look for similar patterns and structures. Such similarities most likely derive from an ancestor that the species have in common. For example, at some time during development, all vertebrate embryos have a tail. *Vertebrates* are animals that have backbones.

› **Reading Check** ***Why is the fossil record incomplete?***

**Figure 9** Although they look very different from one another on the outside, the forelimbs of most tetrapods (vertebrates that have four limbs) include a similar group of bones. ❯ **What hypothesis does this observation support?**

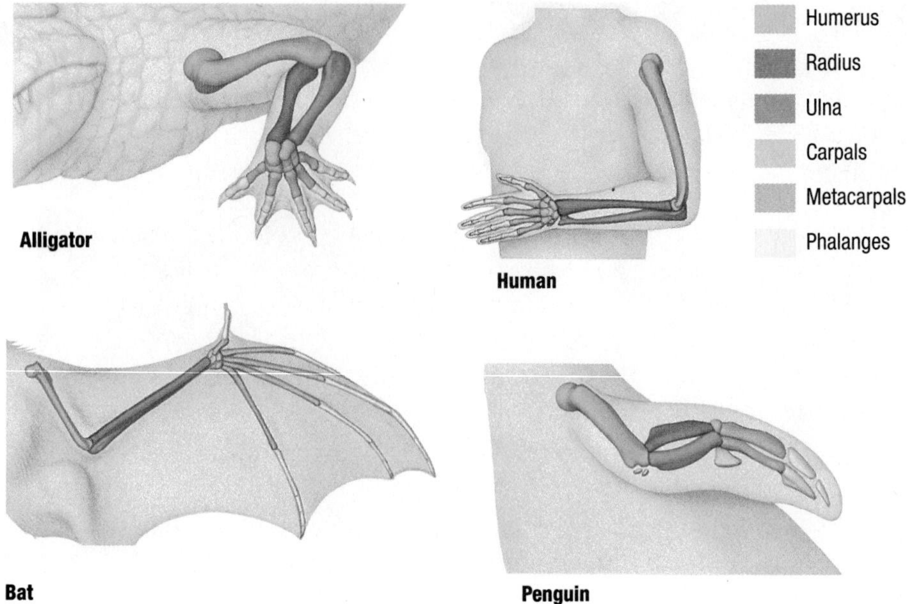


**Anatomy** Another place to observe the results of evolution is inside the bodies of living things. The bodily structure, or *anatomy,* of different species can be compared. Many internal similarities are best explained by evolution and are evidence of how things are related.

For example, the hypothesis that all vertebrates descended from a common ancestor is widely accepted. Observations of the anatomy of both fossil and living vertebrates support this hypothesis. When modern vertebrates are compared, the difference in the size, number, and shape of their bones is clear. Yet the basic pattern of bones is similar. In particular, the forelimbs of many vertebrates are composed of the same basic groups of bones, as **Figure 9** shows. This pattern of bones is thought to have originated in a common ancestor. So, the bones are examples of **homologous** structures, characteristics that are similar in two or more species and that have been inherited from a common ancestor of those species.

**Hemoglobin Comparison**

| Animal with hemoglobin | Amino acids that differ from human hemoglobin |
|---|---|
| Gorilla | 1 |
| Rhesus monkey | 8 |
| Mouse | 27 |
| Chicken | 45 |
| Frog | 67 |
| Lamprey | 125 |

**Figure 10** Scientists have compared the amino acids that make up hemoglobin proteins in several species. Organisms that have fewer differences are more likely to be closely related. ❯ **How does this pattern relate to genetic change?**

**Biochemistry** To explain the patterns of change seen in anatomy, scientists make testable predictions. For example, if species have changed over time, the genes that determine their characteristics should also have changed. Recall that genes can change by mutation and that such change can make new varieties appear. Then, natural selection may "select against" some varieties and so "favor" others.

Scientists have observed that genetic changes occur over time in all natural populations. A comparison of DNA or amino-acid sequences shows that some species are more genetically similar than others. These comparisons, like those in anatomy, are evidence of hereditary relationships among the species. For example, comparing one kind of protein among several species reveals the pattern shown in **Figure 10.** The relative amount of difference is consistent with hypotheses based on fossils and anatomy.

❯ **Reading Check** ***What explains similarities in bone structure?***

## Evaluating Darwin's Ideas

Why was Darwin such an important scientist? ❯ **Darwin's work had three major strengths: evidence of evolution, a mechanism for evolution, and the recognition that variation is important.** Today, Darwin is given credit for starting a revolution in biology.

**Strengths** Darwin was *not* the first to come up with the idea that evolution happens, but he was the first to gather so much evidence about it. He described his most famous book as "one long argument" that evolution is possible. Before publishing, Darwin collected and organized many notes, observations, and examples, such as the illustration shown in **Figure 11.** So, one strength of Darwin's work is that it is supported by, and helps explain, so much data.

Darwin also presented a logical and testable mechanism that could account for the process of evolution. His theory of natural selection was well thought out and convincing to scientists of his time as well as today. It has since become a foundation of biology.

Finally, Darwin changed the way scientists thought about the diversity of life. Before Darwin, most scientists saw species as stable, unchanging things. They classified species based on average appearances and ignored variation. But Darwin showed that variation was everywhere and could serve as the starting point for evolution.

**Weaknesses** Darwin's explanations were incomplete in one major way: He knew very little about genetics. ❯ **Inherited variation was crucial to Darwin's theory of natural selection, yet his theory lacked a clear mechanism for inheritance.** At different times, Darwin proposed or accepted several ideas for such a mechanism, but none of them were correct. He thought about this problem for much of his life.

Darwin never knew it, but Gregor Mendel had begun to solve this problem. However, Mendel's findings about heredity were not widely published until 1900. Those findings opened the door to a new age in the study of evolution. Today, an understanding of genetics is essential to understanding evolution.

❯ **Reading Check** ***What did Darwin do before publishing his ideas?***

**Figure 11** This drawing of a rhea was printed in one of Darwin's books. Darwin collected and organized a large amount of data to help explain his ideas. ❯ **How else did Darwin support his main theory?**

**homologous** (hoh MAHL uh guhs) describes a character that is shared by a group of species because it is inherited from a common ancestor

## Section 2 Review

### ❯ KEY IDEAS

1. **Outline** Darwin's theory of evolution by natural selection. Be sure to include four logical steps.
2. **List** the kinds of data that Darwin helped explain.
3. **Compare** the strengths and weaknesses of Darwin's ideas.

### CRITICAL THINKING

4. **Applying Information** Use the theory of natural selection to explain how the average running speed of a population of zebras might increase over time.
5. **Elaborating on Explanations** Describe how a single pair of seed-eating bird species could have arrived on an island and evolved into an insect-eating species. (Hint: Consider the food available.)

### USING SCIENCE GRAPHICS

6. **Process Cartoon** Create your own version of **Figure 6** in the form of a four-panel cartoon. Choose a unique type of organism to represent the population undergoing natural selection. Also, depict a unique set of traits and limiting conditions for the population.

Section

# 3 Beyond Darwinian Theory

| Key Ideas | Key Terms | Why It Matters |
|---|---|---|
| ➤ How has Darwin's theory been updated?<br>➤ At what scales can evolution be studied? | speciation | The study of evolution was new in Darwin's day, but it is essential to biology today. |

*The Living Environment*
**Standard 4**

**3.1b** New inheritable characteristics can result from new combinations of existing genes or from mutations of genes in reproductive cells.

**3.1f** Species evolve over time. Evolution is the consequence of the interactions of (1) the potential for a species to increase its numbers, (2) the genetic variability of offspring due to mutation and recombination of genes, (3) a finite supply of the resources required for life, and (4) the ensuing selection by the environment of those offspring better able to survive and leave offspring.

**3.1g** Some characteristics give individuals an advantage over others in surviving and reproducing, and the advantaged offspring, in turn, are more likely than others to survive and reproduce. The proportion of individuals that have advantageous characteristics will increase.

**3.1k** Evolution does not necessitate long-term progress in some set direction. Evolutionary changes appear to be like the growth of a bush: Some branches survive from the beginning with little or no change, many die out altogether, and others branch repeatedly, sometimes giving rise to more complex organisms.

Does modern evolutionary theory differ from Darwin's theory? Yes and no. Darwin observed and explained much about the large-scale patterns of biology, but some patterns have yet to be explained. He proposed a logical process (natural selection) for evolution, even though he could not explain evolution at the genetic level. Biology has made great progress since Darwin's time. Modern evolutionary theory relates patterns and processes at many levels.

## Darwin's Theory Updated

Since Darwin's work was published, his theory has been thoroughly investigated. ➤ **Discoveries since Darwin's time, especially in genetics, have been added to his theory to explain the evolution of species.** Some parts of Darwin's theory have been modified, and new parts have been added. But mostly, Darwin's theory has been supported.

The first major advance beyond Darwin's ideas was the rediscovery, in 1900, of Mendel's *laws of heredity*. These ideas opened the door for a genetic explanation of evolution. By the 1940s, scientists began to weave Darwin's theory together with newer studies of fossils, anatomy, genetics, and more. This unification is called the *modern synthesis* of evolutionary theory.

In particular, biologists have learned that evolution can result from processes other than natural selection. For example, survival and reproduction can be limited by chance or by the way that genes work. In the modern view, any or all of these forces may combine with natural selection (as described by Darwin). This synthesis helps explain some of the patterns of evolution that were unexplained by natural selection alone.

**Figure 12** Modern genetic science and Darwin's theory have been united. ➤ **How could this genetic scientist study evolution?**

**Remaining Questions** Some of the most important questions about evolution have been asked only recently. So, many questions are still being investigated, as shown in **Figure 12.** Modern biologists have tentative answers to the following questions:

- **Can an individual evolve?** Darwin correctly inferred that individuals do not evolve. They may respond to outside forces, but individuals do not pass on their responses as heritable traits. Rather, populations evolve when natural selection acts (indirectly) on genes.

Hands-On

# QuickLab

15 min

## Selection Model

In this lab, you will model the process of natural selection. Can you predict the outcome?

### Procedure

1. Work with a partner. Spread out a **handful of small, colored candies** onto a **piece of cloth or paper that has a colorful design.** One person should act as "predator" of the candies while the other uses a **stopwatch** to monitor time and then records the results.
2. The "predator" should use **tweezers** to try to "capture" as many candies as possible within 10 s.
3. Record the results, and switch roles. Repeat 10 times.

### Analysis

1. **Graph** the total number of each color of candy that was "captured." Use a bar graph.
2. CRITICAL THINKING **Evaluating Results** Explain why some colors were "captured" more often than others.
3. CRITICAL THINKING **Forming Hypotheses** Predict the outcome if the background is changed to solid red.

- **Is evolution the survival of the fittest?** Natural selection can act only on the heritable variation that exists in a population. Chance variations do not always provide the best adaptation for a given time and place. So, evolution does not always produce the "fittest" forms, just those that "fit" well enough to leave offspring.
- **Is evolution predictable?** Evolution sometimes results in larger or more-complex forms of life, but this result cannot be predicted. Many forms of life are simple yet successful. For example, bacteria have been abundant for billions of years. In contrast, some complex organisms, such as dinosaurs, have appeared, been successful for a time, and then almost completely disappeared. Mostly, scientists cannot predict the exact path that evolution will take.

## Studying Evolution at All Scales

**Because it affects every aspect of biology, scientists can study evolution at many scales. Generally, these scales range from microevolution to macroevolution, with speciation in between.** Informally, *microevolution* refers to evolution as a change in the genes of populations, whereas *macroevolution* refers to the appearance of new species over time.

**Speciation** The link between microevolution and macroevolution is speciation. **Speciation,** the formation of new species, can be seen as a process of genetic change or as a pattern of change in the form of organisms. Recall that a *species* is a group of organisms that are closely related and that can mate to produce fertile offspring. So, speciation can begin with the separation of populations of the same species. For example, the two kinds of squirrels shown in **Figure 13** seem to be evolving from one species into two because of separation.

**Reading Check** *At what scales can evolution be studied?*

**speciation** (SPEE shee AY shuhn) the formation of new species as a result of evolution

**Figure 13** These squirrels are closely related but are almost different enough to be unique species. Their populations are separated by the Grand Canyon.

**Processes of Microevolution** To study microevolution, we look at the processes by which inherited traits change over time in a population. Five major processes can affect the kinds of genes that will exist in a population from generation to generation. These processes are summarized below. Notice that natural selection is only one of the five. You will learn more about these processes soon.

- **Natural Selection** As you have learned, natural selection can cause an increase or decrease in certain alleles in a population.
- **Migration** *Migration* is the movement of individuals into, out of, or between populations. Migration can change the numbers and types of alleles in a population.
- **Mate Choice** If parents are paired up randomly in a population, a random assortment of traits will be passed on to the next generation. However, if parents are limited or selective in their choice of mates, a limited set of traits will be passed on.
- **Mutation** Mutation can change the numbers and types of alleles from one generation to the next. However, such changes are rare.
- **Genetic Drift** The random effects of everyday life can cause differences in the survival and reproduction of individuals. Because of these differences, some alleles may become more or less common in a population, especially in a small population.

**ACADEMIC VOCABULARY**

**random** without aim or plan; purposeless

**Patterns of Macroevolution** To study macroevolution, we look at the patterns in which new species evolve. We may study the direction, diversity, or speed of change. Patterns of change are seen when relationships between living and fossil species are modeled.

- **Convergent Evolution** If evolution is strongly directed by the environment, then species living in similar environments should evolve similar adaptations. Many examples of this pattern were observed by Darwin and can be seen today.
- **Coevolution** Organisms are part of one other's environment, so they can affect one another's evolution. Species that live in close contact often have clear adaptations to one another's existence, as shown in **Figure 14.**

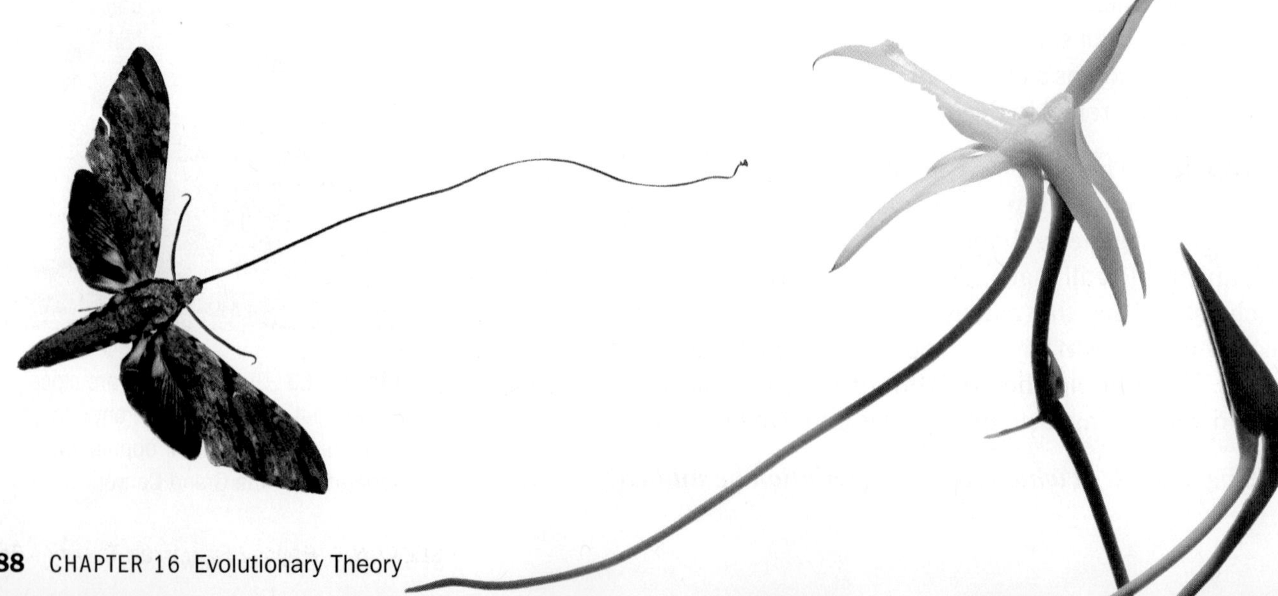

**Figure 14** This moth species and this orchid species have coevolved in a close relationship. The moth feeds exclusively on the orchid, and the orchid's pollen is spread by the moth.

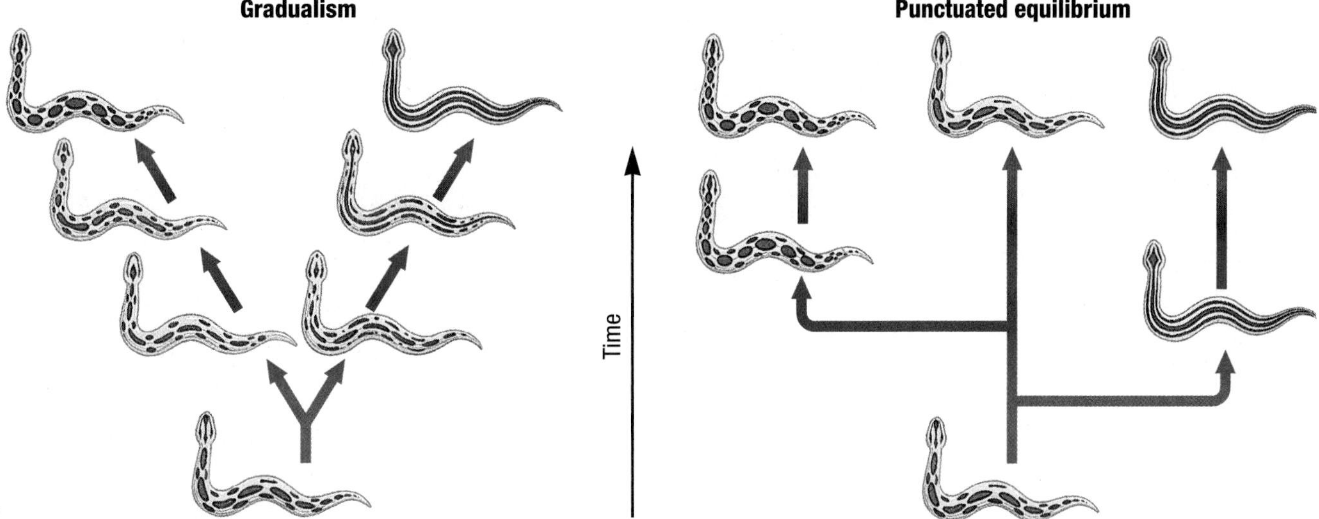


- **Adaptive Radiation** Over time, species may split into two or more lines of descendants, or *lineages*. As this splitting repeats, one species can give rise to many new species. The process tends to speed up when a new species enters an environment that contains few other species. In this case, the pattern is called *adaptive radiation*.
- **Extinction** If all members of a lineage die off or simply fail to reproduce, the lineage is said to be *extinct*. The fossil record shows that many lineages have arisen and radiated, but only a few of their descendants survived and evolved into the species present today.
- **Gradualism** In Darwin's day, the idea of slow, gradual change was new to geology as well as biology. Darwin had argued that large-scale changes, such as the formation of new species, must require many small changes to build up gradually over a long period of time. This model is called *gradualism* and is shown in **Figure 15.**
- **Punctuated Equilibrium** Some biologists argue that species do not always evolve gradually. Species may remain stable for long periods until environmental changes create new pressures. Then, many new species may "suddenly" appear. This model is called *punctuated equilibrium* and is shown in **Figure 15.**

**Figure 15** Two differing models of the pace of evolution have been proposed. **❯ Do these models show microevolution or macroevolution?**

**Taking Notes** Complete your notes summarizing the major concepts from this chapter. Be sure to include microevolution and macroevolution.

## Section 3 Review

### ❯ KEY IDEAS

1. **Describe** how Darwin's ideas have been updated. Be sure to mention the role of natural selection in modern evolutionary theory.
2. **List** the scales at which evolution can be studied, and list the patterns and processes studied.

### CRITICAL THINKING

3. **Arguing Logically** A classmate states that because land animals evolved from fishes and then flying things evolved from walking things, we can predict that future life will evolve to travel in outer space. Write a logical argument against this statement. Be sure to support your argument with examples.

### ALTERNATIVE ASSESSMENT

4. **Who's Who** Make a brochure or poster entitled "Who's Who of Evolutionary Theory." Use reference sources to find basic facts about major evolutionary scientists that lived during or after Darwin's lifetime.

Skills Practice

# Chapter 16 Lab

## Objectives

- Model natural selection.
- Relate favorable mutations to selection and evolution.

## Materials

- construction paper
- meterstick or tape measure
- scissors
- cellophane tape
- soda straws
- marker, felt-tip
- penny or other coin
- die, six-sided

## Safety

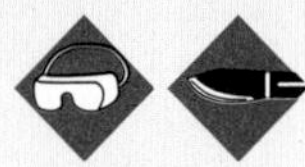

# Natural Selection Simulation

In this lab, you will use a paper model of a bird to model the selection of favorable traits in a new generation. This imaginary bird, the Egyptian origami bird (*Avis papyrus*), lives in dry regions of North Africa. Imagine that the birds must fly long distances between water sources in order to live and reproduce successfully.

## Procedure

### Model Parental Generation

1. Cut a sheet of paper into two strips that are 2 cm × 20 cm each. Make a loop with one strip of paper. Let the paper overlap by 1 cm, and tape the loop closed. Repeat for the other strip.
2. Tape one loop 3 cm from one end of the straw and one loop 3 cm from the other end, as pictured. Use a felt-tip marker to mark the front end of the "bird." This bird represents the parental generation.
3. Test how far your parent bird can fly by releasing it with a gentle overhand pitch. Test the bird twice. Record the bird's average flight distance in a data table like the one shown.

### Model First ($F_1$) Generation

4. Each origami bird lays a clutch of three eggs. Assume that one of the chicks is identical to the parent. Use the parent data to fill in your data table for the first new chick (Chick 1).
5. Make two more chicks (Chick 2 and Chick 3). Assume that these chicks have mutations. Follow Steps A through C for each chick to determine the effects of each mutation.

*Data for All Generations*

| Bird | Coin flip (H or T) | Die throw (1-6) | Anterior wing (cm) | | | Posterior wing (cm) | | | Average distance flown (m) |
|---|---|---|---|---|---|---|---|---|---|
| | | | Width | Circum. | Distance from front | Width | Circum. | Distance from back | |
| Parent | NA | NA | 2 | 19 | 3 | 2 | 19 | 3 | |
| Generation 1 | | | | | | | | | |
| Chick 1 | | | | | | | | | |
| Chick 2 | | | | | | | | | |
| Chick 3 | | | | | | | | | |
| Generation 2 | | | | | | | | | |
| Chick 1 | | | | | | | | | |

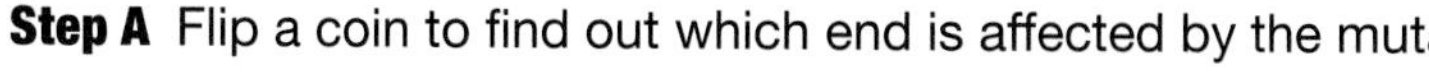

**Step A** Flip a coin to find out which end is affected by the mutation.

Heads = Front wing is affected.

Tails = Back wing is affected.

**Step B** Throw a die to find out how the mutation affects the wing.

⚀ = Wing position moves 1 cm toward the end of the straw.

⚁ = Wing position moves 1 cm toward the middle.

⚂ = Wing circumference increases by 2 cm.

⚃ = Wing circumference decreases by 2 cm.

⚄ = Wing width increases by 1 cm.

⚅ = Wing width decreases by 1 cm.

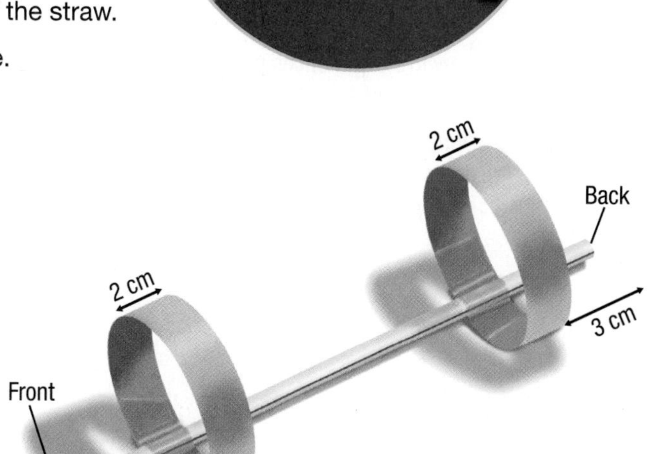


**Step C** If a mutation causes a wing to fall off the straw or makes a wing's circumference smaller than the circumference of the straw, the chick cannot "survive." If such a mutation occurs, record it as "lethal," and then produce another chick.

6. For each new chick, record the mutation and the new dimensions of each wing.

7. Test each bird twice by releasing it with a gentle overhand pitch. Release the bird as uniformly as possible. Record the distance that each bird flies. The most successful bird is the one that flies the farthest.

### Model Subsequent Generations

8. Assume that the most successful bird in the previous generation is the sole parent of the next generation. Using this bird, repeat steps 4–7.

9. Continue to produce chicks and to test and record data for eight more generations.

### Clean Up and Dispose

10. Clean up your work area and all lab equipment. Return lab equipment to its proper place. Dispose of paper scraps in the designated waste container. Wash your hands thoroughly before you leave the lab and after you finish all work.

## Analyze and Conclude

1. **Summarizing Results** Describe any patterns in the evolution of the birds in your model.
2. **Evaluating Models** How well does this lab model natural biological processes? What are the limitations of this model?
3. **Analyzing Data** Compare your data with your classmates' data. Identify any similarities and differences. Try to explain any trends that you notice in terms of the theory of natural selection.

## Extensions

4. **Design an Experiment** Propose a new hypothesis about natural selection that you could test by observing real organisms. Write a brief proposal describing an experiment that could test this hypothesis. Be sure to give your prediction, explain your methods, identify variables, and plan for control groups.

# Chapter 16 Summary

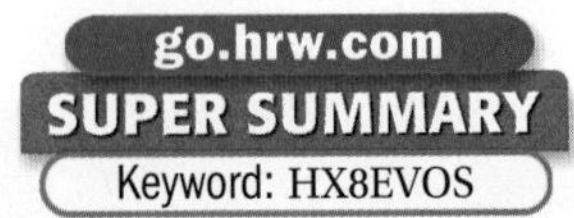


| Key Ideas | Key Terms |
|---|---|
| **1 Developing a Theory** | evolution (375)<br>artificial selection (377) |
| **2 Applying Darwin's Ideas** | natural selection (380)<br>adaptation (381)<br>fossil (382)<br>homologous (384) |
| **3 Beyond Darwinian Theory** | speciation (387) |

## 1 Developing a Theory

- Modern evolutionary theory began when Darwin presented evidence that evolution happens and offered an explanation of how evolution happens.
- Darwin's experiences provided him with evidence of evolution at work.
- Darwin was influenced by ideas from the fields of natural history, economics, and geology.

**Key Terms:** evolution (375), artificial selection (377)

## 2 Applying Darwin's Ideas

- Darwin's theory of evolution by natural selection predicts that over time, the number of individuals that carry advantageous traits will increase in a population.
- Darwin presented a unifying explanation for data from multiple fields of science.
- The strengths of Darwin's work—evidence of evolution, a mechanism for evolution, and the recognition that variation is important—placed Darwin's ideas among the most important of our time. However, Darwin lacked a mechanism for inheritance.

**Key Terms:** natural selection (380), adaptation (381), fossil (382), homologous (384)

## 3 Beyond Darwinian Theory

- Discoveries since Darwin's time, especially in genetics, have been added to his theory to explain the evolution of species.
- Because it affects every aspect of biology, scientists can study evolution at many scales. Generally, these scales range from microevolution to macroevolution, with speciation in between.

**Key Terms:** speciation (387)

Chapter 16

The Living Environment

# Regents Exam Practice

**PART A: Answer all questions in this part.**

*Directions:* For each statement or question, write on your separate answer sheet the number of the word or expression that best completes the statement or answers the question.

**1** The illustration below shows an insect resting on some green leaves. The size, shape, and green color of this insect are adaptations that would most likely help the insect to

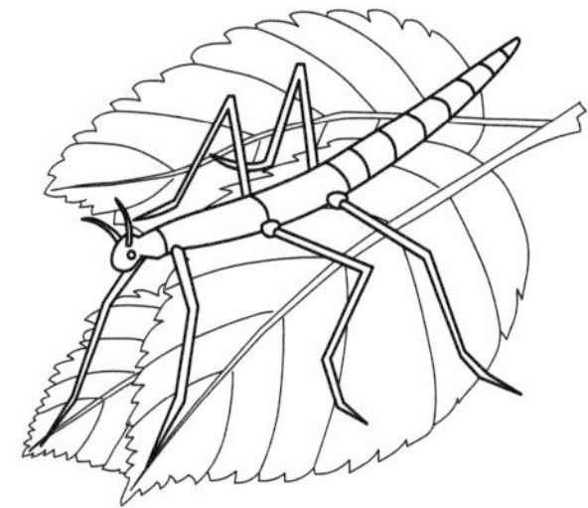

(1) compete successfully with all birds
(2) make its own food
(3) hide from predators
(4) avoid toxic waste materials

**2** Natural selection and its evolutionary consequences provide a scientific explanation for each of the following except

(1) the fossil record
(2) protein and DNA similarities between different organisms
(3) similar structures among different organisms
(4) a stable physical environment

**3** Which factor is least likely to contribute to an increase in the rate of evolution?

(1) presence of genetic variations in a population
(2) environmental selection of organisms best adapted to survive
(3) chromosomal recombinations
(4) a long period of environmental stability

**4** A new chemical was discovered and introduced into a culture containing one species of bacteria. Within a day, most of the bacteria were dead, but a few remained alive. Which statement best explains why some of the bacteria survived?

(1) They had a genetic variation that gave them resistance to the chemical.
(2) They were exposed to the chemical long enough to develop a resistance to it.
(3) They mutated and became a different species after exposure to the chemical.
(4) They absorbed the chemical and broke it down in their digestive systems.

**5** Thousands of years ago, giraffes with short necks were common within giraffe populations. Nearly all giraffe populations today have long necks. This difference could be due to

(1) giraffes stretching their necks to keep their heads out of reach of predators
(2) giraffes stretching their necks so they could reach food higher in the trees
(3) a mutation in genetic material controlling neck size occurring in some skin cells of a giraffe
(4) a mutation in genetic material controlling neck size occurring in the reproductive cells of a giraffe

**6** The teeth of carnivores are pointed and are good for puncturing and ripping flesh. The teeth of herbivores are flat and are good for grinding and chewing. Which statement best explains these observations?

(1) Herbivores have evolved from carnivores.
(2) Carnivores have evolved from herbivores.
(3) The two types of teeth most likely evolved as a result of natural selection.
(4) The two types of teeth most likely evolved as a result of the needs of an organism.

**7** Which factor contributed most to the extinction of many species?

(1) changes in the environment
(2) lethal mutations
(3) inability to evolve into simple organisms
(4) changes in migration patterns

## PART B

**Base your answers to questions 8 and 9 on the diagram below and on your knowledge of biology. Letters *A* through *J* represent different species of organisms. The vertical distances between the dotted lines represent long periods of time in which major environmental changes occurred.**

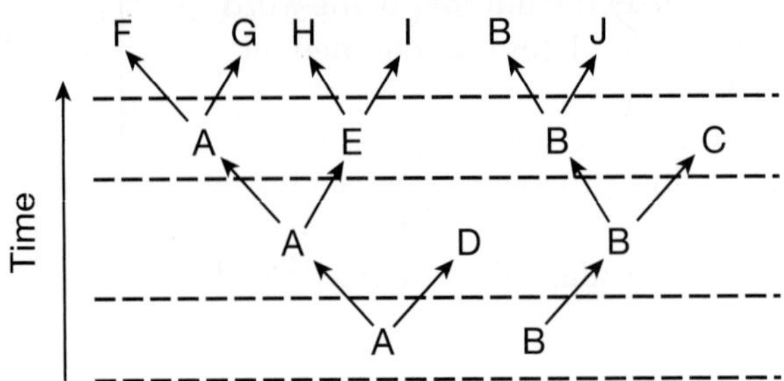


**8** Which species appears to have been most successful in surviving changes in the environment over time?

(1) A
(2) B
(3) C
(4) H

**9** Which species was the first to become extinct?

(1) E
(2) J
(3) C
(4) D

## PART C

**10** Growers of fruit trees have always had problems with insects. Insects can cause visible damage to fruits, making them less appealing to consumers. As a result of this damage, much of the fruit cannot be sold. Insecticides have been useful for controlling these insects, but in recent years, some insecticides have been much less effective. In some cases, insecticides do nothing to stop the insect attacks. Provide a biological explanation for this loss of effectiveness of the insecticides. In your answer, be sure to:

- identify the original event that resulted in the evolution of insecticide resistance in some insects
- explain why the percentage of resistant insects in the population has increased
- describe one alternative form of insect control, other than using a different insecticide, that fruit growers could use to protect their crops from insect attack

**Base your answers to questions 11 and 12 on the information below and on your knowledge of biology.**

A small village was heavily infested with mosquitoes. The village was sprayed weekly with an insecticide for a period of several months. The results of daily counts of the mosquito population are shown in the graph below.

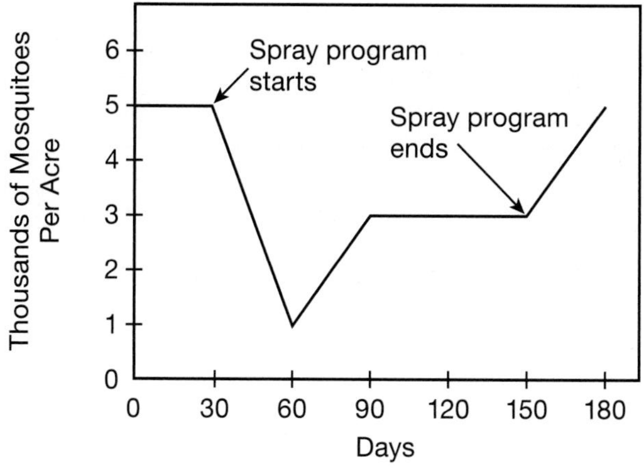


**11** Which statement best explains the decreased effectiveness of the insecticide?

(1) The insecticide caused mutations that resulted in immunity in the mosquito.

(2) Mosquitoes resistant to the insecticide lived and produced offspring.

(3) The insecticide reacted chemically with the DNA of the mosquitoes and was destroyed.

(4) All of the mosquitoes produced antibodies that activated the insecticide.

**12** Which statement best explains why some mosquitoes survived after the first spraying?

(1) Some mosquitoes were adapted to the climatic change that occurred over the several-month period of spraying.

(2) All of the mosquitoes contained DNA unique to the species.

(3) The spraying of the insecticide represented a change in the environment to which all adult mosquitoes were adapted.

(4) A natural variation existed within the mosquito population.

# Chapter 17

# Population Genetics and Speciation

## Preview



## Why It Matters

The fields of ecology, genetics, and evolutionary theory are brought together to understand how genetic changes in populations result in changes to species over time.

Every population, such as this group of banded wood snails, contains variation. Some of this variation can be seen, but much is hidden in DNA.

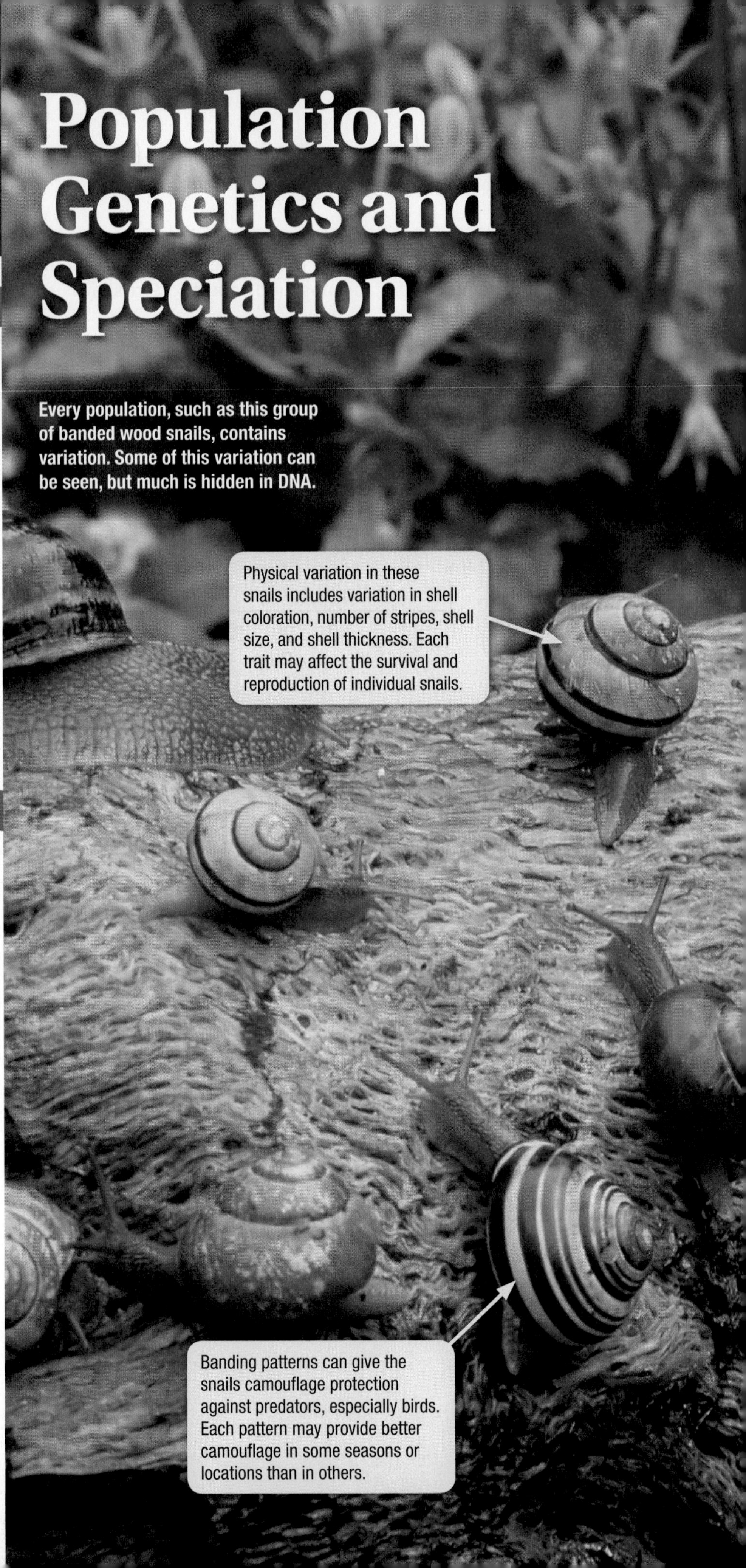

Physical variation in these snails includes variation in shell coloration, number of stripes, shell size, and shell thickness. Each trait may affect the survival and reproduction of individual snails.

Banding patterns can give the snails camouflage protection against predators, especially birds. Each pattern may provide better camouflage in some seasons or locations than in others.

***The Living Environment***

**Standard 4** Students will understand and apply scientific concepts, principles, and theories pertaining to the physical setting and living environment and recognize the historical development of ideas in science.

**Key Idea 2** Organisms inherit genetic information in a variety of ways that result in continuity of structure and function between parents and offspring. ***Major Understandings* - 2.1h**

**Key Idea 3** Individual organisms and species change over time. ***Major Understandings* - 3.1b, 3.1c, 3.1d, 3.1f, 3.1g, 3.1i, 3.1l**

# InquiryLab

15 min

## Normal Variation

4.3.1f

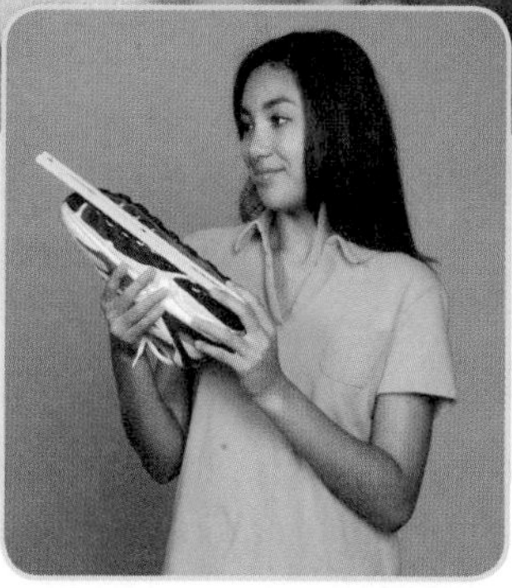

Variation is normal and is evident in all populations. Just look down.

### Procedure

1. Read step 2, and prepare a table for the class data.
2. Use a **ruler or tape-measure** to measure the length of one of **your shoes** to the nearest centimeter. Record this number, as well as your shoe size and gender. Share these data with the class.
3. Make a table of the shoe lengths of everyone in your class. In the first column, record the name of each student. In the second column, record each shoe length.
4. Make a tally of the numbers of each shoe size in your class.

### Analysis

1. **Compare** the table that you made in step 3 to the tally that you made in step 4.
2. **Describe** how the table you made in step 3 could be converted into a tally like that of step 4.
3. **Propose** additional methods by which these kinds of data could be collected and analyzed.
4. **Predict** how the tally that you made in step 4 would change if the data for males were deleted.

Banded wood snails (also called *grovesnails*) eat plant parts and are very common in gardens and moist habitats.

These reading tools can help you learn the material in this chapter. For more information on how to use these and other tools, see **Appendix: Reading and Study Skills.**

## Using Words

**Everyday Words in Science** Many words that we use every day have special meanings in science. For example, *matter* in everyday use is a topic, issue, or problem. In science, *matter* is the substance of which all things are made.

**Your Turn** Make a table like the one shown here.

1. Before you read, write in your own words the everyday meaning of the terms in the table.
2. As you read, fill in the scientific meaning for the terms in the table.

**Everyday Words in Science**

| Word | Everyday Meaning | Science Meaning |
|---|---|---|
| *normal* | | |
| *distribution* | | |
| *drift* | | |
| *fitness* | | |

## Using Language

**General Statements** A general statement often summarizes the features of a group or describes an average or typical feature of members of the group. But if many features are summarized, some individuals in the group probably do not share all of those features. And if an average feature is described, some members of the group will not match the average. So, general statements may be true most of the time, but not always.

**Your Turn** Use what you know about general statements to complete the following tasks.

1. Write a general statement about apples, bananas, tomatoes, and peanuts.
2. List exceptions to the statement "Humans are bigger than monkeys."

## Taking Notes

**Outlining** Outlining is a note-taking skill that helps you organize information. An outline can give you an overview of the topics in a chapter and help you understand how the topics are related.

**Your Turn** Create outlines for each section of this chapter. Start with the example shown here.

1. Copy all of the headings for a section, in order, on a piece of paper.
2. Leave plenty of space between each heading.
3. As you read the material under each heading of a section, write the important facts under that heading on your outline.

*Population Genetics and Speciation*

*Genetic Variation*
- *Population Genetics*
- *Phenotypic Variation*
- *Measuring Variation and Change*
  - *Studying Alleles*
  - *Allele Frequencies*
- *Sources of Genetic Variation*

*Genetic Change*
- *Equilibrium and Change*

Section 1

# Genetic Variation

| Key Ideas | Key Terms | Why It Matters |
|---|---|---|
| ❯ How is microevolution studied?<br>❯ How is phenotypic variation measured?<br>❯ How are genetic variation and change measured?<br>❯ How does genetic variation originate? | population genetics<br>normal distribution | Without variation, evolution cannot occur. |

One of Charles Darwin's contributions to biology was his careful study of variation in characteristics, such as the many flower colors shown in **Figure 1.** As you have learned, Darwin knew that heredity influences characteristics, but he did not know about genes. We now know a great deal about genes. We are able to study and predict the relationships between genotypes and phenotypes. We can also study the genetic variation and change that underlie evolution.

***The Living Environment***
**Standard 4**
**2.1h** Genes are segments of DNA molecules. Any alteration of the DNA sequence is a mutation. Usually, an altered gene will be passed on to every cell that develops from it.
**3.1b** New inheritable characteristics can result from new combinations of existing genes or from mutations of genes in reproductive cells.
**3.1c** Mutation and the sorting and recombining of genes during meiosis and fertilization result in a great variety of possible gene combinations.
**3.1d** Mutations occur as random chance events. Gene mutations can also be caused by such agents as radiation and chemicals. When they occur in sex cells, the mutations can be passed on to offspring; if they occur in other cells, they can be passed on to other body cells only.
**3.1f** Species evolve over time. Evolution is the consequence of the interactions of (1) the potential for a species to increase its numbers, (2) the genetic variability of offspring due to mutation and recombination of genes, (3) a finite supply of the resources required for life, and (4) the ensuing selection by the environment of those offspring better able to survive and leave offspring.

## Population Genetics

Recall that evolution can be studied at different scales, from that of microevolution to macroevolution. And recall that *microevolution* is evolution at the level of genetic change in populations. **❯ Microevolution can be studied by observing changes in the numbers and types of alleles in populations.** The study of microevolution in this sense is **population genetics**. Thus, the studies of genetics and evolution are advancing together. Furthermore, the link from micro-evolution to macroevolution—*speciation*—can be studied in detail.

**population genetics** the study of the frequency and interaction of alleles and genes in populations

**❯ Reading Check** ***What do we now know about heredity that Darwin did not know? (See the Appendix for answers to Reading Checks.)***

**Figure 1** Genetic variation is found in all living things and forms the basis on which evolution acts. **❯ What kinds of variation can be seen in this photograph?**

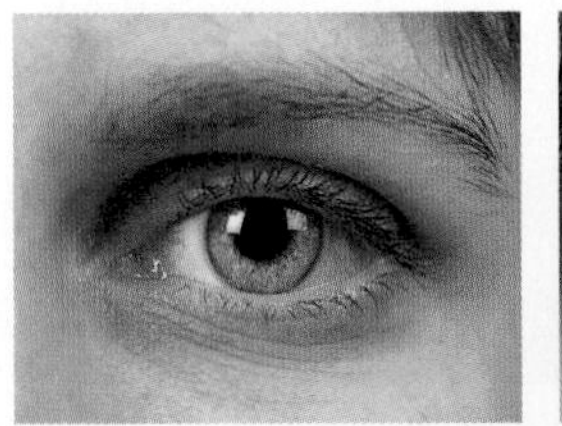
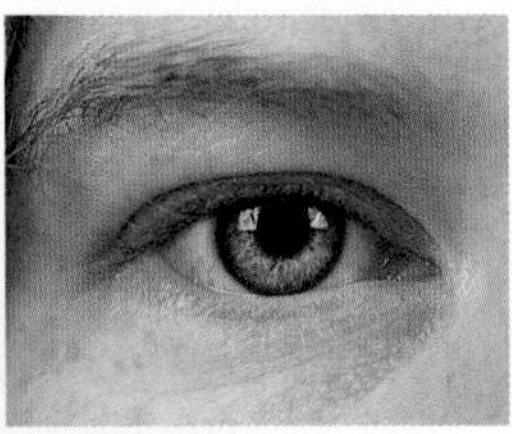
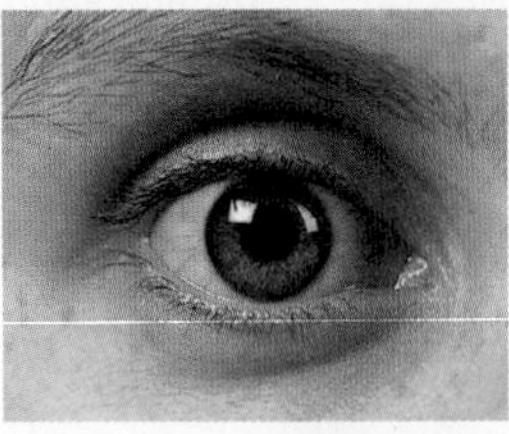
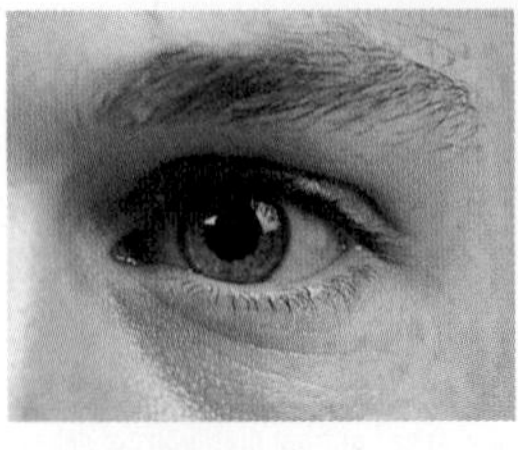
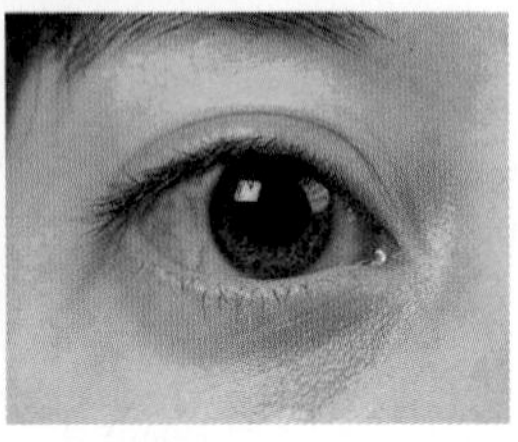

**Figure 2** Eye color is a polygenic character. Different genes control different pigments, which combine to produce various shades of blue, green, or brown.

## Phenotypic Variation

Before anyone understood genetics, the only kind of variation that could be observed and measured was phenotypic variation. Gregor Mendel was the first to suspect that some kind of inherited units determined the various phenotypes that he observed. (In Mendel's day, the term *phenotype* was not used.) We now know that the inherited units are alleles. Mendel used his data on phenotypes to mathematically deduce the ratio of alleles in each individual. Today, we call these ratios *genotypes*.

Mendel's work was made simple by the fact that he studied pea plants with only two phenotypes for each character. As you have learned, genetics is rarely so simple. For example, listing every possible phenotype for height in humans would be difficult. If you compare many humans, you find a range of possible heights, with many slight variations.

The variety of phenotypes that exist for a given character depends on how many genes affect that character. Recall that a character that is influenced by several genes is a *polygenic* character. Human height and human eye color, for example, are polygenic. Polygenic characters may exist as a variety of traits, as shown in **Figure 2,** or a range of trait values, as shown in **Figure 3.**

**❯ Biologists study polygenic phenotypes by measuring each individual in the population and then analyzing the distribution of the measurements.** A *distribution* is an overview of the relative frequency and range of a set of values. Mathematically, a distribution is a tally or a histogram with a smooth line to show the overall pattern of the values.

Often, some values in a range are more common than others. For example, suppose that you were to collect one shoe from each student in your class. If you ordered and grouped the shoes by size, you would probably form a hill-shaped curve such as the one shown in **Figure 3.** This pattern of distribution is called a **normal distribution** or a *bell curve*. "Normal" in this case simply means a tendency to cluster around an average value (mean, median, or mode).

**❯ Reading Check** ***Why do polygenic characters vary so much?***

**Figure 3** Measurements of characters that have a wide range of variation, such as shoe size, can be arranged into a histogram and are likely to form a bell curve. **❯ How do the number of genes for a character relate to its variation?**

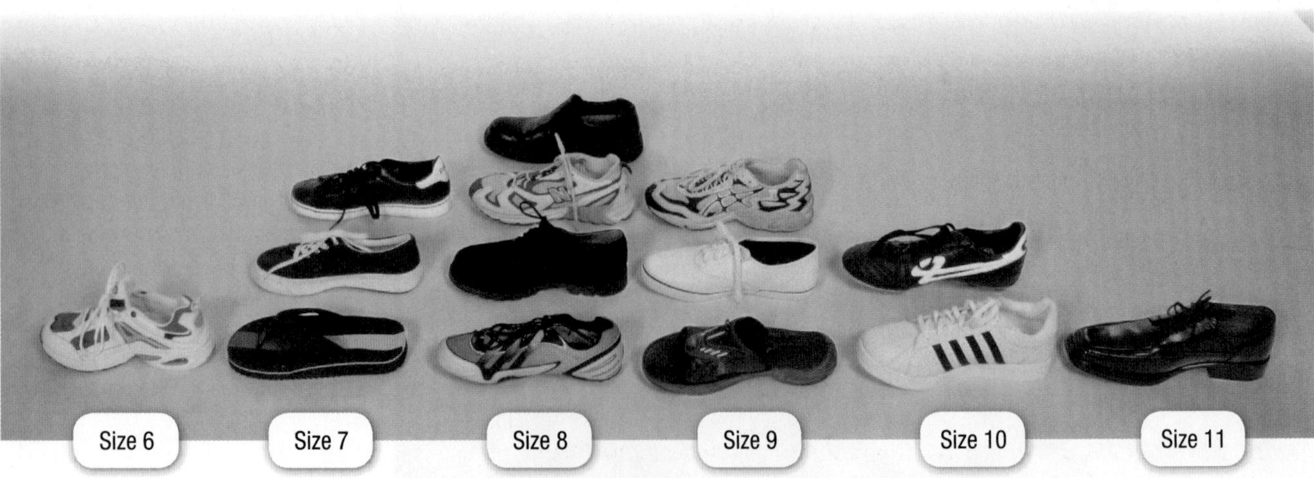

## Math Skills Histograms and Distributions

Suppose that you were to measure the height of every student in your school. You would probably gather a wide range of data. The best way to graph this data would be to use a histogram. A *histogram* is a special kind of bar graph for displaying a range of values. The histogram clearly shows the range of values as well as the values that are most common.

To make a histogram, list the values in order from smallest to largest. Then, determine the *range* from the smallest value to the largest. Draw the *x*-axis of the histogram to cover this range. Then, group the values into convenient intervals. For example, values for height in meters could be grouped into intervals of 0.2 m each, as shown here.

Next, count the number of values that fall within each interval. (Hint: Making a tally of the counts is helpful.) Draw the *y*-axis of the histogram to allow for the highest count in any one interval. Finally, draw bars to show the count for each interval. The bars should touch each other because the graph is showing a continuous range of data.

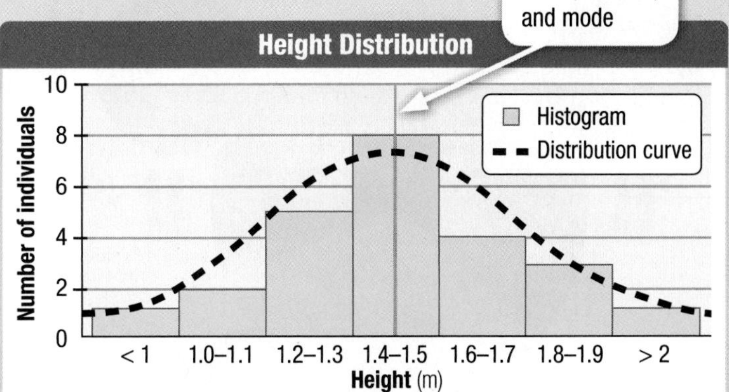


You can use math software to make a histogram and further analyze these kinds of data. For example, you can "fit a curve" to the data, adding a line through the bars to show the general shape, or *distribution*, of the data. You can group the data into smaller or larger intervals, or add or subtract values, and then see changes in the shape of the curve. Finally, you can find the mean, median, and mode(s) of the data. A *normal distribution* will have similar values for the mean, median, and mode.

## Measuring Variation and Change

To study population genetics, we need to study how genes in populations change over time. To measure these changes, we must look at how alleles are passed on from generation to generation as organisms mate and produce offspring. The particular combination of alleles in a population at any one point in time makes up a *gene pool*.

**Studying Alleles** To study genetic variation, we need to estimate the number of alleles in a population. For characters with simple Mendelian inheritance, we can estimate by using simple math combined with our knowledge of genetics. For example, we may start by counting the number of individuals in the population and recording the phenotype of each. Then, we can deduce each genotype.

As you have learned, to keep track of alleles, we can represent alleles with letters. For example, a particular gene may have two alleles, *R* and *r*. In addition, we represent genotypes as combinations of alleles. So, if two alleles exist for a particular gene, then there are three genotypes: *RR*, *Rr*, and *rr*. To compare the numbers of alleles or genotypes, we measure or calculate the frequency of each. **› Genetic variation and change are measured in terms of the frequency of alleles in the gene pool of a population.** A *frequency* is the proportion or ratio of a group that is of one type.

**› Reading Check** *What is the main measure of genetic variation?*

**normal distribution** a line graph showing the general trends in a set of data of which most values are near the mean

**Everyday Words in Science** The word *normal* in science and math is often used to describe measurements that fit within a normal distribution. What does a doctor mean when talking about "normal height" for a person of your age?

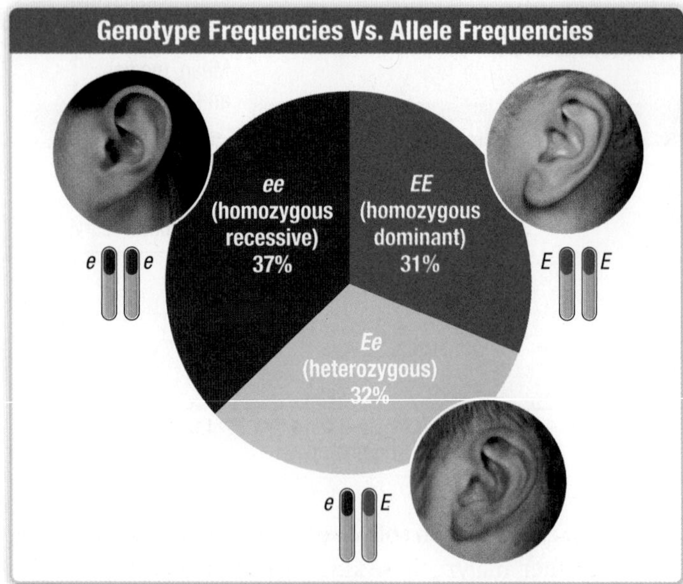


**Figure 4** You cannot see alleles, and you cannot always tell genotype based on phenotype. You have to use math and know dominance patterns to calculate allele frequencies. **Is the dominant allele always the most frequent?**

**Tracking Frequencies** To study genetic change, biologists want to keep track of the frequency of each allele in a population over time. They can keep track in several ways. A direct way would be to detect and count every allele in every individual, which is rarely practical. An indirect way is to use mathematics along with a knowledge of how alleles combine. Recall that alleles combine to form genotypes that, in turn, produce recognizable phenotypes.

To understand the basic mathematics of allele frequencies, consider the simple example shown in **Figure 4.** Human ear lobes have two phenotypes: unattached (free hanging) or attached at the base. The ear lobe character is thought to be controlled by a single gene, and the unattached trait is thought to be dominant. So, the unattached allele is represented as *E,* and the attached allele is represented as *e*. People with attached ear lobes are homozygous recessive, or genotype *ee*. People with unattached ear lobes are either homozygous dominant (*EE*) or heterozygous (*Ee*).

**Genotype Frequencies** Notice how genotype frequencies differ from allele frequencies. Suppose that the population in **Figure 4** consists of 100 people. In this case, 37% of the population, or 37 people, are genotype *ee*; 32 are *Ee*; and 31 are *EE*. Keep in mind that in ratios and percentages, all of the parts add up to one whole, or 100%. So, the sum of genotype frequencies in a population should always be equal to 1 (or 100%). This fact leads to the following equation:

$$(\text{frequency of } EE) + (\text{frequency of } Ee) + (\text{frequency of } ee) = 1$$

Using the numbers in our example, the equation proceeds as follows:

$$0.31 + 0.32 + 0.37 = 1$$

**Allele Frequencies** Similarly, the sum of allele frequencies for any gene must equal 1, as in the following equation:

$$(\text{frequency of } E) + (\text{frequency of } e) = 1$$

or

$$\frac{(\text{count of } E)}{(\text{total})} + \frac{(\text{count of } e)}{(\text{total})} = 1$$

In our example population, there are 94 *E* alleles and 106 *e* alleles, and the total is 200 alleles. The equation proceeds as follows:

$$\frac{94}{200} + \frac{106}{200} = 0.47 + 0.53 = 1$$

As you can see, the frequency of the *E* allele is 0.47, and the frequency of the *e* allele is 0.53. Notice that the dominant allele is not necessarily the most frequent! Also keep in mind that you often cannot tell genotypes by looking at phenotypes. However, you will soon learn how these equations can be used to track changes in populations.

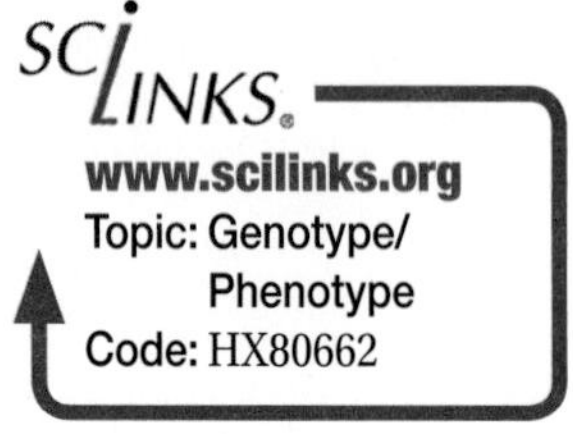

SCINKS.
www.scilinks.org
Topic: Genotype/
Phenotype
Code: HX80662


**Reading Check** ***What is the sum of all allele frequencies for any one gene?***

Hands-On

# QuickLab

15 min

## Alleles: The Next Generation 4.3.1b

Model the allele frequencies in a population over time.

### Procedure

1. Work in a group, which will represent a population. Obtain two colors of marbles (one pair) for each member in the group. Each color will represent a unique allele. Choose one color to be "dominant."
2. Mix the marbles. Each member of the "population" should randomly take two "alleles." Record the resulting genotype and phenotype of each member.
3. Each member should hide one marble in each hand and then randomly exchange one of these "alleles" with another member. Record the resulting genotypes and phenotypes of each member.
4. Repeat the steps to model four more "generations."

### Analysis

1. **Determine** the genotype and phenotype ratios for each "generation." Do the ratios change over time?
2. **Propose** a way to change the ratios in your population from one generation to the next. Propose a way that this change could happen in a real population.

## Sources of Genetic Variation

Evolution cannot proceed if there is no variation. As you have learned, this variation must originate as new alleles. **› The major source of new alleles in natural populations is mutation in germ cells.**

Mutation is important, but it generates new alleles at a slow rate. New alleles first arise in populations as changes to DNA in the sperm and ova (called *germ* cells) of individuals. If a germ cell with a mutation goes on to form offspring, then a new allele is added to the gene pool. Mutations can also occur in nongerm cells (called *somatic* cells), but these mutations are not passed on to offspring.

**Academic Vocabulary**

**generate** produce; bring into being; cause to be

› **Reading Check** ***Why is mutation so important?***

## Section 1 Review

### › KEY IDEAS

1. **Describe** the scope of population genetics.
2. **Explain** how polygenic phenotypes are studied.
3. **Describe** how genetic variation and change can be measured.
4. **Identify** the major source of genetic variation in a population.

### CRITICAL THINKING

5. **Analyzing Concepts** Even in cases of simple Mendelian inheritance within a population, the ratio of phenotypes of a specific character is rarely the same as the ratio of alleles for that character. Explain why these ratios differ.
6. **Applying Logic** Can an individual organism evolve in the Darwinian sense? Explain your answer in terms of genetic variation within populations.

### MATH SKILLS

7. **Distribution Curves** Suppose that **Figure 3** represents the distribution of shoe sizes in a class of twelfth graders. How might the distribution change if the shoes of a class of first graders were added to those of the twelfth graders? Explain your answer.

Section 2

# Genetic Change

| Key Ideas | Key Terms | Why It Matters |
|---|---|---|
| › What does the Hardy-Weinberg principle predict?<br>› How does sexual reproduction influence evolution?<br>› Why does population size matter?<br>› What are the limits of the force of natural selection?<br>› What patterns can result from natural selection? | genetic equilibrium | The mathematics of genetics can be used to make predictions about future generations. |

***The Living Environment***
**Standard 4**

**3.1b** New inheritable characteristics can result from new combinations of existing genes or from mutations of genes in reproductive cells.

**3.1c** Mutation and the sorting and recombining of genes during meiosis and fertilization result in a great variety of possible gene combinations.

**3.1f** Species evolve over time. Evolution is the consequence of the interactions of (1) the potential for a species to increase its numbers, (2) the genetic variability of offspring due to mutation and recombination of genes, (3) a finite supply of the resources required for life, and (4) the ensuing selection by the environment of those offspring better able to survive and leave offspring.

**3.1g** Some characteristics give individuals an advantage over others in surviving and reproducing, and the advantaged offspring, in turn, are more likely than others to survive and reproduce. The proportion of individuals that have advantageous characteristics will increase.

**3.1i** Behaviors have evolved through natural selection. The broad patterns of behavior exhibited by organisms are those that have resulted in greater reproductive success.

You might think that a dominant trait would always be the most common trait in a population. When biologists began to study population genetics, they found that this was not always true.

## Equilibrium and Change

In 1908, the English mathematician G. H. Hardy and the German physician Wilhelm Weinberg began to model population genetics by using algebra and probabilities. They showed that in theory, the frequency of alleles in a population should not change from one generation to the next. Moreover, the ratio of heterozygous individuals to homozygous individuals (the genotype frequencies) should not change. Such a population, in which no genetic change occurred, would be in a state of **genetic equilibrium.**

**Measuring Change** Genetic change in a population can be measured as a change in genotype frequency or allele frequency. A change in one does not necessarily mean a change in the other. For example, as shown in **Figure 5,** the genotype frequencies changed between generations, but the allele frequencies did not.

**Figure 5** Allele frequencies can remain stable while genotype frequencies change.

**Allele Frequencies in Two Generations**

| Genotype frequency | Allele frequency | Generation |
|---|---|---|
| *RR* (red) = 0.5<br>*Rr* (pink) = 0.5<br>*rr* (white)= 0 | *R* = 0.75<br>*r* = 0.25 | 1<br>*RR* *RR* *Rr* *Rr* *RR* *Rr* *Rr* *RR* |
| *RR* (red) = 0.625<br>*Rr* (pink) = 0.25<br>*rr* (white)= 0.125 | *R* = 0.75<br>*r* = 0.25 | 2<br>*RR* *Rr* *rr* *RR* *RR* *Rr* *RR* *RR* |

## Math Skills Hardy-Weinberg Equation

The Hardy-Weinberg principle can be expressed as an equation that can be used to predict stable genotype frequencies in a population.

The equation is usually written as follows:

$$p^2 + 2pq + q^2 = 1$$

| $p^2$ | $2pq$ | $q^2$ | $1$ |
|---|---|---|---|
| (frequency of *RR* individuals) | (frequency of *Rr* individuals) | (frequency of *rr* individuals) | (sum of all frequencies) |

Recall that the sum of the genotype frequencies in a population must always equal 1.

By convention, the frequency of the more common of the two alleles is referred to as $p$, and the frequency of the rarer allele is referred to as $q$.

Individuals that are homozygous for allele *R* occur at a frequency of $p$ times $p$, or $p^2$. Individuals that are homozygous for allele *r* occur at the frequency of $q$ times $q$, or $q^2$.

Heterozygotes have one copy of *R* and one copy of *r*, but heterozygotes can occur in two ways—*R* from the father and *r* from the mother, or *r* from the father and *R* from the mother. Therefore, the frequency of heterozygotes is $2pq$.

**Hardy-Weinberg Principle** Hardy and Weinberg made a mathematical model of genetic equilibrium. This model is the basis of the *Hardy-Weinberg principle.* **› The Hardy-Weinberg principle predicts that the frequencies of alleles and genotypes in a population will not change unless at least one of five forces acts upon the population.**

**genetic equilibrium** a state in which the allele frequencies of a population remain in the same ratios from one generation to the next

**Forces of Genetic Change** In reality, populations are subject to many forces and undergo genetic change constantly. **› The forces that can act against genetic equilibrium are gene flow, nonrandom mating, genetic drift, mutation, and natural selection.**

**Gene Flow** *Gene flow* occurs when genes are added to or removed from a population. Gene flow can be caused by *migration,* the movement of individuals from one population to another, as shown in **Figure 6.** Each individual carries genes into or out of the population, so genetic frequencies may change as a result.

**Nonrandom Mating** In sexually reproducing populations, any limits or preferences of mate choice will cause nonrandom mating. If a limited set of genotypes mates to produce offspring, the genotype frequencies of the population may change.

**Genetic Drift** Chance events can cause rare alleles to be lost from one generation to the next, especially when populations are small. Such random effects on allele frequencies are called *genetic drift.* The allele frequencies are changed directly and genotype frequencies change as a result.

**Mutation** A mutation can add a new allele to a population. Allele frequencies are changed directly, if only slightly.

**Natural Selection** Natural selection acts to eliminate individuals with certain traits from a population. As individuals are eliminated, the alleles for those traits may become less frequent in the population. Thus, both allele and genotype frequencies may change.

**› Reading Check** *What can cause gene flow?*

**Figure 6** These caribou are migrating from one place to another. If they meet other groups of caribou and interbreed, gene flow may occur.

Figure 7 Sexual selection favors the development of extreme phenotypic traits in some species. The vibrant red stripe on the blue muzzle of this male mandrill baboon does not appear in females.

## Sexual Reproduction and Evolution

Recall that sexual reproduction creates chances to recombine alleles and thus increase variation in a population. So, sexual reproduction has an important role in evolution. **Sexual reproduction creates the possibility that mating patterns or behaviors can influence the gene pool of a population.** For example, in animals, females sometimes select mates based on the male's size, color, ability to gather food, or other characteristics, as shown in **Figure 7.** This kind of behavior is called *sexual selection* and is an example of nonrandom mating.

Another example of nonrandom mating is *inbreeding*, in which individuals either self-fertilize or mate with others like themselves. Inbreeding tends to increase the frequency of homozygotes, because a smaller pool of alleles is recombined. For example, populations of self-fertilizing plants consist mostly of homozygotes. However, inbreeding does not change the overall frequency of alleles. Inbreeding is more likely to occur if a population is small.

## Population Size and Evolution

Population size strongly affects the probability of genetic change in a population. **Allele frequencies are more likely to remain stable in large populations than in small populations.** In a small population, the frequency of an allele can be quickly reduced by a chance event. For example, a fire or drought can reduce a large population to a few survivors. At that point, each allele is carried in a few individuals. The loss of even one individual from the population can severely reduce an allele's frequency. So, a particular allele may disappear in a few generations, as shown in **Figure 8.** This kind of change is called *genetic drift* because allele frequencies drift around randomly. The force of genetic drift is strongest in small populations. In a larger population, alleles may increase or decrease in frequency, but the alleles are not likely to disappear.

**Reading Check** *What is the genetic effect of inbreeding?*

Figure 8 Alleles are more likely to be lost from smaller populations. So, variation tends to decrease over time in smaller populations but not in larger populations.

go.hrw.com

interact online

Keyword: HX8POPF8

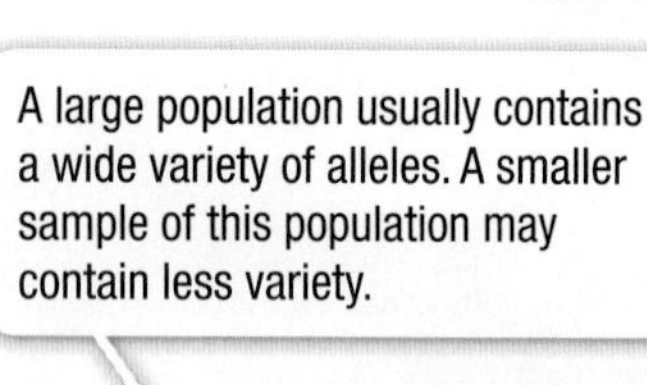

A large population usually contains a wide variety of alleles. A smaller sample of this population may contain less variety.

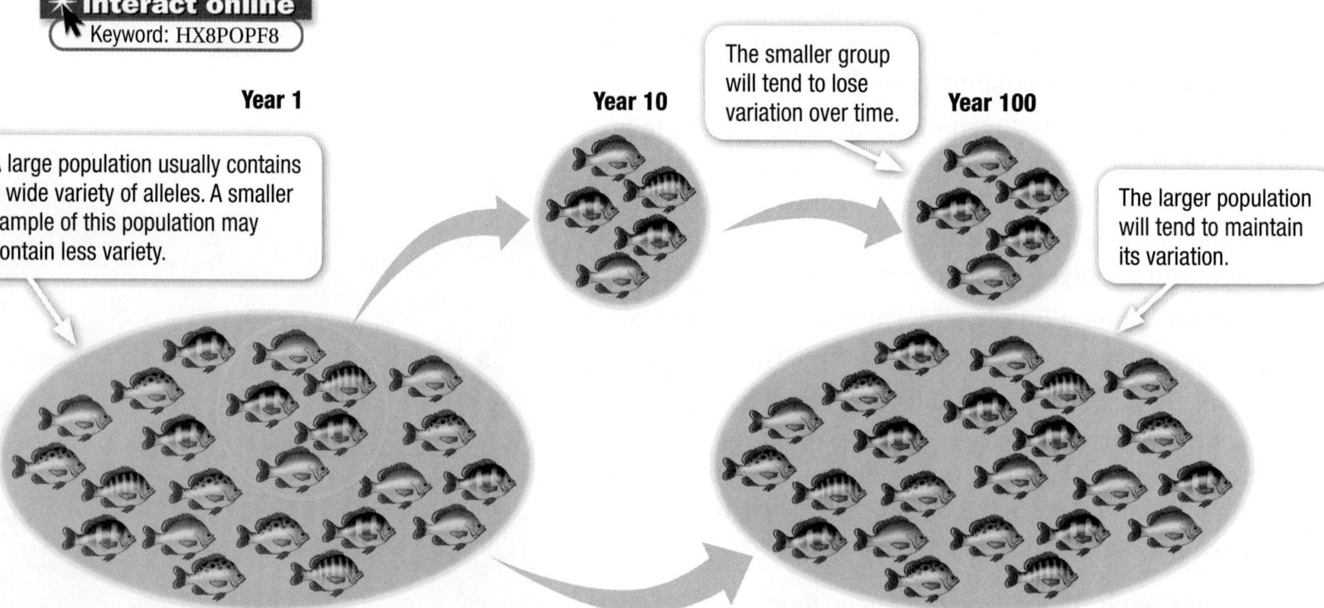

Year 1
Year 10
The smaller group will tend to lose variation over time.
Year 100
The larger population will tend to maintain its variation.

Data

QuickLab

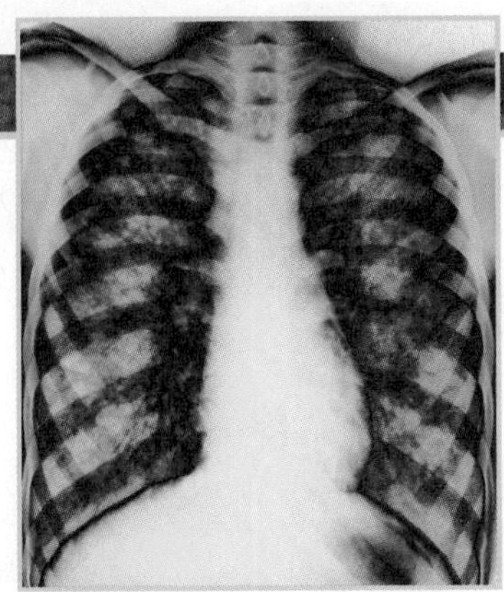
Lungs of a person with cystic fibrosis

15 min

## Genetic Risk Assessment  4.2.2e

How can the Hardy-Weinberg equation be used? It can be used to predict the risk of genetic disorders in a population. For example, medical professionals may know how many people have been diagnosed with a genetic disorder. From this information, they can predict how many people are at risk of passing on the disorder.

### Procedure

1. Consider these facts: Cystic fibrosis (CF) is a disorder that occurs in 1 out of every 2,500 Caucasians in North America. CF is caused by a recessive allele.
2. Use the Hardy-Weinberg equation to predict the percentage of carriers of the allele that causes CF.

### Analysis

1. **Calculate** the frequency of the recessive allele.
2. **Calculate** the frequency of the dominant allele.
3. **Calculate** the frequency of carriers (heterozygotes).
4. **Determine** how many of every 1,000 Caucasian North Americans are likely to carry the cystic fibrosis allele.

## Natural Selection and Evolution

Recall that Charles Darwin proposed natural selection as a mechanism that could drive evolution. Scientists have studied many examples of natural selection in action.

**How Selection Acts** Keep in mind that the process of natural selection is a result of the following facts.

- **All populations have genetic variation.** Any population has an array of individuals that differ slightly from one another in genetic makeup. Although this variation may be obvious in humans, variation also exists in species whose members may appear identical, such as a species of bacteria.
- **Individuals tend to produce more offspring than the environment can support.** Individuals of a population often struggle to survive, whether competing with one another or not.
- **All populations depend upon the reproduction of individuals.** Some biologists have noted that "evolutionary fitness is measured in grandchildren." The statement means that an individual must survive to reproduce, and also produce offspring that can reproduce, to pass its genes on to future generations.

**Genetic Results of Selection** The result of natural selection is that the frequency of an allele may increase or decrease depending on the allele's effects on survival and reproduction. Natural selection causes deviations from genetic equilibrium by directly changing the frequencies of alleles. Although natural selection is not the only force of evolution, it is a powerful force.

**Reading Check** *How is "fitness" measured in evolutionary terms?*

SCILINKS.
www.scilinks.org
Topic: Natural Selection
Code: HX81016

**ACADEMIC VOCABULARY**

**deviate** to turn aside; to diverge or differ

**Figure 9** Crayfish species exist in a variety of colorations. In many cases, the coloration helps the crayfish hide from predators or attract mates. But for crayfish species that live in lightless caves, having color gives no fitness advantage. ❯ **What might happen to a colorless crayfish placed in a well-lit pond?**

**Why Selection Is Limited** The key lesson that scientists have learned about evolution by natural selection is that the environment does the selecting. If the environment changes in the future, the set of characteristics that are most adaptive may change. For example, each of the animals shown in **Figure 9** is adapted to a specific environment and may not be able to survive if placed in another environment.

Natural selection is limited by nature. ❯ **Natural selection acts only to change the relative frequency of alleles that exist in a population.** Natural selection cannot direct the creation of new alleles, nor will it necessarily delete every allele that is not adaptive. So, natural selection does not create perfectly adapted organisms.

**Indirect Force** Natural selection does not act directly on genes. It merely allows individuals who express favorable traits to reproduce and pass those traits on to their offspring. Darwin's idea of natural selection, stated in modern terms, is that ❯ **natural selection acts on genotypes by removing unsuccessful phentoypes from a population.** Biologists say that certain phenotypes are "selected against" and that certain genotypes are thus "favored."

**Role of Mutation** Think about how natural selection might operate on a new allele that has arisen by mutation. At first, the mutation may make no difference. Even if the mutation results in a nonfunctional protein, the cell may have a functional copy of the original gene as its second allele. However, the new, nonfunctioning version could be passed on as a recessive allele. This kind of mutation is the probable origin of many recessive genetic disorders. Genetic disorders can persist in populations because only those traits that are expressed can be targets of natural selection.

**General Statements** List possible exceptions to the statement "Natural selection removes unsuccessful phenotypes from a population."

**Natural Selection and Behavior** Behaviors can evolve in much the same way that physical traits do. Natural selection will favor behaviors that are influenced by genes and that help individuals to survive, reproduce, and pass on their genes. The effects of selection can often be seen in behaviors related to courtship, mating, and caring for offspring and close relatives. Selection will favor any behavior that helps an individual to pass on genes to future generations.

## Patterns of Natural Selection

Recall that many traits, such as human height, have a bell-curve distribution in natural populations. When natural selection acts on polygenic traits, it essentially acts to eliminate some part of the bell curve.

**› Three major patterns are possible in the way that natural selection affects the distribution of polygenic characters over time. These patterns are directional selection, stabilizing selection, and disruptive selection, as Figure 10 illustrates.**

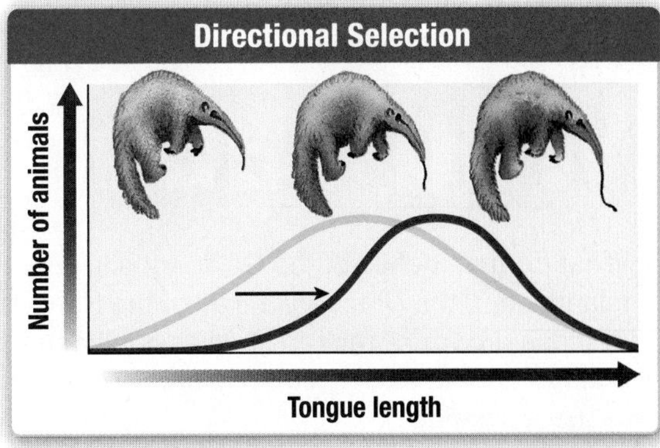


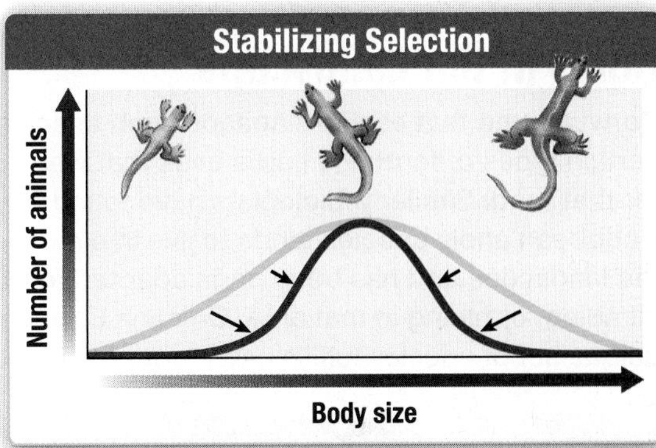


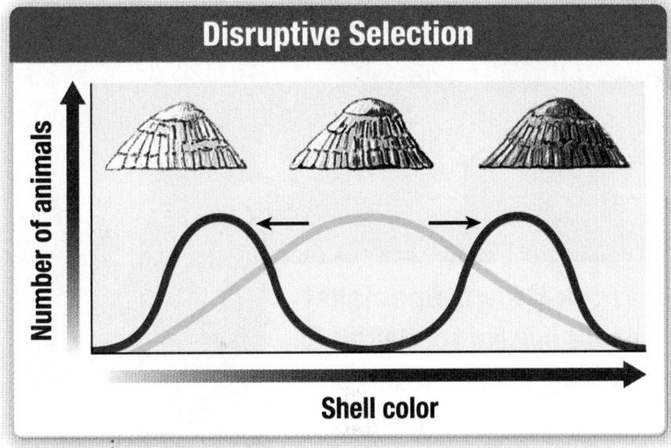


**Figure 10** Selection can shift a distribution from an original bell curve (green) toward a new shape (purple).

**Directional Selection** In *directional selection,* the "peak" of a normal distribution moves in one direction along its range. In this case, selection acts to eliminate one extreme from a range of phenotypes. Thus, the alleles for the extreme phenotype become less common in the population. This pattern of selection is often seen in the evolution of single-gene traits, such as pesticide resistance in insects.

**Stabilizing Selection** In *stabilizing selection,* the bell-curve shape becomes narrower. In this case, selection eliminates individuals that have alleles for any extreme type. So, the ratio of intermediate phenotypes increases. In other words, this pattern of selection tends to "stabilize" the average by favoring a narrow range of phenotypes. Stabilizing selection is very common in nature.

**Disruptive Selection** In *disruptive selection,* the bell curve is "disrupted" and pushed apart into two peaks. In this case, selection acts to eliminate individuals with average phenotype values. Each peak is pushed in an opposite direction, away from the average. The result is increasingly distinct or variable phenotypes in the population. Mathematically, the new distribution is said to have two mode values, each of which differs from the mean value.

**› Reading Check** ***Which form of selection increases the range of variation in a distribution?***

### Section 2 Review

**› KEY IDEAS**

1. **Restate** the Hardy-Weinberg principle in your own terms.
2. **Relate** sexual reproduction to evolutionary forces.
3. **Explain** why a small population is subject to genetic drift.
4. **Describe** the limits of the force of natural selection.
5. **List** the patterns that can result from natural selection acting on polygenic traits.

**CRITICAL THINKING**

6. **Comparing Concepts** In what way is the genetic effect of nonrandom mating similar to the genetic effect of gene flow?
7. **Reasoning Opinions** Are all organisms perfectly adapted for their habitat? Explain.

**USING SCIENCE GRAPHICS**

8. **Prediction** Redraw each of the graphs in **Figure 10.** Use as examples birds with a range of beak sizes. Describe possible situations that would cause each pattern of selection.

Why It Matters

# Wild Laboratories

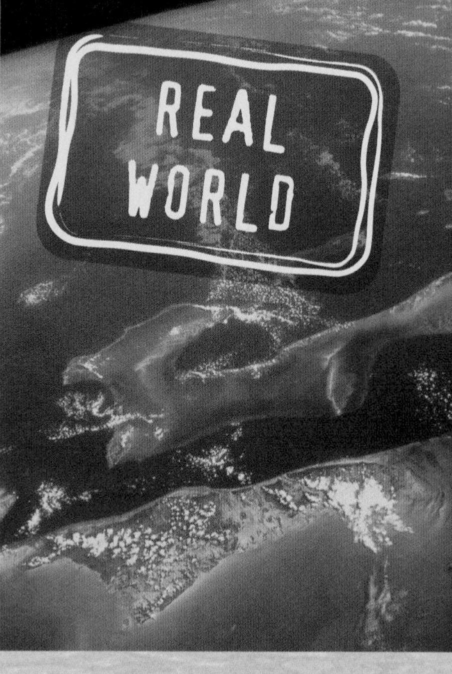


What do the finches of the Galápagos Islands, the anole lizards of the Caribbean Islands, and the *Drosophila* flies of the Hawaiian Islands have in common? Each of these groups of related species has been extensively studied by evolutionary biologists. And each group has undergone a similar pattern of evolution on each group of islands.

## Roles in the Landscape

Darwin found that each Galápagos finch species ate certain types of food and had a beak that was adapted for that food. Similarly, biologists have found that each Caribbean anole species tends to live in a certain part of the landscape and has body parts adapted for running, climbing, or hiding in that area. On each Caribbean island, a unique set of species fulfills each "specialist" role.

**Trunk-Ground Specialist** *Anolis lineatopus* specializes in running along tree trunks and the ground.

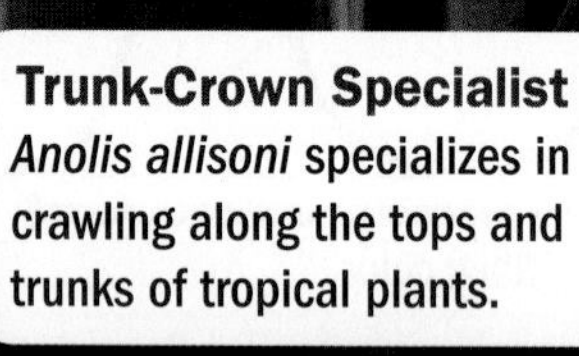

**Trunk-Crown Specialist** *Anolis allisoni* specializes in crawling along the tops and trunks of tropical plants.

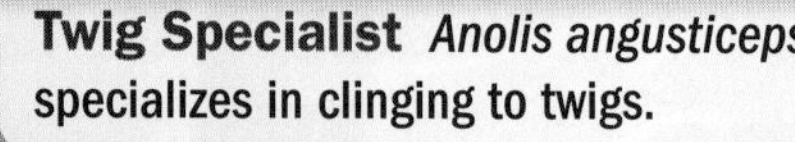

**Twig Specialist** *Anolis angusticeps* specializes in clinging to twigs.

**Grass-Bush Specialist** *Anolis bahorucoensis* specializes in clinging to grass and stems.

**Quick Project** Find out how many species of anoles have been identified in the Carribbean islands as compared with the total number of anole species worldwide. Likewise, find out the number of Hawaiian species of flies in the family Drosophilidae.

Section
# 3 Speciation

| Key Ideas | Key Terms | Why It Matters |
|---|---|---|
| ❯ How can species be defined?<br>❯ How do we know when new species have been formed?<br>❯ Why is studying extinction important to understanding evolution? | reproductive isolation<br>subspecies | How we define species relates to how we study evolution and ecology. |

All of the beetles in **Figure 11** belong to the same species, but each looks different. Identifying species or telling species apart is often difficult. Part of the difficulty lies in the very definition of *species*.

***The Living Environment***
**Standard 4**
**3.1l** Extinction of a species occurs when the environment changes and the adaptive characteristics of a species are insufficient to allow its survival. Fossils indicate that many organisms that lived long ago are extinct. Extinction of species is common; most of the species that have lived on Earth no longer exist.

## Defining Species

Since the days of Darwin, scientists have understood that species are not permanent, stable things. And thanks to Mendel, scientists have learned that genetics underlie the variation and change in species. With this knowledge, they have reconsidered the very definition of *species*. ❯ **Today, scientists may use more than one definition for *species*. The definition used depends on the organisms and field of science being studied.** Increasingly, scientists want to do more than name and describe things—they want to know how things are related.

As you have learned, a *species* is generally defined as a group of natural populations that can interbreed. This definition is based on the *biological species concept*, which adds the requirement that the interbreeding produce healthy, fertile offspring. Applying this concept, any populations that do not share future offspring could be considered separate species.

However, the biological species concept cannot be applied to all organisms. It does not apply to those that reproduce asexually or that are known only from fossils. And any form of reproduction may be difficult to confirm. So, species may instead be defined based on their physical features, their ecological roles, and their genetic relatedness.

❯ **Reading Check** *Why is a species hard to define?*

**Figure 11** How many species of beetles are in this photo? Just one!
❯ **What problems arise when defining species based on appearances?**

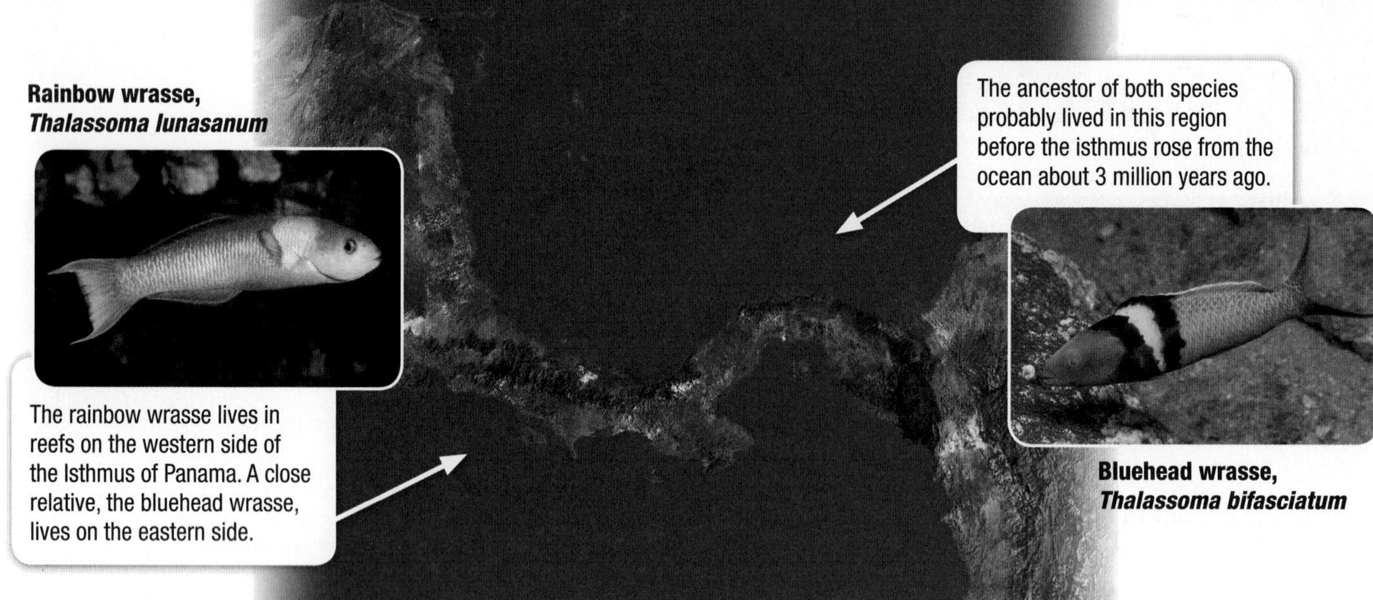

Rainbow wrasse,
*Thalassoma lunasanum*
The ancestor of both species probably lived in this region before the isthmus rose from the ocean about 3 million years ago.
The rainbow wrasse lives in reefs on the western side of the Isthmus of Panama. A close relative, the bluehead wrasse, lives on the eastern side.
Bluehead wrasse,
*Thalassoma bifasciatum*


**Figure 12** These two species probably evolved from a single species that was separated into two groups by geographic change. **❯ What other mechanisms can isolate species?**

## Forming New Species

Each population of a single species lives in a different place. In each place, natural selection acts on the population and tends to result in offspring that are better adapted to the environment. If the environments differ, the adaptations may differ. The accumulation of differences between populations is called *divergence* and can lead to the formation of new species.

Recall that *speciation* is the process of forming new species by evolution from preexisting species. Speciation rarely occurs overnight; it usually occurs in stages over generations. **❯ Speciation has occurred when the net effects of evolutionary forces result in a population that has unique features and is reproductively isolated.**

**reproductive isolation** a state in which a population can no longer interbreed with other populations to produce future generations

**subspecies** a taxonomic classification below the level of species; refers to populations that differ from, but can interbreed with, other populations of the same species

**Reproductive Isolation** Recall that the biological species concept defines species as interbreeding groups. Thus, if two groups stop interbreeding, they take a step toward speciation. **Reproductive isolation** is a state in which two populations can no longer interbreed to produce future offspring. From this point on, the groups may be subject to different forces, so they will tend to diverge over time.

Through divergence over time, populations of the same species may differ enough to be considered subspecies. **Subspecies** are simply populations that have taken a step toward speciation by diverging in some detectable way. This definition is imprecise because reproductive isolation is only apparent after the passage of time.

**Mechanisms of Isolation** Divergence and speciation can happen in many ways. Any of the following mechanisms may contribute to the reproductive isolation of populations.

- **Geography** A physical barrier, such as the one shown in **Figure 12,** may arise between populations. Such a barrier could prevent interbreeding. Over time, if the populations diverge enough, they will probably not interbreed even if the barrier is removed.

- **Ecological Niche** Recall that the *niche* of a species is the role that the species has in its environment, including all of its interactions with other species. Divergence can occur when populations use different niches. The divergence of multiple lineages into many new species in a specific area and time is called *adaptive radiation.*
- **Mating Behavior and Timing** Many species that sexually reproduce have specific behaviors for attracting mates, such as a pattern of sounds or actions. Some undergo mating at specific times or in response to environmental events. If two populations develop differences in these behaviors, they may no longer attract each other for mating. This mechanism seems to be responsible for the species divergence shown in **Figure 13.**
- **Polyploidy** Recall that a *polyploid* organism has received a duplicate set of chromosomes by accident. A polyploid individual may be reproductively isolated because it cannot pair gametes with others from the original population. However, it may reproduce by vegetative growth, self-fertilize, or find a polyploid mate. In these cases, a new species can arise rapidly. Polyploidy has been observed in many plant species.
- **Hybridization** In some cases, two closely related species may come back into contact with each other and attempt to mate. The offspring of such a mating are called *hybrids.* In cases in which the two parent species are sufficiently diverged from each other, their offspring may be sterile. For example, a mule is a sterile hybrid of a horse and a donkey. Another possibility is that hybrid offspring may not be well adapted to the environment of either parent. Finally, if the parents have many genetic differences, the offspring may not develop successfully. However, there are also many cases in which hybridization leads to new and successful species.

**› Reading Check** ***Is hybridization always successful?***

**Outlining** Complete your outline for this chapter. Be sure to include each of the headings on this page, such as "Polyploidy" and "Hybridization." When you finish the chapter, review your outline and add notes to any heading whose meaning is unclear to you.

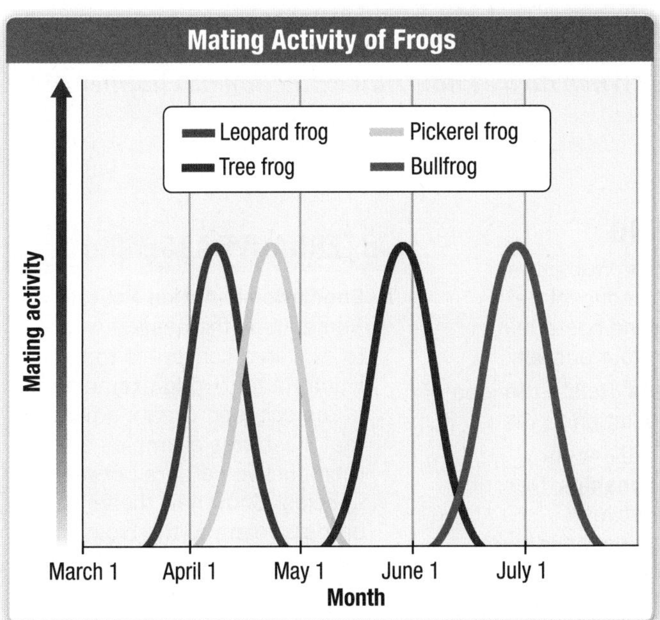


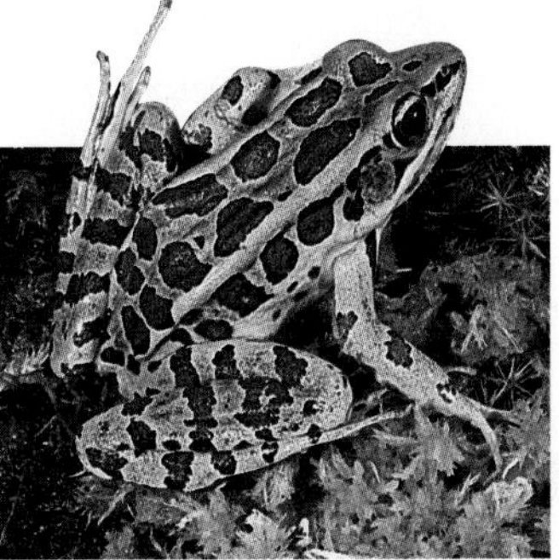

Pickerel frog, *Rana palustris*

Leopard frog, *Rana pipiens*

**Figure 13** The pickerel frog and the leopard frog are closely related species. Differences in mating times may have caused their reproductive isolation. **› What other aspects of mating can push populations to diverge?**

**Figure 14** The Tasmanian wolf was driven to extinction by ranchers and dogs in Australia in the early 1900s. **› What is the role of extinction in evolution?**

## Extinction: The End of Species

*Extinction* occurs when a species fails to produce any more descendants. The animal in **Figure 14** is extinct. Extinction, like speciation, can be detected only after it is complete. And extinction is as much a part of evolution as speciation is. Scientists estimate that more than 99% of all of the species that have ever lived on Earth have become extinct. **› The species that exist at any time are the net result of both speciation and extinction.** If you think of speciation as a branching of a "family tree," then extinction is like the loss of one of the branches.

As you will learn, many cases of extinction are the result of environmental change. Almost all of the dinosaurs died off because of some combination of meteorite impacts, volcanism, and climate change on Earth millions of years ago. Anytime that an environment changes, species that were once well adapted may become poorly adapted. If the environment changes more rapidly than new adaptations arise within a species, the species may be driven to extinction.

SCILINKS.
**www.scilinks.org**
Topic: Extinction
Code: HX80558

**› Reading Check** ***When do we know that extinction has happened?***

## Section 3 Review

### › KEY IDEAS

1. **Identify** two definitions of *species* used in evolutionary biology.
2. **Summarize** a general process by which one species can evolve into two species.
3. **Relate** extinction to changes that occur in the numbers and types of species over time.

### CRITICAL THINKING

4. **Making Inferences** Would the biological species concept be useful for classifying bacterial species? Explain your answer.
5. **Relating Concepts** Relate the idea of reproductive isolation to the biological species concept.
6. **Describing Relationships** Describe the relationship between speciation and extinction in terms of a "family tree" of descent.

### ALTERNATIVE ASSESSMENT

7. **Speciation-in-Action Poster** Sometimes, the easiest way to explain a concept is to illustrate real-world examples of the concept. Create a poster that illustrates examples of reproductive barriers between species. Show how these barriers relate to the biological species concept. Present your poster to the class.

Inquiry

# Chapter 17 Lab

1.3.2, 4.3.1f

45 min

## Objectives

- Investigate the effect of population size on genetic drift.
- Analyze the mathematics of the Hardy-Weinberg principle.

## Materials

- buttons, blue (10 to 100)
- buttons, red (10 to 100)
- buttons, white (10 to 100)
- jar or beaker, large, plastic

Possible alleles

| Possible alleles | $I^A$ | $I^B$ | $i$ |
|---|---|---|---|
| $I^A$ | $I^AI^A$ Type A | $I^AI^B$ Type AB | $I^Ai$ Type A |
| $I^B$ | $I^AI^B$ Type AB | $I^BI^B$ Type B | $I^Bi$ Type B |
| $i$ | $I^Ai$ Type A | $I^Bi$ Type B | $ii$ Type O |

**Blood type molecules**

- Molecule A
- Molecule B

# Genetic Drift

Random chance affects the frequencies of alleles in a population over time. This effect, called *genetic drift,* also depends on population size.

## Preparation

1. SCIENTIFIC METHODS **State the Problem** How does population size affect allele frequencies? Read the procedure to see how you will test this.
2. SCIENTIFIC METHODS **Form a Hypothesis** Form a hypothesis that predicts the results of this procedure for three different population sizes.

## Procedure

1. Prepare to model the populations. First, assign each color button to one of the alleles ($I^A$, $I^B$, or $i$) of the ABO blood types. Notice how each possible pairing of alleles matches one of the four types (A, B, AB, or O). Then, choose three different population sizes. Also choose one ratio of alleles at which to start all three populations (for example, $I^A$:$I^B$:$i$ = 2:2:1). Create tables for your data.
2. Represent the first population's alleles by placing the appropriate number of blue, red, and white buttons in a jar.
3. Randomly select two buttons from the jar to represent one person. Record this person's genotype and phenotype. Place the buttons back into the jar.
4. Repeat step 3 until you have modeled the appropriate number of people in the population. Tally the total number of each allele within this generation.
5. Empty the jar. Refill it with the number and color of buttons that matches the tallies recorded in step 4.
6. Repeat steps 3 through 5 until you have modeled four generations.
7. Repeat steps 2 through 6 to model two more populations.

## Analyze and Conclude

1. **Analyzing Data** Describe any changes in genotype and phenotype ratios within each population over time.
2. **Explaining Results** Did any population maintain genetic equilibrium? Explain how you can tell.
3. SCIENTIFIC METHODS **Analyzing Results** Which popultion showed the greatest amount of genetic drift? Explain.

# Chapter 17 Summary

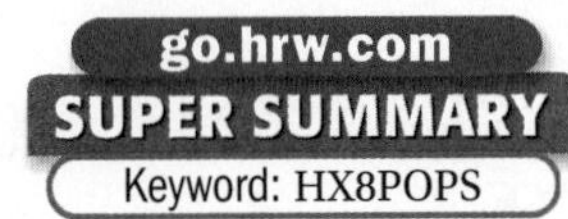

| Key Ideas | Key Terms |
|---|---|
| **1 Genetic Variation**<br>› Microevolution can be studied by observing changes in the numbers and types of alleles in populations.<br>› Biologists study polygenic phenotypes by measuring each individual in the population and then analyzing the distribution of the measurements.<br>› Genetic variation and change are measured in terms of the frequency of alleles in the gene pool of a population.<br>› The major source of new alleles in natural populations is mutation in germ cells. | **population genetics** (399)<br>**normal distribution** (400) |
| **2 Genetic Change**<br>› The Hardy-Weinberg principle predicts that the frequencies of alleles and genotypes in a population will not change unless at least one of five forces acts upon the population. The forces that can act against genetic equilibrium are gene flow, nonrandom mating, genetic drift, mutation, and natural selection.<br>› Sexual reproduction creates the possibility that mating patterns or behaviors can influence the gene pool of a population.<br>› Allele frequencies are more likely to remain stable in large populations than in small populations.<br>› Natural selection acts only to change the relative frequency of alleles that exist in a population. Natural selection acts on genotypes by removing unsuccessful phenotypes from a population.<br>› Three major patterns are possible in the way that natural selection affects a distribution of polygenic characters over time. These patterns are directional selection, stabilizing selection, and disruptive selection. | **genetic equilibrium** (404) |
| **3 Speciation**<br>› Today, scientists may use more than one definition for species. The definition used depends on the organisms and field of science being studied.<br>› Speciation has occurred when the net effects of evolutionary forces result in a population that has unique features and is reproductively isolated.<br>› The species that exist at any time are the net result of both speciation and extinction. | **reproductive isolation** (412)<br>**subspecies** (412) |

Chapter 17

The Living Environment

# Regents Exam Practice

**PART A: Answer all questions in this part.**

*Directions:* For each statement or question, write on your separate answer sheet the number of the word or expression that best completes the statement or answers the question.

**1** Which factor could be the cause of the other three in an animal species?
(1) the inability of the species to adapt to changes
(2) a lack of genetic variability in the species
(3) extinction of the species
(4) a decrease in the survival rate of the species

**2** Which statement describing a cause of extinction includes the other three?
(1) Members of the extinct species were unable to compete for food.
(2) Members of the extinct species were unable to conceal their presence by camouflage.
(3) Members of the extinct species lacked adaptations essential for survival.
(4) Members of the extinct species were too slow to escape from predators.

**3** Which process is least likely to add to the variety of traits in a population?
(1) deletion of bases from DNA
(2) genetic engineering
(3) accurate replication of DNA
(4) exchange of segments between chromosomes

**4** Which of the following is a reason why natural selection is limited in its influence on evolution?
(1) Natural selection cannot direct the creation of new alleles.
(2) All populations depend on the reproduction of individuals.
(3) Natural selection eliminates certain genotypes from populations.
(4) Individuals tend to produce more offspring than the environment can support.

**5** The diagram below shows the evolution of some different species of flowers. Which statement about the species is correct?

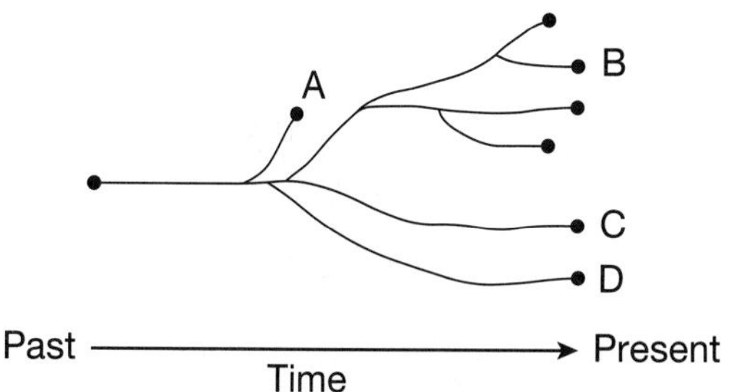


(1) Species A, B, C, and D came from different ancestors.
(2) Species C evolved from species B.
(3) Species A, B, and C can interbreed successfully.
(4) Species A became extinct.

**6** In order for new species to develop, there must be a change in the
(1) temperature of the environment.
(2) migration patterns within a population.
(3) genetic makeup of a population.
(4) rate of succession in the environment.

**7** In evolution, extinction describes the end of
(1) an allele.
(2) a single species.
(3) an individual organism.
(4) a population of organisms.

**8** Which of the following is an example of nonrandom mating?
(1) Genes are removed from the population when individuals migrate.
(2) A change in a population's allele frequency is due to chance.
(3) An individual chooses a mate that has the brightest coloration.
(4) An individual is eliminated from the gene pool by natural selection.

**Base your answers to the following questions on the diagram below and on your knowledge of biology.**

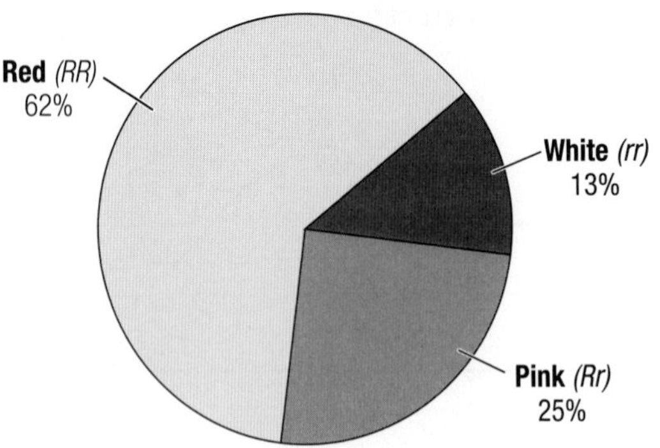


**9** In this population, which genotype has the lowest frequency?

(1) RR (3) red
(2) rr (4) white

**10** In this population, what is the frequency of heterozygotes?

(1) 13% (3) 38%
(2) 25% (4) 62%

**11** The diagram represents which form of selection?

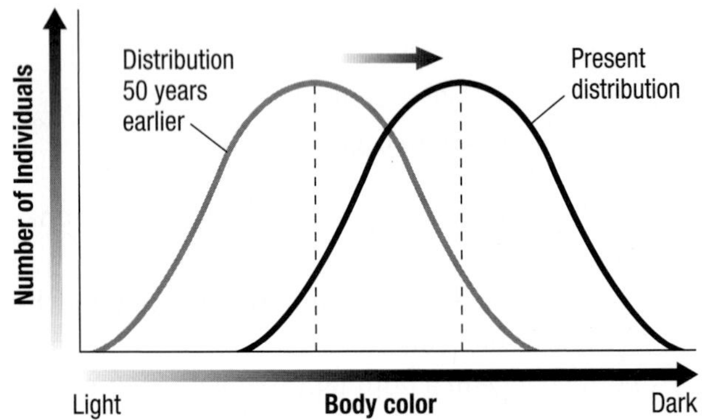


(1) sexual selection
(2) stabilizing selection
(3) disruptive selection
(4) directional selection

**12** The Florida panther, a member of the cat family, has a population of fewer than 100 individuals and has limited genetic variation. Which inference based on this information is valid?

(1) These animals will begin to evolve rapidly.
(2) Over time, these animals will become less likely to survive in a changing environment.
(3) These animals are easily able to adapt to the environment.
(4) Over time, these animals will become more likely to be resistant to disease.

**13** Which process is correctly matched with its explanation?

| | Process | Explanation |
|---|---|---|
| (1) | extinction | adaptive characteristics of a species are not adequate |
| (2) | natural selection | the most complex organisms survive |
| (3) | gene recombination | genes are copied as a part of mitosis |
| (4) | mutation | overproduction of offspring takes place within a certain population |

(1) row 1 (3) row 3
(2) row 2 (4) row 4

**14** Genetic drift has the greatest impact on

(1) large populations.
(2) small populations.
(3) growing populations.
(4) migrating populations.

**15** Population genetics is the study of

(1) how individuals evolve.
(2) how populations interact.
(3) how genes determine traits.
(4) how alleles change within populations.

## PART B

**Base your answers to the following questions on the information below and on your knowledge of biology.**

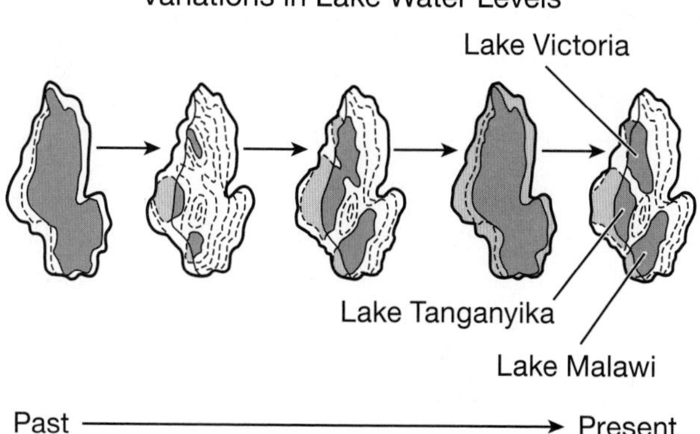


The three great lakes in Africa (Victoria, Tanganyika, and Malawi) contain a greater number of fish species than any other lakes in the world. Lake Malawi alone has 200 species of cichlid fish. The diversity of cichlid species in these African lakes could have been caused by changes in water level over thousands of years.

According to one hypothesis, at one time the three lakes were connected as one large lake and all the cichlids could interbreed. When the water level fell, groups of cichlids were isolated in smaller lakes as shown in the diagram. Over time, the groups of cichlids developed genetic differences. When the water levels rose again, the isolated populations were brought back into contact. Due to significant genetic differences, these populations were unable to interbreed. Variations in water level over thousands of years resulted in today's diversity of cichlid species.

**16** Which discovery would support this explanation of cichlid diversity?

(1) The water level changed little over time.

(2) The local conditions in each of the small lakes were very different.

(3) Differences between cichlid species are small and interbreeding is possible.

(4) Once formed, the lakes remained isolated from each other.

**17** As the water level of the lakes changed, many species of cichlids survived while others became extinct. State why some species survived while others became extinct.

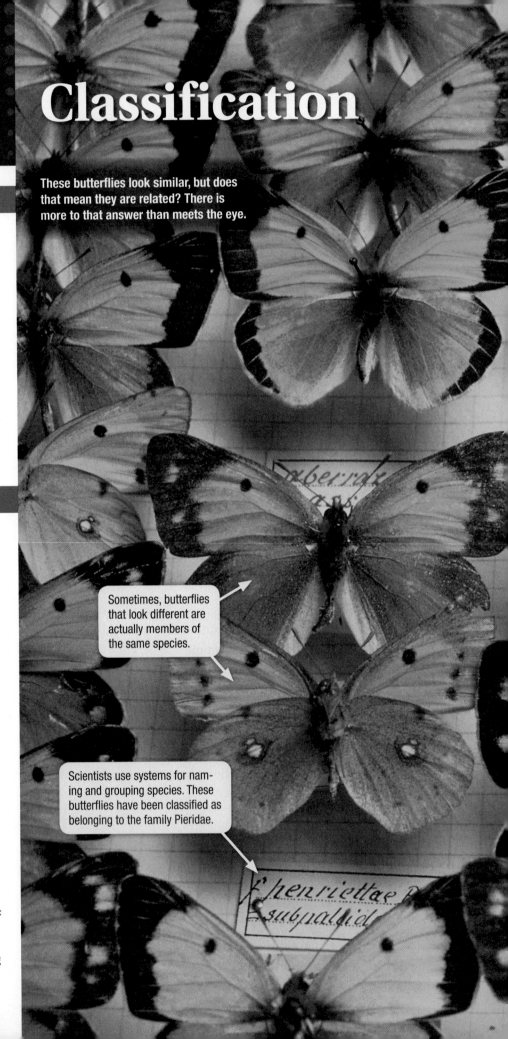

# Chapter 18 Classification

These butterflies look similar, but does that mean they are related? There is more to that answer than meets the eye.

Sometimes, butterflies that look different are actually members of the same species.

Scientists use systems for naming and grouping species. These butterflies have been classified as belonging to the family Pieridae.

## Preview



## Why It Matters

More than one million species on Earth have been given scientific names, but many more species exist that have not been identified.

***The Living Environment***

**Standard 1** Students will use mathematical analysis, scientific inquiry, and engineering design, as appropriate, to pose questions, seek answers, and develop solutions.

**Key Idea 1** The central purpose of scientific inquiry is to develop explanations of natural phenomena in a continuing and creative process. ***Major Understandings* - 1.3b**

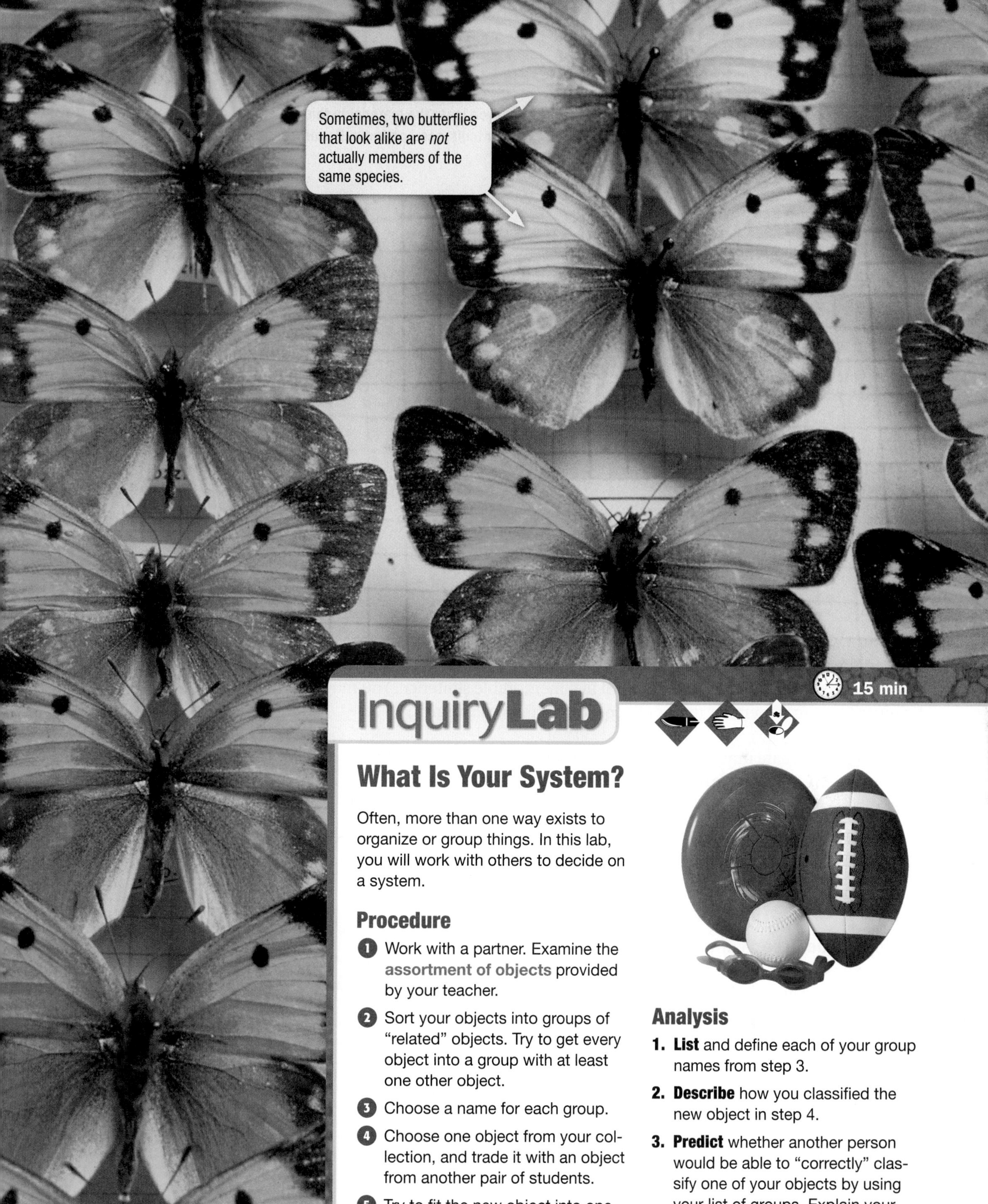

Sometimes, two butterflies that look alike are *not* actually members of the same species.


# InquiryLab

15 min

## What Is Your System?

Often, more than one way exists to organize or group things. In this lab, you will work with others to decide on a system.

### Procedure

1. Work with a partner. Examine the **assortment of objects** provided by your teacher.
2. Sort your objects into groups of "related" objects. Try to get every object into a group with at least one other object.
3. Choose a name for each group.
4. Choose one object from your collection, and trade it with an object from another pair of students.
5. Try to fit the new object into one of your groups.

### Analysis

1. **List** and define each of your group names from step 3.
2. **Describe** how you classified the new object in step 4.
3. **Predict** whether another person would be able to "correctly" classify one of your objects by using your list of groups. Explain your reasoning.

These reading tools can help you learn the material in this chapter. For more information on how to use these and other tools, see **Appendix: Reading and Study Skills.**

## Using Words

**Word Origins** Many scientific words derive their parts from Greek or Latin words. Learning the meanings of some Greek and Latin word parts can help you understand the meaning of many scientific words.

**Your Turn** Answer the following questions.

1. What do taxonomists probably do?
2. What role might nomenclature have in taxonomy?

**Word Parts**

| Word part | Origin | Meaning |
|---|---|---|
| *tax* | Greek | arrangement, order, movement |
| *nom* | Greek; Latin | law, order, system; name |
| *clatur* | Latin | calling, naming |
| *clad* | Greek | shoot, branch, twig |
| *phyl* | Greek | tribe, race, class, clan |
| *gram* | Greek | write, a written record |
| *gen* | Greek, Latin | birth, descent, origin, creation |
| *morph* | Greek | shape, form, appearance |

## Using Language

**Mnemonics** Mnemonic devices are tools that help you remember lists or parts in their proper order. Use the first letter of every word that you want to remember as the first letter of a new word in a memorable sentence. You may be more likely to remember the sentence if the sentence is funny.

**Your Turn** Create mnemonic devices that could help you remember all of the parts of the following groups of items.

1. the names of all of your teachers
2. the 12 months of the year

## Using Science Graphics

**Phylogenetic Tree** A phylogenetic tree shows the relationships of different groups of organisms to each other. The groups that are most closely related appear on branches that lie close together. Branch points represent a point in time where groups became separated and speciation began. Time is represented as moving forward from the bottom (or trunk) toward the top (or branches) of the tree.

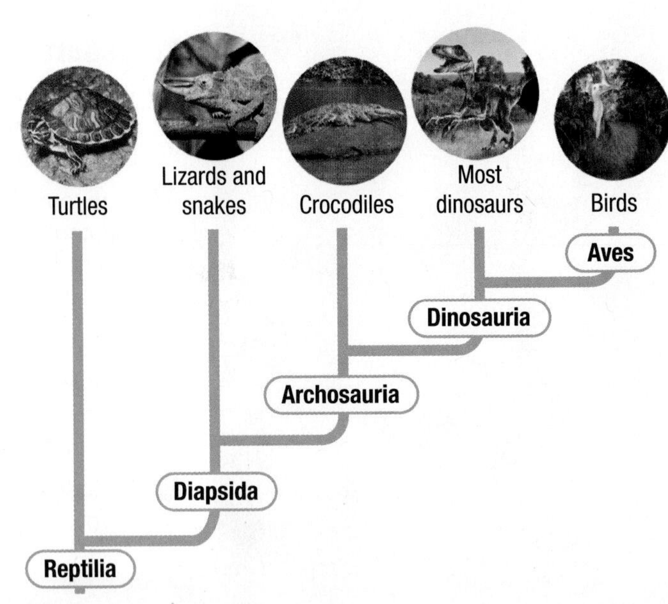


**Your Turn** Use this phylogenetic tree to answer the following questions.

1. Which group is most closely related to extinct dinosaurs?
2. Which group existed before the other groups did?

Section 1

# The Importance of Classification

| Key Ideas | Key Terms | Why It Matters |
|---|---|---|
| ❯ Why do biologists have taxonomic systems?<br>❯ What makes up the scientific name of a species?<br>❯ What is the structure of the modern Linnaean system of classification? | taxonomy<br>genus<br>binomial nomenclature | In order to study and make use of living things, we need a name for each specific thing. |

The number of species that exist in the world is much greater than the number known. About 1.7 million species have been named and described by scientists. But scientists think that millions more are undiscovered. We have little knowledge of Earth's variety of species.

## The Need for Systems

In biology, the practice of naming and classifying organisms is called **taxonomy.** Scientists use a logical system of classification to manage large amounts of information. Similarly, a library uses a system for organizing books. ❯ **Biologists use taxonomic systems to organize their knowledge of organisms. These systems attempt to provide consistent ways to name and categorize organisms.**

Common names of organisms are not organized into a system. One species may have many common names, and one common name may be used for more than one species. For example, the bird called a *robin* in Great Britain is a different bird from the bird called a *robin* in North America. To avoid confusion, biologists need a way to name organisms that does not depend on language or location.

Biologists also need a way to organize lists of names. A system that has categories is more efficient than a simple list. So, biologists group organisms into large categories as well as smaller and more specific categories. The general term for any one of these categories is a *taxon* (plural, *taxa*).

**taxonomy** (taks AHN uh mee) the science of describing, naming, and classifying organisms

❯ **Reading Check** ***What is the problem with common names of species? (See the Appendix for answers to Reading Checks.)***

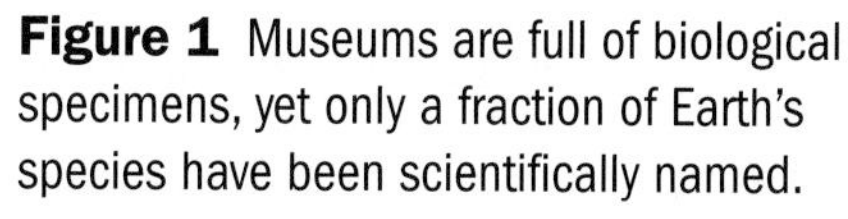

**Figure 1** Museums are full of biological specimens, yet only a fraction of Earth's species have been scientifically named.

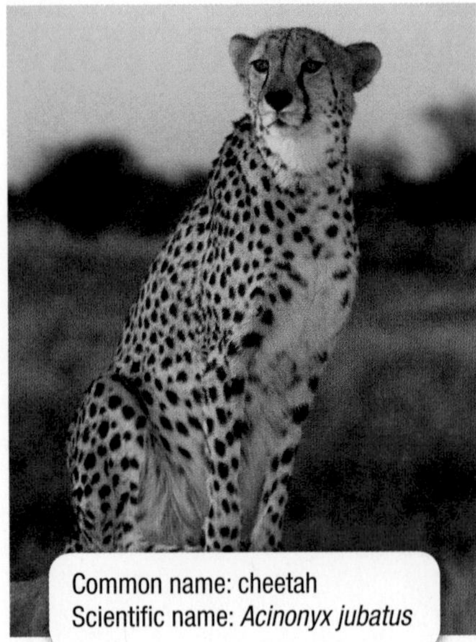

Common name: cheetah
Scientific name: *Acinonyx jubatus*

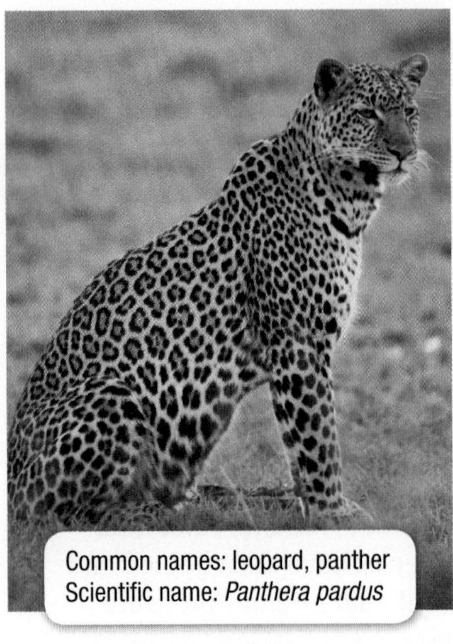

Common names: leopard, panther
Scientific name: *Panthera pardus*

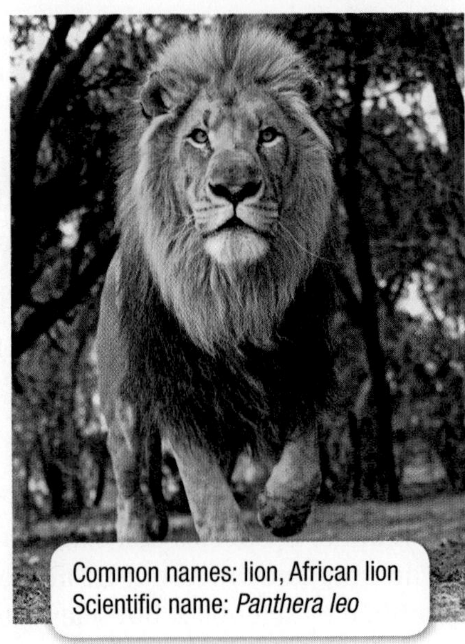

Common names: lion, African lion
Scientific name: *Panthera leo*

**Figure 2** Each species may have many common names but only one scientific name. The scientific name is made up of a genus name and a species identifier. Each genus is a group of closely related species. **❯ To what genus do both lions and leopards belong?**

## Scientific Nomenclature

As biology became established as a science, biologists began to create systems for naming and classifying living things. A major challenge was to give each species a unique name.

**Early Scientific Names** In the early days of European biology, various naming systems were invented. Some used long, descriptive Latin phrases called *polynomials*. Names for taxa were inconsistent between these systems. The only taxon that was somewhat consistent was the **genus,** which was a taxon used to group similar species.

A simpler and more consistent system was developed by the Swedish biologist Carl Linnaeus in the 1750s. He wanted to catalog all known species. He wrote books in which he used the polynomial system but added a two-word Latin name for each species. His two-word system is called **binomial nomenclature.** For example, his two-part name for the European honeybee was *Apis mellifera,* the genus name followed by a single descriptive word for each species. **Figure 2** shows the binomial names of three other animals.

**genus** (JEE nuhs) a level of classification that contains similar species

**binomial nomenclature** (bie NOH mee uhl NOH muhn KLAY chuhr) a system for giving each organism a two-word scientific name that consists of the genus name followed by the species name

**Naming Rules** In the years since Linnaeus created his system, his basic approach has been universally adopted. The unique two-part name for a species is now called a *scientific name.* Scientific names must conform to rules established by an international commission of scientists. No two species can have the same scientific name.

**❯ All scientific names for species are made up of two Latin or Latin-like terms.** All of the members of a genus share the genus name as the first term. The second term is called the *species identifier* and is often descriptive. For example, in the name *Apis mellifera,* the term *mellifera* derives from the Latin word for "honey." When you write the scientific name, the genus name should be capitalized and the species identifier should be lowercased; both terms should be italicized.

**❯ Reading Check** ***Why did Linnaeus devise a new naming system?***

SCILINKS.
**www.scilinks.org**
Topic: Carl Linnaeus
Code: HX80226

## The Linnaean System

In trying to catalog every known species, Linnaeus devised more than just a naming system. He devised a system to classify all plants and animals that were known during his time. His system formed the basis of taxonomy for centuries. ❯ **In the Linnaean system of classification, organisms are grouped at successive levels of a hierarchy based on similarities in their form and structure.** Since Linnaeus's time, many new groups and some new levels have been added, as **Figure 3** shows. ❯ **The eight basic levels of modern classification are domain, kingdom, phylum, class, order, family, genus, and species.**

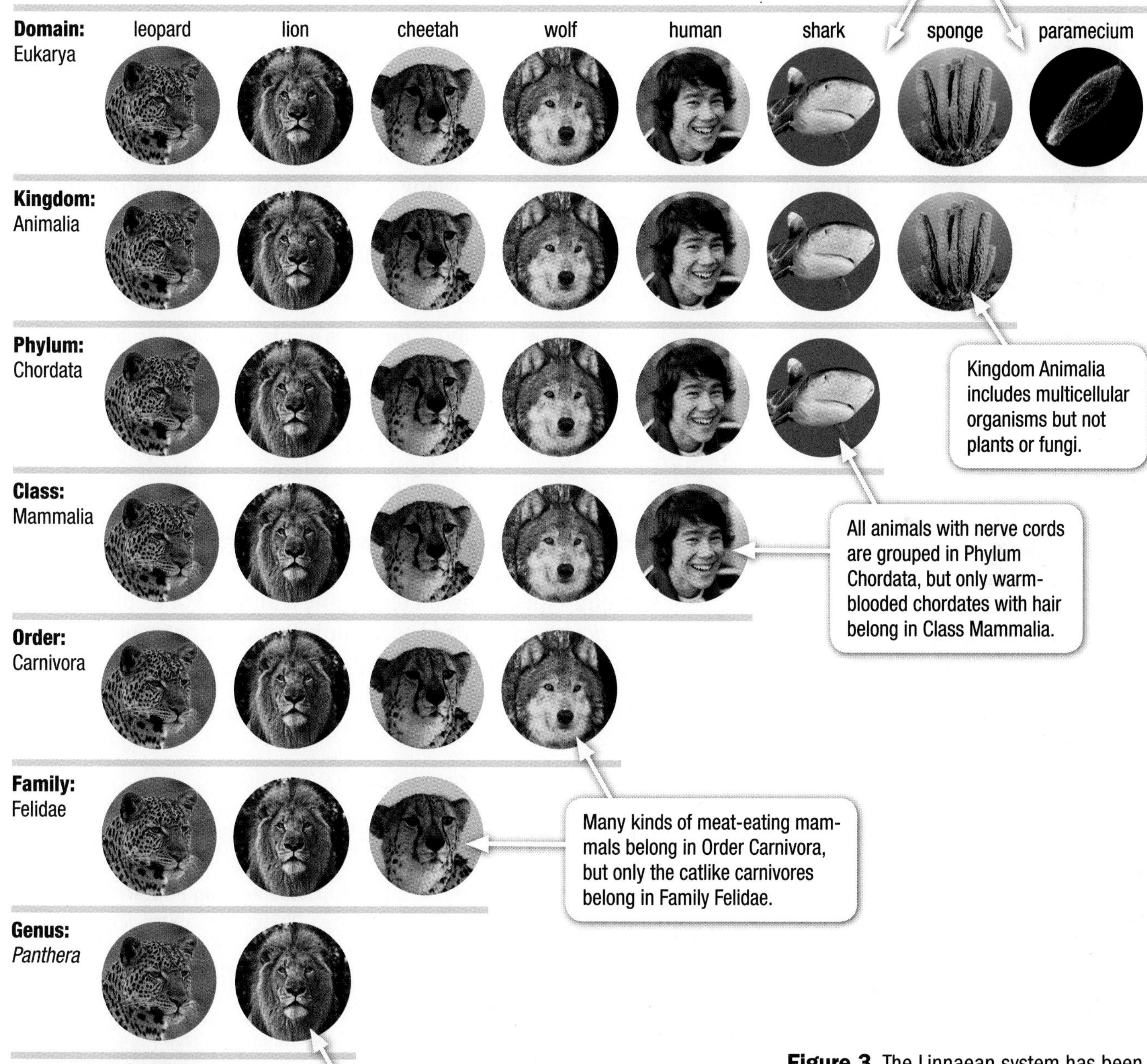
Domain Eukarya includes a wide diversity of eukaryotes but no prokaryotes.
Domain: Eukarya
leopard
lion
cheetah
wolf
human
shark
sponge
paramecium
Kingdom: Animalia
Phylum: Chordata
Kingdom Animalia includes multicellular organisms but not plants or fungi.
Class: Mammalia
All animals with nerve cords are grouped in Phylum Chordata, but only warm-blooded chordates with hair belong in Class Mammalia.
Order: Carnivora
Family: Felidae
Many kinds of meat-eating mammals belong in Order Carnivora, but only the catlike carnivores belong in Family Felidae.
Genus: *Panthera*
Species: *Panthera pardus*
The leopard is a unique species, but it is closely related to the lion. So, the two species are placed in Genus *Panthera*.

**Figure 3** The Linnaean system has been updated and now includes eight levels, from domain to species. ❯ **Which level includes the greatest number of species?**

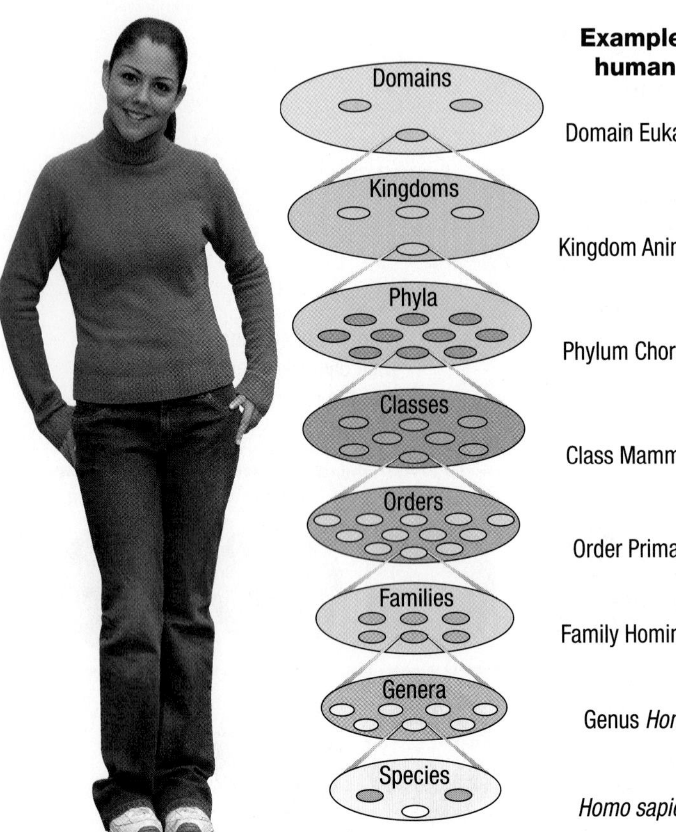


**Figure 4** A species can be classified at each level of the Linnaean system.

### Levels of the Modern Linnaean System

Each level has its own set of names for taxa at that level. Each taxon is identified based on shared traits. Similar species are grouped into a genus; similar genera are grouped into a family; and so on up to the level of domain. **Figure 4** shows the classification of humans in this system.

- **Domain** Since Linnaeus's time, the category *domain* has been invented in order to recognize the most basic differences among cell types. All living things are now grouped into one of three domains. For example, humans belong to the domain Eukarya.
- **Kingdom** The category *kingdom* encompasses large groups such as plants, animals, or fungi. Six kingdoms fit within the three domains.
- **Phylum** A *phylum* is a subgroup within a kingdom. Many phyla exist within each kingdom. Humans belong to the phylum Chordata.
- **Class** A *class* is a subgroup within a phylum.
- **Order** An *order* is a subgroup within a class.
- **Family** A *family* is a subgroup within an order. Humans belong to the family Hominidae.
- **Genus** A *genus* (plural, *genera*) is a subgroup within a family. Each genus is made up of species with uniquely shared traits, such that the species are thought to be closely related. Humans belong to the genus *Homo*.
- **Species** A *species* is usually defined as a unique group of organisms united by heredity or interbreeding. But in practice, scientists tend to define species based on unique features. For example, *Homo sapiens* is recognized as the only living primate species that walks upright and uses spoken language.

**READING TOOLBOX**

**Mnemonics** To remember the eight levels in their proper order, use a phrase, such as "Do Kindly Pay Cash Or Furnish Good Security," to represent *Domain, Kingdom, Phylum, Class, Order, Family, Genus,* and *Species.*

**› Reading Check** ***How many kingdoms are in the Linnaean system?***

## Section 1 Review

### › KEY IDEAS

1. **Explain** why biologists have systems for naming and grouping organisms.
2. **Describe** the structure of a scientific name for a species.
3. **List** the categories of the modern Linnaean system of classification in order from general to specific.

### CRITICAL THINKING

4. **Logical Reasoning** Describe additional problems that might occur for biologists without a logical taxonomic system.
5. **Anticipating Change** Although the basic structure of the system that Linnaeus invented is still in use, many aspects of this system have changed. Suggest some possible ways that the system may have changed.

### ALTERNATIVE ASSESSMENT

6. **Classification Poster** Create a poster that shows the major levels of classification for your favorite organism. Write a description of the general characteristics of the organism at each level. For each level, include a list of other organisms that belong to the same taxon.

Section 2

# Modern Systematics

| Key Ideas | Key Terms | Why It Matters |
|---|---|---|
| ❯ What problems arise when scientists try to group organisms by apparent similarities?<br>❯ Is the evolutionary past reflected in modern systematics?<br>❯ How is cladistics used to construct evolutionary relationships?<br>❯ What evidence do scientists use to analyze these relationships? | phylogeny<br>cladistics | Modern systematics unites evolutionary science with traditional studies of anatomy. |

Have you ever wondered how scientists tell one species from another? For example, how can you tell a mushroom that is harmless from a mushroom that is poisonous? Identification is not easy, even for experts. The experts often revise their classifications as well as their procedures. This field of expertise is known as *systematics*.

## Traditional Systematics

Linnaeus's system was based on his judgment of the importance of various similarities among living things. ❯ **Scientists traditionally have used similarities in appearance and structure to group organisms. However, this approach has proven problematic.** Some groups look similar but turn out to be distantly related. Other groups look different and turn out to be closely related. Often, new data or new analyses suggest relationships between organisms that were not apparent before.

For example, dinosaurs were once seen as a group of reptiles that became extinct millions of years ago. And birds were seen as a separate, modern group that was not related to any reptile group. However, fossil evidence has convinced scientists that birds evolved from one of the many lineages of dinosaurs. Some scientists now classify birds as a subgroup of dinosaurs, as described in **Figure 5.**

❯ **Reading Check** *What is systematics?*

**Figure 5** In a sense, birds are dinosaurs. Scientists think that modern birds are descended from a subgroup of dinosaurs called *theropods.* This inference is based on thorough comparisons of modern birds and fossilized theropods.

**Deinonychus** This is a model of an extinct theropod dinosaur.

**Cassowary** This is a modern bird species.

## Phylogenetics

Today, scientists who study systematics are interested in **phylogeny,** or the ancestral relationships between species. ❯ **Grouping organisms by similarity is often assumed to reflect phylogeny, but inferring phylogeny is complex in practice.** Reconstructing a species' phylogeny is like trying to draw a huge family tree that links ancestors and descendants across thousands or millions of generations.

**phylogeny** the evolutionary history of a species or taxonomic group

**cladistics** a phylogenetic classification system that uses shared derived characters and ancestry as the sole criterion for grouping taxa

**Misleading Similarities** Inferring phylogenies from similarities can be misleading. Not all similar characters are inherited from a common ancestor. Consider the wings of a bird and of an insect. Both types of wings enable flight, but the structures of the two kinds of wings differ. Moreover, fossil evidence shows that insects with wings existed long before birds with wings appeared. Through the process called *convergent evolution,* similarities may evolve in groups that are not closely related to one another, often because the groups become adapted to similar habitats or lifestyles. Similarities that arise through convergent evolution are called *analogous* characters.

**Judging Relatedness** Another problem is that grouping organisms by similarities is subjective. Are all characters equally important, or are some more important than others? Often, different scientists may give different answers to these questions.

For example, systematists historically placed birds in a separate class from reptiles, giving importance to characters such as feathers, as **Figure 6** shows. But more recently, fossil evidence and detailed studies of bird and dinosaur anatomy have changed the view of these groups. **Figure 6** shows that birds are now considered part of the "family tree" of dinosaurs. This family tree, or *phylogenetic tree,* represents a hypothesis of the relationships between several groups.

**Figure 6** Traditional systematics grouped birds separately from other reptiles by emphasizing the unique features of birds. However, modern phylogenetics places birds as a subgroup of reptiles on a phylogenetic tree. ❯ **How do these two systems differ in structure?**

**Linnaean Classification**

| Classes of Animals | |
|---|---|
| **Class Reptilia** | **Class Aves** |
| egg-laying, exothermic, scales | egg-laying, endothermic, feathers |
| lizards, snakes, turtles, crocodiles, and dinosaurs | birds |

**Modern Phylogeny**

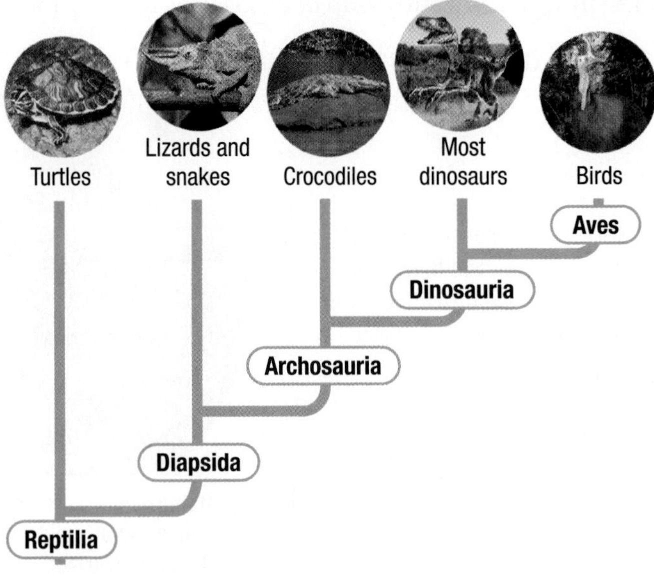

## Cladistics

To unite systematics with phylogenetics, scientists need an objective way to sort out relatedness. Today, the preferred method is cladistics. **Cladistics** is a method of analysis that infers phylogenies by careful comparisons of shared characters. ❯ **Cladistic analysis is used to select the most likely phylogeny among a given set of organisms.**

**Comparing Characters** Cladistics focuses on finding characters that are *shared* between different groups of organisms because of shared ancestry. With respect to two groups, a shared character is defined as *ancestral* if it is thought to have evolved in a common ancestor of both groups. In contrast, a *derived* character is one that evolved in one group but not in the other group. Cladistics infers relatedness by identifying shared derived and shared ancestral characters among groups while avoiding the use of analogous characters.

For example, consider the relationship between flowering plants and conifers. The production of seeds is a character that is present in all living conifers and flowering plants and in some prehistoric plants. So, it is a shared ancestral character among these groups. The production of flowers, however, is a derived character that is shared only among flowering plants. Flowers evolved in some ancestor of flowering plants but did not evolve in the group that led to conifers.

**Constructing Cladograms** Cladistics uses a strict comparison of many characters among several groups in order to construct a cladogram. A *cladogram* is a phylogenetic tree that is drawn in a specific way, as **Figure 7** shows. Organisms are grouped together through identification of their shared derived characters. All groups that arise from one point on a cladogram belong to a clade. A *clade* is a set of groups that are related by descent from a single ancestral lineage.

Each clade in a tree is usually compared with an *outgroup,* or group that lacks some of the shared characters. For example, **Figure 7** shows that flowering plants and conifers share a character with each other that they do not share with ferns. So, conifers and flowering plants form a clade, and ferns form the outgroup.

❯ **Reading Check** ***What does a cladogram show?***

### Academic Vocabulary

**objective** independent of the mind; without bias

### Reading Toolbox

**Word Origins** The word root *clad* means "shoot, branch or twig" and the word root *gram* means "to write or record." Use this information to analyze the meaning of the term *cladogram.*

**Figure 7** This cladogram organizes plants by using a strict comparison of the characters shown in the table. Each clade is united by a specific shared derived character. ❯ **Which groups are united by having seeds?**

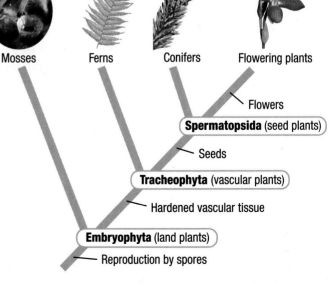

**Characters in Plants**

| Type of plants | Vascular tissue | Seeds | Flowers |
|---|---|---|---|
| Mosses | no | no | no |
| Ferns | yes | no | no |
| Conifers | yes | yes | no |
| Flowering plants | yes | yes | yes |

Data

# QuickLab

## Cladogram Construction

Use this table of shared characters to construct a cladogram. Use the other cladograms in this section to help you draw your cladogram.

**Characters in Vertebrates**

| | Four legs | Amniotic egg | Hair |
|---|---|---|---|
| Tuna | no | no | no |
| Frog | yes | no | no |
| Lizard | yes | yes | no |
| Cat | yes | yes | yes |

### Analysis

1. **Identify** the outgroup. The outgroup is the group that does not share any of the characters in this list. Draw a diagonal line and then a single branch from its base. Write the outgroup at the tip of this first branch.
2. **Identify** the most common character. Just past the "fork" of the first branch, write the most common derived character. This character should be present in all of the subsequent groups added to the tree.
3. **Complete** the tree. Repeat step 2 for the second most-common character. Repeat until the tree is filled with all of the groups and characters from the table.
4. CRITICAL THINKING **Applying Concepts** What is a shared derived character of cats and lizards?
5. CRITICAL THINKING **Applying Concepts** What character evolved in the ancestor of frogs but not in that of fish?

SCILINKS.
www.scilinks.org
Topic: Phylogenetic Tree
Code: HX81141


## Inferring Evolutionary Relatedness

As you have seen, phylogenetics relies heavily on data about characters that are either present or absent in taxa. But other kinds of data are also important. **Biologists compare many kinds of evidence and apply logic carefully in order to infer phylogenies.** They constantly revise and add details to their definitions of taxa.

**Morphological Evidence** *Morphology* refers to the physical structure or anatomy of organisms. Large-scale morphological data are most obvious and have been well studied. For example, the major characters used to define plant groups—vascular tissue, seeds, and flowers—were recognized long ago. But because convergent evolution can lead to analogous characters, scientists must consider many characters and look carefully for similarities and differences. For example, many animals have wings that are merely analagous.

An important part of morphology in multicellular species is the pattern of development from embryo to adult. Organisms that share ancestral genes often show additional similarities during the process of development. For example, in all vertebrate species, the jaw of an adult develops from the same part of an embryo. In many cases, studies of embryos bring new information to phylogenetic debates.

**Molecular Evidence** In recent decades, scientists have used genetic information to infer phylogenies. Recall that as genes are passed on from generation to generation, mutations occur. Some mutations may be passed on to all species that descend from a common ancestor. So, DNA, RNA, and proteins can be compared in the same manner as morphology is compared to infer phylogenies.

**Reading Check** *What is an example of morphological data?*

**Sequence Data** Today, genetic sequence data are widely used for cladistic analysis. First, the sequence of DNA bases in a gene (or of amino acids in a protein) is determined for several species. Then, each letter (or amino acid) at each position in the sequence is compared. Such a comparison can be laid out in a large table, but computers are best able to calculate the relative similarity of many sequences.

**Genomic Data** At the level of genomes, alleles may be added or lost over time. So, another form of molecular evidence is the presence or absence of specific alleles—or the proteins that result from them. Finally, the relative timing between genetic changes can be inferred.

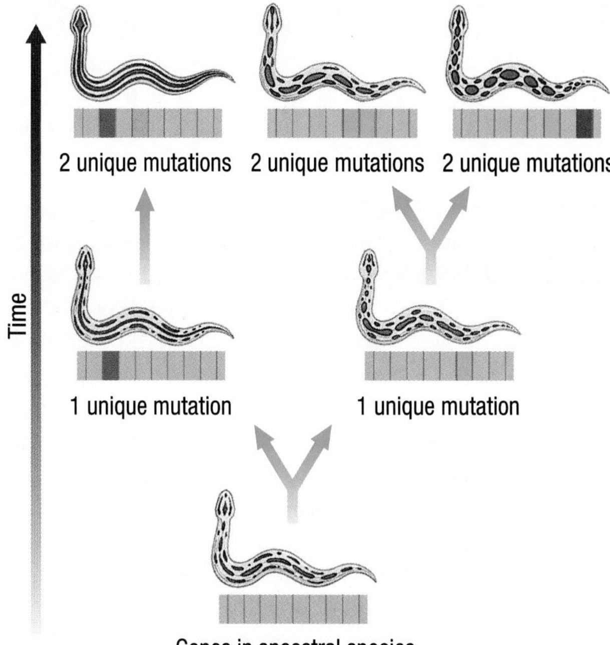


**Figure 8** Because mutation occurs randomly at any time, an average rate of mutation can be measured and used as a "clock" to estimate the time any two species took to accumulate a number of genetic differences.

**Evidence of Order and Time** Cladistics can determine only the relative order of divergence, or branching, in a phylogenetic tree. To infer the actual time when a group may have begun to "branch off," extra information is needed. Often, this information comes from the fossil record. For example, by using cladistics, scientists have identified lancelets as the closest relative of vertebrates. The oldest known fossils of vertebrates are about 450 million years old, but the oldest lancelet fossils are 535 million years old. So, these two lineages must have diverged more than 450 million years ago.

More recently, scientists have noticed that most DNA mutations occur at relatively constant rates. So, genetic change can be used as an approximate "molecular clock," as **Figure 8** shows. Scientists can measure the genetic differences between taxa and then estimate the time at which the taxa began to diverge.

**Inference Using Parsimony** Modern systematists use the *principle of parsimony* to construct phylogenetic trees. This principle holds that the simplest explanation for something is the most reasonable, unless strong evidence exists against the simplest explanation. So, given two possible cladograms, the one that implies the fewest character changes between branch points is preferred.

**› Reading Check** *What kinds of molecular data inform cladistics?*

## Section 2 Review

### › KEY IDEAS

1. **Identify** the kinds of problems that arise when scientists try to group organisms by similarities.
2. **Relate** classification to phylogeny.
3. **Describe** the method of cladistics.
4. **Identify** the kinds of evidence used to infer phylogenies.

### CRITICAL THINKING

5. **Justifying Reasoning** Some scientists who study dinosaurs have stated that dinosaurs are not extinct. How could this statement be justified?
6. **Analyzing Relationships** Explain how the outgroup in a cladogram relates to the difference between ancestral and derived characters.

### METHODS OF SCIENCE

7. **Taxonomic Challenge** In the past, mammals were identified as animals that have fur and give birth to live offspring, and reptiles were identified as animals that have scales and lay eggs. Then, an animal was found that has fur and lays eggs. How might this problem have been resolved?

Why It Matters

# New Species

REAL WORLD

The work of biology is never finished. Indeed, the work of finding, naming, and classifying all living species has barely begun. Scientists have estimated that 1 km² of rain forest may contain hundreds or thousands of species, most of which are currently unknown to science. In fact, new species are "discovered" all of the time, all around the world.

Mantophasmatodea—a new order of insects

## When is a species "new"?

What does discovering a new species mean? Typically, it means collecting a specimen, giving it a name, and classifying it for the first time by using modern taxonomy. Although truly new species may be evolving at any time, most new species are simply new to science.

**Big, Small, Far, Near**
Undiscovered species are everywhere! Even mammals, such as this monkey, are still being discovered. Of course, we may never find all of the tiny bugs and microbes in the world.

**Biodiversity Hot Spots**
Some parts of the world, such as tropical rain forests, contain an extreme diversity of species. This frog is from a region of Sri Lanka that is home to many amphibian species.

**Undiscovered Worlds**
In 2005, an expedition went into a "lost world" of rain forest in New Guinea that was previously unexplored by scientists. The expedition quickly found dozens of new species, such as this honeyeater bird.

Lemur from Madagascar

**Quick Project** Find out if any new species have been discovered in your local area in the last few decades. Try to find the name of the new species, the story behind the name, and a photo of the species.

Section 3

# Kingdoms and Domains

| Key Ideas | Key Terms | Why It Matters |
| --- | --- | --- |
| ❯ Have biologists always recognized the same kingdoms?<br>❯ What are the domains and kingdoms of the three-domain system of classification? | bacteria<br>archaea<br>eukaryote | The three-domain system is one of the latest revolutions in biology. |

If you read old books or stories, you might read about plants and animals, or "flora and fauna," but probably not "fungi" or "bacteria."

***The Living Environment***
**Standard 1**
**1.3b** All scientific explanations are tentative and subject to change or improvement. Each new bit of evidence can create more questions than it answers. This leads to increasingly better understanding of how things work in the living world.

## Updating Classification Systems

For many years after Linnaeus created his system, scientists recognized only two kingdoms: Plantae (plants) and Animalia (animals). Relatively few of Earth's species were known, and little was known about them. ❯ **Biologists have added complexity and detail to classification systems as they have learned more.** Throughout history, many new taxa have been proposed and some groups have been reclassified.

For example, **Figure 9** shows sponges, which were first classified as plants. Then, the invention of the microscope allowed scientists to look at cells. Scientists learned that sponges have cells that are much more like animal cells than like plant cells. So today, sponges are classified as animals. The microscope prompted many such changes.

**From Two to Five Kingdoms** In the 1800s, scientists added Kingdom Protista as a taxon for unicellular organisms. Soon, they noticed the differences between prokaryotic cells and eukaryotic cells. So, scientists created Kingdom Monera for prokaryotes and left single-celled eukaryotes in Kingdom Protista. By the 1950s, five kingdoms were used: Monera, Protista, Fungi, Plantae, and Animalia.

**Six Kingdoms** In the 1990s, Kingdom Monera came into question. Genetic data suggested two major groups of prokaryotes. So, Kingdom Monera was split into two new kingdoms: Eubacteria and Archaebacteria.

❯ **Reading Check** ***What were the original Linnaean kingdoms?***

**Figure 9** Early scientists classified sponges as plants because sponges are attached to the sea floor. Further study and microscopic views in particular led to a reclassification of sponges as animals. ❯ **What features of sponges might have led to this reclassification?**

**Characteristics of Domains and Kingdoms**

| Domain | Bacteria | Archaea | Eukarya | | | |
|---|---|---|---|---|---|---|
| **Kingdom** | Eubacteria | Archae-bacteria | Protista | Fungi | Plantae | Animalia |
| **Example** | *Streptococcus pneumoniae* | *Staphylo-thermus marinus* | paramecium | spore cap mushroom | Texas paintbrush | white-winged dove |
| **Cell type** | prokaryote | | eukaryote | | | |
| **Cell walls** | cell walls with peptidoglycan | cell walls with unique lipids | some species with cell walls | cell walls with chitin | cell walls with cellulose | no cell walls |
| **Number of cells** | unicellular | | unicellular or multicellular | mostly multicellular | mostly multicellular | multicellular |
| **Nutrition** | autotroph or heterotroph | | | heterotroph | autotroph | heterotroph |

**Figure 10** This table shows the major characteristics used to define the domains and kingdoms of the modern Linnaean system. **› What other kind of characteristic differs between kingdoms?**

## The Three-Domain System

As biologists began to see the differences between the two kinds of prokaryotes, they also saw the similarities among all eukaryotes. So, a new system was proposed that divides all organisms into three domains: Bacteria, Archaea, and Eukarya. **› Today, most biologists tentatively recognize three domains and six kingdoms. Figure 10** shows the major characteristics of these taxa.

**Major Characteristics** Major taxa such as kingdoms are defined by major characteristics. These characteristics include:

- **Cell Type** The cells may be either *prokaryotic* or *eukaryotic.*
- **Cell Walls** The cells may either have a cell wall or lack a cell wall.
- **Body Type** An organism is either *unicellular* or *multicellular.*
- **Nutrition** An organism is either an *autotroph* (makes nutrients from inorganic materials) or a *heterotroph* (gets nutrients from other organisms). Some taxa have unique means of nutrition.
- **Genetics** As you have learned, related groups of organisms will have similar genetic material and systems of gene expression. So, organisms may have a unique system of DNA, RNA, and proteins.

**Domain Bacteria** **› Domain Bacteria is equivalent to Kingdom Eubacteria.** The common name for members of this domain is *bacteria.* **Bacteria** are prokaryotes that have a strong exterior cell wall and a unique genetic system. However, bacteria have the same kind of cell membrane lipid as most eukaryotes do.

Hands-On

## QuickLab

20 min

### Field Guides

Have you ever used field guides to identify animals or plants? Do you know how these guides are organized? Take a few guides outside, and take a closer look.

#### Procedure

1. Gather several different field guides for plants or other organisms in your area. Also gather a magnifying glass and a specimen jar. Take these items with you to a local natural area.
2. CAUTION: **Do not touch or disturb any organisms without your teacher's permission; leave all natural items as you found them.** Try to find and identify at least two organisms that are listed in your field guides. Make notes to describe each organism.

#### Analysis

1. **Analyzing Methods** How difficult was identifying your organisms? How certain are you of your identification?
2. **Comparing Systems** How are the field guides organized? What other ways could they be organized?

All bacteria are similar in physical structure, with no internal compartments. Traditionally, bacteria have been classified according to their shape, the nature of their cell wall, their type of metabolism, or the way that they obtain nutrients. Bacteria are the most abundant organisms on Earth and are found in almost every environment.

**Domain Archaea** › **Domain Archaea is equivalent to Kingdom Archaebacteria.** The common name for members of this domain is *archaea.* **Archaea** have a chemically unique cell wall and membranes and a unique genetic system. The genetic systems of archaea share some similarities with those of eukaryotes that they do not share with those of prokaryotes. Scientists think that archaea began to evolve in a separate lineage from bacteria early in Earth's history and that some archaea eventually gave rise to eukaryotes.

Archaea were first found by scientists in extreme environments, such as salt lakes, the deep ocean, or hot springs that exceed 100°C. These archaea are called *extremophiles.* Other archaea called *methanogens* live in oxygen-free environments. However, some archaea live in the same environments as many bacteria do.

**Domain Eukarya** › **Domain Eukarya is made up of Kingdoms Protista, Fungi, Plantae, and Animalia.** Members of the domain Eukarya are **eukaryotes,** which are organisms composed of eukaryotic cells. These cells have a complex internal structure. This structure enabled the cells to become larger than the earliest cells and enabled the evolution of multicellular life. While eukaryotes vary in many fundamental respects, they share several key features.

› **Reading Check** *Which kingdoms are prokaryotic?*

**bacteria** (bak TIR ee uh) extremely small, single-celled organisms that usually have a cell wall and that usually reproduce by cell division; members of the domain Bacteria

**archaea** (ahr KEE uh) prokaryotes that are distinguished from other prokaryotes by differences in their genetics and in the makeup of their cell wall; members of the domain Archaea

**eukaryote** an organism made up of cells that have a nucleus enclosed by a membrane, multiple chromosomes, and a mitotic cycle; members of the domain Eukarya

Protists

Bacteria Archaea Mosses Ferns Conifers Flowering plants Fungi Sponges Cnidarians

Plantae (plants)

Fungi (fungi)

Eubacteria (bacteria)

Protista (protists)

Animalia (animals)

Archaebacteria (archaea)

Eukarya (eukaryotes)

**Figure 11** This tree of life shows current hypotheses of the relationships between all major groups of organisms. For updates on phylogenetic information, visit **go.hrw.com** and enter the keyword **HX8 Phylo.** ❯ **Why might this type of model be revised?**

**Phylogenetic Tree** Look carefully at **Figure 11.** Try to identify which groups are most closely related to each other. Which label includes lineages that do not share a unique common ancestor?

**Characteristics of Eukaryotes** Eukaryotes have highly organized cells. All eukaryotes have cells with a nucleus and other internal compartments. Also, true multicellularity and sexual reproduction occur only in eukaryotes. True multicellularity means that the activities of individual cells are coordinated and the cells themselves are in contact. Sexual reproduction means that genetic material is recombined when parents mate. Sexual reproduction is an important part of the life cycle of most eukaryotes.

**Kinds of Eukaryotes** The major groups of eukaryotes are defined by number of cells, body organization, and types of nutrition.

- **Plantae** Almost all plants are autotrophs that produce their own food by absorbing energy and raw materials from their environment. This process is *photosynthesis,* which occurs inside chloroplasts. The cell wall is made of a rigid material called *cellulose.* More than 270,000 known species of plants exist.
- **Animalia** Animals are multicellular heterotrophs. Their bodies may be simple collections of cells or highly complex networks of organ systems. Animal cells lack the rigid cell walls that plant cells have. More than 1 million known species of animals exist.
- **Fungi** Fungi are heterotrophs and are mostly multicellular. Their cell wall is made of a rigid material called *chitin.* Fungi are considered to be more closely related to animals than to any other kingdom. More than 70,000 known species of fungi exist.

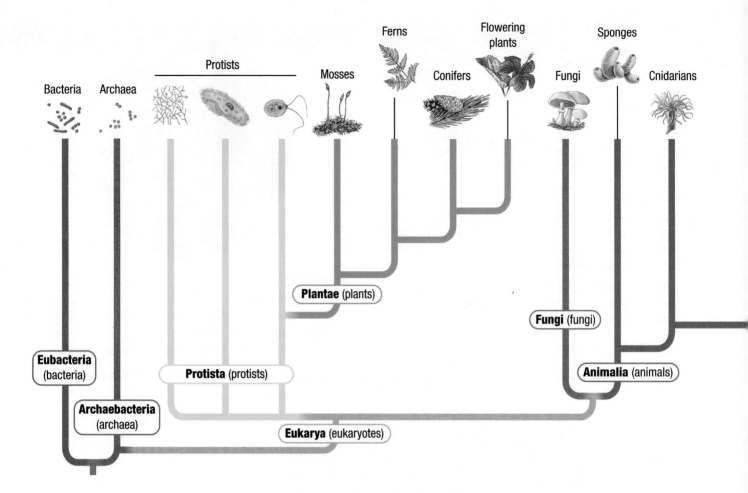

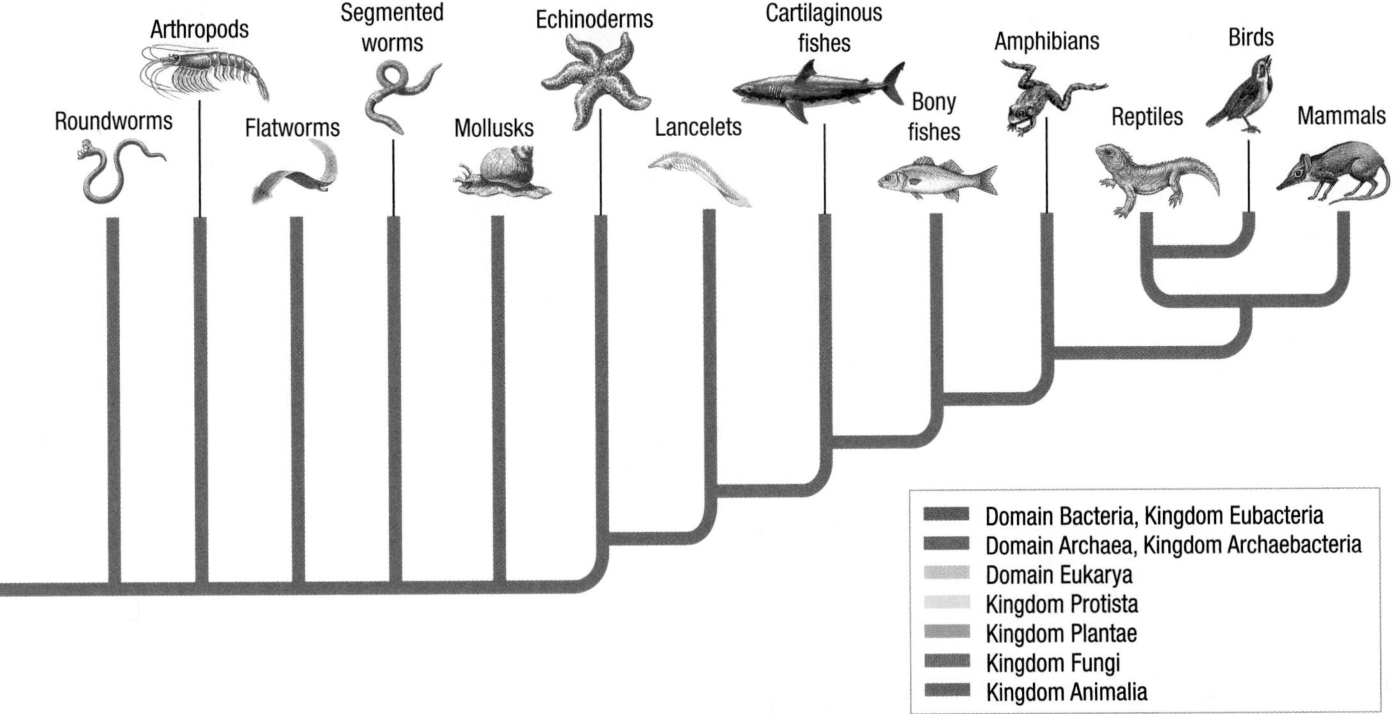

- **Protista** Kingdom Protista is a diverse group. Unlike the other three Kingdoms of Eukarya, Protista is not a natural group but rather a "leftover" taxon. Any single-celled eukaryote that is *not* a plant, animal, or fungi can be called a *protist*. Protists did not descend from a single common ancestor.

  For many years , biolgists recognized four major groups of protists: flagellates, amoebas, algae, and parasitic protists. More recently, biologists have proposed to replace Protista with several new kingdoms. These kingdoms would classify protists that seem to be unrelated to any other groups. However, some protists are being reclassified into other kingdoms. For example, algae that have chloroplasts are thought to be most closely related to plants, as shown in **Figure 11.** Biologists have not yet agreed how to resolve all of these issues.

**› Reading Check** ***Which kingdoms contain only heterotrophs?***

## Section 3 Review

### › KEY IDEAS

1. **Outline** how biologists have changed the major levels of the Linnaean system over time.
2. **List** the three domains, identify the kingdoms that align with each domain, and list the major characteristics of each kingdom.

### CRITICAL THINKING

3. **Finding Evidence** The *theory of endosymbiosis* proposes that eukaryotes descended from a primitive combination of both archaea and bacteria. What evidence supports this theory?
4. **Science and Society** Microscopes led scientists to recognize new kingdoms. What other technology has impacted classification?

### ALTERNATIVE ASSESSMENT

5. **Tree of Life Poster** Make a poster of the tree of life. At appropriate places on the tree, add images of representative organisms, along with labels. Include all domains and kingdoms as well as at least three major taxa within each kingdom.

Skills Practice

# Chapter 18 Lab

## Objectives

- Identify objects by using a dichotomous key.
- Design a dichotomous key for a group of objects.

## Materials

- objects, common (6 to 10)
- labels, adhesive
- pencil

## Safety

# Dichotomous Keys

One way to identify an unknown organism is to use an identification key, which contains the major characteristics of groups of organisms. A dichotomous key is an identification key that contains pairs of contrasting descriptions. After each description, a key either directs the user to another pair of descriptions or identifies an object. In this lab, you will design and use a dichotomous key. A dichotomous key can be written for any group of objects.

## Procedure

### Use a Dichotomous Key

1. Work with a small group. Use the dichotomous key to identify the tree that produced each of the leaves shown here. Identify one leaf at a time. Always start with the first pair of statements (1a and 1b). Follow the direction beside the statement that describes the leaf.
2. Proceed through the key until you get to the name of a tree. Record your answer for each leaf shown.

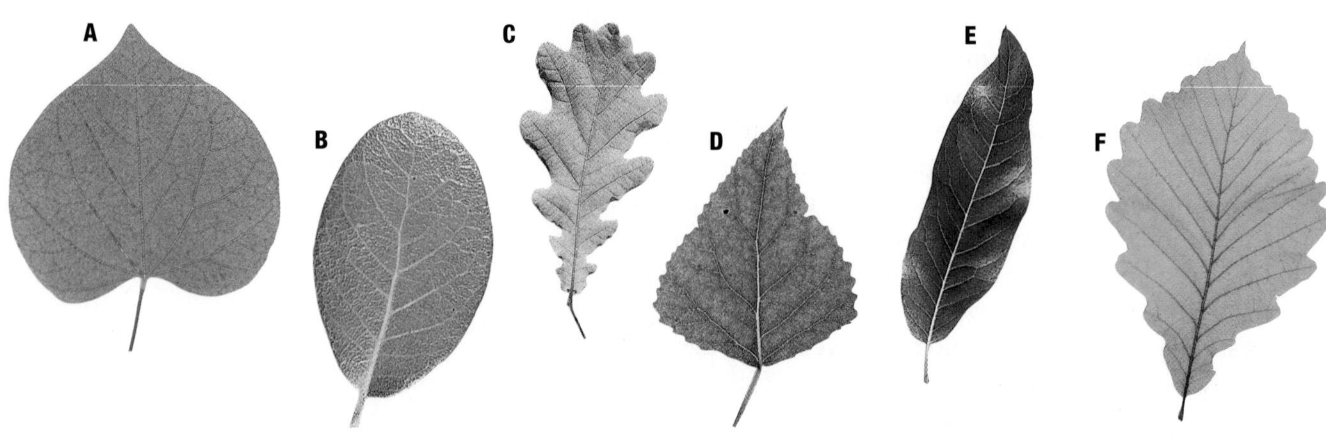


**Key to Forest Trees**

| | | |
|---|---|---|
| 1a | Leaf edge is smooth or barely curved. | go to 2 |
| 1b | Leaf edge has teeth, waves, or lobes. | go to 3 |
| 2a | Leaf has a sharp bristle at its tip. | shingle oak |
| 2b | Leaf has no bristle at its tip. | go to 4 |
| 3a | Leaf edge has small, shallow teeth. | Lombardy poplar |
| 3b | Leaf edge has deep waves or lobes. | go to 5 |
| 4a | Leaf is heart shaped. | eastern redbud |
| 4b | Leaf is not heart shaped. | live oak |
| 5a | Leaf edge has less than 20 large lobes. | English oak |
| 5b | Leaf edge has more than 20 waves. | chestnut oak |

 45 min

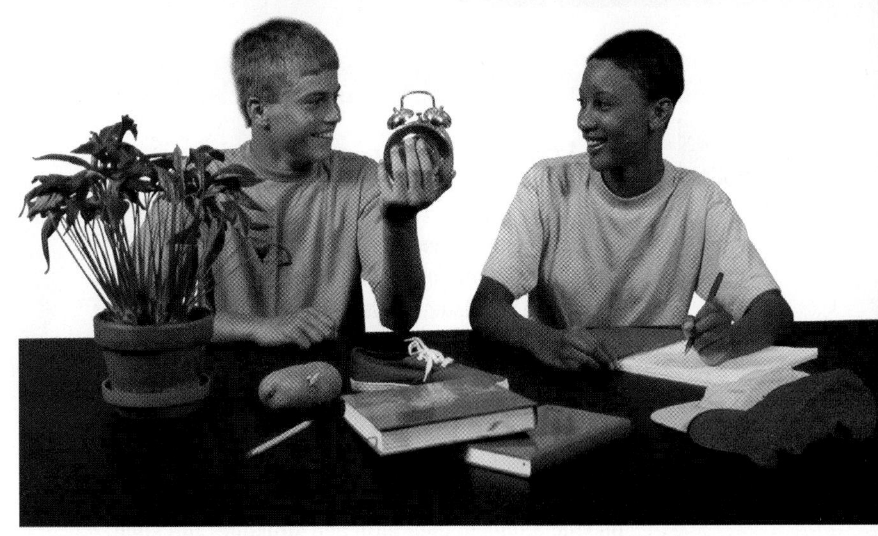

### Design a Dichotomous Key

**3** Put on safety goggles, gloves, and a lab apron.Choose 6 to 10 objects from around the classroom or from a collection supplied by your teacher. Before you go to the next step, have your teacher approve the objects your group has chosen.

**4** Study the structure and organization of the dichotomous key, which includes pairs of contrasting descriptions that form a "tree" of possibilities. Use this key as a model for the next step.

**5** Work with the members of your group to design a new dichotomous key for the objects that your group selected. Be sure that each part of the key leads to either a definite identification of an object or another set of possibilities. Be sure that every object is included.

**6** Test your key by using each one of the objects in your collection.

### Exchange and Test Keys

**7** After each group has completed the steps above, exchange your key and your collection of objects with another group. Use the key you receive to identify each of the new objects. If the new key does not work, return it to the group so that corrections can be made.

### Cleanup

**8** Clean up your work area and return or dispose of materials as directed by your teacher. Wash your hands thoroughly before you leave the lab and after you finish all of your work.

SCILINKS.
**www.scilinks.org**
Topic: Classification
Code: HX80295

## Analyze and Conclude

1. **Summarizing Data** List the identity of the tree for each of the leaves that you analyzed in step 2.
2. SCIENTIFIC METHODS **Critiquing Procedures** What other characteristics might be used to identify leaves by using a dichotomous key?
3. **Analyzing Results** What challenges did your group face while making your dichotomous key?
4. **Evaluating Results** Were you able to use another group's key to identify the group's collection of objects? Describe your experience.
5. SCIENTIFIC METHODS **Analyzing Methods** Does a dichotomous key begin with general descriptions and then proceed to more specific descriptions, or vice versa? Explain your answer by using examples.
6. SCIENTIFIC METHODS **Evaluating Methods** Is a dichotomous key the same as the Linnaean classification system? Explain your answer.

## Extension

7. **Research** Do research in the library or media center to find out what types of methods, other than dichotomous keys, are used to identify organisms.

# Chapter 18 Summary

| Key Ideas | Key Terms |
|---|---|
| **1 The Importance of Classification**<br>› Biologists use taxonomic systems to organize their knowledge of organisms. These systems attempt to provide consistent ways to name and categorize organisms.<br>› All scientific names for species are made up of two Latin or Latin-like terms.<br>› In the Linnaean system of classification, organisms are grouped at successive levels of a hierarchy based on similarities in their form and structure. The eight levels of modern classification are domain, kingdom, phylum, class, order, family, genus, and species. | **taxonomy** (423)<br>**genus** (424)<br>**binomial nomenclature** (424) |
| **2 Modern Systematics**<br>› Scientists traditionally have used similarities in appearance and structure to group organisms. However, this approach has proven problematic.<br>› Grouping organisms by similarity is often assumed to reflect phylogeny, but inferring phylogeny is complex in practice.<br>› Cladistic analysis is used to select the most likely phylogeny among a given set of organisms.<br>› Biologists compare many kinds of evidence and apply logic carefully in order to infer phylogenies. | **phylogeny** (428)<br>**cladistics** (429) |
| **3 Kingdoms and Domains**<br>› Biologists have added complexity and detail to classification systems as they have learned more.<br>› Today, most biologists tentatively recognize three domains and six kingdoms. Domain Bacteria is equivalent to Kingdom Eubacteria. Domain Archaea is equivalent to Kingdom Archaebacteria. Domain Eukarya is made up of Kingdoms Protista, Fungi, Plantae, and Animalia. | **bacteria** (434)<br>**archaea** (435)<br>**eukaryote** (435) |

# Chapter 18 The Living Environment
# Regents Exam Practice

**PART A: Answer all questions in this part.**

*Directions:* For each statement or question, write on your separate answer sheet the number of the word or expression that best completes the statement or answers the question.

**1** The evolutionary pathways of ten different species are represented in the diagram below. Which two species are the most closely related?

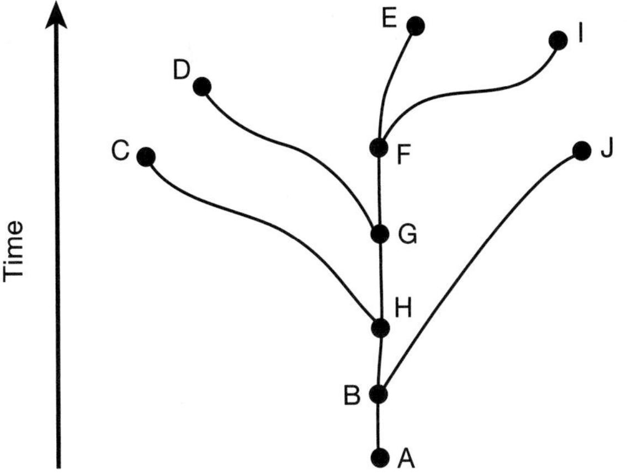


(1) C and D
(2) E and I
(3) G and J
(4) A and F

**2** A current proposal in the field of classification divides life into three broad categories called domains. This idea is illustrated below. Which concept is best supported by this diagram?

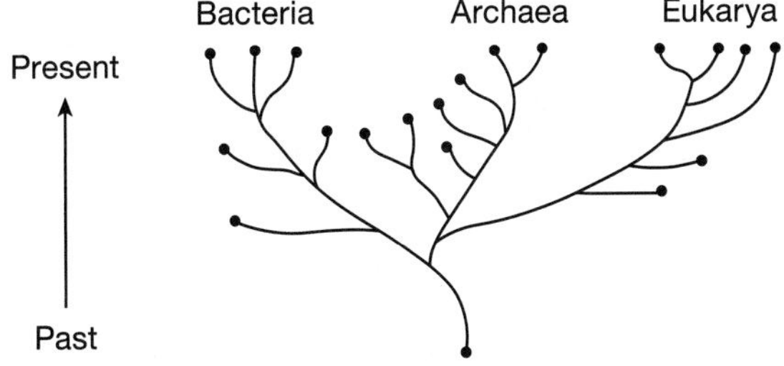


(1) Evolutionary pathways proceed only in one set direction over a short period of time.
(2) All evolutionary pathways will eventually lead to present-day organisms.
(3) All evolutionary pathways are the same length and they all lead to present-day organisms.
(4) Evolutionary pathways can proceed in several directions with only some pathways leading to present-day organisms.

**3** The bones in the forelimbs of three mammals are shown below. For these mammals, the number, position, and shape of the bones most likely indicates that they may have

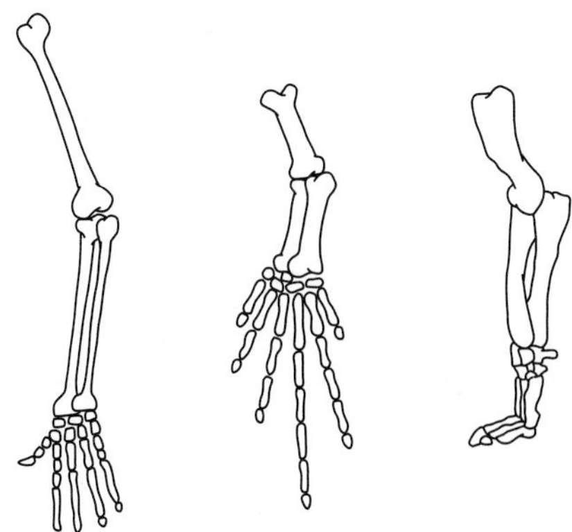

(1) developed in a common environment.
(2) developed from the same earlier species.
(3) identical genetic makeup.
(4) identical methods of obtaining food.

**4** The evolutionary pathways of seven living species are shown in the diagram below. Which two species are likely to have the most similar DNA base sequences?

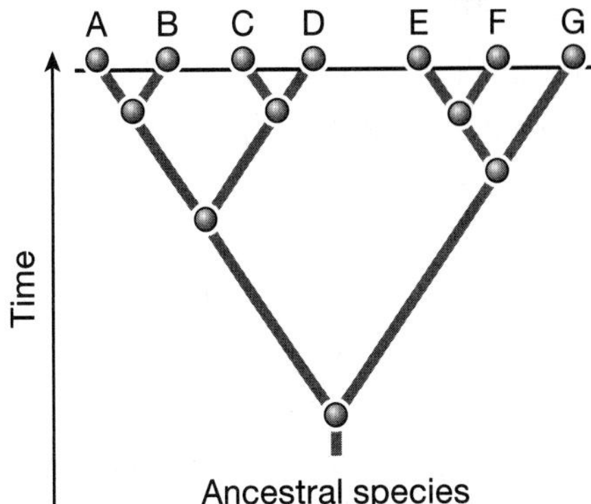


(1) B and G
(2) E and G
(3) B and C
(4) C and D

5 According to some scientists, patterns of evolution can be illustrated by the diagrams below. Which statement best explains the patterns seen in these diagrams?

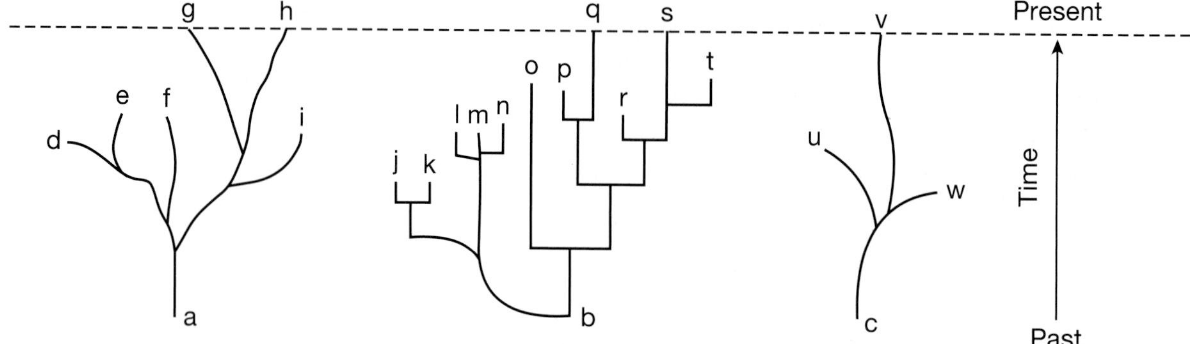


(1) The organisms at the end of each branch can be found in the environment today.
(2) The organisms that are living today have all evolved at the same rate and have undergone the same kinds of changes.
(3) Evolution involves changes that give rise to a variety of organisms, some of which continue to change through time while others die out.
(4) These patterns cannot be used to illustrate the evolution of extinct organisms.

**PART B**

**Base your answers to questions 6 and 7 on the diagram below that shows some evolutionary pathways. Each letter represents a different species.**

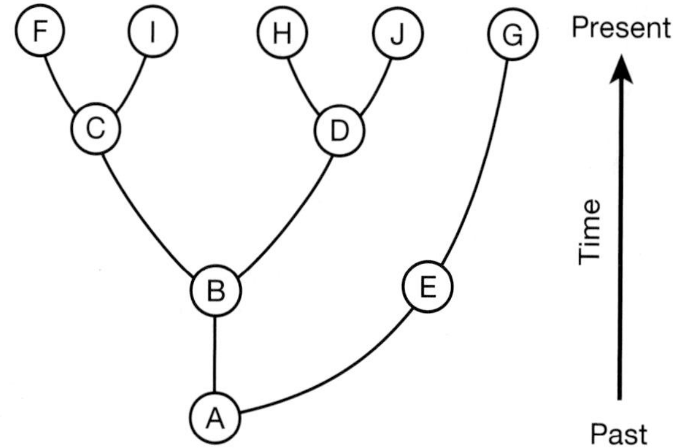


6 The most recent ancestor of organisms D and F is

(1) A
(2) B
(3) C
(4) I

7 Which two organisms are most closely related?

(1) F and I
(2) F and H
(3) A and G
(4) G and J

**8** According to the diagram below, which three species lived on Earth during the same time period?

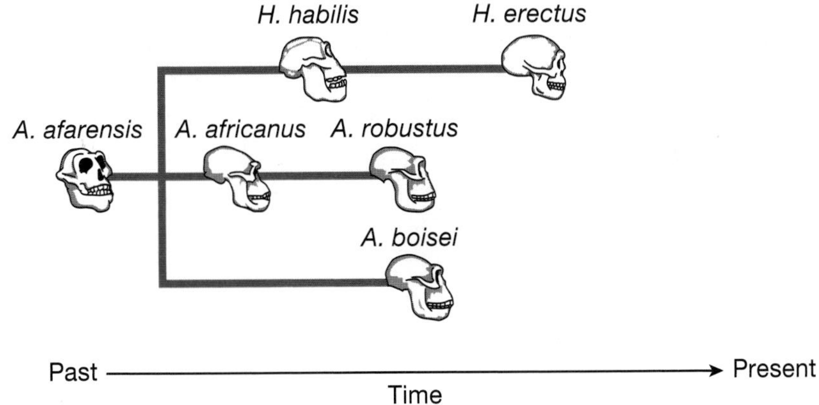


(1) robustus, africanus, afarensis
(2) habilis, erectus, afarensis
(3) habilis, robustus, boisei
(4) africanus, boisei, erectus

**PART D**

**Base your answers to the questions on the information below and on your knowledge of biology.**

Scientists found members of a plant species they did not recognize. They wanted to determine if the unknown species was related to one or more of four known species, A, B, C, and D. The relationship between species can be determined most accurately by comparing the results of gel electrophoresis of the DNA from different species. The chart below represents the results of gel electrophoresis of the DNA from the unknown plant species and the four known species.

Results of Gel Electrophoresis of DNA from Five Plant Species

| Unknown Species | Species A | Species B | Species C | Species D |
|---|---|---|---|---|
| — | | | — | — |
| | | — | | |
| — | — | | — | — |
| — | | | — | |
| | | — | | |
| | | — | | |
| — | | | | |
| — | — | | — | — |
| | — | | | |

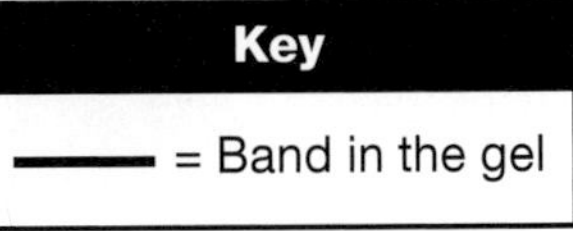


**9** The unknown species is most closely related to which of the four known species? Support your answer.

# Chapter 19

# History of Life on Earth

## Preview



## Why It Matters

The history of life on Earth is like a puzzle; scientists continue to search for evidence and to put it together into a cohesive theory.

**The Fly Geysers of the Black Rock Desert in Nevada are surrounded by a pool of water in which many different types of minerals are dissolved.**

The geyser was created in the 1960s when farmers drilled into the earth to locate water. Boiling water spewed from the ground, and the molecules in the water created colorful deposits.

***The Living Environment***

**Standard 4** Students will understand and apply scientific concepts, principles, and theories pertaining to the physical setting and living environment and recognize the historical development of ideas in science.

**Key Idea 3** Individual organisms and species change over time. ***Major Understandings* - 3.1j, 3.1l**

**Key Idea 6** Plants and animals depend on each other and their physical environment. ***Major Understandings* - 6.2a**

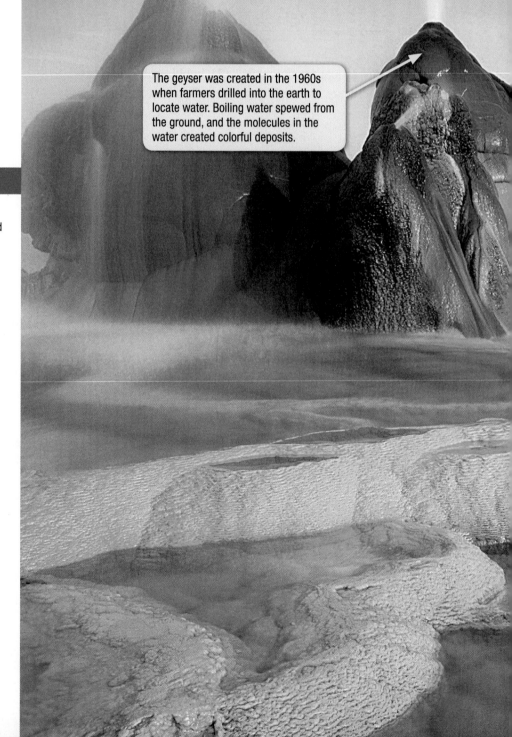

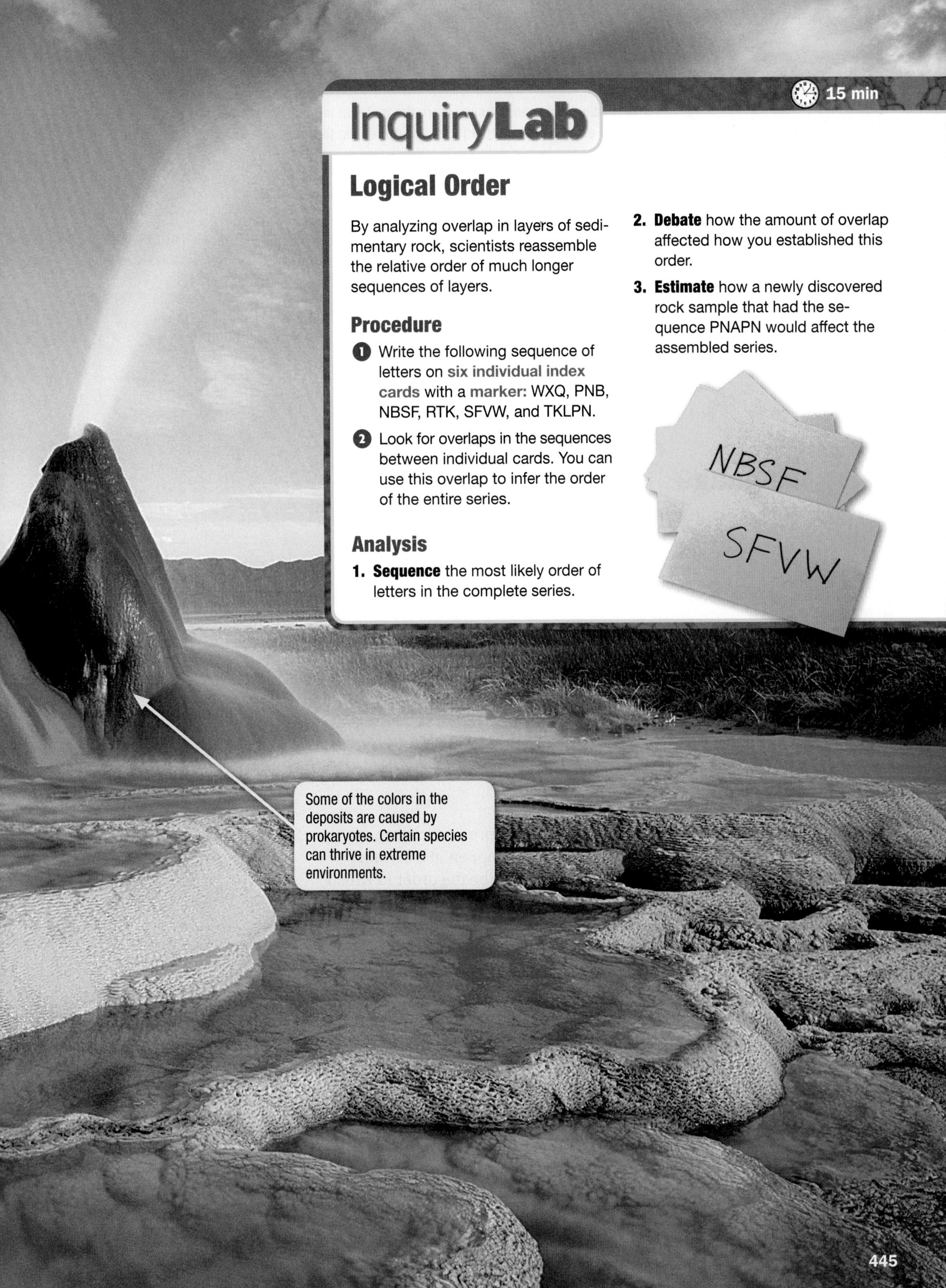


# InquiryLab

## Logical Order

By analyzing overlap in layers of sedimentary rock, scientists reassemble the relative order of much longer sequences of layers.

### Procedure

1. Write the following sequence of letters on **six individual index cards** with a **marker:** WXQ, PNB, NBSF, RTK, SFVW, and TKLPN.
2. Look for overlaps in the sequences between individual cards. You can use this overlap to infer the order of the entire series.

### Analysis

1. **Sequence** the most likely order of letters in the complete series.
2. **Debate** how the amount of overlap affected how you established this order.
3. **Estimate** how a newly discovered rock sample that had the sequence PNAPN would affect the assembled series.

Some of the colors in the deposits are caused by prokaryotes. Certain species can thrive in extreme environments.

These reading tools can help you learn the material in this chapter. For more information on how to use these and other tools, see **Appendix: Reading and Study Skills.**

## Using Words

**Word Parts** You can tell a lot about a word by taking it apart and examining its prefix and root.

**Your Turn** Use the information in the table to write your own definition for the following terms.

1. *microsphere*
2. *lithosphere*
3. *paleolithic*

**Word Parts**

| Word part | Type | Meaning |
|---|---|---|
| *micro-* | prefix | small |
| *paleo-* | prefix | ancient |
| *lith* | root | rock, stone |
| *sphere* | root | ball-shaped object |

## Using Language

**Describing Time** Certain words and phrases can help you get an idea of when something happened and for how long it happened. These phrases are called *specific time markers.* Specific time markers include phrases such as 1 hour, yesterday, the 20th century, and 30 years later.

**Your Turn** Read the sentences below, and write the specific time markers.

1. Jennifer celebrated her 16th birthday on Saturday two weeks ago.
2. Dinosaurs became extinct about 65 million years ago, at the end of the Cretaceous Period.

## Using Science Graphics

**Process Chart** Process charts show the steps that a process takes to get from one point to another point. Events in a process happen in a certain order. There are many words that can be used to describe the order in which things happen. Some of these words include *first, next, then,* and *last.*

**Your Turn** Use the diagram to answer the following questions.

1. Which event happens second?
2. Which event follows RNA self-replication?
3. Describe the process illustrated in this chart in paragraph form. Use sequence words to indicate in what order things happen.

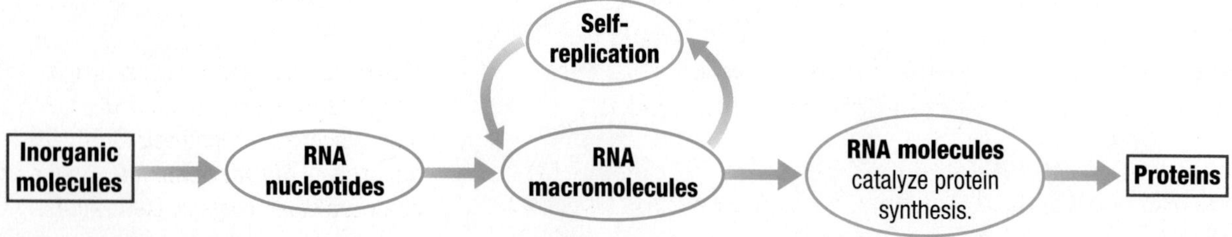

Section 1

# How Did Life Begin?

| Key Ideas | Key Terms | Why It Matters |
|---|---|---|
| › What did the Miller-Urey experiment show about the formation of the basic molecules of life?<br>› What are two theories that propose where the building blocks of life originated on early Earth?<br>› How could molecules have become packaged into cells that contain heritable cellular instructions? | microsphere<br>ribozyme | Studying the origin of life on Earth allows scientists to discover key biological and chemical processes. |

Most scientists think that life on Earth evolved through natural processes. The point when life started likely involved simple chemicals.

## The Basic Chemicals of Life

In the 1920s, Russian scientist Aleksandr I. Oparin and British scientist John B. S. Haldane suggested that Earth's early oceans contained large amounts of organic molecules. They proposed that these molecules formed spontaneously in chemical reactions that were activated by energy from the sun, volcanic eruptions, and lightning.

Oparin and American scientist Harold Urey, along with other scientists, hypothesized that the early atmosphere was rich in hydrogen gas, $H_2$, and hydrogen-containing gases, such as water vapor, $H_2O$, ammonia, $NH_3$, and methane, $CH_4$. They thought that if the atmosphere lacked oxygen gas, a variety of organic compounds made up of the elements found in these gases could form. This hypothesis was tested in the 1950s by Urey and American scientist Stanley Miller.

**The Miller-Urey Experiment** Urey and Miller placed the gases into a device like the one in **Figure 1.** To simulate lightning, they used electrical sparks. After a few days, they found organic molecules in the device, which included some of life's basic building blocks: amino acids, fatty acids, and other hydrocarbons (molecules made of carbon and hydrogen). **› The Miller-Urey experiment showed that, under certain conditions, organic compounds could form from inorganic molecules.**

We now know that the molecules used in the Miller-Urey experiment could not have existed in abundance on early Earth. Four billion years ago, shortly after Earth formed, it did not have a protective layer of ozone gas. Ultraviolet radiation from the sun would have destroyed any ammonia and methane in the atmosphere when the ozone layer did not exist. When ammonia and methane gases are absent from the Miller-Urey experiment, key biological molecules are not made. However, the Miller-Urey experiment clearly shows that complex biological compounds can form from simple building blocks.

› **Reading Check** *What compounds were formed in the Miller-Urey experiment? (See the Appendix for answers to the Reading Checks.)*

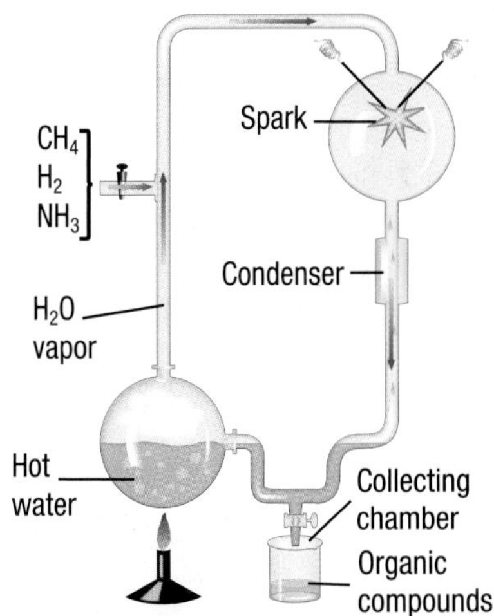


**Figure 1** Urey and Miller simulated an atmosphere that Oparin and others incorrectly hypothesized as the atmosphere of early Earth. The experiment produced several organic compounds.

## Life's Building Blocks

Scientists agree that the building blocks of life formed under special conditions. They research environments that could have made these molecules. **❯ Among the hypotheses that address the origin of life, one states that early biological molecules formed close to hydrothermal vents. Organic molecules may also have arrived on early Earth in meteorites.**

**Hydrothermal Vents** Some scientists think that the chemical reactions that produced the first biological molecules occurred in the oceans of early Earth. The heat from hydrothermal vents, shown in **Figure 2,** could have provided energy for chemical reactions. Within the sea, biological molecules also would have been protected from potentially harmful solar radiation.

**Space** Some scientists think that organic molecules could have arrived on Earth on meteorites or comets. For example, the meteorite shown in **Figure 2** contains amino acids. Organic molecules likely arrived on early Earth from outside of our atmosphere. It is unknown, however, whether these chemicals influenced the history of life on Earth. But we know that such impacts were more frequent in the early history of Earth than they are now.

**ACADEMIC VOCABULARY**

**impact** collision

## The First Cells

Research continues that might provide clues to how biological molecules first began to group together and become packaged into cells. For example, how did amino acids link to form proteins? There are major differences between simple organic molecules and the large organic molecules found in living cells. Research has shown that amino acids can form proteins under certain conditions.

**Forming a Cell** How did molecules become packaged together inside a cell membrane? To answer this question, scientists have studied the behavior of organic molecules in water. Lipids, which make up cell membranes, tend to combine in water. Certain lipids, when combined with other molecules, can form a tiny droplet that has a surface that resembles a cell membrane.

**Figure 2** Scientists have suggested that the basic chemicals of life could have originated in deep-sea vents or from outside our atmosphere. **❯ Why do scientists study the conditions around hydrothermal vents?**

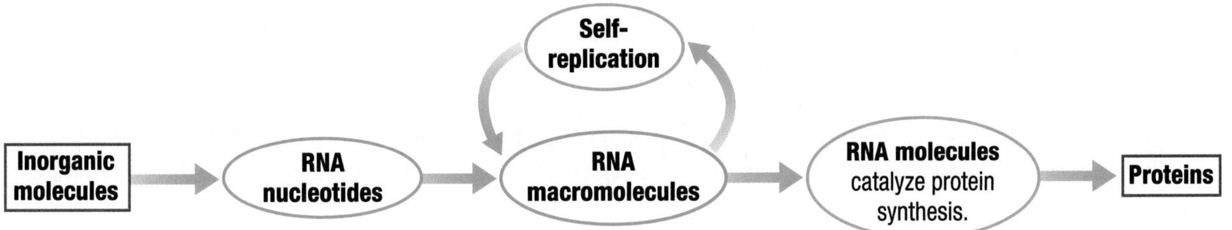


**Figure 3** In this proposed model of protein formation, chemical reactions between inorganic molecules formed RNA nucleotides. The nucleotides assembled into large RNA molecules which were able to replicate and to catalyze the formation of proteins.

Further research has shown that, in water, lipids can form tiny spherical structures called **microspheres** that act like a membrane. **› Many scientists think that the formation of microspheres may have been the first step toward cellular organization.** Microspheres could not be considered cells, however, unless they had characteristics of living things, including heredity.

**Origin of Heredity** How did heredity begin? Recall that our DNA contains instructions for making proteins. DNA is also passed on from one generation to the next. In the laboratory, scientists have not been able to make most proteins or DNA form spontaneously in water. However, scientists have been able to form short chains of RNA, the nucleic acid that helps carry out the instructions of DNA, in water.

Scientists now know that RNA molecules perform many tasks in a cell. There are several types of RNA that accomplish these tasks. Each type of RNA has a unique structure that relates to its function. In the 1980s, American scientists Thomas Cech and Sidney Altman found that a certain type of RNA molecule, called a **ribozyme,** can act like an enzyme. Also, they showed that RNA can form spontaneously in water, without DNA. Other scientists have hypothesized that RNA was the first self-replicating molecule that stored information and that catalyzed the formation of the first proteins. One idea of how RNA could have been involved in protein synthesis is shown in **Figure 3.** It was further hypothesized that RNA could have changed—evolved—from one generation to the next. Scientists hypothesize that DNA and proteins eventually took over these roles in the cell.

**› Reading Check** ***Explain how RNA could have existed before DNA.***

**Process Chart** Use the process chart in **Figure 3** to understand the hypothesis about how proteins were created. What is the significance of the loop at the self-replication step?

**microsphere** (MIE kroh SFIR) a hollow microscopic spherical structure that is usually composed of proteins or a synthetic polymer

**ribozyme** (RIE buh ZIEM) a type of RNA that can act as an enzyme

## Section 1 Review

### › KEY IDEAS

1. **State** what the Miller-Urey experiment demonstrated.
2. **Describe** two theories that address where the building blocks of life evolved.
3. **Explain** a prevailing theory of how cells evolved.

### CRITICAL THINKING

4. **Evaluating Conclusions** People once believed fish could form from the mud in a pond that sometimes dried up. How could you demonstrate that this conclusion is false?
5. **Inferring Conclusions** How might the hypothesis about the origin of heredity change if DNA could form spontaneously in water?

### USING SCIENCE GRAPHICS

6. **Analyzing Models** Using **Figure 1,** determine what changes to the apparatus used by Miller and Urey would be necessary to model the production of amino acids and other organic compounds near hydrothermal vents.

Section

# 2 The Age of Earth

| Key Ideas | Key Terms | Why It Matters |
|---|---|---|
| ❯ How is the fossil record used to chronicle the history of life?<br>❯ How do paleontologists date fossils?<br>❯ What evidence was used to make the geologic time scale? | fossil record<br>relative dating<br>radiometric dating<br>half-life<br>geologic time scale<br>mass extinction | The fossil record is used to understand the diversity of life on Earth. |

*The Living Environment*
**Standard 4**
**3.1l** Extinction of a species occurs when the environment changes and the adaptive characteristics of a species are insufficient to allow its survival. Fossils indicate that many organisms that lived long ago are extinct. Extinction of species is common; most of the species that have lived on Earth no longer exist.

Scientists think Earth formed more than 4.5 billion years ago. Fossil evidence indicates that for much of that long history, Earth has been the home of living things.

## The Fossil Record

The **fossil record** includes all fossil remains of living things on Earth. **❯ Both the geographical distribution of organisms and when they lived on Earth can be inferred from the fossil record. It chronicles the diversity of life on Earth.** The fossil record also provides evidence of intermediate forms of life and suggests how organisms are related to each other. Although our examination of the fossil record will never be complete, it presents strong evidence that evolution has taken place.

**How Fossils Form** Most fossils are found in sedimentary rock. These fossils form when organisms and traces of organisms are rapidly buried in fine sediments that are deposited by water, wind, or volcanic eruptions. The formation of one kind of fossil from a marine animal is shown in **Figure 4.** Environments that often cause fossil formation are wet lowlands, slow-moving streams, lakes, shallow seas, and areas near volcanoes that spew volcanic ash. However, many species have lived in environments where fossils do not form. Even if an organism lives in an environment where fossils can form, its dead body might not be buried in sediment before it decays or is eaten.

**Figure 4** Fossils can form in several ways. The most common way is when an organism dies and is buried in sediment. **❯ What happens when an organism is covered by sediment?**

❶ This trilobite dies and becomes buried under layers of sediment that are deposited by water.

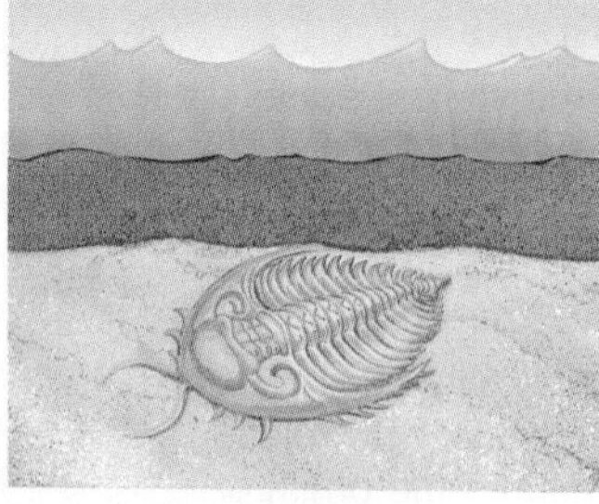
❷ The organism gradually dissolves and leaves a hollow impression, or mold, in the sediment.

❸ Over time, the mold may fill with minerals, which forms a cast of the organism.

## Analyzing Fossil Evidence

Earth's surface changes constantly. Rocks are eroding and are laid down as sediment. This sediment forms layers of sedimentary rock called *strata,* shown in **Figure 5.** According to the *principle of superposition,* older strata are covered by younger strata. However, geologic events such as earthquakes can affect how the strata are arranged. **❯ In order to analyze fossil evidence, paleontologists use both relative and absolute dating methods to date fossils.**

**fossil record** the history of life in the geologic past as indicated by the traces or remains of living things

**relative dating** a method of determining whether an event or object, such as a fossil, is older or younger than other events or objects

**Types of Fossils** The most common types of fossils are little-altered mineral shells of animals. In some cases, as shown in **Figure 4,** an organism breaks down, leaving a hollow space. This mold may fill with minerals. In other cases, the pores of the organism are filled with minerals, preserving the shape of the organism. An example of a mineralized fossil is shown in **Figure 5.** In rare cases, fossils are preserved in hardened plant sap, or amber. In these fossils, soft parts of the tissue are preserved in detail.

**Word Parts** The suffix *-ologist* means "one who studies." What do you think a paleontologist does?

**Relative Age** A process called **relative dating** is used to estimate ages of fossils found within strata. Relative dating cannot reveal a fossil's age, in years. But it can reveal the order that strata and the fossils within them were laid down over time. Paleontologists organize fossils into a sequence based on the relative age of the strata in which the fossil was found.

**Index Fossils** An *index fossil* is a fossil of an organism that was common and had widespread geographical distribution during a certain time in Earth's history. Index fossils are used to estimate the age of other strata that contain the same type of fossil. Scientists have compared patterns of strata and the index fossils within them to make the geologic time scale.

**❯ Reading Check** ***What is the principle of superposition?***

**Figure 5** Rock strata are easily visible in the Grand Canyon. Gastropod fossils like this one have been found in the region.

Strata on top formed more recently than strata beneath them.

Older strata are underneath younger strata.

Hands-On

# QuickLab

15 min

## Radioactive Decay

You can use pennies to model radioactive decay.

### Procedure

1. Work in pairs. Make a data table like the one shown.
2. Place 100 pennies into a box that has a lid.
3. Shake the box gently. Remove the pennies showing heads. This process models one half-life. Record the number of coins remaining in the box.
4. Repeat step 3 until every coin has been removed.
5. Make a line graph of your data. Label "Half-life" on the x-axis and "Coins remaining" on the y-axis.

| Half-life | Number of coins remaining |
|---|---|
| 1 | |
| 2 | |
| 3 | |

### Analysis

1. **Identify** what "Number of coins remaining" represents.
2. **Calculate** the age of your sample if 25 coins remained. Assume that each half-life equals 5,730 years.
3. CRITICAL THINKING **Evaluating Models** Describe how this model illustrates radioactive decay.

**radiometric dating** a method of determining the absolute age of an object, often by comparing the relative percentages of a radioactive (parent) isotope and a stable (daughter) isotope

**half-life** the time required for half of a sample of a radioactive substance to decay

**geologic time scale** the standard method used to divide Earth's long natural history into manageable parts

**mass extinction** an episode during which large numbers of species become extinct

**Absolute Age** Relative dating can show only whether an object is older or younger than another object. **Radiometric dating** estimates the age in years of an object by measuring certain radioactive isotopes that the igneous rock that surrounds the object contains. An *isotope* is a form of an element whose atomic mass differs from that of other atoms of the same element. Radioactive isotopes, or *radioisotopes,* are unstable isotopes that break down and give off energy in the form of charged particles, or radiation. This breakdown is called *radioactive decay.*

When the radioactive isotope, called a "parent," decays, it produces new isotopes—*daughter* isotopes—that are smaller and more stable. The time required for half of a sample of parent radioisotope to decay into a daughter isotope is the isotope's **half-life. Figure 6** shows this concept. Each radioisotope has a specific half-life, and the rate at which a radioisotope decays is not affected by external factors.

**Measuring Age** As the parent radioisotope decays, the amount of the daughter radioisotope increases. By comparing the amounts of certain radioisotopes and their daughter isotopes, scientists can calculate how many half-lives have passed since a material formed. One radioisotope that is widely used to date organic materials, such as mummified remains, is carbon-14. The half-life of carbon-14 is relatively short—5,730 years. Carbon-14 is used to measure the age of carbon-containing materials that are younger than 75,000 years old. Older materials have too little isotope remaining for scientists to accurately measure the age of the materials. To find the age of the older materials, scientists have to measure other radioisotopes.

**Figure 6** This graph shows the rate of decay of a radioactive isotope.

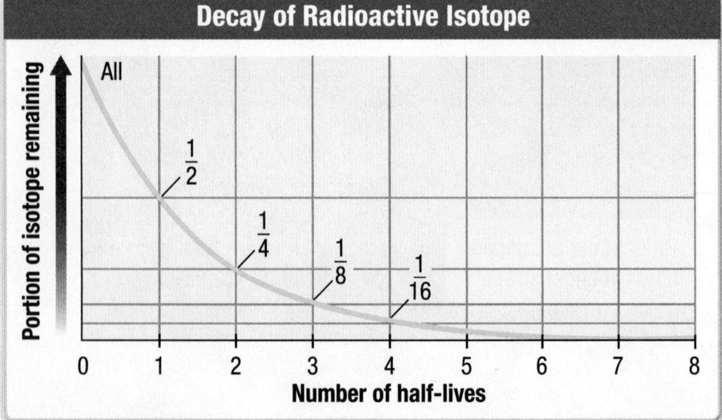

## Describing Geologic Time

The **geologic time scale** organizes geologic and evolutionary events. **› The geologic time scale is based on evidence in the fossil record and has been shaped by mass extinctions.** A shortened geologic time scale is shown in **Figure 7.**

**Divisions of Geologic Time** Earth has existed for more than 4 billion years. From the beginning of Earth to about 542 million years ago is often referred to as Precambrian time. From the end of Precambrian time to the present, Earth's history is divided into three *eras*—the Paleozoic Era, the Mesozoic Era, and the Cenozoic Era. These three eras are further divided into periods. Humans appeared during the Quaternary Period.

**Mass Extinction** Recall that the extinction of a species is the death of all members of that species. When large numbers of species become extinct, the event is called a **mass extinction.** The fossil record indicates that many mass extinctions have occurred during Earth's history. Evidence indicates that worldwide geologic and climate changes are common factors that contribute to mass extinctions. Mass extinctions may have contributed to overall biodiversity on Earth. After a mass extinction, opportunities open for new life-forms to emerge.

Mass extinctions have been used to mark the divisions of geologic time. Large mass extinctions mark the boundaries between eras, as shown on **Figure 7.** For example, mass extinctions occurred at the end of Precambrian time, at the end of the Paleozoic Era, and at the boundary between the Mesozoic Era and Cenozoic Era. Smaller mass extinctions mark the divisions between periods.

**› Reading Check** *What evidence shows that mass extinctions occur?*

**Geologic Time Scale**

| Era | Period | Time* |
|---|---|---|
| Cenozoic | Quaternary | 1.8 |
| | Tertiary | 65.5 |
| MASS EXTINCTION | | |
| Mesozoic | Cretaceous | 146 |
| | Jurassic | 200 |
| | Triassic | 251 |
| MASS EXTINCTION | | |
| Paleozoic | Permian | 299 |
| | Carboniferous | 359 |
| | Devonian | 416 |
| | Silurian | 444 |
| | Ordovician | 488 |
| | Cambrian | 542 |
| MASS EXTINCTION | | |
| Precambrian time | | >4,500 |

*indicates how many millions of years ago the period began

**Figure 7** The geologic time scale is based on fossil evidence. The time in the scale refers to the number of years ago that the time period started. **› How long did the Permian period last?**

## Section 2 Review

**› KEY IDEAS**

1. **Describe** how the fossil record chronicles the history of life.
2. **Explain** how dating methods are used to analyze fossil evidence.
3. **State** the evidence that scientists have used to create the geologic time scale.

**CRITICAL THINKING**

4. **Constructing Explanations** Why might the fossil record give an inaccurate picture of the history of biodiversity? Explain your answer.
5. **Explaining Relationships** How could index fossils in two different rock strata in a series help a paleontologist to estimate the absolute age of fossils in a layer of rock between them? Explain your reasoning.

**METHODS OF SCIENCE**

6. **Describing Methods** You are a paleontologist who is digging for fossils in a remote area. Describe the methods you would use on the dig to make sure that you could estimate the age of the fossils.

Section

# 3 Evolution of Life

| Key Ideas | Key Terms | Why It Matters |
|---|---|---|
| ❯ What major evolutionary developments occurred during Precambrian time?<br>❯ What dominant organisms evolved during the Paleozoic Era?<br>❯ What dominant organisms evolved during the Mesozoic Era and the Cenozoic Era? | cyanobacteria<br>endosymbiosis | Knowing the order in which life-forms evolved helps scientists form new hypotheses of how life forms are related. |

***The Living Environment***
**Standard 4**

**3.1j** Billions of years ago, life on Earth is thought by many scientists to have begun as simple, single-celled organisms. About a billion years ago, increasingly complex multicellular organisms began to evolve.

**3.1l** Extinction of a species occurs when the environment changes and the adaptive characteristics of a species are insufficient to allow its survival. Fossils indicate that many organisms that lived long ago are extinct. Extinction of species is common; most of the species that have lived on Earth no longer exist.

**6.2a** As a result of evolutionary processes, there is a diversity of organisms and roles in ecosystems. This diversity of species increases the chance that at least some will survive in the face of large environmental changes. Biodiversity increases the stability of the ecosystem.

**cyanobacteria**
(SIE uh noh bak TIR ee uh) bacteria that carry out photosynthesis; blue-green algae

When did life first evolve on Earth? To find out, scientists study fossils and other evidence of early life, such as "signatures" of certain isotopes in rock. These isotopes are associated with living things.

## Precambrian Time

Precambrian time spanned between about 4.5 billion and 542 million years ago. Many critical events occurred during this long period of Earth's history. ❯ **Single-celled prokaryotes and later, eukaryotes, evolved and flourished in Precambrian time. The evolution of multicellular organisms set the stage for the evolution of modern organisms. The accumulation of atmospheric oxygen allowed organisms to become larger and live on land.**

Early Earth was a dangerous place. Meteors bombarded the planet in large numbers. This activity heated Earth's surface repeatedly and made our planet a hostile place for living things. Eventually, fewer meteor impacts occurred, which allowed early cells to evolve.

**Prokaryotic Life** Recall that organisms on Earth are divided into three groups: eukaryotes and Archaea and bacteria, the prokaryotes. Living examples from these two groups are shown in **Figure 8.** The close relationship of some eukaryotic genes to those of archaeans suggests that archaea played a role in eukaryote evolution.

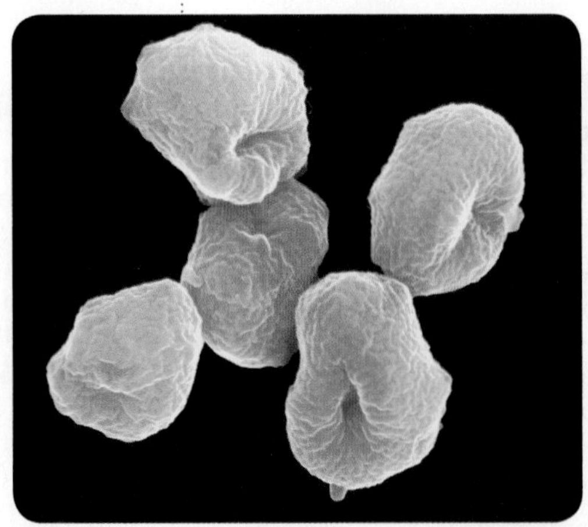

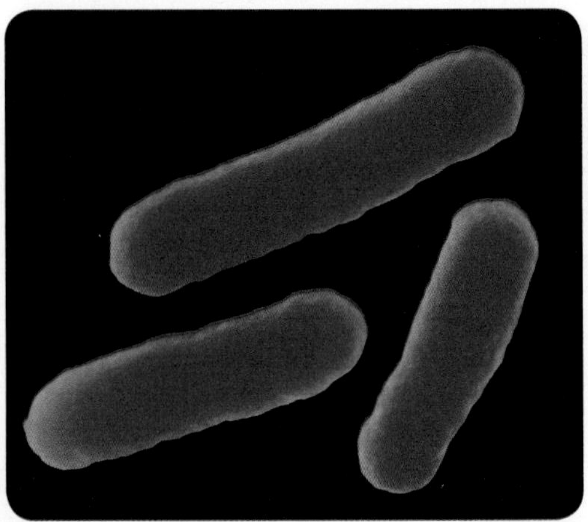

**Figure 8** *Sulfolobus* (left) is a living example of archaea. *Escherichia coli* (right) is a living example of bacteria. Both archaea and bacteria are groups of organisms that have existed since ancient times.

**Figure 9** Fossilized mats of cyanobacteria, called *stromatolites,* are the most common Precambrian fossils. These modern stromatolites are similar to stromatolites that existed during Precambrian time.

Recall that most prokaryotes are single-celled organisms that lack membrane-bound organelles. The oldest presumed fossils, which are microscopic fossils of prokaryotes, come from rock that is about 3.5 billion years old. The earliest common fossils are those of marine cyanobacteria. **Cyanobacteria** are photosynthetic prokaryotes. Modern cyanobacteria, clustered in layered structures called *stromatolites* are shown in **Figure 9.**

**Formation of Oxygen** About 2.4 billion years ago, the chemistry of rock layers changed markedly. Because of this, scientists think that cyanbacteria began adding oxygen to the atmosphere at this time. Before cyanobacteria appeared, oxygen gas was scarce on Earth. But as ancient cyanobacteria carried out photosynthesis, they released oxygen gas into Earth's oceans. This oxygen eventually escaped into the air. The increase of oxygen in the ocean destroyed many marine prokaryotes. These organisms had evolved to live without oxygen, which was a poison to them.

As oxygen reached Earth's upper atmosphere, the sun's rays caused some of the oxygen gas, $O_2$, to chemically react and form molecules of ozone, $O_3$. In the upper atmosphere, the ozone layer blocks some of the ultraviolet radiation of the sun. The sun provides life-giving light, but overexposure to ultraviolet radiation is dangerous to living things. Organisms on the very early Earth could not survive on land because ultraviolet radiation damaged their DNA. After millions of years however, enough ozone had accumulated to make land a safe place for organisms to live. The first organisms to live on land were prokaryotes.

**Eukaryotic Life** Later in Precambrian time, the first eukaryotes appeared. Most eukaryotic cells are much larger than prokaryotic cells are. Eukaryotes have a complex system of internal membranes, and their DNA is enclosed within a nucleus. Most eukaryotes have mitochondria. Plants and some protists also have chloroplasts, which carry out photosynthesis. Mitochondria and chloroplasts are the size of prokaryotes, and they contain their own DNA, which is similar to that of prokaryotes.

**Describing Time** Scientists describe events in Earth's history in terms of geologic time. Look for references to time in this section, and construct a table of their meanings.

**ACADEMIC VOCABULARY**

**accumulate** to collect, especially over a period of time

**endosymbiosis** (EN doh SIM bie OH ses) a mutually beneficial relationship in which one organism lives within another

**Origin of Energy-Releasing Organelles** Mitochondria and chloroplasts likely originated as described by the endosymbiotic theory proposed by Lynn Margulis, which is illustrated in **Figure 10.** **Endosymbiosis** is a mutually beneficial relationship in which one organism lives within another. Endosymbiotic theory proposes that larger cells engulfed smaller cells, which then began to live inside larger cells. According to this theory, mitochondria are the descendants of symbiotic, aerobic (oxygen-requiring) bacteria. Likewise, scientists think that chloroplasts are thought to be the descendants of symbiotic, photosynthetic bacteria. The following observations support the theory that mitochondria and chloroplasts descended from bacteria:

- **Size and Structure** Mitochondria are the same size as most bacteria. Chloroplasts are the same size as some cyanobacteria.
- **Genetic Material** Both chloroplasts and mitochondria contain genes that are different from those found in the nucleus of the host cell and that are closely related to bacterial genes.
- **Ribosomes** Mitochondrial and chloroplast ribosomes are similar in size and structure to bacterial ribosomes.
- **Reproduction** Like bacteria, chloroplasts and mitochondria reproduce by simple fission. This replication takes place independently of the cell cycle of the host cell.

SciLinks. www.scilinks.org
Topic: Endosymbiosis
Code: HX80506

**Multicellularity** *Volvox,* a colonial protist, is shown in **Figure 11.** Colonies differ from true multicellular organisms. In true multicellularity, cells communicate with one another and differentiate to form different cell types. The development of multicellular organisms marked an important step in the evolution of life-forms that are familiar to us. Multicellularity first developed in protists in Precambrian time. Scientists think that the first multicellular organisms began as clusters of single-celled organisms. Eventually these cells took on specialized functions.

**Figure 10** The theory of endosymbiosis states that energy-releasing organelles evolved from ancestors of bacteria.
**› What genetic evidence supports the theory of endosymbiosis?**

go.hrw.com
interact online
Keyword: HX8LIFF10

**Endosymbiotic Theory**

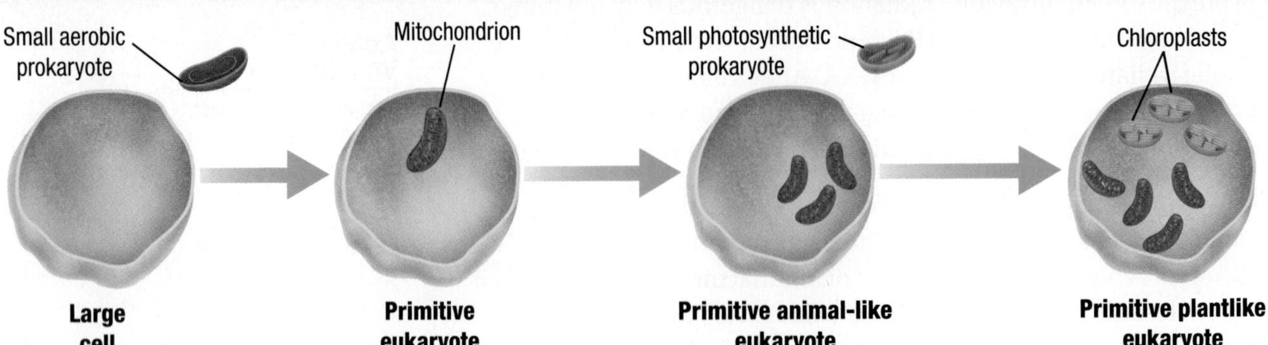


1. Large prokaryotes and small aerobic or photosynthetic prokaryotes exist as separate cells.
2. Aerobic prokaryotes enter the large prokaryotic cell either as parasites or as undigested prey.
3. Instead of being digested, the small prokaryotes survived and began to live inside the host cell.
4. The internalized prokaryotes eventually performed either cellular respiration (mitochondria) or photosynthesis (chloroplasts).

Hands-On

# QuickLab

15 min

## Timeline of Earth 4.3.1j, 4.3.1l

Using some calculations, you can create your own timeline of Earth's history.

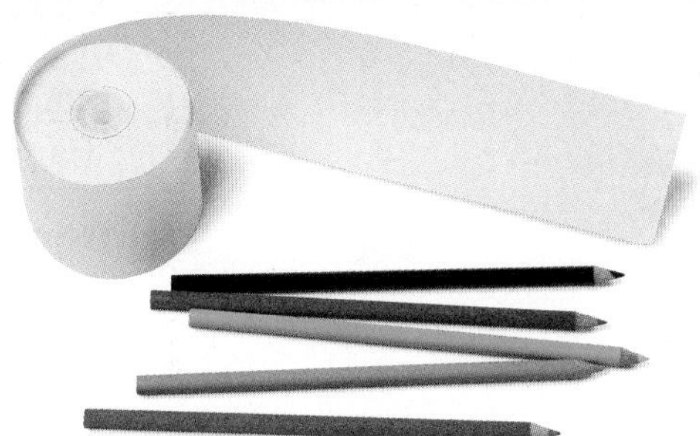

### Procedure

1. Copy the table shown onto a **piece of paper.**
2. Complete the table by using this scale: 1 cm is equal to 10 million years.
3. Lay a **5 m strip of adding-machine paper** flat on a hard surface. Use a **meterstick,** a **metric ruler,** and a **pencil** to mark off the beginning and end of Precambrian time according to the time scale that you calculated. Do the same for the three eras. Label each division of time, and make each a different color with **colored pencils.**
4. Refer to the geologic time scale shown in **Figure 7.** Using the same scale as in step 2, calculate the scale length for each period listed. Mark the boundaries of each period on the paper strip, and label them.
5. Decorate your strip by adding names or drawings of the organisms that lived in each division of time.

| Era | Length of time (years) | Scale length |
|---|---|---|
| Precambrian | 4,058,000,000 | |
| Palezoic | 291,000,000 | |
| Mesozoic | 185,500,000 | |
| Cenozoic | 65,500,000 (to present) | |

### Analysis

1. **Identify** in which period humans appeared.
2. **Calculate** the length from the period in which humans appeared to the present.
3. CRITICAL THINKING **Interpreting Graphics** What percentage of the geologic time scale do these eras combined represent? What percentage of the geologic time scale does Precambrian time represent?

**Dominant Life** For most of Precambrian time, life probably was limited to prokaryotes and protists, which are eukaryotes. Recent evidence suggests that the oldest known fossils of multicellular eukaryotes have been found in rock that is about 1 billion years old. The first known fossils of true multicellular animals are about 632 million years old. Very early animal fossils are scarce because most animals at that time had soft body parts that did not fossilize well. Fossils of marine animals similar to modern sea anemones and snail-like animals are dated to late Precambrian time.

**Mass Extinctions** The first known mass extinction in Precambrian time killed many microorganisms, including cyanobacteria and other types of bacteria. A second mass extinction, late in Precambrian time, killed off many animals that had recently evolved. This mass extinction opened up new ecological niches, and preceded a burst of diversification in animals. The animals, with their hard exoskeletons and shells, that evolved after this extinction have left a rich fossil record as evidence of evolution.

› **Reading Check** ***Why is the evolution of colonial organisms an important step in evolution?***

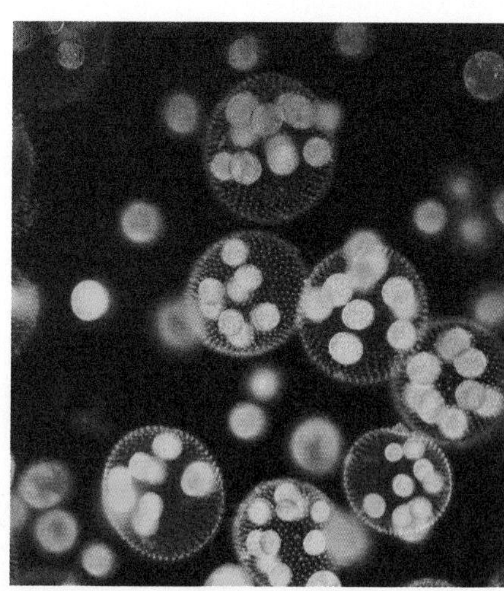

**Figure 11** *Volvox* is a colonial protist. Cells in a colony remain attached after dividing. But they are not truly multicellular.

## Paleozoic Era

The Cambrian Period, the first period in the Paleozoic Era, was a time of great evolutionary expansion. The rapid diversification of animals that appeared in the fossil record is sometimes referred to as the "Cambrian explosion," though it occurred over several million years.

**Dominant Life** The Paleozoic Era was a time of great evolutionary expansion. ❯ **During the Paleozoic Era, marine invertebrates diversified, and marine vertebrates evolved. The first land plants evolved. Some arthropods, and then some vertebrates, left the oceans to colonize land.**

**Plants and Fungi on Land** The first multicellular organisms to live on land may have been fungi living together with plants or algae. Plants and fungi began living together on the surface of the land about 475 million years ago. Eventually, great forests, illustrated in **Figure 12,** covered much of Earth's landscape.

Plant life from the Paleozoic Era still has an impact on our lives. In the great coal swamps of the Carboniferous Period, organic materials were subjected to pressure from overlying earth. Over millions of years this produced fossil fuels—beds of coal and reservoirs of oil. Humans now burn both oil and coal to release stored energy.

**Arthropods** An arthropod is an animal that has a hard outer skeleton, a segmented body, and paired, jointed limbs. Although many arthropods continued to live in the oceans, the first animals to successfully live on land were also arthropods. An important terrestrial arthropod—the insect—evolved in the late Devonian.

**Vertebrates** A vertebrate is an animal with a backbone. According to the fossil record, the first vertebrates were small, jawless fishes that evolved in the oceans about 530 million years ago. Fishes that have jaws appeared about 430 million years ago. For over one hundred million years, vertebrates lived only in the sea. The first land vertebrates, amphibians, came out of the sea about 370 million years ago. Reptiles evolved from amphibian ancestors about 340 million years ago.

**Figure 12** The Devonian Period, which began about 416 million years ago, was dominated by large forests, such as the one shown in this illustration.

**Mass Extinctions** The fossil record indicates that mass extinctions occurred both at the end of the Ordovician Period (440 million years ago) and just before the end of the Devonian Period (375 million years ago). These events eliminated about 70% of all of the species on Earth. The most devastating of all mass extinctions occurred at the end of the Permian Period, about 252 million years ago. More than 90% of all animals species living at the time became extinct.

## Mesozoic and Cenozoic Eras

Many of the dominant life-forms on our planet diverged during the Mesozoic and Cenozoic Eras. › **Reptiles, dinosaurs, and birds were the dominant animals during the Mesozoic Era, and mammalian animals dominated the Cenozoic Era.**

**Dominant Life** During the Mesozoic Era, dinosaurs and other reptiles evolved to be the dominant life-forms. Therapsids, which were mammal-like reptiles, gave rise to modern mammals at about the same time that dinosaurs evolved, during the Triassic Period. Scientists think that birds evolved from feathered dinosaurs during the Jurassic Period. Flowering plants evolved during the Cretaceous Period of the Mesozoic Era. The Cenozoic Era is the current era. During this era, mammals, such as the woolly mammoth shown in **Figure 13,** became the dominant life-form on land. The first hominids (early human ancestors) evolved during the Tertiary Period. Modern humans did not appear until the Quaternary Period.

**Figure 13** This woolly mammoth is an example of an animal that lived during the Quaternary Period. › **Did woolly mammoths live before or after the K-T extinction?**

**Mass Extinction** A mass extinction 65 million years ago included about two-thirds of all land species, including the dinosaurs. This mass extinction is often called the K-T extinction, because it marks the boundary between the Cretaceous Period (K) of the Mesozoic Era and the Tertiary Period (T) of the Cenozoic Era. Scientists think that this mass extinction was caused by a catastrophic event that had widespread effects.

## Section 3 Review

### › KEY IDEAS

1. **Describe** the major events that occurred during Precambrian time.
2. **Name** the types of life-forms that evolved during the Paleozoic Era.
3. **Describe** the dominant life-forms that evolved during the Mesozoic and Cenozoic eras.

### CRITICAL THINKING

4. **Justifying Conclusions** A classmate states that mitochondria and chloroplasts descended from the same type of bacteria. Does the evidence support this? Explain your reasoning.
5. **Evaluating an Argument** Defend the argument that fossil fuels are *not* a renewable resource.

### CONNECTING KEY IDEAS

6. **Evaluating Viewpoints** Several scientists have said that if a large asteroid struck Earth, the impact could result in a mass extinction. If an asteroid impact did not kill all organisms, would evolution continue or stop? Explain your reasoning.

# Nearing the End

Sixty-five million years ago a mass extinction occurred on Earth. The dinosaurs and more than 50% of other species became extinct. What could have caused this worldwide extinction? In 1980, a group of scientists reported evidence that suggested that a huge asteroid 10 km in diameter struck Earth and triggered the mass extinction.

## Effects of Impact

A 10 km asteroid would hit Earth with the force of 100,000 billion metric tons of TNT. This impact would generate an earthquake 1,000 times stronger than the strongest recorded earthquake and winds of more than 400 km/h. Long-term effects would be more deadly. Debris blasted upward would reenter the atmosphere at high speeds, heating it and igniting forest fires across the globe.

**What Died?** The most affected organisms were in the oceans, where 90% of the plankton was killed, which led to the collapse of the oceanic food chain. On land, dinosaurs became extinct but mammals and most non-dinosaur reptiles did not go extinct.

**Research** Conduct research on the Internet to discover why mammals and most non-dinosaur reptiles survived the KT extinction.

Skills Practice

# Chapter 19 Lab

30 min

## Objectives

- Model the formation and analysis of strata.
- Apply the criteria used to identify index fossils to the strata model.
- Evaluate the effectiveness of the model to illustrate relative fossil age.

## Materials

- graduated cylinder, 100 mL
- water, tap
- aquarium gravel, four distinct colors
- dish, small (8 per group)
- tablespoon
- beans, dried (navy, black, pinto)

## Safety

# Model of Rock Strata

Sedimentary strata are arranged so that, if they remain undisturbed, any layer is older than the strata on top of it but younger than the strata beneath it. One way to study strata and the fossils within them is to take core samples through the earth and compare them to samples taken at different locations. Paleontologists can determine the original order of strata by comparing multiple samples from many locations. In this lab, you will model how strata are formed and how they can be used to construct a record of Earth's geologic and biologic history.

## Procedure

1. Work in groups of three or four. Each student in the group should make a separate model. You will build up a series of layers in a column. You will model eight periods of time using different colors of gravel and different beans. The gravel represents sediment and the beans represent fossils. One tablespoon represents deposition that occurs over a 10,000-year period.
2. **CAUTION: Glass items such as graduated cylinders are fragile and may break.** Add 30 mL of tap water to the graduated cylinder.
3. For the first time period, choose a color. Have each member of the group add 1 Tbsp of that gravel color to their column. Randomly choose one member of the group to omit this layer.
4. Repeat step 3 using another color of your choice until you have modeled eight time periods. At the third time period, insert some navy beans; at the fifth time period, insert pinto beans; at the seventh time period, insert black beans. Record the strata order used by your group. Keep this record as a key to your models.
5. Exchange the models from your group with those of another group. Try to determine the order of strata used by that group.
6. Clean up your lab materials according to your teacher's instructions. Wash your hands before leaving the lab.

## Analyze and Conclude

1. **Recognizing Relationships** Explain how this model relates to how sedimentary strata are formed.
2. SCIENTIFIC METHODS **Analyzing Conclusions** Describe your success at inferring the other group's strata order.
3. SCIENTIFIC METHODS **Inferring Conclusions** Compare the occurrence of the three types of "fossils" across the models from each group. What is the significance of these fossils? Explain your reasoning.
4. **Analyzing Models** If the same fossils are contained within different kinds of strata, can they be classified as index fossils? Explain.

# Chapter 19 Summary

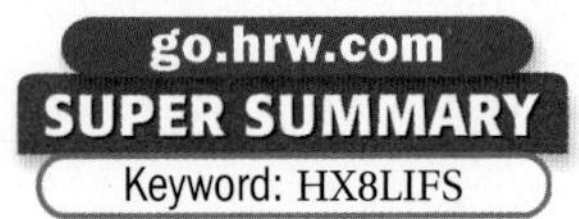


**Key Ideas** | **Key Terms**

## 1 How Did Life Begin?

- The Miller-Urey experiment showed that, under certain conditions, organic compounds could form from inorganic molecules.
- Among the scientific theories that address the origin of life, one suggests that life began close to hydrothermal vents, and another proposes that organic molecules arrived on early Earth from a meteorite.
- The formation of microspheres might have been the first step toward cellular organization.

**Key Terms:**
**microsphere** (449)
**ribozyme** (449)

## 2 The Age of Earth

- Both the geographical distribution of organisms and when organisms lived on Earth can be inferred by examining the fossil record.
- In order to analyze fossil evidence, paleontologists use both relative and absolute dating methods to date fossils.
- The geologic time scale is based on evidence in the fossil record and has been shaped by mass extinctions.

**Key Terms:**
**fossil record** (450)
**relative dating** (451)
**radiometric dating** (452)
**half-life** (452)
**geologic time scale** (453)
**mass extinction** (453)

## 3 Evolution of Life

- Prokaryotes and later, eukaryotes, evolved in the Precambrian. The evolution of multicellular life preceded the evolution of modern life-forms. Atmospheric oxygen allowed life to survive on land.
- During the Paleozoic Era, marine invertebrates diversified, and marine vertebrates evolved. The first land plants evolved. Some arthropods, and then some vertebrates, colonized the land.
- Reptiles, dinosaurs, and birds were the dominant animals in the Mesozoic Era, and mammalian animals were dominant in the Cenozoic Era.

**Key Terms:**
**cyanobacteria** (455)
**endosymbiosis** (456)

# Chapter 19 The Living Environment
# Regents Exam Practice

**PART A: Answer all questions in this part.**

*Directions:* For each statement or question, write on your separate answer sheet the number of the word or expression that best completes the statement or answers the question.

**1** Organism X appeared on Earth much earlier than organism Y. Many scientists believe organism X appeared between 3 and 4 billion years ago, and organism Y appeared approximately 1 billion years ago. Which row in the chart below most likely describes organisms X and Y?

| Row | Organism X | Organism Y |
|---|---|---|
| (1) | simple multicellular | unicellular |
| (2) | complex multicellular | simple multicellular |
| (3) | unicellular | simple multicellular |
| (4) | complex multicellular | unicellular |

(1) row 1
(2) row 2
(3) row 3
(4) row 4

**Base your answer to question 2 on the diagram below that shows some evolutionary pathways. Each letter represents a different species.**

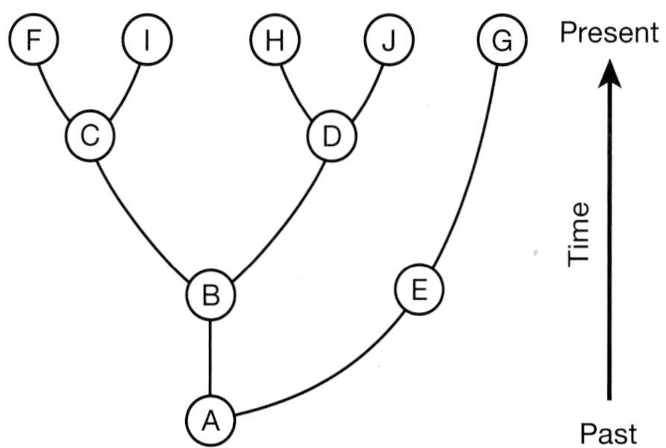


**2** If A represents a simple multicellular heterotrophic organism, B would most likely represent
(1) a single-celled photosynthetic organism
(2) an autotrophic mammal
(3) a complex multicellular virus
(4) another type of simple multicellular heterotroph

**Base your answer to question 3 on the chart below and on your knowledge of biology.**

| A | B | C |
|---|---|---|
| The diversity of multicellular organisms increases. | Simple, single-celled organisms appear. | Multicellular organisms begin to evolve. |

**3** According to most scientists, which sequence best represents the order of biological evolution on Earth?
(1) A → B → C
(2) B → C → A
(3) B → A → C
(4) C → A → B

**4** The first multicellular organisms to invade land were
(1) reptiles.
(2) mammals.
(3) amphibians.
(4) fungi and plants.

**5** Cell specialization came about as a result of
(1) endosymbiosis.
(2) archaebacteria.
(3) the Cambrian period.
(4) multicellularity.

**6** Which ancient organisms were most likely responsible for the development of the ozone layer?
(1) protists
(2) sulfur bacteria
(3) cyanobacteria
(4) plantlike eukaryotes

**7** In the Miller-Urey experiment, which of the following substances were formed after electricity activated chemical reactions?
(1) ozone
(2) methane
(3) hydrocarbons
(4) inorganic molecules

**8** What is the function of a ribozyme?

(1) to form microspheres
(2) to catalyze protein assembly
(3) to catalyze RNA formation
(4) to store genetic information

**Base your answers to question 9 and 10 on the table below and on your knowledge of biology.**

**9** Which element is found in a greater abundance on Earth than in meteorites?

**Estimated Abundance of Elements**

| Element | Percentage of total mass of Earth | Percentage of total mass of meteorites |
|---|---|---|
| Iron | 36.0 | 27.2 |
| Oxygen | 28.7 | 33.2 |
| Magnesium | 13.6 | 17.1 |
| Silicon | 14.8 | 14.3 |
| Sulfur | 1.7 | 1.9 |

(1) iron
(2) sulfur
(3) oxygen
(4) magnesium

**10** If this table is typical of the abundance of all elements on Earth, in meteorites, and on other planets, which statement would be supported?

(1) Earth and meteorites have similar origins.
(2) Earth and meteorites have different origins.
(3) All meteorites formed from parts of Earth.
(4) All elements on Earth come from meteorites.

**11** Which of the following environments is least likely to cause fossil formation?

(1) stream
(2) desert plain
(3) wet lowland
(4) area near a volcano

**12** Most scientists believe that mitochondria are formed from

(1) aerobic bacteria.
(2) photosynthetic bacteria.
(3) aerobic eukaryotes.
(4) anaerobic archaea.

**13** What were the first vertebrates?

(1) reptiles
(2) jawed fishes
(3) amphibians
(4) jawless fishes

**Base your answers to question 14 on the diagram below and on your knowledge of biology.**

**Decay of Radioactive Isotope**

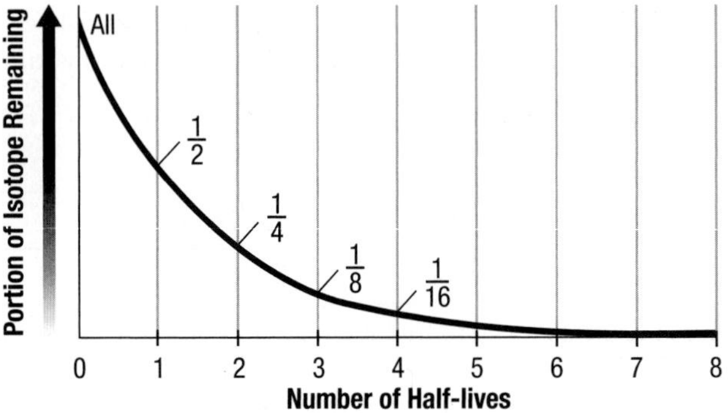


**14** If the half-life of carbon-14 is 5,730 years, how many years would it take for 7/8 of the original amount of carbon-14 in the sample to decay?

(1) 5,014 years
(2) 11,460 years
(3) 17,190 years
(4) 22,920 years

**15** Which gases did Oparin and Urey think were in the atmosphere of early Earth?

(1) water vapor, ammonia, and ozone
(2) oxygen gas, ozone, and water vapor
(3) hydrogen gas, ammonia, and methane
(4) methane, oxygen gas, and hydrogen gas

**16** In an area that has not been disturbed, which rock layer is the oldest?

(1) the layer closest to Earth's surface
(2) the layer closest to Earth's crust
(3) the layer deepest within Earth's crust
(4) the layer that contains fossils

## PART C

**17** If the building blocks for life came to Earth on a meteorite, under what conditions might those building blocks have formed in space?

---

**Base your answers to questions 18 and 19 on the table below and on your knowledge of biology.**

**Radioactive Isotope Half-Life**

| Number of half-lives | Parent isotope | Daughter isotope |
|---|---|---|
| 0 | 100,000 g | 0 g |
| 1 | 50,000 g | 50,000 g |
| 2 | 25,000 g | 75,000 g |
| 3 | 12,500 g | 87,500 g |
| 4 | 6,250 g | 93,750 g |
| 5 | 3,125 g | 96,875 g |

**18** How many half-lives have passed when there is three times more daughter isotope than parent isotope?

**19** How many grams of the parent isotope are left in the sample after three half-lives?

**20** Justify the argument that today's organisms would not exist if mass extinction had not occurred.

**21** Propose a hypothesis for the appearance of all animal phyla on Earth within a relatively short period during late Precambrian time and the early Cambrian Period.

**22** Some forms of air pollution reduce the thickness of Earth's ozone layer. How might this change affect modern life?

# UNIT 6 Humans

**The Living Environment**

**Standard 4** Students will understand and apply scientific concepts, principles, and theories pertaining to the physical setting and living environment and recognize the historical development of ideas in science.

**Key Idea 1** Living things are both similar to and different from each other and from nonliving things.

**Key Idea 2** Organisms inherit genetic information in a variety of ways that result in continuity of structure and function between parents and offspring.

**Key Idea 4** The continuity of life is sustained through reproduction and development.

**Key Idea 5** Organisms maintain a dynamic equilibrium that sustains life.

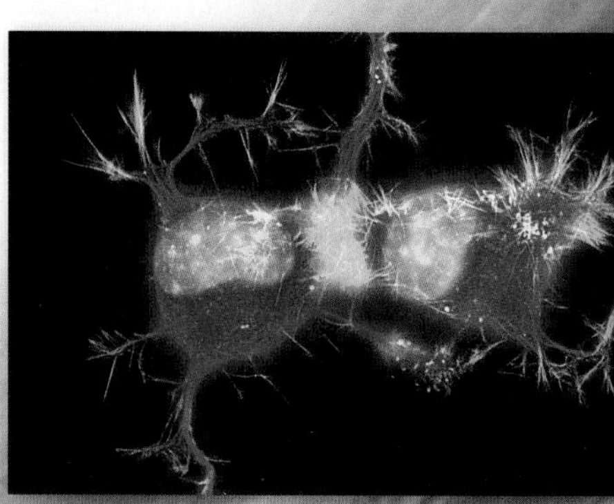

New growth (green) on nerve cells

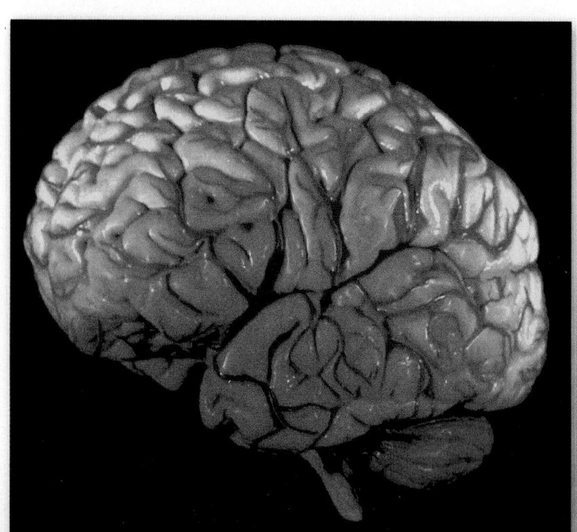

Magnetic resonance imaging (MRI) scan of a human brain

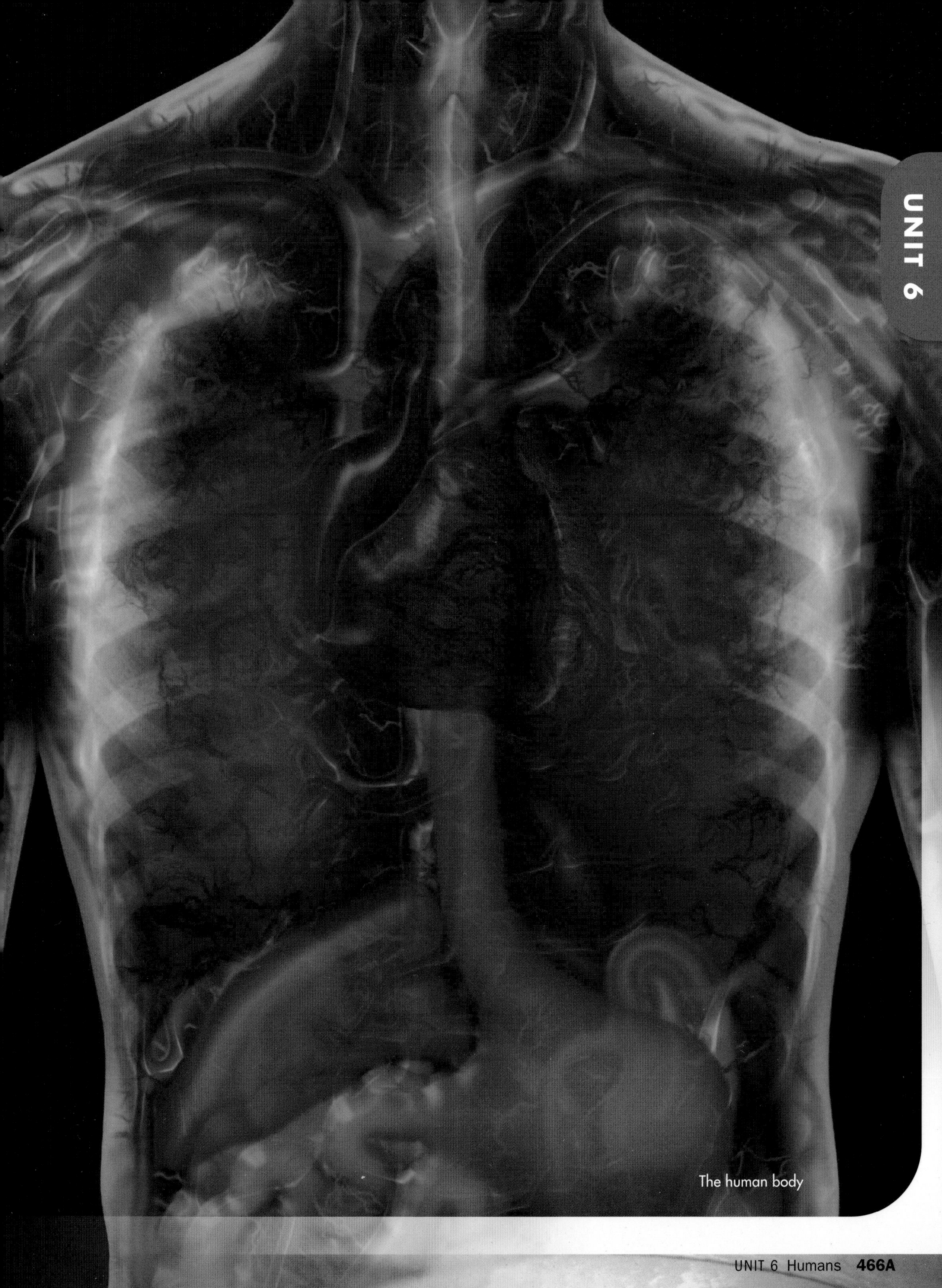

The human body

# Medical Advances

## 400 BCE

Hippocrates writes the oath taken by physicians—to treat all patients with honesty, understanding, and confidentiality.

Hippocrates

## 910 CE

A Persian physician and pharmacist, al-Razi, known as Rhazes, publishes his comprehensive medical book, *Kitab-al-hawi*. The book includes the earliest description of smallpox and, once translated into Latin, becomes an influential medical text in Europe.

## 1552

An anonymous Aztec artist creates *The Badianus Manuscript,* which describes Aztec medical practices. The manuscript includes information about the effective uses of medicinal herbs; the cleaning, suturing, and dressing of wounds; preventive dental hygiene; and the setting of broken bones.

## 1628

William Harvey, an English physician, describes how blood circulates and how the heart acts as a pump. He challenges the belief that the liver creates blood from food.

Human heart

## 1846

In Boston, a dentist named W.T.G. Morton performs the first public demonstration of ether anesthesia on a person during a surgical procedure. Ether had been used as an anesthetic as early as 1842.

## 1895

X rays are discovered by Wilhelm Röntgen. The first "röntgenogram" ever taken was of Röntgen's wife's hand.

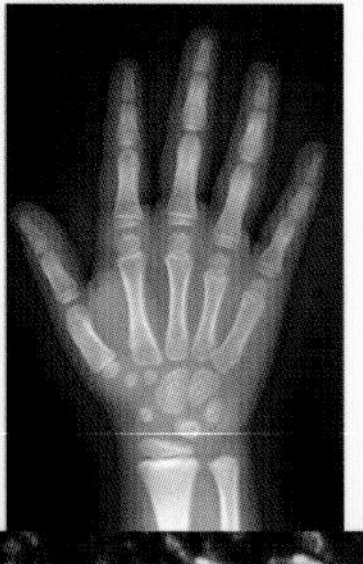

X ray

## 1982

Dr. William DeVries implants an artificial heart into Barney Clark. The heart, a Jarvik-7, is designed by Dr. Robert Jarvik. Barney Clark lives 117 days with the artificial heart.

## 2005

Claudia Mitchell becomes the first woman to be fitted with a computerized ("bionic") prosthetic arm.

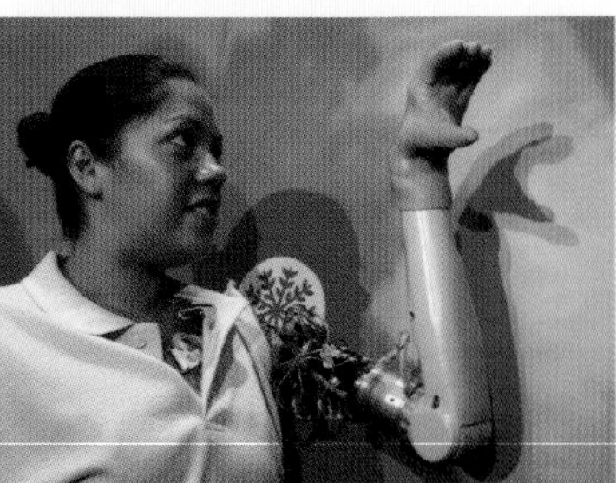

Claudia Mitchell using bionic limb

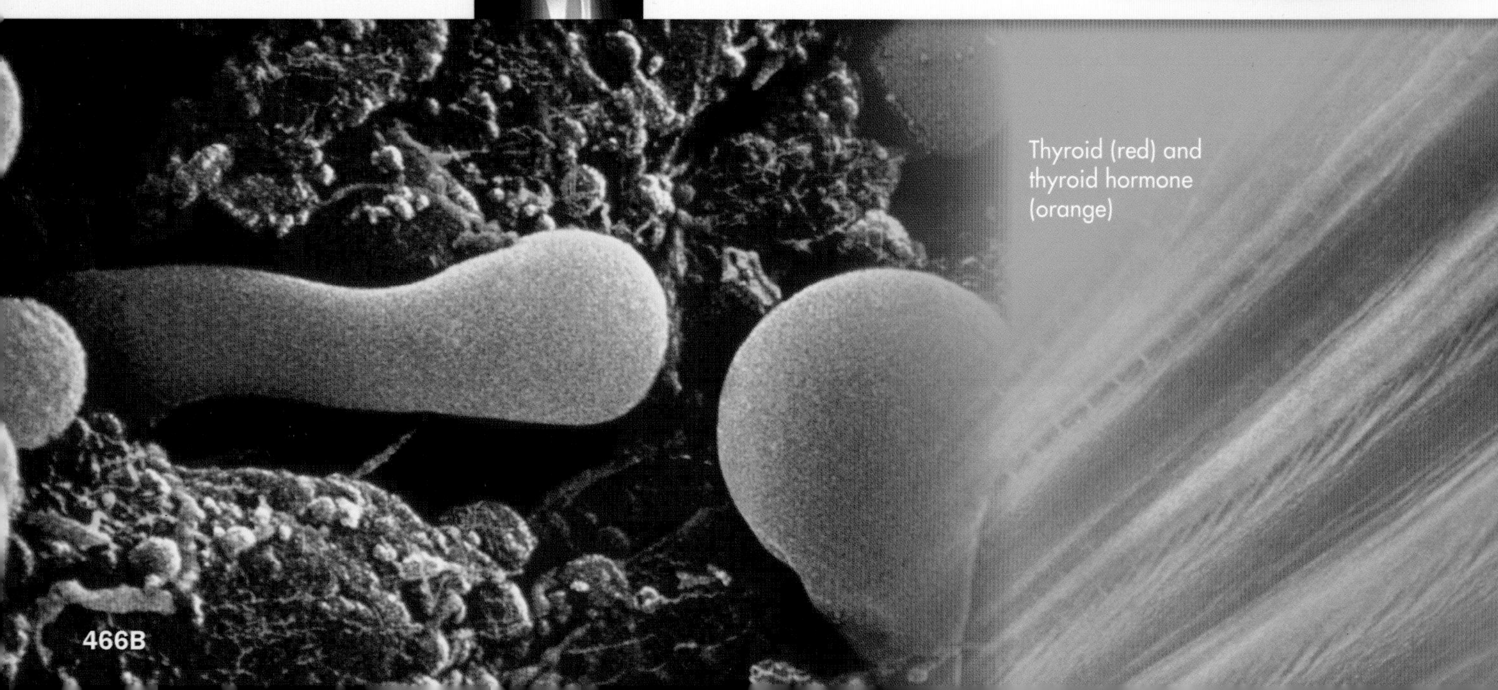

Thyroid (red) and thyroid hormone (orange)

# BIOLOGY CAREER

UNIT 6

## Administrator

**Ellen Mandel**

Ellen Mandel is the assistant principal and supervisor for Science at a New York City public high school. She is also a New York Biology Mentor, president of the Science Supervisors' Association of New York City, and executive board member of the Science Council of New York.

Mandel's favorite part of teaching is opening students' minds to science and to the importance of science in people's daily lives.

Mandel loves to cook and enjoys reading, gardening, needlepoint, and shopping.

## Teacher

**Alan Seidman**

Alan Seidman teaches biology, chemistry, and a class on current topics in science at Margaretville Central School in Margaretville, New York. He is also a Fellow of the Science Teachers Association of New York State.

Seideman loves seeing faces light up when students grasp a new idea or discover that they are good scientists. He feels his most significant accomplishment is having inspired students to pursue science careers.

Seidman is an avid gardener, reader, hiker, and biker. He and his wife enjoy raising dairy goats.

# Chapter 20 Homeostasis and Human Body Systems

## Preview



## Why It Matters

Your body is made of a network of organ systems that work together to maintain a stable internal environment, no matter where you go or what you do.

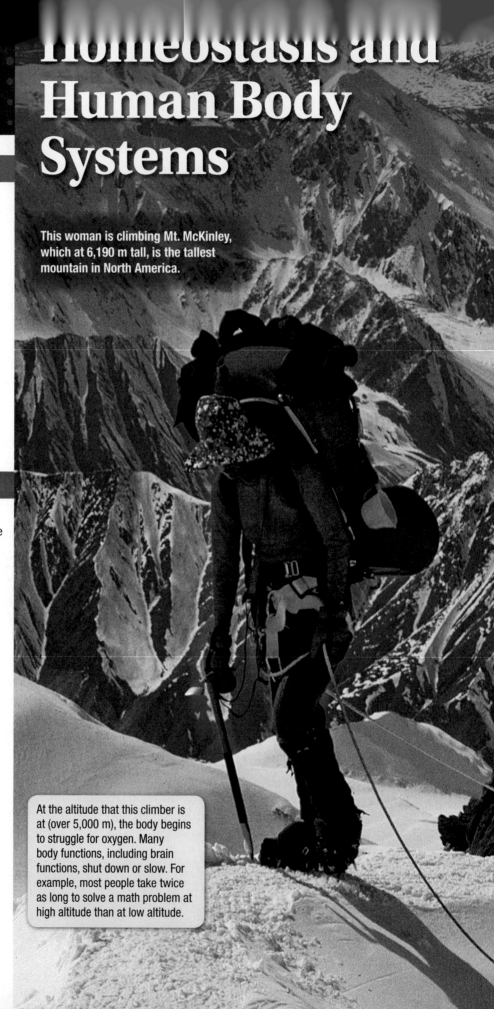

This woman is climbing Mt. McKinley, which at 6,190 m tall, is the tallest mountain in North America.

At the altitude that this climber is at (over 5,000 m), the body begins to struggle for oxygen. Many body functions, including brain functions, shut down or slow. For example, most people take twice as long to solve a math problem at high altitude than at low altitude.

***The Living Environment***

**Standard 4** Students will understand and apply scientific concepts, principles, and theories pertaining to the physical setting and living environment and recognize the historical development of ideas in science.

**Key Idea 1** Living things are both similar to and different from each other and from nonliving things. ***Major Understandings* - 1.2a, 1.2b, 1.2c, 1.2d, 1.2e**

**Key Idea 5** Organisms maintain a dynamic equilibrium that sustains life. ***Major Understandings* - 5.2a, 5.3a, 5.3b**

15 min

# InquiryLab

## Blood Pressure and Homeostasis  4.1.2b, 4.1.2c, 4.5.3a, 4.5.3b

Blood pressure is a measurement of the force that blood applies to artery walls. Many factors can affect blood pressure, so the body must work to maintain homeostasis and keep blood pressure within an acceptable range.

### Procedure

1. Working in a group, familiarize yourself with the operation of a **digital blood-pressure monitor.**
2. Have each group member lay down for 5 min. Take and record everybody's blood pressure.
3. Have members stand up, and immediately retake and record each person's blood pressure.
4. Have members continue standing for 5 min. After the 5 min have passed, retake and record each person's blood pressure.

### Analysis

1. **Draw** a line graph that illustrates how the blood pressure of the test subjects changed over the course of the lab. Be sure to plot all of the readings on your graph.
2. **Explain** what you think caused any changes in blood pressure that you observed.

To compensate for the low levels of oxygen at high altitude, the body begins to make more red blood cells, the heart beats faster, and breathing rate increases.

At Mt. McKinley's peak, the air temperature is usually well below 0°C. Climbers must wear special clothing to deal with the frigid temperatures. Without this special clothing, they could lose body heat so rapidly that death could result in less than an hour.

These reading tools can help you learn the material in this chapter. For more information on how to use these and other tools, see **Appendix: Reading and Study Skills.**

## Using Words

**Word Origins** Many common English words derive from Greek or Latin words. Learning the meanings of some Greek or Latin words can help you understand the meaning of many modern English words.

**Your Turn** Answer the following questions.

**1.** What do you think *homeostasis* might mean?

**2.** How might your body benefit from homeostasis?

**Word Origins**

| Word part | Origin | Meaning |
|---|---|---|
| *homeo-* | Greek | same |
| *-stasis* | Greek | standing still |

## Using Language

**Analogies** Analogies compare words that have similar relationships. You can write analogies with words or with colons. For example, the analogy "up is related to down in the same way that top is related to bottom" can be written "up : down :: top : bottom". To answer an analogy problem, you must figure out how the words are related. In the example given, up is above down and top is above bottom.

**Your Turn** Use information found in the chapter to complete the following analogies.

**1.** heart : pump :: kidney : _____

**2.** nervous system: nerves :: endocrine system : _____

## Taking Notes

**Outlining** Outlining is a note-taking skill that helps you organize information. You can create a simple outline of a section in this chapter by copying all of the headings for that section, in order, on a piece of paper. Leave plenty of space between each heading. As you read the material under a heading of the chapter, write the important facts under that heading on your outline.

**Your Turn** Create outlines for each section of this chapter.

*Homeostasis and Human Body Systems*

*I. Homeostasis*

*A. A Changing Environment*

*1. The environment around an organism is constantly changing.*

*2. Organisms must respond to these changes in order to survive.*

*B. Responses to Change*

Section 1
# Homeostasis

| Key Ideas | Key Terms | Why It Matters |
| --- | --- | --- |
| ❯ How does a change in the external environment affect an organism?<br>❯ How does an organism respond to changes, and what happens if the organism fails to respond to the changes?<br>❯ What organ systems do humans need in order to survive? | homeostasis | When things don't change, it may not seem as if anything interesting is going on. But failure to maintain a 'steady state' can result in disease or death. |

Many people would find the idea of frogs hopping around the Arctic strange, but one type of frog—the wood frog—is able to survive in the Arctic Circle. When temperatures drop, the frog goes into hibernation and about 65% of its body freezes solid. An antifreeze-like chemical that is made by the frog's liver keeps the other 35% of the frog thawed so that the frog's tissues are not frostbitten.

## A Changing Environment

A wood frog's ability to keep part of its body from freezing is one of the many adaptations that enable the frog to react to environmental changes. ❯ **The external environment around an organism is constantly changing. These changes threaten the stability of an organism's internal environment.** The maintenance of a relatively stable internal environment is called **homeostasis.** Almost any kind of change in the external environment, such as a change in seasons, light levels, or water availability, can result in a change to an organism's internal environment. In addition, an organism's internal environment can also be a source of change. For example, if waste products build up inside an organism, they can cause an internal chemical imbalance.

Different organisms may respond to similar environmental changes in different ways. For example, when the environment changes by getting colder, the wood frog maintains its homeostasis by hibernating and thus conserving energy. The pine grosbeak shown in **Figure 1,** on the other hand, responds to a colder environment by eating more food, flying to warmer areas, and puffing out its feathers, as the photograph shows. All organisms, including humans, need ways to respond to change.

❯ **Reading Check** ***How is homeostasis related to environmental change? (See the Appendix for answers to Reading Checks.)***

***The Living Environment***
**Standard 4**

**1.2c** The components of the human body, from organ systems to cell organelles, interact to maintain a balanced internal environment. To successfully accomplish this, organisms possess a diversity of control mechanisms that detect deviations and make corrective actions.
**1.2d** If there is a disruption in any human system, there may be a corresponding imbalance in homeostasis.
**1.2.e** The organs and systems of the body help to provide all the cells with their basic needs. The cells of the body are of different kinds and are grouped in ways that enhance how they function together.
**1.3a** The structures present in some single-celled organisms act in a manner similar to the tissue and systems found in multicellular organisms, thus enabling them to perform all of the life processes needed to maintain homeostasis.
**5.2a** Homeostasis in an organism is constantly threatened. Failure to respond effectively can result in disease or death.
**5.3a** Dynamic equilibrium results from detection of and response to stimuli. Organisms detect and respond to change in a variety of ways both at the cellular level and at the organismal level.

**homeostasis** the maintenance of a constant internal state in a changing environment

These puffed-out feathers trap air and help keep the bird warm.

**Figure 1** Feathers insulate this pine grosbeak from cold weather and help it maintain a stable body temperature.

## Responses to Change

Organisms carry out many different chemical reactions to grow, obtain energy, and reproduce. Many organisms also move, breathe, produce heat, and do other tasks. However, none of these activities can happen unless the organism can maintain a relatively stable internal environment. For example, photosynthesis and cellular respiration can take place only inside a cell that is within a certain temperature and pH range. Thus, an organism must be able to detect and respond to changes in both its internal and external environment so that the temperature and the pH stay within a favorable range. **› Organisms detect and respond to change in a variety of ways: both at the cellular level and at the organismal level. Failure to respond to change can result in an organism's death.**

**Academic Vocabulary**

**internal** located within something

**From Cells to Organ Systems** Every organism, even organisms as small as a single-celled bacterium, responds to changes in the environment. The organelles present in some single-celled organisms work in a way that is similar to the way tissues and systems in multicellular organisms work. Thus, single-celled organisms are able to perform all of the life processes needed to maintain homeostasis. For example, suppose you place a member of the genus *Euglena,* a single-celled photosynthetic protist, in a darkened tank of water. You then turn on a light at one end of the tank. The protist's eyespot, which is a light-sensing organelle, will detect the light. In response, the protist's long flagellum will begin to propel the protist toward the light. The chloroplasts inside the protist's cell will then be able to use the light to perform photosynthesis. By moving toward the light, the protist is able to produce enough energy for its cell to maintain homeostasis and stay healthy.

**Figure 2** The surface of a leaf has many pores, each of which is surrounded by a pair of guard cells. **› Is the plant from which this leaf was taken trying to conserve water? How can you tell?**

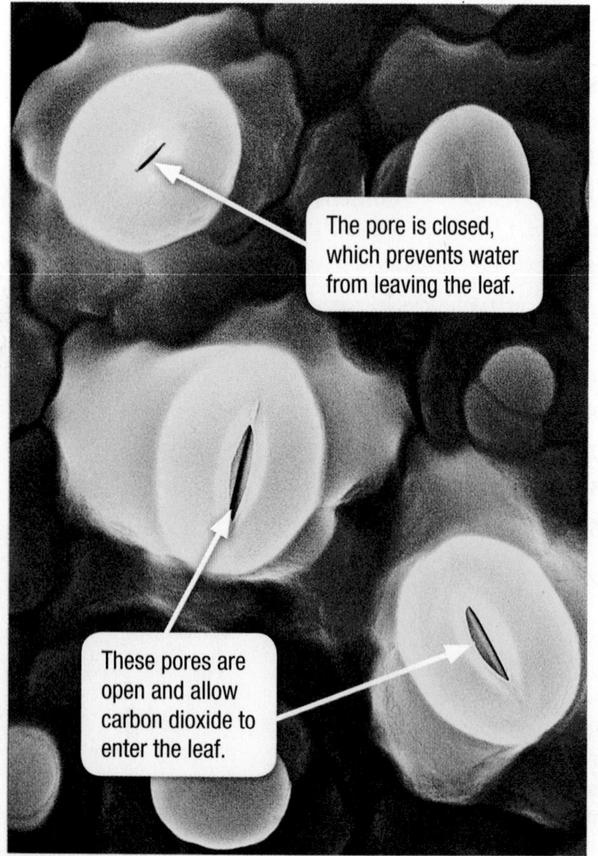

The pore is closed, which prevents water from leaving the leaf.
These pores are open and allow carbon dioxide to enter the leaf.

**Response in Multicellular Organisms** Multicellular organisms also respond to environmental changes at the cellular level. However, multicellular organisms can respond at the tissue, organ system, or organismal levels, too. The way that plants regulate water loss is a good example of how a multicellular organism responds to change. The pores on a plant's leaf help the plant regulate water loss and gas exchange. As **Figure 2** shows, guard cells on either side of a pore enlarge or shrink to open or close pores. During the day, tissues in the leaf perform photosynthesis. The guards cells near the active tissues react by swelling with water. The swollen cells bow apart, which causes the pore to open. Carbon dioxide, a gas necessary for photosynthesis, can then enter the leaf. Likewise, water can exit the leaf. More water is then drawn up to the leaf by the plant's vascular system. At night, when photosynthesis slows, water exits the guard cells. The cells then shrink and the pore closes. This response allows the leaf to prevent excess water loss at night.

**› Reading Check** ***Give an example of an organism reacting to a change in its environment.***

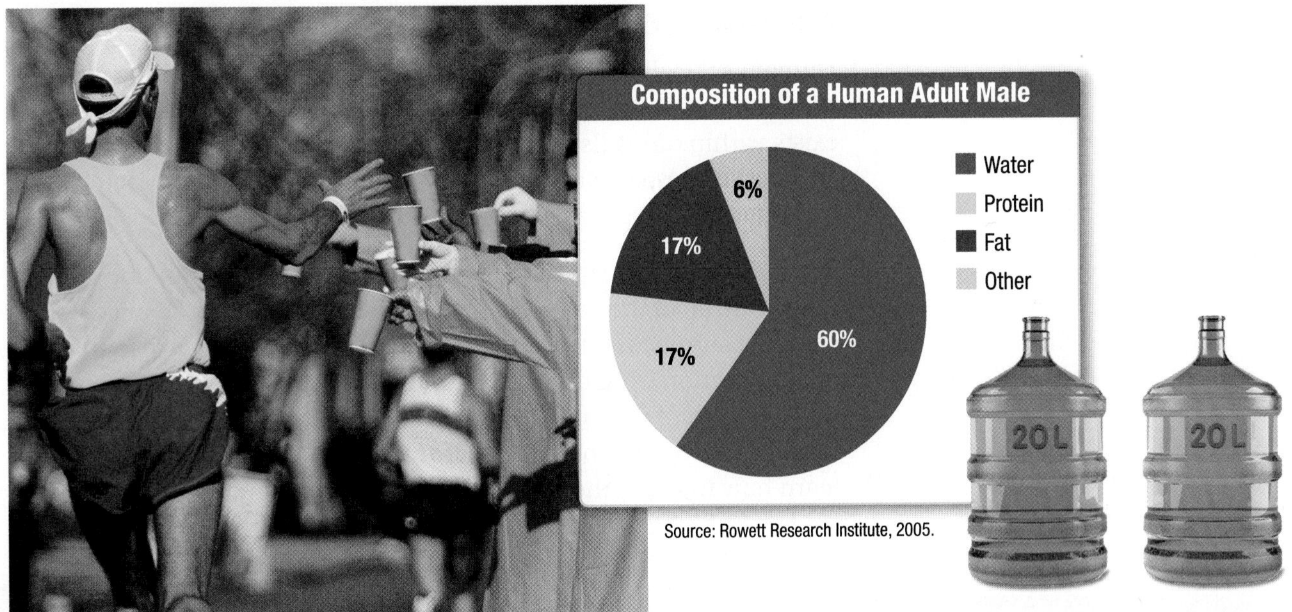


**Figure 3** A healthy adult male's body contains approximately 40 L of water.
**❯ If an athlete loses 2 L of water by sweating, how much water does he need to drink to maintain his homeostasis?**

**Failure to Respond** If an organism is not able to respond to changes in its environment, disease or death can result. To understand why homeostasis is so important, consider what would happen to a plant if its guard cells could not slow water loss. When the amount of water in a plant's tissues gets too low, the plant wilts. This loss of cell pressure, or turgor, can lead to a plant cell collapsing in on itself and dying. Unless water is added, more cells will collapse and die, until the entire organism is at risk of dying.

**Water Balance in Humans** Although very different from plants, humans must also control internal water levels. As **Figure 3** shows, about 2/3 of a human body is made up of water. If a person loses too much water by sweating or urinating, dehydration will occur unless the water is replaced. As in plants, dehydration in humans involves a drop in cell turgor. In addition, dehydration causes blood pressure to significantly decrease until death results.

**Water Pressure and Deep-Sea Fish** Of course, the correct body composition is just one way that homeostasis is maintained. There are many other factors involved. One example is the coelacanth, a fish that lives in very deep waters off the coast of Africa. At the depth of the fish's usual environment, the water pressure is several hundred times greater than the water pressure at the ocean's surface. If a person tried to swim to this depth without any special equipment, the enormous pressure would crush the person's body. Similarly, if a coelacanth was brought to the surface, the lack of pressure would cause the fish's death. Without the high pressure, dissolved gases would bubble out of the fish's bloodstream. The gas bubbles would join and form larger bubbles, until some were big enough to block blood flow through the fish's heart. Because of this need for high pressure, each coelacanth that has been caught has died shortly after being brought to the surface.

## Humans and Homeostasis

Humans, like all other organisms, are constantly subjected to environmental stresses that threaten to upset the delicate balance that exists within our cells and tissues. **Humans require multiple systems for digestion, respiration, reproduction, circulation, movement, coordination, and immunity. The systems interact to maintain homeostasis.**

**Body Systems** The organs and systems of the human body help to provide all of the cells with their basic needs. Each cell needs a constant supply of nutrients and oxygen, removal of waste materials, and protection from disease. With the exception of the reproductive system, each of the human body systems performs a task that helps stabilize the body's internal environment. In the next section, you will learn how many of the body systems work to maintain homeostasis.

**Figure 4** The table below lists the major structures and functions of the organ systems of the body. **Which organs function in more than one system?**

**Major Organ Systems of the Body**

| System | Major structures | Functions |
|---|---|---|
| Circulatory system | heart, blood vessels, blood, lymph nodes and vessels, and lymph | to transport nutrients, wastes, hormones, and gases |
| Digestive system | mouth, throat, esophagus, stomach, liver, pancreas, and small and large intestines | to absorb nutrients from food; to remove wastes; to maintain water and chemical balances |
| Endocrine system | hypothalamus, pituitary gland, pancreas, testis, ovaries, and many other glands | to regulate body temperature, metabolism, development, and reproduction; to maintain homeostasis; to regulate other organ systems |
| Urinary system | kidneys, urinary bladder, ureters, and urethra | to remove wastes from blood; to regulate concentration of body fluids |
| Immune system | white blood cells, lymph nodes and vessels, and skin | to defend against pathogens and disease |
| Integumentary system | skin, nails, and hair | to protect against injury, infection, and fluid loss; to help regulate body temperature |
| Muscular system | skeletal, smooth, and cardiac muscle tissues; tendons | to move limbs and trunk; to move substances through the body; to provide structure and support |
| Nervous system | brain, spinal cord, nerves, and sense organs | to regulate behavior; to maintain homeostasis; to regulate all other organ systems; to control senses and movement |
| Reproductive system | testes, penis, ovaries, uterus, and breasts | to produce gametes (eggs and sperm) and offspring |
| Respiratory system | nose, mouth, trachea, bronchi, and lungs | to move air into and out of lungs; to control gas exchange between blood and lungs |
| Skeletal system | bones, ligaments, and cartilage | to protect and support the body and organs; to work with skeletal muscles; to produce red blood cells, white blood cells, and platelets |

### Main Components of Homeostasis

In the human body, the main components of homeostasis are the following:

- the concentration of salts
- the pH of the internal environment
- the concentrations of nutrients and waste products
- the concentrations of oxygen and carbon dioxide
- the volume and pressure of extracellular fluid, which includes blood and the fluids surrounding body cells

When these five components are adequately controlled, homeostasis is maintained and the body is most likely healthy. No organ system can maintain homeostasis by itself. Organ systems must work together in a synchronized manner. For example, the concentrations of oxygen and carbon dioxide are controlled by four different body systems. First, the respiratory system brings oxygen into and carbon dioxide out of the body. The circulatory system distributes the oxygen to all of the body's tissues and picks up carbon dioxide. If the level of carbon dioxide gets too high, the nervous system instructs the muscular system to make the muscles around the rib cage work harder. This action allows the lungs of the respiratory system to breathe faster in order to rid the body of the excess carbon dioxide. Later in this chapter, you will learn more about how the concentrations of oxygen and carbon dioxide are maintained by the body systems.

**› Reading Check** ***List the five main components of homeostasis in the human body.***

Hands-On

# QuickLab

15 min

## Investigation of Homeostasis 4.1.2c

The human body maintains a fairly constant internal temperature of about 37 °C (98.6 °F). You can test this fact by taking your temperature in a variety of conditions.

### Procedure

1. Use a **thermometer** to take the air temperature inside your classroom, and record it. Use an **oral thermometer** to take your temperature, and record it.
2. Move to a location that is warmer or colder than your classroom. Record the air temperature. After 10 min, take your temperature and record it.

### Analysis

1. **Explain** what happened to your body temperature when you went from your classroom to a warmer or colder place.
2. CRITICAL THINKING **Recognizing Relationships** The body produces heat through metabolism. So, why can people freeze to death?

**Outlining** In your outline, list the main components of homeostasis in the human body.

## Section 1 Review

### › KEY IDEAS

1. **Describe** how the change in seasons affects an organism familiar to you.
2. **Summarize** how plants respond to water loss at the cellular level.
3. **Explain** how the human body works to maintain homeostasis.

### CRITICAL THINKING

4. **Forming Explanations** Use what you know about homeostasis to explain why many species of birds migrate to warmer climates during the winter.
5. **Making Inferences** Many species of bacteria die quickly in very salty environments. Infer how this is related to a bacterium's need to maintain its water level.

### ALTERNATIVE ASSESSMENT

6. **Fictional Writing** Write a short story in which you describe how a change in the external environment affects a certain organism and how the organism responds to the change. Remember that your story is fictitious, so you may want to use humor or illustrations to help tell your story.

Section 2

# Human Body Systems

| Key Ideas | Key Terms | Why It Matters |
|---|---|---|
| › How do the skeletal and muscular systems help the body maintain homeostasis?<br>› How does the integumentary system help the body maintain homeostasis?<br>› How do the nervous and endocrine systems help the body maintain homeostasis?<br>› How do the digestive and excretory systems help the body maintain homeostasis?<br>› How do the circulatory and respiratory systems help the body maintain homeostasis? | tendon<br>epidermis<br>hormone<br>endocrine gland<br>digestion<br>excretion<br>alveoli<br>capillary<br>lymph | Like all humans, you are a very complex organism. Your body contains many systems that must work together to maintain a healthy dynamic equilibrium within the body. |

Even when you are sitting still, your body systems constantly react to changes within and around you to maintain homeostasis.

## Skeletal and Muscular Systems

**› The skeletal and muscular systems enable movement and provide support and protection for tissues and organs.** Bones and muscles work together to make movement possible. This ability increases the chance of survival by allowing a person to gather food, seek shelter, and escape from danger. As **Figure 5** shows, the skeleton provides an anchor for the muscles that move the body. **Tendons** attach muscles to bones. When muscles contract, tendons pull on bones to cause movement. Other types of muscles, known as involuntary muscle, move material within the body. This type of muscle surrounds some blood vessels' inner walls and makes up organs such as the stomach and heart. A heartbeat occurs when this type of muscle contracts rhythmically.

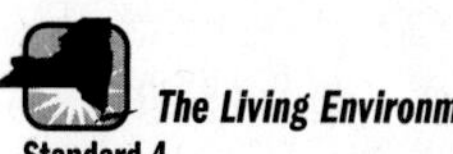


**Standard 4**

**1.2a** Important levels of organization for structure and function include organelles, cells, tissues, organs, organ systems, and whole organisms.

**1.2b** Humans are complex organisms. They require multiple systems for digestion, respiration, reproduction, circulation, excretion, movement, coordination, and immunity. The systems interact to perform the life functions.

**1.2c** The components of the human body, from organ systems to cell organelles, interact to maintain a balanced internal environment. To successfully accomplish this, organisms possess a diversity of control mechanisms that detect deviations and make corrective actions.

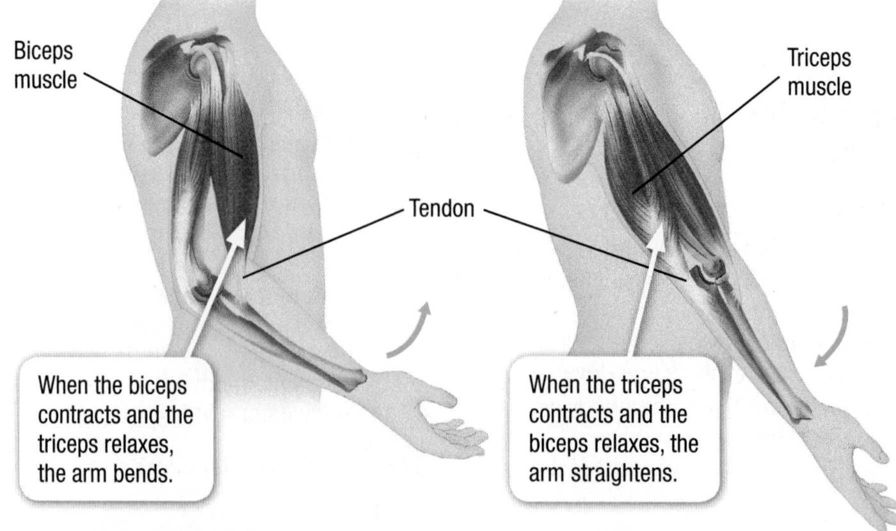

Biceps muscle
Triceps muscle
Tendon
When the biceps contracts and the triceps relaxes, the arm bends.
When the triceps contracts and the biceps relaxes, the arm straightens.

**Figure 5** Pairs of opposing muscles work together to move bones at joints. When one muscle in the pair contracts, the other muscle relaxes to produce movement.

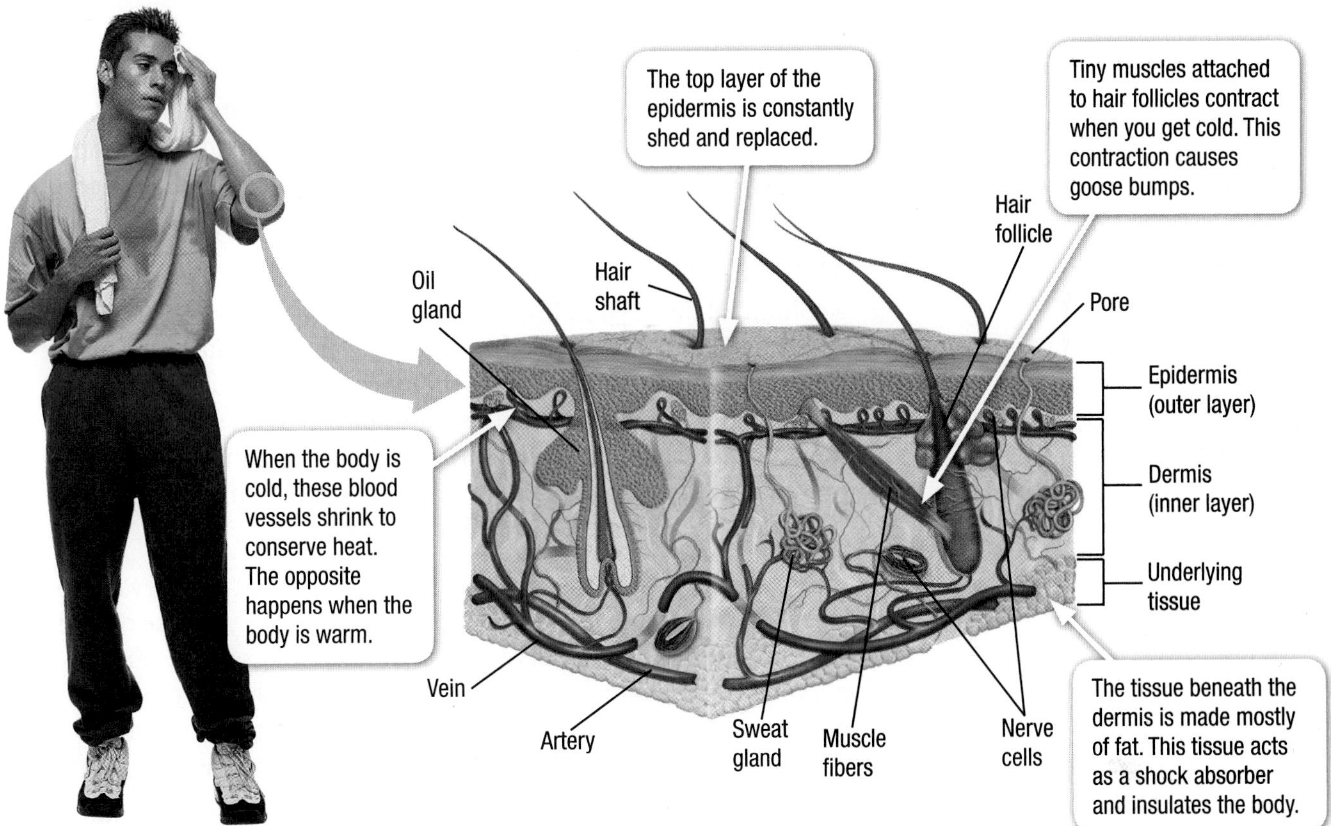

The top layer of the epidermis is constantly shed and replaced.
Tiny muscles attached to hair follicles contract when you get cold. This contraction causes goose bumps.
Hair follicle
Oil gland
Hair shaft
Pore
Epidermis (outer layer)
Dermis (inner layer)
Underlying tissue
When the body is cold, these blood vessels shrink to conserve heat. The opposite happens when the body is warm.
Vein
Artery
Sweat gland
Muscle fibers
Nerve cells
The tissue beneath the dermis is made mostly of fat. This tissue acts as a shock absorber and insulates the body.

**Figure 6** The epidermis and dermis keep water inside the body and harmful bacteria out. **› What is the function of the tissue beneath the dermis?**

## Integumentary System

Skin is the largest organ of the human body. It makes up about 7% of your total body weight. The skin, along with the hair and nails, form the integumentary system. **› The integumentary system protects the body from injury and UV radiation, defends against disease, helps regulate body temperature, and prevents the body from drying out.**

**Waterproofing** The **epidermis,** shown in **Figure 6,** is the outermost layer of the skin. It is made of flattened, dead cells composed of a protein called *keratin.* This protein is also found in hair and nails. Keratin makes the skin tough and waterproof. Glands in the *dermis,* the layer of skin under the epidermis, secrete oil that lubricates the skin. Without the protection of keratin and oil, our bodies would lose water through evaporation or absorb water from the environment.

**Disease Prevention** The epidermis forms a tight barrier that keeps bacteria out and protects the body from disease. Damage to large areas of skin allows bacteria to enter the body freely. This lack of protection is one reason why severe burns are so dangerous.

**UV Protection** The lower layers of the epidermis contain cells that make *melanin,* a pigment that absorbs ultraviolet (UV) radiation. This absorption prevents DNA damage, which can cause skin cancer.

**Temperature Regulation** A network of blood vessels and nerves in the dermis helps regulate body temperature. Sweat glands also help remove excess body heat through the evaporation of sweat.

**› Reading Check** ***How does your skin protect you from diseases?***

**tendon** a tough connective tissue that attaches a muscle to a bone or another body part

**epidermis** the outer surface layer of skin cells

**Word Origin** Use a dictionary to find out the origin of the word *epidermis.*

## Nervous and Endocrine Systems

**➤ The nervous system is composed of signaling cells that collect and respond to information about the body's internal and external environment.** There are two main parts of the nervous system—the central nervous system (CNS) and the peripheral nervous system (PNS).

SCILINKS.
www.scilinks.org
Topic: The Human Brain
Code: HX80190

**CNS** The CNS includes the brain and spinal cord. The spinal cord is a column of nerves that links the brain to most of the PNS. The brain, shown in **Figure 7,** is the body's main processing center. This organ coordinates the body's efforts to maintain homeostasis. Sensory information from all parts of the body converges on the brain's thalamus. The thalamus relays the information to the cerebrum for processing. At the base of the brain is the brainstem, which regulates heart rate, breathing rate, and blood pressure.

**PNS** The PNS contains sensory and motor nerves. Sensory nerves carry information to the central nervous system from sense organs such as the skin. Motor nerves carry commands from the central nervous system to muscles and other organs, such as glands. These motor nerves are grouped into two independent systems—the autonomic nervous system and the somatic nervous system.

**Autonomic Nervous System** Motor nerves that are not in our conscious control are part of the autonomic nervous system. Some ways that the autonomic nervous system maintains homeostasis include stimulating digestion after a meal, slowing down the heart rate after exercise, and preparing the body to respond in stressful situations.

**Somatic Nervous System** The motor nerves under our conscious control, such as the nerves we use to signal our legs to walk, are part of the somatic nervous system. The somatic system also operates without conscious control, as it does to help us maintain balance.

**Figure 7** The cerebrum is the largest part of the brain. It controls most sensory and motor processing. **➤ Which part of the brain regulates body temperature?**

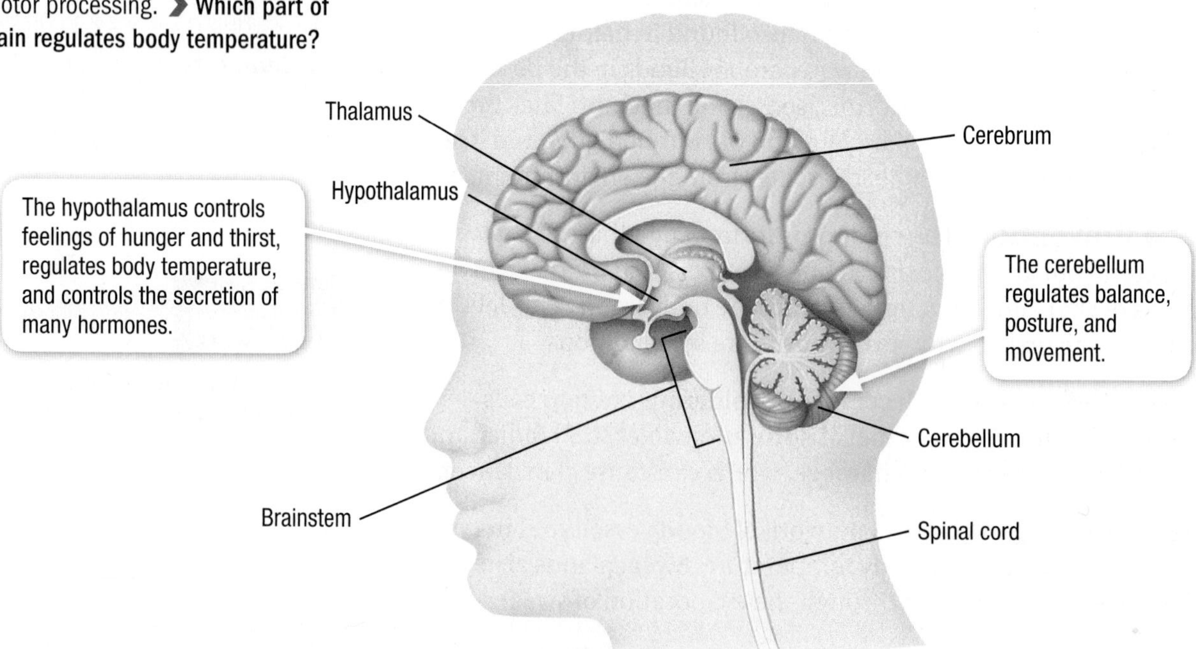

Thalamus
Hypothalamus
Cerebrum
The hypothalamus controls feelings of hunger and thirst, regulates body temperature, and controls the secretion of many hormones.
The cerebellum regulates balance, posture, and movement.
Cerebellum
Brainstem
Spinal cord

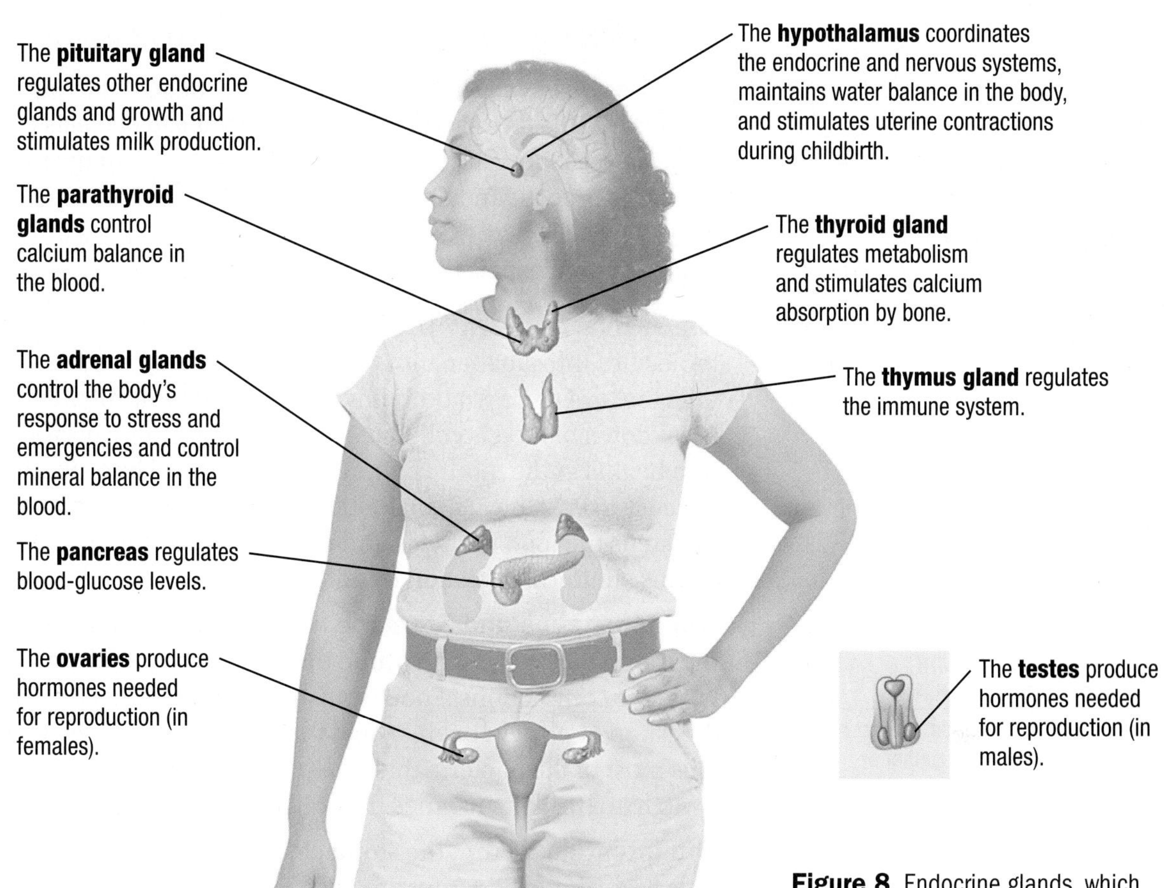

The pituitary gland regulates other endocrine glands and growth and stimulates milk production.
The hypothalamus coordinates the endocrine and nervous systems, maintains water balance in the body, and stimulates uterine contractions during childbirth.
The parathyroid glands control calcium balance in the blood.
The thyroid gland regulates metabolism and stimulates calcium absorption by bone.
The adrenal glands control the body's response to stress and emergencies and control mineral balance in the blood.
The thymus gland regulates the immune system.
The pancreas regulates blood-glucose levels.
The ovaries produce hormones needed for reproduction (in females).
The testes produce hormones needed for reproduction (in males).

**Figure 8** Endocrine glands, which secrete hormones, are located throughout the human body. Many organs that are not shown also have tissues that secrete hormones.

**Endocrine System** Like the nervous system, the endocrine system sends messages to the body's cells. However, endocrine signals act over a longer period of time than nerve signals do. When the body calls for an immediate reaction, those messages are sent along the nervous system. When the body needs to bring about a more long-term change, the endocrine system does the task. **› The endocrine system regulates metabolism; maintains salt, water, and nutrient balance in the blood; controls the body's responses to stress; and regulates growth, development, and reproduction.**

The endocrine system uses chemical messengers called **hormones.** Hormones are made in one part of the body and cause change in another part of the body. Hormones cause cells to change their activities. For example, as people sweat, they lose water and salts. A hormone signals the kidneys to make less urine and conserve water. Another hormone signals the kidneys to reabsorb salt from urine and the sweat glands to decrease the amount of salt in sweat.

Hormones are produced by special cells. Often, these cells are part of an **endocrine gland,** an organ that produces and releases hormones directly into the bloodstream or into the fluid around cells. The major endocrine glands are shown in **Figure 8.**

**› Reading Check** ***How do hormones help maintain homeostasis?***

**hormone** a substance that is made in one cell or tissue and that causes a change in another cell or tissue located in a different part of the body

**endocrine gland** (EN doh KRIN) a ductless gland that secretes hormones into the blood

## Digestive and Excretory Systems

**digestion** the breaking down of food into chemical substances that can be used for energy

**excretion** the process of eliminating metabolic wastes

Suppose you have just eaten your favorite meal. What happens to the food? **The digestive system converts food into nutrients that a body's cells can use.** Some nutrients are used to provide energy for metabolic reactions or to aid metabolism in other ways. Others are used to build new cells. The excretory system removes wastes from metabolic reactions, and expels them from the body.

**Digestive System** **Digestion** is the breaking down of large food molecules into smaller, more-usable ones. Large food molecules must be broken down both physically and chemically. The physical breakdown of food is called *mechanical digestion.* This form of digestion begins in the mouth, where food is chewed into small pieces that are easy to swallow. As the food is chewed, it mixes with saliva. Saliva moistens the food particles and makes them easier to swallow. It also begins chemical digestion by adding digestive enzymes to the food.

**Academic Vocabulary**

**contraction** the act of drawing together or shrinking

**The Esophagus and Stomach** When food is swallowed, it enters the esophagus, a muscular tube that pushes the food along with wavelike contractions. Food is pushed into the stomach, where the digestion of protein begins. Acid that is produced in the stomach kills most of the bacteria that entered with the food, and it acts as a 'switch' to turn on enzymes that will continue chemical digestion.

**The Intestines** From the stomach, food is pushed into the small intestine. There, bile from the liver and enzymes made by the small intestine and pancreas complete digestion. The proteins are reduced to amino acids, complex carbohydrates are changed into simple sugars, and lipids are changed to fatty acids and glycerol. The nutrients can then be absorbed into the blood and the lymph. Millions of tiny, fingerlike projections, called *villi,* line the small intestine. The villi, shown in **Figure 9,** increase the small intestine's surface area so that most nutrients are absorbed by the time the food reaches the large intestine. The undigested material enters the large intestine, where water, some vitamins, and minerals are absorbed into the bloodstream. The remaining materials exit the body through the anus.

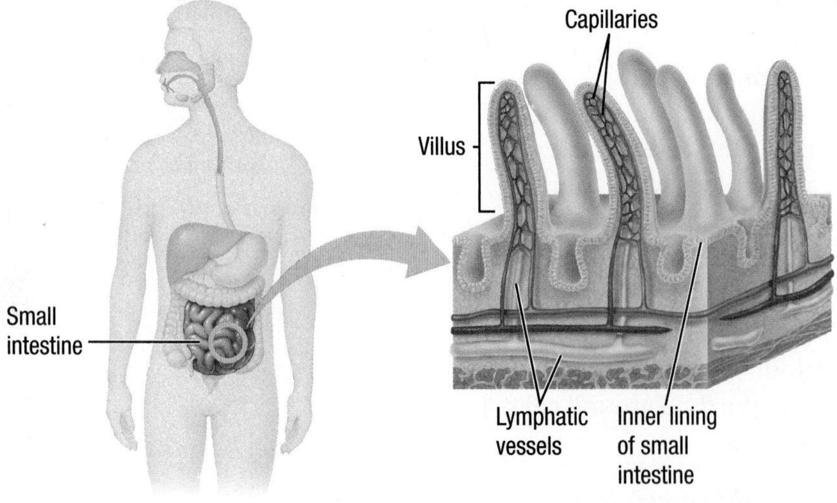


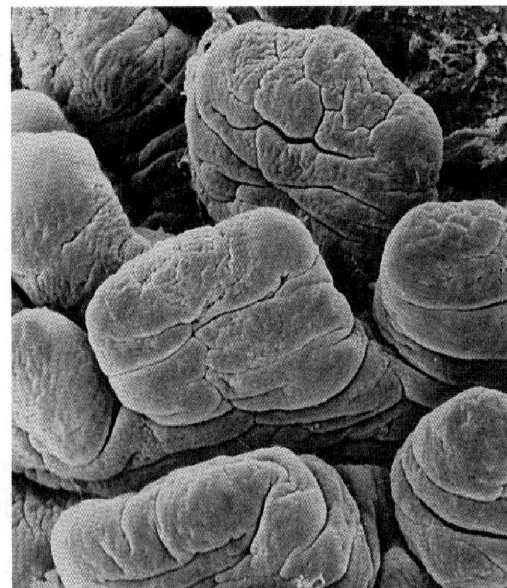

**Figure 9** Villi, as shown in the SEM (137×) and the diagram, expand the surface area of the small intestine to allow greater absorption of nutrients.

Data

# QuickLab

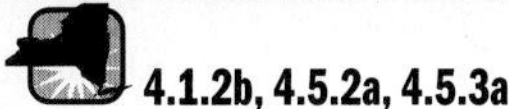

4.1.2b, 4.5.2a, 4.5.3a

15 min

## Filtration Rate in the Kidneys

A human kidney filters fluid from the blood at the rate of about 125 mL/min. However, only a small percentage of this fluid is excreted as urine. Use this information to answer the questions below.

### Analysis

1. **Calculate** how many milliliters of fluid the human kidneys filter each hour.
2. **Calculate** how many milliliters of fluid the kidneys filter each day.
3. CRITICAL THINKING **Analyzing Data** Convert your answer in item 2 from milliliters to liters.
4. CRITICAL THINKING **Predicting Outcomes** What would happen if the kidneys could not return water to the body?

**Excretory System** The human body must remove wastes that are produced by metabolism in a process known as **excretion.** **By removing wastes and toxic chemicals, excretion enables the body to maintain its osmotic and pH balance.** When you sweat, your skin excretes excess water, salts, and some nitrogen wastes. Carbon dioxide and water are excreted as you exhale. The blood also carries other cellular wastes to the kidneys, the primary organs of excretion.

**The Kidneys** The body uses a two-step process to maintain a healthy level of salts and other substances in the blood. Each kidney, shown in **Figure 10,** is composed of nearly one million microscopic filtration units called *nephrons.* At one end of the nephron is the Bowman's capsule, a cup-shaped structure. As blood flows through capillaries in the capsule, blood pressure forces fluid out of the capillaries into the capsule. This fluid is made of water, salt, glucose, amino acids, urea, and other substances. *Urea* is a nitrogen-containing waste product that is released into the blood by the liver. The fluid passes into a narrow tubule, which is surrounded by capillaries. There, glucose and some other molecules in the fluid reenter the bloodstream, which allows the body to take back useful molecules that were removed during filtration. The remaining fluid then passes out of the nephron through collecting ducts, where much of the water is removed. The remaining solution is now called *urine.*

**The Urinary Bladder** Urine flows from the kidneys through a ureter to the urinary bladder, where the urine is collected and stored. When the bladder's muscular walls contract, urine exits through the urethra.

**Reading Check** ***Summarize how blood is filtered.***

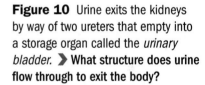

**Figure 10** Urine exits the kidneys by way of two ureters that empty into a storage organ called the *urinary bladder.* **What structure does urine flow through to exit the body?**

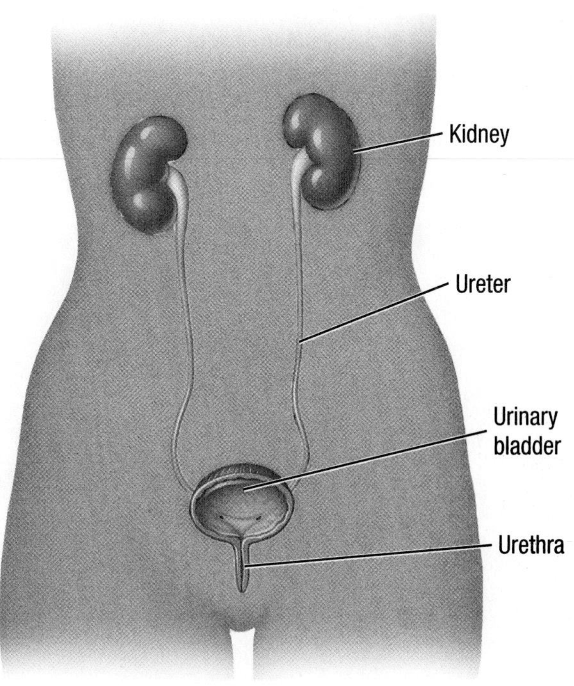

**Figure 11** Concentration gradients allow oxygen and carbon dioxide to diffuse across the alveoli and capillary walls.
**❯ In which direction does an oxygen molecule diffuse in the lungs?**

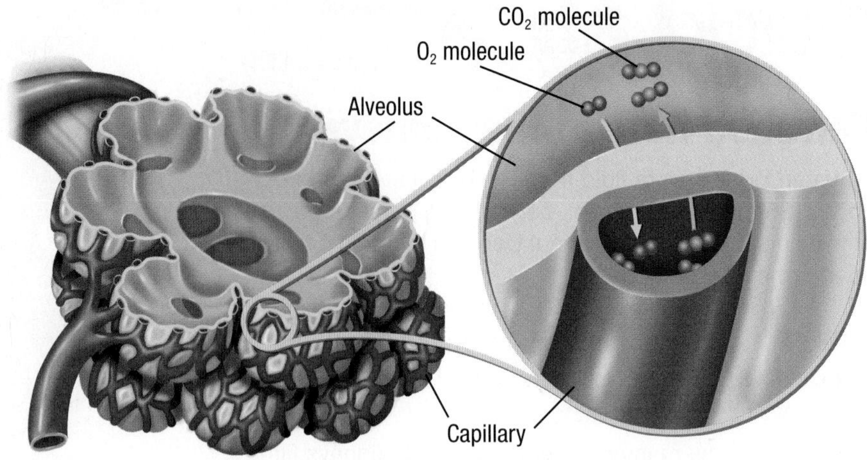


## Respiratory and Circulatory Systems

The respiratory system and circulatory system function together to ensure that oxygen reaches all cells of the body. As you can see in **Figure 11,** the two systems are interwoven within the tissues of the lungs, where the exchange of respiratory gases takes place.

**alveolus** (al VEE uh luhs) any of the tiny air sacs of the lungs where oxygen and carbon dioxide are exchanged

**capillary** (KAP uh LER ee) a tiny blood vessel that allows an exchange between blood and cells in tissue

**lymph** (LIMF) the fluid that is collected by the lymphatic vessels and nodes

**Respiratory System ❯ The respiratory system brings oxygen, $O_2$, into the body and carries carbon dioxide, $CO_2$, a waste product of cellular respiration, out of the body.** Air enters the respiratory system when you inhale through your nose or mouth. Inhalation occurs when muscles around the chest area contract and expand the rib cage. Inhaled air passes through a series of tubes to reach the lungs. Within each lung, the tubes carrying the air split into smaller and smaller tubes, called *bronchioles.* The smallest bronchioles end in groups of tiny air sacs called **alveoli** (singular, *alveolus*), which are surrounded by blood vessels. The actual exchange of gases takes place across the thin, moist membranes of the alveoli. Oxygen leaves the alveoli and enters the blood, while $CO_2$ leaves the blood and enters the alveoli.

**Circulatory System ❯ The circulatory system carries nutrients, oxygen, hormones, and wastes through the body and distributes heat to maintain homeostasis.** Together, the cardiovascular system and the lymphatic system make up the body's circulatory system.

**Figure 12** The exchange of materials across capillary walls is possible because capillary walls are only one cell thick, which allows molecules to easily pass through them.

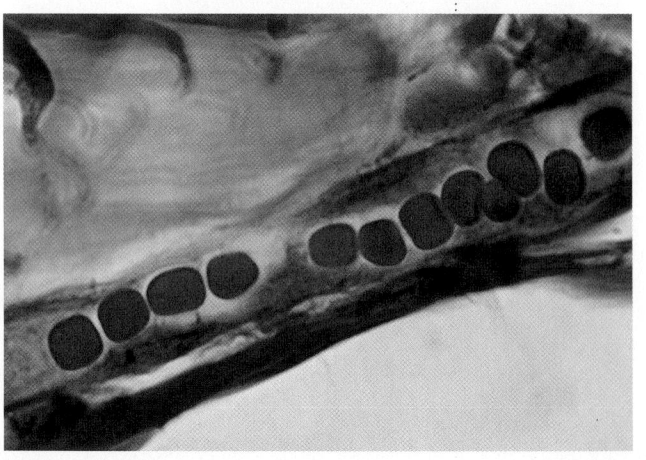

**Cardiovascular System** Blood, blood vessels, and the heart—a muscular organ that acts like a pump—make up the cardiovascular system. This system acts like a network of highways that transports materials to and from the body's cells. The network is made up of three kinds of vessels: arteries, capillaries, and veins. *Arteries* have thick, muscular walls to withstand the force of the blood pumped out of the heart. Arteries carry blood to the capillaries. A **capillary,** shown in **Figure 12,** has an extremely thin wall that allows gases and nutrients in the blood to pass across it into the fluid around body cells. From the capillaries, blood enters the *veins,* which return blood to the heart.

**Blood** Blood moves through blood vessels and interacts with every body system. It brings the materials a body system needs and carries away the products the system makes. Blood also carries wastes away from a system. About 45% of blood is cells and cell fragments. The remaining 55% is plasma, the liquid portion of blood. Plasma is a solution made of about 90% water and 10% solutes. The solutes include nutrients, wastes, and salts. The salts have many functions, including maintaining osmotic balance with the fluids inside of cells and regulating the pH of the blood.

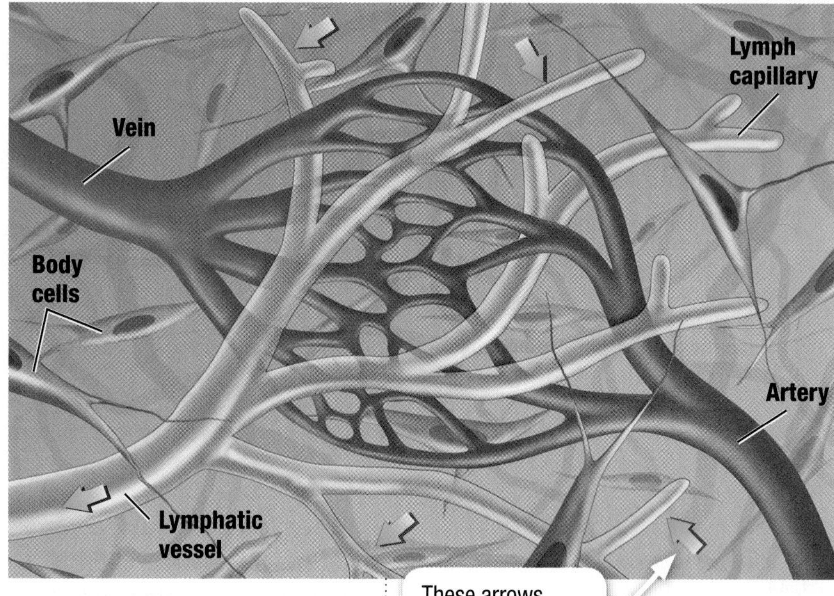


**Figure 13** Skeletal muscles squeeze lymph vessels and thus force the lymph through the lymphatic system. **› What might happen if a lymphatic vessel becomes blocked?**

In addition to carrying materials, blood distributes body heat, which helps the body maintain a steady temperature. When the body is warm, blood vessels in the skin widen. More blood pumps through the skin and allows heat to leave the body. When the body is cold, blood vessels in the skin narrow. This change helps the body conserve heat by diverting more of the blood to deeper tissues so that less heat will escape.

**Lymphatic System** Every time the heart pumps, some of the fluid in blood is forced out of the capillaries. The escaped fluid collects in spaces around the body's cells. As **Figure 13** shows, this fluid, called **lymph,** is picked up by the lymphatic system and returned to the blood. The lymphatic system is made up of a network of vessels, tiny bean-shaped structures called *lymph nodes,* and lymph tissue. Lymph vessels collect lymph and return it to two large veins in the neck. As lymph moves through lymph vessels, the fluid passes through lymph nodes, where white blood cells collect. The white blood cells destroy any bacteria or other dangerous materials in the lymph. In this way, the lymphatic system helps the body fight infection.

**› Reading Check** *What are two functions of the lymphatic system?*

## Section 2 Review

### › KEY IDEAS

1. **Explain** how the skeletal and muscular systems work together to produce movement.
2. **List** four functions of the integumentary system.
3. **Summarize** how the brain controls the maintenance of the body's homeostasis.
4. **Describe** how the excretory system helps the body maintain homeostasis.
5. **Relate** the function of the respiratory system with that of the cardiovascular system.

### CRITICAL THINKING

6. **Recognizing Relationships** Why is a third-degree burn, which destroys the epidermis and dermis of the skin, a serious injury?

### METHODS OF SCIENCE

7. **Formulating Hypotheses** Choose one of the body systems discussed in this section, and write a short paragraph in which you hypothesize how homeostasis would most likely be disrupted if that body system stopped functioning properly.

Section

# 3 Feedback Mechanisms

| Key Ideas | Key Terms | Why It Matters |
|---|---|---|
| ❯ How do feedback mechanisms help maintain homeostasis?<br>❯ How does a feedback mechanism control a person's breathing rate?<br>❯ How does a feedback mechanism maintain the concentration of glucose in the bloodstream? | feedback mechanism | The human body must be able to detect changes in its internal environment and quickly react to maintain the body's homeostasis. |

***The Living Environment***
**Standard 4**

**1.2c** The components of the human body, from organ systems to cell organelles, interact to maintain a balanced internal environment. To successfully accomplish this, organisms possess a diversity of control mechanisms that detect deviations and make corrective actions.

**1.2.e** The organs and systems of the body help to provide all the cells with their basic needs. The cells of the body are of different kinds and are grouped in ways that enhance how they function together.

**5.3b** Feedback mechanisms have evolved that maintain homeostasis. Examples include the changes in heart rate or respiratory rate in response to increased activity in muscle cells, the maintenance of blood sugar levels by insulin from the pancreas, and the changes in openings in the leaves of plants by guard cells to regulate water loss and gas exchange.

Have you ever walked across a balance beam? When you feel yourself falling toward the right, you shift your weight to the left. Your body maintains its internal balance, or homeostasis, in a similar way.

## Mechanisms of Control

The word *homeostasis* is derived from Greek words that mean "to stay the same," but this definition can be misleading. A body's internal state does not stay exactly the same. Instead, as **Figure 14** shows, it varies around a certain average value. Homeostasis maintains a dynamic equilibrium. ❯ **To maintain homeostasis, your body has a diversity of feedback mechanisms that detect deviations in the body's internal environment and make corrective actions.** A **feedback mechanism** is a mechanism in which the last step in a series of events controls the first step. A feedback mechanism has three parts. First, a receptor, such as a nerve, detects change in the internal or external environment. Second, a control center, such as the brain, selects a response to the information from the receptor. Third, an effector, such as a muscle or gland, carries out the response, and this effect is detected by the receptor, which starts the process again.

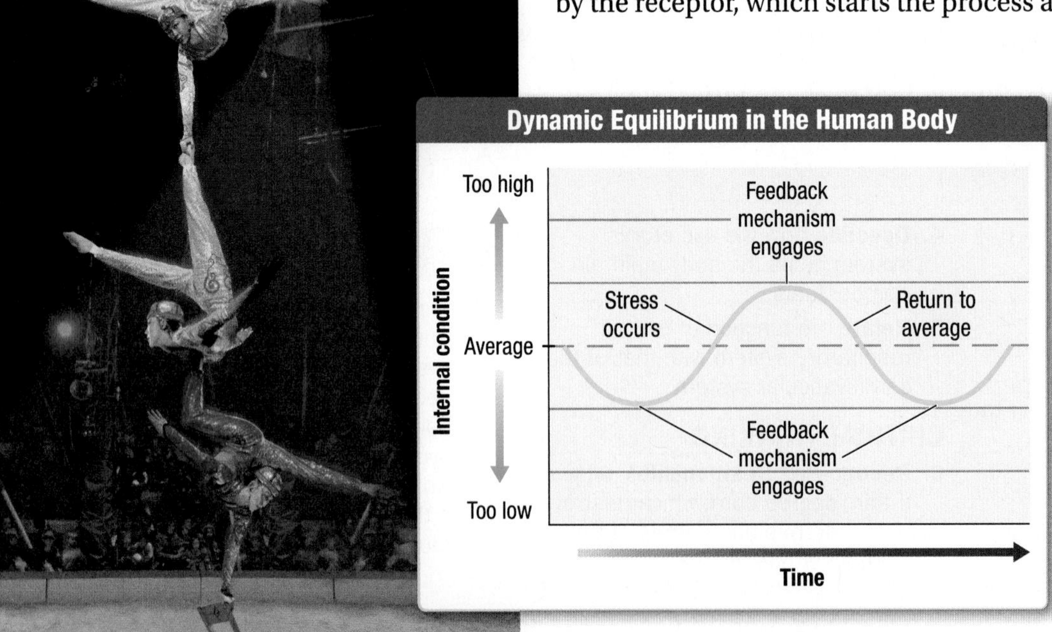


**Figure 14** Just as acrobats use their sense of balance to keep from falling, feedback mechanisms are used to keep the body functioning within a normal range. ❯ **What causes the body's internal environment to deviate from its average state?**

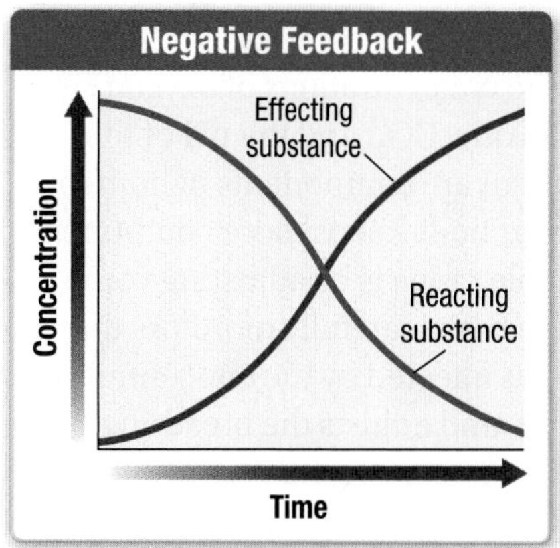


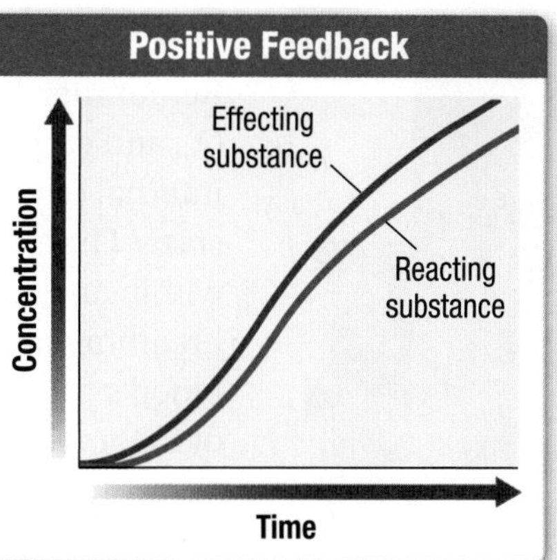


**Figure 15** In negative feedback, an effecting substance causes the body to stop making a reacting substance. In positive feedback, an effecting substance causes the body to make more of the reacting substance. **› Summarize how negative feedback differs from positive feedback.**

**Negative Feedback** The two main types of feedback mechanisms, negative feedback and positive feedback, are illustrated in **Figure 15.** Homeostasis is maintained mostly through negative feedback. In negative feedback, the final step in a series of events inhibits the first step in the series. Negative feedback works like a home heating system that is controlled by a thermostat. When the room temperature drops below a set point, the thermostat activates the heater to warm the room. When room temperature reaches the set point, the thermostat shuts off the heater. These actions maintain the temperature within a narrow range.

**Positive Feedback** In positive feedback, a change in the body causes even more change in the same direction. During positive feedback, the production of a hormone causes the release of another hormone. This process usually progresses until a specific event triggers hormone production to stop. For example, positive feedback occurs in blood clotting, where one clotting factor activates another in a cascade that leads quickly to the formation of a clot. In another example, the hormone that causes a female's ovary to release an egg works through positive feedback. Rising levels of the main female sex hormone, estrogen, cause another hormone to be secreted until an egg is released from one of the two ovaries. You will learn more about this feedback mechanism in Chapter 23.

**feedback mechanism** a cycle of events in which information from one step controls or affects a previous step

**Antagonistic Hormones** Some hormones work in opposing pairs to control levels of important substances. Hormones that work in this way are called *antagonistic hormones* because their actions have opposite effects. The release of each hormone of the pair is regulated by negative feedback. The idea of the thermostat can also apply to antagonistic hormones. Suppose that, instead of just a heater that turns on when the air temperature drops below a certain level, there is also an air conditioner that turns on when the air temperature rises above a certain level. The paired functions of the heater and the air conditioner, each controlled by negative feedback, can maintain a nearly constant air temperature.

**› Reading Check** ***How does the body use feedback mechanisms to maintain homeostasis?***

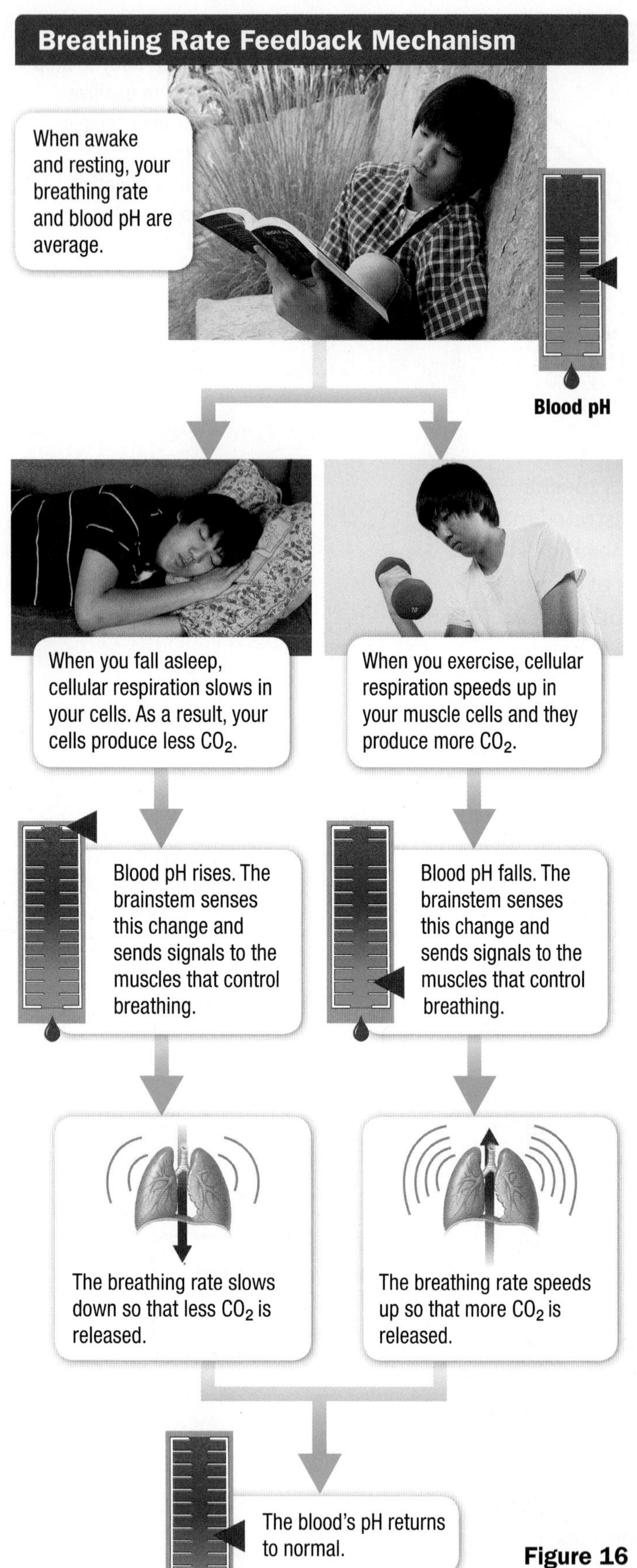

Breathing Rate Feedback Mechanism
When awake and resting, your breathing rate and blood pH are average.
Blood pH
When you fall asleep, cellular respiration slows in your cells. As a result, your cells produce less $CO_2$.
When you exercise, cellular respiration speeds up in your muscle cells and they produce more $CO_2$.
Blood pH rises. The brainstem senses this change and sends signals to the muscles that control breathing.
Blood pH falls. The brainstem senses this change and sends signals to the muscles that control breathing.
The breathing rate slows down so that less $CO_2$ is released.
The breathing rate speeds up so that more $CO_2$ is released.
The blood's pH returns to normal.


**Figure 16** The amount of $CO_2$ in your blood directly affects your breathing rate. ❯ **Why does exercise decrease the blood's pH?**

## Controlling Breathing Rate

Remember that the concentrations of oxygen, $O_2$, and carbon dioxide, $CO_2$, and the pH of the internal environment are components of homeostasis. One way your body keeps these components within an acceptable range is by adjusting your breathing rate. The brain carefully monitors the blood's pH, which is affected by the concentration of $CO_2$ in the blood, and adjusts the breathing rate accordingly. This feedback mechanism is illustrated in **Figure 16.**

**Blood pH** Each breath that you take is initiated by nerve cells in the respiratory control center of the brainstem. ❯ **When the brainstem senses a change in the blood's pH, it adjusts the breathing rate.** But what causes the blood's pH to fluctuate? Suppose a person has a normal blood pH. If that person then begins to exercise, the amount of activity in his or her muscle cells will increase. The muscle cells will need more energy to handle the increased activity. Therefore, the mitochondria in the muscle cells will begin to perform cellular respiration at a faster rate. The waste products of cellular respiration are $CO_2$ and water. These two molecules will exit the muscle cells and be absorbed through capillary walls into the bloodstream.

When $CO_2$ enters the bloodstream, a chemical reaction occurs and most of the $CO_2$ becomes part of a bicarbonate ion molecule, $HCO_3^-$. These ions form in the presence of an enzyme that catalyzes the reaction of carbon dioxide and water to form carbonic acid, $H_2CO_3$, as the equation below shows. The carbonic acid breaks up to form a bicarbonate ion and a hydrogen ion, $H^+$:

$$\underset{\text{(water)}}{H_2O} + \underset{\text{(carbon dioxide)}}{CO_2} \longrightarrow \underset{\text{(carbonic acid)}}{H_2CO_3} \longrightarrow \underset{\text{(bicarbonate ion)}}{HCO_3^-} + \underset{\text{(hydrogen ion)}}{H^+}$$

The higher the concentration of the hydrogen ion in the bloodstream, the more acidic the blood becomes. Thus, the reaction that forms the hydrogen ion results in a decrease in the blood's pH.

Hands-On

# QuickLab

15 min

## Blood pH and Homeostasis 4.1.2d

You can use pH indicator paper, water, and baking soda to model the role of bicarbonate ions in maintaining blood pH levels in the presence of carbon dioxide.

### Procedure

1. Label one beaker "A," and label another beaker "B." Fill each beaker halfway with distilled water.
2. Add 1.4 g of baking soda to beaker B, and stir well.
3. Use pH indicator paper to test and record the pH of the contents of each beaker.
4. Gently blow through a straw into the water in beaker A. Test and record the pH of the resulting solution.
5. Repeat step 4 for beaker B.

### Analysis

1. **Describe** what happened to the pH in the two beakers during the experiment.
2. **State** the chemical name for baking soda.
3. **Propose** the chemical reaction that may have caused a change in pH in beaker A.
4. **Summarize** the effect of the baking soda on the pH of the solution in beaker B after blowing through a straw.
5. CRITICAL THINKING **Analyzing Information** Relate what happened in beaker B to what happens in the bloodstream.

**The Brainstem** Cells on the surface of the brainstem are sensitive to the acidity of the fluid that bathes the brain. In turn, the acidity of this fluid is strongly affected by the blood's acidity. Through this chain of connections, the brainstem's cells are responding to the acidity of the blood, which is directly related to the concentration of carbon dioxide. When this concentration is high, nerve centers in the brainstem signal muscles that control breathing to contract at a faster rate. As the muscles contract faster, the breathing rate increases. As a result, the lungs are able to exhale more carbon dioxide. Thus, excess $CO_2$ is removed from the bloodstream. Less $CO_2$ in the blood (and thus fewer hydrogen ions) results in the rise of the blood's pH level. When the blood's pH returns to normal, the brainstem will signal the muscles that control breathing to slow down.

**Oxygen Levels** Even though oxygen is essential for every cell's survival, the amount of oxygen in the blood does not affect a person's breathing rate unless oxygen levels fall dangerously low. Receptors in the arteries that connect the heart to the lungs are sensitive to the concentration of oxygen in the blood. If these receptors detect a sharp decrease in oxygen concentration, they send an emergency signal to the brainstem to speed the breathing rate. If a faster breathing rate does not increase the amount of oxygen in the blood quickly enough, then brain cells will begin to die. Because even small decreases in oxygen levels can kill brain cells, the body relies on carbon dioxide levels to control the breathing rate.

› **Reading Check** *How does the body control its breathing rate?*

**Analogies** After reading this section, complete the following analogy. Breathing rate : brainstem :: blood-glucose level : _____.

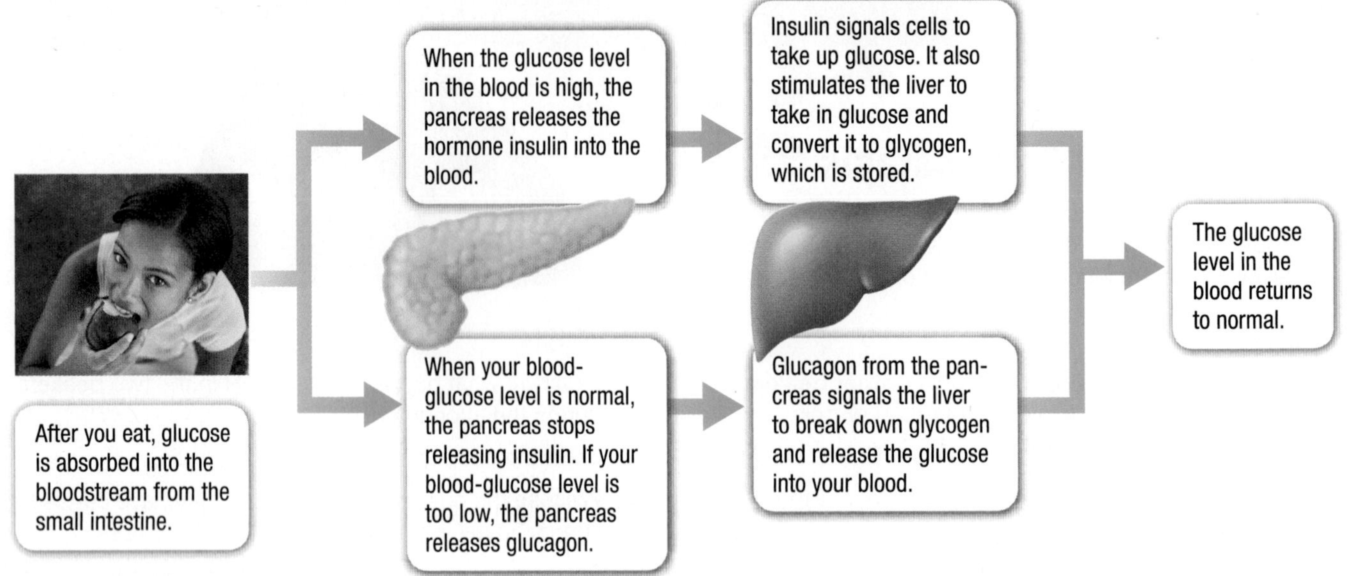


**Figure 17** After eating a meal, a person's blood-glucose level increases. **› Which two organs are primarily responsible for maintaining your blood-glucose level?**

## Controlling Blood-Glucose Level

Your body's cells need glucose in order to perform cellular respiration. When you digest a big meal, you introduce a large amount of glucose into your body in a short period of time. What prevents the level of glucose in your blood from quickly rising to a high level? **› Two hormones released by the pancreas, insulin and glucagon, control the level of glucose in a person's bloodstream.** Insulin and glucagon act antagonistically to regulate the blood-glucose level. Insulin lowers blood glucose levels by communicating with the liver to convert glucose into glycogen that can be stored for future use. Between meals, when glucose levels in the blood fall below the normal range, glucagon stimulates the liver to break down glycogen in order to add more glucose to the bloodstream. Thus, the glucose levels in the blood do not stay very high immediately after a meal and do not drop too low between meals. The feedback mechanism that controls the level of glucose in the blood is shown in **Figure 17.**

**Academic Vocabulary**

**regulate** to control or direct according to a rule

**› Reading Check** *What are the functions of insulin and glucagon?*

## Section 3 Review

**› KEY IDEAS**

1. **Identify** how feedback mechanisms are used to help the body maintain homeostasis.
2. **Explain** why you begin to breathe faster when you are exercising.
3. **Describe** how your body maintains its blood-glucose level after you have eaten a large meal.

**CRITICAL THINKING**

4. **Recognizing Relationships** How do you think the endocrine system and the nervous system work together to maintain the body's homeostasis?
5. **Making Inferences** Infer how the health of a person would be affected if the person's brainstem became insensitive to the pH of the fluid surrounding the brain.

**USING SCIENCE GRAPHICS**

6. **Drawing Diagrams** Research a feedback mechanism that is used by the body to maintain homeostasis. For example, you could research the mechanism that controls body temperature. Draw a diagram similar to Figures 16 and 17 to show how the feedback mechanism works.

Why It Matters

# Diabetes

REAL WORLD

Diabetes mellitus is the most common disorder of the endocrine system. Nine out of 10 diabetics have type 2 diabetes, and 90% of those affected are obese. In type 2 diabetes, cells stop responding to insulin. Type 2 diabetes usually begins in adults, but it is possible to develop in childhood.

## Type 1 or Type 2?

In diabetes, cells are unable to take up enough glucose from the blood, which results in high blood-glucose levels. Symptoms of diabetes include weight loss, increased urination, and thirst. In type 1 diabetes, the immune system destroys insulin-producing cells in the pancreas. In type 2 diabetes, cells stop responding to insulin. Many people are unaware they have the disease. In both types, the kidneys excrete excess glucose and water, which results in large amounts of urine and persistent thirst. Glucose-starved cells use the body's supply of fats and proteins for energy.

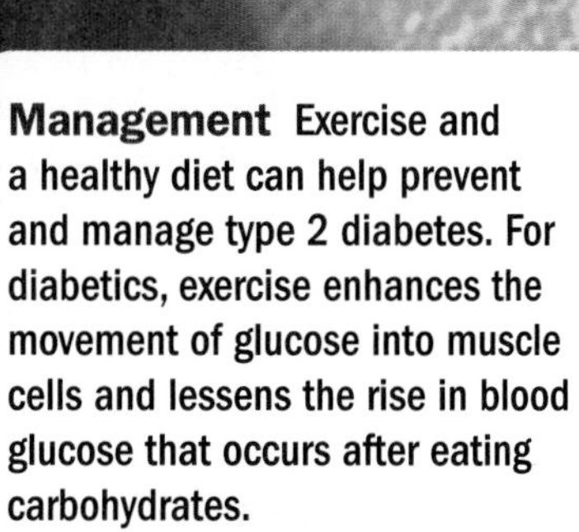

**Management** Exercise and a healthy diet can help prevent and manage type 2 diabetes. For diabetics, exercise enhances the movement of glucose into muscle cells and lessens the rise in blood glucose that occurs after eating carbohydrates.

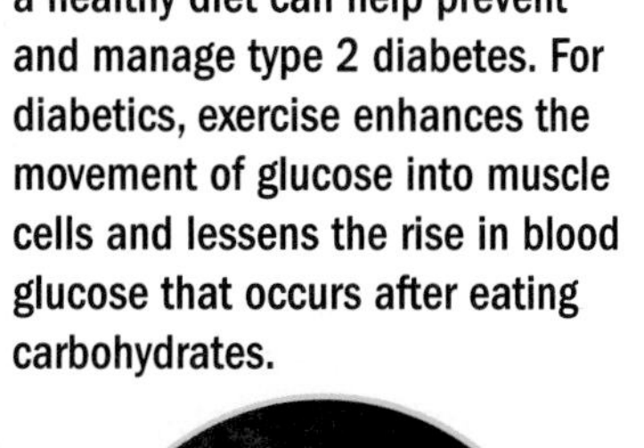

**Treatment** Most diabetics monitor their blood-glucose levels by using small testing devices. Diabetics who cannot make insulin receive it in an injection or from an insulin pump, a device that is worn by the patient and delivers a preset dose of insulin.

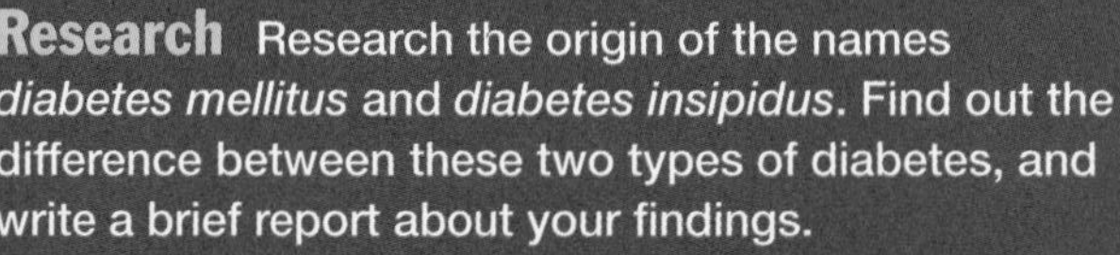

**Research** Research the origin of the names *diabetes mellitus* and *diabetes insipidus*. Find out the difference between these two types of diabetes, and write a brief report about your findings.

Inquiry

# Chapter 20 Lab

4.5.3b

## Objectives

- Measure the heart rate of daphnia.
- Observe the effect of the hormone epinephrine on heart rate in daphnia.
- Determine the threshold concentration for the effects of epinephrine on daphnia.

## Materials

- medicine dropper
- daphnia
- daphnia culture water
- depression slide
- petroleum jelly
- coverslip
- compound microscope
- watch or clock with second hand
- paper towels
- beaker, 100 mL
- graduated cylinder, 10 mL
- epinephrine solutions, 0.001%, 0.0001%, 0.00001%, and 0.000001%

## Safety

# Epinephrine and Heart Rate

Epinephrine is a hormone that increases blood pressure, blood-glucose level, and heart rate (HR). The lowest concentration that stimulates a response is called the *threshold concentration*.

In this lab, you will design an experiment to investigate the threshold concentration of epinephrine that affects heart rate. To do this, you will observe heart rate of the crustacean daphnia under experimental conditions that you determine.

## Preparation

1. SCIENTIFIC METHODS **State the Problem** What is the threshold concentration of epinephrine that affects the heart rate of daphnia?
2. SCIENTIFIC METHODS **Form a Hypothesis** Form a testable hypothesis that explains how epinephrine might affect the heart rate of daphnia. Record your hypothesis.

## Procedure

### Observe Heart Rate in Daphnia

1. Put on safety goggles, gloves, and a lab apron.
2. **CAUTION: Do not touch your face while handling microorganisms.** Use a clean medicine dropper to transfer one daphnia to the well of a clean depression slide. Place a dab of petroleum jelly in the well. Add a coverslip. Observe the daphnia with a compound microscope under low power.
3. Count the daphnia's heartbeats for 10 s. Divide this number by 10 to find the HR in beats per second. Record your observations in a data table as Trial 1. Turn off the microscope light, and wait 20 s. Repeat this step two times, and record your observations as Trials 2 and 3.
4. Calculate the average HR in beats per second. Then, calculate the average heart rate in beats per minute using the following formula:

$$\text{Average HR (beats per minute)} = \text{Average HR (beats per second)} \times 60 \text{ s/min.}$$

*Daphnia Heart Rate*

| Solution | HR (beats per second) Trial 1 (A) | HR (beats per second) Trial 2 (B) | HR (beats per second) Trial 3 (C) | Average HR (beats per second) [(A+B+C)/3] | Average HR (beats per minute) |
|---|---|---|---|---|---|
| | | | | | |

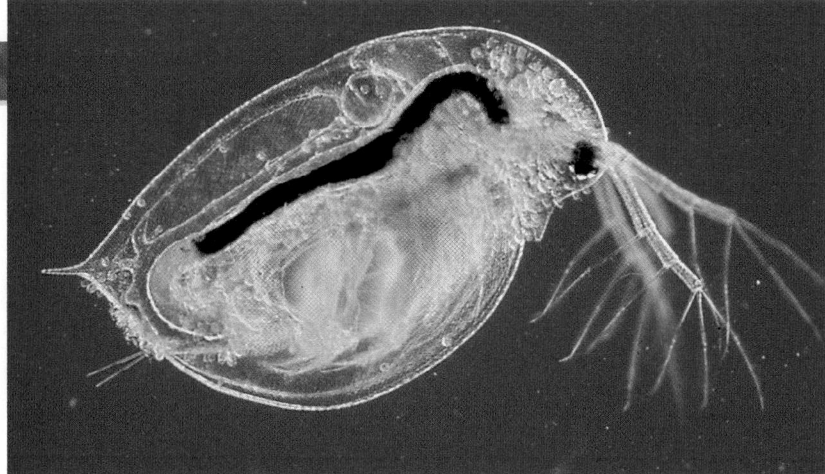

Daphnia

### Design an Experiment

5 Design an experiment that tests your hypothesis and that uses the materials listed for this lab. Predict what will happen during your experiment if your hypothesis is supported.

6 **CAUTION: Handle animals carefully and with respect.** Write a procedure for your experiment. Identify the dependent variables and the independent variables. Construct any tables that you will need to record your data. Make a list of all of the safety precautions that you will take. Have your teacher approve your procedure and safety precautions before you begin.

### Conduct Your Experiment

7 **CAUTION: Glassware such as coverslips and slides are fragile. Notify your teacher of broken glass or cuts.** To add a solution to a prepared slide, first place a drop of the solution at the edge of the coverslip. Then, place a piece of paper towel along the opposite edge to draw the solution under the coverslip. Wait 1 min for the solution to take effect.

8 **CAUTION: Epinephrine is toxic and is absorbed through the skin. Wear gloves at all times during this experiment. Notify your teacher of any spills.** Perform your experiment. Record your observations in a data table.

9 Clean up your lab materials according to your teacher's instructions. Wash your hands before leaving the lab.

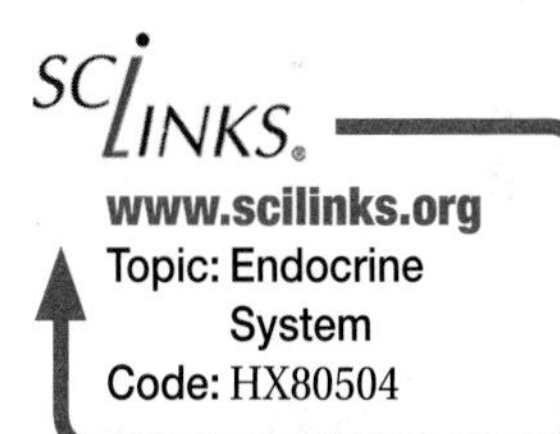

SCILINKS.
www.scilinks.org
Topic: Endocrine System
Code: HX80504


## Analyze and Conclude

1. **Summarizing Results** Make a graph of your data. Plot "Epinephrine concentration (%)" on the *x*-axis. Plot "Average heart rate (beats per minute)" on the *y*-axis.
2. SCIENTIFIC METHODS **Analyzing Data** Which solutions affected the heart rate of daphnia?
3. SCIENTIFIC METHODS **Interpreting Data** What was the threshold concentration of epinephrine?
4. **Making Predictions** Based on the information that you have and based on your data, predict how epinephrine concentration would affect heart rates in humans.

## Extensions

5. **Inferring Relationships** Research anaphylactic shock. Explain why epinephrine is used to treat anaphylactic shock.
6. **Further Inquiry** Write a new question about hormones that could be explored with another investigation.

# Chapter 20 Summary

| Key Ideas | Key Terms |
|---|---|
| **1 Homeostasis** | homeostasis (471) |
| ❯ The external environment around an organism is constantly changing. These changes threaten the stability of an organism's internal environment. ❯ Organisms detect and respond to change in a variety of ways: both at the cellular level and at the organismal level. Failure to respond to change can result in an organism's death. ❯ Humans require multiple systems for digestion, respiration, reproduction, circulation, movement, coordination, and immunity. The systems interact to maintain homeostasis. |  |
| **2 Human Body Systems** | tendon (476)<br>epidermis (477)<br>hormone (479)<br>endocrine gland (479)<br>digestion (480)<br>excretion (481)<br>alveoli (482)<br>capillary (482)<br>lymph (483) |
| ❯ The skeletal and muscular systems enable movement and provide support and protection for tissues and organs. ❯ The integumentary system protects the body from injury and UV radiation, defends against disease, helps regulate body temperature, and prevents the body from drying out. ❯ The nervous system collects and responds to information about the body's internal and external environment. The endocrine system regulates metabolism; maintains salt, water, and nutrient balance in the blood; and regulates growth, development, and reproduction. ❯ The digestive system converts food into nutrients that a body's cells can use. Excretion enables the body to maintain its osmotic and pH balance. ❯ The respiratory system brings oxygen, $O_2$, into the body and carries carbon dioxide, $CO_2$, out of the body. The circulatory system carries nutrients, oxygen, hormones, and wastes through the body and distributes heat to maintain homeostasis. | |
| **3 Feedback Mechanisms** | feedback mechanism (484) |
| ❯ To maintain homeostasis, your body has a diversity of feedback mechanisms that detect deviations in the body's internal environment and make corrective actions. ❯ When the brainstem senses a change in the blood's pH, it adjusts the breathing rate. ❯ Two hormones that are released by the pancreas, insulin and glucagon, control the level of glucose in a person's bloodstream. 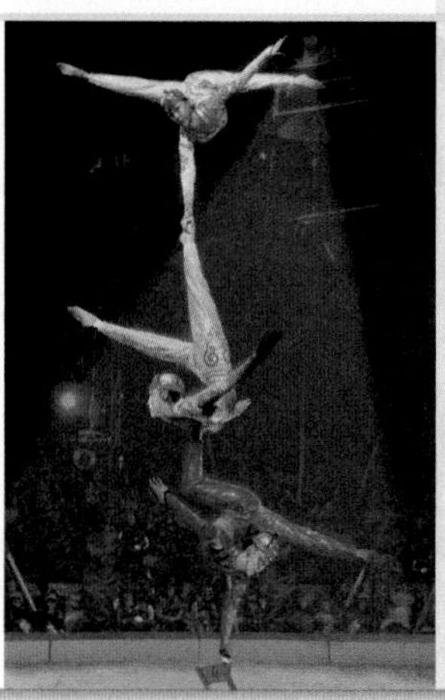 | |

Chapter 20

The Living Environment

# Regents Exam Practice

**PART A: Answer all questions in this part.**

*Directions*: For each statement or question, write on your separate answer sheet the number of the word or expression that best completes the statement or answers the question.

**1** When a person does strenuous exercise, small blood vessels (capillaries) near the surface of the skin increase in diameter. This change allows the body to be cooled. These statements best illustrate

(1) synthesis
(2) homeostasis
(3) excretion
(4) locomotion

**2** Some human body cells are shown in the diagrams below. These groups of cells represent different

Cells from skin

Blood cells

Cells from lining of bladder

Cells from lining of trachea

(1) tissues in which similar cells function together.
(2) organs that help to carry out a specific life activity.
(3) systems that are responsible for a specific life activity.
(4) organelles that carry out different functions.

**3** Which statement does *not* describe an example of a feedback mechanism that maintains homeostasis?

(1) The guard cells close the openings in leaves, preventing excess water loss from a plant.
(2) White blood cells increase the production of antigens during an allergic reaction.
(3) Increased physical activity increases heart rate in humans.
(4) The pancreas releases insulin, helping humans to keep blood sugar levels stable.

**4** Feedback interactions in the human body are important because they

(1) determine the diversity necessary for evolution to occur
(2) direct the synthesis of altered genes that are passed on to every cell in the body
(3) regulate the shape of molecules involved in cellular communication
(4) keep the internal body environment within its normal range

**5** Which situation is *not* an example of the maintenance of a dynamic equilibrium in an organism?

(1) Guard cells contribute to the regulation of water content in a geranium plant.
(2) Water passes into an animal cell causing it to swell.
(3) The release of insulin lowers the blood sugar level in a human after eating a big meal.
(4) A runner perspires while running a race on a hot summer day.

**6** The most immediate response to a high level of blood sugar in a human is an increase in the

(1) muscle activity in the arms
(2) blood flow to the digestive tract
(3) activity of all cell organelles
(4) release of insulin

**7** The pancreas produces one hormone that lowers blood sugar level and another that increases blood sugar level. The interaction of these two hormones most directly helps humans to

(1) maintain a balanced internal environment
(2) digest needed substances for other body organs
(3) dispose of wastes formed in other body organs
(4) increase the rate of cellular communication

**8** The central nervous system includes

(1) only the brain.
(2) the brain and the spinal cord.
(3) the brain, the spinal cord, and the cranial nerves.
(4) the brain, the spinal cord, the cranial nerves, and the spinal nerves.

**9** When a certain plant is without water for an extended period of time, guard cells close openings in the leaves of the plant. This activity conserves water and illustrates

(1) cellular communication involving the action of nerve cells and receptor sites
(2) an increase in rate of growth due to a low concentration of water
(3) maintenance of a dynamic equilibrium through detection and response to stimuli
(4) a response to one biotic factor in the environment

**10** What is the function of the lymphatic system?

(1) It opens two-way vessels.
(2) It helps the body fight infections.
(3) It interacts with the respiratory system.
(4) It transports fluids away from the heart.

**11** In the diagram of a single-celled organism shown below, the arrows indicate various activities taking place.

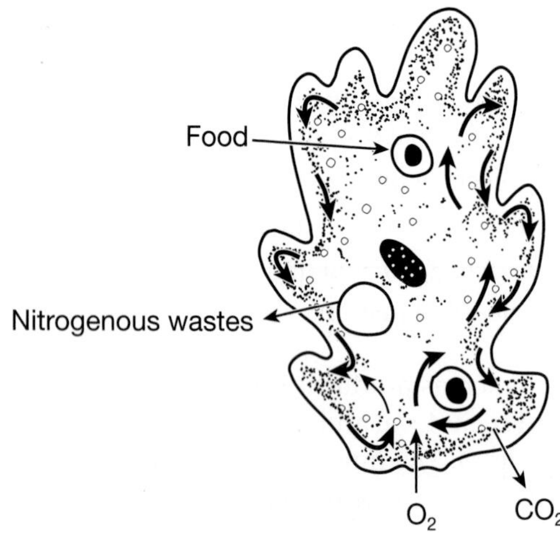


Which systems perform these same activities in humans?

(1) digestive, circulatory, and immune
(2) excretory, respiratory, and reproductive
(3) respiratory, excretory, and digestive
(4) respiratory, nervous, and endocrine

**12** Which process illustrates a feedback mechanism in plants?

(1) Chloroplasts take in more nitrogen, which increases the rate of photosynthesis.
(2) Chloroplasts release more oxygen in response to a decreased rate of photosynthesis.
(3) Guard cells change the size of leaf openings, regulating the exchange of gases.
(4) Guard cells release oxygen from the leaf at night.

**Part B**

**13** Distinguish between a positive feedback mechanism and a negative feedback mechanism.

**14** Describe the relationship between the kidney and the nephron.

**15** List three major types of activities in the body that are regulated by the endocrine system.

**16** Why does exchange of gases between the blood and body tissues not occur through the walls of arteries?

**17** Distinguish between the chemical digestion that occurs in the mouth and in the stomach.

**Part C**

**18** Describe how the endocrine system regulates hormone levels.

**19** X and Y are hormones. X stimulates the secretion of Y. Y exerts negative feedback on the cells that secrete X. What happens when the level of Y in the blood decreases?

**20** Why is it important that the large intestine reabsorb water and not eliminate it?

**21** Relate the similarities in the components and fluids of the cardiovascular and lymphatic systems.

**22** Prostaglandins are hormones that cause the body to feel pain when the body is injured. Why might it be important for the body to feel pain after an injury?

**23** The liver and pancreas are accessory organs of the digestive tract. In what two ways do the liver and pancreas differ from other digestive organs?

**24** One of your classmates states a hypothesis that all organisms must have organ systems. Is your classmate's hypothesis valid? Explain your answer.

**Part D**

**25** A student measures his pulse rate while he is watching television and records it. Next, he walks to a friend's house nearby and when he arrives, measures and records his pulse rate again. He and his friend then decide to run to the mall a few blocks away. On arriving at the mall, the student measures and records his pulse rate once again. Finally, after sitting and talking for a half hour, the student measures and records his pulse rate for the last time.

Which graph below best illustrates the expected changes in his pulse rate according to the activities described above?

A = after watching television
B = after walking to a friend's house
C = after running to the mall
D = after sitting and talking

(1)
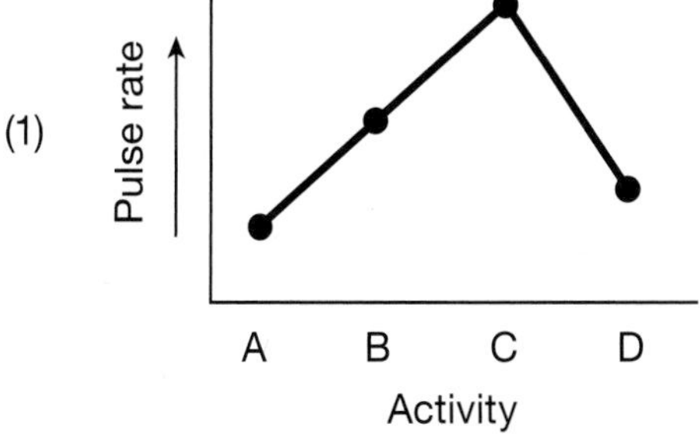


(3)
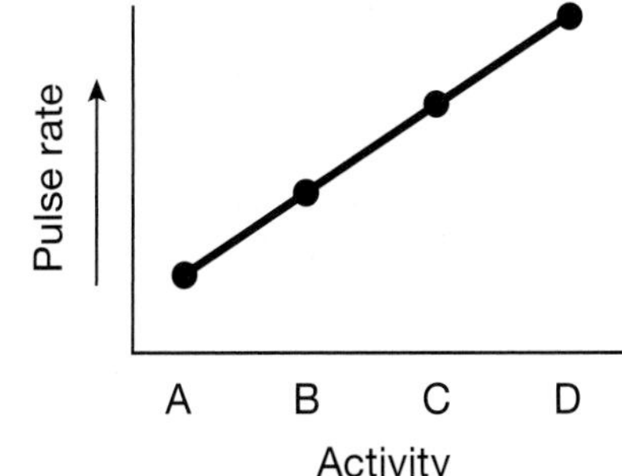


(2)
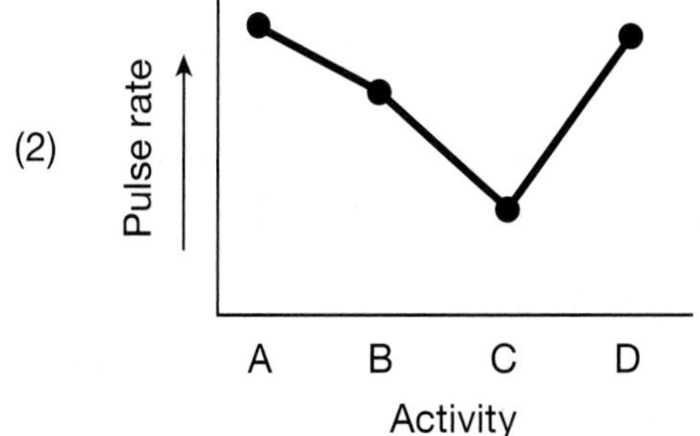


(4)
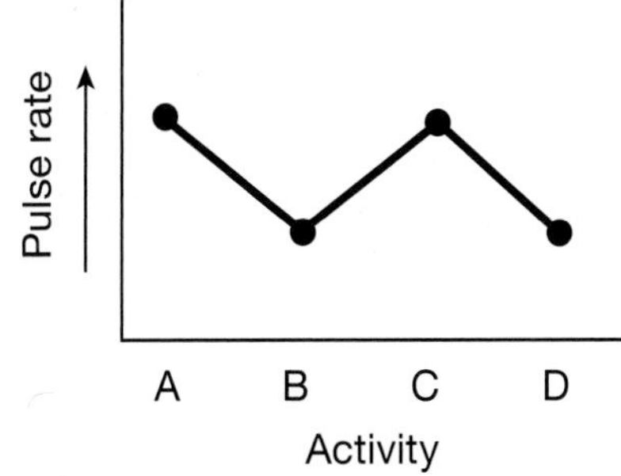

# Chapter 21 Homeostasis and Human Diseases

## Preview

1 **Disease**
The Cause of Disease
The Spread of Pathogens
Avoiding Disease

2 **Infectious Diseases**
Bacteria
Viruses
Fungi
Parasitic Worms
Protists

3 **Noninfectious Diseases**
Personal Behavior
Inheritance
Organ Malfunction
Poor Nutrition
Toxic Substances

## Why It Matters

Disease can result when your body's homeostasis is disrupted. Understanding the link between homeostasis and disease can help you stay healthy.

***The Living Environment***

**Standard 4** Students will understand and apply scientific concepts, principles, and theories pertaining to the physical setting and living environment and recognize the historical development of ideas in science.

**Key Idea 1** Living things are both similar to and different from each other and from nonliving things. ***Major Understandings*** **- 1.2d**

**Key Idea 2** Organisms inherit genetic information in a variety of ways that result in continuity of structure and function between parents and offspring. ***Major Understandings*** **- 2.2e**

**Key Idea 5** Organisms maintain a dynamic equilibrium that sustains life. ***Major Understandings*** **- 5.2a, 5.2b, 5.2h, 5.2j**

This X ray of a hand shows a cancerous tumor growing on a metacarpal, one of the bones that form the hand's palm.

Healthy bone can support more than 5,000 kg of pressure per square inch. Cancerous bone is so weakened that it can break from stress as slight as the pressure of a firm handshake.

Primary bone cancer, or cancer that starts in a bone rather than in another organ, is very rare. It accounts for less than 0.2% of all cancer cases.

# InquiryLab

## Cigarette Smoke and Disease 4.5.2h

15 min

By causing alveoli in the lungs to lose elasticity, cigarette smoke makes the alveoli more likely to tear and form larger and less efficient alveoli. The result is the disease emphysema.

### Procedure

1. Use a **microscope** to examine a **slide of healthy lung tissue.** Note the number and size of the alveoli. Draw what you see.
2. Examine a **slide of lung tissue exhibiting emphysema,** and compare it to the first slide. Draw what you see.
3. In both specimens, locate and compare the capillaries that surround the alveoli.
4. Switch to high power. Examine both specimens, and identify their similarities and differences.

### Analysis

1. **Contrast** the healthy tissue and diseased tissue in terms of their capillaries, the number of alveoli, and the size of the alveoli.
2. **Explain** why a large alveolus exchanges gas less efficiently than a small alveolus does.

Bone cancer disrupts homeostasis by constricting nearby tissues, such as blood vessels and nerves. As a result, movement in the affected area is painful or difficult.

These reading tools can help you learn the material in this chapter. For more information on how to use these and other tools, see **Appendix: Reading and Study Skills.**

## Using Words

**Key-Term Fold** A key-term fold is a useful tool for studying definitions of key terms in a chapter. Each tab can contain a key term on one side and its definition on the other.

**Your Turn** Use the key-term fold to quiz yourself on the definitions of the key terms in a chapter. Fold a sheet of lined notebook paper in half from left to right. Using scissors, cut along every third line from the right edge of the paper to the center fold to make tabs.

## Using Language

**Classification** As you read the chapter, identify general words that describe categories of something and specific words that describe individuals within a category. Often, the general category will be named in a large heading, and the smaller headings will describe individuals in the category.

**Your Turn** Answer the following questions by using information that you read in the chapter.

**1.** What are two major classifications of disease?

**2.** What are five diseases that are often caused by personal behavior?

## Taking Notes

**Two-Column Notes** Two-column notes can help you learn the key ideas from each section.

**Your Turn** Create a two-column notes table for this chapter.

**1.** Write the key ideas in the left column. The key ideas are listed at the beginning of each section. Include one key idea in each row.

**2.** As you read the section, add detailed notes and examples in the right column. Be sure to put these details and examples in your own words.

*Infectious Diseases*

| *Key Idea* | *Supporting Details* |
|---|---|
| | |
| | |
| | |

Section 1

# Disease

| Key Ideas | Key Terms | Why It Matters |
|---|---|---|
| › What causes disease?<br>› How are pathogens spread?<br>› What can you do to help avoid diseases? | noninfectious disease<br>infectious disease<br>pathogen<br>vector | When you're sick, you probably wish you could have prevented your illness. By understanding disease, you may avoid getting sick. |

In May 1720, a ship loaded with silk and other fine cloth arrived at the French port city of Marseille. The ship's captain warned city officials that several passengers were violently ill, but the city's merchants were eager for the cloth. So, the ship was unloaded swiftly, and within days, a disease—bubonic plague—was racing through the city. Within two years, more than half of the city's population was dead. **Figure 1** shows a painting in which the citizens of Marseille are burying plague victims in mass graves.

**Standard 4**

**1.2d** If there is a disruption in any human system, there may be a corresponding imbalance in homeostasis.

**5.2a** Homeostasis in an organism is constantly threatened. Failure to respond effectively can result in disease or death.

**5.2b** Viruses, bacteria, fungi, and other parasites may infect plants and animals and interfere with normal life functions.

**5.2h** Disease may also be caused by inheritance, toxic substances, poor nutrition, organ malfunction, and some personal behavior. Some effects show up right away; others may not show up for many years.

**5.2j** Biological research generates knowledge used to design ways of diagnosing, preventing, treating, controlling, or curing diseases of plants and animals.

## The Cause of Disease

What causes bubonic plague or, for that matter, any other disease? › **Disease is caused by a disruption in a human body system that leads to a corresponding disruption in homeostasis.** Once homeostasis has been disrupted and a person is ill, the disruption may result in further imbalances in other body systems. If the imbalances continue, the end result may be death.

Diseases fall into two categories. **Noninfectious diseases** are diseases that cannot be transmitted from one organism to another. Examples include genetic disorders, heart disease, and most cancers. Diseases that can be transmitted from one organism to another are known as **infectious diseases.** Bubonic plague, for instance, is an infectious disease. It is caused by a **pathogen,** which is a virus, a microorganism, or other organism that causes illness.

**noninfectious disease** a disease that cannot spread from one individual to another

**infectious disease** a disease that is caused by a pathogen and that can be spread from one individual to another

**pathogen** a microorganism, another organism, a virus, or a protein that causes disease; an infectious agent

› **Reading Check** *What causes infectious diseases? (See the Appendix for answers to Reading Checks.)*

**Figure 1** The Great Plague of Marseille in the 1720s was caused by the bacterium *Yersinia pestis.* Fleas spread this bacterium throughout the city.

**Key-Term Fold** As you read this section, record all of the highlighted terms, such as the word *vector,* in your key-term fold.

## The Spread of Pathogens

There are many types of pathogens, including bacteria, viruses, protists, fungi, and parasitic worms. **❯ Pathogens can be spread through the air, through contact with contaminated objects or an infected organism, through the ingestion of contaminated food or water, or through vectors.**

**Air** As **Figure 2** shows, when an infected person coughs or sneezes, thousands of pathogen-carrying droplets can be released into the air. These pathogens then can infect a new host through the nose, mouth, or eyes. The common cold, influenza, strep throat, and tuberculosis are spread through the air.

**Contaminated Objects or Infected Organisms** When an object, such as the syringe needle in **Figure 2,** becomes contaminated with pathogens, the object can transmit the pathogens to a host. Objects that commonly transmit pathogens include eating utensils, hairbrushes, and doorknobs. Pathogens are also transmitted by infected organisms. For example, humans can get rabies from an infected dog or cat. Also, direct person-to-person contact, such as shaking hands, kissing, or sexual intercourse, can spread pathogens.

**vector** an intermediate host that transfers a pathogen or a parasite to another organism

**Contaminated Food or Water** Food and water may carry pathogens. For instance, raw chicken can be covered in salmonellae, bacteria that can cause food poisoning. In addition, if a water line breaks or a water treatment plant becomes flooded, pathogens can enter the public water supply and cause diseases such as cholera.

**Vectors** A **vector** is an intermediate organism that transfers pathogens between humans or from animals to humans. Vectors usually do not get ill from the pathogen. The mosquito is the most common vector for humans. Mosquitoes can transmit malaria and West Nile virus. Fleas, ticks, and rodents are also vectors for pathogens such as the bacteria that cause bubonic plague.

**❯ Reading Check** ***How might you prevent the spread of a pathogen?***

**Figure 2** A sneeze can force thousands of pathogens out of your body at up to 160 km/h. These pathogens may land on and contaminate solid surfaces, such as the tip of an unsterilized syringe, shown on the right. **❯ How might the bacteria on this syringe be transmitted to your body?**

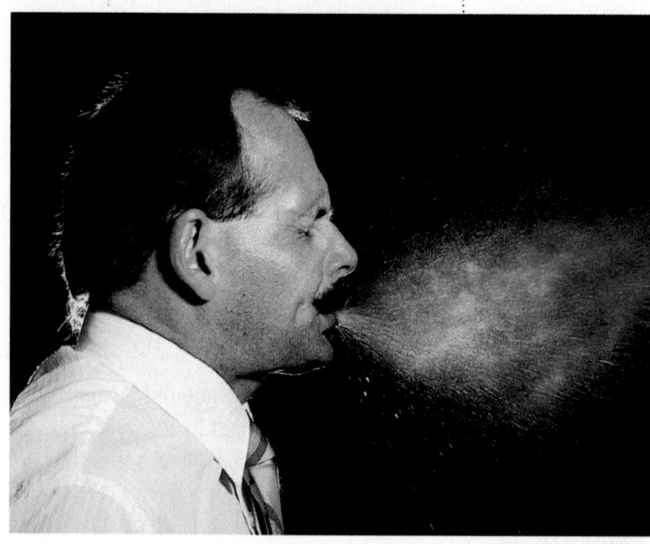

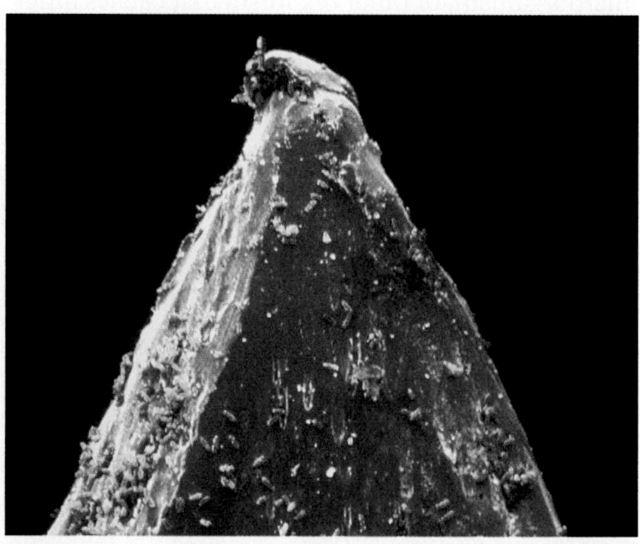

## Avoiding Disease

Whether infectious or noninfectious, disease results from the same general condition: a disruption of homeostasis. If an individual could avoid the disruption of homeostasis, his or her health would not deteriorate. Therefore, actions that help you maintain your body's homeostasis will also help you maintain your overall health. **› You can maintain your homeostasis and can avoid many diseases by practicing good hygiene, avoiding close contact with infected organisms, maintaining a healthy diet, and exercising on a regular basis.**

**Good Hygiene** Pathogens disrupt your homeostasis by damaging cells, tissues, or organs. You can decrease the chance of being infected by a pathogen by practicing good hygiene. Consider all of the ways in which pathogens can be transmitted, and take precautions against these modes of transmission. For example, wash your hands thoroughly and frequently to lower dramatically your risk of being infected by a pathogen. In addition, avoid contact with infected animals or people.

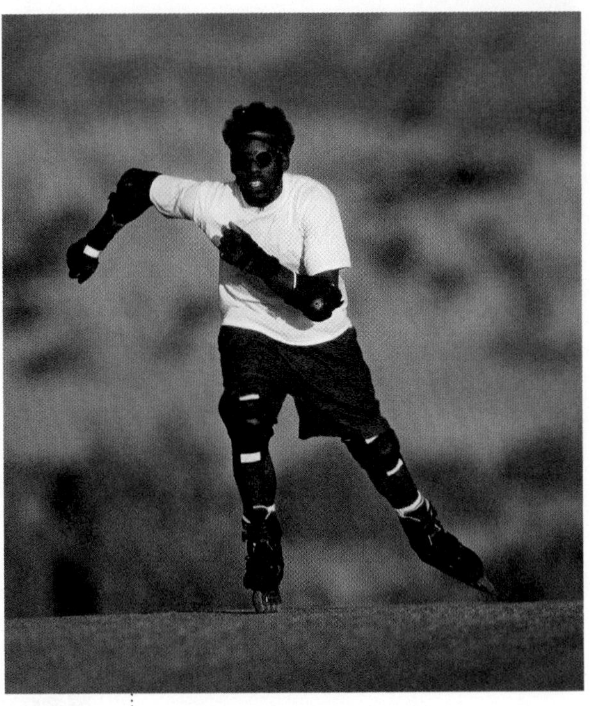

**Figure 3** Exercise increases the health and strength of many of your body systems. **› How does exercise help you avoid disease?**

**A Healthy Lifestyle** To maintain homeostasis, your body needs a regular supply of nutrients, such as protein, vitamins, and minerals. Nutrients are used to power healthy cells, repair damaged cells, and replace dead cells. By eating a balanced diet that supplies all of the nutrients that your body needs, you are supporting the health of all of your tissues and organs. Thus, your body will be better able to resist pathogens and noninfectious diseases. Exercise is also very important for maintaining your body's homeostasis. People who engage in regular physical activity, such as the student shown in **Figure 3,** improve their muscle strength, flexibility, cardiovascular health, and immune system response. People who exercise also strengthen their bones and improve the efficiency of their respiratory system.

**› Reading Check** ***Explain why a healthy diet is necessary for maintaining the body's homeostasis.***

SCILINKS.
**www.scilinks.org**
Topic: Disease
Code: HX80413

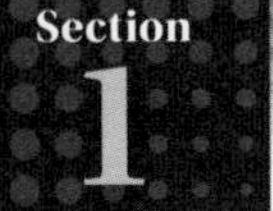

## Section 1 Review

### › KEY IDEAS

1. **Describe** what happens when the internal balance of human body systems is disrupted.
2. **Identify** three ways in which pathogens can be transmitted to humans.
3. **List** the actions that people can take to avoid many kinds of diseases.

### CRITICAL THINKING

4. **Compare and Contrast** What do infectious diseases and noninfectious diseases have in common? What are their main differences?
5. **Inferring Relationships** Describe the relationship between a person's lifestyle and the ability of the person's body systems to maintain homeostasis.

### CONNECTING KEY IDEAS

6. **Relating Concepts** Suppose that you touch an object that is contaminated by a pathogen. Explain how your skin can help your body maintain its homeostasis by providing protection from the pathogen.

Section 2

# Infectious Diseases

| Key Ideas | Key Terms | Why It Matters |
|---|---|---|
| ❯ How do pathogenic bacteria cause disease?<br>❯ Why do viruses cause damage to their hosts?<br>❯ How are pathogenic fungi similar to pathogenic bacteria?<br>❯ How do parasitic worms cause disease?<br>❯ What diseases are caused by protists? | toxin | You may not realize that your body is constantly under attack by other organisms. If they succeed in infecting you, your homeostasis and your health will suffer. |

**Standard 4**
**5.2b** Viruses, bacteria, fungi, and other parasites may infect plants and animals and interfere with normal life functions.

The term *pathogen* derives from Greek words that mean "the birth of pain." In this section, you will learn why pathogens have received such an ominous name.

## Bacteria

Most bacteria are harmless to humans. Many are even helpful. However, a few bacteria can cause diseases that are as minor as acne or as deadly as anthrax. ❯ **Pathogenic bacteria cause disease by producing toxins and by destroying body tissues.** **Toxins** are poisonous chemicals. Most bacterial diseases, including several of the diseases listed in **Figure 4,** are caused when pathogenic bacteria release toxins inside their host. For example, botulism can occur when food is not heated enough during canning to kill the bacterium *Clostridium botulinum.* The bacteria release a toxin, that when eaten, destroys the tips of nerve cells. Paralysis can result.

A second way that bacteria cause disease is by producing enzymes that break down the host's tissues into nutrients that the bacteria can use. Tuberculosis, discussed on the next page, is an example of a disease caused by bacteria that break down tissue for nutrients.

**Figure 4** Many bacterial diseases, such as tooth decay, are very common. ❯ **Which bacterial disease listed in the table can lead to hearing loss?**

**Some Bacterial Diseases**

| Disease | Description |
|---|---|
| Bacterial meningitis | infection of the fluid surrounding the brain and spinal cord; results in high fever, headache, and stiff neck and may lead to brain damage or hearing loss |
| Cholera | infection of the intestine by *Vibrio cholerae;* results in acute diarrhea, vomiting, and leg cramps and may lead to dehydration, shock, and death if not treated |
| Stomach ulcer | sore in the lining of the stomach; is usually caused by *Helicobacter pylori* and results in burning pain in the abdomen |
| Tetanus | body rigidity and convulsive spasms of the skeletal muscles caused by *Clostridium tetani* |
| Tooth decay | a hole (cavity) in the tooth formed by bacteria that live in dental plaque and produce acids that demineralize tooth enamel |

**Tuberculosis** About 2 million people die from tuberculosis every year. Tuberculosis is a disease caused by the bacterium *Mycobacterium tuberculosis.* This bacterium can attack any organ, but it usually infects the lungs. As the bacteria feed off of nutrients in the lung tissue, they can make a hole in the alveoli. As a result, the lungs' efficiency in gas exchange decreases, and homeostasis is disrupted. The lungs must then work harder to obtain the oxygen needed by the body's cells. Yet because tuberculosis often causes coughing and painful breathing, it is difficult for the lungs to work harder. In the end, the body is not able to get as much oxygen as it needs. The effects of this oxygen shortage are fatigue and, in some cases, a loss in appetite. In turn, other body systems become weakened. The infection may spread to other tissues in the body and may cause damage similar to the damage that the bacteria cause in the lungs. If the infection is not treated, the person eventually may die.

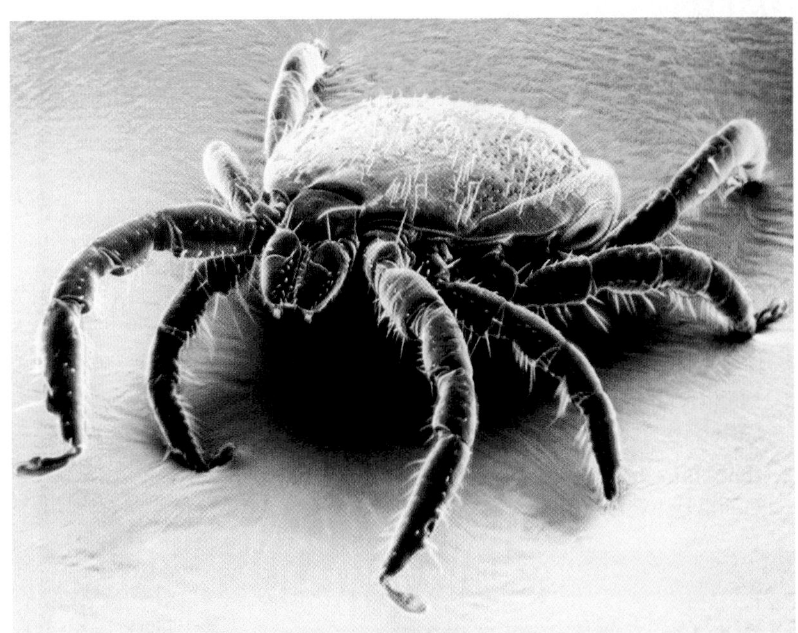

**Figure 5** When this blacklegged tick feeds on the blood of a mouse, a squirrel, or another animal infected with the bacteria that cause Lyme disease, the tick takes the bacteria into its body.

**Lyme Disease** Lyme disease is the most common insect-borne disease in the United States and is caused by the bacterium *Borrelia burgdorferi*. The main vector of the bacterium is the blacklegged tick, such as the one shown in **Figure 5.** Like the bacterium that causes tuberculosis, the bacterium that causes Lyme disease feeds off of the tissues of its host. The bacterium mostly attacks the nervous system and the blood vessels that supply this system. Acute symptoms include a fever and characteristic target-shaped rash. If left untreated, symptoms include concentration problems, loss of memory, muscle weakness or paralysis, tingling and numbness in the arms, headaches, and severe joint pain. None of these symptoms is severe enough to cause death, but the disease does disrupt homeostasis and makes physical activity difficult. A lack of physical activity can cause a decline in the health of other body systems.

**toxin** a substance that is produced by one organism and that is poisonous to other organisms

**Acne** Acne is not as serious as tuberculosis or Lyme disease, but it is probably a bacterial infection with which you are familiar. Acne results when hair follicles become clogged with oil, dead skin cells, and bacteria. These bacteria produce toxins that attract white blood cells. The white blood cells cause the tissue around the follicle to become inflamed, as **Figure 6** shows. A pimple or cyst can form around the inflamed follicle. When the pimple or cyst bursts, the skin may scar. In addition, if the bursting causes an open wound on the skin, other pathogens may enter the body. Thus, it is important that people with acne avoid deliberately bursting their acne lesions.

**Figure 6** Oil glands are especially active during adolescence. Therefore, teenagers are more likely to suffer from acne than adults are.

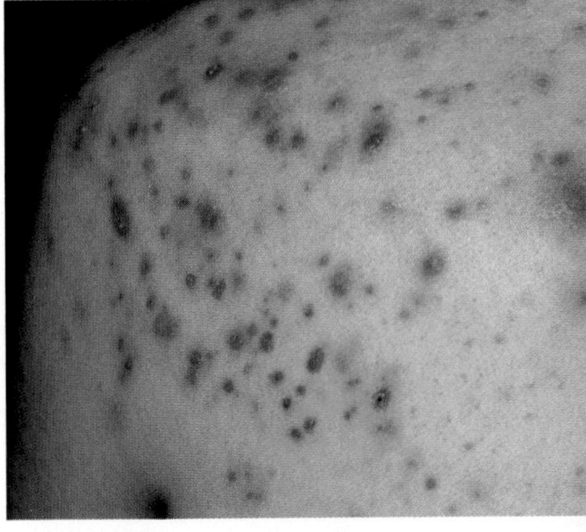

**Reading Check** ***Compare the causes of, symptoms of, and organs affected by tuberculosis and Lyme disease.***

Data

# QuickLab

## Emergence of Bird Flu 4.5.2a

Although bird flu infection is rare in humans, the disease has emerged in several countries. This graph identifies the onset of new cases in the first half of 2006.

### Analysis

1. **Identify** the countries in which new cases of humans infected with bird flu appeared in March 2006.
2. **Calculate** the total number of new cases that appeared in China between January and April 2006.

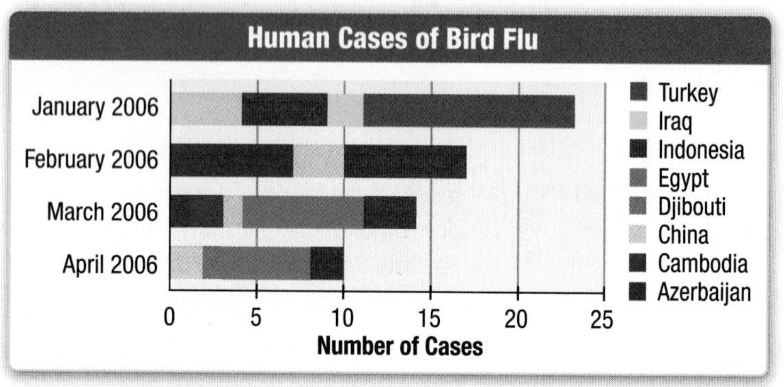


## Viruses

Viruses cause many diseases, such as flu, chickenpox, and viral hepatitis, in humans. Typically, a virus infects a specific organ of the body. For example, flu infects the lungs, and hepatitis viruses infect the liver. Viruses are passed to humans by sneezing or coughing, sexual contact, sharing blood products, or the bite of insect vectors, such as mosquitoes.

Viruses cannot reproduce on their own. › **Instead, viruses must use a living cell to reproduce. This process damages or destroys the living cell.** A viral infection begins when the virus's genetic material enters a host cell. The virus then uses the host's organelles to replicate the virus's genetic material and to make proteins. The proteins are then assembled with the viral genetic material to form new complete viruses. The host cell dies and breaks open, and the newly made viruses are released. If the new viruses infect other cells, they may kill the cells and spread the infection. A viral infection disrupts homeostasis if it destroys cells faster than the body can replace them.

**HIV** In an HIV infection, the destruction of the T cells of the immune system results in the disruption of the body's homeostasis. T cells, a type of white blood cells, normally defend the body against pathogens. If enough T cells are destroyed, the body cannot defend itself against infection. The person who has an HIV infection often becomes ill from other infectious diseases until his or her body systems are overwhelmed and cease to function. You can read more about how HIV infects and destroys T cells in the Up Close feature.

**Bird Flu** Bird flu is an infection caused by avian influenza viruses. These viruses generally infect birds. So far, bird flu does not seem to be spread from one person to another. However, because many viruses mutate easily, this situation could change and result in a global flu epidemic. In 2005, a new form of bird flu appeared in Asia and then spread to other parts of the world. The symptoms of this form of bird flu are similar to those of the common flu but are much more severe. Like the common flu, bird flu infects the respiratory tract. For an unknown reason, though, the bird flu virus sets off a violent immune response. The body's airways become highly inflamed, so breathing becomes very difficult. Without immediate medical attention, the person may suffocate and die.

SCILINKS.
www.scilinks.org
Topic: Emerging Viruses
Code: HX80499

› **Reading Check** *How does viral reproduction damage a host cell?*

# Up Close HIV Reproduction

Human immunodeficiency virus (HIV) is the virus that causes acquired immune deficiency syndrome (AIDS). HIV is considered to be a pandemic, a worldwide epidemic. About 22 million people have died as a result of AIDS. Currently, an estimated 33 million to 46 million people worldwide are living with HIV. Several drugs are effective in slowing HIV, but there is no cure.

**HIV**

**Full name:** human immunodeficiency virus
**Size:** 110 to 128 nm
**Habitat:** human CD4+ T lymphocyte
**Diet:** none
**Mode of nutrition:** none

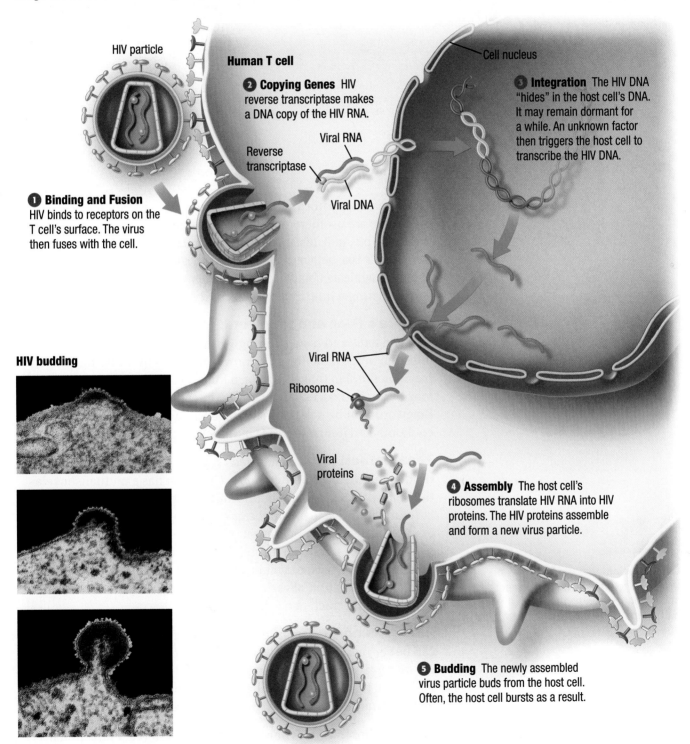

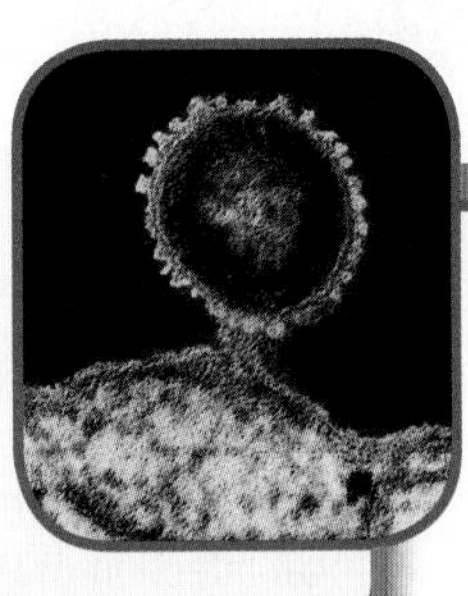



**1 Binding and Fusion** HIV binds to receptors on the T cell's surface. The virus then fuses with the cell.

**2 Copying Genes** HIV reverse transcriptase makes a DNA copy of the HIV RNA.

**3 Integration** The HIV DNA "hides" in the host cell's DNA. It may remain dormant for a while. An unknown factor then triggers the host cell to transcribe the HIV DNA.

**4 Assembly** The host cell's ribosomes translate HIV RNA into HIV proteins. The HIV proteins assemble and form a new virus particle.

**5 Budding** The newly assembled virus particle buds from the host cell. Often, the host cell bursts as a result.

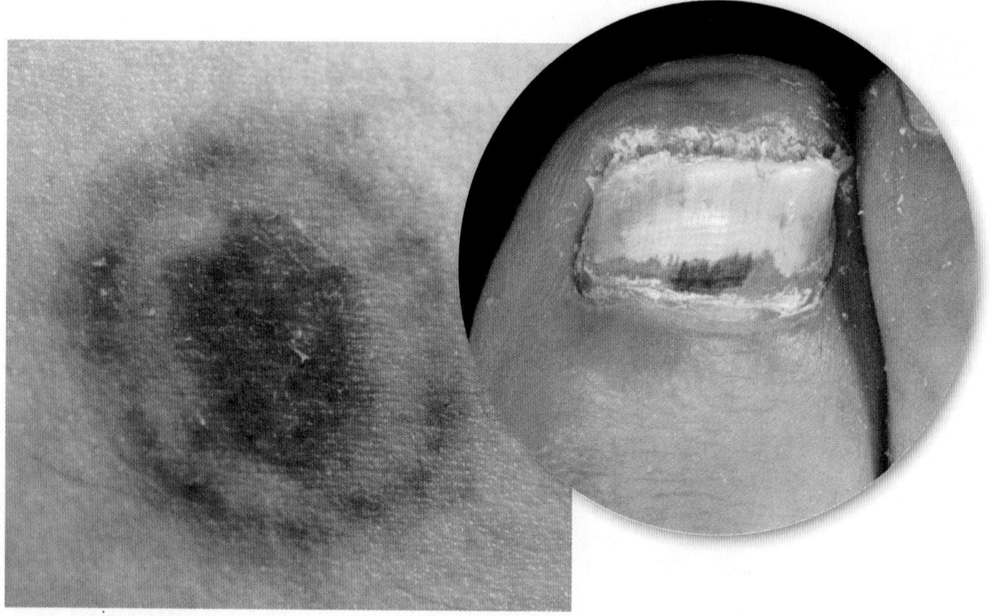

**Figure 7** Ringworm is a fungal infection of the skin. The dried skin that falls off a sore is contaminated with fungal spores. These spores can infect other people or other areas of the body, such as the toenails. **❯ Which body system does ringworm infect?**

## Fungi

The human body normally hosts a variety of fungi. Some of these organisms are useful to the body. Others are pathogenic and, if they multiply, may disrupt the body's homeostasis and may cause a disease. **❯ Like pathogenic bacteria, pathogenic fungi cause disease by absorbing nutrients from the cells of the body and producing toxins.** Some common fungal infections are discussed below.

**Athlete's Foot and Ringworm** Tinea is a fungus that infects the skin and nails and results in ringworm. Athlete's foot is a ringworm infection of the foot. **Figure 7** shows the red, itchy, and ring-shaped patch on the skin that a ringworm infection causes. These patches may blister and ooze. If the nails are infected, they may crumble. Ringworm can be passed via contact with an infected person or contaminated items, such as combs, clothing, towels, or showers.

**ACADEMIC VOCABULARY**

**via** by way of

**Yeast Infection** A yeast called *Candida albicans* is a normal resident of a healthy human body. This yeast has a mutualistic relationship with humans. It obtains nutrients from the food we eat, and in return, it makes toxins that can kill pathogens. Beneficial bacteria in the body keep the population of yeast in check. However, if these beneficial bacteria are disturbed or killed (for example, by taking antibiotics), the yeast may then grow out of control. The toxins made by a large population of yeast can cause diarrhea, sores on the skin or in the digestive tract, or a vaginal infection.

**Classification** Use the headings on this page to classify histoplasmosis and elephantiasis by the types of pathogens that causes these two diseases.

**Histoplasmosis** Fungal diseases that affect the internal organs can be very serious. Histoplasmosis is caused by *Histoplasma capsulatum,* which is found in soil, especially soil mixed with bat and bird feces. If the spores are inhaled, they cause severe respiratory illness and may infect the liver, heart, and central nervous system, too.

**❯ Reading Check** ***How is homeostasis related to yeast infections?***

## Parasitic Worms

**› Flukes, tapeworms, and many species of roundworms are parasitic to humans. These worms cause disease by feeding off of the body and damaging tissues.** Several serious diseases, including the three diseases discussed below, are caused by parasitic worms.

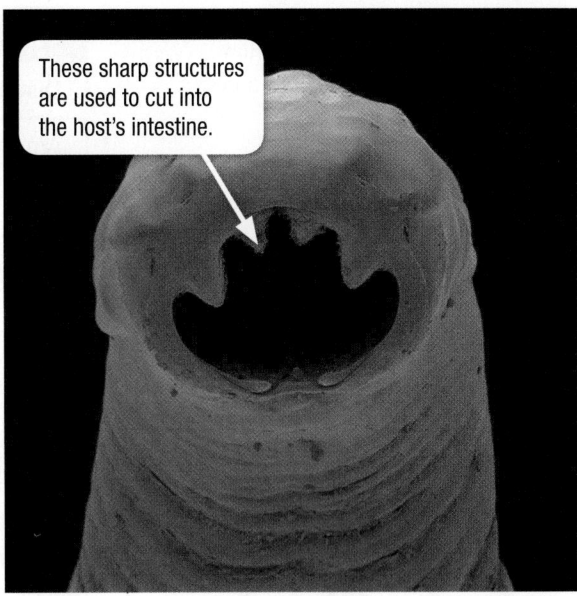

These sharp structures are used to cut into the host's intestine.

**Figure 8** A hookworm attaches itself to the wall of its host's intestine and feeds on the blood that oozes from the cut.

**Hookworm Infection** About 1 billion people are infected with hookworm, an intestinal parasite. Infection occurs when a person walks barefoot on soil that contains the worms' larvae. The larvae can penetrate the soles of the person's feet, enter the blood vessels, and be carried to the lungs. From the lungs, they migrate through tissue to the mouth and are swallowed. After reaching the small intestine, the larvae mature into adults and use sharp, teethlike structures on their mouth, shown in **Figure 8,** to latch onto the wall of the intestine. The worms then get their nourishment by sucking blood from the intestinal lining.

Symptoms of hookworm infection are cramps and mild diarrhea. Diarrhea, a symptom of many digestive tract diseases, is a way in which the body attempts to expel the pathogen and maintain homeostasis. Diarrhea can be dangerous to the body's homeostasis, though, because it causes the body to lose a large amount of water. However, in hookworm infections, the host rarely becomes dangerously dehydrated from diarrhea. It is more common for the host to develop anemia, a decrease in red blood cells that leads to fatigue and stress on body organs. Anemia is caused by blood loss to the worms.

**Schistosomiasis** *Schistosoma* flukes cause the disease schistosomiasis. This disease is common in tropical regions of Asia, Africa, and South America. Infection occurs when people use or wade in water contaminated by human feces or urine that contains the larvae of the *Schistosoma* flukes. First, the larvae bore through the skin. Then, they migrate via blood vessels to the lungs, intestines, bladder, or liver, where they mature and the females lay eggs. The eggs may block blood vessels in the affected organs. The eggs may also cause irritation, bleeding, and tissue decay in these organs. In rare cases, eggs may be laid in the blood vessels of the brain or spinal cord, and seizures or paralysis could result.

**Figure 9** Elephantiasis is caused by the breakdown of the lymphatic system.
**› How is the breakdown of this woman's lymphatic system related to the swelling of her leg?**

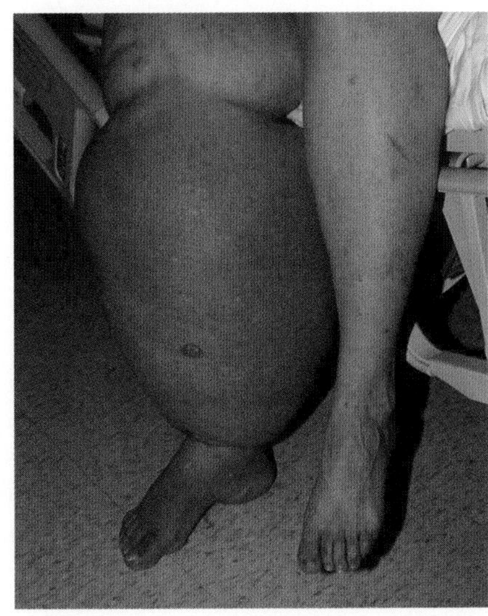

**Elephantiasis** Elephantiasis, shown in **Figure 9,** is the chronic, extreme swelling of the arms, breasts, legs, or male genitals and the hardening of nearby skin tissues. It is caused by years of repeated infections of the lymphatic system by small parasitic worms, known as *filarial worms*. The filiarial worms that cause elephantiasis are transmitted by the bite of an infected mosquito. The worms' larvae migrate into lymph vessels, where they mature into adults, mate, and produce many eggs. Over time, the lymph vessels become blocked and cannot function properly anymore. Because fluids in the area of the blocked vessels cannot drain, the surrounding tissues swell.

**› Reading Check** *How do* Schistosoma *flukes harm humans?*

**Figure 10** This table lists three common diseases caused by protists. **❯ How could amebic dysentery disrupt a body's homeostasis?**

| Some Diseases Caused by Protists | |
|---|---|
| **Disease** | **Description and cause** |
| Amebic dysentery | bowel infection that is caused by amoebas and that results in diarrhea and intestinal sores |
| Chagas' disease | infection by *Trypanosoma cruzi,* which leads to heart disease and digestive abnormalities |
| Cryptosporidiosis | infection of the small intestine that is caused by *Cryptosporidium* sp. and that results in diarrhea |

**Figure 11** *Toxoplasma gondii* is commonly found in cat feces. **❯ How can you avoid contracting toxoplasmosis?**

# Protists

**❯ Protists cause a number of human diseases, including giardiasis, amebic dysentery, toxoplasmosis, and malaria.** Some pathogenic protists cause few or no symptoms. Others can cause diseases such as the ones in **Figure 10,** which can devastate body systems and kill a human host.

**Giardiasis** Giardiasis is a disease caused by intestinal parasites of the genus *Giardia.* The parasite enters the body when a person consumes contaminated food or water. The parasite then moves through the small intestine toward the large intestine. Symptoms are severe diarrhea and intestinal cramps. Though rarely fatal, the disease can affect one's homeostasis by disrupting one's water and salt balance.

**Toxoplasmosis** Toxoplasmosis, caused by *Toxoplasma gondii,* is spread by cysts. They can enter a body if one eats undercooked meat infected with cysts, consumes contaminated soil, or has frequent contact with cats. Infected cats, such as the one in **Figure 11,** have spores in their feces. Adults who have healthy immune systems are usually not affected by contact with the spores. In rare cases, flulike symptoms occur, and the nerves, brain, or eyes are damaged. A pregnant woman without symptoms can pass the infection to a fetus. The infant may develop central nervous system disorders, brain or eye damage, mental retardation, or an enlarged spleen and liver.

## Section 2 Review

### ❯ KEY IDEAS

1. **Describe** how pathogenic bacteria can cause disease.
2. **Relate** viral reproduction to the pathogenic nature of viruses.
3. **Summarize** how pathogenic fungi are detrimental to human health.
4. **Describe** the path that a hookworm takes through the body when the worm infects a human.
5. **List** three protist diseases whose symptoms include diarrhea.

### CRITICAL THINKING

6. **Integrating Information** Why are people infected with HIV more likely to contract other infectious diseases?
7. **Predicting Outcomes** What would happen to disease transmission if all drinking water were filtered and chlorinated and all people maintained good hygiene, cooked food thoroughly, and wore shoes?

### ALTERNATIVE ASSESSMENT

8. **Communicating Information** Research an infectious disease. Then, make a brochure that explains the cause and symptoms of the disease, identifies where the disease commonly occurs, describes how the disease disrupts homeostasis, and lists some preventive measures that people can take to avoid contracting the disease.

Why It Matters

# Protist Plague

WEIRD SCIENCE

Malaria was eradicated from the United States in the 1950s. Yet today it is the third most deadly disease in the world. Up to 500 million people are infected. Up to 3 million die every year. A child dies from malaria every 30 seconds.

## Malaria

Malaria is caused by several types of sporozoans of the genus *Plasmodium.* It is spread by the bite of the *Anopheles* mosquito. When an infected mosquito bites a human, it injects saliva containing the parasite.

The first stage of the malaria parasite, called a *sporozoite,* infects and destroys the liver's cells as it makes millions of copies of the second stage, called a *merozoite.* Merozoites infect red blood cells, in which they divide to make 8 to 24 more merozoites that burst out and destroy the cell. The new merozoites repeat the cycle of invading and destroying red blood cells every 48 to 72 hours.

The death of red blood cells causes anemia and cycles of fever. If left untreated, malaria can cause rupture of the spleen, kidney failure, coma, brain damage, and death.

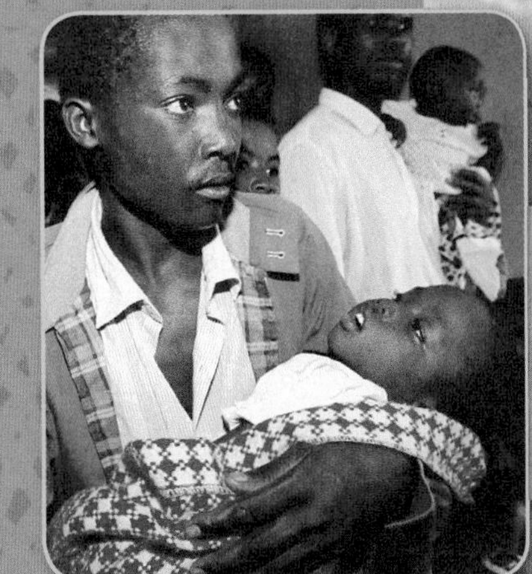

**The Price of Life** The cost of potentially life-saving treatment is as low as 13 cents per dose. However, medicines are not always available.

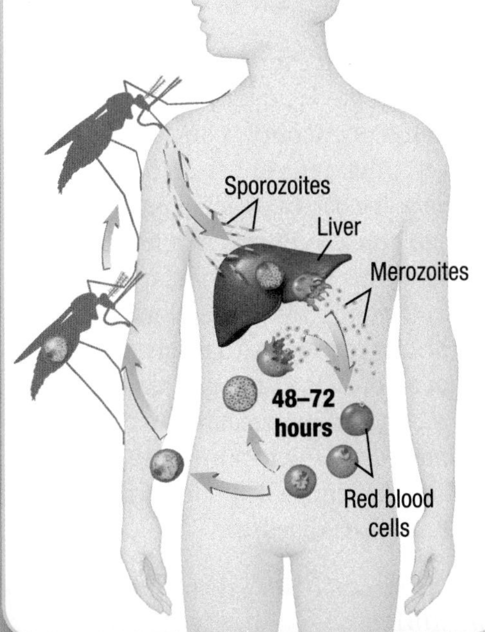


**Stopping a Killer** Research is underway to create a malaria vaccine. Other efforts to control the disease include fumigation to kill mosquitoes and distribution of mosquito nets.

go.hrw.com
interact online
Keyword: HX8PRTWIM

**Research** Use library and Internet sources to find out more about the efforts to eradicate malaria worldwide.

Section
# 3 Noninfectious Diseases

| Key Ideas | Key Terms | Why It Matters |
|---|---|---|
| › How does personal behavior affect a person's health?<br>› How are genetic disorders transmitted?<br>› Why do some organs malfunction?<br>› What causes a nutritional disease?<br>› Why are toxic substances dangerous? | heart attack<br>stroke | Who wouldn't avoid getting sick if they knew how? Many of the diseases that Americans have are noninfectious and can be avoided or managed by making healthier lifestyle choices. |

**Standard 4**

**2.2e** Knowledge of genetics is making possible new fields of health care; for example, finding genes which may have mutations that can cause disease will aid in the development of preventive measures to fight disease. Substances, such as hormones and enzymes, from genetically engineered organisms may reduce the cost and side effects of replacing missing body chemicals.

**5.2a** Homeostasis in an organism is constantly threatened. Failure to respond effectively can result in disease or death.

**5.2h** Disease may also be caused by inheritance, toxic substances, poor nutrition, organ malfunction, and some personal behavior. Some effects show up right away; others may not show up for many years.

Take a look at **Figure 12,** which shows the major causes of death in the United States. The top four causes of death—heart disease, cancer, stroke, and respiratory disease—are noninfectious diseases. Personal behavior greatly influences the onset and course of all four of these diseases. Noninfectious diseases can also be caused by genetic diseases, organ malfunction, poor nutrition, or toxic substances in the environment.

## Personal Behavior

**› The majority of Americans die from heart disease, lung cancer, or other noninfectious diseases that are linked to personal behavior.** These diseases can be avoided or minimized by leading a healthy lifestyle. For example, the diet you maintain, the amount of exercise you do, and other personal choices directly affect the state of your health.

**Alcoholism** One personal choice that every person must face is whether to use drugs. Several drugs are legal for adults to use, but they still pose serious health dangers. Alcohol is one of these drugs. Currently, more than 17 million Americans abuse alcohol or suffer from alcoholism. Alcoholism is a disease in which a person has a strong need to drink despite bad consequences. Alcohol acts on the brain's neurons and thus disrupts cellular function. This disruption in function slows reaction times and decreases one's ability to judge situations. Therefore, it is no surprise that alcohol is a factor in almost half of all U.S. traffic deaths. Alcohol abuse can also cause long-term damage. Heavy drinking can increase the risk for certain cancers and can cause liver cirrhosis, hypertension, dementia, and heart disease.

**› Reading Check** ***How can drinking alcohol affect the state of your health?***

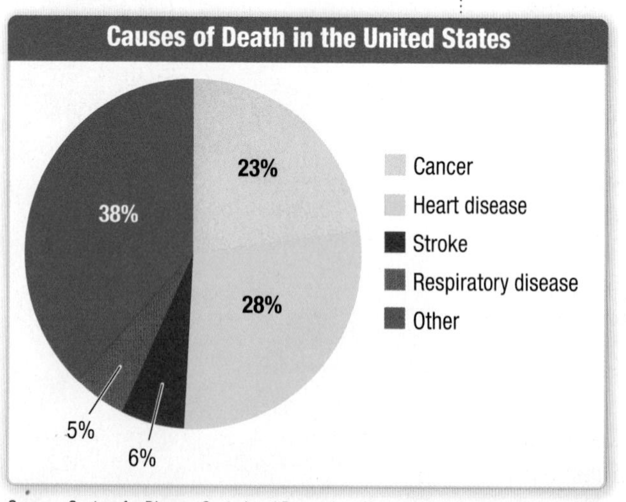


Source: Centers for Disease Control and Prevention, *National Vital Statistics Report*, 2003.

**Figure 12** Heart disease is the leading cause of death in the United States. **› What percentage of deaths in the United States are caused by heart disease?**

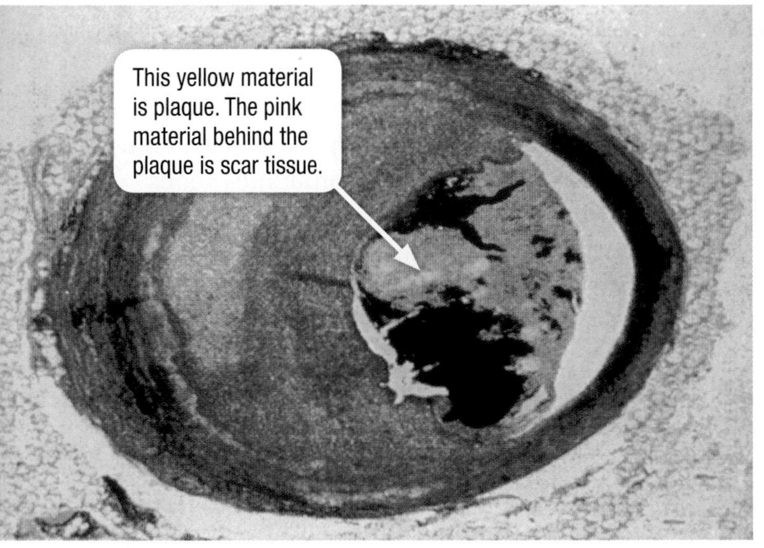

This yellow material is plaque. The pink material behind the plaque is scar tissue.
Artery wall

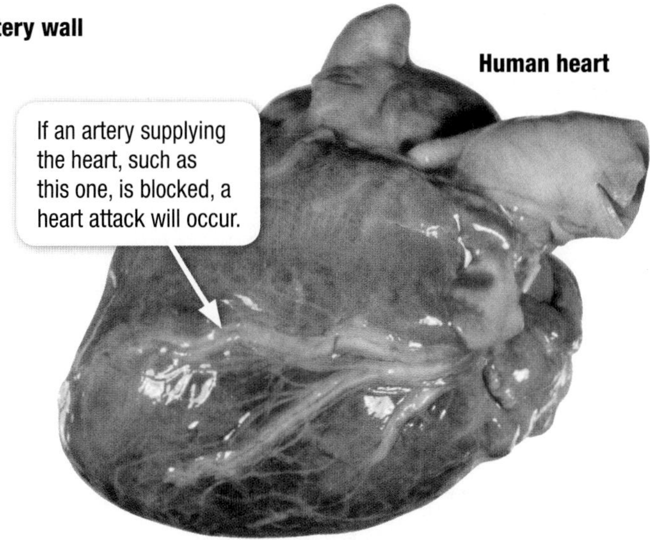

Human heart
If an artery supplying the heart, such as this one, is blocked, a heart attack will occur.

**Figure 13** Heart attacks and most strokes occur when a vessel supplying the heart or brain becomes blocked with plaque.

**Cardiovascular Disease** The causes of cardiovascular disease include alcohol and tobacco use, a diet high in fat, and a genetic predisposition. Cardiovascular disease is so deadly because it can result in the blood supply being cut off to part of the heart, an event called a **heart attack,** or to part of the brain, an event called a **stroke.** Unlike many other diseases, which slowly disrupt homeostasis, a heart attack or stroke immediately disables the heart or part of the brain and thus causes a sudden threat to all other systems in the body. Without the heart pumping blood through the body, tissues can suffocate in minutes. Without the brain acting as a control center, feedback mechanisms quickly break down.

Most heart attacks and strokes are the result of high blood pressure and the buildup of plaque (deposits of fats and other materials) on vessel walls. By causing the heart to work harder than it normally does, high blood pressure weakens the heart and damages arteries. As **Figure 13** shows, plaque can narrow artery walls. If a blood clot breaks off from a blood vessel wall, it may get stuck in a narrow blood vessel. The stuck clot may cut off blood flow to part of the body. If a blood clot gets stuck in the vessels of the heart, a heart attack occurs. If a clot blocks blood supply to the brain, a stroke occurs.

**heart attack** the death of heart tissues due to a blockage of their blood supply

**stroke** a sudden loss of consciousness or paralysis that occurs when the blood flow to the brain is interrupted

**Emphysema and Lung Cancer** A heart attack kills by depriving cells of oxygen. Most lung diseases kill in the same way—but at a slower rate. One reason that lung diseases are more common today than 100 years ago is that more people smoke now. In fact, smoking causes up to 90% of all cases of emphysema and lung cancer.

In emphysema, the lungs' normally elastic alveoli become brittle and break. Over time, the alveoli become larger and less efficient. The lack of oxygen that results leads to fatigue and breathlessness.

In lung cancer, which causes about 28% of all deaths due to cancer in the United States, lung cells begin to grow at an abnormal rate. The abnormal cell growth causes tumors, which take away resources from the body. A tumor is shown in **Figure 14.**

**Figure 14** This tumor was surgically removed from a lung cancer victim. Only about 15% of lung cancer victims live more than five years after diagnosis.

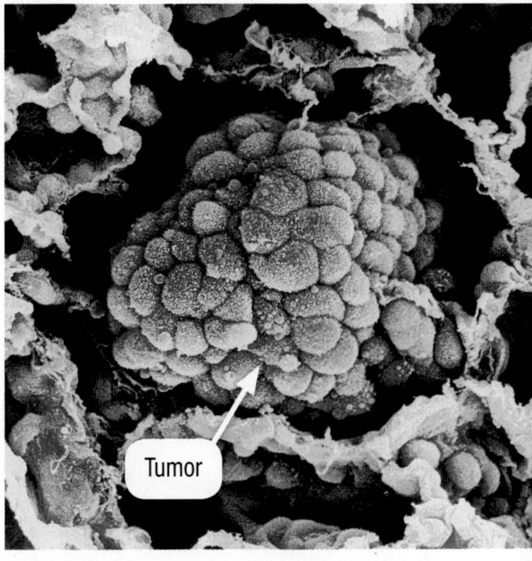

## Inheritance

As previous chapters have explained, for a person to develop and function normally, the proteins encoded by his or her genes must work correctly. Proteins that do not perform their jobs properly compromise the body's homeostasis. Unfortunately, sometimes genes are damaged or copied incorrectly. These faulty genes may cause a genetic disease. ❯ **Genetic diseases are passed on through heredity rather than through a pathogen.** Two common genetic diseases—cystic fibrosis and sickle cell disease—are discussed below.

SCILINKS. www.scilinks.org
Topic: Genetic Diseases
Code: HX80650

**Cystic Fibrosis** Cystic fibrosis is one of the most common fatal genetic diseases among Caucasians. About 1 in 2,500 Caucasian infants is born with the illness. Cystic fibrosis occurs when a person inherits two copies of a defective gene for a certain protein. One copy comes from the mother; the other, from the father. Ordinarily, this protein moves salt into and out of cells. In people with two copies of the defective gene for this protein, the body's cells make a thick, sticky mucus. The mucus builds up in the pancreas and in breathing passages of the lungs. When mucus clogs the pancreas, the pancreas cannot perform its role in food digestion. Malnutrition, bowel problems, and weight loss may result. When mucus clogs the lungs, the results are respiratory system problems, lung damage, and infections.

**Sickle Cell Disease** Red blood cells (RBCs) are normally disk shaped. However, in people who have sickle cell disease, the RBCs often become crescent (sickle) shaped. The sickling is caused by a mutation in the gene that produces hemoglobin, a protein that enables RBCs to carry oxygen. The mutated gene produces defective hemoglobin that sticks together inside of a RBC to form long chains of the protein. By stretching out the RBC, the chains cause the RBC to sickle, as **Figure 15** shows. The sickle-shaped cell can get lodged in small vessels and can disrupt blood flow. Without enough blood, tissues in the affected region can become damaged. When blood flow is interrupted repeatedly, damage to many body systems can occur.

The long chains of hemoglobin can cause other problems, as well. When the chains stretch and pull the RBC's cell membrane, they can cause the membrane to weaken and to leak nutrients. This weakening leads to the cell's early death. While normal RBCs live about 120 days, sickle-cell RBCs live only about 16 days. A person who has sickle cell disease develops a severe anemia because too few RBCs are in the bloodstream to meet the oxygen needs of all of the body's cells.

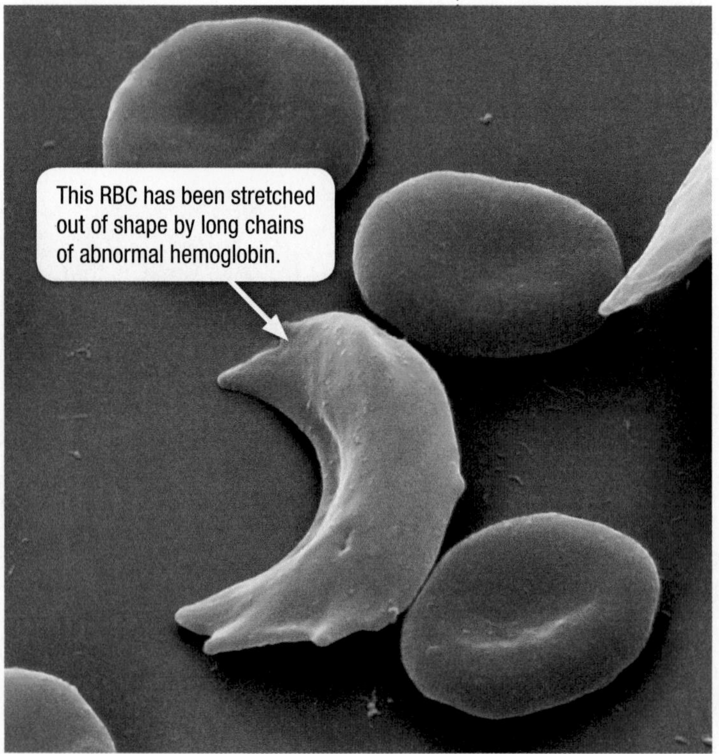

This RBC has been stretched out of shape by long chains of abnormal hemoglobin.

**Figure 15** One out of every 500 African Americans has sickle cell disease, which is caused by a gene mutation that produces a defective form of hemoglobin. ❯ **Why is a sickle-shaped red blood cell more likely to block a capillary than a normal red blood cell is?**

❯ **Reading Check** ***How might sickle cell disease disrupt a body's homeostasis?***

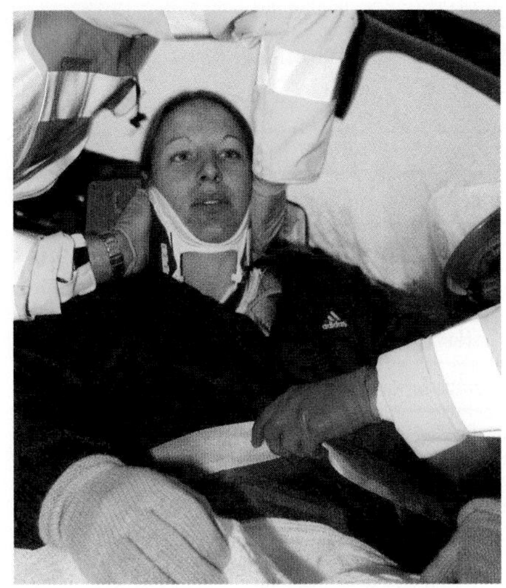

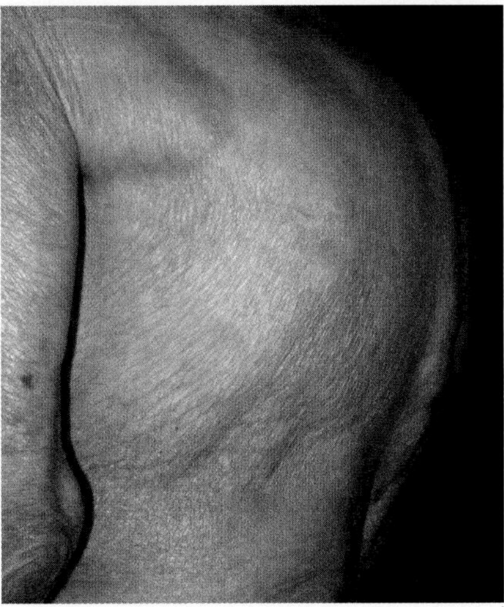

**Figure 16** Organ malfunctions can be caused by a variety of factors, including trauma and aging. ❯ **How do you think osteoporosis caused this man's spine to become humped?**

## Organ Malfunction

Homeostasis is dependent upon all of the body or organ systems working together. What affects one system will affect others, which in turn affect still other organ systems. Thus, your organs are very important to homeostasis and your well-being. ❯ **Organs malfunction for a variety of reasons, including birth defects, trauma, and aging.**

**Birth Defects** A birth defect is an abnormality of structure, function, or metabolism and is present at birth. Some birth defects are caused by genetic disorders, but birth defects can also be caused by environmental factors, such as drug or alcohol abuse by a pregnant woman. For example, when a pregnant woman drinks alcohol, the development of her baby's body systems may be affected. The baby may develop fetal alcohol syndrome (FAS). FAS is characterized by a cluster of related problems, including abnormal facial features, faulty enamel on teeth, heart defects, bones that are deformed, nearsightedness, and behavioral problems.

**Trauma** Trauma, such as what happens in an automobile accident or a fall, can damage the body's organs. In a serious motor vehicle accident, injury to the brain and spinal cord are common and can be devastating. Brain damage, coma, paralysis, concussion, and death are possible. The body may also collide with the steering wheel. Such a collision may cause blunt force trauma to internal organs and the skeletal system. Wearing a seat belt and driving a car equipped with air bags help make severe injury less likely.

**Aging** Machinery, such as a car, becomes less efficient as it ages. So do the organs of the human body. Older people are not as strong and flexible and do not heal as well as younger people. Because of this, aging can lead to many diseases. Osteoporosis, for example, is a disease associated with aging. It is characterized by the thinning and weakening of bones. Osteoporosis increases the risk of bone fractures. The man in **Figure 16** is suffering from osteoporosis.

❯ **Reading Check** *How can trauma affect the body's organs?*

**Two-Column Notes** Use the headings on this page to find examples that support the key idea.

Data

# QuickLab

15 min

## The Nutrition Facts Label

The Nutrition Facts label provides a convenient source of nutritional information about foods and can help you see how a food fits into your daily diet. It lists the number of Calories and quantity of nutrients per serving size. Nutrients are listed by weight and as a percentage of the daily values for a 2,000 Cal diet. Daily values (DVs) are recommended daily amounts of nutrients.

| Nutrition Facts | Amount/serving | %DV* | Amount/serving | %DV* |
|---|---|---|---|---|
| | **Total fat** 1g | 1% | **Total carb.** 43g | 14% |
| Serv. size 2 oz (56g/ box) | Saturated fat 0g | 0% | Dietary fiber 2g | 8% |
| Servings per container 8 | *Trans* fat 0g | | Sugars 3g | |
| **Calories** 210 Fat Cal. 10 | **Cholesterol** 0mg | 0% | **Protein** 6g | |
| | **Sodium** 0mg | 0% | | |
| *Percent Daily Values (DV) are based on a 2,000 Calorie diet. | Vitamin A 0% • Vitamin C 0% • Calcium 2% • Iron 10% Thiamin 30% • Riboflavin 10% • Niacin 15% | | | |

### Analysis

1. **Calculate** the percentage of the food's total Calories that come from fat according to the label shown here.

2. CRITICAL THINKING **Applying Information** If your diet requires 30 g of fiber, what percentage of the daily value for fiber does one serving of this food provide?

## Poor Nutrition

Your body needs a great deal of energy to maintain its temperature, which is an important aspect of homeostasis. Food supplies this energy. Food also supplies the building blocks needed to build your cells and tissues. For you to stay healthy, your body requires specific amounts of certain nutrients. › **If you ingest too few or too many of the necessary nutrients, you could develop a nutritional disease.**

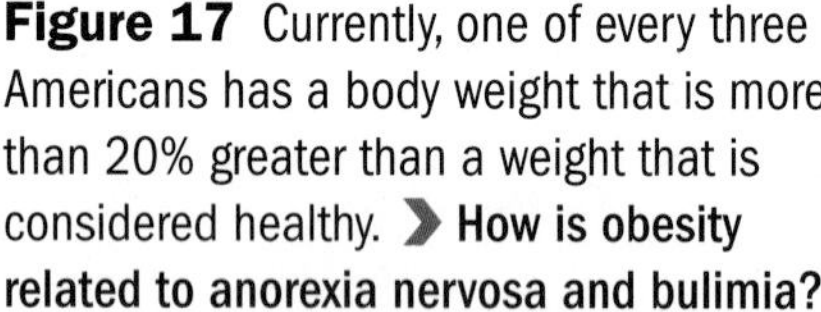

**Figure 17** Currently, one of every three Americans has a body weight that is more than 20% greater than a weight that is considered healthy. › **How is obesity related to anorexia nervosa and bulimia?**

**Eating Disorders** Eating disorders are extremely common among Americans. The most common eating disorder by far is overeating, which leads to obesity. The extra weight carried by people who are obese, such as the woman in **Figure 17,** increases the risk of heart disease and diabetes. Two other eating disorders are bulimia and anorexia nervosa. In bulimia, a person avoids weight gain by purging the food that he or she eats. Damage to the digestive system results. In anorexia nervosa, a person undereats to maintain a below-average weight. This disorder causes anemia, a weakened immune system, and, in some cases, kidney failure.

**Vitamin Deficiencies** Vitamins are needed for metabolic reactions. Most vitamins are obtained from food. If your diet lacks the right vitamins, some metabolic reactions will slow or stop. Homeostasis will be disturbed, and you may fall ill. One disease caused by a vitamin deficiency is scurvy. Specifically, scurvy is due to a diet low in vitamin C. Without vitamin C, one's tissues begin to break down. Early symptoms of scurvy include bleeding gums and joint pain.

› **Reading Check** ***Relate eating disorders to a person's personal behavior.***

## Toxic Substances

Many common substances, such as the mouthwash shown in **Figure 18,** can be toxic to humans. ❯ **Toxic substances have the ability to damage cells, tissues, organs, or entire body systems.** Most toxins enter the body through the mouth. From the mouth, the toxins travel to the stomach, where they may be absorbed into the bloodstream. In this way, toxins can travel throughout the body and can damage or interfere with every body system. Sometimes, the damage to a body system is so severe that death occurs. Toxic substances can be found everywhere. For instance, toxins are present in many types of household chemicals and even in some kinds of fungi.

**Figure 18** If swallowed, mouthwash that contains alcohol is toxic to children. Each year, about 250 cases of mouthwash poisoning occur in the United States.

**Household Chemicals** Substances around your house may contain toxic chemicals. For example, many homes have lead-based paints. Exposure to lead can cause high blood pressure, fertility problems, and nervous system disorders. Pesticides and weed killers also contain many toxic ingredients. These chemicals can harm humans by damaging the nervous system, irritating the skin or eyes, affecting the endocrine system, or causing cancer.

**Toxic Fungi** Many houses have damp areas, such as basements. In these areas, various types of molds can grow. Some of these molds may release spores that are toxic to humans. Asthma, bronchitis, and various other diseases are linked to inhaling toxic mold spores. Molds, mushrooms, and other fungi may also be toxic if they are eaten. For example, many species of the genus *Amanita* resemble edible mushrooms. However, they contain extremely dangerous toxins that quickly destroy a person's liver. Liver failure severely disrupts digestion and causes excessive bleeding because the liver no longer makes essential blood-clotting compounds.

❯ **Reading Check** ***Explain how eating a mushroom of the genus*** **Amanita** ***can affect a person's homeostasis.***

## Section 3 Review

### KEY IDEAS

1. **List** three behaviors that can affect a person's health.
2. **Describe** the role that genes play in genetic disorders.
3. **Summarize** three ways in which organ malfunction can occur.
4. **Relate** the role of diet to nutritional diseases.
5. **State** the ways in which toxic substances may cause illness.

### CRITICAL THINKING

6. **Comparing Effects** Explain how lifestyle choices can be important to the health of a person who has heart disease and to the health of a person who has diabetes.
7. **Relating Concepts** Can alcohol be considered a toxic substance in the same way that pesticides and poisonous mushrooms are? Explain your answer.

### WRITING FOR SCIENCE

8. **Oral Report** Research a genetic disorder, such as polycystic kidney disease, familial dysautonomia, Huntington's disease, or hemophilia. Prepare a brief oral report. Discuss the genetic cause, the symptoms, the organ systems affected, and the treatment.

Skills Practice

# Chapter 21 Lab

## Objectives

- Study the effect of cigarette tobacco on leaves of tomato plants.
- Observe how a viral infection affects plant tissues.

## Materials

- lab apron
- protective gloves
- safety goggles
- tomato plants (2)
- glass-marking pencil
- tobacco from several brands of cigarettes
- mortar and pestle
- dibasic potassium phosphate solution, 0.1 M (10 mL)
- beaker, 100 mL
- cotton swabs
- carborundum powder, 400 grit

## Safety

# Tobacco Mosaic Virus

The tobacco mosaic virus (TMV) infects tobacco as well as other plants. Plants damaged by wind, low temperatures, injury, or insects are more susceptible to plant viruses than healthy plants are. Plants that are infected with TMV have lesions and yellow patches on their leaves. In this lab, you will study how a tomato plant can be infected with TMV and how the infection affects the plant.

## Procedure

### Set Up the Experiment

1. Put on a lab apron, gloves, and goggles before beginning this investigation.
2. Obtain two tomato plants that have not been infected with TMV. Label one plant "Control plant" and the other plant "Experimental plant."
3. **CAUTION: Use poisonous chemicals with extreme caution.** Keep your hands away from your face when handling plants or chemicals. Place pinches of tobacco from different brands of cigarettes into a mortar. Add 5 mL of dibasic potassium phosphate solution, and grind the mixture with a pestle as shown in the figure.
4. Pour the mixture into a labeled beaker. This mixture can be used to test whether cigarette tobacco can infect plants with TMV.
5. Wash your hands and all laboratory equipment used in the previous steps with soap and water to avoid the accidental spread of the virus.

6 Moisten a sterile cotton swab with the mixture, and sprinkle a small amount of carborundum powder onto the moistened swab. Apply the mixture to two leaves on the experimental plant by swabbing the surface of the leaves several times. Why might swabbing the leaves with carborundum powder facilitate infection?

7 Moisten a clean swab with dibasic potassium phosphate solution, and sprinkle a small amount of carborundum powder onto the moistened swab. This swab should *not* come into contact with the mixture of cigarette tobacco. Swab over the surface of two leaves on the control plant several times.

8 Do not allow the control plants to touch the experimental plants. Keep both plants away from other plants that may be in your investigation area, such as houseplants or garden plants. Wash your hands after handling each plant to avoid the accidental spread of TMV.

9 Treat both plants in precisely the same manner. The only difference between the two plants should be the experimental factor—exposure to cigarette tobacco. Both plants should receive the same amount of light and the same amount of water.

10 Clean up your materials according to your teacher's instructions, and wash your hands before leaving the lab.

### Collect Data

11 In your lab report, create a data table similar to the table shown. Allow plenty of space to record your observations of each plant.

12 Check the control and experimental plants each day for one week. Record your observations of each plant in your lab report. To prevent contaminating your results, wash your hands after handling each plant.

**Observations of Tomato Plants**

| Day | Control plant | Experimental plant |
|---|---|---|
| 1 | | |
| 2 | | |
| 3 | | |
| 4 | | |
| 5 | | |
| 6 | | |
| 7 | | |

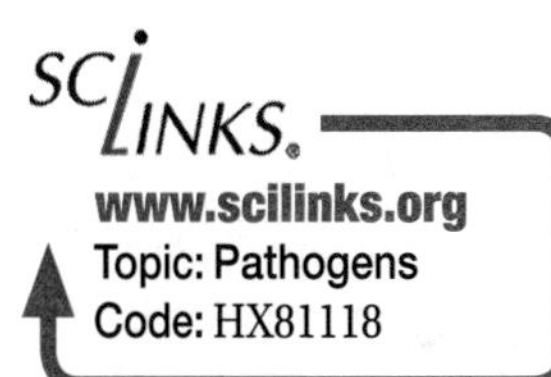

SCILINKS.
www.scilinks.org
Topic: Pathogens
Code: HX81118


## Analyze and Conclude

1. SCIENTIFIC METHODS **Making Systematic Observations** What differences, if any, did you detect in the two plants after one week?
2. **Interpreting Observations** Did the plants exposed to cigarette tobacco become infected with the tobacco mosaic virus?
3. SCIENTIFIC METHODS **Critiquing Procedures** What are some possible sources of error in the experiment?
4. **Drawing Conclusions** Examine a plant that contracted TMV. How might the virus be affecting the plant's homeostasis?
5. SCIENTIFIC METHODS **Using Evidence to Support Arguments** Greenhouse operators generally do not allow smoking in their greenhouses for various reasons, including health and safety reasons. How might your results also support this practice?

## Extensions

6. **Making Inferences** Why was it necessary to use tobacco from different brands of cigarettes?
7. **Designing Experiments** The tobacco mosaic virus is capable of infecting various species of plants. Design an experiment to determine which of several types of plants are susceptible to the tobacco mosaic virus.

# Chapter 21 Summary

| Key Ideas | Key Terms |
|---|---|

## 1 Disease

- Disease is caused by a disruption in a human body system that leads to a corresponding disruption in homeostasis.
- Pathogens can be spread through the air, through contact with contaminated objects or an infected organism, through the ingestion of contaminated food or water, or through vectors.
- You can maintain your homeostasis and can avoid many diseases by practicing good hygiene, avoiding close contact with infected organisms, maintaining a healthy diet, and exercising on a regular basis.

**Key Terms:**
**noninfectious disease** (499)
**infectious disease** (499)
**pathogen** (499)
**vector** (500)

## 2 Infectious Diseases

- Pathogenic bacteria cause disease by producing toxins and by destroying body tissues.
- Viruses must use a living cell to reproduce. This process damages or destroys the living cell.
- Like pathogenic bacteria, pathogenic fungi cause disease by absorbing nutrients from the cells of the body and producing toxins.
- Flukes, tapeworms, and many species of roundworms are parasitic to humans. These worms cause disease by feeding off of the body and damaging tissues.
- Protists cause a number of human diseases, including giardiasis, amebic dysentery, toxoplasmosis, and malaria.

**Key Terms:**
**toxin** (502)

## 3 Noninfectious Diseases

- The majority of Americans die from heart disease, lung cancer, or other noninfectious diseases that are linked to personal behavior.
- Genetic diseases are passed on through heredity rather than through a pathogen.
- Organs malfunction for a variety of reasons, including birth defects, trauma, and aging.
- If you ingest too few or too many of the necessary nutrients, you could develop a nutritional disease.
- Toxic substances have the ability to damage cells, tissues, organs, or entire body systems.

**Key Terms:**
**heart attack** (511)
**stroke** (511)

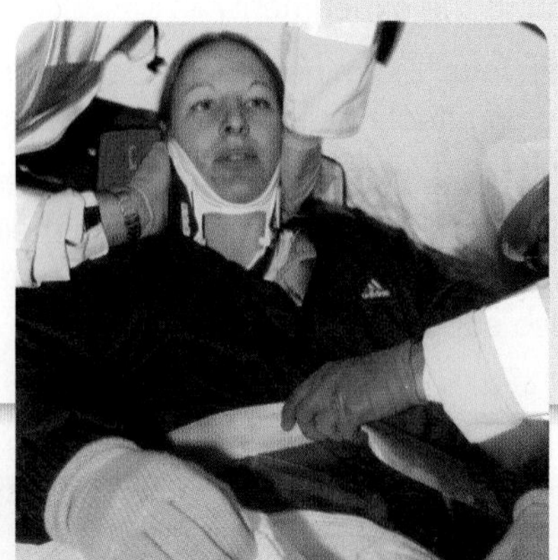

Chapter 21

The Living Environment

# Regents Exam Practice

**PART A: Answer all questions in this part.**

*Directions*: For each statement or question, write on your separate answer sheet the number of the word or expression that best completes the statement or answers the question.

**1** The presence of parasites in an animal will usually result in
(1) an increase in meiotic activity within structures of the host
(2) the inability of the host to maintain homeostasis
(3) the death of the host organism within twenty-four hours
(4) an increase in genetic mutation rate in the host organism

**2** Blood can be tested to determine the presence of the virus associated with the development of AIDS. This blood test is used directly for
(1) cure.
(2) treatment.
(3) diagnosis.
(4) prevention.

**3** The diagram below represents two single-celled organisms. These organisms carry out the activities needed to maintain homeostasis by using specialized internal

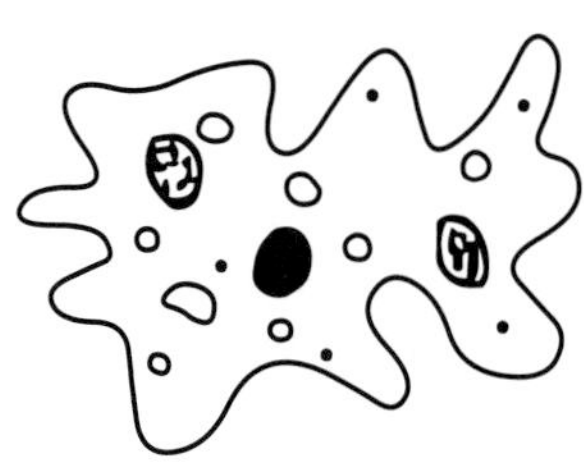

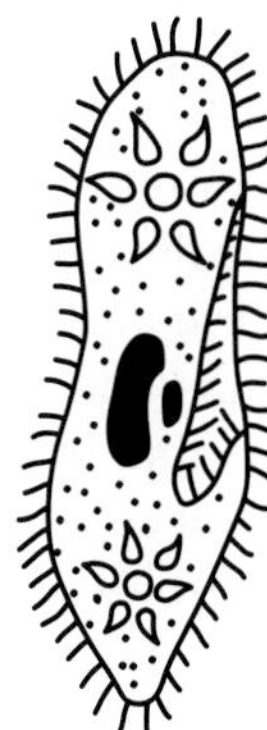

(1) tissues.
(2) organelles.
(3) systems.
(4) organs.

**4** The use of a vaccine to stimulate the immune system to act against a specific pathogen is valuable in maintaining homeostasis because
(1) once the body produces chemicals to combat one type of virus, it can more easily make antibiotics.
(2) the body can digest the weakened microbes and use them as food.
(3) the body will be able to fight invasions by the same type of microbe in the future.
(4) the more the immune system is challenged, the better it performs.

**5** Botulism can cause paralysis because a toxin
(1) can poison the blood.
(2) can damage the heart.
(3) can destroy the tips of nerve cells.
(4) can stress the body and can enable other infectious agents to grow.

**6** Which two fungal infections are caused by the same type of fungus?
(1) athlete's foot and histoplasmosis
(2) athlete's foot and hookworm
(3) athlete's foot and ringworm
(4) hookworm and ringworm

**7** Causes of cardiovascular disease include all of the following *except*
(1) fungal infection.
(2) tobacco use.
(3) genetic predisposition.
(4) a high-fat diet.

**8** Which of the following is *not* a lifestyle choice that can help you maintain your body's homeostasis and avoid many diseases?
(1) avoiding close contact with infected animals or people
(2) exercising regularly and maintaining a healthy diet
(3) practicing good hygiene, such as washing hands often
(4) drinking alcohol heavily and using tobacco products

**9** The data in the graph below show evidence of disease in the human body. A disruption in dynamic equilibrium is indicated by the temperature change between points

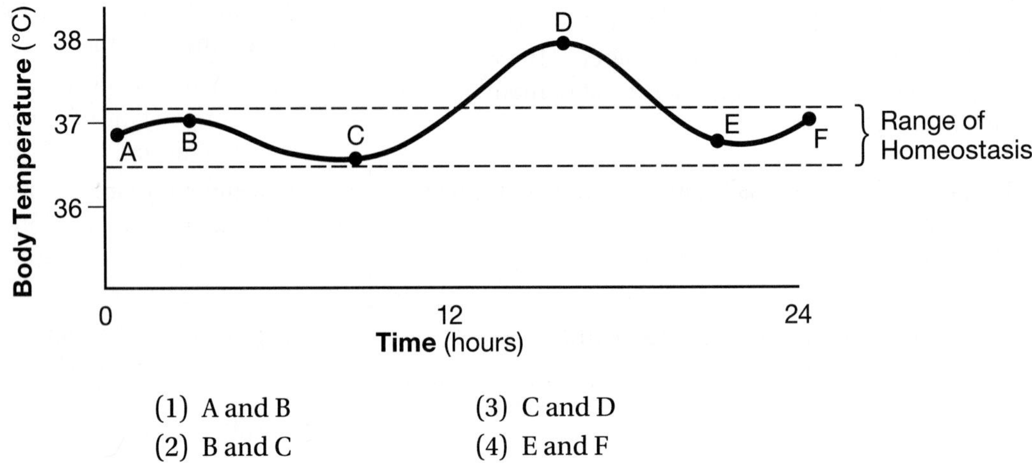


(1) A and B
(2) B and C
(3) C and D
(4) E and F

**PART B**

**Base your answer to question 10 on the passage below and on your knowledge of biology.**

. . . Some of the most common and deadly bacteria do their mischief by forming a sticky scum called biofilm. Individually, the microbes are easy to control, but when they organize themselves into biofilms they can become deadly, said Dr. Barbara Iglewski of the University of Rochester. . . .

Biofilms are actually intricately organized colonies of billions of microbes, all working in a coordinated way to defend against attack and to pump out a toxin that can be deadly.

Once they are organized, the bacteria are highly resistant to antibiotics and even strong detergents often cannot wash them away or kill them.

Iglewski and colleagues from Montana State University and the University of Iowa report in *Science* that they discovered how the microbes in the colonies communicate and found that once this conversation is interrupted, the deadly bugs can be easily washed away.

Using *Pseudomonas aeruginosa,* a common bacteria that is a major infection hazard in hospitals and among cystic fibrosis patients, the researchers isolated a gene that the bacteria uses to make a communications molecule. The molecule helps the microbes organize themselves into a biofilm — a complex structure that includes tubes to carry in nutrients and carry out wastes, including deadly toxins.

In their study, the researchers showed that if the gene that makes the communications molecule was blocked, the *Pseudomonas aeruginosa* could form only wimpy [weak], unorganized colonies that could be washed away with just a soap that has no effect on a healthy colony. . . .

Adapted from: Paul Recer, "Researchers find new means to disrupt attack by microbes," *The Daily Gazette,* April 26, 1998.

**10** The tubes in biofilms function much like the human
(1) muscular and nervous systems.
(2) circulatory and excretory systems.
(3) digestive and endocrine systems.
(4) reproductive and respiratory systems.

**PART C**

**11** Biological research has generated knowledge used to diagnose genetic disorders in humans. Explain how a specific genetic disorder can be diagnosed. Your answer must include at least:

- the name of a genetic disorder that can be diagnosed
- the name or description of a technique used to diagnose the disorder
- a description of one characteristic of the disorder

**12** Select one human body system from the list below.

*Body Systems*
Digestive
Circulatory
Respiratory
Excretory
Nervous

Describe a malfunction that can occur in the system chosen. Your answer must include at least:

- the name of the system and a malfunction that can occur in this system
- a description of a possible cause of the malfunction identified
- an effect this malfunction may have on any other body system

**13** Not all diseases are caused by pathogenic organisms. Other factors, such as inheritance, poor nutrition, and toxic substances, may also cause disease. Describe a disease or disorder that can occur as a result of one of these other factors. Your answer must include at least:

- the name of the disease
- one specific factor that causes this disease
- one major effect of this disease on the body, other than death
- one way this disease can be prevented, treated, or cured

**PART D**

**Base your answers to the following questions on your knowledge of biology.**

**14** How might the current epidemic of obesity in the United States be related to the increases in portion sizes served at restaurants?

**15** The drug AZT works by blocking the enzyme reverse transcriptase. Explain how AZT can help patients infected with HIV.

# Chapter 22 The Body's Defenses

## Preview



## Why It Matters

Each day, your body is assaulted by millions of different bacteria, viruses, and other disease-causing agents. Fortunately, your body has ways to defend against these invaders. These defenses prevent you from getting sick and help heal the body if you do get sick.

Parasitic worms can invade the body and cause disease. This image shows the immune system at work against a parasite.

This microfilaria, the larval form of a parasitic worm, can infect the lymphatic system. It can enter the body through the bites of infected organisms, such as mosquitoes.

***The Living Environment***

**Standard 4** Students will understand and apply scientific concepts, principles, and theories pertaining to the physical setting and living environment and recognize the historical development of ideas in science.

**Key Idea 1** Living things are both similar to and different from each other and from nonliving things. ***Major Understandings*** **- 1.2b**

**Key Idea 5** Organisms maintain a dynamic equilibrium that sustains life. ***Major Understandings*** **- 5.1g, 5.2c, 5.2d, 5.2e, 5.2f, 5.2g**

15 min

# InquiryLab

## Barrier Breaking

Your skin is your first line of defense against harmful microorganisms. In this activity, you will use a protective glove to model skin.

### Procedure

1. Put on **gloves** and a **lab apron.**
2. Fill a **mixing bowl** half full with **water.** Add **20 mL of vinegar** to the water. Gently swirl to mix.
3. Fill a **protective glove** half full with water. Add **several drops of bromothymol blue** to the water in the glove.
4. Knot the open end of the glove.
5. Place the glove in the bowl of water.
6. Let stand for 2 minutes. Record your observations.
7. Use **scissors** to make a 1 cm cut in one of the glove fingers. Put the glove back in the bowl.
8. Let stand for 3 to 5 minutes. Record your observations.

### Analysis

1. **Describe** how the glove models skin.
2. **Explain** what happens when the glove is cut.
3. **Summarize** how cutting the glove modeled a real-world event.

This immune cell is called a *macrophage.* Macrophages are special types of white blood cells that ingest and kill disease-causing agents that enter the body.

These reading tools can help you learn the material in this chapter. For more information on how to use these and other tools, see **Appendix: Reading and Study Skills.**

## Using Words

**Word Parts** Knowing the meanings of word parts can help you figure out the meanings of words that you do not know.

**Your Turn** Use the table to answer the following questions.

1. Define *inflammation* in your own words.
2. What do you think the word *cytotoxic* means? Use your dictionary to find out if your guess is correct.

**Word Parts**

| Part | Type | Meaning |
|---|---|---|
| *in-, en-* | prefix | cause, make, enable |
| *flam* | root | burn, flame |
| *cyto-* | prefix | cell |
| *toxic* | root | poison |

## Using Language

**Mnemonics** Mnemonic devices are tools that can help you memorize words, steps, concepts that go together. Use the first letter of every word you want to remember as the first letter of a new word, in a sentence that is easy to remember. For example, the trees *maple, dogwood, ash,* and *sycamore* can be remembered by the mnemonic "My Dear Aunt Sally."

**Your Turn** Create mnemonic devices to help you remember the following groups of words.

1. The four parts of blood: *red cells, white cells, platelets,* and *plasma*
2. The four major tissue types: *epithelial, nervous, connective,* and *muscle*

## Using Graphic Organizers

**Pattern Puzzles** A pattern puzzle is useful for organizing and remembering the steps of a process. Pattern puzzles can help you understand how the steps of a process fit together.

**Your Turn** Use a pattern puzzle to learn the steps of the inflammatory immune response.

1. Write the steps of the inflammatory immune response in your own words. Write one step per line. Do not number the steps.
2. Cut the sheet of paper so that there is one step per strip of paper.
3. Shuffle the paper strips so that they are out of sequence.
4. Place the strips in their proper sequence.
5. Confirm the order of the process by checking your text or class notes.
6. Use this exercise to model another immune response.

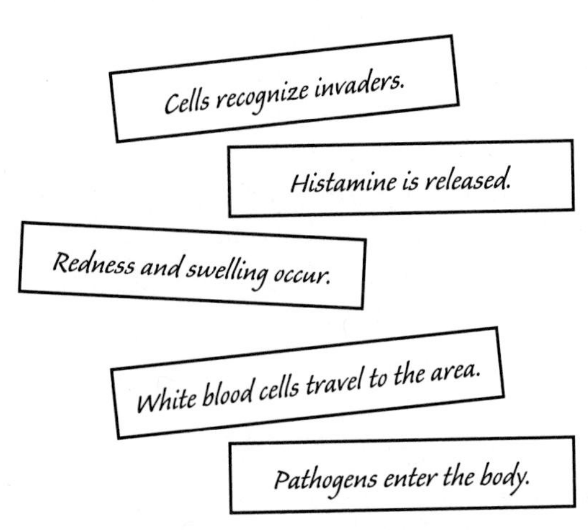

Cells recognize invaders.
Histamine is released.
Redness and swelling occur.
White blood cells travel to the area.
Pathogens enter the body.

Section 1

# Protecting Against Disease

| Key Ideas | Key Terms | Why It Matters |
|---|---|---|
| ❯ What physical barriers protect the human body?<br>❯ What are three general defense mechanisms that the body uses to fight pathogens?<br>❯ How does the body respond to pathogens that have infected a cell? | pathogen<br>mucous membrane<br>inflammation<br>histamine<br>antigen<br>macrophage | To survive, the body must protect itself from infections. The body has both general and specific responses to prevent and fight infections. |

Microorganisms are everywhere! Some are harmless, but others can cause illness by invading your body and infecting your cells. Disease-causing microorganisms and viruses are called **pathogens.** Your body protects against disease by preventing pathogens from entering the body, or by fighting pathogens if they do enter.

## Preventing Entry

**❯ Skin and mucous membranes form strong barriers that prevent pathogens from entering the body.** Your skin is the first line of defense against pathogens. Oil makes the skin's surface acidic, which inhibits the growth of many pathogens. Sweat also contains enzymes that digest bacterial cell walls and kill the bacteria. Mucous membranes form a second barrier to pathogens. **Mucous membranes** are layers of epithelial tissue that produce a sticky, viscous fluid called *mucus.* They cover many internal body surfaces, including the linings of the digestive, respiratory, and reproductive tracts. Mucus traps pathogens before they can cause infections.

Sometimes pathogens cross one of these two physical barriers. Cuts and abrasions allow pathogens to enter through the skin. Tears in the epithelium allow pathogens to cross mucous membranes. Airborne pathogens, shown in **Figure 1,** can enter the body through the respiratory system. You can ingest pathogens via contaminated food or water. Some pathogens can cross mucous membranes of the reproductive tract during sexual contact. Sometimes, pathogens are injected directly into the bloodstream. This can occur through insect bites or through the use of contaminated needles.

**❯ Reading Check** ***How do physical barriers prevent pathogens from entering the body? (See the Appendix for answers to Reading Checks.)***

***The Living Environment***
**Standard 4**

**1.2b** Humans are complex organisms. They require multiple systems for digestion, respiration, reproduction, circulation, excretion, movement, coordination, and immunity. The systems interact to perform the life functions.

**5.2c** The immune system protects against antigens associated with pathogenic organisms or foreign substances and some cancer cells.

**5.2d** Some white blood cells engulf invaders. Others produce antibodies that attack them or mark them for killing. Some specialized white blood cells will remain, able to fight off subsequent invaders of the same kind.

**pathogen** a microorganism, another organism, a virus, or a protein that causes disease; an infectious agent

**mucous membrane** (MYOO kuhs) the layer of epithelial tissue that covers internal surfaces of the body and that secretes mucus

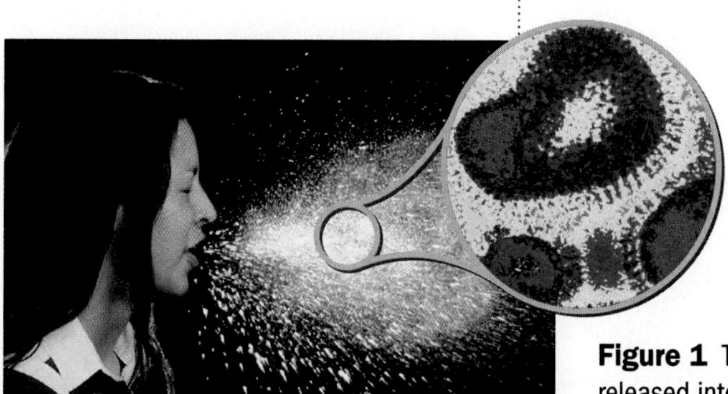

**Figure 1** The flu virus can be released into the air through a cough or sneeze and can infect another person who inhales the air.

**Word Parts** The word part *path-* means "disease." The suffix *-gen* means "to bring forth." Write a sentence explaining how pathology and pathogens are related.

**inflammation** a protective response of tissues affected by disease or injury

**histamine** (HIS tuh MEEN) a chemical that stimulates the dilation of capillaries

**antigen** a substance that stimulates an immune response

**macrophage** an immune system cell that engulfs pathogens and other materials

## Nonspecific Immune Responses

**When pathogens break through the body's physical barriers, the body quickly responds with second-line defenses. These defenses are fever, inflammation, and the activation of special proteins that kill or inhibit pathogens.** These second-line defenses depend on your body's ability to know its own cells and proteins and to separate these "self" cells and proteins from outside invaders.

**Fever** The body's temperature, normally 36.5 °C to 37.2 °C (97.8 °F to 99 °F), rises several degrees as the body begins to fight against an invading pathogen. High body temperature, or fever, is a common symptom of sickness. Higher temperatures are harmful to many bacterial pathogens, so fever helps the body fight infection. However, fever can be dangerous. Fever above 39 °C (103 °F) can destroy the body's cellular proteins, and fever above 41 °C (105 °F) can be fatal.

**Inflammation** An injury or local infection stimulates inflammation, shown in **Figure 2.** During **inflammation,** chemicals and cells that attack and destroy pathogens gather around the area of injury or infection. **1** When the skin is damaged, pathogens can enter the body. **2** Infected or injured cells recognize the "nonself" invaders and release chemicals such as histamine. **Histamine** causes local blood vessels to dilate, which increases blood flow to the area and causes swelling and redness. **3** White blood cells travel to the infection site to attack pathogens. The whitish liquid, or pus, connected with many infections is filled with white blood cells, dead body cells, and dead pathogens. Three types of white blood cells play a role in this response: macrophages, neutrophils, and natural killer cells. These cells are described in **Figure 3.**

**Figure 2** When pathogens enter your body, an inflammatory response is triggered. **Which cells are activated by the inflammatory response?**

go.hrw.com
interact online
Keyword: HX8IMNF2

### Inflammation

**1** When skin is damaged, such as from a puncture wound, pathogens enter the body.

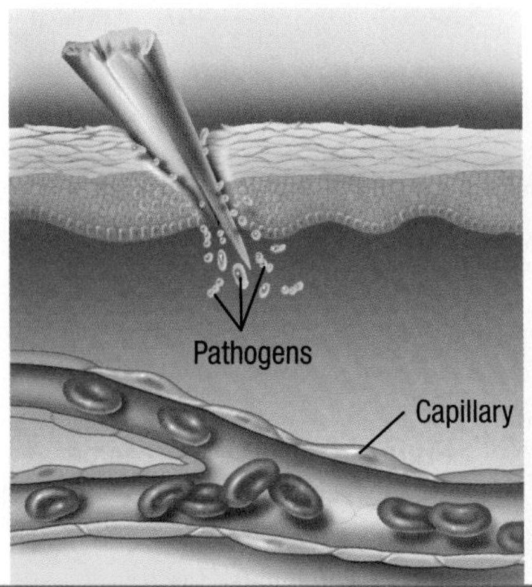


**2** Increased blood flow to the area causes swelling and redness.

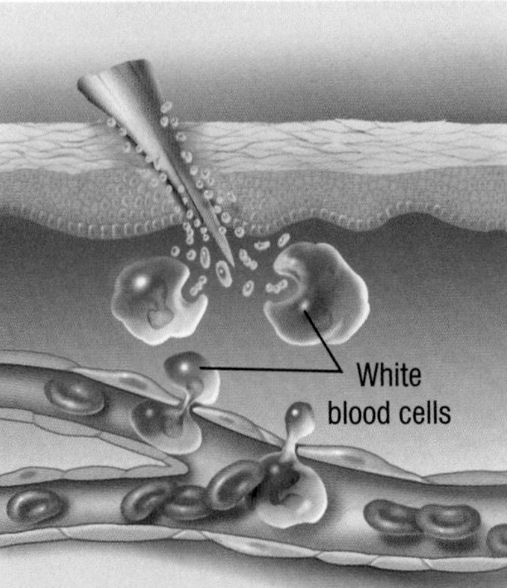


**3** White blood cells attack and destroy the pathogens.

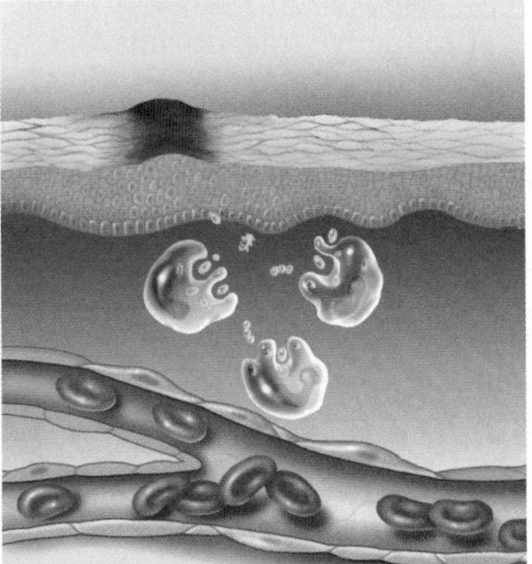

| White Blood Cells Involved in Inflammation | | |
|---|---|---|
| **Macrophage** | **Neutrophil** | **Natural Killer Cell** |
| Target: pathogens, dead cells, and cellular debris | Target: pathogens | Target: cells infected with pathogens and cancer cells |
| Method of action: ingests and kills pathogens | Method of action: ingests and kills pathogens | Method of action: punctures an infected cell membrane, and causes water to rush in and burst the cell |
| Location: lymph and fluid between cells, concentrated in the spleen and lungs | Location: blood and fluid between cells and in the walls of capillaries | Location: lymph nodes and other tissues |

**Figure 3** Different types of white blood cells (each shown in yellow) help defend the body against pathogens.

**Protein Activation** Some pathogens activate proteins that boost the body's general responses to infection. Complement proteins attack cellular pathogens, such as bacteria, by punching holes in the cell membranes and causing the contents to leak out. Interferons, another group of proteins, are released by cells infected with viruses. These proteins prevent viruses from making proteins and RNA.

## Specific Immune Responses

Most pathogens are destroyed by the general, nonspecific defenses that have been looked at so far. But what happens if an invader gets past these responses? The third line of defense is the specific immune response, in which special white blood cells target a particular invader. **> When a pathogen infects a cell, the body produces immune cells that specialize in detecting and destroying that specific pathogen.**

**Antigen Display** **Macrophages** are one type of white blood cell that destroys pathogens. Pathogens have unique proteins on their surfaces that help your body identify them as "nonself." These proteins, called **antigens,** identify the cell as foreign and start an immune response. After a macrophage or similar cell swallows up and destroys a pathogen, pieces of the pathogen that contain its antigens move to the surface of the macrophage. This "display" of antigens changes the cell surface markers on the macrophage. The antigen display alerts the immune system to an invader and the immune system cells are put into action.

Every antigen has its own receptor, which is located on the surface of an immune cell. The shape of antigen receptors allows the immune system to be specific to certain antigens. As **Figure 4** shows, antigen receptors bind to antigens that match their shape exactly, in the same way that two pieces of a puzzle fit together. The body produces a great variety of immune cells, each of which has receptors for a different antigen. This variety allows the immune system to respond to millions of different antigens.

**> Reading Check** ***How does the body recognize "nonself" invaders?***

Complementary shapes bind.

**Figure 4** Specific antigens (green) located on foreign cells (yellow) bind to antigen receptors (red) that are located on immune system cells (purple).

30 min

## Antigen Binding

In this lab, you will observe what happens when receptors in blood-typing serum bind to the antigens on simulated red blood cells.

### Procedure

1. Put on safety goggles, a lab apron, and gloves.
2. Use only simulated blood provided by your teacher. Place three or four drops of type AB simulated blood into each well of a clean blood-typing tray.
3. Add three drops of anti-A blood-typing serum to one well. Stir the mixture with a toothpick for 30 s.
4. Add three drops of anti-B serum to the other well. Stir the mixture with a new toothpick. Look for clumps separating from the mixtures.
5. Using type O simulated blood, repeat steps 1–4.

### Analysis

1. **Determine** which blood type has antigens that are recognized by the blood-typing serums.
2. **Evaluating Results** What does the clumping of the blood mixtures indicate?
3. CRITICAL THINKING **Predicting Outcomes** What would happen if you used type A, type B, and type O simulated blood in the same experiment? Explain your answer.

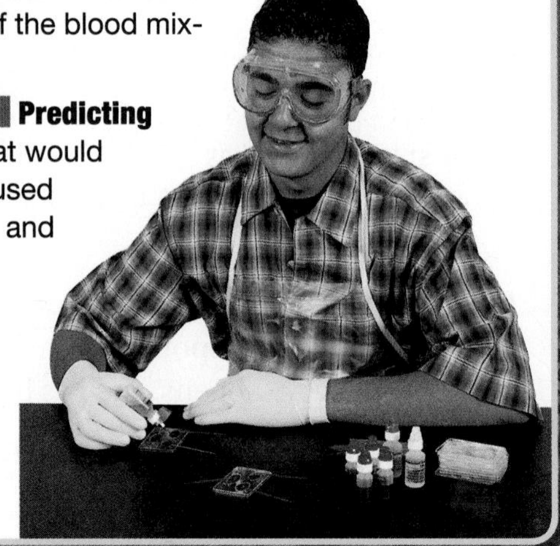

SCILINKS. www.scilinks.org Topic: Immune Systems Code: HX80786

**Two-Part Assault** When a displayed antigen binds to its antigen receptor on an immune cell, another response is triggered—more immune cells are produced that have the same antigen receptor. These immune cells carry out two processes at the same time. One process destroys a person's body cells that are no longer normal. These cells may be infected by pathogens or may be other altered body cells, such as cancer cells. The other process removes extracellular pathogens, pathogens that have not entered body cells. Together, these two processes form an integrated response to an infection. These two immune processes will be described in more detail in the next section.

## Section 1 Review

### KEY IDEAS

1. **Summarize** how the skin and mucous membranes help prevent infection by a pathogen.
2. **Identify** the three general defense mechanisms that protect the body from infection.
3. **Describe** how a cell responds to pathogens.

### CRITICAL THINKING

4. **Relating Concepts** Identify the process that would occur immediately if you cut your foot on a piece of glass, and describe how it would help keep the cut from getting infected.
5. **Drawing Conclusions** In the disease leukemia, abnormal white blood cells are produced. Why are people who have leukemia at greater risk for infections than other people are?

### WRITING FOR SCIENCE

6. **Short Story** Imagine that you are a pathogen trying to get into a human body. Write a short story that describes the challenges that you face as you attempt to get past the body's defenses. Be sure to include at least three different types of immune system defenses.

Section

# 2 Eliminating Invaders

| Key Ideas | Key Terms | | Why It Matters |
|---|---|---|---|
| ❯ How is the specific immune response activated?<br>❯ How does the body eliminate intracellular pathogens?<br>❯ How does the body eliminate extracellular pathogens?<br>❯ How does the immune system protect the body from repeated infection by the same pathogen? | helper T cell<br>cytotoxic T cell<br>B cell<br>plasma cell<br>antibody | memory cell<br>immunity<br>vaccine | At the same time that the immune system is fighting an infection, it is creating a reserve army of cells to fight the same pathogen in the future. |

The immune system consists of many types of white blood cells, including macrophages, T cells, and B cells. The first time your body meets a particular pathogen, the immune response launches an attack on the invader. The coordinated effort of all of the immune system cells not only destroys invading pathogens but also provides protection against future infection by a similar pathogen.

***The Living Environment***
**Standard 4**

**1.2b** Humans are complex organisms. They require multiple systems for digestion, respiration, reproduction, circulation, excretion, movement, coordination, and immunity. The systems interact to perform the life functions.
**5.1g** Enzymes and other molecules, such as hormones, receptor molecules, and antibodies, have specific shapes that influence both how they function and how they interact with other molecules.
**5.2c** The immune system protects against antigens associated with pathogenic organisms or foreign substances and some cancer cells.
**5.2d** Some white blood cells engulf invaders. Others produce antibodies that attack them or mark them for killing. Some specialized white blood cells will remain, able to fight off subsequent invaders of the same kind.
**5.2e** Vaccinations use weakened microbes (or parts of them) to stimulate the immune system to react. This reaction prepares the body to fight subsequent invasions by the same microbes.

## Activating a Specific Immune Response

As part of the body's general immune response, macrophages engulf and destroy pathogens. The result is the display of antigens on the surface of infected cells. These "altered" cells now become a target of the specific immune response. **❯ A specialized white blood cell called a *helper T cell* activates the immune system. These cells coordinate two responses: destroying cells that have been infected by a pathogen, and cleaning up pathogens at large in the body.**

**helper T cell** a white blood cell necessary for B cells to develop normal levels of antibodies

**Helper T Cells** Helper T cells, shown in **Figure 5,** are white blood cells that regulate the function of other cells in the immune system. Recall that helper T cells have specific antigen receptors on their surfaces that bind to specific antigens that are displayed on the surface of a macrophage. The binding of receptor to the antigen activates the helper T cell, which causes the release of chemical signals.

Activated helper T cells do not directly attack infected body cells or pathogens. Instead, they grow and divide to produce more helper T cells that have identical receptors on their surfaces. The helper T cells activate the two processes of the specific immune response: the destruction of infected cells by cytotoxic T cells and the removal of extracellular pathogens from the body by B cells.

**Figure 5** Some white blood cells, such as helper T cells and cytotoxic T cells, are produced in bone marrow and mature in the thymus.

cytotoxic T cell a type of T cell that recognizes and destroys cells infected by viruses

B cell a white blood cell that matures in bones and makes antibodies

plasma cell a type of white blood cell that produces antibodies

antibody a protein that reacts to a specific antigen or that inactivates or destroys toxins

## Destroying Infected Cells

Helper T cells produce chemical signals that activate the second kind of T cell, called a *cytotoxic T cell.* **Cytotoxic T cells** are white blood cells that carry pathogen-specific receptors on their surfaces. **❯ Cytotoxic T cells destroy cells that have been infected by pathogens.** They can also kill cancer cells and attack foreign tissues, such as tissues that are received during an organ transplant. The cytotoxic T cell response is summarized in **Figure 7.**

**Activating Cytotoxic T Cells** Recall that when a body cell becomes infected by a virus, it displays specific antigens on its surface. These antigens activate matching antigen receptors on helper T cells. The activated helper T cells then turn on the production of cytotoxic T cells that will have the same antigen receptor. As a result, the new cytotoxic T cells will bind to matching antigens on the surface of infected cells. When they bind, the cytotoxic T cells release chemicals that punch holes in the membranes of the infected cells. The infected cells die when water enters them and splits them open.

**Pattern Puzzles** Make a pattern puzzle to help you remember the steps of the immune response system.

## Removing Pathogens at Large

Helper T cells also activate the second part of the specific immune response, which is carried out by B cells. **B cells** are white blood cells that produce proteins that bind to pathogens outside of body cells. This action tags the pathogens for destruction by macrophages. **❯ The B cell response removes extracellular pathogens from the body and prevents further infection.** This response is summarized in **Figure 7.**

**Activating B Cells** The B cell response is triggered when B cells are activated by helper T cells, as shown in **Figure 6.** Like T cells in the T cell response, only B cells that have antigen receptors matching a specific antigen are activated. Activated B cells produce **plasma cells,** which are white blood cells that produce and release antibodies. **Antibodies** are Y-shaped protein molecules that bind to the specific antigen that they match.

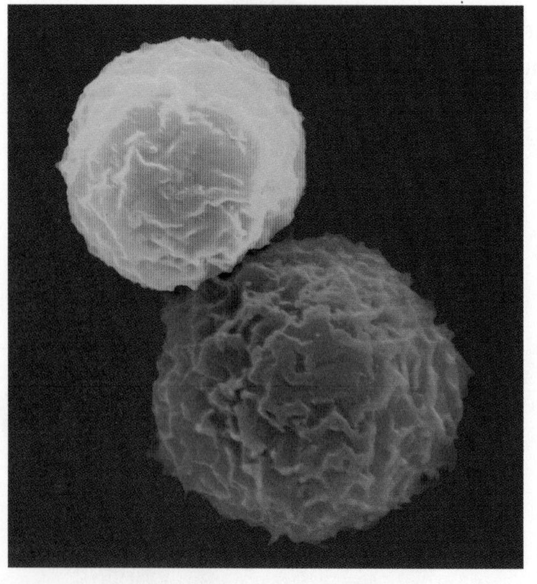

**Figure 6** When a helper T cell (blue) activates a B cell (purple), they come in close contact with each other.

**Antibody Binding** Antibodies are released by plasma cells and circulate in the blood and lymph fluid. When antibodies encounter extracellular pathogens that they match, they attach to the pathogens. This binding is like the specific binding of cytotoxic T cells to matching infected body cells. However, antibodies do not remain attached to the plasma cells that produced them.

Each Y-shaped antibody has two binding sites, which are located at the tips of the Ys. Antibodies can either bind to two antigens on the surface of a single pathogen cell or to single antigens on two pathogen cells. The binding of multiple antibodies to pathogens forms an antigen-antibody complex. These complexes are then destroyed by general defense mechanisms, such as macrophages or defense proteins that puncture the pathogen membranes.

**❯ Reading Check** ***Which cells produce antibodies?***

go.hrw.com
interact online
Keyword: HX8IMNF7

## The Immune Response System

**Figure 7** Antigens (small green knobs), such as those from a virus (yellow), activate helper T cells. Helper T cells then activate both the intracellular response (by stimulating T cells) and the extracellular response (by stimulating B cells).

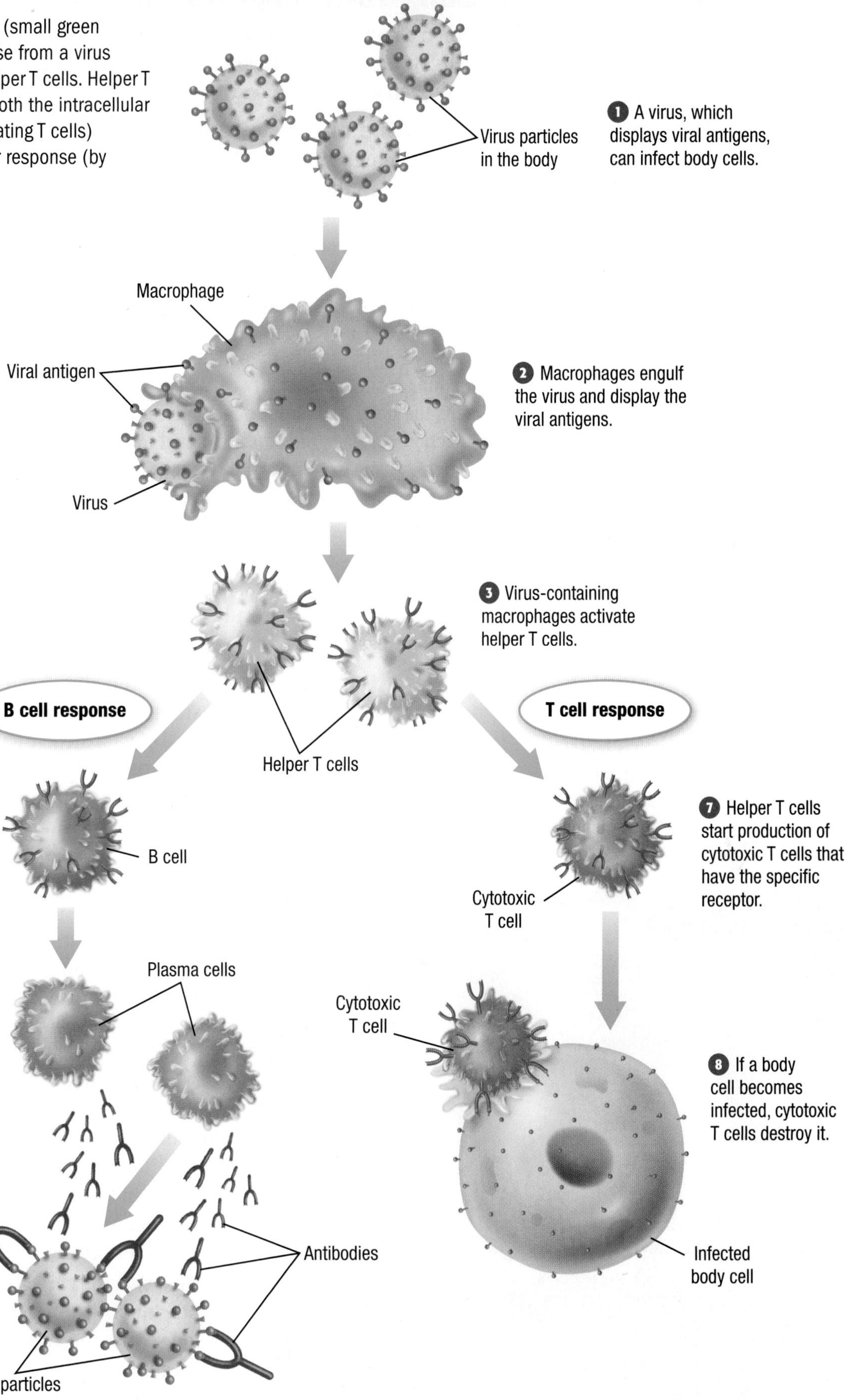

Virus particles in the body

1 A virus, which displays viral antigens, can infect body cells.

Macrophage

Viral antigen

Virus

2 Macrophages engulf the virus and display the viral antigens.

3 Virus-containing macrophages activate helper T cells.

Helper T cells

B cell response

T cell response

4 Helper T cells start production of B cells that have the specific receptor.

B cell

5 B cells form specific plasma cells.

Plasma cells

6 Plasma cells make and release antibodies that bind to the viral antigens. This action tags the virus for destruction.

Antibodies

Virus particles

7 Helper T cells start production of cytotoxic T cells that have the specific receptor.

Cytotoxic T cell

Cytotoxic T cell

8 If a body cell becomes infected, cytotoxic T cells destroy it.

Infected body cell

## Long-Term Protection

When a pathogen has been destroyed, the specific T cells, plasma cells, and antibodies involved are no longer needed. But if the same pathogen invades the body again, the immune system is prepared.

**memory cell** an immune system B cell or T cell that does not respond the first time that it meets with an antigen or an invading cell but that recognizes and attacks the antigen or invading cell during subsequent infections

**immunity** the ability to resist or recover from an infectious disease

**vaccine** a substance prepared from killed or weakened pathogens and introduced into a body to produce immunity

**Activating Memory Cells** Recall that when the body first meets a pathogen, B cells make plasma cells that produce antibodies to that pathogen. At the same time, activated B cells also produce another kind of white blood cell called a *memory cell.* Like plasma cells, **memory cells** carry antigen receptors to the target antigen. These cells also continue to patrol the body's tissues, in some cases for the rest of a person's life. If the same pathogen invades the body again, the memory cells rapidly divide and produce a group of immune cells—helper T cells, cytotoxic T cells, and plasma cells. **❯ After an immune response, memory cells continue to protect the body from pathogens the body had already encountered. An individual who recovers from an infectious disease becomes resistant to that particular pathogen.**

The secondary immune response that is started by memory cells is called *immunity.* **Immunity** is a long-lasting resistance that is usually effective only against the specific pathogen that triggered the response. This secondary response starts much more quickly than when the body first faced the pathogen. It also produces many more specialized cells. As a result, the invader is stopped before it can cause illness.

**Vaccination** Infection by a pathogen allows the body to gain immunity to that particular pathogen. However, the body can also become immune through the use of vaccines. A **vaccine** is a solution that contains a dead or weakened form of a pathogen. They are typically injected into the bloodstream so that the pathogens can get past the general defenses of the immune system. Vaccines are available for many serious and deadly diseases.

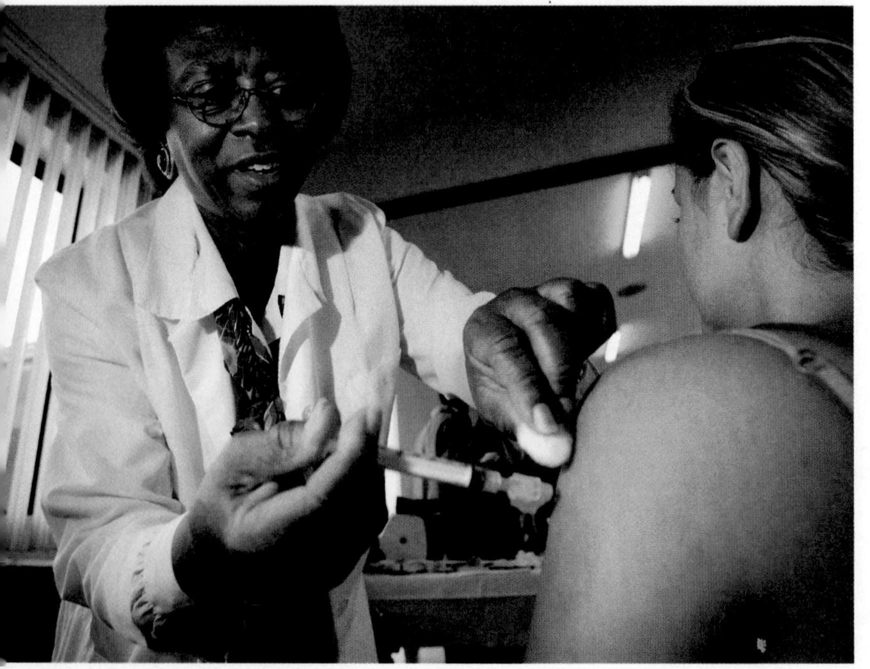

**Figure 8** This young person is receiving a vaccination shot. A vaccine is produced from a killed or weakened pathogen. **❯ Vaccines trigger which type of immune response?**

A vaccine triggers an immune response against a pathogen without causing symptoms. How? Vaccines carry surface antigens from the pathogen that the body recognizes as harmful. This recognition triggers the immune response and forms memory cells against the pathogen. However, the genetic material in a vaccine is weakened or destroyed so that the pathogen cannot cause illness. In this way, immunity is built against the disease without the disease occurring in the body. Future contact with the pathogen will trigger the immune system to respond.

Most vaccines are given as a shot directly into the bloodstream. This method is used so that the vaccine can get past the body's general defenses. Vaccination is shown in **Figure 8.**

Data

# QuickLab

15 min

## The Eradication of Polio  4.5.2e

The graph shows the global incidence of polio, and the percent of the population covered by polio vaccines.

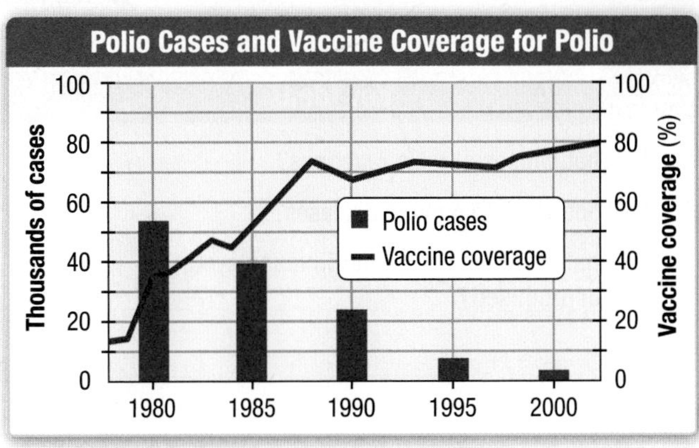

Source: World Health Organization.

### Analysis

1. **Determine** how many cases of polio were reported globally in 1980. In 2000?
2. **Determine** what percent of the population was covered by protective polio vaccine in 1980. In 2000?
3. **Describe** the relationship between the number of polio cases and the coverage by preventative vaccine.
4. **Name** the two-year period over which the greatest drop in cases occurred. Explain this decrease.
5. CRITICAL THINKING **Inferring Conclusions** What might cause a sudden yearly increase in the number of polio cases?

**How Pathogens Evade Immunity** Microorganisms have short life cycles. Several generations can be produced in as little as an hour. Also, changes in the genetic material of a microorganism often occur. These genetic changes may cause *antigen shifting,* an abrupt change in a pathogen's antigens. This process can allow a pathogen to avoid being recognized by the immune system of a person who had already become immune to the pathogen.

Influenza viruses are well known for frequent antigen shifts. New forms of the flu appear rapidly, and people at risk of serious complications from the flu must receive new vaccines annually. Human immunodeficiency virus (HIV) also undergoes antigen shifts. As a result, making a vaccine against HIV is very difficult. Antigen shifting also causes the virus to become resistant to drugs that are used to treat HIV in fection.

› **Reading Check** *What causes antigen shifting?*

## Section 2 Review

### › KEY IDEAS

1. **Describe** the role of helper T cells in fighting an infection.
2. **Explain** how cytotoxic T cells destroy infected body cells.
3. **Sequence** how B cells fight an infection.
4. **Explain** how memory cells ensure immunity to a specific pathogen.

### CRITICAL THINKING

5. **Drawing Conclusions** In the first vaccine developed, cowpox virus was used to protect against smallpox. This fact seems to contradict the high specificity that characterizes immune responses. What conclusion can you draw about the cowpox virus in relation to the smallpox virus?

### WRITING FOR SCIENCE

6. **Short Essay** Scientists have created an effective vaccine for smallpox but have not been able to do so for HIV. What does this fact suggest about the rate of mutation of the smallpox virus? Write a short essay to explain your reasoning.

Section

# 3 Immune System Dysfunctions

| Key Ideas | Key Terms | Why It Matters |
|---|---|---|
| ❯ What causes allergic reactions?<br>❯ What are autoimmune diseases?<br>❯ What happens when your immune system is compromised? | allergy<br>allergen<br>autoimmune disease<br>AIDS<br>HIV | Only when the immune system breaks down do we realize how important it is to our survival. |

*The Living Environment*
**Standard 4**
**5.2f** Some viral diseases, such as AIDS, damage the immune system, leaving the body unable to deal with multiple infectious agents and cancerous cells.
**5.2g** Some allergic reactions are caused by the body's immune responses to usually harmless environmental substances. Sometimes the immune system may attack some of the body's own cells or transplanted organs.

The immune system protects us from a wide variety of diseases. When the immune system malfunctions, the results are usually very serious and often fatal. Allergies, autoimmune disorders, and inherited or acquired immunodeficiency disorders are all examples of what can happen when the immune system does not work properly.

## Allergies

If you suffer from hay fever, you experience an immune response to pollen antigens. **Allergies** are immune responses to antigens to which most people do not react. These weak antigens are called **allergens.** ❯ **An allergic reaction is the immune system's excessive response to a normally harmless antigen.** Common allergens include pollen, dust, fungal spores, the feces of dust mites, and materials found in some foods and drugs. Some allergens are shown in **Figure 9.**

In a sensitive person, exposure to an allergen causes histamine release. This event can cause swelling, redness, high mucus production, a runny or stuffy nose, and itchy eyes. Most allergy medicines contain antihistamines, drugs that prevent the action of histamine. Most allergic reactions are just uncomfortable. However, severe allergic reactions can be life threatening if they are not treated immediately.

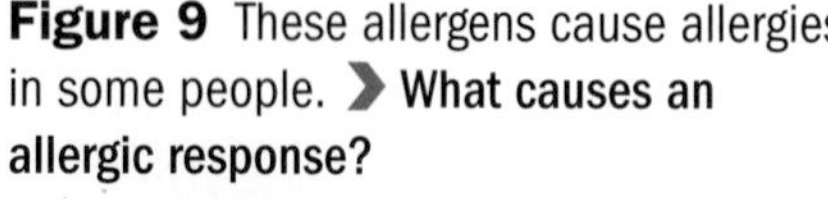

**Figure 9** These allergens cause allergies in some people. ❯ **What causes an allergic response?**

Hands-On

# QuickLab

15 min

## Constricted Airways

During an asthma attack, muscles surrounding the airways contract and restrict airflow into the lungs.

### Procedure

1. Get three clean straws and three rubber bands. Slip one rubber band near one end of a straw. Coil the rubber band around the straw so that it does not change the shape of the straw.
2. Wrap another rubber band around the end of a second straw so that the straw is slightly crushed.
3. Wrap the third rubber band around the last straw so that the straw is almost sealed.
4. Breathe through each of the straws. Only breathe through your own straws. Compare the straws in terms of how easily you can breathe through them.

### Analysis

1. **Describe** what the straw and rubber band represent.
2. **State** which straw represented an unrestricted airway.
3. **Describe** how this activity models an asthma attack.
4. CRITICAL THINKING **Predicting Outcomes** How might you reduce the prevalence of allergen-induced asthma attacks?

**Asthma** Asthma is an inflammation of the respiratory tract and is often caused by an allergic reaction to particles in the air. Asthma symptoms include coughing, wheezing, and difficulty in breathing. Asthma affects nearly 20 million Americans and causes more than 4,000 deaths each year.

**Other Allergies** Some foods that cause allergies are eggs, peanuts, milk, and shellfish. Food allergies may cause vomiting, diarrhea, and hives. They may be so severe that they cause a person to stop breathing and go into shock. Allergies to some detergents, cosmetics, or plants such as poison ivy can cause itchy red rashes and blisters. Some people are allergic to the stings of bees and other insects. Their reaction to a sting may include hives, difficulty in breathing, and loss of consciousness.

**allergy** a physical response to an antigen, which can be a common substance that produces little or no response in the general population

**allergen** a substance that causes an allergic reaction

› **Reading Check** *Why is asthma classified as an allergy?*

Mold

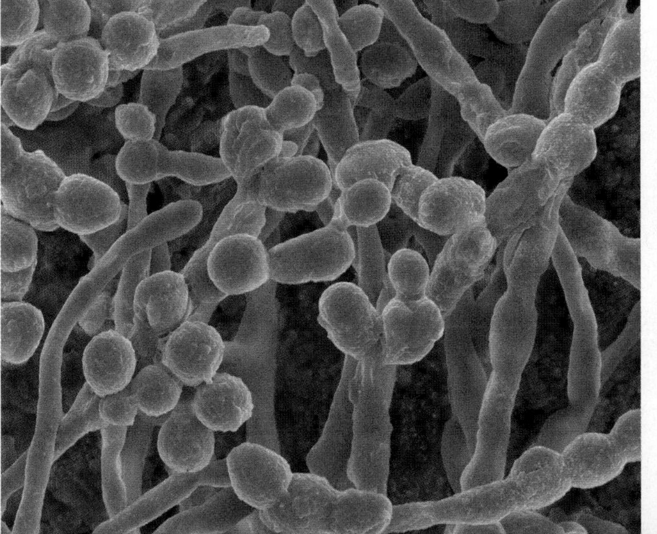

Dust mite

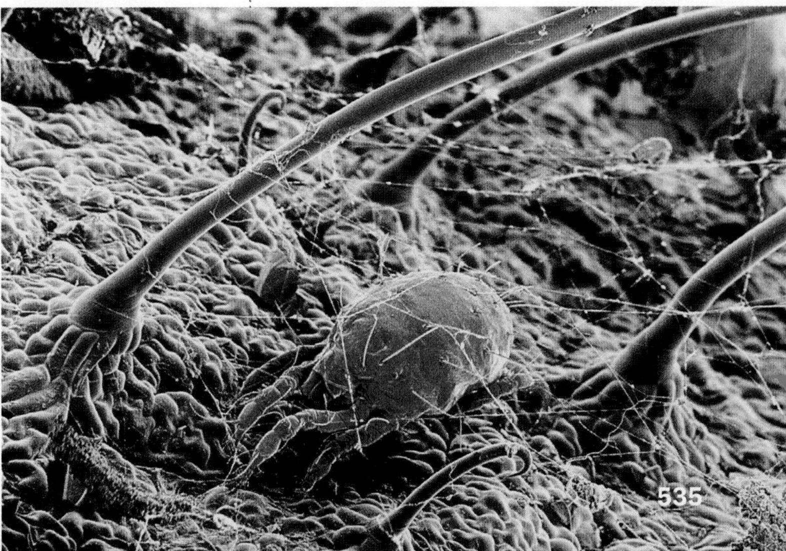

Why It Matters

# Allergies & Culture

The number of people in the United States suffering from asthma today is 1.75 times higher than in 1980. What is the reason for this trend? One interesting explanation, known as the *hygiene hypothesis,* suggests that improved sanitation conditions can lead to higher rates of asthma, allergies, and autoimmune disorders.

## Immune System in Training

As sanitation conditions improve in industrialized nations, children are exposed to far fewer microorganisms. The hygiene hypothesis argues that when a child's immune system is not exposed to common microorganisms, it can become unbalanced and can trigger allergic responses to harmless substances.

The hygiene hypothesis proposes that an imbalance exists between helper T cells and cytotoxic T cells. A newborn child depends primarily on helper T cells to prevent infection. The cytotoxic T cell system grows stronger as a child is exposed to microbes in the environment. The hygiene hypothesis suggests that if a developing child is not exposed to a variety of microbes, the cytotoxic T cell system does not develop properly and helper T cells can become dominant.

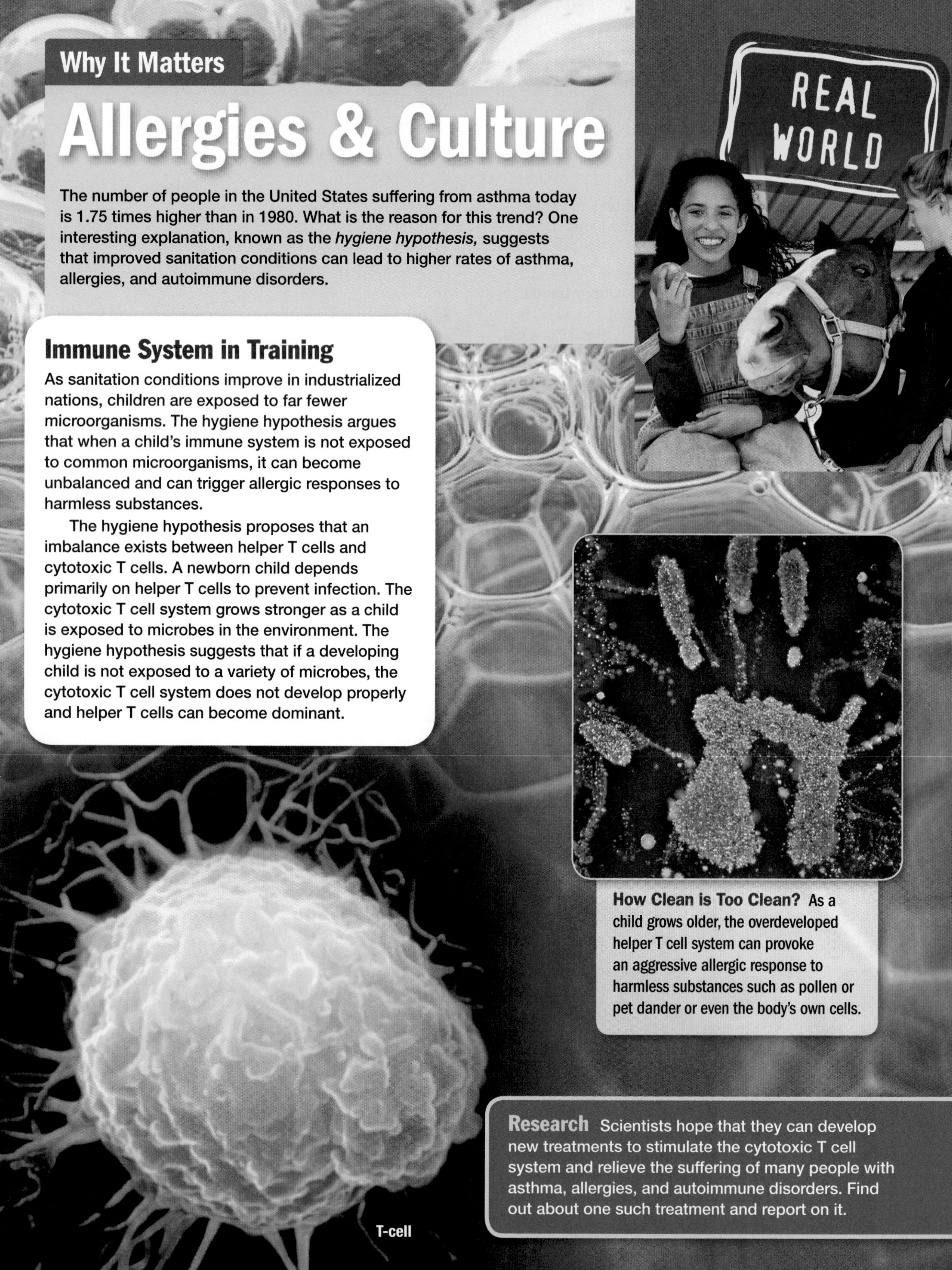


**How Clean is Too Clean?** As a child grows older, the overdeveloped helper T cell system can provoke an aggressive allergic response to harmless substances such as pollen or pet dander or even the body's own cells.

T-cell

**Research** Scientists hope that they can develop new treatments to stimulate the cytotoxic T cell system and relieve the suffering of many people with asthma, allergies, and autoimmune disorders. Find out about one such treatment and report on it.

## Autoimmune Diseases

The ability of the immune system to distinguish between "self" substances, which it ignores, and "nonself" molecules, which it attacks, is crucial to protecting the body from pathogens. Sometimes, the immune system loses its tolerance for "self," attacks certain cells of the body, and thus causes one of many **autoimmune diseases.** **In an autoimmune disease, the body launches an immune response, such that body cells are attacked as if they were pathogens.** Autoimmunity causes a wide range of disorders, some of which are shown in **Figure 11.** In all of these diseases, the immune system attacks the very organs that it is programmed to protect.

**Common Autoimmune Disorders** Diabetes is a disease in which the body does not produce or properly use the hormone insulin. This hormone allows glucose to enter body cells. Type 1 diabetes (or insulin dependent diabetes) is an example of an autoimmune disease. When a person has type 1 diabetes, the body does not produce or properly use insulin, the hormone that allows glucose to enter body cells. His or her immune cells attack the cells of the pancreas that produce insulin. As a result, he or she produces very little insulin, and the body cells starve for glucose while it accumulates in the blood. Type 1 diabetes is treated with insulin through injections or an insulin pump, shown in **Figure 10.**

Multiple sclerosis is an autoimmune disease in which the immune system targets the insulating material that covers nerves. This result is numbness, weakness, paralysis of one or more limbs, poor coordination, and vision impairment.

Autoimmune diseases affect 5% to 7% of the U.S. population and are three times more common in women than men. These diseases are not curable, but they are treatable to some extent. The causes of autoimmune diseases are not well understood but likely involve factors including genetics, environmental factors, or pathogens.

**Figure 10** This insulin pump is used to treat type 1 diabetes. **How is the immune system involved in type 1 diabetes?**

**autoimmune disease** a disease in which the immune system attacks the organism's own cells

**Examples of Autoimmune Diseases**

| Disease | Areas affected | Symptoms |
|---|---|---|
| Graves' disease | thyroid gland | weakness, irritability, heat intolerance, increased sweating, weight loss, and insomnia |
| Systemic lupus erythematosus (SLE) | connective tissue, joints, and kidneys | facial skin rash, painful joints, fever, fatigue, kidney problems, and weight loss |
| Rheumatoid arthritis | joints | severe pain, fatigue, and disabling inflammation of joints |
| Psoriasis | skin | dry, scaly, red skin patches |
| Crohn's disease | digestive system | abdominal pain, nausea, vomiting, and weight loss |

**Figure 11** Autoimmune diseases can affect organs and tissues in various areas of the body.

AIDS acquired immune deficiency syndrome, a disease caused by HIV, an infection that results in an ineffective immune system

HIV human immunodeficiency virus, the virus that causes AIDS

## Immune Deficiency

A strong immune system works so well and so quietly that we often don't realize how many times it has saved our lives. However, some people have a deficiency in which part of the immune system is missing or does not work properly. **When the immune system does not function, the body is unable to fight and survive infections by pathogens that do not cause any problems for a robust immune system.** Immune deficiencies can be inherited, acquired through infection, or even produced as an unintended side effect of a drug. They can affect antibodies, T cells, B cells, macrophages, or other substances normally produced by the immune system.

People who have immunodeficiency tend to have one infection after another. The infections are severe, and they last longer than they do in other people. Infections of the skin and the membranes lining the mouth, eyes, and digestive tract are common. The pathogens that cause infection are often ones that do not cause disease when present in the bodies of people who have healthy immune systems. Diseases caused by such agents are called *opportunistic infections.* These infections take advantage of the "opportunity" to infect a person who has a weakened immune system.

**Mnemonics** Create a mnemonic device to help you remember the types of immune system dysfunctions described in this section.

**Innate Immune Deficiency** Some people are born with immune deficiencies. These deficiences are usually inherited but are occasionally caused by problems during pregnancy. B cell and antibody defects are the most common kinds of innate immune deficiency. People who have these conditions are prone not only to infections but also to autoimmune disorders. Often, they do not develop immunity following vaccination. T cell defects are less common but more severe than B cell defects. Individuals fail to grow and develop normally, and they tend to develop overwhelming infections. In rare cases, neither the B cell nor the T cell response works. This condition is called *severe combined immunodeficiency (SCID).* Babies who have SCID usually develop severe or even life-threatening infections.

**Figure 12** Family members like these two sisters are often donors for organ transplants.

**Immune Suppression** Sometimes, there is a medical reason to suppress the immune response. For example, after having an organ transplant, a person is given drugs that suppress immune function. Because the body does not recognize the transplanted organ as "self," these drugs are needed to keep the immune system from attacking the organ. The organ transplant recipient shown in **Figure 12** will need to take immunosuppressant drugs for life. Some drugs suppress the immune system as a side effect. Chemotherapy often causes supression of the immune system. People who have suppressed immune systems are more susceptible to opportunistic infections than people with healthy immune systems.

**AIDS** The best-known acquired immune deficiency disease is **AIDS,** or acquired immune deficiency syndrome. In AIDS, a virus infects and kills helper T cells, shown in **Figure 13.** People who have AIDS are very susceptible to infections. Because only a few helper T cells are left in the body, neither the T cell nor the B cell response is triggered.

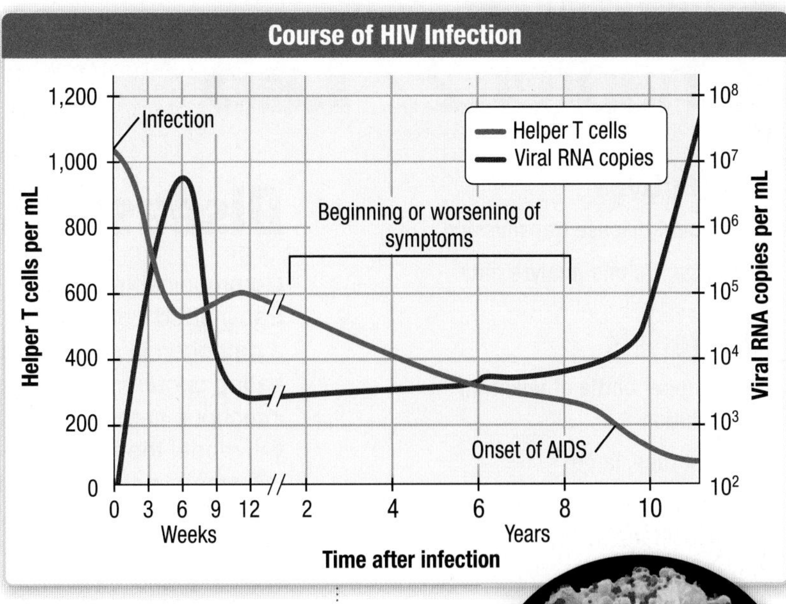


The virus that causes AIDS is called **HIV,** or human immunodeficiency virus. HIV is most commonly transmitted through human body fluids, such as semen, blood, and breast milk. Although HIV has been found in saliva, tears, and urine, these body fluids usually contain too few HIV particles to cause an infection. HIV is not transmitted through the air, on toilet seats, by kissing or handshaking, or by other forms of casual contact. Mosquitoes and ticks do not transmit HIV.

Once inside helper T cells, HIV is protected from the normal processes that would destroy it. The virus also uses the organelles of the host cell to produce copies of itself. Helper T cells that are loaded with HIV particles burst open, which releases large numbers of viruses into the bloodstream that can infect new cells. Initially, the immune system responds to the viruses. Antibodies to HIV can be detected in the blood. Someone whose blood contains antibodies to HIV is said to be HIV positive. As the infection progresses, the number of helper T cells decreases and the number of HIV particles increases, as shown in **Figure 13.** It takes an average of 10 years for HIV infection to progress to AIDS. AIDS is fatal in nearly every case. Currently, there is no vaccine or cure for HIV. However, some drugs can slow the progression from HIV infection to AIDS.

**Figure 13** The graph plots the amount of helper T cells and viral RNA copies in the blood during HIV infection. In the micrograph, small HIV particles (orange) surround a helper T cell (white).

› **Reading Check** ***Which immune cells does HIV destroy, and how does the virus destroy them?***

## Section 3 Review

### › KEY IDEAS

1. **Describe** what causes an allergic reaction.
2. **Define** what an autoimmune disease is and give an example of one.
3. **List** the causes of immune deficiency.

### CRITICAL THINKING

4. **Drawing Conclusions** Would a person who has asthma be able to launch a normal immune response following exposure to an influenza virus? What about a person who has multiple sclerosis?
5. **Determining Factual Accuracy** Why are allergic reactions often referred to as inappropriate responses of the immune system? Explain your reasoning.

### USING SCIENCE GRAPHICS

6. **Identifying Variables** In the graph in **Figure 13,** there are many different variables to track. Identify which variables are the dependent variables, and which are the independent variables. Describe the relationships between these variables.

Skills Practice

# Chapter 22 Lab

## Objectives

- Model disease transmission.
- Organize and analyze data.

## Materials

- dropper bottle of unknown solution
- test tube, large
- dropper bottle of indophenol indicator

## Safety

# Disease Transmission Model

Communicable diseases are caused by pathogens and can be transmitted from one person to another. You can become infected by a pathogen in several ways, including by drinking contaminated water, eating contaminated foods, receiving contaminated blood, and inhaling infectious aerosols (droplets from coughs or sneezes). In this lab, you will model the transmission of a communicable disease. To do this, you will create a simulation of disease transmission. After the simulation, you will try to identify the person who was originally infected in the closed class population.

## Procedure

### Simulate Disease Transmission

1. Make two data tables similar to the ones shown.

*Disease Transmission*

| Round number | Partner's name |
|---|---|
| | |

*Disease Source*

| | Names of infected person's partners | | |
|---|---|---|---|
| Name of infected person | Round 1 | Round 2 | Round 3 |
| | | | |

2. Put on disposable gloves, a lab apron, and safety goggles.
3. **CAUTION: Do not touch or taste any chemicals. Exercise caution when working with glassware such as a test tube.** You will be given a dropper bottle of an unknown solution. When your teacher says to begin, transfer three droppersful of your solution to a clean test tube.
4. Select a partner for Round 1. Record the name of this partner in your Disease Transmission table.

5 Together, you and your partner have two test tubes. Pour the contents of one of the test tubes into the other test tube. Then, pour half of the solution back into the first test tube. You and your partner now share any pathogens either of you might have.

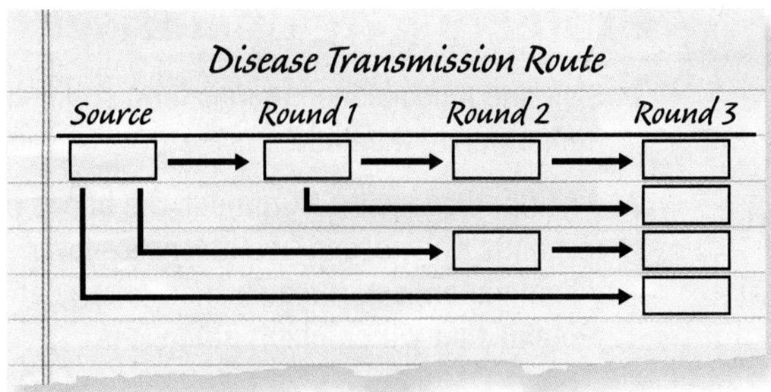


6 On your teacher's signal, select a new partner for Round 2. Record this partner's name in your Disease Transmission table. Repeat step 5.

7 On your teacher's signal, select a new partner for Round 3. Record this partner's name in your Disease Transmission table. Repeat step 5.

8 Add one dropperful of indophenol indicator to your test tube. "Infected" solutions will be colorless or will turn light pink. "Uninfected" solutions will turn blue. Record the results of your test.

### Trace the Disease Source

9 If you are infected, write your name and the name of your partner in each round on the board or on an overhead projector. Mark your infected partners. Record all of the data for your class in your Disease Source table.

10 To trace the source of the infection, cross out the names of the uninfected partners in Round 1. There should be only two names left. One is the name of the original disease carrier. To find the original disease carrier, place a sample from his or her dropper bottle in a clean test tube, and test it with indophenol indicator.

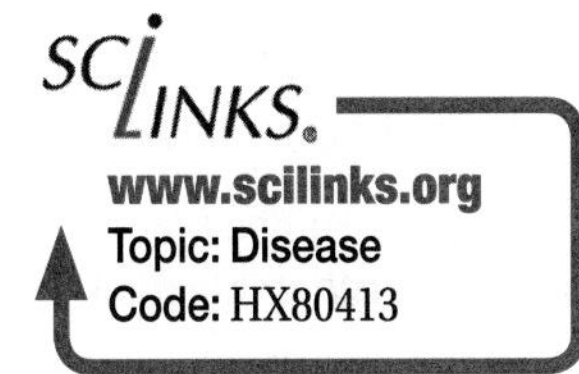


11 To show the disease transmission route, make a diagram similar to the one labeled "Disease Transmission Route." Show the original disease carrier and the people each disease carrier infected.

12 Clean up your lab materials according to your teacher's instructions. Wash your hands thoroughly before leaving the lab.

## Analyze and Conclude

1. SCIENTIFIC METHODS **Interpreting Data** After Round 3, how many people were infected? Express this number as a percentage of your class.
2. **Relating Concepts** What do you think the clear fluids each student started with represent? Explain your response.
3. **Drawing Conclusions** Can someone who does not show any symptoms of a disease transmit that disease? Explain.
4. SCIENTIFIC METHODS **Further Inquiry** Write a new question about disease transmission that could be explored with another investigation.

## Extensions

5. **On the Job** Public health officials, such as food inspectors, research and work to prevent the spread of diseases in human populations. Do research to find out how public health officials trace the origin of communicable diseases.

# Chapter 22 Summary

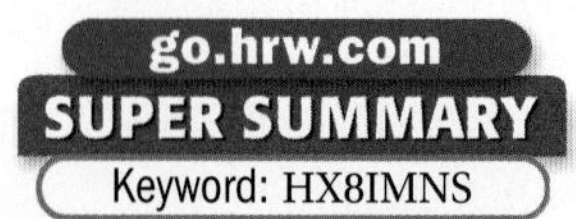


| Key Ideas | Key Terms |
|---|---|

## 1 Protecting Against Disease

- Skin and mucous membranes form strong barriers that prevent pathogens from entering the body.
- When pathogens break through the body's physical barriers, the body quickly responds with second-line defenses—fever, inflammation, and the activation of special proteins that kill or inhibit pathogens.
- When a pathogen infects a cell, the body produces immune cells that specialize in detecing and destroying that specific pathogen.

**Key Terms:** **pathogen** (525), **mucous membrane** (525), **inflammation** (526), **histamine** (526), **antigen** (526), **macrophage** (526)

## 2 Eliminating Invaders

- A specialized white blood cell called a helper T cells activates the specific immune response. These cells coordinate two responses; the destruction of cells that have been infected by a pathogen, and the removal of pathogens at large in the body.
- Cytotoxic T cells attack and kill cells that have been infected by pathogens.
- The B cell response removes extracellular pathogens from the body and prevents further infection.
- After an immune response, memory cells continue to protect the body from previously encountered pathogens.

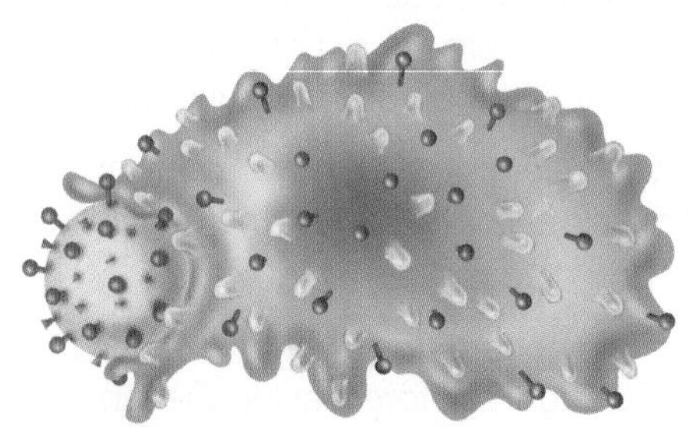

**Key Terms:** **helper T cell** (529), **cytotoxic T cell** (530), **B cell** (530), **plasma cell** (530), **antibody** (530), **memory cell** (532), **immunity** (532), **vaccine** (532)

## 3 Immune System Dysfunctions

- An allergic reaction is an excessive immune response to a normally harmless antigen.
- In an autoimmune disease, the body launches an immune response so that body cells are attacked as if they were pathogens.
- When the immune system does not function, the body is unable to fight and survive infections by pathogens that do not cause problems for a robust immune system.

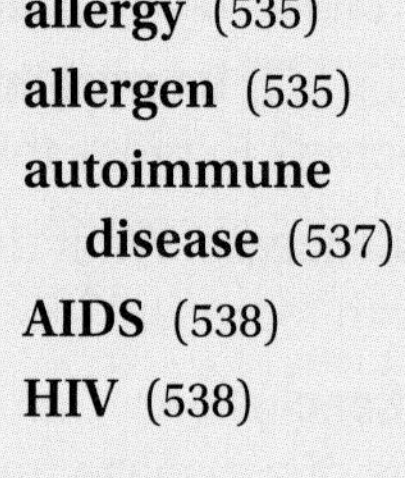

**Key Terms:** **allergy** (535), **allergen** (535), **autoimmune disease** (537), **AIDS** (538), **HIV** (538)

Chapter 22

The Living Environment

# Regents Exam Practice

**PART A: Answer all questions in this part.**

*Directions:* For each statement or question, write on your separate answer sheet the number of the word or expression that best completes the statement or answers the question.

**1** The purpose of introducing weakened microbes into the body of an organism is to stimulate the
(1) production of living microbes that will protect the organism from future attacks.
(2) production of antigens that will prevent infections from occurring.
(3) immune system to react and prepare the organism to fight future invasions by these microbes.
(4) replication of genes that direct the synthesis of hormones that regulate the number of microbes.

**2** Certain microbes, foreign tissues, and some cancerous cells can cause immune responses in the human body because all three contain
(1) antigens.
(2) enzymes.
(3) fats.
(4) cytoplasm.

**3** Which activity would stimulate the human immune system to provide protection against an invasion by a microbe?
(1) receiving antibiotic injections after surgery
(2) choosing a well-balanced diet and following it throughout life
(3) being vaccinated against chicken pox
(4) receiving hormones contained in mother's milk while nursing

**4** Many vaccinations stimulate the immune system by exposing it to
(1) antibodies
(2) enzymes
(3) mutated genes
(4) weakened microbes

**Base your answer to question 5 on the graph below and on your knowledge of biology.**

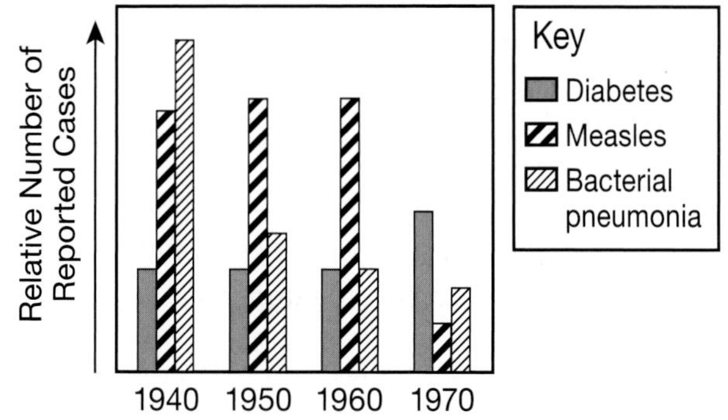


**5** Which statement best explains a change in the incidence of disease in 1970?
(1) Children were vaccinated against measles.
(2) New drugs cured diabetes.
(3) The bacteria that cause pneumonia developed a resistance to drugs.
(4) New technology helped to reduce the incidence of all three diseases.

**6** Vaccinations help prepare the body to fight invasions of a specific pathogen by
(1) inhibiting antigen production
(2) stimulating antibody production
(3) inhibiting white blood cell production
(4) stimulating red blood cell production

**7** The immune system of humans may respond to chemicals on the surface of an invading organism by
(1) releasing hormones that break down these chemicals
(2) synthesizing antibodies that mark these organisms to be destroyed
(3) secreting antibiotics that attach to these organisms
(4) altering a DNA sequence in these organisms

8 Some human white blood cells help destroy pathogenic bacteria by

(1) causing mutations in the bacteria
(2) engulfing and digesting the bacteria
(3) producing toxins that compete with bacterial toxins
(4) inserting part of their DNA into the bacterial cells

9 Fever can indicate that

(1) the pathogen remains on the skin
(2) the body is responding to an infection
(3) a pathogen has been trapped by mucous
(4) the body has recovered from an infection

10 Allergic reactions usually occur when the immune system produces

(1) antibiotics against usually harmless antigens
(2) antigens against usually harmless antibodies
(3) antibodies against usually harmless antigens
(4) enzymes against usually harmless antibodies

11 Which activity is not a function of white blood cells in response to an invasion of the body by bacteria?

(1) engulfing these bacteria
(2) producing antibodies to act against this type of bacteria
(3) preparing for future invasions of this type of bacteria
(4) speeding transmissions of nerve impulses to detect these bacteria

12 Which statement best describes what will most likely happen when an individual receives a vaccination containing a weakened pathogen?

(1) The ability to fight disease will increase due to antibodies received from the pathogen.
(2) The ability to fight the disease caused by the pathogen will increase due to antibody production.
(3) The ability to produce antibodies will decrease after the vaccination.
(4) The ability to resist most types of diseases will increase.

13 A part of the Hepatitis B virus is synthesized in the laboratory. This viral particle can be identified by the immune system as a foreign material but the viral particle is not capable of causing disease. Immediately after this viral particle is injected into a human it

(1) stimulates the production of enzymes that are able to digest the Hepatitis B virus.
(2) triggers the formation of antibodies that protect against the Hepatitis B virus.
(3) synthesizes specific hormones that provide immunity against the Hepatitis B virus.
(4) breaks down key receptor molecules so that the Hepatitis B virus can enter body cells.

**Base your answer to question 14 on the graph below and on your knowledge of biology.**

14 A diagnosis of AIDS is made when the helper T cell count is less than 200 cells per mL of blood. How many months after infection did the onset of AIDS occur?

(1) 18
(2) 39
(3) 54
(4) 69

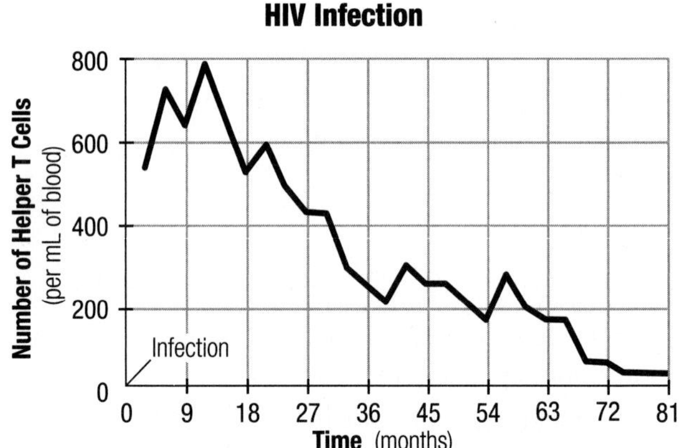


15 HIV causes AIDS by attacking and destroying

(1) B cells.
(2) helper T cells.
(3) neutrophils.
(4) natural killer cells.

**16** The diagram below represents one possible immune response that can occur in the human body. The structures that are part of the immune system are represented by

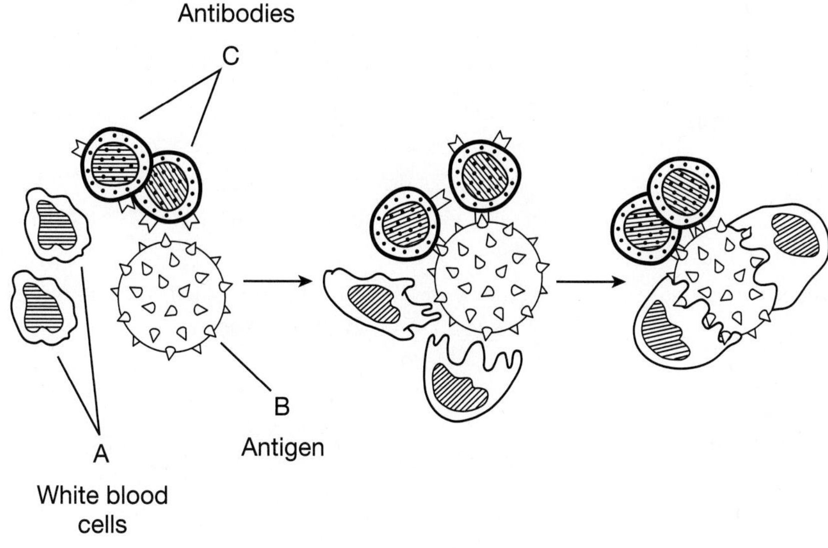


(1) A, only
(2) A and C, only
(3) B and C, only
(4) A, B, and C

**Part C**

**17** Many people become infected with the chicken pox virus during childhood. After recovering from chicken pox, these people are usually immune to the disease for the rest of their lives. However, they may still be infected by viruses that cause other diseases, such as measles.

Discuss the immune response to the chicken pox virus. In your answer, be sure to include:

- the role of antigens in the immune response
- the role of white blood cells in the body's response to the virus
- an explanation of why recovery from an infection with the chicken pox virus will not protect a person from getting a different disease, such as measles
- an explanation of why a chicken pox vaccination usually does not cause a person to become ill with chicken pox

**18** A person who has a defect in the production of B cell or antibodies often does not develop immunity following vaccination. Given what you know about the immune response, explain why this problem occurs.

Chapter 23

# Reproduction and Development

## Preview



## Why It Matters

All people start life as a single fertilized egg. Thus, the story of a fertilized egg's formation and development is the story of how your own life began.

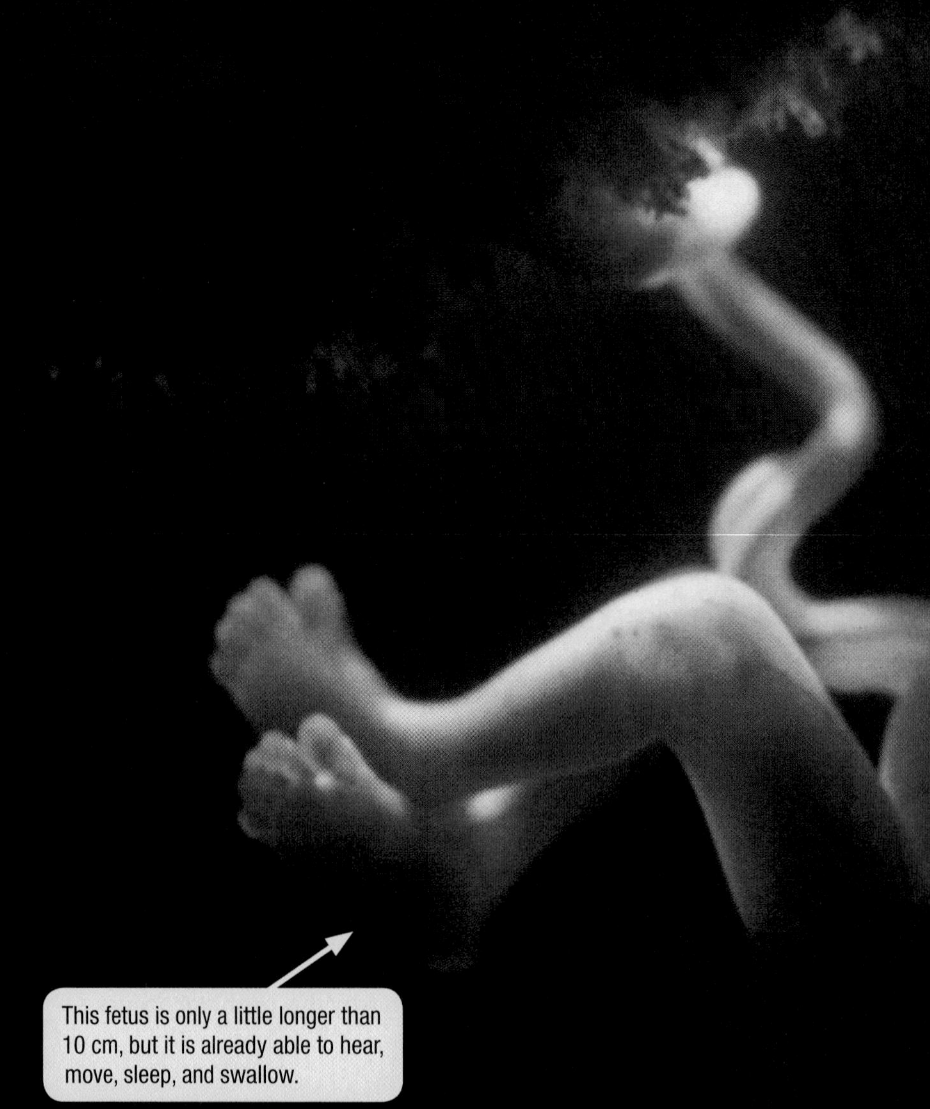

This human fetus has been developing inside its mother for four months.

This fetus is only a little longer than 10 cm, but it is already able to hear, move, sleep, and swallow.

***The Living Environment***

**Standard 4** Students will understand and apply scientific concepts, principles, and theories pertaining to the physical setting and living environment and recognize the historical development of ideas in science.

**Key Idea 4** The continuity of life is sustained through reproduction and development. ***Major Understandings* - 4.1c, 4.1d, 4.1e, 4.1f, 4.1g, 4.1h**

**Key Idea 5** Organisms maintain a dynamic equilibrium that sustains life. ***Major Understandings* - 5.2b, 5.2f**

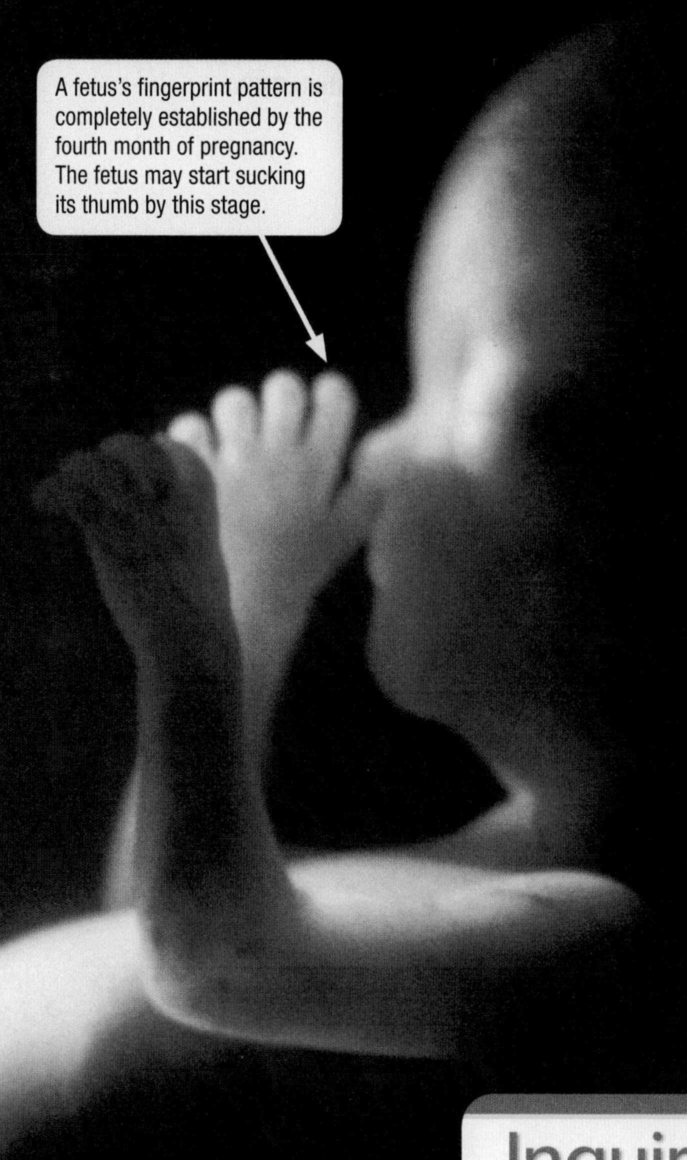

A fetus's fingerprint pattern is completely established by the fourth month of pregnancy. The fetus may start sucking its thumb by this stage.

A four-month-old fetus weighs approximately 454 g. Its eyebrows, eyelashes, and fingernails have formed by this time.

15 min

# InquiryLab

## A Closer Look at Gametes

4.4.1c, 4.4.1f, 4.4.1g

In this lab, you will examine a mammalian ovary and sperm.

### Procedure

1. Place a **human spermatozoa slide** on a **microscope** stage. Examine the smear with low power. Record what you see.
2. Switch to high power. Examine a single sperm. Draw a picture of it.
3. Place a **cross section of the ovary slide** on the microscope stage. Examine it with low power. Locate the circular compartments that are surrounded by a distinct layer of cells.
4. Locate a separate circular mass within these chambers. The mass is the developing egg cell. Draw a picture of this cell.

### Analysis

1. **Compare** the sperm cell's size with the developing egg cell's size.
2. **Explain** how the sperm cell's shape is related to its function.

These reading tools can help you learn the material in this chapter. For more information on how to use these and other tools, see **Appendix: Reading and Study Skills.**

## Using Words

**Word Families** Word families are terms that share a root. The meanings of words within a family differ according to the suffixes, prefixes, and other roots which have been added to the roots.

**Your Turn** Use the information in the table to answer the questions below.

1. What do you think is carried through an oviduct?
2. Who do you think are more likely to get ovarian cancer, men or women?

**Word Parts**

| Word | Part of speech | Meaning |
|---|---|---|
| *ovum* | noun | egg |
| *ovary* | noun | organ that produces eggs |
| *ovulate* | verb | to release an egg from the ovary |

## Using Language

**Recognizing Main Ideas** A main idea is a sentence that states the main point of a paragraph. The main idea is often, but not always, one of the first few sentences of a paragraph. All the other sentences of the paragraph give support to the main idea.

**Your Turn** Find the main idea in the paragraph below.

*Disease-causing pathogens are transmitted in many ways. Some pathogens can be passed by drinking contaminated water. Other pathogens are present in body fluids such as semen. These pathogens can be passed from one person to another through sexual contact.*

## Using FoldNotes

**Pyramid** A pyramid is a unique method for taking notes. The three sides of the pyramid can summarize information in three categories.

**Your Turn** Create a pyramid to summarize the development of a human fetus during the three trimesters.

1. Start with a square sheet of paper. Fold the paper in half diagonally to form a triangle.
2. Fold the triangle in half to form a smaller triangle.
3. Open the paper. The creases of the two folds will have created an X.
4. Using scissors, cut along one of the creases. Start from any corner, and stop at the center point to create two flaps.
5. Use tape or glue to attach one flap on top of the other flap.

Section 1

# The Male Reproductive System

| Key Ideas | Key Terms | Why It Matters |
|---|---|---|
| › Where are male gametes produced?<br>› What path do sperm take to exit the body?<br>› What occurs as sperm move into the urethra?<br>› What happens to sperm after they exit the body? | testis<br>seminiferous tubules<br>epididymis<br>vas deferens<br>prostate gland<br>semen<br>penis | When humans reproduce, they pass their genes to their children. You have about half of your father's genes and half of your mother's genes. |

Humans reproduce sexually by internal fertilization. The roles of the male reproductive system are to produce sperm and to deliver sperm to the female reproductive system.

***The Living Environment***

**Standard 4**

**4.1e** Human reproduction and development are influenced by factors such as gene expression, hormones, and the environment. The reproductive cycle in both males and females is regulated by hormones such as testosterone, estrogen, and progesterone.

**4.1g** The structures and functions of the human male reproductive system, as in other mammals, are designed to produce gametes in testes and make possible the delivery of these gametes for fertilization.

## Sperm Production

**› The male reproductive system has two testes (testicles) that produce the male gametes, *sperm*, and the primary male sex hormone, testosterone.** The **testes** are inside the *scrotum,* a sac that hangs from the body. Normal body temperature, 37 °C, is too high for proper sperm development. The temperature in the scrotum is about 3 °C lower than normal body temperature, so it is ideal for sperm production.

**Seminiferous Tubules** As **Figure 1** shows, testes have hundreds of compartments packed with tightly coiled tubes called **seminiferous tubules.** Sperm cells are produced through meiosis in the seminiferous tubules. Thus, human sperm cells have only 23 chromosomes (the haploid number) instead of the usual 46 chromosomes (the diploid number) found in other body cells. Two hormones released by the pituitary, luteinizing hormone (LH) and follicle-stimulating hormone (FSH), regulate the functioning of the testes. LH causes cells surrounding the seminiferous tubules to secrete testosterone. This hormone, along with FSH, stimulates sperm production. Testosterone also stimulates the growth of facial hair and other male features.

**› Reading Check** ***Describe how hormones regulate sperm production. (See the Appendix for answers to Reading Checks.)***

**testis** (TES TEEZ) the primary male reproductive organ, which produces sperm cells and testosterone

**seminiferous tubule** (sem uh NIF uhr uhs) one of the many tubules in the testis where sperm are produced

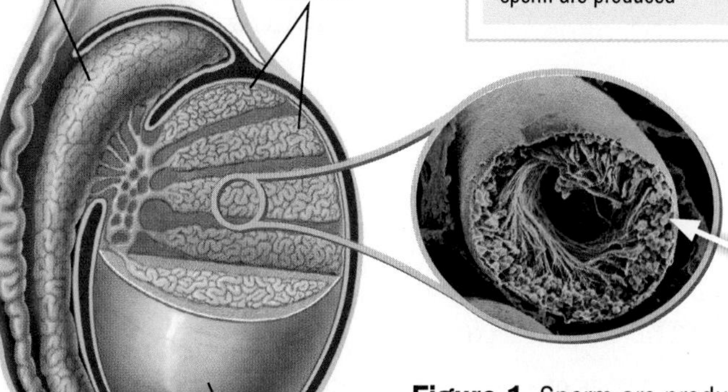


**Figure 1** Sperm are produced in the testes' seminiferous tubules. If these tubules were uncoiled, they would extend the length of six football fields!

Figure 2 The arrows show the path that sperm take as they exit the body. › **After leaving the testes, what structures do sperm move through?**

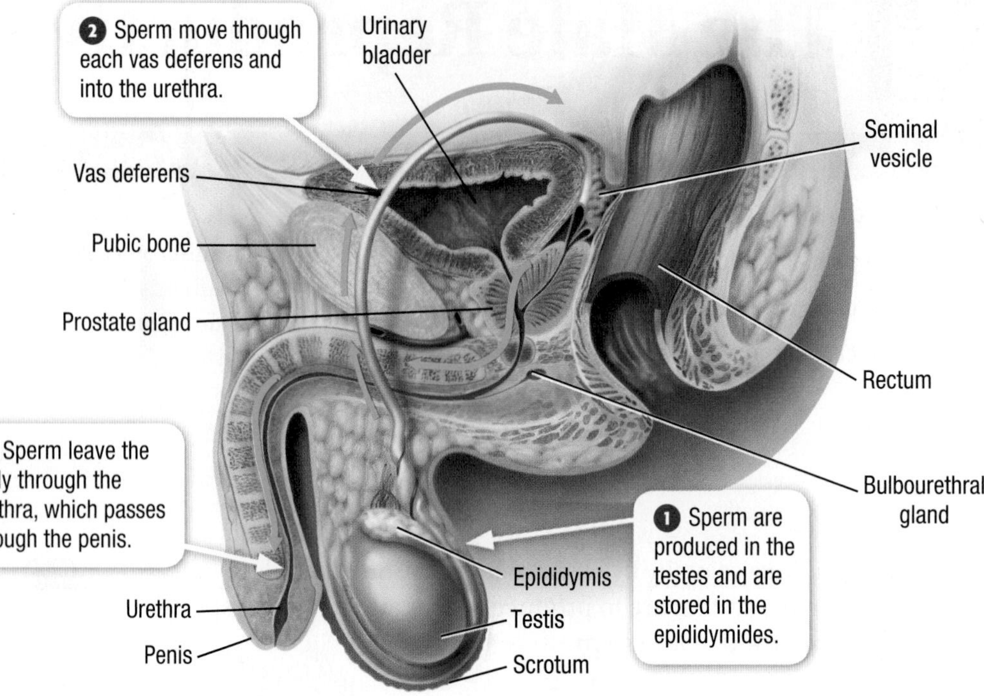

2 Sperm move through each vas deferens and into the urethra.
Urinary bladder
Seminal vesicle
Vas deferens
Pubic bone
Prostate gland
Rectum
3 Sperm leave the body through the urethra, which passes through the penis.
Bulbourethral gland
1 Sperm are produced in the testes and are stored in the epididymides.
Epididymis
Urethra
Testis
Penis
Scrotum

## Sperm's Path Through the Body

Sperm production starts during puberty and continues throughout adulthood. A typical adult male produces several hundred million sperm cells each day. The path sperm travel through the male reproductive system is illustrated in **Figure 2.** When sperm first form in the seminiferous tubules, they are not capable of swimming or of fertilizing an egg. The immature sperm travel along tubes to the epididymis. The **epididymis** is a long coiled tube attached to the top of each testis. Within each of these tubes, the sperm mature and are stored for up to two weeks. From the epididymis, sperm move to another long tube, the **vas deferens.** › **The vas deferens carries sperm into the urethra. Sperm leave the body by passing through the urethra, the same duct through which urine exits the body.** A valve at the bladder-urethra connection prevents urine from entering the urethra when sperm are moving through it.

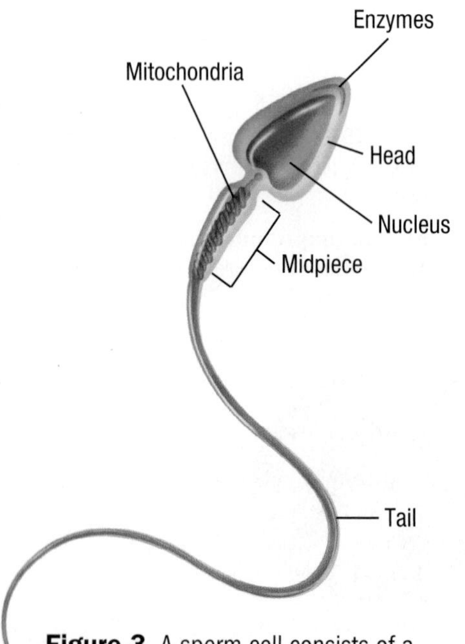

Enzymes
Mitochondria
Head
Nucleus
Midpiece
Tail

Figure 3 A sperm cell consists of a head, a midpiece, and a tail. › **Which part of the sperm cell is able to fertilize an egg?**

**Structure of Mature Sperm** As **Figure 3** shows, a mature sperm cell has a head with very little cytoplasm, a midpiece, and a long tail. Enzymes produced at the tip of the head help the sperm cell to penetrate an egg cell during fertilization. The midpiece contains many mitochondria that supply sperm with the energy they need to propel themselves through the female reproductive system. The tail of a sperm cell is a powerful flagellum that whips back and forth. This whipping motion allows the sperm cell to move. ATP produced within the mitochondria powers the movements of the tail. During fertilization, only the head of a sperm cell enters an egg. As a result, a male's mitochondria are not passed to his offspring.

› **Reading Check** *Why does a sperm cell need mitochondria?*

## Semen

**› As sperm cells move into the urethra, they mix with fluids secreted by the seminal vesicles, the prostate gland, and the bulbourethral glands.** As you can see in **Figure 4,** these fluids nourish the sperm and aid their passage through the female reproductive system. The *seminal vesicles* lie between the bladder and the rectum. These exocrine glands produce a fluid rich in sugars that sperm use for energy. The **prostate gland** is located just below the bladder. This gland secretes an alkaline fluid that helps to balance the acidic pH in the female reproductive system. Fluid from the *bulbourethral glands* neutralizes traces of acidic urine in the urethra and lubricates the path as sperm leave the body. The mixture of these fluids that are secreted with sperm is called **semen.**

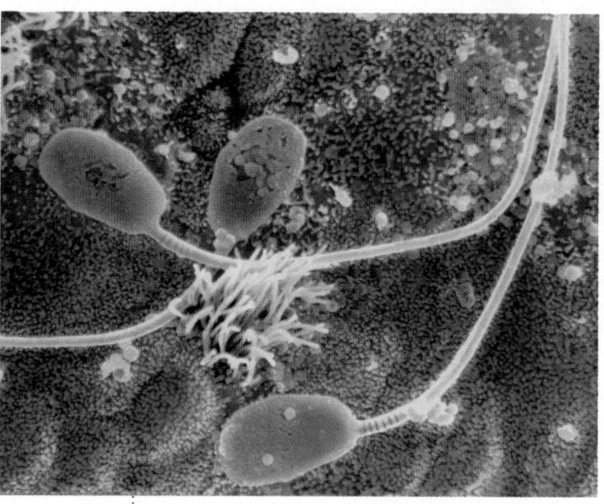

**Figure 4** These sperm are swimming in a mixture of fluids that nourish, protect, and lubricate the sperm.

## Sperm Delivery

The urethra passes through the **penis,** the male organ that deposits sperm into the female reproductive system during sexual intercourse. During arousal, blood flow to the penis increases. The penis contains a high volume of spongy tissue. Small spaces separate the cells of the spongy tissue. Blood collects within these spaces, which causes the penis to become erect. Muscles around each vas deferens contract, moving sperm into the urethra. The ejection of semen out of the penis through the urethra is called *ejaculation.*

**› After semen is deposited in the female reproductive system, sperm swim until they encounter an egg cell or until they die.** If sperm cells are unable to reach an egg, fertilization does not occur. About 3.5 mL of semen, which contains 300–400 million sperm, are expelled during ejaculation. Many sperm die in the acidic environment of the female reproductive system. In order for even one sperm cell to reach and penetrate an egg, the sperm count (sperm per mL of semen) must be high. Males with fewer than 20 million sperm per mL of semen are generally considered sterile.

**› Reading Check** ***Explain why a high sperm count is necessary for fertilization.***

**epididymis** (ep uh DID i mis) the long, coiled tube that is on the surface of a testis and in which sperm mature

**vas deferens** (vas DEF uh renz) a duct through which sperm move from the epididymis to the ejaculatory duct at the base of the penis

**prostate gland** (PRAHS TAYT) a gland in males that contributes to the seminal fluid

**semen** (SEE muhn) the fluid that contains sperm and various secretions produced by the male reproductive organs

**penis** the male organ that transfers sperm to a female and that carries urine out of the body

## Section 1 Review

### › KEY IDEAS

1. **Describe** the testes' function.
2. **State** where sperm go after leaving the epididymis.
3. **List** the components of semen.
4. **Explain** what happens to sperm when they enter a female's body.

### CRITICAL THINKING

5. **Recognizing Relationships** How do secretions by exocrine glands help the delivery of sperm to the female reproductive system? Explain your reasoning.
6. **Inferring Relationships** If a male's left vas deferens is blocked by scar tissue, how will his sperm count most likey be affected? Explain your answer.

### PROBLEM SOLVING

7. **Applying Concepts** Sperm cells contain many more mitochondria than most other types of cells. Why do you think sperm have such a large number of mitochondria?

Section 2

# The Female Reproductive System

| Key Ideas | Key Terms | | Why It Matters |
|---|---|---|---|
| ❯ What are the functions of the ovaries?<br>❯ How does the female body prepare for pregnancy?<br>❯ What changes occur in the female's body when an ovum is not fertilized? | ovary<br>ovum<br>fallopian tube<br>uterus<br>vagina | ovulation<br>menstrual cycle<br>menstruation | Human babies develop inside the female reproductive system. |

***The Living Environment***

**Standard 4**

**4.1e** Human reproduction and development are influenced by factors such as gene expression, hormones, and the environment. The reproductive cycle in both males and females is regulated by hormones such as testosterone, estrogen, and progesterone.

**4.1f** The structures and functions of the human female reproductive system, as in almost all other mammals, are designed to produce gametes in ovaries, allow for internal fertilization, support the internal development of the embryo and fetus in the uterus, and provide essential materials through the placenta, and nutrition through milk for the newborn.

Each month, the female reproductive system prepares for a possible pregnancy by producing a mature egg cell—the female gamete. The mature egg is called an *ovum.* If the ovum is fertilized by a sperm cell, and if the fertilized ovum implants in the uterus, a pregnancy will begin. The fertilized egg will be fed and protected through nine months of development.

## Egg Production

Two **ovaries,** shown in **Figure 5,** are found within the female's abdomen. ❯**The ovaries produce egg cells. Ovaries also secrete estrogen and progesterone, the female sex hormones.** The ovaries of a newborn female contain about 2 million immature egg cells. Egg cells have 23 chromosomes (the haploid number) because eggs, like sperm, are formed through meiosis. This process begins in the egg cells of a female before she is born, but it becomes stalled in prophase of the first meiotic division. When a female reaches puberty, the levels of sex hormone rises. This event allows meiosis to start again. However, only one egg cell completes development each month inside one of an adult female's ovaries.

**Figure 5** The ovaries of the female reproductive system produce egg cells. The uterus nurtures the fetus during pregnancy.

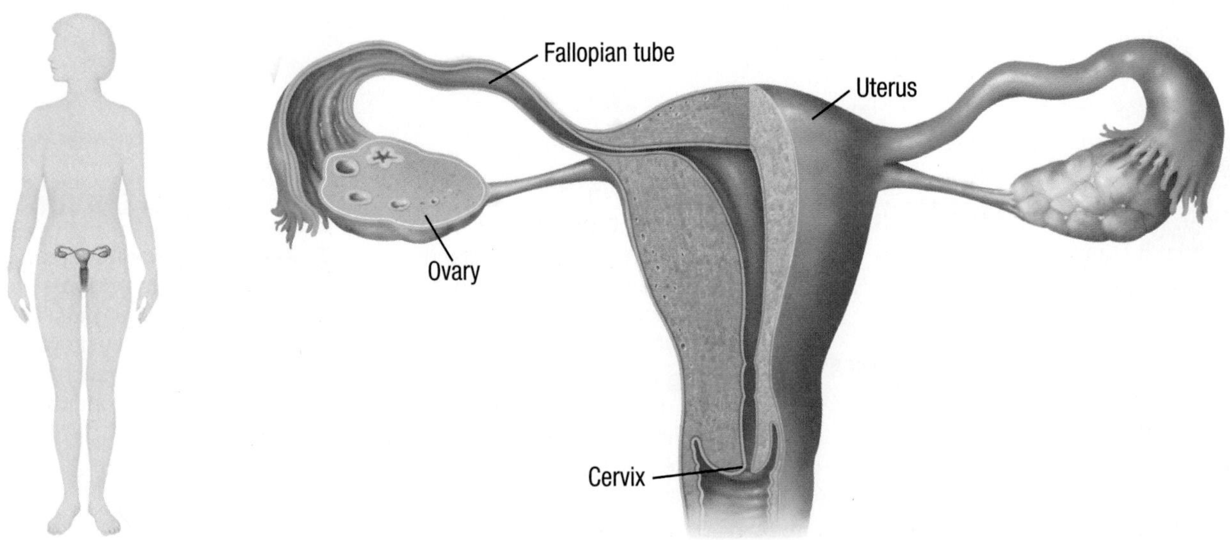

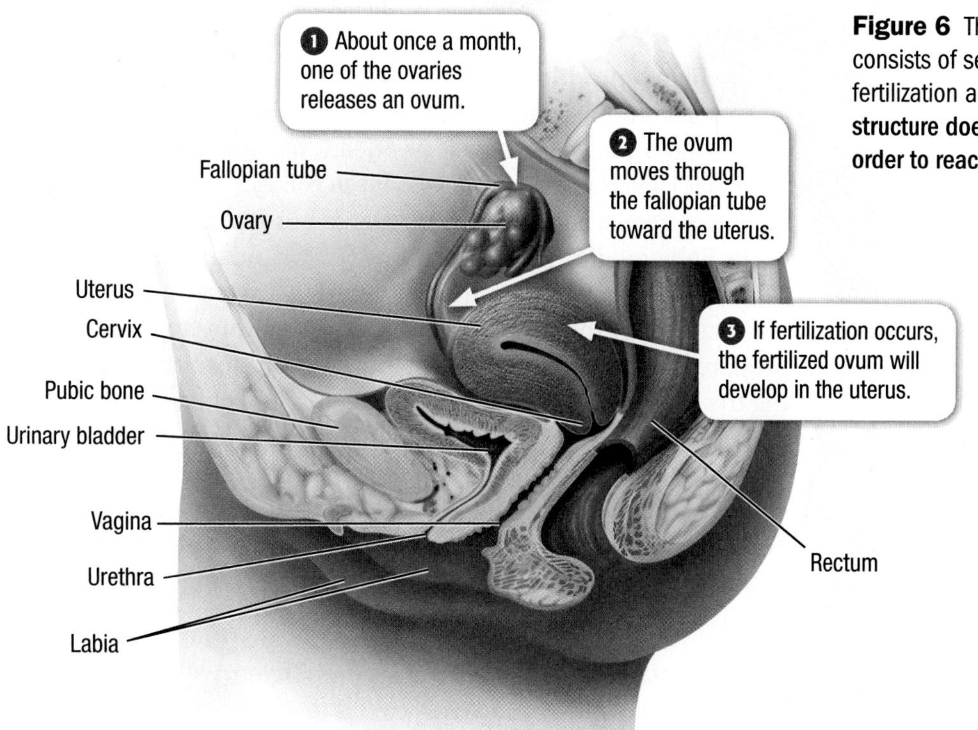

1 About once a month, one of the ovaries releases an ovum.
2 The ovum moves through the fallopian tube toward the uterus.
3 If fertilization occurs, the fertilized ovum will develop in the uterus.
Fallopian tube
Ovary
Uterus
Cervix
Pubic bone
Urinary bladder
Vagina
Urethra
Labia
Rectum

**Figure 6** The female reproductive system consists of several structures that enable fertilization and development. **› What structure does an ovum move through in order to reach the uterus?**

**The Egg's Path** In contrast to the male reproductive system, which produces millions of gametes each day, the female reproductive system produces about one viable egg each month. Although a female is born with about 2 million eggs in her ovaries, only 300–400 egg cells will mature in her lifetime. When an egg cell matures, it is called an **ovum.** An ovum is about 75,000 times larger than a sperm cell and can be seen with the unaided eye.

After an ovum is released from an ovary, cilia sweep the ovum into a fallopian tube. The **fallopian tube,** shown in **Figures 5 and 6,** is a passageway through which an ovum moves from an ovary to the uterus. Rhythmic contractions of the smooth muscles lining the fallopian tube move the ovum down the tube and toward the uterus. An ovum's journey through a fallopian tube usually takes three or four days to complete. If sperm are present in the fallopian tube during this time, the ovum may become fertilized.

**The Vagina and Uterus** The external structures of the female reproductive system are collectively called the *vulva.* The vulva includes the *labia,* which are folds of skin and mucous membranes that cover and protect the opening of the vagina. The **vagina** is a muscular tube that leads from the vulva to the entrance to the uterus, the *cervix.* A sphincter muscle in the cervix controls the opening to the uterus. The **uterus** is a muscular, triangle-shaped organ that is about the size of a small fist. During sexual intercourse, sperm are deposited inside the vagina. If fertilization occurs, the zygote develops into a baby inside the uterus. During childbirth, a baby passes through the cervix and leaves the mother's body through the vagina.

**› Reading Check** ***Where does an ovum become fertilized?***

**ovary** (OH vuh ree) an organ that produces eggs in the female reproductive system

**ovum** (OH vuhm) a mature egg cell

**fallopian tube** (fuh LOH pee uhn) a tube through which eggs move from the ovary to the uterus

**vagina** (vuh JIE nuh) the female reproductive organ that connects the outside of the body to the uterus and that receives sperm during reproduction

**uterus** (YOOT uhr uhs) in female mammals, the hollow, muscular organ in which an embryo embeds itself and develops into a fetus

**Finding Main Ideas** Read the first paragraph on this page. What is the main idea of that paragraph?

## Preparation for Pregnancy

The female reproductive organs are structured to prepare a fertilized egg for development into a baby. This process is called *pregnancy.* **Throughout a female's reproductive years, her body undergoes a hormonal cycle that causes periodic changes. These changes prepare the body in the event that an egg is fertilized.** Two sets of hormones control the female cycle. Follicle-stimulating hormone (FSH) and luteinizing hormone (LH) are secreted by the pituitary gland. Estrogen and progesterone are secreted by the ovaries. All of these hormones tell the body to prepare for fertilization. Each of these hormones has a role in preparing the body for a pregnancy. If fertilization occurs, some of these hormones continue to be released. This process keeps the body from producing another egg and ovulating while a fertilized egg is developing. If fertilization does not occur, production of progesterone and estrogen slows and eventually stops. Thus, the hormonal cycle is complete for that month. After the uterine lining is shed, the cycle begins again.

**ovulation** (AHV yoo LAY shuhn) the release of an ovum from a follicle of the ovary

**The Ovarian Cycle** The ovaries prepare and release an ovum in a series of events collectively called the *ovarian cycle.* This cycle has three parts: the follicular phase, ovulation, and the luteal phase. All three phases are regulated by changes in the levels of the female hormones. The release of an ovum from an ovary is called **ovulation.** **Figure 7** illustrates the process of ovulation. After ovulation, the ovum is drawn into the fallopian tube and begins to move toward the uterus. The lining of the uterus becomes enriched with nutrients and liquids. Although the duration of the ovarian cycle varies, the cycle generally lasts about 28 days.

**Figure 7** Ovulation occurs about midway through the 28-day ovarian cycle.
**What is the function of the follicle?**

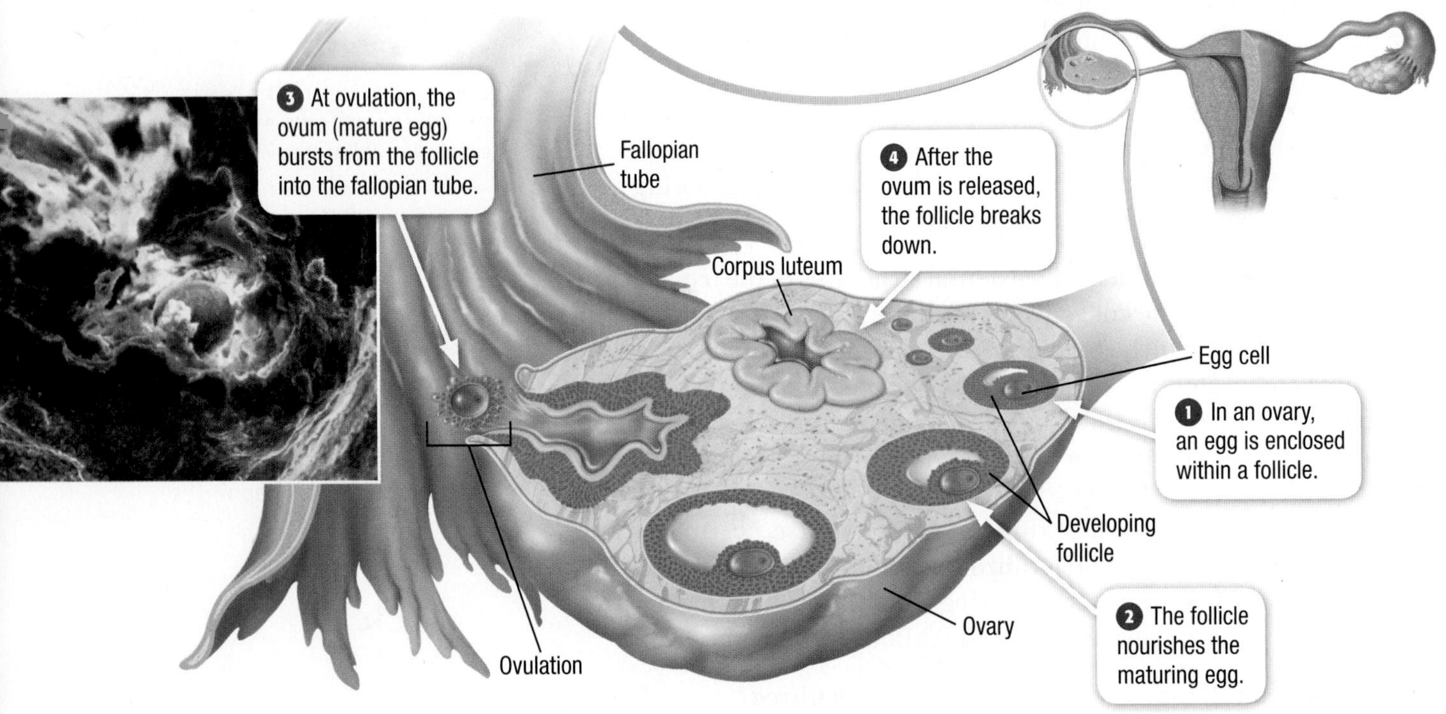

3 At ovulation, the ovum (mature egg) bursts from the follicle into the fallopian tube.
Fallopian tube
4 After the ovum is released, the follicle breaks down.
Corpus luteum
Egg cell
1 In an ovary, an egg is enclosed within a follicle.
Developing follicle
Ovary
2 The follicle nourishes the maturing egg.
Ovulation

**Follicular Phase** In an ovary, egg cells mature within follicles. A *follicle* is a cluster of cells that surrounds an immature egg cell and provides the egg with nutrients. The follicular phase, shown in **Figure 8,** marks the beginning of the ovarian cycle. Levels of hormones in the blood control the maturation of the egg. The egg begins to mature when the pituitary releases FSH into the bloodstream. FSH causes the follicle to develop and to produce estrogen. Estrogen does many things during this phase. First, it aids in the growth of the follicle. Second, it stimulates the lining of the uterus to thicken. Finally, it causes the anterior pituitary to secrete more LH. The rise in LH leads to ovulation.

**Ovulation** Ovulation occurs when a mature egg bursts out of a follicle. At first, a small increase in the level of estrogen slows the release of FSH from the pituitary. This kind of interaction, in which an increase in one hormone results in a decrease in another hormone, is called *negative feedback.* As the follicle nears maturity, it secretes larger and larger amounts of estrogen. The pituitary responds to the rising level of estrogen in the blood by causing the anterior pituitary gland to secrete more LH. This interaction, in which an increase in one hormone results in an increase in another hormone, is called *positive feedback.* The large amount of LH in the bloodstream causes the egg cell to complete its first meiotic division. LH also causes the follicle to burst. Ovulation occurs when the follicle bursts and the ovum is released.

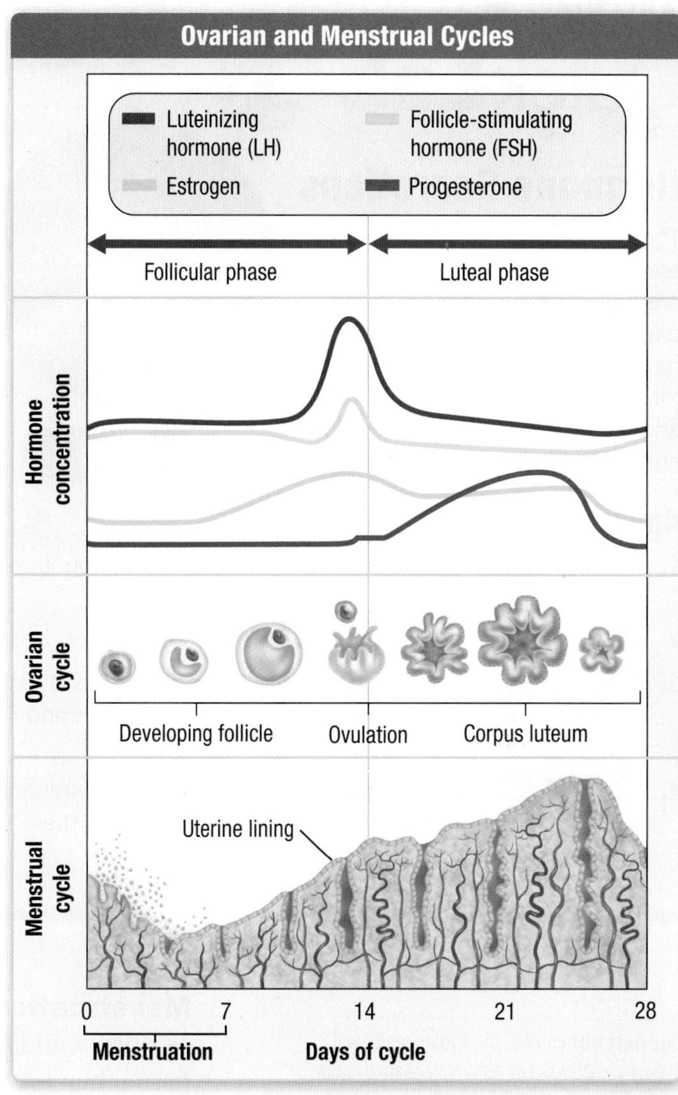


**Figure 8** The ovarian cycle is regulated by hormones produced by the hypothalamus and the pituitary gland. The menstrual cycle is regulated by hormones produced by the follicle and the corpus luteum. **During which stage of the ovarian cycle does the corpus luteum form?**

**Luteal Phase** After ovulation, LH causes the cells of the ruptured follicle to grow and fill the cavity of the follicle. The new structure which forms is called a *corpus luteum.* Therefore, this stage of the ovarian cycle is called the *luteal phase.* The corpus luteum is a mass of follicle cells that acts like an endocrine gland. This mass of cells secretes estrogen and progesterone. These hormones turn on the growth of new blood vessels in the uterus. They also stimulate the storage of fluids and nutrients in the lining of the uterus, which causes the lining to thicken further. In addition, the estrogen and progesterone inhibit the release of more FSH and LH by the pituitary by negative feedback. Levels of FSH and LH in the blood fall, which prevents the formation of new follicles (and a second opportunity for fertilization) within a single ovarian cycle. The luteal phase lasts about 14 days. If an egg does not become embedded in the lining of the uterus during this period, the lining will be shed in a process known as *menstruation.*

**ACADEMIC VOCABULARY**

**mature** to reach full growth or development

**Reading Check** ***What event causes the ovarian cycle to enter the luteal phase?***

Data

# QuickLab

15 min

4.4.1e, 4.4.1f

## Hormone Secretions

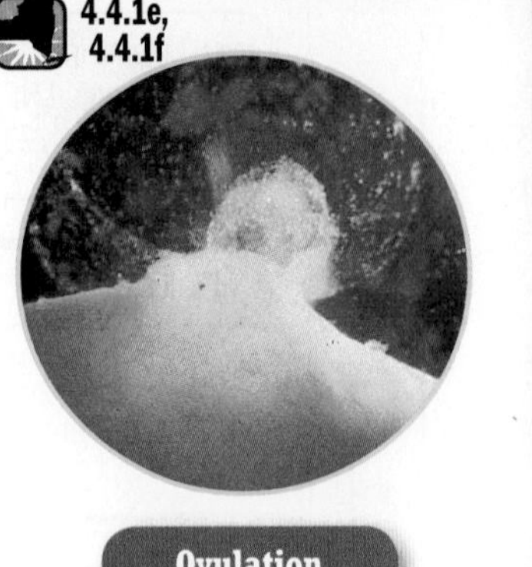
Ovulation

The ovarian and menstrual cycles are regulated by hormones secreted by the hypothalamus, the pituitary, and the ovaries. Feedback mechanisms play a major role in these cycles. Use **Figure 8** and the explanation in the text to answer the following questions.

### Analysis

1. **Identify** the hormones that are secreted in large amounts prior to ovulation.
2. **Describe** the effect of estrogen on the secretion of LH.
3. CRITICAL THINKING **Analyzing Concepts** What type of feedback mechanism causes a decrease in the secretion of LH and FSH during the luteal phase?
4. CRITICAL THINKING **Analyzing Concepts** What type of feedback mechanism causes the surge of LH secretion during the follicular phase?

## Menstrual Cycle

The series of changes that prepares the egg for fertilization is the ovarian cycle. The series of changes that prepares the uterus for a possible pregnancy is the **menstrual cycle.** The menstrual cycle lasts about 28 days and is driven by the changing levels of estrogen and progesterone during the ovarian cycle. Before ovulation, increasing levels of estrogen cause the lining of the uterus to thicken with blood vessels. This prepares the uterus for the possible implantation of a fertilized egg. The blood vessels will nourish the egg as it develops into an embryo.

After ovulation, high levels of both estrogen and progesterone cause further development and maintenance of the uterine lining. **› If pregnancy does not occur, the levels of estrogen and progesterone fall. This decrease causes the lining of the uterus to be shed.** The menstrual cycle ends at the same time as the hormonal cycle ends. Both cycles then begin again. Every month, the uterus is preparing for pregnancy.

**menstrual cycle** the female reproductive cycle, characterized by a monthly change of the lining of the uterus and the discharge of blood

**menstruation** the discharge of blood and discarded tissue from the uterus during the menstrual cycle

**Menstruation** When the lining of the uterus is shed, blood vessels break and bleeding results. A mixture of blood and discarded tissue then leaves the body through the vagina. This process, called **menstruation,** usually begins about 14 days after ovulation and lasts for three to five days. The ovarian and menstrual cycles eventually stop, usually when a woman is between the ages of 45 and 55. The end of menstruation, called *menopause,* marks the end of the child-bearing phase of a woman's life.

**› Reading Check** ***What causes menstruation to occur?***

## Section 2 Review

### › KEY IDEAS

1. **Identify** the functions of the ovaries.
2. **Summarize** the path of an egg through the female reproductive system.
3. **Compare** the roles of LH and FSH in the ovarian cycle.
4. **Explain** how the menstrual cycle is related to the ovarian cycle.

### CRITICAL THINKING

5. **Recognizing Relationships** What causes the lining of the uterus to thicken and then to be shed during the menstrual cycle?
6. **Relating Concepts** How could the maturation of an egg cell in an ovary be halted?

### MATH SKILLS

7. **Problem Solving** A woman does not ovulate while she is pregnant. Pregnancy generally lasts nine months. If a woman goes through three pregnancies, how many fewer mature eggs will she release in her lifetime than if she never became pregnant?

Section

# 3 Human Development

| Key Ideas | Key Terms | Why It Matters |
|---|---|---|
| ❯ How does fertilization occur?<br>❯ What important events occur in the first trimester of pregnancy?<br>❯ What important event occurs at the end of the third trimester of pregnancy? | embryo<br>implantation<br>fetus | All humans go through the same developmental stages as they change from a single fertilized egg into a complex organism composed of billions of cells. |

Development begins with a single diploid cell. Billions of other cells arise from this one cell. During pregnancy, the uterus provides protection and nourishment to the developing human being.

## Fertilization

If sperm are present in the female reproductive system within a few days after ovulation, fertilization may occur. To fertilize an ovum, a sperm cell must move up into a fallopian tube. ❯ **During fertilization, a sperm cell penetrates an ovum by releasing enzymes from the tip of its head. These enzymes break down the jellylike outer layers of the ovum. The head of the sperm enters the ovum, and the nuclei of the ovum and sperm fuse together.** This fusion produces a diploid cell called a *zygote.*

**Cleavage and Implantation** The zygote undergoes a series of mitotic divisions known as cleavage, as **Figure 9** shows. Cleavage produces many smaller cells—first two cells, then four, then eight, and so on. The resulting clump of cells is called an **embryo.** Cleavage continues as the embryo moves toward the uterus. By the time it reaches the uterus, the embryo is a hollow ball of cells called a *blastocyst.* About six days after fertilization, the blastocyst burrows into the lining of the uterus in an event called **implantation.**

***The Living Environment***
**Standard 4**

**4.1c** The processes of meiosis and fertilization are key to sexual reproduction in a wide variety of organisms. The process of meiosis results in the production of eggs and sperm which each contain half of the genetic information. During fertilization, gametes unite to form a zygote, which contains the complete genetic information for the offspring.

**4.1d** The zygote may divide by mitosis and differentiate to form the specialized cells, tissues, and organs of multicellular organisms.

**4.1f** The structures and functions of the human female reproductive system, as in almost all other mammals, are designed to produce gametes in ovaries, allow for internal fertilization, support the internal development of the embryo and fetus in the uterus, and provide essential materials through the placenta, and nutrition through milk for the newborn.

**4.1h** In humans, the embryonic development of essential organs occurs in early stages of pregnancy. The embryo may encounter risks from faults in its genes and from its mother's exposure to environmental factors such as inadequate diet, use of alcohol/drugs/tobacco, other toxins, or infections throughout her pregnancy.

**embryo** (EM bree OH) an organism in an early stage of development; in humans, a developing individual from first cleavage through the next eight weeks

**implantation** the process by which a blastocyst embeds itself in the lining of the uterus

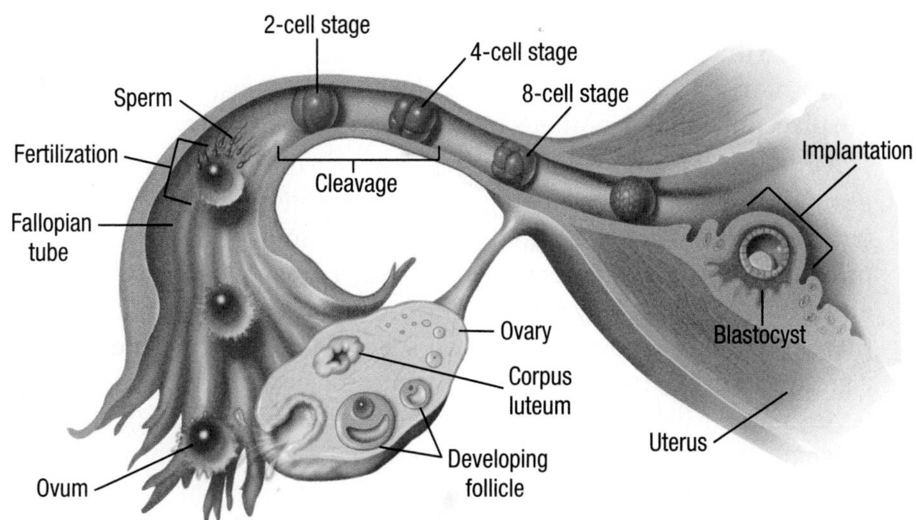


**Figure 9** Fertilization, cleavage, and implantation may occur after ovulation. ❯ **What has the embryo become by the time it reaches the uterus?**

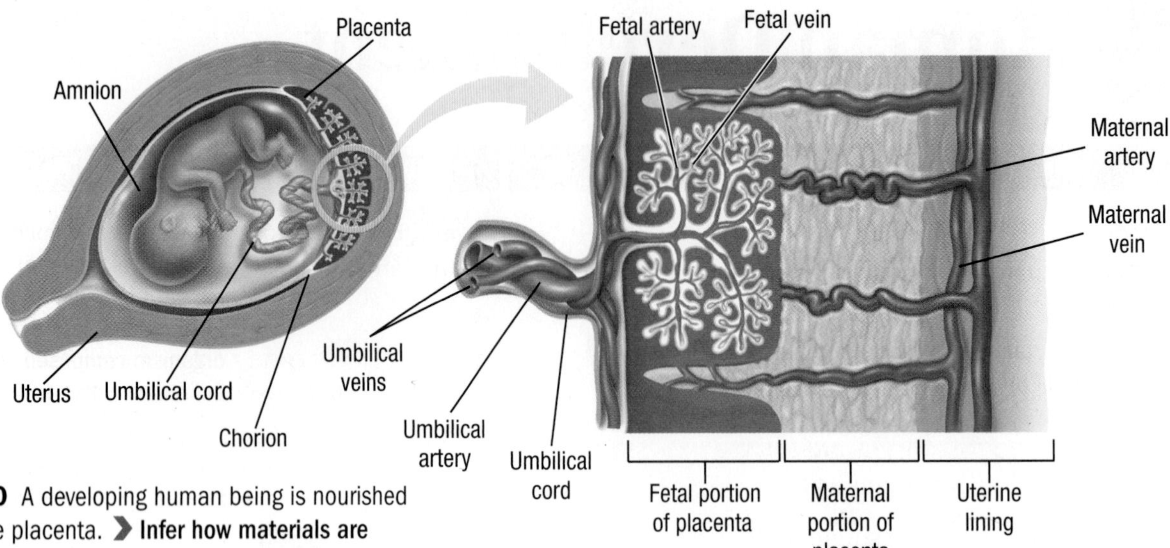


**Figure 10** A developing human being is nourished through the placenta. **Infer how materials are exchanged in the placenta.**

## First Trimester

Human development takes about nine months—a period known as *gestation,* or pregnancy. Pregnancy begins when the embryo implants itself in the wall of the uterus. The nine months of pregnancy are typically divided into three *trimesters,* or three-month periods. The most important events of development occur in the first trimester. **All of the embryo's organ systems, as well as the supportive membranes that feed and protect the embryo, develop during the first trimester of pregnancy.**

**fetus** a developing human from the end of the eighth week after fertilization until birth

**Supportive Membranes** Membranes that will protect and feed the embryo begin to develop very shortly after implantation. One membrane, the *amnion,* encloses and protects the embryo. Another membrane, the *chorion,* interacts with the uterus to form the placenta. The umbilical cord connects the amnion with the placenta. The placenta, shown in **Figure 10,** is the structure through which the mother feeds the embryo. The placenta forms by the third week of pregnancy. The mother's blood does not mix with the blood of the embryo. Instead, nutrients in the mother's blood diffuse through the placenta. The nutrients are carried to the embryo through blood vessels in the umbilical cord, which is fully formed by the sixth week of pregnancy. The waste products of the embryo diffuse back through the placenta into the mother's blood.

Other substances, including drugs, can also diffuse through the placenta. Thus, if the mother ingests any harmful substances, the embryo is also affected. Pregnant women who smoke may have premature births and underweight babies. Pregnant women who abuse alcohol, especially during early pregnancy, may have babies that suffer from fetal alcohol syndrome. Fetal alcohol syndrome is a group of birth defects which may include facial deformation and severe mental, behavioral, and physical retardation. All drugs that are inappropriate for infants should be avoided, or used only with a physician's prescription, throughout pregnancy.

**Recognizing Main ideas** How do the text heads on this page relate to the main ideas of the paragraphs following the heads? Which sentence states the main idea for each paragraph?

**Embryonic Development** As the placenta takes shape, the inner cells of the blastocyst form the three primary tissue layers of the embryo—endoderm, mesoderm, and ectoderm. By the end of the third week, blood vessels and the digestive system begin to develop. The embryo is about 2 mm long. In the fourth week, arm and leg buds form. By the end of the fourth week, all of the major organs begin to form, and the heart begins to beat. The embryo has more than doubled its length. During the second month, the final stages of embryonic development take place. The arms and legs take shape. By the end of the second month, the embryo is about 25 mm long and weighs about 1 g.

**Fetal Development** From the end of the eighth week after fertilization until childbirth, the developing human is called a **fetus.** By the end of the first trimester, the sex of the fetus can be distinguished. The fetus has recognizable body features, as **Figure 11** shows. The fetus's major organ systems continue to develop.

Hands-On

## QuickLab

15 min

### An Amniotic Shock Absorber 4.4.1f

In this lab, you will model how amniotic fluid serves as a shock absorber for a developing fetus.

#### Procedure

1. Stand a paper clip upright in a base of clay. Tap the top of the clip to see how much force is needed to topple it.
2. Fill a sandwich bag with water. Place the clip within its clay base at the center of the water-filled bag, and seal the bag. Gently tap the bag. Does this impact topple the clip?

#### Analysis

1. **Compare** the parts of this model to an actual amnion.
2. CRITICAL THINKING **Analyzing Concepts** Explain how the water-filled bag affected the force needed to topple the paper clip.

> **Reading Check** *During which trimester do the embryo's organs begin to form?*

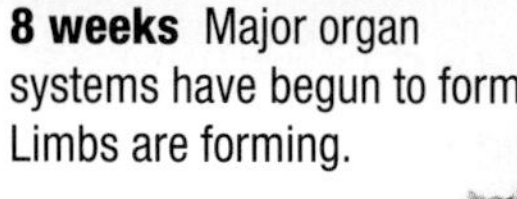

**8 weeks** Major organ systems have begun to form. Limbs are forming.

**12 weeks** Skin and nails form. Organs are developing.

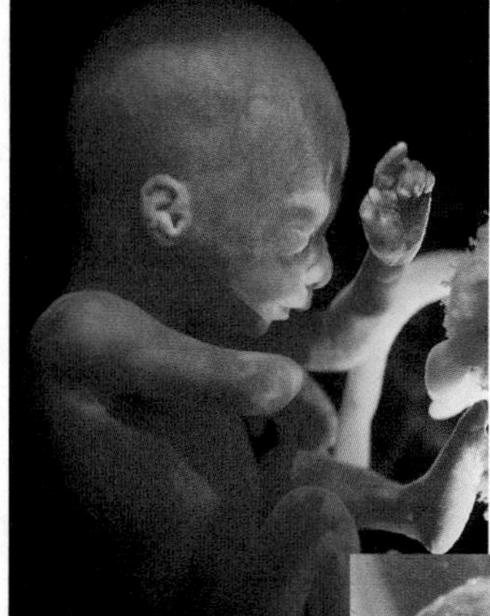

**21 weeks** Hair forms on body and head. Facial features are developing.

**8 months** Subcutaneous tissue is forming. Fetal development nears completion.

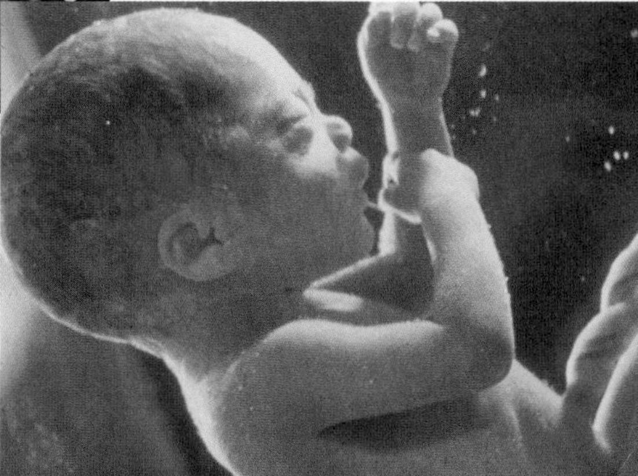

**Figure 11** Near the end of the third trimester, a fetus doubles and then triples in size. > **How does the 8-week-old fetus compare with the 12-week-old fetus?**

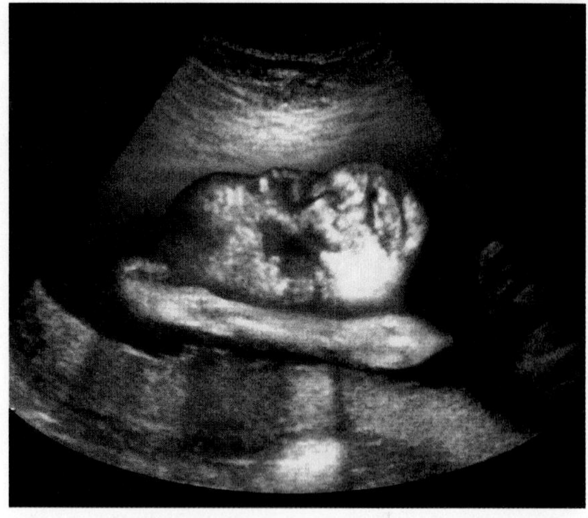

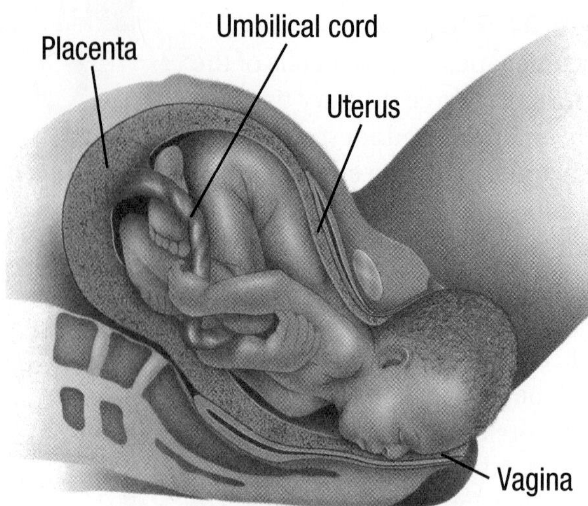


**Figure 12** Doctors use ultrasound imaging to monitor a fetus's growth. The fetus shown in this ultrasound (left) is near birth. During childbirth (right), the fetus exits the mother's body through the vagina. **Why is it important that the baby exit the mother head first?**

## Second and Third Trimesters

During the second trimester (4–6 months) the fetus grows to about 15 cm in length. Bone development continues. Toenails and fingernails form. The brain develops and begins to control muscle responses. By the end of the fifth month, the fetus begins to move. It stretches its arms and legs, and may even suck its thumb. The mother may be able to feel these movements. The fetus has a fast heartbeat. Doctors may use ultrasound images, such as the one shown in **Figure 12,** to monitor the fetus's growth.

In the third trimester (7–9 months) the fetus gains about 2.5 kg. The brain and nerves develop. The fetus can hear, smell, and see light. The lungs mature. The fetus moves into a head down position during the ninth month, and becomes less active. **By the end of the third trimester, the fetus is able to live outside the mother's body. The fetus leaves the mother's body in a process called labor, which usually lasts several hours.** During labor, the walls of the uterus contract and expel the fetus from the uterus, as shown in **Figure 12.** The fetus leaves the mother's body through the vagina. Further contractions of the uterus expel the placenta and the umbilical cord.

SCLINKS.
www.scilinks.org
Topic: Before Birth
Code: HX80140

**Reading Check** *How does the fetus change in the third trimester?*

## Section 3 Review

**KEY IDEAS**

1. **Summarize** the events in development that occur during fertilization.
2. **Explain** what important events occur in the first trimester of pregnancy.
3. **Describe** the events that occur at the end of the third trimester.

**CRITICAL THINKING**

4. **Relating Concepts** Why can some drugs be harmful to a fetus if the mother takes them while she is pregnant?
5. **Predicting Outcomes** What might happen if more than one egg were released from the ovaries prior to fertilization?

**ALTERNATIVE ASSESSMENT**

6. **Sequencing Events** Draw a timeline that illustrates the developmental changes that occur during each of the three trimesters of pregnancy. Use photos, drawings, and/or charts to illustrate your timeline.

Section 4

# Sexually Transmitted Infections

| Key Ideas | Key Terms | Why It Matters |
|---|---|---|
| ❯ How can you avoid being infected by an STI?<br>❯ What are some common STIs in the United States? | **genital herpes**<br>**pelvic inflammatory disease** | STIs are some of the most common infectious diseases in the world. |

Diseases spread by sexual contact are called sexually transmitted infections (STIs). Some of the most common STIs in the United States are listed in **Figure 13.**

*The Living Environment*
**Standard 4**
**5.2b** Viruses, bacteria, fungi, and other parasites may infect plants and animals and interfere with normal life functions.
**5.2f** Some viral diseases, such as AIDS, damage the immune system, leaving the body unable to deal with multiple infectious agents and cancerous cells.

## STI Transmission and Treatment

Disease-causing pathogens are transmitted in many ways. Pathogens present in body fluids, such as semen, can be passed from one person to another through sexual contact. STIs can be caused by both viruses and bacteria. ❯ **Abstinence is the only sure way to protect yourself from contracting an STI.** Early detection and treatment are necessary to prevent serious consequences that can result from infection. Some viral STIs can be treated with antiviral medication. Many bacterial STIs can be treated and cured with antibiotics. However, early symptoms of most bacterial STIs are very mild and often are not detected. Untreated bacterial STIs can cause sterility in both men and women.

❯ **Reading Check** *How are different kinds of STIs treated?*

**Figure 13** The table shows the estimated new cases of STIs per year for the entire American population.

**Sexually Transmitted Infections**

| Infection | New cases per year | Symptoms |
|---|---|---|
| Genital HPV | 5,500,000 | warts on genital or anal region |
| Trichomoniasis | 5,000,000 | often no symptoms in males; yellow-green vaginal discharge with strong odor in females |
| Chlamydia | 3,000,000 | painful urination and penile discharge in males; abdominal pain and vaginal discharge in females |
| Genital herpes | 1,000,000 | painful blisters around the genital region; flulike symptoms |
| Gonorrhea | 650,000 | painful urination and penile discharge in males; abdominal pain and vaginal discharge in females |
| Hepatitis B | 120,000 | flulike symptoms and yellowing of skin |
| Syphilis | 70,000 | sores on penis in males; sores in vagina or on cervix in females; fever and rash; destruction of body tissue |
| HIV/AIDS | 40,000 | immune-system failure and susceptibility to infections |

Source: Centers for Disease Control and Prevention

Data

# QuickLab

15 min

## STI Rates 4.5.2f

STIs are the most widespread type of infection in the United States. Use **Figure 13** and the explanation in the text to complete the following activities.

### Analysis

1. **Draw** a bar graph showing new cases of STIs.
2. **Identify** the name of the pathogen that causes the most common STI.
3. CRITICAL THINKING **Predicting Patterns** Calculate the number of Americans that each of the STIs shown in **Figure 13** will infect within five years if the estimated number of new cases per year remains constant.
4. CRITICAL THINKING **Analyzing Data** Genital herpes is not the STI with the most new cases per year, but it is the most common STI in the United States. Suggest a possible reason for this.

SCILINKS.
www.scilinks.org
Topic: Sexually Transmitted Diseases
Code: HX81388

## Common STIs

**The most common STIs include genital herpes, genital HPV, trichomoniasis, AIDS, hepatitis B, chlamydia, and gonorrhea.** For example, around one in every five Americans has had a genital herpes infection.

**Genital Herpes** At a rate of 22,300 cases per 100,000 Americans, **genital herpes** is the most common STI in the United States. This STI is caused by herpes simplex virus (HSV). About 70% of genital herpes infections are caused by HSV-2. The rest are caused by HSV-1, which more commonly causes cold sores around and inside the mouth. Symptoms of genital herpes include periodic outbreaks of painful blisters, such as those shown in **Figure 14.** Symptoms may also include flulike aches and fever. Antiviral drugs can temporarily get rid of the blisters caused by genital herpes, but they cannot remove HSV from the body. Although genital herpes is not life threatening, it can have serious consequences. Women who have genital herpes have a greater risk of developing cervical cancer.

**Figure 14** The blisters of genital herpes may appear on or near the genitals.

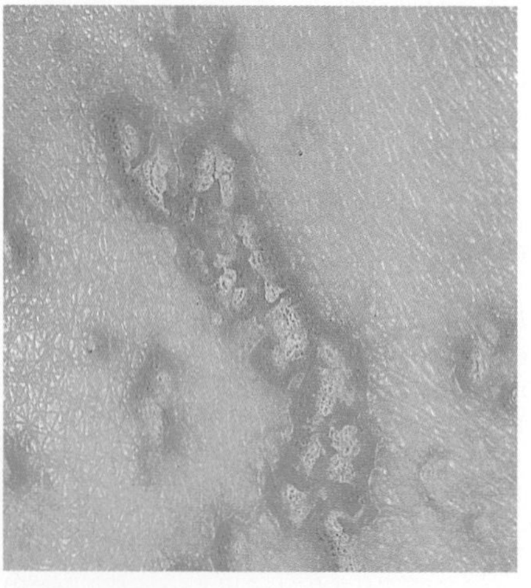

**Genital HPV** Human papilloma virus (HPV) causes genital warts and other symptoms. Current statistics indicate that 50% of all Americans will be infected by genital HPV at some point in their lives. Most people who are infected with HPV show no symptoms and do not know that they are infected. Some people who have HPV infections get genital warts. Some experience cell changes in the cervix, which could lead to cancer. No therapy has been shown to get rid of the virus; the infection often comes back following treatment.

**Trichomoniasis** Trichomoniasis is the only major STI caused by a protistan parasite rather than by a virus or a bacterium. Some men with this infection have a mild discharge and temporary irritation inside the penis. Most men, though, have no symptoms. Women with trichomoniasis often have vaginal itching and a yellow-green vaginal discharge with a strong odor. Trichomoniasis can usually be cured with medication.

**AIDS** AIDS is a fatal disease caused by the human immunodeficiency virus (HIV). HIV infection occurs most commonly through sexual contact. HIV attacks the immune system by destroying white blood cells. People who have AIDS usually die from infections that generally affect only people who have weakened immune systems.

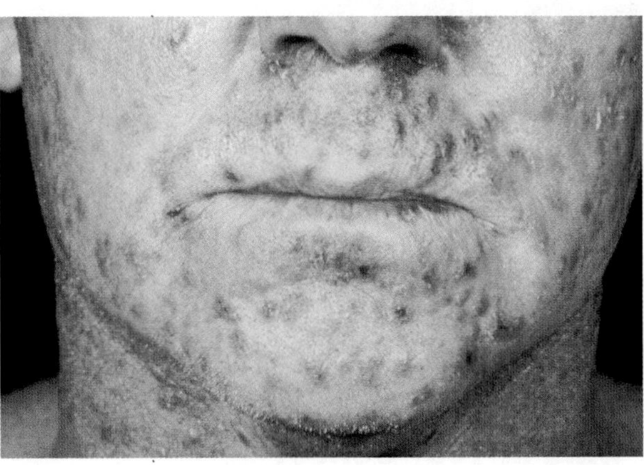

**Figure 15** The sores on this man's face are caused by syphilis. Syphilis also eats away at other body tissues, including skeletal tissue.

**Hepatitis B** Of the five forms of hepatitis, form B is the most common in the United States. Like HIV, hepatitis B is a viral STI that is transmitted typically through sexual contact or contaminated needles. The virus infects the liver and damages liver cells. Any injury to the liver is a problem, because the liver fights infections and removes poisons from the body. A vaccine is available for hepatitis B, and can give unexposed people immunity to the virus. The vaccine also helps to treat people who have been exposed to the virus. However, the vaccine cannot cure hepatitis B.

**Academic Vocabulary**

**available** that can be used

**Chlamydia and Gonorrhea** Chlamydia and gonorrhea are the most common bacterial STIs in the United States. Some people show no symptoms. Some men experience painful urination, and some women experience vaginal discharge. Gonorrhea may cause pus to discharge from the penis. Chlamydia (and less often, gonorrhea) can cause scar tissue to form inside the fallopian tubes.

**Pelvic Inflammatory Disease** Most cases of **pelvic inflammatory disease** (PID) result from gonorrhea or chlamydia infections. A normal fallopian tube has a highly-folded lining and many spaces through which gametes can pass. The spaces in a fallopian tube of a woman who has PID may become blocked with scar tissue.

**Syphilis** Syphilis is a serious bacterial STI that has a low incidence level in the United States, but is still common in much of the rest of the world. Syphilis usually begins with the appearance of a small sore on the genitals a few weeks after infection. Fever and rash are also common symptoms. These symptoms disappear without treatment. Years later, however, untreated syphilis begins to destroy body tissues, including bone and skin tissue, as you can see in **Figure 15.**

**genital herpes** a sexually transmitted infection that is caused by a herpes simplex virus

**pelvic inflammatory disease** a sexually transmitted infection of the upper female reproductive system, including the uterus, ovaries, fallopian tubes, and other structures

## Section 4 Review

### KEY IDEAS

1. **State** the best way to avoid becoming infected by an STI.
2. **List** three symptoms of genital herpes.
3. **Identify** which bacterial STIs are the most common in the United States.

### CRITICAL THINKING

4. **Making Inferences** Why is a symptomless STI just as dangerous as an STI that exhibits symptoms? Explain your answer.
5. **Applying Information** Do you think that an STI can be transmitted from a mother to her fetus? Explain your answer.

### ALTERNATIVE ASSESSMENT

6. **Making Bar Graphs** Research the rate of incidence of STIs among teenagers compared to the rate of incidence in the rest of the population. Use the information you discover to construct a bar graph.

Why It Matters

# Seeing Double

REAL WORLD

Multiple births occur when two or more children are carried during the same pregnancy. In humans, the most common type of multiple births occurs when the mother gives birth to two children, which are also known as twins. About 3% of all births in the United States result in twins.

## Twins in Your Genes?

There are two types of twins: identical and fraternal. While there does not seem to be any genetic basis for identical twins, fraternal twins are another matter. Women with fraternal twins in their families are more likely to give birth to fraternal twins. Also, the frequency of fraternal twinning has increased over the last 20 years, probably due to the increased use of fertility drugs.

**Identical Twins** Identical twins form when a single sperm fertilizes a single egg. The developing embryo then divides in two. Identical twins are always the same gender and are genetically identical.



**Fraternal Twins** Fraternal twins form when two sperm fertilize two separate eggs. Fraternal twins can be the same or different genders and are as different genetically as any ordinary siblings.

**Triplets** While twinning is the most common type of multiple birth, other multiples do occur. About 0.1% of all births are triplets.

**Research** It is common for twins to develop their own language. Find out more about this occurence, which is known as cryptophasia or idioglossia.

Inquiry

# Chapter 23 Lab

15 min

## Objectives

- Analyze how different materials affect the pattern of water waves.
- Form a hypothesis about how a viscous fluid alters the wave.

## Materials

- lab apron
- shallow pan
- metric ruler
- water, tap
- corn syrup
- timer
- large spoon
- various objects such as a wooden block, a domino, and paper clips

## Safety

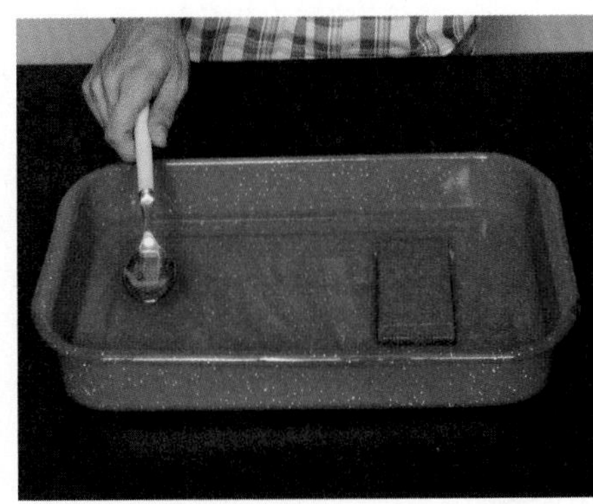

# Sonography

Sonography is a medical technique that is frequently used to obtain images of a developing fetus. During this process, ultrasonic waves are directed into the uterus. Upon hitting hard surfaces, the waves reflect. These returning waves produce a distinct pattern, which is used to generate an image of the fetus. In this lab, you will explore the reflection and bending of water waves. You will use your data to develop a better understanding of sonography as a tool in prenatal observation.

## Preparation

1. SCIENTIFIC METHODS **State the Problem** How does a viscous fluid affect the wave's pattern in a model of a sonogram?
2. SCIENTIFIC METHODS **Form a Hypothesis** Form a testable hypothesis that explains how corn syrup affects the wave pattern of the model.

## Procedure

1. Put on a lab apron. Place a shallow pan on a flat, level surface. Carefully fill it with water to a depth of about 0.5 cm.
2. Position a spoon at one end of the tray. Keeping the spoon level over the water's surface, gently tap down once on the water. Be sure that your fingertips don't touch the water. What do you observe? Continue tapping to form a regular rhythm.
3. Place a domino or other target with a flat edge midway in the tray. Tap out a regular rhythm. What do you observe?
4. Alter the distance between the target and the spoon. Tap again.
5. Use a variety of targets with different shapes including curved and angular edges. Note how these targets affect the return wave.
6. Place several drops of corn syrup in the center of the tray. Observe how this more dense liquid affects the waves that pass through it.
7. Clean up your materials according to your teacher's instructions. Wash your hands before leaving the lab.

## Analyze and Conclude

1. **Describing Observations** What happened to the wave when it struck a hard surface? Did the wave vary with the type of object?
2. SCIENTIFIC METHODS **Drawing Conclusions** How did the distance to the target affect the wave's return?
3. **Evaluating Models** How does this activity model the use of sonography in prenatal observation?
4. SCIENTIFIC METHODS **Analyzing Results** How did traveling though the corn syrup affect the wave? How might this be applied to sonography?

# Chapter 23 Summary

| Key Ideas | Key Terms |
|---|---|

## 1 The Male Reproductive System

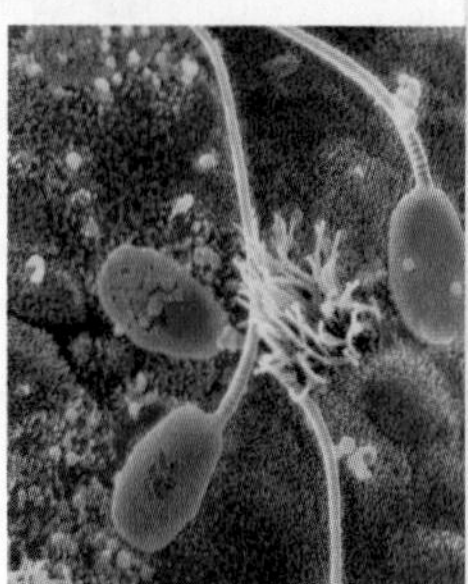

- The male reproductive system has two testes that produce sperm and testosterone.
- The vas deferens carries sperm into the urethra. Sperm leave the body by passing through the urethra.
- As sperm cells move into the urethra, they mix with fluids secreted by three exocrine glands: the seminal vesicles, the prostate gland, and the bulbourethral glands.
- After the semen is deposited in the female reproductive system, sperm swim until they encounter an egg cell or until they die.

**Key Terms:** **testis** (549), **seminiferous tubule** (549), **epididymis** (550), **vas deferens** (550), **prostate gland** (551), **semen** (551), **penis** (551)

## 2 The Female Reproductive System

- The ovaries produce egg cells. Ovaries also secrete estrogen and progesterone.
- During the reproductive years, the female body undergoes a hormonal cycle that causes periodic changes. These changes prepare the body in the event that an egg is fertilized.
- If pregnancy does not occur, levels of estrogen and progesterone fall. The decrease in these two hormones causes the lining of the uterus to be shed during menstruation.

**Key Terms:** **ovary** (552), **ovum** (553), **fallopian tube** (553), **uterus** (553), **vagina** (553), **ovulation** (554), **menstrual cycle** (556), **menstruation** (556)

## 3 Human Development

- When a sperm cell encounters an ovum, the sperm cell releases enzymes that break down the outer layers of the ovum. The head of the sperm enters the ovum, and the nuclei of the ovum and sperm fuse. This process, from encounter to fusion, is called fertilization.
- All of the embryo's organ systems, as well as the supportive membranes that feed and protect the embryo, develop during the first trimester of pregnancy.
- By the end of the third trimester, a fetus is able to live outside the mother's body. A baby leaves the mother's body after labor.

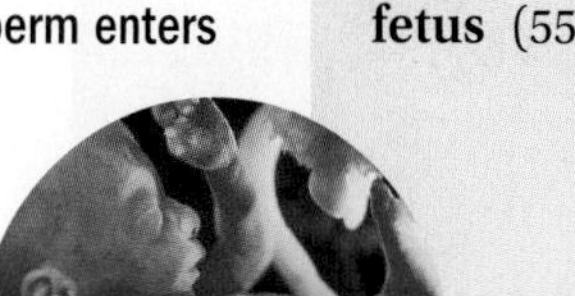

**Key Terms:** **embryo** (557), **implantation** (557), **fetus** (559)

## 4 Sexually Transmitted Infections

- Abstinence is the only sure way to protect yourself from contracting an STI.
- Common STIs include genital herpes, genital HPV, trichomoniasis, AIDS, hepatitis B, chlamydia, and gonorrhea.

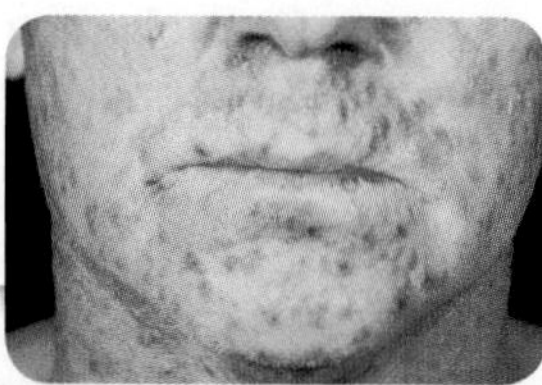

**Key Terms:** **genital herpes** (562), **pelvic inflammatory disease** (563)

# Chapter 23

The Living Environment

# Regents Exam Practice

**PART A: Answer all questions in this part.**

*Directions:* For each statement or question, write on your separate answer sheet the number of the word or expression that best completes the statement or answers the question.

**1** Toxins can harm a developing fetus. They usually enter the fetus by the process of

(1) blood flow from the mother to the fetus
(2) active transport from the ovary
(3) diffusion across placental membranes
(4) recombination of genes from the fetus and mother

**2** Which substance usually passes in the greatest amount through the placenta from the blood of the fetus to the blood of the mother?

(1) oxygen
(2) carbon dioxide
(3) amino acids
(4) glucose

**3** Removal of one ovary from a human female would most likely

(1) affect the production of eggs.
(2) make fertilization impossible.
(3) make carrying a fetus impossible.
(4) decrease her ability to provide essential nutrients to an embryo.

**4** Which reproductive structure is correctly paired with its function?

(1) uterus—usual site of fertilization
(2) testis—usual location for egg development
(3) ovary—delivers nutrients to the embryo
(4) sperm—transports genetic material

**5** The reproductive cycle of a human is usually regulated by

(1) gametes
(2) hormones
(3) natural selection
(4) immune responses

**6** Some body structures of a human male are represented in the diagram below. An obstruction in the structures labeled X would directly interfere with the

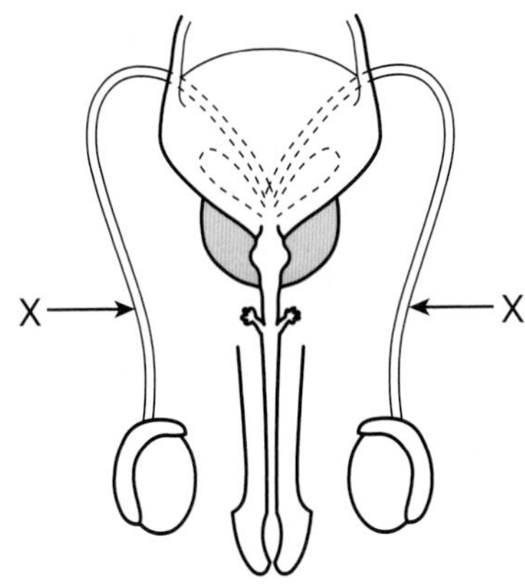


(1) transfer of sperm to a female.
(2) production of sperm.
(3) production of urine.
(4) transfer of urine to the external environment.

**7** One function of the placenta in a human is to

(1) surround the embryo and protect it from shock.
(2) allow for mixing of maternal blood with fetal blood.
(3) act as the heart of the fetus, pumping blood until the fetus is born.
(4) permit passage of nutrients and oxygen from the mother to the fetus.

**8** The characteristics of a developing fetus are most influenced by

(1) gene combinations and their expression in the embryo.
(2) hormone production by the father.
(3) circulating levels of white blood cells in the placenta.
(4) milk production in the mother.

**9** A diagram of human female reproductive structures is shown below. Which structure is correctly paired with its function?

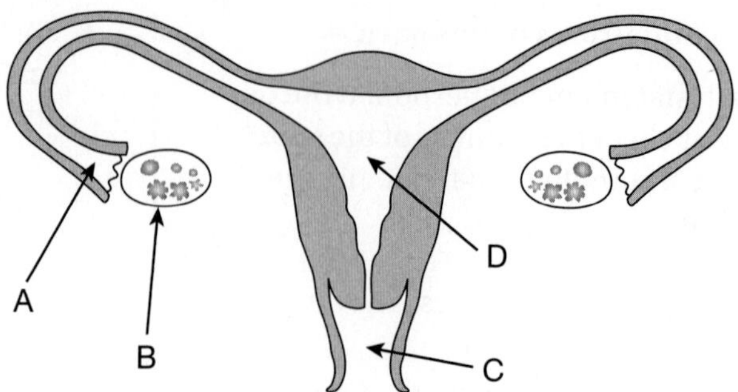


(1) A — releases estrogen and progesterone
(2) B — produces and releases the egg
(3) C — provides the usual site for fertilization
(4) D — nourishes a developing embryo

**PART B**

**The diagrams below represent organs of two individuals. The diagrams are followed by a list of sentences. For each phrase in questions 10 through 11, select the sentence from the list below that best applies to that phrase. Then record the number in the space provided.**

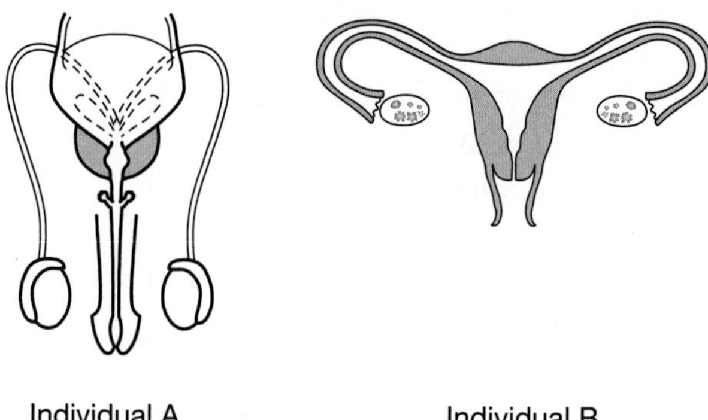

Individual A

Individual B

*Sentences*

1. The phrase is correct for both Individual *A* and Individual *B*.
2. The phrase is not correct for either Individual *A* or Individual B.
3. The phrase is correct for Individual *A*, only.
4. The phrase is correct for Individual *B*, only.

**10** Contains a structure in which a zygote divides by mitosis

**11** Contains organs involved in internal fertilization

12 Part of embryonic development in a species is illustrated in the diagram below. Which set of factors plays the most direct role in controlling the events shown in the diagram?

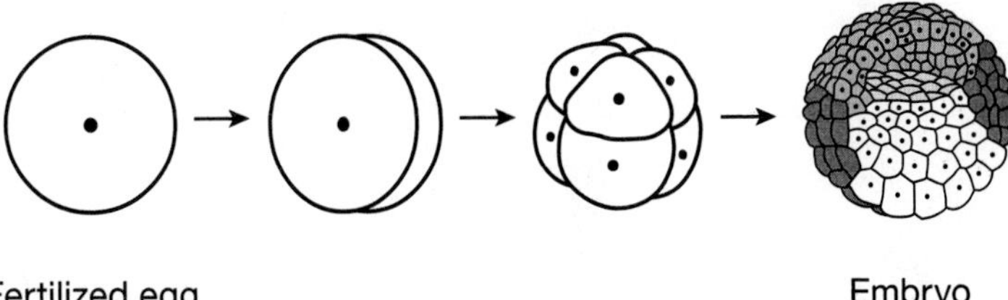


(1) genes, hormones, and cell location
(2) antibodies, insulin, and starch
(3) ATP, amino acids, and inorganic compounds
(4) abiotic resources, homeostasis, and selective breeding

**PART C**

**Base your answers to questions 13 and 14 on the statement and diagram below and on your knowledge of biology.**

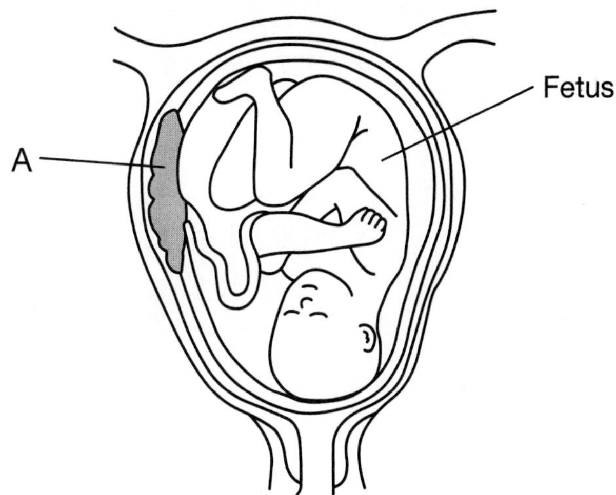


Women are advised to avoid consuming alcoholic beverages during pregnancy.

13 Identify the structure labeled A and explain how the functioning of structure A is essential for the normal development of the fetus.

14 Explain why consumption of alcoholic beverages by a pregnant woman is likely to be more harmful to her fetus than to herself.

# Appendix Table of Contents

# FoldNotes

FoldNotes are a useful study tool that you can use to organize concepts. One FoldNote focuses on a few main concepts. By using a FoldNote, you can learn how concepts fit together. FoldNotes are designed to make studying concepts easier, so you can remember the ideas for tests.

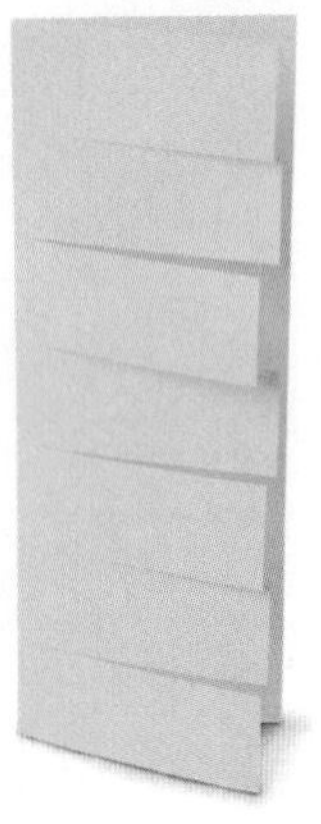

## Key-Term Fold

A key-term fold is useful for studying definitions of key terms in a chapter. Each tab can contain a key term on one side and its definition on the other. Use the key-term fold to quiz yourself on the definitions of the key terms in a chapter.

1. Fold a **sheet of lined notebook paper** in half from left to right.
2. Using **scissors**, cut along every third line from the right edge of the paper to the center fold to make tabs.

## Double-Door Fold

A double-door fold is useful when you want to compare the characteristics of two topics. The double-door fold can organize characteristics of the two topics side by side under the flaps. Similarities and differences between the two topics can then be easily identified.

1. Fold a **sheet of paper** in half from the top to the bottom. Then, unfold the paper.
2. Fold the top and bottom edges of the paper to the center crease.

## Four-Corner Fold

A four-corner fold is useful when you want to compare the characteristics of four topics. The four-corner fold can organize the characteristics of the four topics side by side under the flaps. Similarities and differences between the four topics can then be easily identified.

1. Fold a **sheet of paper** in half from top to bottom. Then, unfold the paper.
2. Fold the top and bottom of the paper to the crease in the center of the paper.
3. Fold the paper in half from side to side. Then, unfold the paper.
4. Using **scissors**, cut the top flap creases made in step 3 to form four flaps.

## Booklet

A booklet is a useful tool for taking notes as you read a chapter. Each page of the booklet can contain a main topic from the chapter. Write details of each main topic on the appropriate page to create an outline of the chapter.

1. Fold a **sheet of paper** in half from top to bottom.
2. Fold the sheet of paper in half again from left to right.
3. Fold the sheet of paper one more time from top to bottom.
4. Completely unfold the paper.
5. Refold the paper from top to bottom. Using **scissors**, cut a slit along the vertical crease of the sheet from the folded edge to the horizontal crease in the middle of the folded paper. Do not cut the entire sheet in half. Unfold the paper.
6. Fold the sheet of paper in half from left to right. While holding the bottom and top edges of the paper, push the bottom and top edges together so that the center collapses at the center slit. Fold the four flaps to form a four-page book.

## Layered Book

A layered book is a useful tool for taking notes as you read a chapter. The four flaps of the layered book can summarize information into four categories. Write details of each category on the appropriate flap to create a summary of the chapter.

1. Lay one **sheet of paper** on top of **another sheet**. Slide the top sheet up so that 2 cm of the bottom sheet is showing.
2. Holding the two sheets together, fold down the top of the two sheets so that you see four 2 cm tabs along the bottom.
3. Using a stapler, staple the top of the FoldNote.

## Pyramid

A pyramid provides a unique way for taking notes. The three sides of the pyramid can summarize information into three categories. Use the pyramid as a tool for studying information in a chapter.

1. Place a **sheet of paper** in front of you. Fold the lower left-hand corner of the paper diagonally to the opposite edge of the paper.
2. Cut off the tab of paper created by the fold (at the top).
3. Open the paper so that it is a square. Fold the lower right-hand corner of the paper diagonally to the opposite corner to form a triangle.
4. Open the paper. The creases of the two folds will have created an X.
5. Using **scissors**, cut along one of the creases. Start from any corner, and stop at the center point to create two flaps. Use **tape** or **glue** to attach one of the flaps on top of the other flap.

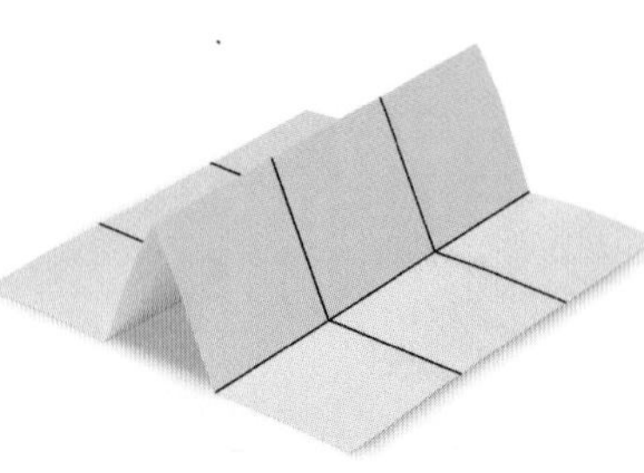

## Table Fold

A table fold is a useful tool for comparing the characteristics of two or three topics. In a table fold, all topics are described in terms of the same characteristics so that you can easily make a thorough comparison.

1. Fold a **piece of paper** in half from the top to the bottom. Then, fold the paper in half again.
2. Fold the paper in thirds from side to side.
3. Unfold the paper completely. Carefully trace the fold lines by using a pen or pencil.

## Tri-Fold

A tri-fold is a useful tool that helps you track your progress. By organizing the chapter topic into what you know, what you want to know, and what you learn, you can see how much you have learned after reading a chapter.

1. Fold a piece a paper in thirds from the top to the bottom.
2. Unfold the paper so that you can see the three sections. Then, turn the paper sideways so that the three sections form vertical columns.
3. Trace the fold lines by using a **pen** or **pencil**. Label the columns "Know," "Want," and "Learn."

## Three-Panel Flip Chart

A three-panel flip chart is useful when you want to compare the characteristics of three topics. The three-panel flip chart can organize the characteristics of the three topics side by side under the flaps. Similarities and differences between the three topics can then be easily identified.

1. Fold a **piece of paper** in half from the top to the bottom.
2. Fold the paper in thirds from side to side. Then, unfold the paper so that you can see the three sections.
3. From the top of the paper, cut along each of the vertical fold lines to the fold in the middle of the paper. You will now have three flaps.

## Two-Panel Flip Chart

A two-panel flip chart is useful when you want to compare the characteristics of two topics. The two-panel flip chart can organize the characteristics of the two topics side by side under the flaps. Similarities and differences between the two topics can then be easily identified.

1. Fold a **piece of paper** in half from the top to the bottom.
2. Fold the paper in half from side to side. Then, unfold the paper so that you can see the two sections.
3. From the top of the paper, cut along the vertical fold line to the fold in the middle of the paper. You will now have two flaps.

# Word Origins

## Determining the Meanings of Words

The challenge of understanding a new word can often be simplified by carefully examining the word. Many words can be divided into three parts: a prefix, root, and suffix. The prefix consists of one or more syllables placed in front of a root. The root is the main part of the word. The suffix consists of one or more syllables at the end of a root. Prefixes and suffixes modify or add to the meaning of the root. A knowledge of common prefixes, roots, and suffixes can give you clues to the meaning of unfamiliar words and can help make learning new words easier. For example, each of the word parts in **Table 1** can be combined with the root *derm* to form a word.

**Table 2** lists prefixes and suffixes commonly used in biology. Each word part is followed by its common meaning, an example of a word in which the word part is used, and a definition of that word. Examine the word meaning and the example. Decide whether each word part in the first column is a prefix or suffix, depending on how the word part is used in the example.

Use **Table 1** to form five words using the root *derm.*

**Table 1 Word Parts**

| Prefix | Root | Suffix |
|---|---|---|
| *hypo-* | *derm* | *-ic* |
| *pachy-* | *derm* | |
| | *derm* | *-atology* |
| | *derm* | *-atologist* |
| | *derm* | *-atitis* |

Then, use the list of word parts and their meanings to write what you think each word that you formed means. An example is shown below.

**Example:** **dermatologist**
*derm* (root): skin
*-logy* (suffix): the study of
*-ist* (suffix): someone who practices or deals with something
*dermatologist:* someone who studies or deals with skin

**Table 2 Word Prefixes and Suffixes**

| Prefix or suffix | Meaning | Example |
|---|---|---|
| *a-* | not, without | asymmetrical: not symmetrical |
| *ab-* | away, apart | abduct: move away from the middle |
| *-able* | able | viable: able to live |
| *ad-* | to, toward | adduct: move toward the middle |
| *amphi-* | both | amphibian: type of vertebrate that lives both on land and in water |
| *ante-* | before | anterior: front of an organism |
| *anti-* | against | antibiotic: substance, such as penicillin, capable of killing bacteria |
| *arche-* | ancient | Archaeopteryx: a fossilized bird |
| *arthro-* | joint | arthropod: jointed-limbed organism belonging to the phylum Arthropoda |
| *auto-* | self, same | autotrophic: able to make its own food |
| *bi-* | two | bivalve: mollusk with two shells |
| *bio-* | life | biology: the study of life |
| *blast-* | embryo | blastula: hollow ball stage in the development of an embryo |
| *carcin-* | cancer | carcinogenic: cancer-causing |
| *cereb-* | brain | cerebrum: part of the vertebrate brain |
| *chloro-* | green | chlorophyll: green pigment in plants that is needed for photosynthesis |

**Table 2 Word Prefixes and Suffixes, con't.**

| Word part | Meaning | Example |
|---|---|---|
| *chromo-* | color | chromosome: structure found in eukaryotic cells that contains DNA |
| *chondro-* | cartilage | Chondrichthyes: cartilaginous fish |
| *circ-* | around | circulatory: system for moving fluids through the body |
| *-cide* | kill | insecticide: a substance that kills insects |
| *co-, con-* | with, together | conjoined twins: identical twins physically joined by a shared portion of anatomy at birth |
| *-cycle* | circle | pericycle: layer of plant cells |
| *cyt-* | cell | cytology: the study of cells |
| *de-* | remove | dehydration: removal of water |
| *derm-* | skin | dermatology: study of the skin |
| *di-* | two | diploid: full set of chromosomes |
| *dia-* | through | dialysis: separating molecules by passing them through a membrane |
| *ecol-* | dwelling, house | ecology: the study of living things and their environments |
| *ecto-* | outer, outside | ectoderm: outer germ layer of developing embryo |
| *-ectomy* | removal | appendectomy: removal of the appendix |
| *endo-* | inner, inside | endoplasm: cytoplasm within the cell membrane |
| *epi-* | upon, over | epiphyte: plant growing upon another plant |
| *ex-, exo-* | outside of | exobiology: the search for life elsewhere in the universe |
| *gastro-* | stomach | gastropod: type of mollusk |
| *-gen* | type | genotype: genes in an organism |
| *-gram* | write or record | climatogram: report depicting the annual precipitation and temperature for an area |
| *hemi-* | half | hemisphere: half of a sphere |
| *hetero-* | different | heterozygous: different alleles inherited from parents |
| *hist-* | tissue | histology: the study of tissues |
| *homeo-* | the same | homeostasis: the maintenance of a constant condition |
| *hydro-* | water | hydroponics: growing plants in water instead of soil |
| *hyper-* | above, over | hypertension: blood pressure that is higher than normal |
| *hypo-* | below, under | hypothalamus: part of the brain located below the thalamus |
| *-ic* | of or pertaining to | hypodermic: pertaining to under the skin |
| *inter-* | between, among | interbreed: breed within a family or strain |
| *intra-* | within | intracellular: inside a cell |
| *iso-* | equal | isogenic: having the same genotype |
| *-ist* | practices or deals | biologist: someone who studies life |
| *-logy* | study of | biology: the study of life |
| *macro-* | large | macromolecule: large molecule, such as DNA or proteins |
| *mal-* | bad | malnourishment: poor nutrition |

| Table 2 Word Prefixes and Suffixes, con't. | | |
|---|---|---|
| **Word part** | **Meaning** | **Example** |
| *mega-* | large | megaspore: larger of two types of spores produced by some ferns and flowering plants |
| *meso-* | in the middle | mesoglea: jellylike material found between outer and inner layers of coelenterates |
| *meta-* | change | metamorphosis: change in form |
| *micro-* | small | microscopic: too small to be seen with unaided eye |
| *mono-* | one, single | monoploid: one set of alleles |
| *morph-* | form | morphology: study of the form of organisms |
| *neo-* | new | neonatal: newborn |
| *nephr-* | kidney | nephron: functional unit of the kidneys |
| *neur-* | neuron | neurotransmitter: chemical released by a neuron |
| *oo-* | egg | oogenesis: gamete formation in female diploid organisms |
| *org-* | living | organism: living thing |
| *-oma* | swelling | carcinoma: cancerous tumor |
| *orth-* | straight | orthodontics: the practice of straightening teeth |
| *pachy-* | thick | pachyderm: thick-skinned animal, such as an elephant |
| *para-* | near, on | parasite: organism that lives on and gets nutrients from another organism |
| *path-* | disease | pathogen: disease-causing agent |
| *peri-* | around | pericardium: membrane around the heart |
| *photo-* | light | phototropism: bending of plants toward light |
| *phyto-* | plants | phytoplankton: plankton that consists of plants |
| *poly-* | many | polypeptide: sequence of many amino acids joined together to form a protein |
| *-pod* | foot | pseudopod: false foot that projects from the main part of an amoeboid cell |
| *pre-* | before | prediction: a forecast of events before they take place |
| *-scope* | instrument used | microscope: instrument used to see very small objects |
| *semi-* | partially | semipermeable: allowing some particles to move through |
| *-some* | body | chromosome: structure found in eukaryotic cells that contains DNA |
| *sub-* | under | substrate: molecule on which an enzyme acts |
| *super-, supra-* | above | superficial: on or near the surface of a tissue or organ |
| *syn-* | with | synapse: junction of a neuron with another cell |
| *-tomy* | to cut | appendectomy: operation in which the appendix is removed |
| *trans-* | across | transformation: the transfer of genetic material from one organism to another |
| *ur-* | referring to urine | urology: study of the urinary tract |
| *visc-* | organ | viscera: internal organs of the body |

# Scientific Research

## The Process of Science

The word *research* is derived from the French word *recherché,* which means "to investigate thoroughly." Nearly all of us have done some kind of research, but scientific research has special characteristics. At its core is systematic observation and objective recording of these observations. The goals of scientific research are the understanding of the natural world and the application of this understanding to benefit people and the world in which we live.

Science is a process of gaining knowledge about the world around us. The state of scientific knowledge is always changing. Any conclusion drawn from scientific research is subject to change if further research uncovers new information or new insights.

Scientific research is also a collaborative process. It relies on open communcation and cooperation between scientists. The results of one scientist's research are supported only when other scientists reproduce the studies and obtain the same results.

A scientist works in a greenhouse lab.

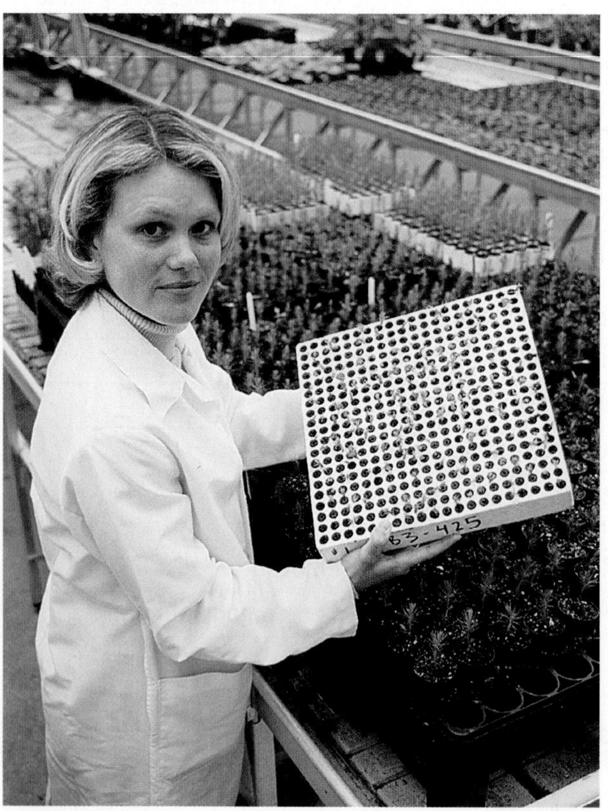

### Preparation for Scientific Research

Before beginning a scientific study, it is important to learn about research that has already been conducted on the subject. Scientists learn about the latest discoveries in their fields by reading the "primary" literature on the subject. Primary literature consists of articles that are published in scientific journals and that have been reviewed by other scientists in the same field. (By comparison, textbooks, encyclopedias, and similar types of publications are referred to as "secondary" literature.) Today, many scientific journals publish online versions of their articles.

### Types of Scientific Research

Scientific research typically involves asking very specific questions and then designing studies to collect answers to these questions. There are two broad styles of scientific research: experimental and observational.

In an experiment, some aspect of an organism, an object, or part of the environment is deliberately changed. The researcher then observes the effects of this change. For example, a scientist might study the effects of adding different amounts of nitrogen fertilizer to the soil in which a crop is grown.

Sometimes, it is not possible or desirable to perform an experiment. Observational research uses the senses, such as sight and hearing, to take in information. Scientific observation may also make use of instruments such as microscopes that allow us to see small things and balances that weigh objects. During scientific observation, a scientist observes but usually does not disturb or change his or her subject. For example, for a study of bird song, a scientist might quietly observe birds by recording their songs to be analyzed later in a laboratory.

The application of science for a specific purpose is referred to as *technology.* Pure scientific inquiry and research related to technology have different purposes. Scientific inquiry is conducted to advance our knowledge about the natural world. In contrast, research related to technology may be founded on prior scientific inquiry and is generally aimed at solving problems and meeting the needs of society. Scientific inquiry on the structure and function of DNA, for example, paved the way for technology that is aimed at preventing or curing diseases and improving crops.

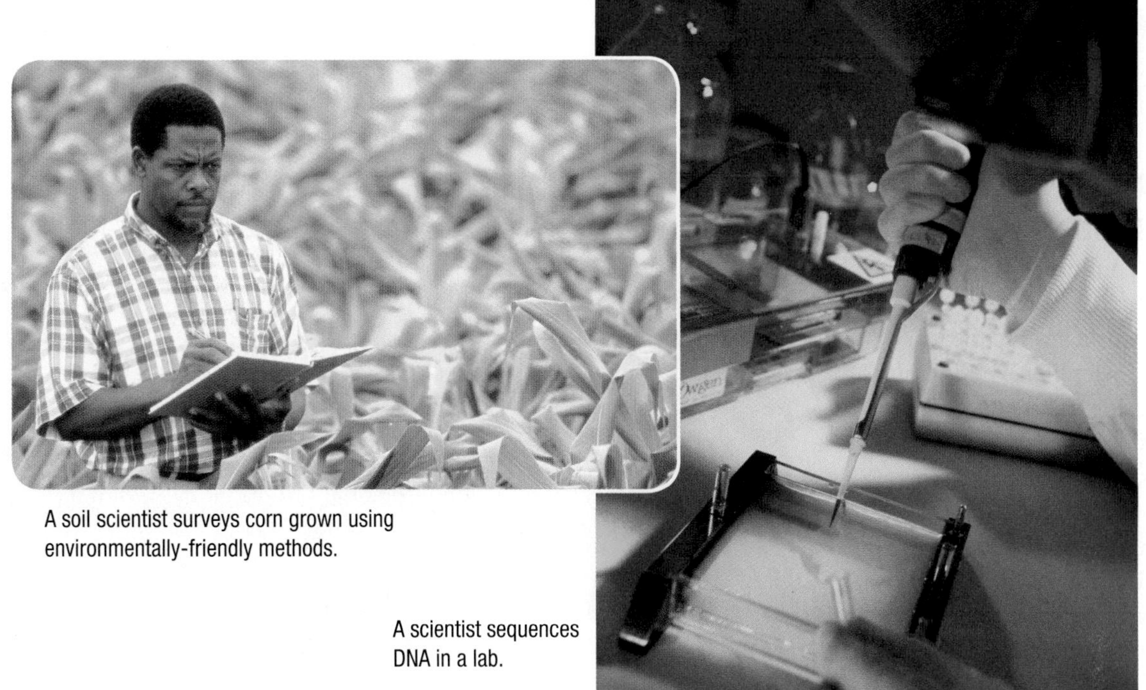

A soil scientist surveys corn grown using environmentally-friendly methods.

A scientist sequences DNA in a lab.



### Conclusions of Scientific Research

Scientific research relies upon the evaluation of hypotheses, which are testable explanations for observations. If a hypothesis cannot be tested, then it cannot be studied using the tools of science.

Scientific investigation cannot prove that a hypothesis is correct. Rather, it can provide evidence that supports a hypothesis or it can disprove the hypothesis. Hypotheses can be supported but are never proven because scientists cannot be sure that there is not another hypothesis that could better explain their results.

An example of a testable hypothesis is that poinsettia plants flower when the day length is less than 12 hours. This hypothesis about flowering was accepted until scientists discovered that poinsettias would not bloom if they were exposed to day lengths shorter than 12 hours and nights that were interrupted with a period of light. The currently accepted hypothesis is that poinsettias will flower when the length of the night is at least 12 hours.

Scientists are human. They are disappointed if a hypothesis that they favored is disproved or replaced. But scientists are bound by ethics and service to the truth. They must be truthful about their methods and results. They must open their work to the scrutiny of their peers, and they must share their work with the scientific community for the common good.

## Science, Technology and Society

Science is part of society. You have read how science and technology can affect society. In a similar way, society can directly affect progress in science and in technology through laws and by giving or withholding government or private funding for research. Certain healthcare issues, such as the use of human embryonic stem cells, are subject to public debate and to governmental control. The progress made in understanding and curing certain diseases can partly depend upon funding for research.

Pure scientific inquiry often drives technological developments. Technology, in turn, enables scientists to conduct experiments that could not otherwise be done. One large difference between the two is that scientific knowledge is made freely available to the scientific community by publication in peer-reviewed scientific journals. Technology, on the other hand, is often funded by private companies. Technological advances may be closely guarded secrets, which may be patented or sold.

The use of science and technology for the benefit of society is subject to political, economic, and ethical concerns. It is the responsibility of all citizens to remain aware of these issues in order to make informed, sound decisions about science, technology, and society.

# Experimental Design



## Before Experiments

Scientists conduct experiments in order to explore and better understand the world around us. A key element of scientific experiments is that they address very specific questions. Scientists first ask the questions, then propose answers, and then test these possible answers using objective methods that can be repeated by other scientists.

This scientific method, as it is called, is often thought to consist of a rigid set of steps and related rules. In fact, the ways that experiments are carried out do not always fit this mold. Nevertheless, experiments must be done and explained in such a way that other scientists can repeat the procedures and obtain the same results. Producing consistent results between trials of the same experiment allows scientists to verify their conclusions.

### Making Observations

An experiment always starts with an observation—something that has made someone wonder. When scientists, or any of us, wonder about something, we ask questions. How do bats catch their prey in the dark? Why do all nests from a single species of bird look the same? Why do I feel cold when I have a fever?

The questions, like these questions, are rather broad at first. But they become very focused as the investigator prepares to systematically study the subject. At this stage, scientists also typically collect and study other information on the subject, such as articles published in scientific journals.

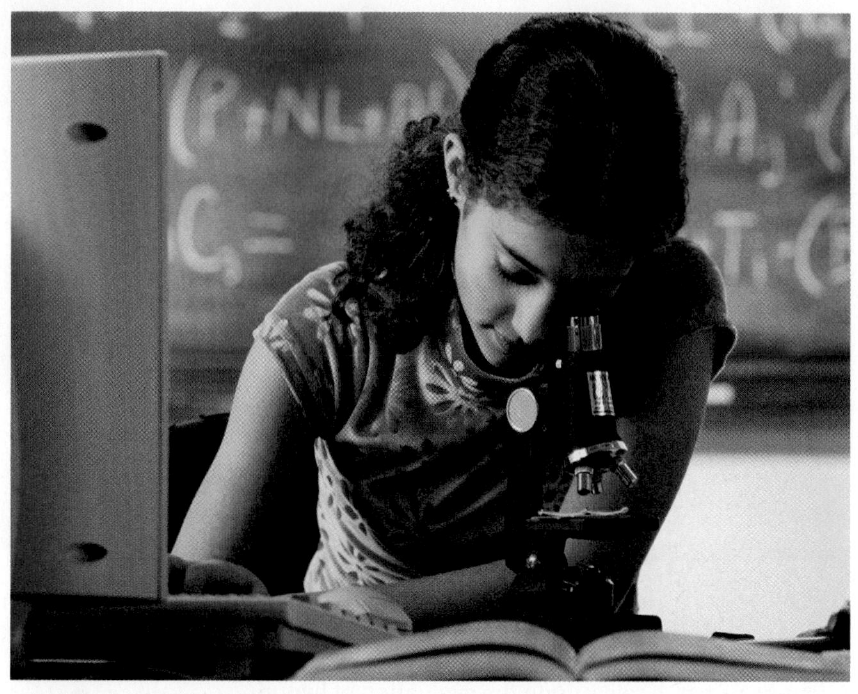

### Forming a Hypothesis

The first step a scientist takes in answering a question is to develop a possible explanation for what he or she has observed. This explanation is essentially an educated guess that is based on the evidence that the scientist has collected. The critical feature of this educated guess is that it can be tested. These educated guesses are **hypotheses.**

For example, a plant biologist (a botanist) observes that healthy plants often grow in nitrogen-rich soil. The botanist might hypothesize that nitrogen is important for plant growth. Hypotheses allow scientists to develop **predictions,** or specific expectations about what should occur if a hypothesis is true. Although it might not be worded exactly as such, a prediction takes the form of an if-then statement. The botanist might predict that if most soils do not contain a lot of nitrogen, then adding nitrogen to soil will enhance plant growth.

In addition to being testable, a scientific hypothesis must also be falsifiable. That is, an experiment is designed so that it will show the hypothesis to be false, if indeed it is. Scientists often have several alternative hypotheses that they consider when they conduct an experiment or a series of experiments.

### Designing an Experiment

Next, the scientist carefully designs an experiment to test the hypothesis. He or she might grow plants in soils that contain different amounts of nitrogen. In a scientific experiment, only one factor, or *variable,* is changed. This factor that changes is the **independent variable.** The independent variable in this experiment would be the nitrogen level in the soil.

### Types of Variables

Other factors must be kept constant in the experiment. These factors are **controlled variables.** Some of the variables that could affect plant growth are air temperature and the amount of rainfall and sunlight.

The factor that changes in response to a change in the independent, or tested, variable is the **dependent variable.** In the soil-nitrogen experiment, the size of plants is the dependent variable.

An experiment that has controlled variables is called a *controlled experiment.* Controlled experiments such as this one allow researchers to conclude that changes in the dependent variable are due only to changes in the independent variable.

## Performing the Experiment

Once a reliable experimental design is in place, performing the experiment is often easy. It is important that researchers carefully collect data and record all of their measurements and other observations.

### Analyzing Data

When an experiment has been completed, the scientist analyzes the data collected. He or she makes computations, creates tables, draws graphs, and often does statistical analyses. The primary goal of the analysis is to organize and interpret the data so that conclusions can be drawn from them. The scientist also evaluates the procedures and results for possible sources of error—human mistakes, problems with equipment, or unexpected interferences, such as bad weather.

### Drawing Conclusions

The final task in an experiment is to determine whether or not the results support the tested hypothesis. If the hypothesis is supported by the findings, the researcher details the supporting evidence and notes any inconsistencies. If the hypothesis is not supported, the researcher offers possible explanations. In either case, the researcher might also discuss alternative hypotheses. These hypotheses might include new ones that have occurred to the scientist during the course of the experiments. One or more hypotheses may be falsified by the experiments, and one or more may be supported. Usually, a single hypothesis emerges that is best supported by the experimental evidence. The scientist also generally compares his or her results to those obtained by other researchers conducting related experiments.

### Follow-up Experiments

Scientists usually repeat their experiments, even multiple times, to verify their findings. They also distribute their findings to other scientists, often in the form of articles published in scientific journals. The scientists may also conduct related experiments to test other hypotheses.

# Microscopy

## Parts of the Compound Light Microscope

- The **eyepiece** magnifies the image, usually 10x.
- The **low-power objective** further magnifies the image, up to 4x.
- The **high-power objectives** further magnify the image, from 10x to 43x.
- The **nosepiece** holds the objectives and can be turned to change from one objective to another.
- The **body tube** maintains the correct distance between the eyepiece and the objectives. This distance is usually about 25 cm, the normal distance for reading and viewing objects with the unaided eye.
- The **coarse adjustment** moves the stage up and down in large increments to allow gross positioning and focusing of the objective lens.
- The **fine adjustment** moves the stage slightly to bring the image into sharp focus.
- The **stage** supports a slide that contains the viewed specimen.
- The **stage clips** secure the slide in position for viewing.
- The **diaphragm** (not labeled), located under the stage, controls the amount of light allowed to pass through the object being viewed.
- The **light source** provides light for viewing the image. It can be either a light reflected with a mirror or an incandescent light from a small lamp. Never use reflected direct sunlight as a light source.
- The **arm** supports the body tube.
- The **base** supports the microscope.



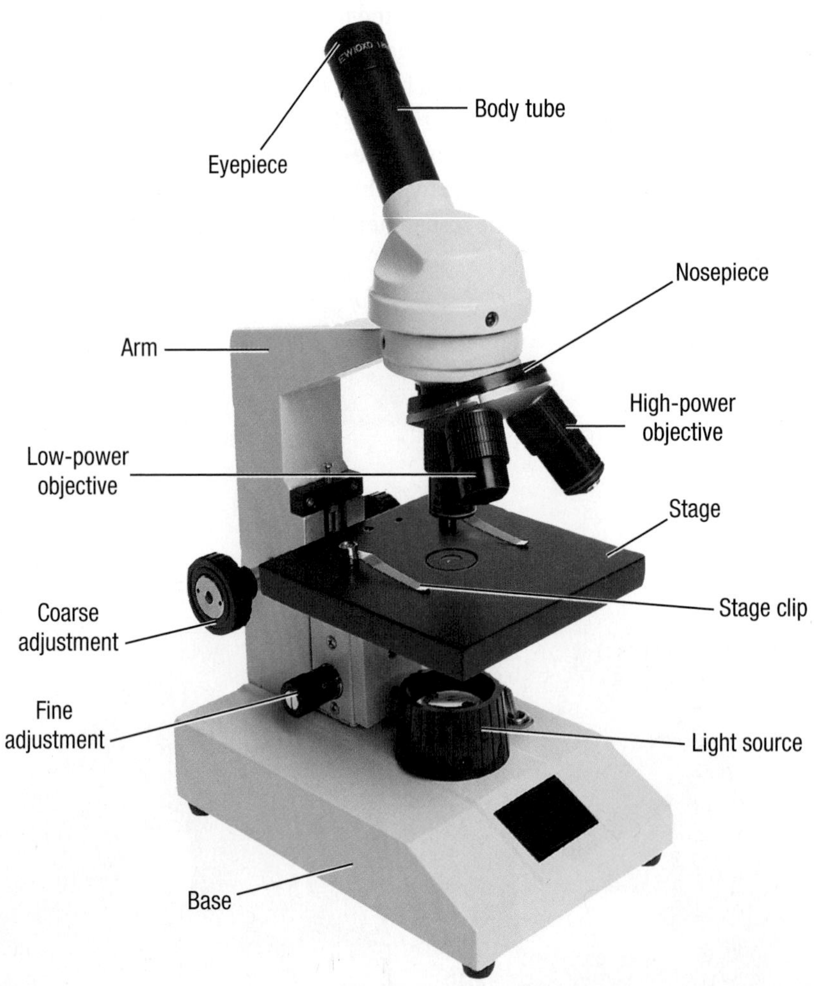

## Proper Handling and Use of the Compound Light Microscope

1. Carry the microscope to your lab table using both hands, one supporting the base and the other holding the arm of the microscope. Hold the microscope close to your body.
2. Place the microscope on the lab table at least 5 cm from the edge of the table.
3. Check to see what type of light source the microscope has. If the microscope has a lamp, plug it in, making sure that the cord is out of the way. If the microscope has a mirror, adjust it to reflect light through the hole in the stage.

   **CAUTION: If your microscope has a mirror, do not use direct sunlight as a light source. Using direct sunlight can damage your eyes.**
4. Adjust the revolving nosepiece so that the low-power objective is aligned with the body tube.
5. Place a prepared slide over the hole in the stage, and secure the slide with the stage clips.
6. Look through the eyepiece, and move the diaphragm to adjust the amount of light that passes through the specimen.
7. Now look at the stage at eye level. Slowly turn the coarse adjustment to raise the stage until the objective almost touches the slide. Do not allow the objective to touch the slide.
8. While looking through the eyepiece, turn the coarse adjustment to lower the stage until the image is in focus. Never focus objectives downward. Use the fine adjustment to achieve a sharply focused image. Keep both eyes open while viewing a slide.
9. Make sure that the image is exactly in the center of your field of vision. Then switch to the high-power objective. Focus the image with the fine adjustment. Never use the coarse adjustment at high power.
10. When you are finished using the microscope, remove the slide. Clean the eyepiece and objectives with lens paper, and return the microscope to its storage area.

## Procedure for Making a Wet Mount

1. Use lens paper to clean a glass slide and coverslip.

   **CAUTION: Glass slides and coverslips break easily. Handle them carefully. Notify your teacher if you break a slide or coverslip.**
2. Place the specimen that you wish to observe in the center of the slide.
3. Using a medicine dropper, place one drop of water on the specimen.
4. Position the coverslip so that it is at the edge of the drop of water and at a 45° angle to the slide. Make sure that the water runs along the edge of the coverslip.
5. Lower the coverslip slowly to avoid trapping air bubbles.
6. If a stain or solution will be added to a wet mount, place a drop of the staining solution on the microscope slide along one side of the coverslip. Place a small piece of paper towel on the opposite side of the coverslip to draw the stain under the coverslip.
7. As the water evaporates from the slide, add another drop of water by placing the tip of the medicine dropper next to the edge of the coverslip, just as you would when adding stains or solutions to a wet mount. If the slide is too wet, remove the excess water by using the corner of a paper towel as a blotter. Do not lift the coverslip to add or remove water.

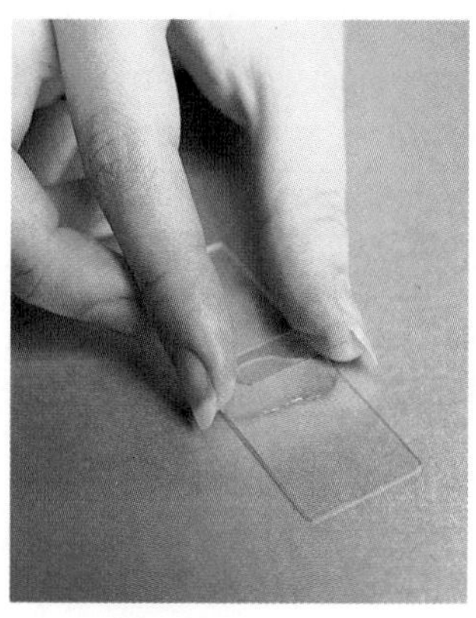

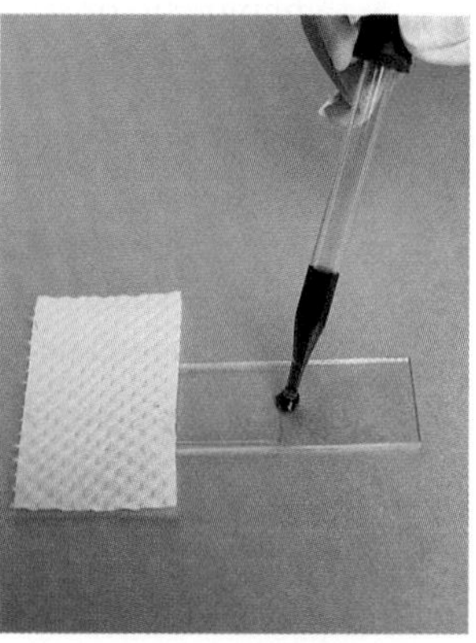

# Determining Mass and Temperature

## Reading a Balance

A **single-pan balance,** such as the one shown at right, has one pan and three or four beams. The scale of measure for each beam depends on the model of the balance. When an object is placed on the pan, the riders are moved along the beams until the mass on the beams equals the mass of the object in the pan.



**Measuring Mass** When determining the mass of a chemical or powder, use weighing or filter paper. Determine the mass of the paper, and subtract that mass from the total mass of the paper and the sample. Use the following procedure for determining an object's mass:

1. Make sure the balance is on a level surface and the pan is allowed to move freely. Position all riders at zero. If the pointer does not come to rest in the middle of the scale, calibrate the balance by using the adjustment knob (usually located under and to the left of the pan).

   **CAUTION: Never place a hot object or chemical directly on a balance pan.**

2. Place the object on the pan.

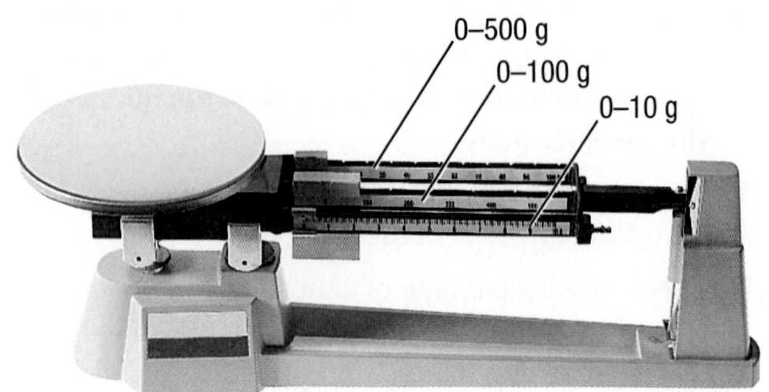


3. Move the largest rider along the beam to the right until it is at the last notch that does not move the pointer below the zero point in the middle of the scale.
4. Follow the same procedure with the next rider.
5. Move the smallest rider until the pointer rests at zero in the middle of the scale.
6. Add up the readings on all of the beams to determine the mass of the object.

**Your Turn** **Complete the following exercises.**

1. Determine the mass of each of the following items by using a single-pan balance:
   a. an empty 250 mL beaker
   b. 250 mL beaker filled with 100 mL of water
   c. 250 mL beaker filled with 100 mL of vegetable oil
   d. a house key
   e. a small book
   f. a paper clip or small safety pin
2. Determine the mass of each object represented by the balance readings shown.

a.

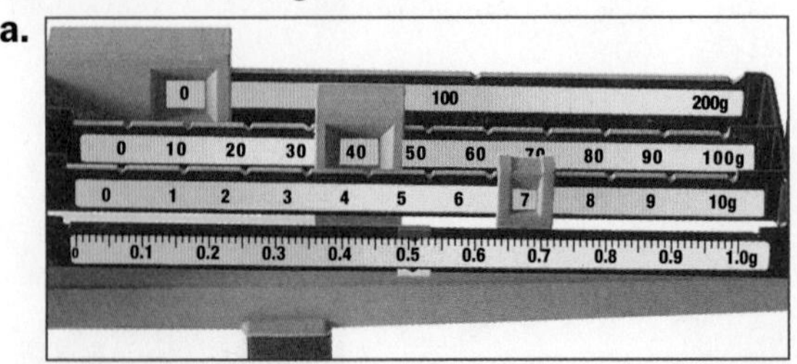


b.

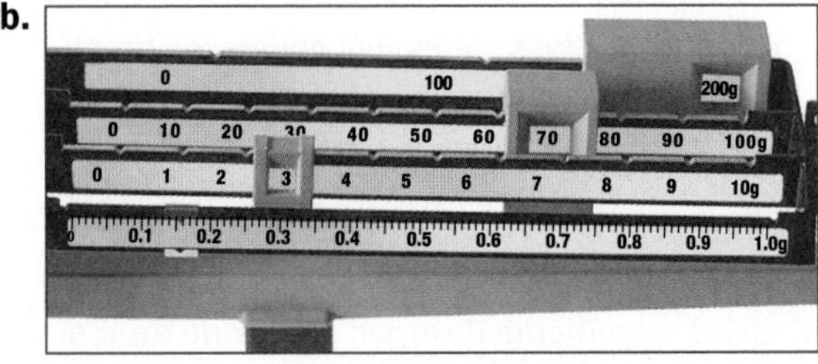


c.

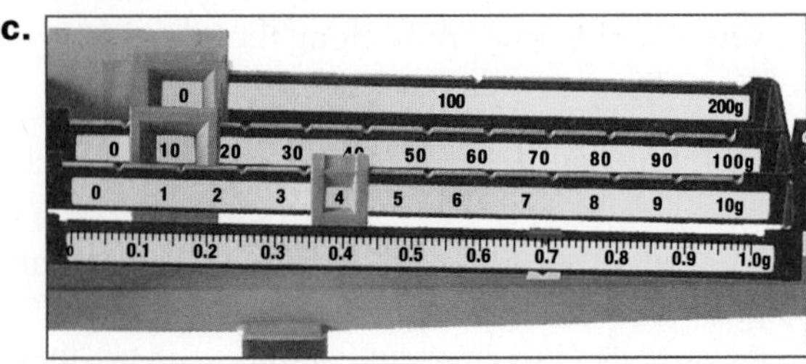

## Reading a Thermometer

Many laboratory thermometers are the bulb-type shown below. The sensing bulb of the thermometer is filled with a colored liquid (alcohol) that expands when heated. When the liquid expands, it moves up the stem of the thermometer through the capillary tube. Thermometers usually measure temperature in degrees Celsius (°C).

**Measuring Temperature** Use the following procedure when measuring the temperature of a substance.

1. Carefully lower the bulb of the thermometer into the substance. The stem of the thermometer may rest against the side of the container, but the bulb should never rest on the bottom, where heat is being applied. If the thermometer has an adjustable clip for the side of the container, the thermometer can be suspended in the liquid.

   **CAUTION: Do not hold a thermometer in your hand while measuring the temperature of a heated substance.**

2. Gently rotate the thermometer in the clip. Watch the rising colored liquid in the capillary tube. When the liquid in the capillary tube stops rising, note the whole-degree increment nearest the top of the liquid column. If your thermometer is marked in whole degrees, report temperature to the nearest half degree. For example, if the top of the colored liquid column is closest to the 52 °C mark but somewhat above it, as shown at right, what is the accurate temperature reading? Because the top of the column is slightly but not halfway above the 52 °C mark, the temperature is read as 52 °C.

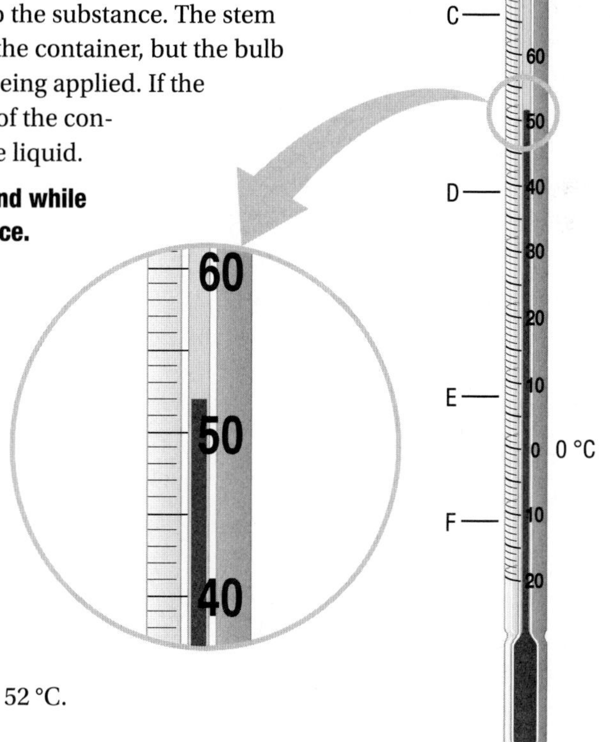


**Your Turn** **Use the thermometer shown above to answer the following questions:**

1. Identify the scale used for this thermometer.
2. Determine whether this thermometer is marked only in whole degrees or in tenths of degrees.
3. Estimate the temperature reading shown on this thermometer.
4. **Interpreting Variables** What would be the temperature reading if the top of the column were resting at each of the following points?

   **a.** A
   **b.** B
   **c.** C
   **d.** D
   **e.** E
   **f.** F

# SI Measurement

## SI Units

Scientists throughout the world use the metric system. The metric system is now officially known as the Système International d'Unités, or the International System of Units. It is usually referred to simply as the SI. Most measurements in this book are expressed in SI units. You will always use SI units when you take measurements in the lab.



**SI Prefixes** The SI is a decimal system; that is, all relationships between SI units are based on powers of 10. Most units have a prefix that indicates the relationship of a particular unit to a base unit. For example, the SI base unit for length is the meter. A meter equals 100 centimeters (cm), or 1,000 millimeters (mm). A meter also equals 0.001 kilometer (km). **Table 1** summarizes the prefixes used in SI units.

**Conversion Factors** Conversion between SI units requires a conversion factor. For example, to convert from meters to centimeters, you need to know the relationship between meters and centimeters.

$$1\ \text{cm} = 0.01\ \text{m} \quad \text{and} \quad 1\ \text{m} = 100\ \text{cm}$$

**Table 1 SI Prefixes**

| Prefix | Symbol | Factor of base unit |
|---|---|---|
| *giga-* | G | 1,000,000,000 |
| *mega-* | M | 1,000,000 |
| *kilo-* | k | 1,000 |
| *hecto-* | h | 100 |
| *deka-* | da | 10 |
| *deci-* | d | 0.1 |
| *centi-* | c | 0.01 |
| *milli-* | m | 0.001 |
| *micro-* | μ | 0.000001 |
| *nano-* | n | 0.000000001 |
| *pico-* | p | 0.000000000001 |

If you need to convert 15.5 cm to meters, you could do either of the following:

$$15.5\ \text{cm} \times \frac{1\ \text{m}}{100\ \text{cm}} = 0.155\ \text{m}$$

or

$$15.5\ \text{cm} \times \frac{0.01\ \text{m}}{1\ \text{cm}} = 0.155\ \text{m}$$

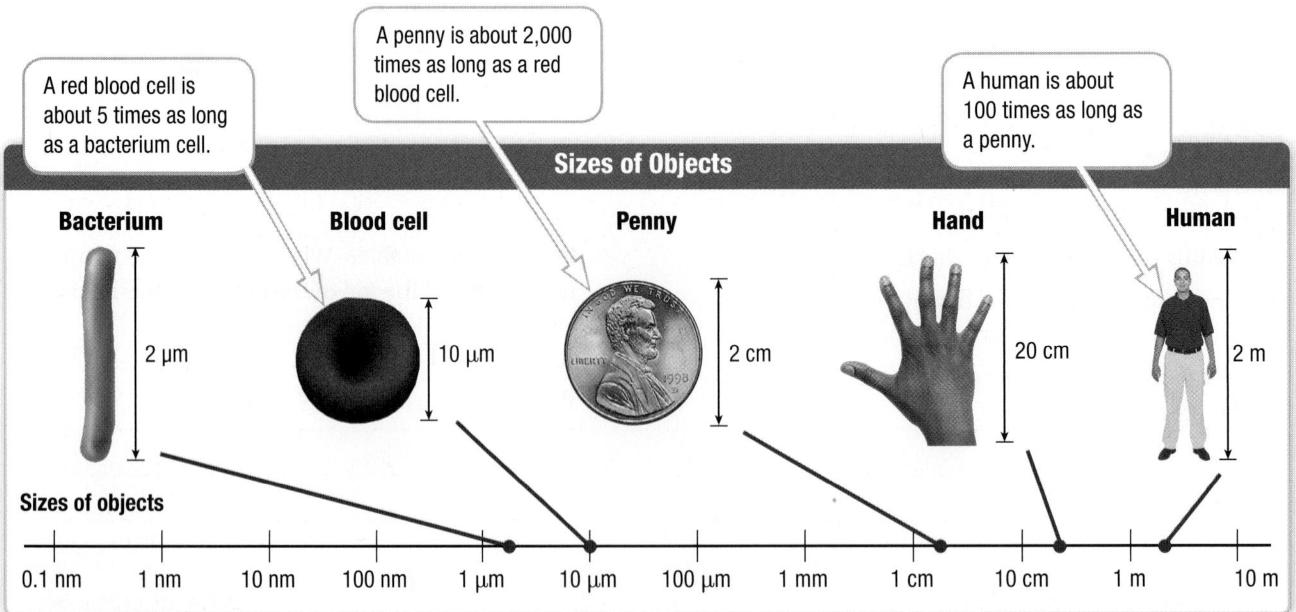

**Base Units** In this book, you will see three fundamental quantities represented by base units in SI: mass, length, and time. The base units of these quantities are the kilogram (kg), the meter (m), and the second (s). These quantities, their base units and symbols, and some unit conversions are listed in **Table 2.**

**Derived Units** Other quantities, such as area and liquid volume, are expressed in derived units. A derived unit is a combination of one or more base units. Like base units, derived units can be expressed by using SI prefixes. Some SI-derived units, including their symbols and common unit conversions, are listed in **Table 3.**

| Table 2 Conversions for SI Base Units |
|---|
| **Mass: unit = kilogram (kg)** |
| 1 kilogram (kg) = 1,000 g |
| 1 gram (g) = 0.001 kg |
| 1 milligram (mg) = 0.001 g |
| 1 microgram (μg) = 0.000001 g |
| **Length: unit = meter (m)** |
| 1 kilometer (km) = 1,000 m |
| 1 meter (m) = 100 cm |
| 1 centimeter (cm) = 0.01 m |
| 1 millimeter (mm) = 0.001 m |
| 1 micrometer (μm) = 0.000001 m |
| **Time: unit = second (s)** |
| 1 minute (min) = 60 s |
| 1 hour (h) = 3,600 s = 60 min |
| 1 day (d) = 24 h |

| Table 3 Conversions for SI-Derived Units |
|---|
| **Area: unit = square meter ($m^2$)** |
| 1 square kilometer ($km^2$) = 100 ha |
| 1 hectare (ha) = 10,000 $m^2$ |
| 1 square meter ($m^2$) = 10,000 $cm^2$ |
| 1 square centimeter ($cm^2$) = 100 $mm^2$ |
| **Liquid volume: unit = cubic meter ($m^3$)** |
| 1 cubic meter ($m^3$) = 1 kL |
| 1 kiloliter (kL) = 1,000 L |
| 1 liter (L) = 1,000 mL |
| 1 milliliter (mL) = 0.001 L |
| 1 cubic centimeter ($cm^3$) = 1 mL |
| **Mass density: unit = kilograms per cubic meter ($kg/m^3$)** |
| **Temperature: unit = degrees Celsius (°C)** |
| **Velocity: unit = meters per second (m/s)** |

## Temperature

Though not part of the SI, the Celsius scale is commonly used to express temperature. In the Celsius scale, 0 °C is the freezing point of water, and 100 °C is the boiling point of water. You can use the temperature scale shown below to convert between the Celsius scale and the Fahrenheit scale, which is commonly used in the United States. You can also use the following equation to convert between degrees Celsius ($T_C$) and degrees Fahrenheit ($T_F$):

$$T_F = \frac{9}{5}T_C + 32$$

For example, to convert 0 °C to degrees Fahrenheit, perform the following calculation:

$$T_F = \frac{9}{5}(0\text{ °C}) + 32\text{ °F} = 0 + 32\text{ °F} = 32\text{ °F}$$

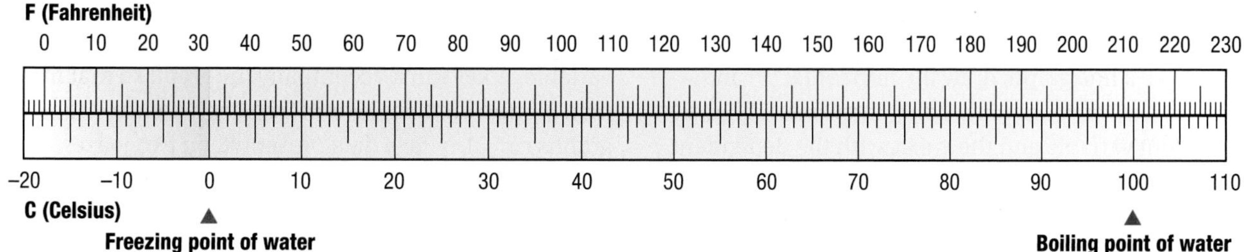

# Graphing

## Constructing Graphs

After finishing an experiment, scientists often illustrate experimental data in graphs. There are three main types of graphs: line graphs, bar graphs, and pie graphs. Organizing data visually helps us identify relationships between variables—factors that change.

The data table shows data collected by a researcher who has hypothesized that increased salt intake will cause an increase in blood pressure. In this experiment, the independent variable was daily salt intake. Recall that the **independent variable** is the one that is changed by the researcher. You can see in the data table that the researcher varied daily salt intake between 0 and 30 g.

Recall that the **dependent variable** is the one that is observed to determine if it is affected by changes in the independent variable. The dependent variable in this experiment was systolic pressure. You can see that in this case, an increase in salt intake corresponds to an increase in systolic pressure. These data support the hypothesis that increases in salt intake cause a rise in blood pressure.

**Data Table**

| Systolic pressure (mm Hg) | Daily salt intake (g) |
|---|---|
| 110 | 0 |
| 120 | 10 |
| 140 | 20 |
| 165 | 30 |

This last data pair is plotted here on the graph.
The dependent variable is graphed on the vertical (y) axis.
Salt Intake and Blood Pressure
Systolic pressure (mm Hg)
170
160
150
140
130
120
110
0
0
10
20
30
Daily salt intake (g)
The independent variable is graphed on the horizontal (x) axis.

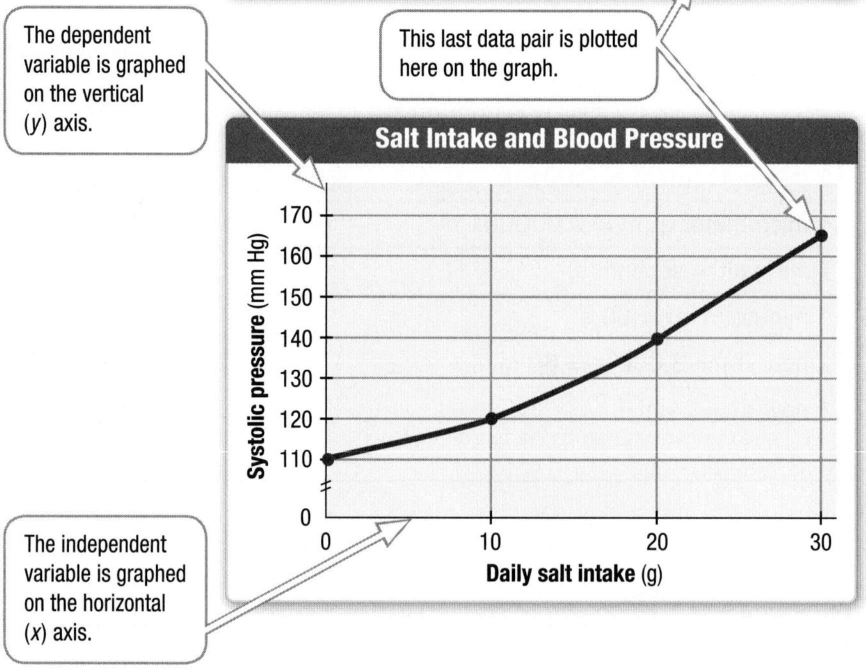

## Line Graphs

Line graphs, such as the one shown above, are most often used to compare or relate one or more sets of data that show continuous change. Each set of data—the independent variable and its corresponding dependent variables—is called a *data pair.*

To make a line graph, draw the horizontal ($x$) and vertical ($y$) axes of your graph. Label the $y$-axis with the independent variable and the $x$-axis with the dependent variable. (Refer to your data table to determine the scale and appropriate units for each axis). Plot each data pair, and then connect the data points to make a line, or curve. Finally, give the graph a title that clearly indicates the relationship between the data shown by the graph.

Sometimes, line graphs can be more complex than the one shown. When a line graph has more than one line, each extra line illustrates another dependent variable. A key must accompany the graph so that the data plotted on the two or more lines are clear. Line graphs can also have data presented on two $y$-axes, which may have different units. In these graphs, the effect of the independent variable can be observed on two dependent variables.

## Bar Graphs

Sometimes, it is not appropriate to use a line graph to represent data. A bar graph can clearly display data that are not continuous. A bar graph is a good indicator of trends if the data are taken over a sufficiently long period of time. For example, studying color variations in moths requires that data be collected over a long period of time. Even after years of study, predictions can still be difficult to make with certainty. Notice that a bar graph is also useful in comparing multiple sets of data, such as those for the light and dark moths found in the woods near Birmingham and Dorset.

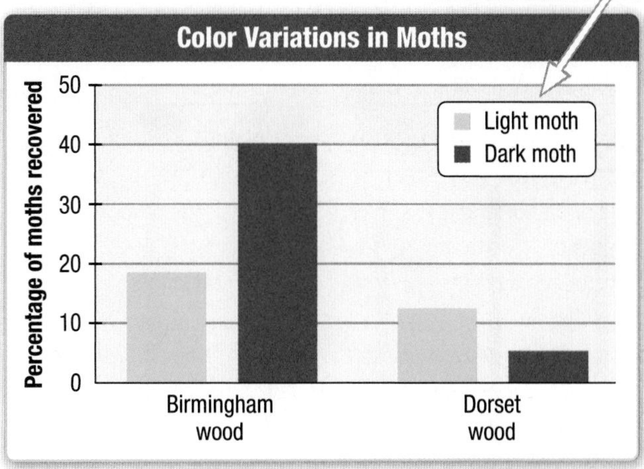




## Pie Graphs

Pie graphs are an easy way to visualize the composition of a whole. Frequently, pie graphs are made from percentage data. For example, you could create a pie graph showing the percentage of known insect species that various insect groups represent. To create a pie graph from data in a table, begin by drawing a circle to represent the whole, or total. Then, imagine dividing the circle into 100 equal sections to represent 100%. Shade in the number of consecutive sections that are represented by each group, and label the slice with the name of that group.

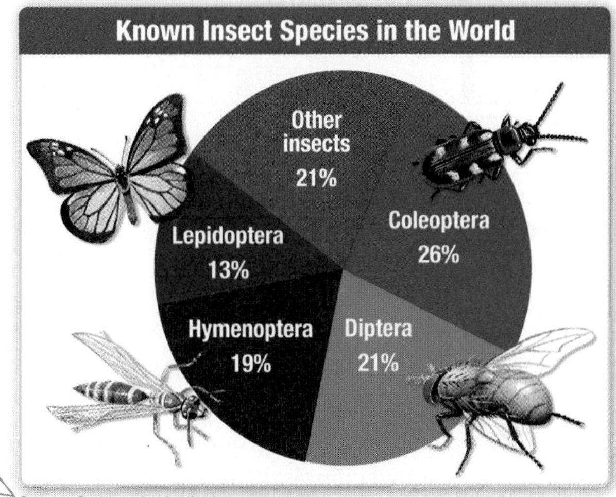


Source: Smithsonian Institution.

## Using Graphs to Make Predictions

Graphs show trends in data that allow us to make predictions. For example, how might taking in 40 g of salt per day affect blood pressure? Referring to the graph of blood pressure and salt intake, you might estimate that systolic pressure could be 190 mm Hg or more. Using a trend in a range of data to estimate values beyond that range is called **extrapolation.**

Likewise, we can use graphs to estimate values that are untested but that lie *within* the range of our data. How might taking in 15 g of salt per day affect blood pressure? You might use the graph to estimate that blood pressure would be about 130 mm Hg. Using a trend in a range of data to estimate values missing from that range is called **interpolation.**

Some data, such as the values for salt intake and blood pressure, interact in an expected way and seem to indicate a causal relationship. But beware of hastily drawing conclusions based on a graph of two variables that change together. In September, the number of school buses on the road and the number of trees turning fall colors rise. But school buses do not make leaves change color! Both are affected by the time of year.

# Classification

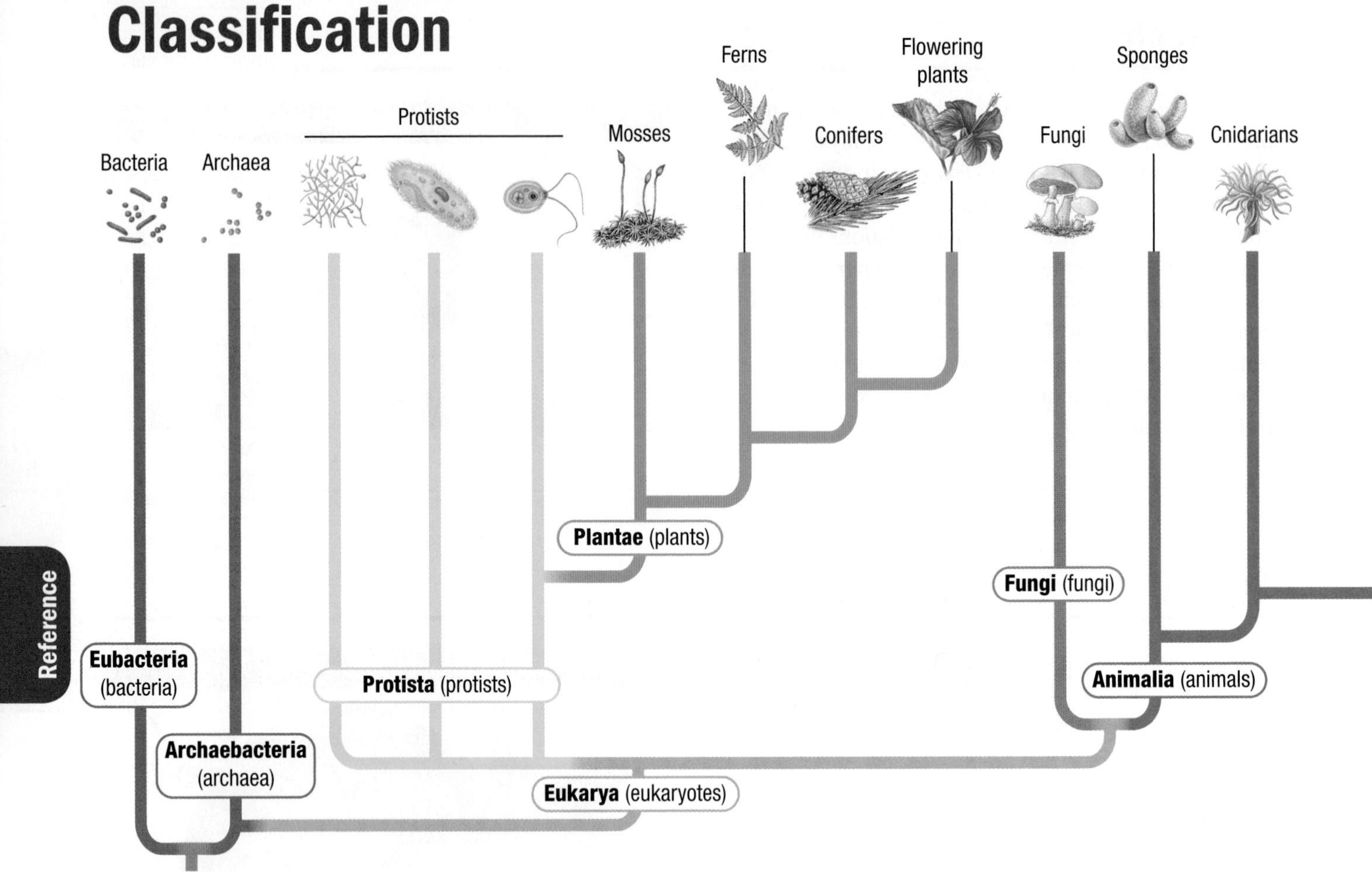


**How Organisms Are Classified** Like many areas of science, the classification of organisms is an active and ever-changing endeavor. Throughout history, many new taxa have been proposed, and some taxa have been reclassified. Biologists have added complexity and detail to their classification systems as they have learned more about organisms. Scientists are unlikely to discover and name all species, much less to agree on the exact relationships between all species.

Today, most biologists use and recognize the Linnaean system, shown here, which consists of three domains and six kingdoms. Also, there is general agreement on the relationships between most of the groups shown in this phylogenetic tree. However, many groupings remain the subject of strong debate and active investigation.

In particular, the relationships between protists are poorly understood, and many scientists are beginning to agree that "Protista" should no longer be considered a single, related taxon. The relationships between invertebrates, such as worms, arthropods, and mollusks, are also strongly debated. For these reasons, this phylogenetic tree does not indicate any particular relationships between these groups.

Any part of a phylogenetic tree—and any taxonomic name—may be revised when scientists gather enough evidence and agree upon revisions. In fact, the entire Linnaean system may someday be replaced with another system that is based on phylogenetic trees rather than lists and tables.

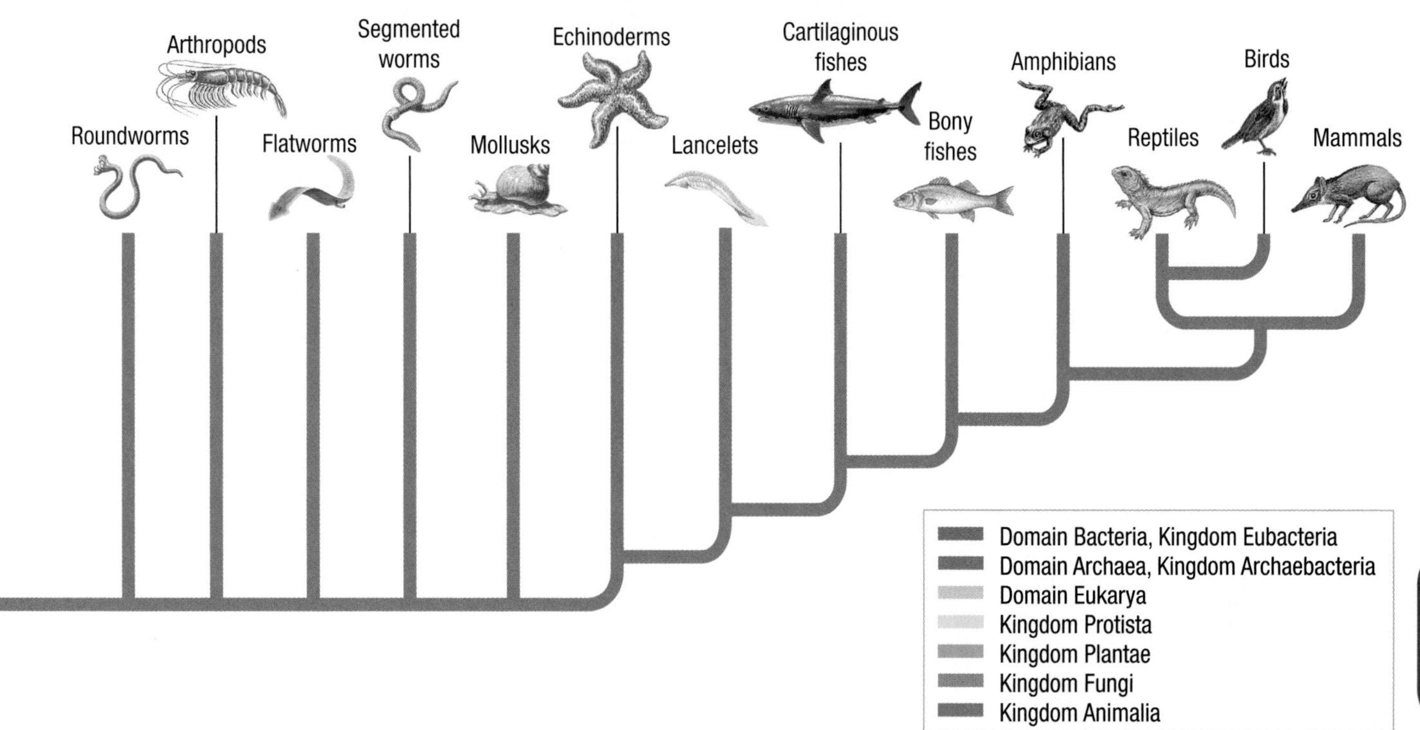




**Characteristics of Domains and Kingdoms**

| Domain | Bacteria | Archaea | Eukarya | | | |
|---|---|---|---|---|---|---|
| **Kingdom** | Eubacteria | Archae-bacteria | Protista | Fungi | Plantae | Animalia |
| **Example** | *Streptococcus pneumoniae* | *Staphylo-thermus marinus* | paramecium | spore cap mushroom | Texas paintbrush | white-winged dove |
| | | | | | | |
| **Cell type** | prokaryotic | | eukaryotic | | | |
| **Cell walls** | cell walls with peptidoglycan | cell walls with unique lipids | cell walls in some species | cell walls with chitin | cell walls with cellulose | no cell walls |
| **Number of cells** | unicellular | | unicellular or multicellular | mostly multicellular | mostly multicellular | multicellular |
| **Nutrition** | autotroph or heterotroph | | | heterotroph | autotroph | heterotroph |

# The Biologist's Periodic Table of Elements

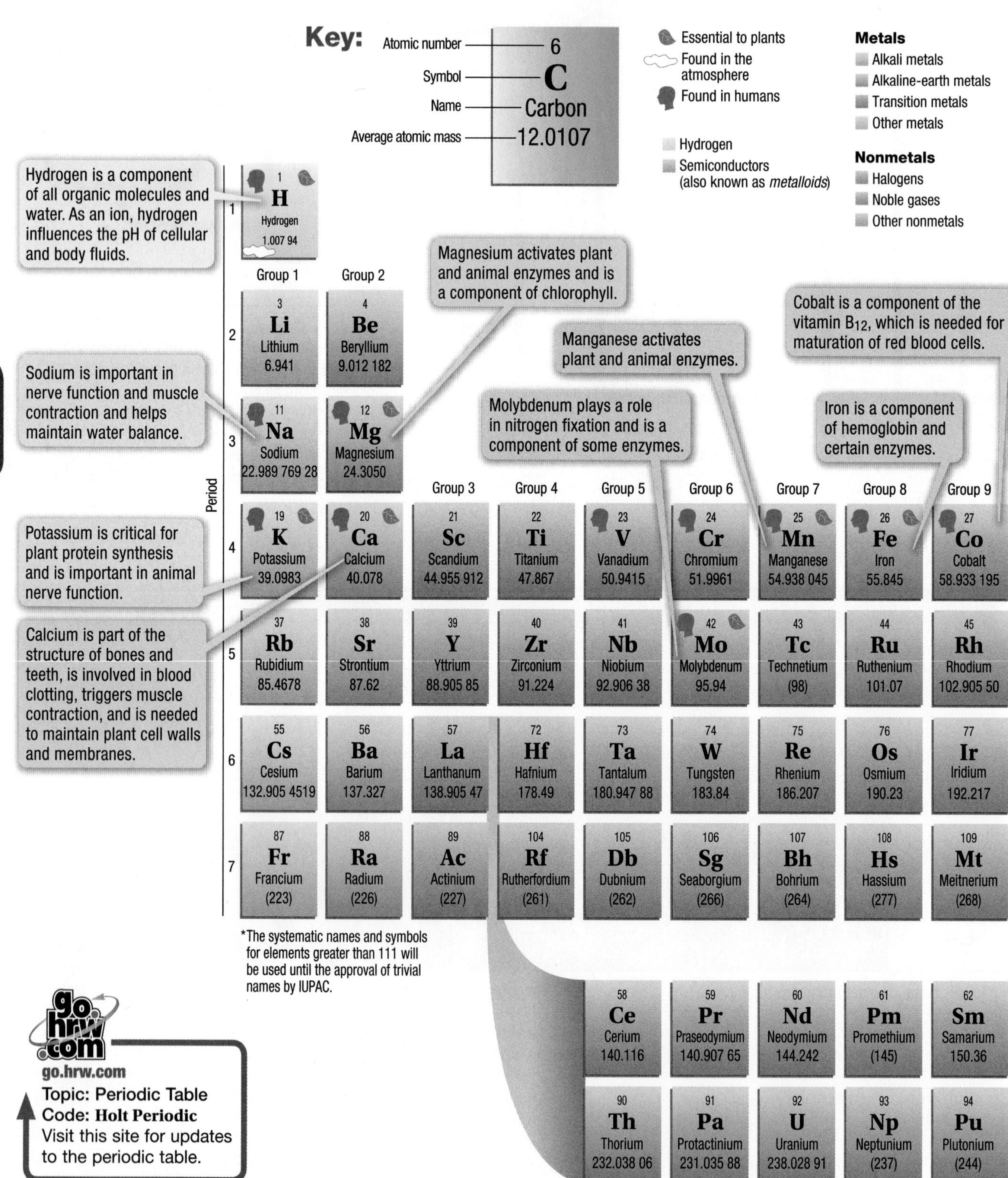

Key:
Atomic number
Symbol
Name
Average atomic mass
6
C
Carbon
12.0107
Essential to plants
Found in the atmosphere
Found in humans
Hydrogen
Semiconductors (also known as *metalloids*)
Metals
Alkali metals
Alkaline-earth metals
Transition metals
Other metals
Nonmetals
Halogens
Noble gases
Other nonmetals
Hydrogen is a component of all organic molecules and water. As an ion, hydrogen influences the pH of cellular and body fluids.
Sodium is important in nerve function and muscle contraction and helps maintain water balance.
Potassium is critical for plant protein synthesis and is important in animal nerve function.
Calcium is part of the structure of bones and teeth, is involved in blood clotting, triggers muscle contraction, and is needed to maintain plant cell walls and membranes.
Magnesium activates plant and animal enzymes and is a component of chlorophyll.
Molybdenum plays a role in nitrogen fixation and is a component of some enzymes.
Manganese activates plant and animal enzymes.
Iron is a component of hemoglobin and certain enzymes.
Cobalt is a component of the vitamin $B_{12}$, which is needed for maturation of red blood cells.
Period
1
2
3
4
5
6
7
Group 1
Group 2
Group 3
Group 4
Group 5
Group 6
Group 7
Group 8
Group 9
1 H Hydrogen 1.007 94
3 Li Lithium 6.941
4 Be Beryllium 9.012 182
11 Na Sodium 22.989 769 28
12 Mg Magnesium 24.3050
19 K Potassium 39.0983
20 Ca Calcium 40.078
21 Sc Scandium 44.955 912
22 Ti Titanium 47.867
23 V Vanadium 50.9415
24 Cr Chromium 51.9961
25 Mn Manganese 54.938 045
26 Fe Iron 55.845
27 Co Cobalt 58.933 195
37 Rb Rubidium 85.4678
38 Sr Strontium 87.62
39 Y Yttrium 88.905 85
40 Zr Zirconium 91.224
41 Nb Niobium 92.906 38
42 Mo Molybdenum 95.94
43 Tc Technetium (98)
44 Ru Ruthenium 101.07
45 Rh Rhodium 102.905 50
55 Cs Cesium 132.905 4519
56 Ba Barium 137.327
57 La Lanthanum 138.905 47
72 Hf Hafnium 178.49
73 Ta Tantalum 180.947 88
74 W Tungsten 183.84
75 Re Rhenium 186.207
76 Os Osmium 190.23
77 Ir Iridium 192.217
87 Fr Francium (223)
88 Ra Radium (226)
89 Ac Actinium (227)
104 Rf Rutherfordium (261)
105 Db Dubnium (262)
106 Sg Seaborgium (266)
107 Bh Bohrium (264)
108 Hs Hassium (277)
109 Mt Meitnerium (268)
*The systematic names and symbols for elements greater than 111 will be used until the approval of trivial names by IUPAC.
58 Ce Cerium 140.116
59 Pr Praseodymium 140.907 65
60 Nd Neodymium 144.242
61 Pm Promethium (145)
62 Sm Samarium 150.36
90 Th Thorium 232.038 06
91 Pa Protactinium 231.035 88
92 U Uranium 238.028 91
93 Np Neptunium (237)
94 Pu Plutonium (244)
go.hrw.com
go.hrw.com
Topic: Periodic Table
Code: Holt Periodic
Visit this site for updates to the periodic table.

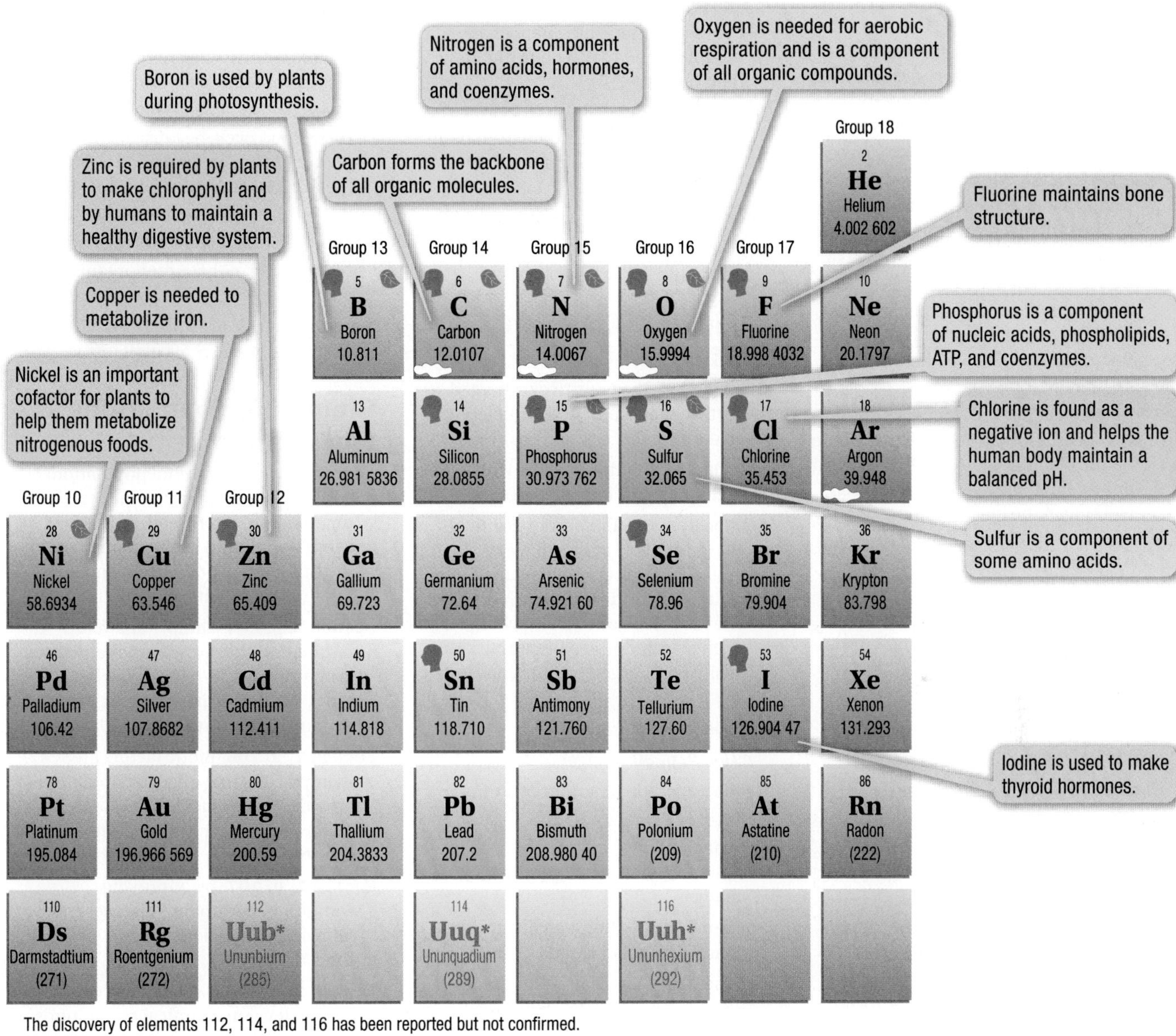


The discovery of elements 112, 114, and 116 has been reported but not confirmed.

| 63 Eu Europium 151.964 | 64 Gd Gadolinium 157.25 | 65 Tb Terbium 158.925 35 | 66 Dy Dysprosium 162.500 | 67 Ho Holmium 164.930 32 | 68 Er Erbium 167.259 | 69 Tm Thulium 168.934 21 | 70 Yb Ytterbium 173.04 | 71 Lu Lutetium 174.967 |
|---|---|---|---|---|---|---|---|---|
| 95 Am Americium (243) | 96 Cm Curium (247) | 97 Bk Berkelium (247) | 98 Cf Californium (251) | 99 Es Einsteinium (252) | 100 Fm Fermium (257) | 101 Md Mendelevium (258) | 102 No Nobelium (259) | 103 Lr Lawrencium (262) |

The atomic masses listed in this table reflect the precision of current measurements. (Each value listed in parentheses is the mass number of that radioactive element's most stable or most common isotope.)

## Chapter 1 Biology and You

**Section 1, p. 8** Sample answer: If a scientist falsely claims to have found a cure for a disease, people who have that disease may try to use the false cure and may be harmed.

**Section 2, p. 13** Sample answer: In science, the word *theory* describes a well-tested, generally accepted principle. In general use, the word *theory* describes a good guess.

**Section 3, p. 14** Most SI units have a prefix that indicates the relationship of that unit to a base unit.

**Section 3, p. 15** Sterile technique is used in a lab when one is trying to avoid contaminating a specimen or is trying to grow only a certain type of microorganism.

**Section 3, p. 16** Sample answer: Listen to your teacher, and follow all instructions. Read your lab procedure before beginning the lab. Always wear any needed safety equipment when working in the lab. Measure chemicals precisely. Do not use damaged or defective equipment.

**Section 4, p. 19** Sample answer: Evolution is the change in inherited characteristics in a population over generations.

## Chapter 2 Applications of Biology

**Section 1, p. 29** It causes disease.

**Section 1, p. 30** Warm water causes the copepod host to mature more quickly. As a result, the cholera bacteria also increase in number.

**Section 1, p. 31** Vaccines allow one's immune system to develop resistance to a pathogen without contracting it.

**Section 1, p. 32** a bionic limb

**Section 2, p. 35** Relative to the eyes of other animals, lobster eyes focus light waves in a unique way. The lobster eye telescope incorporated this technology to focus X-rays, something that other telescopes cannot do.

**Section 2, p. 36** DNA fingerprinting is an identification technique based on a pattern of DNA that represents the total of an organism's genetic material. It uses DNA material, such as skin cells, to identify someone.

**Section 2, p. 37** Some people are concerned that eating genetically modified food may be harmful to their health.

**Section 3, p. 39** A GIS allows researchers to access data from many different studies so that they can work together.

**Section 3, p. 40** to help students understand the natural world through hands-on activities

## Chapter 3 Chemistry of Life

**Section 1, p. 51** a positively charged particle that is part of the nucleus of an atom

**Section 1, p. 52** the attractive force that holds atoms or ions together

**Section 1, p. 54** The partial positive charge of the H atoms in water molecules attracts the negatively charged chloride ions in salt crystals. The partial negative charge of the O atom of water molecules attracts the positively charged sodium ions in salt crystals.

**Section 2, p. 59** carbon

**Section 2, p. 60** a sugar

**Section 2, p. 62** the order of amino acids

**Section 3, p. 64** a change that occurs when the identity of the substance changes

**Section 3, p. 65** their negatively charged electron clouds

**Section 3, p. 67** because the shape of the active site determines which reactant will bind to the active site

## Chapter 4 Ecosystems

**Section 1, p. 80** Sample answer: water, sunlight, and oxygen

**Section 1, p. 81** Pioneer species change the habitat so that other species can live in that habitat.

**Section 1, p. 83** low latitudes

**Section 1, p. 84** marine communities and estuaries

**Section 2, p. 86** Consumers get their energy by eating producers or other consumers. Ultimately, all living organisms get their energy from the sun.

**Section 2, p. 88** Ninety percent of the energy in a predator's prey is lost to the environment as heat as the predator burns the energy to do work, such as breathing and running.

**Section 3, p. 91** Respiration is part of the carbon cycle because it is a process in which oxygen and carbon are exchanged between living organisms and their environment.

**Section 3, p. 92** Bacteria breaks down $N_2$ into a form that other organisms can use.

**Section 3, p. 93** Phosphorus is absorbed by the roots of plants.

## Chapter 5 Populations and Communities

**Section 1, p. 103** A zebra population consists of a group of zebras that live together and interbreed. A different zebra population lives separately from the other zebra population and does not interbreed with that population.

**Section 1, p. 104** Sample answer: A population that grows exponentially grows slowly when it is small but grows quickly as it gets larger. An exponential growth curve is J shaped.

**Section 1, p. 106** Biotic factors are living factors that affect a population's growth. Abiotic factors are nonliving factors that affect a population's growth.

**Section 1, p. 107** by improving sanitation, controlling disease, and allowing for efficient production of food

**Section 2, p. 110** Sample answer: Plants develop chemical compounds that make the plants taste terrible to the herbivores. The herbivores develop defenses against the toxic compounds so that they may eat the plants.

**Section 2, p. 111** Mutualism is a relationship in which both species benefit. Commensalism is a relationship in which one species benefits and the other species is not harmed.

**Section 3, p. 112** A niche is the function of a species in a community. A habitat is the place where the species lives.

**Section 3, p. 113** because they usually have to compete with other species for limited resources

**Section 3, p. 114** by feeding in slightly different ways or slightly different areas

**Section 3, p. 115** Sample answer: Competition between species and high biodiversity contribute to the stability of an ecosystem.

## Chapter 6 The Environment

**Section 1, p. 125** Humans and other organisms are part of the environment and depend on resources from the environment to survive. In turn, the environment is affected by the actions of humans and other organisms.

**Section 1, p. 126** It takes millions of years for natural gas to form.

**Section 2, p. 129** The burning of fossil fuels releases $CO_2$ into the atmosphere. An increase in $CO_2$ in the atmosphere due to the burning of fossil fuels may be responsible for an increase in global temperatures.

**Section 2, p. 130** Sample answer: runoff from roads, leaking underground septic tanks, and pesticides that run off from farms

**Section 2, p. 131** Erosion causes soil to be washed away. Without soil, crops cannot be grown.

**Section 2, p. 133** The zebra mussel clogs treatment facilities and causes millions of dollars in damage.

**Section 3, p. 134** Restoration involves cleaning up and restoring a damaged ecosystem. Conservation involves protecting an existing ecosystem.

**Section 3, p. 135** Sample answer: I can reduce resource use by using recycled materials, low-flow toilets, and low-flow shower heads.

**Section 3, p. 136** by releasing less pollution into the atmosphere than the average car does

**Section 3, p. 137** by having people become more aware of the problems and by motivating people to help solve the problems

**Section 3, p. 138** because we can avoid damage to the environment

## Chapter 7 Cell Structure

**Section 1, p. 151** Hooke's microscope could magnify objects to 30 times their normal size.

**Section 1, p. 153** Smaller cells can exchange substances more efficiently than larger cells of the same shape can.

**Section 1, p. 154** a cellular structure on which proteins are made

**Section 2, p. 157** proteins that remain in the cell, such as proteins that build new organelles or enzymes to speed chemical reactions

**Section 2, p. 161** Nearly all eukaryotic cells, including plant cells, contain mitochondria.

**Section 3, p. 163** long, threadlike structures that rotate quickly to move an organism through its environment

**Section 3, p. 166** the process by which cells of a multicellular organism develop specialized forms and functions

## Chapter 8 Cells and Their Environment

**Section 1, p. 175** The cell membrane provides structural support to the cytoplasm, recognizes foreign material, communicates with other cells, and helps transport substances.

**Section 1, p. 176** Small, nonpolar molecules, ions, and most polar molecules are repelled by the nonpolar interior of the lipid bilayer.

**Section 2, p. 179** because its concentration is higher outside the cell than it is inside the cell

**Section 2, p. 183** lipid bilayer

**Section 3, p. 184** Both signals have long-distance targets. Hormones are distributed widely but affect only certain cells; nerve cells' signals are not widely distributed and instead affect cells in certain locations.

**Section 3, p. 186** Transport proteins open or close in response to signals.

## Chapter 9 Cellular Respiration and Photosynthesis

**Section 1, p. 197** in order to maintain homeostasis

**Section 1, p. 198** Solar energy powers part of the carbon cycle by providing the energy needed for autotrophs to convert carbon dioxide into glucose.

**Section 1, p. 200** ATP is used as an energy source for cellular processes. When the cell needs to perform an activity, ATP can be broken down in order to release energy.

**Section 2, p. 202** A chloroplast has an outer membrane and an inner membrane. The space inside the inner membrane is the stroma. Within the stroma lies the thylakoid membrane, which contains stacks of thylakoids.

**Section 2, p. 205** Pigment molecules in the thylakoids of chloroplasts absorb light energy. Electrons in the pigments are excited by light and move through electron transport chains in thylakoid membranes. These chains generate both ATP and NADPH for the final stage of photosynthesis. Enzymes remove electrons from water to form $O_2$. These electrons replace the excited electrons that passed through the electron transport chains.

**Section 2, p. 207** Temperatures that are too high or too low could inactivate enzymes that are used to perform photosynthesis, which would slow or stop the process.

**Section 3, p. 209** pyruvate, ATP, and NADH

**Section 3, p. 211** Glycolysis breaks down glucose into pyruvate, which is small enough to diffuse across mitochondrial membranes into the mitochondria, where the Krebs cycle takes place.

**Section 3, p. 212** Electrons carried by NADH are transferred to pyruvate produced during glycolysis.

## Chapter 10 Cell Growth and Division

**Section 1, p. 225** A chromatid is a strand of a duplicated and condensed chromosome and is made of a single, long molecule of DNA.

**Section 1, p. 226** between the two DNA copies, where a new cell membrane forms

**Section 2, p. 229** $G_1$, S, and $G_2$

**Section 2, p. 231** a network of several spindle fibers (microtubules)

**Section 2, p. 232** a large, membrane-bound cell wall that forms across the middle of a dividing plant cell (and other cells that have cell walls)

**Section 3, p. 233** protein signals within the cell; signals from other cells; environmental signals/conditions

**Section 3, p. 234** The cell checks for and corrects any mistakes in the copied DNA. Proteins check that the cell is large enough to divide.

**Section 3, p. 235** damage to a cell's DNA, especially genes that control the cell cycle

## Chapter 11 Meiosis and Sexual Reproduction

**Section 1, p. 247** Fragmentation is a kind of reproduction in which the body breaks into several pieces.

**Section 1, p. 248** Germ cells produce gametes, which are reproductive cells.

**Section 2, p. 251** in prophase 1

**Section 2, p. 252** Meiosis produces haploid cells that contain only one set of chromosomes. Mitosis produces diploid cells that contain two sets of chromosomes.

**Section 2, p. 253** Crossing-over increases genetic variation because pieces of two chromatids exchange material during meiosis.

**Section 3, p. 257** One gamete is formed from one female germ cell.

## Chapter 12 Mendel and Heredity

**Section 1, p. 267** Mendel crossed different types of pea plants and recorded the number of each type of offspring.

**Section 1, p. 268** A character is a physical feature that is inherited. A trait is one of several possible forms of a character.

**Section 1, p. 269** a cross that is done to study one pair of contrasting traits

**Section 1, p. 270** In the $F_1$ generation, all of the plants expressed the same trait for a given character. In the $F_2$ generation, the missing trait reappeared.

**Section 2, p. 272** The blending hypothesis states that traits of offspring are always a blend of the traits from parents.

**Section 2, p. 275** A dihybrid cross is a cross involving two characters.

**Section 3, p. 277** Each box inside a Punnett square shows a possible genotype from a given cross.

**Section 3, p. 279** 1/4

**Section 3, p. 280** Traits that are not expressed equally in both sexes are commonly sex-linked traits.

**Section 4, p. 283** Codominance is a condition in which both alleles for the same gene are fully expressed. Incomplete dominance occurs when a phenotype that is intermediate between the two traits is expressed.

**Section 4, p. 284** linked

## Chapter 13 DNA, RNA, and Proteins

**Section 1, p. 293** DNA

**Section 1, p. 297** by weak hydrogen bonds

**Section 1, p. 299** X-ray diffraction studies suggested that DNA's structure resembled a tightly coiled helix.

**Section 2, p. 301** It reduces the number of replication errors.

**Section 2, p. 303** Two distinct replication forks form at each start site, and replication occurs in opposite directions.

**Section 3, p. 305** RNA is composed of one strand of nucleotides instead of two, and it has a ribose backbone rather than a deoxyribose backbone. In RNA, adenine pairs with uracil rather than thymine.

**Section 3, p. 306** The promoter is the "start" site on a sequence of DNA.

**Section 3, p. 309** Codons are the three-nucleotide sequence of mRNA that is created during transcription. An anticodon is the complementary three-nucleotide sequence that is assembled during translation.

## Chapter 14 Genes in Action

**Section 1, p. 319** from mutations of existing genes

**Section 1, p. 321** A point mutation is often silent because the genetic code is redundant; a single nucleotide letter in a codon can change without changing the amino acid that is coded for.

**Section 1, p. 323** Cancer is the uncontrolled growth of tumors, which may be caused by mutations in somatic cells.

**Section 1, p. 324** When the sister chromatids in one of the parent gametes fail to separate, the gamete passes on both copies instead of one.

**Section 2, p. 325** no; The expression of many genes may be turned on or off.

**Section 2, p. 327** almost all parts (before and after transcription and after translation)

**Section 2, p. 329** the sequence of amino acids that forms the protein

**Section 3, p. 331** plants

**Section 3, p. 332** Both consist of DNA or RNA, carry a small set of genes, and move around within and between genomes.

**Section 3, p. 333** a DNA sequence that codes for a DNA-binding domain of a regulatory protein

**Section 3, p. 334** CDK and cyclin act as the engine and gears of the protein cycle.

## Chapter 15 Gene Technologies and Human Applications

**Section 1, p. 345** 3.2 billion base pairs (although much of human DNA is noncoding!)

**Section 1, p. 346** when they are considering having children

**Section 1, p. 347** because insulin is not produced by the person's body (because a gene is defective)

**Section 1, p. 348** It seems to be affected by many genes as well as by the environment; we are not likely to find a simple cure.

**Section 2, p. 350** a genetically modified organism, or an organism that had recombinant genes

**Section 2, p. 351** to cause a plant to produce an insecticide

**Section 2, p. 353** adult and embryonic

**Section 2, p. 354** issues of who should get the information and what decisions should be made based on the information

**Section 3, p. 355** restriction enzymes and plasmids

**Section 3, p. 356** It is semisolid, so molecules can travel through it.

**Section 3, p. 358** transferring genetic samples from one surface or medium to another

**Section 3, p. 359** in the first step, to start copying the template sequence

**Section 3, p. 360** a structure such as a virus or plasmid that can carry and transfer DNA between cells

**Section 3, p. 361** identifying specific genes and mapping their locations

**Section 3, p. 363** genomic and EST

## Chapter 16 Evolutionary Theory

**Section 1, p. 375** the development of new species over time

**Section 1, p. 377** when he visited the Galápagos Islands during his voyage on the *Beagle*

**Section 1, p. 379** that traits acquired during a lifetime could be passed on to offspring

**Section 1, p. 381** No, natural selection is a mechanism that can cause evolution.

**Section 2, p. 383** because not all organisms leave fossils and not all fossils are found

**Section 2, p. 384** descent from a common ancestor

**Section 2, p. 385** carefully collect and consider a great deal of data

**Section 3, p. 387** small-scale genetic changes in populations (microevolution) to large-scale changes in species (macroevolution)

## Chapter 17 Population Genetics and Speciation

**Section 1, p. 399** We know about genetics, such as how genotype relates to phenotype.

**Section 1, p. 400** because many unique combinations of alleles are possible

**Section 1, p. 401** frequency of alleles

**Section 1, p. 402** 1 (or 100%)

**Section 1, p. 403** because it is the source of variation in populations

**Section 2, p. 405** migration

**Section 2, p. 406** increased homozygosity

**Section 2, p. 407** success in leaving future generations of offspring

**Section 2, p. 408** by remaining unexpressed, recessive alleles can be inherited and yet not acted upon by selection

**Section 2, p. 409** disruptive selection

**Section 3, p. 411** because not all species reproduce the same way and the definition of *species* depends on why the species are being studied

**Section 3, p. 413** no; It sometimes results in sterile, unhealthy, or poorly adapted offspring.

**Section 3, p. 414** when it's over!

## Chapter 18 Classification

**Section 1, p. 423** Common names have no system.

**Section 1, p. 424** He wanted to catalog all known species.

**Section 1, p. 426** six

**Section 2, p. 427** the field of classifying species and revising systems of classification

**Section 2, p. 429** It shows relatedness and shared characters between groups of organisms.

**Section 2, p. 430** Sample answer: embryonic development pattern

**Section 2, p. 431** comparisons between DNA, RNA, and proteins

**Section 3, p. 433** Plantae (plants) and Animalia (animals)

**Section 3, p. 435** Archaebacteria and Eubacteria

**Section 3, p. 437** Animalia and Fungi

## Chapter 19 History of Life on Earth

**Section 1, p. 447** simple organic compounds, such as amino acids, fatty acids, and other hydrocarbons

**Section 1, p. 449** RNA can form spontaneously in water, and DNA cannot. RNA can also perform many functions that DNA performs in cells.

**Section 2, p. 451** As layers of sedimentary rock form, layers that are older form beneath layers that are younger.

**Section 2, p. 453** fossil evidence

**Section 3, p. 457** Colonial organisms developed the first example of separate functions being performed by different parts in a larger unit.

## Chapter 20 Homeostasis and Human Body Systems

**Section 1, p. 471** Homeostasis is the tendency of an organism to attempt to maintain a stable internal environment as the environment around the organism changes.

**Section 1, p. 472** Sample answer: A plant's cells react to an increase in light in the plant's environment by performing photosynthesis.

**Section 1, p. 475** (1) concentration of oxygen and carbon dioxide, (2) pH of the internal environment, (3) concentration of nutrients and waste products, (4) Concentration of salts, and (5) volume and pressure of extracellular fluid

**Section 2, p. 477** The epidermis forms a tight barrier that keeps bacteria out.

**Section 2, p. 479** Hormones are used to regulate metabolism; maintain salt, water, and nutrient balance in the blood; control the body's responses to stress; and regulate growth and development.

**Section 2, p. 481** As blood flows through capillaries in the Bowman's capsule, fluid is forced out of the blood into the capsule. This fluid is composed of water, salt, glucose, amino acids, and urea. The fluid passes into a tubule, where glucose and some other molecules in the fluid reenter the bloodstream.

**Section 2, p. 483** to return fluids to the bloodstream and to help the body fight infections

**Section 3, p. 485** Feedback mechanisms are designed to detect changes in the body's internal environment and bring about corrective actions so that the body returns to its normal state.

**Section 3, p. 487** The brainstem detects changes in the amount of carbon dioxide in the bloodstream and signals the muscles that control breathing to speed up or slow down in order to return the carbon dioxide levels to normal.

**Section 3, p. 488** Insulin is the hormone that lowers the blood glucose level by telling the liver to take in glucose and convert it into glycogen. Glucagon is the hormone that raises the blood glucose level between meals by signaling the liver to break down glycogen into glucose to be released into the bloodstream.

## Chapter 21 Homeostasis and Human Diseases

**Section 1, p. 499** pathogens

**Section 1, p. 500** Sample answer: by covering my mouth when I sneeze, washing my hands before eating, washing and cooking food thoroughly, and avoiding contact with infected organisms

**Section 1, p. 501** A healthy diet ensures that your body has the building blocks needed to power healthy cells, repair damaged cells, and replace dead cells.

**Section 2, p. 503** Both diseases are caused by bacteria that cause disease by feeding off of tissues. Fatigue is a symptom of both diseases. The diseases differ in the areas of the body that they typically infect. The bacteria that case tuberculosis typically infect the lungs, while the bacteria that cause Lyme disease typically infect the nervous system and related tissues.

**Section 2, p. 504** Viruses use their host cell to reproduce. When they exit the cell, they often cause the host cell to burst, which results in its death.

**Section 2, p. 506** Yeast infection can occur when the homeostasis of other microorganisms in the body, such as bacteria, is disrupted.

**Section 2, p. 507** The flukes lay eggs in the blood vessels lining the walls of organs. The eggs block the vessels and cause the organs to be damaged.

**Section 3, p. 510** Drinking alcohol can lead to dangerous behavior and can cause serious diseases, such as liver cirrhosis.

**Section 3, p. 512** The disease causes tissue damage through oxygen deprivation and blood clotting. The damaged tissue cannot perform its job as well, which leads to an imbalance in homeostasis.

**Section 3, p. 513** Trauma can damage large parts of an organ. As a result, the organ may be unable to function efficiently or may stop functioning altogether.

**Section 3, p. 514** People choose what they eat and how much they eat. If they make unhealthy choices, an eating disorder may develop.

**Section 3, p. 515** Eating an amanita mushroom can cause liver failure, which will decrease the ability of the blood to clot. As a result,a person could bleed to death. In addition, liver failure severely disrupts digestion and thus leads to an overall weakening of every cell in the body due to malnutrition.

## Chapter 22 The Body's Defenses

**Section 1, p. 525** Skin prevents many pathogens from invading the body (unless there is a tear in the skin).

**Section 1, p. 9527** Viruses display antigens on their cell surfaces, which tells the body that the viral cells are different from "self" cells.

**Section 2, p. 530** plasma cells

**Section 2, p. 533** Antigen shifting is caused by the mutation of viral cells.

**Section 3, p. 535** because the body is launching a strong immune response against harmless airborne particles

**Section 3, p. 539** HIV destroys helper T cells by infecting them and causing them to burst open.

## Chapter 23 Reproduction and Development

**Section 1, p. 549** The anterior pituitary releases LH, which stimulates the production of testosterone. Testosterone, along with FSH, stimulates sperm production.

**Section 1, p. 550** The mitochondria supply sperm with the energy that the sperm need to propel themselves through the female reproductive system.

**Section 1, p. 551** Many sperm die in the acidic environment of the female reproductive system.

**Section 2, p. 553** The ovum is fertilized in a fallopian tube.

**Section 2, p. 555** Elevated levels of LH cause the corpus luteum to secrete estrogen and progesterone, sex hormones.

**Section 2, p. 556** If a fertilized egg does not implant on the wall of the uterus, the levels of estrogen and progesterone will fall. The thick uterine lining will no longer be maintained and will be shed.

**Section 3, p. 559** by the end of the fourth week of pregnancy

**Section 3, p. 560** The fetus gains a great deal of weight, and all of its organ systems become developed enough such that it can live outside of the mother.

**Section 4, p. 561** Some viral STDs can be treated with antiviral medication. Many bacterial STDs can be treated and cured with antibiotics.

**abiotic** (AY bie AHT ik) describes the nonliving part of the environment, including water, rocks, light, and temperature (80)
**abiótico** término que describe la parte sin vida del ambiente, incluyendo el agua, las rocas, la luz y la temperatura (80)

**abiotic factor** (AY bie AHT ik FAK tuhr) an environmental factor that is not associated with the activities of living organisms (106)
**factor abiótic** un factor ambiental que no está asociado con las actividades de los seres vivos (106)

**acid** any compound that increases the number of hydronium ions when dissolved in water; acids turn blue litmus paper red and react with bases and some metals to form salts (56)
**ácido** cualquier compuesto que aumenta el número de iones de hidrógeno cuando se disuelve en agua; los ácidos cambian el color del papel tornasol a rojo y forman sales al reaccionar con bases y con algunos metales (56)

**acid rain** precipitation that has a pH below normal and has an unusually high concentration of sulfuric or nitric acids, often as a result of chemical pollution of the air from sources such as automobile exhausts and the burning of fossil fuels (128)
**lluvia ácida** precipitación con un pH inferior al normal, que tiene una concentración inusualmente alta de ácido sulfúrico y ácido nítrico como resultado de la contaminación química del aire por fuentes tales como los escapes de los automóviles y la quema de combustibles fósiles (128)

**activation energy** the minimum amount of energy required to start a chemical reaction (65)
**energía de activación** la cantidad mínima de energía que se requiere para iniciar una reacción química (65)

**active site** on an enzyme, the site that attaches to a substrate (66)
**sitio activo** el sitio en una enzima que se une al sustrato (66)

**active transport** the movement of chemical substances, usually across the cell membrane, against a concentration gradient; requires cells to use energy (178)
**transporte activo** el movimiento de sustancias químicas, normalmente a través de la membrana celular, en contra de un gradiente de concentración; requiere que la célula gaste energía (178)

**adaptation** (AD uhp TAY shuhn) the process of becoming adapted to an environment; an anatomical, physiological, or behavioral change that improves a population's ability to survive (381)
**adaptación** el proceso de adaptarse a un ambiente; un cambio anatómico, fisiológico o en la conducta que mejora la capacidad de supervivencia de una población (381)

**adaptive radiation** (uh DAP tiv RAY dee AY shuhn) an evolutionary pattern in which many species evolve from a single ancestral species (389, 413)
**radiación adaptativa** un patrón evolucionista en el cual muchas especies evolucionan a partir de una sola especie ancestral (389, 413)

**adenine** (AD uh NEEN) one of the four bases that combine with sugar and phosphate to form a nucleotide subunit of DNA; adenine pairs with thymine (297)
**adenina** una de las cuatro bases que se combinan con un azúcar y un fosfato para formar una de las subunidades de nucleótidos del ADN; la adenina se une a la timina (297)

**adhesion** (ad HEE zhuhn) the attractive force between two bodies of different substances that are in contact with each other (55)
**adhesión** la fuerza de atracción entre dos cuerpos de diferentes sustancias que están en contacto (55)

**aerobic** (er OH bik) describes a process that requires oxygen (209)
**aeróbico** término que describe un proceso que requiere oxígeno (209)

**AIDS** (AYDZ) acquired immune deficiency syndrome, a disease caused by HIV, an infection that results in an ineffective immune system (539)
**SIDA** síndrome de inmunodeficiencia adquirida, enfermedad causada por una infección de VIH, la cual resulta en un sistema inmunológico ineficiente (539)

**alcoholic fermentation** (FUHR muhn TAY shuhn) the anaerobic process by which yeasts and other microorganisms break down sugars to form carbon dioxide and ethanol (212)
**fermentación alcohólica** el proceso anaeróbico por medio del cual las levaduras y otros microorganismos descomponen los azúcares para formar dióxido de carbono y alcohol etílico (212)

**allele** (uh LEEL) one of the alternative forms of a gene that governs a characteristic, such as hair color (272)
**alelo** una de las formas alternativas de un gene que rige un carácter, como por ejemplo, el color del cabello (272)

**allergen** (AL uhr juhn) a substance that causes an allergic reaction (534)
**alergeno** una sustancia que causa una reacción alérgica (534)

**allergy** (AL uhr jee) a physical response to an antigen, which can be a common substance that produces little or no response in the general population (534)
**alergia** una reacción física a un antígeno, el cual puede ser una sustancia común que produce una reacción ligera o que no produce ninguna reacción en la población general (534)

**alveolus** (al VEE uh luhs) any of the tiny air sacs of the lungs where oxygen and carbon dioxide are exchanged (482)
**alveolo** cualquiera de las diminutas bolsas de aire de los pulmones, en donde ocurre el intercambio de oxígeno y dióxido de carbono (482)

**amino acid** (uh MEE noh) a compound of a class of simple organic compounds that contain a carboxyl group and an amino group and that combine to form proteins (62)
**aminoácido** un compuesto de una clase de compuestos orgánicos simples que contienen un grupo carboxilo y un grupo amino y que al combinarse forman proteínas (62)

**ammonification** (uh MAHN i fi KAY shuhn) the formation of ammonia compounds in the soil by the action of bacteria on decaying matter (92)
**amonificación** la formación compuestos de amoniaco en el suelo debido a la acción de las bacterias en la materia en descomposición (92)

**amnion** (AM nee uhn) the membrane that contains a developing embryo and its surrounding fluid (558)
**membrana amniótica** la membrana que contiene al embrión en desarrollo y el líquido que lo rodea (558)

**anaerobic** (AN uhr OH bik) describes a process that does not require oxygen (209)
**anaeróbico** término que describe un proceso que no requiere oxígeno (209)

**analogous** (uh NAL uh guhs) in comparisons of different organisms, describes features that are similar in function and appearance but not in structure or origin (428)
**análogo** en comparaciones de diferentes organismos, término que describe características que son similares en función y apariencia, pero no en estructura u origen (428)

**anatomy** (uh NAT uh mee) the bodily structure of an organism (384)
**anatomía** la estructura corporal de un organismo (384)

**antibody** (AN ti BAHD ee) a protein that reacts to a specific antigen or that inactivates or destroys toxins (530)
**anticuerpo** una proteína que reacciona ante un antígeno específico o que inactiva o destruye toxinas (530)

**anticodon** (ANT ie KOH DAHN) a region of a tRNA molecule that consists of a sequence of three bases that is complementary to an mRNA codon (308)
**anticodón** una región de una molécula de ARNt formada por una secuencia de tres bases que complementan el codón del ARNm (308)

**antigen** (AN tuh juhn) a substance that stimulates an immune response (527)
**antígeno** una sustancia que estimula una respuesta inmunológica (527)

**antigen shifting** the production of new antigens by a virus as it mutates over time (533)
**cambio antigénico** la producción de antígenos nuevos por un virus cuando éste muta con el paso del tiempo (533)

**apoptosis** (AP uhp TOH sis) in multicellular organisms, a genetically controlled process that leads to the death of a cell; programmed cell death (334)
**apoptosis** en los organismos pluricelulares, un proceso controlado genéticamente que lleva a la muerte de una célula; la muerte programada de una célula (334)

**archaea** (ahr KEE uh) prokaryotes (most of which are known to live in extreme environments) that are distinguished from other prokaryotes by differences in their genetics and in the makeup of their cell wall; members of the domain Archaea (singular, *archaeon*) (435)
**arqueas** procariotes (la mayoría de los cuales viven en ambientes extremos) que se distinguen de otros procariotes por diferencias genéticas y por la diferente composición de su pared celular; miembros del dominio Archaea (435)

**artery** (AHRT uhr ee) a blood vessel that carries blood away from the heart to the body's organs (482)
**arteria** un vaso sanguíneo que transporta sangre del corazón a los órganos del cuerpo (482)

**artificial selection** the human practice of breeding animals or plants that have certain desired traits (377)
**selección artificial** la práctica humana de criar animales o cultivar plantas que tienen ciertos caracteres deseados (377)

**asexual reproduction** (ay SEK shoo uhl) reproduction that does not involve the union of gametes and in which a single parent produces offspring that are genetically identical to the parent (247)
**reproducción asexual** reproducción que no involucra la unión de gametos, en la que un solo progenitor produce descendencia que es genéticamente igual al progenitor (247)

**atom** the smallest unit of an element that maintains the chemical properties of that element (51)
**átomo** la unidad más pequeña de un elemento que conserva las propiedades químicas de ese elemento (51)

**ATP** adenosine triphosphate, an organic molecule that acts as the main energy source for cell processes; composed of a nitrogenous base, a sugar, and three phosphate groups (63, 198)
**ATP** adenosín trifosfato; molécula orgánica que funciona como la fuente principal de energía para los procesos celulares; formada por una base nitrogenada, un azúcar y tres grupos fosfato (63, 198)

**ATP synthase** (SIN THAYZ) an enzyme that catalyzes the synthesis of ATP (201)
**ATP sintetasa** una enzima que cataliza la síntesis del ATP (201)

**autoimmune disease** (AWT oh i MYOON) a disease in which the immune system attacks the organism's own cells (537)
**enfermedad autoinmune** una enfermedad en la que el sistema inmunológico ataca las células del propio organismo (537)

**autosome** (AWT uh SOHM) any chromosome that is not a sex chromosome (249)
**autosoma** cualquier cromosoma que no es un cromosoma sexual (249)

**autotroph** (AWT oh TRAHF) an organism that produces its own nutrients from inorganic substances or from the environment instead of consuming other organisms (197, 434, 437)
**autótrofo** un organismo que produce sus propios nutrientes a partir de sustancias inorgánicas o del ambiente, en lugar de consumir otros organismos (197, 434, 437)

**bacteria** (bak TIR ee uh) extremely small, single-celled organisms that usually have a cell wall and that usually reproduce by cell division (singular, *bacterium*) (435)
**bacterias** organismos extremadamente pequeños, unicelulares, que normalmente tienen pared celular y se reproducen por división celular (435)

**base** any compound that increases the number of hydroxide ions when dissolved in water; bases turn red litmus paper blue and react with acids to form salts (56)
**base** cualquier compuesto que aumenta el número de iones de hidróxido cuando se disuelve en agua; las bases cambian el color del papel tornasol a azul y forman sales al reaccionar con ácidos (56)

**base pairing rules** the rules stating that in DNA cytosine pairs with guanine and adenine pairs with thymine and that in RNA cytosine pairs with guanine and adenine pairs with uracil (297)
**regla de apareamiento de las bases** las reglas que establecen que en el ADN, la citosina se une a la guanina y la adenina se une a la timina, y que en el ARN, la citosina se une a la guanina y la adenina se une al uracilo (297)

**B cell** a white blood cell that matures in bones and makes antibodies (530)
**célula B** un glóbulo blanco de la sangre que madura en los huesos y fabrica anticuerpos (530)

**bell curve** a symmetrical frequency curve (400)
**curva de campana** una curva simétrica de frecuencia (400)

**benign tumor** (bi NIEN TOO muhr) an abnormal but noncancerous cell mass or growth (235)
**tumor benigno** un bulto o masa de células anormal, pero que no es cancerosa (235)

**binary fission** (BIE nuh ree FISH uhn) a form of asexual reproduction in single-celled organisms by which one cell divides into two cells of the same size (247)
**fisión binaria** una forma de reproducción asexual de los organismos unicelulares, por medio de la cual la célula se divide en dos células del mismo tamaño (247)

**binomial nomenclature** (bie NOH mee uhl NOH muhn KLAY chuhr) a system for giving each organism a two-word scientific name that consists of the genus name followed by the species name (424)
**nomenclatura binomial** un sistema para darle a cada organismo un nombre científico de dos palabras, el cual está formando por el género seguido de la especie (424)

**biodiversity** (BIE oh duh VUHR suh tee) the variety of organisms in a given area, the genetic variation within a population, the variety of species in a community, or the variety of communities in an ecosystem (80, 132)
**biodiversidad** la variedad de organismos que se encuentran en un área determinada, la variación genética dentro de una población, la variedad de especies en una comunidad o la variedad de comunidades en un ecosistema (80, 132)

**biogeography** (BIE oh jee AH gruh fee) the study of the geographical distribution of living organisms and fossils on Earth (383)
**biogeografía** el estudio de la distribución geográfica de los seres vivos y los fósiles en la Tierra (383)

**bioinformatics** (BIE oh in fuhr MA tiks) the application of information technologies in biology, especially in genetics (361)
**bioinformática** la aplicación de las tecnologías de la información en la biología, especialmente la genética (361)

**biological species concept** the principle that defines a species as a group of organisms whose members can interbreed to produce offspring (411)
**concepto de especie biológica** el principio que define a una especie como un grupo de organismos que pueden producir descendencia al cruzarse entre ellos (411)

**biology** the scientific study of living organisms and their interactions with the environment (17)
**biología** el estudio científico de los seres vivos y sus interacciones con el medio ambiente (17)

**biome** (BIE OHM) a large region characterized by a specific type of climate and certain types of plant and animal communities (82)
**bioma** una región extensa caracterizada por un tipo de clima específico y ciertos tipos de comunidades de plantas y animales (82)

**biometrics** (BIE oh ME triks) the statistical analysis of biological data; especially the measurement and analysis of unique physical or behavioral characteristics to verify the identity of a person (36)
**biométrica** el análisis estadístico de datos biológicos, especialmente la medición y el análisis de características físicas o características de conducta únicas para verificar la identidad de una persona (36)

**bioremediation** (BIE oh ri MEE dee AY shuhn) the biological treatment of hazardous waste by natural or genetically engineered microorganisms (349)
**bioremediación** el tratamiento biológico de desechos peligrosos por medio de microorganismos naturales o modificados genéticamente (349)

**biotic** (bie AHT ik) describes living factors in the environment (79)
**biótico** término que describe los factores vivientes del ambiente (79)

**biotic factor** an environmental factor that is associated with or results from the activities of living organisms (106)
**factor biótico** un factor ambiental que está asociado con las actividades de los seres vivos o que resulta de ellas (106)

**blastocyst** (BLAS toh SIST) in placental mammals, a developing embryo that consists of a hollow ball of cells surrounding an inner cell mass (557)
**blastoquistela** en los mamíferos placentarios, un embrión en desarrollo que consiste en una bola hueca de células que rodean una masa de células interna (557)

**budding** asexual reproduction in which a part of the parent organism pinches off and forms a new organism (247)
**yemación** reproducción asexual en la que una parte del organismo progenitor se separa y forma un nuevo organismo (247)

**buffer** (BUHF uhr) a solution made from a weak acid and its conjugate base that neutralizes small amounts of acids or bases added to it (57)
**búfer** una solución que contiene un ácido débil y su base conjugada y que neutraliza pequeñas cantidades de ácidos y bases que se le añaden (57)

**bulbourethral gland** (BUHL boh yoo REE thruhl) one of the two glands in the male reproductive system that add fluid to the semen during ejaculation (551)
**glándula bulbouretral** una de las dos glándulas del aparato reproductor masculino que añaden líquido al semen durante la eyaculación (551)

**Calvin cycle** (KAL vin) a biochemical pathway of photosynthesis in which carbon dioxide is converted into glucose using ATP (206)
**ciclo de Calvin** una vía bioquímica de la fotosíntesis en la que el dióxido de carbono se convierte en glucosa usando ATP (206)

**cancer** a type of disorder of cell growth that results in invasion and destruction of surrounding healthy tissue by abnormal cells (235, 323)
**cáncer** un tipo de trastorno del crecimiento celular en el que células anormales invaden y destruyen los tejidos sanos que las rodean (235, 323)

**capillary** (KAP uh LER ee) a tiny blood vessel that allows an exchange between blood and cells in tissue (482)
**capilar** diminuto vaso sanguíneo que permite el intercambio entre la sangre y las células de los tejidos (482)

**capsule** in mosses, the part that contains spores; in bacteria, a protective layer of polysaccharides around the cell wall (154)
**cápsula** en los musgos, la parte que contiene las esporas; en las bacterias, una capa protectora de polisacáridos que se encuentra alrededor de la pared celular (154)

**carbohydrate** (KAHR boh HIE drayt) a class of molecules that includes sugars, starches, and fiber; contains carbon, hydrogen, and oxygen (60)
**carbohidrato** una clase de moléculas entre las que se incluyen azúcares, almidones y fibra; contiene carbono, hidrógeno y oxígeno (60)

**carbon cycle** the movement of carbon from the nonliving environment into living things and back (91)
**ciclo del carbono** el movimiento del carbono del ambiente sin vida a los seres vivos y de los seres vivos al ambiente (91)

**carnivore** (KAHR nuh VAWR) an organism that eats animals (87)
**carnívoro** un organismo que se alimenta de animales (87)

**carrier** in biology, an individual who has one copy of a recessive autosomal allele that causes disease in the homozygous condition (323)
**portador** en biología, un individuo que tiene una copia de un alelo recesivo autosómico, el cual causa enfermedades en la condición homocigótica (323)

**carrier protein** a protein that transports substances across a cell membrane (179)
**proteína transportadora** una proteína que transporta sustancias a través de la membrana celular (179)

**carrying capacity** (kuh PAS i tee) the largest population that an environment can support at any given time (104)
**capacidad de carga** la población más grande que un ambiente puede sostener en cualquier momento dado (104)

**cell** in biology, the smallest unit that can perform all life processes; cells are covered by a membrane and contain DNA and cytoplasm (18, 151)
**célula** en biología, la unidad más pequeña que puede realizar todos los procesos vitales; las células están cubiertas por una membrana y tienen ADN y citoplasma (18, 151)

**cell cycle** the life cycle of a cell; in eukaryotes, it consists of a cell-growth period in which DNA is synthesized and a cell-division period in which mitosis takes place (228, 334)
**ciclo celular** el ciclo de vida de una célula; en los eucariotes, consiste de un período de crecimiento celular en el que el ADN se sintetiza, y un período de división celular en el que ocurre la mitosis (228, 334)

**cell differentiation** (DIF uhr EN shee AY shuhn) the process by which a cell becomes specialized for a specific structure or function during multicellular development (333)
**diferenciación celular** el proceso por medio del cual una célula se especializa en una estructura o función específica durante el desarrollo pluricelular (333)

**cell membrane** (MEM BRAYN) a phospholipid layer that covers a cell's surface and acts as a barrier between the inside of a cell and the cell's environment (154)
**membrana celular** una capa de fosfolípidos que cubre la superficie de la célula y funciona como una barrera entre el interior de la célula y el ambiente de la célula (154)

**cell theory** the theory that states that all living things are made up of cells, that cells are the basic units of organisms, that each cell in a multicellular organism has a specific job, and that cells come only from existing cells (152)
**teoría celular** la teoría que establece que todos los seres vivos están formados por células, que las células son las unidades fundamentales de los organismos y que las células provienen únicamente de células existentes (152)

**cellular respiration** (SEL yoo luhr RES puh RAY shuhn) the process by which cells produce energy from carbohydrates; atmospheric oxygen combines with glucose to form water and carbon dioxide (198)
**respiración celular** el proceso por medio del cual las células producen energía a partir de los carbohidratos; el oxígeno atmosférico se combina con la glucosa para formar agua y dióxido de carbono (198)

**cellulose** (SEL yoo LOHS) a carbohydrate that consists of linked glucose units and that adds rigidity to the cell walls in plants, many algae, and some fungi; it is a component of dietary fiber (60, 437)
**celulosa** un carbohidrato compuesto por unidades de glucosa ligadas que agrega rigidez a las paredes celulares de las plantas, de muchas algas y de algunos hongos; es un componente de la fibra dietaria (60, 437)

**central vacuole** (VAK yoo OHL) a large cavity or sac that is found in plant cells or protozoans and that contains air or partially digested food (160)
**vacuola central** una cavidad o bolsa grande que se encuentra en las células vegetales o en los protozoarios y que contiene aire o alimentos parcialmente digeridos (160)

**centromere** (SEN troh MIR) the region of the chromosome that holds the two sister chromatids together during mitosis (225)
**centrómero** la región de un cromosoma que mantiene unidas las dos cromátidas hermanas durante la mitosis (225)

**centrosome** (SEN truh SOHM) an organelle that contains the centrioles and is the center of dynamic activity in mitosis (230)
**centrosoma** un organelo que contiene los centríolos y es el centro de actividad dinámica en la mitosis (230)

**cervix** (SUHR VIKS) the inferior portion of the uterus (553)
**cuello del útero** la porción inferior del útero (553)

**character** (KAR uhk tuhr) a recognizable inherited feature or characteristic of an organism; in Mendelian heredity, a feature that exists in one of two or more possible variations called *traits* (268)
**carácter** un elemento o característica heredada reconocible de un organismo; en la herencia mendeliana, una característica que existe en una de dos o más variaciones posibles llamadas *rasgos* (268)

**chemical bond** the attractive force that holds atoms or ions together (52)
**enlace químico** la fuerza de atracción que mantiene unidos a los átomos o iones (52)

**chitin** (KIE tin) a carbohydrate that forms part of the cell walls of fungi and part of the exoskeleton of arthropods, such as insects and crustaceans (60, 437)
**quitina** un carbohidrato que forma parte de la pared celular de los hongos y del exoesqueleto de los artrópodos, como por ejemplo los insectos y los crustáceos (60, 437)

**chlorofluorocarbons** (KLAWR oh FLUR uh KAWR buhnz) hydrocarbons in which some or all of the hydrogen atoms are replaced by chlorine and fluorine; used in coolants for refrigerators and air conditioners and in cleaning solvents; their use is restricted because they destroy ozone molecules in the stratosphere (abbreviation, CFCs) (128)
**clorofluorocarbonos** hidrocarburos en los que algunos o todos los átomos de hidrógeno son reemplazados por cloro y flúor; se usan en líquidos refrigerantes para refrigeradores y aires acondicionados y en solventes para limpieza; su uso está restringido porque destruyen las moléculas de ozono de la estratosfera (abreviatura: CFC) (128)

**chlorophyll** (KLAWR uh FIL) a green pigment that is present in most plant and algae cells and some bacteria, that gives plants their characteristic green color, and that absorbs light to provide energy for photosynthesis (203)
**clorofila** un pigmento verde presente en la mayoría de las células de las plantas y las algas y en algunas bacterias, que les da a las plantas su color verde característico y que absorbe luz para brindar energía para la fotosíntesis (203)

**chloroplast** (KLAWR uh PLAST) an organelle found in plant and algae cells where photosynthesis occurs (161)
**cloroplasto** un organelo que se encuentra en las células vegetales y en las células de las algas, en el cual se lleva a cabo la fotosíntesis (161)

**chorion** (KAWR ee AHN) the outer membrane that surrounds an embryo (558)
**membrana coriónica** la membrana exterior que rodea al embrión (558)

**chromatid** (KROH muh TID) one of the two strands of a chromosome that become visible during meiosis or mitosis (225)
**cromátida** una de las dos hebras de un cromosoma que se vuelve visible durante la meiosis o mitosis (225)

**chromatin** (KROH muh TIN) the substance that composes eukaryotic chromosomes; it consists of specific proteins, DNA, and small amounts of RNA (224)
**cromatina** la sustancia que compone los cromosomas eucarióticos; contiene proteínas específicas, ADN y pequeñas cantidades de ARN (224)

**chromosome** (KROH muh SOHM) in a eukaryotic cell, one of the structures in the nucleus that are made up of DNA and protein; in a prokaryotic cell, the main ring of DNA (224, 249, 251, 302)
**cromosoma** en una célula eucariótica, una de las estructuras del núcleo que está hecha de ADN y proteína; en una célula procariótica, el anillo principal de ADN (224, 249, 251, 302)

**clade** a group of organisms that includes all of the evolutionary descendants of a common ancestral lineage (429)
**clado** un grupo de organismos que incluye a todos los descendientes evolutivos de un linaje ancestral en común (429)

**cladistics** (kluh DIS tiks) a phylogenetic classification system that uses shared derived characters and ancestry as the sole criterion for grouping taxa (428)
**cladística** un sistema de clasificación filogénica en el que los únicos criterios de agrupación de los taxa son los caracteres comunes derivados y la ascendencia (428)

**cladogram** (KLAD uh GRAM) a diagram that is based on patterns of shared, derived traits and that shows the evolutionary relationships between groups of organisms (429)
**cladograma** un diagrama basado en modelos de caracteres comunes derivados, que muestra las relaciones evolutivas entre grupos de organismos (429)

**class** a taxonomic category containing orders with common characteristics (426)
**clase** una categoría taxonómica que contiene órdenes con características comunes (426)

**climate** the average weather conditions in an area over a long period of time (82)
**clima** las condiciones promedio del tiempo en un área durante un largo período de tiempo (82)

**clone** an organism, cell, or piece of genetic material that is genetically identical to one from which it was derived; to make a genetic duplicate (352)
**clon** un organismo, una célula o una muestra de material genético que es genéticamente idéntico a aquél del cual deriva; hacer un duplicado genético (352)

**codominance** (koh DAHM uh nuhns) a condition in which both alleles for a gene are fully expressed (283)
**codominancia** una condición en la que los dos alelos de un gene están totalmente expresados (283)

**codon** (KOH DAHN) in DNA and mRNA, a three-nucleotide sequence that encodes an amino acid or signifies a start signal or a stop signal (307)
**codón** en el ADN y el ARN, una secuencia de tres nucleótidos que codifica un aminoácido o indica una señal de inicio o una señal de terminación (307)

**coevolution** (KOH ev uh LOO shuhn) the evolution of two or more species that is due to mutual influence, often in a way that makes the relationship more mutually beneficial (109)
**coevolución** la evolución de dos o más especies que se debe a su influencia mutua, a menudo de un modo que hace que la relación sea más mutuamente beneficiosa (109)

**cohesion** (coh HEE zhuhn) the force that holds molecules of a single material together (55)
**cohesión** la fuerza que mantiene unidas a las moléculas de un solo material (55)

**colonial organism** (kuh LOH nee uhl) a collection of genetically identical cells that are permanently associated but in which little or no integration of cell activities occurs (165)
**organismo colonial** un conjunto de células genéticamente idénticas que están asociadas permanentemente, pero en el que no se da una gran integración de las actividades celulares (165)

**combustion** (kuhm BUHS chuhn) the burning of a substance (91)
**combustión** fenómeno que ocurre cuando una sustancia se quema (91)

**commensalism** (kuh MEN suhl IZ uhm) a relationship between two organisms in which one organism benefits and the other is unaffected (110)
**comensalismo** una relación entre dos organismos en la que uno se beneficia y el otro no es afectado (110)

**community** a group of various species that live in the same habitat and interact with each other (79)
**comunidad** un grupo de varias especies que viven en el mismo hábitat e interactúan unas con otras (79)

**competitive exclusion** (eks KLOO zhuhn) the exclusion of one species by another due to competition (114)
**exclusión competitiva** la exclusión de una especie por otra debido a la competencia (114)

**compound** a substance made up of atoms of two or more different elements joined by chemical bonds (52)
**compuesto** una sustancia formada por átomos de dos o más elementos diferentes unidos por enlaces químicos (52)

**concentration** (KAHN suhn TRAY shuhn) the amount of a particular substance in a given quantity of a mixture, solution, or ore (178)
**concentración** la cantidad de una cierta sustancia en una cantidad determinada de mezcla, solución o mena (178)

**concentration gradient** a difference in the concentration of a substance across a distance (178)
**gradiente de concentración** una diferencia en la concentración de una sustancia a través de una distancia (178)

**condensation** (KAHN duhn SAY shuhn) the change of state from a gas to a liquid (90)
**condensación** el cambio de estado de gas a líquido (90)

**consumer** an organism that eats other organisms or organic matter instead of producing its own nutrients or obtaining nutrients from inorganic sources (86)
**consumidor** un organismo que se alimenta de otros organismos o de materia orgánica, en lugar de producir sus propios nutrientes o de obtenerlos de fuentes inorgánicas (86)

**contractile vacuole** (kunh TRAK til VAK yoo OHL) in protozoans, an organelle that accumulates water and then releases it periodically to maintain osmotic pressure (181)
**vacuola contráctil** en los protozoarios, un organelo que acumula agua y luego la libera periódicamente para mantener la presión osmótica (181)

**control group** in an experiment, a group that serves as a standard of comparison with another group to which the control group is identical except for one factor (11)
**grupo de control** en un experimento, un grupo que sirve como estándar de comparación con otro grupo, al cual el grupo de control es idéntico excepto por un factor (11)

**convergent evolution** (kuhn VUHR juhnt) the process by which unrelated species become more similar as they adapt to the same kind of environment (428)
**evolución convergente** el proceso por medio del cual especies no relacionadas se vuelven más parecidas a medida que se adaptan al mismo tipo de ambiente (428)

**corpus luteum** (KAWR puhs LOOT ee uhm) the structure that forms from the ruptured follicle in the ovary after ovulation; it releases hormones (555)
**cuerpo lúteo** la estructura que se forma a partir de los folículos rotos del ovario después de la ovulación; libera hormonas (555)

**covalent bond** (koh VAY luhnt) a bond formed when atoms share one or more pairs of electrons (52)
**enlace covalente** un enlace formado cuando los átomos comparten uno o más pares de electrones (52)

**crossing-over** the exchange of genetic material between homologous chromosomes during meiosis; can result in genetic recombination (251)
**recombinación** el intercambio de material genético entre cromosomas homólogos durante la meiosis; puede resultar en la recombinación genética (251)

**cross-pollination** (PAHL uh NAY shuhn) a reproductive process in which pollen from one plant is transferred to the stigma of another plant (268)
**polinización cruzada** un proceso reproductor en el que el polen de una planta es transferido al estigma de otra (268)

**cyanobacterium** (SIE uh noh bak TIR ee uhm) a bacterium that carries out photosynthesis; a blue-green alga (455)
**cianobacteria** una bacteria que efectúa la fotosíntesis; un alga verdiazul (455)

**cytokinesis** (SIET oh ki NEE sis) the division of the cytoplasm of a cell; cytokinesis follows the division of the cell's nucleus by mitosis or meiosis (229)
**citoquinesis** la división del citoplasma de una célula; la citoquinesis ocurre después de que el núcleo de la célula se divide por mitosis o meiosis (229)

**cytoplasm** (SIET oh PLAZ uhm) the region of the cell within the membrane that includes the fluid, the cytoskeleton, and all of the organelles except the nucleus (154)
**citoplasma** la región de la célula dentro de la membrana, que incluye el líquido, el citoesqueleto y los organelos, pero no el núcleo (154)

**cytosine** (SIET oh SEEN) one of the four bases found in DNA and RNA; cytosine pairs with guanine (297)
**citosina** una de las cuatro bases que se encuentran en el ADN y ARN; la citosina se une con la guanina (297)

**cytoskeleton** (SIET oh SKEL uh tuhn) the cytoplasmic network of protein filaments that plays an essential role in cell movement, shape, and division (156)
**citoesqueleto** la red citoplásmica de filamentos de proteínas que juega un papel esencial en el movimiento, forma y división de la célula (156)

**cytosol** (SIE tuh SAWL) the soluble portion of the cytoplasm, which includes molecules and small particles, such as ribosomes, but not the organelles covered with membranes (154)
**citosol** la porción soluble del citoplasma, que incluye moléculas y partículas pequeñas, tales como los ribosomas, pero no los organelos que están cubiertos por membranas (154)

**cytotoxic T cell** (SIE tuh TAHK sik) a type of T cell that recognizes and destroys cells infected by virus (530)
**célula T citotóxica** un tipo de célula T que reconoce y destruye las células infectadas por un virus (530)

**decomposer** (DEE kuhm POH zuhr) an organism that feeds by breaking down organic matter from dead organisms; examples include bacteria and fungi (86)
**descomponedor** un organismo que desintegra la materia orgánica de organismos muertos y se alimenta de ella; entre los ejemplos se encuentran las bacterias y los hongos (86)

**deforestation** (dee FAWR i STAY shuhn) the process of clearing forests (132)
**deforestación** el proceso de talar bosques (132)

**denitrification** (dee NIE truh fi KAY shuhn) the liberation of nitrogen from nitrogen-containing compounds by bacteria in the soil (92)
**desnitrificación** ocurre cuando las bacterias liberan nitrógeno contenido en compuestos que se encuentran en el suelo (92)

**density-dependent factor** a variable affected by the number of organisms present in a given area (105)
**factor dependiente de la densidad** una variable afectada por el número de organismos presentes en un área determinada (105)

**density-independent factor** a variable that affects a population regardless of the population density, such as climate (105)
**factor independiente de la densidad** una variable que afecta a una población independientemente de la densidad de la población, por ejemplo, el clima (105)

**deoxyribose** (dee AHKS ee RIE bohs) a five-carbon sugar that is a component of DNA nucleotides (296)
**desoxirribosa** azúcar de cinco carbonos que es un componente de los nucleótidos de ADN (296)

**dermis** (DUHR mis) the layer of skin below the epidermis (477)
**dermis** la capa de piel que está debajo de la epidermis (477)

**diffusion** (di FYOO zhuhn) the movement of particles from regions of higher density to regions of lower density (178)
**difusión** el movimiento de partículas de regiones de mayor densidad a regiones de menor densidad (178)

**digestion** (die JES chuhn) the breaking down of food into chemical substances that can be used for energy (480)
**digestión** la descomposición de la comida en sustancias químicas que se usan para generar energía (480)

**dihybrid cross** (die HIE brid) a cross between individuals that have different alleles for the same gene (275)
**cruza dihíbrida** un cruzamiento entre individuos que tienen diferentes alelos para el mismo gene (275)

**diploid** (DIP LOYD) a cell that contains two haploid sets of chromosomes (249)
**diploide** una célula que contiene dos juegos de cromosomas haploides (249)

**directional selection** a natural selection process in which one genetic variation is selected and that causes a change in the overall genetic composition of the population (409)
**selección direccional** un proceso de selección natural en el cual se selecciona una variación genética que origina un cambio en la composición genética global de la población (409)

**disaccharide** (die SAK uh RIED) a sugar formed from two monosaccharides (60)
**disacárido** un azúcar formada a partir de dos monosacáridos (60)

**disruptive selection** a type of natural selection in which two extreme forms of a trait are selected (409)
**selección disruptiva** un tipo de selección natural en el cual se seleccionan dos formas extremas de un carácter (409)

**distribution** (DIS tri BYOO shuhn) the relative arrangement of the members of a statistical population; usually shown in a graph (400)
**distribución** la organización relativa de los miembros de una población estadística; normalmente se muestra en una gráfica (400)

**DNA** deoxyribonucleic acid, the material that contains the information that determines inherited characteristics (63, 293)
**ADN** ácido desoxirribonucleico, el material que contiene la información que determina las características que se heredan (63, 293)

**DNA fingerprint** a pattern of DNA characteristics that is unique, or nearly so, to an individual organism (347, 358)
**huella de ADN** un patrón de características del ADN que pertenece exclusivamente, o casi exclusivamente, a un organismo individual (347, 358)

**DNA helicase** (HEEL uh KAYS) an enzyme that unwinds the DNA double helix during DNA replication (301)
**helicasa ADN** una enzima que separa las hebras de la doble hélice del ADN durante la replicación del ADN (301)

**DNA polymerase** (puh LIM uhr AYS) an enzyme that catalyzes the formation of the DNA molecule (301)
**polimerasa ADN** una enzima que actúa como catalizadora en la formación de la molécula de ADN (301)

**DNA polymorphisms** (PAHL ee MAWR FIZ uhmz) variations in DNA sequences; can be used as a basis for comparing genomes (356)
**polimorfismos de ADN** variaciones en las secuencias de ADN; puede usarse como base para comparar genomas (356)

**DNA replication** (REP luh KAY shuhn) the process of making a copy of DNA (300)
**replicación del ADN** el proceso de hacer una copia del ADN (300)

**DNA sequencing** (SEE kwuhns ing) the process of determining the order of every nucleotide in a gene or genetic fragment; also referred to as *gene sequencing* (345, 359)
**secuenciación de ADN** el proceso de determinar el orden de cada nucleótido de un gene o un fragmento genético; también conocido como *secuenciación de genes* (345, 359)

**domain** in a taxonomic system based on rRNA analysis, one of the three broad groups that all living things fall into; in a protein, a functional unit that has a distinctive pattern of structural folding (329, 426)
**dominio** en el sistema taxonómico basado en el análisis de ARNr, uno de los tres amplios grupos al que pertenecen todos los seres vivos; en una proteína, una unidad funcional que tiene un patrón distintivo de plegamiento estructural (329, 426)

**dominant** (DAHM uh nuhnt) in genetics, describes an allele that is fully expressed whenever the allele is present in an individual (273)
**dominante** en la genética, término que describe a un alelo que se expresa por completo siempre que el alelo está presente en un individuo (273)

**double helix** (HEE LIKS) the spiral-staircase structure characteristic of the DNA molecule (296)
**doble hélice** la estructura en forma de escalera en espiral característica de la molécula del ADN (296)

**Down syndrome** (SIN DROHM) a disorder caused by an extra 21st chromosome and characterized by a number of physical and mental abnormalities; also called *trisomy-21* (324)
**síndrome de Down** un trastorno producido por un cromosoma 21 adicional y caracterizado por una variedad de anormalidades físicas y mentales; también se llama *trisomía-21* (324)

**ecology** (ee KAHL uh jee) the study of the interactions of living organisms with one another and with their environment (38)
**ecología** el estudio de las interacciones de los seres vivos entre sí mismos y entre sí mismos y su ambiente (38)

**ecosystem** (EE koh SIS tuhm) a community of organisms and their abiotic environment (79)
**ecosistema** una comunidad de organismos y su ambiente abiótico (79)

**ecotourism** (EK oh TUR IZ uhm) a form of tourism that supports the conservation and sustainable development of ecologically unique areas (137)
**ecoturismo** una forma de turismo que apoya la conservación y desarrollo sustentable de áreas ecológicamente únicas (137)

**ejaculation** (ee JAK yoo LAY shuhn) the expulsion of seminal fluids from the urethra of the penis during sexual intercourse (551)
**eyaculación** la expulsión de fluidos seminales de la uretra del pene durante las relaciones sexuales (551)

**electron** (ee LEK TRAHN) a subatomic particle that has a negative charge (51)
**electrón** una partícula subatómica que tiene carga negativa (51)

**electron cloud** a region around the nucleus of an atom where electrons are likely to be found (51)
**nube de electrones** una región que rodea al núcleo de un átomo en la cual es probable encontrar a los electrones (51)

**electron transport chain** a series of molecules, found in the inner membranes of mitochondria and chloroplasts, through which electrons pass in a process that causes protons to build up on one side of the membrane (201)
**cadena de transporte de electrones** una serie de moléculas que se encuentran en las membranas internas de las mitocondrias y cloroplastos y a través de las cuales pasan los electrones en un proceso que hace que los protones se acumulen en un lado de la membrana (201)

**electrophoresis** (ee LEK troh fuh REE sis) the process by which electrically charged particles suspended in a liquid move through the liquid because of the influence of an electric field (356)
**electroforesis** el proceso por medio del cual las partículas con carga eléctrica que están suspendidas en un líquido se mueven por todo el líquido debido a la influencia de un campo eléctrico (356)

**element** a substance that cannot be separated or broken down into simpler substances by chemical means; all atoms of an element have the same atomic number (51)
**elemento** una sustancia que no se puede separar o descomponer en sustancias más simples por medio de métodos químicos; todos los átomos de un elemento tienen el mismo número atómico (51)

**embryo** (EM bree OH) in plants and animals, one of the early stages of development of an organism (557)
**embrión** en las plantas y los animales, un organismo en una de las primeras etapas del desarrollo (557)

**embryology** (EM bree AHL uh jee) the study of the development of an animal from the fertilized egg to the new adult organism; sometimes limited to the period between fertilization of the egg and hatching or birth (383)
**embriología** el estudio del desarrollo de un animal desde el óvulo fecundado hasta el nuevo organismo adulto; a veces se limita al período entre la fecundación del óvulo y la salida del cascarón o el nacimiento (383)

**emigration** (EM i GRAY shuhn) the movement of an individual or group out of its native area (104)
**emigración** la salida de un individuo o grupo de la región de la que es originario (104)

**endocrine gland** (EN doh KRIN) a ductless gland that secretes hormones into the blood (479)
**glándula endocrina** una glándula sin conductos que secreta hormonas a la sangre (479)

**endocytosis** (EN doh sie TOH sis) the process by which a cell membrane surrounds a particle and encloses the particle in a vesicle to bring the particle into the cell (183)
**endocitosis** el proceso por medio del cual la membrana celular rodea una partícula y la encierra en una vesícula para llevarla al interior de la célula (183)

**endoplasmic reticulum** (EN doh PLAZ mik ri TIK yuh luhm) a system of membranes that is found in a cell's cytoplasm and that assists in the production, processing, and transport of proteins and in the production of lipids (158)
**retículo endoplásmico** un sistema de membranas que se encuentra en el citoplasma de la célula y que tiene una función en la producción, procesamiento y transporte de proteínas y en la producción de lípidos (158)

**endosymbiosis** (EN doh SIM bie OH ses) a mutually beneficial relationship in which one organism lives within another (456)
**endosimbiosis** una relación mutuamente beneficiosa en la que un organismo vive dentro de otro (456)

**endosymbiotic theory** a theory that some cell organelles (mainly mitochondria and chloroplasts) are descended from prokaryotic cells that came to live within other cells during early evolutionary history (331)
**teoría endosimbiótica** una teoría según la cual los organelos celulares (principalmente las mitocondrias y los cloroplastos) descienden de células procarióticas que comenzaron a vivir dentro de otras células al comienzo de la historia evolutiva (331)

**energy** the capacity to do work (64)
**energía** la capacidad de realizar un trabajo (64)

**energy pyramid** a triangular diagram that shows an ecosystem's loss of energy, which results as energy passes through the ecosystem's food chain; each row in the pyramid represents a trophic (feeding) level in an ecosystem, and the area of a row represents the energy stored in that trophic level (89)
**pirámide de energía** un diagrama con forma de triángulo que muestra la pérdida de energía que ocurre en un ecosistema a medida que la energía pasa a través de la cadena alimenticia del ecosistema; cada hilera de la pirámide representa un nivel trófico (de alimentación) en el ecosistema, y el área de la hilera representa la energía almacenada en ese nivel trófico (89)

**environmental science** (en VIE ruhn MENT'l) the study of the air, water, and land surrounding an organism or a community, which ranges from a small area to Earth's entire biosphere; it includes the study of the impact of humans on the environment (38, 125)
**ciencias ambientales** el estudio del aire, agua y tierra circundantes en relación con un organismo o comunidad, desde un área pequeña de la Tierra hasta la biosfera completa; incluye el estudio del impacto que los seres humanos tienen en el ambiente (38, 125)

**enzyme** (EN ZIEM) a molecule, either protein or RNA, that acts as a catalyst in biochemical reactions (66)
**enzima** una molécula, ya sea una proteína o ARN, que actúa como catalizador en las reacciones bioquímicas (66)

**epidemiology** (EP uh DEE mee AHL uh jee) the study of the distribution of diseases in populations and the study of factors that influence the occurrence and spread of disease (31)
**epidemiología** el estudio de la distribución de las enfermedades en poblaciones y el estudio de los factores que influyen en la incidencia y propagación de las enfermedades (31)

**epidermis** (EP uh DUHR mis) the outer surface layer of cells of a plant or animal (477)
**epidermis** la superficie externa de las células de una planta o animal (477)

**epididymis** (EP uh DID i mis) the long, coiled tube that is on the surface of a testis and in which sperm mature (550)
**epidídimo** el conducto largo y enrollado que se encuentra en la superficie de los testículos, en el que los espermatozoides maduran (550)

**equilibrium** (EE kwi LIB ree uhm) in biology, a state that exists when the concentration of a substance is the same throughout a space (178)
**equilibrio** en biología, un estado que existe cuando la concentración de una sustancia es la misma en un espacio dado (178)

**era** a unit of geologic time that includes two or more periods (453)
**era** una unidad de tiempo geológico que incluye dos o más períodos (453)

**erosion** (ee ROH zhuhn) a process in which the materials of Earth's surface are loosened, dissolved, or worn away and transported from one place to another by a natural agent, such as wind, water, ice, or gravity (131)
**erosión** un proceso por medio del cual los materiales de la superficie de la Tierra se aflojan, disuelven o desgastan y son transportados de un lugar a otro por un agente natural, como el viento, el agua, el hielo o la gravedad (131)

**estrogen** (ES truh juhn) a hormone that regulates the sexual development and reproductive function of females (554)
**estrógeno** una hormona que regula el desarrollo sexual y la función reproductiva en las hembras (554)

**estuary** (ES tyoo er ee) an area where fresh water from rivers mixes with salt water from the ocean; the part of a river where the tides meet the river current (84)
**estuario** un área donde el agua dulce de los ríos se mezcla con el agua salada del océano; la parte de un río donde las mareas se encuentran con la corriente del río (84)

**eukaryote** (yoo KAR ee OHT) an organism made up of cells that have a nucleus enclosed by a membrane, multiple chromosomes, and a mitotic cycle; eukaryotes include protists, animals, plants, and fungi but not archaea or bacteria (155, 436)
**eucariote** un organismo cuyas células tienen un núcleo contenido en una membrana, varios cromosomas y un ciclo mitótico; entre los eucariotes se encuentran protistas, animales, plantas y hongos, pero no arqueas ni bacterias (155, 436)

**evaporation** (ee VAP uh RAY shuhn) the change of state from a liquid to a gas (90)
**evaporación** el cambio de estado de líquido a gas (90)

**evolution** (EV uh LOO shuhn) generally, in biology, the process of change by which new species develop from preexisting species over time; at the genetic level, the process in which inherited characteristics within populations change over time; the process defined by Darwin as "descent with modification" (19, 375)
**evolución** generalmente, en biología, el proceso de cambio por el cual se desarrollan nuevas especies a partir de especies preexistentes a lo largo del tiempo; a nivel genético, el proceso por el cual las características heredadas dentro de las poblaciones cambian con el tiempo; el proceso que Darwin llamó "descendencia con modificación" (19, 375)

**excretion** (eks KREE shuhn) the process of eliminating metabolic wastes (481)
**excreción** el proceso de eliminar desechos metabólicos (481)

**exocytosis** (EK soh sie TOH sis) the process by which a substance is released from the cell through a vesicle that transports the substance to the cell surface and then fuses with the membrane to let the substance out (183)
**exocitosis** el proceso por medio del cual una sustancia se libera de la célula a través de una vesícula que la transporta a la superficie de la célula en donde se fusiona con la membrana para dejar salir a la sustancia (183)

**exon** (EK sahn) one of several nonadjacent nucleotide sequences that are part of one gene and that are transcribed, joined together, and then translated (329)
**exón** una de las varias secuencias de nucleótidos no adyacentes que forman parte de un gene y que se transcriben, se unen y luego se traducen (329)

**experiment** (ek SPER uh muhnt) a procedure that is carried out under controlled conditions to discover, demonstrate, or test a fact, theory, or general truth (11)
**experimento** un procedimiento que se lleva a cabo bajo condiciones controladas para descubrir, demostrar o probar un hecho, teoría o verdad general (11)

**exponential growth** (EKS poh NEN shuhl) logarithmic growth, or growth in which numbers increase by a certain factor in each successive time period (104, 379)
**crecimiento exponencial** crecimiento logarítmico o crecimiento en el que los números aumentan en función de un cierto factor en cada período de tiempo sucesivo (104, 379)

**extinct** (ek STINGKT) describes a species that has died out completely (389)
**extinto** término que describe a una especie que ha desaparecido por completo (389)

**extinction** (ek STINGK shuhn) the death of every member of a species (133, 389, 414)
**extinción** la muerte de todos los miembros de una especie (133, 389, 414)

**$F_1$ generation** the first generation of offspring obtained from an experimental cross of two organisms (269)
**generación $F_1$** la primera generación de descendencia que se obtiene de la cruza experimental de dos organismos (269)

**$F_2$ generation** the second generation of offspring, obtained from an experimental cross of two organisms; the offspring of the $F_1$ generation (269)
**generación $F_2$** la segunda generación de descendencia que se obtiene de la cruza experimental de dos organismos de una generación $F_1$ (269)

**facilitated diffusion** (fuh SIL uh TAYT id di FYOO zhuhn) the transport of substances through a cell membrane along a concentration gradient with the aid of carrier proteins (179)
**difusión facilitada** el transporte de sustancias a través de la membrana celular de una región de mayor concentración a una de menor concentración con la ayuda de proteínas transportadoras (179)

**fallopian tube** (fuh LOH pee uhn) a tube through which eggs move from the ovary to the uterus (553)
**trompa de Falopio** un conducto a través del cual se mueven los óvulos del ovario al útero (553)

**family** the taxonomic category below the order and above the genus (426)
**familia** la categoría taxonómica debajo del orden y arriba del género (426)

**feedback mechanism** (MEK uh NIZ uhm) a cycle of events in which information from one step controls or affects a previous step (484)
**mecanismo de retroalimentación** un ciclo de sucesos en el que la información de una etapa controla o afecta a una etapa anterior (484)

**fermentation** the breakdown of carbohydrates by enzymes, bacteria, yeasts, or mold in the absence of oxygen (212)
**fermentación** la descomposición de carbohidratos por enzimas, bacterias, levaduras o mohos, en ausencia de oxígeno (212)

**fertilization** (FUHR'tl i ZAY shuhn) the union of a male and female gamete to form a zygote (248)
**fecundación** la unión de un gameto masculino y femenino para formar un cigoto (248)

**fetus** (feetus) a developing human from the end of the eighth weeks after fertilization until birth (559)
**feto** un ser humano en desarrollo, desde el final de la octava semana después de la fecundación hasta el nacimiento (559)

**flagellum** (fluh JEL uhm) a long, hairlike structure that grows out of a cell and enables the cell to move (162)
**flagelo** una estructura larga parecida a una cola, que crece hacia el exterior de una célula y le permite moverse (162)

**follicle** (FAHL i kuhl) a small, narrow cavity or sac in an organ or tissue, such as the ones on the skin that contain hair roots or the ones in the ovaries that contain the developing eggs (555)
**folículo** una bolsa o cavidad angosta y pequeña en un órgano o tejido, como las que se encuentran en la piel y contienen las raíces de los pelos, o las que se encuentran en los ovarios y contienen los óvulos en desarrollo (555)

**food chain** the pathway of energy transfer through various stages as a result of the feeding patterns of a series of organisms (87)
**cadena alimenticia** la vía de transferencia de energía través de varias etapas, que ocurre como resultado de los patrones de alimentación de una serie de organismos (87)

**food web** a diagram that shows the feeding relationships between organisms in an ecosystem (87)
**red alimenticia** un diagrama que muestra las relaciones de alimentación entre los organismos de un ecosistema (87)

**fossil** (FAHS uhl) the trace or remains of an organism that lived long ago, most commonly preserved in sedimentary rock (382)
**fósil** los indicios o los restos de un organismo que vivió hace mucho tiempo, comúnmente preservados en las rocas sedimentarias (382)

**fossil fuel** a nonrenewable energy resource formed from the remains of organisms that lived long ago; examples include oil, coal, and natural gas (126)
**combustible fósil** un recurso energético no renovable formado a partir de los restos de organismos que vivieron hace mucho tiempo; algunos ejemplos incluyen el petróleo, el carbón y el gas natural (126)

**fossil record** the history of life in the geologic past as indicated by the traces or remains of living things (382, 450)
**registro fósil** la historia de la vida en el pasado geológico según la indican los rastros o restos de seres vivos (382, 450)

**frameshift mutation** a mutation, such as the insertion or deletion of a nucleotide in a coding sequence, that results in the misreading of the code during translation because of a change in the reading frame (320)
**mutación de desplazamiento del marco** una mutación, tal como la inserción o supresión de un nucleoide en una secuencia de codificación, que tiene como resultado una lectura equivocada del código durante la traducción debido a un cambio en el marco de lectura (320)

**frequency** (FREE kwuhn see) the number of cycles or vibrations per unit of time; *also* the number of waves produced in a given amount of time (401)
**frecuencia** el número de ciclos o vibraciones por unidad de tiempo; *también,* el número de ondas producidas en una cantidad de tiempo determinada (401)

**fundamental niche** (FUHN duh MENT'l NICH) the largest ecological niche where an organism or species can live without competition (113)
**nicho fundamental** el nicho ecológico más grande en el que un organismo o especie vive sin experimentar competencia (113)

## G

**gamete** (GAM eet) a haploid reproductive cell that unites with another haploid reproductive cell to form a zygote (248)
**gameto** una célula reproductiva haploide que se une con otra célula reproductiva haploide para formar un cigoto (248)

**gametophyte** (guh MEET uh FIET) in alternation of generations, the phase in which gametes are formed; a haploid individual that produces gametes (258)
**gametofito** en generaciones alternadas, la fase en la que los gametos se forman; un individuo haploide que produce gametos (258)

**gene** (JEEN) the most basic physical unit of heredity; a segment of nucleic acids that codes for a functional unit of RNA and/or a protein (224, 293)
**gene** la unidad física más básica de la herencia; un segmento de ácidos nucleicos que codifica una unidad funcional de ARN y/o una proteína (224, 293)

**gene expression** (eks PRESH uhn) the manifestation of the genetic material of an organism in the form of specific traits (304)

**expresión de los genes** la manifestación del material genético de un organismo en forma de caracteres específicos (304)

**gene flow** the movement of genes into or out of a population due to interbreeding (405)

**flujo de genes** el movimiento de genes a una población o fuera de ella debido al entrecruzamiento (405)

**gene pool** the total set of genes, including all alleles, that are present in a population at any one point in time (401)

**fondo común de genes** el conjunto total de genes, incluyendo todos los alelos, que están presentes en una población en un momento determinado (401)

**generation** (JEN uhr AY shuhn) the entire group of offspring produced by a given group of parents (269)

**generación** el grupo completo de descendientes producido por un grupo determinado de progenitores (269)

**gene technology** any of a wide range of procedures that analyze, decipher, or manipulate the genetic material of organisms (350)

**tecnología genética** cualquiera de una gran variedad de procedimientos para analizar, descifrar o manipular el material genético de los organismos (350)

**gene therapy** a technique that places a gene into a cell to correct a hereditary disease or to improve the genome (347)

**terapia genética** una técnica que coloca un gene en una célula para corregir una enfermedad hereditaria o para mejorar el genoma (347)

**genetically modified organism** an organism containing genetic material that has been artificially altered so as to produce a desired characteristic (abbreviation, GMO) (350)

**organismo modificado genéticamente** un organismo que contiene material genético que ha sido alterado en forma artificial para producir una característica deseada (abreviatura: OMG) (350)

**genetic code** the rule that describes how a sequence of nucleotides, read in groups of three consecutive nucleotides (triplets) that correspond to specific amino acids, specifies the amino acid sequence of a protein (63, 307)

**código genético** la regla que describe la forma en que una secuencia de nucleótidos, leídos en grupos de tres nucleótidos consecutivos (triplete) que corresponden a aminoácidos específicos, especifica la secuencia de aminoácidos de una proteína (63, 307)

**genetic counseling** the process of testing and informing potential parents about their genetic makeup and the likelihood that they will have offspring with genetic defects or hereditary diseases (346)

**orientación genética** el proceso de hacer pruebas e informar a una pareja de padres potenciales acerca de su constitución genética y acerca de la posibilidad de que tengan hijos con defectos genéticos o enfermedades hereditarias (346)

**genetic disorder** an inherited disease or disorder that is caused by a mutation in a gene or by a chromosomal defect (280, 323)

**trastorno genético** una enfermedad o trastorno hereditario que es causado por una mutación en un gene o por un defecto cromosómico (280, 323)

**genetic drift** the random change in allele frequency in a population (405)

**desviación genética** el cambio aleatorio en la frecuencia de los alelos de una población (405)

**genetic engineering** a technology in which the genome of a living cell is modified for medical or industrial use (33, 346, 350)

**ingeniería genética** una tecnología en la que el genoma de una célula viva se modifica con fines médicos o industriales (33, 346, 350)

**genetic equilibrium** (EE kwi LIB ree uhm) a state in which the allele frequencies of a population remain in the same ratios from one generation to the next (404)

**equilibrio genético** un estado en el que las frecuencias de los alelos de una población permanecen en la misma proporción de generación en generación (404)

**genetic library** a collection of genetic sequence clones that represent all of the genes in a given genome (363)

**biblioteca genética** un grupo de clones de secuencia genética que representan a todos los genes de un genoma determinado (363)

**genetic marker** a gene whose phenotype is easily identified (362)

**marcador genético** un gene cuyo fenotipo se identifica fácilmente (362)

**genetics** (juh NET iks) the science of heredity and of the mechanisms by which traits are passed from parents to offspring (31)

**genética** la ciencia de la herencia y de los mecanismos por los cuales los caracteres son transmitidos de padres a hijos (31)

**genital herpes** (JEN i tuhl HUHR PEEZ) a sexually transmitted infection that is caused by a herpes simplex virus (562)

**herpes genital** una infección de transmisión sexual causada por el virus herpes simplex (562)

**genome** (JEE NOHM) the complete genetic material contained in an individual or species (31, 330)
**genoma** el material genético completo contenido en un individuo o especie (31, 330)

**genome mapping** the process of determining the relative position of genes in a genome (362)
**mapeo genómico** el proceso de determinar la posición relativa de los genes en un genoma (362)

**genomics** (juh NOH miks) the study of entire genomes, especially by using technology to compare genes within and between species (345)
**genómica** el estudio de genomas completos, en especial mediante el uso de tecnología para comparar genes dentro de las especies y entre ellas (345)

**genotype** (JEE nuh TIEP) the entire genetic makeup of an organism; *also* the combination of genes for one or more specific traits (274, 400)
**genotipo** la constitución genética completa de un organismo; *también,* la combinación de genes para uno o más caracteres específicos (274, 400)

**genus** (JEE nuhs) the level of classification that comes after family and that contains similar species (424)
**género** el nivel de clasificación que viene después de la familia y que contiene especies similares (424)

**geologic time scale** the standard method used to divide Earth's long natural history into manageable parts (453)
**escala de tiempo geológico** el método estándar que se usa para dividir la larga historia natural de la Tierra en partes razonables (453)

**geology** (jee AHL uh jee) the scientific study of the origin, history, and structure of Earth and the processes that shape Earth (379)
**geología** el estudio científico del origen, la historia y la estructura del planeta Tierra y los procesos que le dan forma (379)

**germ cell** in a multicellular organism, any reproductive cell (as opposed to a somatic cell) (248, 322, 403)
**célula germinal** en un organismo pluricelular, cualquier célula reproductiva (en contraposición a una célula somática) (248, 322, 403)

**gestation** (jes TAY shuhn) in mammals, the process of carrying young from fertilization to birth (558)
**gestación** en los mamíferos, el proceso de llevar a las crías de la fecundación al nacimiento (558)

**global warming** a gradual increase in average global temperature (128)
**calentamiento global** un aumento gradual de la temperatura global promedio (128)

**glycolysis** (glie KAHL i sis) the anaerobic breakdown of glucose to pyruvic acid, which makes a small amount of energy available to cells in the form of ATP (209)
**glicólisis** la descomposición anaeróbica de glucosa en ácido pirúvico, la cual hace que una pequeña cantidad de energía en forma de ATP esté disponible para las células (209)

**glycoprotein** (GLIE koh PROH TEEN) a protein to which carbohydrate molecules are attached (177)
**glicoproteína** una proteína que tienen unidas moléculas de carbohidratos (177)

**Golgi apparatus** (GOHL jee AP uh RAT uhs) a cell organelle that helps make and package materials to be transported out of the cell (158)
**aparato de Golgi** un organelo celular que ayuda a hacer y a empacar los materiales que serán transportados al exterior de la célula (158)

**gradualism** (GRA joo uhl IZ uhm) a model of evolution in which gradual change over a long period of time leads to biological diversity (389)
**gradualismo** un modelo de evolución en el que un cambio gradual a través de un largo período de tiempo conlleva a la diversidad biológica (389)

**greenhouse effect** the warming of the surface and lower atmosphere of Earth that occurs when carbon dioxide, water vapor, and other gases in the air absorb and reradiate infrared radiation (129)
**efecto invernadero** el calentamiento de la superficie terrestre y de la parte más baja de la atmósfera, el cual se produce cuando el dióxido de carbono, el vapor de agua y otros gases del aire absorben radiación infrarroja y la vuelven a irradiar (129)

**guanine** (GWAH NEEN) one of the four bases that combine with sugar and phosphate to form a nucleotide subunit of DNA; guanine pairs with cytosine (297)
**guanina** una de las cuatro bases que se combinan con el azúcar y fosfato para formar una subunidad de nucleótidos del ADN; la guanina se une con la citosina (297)

**habitat** the place where an organism usually lives (80, 112)
**hábitat** el lugar donde un organismo vive normalmente (80, 112)

**half-life** the time required for half of a sample of a radioactive isotope to break down by radioactive decay to form a daughter isotope (452)
**vida media** el tiempo que se requiere para que la mitad de una muestra de un isótopo radiactivo se descomponga por desintegración radiactiva y forme un isótopo hijo (452)

**haploid** (HAP LOYD) describes a cell, nucleus, or organism that has only one set of unpaired chromosomes (249)
**haploide** término que describe a una célula, núcleo u organismo que tiene sólo un juego de cromosomas que no están asociados en pares (249)

**Hardy-Weinberg principle** (HAHR dee WIEN BUHRG) the principle that states that the frequency of alleles in a population does not change unless evolutionary forces act on the population (405)
**principio de Hardy-Weinberg** el principio que establece que la frecuencia de alelos en una población no cambia a menos que fuerzas evolutivas actúen en la población (405)

**heart attack** the death of heart tissues due to a blockage of their blood supply (511)
**ataque cardíaco** la muerte de los tejidos del corazón debido a una obstrucción de su suministro sanguíneo (511)

**helper T cell** a white blood cell necessary for B cells to develop normal levels of antibodies (529)
**célula T auxiliar** un glóbulo blanco de la sangre necesario para que las células B desarrollen niveles normales de un anticuerpo (529)

**heredity** (huh RED i tee) the passing of genetic traits from parent to offspring (19)
**herencia** la transmisión de caracteres genéticos de padres a hijos (19)

**heterotroph** (HET uhr uh TROHF) an organism that obtains organic food molecules by eating other organisms or their byproducts and that cannot synthesize organic compounds from inorganic materials (434)
**heterótrofo** un organismo que obtiene moléculas de alimento al comer otros organismos o sus productos secundarios y que no puede sintetizar compuestos orgánicos a partir de materiales inorgánicos (434)

**heterozygous** (HET uhr OH ZIE guhs) describes an individual that carries two different alleles of a gene (275)
**heterocigoto** término que describe un individuo que tiene dos alelos diferentes para un gene (275)

**histamine** (HIS tuh MEEN) a chemical that stimulates the autonomous nervous system, secretion of gastric juices, and dilation of capillaries (526)
**histamina** una sustancia química que estimula el sistema nervioso autónomo, la secreción de jugos gástricos y la dilatación de capilares (526)

**histone** (HIS TOHN) a type of protein molecule found in the chromosomes of eukaryotic cells but not prokaryotic cells (224, 302)
**histona** un tipo de molécula de proteína que se encuentra en los cromosomas de las células eucarióticas, pero nunca en las procarióticas (224, 302)

**HIV** human immunodeficiency virus, the virus that causes AIDS (539)
**VIH** virus de inmunodeficiencia humana; el virus que causa el SIDA (539)

**homeobox** (HOH mee uh BAHKS) a DNA sequence within a homeotic gene that regulates development in animals (333)
**homeocaja** una secuencia de ADN dentro de un gene homeótico que regula los patrones de desarrollo en los animales (333)

**homeostasis** (HOH mee OH STAY sis) the maintenance of a constant internal state in a changing environment; a constant internal state that is maintained in a changing environment by continually making adjustments to the internal and external environment (19, 471)
**homeostasis** la capacidad de mantener un estado interno constante en un ambiente en cambio; un estado interno constante que se mantiene en un ambiente en cambio al hacer ajustes continuos al ambiente interno y externo (19, 471)

**homeotic gene** (HOH mee AHD ik) a gene that controls the development of a specific adult structure (333)
**gene homeótico** un gene que controla el desarrollo de una estructura específica de la etapa adulta (333)

**homologous** (hoh MAHL uh guhs) describes a character that is shared by a group of species because it is inherited from a common ancestor (384)
**homólogo** término que describe un carácter compartido por un grupo de especies porque es heredado de un ancestro en común (384)

**homologous chromosomes** chromosomes that have the same sequence of genes, that have the same structure, and that pair during meiosis (249)
**cromosomas homólogos** cromosomas con la misma secuencia de genes, que tienen la misma estructura y que se acoplan durante la meiosis (249)

**homozygous** (HOH moh ZIE guhs) describes an individual that has identical alleles for a trait on both homologous chromosomes (274)
**homocigoto** término que describe a un individuo que tiene alelos idénticos para un carácter en los dos cromosomas homólogos (274)

**hormone** (HAWR MOHN) a substance that is made in one cell or tissue and that causes a change in another cell or tissue located in a different part of the body (479)
**hormona** una sustancia que es producida en una célula o tejido, la cual causa un cambio en otra célula o tejido ubicado en una parte diferente del cuerpo (479)

**host** an organism from which a parasite takes food or shelter (110)
**huésped** el organismo del cual un parásito obtiene alimento y refugio (110)

**Human Genome Project** a research effort to sequence and locate the entire collection of genes in human cells (345)
**Proyecto del Genoma Humano** un esfuerzo de investigación para determinar la secuencia y ubicación de todo el conjunto de genes de las células humanas (345)

**hybrid** (HIE brid) in biology, the offspring of a cross between parents that have differing traits; a cross between individuals of different species, subspecies, or varieties (268, 413)
**híbrido** en biología, la descendencia de una cruza entre padres que tienen características diferentes; una cruza entre individuos de especies, subespecies o variedades diferentes (268, 413)

**hydrogen bond** (HIE druh juhn) the intermolecular force occurring when a hydrogen atom that is bonded to a highly electronegative atom of one molecule is attracted to two unshared electrons of another molecule (54)
**enlace de hidrógeno** la fuerza intermolecular producida por un átomo de hidrógeno que está unido a un átomo muy electronegativo de una molécula y que experimenta atracción a dos electrones no compartidos de otra molécula (54)

**hypertonic** (HIE puhr TAHN ik) describes a solution whose solute concentration is higher than the solute concentration inside a cell (180)
**hipertónico** término que describe una solución cuya concentración de soluto es más alta que la concentración del soluto en el interior de la célula (180)

**hypothesis** (hie PAHTH uh sis) a testable idea or explanation that leads to scientific investigation (10)
**hipótesis** una idea o explicación que conlleva a la investigación científica y que se puede probar (10)

**hypotonic** (HIE poh TAHN ik) describes a solution whose solute concentration is lower than the solute concentration inside a cell (180)
**hipotónico** término que describe una solución cuya concentración de soluto es más baja que la concentración del soluto en el interior de la célula (180)

**immigration** (IM uh GRAY shuhn) the movement of an individual or a group to a new community or region (104)
**inmigración** la llegada de un individuo o grupo a una nueva comunidad o región (104)

**immunity** (im MYOON i tee) the ability to resist or recover from an infectious disease (532)
**inmunidad** la capacidad de resistir una enfermedad infecciosa o recuperarse de ella (532)

**implantation** (IM plan TAY shuhn) the process by which a blastocyst embeds itself in the lining of the uterus; occurs about six days after fertilization (557)
**implantación** el proceso por medio del cual la blastoquistela se incrusta en la cubierta interior del útero; ocurre unos seis días después de la fecundación (557)

**inbreeding** (IN BREED ing) the crossing or mating of plants or animals with close relatives (406)
**endogamia** el cruzamiento de plantas o animales con parientes cercanos (406)

**incomplete dominance** a condition in which a trait in an individual is intermediate between the phenotype of the individual's two parents because the dominant allele is unable to express itself fully (282)
**dominancia incompleta** una condición en la que un carácter de un individuo es intermedio entre el fenotipo de los dos padres del individuo porque el alelo dominante no puede expresarse por completo (282)

**independent assortment** the random distribution of the pairs of genes on different chromosomes to the gametes (253)
**distribución independiente** la distribución al azar de pares de genes de diferentes cromosomas a los gametos (253)

**index fossil** a fossil that is used to establish the age of a rock layer because the fossil is distinct, abundant, and widespread and the species that formed that fossil existed for only a short span of geologic time (451)
**fósil guía** un fósil que se usa para establecer la edad de una capa de roca debido a que puede diferenciarse bien de otros, es abundante y está extendido; la especie que formó ese fósil existió sólo por un corto período de tiempo geológico (451)

**infectious disease** a disease that is caused by a pathogen and that can be transmitted from one individual to another(499)
**enfermedad infecciosa** una enfermedad que es causada por un patógeno y que puede transmitirse de un individuo a otro (499)

**inflammation** (IN fluh MAY shuhn) a protective response of tissues affected by disease or injury; characterized by pain, swelling, redness, and heat (526)
**inflamación** una reacción de protección de los tejidos afectados por una enfermedad o lesión (526)

**interphase** (IN tuhr FAYZ) the period of the cell cycle during which activities such as cell growth and protein synthesis occur without visible signs of cell division (228)
**interfase** el período del ciclo celular durante el cual las actividades como el crecimiento celular y la síntesis de proteínas existen sin signos visibles de división celular (228)

**intron** (IN trahn) a nucleotide sequence that is part of a gene and that is transcribed from DNA into mRNA but not translated into amino acids (328)
**intrón** una secuencia de nucleótidos que es parte de un gene y que se transcribe del ADN al ARNm pero no se traduce en aminoácidos (328)

**ion** (IE AHN) an atom, radical, or molecule that has gained or lost one or more electrons and has a negative or positive charge (53)
**ion** un átomo, radical o molécula que ha ganado o perdido uno o más electrones y que tiene una carga negativa o positiva (53)

**ionic bond** (ie AHN ik) the attractive force between oppositely charged ions, which form when electrons are transferred from one atom to another (53)
**enlace iónico** la fuerza de atracción entre iones con cargas opuestas, que se forman cuando se transfieren electrones de un átomo a otro (53)

**isotonic solution** (IE soh TAHN ik) a solution whose solute concentration is equal to the solute concentration inside a cell (180)
**solución isotónica** una solución cuya concentración de soluto es igual a la concentración de soluto en el interior de la célula (180)

**isotope** (IE suh TOHP) an atom that has the same number of protons (or the same atomic number) as other atoms of the same element do but that has a different number of neutrons (and thus a different atomic mass) (51, 452)
**isótopo** un átomo que tiene el mismo número de protones (o el mismo número atómico) que otros átomos del mismo elemento, pero que tiene un número diferente de neutrones (y, por lo tanto, otra masa atómica) (51, 452)

**keystone species** a species that is critical to the functioning of the ecosystem in which it lives because it affects the survival and abundance of many other species in its community (114)
**especie clave** una especie que es crítica para el funcionamiento del ecosistema en el que vive porque afecta la supervivencia y abundancia de muchas otras especies en su comunidad (114)

**kingdom** the highest taxonomic category, which contains a group of similar phyla (426)
**reino** la categoría taxonómica más alta, que contiene un grupo de phyla similares (426)

**Krebs cycle** a series of biochemical reactions that convert pyruvic acid into carbon dioxide and water; it is the major pathway of oxidation in animal, bacterial, and plant cells, and it releases energy (210)
**ciclo de Krebs** una serie de reacciones bioquímicas que convierten el ácido pirúvico en dióxido de carbono y agua; es la vía principal de oxidación en las células animales, bacterianas y vegetales, y libera energía (210)

**labia** (LAY bee uh) liplike structures, usually referring to fleshy folds located on a female's pubis and at the opening of the vagina (553)
**labia** estructuras parecidas a labios, que normalmente se refieren a los pliegues carnosos que se encuentran en el pubis de una hembra a la entrada de la vagina (553)

**lactic acid fermentation** (FUHR muhn TAY shuhn) the chemical breakdown of carbohydrates that produces lactic acid as the main end product (212)
**fermentación del ácido láctico** la descomposición química de los carbohidratos que produce ácido láctico como producto final principal (212)

**law of conservation of energy** the law that states that energy cannot be created or destroyed but can be changed from one form to another (64)
**ley de la conservación de la energía** la ley que establece que la energía ni se crea ni se destruye, sólo se transforma de una forma a otra (64)

**law of conservation of mass** the law that states that mass cannot be created or destroyed in ordinary chemical and physical changes (64)
**ley de la conservación de la masa** la ley que establece que la masa no se crea ni se destruye por cambios químicos o físicos comunes (64)

**law of independent assortment** the law that states that genes separate independently of one another in meiosis (284)
**ley de la distribución independiente** la ley que establece que los genes se separan de manera independiente durante la meiosis (284)

**life cycle** all of the events in the growth and development of an organism until the organism reaches sexual maturity (256)
**ciclo de vida** todos los sucesos en el crecimiento y desarrollo de un organismo hasta que el organismo llega a su madurez sexual (256)

**linked** in genetics, describes two or more genes that tend to be inherited together (275, 284)
**ligado** en genética, término que describe dos o más genes que tienden a heredarse juntos (275, 284)

**lipid** (LIP id) a fat molecule or a molecule that has similar properties; examples include oils, waxes, and steroids (61)
**lípido** una molécula de grasa o una molécula que tiene propiedades similares; algunos ejemplos son los aceites, las ceras y los esteroides (61)

**lipid bilayer** (BIE LAY uhr) the basic structure of a biological membrane, composed of two layers of phospholipids (176)
**bicapa de lípidos** la estructura básica de la membrana biológica, formada por dos capas de fosfolípidos (176)

**logistic growth** (loh JIS tik) population growth that starts with a minimum number of individuals and reaches a maximum depending on the carrying capacity of the region; described by an S-shaped curve (104)
**crecimiento logístico** crecimiento de la población que comienza con un número mínimo de individuos y llega al máximo dependiendo de la capacidad de carga de la región; se describe por medio de una curva en forma de S (104)

**lung** the central organ of the respiratory system in which oxygen from the air is exchanged with carbon dioxide from the blood (482)
**pulmón** el órgano central del aparato respiratorio en el que el oxígeno del aire se intercambia con el dióxido de carbono de la sangre (482)

**luteal phase** (LOOT ee uhl) the menstrual stage in which the corpus luteum develops (555)
**fase luteal** la etapa de la menstruación en la que se desarrolla el corpus luteum (555)

**lymph** (LIMF) the fluid that is collected by the lymphatic vessels and nodes (483)
**linfa** el fluido que es recolectado por los vasos y nodos linfáticos (483)

**lymph node** an organ that filters lymph and that is found along the lymphatic vessels (483)
**nodo linfático** un órgano que filtra la linfa y que se encuentra a lo largo de los vasos linfáticos (483)

## M

**macrophage** (MAK roh FAYJ) an immune system cell that engulfs pathogens and other materials (527)
**macrófago** una célula del sistema inmunológico que envuelve a los patógenos y otros materiales (527)

**malignant tumor** (muh LIG nuhnt) a cancerous mass of cells (235)
**tumor maligno** una masa cancerosa de células (235)

**marine ecosystem** (muh REEN) an ecosystem in the sea (84)
**ecosistema marino** un ecosistema en el mar (84)

**mass extinction** (ek STINGK shuhn) an episode during which large numbers of species become extinct (453)
**extinción masiva** un episodio durante el cual grandes cantidades de especies se extinguen (453)

**meiosis** (mie OH sis) a process in cell division during which the number of chromosomes decreases to half the original number by two divisions of the nucleus, which results in the production of sex cells (gametes or spores) (250)
**meiosis** un proceso de división celular durante el cual el número de cromosomas disminuye a la mitad del número original por medio de dos divisiones del núcleo, lo cual resulta en la producción de células sexuales (gametos o esporas) (250)

**melanin** (MEL uh nin) a pigment that helps determine the color of skin, hair, eyes, fur, feathers, and scales (477)
**melanina** un pigmento que ayuda a determinar el color de la piel, el cabello, los ojos, el pelaje, las plumas y las escamas (477)

**memory cell** an immune system B cell or T cell that does not respond the first time that it meets with an antigen or an invading cell but that recognizes and attacks the antigen or invading cell during subsequent infections (532)
**célula de memoria** un célula B o una célula T del sistema inmunológico que no responde la primera vez que se encuentra con un antígeno o célula invasora, pero que reconoce y ataca al antígeno o célula invasora durante infecciones posteriores (532)

**menopause** (MEN uh PAWZ) the termination of the menstrual cycle; occurs between the ages of 45 and 55 (556)
**menopausia** la terminación del ciclo menstrual; ocurre entre los 45 y 55 años de edad (556)

**menstrual cycle** the female reproductive cycle, characterized by a monthly change of the lining of the uterus and the discharge of blood (556)
**ciclo menstrual** el ciclo reproductor femenino, caracterizado por un cambio mensual en el revestimiento del útero y una descarga de sangre (556)

**menstruation** (MEN STRAY shuhn) the discharge of blood and discarded tissue from the uterus during the menstrual cycle (556)
**menstruación** la descarga de sangre y tejido de desecho del útero durante el ciclo menstrual (556)

**metabolism** (muh TAB uh LIZ uhm) the sum of all chemical processes that occur in an organism (19)
**metabolismo** la suma de todos los procesos químicos que ocurren en un organismo (19)

**methanogen** (muh THAN uh JEN) a microorganism that produces methane gas (435)
**metanógeno** un microorganismo que produce gas metano (435)

**microarray** (MIE kroh uh RAY) a device that contains, in microscopic scale, an orderly arrangement of biomolecules; a device that is used to rapidly test for the presence of a range of similar substances, such as specific DNA sequences (346, 358)
**chip de ADN** un aparato que contiene, a escala microscópica, una organización ordenada de biomoléculas; un aparato que se usa para probar rápidamente la presencia de una variedad de sustancias similares, como secuencias específicas de ADN (346, 358)

**microfilament** (MIE kroh FIL uh muhnt) a fiber found inside eukaryotic cells that is composed mainly of the protein actin and that has a role in cell structure and movement (156)
**microfilamento** una fibra que se encuentra dentro de las células eucarióticas, compuesta principalmente por la proteína actina, y que está relacionada con la estructura y movimiento de la célula (156)

**microsphere** (MIE kroh SFIR) a hollow microscopic spherical structure that is usually composed of proteins or a synthetic polymer (449)
**microesfera** una estructura microscópica esférica y hueca compuesta generalmente por proteínas o por un polímero sintético (449)

**microtubule** (MIE kroh TOO BYOOL) one of the small, tubular fibers composed of the protein tubulin that are found in the cytoplasm of eukaryotic cells, that compose the cytoskeleton, and that play a role in cell structure and movement (156)
**microtúbulo** una de las fibras pequeñas y tubulares compuestas de la proteína tubulina, las cuales se encuentran en el citoplasma de las células eucarióticas, forman el citoesqueleto y están involucradas en el movimiento y estructura de la célula (156)

**migration** (mie GRAY shuhn) in general, any movement of individuals or populations from one location to another; specifically, a periodic group movement that is characteristic of a given population or species (388, 405)
**migración** en general, cualquier movimiento de individuos o poblaciones de un lugar a otro; específicamente, un movimiento periódico en grupo que es característico de una población o especie determinada (388, 405)

**missense mutation** a type of point mutation that converts one codon to another such that the codon specifies a different amino acid (320)
**mutación de sentido erróneo** un tipo de mutación puntual que convierte a un codón en otro de manera que el codón especifica un aminoácido diferente (320)

**mitochondrion** (MIET oh KAHN dree uhn) in eukaryotic cells, the cell organelle that is surrounded by two membranes and that is the site of cellular respiration, which produces ATP (161)
**mitocondria** en las células eucarióticas, el organelo celular rodeado por dos membranas que es el lugar donde se lleva a cabo la respiración celular, la cual produce ATP (161)

**mitosis** (mie TOH sis) in eukaryotic cells, a process of cell division that forms two new nuclei, each of which has the same number of chromosomes (229)
**mitosis** en las células eucarióticas, un proceso de división celular que forma dos núcleos nuevos, cada uno de los cuales posee el mismo número de cromosomas (229)

**mobile genetic element** a genetic sequence that is sometimes removed or copied from one place and inserted into another within chromosomes or genomes; includes plasmids, transposons, and other elements (abbreviation, MGE) (332)
**elemento genético móvil** una secuencia genética que a veces se elimina o se copia de un lugar y se inserta en otro dentro de los cromosomas o genomas; incluye a los plásmidos, los transposones y otros elementos (abreviatura: EGM) (332)

**molecule** (MAHL i KYOOL) a group of atoms that are held together by chemical forces; a molecule is the smallest unit of matter that can exist by itself and retain all of a substance's chemical properties (52)
**molécula** un conjunto de átomos que se mantienen unidos por acción de las fuerzas químicas; una molécula es la unidad más pequeña de la materia capaz de existir en forma independiente y conservar todas las propiedades químicas de una sustancia (52)

**monohybrid cross** (MAHN oh HIE brid) a cross between individuals that involves one pair of contrasting traits (269)
**cruza monohíbrida** una cruza entre individuos que involucra un par de caracteres contrastantes (269)

**monosaccharide** (MAHN oh SAK uh RIED) a simple sugar that is the basic subunit of a carbohydrate (60)
**monosacárido** un azúcar simple que es una subunidad fundamental de los carbohidratos (60)

**morphology** (mawr FAHL uh jee) the study of the structure and form of an organism (430)
**morfología** el estudio de la estructura y forma de un organismo (430)

**mRNA** messenger RNA, a single-stranded RNA molecule that encodes the information to make a protein (305)
**ARNm** ARNm mensajero; una molécula de ARN de una sola hebra que codifica la información para hacer una proteína (305)

**mucous membrane** (MYOO kuhs) the layer of epithelial tissue that covers internal surfaces of the body and that secretes mucus (525)
**membrana mucosa** la capa de tejido epitelial que cubre las superficies internas del cuerpo y que secreta moco (525)

**multicellular** (muhl ti SEL yoo luhr) describes a tissue, organ, or organism that is made of many cells (434)
**pluricelular** término que describe a un tejido, órgano u organismo constituido por muchas células (434)

**multiple alleles** (uh LEELZ) more than two alleles (versions of the gene) for a genetic trait (283)
**alelos múltiples** más de dos alelos (versiones del gene) para un carácter genético (283)

**mutation** (myoo TAY shuhn) a change in the structure or amount of the genetic material of an organism (319)
**mutación** un cambio en la estructura o cantidad del material genético de un organismo (319)

**mutualism** (MYOO choo uhl IZ uhm) a relationship between two species in which both species benefit (110)
**mutualismo** una relación entre dos especies en la que ambas se benefician (110)

**natural selection** the process by which individuals that are better adapted to their environment survive and reproduce more successfully than less well adapted individuals do; a theory to explain the mechanism of evolution (380)
**selección natural** el proceso por medio del cual los individuos que están mejor adaptados a su ambiente sobreviven y se reproducen con más éxito que los individuos menos adaptados; una teoría que explica el mecanismo de la evolución (380)

**negative feedback** a change in one direction of a feedback mechanism that stops further change in that direction (555)
**retroalimentación negativa** un cambio en una dirección o un mecanismo de retroalimentación que detiene otros cambios en esa dirección (555)

**nephron** (NEF RAHN) the functional unit of the kidney (481)
**nefrona** la unidad funcional del riñón (481)

**neutron** (NOO TRAHN) a subatomic particle that has no charge and that is located in the nucleus of an atom (51)
**neutrón** una partícula subatómica que no tiene carga y que está ubicada en el núcleo de un átomo (51)

**niche** (NICH) the unique position occupied by a species, both in terms of its physical use of its habitat and its function within an ecological community (113, 413)
**nicho** la posición única que ocupa una especie, tanto en lo que se refiere al uso de su hábitat como en cuanto a su función dentro de una comunidad ecológica (113, 413)

**nitrification** (NIE truh fi KAY shuhn) the process by which nitrites and nitrates are produced by bacteria in the soil (92)
**nitrificación** el proceso por medio del cual las bacterias del suelo producen nitritos y nitratos (92)

**nitrogen cycle** (NIE truh juhn) the cycling of nitrogen between organisms, soil, water, and the atmosphere (91)
**ciclo del nitrógeno** el ciclado del nitrógeno entre los organismos, el suelo, el agua y la atmósfera (91)

**nitrogen fixation** (NIE truh juhn fiks AY shuhn) the process by which gaseous nitrogen is converted into ammonia, a compound that organisms can use to make amino acids and other nitrogen-containing organic molecules (92)
**fijación de nitrógeno** el proceso por medio del cual el nitrógeno gaseoso se transforma en amoniaco, un compuesto que los organismos utilizan para elaborar aminoácidos y otras moléculas orgánicas que contienen nitrógeno (92)

**nondisjunction** (NAHN dis JUHNK shuhn) the failure of homologous chromosomes to separate during meiosis I or the failure of sister chromatids to separate during mitosis or meiosis II (324)
**no-disyunción** fenómeno que se produce cuando los cromosomas homólogos no se separan durante la meiosis I o cuando las cromátidas hermanas no se separan durante la meiosis II (324)

**noninfectious disease** (NAHN in FEK shuhs di ZEEZ) a disease that cannot spread from one individual to another (499)
**enfermedad no infecciosa** una enfermedad que no se contagia de una persona a otra (499)

**nonsense mutation** a mutation that alters a gene so that a nonsense (or noncoding) codon is inserted; a mutation that usually results in the abnormal termination of an amino-acid chain during translation (321)
**mutación sin sentido** una mutación que altera un gene de modo que se inserta un codón sin sentido (o que no codifica); una mutación que suele tener como resultado la interrupción anormal de una cadena de aminoácidos (321)

**normal distribution** a distribution of numerical data whose graph forms a bell-shaped curve that is symmetrical about the mean (400)
**distribución normal** una distribución de datos numéricos cuya gráfica forma una curva en forma de campana que es simétrica respecto a la media (400)

**nuclear envelope** (NOO klee uhr) the double membrane that surrounds the nucleus of a eukaryotic cell (157)
**envoltura nuclear** la doble membrana que rodea el núcleo de una célula eucariótica (157)

**nucleic acid** (noo KLAY ik) an organic compound, either RNA or DNA, whose molecules are made up of one or two chains of nucleotides and carry genetic information (63)
**ácido nucleico** un compuesto orgánico, ya sea ARN o ADN, cuyas moléculas están formadas por una o más cadenas de nucleótidos y que contiene información genética (63)

**nucleolus** (noo KLEE uh luhs) the part of the eukaryotic nucleus where ribosomal RNA is synthesized (157)
**nucleolo** la parte del núcleo eucariótico donde se sintetiza el ARN ribosomal (157)

**nucleosome** (NOO klee uh SOHM) a eukaryotic structural unit of chromatin that consists of DNA wound around a core of histone proteins (224)
**nucleosoma** una unidad estructural eucariótica de cromatina formada por ADN que rodea un núcleo de proteínas de histona (224)

**nucleotide** (NOO klee oh TIED) an organic compound that consists of a sugar, a phosphate, and a nitrogenous base; the basic building block of a nucleic-acid chain (63, 296)
**nucleótido** un compuesto orgánico formado por un azúcar, un fosfato y una base nitrogenada; el componente básico de una cadena de ácidos nucleicos (63, 296)

**nucleus** (NOO klee uhs) in a eukaryotic cell, a membrane-bound organelle that contains the cell's DNA and that has a role in processes such as growth, metabolism, and reproduction (155)
**núcleo** en una célula eucariótica, un organelo cubierto por una membrana, el cual contiene el ADN de la célula y participa en procesos tales como el crecimiento, metabolismo y reproducción (155)

**observation** (AHB zuhr VAY shuhn) the process of obtaining information by using the senses; the information obtained by using the senses (10)
**observación** el proceso de obtener información por medio de los sentidos; la información que se obtiene al usar los sentidos (10)

**omnivore** (AHM ni VAWR) an organism that eats both plants and animals (87)
**omnívoro** un organismo que come tanto plantas como animales (87)

**operator** (AHP uh RAY tuhr) a short sequence of viral or bacterial DNA to which a repressor binds to prevent transcription (mRNA synthesis) of the adjacent gene in an operon (326)
**operador** una secuencia corta de ADN viral o bacteriano a la que se une un represor para impedir la transcripción (síntesis de ARNm) del gene adyacente en un operón (326)

**operon** (AHP uhr AHN) a unit of adjacent genes that consists of functionally related structural genes and their associated regulatory genes; common in prokaryotes and phages (326)
**operón** una unidad de genes adyacentes formada por genes estructurales de función relacionada y sus genes reguladores asociados; es común en los procariotes y los fagos (326)

**order** the taxonomic category below the class and above the family (426)
**orden** la categoría taxonómica que se encuentra debajo de la clase y arriba de la familia (426)

**organ** a collection of tissues that carry out a specialized function of the body (164)
**órgano** un conjunto de tejidos que desempeñan una función especializada en el cuerpo (164)

**organelle** (AWR guh NEL) one of the small bodies that are found in the cytoplasm of a cell and that are specialized to perform a specific function (155)
**organelo** uno de los cuerpos pequeños que se encuentran en el citoplasma de una célula y que están especializados para llevar a cabo una función específica (155)

**organism** (AWR guh NIZ uhm) a living thing; anything that can carry out life processes independently (17)
**organismo** un ser vivo; cualquier cosa que pueda llevar a cabo procesos vitales independientemente (17)

**organ system** a group of organs that work together to perform body functions (165)
**aparato (o sistema) de órganos** un grupo de órganos que trabajan en conjunto para desempeñar funciones corporales (165)

**osmosis** (ahs MOH sis) the diffusion of water or another solvent from a more dilute solution (of a solute) to a more concentrated solution (of the solute) through a membrane that is permeable to the solvent (180)
**ósmosis** la difusión de agua u otro solvente de una solución más diluida (de un soluto) a una solución más concentrada (del soluto) a través de una membrana que es permeable al solvente (180)

**ovarian cycle** (oh VAHR ee uhn) a series of hormone-induced changes in which the ovaries prepare and release a mature ovum each month (554)
**ciclo ovárico** una serie de cambios inducidos por hormonas en los cuales los ovarios preparan y liberan un óvulo maduro todos los meses (554)

**ovary** (OH vuh ree) in flowering plants, the lower part of a pistil that produces eggs in ovules (552)
**ovario** en las plantas con flores, la parte inferior del pistilo que produce óvulos (552)

**ovulation** (AHV yoo LAY shuhn) the release of an ovum from a follicle of the ovary (554)
**ovulación** la liberación de un óvulo de un folículo del ovario (554)

**ovule** (AHV YOOL) a structure in the ovary of a seed plant that contains an embryo sac and that develops into a seed after fertilization (554)
**óvulo** una estructura del ovario de una planta con semillas que contiene un saco embrionario y se desarrolla para convertirse en una semilla después de la fecundación (554)

**ovum** (OH vuhm) a mature egg cell (553)
**óvulo** una célula sexual madura (553)

**parasitism** (PAR uh SIET IZ uhm) a relationship between two species in which one species, the parasite, benefits from the other species, the host, which is harmed (110)
**parasitismo** una relación entre dos especies en la que una, el parásito, se beneficia de la otra, el huésped, que resulta perjudicada (110)

**parthenogenesis** (PAHR thuh NOH JEN uh sis) reproduction in which a female gamete grows into a new individual without being fertilized by a male (247)
**partenogénesis** reproducción en la cual un gameto femenino se convierte en un nuevo individuo sin ser fecundado por un macho (247)

**passive transport** the movement of substances across a cell membrane without the use of energy by the cell (178)
**transporte pasivo** el movimiento de sustancias a través de una membrana celular sin que la célula tenga que usar energía (178)

**pathogen** (PATH uh juhn) a microorganism, another organism, a virus, or a protein that causes disease; an infectious agent (499, 525)
**patógeno** un microorganismo, otro organismo, un virus o una proteína que causa enfermedades; un agente infeccioso (499, 525)

**pedigree** (PED i GREE) a diagram that shows the occurrence of a genetic trait in several generations of a family (280)
**pedigrí** un diagrama que muestra la incidencia de un carácter genético en varias generaciones de una familia (280)

**pelvic inflammatory disease** (in FLAM uh TAWR ee) a sexually transmitted infection of the upper female reproductive system, including the uterus, ovaries, and fallopian tubes (563)
**enfermedad pélvica inflamatoria** una infección de transmisión sexual del aparato reproductor femenino superior, que incluye el útero, los ovarios y las trompas de Falopio (563)

**penis** (PEE nis) the male organ that transfers sperm to a female and that carries urine out of the body (551)
**pene** el órgano masculino que transfiere espermatozoides a una hembra y que lleva la orina hacia el exterior del cuerpo (551)

**peptide bond** (PEP TIED) the chemical bond that forms between the carboxyl group of one amino acid and the amino group of another amino acid (62)
**enlace peptídico** el enlace químico que se forma entre el grupo carboxilo de un aminoácido y el grupo amino de otro aminoácido (62)

**period** a unit of geologic time that is longer than an epoch but shorter than an era (453)
**período** una unidad de tiempo geológico que es más larga que una época pero más corta que una era (453)

**P generation** parental generation, the first two individuals that mate in a genetic cross (269)
**generación P** generación parental; los primeros dos individuos que se aparean en una cruza genética (269)

**pH** (PEE AYCH) a value that is used to express the acidity or alkalinity (basicity) of a system; each whole number on the scale indicates a tenfold change in acidity; a pH of 7 is neutral, a pH of less than 7 is acidic, and a pH of greater than 7 is basic (57)
**pH** un valor que expresa la acidez o la alcalinidad (basicidad) de un sistema; cada número entero de la escala indica un cambio de 10 veces en la acidez; un pH de 7 es neutro, un pH de menos de 7 es ácido y un pH de más de 7 es básico (57)

**phenotype** (FEE noh TIEP) an organism's appearance or other detectable characteristic that results from the organism's genotype and the environment (274, 400)
**fenotipo** la apariencia de un organismo u otra característica perceptible que resulta debido al genotipo del organismo y a su ambiente (274, 400)

**phospholipid** (FAHS foh LIP id) a lipid that contains phosphorus and that is a structural component in cell membranes (176)
**fosfolípido** un lípido que contiene fósforo y que es un componente estructural de la membrana celular (176)

**phosphorus cycle** (FAHS fuh ruhs) the cyclic movement of phosphorus in different chemical forms from the environment to organisms and then back to the environment (93)
**ciclo del fósforo** el movimiento cíclico del fósforo en diferentes formas químicas del ambiente a los organismos y de regreso al ambiente (93)

**photosynthesis** (FOHT oh SIN thuh sis) the process by which plants, algae, and some bacteria use sunlight, carbon dioxide, and water to produce carbohydrates and oxygen (197)
**fotosíntesis** el proceso por medio del cual las plantas, algas y algunas bacterias utilizan la luz solar, dióxido de carbono y agua para producir carbohidratos y oxígeno (197)

**phylogenetic tree** (FIE loh juh NET ik) a branching diagram that shows how organisms are related through evolution (428)
**árbol filogenético** un diagrama ramificado que muestra cómo se relacionan los organismos a través de la evolución (428)

**phylogeny** (fie LAHJ uh nee) the evolutionary history of a species or taxonomic group (428)
**filogenia** la historia evolutiva de una especie o grupo taxonómico (428)

**phylum** (FIE luhm) the taxonomic group below kingdom and above class (426)
**phylum** el grupo taxonómico que se ubica debajo del reino y arriba de la clase (426)

**pigment** (PIG muhnt) a substance that gives another substance or a mixture its color (203)
**pigmento** una sustancia que le da color a otra sustancia o mezcla (203)

**pioneer species** a species that colonizes an uninhabited area and that starts an ecological cycle in which many other species become established (81)
**especie pionera** una especie que coloniza un área deshabitada y empieza un ciclo ecológico en el cual se establecen muchas otras especies (81)

**placenta** (pluh SEN tuh) the structure that attaches a developing fetus to the uterus and that enables the exchange of nutrients, wastes, and gases between the mother and the fetus (558)
**placenta** la estructura que une al feto en desarrollo con el útero y que permite el intercambio de nutrientes, desechos y gases entre la madre y el feto (558)

**plasma cell** a type of white blood cell that produces antibodies (530)
**célula plasmática** un tipo de glóbulo blanco que produce anticuerpos (530)

**plasmid** (PLAZ mid) a genetic structure that can replicate independently of the main chromosome(s) of a cell; usually, a circular DNA molecule in bacteria (prokaryotes) (331)
**plásmido** una estructura genética que puede duplicarse en forma independiente del cromosoma principal o los cromosomas principales de una célula; generalmente, una molécula de ADN circular de las bacterias (procariotes) (331)

**point mutation** a mutation in which only one nucleotide or nitrogenous base in a gene is changed (320)
**mutación puntual** una mutación en la que sólo cambia un nucleótido o una base nitrogenada en un gene (320)

**polar** (POH luhr) describes a molecule in which the positive and negative charges are separated (54)
**polar** término que describe una molécula en la que las cargas positivas y negativas están separadas (54)

**polar body** one of the small cells that separate from an oocyte during meiosis, that have little cytoplasm, and that are ultimately discarded (255)
**cuerpo polar** una de las células pequeñas que se separan de un oocito durante la meiosis, que tienen poco citoplasma y que finalmente se descartan (255)

**polygenic character** (PAHL uh JEN ik) a character that is influenced by more than one gene (282, 400)
**carácter poligénico** un carácter que es influenciado por más de un gene (282, 400)

**polymerase chain reaction** (PAHL i muhr AYZ) a technique that is used to make many copies of selected segments of DNA (abbreviation, PCR) (357)
**reacción en cadena de la polimerasa** una técnica que se usa para hacer muchas réplicas de segmentos seleccionados de ADN (abreviatura: PCR, por sus siglas en inglés) (357)

**polyploidy** (PAH lee PLOY dee) an abnormal condition of having more than two sets of chromosomes (324)
**poliploidia** la condición anormal de tener más de dos conjuntos de cromosomas (324)

**polysaccharide** (PAHL i SAK uh RIED) one of the carbohydrates made up of long chains of simple sugars; polysaccharides include starch, cellulose, and glycogen (60)
**polisacárido** uno de los carbohidratos formados por cadenas largas de azúcares simples; algunos ejemplos de polisacáridos incluyen al almidón, celulosa y glucógeno (60)

**population** (PAHP yoo LAY shuhn) a group of organisms of the same species that live in a specific geographical area (103, 379)
**población** un grupo de organismos de la misma especie que viven en un área geográfica específica (103, 379)

**population genetics** the study of the frequency and interaction of alleles and genes in populations (399)
**genética de poblaciones** el estudio de la frecuencia e interacción de los alelos y genes en las poblaciones (399)

**positive feedback** in a system, the mechanism by which a cycle of events establishes conditions that favor repetition of the cycle (555)
**retroalimentación positiva** en un sistema, el mecanismo por el cual un ciclo de sucesos establece condiciones que favorecen la repetición del ciclo (555)

**precipitation** (pree SIP uh TAY shuhn) any form of water that falls to Earth's surface from the clouds; includes rain, snow, sleet, and hail (90)
**precipitación** cualquier forma de agua que cae de las nubes a la superficie de la Tierra; incluye a la lluvia, nieve, aguanieve y granizo (90)

**predation** (pree DAY shuhn) an interaction between two organisms in which one organism, the predator, kills and feeds on the other organism, the prey (109)
**depredación** la interacción entre dos organismos en la que un organismo, el depredador, mata a otro organismo, la presa, y se alimenta de él (109)

**pregnancy** (PREG nuhn see) in developmental biology, the period of time in which a woman carries a developing human from fertilization until the birth of the baby (about 266 days, or 38 weeks); in medical practice, this period of time is measured from the first day of a woman's last menstrual period to the delivery of her baby (about 280 days, or 40 weeks) (558)
**embarazo** en biología del desarrollo, el período de tiempo durante el cual una mujer lleva en su interior a un ser humano en desarrollo desde la fecundación hasta el nacimiento del bebé (aproximadamente 266 días, o 38 semanas); en medicina, este período se mide desde el primer día del último período menstrual de una mujer hasta el nacimiento del bebé (aproximadamente 280 días, o 40 semanas) (558)

**primer** (PRIEM uhr) a short, single-stranded fragment of DNA or RNA that is required for the initiation of DNA replication (357)
**cebador** un fragmento corto de una sola hebra de ADN o ARN que se requiere para iniciar la replicación del ADN (357)

**probability** (PRAHB uh BIL uh tee) the likelihood that a possible future event will occur in any given instance of the event; the mathematical ratio of the number of times one outcome of any event is likely to occur to the number of possible outcomes of the event (278)
**probabilidad** término que describe qué tan probable es que ocurra un posible evento futuro en un caso dado del evento; la proporción matemática del número de veces que es posible que ocurra un resultado de cualquier evento respecto al número de resultados posibles del evento (278)

**producer** (proh DOOS uhr) an organism that can make organic molecules from inorganic molecules; a photosynthetic or chemosynthetic autotroph that serves as the basic food source in an ecosystem (86)
**productor** un organismo que elabora moléculas orgánicas a partir de moléculas inorgánicas; un autótrofo fotosintético o quimiosintético que funciona como la fuente fundamental de alimento en un ecosistema (86)

**product** a substance that forms in a chemical reaction (65)
**producto** una sustancia que se forma en una reacción química (65)

**progesterone** (proh JES tuhr OHN) a steroid hormone that is secreted by the corpus luteum of the ovary, that stimulates changes in the uterus to prepare for the implantation of a fertilized egg, and that is produced by the placenta during pregnancy (554)
**progesterona** una hormona esteroide que es secretada por el corpus luteum del ovario, la cual estimula cambios en el útero con el fin de prepararlo para la implantación del óvulo fecundado, y que es producida por la placenta durante el embarazo (554)

**prokaryote** (proh KAR ee OHT) a single-celled organism that does not have a nucleus or membrane-bound organelles; examples are archaea and bacteria (154)
**procariote** un organismo unicelular que no tiene núcleo ni organelos cubiertos por una membrana, por ejemplo, las arqueas y las bacterias (154)

**promoter** (proh MOHT uhr) a nucleotide sequence on a DNA molecule to which an RNA polymerase molecule binds, which initiates the transcription of a specific gene (306, 326)
**promotor** una secuencia de nucleótidos en una molécula de ADN a la cual se une una molécula de ARN polimerasa, lo cual inicia la transcripción de un gene específico (306, 326)

**prostate gland** (PRAHS TAYT) a gland in males that contributes to the seminal fluid (551)
**glándula próstata** una glándula que contribuye al fluido seminal en los machos (551)

**protein** (PROH TEEN) an organic compound that is made of one or more chains of amino acids and that is a principal component of all cells (62)
**proteína** un compuesto orgánico que está hecho de una o más cadenas de aminoácidos y que es el principal componente de todas las células (62)

**protist** (PROH tist) an organism that belongs to the kingdom Protista (436)
**protista** un organismo que pertenece al reino Protista (436)

**proton** (PROH TAHN) a subatomic particle that has a positive charge and that is located in the nucleus of an atom; the number of protons in the nucleus is the atomic number, which determines the identity of an element (51)
**protón** una partícula subatómica que tiene una carga positiva y que está ubicada en el núcleo de un átomo; el número de protones que hay en el núcleo es el número atómico, y éste determina la identidad del elemento (51)

**punctuated equilibrium** (PUHNGK choo AYT id EE kwi LIB ree uhm) a model of evolution in which short periods of drastic change in species, including mass extinctions and rapid speciation, are separated by long periods of little or no change (389)
**equilibrio puntuado** un modelo de evolución en el que períodos cortos en los que ocurren cambios drásticos en una especie (incluyendo extinciones masivas y especiación rápida) están separados por períodos largos en los que ocurren muy pocos cambios o en los que no ocurre ningún cambio (389)

**Punnett square** (PUH nuht) a graphic used to predict the results of a genetic cross (276)
**cuadro de Punnett** una gráfica que se usa para predecir los resultados de una cruza genética (276)

**purine** (PYOOR EEN) a nitrogenous base that has a double-ring structure; one of the two general categories of nitrogenous bases found in DNA and RNA; either adenine or guanine (297)
**purina** una base nitrogenada que tiene una estructura de anillo doble; una de las dos categorías generales de bases nitrogenadas que se encuentran en el ADN y ARN; ya sea la adenina o la guanina (297)

**pyrimidine** (pi RIM uh DEEN) a nitrogenous base that has a single-ring structure; one of the two general categories of nitrogenous bases found in DNA and RNA; thymine, cytosine, or uracil (297)
**pirimidina** una base nitrogenada que tiene una estructura de anillo sencillo; una de las dos categorías generales de bases nitrogenadas que se encuentran en el ADN y ARN; timina, citosina o uracilo (297)

**radiometric dating** (RAY dee oh MET rik) a method of determining the absolute age of an object by comparing the relative percentages of a radioactive (parent) isotope and a stable (daughter) isotope (452)
**datación radiométrica** un método para determinar la edad absoluta de un objeto comparando los porcentajes relativos de un isótopo radiactivo (precursor) y un isótopo estable (hijo) (452)

**reactant** (ree AK tuhnt) a substance or molecule that participates in a chemical reaction (65)
**reactivo** una sustancia o molécula que participa en una reacción química (65)

**realized niche** (REE uh LIEZD NICH) the range of resources that a species uses, the conditions that the species can tolerate, and the functional roles that the species plays as a result of competition in the species' fundamental niche (113)
**nicho realizado** la gama de recursos que una especie usa, las condiciones que la especie tolera y los papeles funcionales que la especie juega como resultado de la competencia en su nicho fundamental (113)

**receptor protein** (ri SEP tuhr) a protein that binds specific signal molecules, which causes the cell to respond (185)
**proteína receptora** una proteína que liga moléculas señal específicas, lo cual hace que la célula responda (185)

**recessive** (ri SES iv) in genetics, describes an allele that is expressed only when no dominant allele is present in an individual (273)
**recesivo** en genética, término que describe un alelo que se expresa sólo cuando no hay un alelo dominante presente en el individuo (273)

**recombinant DNA** (ree KAHM buh nuhnt) DNA molecules that are artificially created by combining DNA from different sources (350)
**ADN recombinante** moléculas de ADN que son creadas artificialmente al combinar ADN de diferentes fuentes (350)

**recycling** (ree SIE kling) the process of recovering valuable or useful materials from waste or scrap; the process of reusing some items (135)
**reciclar** el proceso de recuperar materiales valiosos o útiles de los desechos o de la basura; el proceso de reutilizar algunas cosas (135)

**relative dating** a method of determining whether an event or object, such as a fossil, is older or younger than other events or objects without referring to the object's age in years (451)
**datación relativa** un método para determinar si un acontecimiento u objeto, tal como un fósil, es más viejo o más joven que otros acontecimientos u objetos sin referirse a la edad del objeto en años (451)

**replication fork** (REP luh KAY shuhn) a Y-shaped point that results when the two strands of a DNA double helix separate so that the DNA molecule can be replicated (300)
**bifurcación de replicación** un punto que tiene forma de Y, el cual se produce cuando las dos hebras de una doble hélice de ADN se separan de modo que la molécula de ADN pueda duplicarse (300)

**reproduction** (REE pruh DUHK shuhn) the process of producing offspring (19, 247)
**reproducción** el proceso de producir descendencia (19, 247)

**reproductive isolation** (REE pruh DUHK tiv IE suh LAY shuhn) a state in which a particular set of populations can no longer interbreed to produce future generations of offspring (412)
**aislamiento reproductivo** un estado en el cual un conjunto particular de poblaciones ya no puede reproducirse entre sí para crear generaciones futuras de descendientes (412)

**respiration** (RES puh RAY shuhn) in biology, the exchange of oxygen and carbon dioxide between living cells and their environment; includes breathing and cellular respiration (91)
**respiración** en biología, el intercambio de oxígeno y dióxido de carbono entre células vivas y su ambiente; incluye la respiración y la respiración celular (91)

**restriction enzyme** (ri STRIK shuhn EN ZIEM) an enzyme that cuts double-stranded DNA into fragments by recognizing specific nucleotide sequences and cutting the DNA at those sequences (355)
**enzima de restricción** una enzima que corta en fragmentos las moléculas de doble hebra del ADN reconociendo secuencias de nucleótidos específicas y cortando el ADN en esas secuencias (355)

**retrovirus** (RE troh VIE ruhs) a virus that contains single-stranded RNA and produces a reverse transcriptase, which converts RNA to DNA (332)
**retrovirus** un virus que contiene ARN de una sola hebra y que produce transcriptasa inversa, la cual convierte el ARN en ADN (332)

**ribose** (RIE BOHS) a five-carbon sugar present in RNA (305)
**ribosa** un azúcar de cinco carbonos presente en el ARN (305)

**ribosome** (RIE buh SOHM) a cell organelle composed of RNA and protein; the site of protein synthesis (154, 305)
**ribosoma** un organelo celular compuesto de ARN y proteína; el sitio donde ocurre la síntesis de proteínas (154, 305)

**ribozyme** (RIE buh ZIEM) a type of RNA that can act as an enzyme (449)
**ribozima** un tipo de ARN que puede funcionar como una enzima (449)

**RNA** ribonucleic acid, a natural polymer that is present in all living cells and that plays a role in protein synthesis (63, 304)
**ARN** ácido ribonucleico; un polímero natural que se encuentra en todas las células vivas y que juega un papel en la síntesis de proteínas (63, 304)

**RNA polymerase** (puh LIM uhr AYS) an enzyme that starts (catalyzes) the formation of RNA by using a strand of a DNA molecule as a template (306)
**ARN polimerasa** una enzima que comienza (cataliza) la formación de ARN usando una hebra de una molécula de ADN como plantilla (306)

**rough endoplasmic reticulum** (EN doh PLAZ mik ri TIK yuh luhm) the portion of the endoplasmic reticulum to which ribosomes are attached (158)
**retículo endoplásmico rugoso** la porción del retículo endoplásmico a la que se unen los ribosomas (158)

**rRNA** ribosomal RNA, an organelle that contains most of the RNA in the cell and that is responsible for ribosome function (305)
**ARNr** ARN ribosomal; un organelo que contiene la mayor parte del ARN en la célula y que es responsable del funcionamiento de los ribosomas (305)

**savanna** (suh VAN uh) a plain full of grasses and scattered trees and shrubs; found in tropical and subtropical habitats and mainly in regions with a dry climate, such as East Africa (83)
**sabana** una planicie llena de pastizales y árboles y arbustos dispersos; se encuentra en los hábitats tropicales y subtropicales y, sobre todo, en regiones con un clima seco, como en el este de África (83)

**scrotum** (SKROHT uhm) the sac that contains the testes in most male mammals (549)
**escroto** la bolsa que contiene los testículos en la mayoría de los mamíferos machos (549)

**second messenger** a molecule that is generated when a specific substance attaches to a receptor on the outside of a cell membrane, which produces a change in cellular function (186)
**mensajero secundario** una molécula que se genera cuando una sustancia específica se une a un receptor en el exterior de la membrana celular, lo cual produce un cambio en la función celular (186)

**semen** (SEE muhn) the fluid that contains sperm and various secretions produced by the male reproductive organs (551)
**semen** el fluido que contiene espermatozoides y varias secreciones producidas por los órganos reproductores masculinos (551)

**seminal vesicle** (SEM uh nuhl VES i kuhl) one of two glandular structures in male vertebrates that hold and secrete seminal fluid (551)
**vesícula seminal** una de las dos estructuras glandulares en los vertebrados macho, las cuales acumulan y secretan fluido seminal (551)

**seminiferous tubule** (sem uh NIF uhr uhs) one of the many tubules in the testis where sperm are produced (549)
**túbulo seminífero** uno de los muchos túbulos que hay en los testículos, en donde se producen los espermatozoides (549)

**sex chromosome** one of the pair of chromosomes that determine the sex of an individual (249)
**cromosoma sexual** uno de los dos cromosomas que determinan el sexo de un individuo (249)

**sexual reproduction** reproduction in which gametes from two parents unite (248)
**reproducción sexual** reproducción en la que se unen los gametos de los dos progenitores (248)

**sexual selection** an evolutionary mechanism by which traits that increase the ability of individuals to attract or acquire mates appear with increasing frequency in a population; selection in which a mate is chosen on the basis of a particular trait or traits (406)
**selección sexual** un mecanismo evolutivo por medio del cual los caracteres que aumentan la capacidad de los individuos de atraer o adquirir una pareja aparecen con más frecuencia en una población; selección en la que se elige una pareja con base en un carácter o caracteres particulares (406)

**SI** (ES IE) Le Système International d'Unités, or the International System of Units, which is the measurement system that is accepted worldwide (15)
**SI** Le Système International d'Unités, o el Sistema Internacional de Unidades, que es el sistema de medición que se acepta en todo el mundo (15)

**signal** anything that serves to direct, guide, or warn (184)
**señal** cualquier cosa que sirve para dirigir, guiar o advertir (184)

**silent mutation** an alteration of genetic information that has no apparent effect on the phenotype of an organism (320)
**mutación silenciosa** una alteración de la información genética que no tiene un efecto aparente en el fenotipo de un organismo (320)

**skepticism** (SKEP ti SIZ uhm) a habit of mind in which a person questions the validity of accepted ideas (7)
**escepticismo** un hábito de la mente que hace que la persona cuestione la validez de las ideas aceptadas (7)

**smooth endoplasmic reticulum** (EN doh PLAZ mik ri TIK yuh luhm) the portion of the endoplasmic reticulum that lacks attached ribosomes (158)
**retículo endoplásmico liso** la porción del retículo endoplásmico que no tiene ribosomas adjuntos (158)

**sodium-potassium pump** (SOH dee uhm poh TAS ee uhm) a carrier protein that uses ATP to actively transport sodium ions out of a cell and potassium ions into the cell (182)
**bomba de sodio-potasio** una proteína transportadora que utiliza el ATP para efectuar el transporte activo de iones de sodio hacia el exterior de la célula y de iones de potasio hacia el interior de la célula (182)

**solution** (suh LOO shuhn) a homogeneous mixture throughout which two or more substances are uniformly dispersed (56)
**solución** una mezcla homogénea en la cual dos o más sustancias se dispersan de manera uniforme (56)

**somatic cell** (soh MAT ik) a cell other than a gamete or germ cell; a body cell (248, 322, 403)
**célula somática** una célula que no es un gameto o una célula germinal; una célula del cuerpo (248, 322, 403)

**speciation** (SPEE shee AY shuhn) the formation of new species as a result of evolution (387, 412)
**especiación** la formación de especies nuevas como resultado de la evolución (387, 412)

**species** (SPEE seez) a group of organisms that are closely related and can mate to produce fertile offspring; *also* the level of classification below genus and above subspecies (19, 387, 411, 426)
**especie** un grupo de organismos que tienen un parentesco cercano y que pueden aparearse para producir descendencia fértil; *también,* el nivel de clasificación debajo de género y arriba de subespecie (19, 387, 411, 426)

**sperm** (SPUHRM) the male gamete (sex cell) (549)
**espermatozoide** el gameto masculino (célula sexual) (549)

**spindle** (SPIN duhl) a network of microtubules that forms during mitosis and moves chromatids to the poles (230)
**huso mitótico** una red de microtúbulos que se forma durante la mitosis y que mueve cromátidas a los polos (230)

**sporophyte** (SPOH ruh FIET) in plants and algae that have alternation of generations, the diploid individual or generation that produces haploid spores (258)
**esporofito** en las plantas y algas que tienen generaciones alternas, el individuo o generación diploide que produce esporas haploides (258)

**stabilizing selection** (STAY buh LIEZ ing) a type of natural selection in which the average form of a trait is favored and becomes more common (409)
**selección de estabilización** un tipo de selección natural en la que se favorece la forma promedio de un carácter, el cual se vuelve más común (409)

**stem cell** a cell that can divide repeatedly and can differentiate into specialized cell types (353)
**célula madre** una célula que puede dividirse repetidamente y puede diferenciarse y formar tipos de células especializados (353)

**sticky end** a single-stranded end of a double-stranded DNA molecule; can base-pair with a complementary sticky end (355)
**extremo cohesivo** el extremo de una hebra de la molécula de ADN de doble hebra; puede formar pares de bases con un extremo cohesivo complementario (355)

**stroke** a sudden loss of consciousness or paralysis that occurs when the blood flow to the brain is interrupted (511)
**ataque de apoplejía** una pérdida súbita de la conciencia o parálisis que ocurre cuando se interrumpe el flujo sanguíneo al cerebro (511)

**subspecies** (SUHB SPEE sheez) a taxonomic classification below species that groups organisms that live in different geographical areas, differ morphologically from other populations of the species, but can interbreed with other populations of the species (412)
**subespecie** una clasificación taxonómica que se ubica debajo de la especie y agrupa a organismos que viven en áreas geográficas diferentes y difieren en forma morfológica de otras poblaciones de la especie, pero tienen la capacidad de cruzarse con otras poblaciones de la especie (412)

**substrate** (SUHB STRAYT) a part, substance, or element that lies beneath and supports another part, substance, or element; the reactant in reactions catalyzed by enzymes (66)
**sustrato** una parte, sustancia o elemento que se encuentra debajo de otra parte, sustancia o elemento y lo sostiene; el reactivo en reacciones que son catalizadas por enzimas (66)

**succession** (suhk SESH uhn) the replacement of one type of community by another at a single location over a period of time (81)
**sucesión** el reemplazo de un tipo de comunidad por otro en un mismo lugar a lo largo de un período de tiempo (81)

**symbiosis** (SIM bie OH sis) a relationship in which two different organisms live in close association with each other (110, 331)
**simbiosis** una relación en la que dos organismos diferentes viven estrechamente asociados uno con el otro (110, 331)

**systematics** (SIS tuh MAT iks) the classification of living organisms in terms of their natural relationships; it includes describing, naming, and classifying the organisms (427)
**sistemática** la clasificación de los seres vivos en función de sus relaciones naturales; involucra describir, nombrar y clasificar a los organismos (427)

**taiga** (TIE guh) a region of evergreen, coniferous forest below the arctic and subarctic tundra regions (83)
**taiga** una región de bosques siempreverdes de coníferas, ubicado debajo de las regiones árticas y subárticas de tundra (83)

**target cell** a specific cell to which a hormone is directed to produce a specific effect (184)
**célula blanco** una célula específica a la que se dirige una hormona para producir un efecto específico (184)

**taxon** (TAKS AHN) any named taxonomic group of any rank in the hierarchical classification of organisms; for example, family, genus, or species (423)
**taxón** cualquier grupo taxonómico nombrado de cualquier rango en la clasificación jerárquica de los organismos; por ejemplo: familia, género o especie (423)

**taxonomy** (taks AHN uh mee) the science of describing, naming, and classifying organisms (423)
**taxonomía** la ciencia de describir, nombrar y clasificar organismos (423)

**telomere** (TEL uh MIR) the region at the tip of a chromosome; a region of repeating DNA sequences that forms one of the end points of the DNA segment that makes up a chromosome (334)
**telómero** la región de la punta de un cromosoma; una región de secuencias de ADN repetidas que forma uno de los extremos del segmento de ADN que compone un cromosoma (334)

**temperate grassland** a community (or biome) that is dominated by grasses, has few trees, and is characterized by cold winters and rainfall that is intermediate between that of a forest and a desert (83)
**pradera templada** una comunidad (o bioma) que está dominada por pastos, tiene pocos árboles y se caracteriza por inviernos fríos y precipitación pluvial que es intermedia entre la de un bosque y la de un desierto (83)

**tendon** (TEN duhn) a tough connective tissue that attaches a muscle to a bone or to another body part (476)
**tendón** un tejido conectivo duro que une un músculo con un hueso o con otra parte del cuerpo (476)

**testes** (TES TEEZ) the primary male reproductive organs, which produce sperm cells and testosterone (singular, *testis*) (549)
**testículos** los principales órganos reproductores masculinos, los cuales producen espermatozoides y testosterona (549)

**tetrad** (TE TRAD) the four chromatids in a pair of homologous chromosomes that come together as a result of synapsis during meiosis (252)
**tétrada** las cuatro cromátidas que se encuentran en un par de cromosomas homólogos, las cuales vienen juntas como resultado de la sinapsis durante la meiosis (252)

**theory** (THEE uh ree) a system of ideas that explains many related observations and is supported by a large body of evidence acquired through scientific investigation (13, 375)
**teoría** un sistema de ideas que explica muchas observaciones relacionadas y que está respaldado por una gran cantidad de pruebas obtenidas mediante la investigación científica (13, 375)

**thylakoid** (THIE luh KOYD) a membrane system found within chloroplasts that contains the components for photosynthesis (202)
**tilacoide** un sistema de membranas que se encuentra dentro de los cloroplastos y que contiene los componentes para que se lleve a cabo la fotosíntesis (202)

**thymine** (THIE MEEN) one of the four bases that combine with sugar and phosphate to form a nucleotide subunit of DNA; thymine pairs with adenine (297)
**timina** una de las cuatro bases que se combinan con un azúcar y un fosfato para formar una subunidad de nucleótido de ADN; la timina se une a la adenina (297)

**tissue** (TISH oo) a group of similar cells that perform a common function (164)
**tejido** un grupo de células similares que llevan a cabo una función común (164)

**toxin** a substance that is produced by one organism and that is poisonous to other organisms (502)
**toxina** una sustancia que un organismo produce y que es venenosa para otros organismos (502)

**trait** (TRAYT) a genetically determined characteristic (268)
**carácter** una característica determinada genéticamente (268)

**transcription** (tran SKRIP shuhn) the process of forming a nucleic acid by using another molecule as a template; particularly the process of synthesizing RNA by using one strand of a DNA molecule as a template (305)
**transcripción** el proceso de formar un ácido nucleico usando otra molécula como plantilla; en particular, el proceso de sintetizar ARN usando una de las hebras de la molécula de ADN como plantilla (305)

**transcription factor** an enzyme that is needed to begin and/or continue genetic transcription (327)
**factor de transcripción** una enzima que se necesita para comenzar y/ o continuar la transcripción genética (327)

**transfer RNA** an RNA molecule that transfers amino acids to the growing end of a polypeptide chain during translation (305)
**ARN de transferencia** una molécula de ARN que transfiere aminoácidos al extremo en crecimiento de una cadena de polipéptidos durante la traducción (305)

**transformation** (TRANS fuhr MAY shuhn) the transfer of genetic material in the form of DNA fragments from one cell to another or from one organism to another (294)
**transformación** la transferencia de material genético en forma de fragmentos de ADN de una célula a otra o de un organismo a otro (294)

**transgenic organism** (trans JE nik) an organism that has been transformed by the introduction of novel DNA into its genome (350)
**organismo transgénico** un organismo que ha sido transformado por la introducción de ADN nuevo a su genoma (350)

**translation** (trans LAY shuhn) the portion of protein synthesis that takes place at ribosomes and that uses the codons in mRNA molecules to specify the sequence of amino acids in polypeptide chains (305)
**traducción** la porción de la síntesis de proteínas que tiene lugar en los ribosomas y que usa los codones de las moléculas de ARNm para especificar la secuencia de aminoácidos en las cadenas de polipéptidos (305)

**transpiration** (TRAN spuh RAY shuhn) the process by which plants release water vapor into the air through stomata; *also* the release of water vapor into the air by other organisms (90)
**transpiración** el proceso por medio del cual las plantas liberan vapor de agua al aire por medio de los estomas; *también,* la liberación de vapor de agua al aire por otros organismos (90)

**transposon** (trans POH ZAHN) a genetic sequence that is randomly moved, in a functional unit, to new places in a genome (332)
**transposón** una secuencia genética que se mueve al azar, en una unidad funcional, a lugares nuevos dentro de un genoma (332)

**trophic level** (TRAHF ik) one of the steps in a food chain or food pyramid; examples include producers and primary, secondary, and tertiary consumers (86)
**nivel trófico** uno de los pasos de la cadena alimenticia o de la pirámide alimenticia; entre los ejemplos se encuentran los productores y los consumidores primarios, secundarios y terciarios (86)

**tropical rain forest** (TRAHP i kuhl) a forest or jungle near the equator that is characterized by large amounts of rain and little variation in temperature and that contains the greatest known diversity of organisms on Earth (83)
**selva tropical** un bosque o jungla que se encuentra cerca del ecuador y se caracteriza por una gran cantidad de lluvia y poca variación en la temperatura, y que contiene la mayor diversidad de organismos que se conoce en la Tierra (83)

**true-breeding** describes organisms or genotypes that are homozygous for a specific trait and thus always produce offspring that have the same phenotype for that trait (269)
**variedad pura** término que describe organismos o genotipos que son homocigotos para un carácter específico y, por lo tanto, producen descendencia que tiene el mismo fenotipo para ese carácter (269)

**tumor** (TOO muhr) a growth that arises from normal tissue but that grows abnormally in rate and structure and lacks a function (235, 323)
**tumor** un bulto que surge en un tejido normal, pero que crece anormalmente en tasa y estructura, y carece de función (235, 323)

**tundra** (TUHN druh) a treeless plain that is located in the Arctic or Antarctic and that is characterized by very low winter temperatures; short, cool summers; and vegetation that consists of grasses, lichens, and perennial herbs (83)
**tundra** una llanura sin árboles situada en la región ártica o antártica y se caracteriza por temperaturas muy bajas en el invierno, veranos cortos y frescos y vegetación que consiste en pasto, líquenes y hierbas perennes (83)

**unicellular** (YOON uh SEL yoo luhr) describes an organism that consists of a single cell (434)
**unicelular** término que describe a un organismo que está formado por una sola célula (434)

**uracil** (YOOR uh SIL) one of the four bases that combine with sugar and phosphate to form a nucleotide subunit of RNA; uracil pairs with adenine (305)
**uracilo** una de las cuatro bases que se combinan con un azúcar y un fosfato para formar una subunidad de nucleótido de ADN; el uracilo se une a la adenina (305)

**urea** (yoo REE uh) the principal nitrogenous product of the metabolism of proteins that forms in the liver from amino acids and from compounds of ammonia and that is found in urine and other body fluids (481)
**urea** el principal producto nitrogenado que se obtiene del metabolismo de las proteínas, se forma en el hígado a partir de aminoácidos y compuestos de amoníaco y se encuentra en la orina y otros fluidos del cuerpo (481)

**urine** (YUR in) the liquid excreted by the kidneys, stored in the bladder, and passed through the urethra to the outside of the body (481)
**orina** el líquido que excretan los riñones, se almacena en la vejiga y pasa a través de la uretra hacia el exterior del cuerpo (481)

**uterus** (YOOT uhr uhs) in female placental mammals, the hollow, muscular organ in which an embryo embeds itself and develops into a fetus (553)
**útero** en los mamíferos placentarios hembras, el órgano hueco y muscular en el que el embrión se incrusta y se desarrolla hasta convertirse en feto (553)

**vaccination** (VAK suh NAY shuhn) the administration of treated microorganisms into humans or animals to induce an immune response (31)
**vacunación** la administración a seres humanos o animales de organismos que han sido tratados para inducir una respuesta inmunológica (31)

**vaccine** (vak SEEN) a substance prepared from killed or weakened pathogens and introduced into a body to produce immunity (532)
**vacuna** una sustancia que se prepara a partir de organismos patógenos muertos o debilitados y se introduce al cuerpo para producir inmunidad (532)

**vacuole** (VAK yoo OHL) a fluid-filled vesicle found in the cytoplasm of plant cells or protozoans (160)
**vacuola** una vesícula llena de líquido que se encuentra en el citoplasma de las células vegetales o de los protozoarios (160)

**vagina** (vuh JIE nuh) the female reproductive organ that connects the outside of the body to the uterus and that receives sperm during reproduction (553)
**vagina** el canal de las hembras que se extiende de la vulva al cuello del útero y que recibe al pene durante el coito (553)

**valence electron** (VAY luhns) an electron that is found in the outermost shell of an atom and that determines the atom's chemical properties (52)
**electrón de valencia** un electrón que se encuentra en la capa más externa de un átomo y que determina las propiedades químicas del átomo (52)

**vas deferens** (vas DEF uh renz) a duct through which sperm move from the epididymis to the ejaculatory duct at the base of the penis (550)
**conducto deferente** un conducto a través del cual los espermatozoides se mueven del epidídimo al conducto eyaculatorio que está en la base del pene (550)

**vector** (VEK tuhr) in biology, any agent, such as a plasmid or a virus, that can incorporate foreign DNA and transfer that DNA from one organism to another; an intermediate host that transfers a pathogen or a parasite to another organism (360, 500)
**vector** en biología, cualquier agente, como por ejemplo un plásmido o un virus, que tiene la capacidad de incorporar ADN extraño y de transferir ese ADN de un organismo a otro; un huésped intermediario que transfiere un organismo patógeno o un parásito a otro organismo (360, 500)

**vein** (VAYN) in biology, a vessel that carries blood to the heart (482)
**vena** en biología, un vaso que lleva sangre al corazón (482)

**vertebrate** (VUHR tuh brit) an animal that has a backbone; includes mammals, birds, reptiles, amphibians, and fish (383)
**vertebrado** un animal que tiene columna vertebral; incluye a los mamíferos, aves, reptiles, anfibios y peces (383)

**vesicle** (VES i kuhl) a small cavity or sac that contains materials in a eukaryotic cell; forms when part of the cell membrane surrounds the materials to be taken into the cell or transported within the cell (158)
**vesícula** una cavidad o bolsa pequeña que contiene materiales en una célula eucariótica; se forma cuando parte de la membrana celular rodea los materiales que van a ser llevados al interior la célula o transportados dentro de ella (158)

**virus** (VIE ruhs) a nonliving, infectious particle composed of a nucleic acid and a protein coat; it can invade and destroy a cell (332)
**virus** una partícula infecciosa sin vida formada por un ácido nucleico y una cubierta de proteína; puede invadir una célula y destruirla (332)

**vulva** (VUHL vuh) the external part of the female reproductive organs (553)
**vulva** la parte externa de los órganos reproductores femeninos (553)

**water cycle** the continuous movement of water between the atmosphere, the land, and the oceans (90)
**ciclo del agua** el movimiento continuo del agua entre la atmósfera, la tierra y los océanos (90)

**zygote** (ZIE GOHT) the cell that results from the fusion of gametes; a fertilized egg (248, 557)
**cigoto** la célula que resulta debido a la fusión de los gametos; el óvulo fecundado (248, 557)

Note: Page references followed by *f* refer to illustrative material, such as figures and tables.

Index

Index

Index

Index

# Credits

## Photography

**Abbreviations used:** (t) top, (b), bottom, (c) center, (l) left, (r) right, (bkgd) background

**LABS** (bkgd) Brand X/SuperStock; **UNIT OPENERS** (bkgd), (border) Royalty-Free/Getty Images; **UNIT 1** (section borders) Michael Melford/Royalty-Free/Getty Images; **UNITS 2–4** (section borders) Royalty-Free/Creatas Images; **UNITS 5–6** (section borders) PhotoDisc/Veer

**COVER AND TITLE** © Frank Lane/Parfitt/Getty Images; iii (tl, bl) Andy Christiansen/HRW; (tr, br) Patrick Greene/National Geographic Image Collection; iv (Gaul) Sam Dudgeon/HRW; (Govind) Andy Christiansen/HRW; (Lumsden) Paul Draper/HRW; (Mandel) Andy Christiansen/HRW; (Seidman) Andy Christiansen/HRW; (Zavaleta) Robert Houser; vii (b) Barbara Strnadova/Photo Researchers, Inc.; viii (bl) Stephen Alvarez/National Geographic Image Collection; (tl) James M. Bell/Photo Researchers, Inc.; ix (b) ABPL/Daryl Balfour/Animals Animals/Earth Scenes; x (cl) Dr. Linda Stannard, UCT/Photo Researchers, Inc.; xi (tr) Joe Outland/Alamy; (bl) Dr. Paul Andrews, University of Dundee/Photo Researchers, Inc.; xii (tl) Andrew Leonard/Photo Researchers, Inc.; xiii (cr) Toni Angermayer/Photo Researchers, Inc.; xiv (tl) Sam Dudgeon/HRW; (b) Anatomical Travelogue/Photo Researchers, Inc.; xv (b) Derek Berwin/Getty Images; xvi (t) AP Photo/Katsumi Kasahara; xviii (t) Sam Dudgeon/HRW; xix (b) Sam Dudgon/HRW; 2 (bl) Bill Curtsinger/National Geographic Image Collection; (br) Katherine Feng/Globio/Minden Pictures; (tl) Royalty-Free/Corbis; 2A Bill Hatcher/National Geographic Image Collection; 2B (bl) Meul/ARCO/Nature Picture Library; (tr) (cl) Bettmann/Corbis; (cr) Time & Life Pictures/Getty Images; 3 (tl) (cr) Sam Dudgeon/HRW; (cl) Age Fotostock/SuperStock

**CHAPTER 1:** 4–5 Frans Lanting/Minden Pictures; 7 (br) Deep Light Productions/Photo Researchers, Inc.; (bc) P. Hawtin/University of Southhampton/Photo Researchers, Inc.; 8 (tr) National Optical Astronomy Observatories/Photo Researchers, Inc.; (tl) David Tipling/Nature Picture Library; 9 (tr) Victoria Smith/HRW; 10 (bl) Georgette Douwma/Nature Picture Library; 11 (tr) Sam Dudgeon/HRW; 12 (bl) Millard H. Sharp/Photo Researchers, Inc.; (br) AP Photo/Marcio Jose Sanchez; 13 (tr) Royalty-Free/Corbis; 14 (r) Sam Dudgeon/HRW; (cl) PhotoDisc/Getty Images; (cr), 15 (tr) Victoria Smith/HRW; 16 (tl) Carsten Peter/National Geographic Image Collection; 17 (bl) Phil Schermeister/National Geographic Image Collection; 18 (bl) Stephen Alvarez/National Geographic Image Collection; (tr) Paul Nicklen/National Geographic Image Collection; (c) Douglas Faulkner/Photo Researchers, Inc.; (bkgd) Michael Martin/Photo Researchers, Inc.; 19 (tr) Gabe Palmer/Alamy; 20 Victoria Smith/HRW; 22 (b) Stephen Alvarez/National Geographic Image Collection; (t) P. Hawtin/University of Southhampton/Photo Researchers, Inc.; (tc) Sam Dudgeon/HRW; (bc) PhotoDisc/Getty Images

**CHAPTER 2:** 26–27 Roger Harris/Photo Researchers, Inc.; 29 (b) James M. Bell/Photo Researchers, Inc.; 30 (b) Jeremy Horner/Corbis; (cl) Amit Dave/NewsCom; 31 (tr) Sam Dungeon/HRW; 32 (tl) epa/Corbis; (tr) Vo Trung Dung/Corbis Sygma; 33 (bl) Taxi/Getty Images; (br) Don Farrall/Photographer's Choice RF/Getty Images; 34 (bl) Peter Menzel/Photo Researchers, Inc.; 35 (b) ORNL/Photo Researchers, Inc.; 36 (br) Eric Miller/Getty Images; (bl) Mark Maio/King-Holmes/Photo Researchers, Inc.; 37 (tr) Getty Images; 38 (cl), (br), (cr) David Brabyn/Sipa Photos/NewsCom; 39 (t) Mike Johnson. All rights reserved.; 30 (tl) Courtesy of Dr. Rita Colwell; 40 (t) Andrew Dunn; 41 (tr) Yuriko Nakao/NewsCom; (bl) Jim Sulley/NewsCom; (c) Volker Steger/Photo Researchers, Inc.; (bkgd) Royalty-Free/Corbis; 43 (tr) Sam Dudgeon/HRW; 44 (t) Amit Dave/NewsCom; (c) David Brabyn/NewsCom; (b) Don Farrall/Photographer's Choice RF/Getty Images; 46 (tc) AP Photo/Katsumi Kasahara

**CHAPTER 3:** 48–49 Daniel Boschung/zefa/Corbis; 51 (bl) Victoria Smith/HRW; 52 (tc) blickwinkel/Alamy; 53 (br) Sergio Purtell/Foca/HRW; 55 (bl) Botanica/The Garden Picture Library; 56 (b-all) Sam Dudgeon/HRW; 57 (t) Victoria Smith/HRW; 58 (tr) O.S.F./Animals Animals/Earth Scenes; (cl) Bernard, George/Animals Animals/Earth Scenes; (t-bkgd) PhotoDisc/Getty Images; (cr) Layne Kennedy/Corbis; (b-bkgd) Bernhard Edmaier/SPL/Photo Researchers, Inc.; 59 (br) Andrew Holt/Alamy; (bl) Andy Christiansen/HRW; 60 (bc) Sam Dudgeon/HRW; 61 (t) Sam Dudgeon/HRW; (bl) Suzanne Danegger/NHPA; (br) Tony Hamblin; Frank Lane Picture Agency/Corbis; 62 (br) SuperStock; 64 (b) Victor Ruiz Caballero/AP/Wide World Photos; 68 Sam Dudgeon/HRW; 70 (t) Victoria Smith/HRW; (c) Botanica/The Garden Picture Library; (b) Victor Ruiz Caballero/AP/Wide World Photos; 74 (br) A ROOM WITH VIEWS/Alamy; (bl) FRANS LANTING/Minden Pictures; 74A Doug Perrine/Nature Picture Library; 74B (bl) Mark Moffett/Minden Pictures; (tl) Brand X Pictures; (tr) Royalty-Free/Corbis; (cl) Erich Hartmann/Magnum Photos; (cr) Iain Masterton/Alamy; 75 (tl, cr) Robert Houser; (cl) Heidi & Hans-Jurgen Koch/Minden Pictures

**CHAPTER 4:** 76–77 Ingo Arndt/Nature Picture Library; 79 (b) Kim Taylor/Nature Picture Library; 80 (t) Sam Dungeon/HRW Photo; 81 (l) Ken M. Johns, The National Audubon Society Collection/Photo Researchers; (c) Glenn M. Oliver/Visuals Unlimited; (r) ER Degginger/Color-Pic, Inc.; 82–83 (t) Michael DeYoung/Corbis; 83 (tc) Brenda Tharp/Photo Researchers, Inc.; (tr) ER Degginger/Color-Pic, Inc.; 84 (tl) Tamara Dormier/Seapics; (tr) Mark Conlin/Seapics; 85 (b-bkgd) Jan Baks/Alamy; (tr) Paul Chesley/National Geographic/Getty Images; (t-bkgd) Victoria Smith/HRW; (c) Roger W. Archibald/Animals Animals/Earth Scenes; 86 (l) blickwinkel/Alamy; (cl) B.A.E. Inc./Alamy; (cr) James Carmichael, Jr./NHPA; (r) Tom Vezo/VIREO; 88 (t) Michael Keller/Corbis; 89 (t) Brian Wheeler/VIREO; (c) D. Robert & Lorri Franz/Corbis; (b) Jason Brindel Photography/Alamy Photos; 93, 94, 95 Sam Dudgeon/HRW; 96 (t) Kim Taylor/Nature Picture Library; (b) Michael Keller/Corbis

**CHAPTER 5:** 100–101 Tui De Roy/Minden Pictures; 103 (b) ABPL/Balfour, Daryl/Animals Animals/Earth Scenes; 104 (t) Terry Andrewartha/Nature Picture Library; 105 (b) Frans Lanting/Minden Pictures; 106 (b) Fritz Polking/Peter Arnold, Inc.; 107 (t-bkgd) Janine Wiedel Photolibrary/Alamy; 108 (cl) Yoshikazu Tsuno/AFP/Getty Images; (b-bkgd) SETBOUN/Corbis; (tr) Iain Masterton/Alamy; (t-bkgd) Corbis/PunchStock; 109 (b) Mitsuaki Iwago/Minden Pictures; 110 (tc) Patti Murray/Animals Animals/Earth Scenes; 111 (tl) Doug Perrine/Nature Picture Library; (tr) Clay Perry/Corbis; 112 (b) Ilene MacDonald/Alamy; 114 (tl) Robert Royse/VIREO; (tcl) John Dunning/VIREO; (tc) Bob Steele/VIREO; (tcr) Rob & Ann Simpson/VIREO; (tr) Arthur Morris/VIREO; 115 (t) James D. Watt/Seapics; 117 (tl) Victoria Smith/HRW; (tr) Dr. David B. Fankhouser; 118 (t) Frans Lanting/Minden Pictures; (c) Doug Perrine/Nature Picture Library; (b) James D. Watt/Seapics

**CHAPTER 6:** 122–123 George Steinmetz/Corbis; 123 (br) Victoria Smith/HRW; 125 (br) Cameron Davidson/Getty Images; 126 (br) George Steinmetz/Corbis; (bl) Lester Lefkowitz/Corbis; 127 (tr) Sam Dungeon/HRW; 128 (b) China Photos/Getty Images; 131 (tr) Victoria Smith/HRW; 132 (b) Peter Oxford/Nature Picture Library; 133 (tl) Will Meinderts/Foto Natura/Minden Pictures; (tr) Shin Yoshino/Minden Pictures; 134 (b) Royalty-free/Robert Harding; 135 (tr) Victoria Smith/HRW; 136 (bl) Courtesy Cliff Lerner/HRW; (br) Richard Price/Getty Images; 137 (t) Stuart Westmorland/Corbis; 138 (tr) Image entitled "Fresh Kills Future Parkland" used with permission of the New York City Department of City Planning. All rights reserved; (tl) Louie Psihoyos/Corbis; 139 (cr) Handout-Obvio!/Reuters/Corbis; (tr) Reuters/Corbis; (b) Issei Kato/Reuters/Corbis; (bkgd) Royalty-Free/Corbis; 141 (tr) Sam Dudgeon/HRW; 142 (br) Royalty-free/Robert Harding; (c) Shin Yoshino/Minden Pictures; (tr) Lester Lefkowitz/Corbis; 146 (bl) PHOTOTAKE Inc./Alamy; (br) Andrew Syred/Photo Researchers, Inc.; 146A James Cavallini/Photo Researchers, Inc.; 146B (bl) Jennifer C. Waters/Photo Researchers, Inc.; (tl) Kevin Collins/Visuals Unlimited; (tr) PhotoDisc/Getty Images; (cl) Gary D. Gaugler/Photo Researchers, Inc.; (cr) Paula Lerner/Aurora; 147 (tl, cr) Andy Christiansen/HRW; (cl) Don W. Fawcett/Photo Researchers, Inc.

**CHAPTER 7:** 148–149 Volker Steger/Christian Bardele/Photo Researchers, Inc.;149 (tr) Victoria Smith/HRW;151 (bc) Michael Newman/Photo Edit; (br) Michael Abbey/Visuals Unlimited;152 (br) Andrew Syred/Photo Researchers, Inc.; (c) Laude Nuridsany & Marie Perennou/Photo Researchers, Inc.; (tr) Thomas Deerinck/Visuals Unlimited; (bl), (bkgd) Francois Paquet-Durand/Photo Researchers, Inc.;154 (tr) CNRI/Photo Researchers, Inc.;155 (tl) Dr. Donald Fawcett/Visuals Unlimited;157 (tr) Don Fawcett/Visuals Unlimited;159 (tr), (cr) R. Boldender/D. Fawcett/Visuals Unlimited; (br) Professor Birgit H. Satir;160 (br) Dr. Jeremy Burgess/Photo Researchers, Inc.; 161 (tr) Dr. Don Fawcett/Visuals Unlimited; 162 (bl) Dr. Linda Stannard, UCT/Photo Researchers, Inc.; 164 (cl) Dr. George Chapman/Visuals Unlimited; (c) Clouds Hill Imaging Ltd./Corbis; (cr) Gentl & Hyers/Botanica/Jupiter Images; (bl) Photo Insolite Realite/SPL/Photo Researchers, Inc.; 166 (tl) Lawrence Naylor/Photo Researchers, Inc.; (cl) Eddy Marissen/Foto Natura/Minden Pictures; (tr) Age FotoStock/SuperStock; (br) IT Stock International/Jupiter Images; 167 (tr) E.R. Degginger/Color-Pic, Inc.; 168 (br) Eddy Marissen/Foto Natura/Minden Pictures; (tr) Michael Newman/Photo Edit

**CHAPTER 8:** 172–173 CNRI/Photo Researchers, Inc.; 173 (cr) Runk/Schoenberger/Grant Heilman Photography; 175 (b) Marc Chamberlain/Seapics; 178 (b) Keith Levit/Alamy; 180 (all) Dr. David M. Phillips/Visuals Unlimited; 181 (t) Sam Dudgeon/HRW; (b) Nigel Cattlin/Photo Researchers, Inc.; 184 (b) Bob Daemmrich/PhotoEdit, Inc.; 185 (t) Kevin Schafer/Corbis; 187 (cl, cr) NASA/SPL/Photo Researchers, Inc.; (tr) Meul/ARCO/Nature Picture Library; (tl) PhotoDisc/Getty Images; (bkgd) Dr. Jeremy Burgess/SPL/Photo Researchers, Inc.; (br) Lourens Smak/Alamy; 188 (bl) WARD'S Natural Science; (br) Sam Dudgeon/HRW; 190 (t) Marc Chamberlain/Seapics; (c) Keith Levit/Alamy; (b) Bob Daemmrich/PhotoEdit, Inc.

**CHAPTER 9:** 194–195 Frans Lanting/Minden Pictures; 195 (tr) Sam Dungeon/HRW; 197 (br) Terry W. Eggers/Corbis; 198 (tr) Victoria Smith/HRW; 199 (cr) Michael Newman/PhotoEdit; (cl) Royalty-Free/Corbis; 200 (br) Troy and Mary Parlee/Alamy; 202 (bl) Copyright Dorling Kindersley; 207 (tl) Richard Cummins/Corbis; (tr) Wolfgang Kaehler/Corbis; 208 John Henley/Corbis; 213 (tl) Mike Powell/Allsport Concepts/Getty Images; (tc) David Madison/Getty Images; 214 (bkgd), (tr), (cr) Roger Ressmeyer/Corbis; (b) James Marshall/Corbis; 215 (bl) Victoria Smith/HRW; 216 (t) Richard Cummins/Corbis; (b) David Madison/Getty Images; (t) Troy and Mary Parlee/Alamy

**CHAPTER 10:** 220–221 Dr. Linda Stannard, UCT/Photo Researchers, Inc.; 221 (tr) Carolina Biological Supply/Visuals Unlimited; 223 (b) Pixoi Ltd./Alamy; 224 (t) Victoria Smith/HRW; 225 (br) David M. Philips/Visuals Unlimited; 226 (tl) Visuals Unlimited/Corbis; 227 (c) R. Andrew Odum/Peter Arnold, Inc.; (t-bkgd) Robert Yin/Corbis; (b-bkgd) Doug Perrine/Seapics; (tr) Dwight R. Kuhn; (cl, cr) R. Andrew Odum/Peter Arnold, Inc.; 230–231 (b-all) Dr. Conly L. Rieder and Dr. Alexey

Khodjakov/Visuals Unlimited; 232 (tr) R. Calentine/Visuals Unlimited; (tl) RMF/Visuals Unlimited; 233 (bl) Antonia Reeve/Science Photo Library/Photo Researchers, Inc.; 235 (cr) Steve Gschmeissner/Science Photo Library/Photo Researchers, Inc.; (tr) Jose Luis Pelaez, Inc./Corbis; 237 (tr) Victoria Smith/HRW; (tl) Dr. John D. Cunningham/Visuals Unlimited; 238 (t) Visuals Unlimited/Corbis; (c) Dr. Conly L. Rieder and Dr. Alexey Khodjakov/Visuals Unlimited; (b) Jose Luis Pelaez, Inc./Corbis; 239 (br) David M. Philips/Visuals Unlimited; 242 (br) Steve Paddock, Jim Langeland, Sean Carroll/Visuals Unlimited; (bl) Christian Ziegler/Danita Delimont; 242A Frans Lanting/Minden Pictures; 242B (bl) Ted Horowitz/Corbis; (tl) James King-Holmes/Science Photo Library; (tr) MBL/WHOI Library; (cr) David Parker/Photo Researchers, Inc.; 243 (tl), (cr) Andy Christiansen/HRW Photo; 243 (bl) Dynamic Graphics Value/SuperStock

**CHAPTER 11:** 244–245 Heidi Hans-Jurgen Koch/Minden Pictures; 245 (br) Martin Gabriel/Nature Picture Library; 247 (br) BPA/SS/Photo Researchers, Inc.; 248 (bl) David M. Phillips/Photo Researchers, Inc.; 249 (cr) Frans Lanting/Minden Pictures; (tr) Eye of Science/Photo Researchers, Inc.; 255 (cr) Konrad Wothe/Minden Pictures; (bl) George Bernard/Photo Researchers, Inc.; (br) Tom Brakefield/Corbis; (bkgd) Frank Lukasseck/zefa/Corbis; (tr) Francesco Tomasinelli/Natural Visions; 256 (br) David M. Phillips/Visuals Unlimited; (cl) (c) Image 1999 PhotoDisc, Inc./HRW; (bc) Yorgos Nikas/Tony Stone/Getty Images; (bl) Jason Burns/Ace/Phototake; (cr), (b) Image 1999 PhotoDisc, Inc./HRW; 259 Sam Dudgeon/HRW; 260 (t) David M. Phillips/Photo Researchers, Inc.

**CHAPTER 12:** 263–264 Leszczynski, Zigmund/Animals Animals-Earth Scenes; 265 (tl), (tr) Sam Dudgeon/HRW; 271 (bkgd) Manfred Kage/Peter Arnold, Inc.; (bl) Eye of Science/Photo Researchers, Inc.; (tr) David M. Phillips/Photo Researchers, Inc.; 273 (tl) Picture Press; (tr) Royalty-Free/Alamy Images; 274 (c), (bc) Christian Grzimek/Okapia/Photo Researchers, Inc.; (cr), (br) Barry Runk/Grant Heilman Photography; 277 (t), (b) Lynn M. Stone/DRK Photo; 278 Irving J. Buchbinder/Community Health Services; 279 (tl), (tr) Ken Lax/HRW Photo; 280 Joe Outland/Alamy; 282 Digital Vision/Getty Images; 284 (t) Dan Guravich/Photo Researchers, Inc.; (b) Tom Walker/Tony Stone Images; 285 Victoria Smith/HRW; 286 (br) Digital Vision/Getty Images; 286 (cl) Picture Press

**CHAPTER 13:** 290–291 Alfred Pasieka/Photo Researchers, Inc.; 293 (b) Rick Gomez/Corbis; 297 (tr) Sam Dudgeon/HRW; 299 (cr) SPL/Photo Researchers, Inc.; (tr) A. Barrington Brown/Photo Researchers, Inc.; 300 (bl) Dr. Gopal Murti/SPL/Photo Researchers, Inc.; 303 (tr) Dr Paul Andrews, University Of Dundee/Photo Researchers, Inc.; 309 (br) Alfred Pasieka/Photo Researchers, Inc.; 310 (tr) Dr. Dennis Kunkel/Visuals Unlimited; (tc) John Langford/HRW; 311 (bl) Victoria Smith/HRW; 312 (tr) Rick Gomez/Corbis; (br) Alfred Pasieka/Photo Researchers, Inc; (c) Dr. Gopal Murti/SPL/Photo Researchers, Inc.

**CHAPTER 14:** 316–317 Frans Lanting/Minden Pictures; 317 (tr) Sheila Terry/Photo Researchers, Inc.; 319 Dr. Stanley Flegler/Visuals Unlimited; 321 (tr) Sam Dudgeon/HRW; 322 (bl) Lauren Shear/Photo Researchers, Inc.; (tc) Dr. P. Marazzi/Photo Researchers, Inc.; (br) Biophoto Associates/Science Source/Photo Researchers, Inc.; 323 (b) Custom Medical Stock Photo; (t) Dr. Stanley Flegler/Visuals Unlimited; (c) Simon Fraser/Photo Researchers, Inc.; (bc) Robert Caughey/Visuals Unlimited; (tc) Dr. S. Walkley/Peter Arnold, Inc.; 324 (tr) L. Willatt, East Anglian Regional Genetics Service/Photo Researchers, Inc.; (br) L. Willatt, East Anglian Regional Genetics Service/Photo Researchers, Inc.; (tl) Stockbyte/SuperStock; 325 (bl) Westend61/Royalty-Free/Getty Images; (br) Leslie J. Borg/Photo Researchers, Inc.; 326 (tl) Dr. Dennis Kunkel/Visuals Unlimited; 328 (t) Victoria Smith/HRW; 329 (tr) Corbis; 330 (l) Phototake, Inc./Alamy; (cl) Wally Eberhart/Visuals Unlimited; (cr) Nathalie Pujol/Visuals Unlimited; (r) Hermann Eisenbeiss/Photo Researchers, Inc.; 331 (r) Rubberball/Jupiter Images; (l) Mark Smith/Photo Researchers, Inc.; (cl) Digital Vision Ltd./SuperStock; (cr) PhotoDisc Blue/Royalty-Free/Getty Images; Martha Powell/Visuals Unlimited; 332 (tl) Alix/Photo Researchers, Inc.; (cl) Dr. Dennis Kunkel/Visuals Unlimited; 334 Peter Skinner/Photo Researchers, Inc.; 335 (b) Chris Graythen/Getty Images; (bkgd) Matthias Kulka/zefa/Corbis; (tr) AP Photo/Cristina Quicler; 337 (t) Ward's Natural Science; 338 (b) PhotoDisc Blue/Royalty-Free/Getty Images; (c) Corbis; (t) Lauren Shear/Photo Researchers, Inc.

**CHAPTER 15:** 342–343 Simon Lin/AP Wide World Photos; 345 (br) Roy Morsch/zefa/Corbis; 346 Science VU/Visuals Unlimited; 347 (tr) Courtesy of Cellmark Diagnostics, Inc., Germantown, Maryland; 348 Photo by Russ Morris, The Tech Museum of Innovation; 349 (b) Bettmann/Corbis; (tr), (cr) Reuters/Corbis; (bkgd) Royalty-Free/Corbis; 350 (bl) AFP/Getty Images; 351 (br) Jim Richardson/Corbis; 353 (tl) Andrew Leonard/Photo Researchers, Inc.; (tr) CC Studio/Photo Researchers, Inc.; (tc) Mauro Fermariello/Photo Researchers, Inc.; 354 Wolfgang Flamisch/zefa/Corbis; 356 (tr) Sam Dudgeon/HRW; (bl) Louise Lockley/CSIRO/Photo Researchers, Inc.; 361 (b) Royalty-Free/Corbis; 362 (br) Lisa Peardon/Taxi/Getty Images; 363 (tr) David Parker/Photo Researchers, Inc.; 365 (tr) Tek Image/Photo Researchers, Inc.; 366 (t) Roy Morsch/zefa/Corbis; (c) Jim Richardson/Corbis; (b) Louise Lockley/CSIRO/Photo Researchers, Inc.; 370 (br) Photo by Simon van Noort, courtesy Iziko Museums of Cape Town; (bl) Rob Reijnen/Foto Natura/Minden Pictures; 370A Mark Moffett/Minden Pictures; 370B (tl) Jeff Greenberg/Lonely Planet Images; (tr) John Reader/Photo Researchers, Inc.; (cl) Index Stock Imagery/Newscom; (cr) STR/AFP/Getty Images; 371 (tl), (cr) Andy Christiansen/HRW Photo; (bl) Louie Psihoyos/Corbis; (bl) Edwin L. Wisherd/National Geographic Image Collection/Getty Images

**CHAPTER 16:** 372–373 Paul Osmond/Deep Sea Images; 373 (cr) Victoria Smith/HRW; 375 (c) Bridgeman Art Library, London/New York; 376 (bc) Images & Stories/Alamy; (br) Adrienne Gibson/Animals Animals/Earth Scenes; (b) Reinhard Dirscheri/Peter Arnold, Inc.; (bl) David Hosking/Alamy; 377 (cr) Toni Angermayer/Photo Researchers, Inc.; (b) Carol Kaelson/Animals Animals/Earth Scenes; (bkgd) Sam Dudgeon/HRW; 378 (bl) Markus Boesch/Getty Images; 379 (tr) Russell Wood; 380 (bl) Robert & Linda Mitchell; 382 (br) Bruce Coleman, Inc./Alamy; t Courtesy of Research Casting International and Dr. J. G. M. Thewissen; tc Courtesy of Research Casting International and Dr. J. G. M. Thewissen; 382 bc 1998 Philip Gingerich/Courtesy of the Museum of Paleontology, The University of Michigan; 382 cl 1998 Philip Gingerich/Courtesy of the Museum of Paleontology, The University of Michigan; 382 b Courtesy of Betsy Webb, Pratt Museum, Homer, Alaska; 382 (bl) Courtesy of Betsy Webb, Pratt Museum, Homer, Alaska; 383 (tr) Martin Harvey/Alamy; (tl) Tui De Roy/Minden Pictures; (tc) Gavriel Jecan/Getty Images; 385 (tr) The Natural History Museum, London; 386 (bl) Eurelios/Phototake; 387 (br) Tom & Pat Leeson/DRK Photo; (cr) Tom & Pat Leeson/DRK Photo; (tr) Victoria Smith/HRW; 388 (bl) Robert Clark Photography; (br) Robert Clark Photography; 391 (tr) Tim Fuller/HRW; 392 (tr) Images & Stories/Alamy; (cr) Robert & Linda Mitchell; (br) Eurelios/Phototake

**CHAPTER 17:** 396–397 Wil Meinderts/Foto Natura/Nature Picture Library; 397 (tr) Victoria Smith/HRW; 399 Royalty-Free/Corbis; 400 (b) Victoria Smith/HRW; (tl), (tr), (c), (bl), (br), Sam Dudgeon/HRW; 402 (tl), (tr), (b) Victoria Smith/HRW; 403 Victoria Smith/HRW; 405 (br) Michio Hoshino/Minden Pictures; 406 (tl) Art Wolfe/Getty Images; 407 (tr) ISM/Phototake-All rights reserved; 408 (tl) Barry Mansell/Nature Picture Library; (cl) Mark Smith/Photo Researchers, Inc.; (tr) Gerard Lacz/Animals Animals-Earth Scenes; 410 (bkgd) David Lawrence/Corbis; (tc), (c), (bl), (bc) Jonathan Losos; (tr) NASA/Photo Researchers, Inc.; 411 Barbara Strnadova/Photo Researchers, Inc.; 412 (tl) Norbert Wu; (tc) WorldSat; (tr) Doug Perrine/SeaPics; 413 (b) Gary Mezaros/Visuals Unlimited; (t) Zig Leszczynski/Animals Animals-Earth Scenes; 414 (tr) Tom McHugh/Photo Researchers, Inc.; (tl) Photo Researchers, Inc.; 416 (c) Art Wolfe/Getty Images; (b) Gary Mezaros/Visuals Unlimited; (t) HRW

**CHAPTER 18:** 420–421 Mauro Fermariello/Photo Researchers, Inc.; 421 (br) Sam Dudgeon/HRW; 422 (l) ROBINSON, JAMES/Animals Animals/Earth Scenes; (cl) WATT, JAMES/Animals Animals/Earth Scenes; (c) ERLACH, JOHN/Animals Animals/Earth Scenes; (cr) Roger Harris/Photo Researchers, Inc.; (r) Michael & Patricia Fogden/Minden Pictures; 423 (b) Frans Lanting/Corbis; 424 (tl) Winfried Wisniewski/Foto Natura/Minden Pictures; (tc) Angela Scott/Nature Picture Library; (tr) Martin Harvey/NHPA; 425 (sponge) Doug Perrine/Seapics; (shark) Masa Ushioda/Seapics; (teen) Simon Marcus/Corbis; (wolf) Pryor, Maresa/Animals Animals/Earth Scenes; (cheetah) Winfried Wisniewski/Foto Natura/Minden Pictures; (leopard) Angela Scott/Nature Picture Library; (lion) Martin Harvey/NHPA; (paramecium) Dr. Dennis Kunkel/Visuals Unlimited; 426 (tl) Don Couch/HRW Photo; 427 (br) Michael & Patricia Fogden/Minden Pictures; (bl) Roger Harris/Photo Researchers, Inc.; 428 (turtle) Robinson, James/Animals Animals/Earth Scenes; (chameleon) Watt, James/Animals Animals/Earth Scenes; (crocodile) Erlach, John/Animals Animals/Earth Scenes; (bird-cassowary) Michael & Patricia Fogden/Minden Pictures; (dinosaur) Roger Harris/Photo Researchers, Inc.; (bird-warbler) Robert Royse/VIREO; 429 (bl) H. Taylor/OSF/Animals Animals/Earth Scenes; 429 (bcl) Dani/Jeske/Animals Animals/Earth Scenes; (bcr. br) age fotostock/SuperStock; 432 (c) AP Photo/Courtesy Wild Life Heritage Trust, HO; (bl) Robert Zingg; (tr) Dr. Mike Picker; (ct) AP Photo/Conservation International; (cb) Stephen Richards, Conservation International; (bkgd) COMSTOCK, Inc.; 433 (br) Doug Perrine/Seapics; (bl) Louis De Vos - Free University of Brussels; 434 (Eubacteria) Gary D. Gaugler/Photo Researchers, Inc.; (archaebacteria) Wolfgang Baumeister/Science Photo Library/Photo Researchers, Inc.; (protista) Dr. Dennis Kunkel/PhotoTake; (fungi) Rod Planck/Photo Researchers Inc.; (plantae) Adam Jones/Photo Researchers Inc.; (animalia) Myron Jay Dorf/Corbis; 435 (t) Victoria Smith/HRW; 438 (E) John Gilmore; (C, D) BIOS (Klein/Hubert)/Peter Arnold, Inc.; (A) Runk/Schoenberger/Grant Heilman Photography; (B) Robert & Linda Mitchell; (F) Barry Runk/Grant Heilman Photography; 439 (t) Sam Dudgeon/HRW; 440 (t) Don Couch/HRW Photo; (c) Roger Harris/Photo Researchers, Inc.; (b) Doug Perrine/Seapics

**CHAPTER 19:** 444–445 Jack Dykinga/Stone/Getty Images; 445 (tr) Victoria Smith/HRW; 448 (br) B. Murton/Southhampton Oceanography Centre/Photo Researchers, Inc.; (bl) Breck P. Kent/Animals Animals-Earth Scenes; 450 (br) James L. Amos/Corbis; 451 Theo Allofs/Corbis; (cr) Tom Bean/Corbis; 454 (bl) Eye of Science/Photo Researchers, Inc.; (br) Dr. Dennis Kunkel/Visuals Unlimited; 455 John Reader/SPL/Photo Researchers, Inc.; 457 (tr) John Morrison/Morrison Photography; (br) Spike Walker/Getty Images; 458 Chase Studio/Photo Researchers, Inc.; 459 Jonathan Blair/Corbis; 460 (tr) Reuters/Corbis; (c) Chris Butler/Photo Researchers, Inc.; (bkgd) Robert Harding Picture Library Ltd./Alamy; (b) Mark Garlick/Photo Researchers, Inc.; 461 Victoria Smith/HRW; 462 (t) Breck P. Kent/Animals Animals-Earth Scenes; (c) Theo Allofs/Corbis; (b) Jonathan Blair/Corbis; 466 (bl) FLIP NICKLIN/Minden Pictures; (br) Scimat/Photo Researchers, Inc.; 466A Steve Gschmeissner/Photo Researchers, Inc.; 466B (bl) Steve Axford; (tr) POPPERFOTO/Alamy; (cl) Bettmann/Corbis; (cr) Photo by Erskine Palmer/Time Magazine/Time & Life Pictures/ Getty Images; 467 (all) Andy Christiansen/HRW

**CHAPTER 20:** 468–469 Galen Rowell/CORBIS; 471 (bl) Stephen J. Krasemann/Photo Researchers; 472 (l) Dr. Jeremy Burgess/Science Photo Library/Photo Researchers; 473 (tl) Mario Tama/Getty Images; 474 (cr) Anatomical Travelogue/Photo Researchers; 475 (cr) Stockbyte/Getty Images; 477 (tl) Sergio Purtell/ Foca/HRW; 479 (t) Sam Dudgeon/HRW; 480 (br) P. MOTTA/Department of Anatomy/University La Sapienza, Rome/Photo Researchers; 481 (tr) Sergio Purtell/Foca/ HRW; 482 (bl) Ed Reschke/Peter Arnold; 484 (br) Larry Lilac/Alamy; 486 (all) Sam Dudgeon/HRW; 487 (tr) Sam Dudgeon/HRW; 488 (t) Royalty-Free/CORBIS; 489 (bkgd) CNRI/Photo Researchers; (bc, bl) Justin Hayworth/ Duluth News Tribune/AP/Wide World Photos; (cr) BSIP/ Phototake; (tr) Volker Steger/Science Photo Library/Photo Researchers; 490 (t) M.I. Walker/ Photo Researchers

**CHAPTER 21:** 496–497 CNRI/Photo Researchers; 499 (b) The Bridgeman Art Library/Getty Images; 500 (br) Dr. Tony Brain/Photo Researchers; (bl) Kent Wood/Photo Researchers; 501 (tr) Scott Markewitz/Getty Images; 503 (br) Dr. P. Marazzi/Photo Researchers; (tr) David M. Phillips/Photo Researchers; 505 (bl) Eye of Science/Photo Researchers; 506 (bl) Mediscan/Visuals Unlimited; (tl) Science Photo Library/Photo Researchers; 507 (br) John Greim/Photo Researchers; (tr) Peter Arnold/Peter Arnold; 508 (cl) Tetsu Yamazaki/International Stock Photography; (inset) VEM/Photo Researchers; 509 (bkgd) iStockphoto. com/Luba Nel; (br) AP Photo/Eugene Hoshiko; (cr) REUTERS/Corinne Dufka; (tr) Jack Clark /Animals Animals/Earth Scenes; 511 (br) Moredun Scientific/Photo Reseachers; (tl) GJLP/Photo Researchers; (tr) Morris Huberland/Photo Researchers; 512 (bl) Meckes/Ottawa/ Photo Researchers; 513 (br) SPL/Photo Researchers; (tr) Michael Donne/Photo Researchers; 514 (bl) Dr. Arthur Tucker/Photo Researchers; 515 (tr) Sam Dudgeon/HRW; 516 (bl) Norm Thomas/Photo Researchers; (br) Jeff Smith/fotosmith

**CHAPTER 22:** 522–523 Eye of Science/Photo Researchers, Inc.; 525 (bc) A. Davidhazy/Custom Medical Stock Photo; (br) Gopal Murti/Phototake, Inc./Alamy; 527 (tl), (tc) Dr. Dennis Kunkel/Phototake; (tr) Meckes/Ottawa/ Photo Researchers, Inc.; 528 (tr) Sam Dudgeon/HRW; 529 (br) Victoria Smith/HRW; 530 (bl) Dennis Kunkel/ Phototake; 532 (bl) David McNew/Getty Images; 534 (bl) Sam Dudgeon/HRW; (br) Peter Arnold, Inc./Alamy; (bc) SciMAT/Photo Researchers, Inc.; 535 (br) Derek Berwin/Getty Images; (bl) Dennis Kunkel/Phototake; (tr) Victoria Smith/HRW; 536 (cr) Science Pictures Ltd/Photo Researchers, Inc.; (bl) Steve Jems/Photo Researchers, Inc.; (tr) Brand X Pictures; (bkgd) Luca DiCecco/Alamy; 537 (tr) Animas Corp; 538 (bl) AP Photo/Damian Dovarganes; 539 (cr) NIBSC/Photo Researchers, Inc.; 540 (cl) Tim Fuller/HRW; 542 (tc) A. Davidhazy/Custom Medical Stock Photo; (bc) SciMAT/Photo Researchers, Inc.

**CHAPTER 23:** 546–547 OSF/Derek Bromhall/Animals Animals-Earth Scenes; 549 (br) CNRI/Photo Researchers, Inc.; 551 (tr) Professor P. Motta, Dept. of Anatomy, Rome University/Photo Researchers, Inc.; 554 (bl) Professors P.M. Motta & J. Van Blerkom/Photo Researchers, Inc.; 556 (t) C. Edelmann/La Villette/SS/Photo Researchers, Inc.; 559 (tl), (bl) Lennart Nilsson/Albert Bonniers Firlag; (tr) D. Bromhall/OSF/Animals Animals-Earth Scenes; (br) Petit Format/Nestle/Photo Researchers, Inc.; 560 (tr) Zephyr/Photo Researchers, Inc.; 562 (bl) SPL/Custom Medical Stock Photo; 563 (t) NMSB/Custom Medical Stock Photo; 564 (cl) Big Cheese Photo/Royalty-Free/ Getty Images; (b) Robert W. Ginn/Photo Edit; (cr) Tony Freeman/Photo Edit; (tr) Dr. Najeeb Layyous/Photo Researchers, Inc.; (bkgd) P. Motta/G. Macchiarelli/S. Nottola/Photo Researchers, Inc.; 566 (tr) Professor P. Motta, Dept. of Anatomy, Rome University/Photo Researchers, Inc.; (tr) D. Bromhall/OSF/Animals Animals-Earth Scenes

**Appendix:** 570–571 Mark Conlin/Seapics; 578 (bl) Rob Melnychuk/gettyimages; 579 (tl) Scott Bauer/Agricultural Research Service, USDA; (tr) Tek Image/Photo Researchers, Inc. 580 (t) LWA-Dann Tardif/Corbis; 581 (b) Victoria Smith/HRW; 582 (b) Sergio Purtell/Foca/HRW; 583 (bc), (br) Sergio Purtell/Foca/HRW; 584 (all) Sergio Purtell/Foca/HRW; 586 (cl) Dr. Dennis Kunkel/Phototake; (c), (cr), (br) Sam Dudgeon/HRW; 591 (animalia) Myron Jay Dorf/Corbis; (Eubacteria) © Gary D. Gaugler/Photo Researchers, Inc.; (archaebacteria) Wolfgang Baumeister/ Science Photo Library/Photo Researchers, Inc.; (protista) Dr. Dennis Kunkel/PhotoTake; (fungi) Rod Planck/ Photo Researchers Inc.; (plantae) Adam Jones/Photo Researchers Inc.

## HRW STAFF

The people who contributed to **Holt New York Biology Living Environment** are listed below. They represent editorial, design, production, emedia, marketing, and permissions.

David Alvarado, Karen Arneson, Wesley M. Bain, Kimberly Barr, Soojinn Choi, Martize Cross, Eddie Dawson, Julie Dervin, Lydia Doty, Paul Draper, Sam Dudgeon, Sally Garland, Diana Goetting, Mark Grayson, Frieda Gress, Angela Hemmeter, Timothy Hovde, Jevara Jackson, Simon Key, Jane A. Kirschman, Liz Kline, Michelle Kwan, Denise Mahoney, Richard Metzger, Cathy Murphy, Mercedes Newman, Eric O'Bryant, Cathy Paré, Jenny Patton, Peter Reid, Raegan Remington, Diana Rodriguez, Karen Ross, Michelle Rumpf-Dike, Kathryn Selke, Chris Smith, Victoria Smith, Dawn Marie Spinozza, Jeff Streber, Amy Taulman, Jeannie Taylor, Kathy Towns, David Trevino, Bob Tucek, Heather Tucek, Kira J. Watkins, Aimee Wiley

# The Biologist's Periodic Table of Elements

**Key:**

Atomic number — 6
Symbol — C
Name — Carbon
Average atomic mass — 12.0107

Essential to plants
Found in the atmosphere
Found in humans

Hydrogen
Semiconductors (also known as *metalloids*)

**Metals**
Alkali metals
Alkaline-earth metals
Transition metals
Other metals

**Nonmetals**
Halogens
Noble gases
Other nonmetals

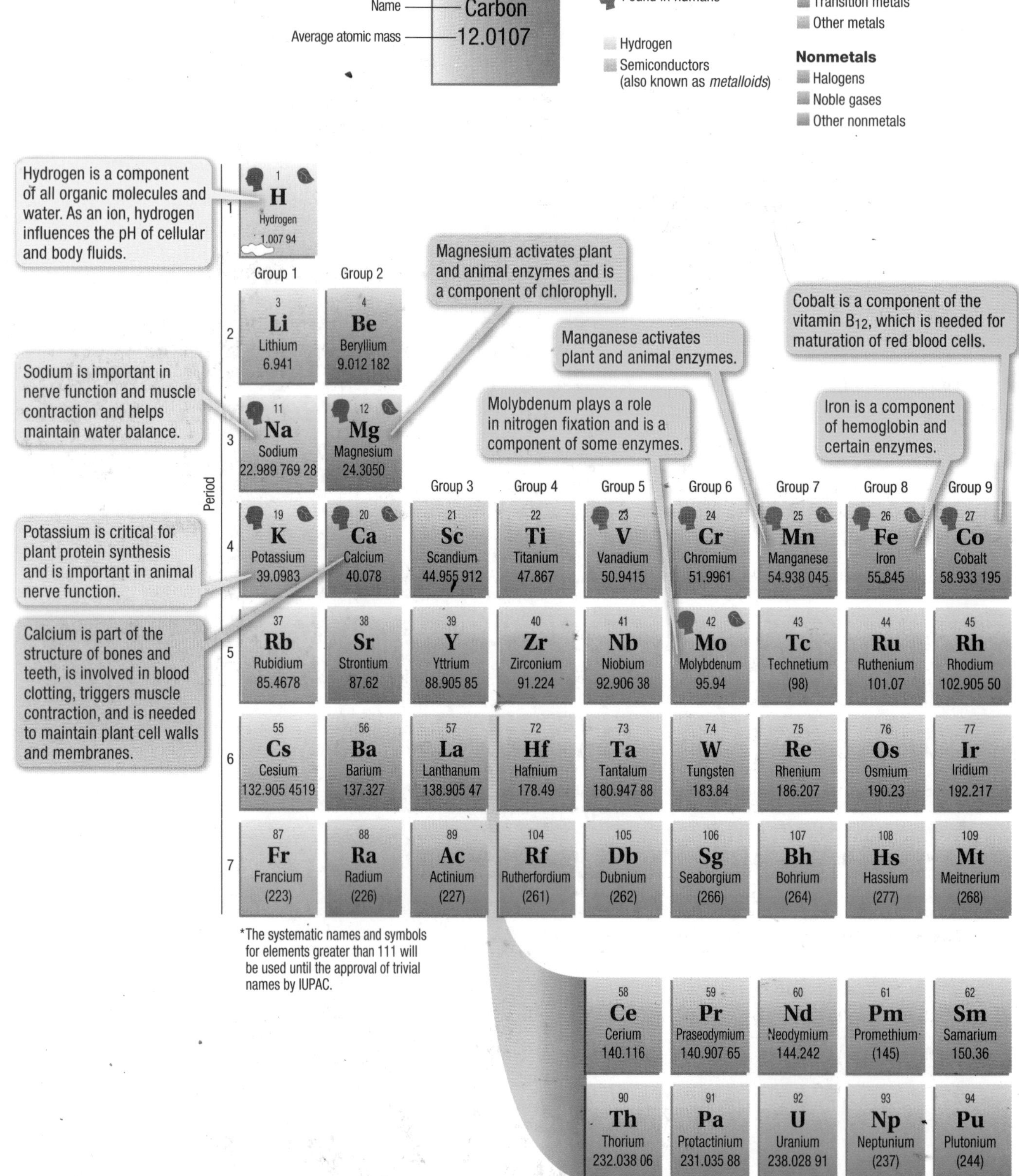
Hydrogen is a component of all organic molecules and water. As an ion, hydrogen influences the pH of cellular and body fluids.
Magnesium activates plant and animal enzymes and is a component of chlorophyll.
Cobalt is a component of the vitamin B12, which is needed for maturation of red blood cells.
Manganese activates plant and animal enzymes.
Sodium is important in nerve function and muscle contraction and helps maintain water balance.
Molybdenum plays a role in nitrogen fixation and is a component of some enzymes.
Iron is a component of hemoglobin and certain enzymes.
Potassium is critical for plant protein synthesis and is important in animal nerve function.
Calcium is part of the structure of bones and teeth, is involved in blood clotting, triggers muscle contraction, and is needed to maintain plant cell walls and membranes.
Period
1
2
3
4
5
6
7
Group 1
Group 2
Group 3
Group 4
Group 5
Group 6
Group 7
Group 8
Group 9
1 H Hydrogen 1.007 94
3 Li Lithium 6.941
4 Be Beryllium 9.012 182
11 Na Sodium 22.989 769 28
12 Mg Magnesium 24.3050
19 K Potassium 39.0983
20 Ca Calcium 40.078
21 Sc Scandium 44.955 912
22 Ti Titanium 47.867
23 V Vanadium 50.9415
24 Cr Chromium 51.9961
25 Mn Manganese 54.938 045
26 Fe Iron 55.845
27 Co Cobalt 58.933 195
37 Rb Rubidium 85.4678
38 Sr Strontium 87.62
39 Y Yttrium 88.905 85
40 Zr Zirconium 91.224
41 Nb Niobium 92.906 38
42 Mo Molybdenum 95.94
43 Tc Technetium (98)
44 Ru Ruthenium 101.07
45 Rh Rhodium 102.905 50
55 Cs Cesium 132.905 4519
56 Ba Barium 137.327
57 La Lanthanum 138.905 47
72 Hf Hafnium 178.49
73 Ta Tantalum 180.947 88
74 W Tungsten 183.84
75 Re Rhenium 186.207
76 Os Osmium 190.23
77 Ir Iridium 192.217
87 Fr Francium (223)
88 Ra Radium (226)
89 Ac Actinium (227)
104 Rf Rutherfordium (261)
105 Db Dubnium (262)
106 Sg Seaborgium (266)
107 Bh Bohrium (264)
108 Hs Hassium (277)
109 Mt Meitnerium (268)
*The systematic names and symbols for elements greater than 111 will be used until the approval of trivial names by IUPAC.
58 Ce Cerium 140.116
59 Pr Praseodymium 140.907 65
60 Nd Neodymium 144.242
61 Pm Promethium (145)
62 Sm Samarium 150.36
90 Th Thorium 232.038 06
91 Pa Protactinium 231.035 88
92 U Uranium 238.028 91
93 Np Neptunium (237)
94 Pu Plutonium (244)